£29-50

Qu4

BIOLOGY
PRINCIPLES AND PROCESSES

D1335812

CONTENTS

Chapter 42   Evolution in evidence 759

Chapter 43   The mechanism of evolution 783

Chapter 44   Major steps in evolution 808

Index 833

Acknowledgements 849

Recommended periodicals

The following periodicals contain articles which are often relevant to advanced level and comparable studies:

Biological Sciences Review

Published five times a year, this visually attractive magazine contains readable articles written by experts specially for A–level syllabuses, Scottish Highers and first year undergraduate courses.

New Scientist

Published weekly, this well known magazine contains a wide range of articles and topical features covering all aspects of science and technology. A good way of keeping up to date on a wide front.

Scientific American

This greatly respected magazine, published monthly, is aimed at university students and lecturers but certain articles are also useful at pre-university level. The articles are written by world authorities.

Nomenclature

Unfortunately biology is beset with ambiguous terms. Often different words are used for the same thing, and sometimes the same word is used for different things. In order to rectify this situation, the Institute of Biology has produced a booklet containing recommendations on nomenclature, units and symbols commonly encountered in school and college biology courses.

In *Biology, Principles and Processes* we have adopted with very few exceptions, the recommendations made in the above booklet.

Biological Nomenclature, Recommendations on Terms, Units and Symbols is available from the Institute of Biology, 20 Queensberry Place, London SW7 2DZ.

A MESSAGE FROM THE AUTHORS

In 1971, *Biology, A Functional Approach* was published as a protest against the then highly traditional syllabuses and their failure to recognise modern biology. The book caught on.

Since then syllabuses have changed radically and topics that were novel then are now in all advanced level and comparable syllabuses. However, a new problem has arisen, namely that syllabuses have become overloaded. Further, the introduction of modular syllabuses and options has tended to emphasise certain topics at the expense of others.

This book presents biology as a single integrated subject. We do not claim to have covered everything – only an encyclopaedia could do that. But by focusing on principles backed up by carefully selected examples we have tried to present a balanced overview of the subject which fulfils the requirements of current syllabuses and examination bodies.

We firmly believe in *learning through understanding*. For this reason we have endeavoured to write with maximum clarity. We hold the view that nothing in biology is too complex to be explained simply and clearly, yet accurately. Our aim has been to provide a readable text, uncluttered by unnecessary detail, which satisfies the enquiring mind and does not leave too many loose ends. In this regard we have been greatly aided by our publisher who has ensured that colour is used effectively and that illustrations are always visible with the relevant text.

As a scientific subject biology has had an impressive past, each discovery paving the way to the next. We have tried to convey something of this progression and the way it has led to the emergence of modern biology. It is an exciting story, particularly when seen in historical perspective. One can't help wondering, for example, what Mendel would think if he heard about the human genome project, or what Darwin would say if he saw Richard Dawkins' computer biomorphs.

We tell the story of biology in our main text, but there are numerous asides. Some of these are presented as 'boxes' which we hope will interest those readers who wish to delve into certain topics in greater depth. The boxes include a number of specially commissioned articles by guest authors who are specialists in their fields.

Today's syllabuses rightly emphasise technology and the social aspects of biology. We do not have special chapters on biotechnology and social biology. Instead, these are recurring themes which run through the whole book.

Each chapter ends with a summary, a set of questions to test knowledge and understanding, and some suggestions for further reading. The book does not include practical work or advice on preparing for examinations as we felt that these were best dealt with separately.

Bearing in mind the burden which students already have to carry, we have exercised considerable restraint in our suggestions for further reading, restricting these mainly to short books and relevant essays in *Biology, Advanced Topics*, the companion volume to *Biology, A Functional Approach*. We have not recommended many specialised articles since new ones are constantly being written. However, a list of suitable periodicals is given on page X and we hope that students will browse through these and use some of the articles to amplify the more general treatment given in our book.

This book has evolved from *Biology, A Functional Approach* and it retains many of the features of that book. But it is a new book with two new authors, and it has benefited from the help and advice of many friends and colleagues. Their names are listed on page IV. We thank them all for giving us their time and expertise. Any faults that remain are our responsibility and we hope that teachers and students will not hesitate to point these out to us.

Finally, it is a pleasure to thank the staff of Thomas Nelson and Sons Ltd, our publisher, for their unfailing courtesy and efficiency at all times.

Michael Roberts
Michael Reiss
Grace Monger

March 1993

GUEST AUTHORS OF BOXES

Patrick Bateson is Professor of Animal Behaviour and Provost of King's College, Cambridge. (Page 538.)

Sir Roy Calne is Professor of Surgery and a Fellow of Trinity Hall, Cambridge. (Page 426.)

Dr Jenny Chapman is a member of the British Antarctic Survey at Cambridge and also works in the Department of Earth Sciences at Oxford. (Page 648.)

Dr Arthur Cruickshank is a research palaeontologist who lectures at the Open University. (Page 777.)

Geoffrey Curtis is a Hearing Aid Consultant for Siemens Hearing Instruments Ltd. (Page 491.)

Dr Richard Dawkins, author of *The Selfish Gene* and other books on evolution, is a Fellow of New College and Reader in Zoology at Oxford. (Page 801.)

Dr Dianne Edwards is a palaeobotanist who lectures in the Department of Geology at the University of Wales, Cardiff. (Page 821.)

Glyn Evans is a Consultant Orthopaedic Surgeon at the Royal Isle of Wight County Hospital and a frequent writer on medical topics. (Pages 512 and 513.)

Jane Goodall founded the Gombe Stream Research Center in Tanzania where she has directed research on chimpanzees and baboons for many years. (Page 543.)

Tim Halliday, ethologist and artist, is Professor of Biology at the Open University. (page 830.)

Dr Geoffrey Harper, formerly a research zoologist and Head of Biology at Watford Grammar School, is now a freelance scientific writer and translator. (Page 76.)

Sir Andrew Huxley, former President of the Royal Society, was Master of Trinity College, Cambridge, until his retirement in 1990. (Page 444.)

Vivian James is Professor of Chemical Pathology and Chemical Endocrinology at St Mary's Hospital Medical School, London. (Page 566.)

Dr Tim King researched in botany and ecology at Oxford and is now Senior Master (Studies) Abingdon School. (Pages 393, 431, 460, 645, 661 and 737.)

Dr Patricia Kohn was a research physiologist and now works as an administrator in an *in vitro* fertilisation clinic in Sheffield. (Pages 359, 382, 407, 450, 457, 467, 469 and 497.)

Dr Peter Kohn is a Lecturer in the Department of Biomedical Science at the University of Sheffield. (Page 195.)

Dr John Land carried out botanical research at Nottingham and Oxford Universities before taking up a teaching post at Marlborough College. (Page 655.)

Dr Henry Leese is a Senior Lecturer in the Department of Biology at the University of York. (Page 629.)

Dr James Lovelock, originator of the Gaia hypothesis, is President of the Marine Biological Association of the United Kingdom. (Page 24.)

Dr Ann McNeil is Programme Manager on smoking education at the Health Education Authority, London. (Page 266.)

Dr James Parkyn is a physician whose career has spanned clinical medicine, research and teaching. (Page 244.)

Anthony Pinching is Professor of Immunology at St Bartholomew's Hospital Medical College, London. (Page 420.)

Anita Roddick founded *The Body Shop*, a cosmetics company whose products do not involve research on animals. (Page 8.)

Baroness Warnock, a philosopher, chaired the government committee on human embryo research and was until recently Mistress of Girton College, Cambridge. (Page 628.)

The nature of biology

The word **biology** comes from Greek: *bios* – 'life', *logos* – 'knowledge'. It is the study of life and living things – or **organisms** as we call them. It is an enormous subject, involving many other allied disciplines such as chemistry, physics, mathematics, geology and psychology. You have only to glance through the current issues of the British scientific journal *Nature*, or its American equivalent *Science*, to appreciate the extent and ramifications of biology. Well over a million original papers are published in the biological (including medical) sciences every year, ranging from descriptions of new species to analyses of complex chemical reactions in organisms (figure 1.1). The sheer volume of information grows at a rate that makes it impossible for any one person to keep up with it all.

With such a flow of information from research laboratories, it is difficult to gain a broad overview of the subject which is essential for understanding the principles. It is therefore the *principles* that we stress in our book. But one cannot appreciate the principles without having some familiarity with the facts on which they are based. The facts must come first, just as the parts of a jigsaw come before the completed picture.

Thankfully, there is no need to know all the facts, only those that are relevant and important. A skill which every student has to acquire is the ability to distinguish between the important and less important facts. In this book we try to help you with this by looking at selected facts within a framework of principles.

There are many ways of approaching biology. For example, one might approach it through the structure of organisms, or perhaps through the environment. Ours is a functional approach, having as a pervading theme the way biological systems work. That is why we have called our book 'Biology – Principles and *Processes*'.

Figure 1.1 Over one million original papers are published in the biological and medical sciences every year. The picture shows the Scientific Periodicals Library at Cambridge University. In 1992 this library was taking 2943 journals in 17 languages from over 50 countries.

The branches of biology

Traditionally biology has been divided into **zoology**, the study of animals, and **botany**, the study of plants. A third subdivision, **microbiology**, embraces a vast assortment of microscopic organisms (micro-organisms) most of which are neither animals nor plants. Within microbiology come such subjects as **bacteriology**, the study of bacteria, and **virology**, the study of viruses.

In the nineteenth and early twentieth centuries biologists were mainly concerned with describing the structure, or **anatomy**, of animals and plants, together with their classification (**taxonomy**). Anatomical studies included the microscopic structure of organs and tissues – **histology** as it is called. Similar descriptive studies were carried out on the stages through which animals developed – **embryology**. In more recent times there has been a shift of interest towards the way organisms function, resulting in the growth of animal and plant **physiology**. Embryological studies have become more functional too as scientists have attempted to discover the mechanisms which direct development. This important area of biology is called **developmental biology**.

In the last 60 years or so, these functional studies have become increasingly chemical, employing the talents of chemists as well as biologists. The first professorship of **biochemistry** in Britain was established at Liverpool University in 1902. London followed in 1912, and Cambridge in 1914. Now biochemistry is very much a subject in its own right with university departments all over the world.

Figure 1.2 The settings are different, but these two biologists share the same basic purpose, to understand life and living organisms.

A A technician is examining a cell harvester. This device is essentially a filter which is used to separate cells from the medium in which they are suspended. Up to 48 samples may be filtered simultaneously. The blue colour in the delivery tubes is caused by a dye that is used to check the cells for viability by only staining dead cells.

B A blue-breasted kingfisher is being examined by Dr Mike Harrison. The ringing of birds enables their movements and habits to be studied and this is important in understanding the environment and conservation of species.

Biochemical studies have shown us that in many respects the traditional division of biology into botany and zoology is an artificial one. Animals and plants – indeed all organisms – are made of **cells**. Research on cells, the study of **cytology** or **cell biology**, has made it clear that in both their structure and functioning all cells have much in common. This similarity is also seen in the way an organism's characteristics are passed on to its offspring, the study of **heredity** or **genetics**.

Genetics is derived from the word **gene**, the term used to describe the physical entities by which inherited characteristics are transmitted from parents to offspring. Research on the structure and properties of molecules in cells has helped us to understand what genes consist of and how they exert their action. This is a relatively new field, in which spectacular advances have been made in recent years. It is known as **molecular biology** and, like biochemistry, is now an established subject in its own right.

So, looking back, there has been a gradual shift of interest from anatomical description of the whole organism to functional studies of cells and their constituent molecules. This does not mean that all modern biologists are engaged in cellular or molecular research. The older, more traditional studies are still pursued and have an important part to play in elucidating the nature of life and living organisms (figure 1.2).

From the earliest times people have been fascinated by the ways and habits of animals and plants – natural history as one would call it. These pursuits are often carried out by enthusiastic amateurs, and they can provide very useful information. At the professional level, such studies fall into two main categories: **behaviour** and **ecology**.

At one time behaviour studies consisted of lengthy descriptions of the activities and responses of various animals, particularly birds. Today behaviour, or **ethology** as it is called, is much more analytical and experimental, involving increasingly the techniques of nerve physiology.

Ecological studies are important partly because they affect the future of the human race, but also because all forms of life have a right to live in a stable and healthy world. Our hopes of reducing global pollution and of sustaining the environment and the world's natural resources will depend on advances in this field. Scientists have taken these matters seriously for years; now politicians are beginning to do so. Ecological studies are demonstrating how humans can derive material benefits from the environment without destroying it: **conservation** as opposed to **exploitation**.

Levels of organisation

This brief survey of the different branches of biology will have convinced you that biology is a diverse subject, broad in scope and varied in approach. The reason is that living organisms can be studied at different levels of organisation (figure 1.3). Thus a molecular biologist studies the organism at the level of its component molecules, a cell biologist at the level of its cells, and a physiologist at the level of its tissues and organs. In contrast, an ecologist studies organisms at the level of populations and communities.

Recognition of these levels of organisation have led scientists and philosophers to look at organisms in two different ways. At one extreme the organism is regarded as a machine made up of a collection of parts – organs, molecules and so on. This is a **mechanistic approach** and it involves **reductionism**, the idea that an organism can be understood by *reducing* it to its component parts. At the other extreme the organism is regarded as having special qualities which make it more than the sum of its parts and which can only be understood by considering the whole organism. This is called the **holistic approach** from the greek word *holos*, 'whole'.

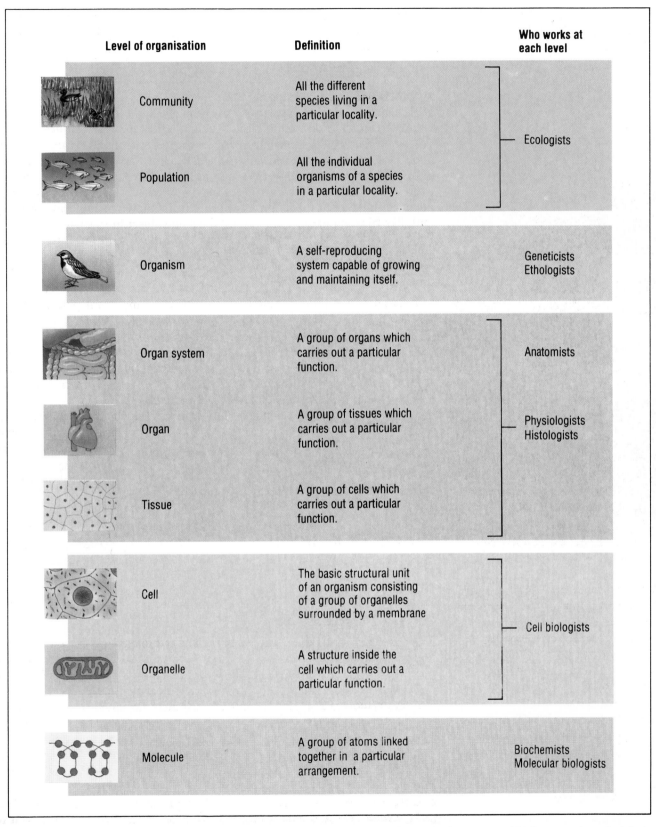

Level of organisation	Definition	Who works at each level
Community	All the different species living in a particular locality.	Ecologists
Population	All the individual organisms of a species in a particular locality.	
Organism	A self-reproducing system capable of growing and maintaining itself.	Geneticists Ethologists
Organ system	A group of organs which carries out a particular function.	Anatomists
Organ	A group of tissues which carries out a particular function.	Physiologists Histologists
Tissue	A group of cells which carries out a particular function.	
Cell	The basic structural unit of an organism consisting of a group of organelles surrounded by a membrane	Cell biologists
Organelle	A structure inside the cell which carries out a particular function.	
Molecule	A group of atoms linked together in a particular arrangement.	Biochemists Molecular biologists

Figure 1.3 The different levels of organisation in biology and who works at each level. The distinctions are not rigid. For example, a physiologist may work on individual cells as well as on tissues and organs, and a geneticist may work on populations as well as on individual organisms. Occasionally an ecologist may venture into the realms of cell biology or biochemistry if the problem being investigated takes a turn in that direction. Can you think of any circumstances in which that might happen?

Methods of enquiry in biology

Whatever level of organisation a biologist is concerned with, all biologists are scientists and, as such, use several well recognised methods in carrying out their investigations. The main methods are these:

- **Observation and description**

Observing and describing natural phenomena is the basis of all biological enquiry from cells to communities. Technological aids are frequently used. For example, the electron microscope has made it possible to describe in great detail the structures found inside cells, and X-ray crystallography has been used to establish the structure of individual molecules.

- **Testing hypotheses by experiment**

Hypotheses, arising from observations, may be tested by controlled experiments in which certain variables are manipulated and others kept constant. This is how, for example, you would investigate the conditions needed for a biological process such as photosynthesis, or the cause of a particular disease.

- **Making correlations**

When experimentation is not feasible, an attempt may be made to find out if two phenomena are in some way connected, i.e. correlated. For example, you might want to see if there is a correlation between smoking and lung cancer. In such investigations statistical analysis is used to evaluate the data.

Using animals in research

The use of animals in research has been an integral part of biology for years. Is it justified? In this box, and the one by Anita Roddick on page 8, this question is addressed.

It is important to realise that there are many types of research that use animals. At one extreme are tests carried out for relatively minor advances of knowledge. One example is the Draize eye test on rabbits, a test which has been widely used since its introduction in 1944. It is usually carried out on albino rabbits because their large eyes don't produce tears and cannot wash the substance away. The rabbits are held in a harness which immobilises them and prevents them from rubbing their eyes with their paws. The substance, such as a new shampoo, is then introduced into one of their eyes and the effects are noted for up to seven days. Pain relief is usually not provided. Effects can include redness, swelling, opacity, ulceration and blindness.

At the other extreme is the testing of new human vaccines or drugs. Here the idea is to study the effects of the vaccine or drug on animals before trials are made on human volunteers. Chimpanzees are sometimes used in such tests because they are our closest relatives and have a physiology very similar to ours.

Supporters of animal research point out that many of the great advances in biomedical knowledge made over the past 40 years have relied on the use of animals. Countless people owe their lives and good health to these studies. To test potential new drugs on human volunteers without first studying their effects on experimental animals would, it is argued, be unethical.

Those opposed to the use of animals in research point out that much research on animals is trivial, such as testing new cosmetics. They also point out that some laboratories do pure research in which animals are caused stress, for instance by submitting them to painful electric shocks. Advocates of a complete ban on the use of animals in research usually argue that to use animals in this way is immoral. What right have we to experiment on animals, whatever the benefits?

Although the two sides may seem poles apart, there is one bit of good news. The last ten years have seen huge advances in cell and tissue culture techniques. This means that procedures that once required the use of animals can now be carried out on laboratory cultures of mammalian cells. Partly as a result of this, the total number of experiments conducted on animals in Great Britain fell from 5 600 000 in 1971, when it reached a peak, to 3 480 000 in 1988.

What is your opinion on the use of animals in research? Do you hold an extreme view or do you take a position somewhere in between? Argue your case.

The characteristics of living organisms

What are the characteristics of living organisms that distinguish them from non-living matter? They are as follows:

- **Reproduction**

Reproduction, the production of new individuals from pre-existing ones, is a basic feature of all living organisms. It takes place in different ways, but it always involves certain giant molecules (macromolecules) producing copies of themselves, in other words **replicating**. Molecular biologists have identified and characterised these molecules. They are **nucleic acids**, the main one being **deoxyribonucleic acid (DNA)**. Encoded in this complex molecule are the instructions required by the cells for all their activities and therefore ultimately for the whole organism. In certain viruses a similar nucleic acid called **ribonucleic acid (RNA)** is used instead of DNA.

- **Respiration**

Respiration, the controlled transfer of energy in living organisms, is essential for life. Everything an organism does is dependent on chemical processes which are ultimately energy-consuming. Energy, the capacity to do work, is obtained by the organism from molecules such as glucose. This does not happen in a single reaction. Rather, the molecules are gradually dismantled, small amounts of energy being transferred at various stages of the process. The energy is used to synthesise molecules of a substance called **adenosine triphosphate (ATP)**. The energy contained in ATP is then used to power a wide range of biochemical processes. ATP is of universal occurrence in living organisms and is itself a basic feature of life.

- **Nutrition**

The molecules which living organisms use as their source of energy are obtained from food in the process of feeding or **nutrition**. Food also provides substances needed for other purposes such as growth, maintenance and repair.

There are two fundamentally different methods of nutrition. Animals and certain other organisms take in ready-made organic substances (**heterotrophic nutrition**). Other organisms, notably plants, take in simple inorganic substances which they then build up into complex organic substances (**autotrophic nutrition**). The main type of autotrophic nutrition is **photosynthesis** in which sunlight is the source of energy.

- **Excretion**

The chemical reactions that occur in organisms result in the formation of waste products, often toxic, which must be disposed of in some way. The disposing of these waste products is what is meant by **excretion**. Usually they are eliminated from the organism. However, plants generally retain their excretory waste, storing it in a harmless form.

- **Growth**

New individuals, produced by reproduction, grow. Of course some inanimate objects grow too – crystals, for example – but the mechanism is different. A crystal grows by new matter being added at the surface. An organism grows from within by taking in substances from outside and incorporating them into its internal structure. This is called **assimilation**. In organisms growth is kept under control so that it occurs in the right places and at the right time.

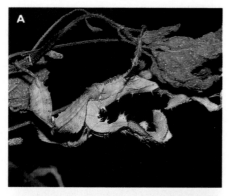

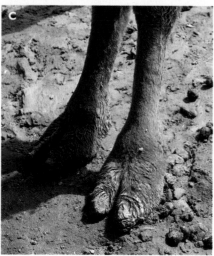

Figure 1.4 Three examples of adaptation in animals.

A The prickly stick insect *Exatosoma tiaratum*, found in Australia, is active at night but during the day it remains stationary in imitation of the twigs and leaves which it closely resembles.

B The Gaboon viper *Bitis gabonica*, characterised by a flattened body, long fangs and extremely poisonous venom, is seen here disguised against a pile of leaves.

C The splayed-out foot of the camel prevents the foot sinking into the soft sand. This is just one of a large number of adaptions which camels possess for living in the desert.

• **Responsiveness**

It is characteristic of living organisms that they react to changes in their surroundings. The changes are called **stimuli** (singular: stimulus) and the reactions are called **responses**. Responses evoked by stimuli range from rapid ones like the withdrawal of one's hand from a hot object, to much slower ones like the growth of a plant towards light.

Although plants tend to respond slowly to stimuli, there are some interesting exceptions: insectivorous plants such as the one in figure 16.13 on page 274 respond very quickly to touch, as do the leaves of the sensitive plant *Mimosa pudica*.

Even seemingly simple organisms respond to stimuli. For instance, single-celled organisms such as *Amoeba* and *Paramecium* move away from noxious substances in their environment.

• **Movement**

Responding to stimuli usually means moving in some way, and this is another characteristic of living organisms. Even plants, which at first appear to be an exception, display movement within their cells. For example, chloroplasts can sometimes be seen circulating round the cells of the Canadian pondweed *Elodea*. This kind of movement cannot be explained by purely physical forces such as diffusion. It is an active, energy-requiring process arising from within the cells.

Evolution, natural selection and variation

The seven characteristics listed above are those traditionally ascribed to living organisms. However, the list leaves out an important feature of living organisms, namely their potential to change or **evolve** over generations. Of course, non-living things change too, but not by the same mechanism. The mechanism by which living organisms evolve is **natural selection**.

We shall have more to say about natural selection later in the book, but for the moment we should note that it is unique to living organisms and may therefore be included as one of their basic characteristics. We shall see that natural selection is made possible by **genetic variation**, and this too should be regarded as a characteristic of living organisms.

The basis of genetic variation and evolution is DNA, and it is therefore not surprising that DNA has been described as the molecule of life.

Some basic concepts

As one looks at organisms, one is struck by the way their structure and physiology seem to suit them for living in their particular environments. We say the organism is **adapted** to its environment. Figure 1.4 shows some particularly striking examples of adaptation, but in fact every species is adapted to its environment to a degree: it must be to survive.

In what ways need an organism be adapted? It must be adapted in such a way that it can defend itself from attack by other organisms, compete successfully for food and other essentials, respond appropriately to changes in its environment, and live long enough to reproduce its kind. In short, the organism must be able to maintain all those processes which we listed earlier as fundamental to living organisms.

We could add one further aspect of adaptation. It must ensure that the organism's cells always experience those conditions which permit efficient functioning. This is achieved by a wide range of mechanisms which together keep the physical and chemical conditions inside the organism constant. This is called **homeostasis**, and it will come up repeatedly in this book.

From the principle of adaptation a further principle arises, namely that the structure of an organism and its component parts are closely related to the functions which they perform. Guts, kidneys, gills, lungs, stems and leaves all demonstrate this close relationship between structure and function (see figure 1.5 for example). This concept is not restricted to the level of whole organisms and organs; it also applies to individual cells and molecules, as we shall see in later chapters.

Adaptation and the close relationship between structure and function can be explained by a further concept: **evolution**. It is generally believed that present-day species have arisen by a process of gradual evolution from pre-existing forms that lived in the past, this being achieved by natural selection.

The theory of evolution by natural selection originated with Charles Darwin and Alfred Russel Wallace in the middle of the nineteenth century. Today it forms the backbone of biology: it makes sense of the discoveries that have been made, and it gives a direction to research. This is not to say that everyone believes in it unquestioningly. Indeed Darwinism comes under attack quite often, sometimes by biologists themselves, and its detailed claims are constantly under review. Nevertheless, its influence is tremendous and it is difficult to imagine biology without it.

Applied biology

Applied biology is the application of the biological sciences to human affairs. Thus defined, applied biology embraces the medical and veterinary sciences, agriculture and horticulture.

For thousands of years micro-organisms have been used for manufacturing bread and alcoholic drinks such as beer and wine. The use of micro-organisms for the benefit of humans is part of **biotechnology**. Nowadays this term has taken on a wider meaning and embraces all aspects of applied biology that have a technological slant.

Figure 1.5 The leaf of the giant water lily of the Amazon, *Victoria amazonica*, illustrates the close relationship between structure and function. The leaves have a diameter of up to 2 metres. The vertical margin round the edge of the large floating leaf, seen in the top picture, prevents flooding over the surface. The thick fibrous ribs on the underside of the leaf, seen in the lower picture, prevent the leaf from collapsing and hold it out flat, exposing it to the sun and maximising photosynthesis. Reminiscent of fan vaulting, this strong construction is said to have been the inspiration for the design of the roof of the Crystal Palace in London. The left hand picture shows a young leaf unfolding on the surface of the water.

Today biotechnology is a rapidly growing branch of industry. Two developments in particular have made this possible. One is the use of enzymes – organic catalysts which speed up chemical reactions in living organisms. Enzymes can be extracted from micro-organisms, purified and then used in a wide range of manufacturing processes. The second development that has given impetus to biotechnology is our ability to manipulate an organism's genes so that the organism produces something useful for us. This is called **genetic engineering** and it is bringing about a revolution in the way many biologically important substances are manufactured.

Advances in applied science give us power – power to control the environment and power to improve the quality of human life. But power can be misused. We see evidence of the misuse of power in pollution, exploitation of our natural resources, and destruction of the environment. At one time these were thought of as essentially local phenomena, but in recent years it has become apparent that they are happening on a global scale. The depletion of the ozone layer, the greenhouse effect and acid rain are three particularly pressing examples. One reason for studying biology is to understand how an ever-expanding human population can survive on this planet without irreparably harming the very environment that gives us life.

Animal testing in the cosmetics industry

Guest author Anita Roddick explains how the use of animals for testing products in the cosmetics industry can be avoided.

'The question is not, can they reason? Nor, can they talk? But, can they suffer?'

That question, from the eighteenth century philosopher Jeremy Bentham, has become a cornerstone of The Body Shop canon. The 'issue' of testing our products on animals – with the risk of inflicting immeasurable suffering on thousands of living creatures – was never an issue with me. It was simply inconceivable, and I never doubted that there would be thousands of people who felt the same. All they needed was to have Bentham's question made more specific.

Testing for medical or pharmaceutical purposes is beyond The Body Shop's terms of reference as a company. We're in the business of making and selling products that cleanse, polish and protect the skin and hair. As someone else engaged in a similar line of work once said,

'We're not talking about a cure for cancer here.' That's why I think there's an inherent obscenity in testing something as irrelevant as a moisture cream on an animal. The governing ethic of the female gender is tied to the nurture of life. But the cosmetic industry, which purports to feed the well-being of women, has been painfully slow to incorporate that ethic into its own code of behaviour.

We object to animal tests in the cosmetic industry on four grounds: they're cruel, irrelevant, unreliable and unnecessary. Anyone else who is interested in making a success of a 'cruelty-free' business could do worse than use those objections to frame their own response.

Cruelty is obviously the most emotional accusation, the one that accounts for the intense public feeling on the question of animal tests in the cosmetic industry (85 per cent of respondents in one MORI poll felt products should not be tested on animals). The other charges make a no less pointed appeal to pure logic.

In the cosmetic industry, animal testing is irrelevant because intensive database examinations of the structure, properties and

suitability of new ingredients and formulae provide safety evaluations for each product. In other words, you know what to expect from a product without testing it on a living organism. Far from clarifying a problem, animal testing may actually obscure it. Our reactions are different from a rabbit's or a guinea pig's. After all, the results of animal testing suggested that thalidomide was safe and cleared it for human use. So results can be unreliable.

And now the tests themselves are unnecessary. Alternatives exist: cell culture tests, computer simulations, tests on human volunteers. The Body Shop has used the common sense accumulated through thousands of years of cosmetic use in societies all over the world to formulate some of its most successful products.

So in the end our ingredients actually *have* been thoroughly tested on animals – us, the animals for whom these products were intended in the first place. And that seems to me to fit perfectly within the natural order.

Do you think Anita Roddick's argument makes sound scientific and commercial sense?

Enjoying science

Here, Sir Hans Krebs, one of the foremost biochemists of the twentieth century, talks about his retirement – or rather his non-retirement, because he continued his scientific research until the end of his life.

In recent years I have sometimes been asked, Why do you carry on with work? Why are you not enjoying yourself? Why are you not now doing all the things you wanted to do earlier in life and could not because you were too busy? I find such questions somewhat irritating. After all, there is work and work. I suspect that many who do ask such questions have never experienced the profound enjoyment one can derive from creative work – enjoyment, fun and intellectual satisfaction. I am one of those lucky people who has always derived deep, lasting satisfaction and pleasure from his work. So I am anxious to carry on as long as I feel my work is still creative and as long as I am permitted to do so.

One of my questioners, knowing that I enjoy music, once argued that I should use the opportunity given by retirement to listen to more and more music. He is a musician and believes there could be no greater pleasure for a music-lover than to listen to good music. I think this view is quite wrong. Even for music-lovers there can be one pleasure still greater – the creating of music. I believe that all artists carry on 'working' as long as they are able to do so. Noel Coward once said, 'Work is fun. There is no fun like work.'

(From *Reminiscences and Reflections* by Hans Krebs in collaboration with Anne Martin, Oxford University Press, 1981)

Summary

1 **Biology**, the study of life and living organisms, is divided into numerous subjects which include **zoology, botany, microbiology, taxonomy, anatomy, physiology, biochemistry, cytology** (cell biology), **heredity** (genetics), **molecular biology, behaviour** (ethology) and **ecology**.

2 Living organisms can be studied at different **levels of organisation**, e.g. the molecular, cellular, organ, organism and population levels.

3 Characteristics shared by all living organisms are:

- **reproduction** (involving the replication of DNA),
- **respiration** (with the use of ATP for transferring energy),
- **nutrition**,
- **excretion**,
- **growth** by assimilation,
- **responsiveness**,
- **movement**.

4 The main methods used in biological investigations are **observation, experimentation** and **correlation**.

5 Basic biological concepts include **survival, adaptation, homeostasis** and **evolution**.

6 **Applied biology** includes **agriculture** and **medicine**. **Biotechnology** is of growing importance in society.

Review questions

1 Why is it useful to identify the features which are characteristic of all living organisms? What further features might be added to the list on pages 5 and 6?

2 Try to define the word 'life'. Does this present any difficulties?

3 To what extent does progress in biology depend on making hypotheses? Suggest some areas of biology where hypothesis-making is relatively unimportant.

4 Look at the photographs in figure 1.4 and select one interesting phenomenon which you can observe. Put forward a hypothesis to explain the phenomenon, and describe how you would test it.

5 Comment on the role of each of the following in biological research: intuition, luck, manual dexterity, numeracy, persistence.

6 Darwinian evolution is the backbone of biology. Do you think it is desirable for a scientific subject such as biology to be so influenced by a single idea?

7 What is biotechnology and why is it important? Can you think of any dangers that it may have?

8 Explain with examples what is meant by adaptation.

9 Give an example of the close relationship between structure and function in biology.

10 What is meant by the term homeostasis?

Further reading

You will find short, readable accounts of the aims and methods of science in *The Art of Scientific Investigation* by W.I.B. Beveridge (Heinemann, 1968) and in *The Common Sense of Science* by J. Bronowski (Heinemann, 1979).

Peter Medawar in his little book *The Limits of Science* (Oxford, 1984) discusses what science can and cannot do.

For an advanced but succinct treatment of experimentation and statistical methods, *Investigation by Experiment* by O.V.S. Heath (Arnold, 1970) is recommended.

The difficulty of defining life, the scientific method and viruses is discussed further in *Biology, Advanced Topics*.

Part I

*E*cology is the study of how organisms interact with each other and with other components of their environment. The word 'ecology' comes from the Greek words *oikos*, meaning 'home' and *logos* meaning 'study' so an ecologist literally studies the homes of organisms.

Ecology takes account of all aspects of an organism's biology. You will find therefore that it keeps coming up throughout this book. Nevertheless, certain topics fall into the subject that is traditionally labelled ecology and it is those that we address in Part I.

We start with the places which organisms inhabit and the species which live in them. We then see how different species interact with each other to give rise to complex communities. The effect of humans on such communities is considered, and this is followed by a study of populations and the way different species associate with each other.

One of the conclusions to emerge from ecological studies is that the number and variety of species inhabiting our planet is immense. In the last two chapters we survey the various forms of life and see how they are classified.

Photograph: The Cascade Mountains in Washington State, USA.

CHAPTER 2 | Biomes to microhabitats

As far as is known, our planet is the only one on which life exists. In this chapter we shall first look at the distribution of organisms around the globe. We will then look in more detail at what is meant by the environment of an organism, paying particular attention to the importance of soil for terrestrial organisms.

The biosphere

If you look at the Earth from space, you can see the blue of the oceans, the white of the clouds and the green and brown of the land (figure 2.1). The part of the Earth and its atmosphere that is inhabited by living things is called the **biosphere**. We can subdivide the biosphere into large areas which, though separate spatially, are linked by a common type of vegetation. These areas are called **biomes**.

Ecologists argue about how many different biomes there are. To some extent it is a matter of opinion and depends on whether you want to combine the world's **flora** (plants) and **fauna** (animals) into a few very large categories or split them into a large number of smaller categories. In any event it is convenient to look at **terrestrial biomes** separately from **aquatic biomes**, as different environmental variables are important for each.

Terrestrial biomes

The two most important environmental variables for life on land are rainfall and temperature. Figure 2.2 shows how much rain falls in different parts of the world. You can see how desert areas such as the Sahara and Central Australia receive little rain, while Central America and Western Central Africa are much wetter. Figure 2.3 shows how hot it is in different parts of the world. Separate diagrams are shown for summer and winter. As you would expect, it gets hotter towards the tropics and colder towards

Figure 2.1 The Earth from space. Meteostat satellite images such as these can reveal changing patterns of land use, for instance loss of forests through burning.

Figure 2.2 Average rainfall in a year in different parts of the world.

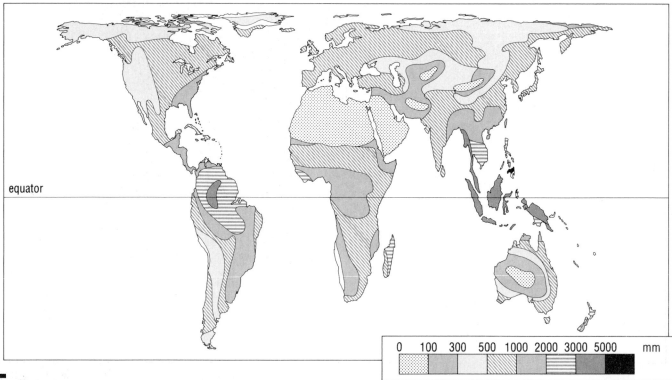

equator

0 100 300 500 1000 2000 3000 5000 mm

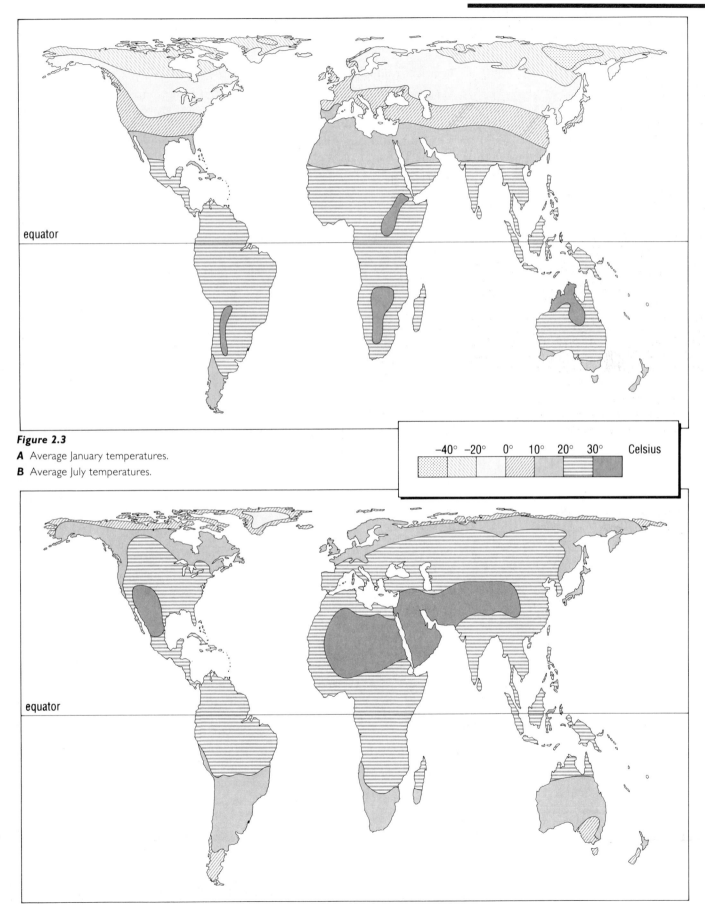

Figure 2.3

A Average January temperatures.

B Average July temperatures.

| −40° | −20° | 0° | 10° | 20° | 30° | Celsius |

the poles. Armed with this information, we can now look at the major terrestrial biomes (figure 2.4).

Tropical rain forest

Tropical rain forests are found wherever it is hot and wet throughout the year. Mean monthly temperatures usually lie between 24 and 28°C and frosts are unknown. The annual rainfall is between about 2000 and 3000 mm and rain falls throughout the year; there is no dry season. This climate is found in South-East Asia, Western Central Africa, the Amazon basin, Indonesia and parts of Australia.

Figure 2.4 The world's major terrestrial biomes. Boreal forest is dominated by evergreen conifers. Schlerophyll vegetation consists of small trees and shrubs with small thick leaves.

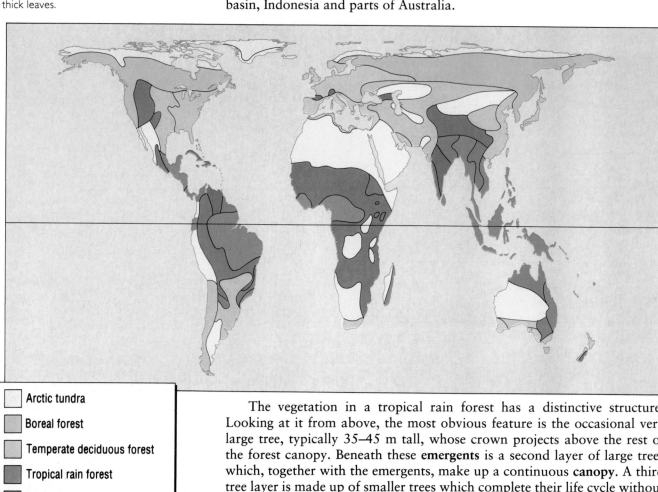

Arctic tundra

Boreal forest

Temperate deciduous forest

Tropical rain forest

Tropical seasonal forest

Temperate grassland

Tropical grassland and scrub

Desert

Broad-leaved sclerophyll

Mountain

The vegetation in a tropical rain forest has a distinctive structure. Looking at it from above, the most obvious feature is the occasional very large tree, typically 35–45 m tall, whose crown projects above the rest of the forest canopy. Beneath these **emergents** is a second layer of large trees which, together with the emergents, make up a continuous **canopy**. A third tree layer is made up of smaller trees which complete their life cycle without ever reaching the main canopy. Still nearer the ground are young trees, palms, vines and herbs. By the time sunlight reaches the forest floor, most of it has already been intercepted so that it is dark with relatively sparse vegetation.

Many organisms live in the canopy. This is one reason why we know so little of the ecology of tropical rain forests. Only recently have ecologists started to climb the trees or use balloons to investigate the canopy, though early in the twentieth century one ingenious botanist used monkeys to collect specimens for him. Once in the canopy, the contrast with the dark forest floor is striking. Here all is colour and noise. Beautiful **epiphytic** orchids grow on the branches of the trees. Colourful insects and birds live here without ever descending to the ground. They feed on the copious flowers and fruits available throughout the year. These flowers and fruits are produced by an impressive variety of trees – a single hectare of tropical rain forest may contain over 100 different tree species!

The leaves of the trees tend to be tough and impossible for most animals to digest. The most successful leaf-eaters in Central and tropical South America are sloths (figure 2.5). A sloth's entire life is organised around eating large quantities of tough leaves. Because their food is so difficult to digest, sloths have huge stomachs which hold cellulose-digesting bacteria. Food may spend up to a month in the stomach before digestion is complete. It takes a sloth so long to obtain nourishment from its food that it has to conserve as much energy as possible. Although sloths are mammals, their body temperature fluctuates, falling several degrees Celsius at night. They also conserve energy by moving very slowly. Consequently they cannot run away from predators. Instead they rely on **camouflage**. Camouflage is provided by cyanobacteria which live in their fur. These organisms give a greenish tinge to the fur and so help the sloths to blend into their background.

Tropical rain forests contain more species than any of the world's other biomes. With their hot, moist climate and great diversity of living organisms, they are extremely productive. However, their soils are generally nutrient poor. This is probably because decomposition occurs very quickly and any available minerals are rapidly taken up by the many plants.

One result of the soil being nutrient poor is that if the trees are cut down and removed or burnt, as often happens to provide agricultural land, the resulting soil is only suitable for a few year's farming. After this, the soil becomes so poor that the land has to be abandoned. In Central America, large areas of tropical rainforest are cut down every year to provide space for cattle ranching, crop-growing and industry. Many of the cattle are subsequently made into beefburgers and sold in fast-food outlets.

Figure 2.5 Two-toed sloth in a Brazilian rain forest. Sloths are adapted for feeding on the leaves of the trees.

Temperate deciduous forest

The north temperate zone lies between the tropic of Cancer and the Arctic Circle. The south temperate zone lies between the tropic of Capricorn and the Antarctic Circle. In these two zones, **temperate deciduous forest** may be found. This type of forest is dominated by broad-leaved trees that lose their leaves in winter. The biome experiences cold winters, warm summers and intermittent rain throughout the year with a peak in summer.

Among the major types of temperate deciduous forest found in Europe are those dominated by lime, those by oak and hazel, those by birch and those by beech (figure 2.6). The location of each type of forest depends on the climate and, to a lesser extent, the soil.

Until the dawn of agriculture, huge areas of temperate deciduous forest existed. However, over the last few thousand years, these forests have been extensively cleared for cultivation and pasture. Those that remain have almost always, at some time in their past, been managed by people for their wood and other products. Indeed, few undisturbed examples of this biome are to be found anywhere. We will look at one particular example of this biome in more detail later (see page 26).

Tundra

Tundra occurs at low altitudes and is characterised by the absence of trees and permanently frozen subsoil. True tundra is found in northern Canada, northern Asia and parts of northern Europe. Here it is impossible for trees to grow because the growing season is too short and the soil is too unstable. For much of the year the soil is frozen. Only in summer does the surface thaw. Beneath the surface is soil with water that never melts. This is called **permafrost**.

Figure 2.6 Mature beech wood. Beech trees intercept so much sunlight that very little reaches the ground. As a result, few plants can grow at ground level in a beech wood.

Figure 2.7 Reindeer grazing on lichens beneath the snow.

For much of the year the tundra appears almost lifeless. Then, during the brief growing season, which may last only six weeks, many plants produce spectacular flowers which attract insects for pollination. The Arctic poppy has flowers which rotate during the day, following the sun. The petals are shaped so as to focus the rays of the sun on to the stigma and stamens. Here insects gather, attracted by the warmth. In the process, the insects transfer pollen from one plant to another and so bring about cross-pollination.

The most abundant large herbivores of this biome are reindeer, which graze on lichens (figure 2.7). Lemmings are also common. Contrary to popular belief, lemmings do not commit mass suicide by flinging themselves into the sea. What happens is that every three to four years their numbers increase to the point at which overcrowding forces large numbers of them to disperse to less populated areas. During this dispersal lemmings will indeed jump into rivers and lakes, but they have exceptionally good long-distance vision and will only jump into water if they can see land at the other side. Once in water they are surprisingly good swimmers and rarely drown.

Tundra-like vegetation is found high up on mountains throughout the world. Again, the short growing season and unstable soil prevent trees from growing. However, there are differences between the climate of the true tundra and that found on mountains. For one thing, at the poles there are times of the year when the sun never rises, and times when it never sets. Another difference is that more rain and snow tend to fall on mountains than in the tundra. These climatic differences affect the organisms found in each area.

Desert

Deserts are found throughout the world. Some famous ones are the Sahara of northern Africa, the Kalahari of southern Africa, the Gobi of Central Asia and the Atacama of Peru and Chile. Rain is scarce – usually less than 50 mm a year. Moreover, what little rain there is falls irregularly throughout the year. Some deserts may get no rain for years, only suddenly to receive a downpour of several centimetres within a few hours.

To survive in a desert, organisms have to be able to take advantage of the sudden rains (figure 2.8). Many of the smaller desert plants survive as seeds. When it rains heavily, they germinate, mature, flower and produce seeds within as little as two weeks. Other plants are perennials, surviving the dry periods in the vegetative state. Some of them, such as the cacti of America and the euphorbias of Africa, are succulents, storing water and possessing features that minimise water loss. They have thick cuticles, a very low surface-volume ratio and sunken stomata which only open at night (see page 304). Some desert perennials survive the long periods of drought as underground bulbs or corms. They produce their leaves only when it rains.

Animals too are faced with the problem of water shortage, but there are also other difficulties with living in a desert. Although it may be very hot during the day, the nights can be surprisingly cold as cloudless skies allow the daytime heat to radiate from the ground. Another difficulty is that sand is hardly an ideal soil. Larger animals need to expend quite a bit of energy in walking over it, while smaller ones find it difficult to maintain burrows.

Some of the physiological adaptations shown by animals to the problems of desert life are remarkable. For example, certain frogs can survive for years without water by burying themselves deep into the sand. When the rains eventually come they dig themselves out, mate and lay their

Figure 2.8 The Namibian desert just days after the rains had come. Notice the profusion of camelthorn flowers. Two days after this photograph had been taken, the flowers had gone and the plants were producing seeds.

eggs in shallow puddles. Here the tadpoles grow very quickly, metamorphosing into adults before the puddles disappear.

Aquatic biomes

The most important variables that operate in aquatic biomes are the salinity, nutrient availability, depth of the water and how permanent it is. Imagine, at one extreme, a puddle in a field. Here the water is not salty. It is shallow and temporary and may well be rich in nutrients. At the other extreme, consider the deep ocean. Here conditions are constant throughout the year. The water is salty, dark, cold and nutrient poor. With these extremes in mind, we shall look at two contrasting aquatic biomes.

Lakes and ponds

The crucial factors that determine the ecology of **lakes** and **ponds** are their size and nutrient content. Small ponds may dry up. This has a profound effect on their ecology. Organisms living in such ponds must be able to survive dry periods in some sort of resting stage. Such organisms tend to be small and they complete their life cycle within a few months or even weeks. For this reason fish are not usually found in temporary ponds. But insects and crustaceans are abundant. Indeed, certain crustaceans such as *Chirocephalus*, the fairy shrimp, actually *require* a period of drought to complete their life cycles.

An important feature of most lakes is that the water of the lake is divided into strata (layers) which tend not to mix. Figure 2.9 shows **thermal stratification** in Gull Lake, Michigan, USA. In the summer the top few metres of the lake are at a temperature of 20 to 24°C, a pleasant temperature for swimming. However, at a depth of 20 m, the temperature may be 15 degrees colder than this. Most humans would die from hypothermia within an hour of being in water this cold. In winter the reverse happens; the surface of the lake is colder than lower down. Stratification can be understood if one remembers that water is densest at 4°C. Consequently, water that is either cooler or warmer than this will rise.

Because the surface and deeper waters of a lake may remain distinct for much of the year, they can differ not only in temperature but also in nutrient concentration and oxygen saturation. This means that even a quite shallow lake can provide places for organisms with very different ecological requirements.

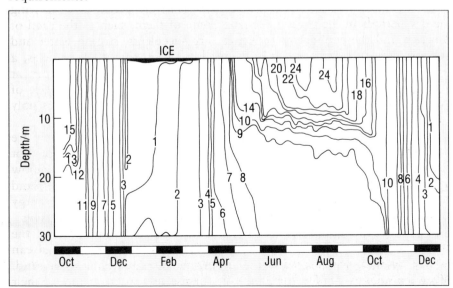

Figure 2.9 Depth-time diagram showing thermal stratification in Gull Lake, Michigan, USA at different times of the year. The temperatures are in degrees Celsius.

The most important environmental variable in permanent freshwater is the amount of nutrients available. Paradoxically, lakes which are low in phosphates and nitrates (**oligotrophic** lakes) contain more species than lakes which have high levels of these nutrients (**eutrophic** lakes). In eutrophic lakes the high levels of nitrates and phosphates promote the growth of large numbers of algae and other small photosynthetic organisms. These in turn support large numbers of aerobic bacteria which decompose the photosynthetic organisms when they die. However, these aerobic bacteria take up so much of the oxygen in the water that the oxygen saturation of the water may fall from nearly 100 per cent to around 60 per cent. Many invertebrates and fish are unable to live unless the oxygen saturation is over 90 per cent.

Marine rocky shore

Marine rocky shores are found on coasts where the waves are too strong to allow the build-up of sand. One of the most characteristic features of rocky shores is **zonation**. Zonation is the occurrence of organisms in bands – or **zones**. On rocky shores zonation occurs because at any one locality the most important environmental variable is the amount of time the organisms are submerged by water (figure 2.10). Low down on the shore, organisms may only be exposed at low spring tides. High up on the shore, they may only be submerged at high spring tides. The seashore therefore exhibits a gradation from the terrestrial to the aquatic.

A classic instance of rocky shore zonation is provided by four seaweeds in parts of North-West Europe. Lowest on the shore, and submerged for most of the time, is saw wrack (*Fucus serratus*); higher up, saw wrack is replaced by bladder wrack (*F. vesiculosus*); still higher, bladder wrack is replaced by spiral wrack (*F. spiralis*). Finally, at the top of the shore, and only occasionally submerged, is the drought-tolerant channelled wrack (*Pelvetia canaliculata*). Experiments show that if the species characteristic of the lower shore are transplanted to areas higher up the shore, they tend to die from desiccation. When the species characteristic of the upper shore are transplanted to areas lower down the shore, they become overgrown by the species that normally grow there because they cannot compete with them.

Animals too may show zonation, especially if they are immobile, like barnacles. *Semibalanus balanoides* and *Chthamalus montagui* are two barnacles commonly found on British shores. *Chthamalus* is more drought resistant than *Semibalanus* and so is found higher up the shore. As with the seaweeds, competition is important lower down the shore. Here *Semibalanus* outcompetes *Chthamalus*, probably because it has a looser and more porous shell which is quicker to produce. This allows young *Semibalanus* to grow faster and so cover and crush the young *Chthamalus*. Higher up the shore, though, the loose porous shell of *Semibalanus* renders it susceptible to desiccation. Here the slower growing *Chthamalus* does better.

Figure 2.10 Rocky coastline showing zonation of seaweeds.

Habitats and microhabitats

Within each biome are numerous **habitats**, specific localities each with a particular set of conditions and associated organisms. A habitat (literally 'it dwells') is therefore the place where an organism lives. Typical habitats include freshwater ponds, slow-flowing streams, rock pools, hedgerows and beech woods.

We can subdivide a habitat into **microhabitats**, small localities each with its own particular conditions. The conditions (or **microclimate**) on the underside of a leaf, in a hedge for instance, will differ from those on the upper side; similarly the lower side of a stone in a stream will be markedly different from the top side. A particular microhabitat will support certain organisms but not others, as can easily be shown by turning over a fallen log in a wood (figure 2.11).

All the ecological units mentioned so far are essentially different localities of varying sizes. Fundamental to all terrestrial localities is soil. Soil forms a link between terrestrial organisms and the rock on which the plants, and therefore the other species in a locality, ultimately depend. For this reason we shall look in some detail at the biology of soil.

Soil

Soils are derived from rocks by **weathering**. Percolating water is especially important in the formation of soils. Young soils are stabilised when they become colonised by plants and animals. Eventually dead organic matter builds up and a mature soil is formed. Although the underlying **parent rock** influences the type of soil formed, the climate and vegetation are just as important.

Soil content

Soils contain inorganic particles, water, air, organic matter and dissolved minerals. The balance of these components varies considerably in different soils. Sand dune soils, for example, are high in sand, air, sodium ions and chloride ions. Usually they are low in organic matter, most dissolved minerals and water. On the other hand, soils in acid peat bogs are very high in organic matter and water, but low in inorganic particles, dissolved minerals and air.

Inorganic particles

The inorganic particles found in soil are classified by their size (table 2.1). Few soils contain particles all of the same size. Usually a range of particle sizes is found. With experience you can tell the composition of a soil just by rubbing it between your fingers. A soil that contains a mixture of sand, silt and clay is called a **loam** and generally this is the best sort of soil for plant growth.

Clay particles are found in most soils and greatly influence the properties of the soil. Clay minerals have a crystalline structure composed of plate-like layers (figure 2.12). Their overall electrical charge is negative and this means that they attract cations such as H^+, K^+, Na^+, Ca^{2+} and Mg^{2+} to their surfaces. Because of this, clay soils tend to hold on tightly to their cations. Clay soils therefore resist **leaching**, the process in which percolating water washes out dissolved minerals.

Figure 2.11 The organisms that live on the underside of a fallen log differ greatly from those found on its upper surface. This is due to the different microhabitats available to the organisms in those two regions.

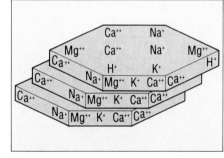

Figure 2.12 Diagrammatic representation of the plate structure of clay minerals. Notice how cations are attracted to exposed surfaces and edges.

Particle diameter	Particle name
< 2 μm	Clay
2 μm – 20 μm	Silt
20 μm – 200 μm	Fine sand
200 μm – 2 mm	Coarse sand
2 mm – 20 mm	Gravel

Table 2.1 Soil particle size classes

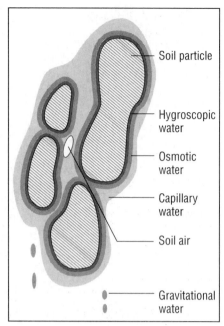

Figure 2.13 The relationship between soil particles, soil air and the four types of soil water.

Property	Sand	Clay
Texture	Coarse	Fine
Structure	'Light'	'Heavy' – forms large clods when wet
Aeration	Good	Poor
Drainage	Fast	Slow
Water retention	Poor	Excellent but may lead to waterlogging
Nutrient content	Poor	Good

Table 2.2 The properties of sand and clay

Sandy soils tend to consist mainly of small particles of silica, SiO_2. A comparison between sand and clay is given in table 2.2. In a loam, individual soil particles become bound together into **soil crumbs**. Crumb formation is due to the binding properties of fungal mycelia and bacterial polysaccharides.

Water

Four types of soil water can be recognised:

- **Hygroscopic water** forms a very thin layer around soil particles. Hygroscopic water is so tightly bound to the particles by surface tension that it is unavailable to plants.
- **Osmotic water** forms a thin layer around hygroscopic water and can be utilised only by the roots of certain plants.
- **Capillary water** is still less tightly bound. It is the most important regular source of water to plants. Capillary water takes its name from its ability to move upwards against gravity under the influence of capillarity, should the surface of the soil start to dry out.
- **Gravitational water** drains out of soil under the influence of gravity. It is therefore only found in the soil after periods of rain, after which it sinks below the water table to join the ground water.

The relationship between these types of soil water is shown in figure 2.13.

The total amount of water that can be held by a soil against the force of gravity is called the **field capacity**. Farmers value soils with high field capacities as such soils effectively store water that can be used by crops. Clays and loams may have a field capacity equivalent to 15 per cent of their mass.

Water plays a crucial part in soil. It is necessary for all the soil organisms, holds dissolved minerals in solution and helps to weather the soil.

Air

Between the soil particles and the crumbs are **pores** which are filled either with liquids or gases. **Soil air** differs from air in the atmosphere. It is usually saturated with water vapour and contains less oxygen, but more carbon dioxide. Ammonia and methane, the products of microbial activity, may also be present.

Organic matter

Dead **organic material** is derived both from soil organisms and from organisms that live above the soil surface. Fungi and bacteria in the soil **decompose** this organic material into **humus**.

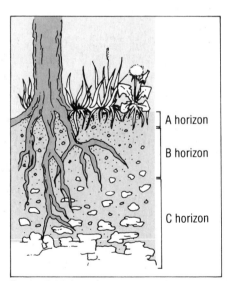

Figure 2.14 Generalised soil profile, showing the A, B and C horizons in relation to surface vegetation and plant roots.

A horizon

B horizon

C horizon

Humus is a complex mixture of many substances. Most of it consists of partly decomposed, insoluble, dark material. Humus is extremely resistant to further decomposition. It is generally acidic and, like clay, holds on to cations. Humus, again like clay, can act as a **colloid**: the particles are so small that they remain suspended in a fluid and do not settle out under the influence of gravity.

For humus to be formed, oxygen must be available as most decomposers are aerobic. Under waterlogged conditions, little oxygen is present and large amounts of undecomposed organic material may accumulate. This is essentially how **peat**, **coal** and **oil** are made.

In addition to dead organic material, soil also contains **soil organisms**. These play a vital role in decomposition. Soil organisms range in size from bacteria and protoctists to fungi, nematodes, insects, earthworms and a few mammals, such as moles.

When present, earthworms help to aerate the soil. Charles Darwin was fascinated by earthworms and wrote a book on them at the end of which he concluded: *'It may be doubted whether there are many other animals which have played so important a part in the history of the world, as have these lowly organized creatures.'* One thing earthworms cannot do is decompose cellulose and lignin, the main chemicals of which wood is made. Cellulose decomposition is carried out mainly by bacteria and fungi. Lignin decomposition is even more difficult and can only be achieved by a few genera of fungi.

Dissolved minerals

The nature of the **dissolved minerals** in soil water depends on the parent rock, the organisms growing in and above the soil, and whether or not aerobic conditions prevail. Chalk soils, for example, are high in calcium carbonate. However, they are low in phosphate, nitrate and iron. In terms of their nutrient availability, chalk soils are rather like oligotrophic lakes (see page 17). Again, as is the case for oligotrophic lakes, species diversity is high. More flowering plants are found in a square metre of chalk grassland than in any other European habitat.

When soils are waterlogged, ions capable of existing in either an oxidised or a reduced state are found in their reduced form. Fe^{2+}, for instance, occurs instead of Fe^{3+}. Some plants are very sensitive to Fe^{2+}, so the vegetation found on waterlogged soils differs from vegetation found in well drained conditions.

Soil pH normally lies within the range 3.0 to 8.0. Bogs often have soils with a pH of less than 4.5. In these acidic conditions, nitrogen and phosphorus become unavailable to plants. On the other hand, the concentration of toxic Al^{3+} ions increases as the pH falls. These factors mean that few plants can grow in acid bogs. Those that do so are often carnivorous and this supplies them with extra nutrients.

Soil types

A vertical section through any soil reveals a series of horizontal layers which constitute the **soil profile**. These layers are called **horizons** (figure 2.14). The top one is called the **A horizon**. This horizon gains organic material from above, but loses material through leaching to layers beneath. Underneath the A horizon is the **B horizon**. The B horizon gains material leached from the A horizon above. Finally, we have the **C horizon**. The C horizon consists of the weathered parent material – broken up pieces of rock. Beneath this is the parent material itself – solid rock. Soils differ in their profiles as shown in figure 2.15.

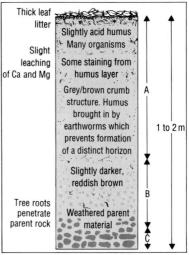

A Typical soil under a deciduous woodland, pH usually 5–7 (England).

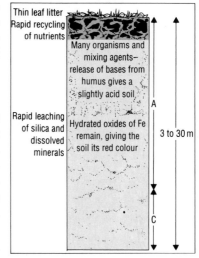

B Typical soil under a tropical rain forest, pH usuallly 4–6 (Hawaii).

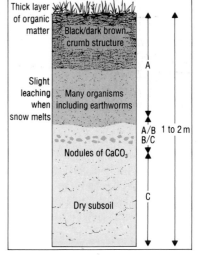

C Typical soil under steppe grassland, pH usually 6–8 (Russia).

Figure 2.15 Profiles of three types of soil.

Figure 2.16 There may well be over thirty species of flowering plants in a square metre of closely grazed chalkland.

Figure 2.17 A butterwort from the Dingle Peninsula, Western Ireland. Like all insectivorous plants, butterworts obtain much of their nitrogen by catching and digesting insects and other small animals. The leaves of the butterwort (close to the ground) bear numerous sticky glands which trap and immobilise small prey. Once the victim is caught, the edges of the leaves fold over, further securing it. Enzymes are then secreted. These digest the prey, allowing nutrients to be absorbed by the plant

The physical environment

Central to ecology is the concept of the **environment** or surroundings of an organism. The environment includes all the conditions in which an organism lives. It can be divided into two sorts: the **physical environment** (also known as the **abiotic environment**) and the **biotic environment**. Here we shall restrict ourselves to a consideration of the physical environment, leaving the biotic environment to subsequent chapters.

Traditionally the physical environment is divided into edaphic, climatic and topographic factors.

Edaphic factors

Edaphic factors are those to do with the soil, such as soil pH and particle size. We have already discussed them in detail. It should be remembered that most aquatic ecosystems contain soil too. Lakes, for instance, have soil at their edges and bottoms. Some marine ecosystems also have soils – for example, mangrove swamps and saltmarshes.

Two soils low in nutrient status are shown in figures 2.16 and 2.17. Figure 2.16 shows a chalk grassland. Here the low levels of available nitrogen and phosphorus mean that no one plant species can dominate the vegetation. As a result, many different species can co-exist, giving rise in summer to a profusion of colour. Figure 2.17 shows an acid bog. Here some plants enhance their mineral uptake by catching insects.

Climate

As we saw in the first part of this chapter, differences in climate are mainly responsible for differences between the world's biomes. Climate should be distinguished from weather. **Climate** refers to the predictable long-term patterns of rainfall, temperature and light. For instance, we talk about Ireland having an oceanic climate, meaning that it is warm and wet for its latitude. **Weather**, though, is more short term. It may be cold, windy and wet one day and warm, calm and dry the next.

Water

In general, water is necessary for all life. For terrestrial organisms the annual rainfall is the most important variable. However, its predictability and pH are also important. Organisms living in dry places usually have specialised mechanisms to reduce water loss (see Chapter 22).

For aquatic organisms, the temperature, salinity, oxygen saturation and nutrient content of the water are vital. In addition, wave action limits the distribution of many aquatic species. Limpets, barnacles and some seaweeds cling on to the rocks, while many organisms living on beaches burrow out of the way during storms. In rivers and streams, the rate at which the current flows is important. It is noticeable that free-floating aquatic plants are absent from most streams and rivers, but are widespread in lakes and ponds.

Temperature

Few organisms can grow if the ambient temperature falls outside the range 0–40°C, though, remarkably, some **thermophilous** (heat-loving) bacteria can complete their entire life cycles at temperatures in excess of 100°C. Emperor penguins breed on the Antarctic ice during the long midwinter darkness when the temperature can get as low as −80°C (figure 2.18). Most organisms, wherever they live, have physiological or behavioural adaptations to avoid extremes of temperature (see Chapter 23).

Light

Light is needed for photosynthesis (see Chapter 17). It is also used by many animals for vision. Light can vary in its wavelength, intensity and daily duration. In temperate regions, changes in daylength (hours of light) are used by many organisms as indicators of the season. Many plants, for example, start to flower when the days exceed a critical length (see Chapter 36). In aquatic environments, the depth to which light can penetrate limits the distribution of photosynthetic organisms.

Atmosphere

One of the most important components of the atmosphere is **oxygen**. Few organisms can live without it. In the atmosphere, oxygen levels remain constant, but in water the concentration of oxygen can vary greatly. Warmth and the presence of aerobic organisms decrease the amount of oxygen carried by water, though plants release oxygen during photosynthesis. When fully saturated, saltwater holds less oxygen than freshwater. Turbulence can increase the oxygen content of water by dissolving oxygen from the air.

When conditions are warm and moist, **carbon dioxide** may limit the rate of photosynthesis. The concentration of carbon dioxide varies little, being present in the atmosphere at a concentration of about 0.035 per cent. Only in the soil are carbon dioxide concentrations often significantly greater than this.

The **relative humidity** of the atmosphere can vary greatly. When it is low, organisms lose more water through evaporation, and therefore face the risk of dehydration. On the other hand, if it is very hot and humid, a low rate of evaporation may be harmful, as evaporation serves to remove heat from an organism and so cool it down.

Winds are the atmospheric equivalents of water currents and waves. Occasional strong winds can flatten trees that are hundreds of years old. Continuous strong winds can prevent trees from becoming established. This is the case, for example, in the Shetland Islands off Scotland. Wind serves a useful function in the pollination and seed dispersal of many plants. Migratory birds may use winds to minimise their transport costs.

Fire

Fire can only burn if organic matter has accumulated. Nowadays fires are often the result of human carelessness. However, in many biomes, fire has always been a natural phenomenon (figure 2.19). In nature, fires are caused by lightning strikes or, more rarely, by volcanoes.

Topography

By **topography** is meant the altitude, slope and aspect of a place. As one climbs a mountain, many features of the physical environment change. It may well become colder, wetter and windier. The air gets thinner, so that oxygen and carbon dioxide become scarcer and more ultraviolet light penetrates.

Slope is important because it reduces the chance of a soil becoming waterlogged. On very steep slopes, soil cannot form, so plants cannot establish themselves.

The aspect of a place is of most importance to sessile (immobile) organisms. In the northern hemisphere, south-facing slopes receive more light and heat energy than north-facing ones (the reverse is the case in the southern hemisphere). This fact is well known to gardeners who position their plants accordingly. It also influences the distribution of plants in the wild.

Figure 2.18 Emperor penguins with their young on ice in the Antarctic.

Figure 2.19 Lodgepole pines on fire in Yellowstone National Park, USA. Such fires are a natural phenomenon in the park. Before this was realised, great efforts were made at Yellowstone Park to eliminate fires. The result was a change in the vegatation, with some of the most interesting plant species being replaced by more common ones. Also, when eventually there was a fire, the build up of dead organic matter over several decades was so large that the fire did far more damage than usual.

The Gaia hypothesis

Guest author, James Lovelock, originator of the Gaia hypothesis, explains his ideas.

The Gaia hypothesis is now 20 years old. Those few scientists who have worked closely with it see it as reasonable science and growing ever more plausible as evidence and models map together. Many other scientists disagree and see Gaia as little more than a metaphor – some even denounce it as anti-science.

Gaia was the Greek word for Mother Earth. The Gaia hypothesis supposes that the Earth is a self-regulating planet, able to keep its climate and chemical composition constant and always favourable for life. The hypothesis arose when the Earth's atmosphere was compared with the atmospheres of Mars and Venus. Astronomical observations in the 1960s showed the atmospheres of Mars and Venus to be constant in composition and close to chemical equilibrium. By contrast the Earth's atmosphere, although stable in composition for long periods, profoundly departs from chemical equilibrium. I first proposed the existence on Earth of a regulatory system in 1972. The Gaia hypothesis was developed over the next few years in collaboration with the biologist Lynn Margulis.

Gaia is the hard science view of a physical chemist with an interest in control theory, and a microbiologist. Neither of its originators have ever proposed a mystical or teleological hypothesis or suggested that the proposed planetary self-regulation is purposeful, or involves foresight or planning by the biota.

Over the past 15 years, sharpened by criticism, Gaia has evolved. It can be seen now as the theory of an evolving system: a system made from the living organisms of the Earth, and from their material environment, the two parts tightly coupled together

and indivisible. Gaia predicts the evolution of this system to proceed gradually during long periods of constancy, punctuated by sudden simultaneous changes in both organisms and environment; changes that move the system to new and different homeostatic states. A significant jump of this kind occurred when oxygen first appeared in the atmosphere some 2.5 billion years ago.

Gaia theory is not contrary to Darwin's theory of natural selection. The step that distinguishes Gaia from Darwinism lies in the tightness of the coupling between the organisms and their physical environment. Almost everyone now accepts that life profoundly influences the environment. It is equally obvious that life is influenced by and adapts to the environment. Therefore life and the environment are a coupled feedback system where changes in one element will affect the other – and this may in turn feed back on the original change. The real debate is then, how important and how tight is the coupling?

Gaia asserts that this close coupling of organisms and their environment is strong enough to have greatly influenced the way in which the life-environment system on Earth, and on other planets with life, has evolved.

Gaia is a theory that can be tested experimentally. It makes predictions such as that oxygen has been held at its current level of 21 per cent for at least the last 200 million years. It predicts that the atmosphere in the archean period over 2.5 billion years ago was chemically dominated by methane, with oxygen as a trace gas at the parts per million level. It successfully predicted that the gases iodomethane and dimethyl sulphide would be found to be the dominant carriers of the elements iodine and sulphur from the oceans to the land surfaces.

Among other insights from Gaia is the recognition that planetary life can never be sparse: a planet with sparse life could never self-regulate. Self-regulation is needed because the geochemical evolution of terrestrial planets is progressive and moves towards states like those of Mars and Venus now. During this evolution there will be a period when conditions are favourable for life. This is a window of opportunity and in it organisms must reach a sufficient abundance to affect and couple in with the geochemical evolution. If they fail, planetary conditions will continue to change inorganically until the point is reached when life is impossible.

Another insight is on glaciations. Pollution with greenhouse gases, and the widespread destruction of natural habitats, are insults to a weakened system. Forced too far, a sudden transition could occur to a new homeostasis, possibly at a much higher global temperature.

In recent years the churches have grown aware that their environmental stance, though appropriate in biblical times, is no longer so in a world of 5 billion. Now that we, and our dependent crops and livestock, occupy so many available habitats of the Earth, theologians begin to wonder if it is right for us to make the whole planet a sty, no matter how hygienic and well-run. In Gaia we are part and partners of a democratic entity. The rules insist, through natural selection, that species that harm the environment are voted out. If we are truly concerned for mankind then we must respect other organisms. If we think of nothing but people and ignore the natural life of the Earth, the scene is set for our own destruction and that of the comfortable Earth we know. Just now we seem like the Gadarene swine, driving our polluting cars down to a sea rising to meet us.

Summary

1 **Ecology** is the study of organisms in relation to their **environment**.

2 The part of the Earth and its atmosphere inhabited by life is called the **biosphere**. The biosphere can be divided into **biomes**.

3 Terrestrial biomes include **tropical rain forest, temperate deciduous forest, tundra, tropical grassland** and **desert**. The most important variables for life on land are the amount of rain and the temperature.

4 Aquatic biomes include **oceans, rivers, lakes, coral reefs** and the **shore**. The most important variables for life in water are the **salinity** of the water, its **depth, permanence** and **nutrient availability**.

5 A **habitat** is a specific locality where an organism lives.

6 A habitat is divided into numerous **microhabitats**, each with its own particular conditions (**microclimates**).

7 For terrestrial organisms, soil is particularly important. All soils contain **inorganic particles, air, organic matter** and **dissolved minerals**. However, soils may differ greatly from one to another.

8 The **environment**, or conditions in which organisms live, can be divided into the **physical** (or **abiotic**) **environment** and the **biotic environment**.

9 The abiotic (physical) environment includes **edaphic factors** (to do with the soil), **climatic factors** (water, temperature, light, atmosphere and fire) and **topographical factors** (altitude, slope and aspect).

Review questions

1 How might scientists try to find out whether life is present on other planets?

2 Why do you think tropical rain forests have so many species?

3 What special features would you expect to see in mammals that live in the tundra?

4 How might you test the hypothesis that in lakes low nutrient levels are associated with high species diversity?

5 What climatic factors would you expect to speed up the formation of soil?

6 How could you investigate the part played by different groups of organisms (e.g. bacteria, fungi and animals) in the decomposition of leaves in a wood?

7 Draw a diagram to show the relationship between the biosphere, biomes, habitats, microhabitats and the environment.

8 Explain the difference between weather and climate. Suggest the roles that each might play in the survival and reproduction of annual plants in a desert.

9 What special features would you expect to see in plants growing on sand dunes close to the sea shore?

10 List the ways in which topography can influence the distribution of plants and other photosynthetic organisms.

Further reading

For a beautifully clear introduction in the world's biomes, climate and soils, consult Howard Miekle's *Patterns of Life* (Unwin Hyman, 1989).

For a fascinating glimpse into the subtlety and complexity of just one habitat, see Andrew Mitchell *The Enchanted Canopy: Secrets from the Rainforest Roof* (Fontana/Collins, 1986).

CHAPTER 3 | Communities and ecosystems

John Donne, the seventeenth century English poet, once wrote 'No man is an Island, entire of itself; every man is a piece of the Continent, a part of the main'. Donne meant that none of us can lead a life totally independent of others. Humans depend on one another. In the same way, no other organism can exist on its own. Without plants, animals would starve through lack of food and in the long term would run short of oxygen. Without bacteria and fungi, decomposition and nutrient cycling would stop. In the absence of animals, many plants would be unable to reproduce. This chapter is about the ways in which organisms depend on each other.

Communities

A **community** is the sum of the organisms found in a habitat. Some communities are named after an obvious feature of the environment – rock pool and sand dune communities for example. Other communities are named after the dominant plants – heathland and pine forest communities for example (figure 3.1).

Careful examination of any community reveals that the species in it interact with each other. Sometimes these interactions benefit both species. For example, many trees produce fruits which are eaten by birds. Clearly the birds benefit; they obtain food from the tree. But the tree benefits too. Its seeds are dispersed by the birds into new areas. There, they may grow into trees. Sometimes the interactions between two species are such that one species benefits at the expense of the other. This is the case when one species eats another.

We will have more to say about the different interactions between organisms in Chapter 6. Here it is enough to note that it is the interactions between organisms that shape a community. With this in mind we will look at the interactions in an oak wood community.

Oak woodland

Most of Europe has been so influenced by agriculture and human settlements that little virgin forest remains. Only in Czechoslovakia, Poland and some other parts of Eastern Europe is truly undisturbed woodland left. A number of European countries, though, have ancient woodland. Ancient woodland is woodland known to have existed for at least several hundred years. Often it has been used by humans, for instance as a source of timber. Nevertheless, these ancient managed woods are similar in structure to the few remaining undisturbed ones.

Much of Europe was once dominated by the pedunculate oak (*Quercus robur*). Oak is usually found with other trees such as lime, elm and ash. The relationship between oak and ash is quite complex. Oak seedlings are intolerant of shade. This means that they only survive in clearings formed by the death and fall of old trees. Unlike oak, ash seedlings are tolerant of shade and can wait many years until an opening in the canopy gives them the light they need to develop further. Paradoxically though, the adult tree is intolerant of shade and so tends, in time, to be replaced by the oak.

Beneath the tall trees in an oak wood is an **understorey** of shrubs such as hazel and small trees such as hawthorn. Lower still is the **herb layer**. This is at its most spectacular early in the year before the leaves of the trees have opened in the late spring. Here are found bluebells, wood anemones and violets among others (figure 3.2).

Figure 3.1 A pine forest community in Scotland.

Figure 3.2 A British oak woodland in spring, with bluebells in flower.

The plants in an oak wood provide food for a rich variety of animals. Many insects and molluscs are found. Oak in particular supports a large number of different insect species. These insects in turn are eaten by a number of birds including great tits and great spotted woodpeckers. Many insects are also eaten by spiders. Other birds take a greater variety of food. The blackbird and song thrush eat berries and earthworms in addition to insects. The smaller of these birds may be hunted by sparrowhawks.

Mammals too are common in oak woods. Shrews make runways through the litter resulting from the fall of dead leaves, and tunnel through the soil. They feed on earthworms, beetles, spiders, centipedes, woodlice, snails and slugs. The bank vole is found in areas with thick cover and feeds mainly on fleshy fruits and seeds. In winter, though, it will eat dead leaves. The wood mouse has a more varied diet, feeding on seedlings, buds, fruits, nuts, snails and arthropods. Another mammal found in oak woods is the stoat. Stoats are carnivorous. They eat rabbits, birds and small rodents such as bank voles and wood mice.

Many other species are found in oak woods. Fungi and bacteria are abundant but easily overlooked. Some break down dead animals and plants; others attack living species. Fungi are at their most obvious in the autumn when their fruiting bodies appear (figure 3.3).

Even this brief description of the organisms in an oak wood should convince you of the complexity of their interactions. We will consider the feeding relationships found in communities in more detail below. However, the organisms in a community interact not just with each other but also with their physical environment. This brings us to the concept of the ecosystem.

Ecosystems

An **ecosystem** consists of all the interacting organisms in an area together with the non-living constituents of their environment. For example, an oak wood ecosystem includes not only the organisms that make up the oak wood community but also the relevant aspects of the physical environment, such as rain, the inorganic components of the soil, sunlight and atmospheric oxygen and carbon dioxide.

Ecosystems are relatively self-contained. Any ecosystem tends to perpetuate itself by the cycling of minerals within that ecosystem. In a wood, for instance, leaves fall and decompose and their nutrients are returned to the soil. In turn, the plants remove these nutrients from the soil and use them in growth. It was the English ecologist Sir Arthur Tansley who first used the term ecosytem in 1935. He realised that organisms and their immediate environment need to be considered together as a functional unit.

Examples of individual ecosystems include saltmarshes, coral reefs and ponds (figure 3.4). Several different ecosystems may be present in one area, as in figure 3.5, and sometimes it is not possible to decide where one ecosystem stops and another one begins. The Amazon rain forest, for instance, is too large to be described as a single ecosystem. Despite this difficulty, the concept of the ecosystem has proved very useful to ecologists.

To give a full account of an ecosystem it is necessary both to list the organisms there and to describe the relevant aspects of their environment. For instance, an adequate description of a lake requires a detailed account of the water there as well as of the species found in it. We would need to look at the temperature of the water at different depths throughout the year. The pH, oxygen and nutrient content are also important, as is the depth to which light penetrates. In terrestrial ecosystems **soil** forms an

Figure 3.3 The fruiting bodies of a fungus on a dead tree, in an oak woodland in autumn.

Figure 3.4 A pond in the forest of Dean, Gloucestershire, England. Notice the way the pond is being colonised by plants. Reeds are particularly evident.

Figure 3.5 View of the Rift Valley in northern Zimbabwe, showing several different ecosystems. In the foreground lichens can be seen having colonised bare rock.

Figure 3.6 Succession on a cleared area of oak-hornbeam forest in southern Poland. From top to bottom the succession has occurred for 7, 30 and 150 years.

important link between organisms and their physical environment.

Analysing an ecosystem involves studying how different species interact in a community. Such studies are known as **synecology**. The first step is to identify the organisms living in the ecosystem, though occasionally this is left till later. Identification can be done with the aid of systematic keys (see Chapter 7). It is then necessary to determine exactly where in the ecosystem the different species are found. Ecologists usually want to know why species occur in some places but not others. Answering this question is rarely easy. It involves trying to see how a species interacts with other species and with the physical environment. Often experiments are needed to test the various hypotheses generated.

Succession

If a lawn is left unmown, the grass soon grows long. If the lawn is left unmown for several years, it will no longer be a lawn. New plants will have invaded it and become established. This is an example of **colonisation**. These plants will probably be taller than the grasses. Because of this, the grasses may become shaded, so that they fail to get enough light. In most parts of the world, a lawn that is left uncut will eventually turn into a wood.

The lawn example illustrates a widespread observation: communities do not remain in the same state indefinitely. They change. This change in a community over time is called **succession**. Three of the easiest examples of succession to interpret are those that occur on bare rock, in a pond and on animal dung.

Succession on bare rock

Think of a bare area of rock, such as might be found at the base of a retreating glacier. At first there are no organisms on the rock, except for the occasional insect blown on to it by the wind. Soon, however, organisms begin to establish themselves.

The first organisms to become established are often lichens, one of the few types of organism that can subsist on bare rock. You can see them in figure 3.5 on page 27. These lichens trap windblown dust particles. They also promote the break-up of the rock surface, so allowing a very shallow and simple soil to accumulate. This simple soil allows mosses to colonise the area and, later, grasses and ferns.

Over the years sufficient soil builds up for various herbaceous perennials to take root. Often these early invaders can fix atmospheric nitrogen, thus compensating for the poor nutrient status of the shallow soil. In time small shrubs colonise the area. Eventually the soil is deep enough to allow the establishment of tall trees (figure 3.6).

Throughout the course of the succession, changes in the animal species accompany changes in the plants. Even mosses have a characteristic fauna. This can be shown by dropping a few drops of water on to a moss tuft, waiting for half an hour and then squeezing the water from the moss. If the water is examined under a microscope, tardigrades and other tiny animals can often be seen.

The progressive colonisation of a previously unoccupied area is called a **primary succession**. Communities found earliest in a succession are typically the simplest. They have the fewest species and the interrelationships between them are usually straightforward. Later communities have more species and may show more complex interactions. For instance, insect pollination is generally more frequent in the later stages of a succession. It may take hundreds or even thousands of years for succession to result in a forest growing on what was once bare ground.

Succession in a pond

Most ponds and lakes have plants growing at their edges. Some of these plants take root in the mud at the bottom and hold their leaves beneath the surface of the water. Other plants, such as bulrushes and reeds, grow at the edge and send their leaves above the water level.

The effect of these plants is to cause a steady accumulation of organic matter at the edge of the pond. This organic matter comes mainly from the dead remains of the plants. In time, the pond becomes shallower due to the accumulation of organic matter, and the rooted plants extend towards the centre. You can see this in figure 3.4 on page 27. Gradually, the pond becomes filled up. Eventually the succession may result in forest, just as is the case for succession on bare ground.

Succession on herbivore dung

The succession from bare ground or open water to forest rarely takes place within a human lifetime. An interesting example of a much more rapid succession is seen in the fungi that colonise herbivore dung (figure 3.7). The first fungi exploit the dung quickly. Their hyphae grow rapidly and utilise any sugars, proteins and starch in the dung. These fungi are similar in appearance to those seen after several days on bread kept moist.

The next fungi to move in are those that can utilise the less digestible hemicelluloses. Finally, certain mushrooms and toadstools (basidiomycetes) appear. These possess the enzymes necessary to break down cellulose and lignin.

Figure 3.7 Fungi growing on elephant dung. The capped fungi visible in the picture represent a stage in the rapid succession which takes place on herbivore dung.

Why does succession occur?

There are two reasons why communities change with time. One is that the organisms themselves cause a change in their environment which in turn makes the environment more suitable for other species. This is what happens, for instance, in the succession from bare ground to forest. The lichens are responsible for the accumulation of a rudimentary soil suitable for mosses. In turn the mosses help generate a soil suitable for vascular plants. This type of change is called **autogenic succession**.

The second reason why communities may change with time is that the physical environment changes for some reason not directly related to the organisms in the community. For instance, at the start of an ice age it gets colder and both the vegetation and the fauna change. This sort of change is called **allogenic succession**.

The result of succession

What happens at the end of a succession? Eventually a **climax community** establishes itself. Across much of the Earth's land surface, forest is the climax community. However, this is not always the case. In the tundra, as discussed on page 15, the climate and soil do not allow trees to grow. Instead, the climax vegetation is a mixture of short grasses, herbs and lichens.

While primary succession starts with an area previously unoccupied by organisms, **secondary succession** begins in an area where at least some organisms are already present. For instance, the successions that occur in a cleared area of forest, on a burnt moorland or in a meadow flooded with river silt are examples of secondary succession. Secondary succession usually takes place more rapidly than primary succession.

Sometimes succession may not proceed to a climax community. For example, many grasslands are maintained as grasslands by a combination of grazing and fire. In the absence of these factors, grassland usually develops into shrubland and then into forest. Instances where natural successions are halted in this way are known as **deflected successions**. Permanent grassland is therefore the result of a deflected succession.

If the cause of a deflected succession is removed, then the succession may proceed towards the climax in the normal way. A classic example of this is provided by the introduction of the myxomatosis virus into Britain in 1953. This was done in an attempt to reduce the number of rabbits, which are generally considered to be agricultural pests. Within two years over 99 per cent of the British rabbit population died from the disease. The grass on chalk downs, until then kept short by rabbit grazing, grew rampant, displacing many low-growing wild flowers. The rabbits had also included hawthorn seedlings in their diet. With the demise of the rabbits, these seedlings soon grew into young trees.

As well as causing large areas of grassland to change into shrubland, myxomatosis had a number of other effects. With the collapse in the rabbit population, foxes, stoats, weasels and buzzards failed to breed in the years immediately after 1953 and declined in numbers. As a result, vole numbers reached an unusually high level in 1956–7, allowing the carnivores to recover in numbers.

Cycling of matter and flow of energy in ecosystems

In almost all ecosystems, the organisms fall into three nutritional groups.

- **Producers:** autotrophic organisms, so called because they can make organic compounds, such as starch and proteins, from inorganic precursors. Producers include plants, some protoctists and certain prokaryotes.

- **Consumers:** heterotrophic organisms, so called because they need to feed on the organic compounds made by autotrophs. Consumers include animals, parasitic fungi, some protoctists and certain bacteria.

- **Decomposers:** heterotrophic organisms, responsible for breaking down the organic waste products and dead remains of organisms into the inorganic substances needed by the producers. Decomposers mainly comprise bacteria and fungi. Such organisms are known as saprotrophs · or **saprobionts**.

Producers, consumers and decomposers are related as shown in figure 3.8. Organic materials synthesised by the producers are eaten and assimilated by the consumers. Thanks to the activities of the decomposers, all the organic materials incorporated into the bodies of the consumers are eventually broken down into inorganic materials. These are then rebuilt into organic compounds by the synthetic activities of the producers. So matter circulates in nature. An individual atom may find itself at one time in a producer, at another time in a decomposer and at another time in water, air or soil. However, there is little overall loss of matter from the system.

Although matter circulates repeatedly around an ecosystem, this is not the case with energy. Instead, energy is continually lost from ecosystems as heat energy. The photosynthetic producers transfer some of the radiant energy of sunlight to chemical energy in plant carbohydrates. By their respiratory activities, the producers, consumers and decomposers transfer this energy to ATP, whose subsequent hydrolysis provides energy for the cells'

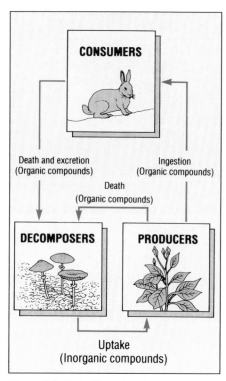

Figure 3.8 Cycle illustrating the interdependence of producers and consumers in an ecosystem. The autotrophic activities of the producers (green plants, etc) produce organic materials which are fed on by the consumers. The saprotrophic activities of the decomposers (mainly certain bacteria and fungi) free inorganic materials from the dead bodies and waste products of the producers and consumers, thereby ensuring a continual supply of raw materials for the producers. The carbon and nitrogen cycles are detailed applications of this general principle.

vital activities (see page 230). Both in the formation of ATP, and in its subsequent usage, a proportion of the energy is lost from an ecosystem as heat energy. Ultimately all the energy in an ecosystem is transferred to heat energy. However, the continual trapping of the energy of sunlight by green plants makes good this loss and maintains the flow of energy.

Nutrient cycles

In order for organisms to maintain themselves, grow and reproduce, they need a supply of the elements of which they are made. These they receive from the cycling of matter, or **nutrient cycles** as they are called.

Nutrient cycles have two components: a biological component showing how the element cycles through organisms, and a geochemical component showing how the element cycles through rocks, water and the atmosphere. For this reason, nutrient cycles are also called **biogeochemical cycles**.

Carbon cycle

The **carbon cycle** is unique among nutrient cycles because it need not involve decomposers. This is because autotrophs take in their carbon as carbon dioxide, and carbon dioxide is given out by all organisms as a result of respiration. Figure 3.9 shows the carbon cycle on a global scale, but even in the absence of any decomposers, carbon would still be able to circulate for some time within an ecosystem.

Not all dead material decays. In anaerobic or highly acidic conditions decomposers may be unable to break down all the remains or waste products of organisms. In such situations these may accumulate to form

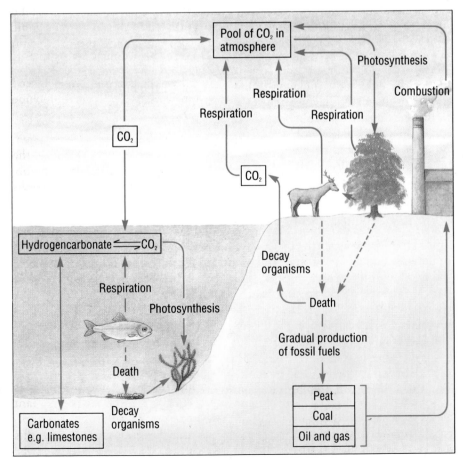

Figure 3.9 The carbon cycle. The amount of carbon dioxide in the atmosphere is maintained by a balance between photosynthesis (which withdraws carbon dioxide from the atmosphere) and respiration and combustion (which add carbon dioxide to the atmosphere). In fact, the level of carbon dioxide in the atmosphere has risen this century for reasons discussed on page 41.

fossil fuels such as peat, coal, oil and their gaseous derivatives. In natural circumstances these deposits represent a **sink**.

Sinks are the diversions from cycles. However, in practice humans use fossil fuels as a source of energy in combustion. But, even in the absence of human activity, the carbon in fossil fuels would eventually return to the carbon cycle when geological processes return these substances to the Earth's surface. Oxidation might then return the carbon to the air as carbon dioxide.

Human activity is currently reducing the amount of carbon trapped in the sinks of the carbon cycle at a speed vastly in excess of that at which fossil fuels are made. As a result, atmospheric levels of carbon dioxide have been rising this century, as discussed in Chapter 4. If we carry on burning fossil fuels at our current rate, the nations of the world will have exhausted their accessible fossil fuel deposits within one to two hundred years. The only two ways for us to postpone or avoid this **energy crisis** (strictly a **fuel crisis**) will be to use far less fuel or obtain energy from other sources, such as the sun (solar power), wind or nuclear power.

Nitrogen cycle

The **nitrogen cycle** is more complex than the carbon cycle and depends on the activities of various bacteria whose metabolic processes are examined in Chapter 17.

The way the nitrogen cycle relates to the biosphere as a whole is illustrated in figure 3.10. Gaseous nitrogen makes up about 80 per cent of the atmosphere where it is in the form N_2. N_2 is a very stable molecule. It can be removed from the atmosphere in only two ways: by lightning and by nitrogen fixation. Nitrogen fixation can be carried out naturally by certain prokaryotes, and in industry by the **Haber process** which is used to make nitrogen-rich fertilisers.

Plants are unable to take in nitrogen from the atmosphere. Most plants can absorb only nitrate (and sometimes ammonium) from the soil. Some plants, though, have nitrogen-fixing bacteria in their roots and can thus grow in soils which have very little nitrate. Either way, nitrogen finishes up in proteins inside the plants.

Animals in turn rely on plants for their source of nitrogen. The nitrogen bound up in animal or plant protein can be converted back to nitrate via ammonia and nitrite by the sequential activities of various bacteria. Superimposed on this conversion of protein to nitrate are a series of reactions carried out by various denitrifying bacteria. These reduce the amount of nitrate in the soil.

In the oceans some of the available nitrogen (as nitrate and ammonium) brought in by rain and the activities of nitrogen-fixing organisms circulates through the plants and animals found there. Some of the available nitrogen, however, sinks beneath the upper 100 m or so to which photosynthetic organisms are confined. It may then sink all the way to the sediments at the bottom of the ocean. Here it is unavailable to most organisms unless it is eventually returned to the atmosphere by volcanic emissions and other processes. This loss of nitrate and other nutrients makes the ocean a relatively impoverished environment. Close to the shore and in estuaries powerful upcurrents bring nutrients to the surface. In these situations plant and animal life is more abundant. This is why fishing is so successful in such regions.

Although the carbon and nitrogen cycles are of particular ecological significance, other elements, such as oxygen, phosphorus and sulphur, also circulate. Water circulates too, though this of course is not an element but a

The chemistry of nitrogen-fixation and other conversions in the nitrogen cycle are dealt with on pages 306–7.

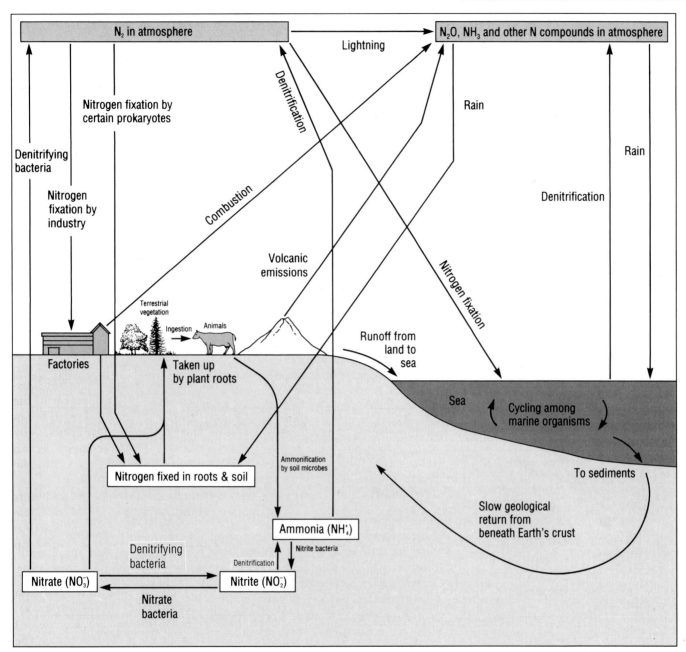

compound made up of two elements. Try drawing the **water cycle**, showing how it relates to terrestrial and aquatic ecosystems.

Having looked at the cycling of matter in ecosystems, we will now go on to examine the feeding relationships of organisms in more detail to see how matter and energy flow through ecosystems.

Food chains

In the cycle shown in figure 3.8 the consumers are shown feeding directly on the producers. In reality the situation is usually more complicated, the producers being eaten by herbivores (**primary consumers**) which are then eaten by carnivores (**secondary consumers**). Moreover, there may be several carnivores in the series, with first level carnivores (secondary consumers) being fed on by second level carnivores (tertiary consumers). Sometimes these second level carnivores are eaten by third level carnivores. Eventually,

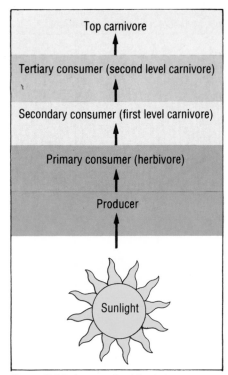

Figure 3.11 A generalised food chain showing the passage of matter and energy through the trophic levels.

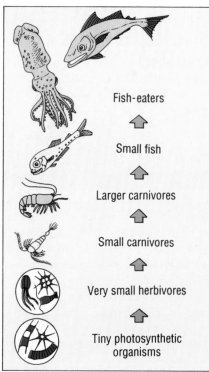

Figure 3.12 A typical food chain in the ocean. Notice the number of trophic levels. The smaller organisms in this food chain make up plankton, the millions of organisms which float or drift in surface water.

top carnivores are reached. These are not preyed upon. Instead they die of old age, disease or injury.

The nutritional sequence that leads from producers to top carnivores is known as a **food chain** (figure 3.11). A food chain shows a series of organisms through which the organic compounds initially produced by plants, or other autotrophs, are transferred. Each organism in the series feeds on, and therefore derives its energy and nutrients from, the preceding one. In turn it is consumed by, and provides nutrients and energy for, the one following it. The levels in a food chain are referred to as **trophic levels**, *trophic* meaning feeding.

Food chains vary in length. In theory an ecosystem could have a food chain consisting of just one producer which was unpalatable or toxic to all herbivores. In practice, the shortest food chains usually consist of at least three levels, as in grass → cow → human, or grass → deer → jaguar.

It is rare to find food chains of more than six levels (figure 3.12). Several different reasons have been suggested for this. One is that there simply is not enough energy in ecosystems to support more than this number of steps. As it is, top carnivores often have to roam over huge areas to find enough food.

A second possible reason is that it is difficult to imagine a species with the hunting abilities necessary to feed on eagles, lions, killer whales or any other existing top carnivores.

A third suggestion is that the more levels in a food chain, the less stable it becomes. Imagine a food chain with 20 levels. Suppose that the numbers of one particular species half-way up the food chain happened to be much lower than usual. The organisms that depended on this species for their food would be threatened with extinction. The more levels in a food chain, the greater this problem would be.

Food webs

If you study a community in detail, you find that simple linear food chains are rare. Instead of a herbivore feeding on only one species of plant, it usually feeds on several. In the same way, herbivores are generally eaten by a number of different predators. A diagram showing such feeding relations in a community is referred to as a **food web**.

In general a food web consists of a number of interconnected food chains. In most ecosystems, food webs are extremely complicated. A typical oak wood, for instance, contains thousands of species of plants, fungi and animals, as well as many different species of bacteria and protoctists. A simplified food web in an oak wood is shown in figure 3.13.

If you study a food web, such as the one in figure 3.13, you will realise how difficult it is to assign organisms to specific trophic levels. To what level, for example, does the wood mouse belong? It eats both herbs and insects. As such it is classified as an **omnivore**. The same applies to the blackbird in figure 3.13. It eats the berries of plants, insects and earthworms, which are respectively producers, primary consumers and decomposers.

Ecological pyramids

Food webs give a useful description of the feeding relationships in a community. However, they are non-quantitative. The first attempt to provide a quantitative account of the feeding relationships in a community was made by the English ecologist Charles Elton.

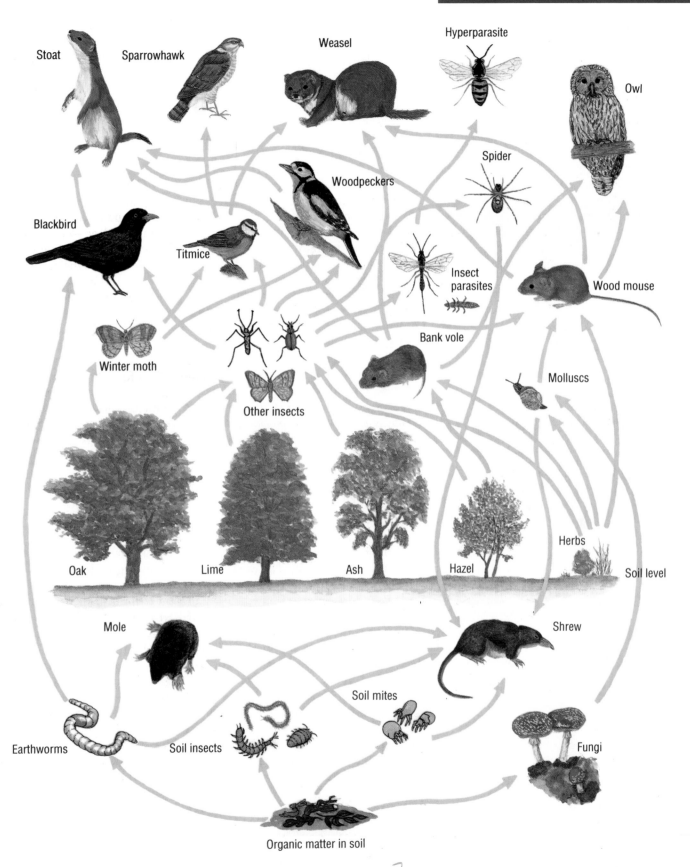

Figure 3.13 Simplified diagram of a food web in an oak wood (Sun not shown). Notice how some species cannot be classified into a single trophic level. Hyperparasites are parasites that attack parasites.

Figure 3.14 Typical pyramid of numbers showing how the number of individuals found at each trophic level decreases as you go up a food chain. The width of each rectangle is indicative of the number of organisms in each trophic level.

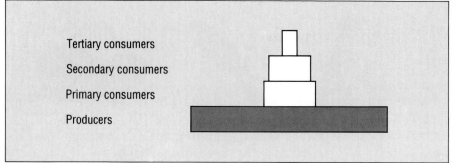

Figure 3.15 Five ticks on the skin of a buffalo.

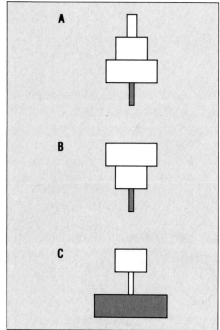

Figure 3.16 Some inverted pyramids of numbers. The producer boxes are shaded.
A The producer is a single plant such as a tree.
B The producer is a single plant which is infected with parasites (primary consumers) and the latter are parasatised by further parasites (hyperparasites).
C A large number of producers are eaten by a single primary consumer which is infected with parasites (secondary consumers).

Pyramids of numbers

In 1927 Elton pointed out that if you study the animals in an oak wood in summer, you find vast numbers of small herbivorous insects like aphids, a large number of spiders and carnivorous ground beetles, a fair number of small birds and only a few hawks. As you go up a food chain there is a progressive drop in the numbers of the organisms found at each trophic level. This progressive drop of numbers is shown in figure 3.14 and is known as a **pyramid of numbers**.

Pyramids of numbers, despite their name, need not always be pyramidal in shape. Consider the situation where a single very large producer, such as a tree, supports a large number of primary consumers. In this case, an **inverted pyramid of numbers** results. Inverted pyramids of numbers can also result when communities contain parasites. Imagine, for instance, a mammal infected with ticks or fleas (figure 3.15). These parasites are in the trophic level above the mammal, yet their numbers will be much greater. Some inverted pyramids of numbers are shown in figure 3.16.

Pyramids of biomass

Another type of ecological pyramid which can be constructed for a community is the **pyramid of biomass**. Here, instead of counting the number of individuals at each trophic level, you measure the total mass of organisms at each level. This is called the **biomass**.

Pyramids of biomass are very time consuming to construct and only a few have ever been determined. As you might expect, those that have been constructed are almost always pyramidal in shape. The greatest mass of organisms is found in the producers. These support a smaller mass of herbivores, which in turn support a smaller mass of carnivores. Although top level carnivores, such as eagles, leopards and wolves, may be large (figure 3.17), they are few in number with the result that top level carnivores always have a relatively low biomass per unit area.

In certain circumstances, however, measurements of the biomass at the various trophic levels in a community may also give an inverted pyramid. For instance, at certain times of year the biomass of the tiny herbivorous organisms that float in lakes and oceans (**zooplankton**) may exceed the biomass of the tiny photosynthetic organisms (**phytoplankton**) on which they feed (figure 3.18). This is because biomass refers to the mass of organisms present at a particular moment, the so-called **standing crop**. However, the organisms which constitute the phytoplankton are smaller than the zooplankton that depend on them. Because of this, the phytoplankton have shorter life cycles. As a result, at any one time the biomass of the phytoplankton may be less than that of the zooplankton, the latter being supported by a tremendous turnover of phytoplankton.

Pyramids of numbers and biomass provide ecologists with a certain amount of useful information. However, to get a fuller understanding of what happens in communities, pyramids of energy are often constructed.

Pyramids of energy

A **pyramid of energy** shows the transfer – or *flow* – of energy through a community. As a result, pyramids of energy are expressed in units of energy per area per time, e.g. kilojoules m^{-2} yr^{-1}. They show the rate at which energy is transferred from one trophic level to another. This dynamic view of a community contrasts with the static picture provided by pyramids of numbers or biomass which are taken at an instant in time rather than over a measured period of time.

Figure 3.19 shows both a generalised pyramid of energy and a specific example. These pyramids can never be inverted, as pyramids of numbers or biomass sometimes are. To understand why, look at figure 3.20. Consider the energy of sunlight which the producers have transferred to photosynthetic products. Three things can happen to this energy: it can be respired by the producers, it can pass to the herbivores or it can pass to the decomposers. In the same way, some of the energy stored in the herbivores will be respired, some will pass to the carnivores and some to the decomposers.

We can see therefore that the energy transferred from the producers to the herbivores must be greater than the energy transferred from the herbivores to the consumers. This is an application of the **Law of Conservation of Energy**, the first law of thermodynamics.

It is worth realising that if you constructed pyramids not of energy flow but of nutrient flow, with units of grams of nitrogen (or whichever nutrient) per square metre per year, these pyramids would also never be inverted. This follows from the Law of Conservation of Mass.

Energy budgets

An **energy budget** for a species shows what percentage of the energy ingested by an individual is assimilated. It then looks at the fate of the assimilated energy. Some of this energy is respired, some is used for growth and building up tissues, and some is used for the production of gametes (reproduction). How much energy is allocated to each of these three functions depends on a number of factors. A juvenile individual, for example, will allocate quite a bit to growth, but nothing to reproduction.

Figure 3.17 Wolves in the mist in the Bavarian Forest National Park, Germany.

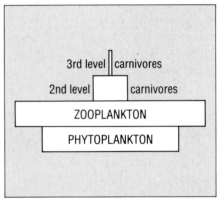

Figure 3.18 An inverted pyramid of biomass, showing how a small mass of phytoplankton can, at some times of the year, support a larger mass of zooplankton.

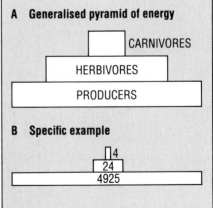

Figure 3.19
A Generalised pyramid of energy, showing how the energy flowing through a trophic level decreases as you go up a food chain.
B Pyramid of energy from the Arctic tundra, Devon Island, Canada. Units are kJ m^{-2} yr^{-1}.

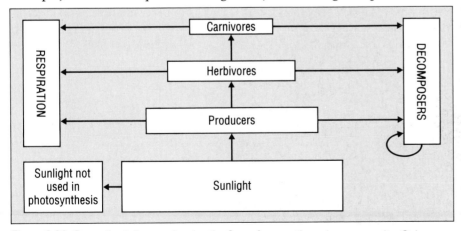

Figure 3.20 Generalised diagram showing the flow of energy through a community. Only some of the energy stored in a trophic level goes to the trophic level above. The rest is respired or passes to the decomposers. This is why pyramids of energy can never be inverted.

Figure 3.21 Silver Springs, Florida, with large mouth bass swimming.

Energy budgets can be constructed either for individual species or for whole communities. It takes a lot of careful experimental work to determine the energy budget for a species. It takes even longer to determine the energy budget for a whole community. Yet such studies can tell us a lot about the dynamics of ecosystems. The first study to investigate the energy budget of a community was carried out by the American ecologist E.P. Odum at Silver Springs, a pool plus its associated five mile river, in Florida (figure 3.21). Odum spent four years painstakingly measuring the energy flow at Silver Springs and his results are summarised in figure 3.22.

Notice from figure 3.22 how little of the sunlight that struck the producers was actually trapped by the chloroplasts and used to fix carbon dioxide. The total amount of light striking the producers (the insolation) was about 7 120 000 kJ m^{-2} yr^{-1}, whereas the energy fixed in photosynthesis was only 87 110 kJ m^{-2} yr^{-1}. From these figures we can calculate the **efficiency of photosynthesis**:

$$\text{Efficiency of photosynthesis} = 87\,110 \text{ kJ m}^{-2}\text{ yr}^{-1} \div 7\,120\,000 \text{ kJ m}^{-2}\text{ yr}^{-1}$$
$$= 1.2\%$$

This figure seems very low, but is similar to that found in many other communities. The highest photosynthetic efficiencies are found in tropical rain forests and in crops growing under intensive agriculture. Even here, the efficiency of photosynthesis is only 3–4 per cent.

Productivity of ecosystems

The total organic material made in photosynthesis is known as the **gross primary production**. However, only some of this is available to herbivores. The remainder is respired. The amount of organic material actually available to the herbivores is called the **net primary production**. If we look at the fate of this net primary production at Silver Springs, we can see from

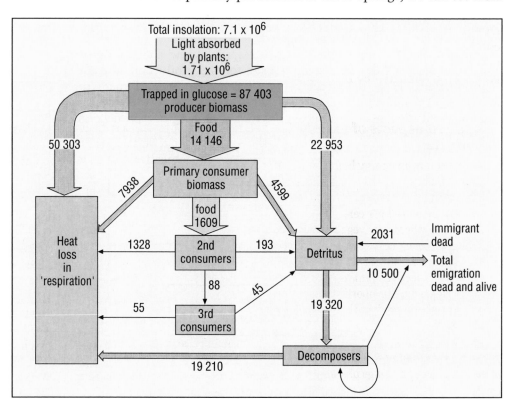

Figure 3.22 The energy flow in the Silver Springs community, Florida. The units are kJ m^{-2} yr^{-1}. Notice how little of the sunlight that strikes the plants (insolation) ends up trapped in glucose.

figure 3.22 that some of it went to the decomposers, some was carried downstream and some was consumed by the herbivores. In turn, some of the energy transferred to the herbivores goes to the first level carnivores, and some of the energy transferred to them goes to the second level carnivores.

The percentage of the energy at one trophic level which ends up in the next trophic level is called the **trophic efficiency**. The trophic efficiency of the herbivores, for instance, equals the percentage of the net primary production that is converted to herbivore production (i.e. to the growth and reproduction of herbivores). Similarly, the trophic efficiency of the first level carnivores equals the percentage of the production of the herbivores that is converted to first level carnivore production (i.e. to the growth and reproduction of first level carnivores).

From the data in figure 3.22 we can calculate these trophic efficiencies:

Trophic efficiency of herbivores	$= 6187$ kJ m^{-2} yr^{-1} ÷ 39 000 kJ m^{-2} yr^{-1}
	$= 16\%$
Trophic efficiency of first level carnivores	$= 280$ kJ m^{-2} yr^{-1} ÷ 6187 kJ m^{-2} yr^{-1}
	$= 5\%$
Trophic efficiency of second level carnivores	$= 25$ kJ m^{-2} yr^{-1} ÷ 280 kJ m^{-2} yr^{-1}
	$= 9\%$

Ecologists have now calculated trophic efficiencies for a number of ecosystems. The measured values range from less than 1 per cent to over 40 per cent. Some of the lowest values are found in ecosystems where most of the animals are birds or mammals. The trophic efficiencies of small mammals, for instance, are generally less than 1 per cent.

Some of the highest trophic efficiencies are found in the oceans. The trophic efficiencies of zooplankton feeding on phytoplankton, for instance, can be over 40 per cent. This means that a pyramid of energy drawn for an ocean ecosystem would have steeper sides than one drawn for a terrestrial ecosystem dominated by birds or mammals. Can you see why?

Applied aspects of energy budgets

Farmers rely on energy budgets to stay in business and provide the rest of us with food. Although plants only convert about 1–3 per cent of incident sunlight into vegetation, sunlight doesn't cost anything and there's a lot of it around. Over the centuries selective plant breeding has increased the proportion of photosynthetic product that is channelled into the part of the plant that we eat. Wheat, for instance, used to stand almost 2 m tall, as can be seen from paintings of medieval harvests. Nowadays, it is less than a third of that height. This means that more of the plant matter ends up in the grain.

Animal farmers want a high proportion of the energy ingested by their flock or herd to go towards production (i.e. growth and reproduction) rather than respiration. They therefore use a variety of techniques to maximise the economic value of their animals. Strategies include:

- Ensuring that food is highly digestible;
- Using young animals (older animals put less of their energy intake into growth);
- Minimising energy expenditure by the animals – for example, by keeping the animals warm and in the dark.

Pigs have the highest growth efficiency of any domestic mammal, transforming up to 15 per cent of the energy they ingest into meat. This is why pork is a relatively inexpensive meat, despite the fact that pigs require more looking after than many other farm animals.

Summary

1 A **community** consists of the organisms found in an area. These organisms interact with one another in a large number of ways.

2 An **ecosystem** consists of the interacting organisms and their **abiotic environment** within an area.

3 The change in the species found in a community over time is known as **succession**.

4 **Primary succession** is the progressive colonisation of a previously unoccupied area, such as bare rock or open water. **Secondary succession** begins in an area which has been previously colonised.

5 The end point of a succession is known as a **climax community**. Over much of Europe, mixed deciduous forest is the climax community.

6 Species can be classified into **producers** (autotrophic organisms), **consumers** (heterotrophic organisms) and **decomposers (saprobionts)**.

7 **Nutrient cycles** show how matter circulates around an ecosystem. They have two components: a biological component and a geochemical component.

8 The nutritional sequence that leads from producers to **top carnivores** is known as a **food chain**. Food chains rarely have more than six **trophic levels**.

9 A **food web** shows the feeding relationships of a community more fully than do food chains. A food web consists of interconnected food chains.

10 A **pyramid of numbers** shows the number of organisms at each trophic level in a community. A **pyramid of biomass** shows the mass of organisms at each trophic level.

11 A **pyramid of energy** shows the rate at which energy flows through the trophic levels of a community.

12 Pyramids of numbers are quite often **inverted**, pyramids of biomass occasionally and pyramids of energy never.

13 The efficiency with which energy is passed from one trophic level to another varies greatly, but is rarely more than 10 per cent.

Review questions

1 What is the difference between a community and an ecosystem?

2 Discuss why the concept of the ecosystem has proved so powerful in ecology.

3 What differences might you expect to develop in the soil during a succession on a sand dune?

4 Suggest two reasons why secondary successions are generally more rapid than primary successions.

5 What might be the ecological consequences in tropical grassland ecosystems if elephants, rhinoceroses, cheetahs and leopards are hunted to extinction?

6 Make a simple diagram of the nitrogen cycle which shows its main features.

7 What significant differences are there between the carbon and nitrogen cycles?

8 Describe how you might determine the food web of a small pond.

9 Into which trophic level would you place an internal parasite such as a tapeworm?

10 With reference to pyramids of energy explain why it takes a smaller area of agricultural land to provide the food for a vegetarian compared to someone with a high meat intake.

Further reading

Oliver Rackham's *The History of the Countryside* (J.M. Dent, 1986) is an award-winning book which provides a comprehensive account of the communities found in Great Britain.

The best introduction to global ecosystems is probably still R.H. Whittaker's *Communities and Ecosystems,* 2nd edn. (Macmillan/Collier Macmillan, 1975).

Biology, Advanced Topics focuses on these specific aspects of ecology: the energetics of food production, energy flow and nutrient cycling in ecosystems, and succession.

Pollution and conservation

In the last two chapters we have concentrated on the natural environments of this planet. We have looked at biomes, ecosystems, communities and habitats largely as if they existed independently of humans. But of course this is not the case. Until a few thousand years ago humans were just one species among countless others, but today there are few areas in the world that have not been influenced by our activities. As we shall see in this chapter, even the ice of the Arctic and Antarctic and the waters of the largest oceans have been significantly affected by our species (figure 4.1).

We will look first at the pollution we cause, and then at efforts to limit the negative effects of our activities by conservation.

Pollution

Pollution is the damaging release by humans of materials or energy into the environment. The materials or energy released are referred to as **pollutants**.

Of course, whether an action is 'damaging' is often a matter of opinion. Is the addition of insecticides to the environment damaging? On the one hand, the pesticide may accumulate in food chains to the point at which it prevents some species from breeding and may be poisonous to humans. In this respect the pesticide is damaging. On the other hand, it may kill organisms that transmit diseases or eat crops, and so be used to our benefit. To understand pollution you need to understand biology, chemistry, economics, sociology and psychology!

A useful distinction can be made between biodegradable and non-biodegradable pollutants. **Biodegradable pollutants** like sewage are broken down by micro-organisms to harmless substances fairly quickly. **Non-biodegradable** pollutants, though, cannot be so readily broken down. They tend to accumulate and are therefore potentially more dangerous. We will look at several specific pollutants and their effects on ecosystems.

Carbon dioxide

It may seem strange to describe this odourless, invisible gas as a pollutant, especially as it is needed for photosynthesis and occurs in the atmosphere at a concentration of less than one part in a thousand. However, on a global scale carbon dioxide may prove to be the most serious pollutant over the next hundred years. This is because it contributes to the so-called **greenhouse effect**.

The greenhouse effect takes its name from the fact that carbon dioxide, along with some other atmospheric components, helps to warm the Earth in much the same way that glass helps to warm a greenhouse (figure 4.2). Measurements of the carbon dioxide concentration of air bubbles trapped in the ice of Antarctica show that from about 500 BC to AD 1880 the carbon dioxide concentration remained fairly steady at about 270 ppm (parts per million). Since then, however, the global carbon dioxide concentration has been rising at a gradually increasing rate and has now reached over 350 ppm, an increase of 30 per cent (figure 4.3).

What has caused this increase in the level of atmospheric carbon dioxide? One answer is that we are burning more and more fossil fuels. This releases carbon dioxide into the atmosphere from coal, oil, gas and peat formed over several hundred million years. A second cause is that the world's forests are being cut down at an ever-increasing rate, thus removing plants that would otherwise take up the carbon dioxide. To some extent,

Figure 4.1 Tropical island off Malaysia. Even here the water contains detectable levels of pollutants, while a rise in sea level, possibly resulting from increased atmospheric levels of carbon dioxide, could destroy such islands.

Light rays

Heat rays

Figure 4.2 The greenhouse effect. Light rays (short wavelength electromagnetic radiation) from the sun pass through the glass into the greenhouse. They strike objects in the greenhouse, warming them. These objects give out heat rays (long wavelength electromagnetic radiation) which cannot get through the glass. So heat energy is held within the greenhouse. The same process happens in the Earth's atmosphere. Light rays from the sun heat up the Earth's surface. Some of the Earth's reflected heat is trapped by carbon dioxide, water vapour and some other gases in the atmosphere. These gases hold heat energy in, just as glass does in a greenhouse.

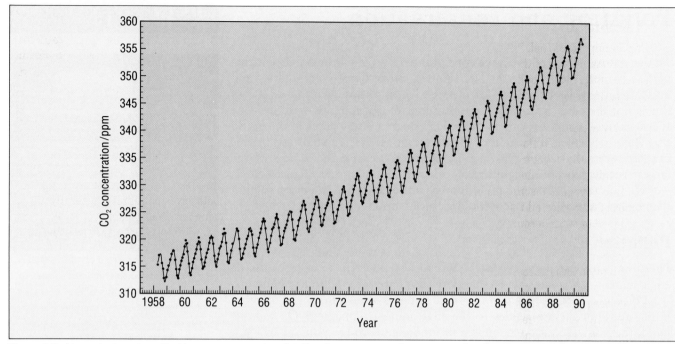

Figure 4.3 Atmospheric carbon dioxide concentrations (four-weekly averages) measured at Mauna Loa Observatory, Hawaii between 1958 and 1990. The monthly fluctuations, caused by seasonal differences in the amount of photosynthesis, are superimposed on a steady upward trend.

negative feedback comes to the rescue. As the amount of carbon dioxide in the atmosphere increases, plants automatically photosynthesise more rapidly. Unfortunately, this only uses up about one-third of the extra carbon dioxide being released into the atmosphere.

What are the likely consequences of the greenhouse effect? Scientists know that during the last hundred years, average world temperatures have risen by between 0.5 and 1.0°C. This may not sound very much, but the warming is greatest at the poles and over a number of years warming by only a few degrees centigrade could lead to much of the ice at the poles melting. There is already some evidence that this has begun to happen.

Scientists still cannot predict with any confidence what the likely consequences of the greenhouse effect will be. However, it is thought that over the next few decades, world temperatures may increase by a further 1 to 5°C. Possible consequences include the flooding of much of the world's coastal land. There may also be more droughts in sub-tropical latitudes (5–35°N).

The greenhouse effect is an example of **global pollution**. No one government on its own can hope to overcome it. International cooperation is needed. There are several possible ways in which the rise in carbon dioxide concentrations could be halted:

- A switch could be made from the burning of fossil fuels to the use of nuclear power.
- The use of alternative energy sources such as solar power and wind power could be expanded.
- More energy-saving measures could be introduced.
- People could stop expecting their standard of living (and therefore energy consumption) to go on rising.
- A massive tree-planting programme could be started, allowing carbon dioxide to be 'locked up' in wood.
- Nutrient enrichment of the oceans might allow huge algal blooms, which would again trap carbon dioxide in organic matter.

It will be interesting to see which, if any, of these measures are adopted in the years ahead.

Oil pollution

Oil is an important fuel, but is found only in certain parts of the world. Because of this, vast amounts of oil are carried every day by supertankers around the globe. Inevitably accidents happen and **oil spills** result. Oil pollution may also occur when ballast water taken into empty tankers to provide stability on the return voyage is discharged, and in times of war when oil refineries are bombed or when a country deliberately spills oil into the sea for military purposes.

Oil is lighter than water and, being non-polar, does not dissolve in it. As a result, large **oil slicks** form on the surface of the water. These may persist for weeks or months, before being washed up on coastlines or eventually dispersing.

The most obvious victims of oil pollution are oceanic birds and other large animals, thousands of which may die as a result of oil spills. However, such damage is only the tip

Damage resulting from the Haven oil spill, Riviera di Ponente, near Genoa, Italy.

of the iceberg. Many other species are killed by the oil which carpets the water, preventing photosynthesis and smothering organisms.

Early attempts to treat oil pollution involved using **detergents** to disperse the oil, much as washing-up liquid helps grease to dissolve in water. However, such treatment often caused more pollution than it prevented, as detergents are themselves pollutants, generally being non-biodegradable.

More recent methods at treating oil pollution involve:

- Using floating booms to prevent slicks from reaching the shore.
- Setting fire to the oil.
- Pumping the oil back into special collection ships.
- Adding naturally occurring bacteria that can digest oil.
- Adding special oil spill cleansers that are relatively non-toxic and more biodegradable than previously used detergents.

Damage to the ozone layer

Ozone, O_3, is found at low concentrations in the Earth's stratosphere, 15 to 50 km up. Here it serves the useful function of intercepting much of the dangerous ultraviolet radiation that would otherwise strike the Earth from the sun and damage the genetic material in cells. During the late 1980s, measurements above Antarctica showed a seasonal collapse in the amount of ozone there. A hole in the ozone layer was appearing and getting bigger each year.

The chemicals found to be damaging the ozone layer were identified as **CFCs** (chlorofluorocarbons). In the atmosphere these break down, releasing atoms of chlorine. The chlorine atoms then react with ozone as follows:

$$Cl + O_3 \rightarrow ClO + O_2$$

The ClO so formed then reacts with an oxygen atom thus:

$$ClO + O \rightarrow Cl + O_2$$

As a result of these two reactions, a molecule of ozone is destroyed without any chlorine being used up. Chlorine atoms can therefore be said to *catalyse* the destruction of ozone. The English scientist Joe Farman, who discovered the hole in the ozone layer, calculates that a single CFC molecule can remove hundreds of thousands of ozone molecules.

Until very recently CFCs were widely used in refrigerators, aerosol sprays and fast-food packaging. Thanks to intensive lobbying by scientists and environmentalists, a number of international measures have now been agreed which hopefully will cut back the use of CFCs. If these measures are not successful, a rise in the number of cases of skin cancer is likely, particularly in countries close to Antarctica, as more ultraviolet radiation gets through to ground level.

Pesticides

Pests are organisms which people consider a nuisance or harmful. **Pesticides** are substances deliberately introduced into the environment to kill pests. The main classes of pesticides are **herbicides** (used to kill weeds), **insecticides** (developed for use against insects) and **fungicides** (which kill fungi).

Herbicides rarely cause serious environmental problems even though they are widely used. Most of them are biodegradable and are only dangerous to humans and other animals when used in fairly high concentrations. Fungicides, however, can be important pollutants. Many of them contain either copper or mercury, as fungi are very sensitive to these two elements. Mercury is toxic to humans. Cases have arisen, for instance in Japan, where people have died as a result of eating fish and molluscs which had accumulated quite high concentrations of mercury.

Many substances, from cyanide and nicotine to synthetic organochlorines, have been used as insecticides. A general problem with many insecticides is that they don't just kill the intended insects. Often the insecticide also kills useful insects which may parasitise, eat or compete with the harmful species. This means that when the time comes for the insecticide to be used a second or third time, the natural checks to the population growth of the pest will have been removed (figure 4.4). A farmer may then become

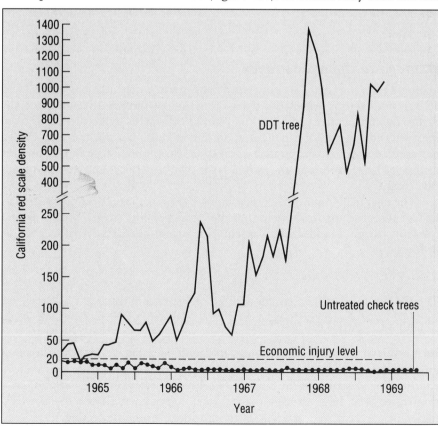

Figure 4.4 Increases in California red scale (*Aonidiella aurantii*) infestation on lemon trees caused by monthly applications of DDT spray. Nearby untreated lemon trees suffered no economic damage because a variety of insect parasites and predators kept the red scale under control.

locked into an expensive dependency on the insecticide, being forced to spray more often than was originally required.

Some of the most widely used insecticides have been the **organochlorines**. These are fairly non-biodegradable. One such compound, 1,1-bis(*p*-chlorophenyl)-2,2,2-trichloroethane, better known as **DDT**, was widely used during and after the Second World War against mosquitoes and other insects. Thanks to its use, millions of people survived who would otherwise have died of malaria or starvation. However, DDT and other organochlorine insecticides get amplified in food chains. This is because they are not very soluble in water, and so tend not to be excreted. Instead, they are stored in fat where they accumulate. Because an animal generally eats *lots* of animals belonging to the preceding trophic level – a single heron eats hundreds of fish for example – the concentration of the insecticide increases as it goes along a food chain.

As organochlorines accumulate in food chains, carnivores are more at risk than herbivores (figure 4.5). In Britain, the peregrine falcon (*Falco peregrinus*) began to decline in numbers in the 1950s. By the 1960s its numbers were less than half of what they had been 25 years earlier. Careful research by the ecologist Derek Ratcliffe established that the decline of the peregrine was due to the accumulation of organochlorine residues. These caused the birds to lay eggs with thinner shells (figure 4.6). These thin shells resulted in the eggs being more likely to get broken. Fortunately, the story has a happy ending. The British government introduced strict restrictions on the use of organochlorine pesticides and by the late 1980s peregrine numbers had completely recovered.

A further problem with pesticides is that pests may evolve **resistance** to them, requiring ever-increasing doses to be applied. We shall return to this issue in a later chapter (see page 798).

Acid rain

In 1851 Robert Smith read a paper to the British Association for the Advancement of Science in which the phenomenon of acid rain was

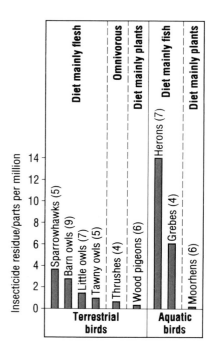

Figure 4.5 Average concentration of organochlorine insecticide residues in the breast muscle of different types of bird. The number of species analysed is given in brackets after the name of each type.

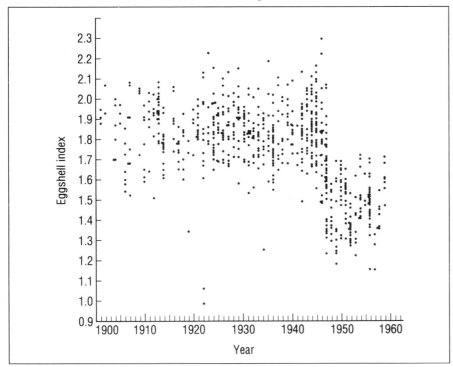

Figure 4.6 Eggshell index, an indication of eggshell thickness, in British peregrine falcons from 1900 to 1960. Notice the sudden decrease in thickness in the late 1940s at just the time when DDT began to be used.

$$\text{Eggshell index} = \frac{\text{mass of egg (mg)}}{\text{length} \times \text{breath (mm)}}$$

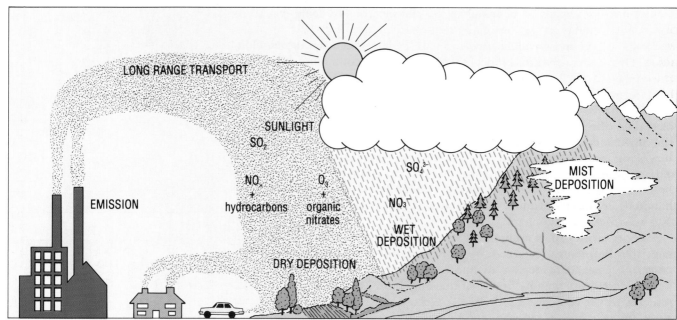

Figure 4.7 Acid rain is caused by the emissions of various gases resulting from the burning of fossil fuels. The principal gases involved are sulphur dioxide (SO_2) and several oxides of nitrogen (NO_x). Dry deposition happens in the absence of rain. The action of sunlight on NO_x and hydrocarbons in the atmosphere can give rise to photochemical smog in which ozone(O_3) and organic nitrates are important secondary pollutants. Wet deposition is particularly severe in upland areas covered with mists for long periods of time.

Figure 4.8 Spruce trees in an acid rain-damaged forest in the Karkonoski National Park, Poland. In 1989, rainfall of pH 1.7 was recorded on one occasion.

described for the first time. **Acid rain** is the result of a variety of processes which together lead to acidic gases being deposited from the atmosphere (figure 4.7). The main sources of these acidic gases are power stations that burn coal or oil, and motor vehicles. The gases involved are sulphur dioxide (SO_2) and various oxides of nitrogen (collectively labelled NO_x). When these gases dissolve in rain water, the rain that falls typically has a pH of between 4.0 and 4.5. Unpolluted rain water has a pH of about 5.6.

Lichens are among the organisms most sensitive to atmospheric sulphur dioxide. Different species of lichen vary in their tolerance to sulphur dioxide, but most are so susceptible that they cannot grow in industrial areas. That is why tree trunks and tombstones in cities often have fewer lichens than in rural areas. The distribution of lichens around major industrial centres shows that sulphur dioxide pollution drifts downwind. Nowadays coal- and oil-fired power stations are equipped with very tall chimneys. These enable the pollutants to be carried hundreds of miles away. Much of Britain's industrial pollutants falls as acid rain on Germany and Scandinavia.

Acid rain probably contributes to the damage of many European and North American forests (figure 4.8). In these forests trees may lose their leaves and even die. It is also thought to be responsible for the fact that during the 1960s and 1970s many of the fish in Scandinavian lakes and rivers died. It has proved difficult to be certain that acid rain is responsible for damage to forests and lakes, but the evidence is highly suggestive. Unfortunately, measures to reduce the emissions of the gases responsible for acid rain are expensive and governments have been slow to pass effective legislation.

Sewage

Sewage is the water-borne waste of society. It includes both domestic and industrial sewage. Domestic sewage contains human faeces and urine, the water used to wash these away and the dirty water that flows from our baths and sinks. Industrial sewage includes the dirty water from industry, hospitals and abattoirs. Agricultural sewage is not allowed to mix with domestic and industrial waste, and is treated separately.

If untreated sewage or agricultural fertilisers are allowed to enter lakes or rivers, **eutrophication** may occur. Eutrophication is the enrichment of water with nutrients when large amounts of organic matter, or nitrogen and phosphorus, enter the water. A chain reaction then occurs, as a result of which the oxygen level of the water falls and many organisms die (figure 4.9).

The degree of eutrophication in a body of water can be determined by measuring the rate at which a sample of the water takes up oxygen in the dark. This is known as the **biological oxygen demand (BOD)**. The higher the BOD, the greater the number of aerobic micro-organisms in the water and the greater the degree of eutrophication. At a sewage treatment works, the BOD of the sewage can be reduced by a factor of over 20. This means that the water discharged into lakes or rivers after treatment is far less likely to cause pollution.

The principles of sewage treatment are outlined in figure 4.10. Two main techniques are available for treating the effluent from the primary treatment tanks. In a **biological filter system** the soluble supernatant from the primary sedimentation tanks is allowed to trickle down through a filter bed under the influence of gravity. This filter bed is usually composed of rock chippings and provides a large surface area for the growth of bacteria and fungi. These microbes support a complex community of protoctists, rotifers, annelids, nematodes, flies, beetles and springtails. Between them, these organisms remove most of the organic matter from the effluent.

The other technique used in sewage treatment is the **activated sludge system**. Here the supernatant fluid from the primary sedimentation tanks is fed into large tanks and mechanically aerated. Again, bacteria and fungi feed off the sewage, but the mechanical agitation prevents the growth of larger invertebrates.

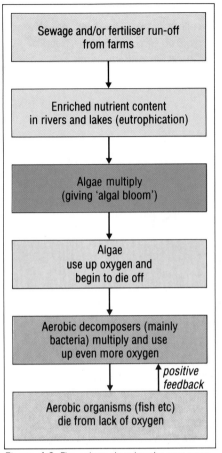

Figure 4.9 Flow chart showing the sequence of events which may result from eutrophication.

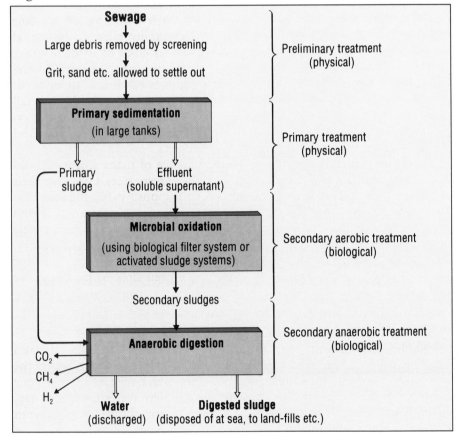

Figure 4.10 Major stages in the treatment of sewage.

Figure 4.11 Diagrammatic representation of the effects of sewage discharge into a river.
A and **B** Physical and chemical changes;
C Changes in micro-organisms;
D Changes in aquatic invertebrates.

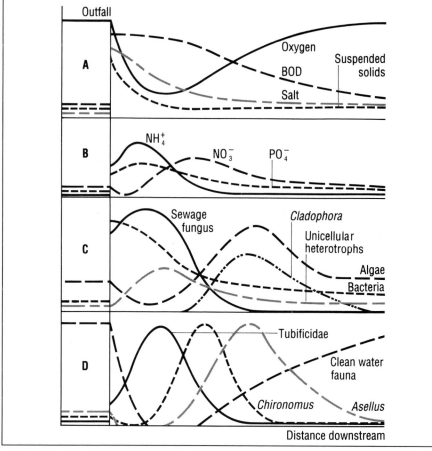

With either system the end result is much the same. The great majority of the organic matter is removed from the sewage by aerobic decomposition. Despite this, the water finally discharged from a sewage works still has lots of nutrients and a biological oxygen demand about six times that of clean river water. Figure 4.11 shows what happens when sewage enters an otherwise unpolluted and well oxygenated river.

Reclaiming colliery spoil

Coal mining often takes place near areas of high human population. When coal is mined, huge mounds of unwanted colliery spoil accumulate near the mine. Plants are often very slow to colonise these spoil tips, with the result that for many years ugly naked heaps scar the landscape.

Restoring land which has been scarred in this kind of way so that it is covered with vegetation is called **reclamation**. Soil analyses show that colliery spoil often has a pH of less than 3.5 and is frequently very low in essential plant nutrients. Reclamation of such spoil usually

first involves liming the area. This helps to neutralise the soil, though as much as 50 tonnes of lime per hectare may be needed. Fertilisers can then be added to provide essential nitrogen and phosphorus.

Seeding is then carried out. The seed added depends on whether or not it is intended to graze the land. If it is to be grazed, a plant like ryegrass (*Lolium perenne*) is often used as this is palatable to grazing animals. If, however, grazing is not envisaged, a plant such as wavy hair grass (*Deschampsia flexuosa*) may be more suitable. Wavy hair grass can grow well on quite acid soil and therefore less lime has to be added.

Legumes are nearly always sown along with the grasses. This is because most legumes can fix atmospheric nitrogen (see Chapter 17). Once established, they reduce the need for further applications of fertiliser, thus making the reclamation operation less expensive.

Although colliery spoils are unsightly and nearly always benefit from reclamation, limestone quarries often make attractive nature reserves if they are left alone once quarrying has finished. The nutrient-poor soil allows a wealth of beautiful chalk-loving plants to colonise the site over the years.

Radioactivity

The average person living in the United Kingdom receives a total radiation dose of about 2 millisieverts per year. About 87 per cent of this is natural radiation which comes either from outer space (e.g. cosmic rays) or from rocks in the Earth's crust that contain radioactive materials. The other 13 per cent of the radiation we receive is the result of human activity (figure 4.12). The great majority of this 13 per cent comes from radioactivity used for medical purposes. This includes radioactivity from X-rays, used for diagnostic purposes, and from **radiotherapy**, used in the treatment of many cancers. Only about 1 per cent of the radioactivity to which we are exposed is due to radiation from nuclear power stations or nuclear weapons.

Advocates of nuclear power use these figures to emphasise how safe nuclear power is. However, most of the worries about nuclear power centre on what would happen if there was a major accident at a nuclear power station. So far the world's worst nuclear accident was the explosion at Chernobyl in South-West Russia on 26 April 1986. This released large quantities of **radionuclides** (radioactive substances) into the atmosphere and led to the Russian authorities having to evacuate 135 000 people from within a 36 km radius of the plant. The radionuclides produced were eventually deposited throughout the northern hemisphere. In Britain the worst affected regions were upland areas in North Wales, Cumbria and Scotland. These areas were severely affected for the simple reason that they receive a lot of rain. The rain washed the radionuclides down and deposited them on the ground.

The radioactive substances in the Chernobyl fallout that proved most significant in the long term were caesium-134 (half-life = 2 years) and caesium-137 (half-life = 32 years). Considerable quantities of iodine-131 were also released but as this has a half-life of only eight days, most of the radioactivity from this source soon disappeared. Measurements on the level of radioactivity present in lamb and mutton led to restrictions on the movement and slaughtering of some British sheep. It is an indication of just how little we understand about pollution from radioactivity that these restrictions were initially introduced for a three-week period, but were still in force three years later (figure 4.13).

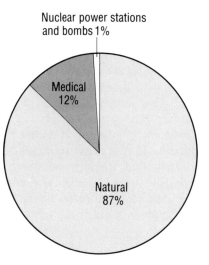

Figure 4.12 Sources of radiation for the average person living in the United Kingdom.

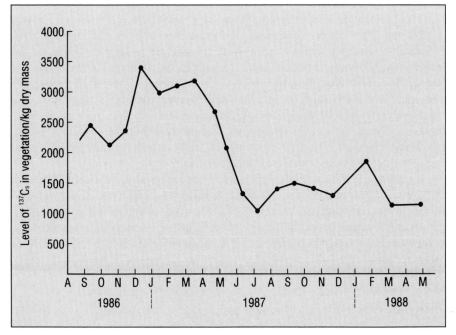

Figure 4.13 Changes in the ^{137}Cs (caesium-137) activity from vegetation on a typical Cumbrian sheep farm in Britain after the explosion at the Chernobyl nuclear power station in South-West Russia in April 1986. The safety level for radiation levels in meat set by the National Radiological Protection Board is 1000 becquerels/kg fresh mass.

Thermal pollution

All the examples of pollution considered so far have involved the release of materials into the environment. Thermal pollution occurs when excessive amounts of heat energy are produced with damaging consequences. It is most noticeable in rivers downstream from industries that use river water for cooling purposes. Once the water has done its job, it is returned – warmed – to the river. In the River Trent temperature rises of over 20°C have been recorded more than 1.5 km downstream of a Central Electricity Generating Board power station.

It might be thought that such warming would have no ill effects. However, as the temperature of water rises, the water holds less dissolved oxygen. At 5°C a litre of water can hold up to 9 cm³ of dissolved oxygen. At 20°C, the same volume of water can hold only 6 cm³ of oxygen. Changes in the temperature of a river can therefore lead to fish and other organisms dying through asphyxiation. The problem is compounded by the fact that the warmer the water, the greater the metabolic rate of the organisms and therefore the greater their oxygen requirements.

Thermal pollution has not yet proved to be much of a problem. However, on a global scale the greenhouse effect is a type of thermal pollution which may prove far more serious than the warming of an occasional river.

In the event of a nuclear war there is little doubt that enormous numbers of people would be killed or horribly injured. Information from the bombs dropped on Hiroshima and Nagasaki at the end of the Second World War shows that radioactivity causes an increase in the incidence of genetic mutation. This means that the effects of a nuclear war would persist for at least two generations. Some people feel that the existence of nuclear bombs has made the world a safer place by reducing the number of conventional (non-nuclear) wars. Others fear that as the number of countries with nuclear weapons increases, their eventual use, if only by terrorists, is inevitable.

Having looked at the problems of pollution we will now turn to the subject of conservation to see what can be done to protect our planet and the organisms that live on it.

Conservation

Garrett Hardin, of the University of California, has put the fundamental need for conservation succinctly in an essay called *The Tragedy of the Commons*.

The 'commons' is a communal pasture available to everyone who wants to use it. Each herder possesses a certain number of grazing animals. Although he realises that the amount of grass on the commons is limited, he feels that if his animals do not eat it someone else's will. So he increases the size of his herd. Not unnaturally this causes one of the other herders to increase *his* herd – and so on. Eventually over-grazing occurs with dire consequences not only for the animals themselves, which cannot get enough food, but for the ecosystem in general. The point is that the pasture – indeed any habitat – has a limited **carrying capacity** which cannot be exceeded without upsetting the ecosystem (figure 4.14).

The tragedy of the commons has been repeated a thousand times in different ecosystems. We cut down too many trees, catch too many fish and shoot too many elephants (figure 4.15). The root problem is human selfishness. **Conservation** involves managing the Earth's resources so as to restore and maintain a balance between the requirements of humans and those of other species.

Why conserve?

There are two main reasons why we should conserve. One is an *ethical* reason, the other a *pragmatic* one. The ethical reason is that we have a

Figure 4.14 Overgrazing by domestic animals can turn a productive area (*above*) into a near-desert (*below*).

moral duty to look after the environment: we have no right to destroy ecosystems or allow species to become extinct. The pragmatic argument says that it is to our advantage to ensure the integrity of our environment: if we preserve the tropical rain forests, the greenhouse effect will be lessened; if we conserve fish stocks, we can get more food from the seas; and if we reduce water pollution, people will be able to swim on unpolluted beaches and fish in clean rivers.

We shall look at the issue of conservation at four levels: the international level, the national level, the local level and finally the individual level.

Conservation at the international level

Conservation at the international level requires the concerted action of many nations. We have already discussed the damage to the ozone layer and the problems of the greenhouse effect. Resolution of both these problems will require cooperation between the major industrial nations of the world. Similarly, measures to reduce the risks of nuclear war require international negotiation.

However, there are other ecological issues which require international agreement. We will focus on the hunting of whales and the preservation of tropical rain forests.

Whale hunting

Whales have been hunted by humans for thousands of years. But it wasn't until the 1700s that whaling became a commercial industry. During the eighteenth and early nineteenth centuries, enormous numbers of right whales were taken by whaling ships from Britain and Holland. This species takes its name from the fact that it swims slowly and floats when dead. This makes it the 'right' whale to hunt. By 1850 right whales had become so rare that it was no longer worth hunting them. Instead, the whalers turned to the sperm whale. Then, in 1868, the explosive harpoon was invented. This made it feasible to hunt the great blue and fin whales of Antarctica (figure 4.16).

The history of whaling has been a saga of one species after another being hunted to near extinction. Two early pieces of evidence suggested that numbers were falling steeply. One was that more effort was required to catch each whale (figure 4.17). The second was that more juveniles were being caught (figure 4.18).

Figure 4.15 Elephant tusks compounded in Kenya.

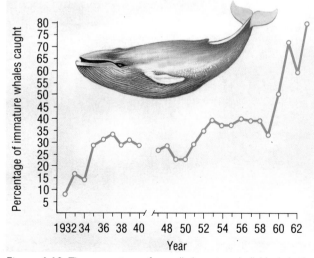

Figure 4.16 A blue whale – the largest animal species ever to have existed on Earth. This one was photographed in the Sea of Cortez, Baja California.

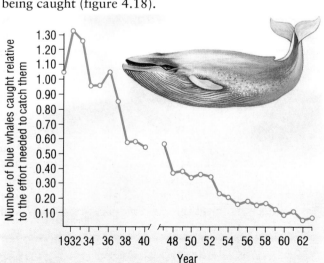

Figure 4.17 The catch per unit effort (measured as the catch per catcher-day's work) of blue whales in the Antarctic from 1931 to 1963.

Figure 4.18 The percentage of sexually immature individuals in the blue whale catch in the Antarctic from 1931 to 1963.

Figure 4.19 Interior of a rain forest in cloud. The Monteverde Forest Reserve, Costa Rica.

In 1946 **the International Whaling Commission (IWC)** was set up to conserve whale stocks by regulating the whaling industry. Since then the Commission has fought a series of battles as country after country has wanted to exceed the catches recommended by scientists. On a positive note, most countries have now stopped whaling. Indeed, commercial whaling ceased in 1988, though a few countries still take whales for 'scientific' or 'cultural' reasons.

Remarkably, no species of whales have yet become extinct, so there is a chance that their populations will recover. However, it is desperately difficult to know for sure just how many whales there still are. In the 1960s, when blue whale hunting stopped, estimates suggested that a total of between 10 000 and 20 000 individuals remained south of the Equator from an original number of nearly 250 000. But 1989 estimates range from 200 to 1100 individuals.

Similarly, until as recently as March 1989 the IWC thought that of the 1 250 000 sperm whales originally living in the southern hemisphere, 950 000 remained. But in June 1989 a figure of between 2000 and 4000 was produced by the IWC Scientific Committee. Commercial fishing of the crustaceans called **krill**, on which many whales feed in the waters around Antarctica, may mean that whale numbers will never recover to their former levels, even in the absence of any hunting.

Two of the countries which still hunt whales are Japan and Iceland. Both countries maintain that whale hunting is an important part of their national culture. This reminds us that not all conservation disputes involve purely economic considerations.

Saving the tropical rain forests

Why should we preserve the world's tropical rain forests? The ethical argument is that they are the most diverse biome in the world (figure 4.19). They contain millions of species completely unknown to us. Most of the species that live in tropical rain forests probably haven't even been named yet. The pragmatic argument states that the tropical rain forests play a vital part in the health of our world. Quite apart from their possible role in averting excessive global warming, many pharmaceutical drugs of immense value are probably obtainable from plants found only in the rain forests.

A second pragmatic reason for preserving the tropical rain forests is that in countries where forests have been extensively cut down (**deforestation**), severe erosion has often followed (figure 4.20). Normally the vegetation prevents heavy rains from washing away the soil. The plants in a rain forest hold on to rain water, rather like a sponge, and only slowly release it

Figure 4.20 Landslide resulting from deforestation, Mount Kaindi, Papua New Guinea.

into rivers. Once this protective blanket is removed, several interrelated changes occur:

- Sheet erosion of surface soils leads to loss of fertility.
- Gully erosion increases the rate at which water runs off, leading to flooding.
- Changes in the amount of light reflected back by the forest into the atmosphere alter patterns of precipitation. The result is heavier and less frequent rain which exacerbates the flooding.

A study in 1989 of an Amazon rain forest in Peru showed that each hectare of the forest produced fruit and latex (rubber) with an annual market value of $700. If, however, the trees are cut down, the total value of their wood is $1000. Now, trees can only be felled once, but fruit and latex can be harvested every year. This study into sustainable management provides a ray of hope for the Amazonian rain forest. If governments can be persuaded that more money can be made from rain forests by exploiting them on a sustainable basis than by destroying them, it may be worth their while to preserve them.

In 1990 in the Amazon rain forest, an area the size of Belgium was burnt. The destruction of the rain forests is an international issue because much of the pressure to cut them down comes from countries such as Japan and the USA. Japan, despite its small size, imports 30 per cent of the world's tropical hardwoods. We should also remember that when countries like Brazil and the Philippines cut down their forests they are only doing what many other countries, such as the USA and those in Europe, have already done over many centuries.

Conservation at the national level

Although some conservation requires international cooperation, there is a tremendous amount that individual countries can do. We will look at one example in Australia.

The problem of introduced species in Australia

Australia has been an island separated from other continents for approximately 55 million years. This has allowed its flora and fauna to evolve in their own unique way. Unfortunately, during the last 200 years a great many animals and plants have been introduced into Australia and these have done untold harm. For instance, the sensitive mimosa bush (*Mimosa pigra*) has been introduced from South America. In Kakadu National Park it is spreading at such a rate that four men employed full time cannot control it. As a result it is turning the wetlands into shrubby heath.

Another example is the bitou bush (*Chrysanthemoides monilifera*). This was introduced from South Africa between 1950 and 1970 to help stabilise sand dunes. However, it is forming vast impenetrable thickets over much of the New South Wales coast, where it is now choking out native vegetation.

Introduced animals also cause great problems in Australia. Rabbits and house mice eat enormous amounts of food, and rats eat the eggs of many native birds. In Chapter 5 we will look at two examples where species introduced into Australia have been brought under control. However, there are many more species that continue to cause great ecological damage. Whether the Australian government is prepared to put in the necessary finance to preserve what is left of Australia's unique fauna and flora remains to be seen.

Figure 4.21 Black-footed ferret. One of the few examples where captive breeding has saved a species from extinction.

Conservation at the local level

It is encouraging just how much can be achieved by local action. We will look at two examples which differ in scale. At one extreme is the rescue from extinction, at a cost of several million dollars, of the black-footed ferret. At the other is churchyard conservation which costs almost nothing.

Saving the black-footed ferret

The black-footed ferret is a large weasel that was once widespread throughout the western prairies of the USA (figure 4.21). It is a specialist carnivore, feeding only on large squirrel-like rodents called prairie dogs. Prairie dogs have been hunted as pests throughout the twentieth century on account of the damage they can cause to crops. As a result, the number of black-footed ferrets has crashed.

By 1986 the total known population of the black-footed ferret was less than 30 individuals. The Wyoming Game and Fish Department made the controversial decision to capture as many of these as possible to try to establish a programme of **captive breeding**. In September 1986 eleven females and six males were trapped; a further male was trapped in February 1987. Fortunately, the ferrets proved easier to breed in captivity than many had feared, and within five years their number had grown to 184 individuals.

The immediate aim of the recovery plan is to build up the population to about 200 individuals and to establish, by the year 2010, ten or more separate populations in the wild, each numbering around 150 ferrets.

Churchyard conservation

In many places, whether urban or rural, churchyards are an oasis of wildlife. Every churchyard is unique and has to be managed as such, but some broad guidelines can be given.

Most churchyards are essentially 'old pasture'. In Britain, for example, they were often used before this century for grazing the priest's sheep. With a bit of care, many churchyards can support over 50 species of native flowering plants, together with a rich fauna of butterflies, moths, other invertebrates, birds and mammals (figure 4.22).

The churchyard should provide a variety of habitats. Some of the grass should be cut regularly, say once a week during the growing season. Other areas should be cut less frequently, including some areas that are cut only once a year in the autumn. Where possible, grass cuttings should be removed to a compost heap.

A corner of the churchyard should be left almost untended. Here, brambles, nettles and native shrubs can grow up. These will provide nesting sites for birds, breeding grounds for butterflies and winter food for many animals. Where possible, one should ensure that the trees and bushes in the churchyard are native. The use of pesticides should be avoided as far as possible.

In Britain, churchyards are the responsibility of individual Parochial Church Councils. Usually they will be only too pleased for the offer of help, provided that access to the church and graves is kept clear. By looking after a churchyard, a small group of people can make a major impact on local conservation within just a few years.

Figure 4.22 A churchyard showing a variety of habitats. The ecological value of this particular churchyard would be increased if some of the grass was kept short. Why do you think this would be beneficial from the conservation point of view? It would certainly be appreciated by people visiting graves and having wedding photographs taken.

Conservation at the individual level

Ultimately, conservation is the responsibility of each of us individually. Even at the international level conservation relies on the pressure exerted by individuals. Here are ten things you can do to help conservation:

1 Belong to one or more conservation organisations.[1]
2 Write constructive letters to politicians about environmental matters.
3 Recycle paper, glass and metal cans.
4 Stop wearing coats made from the furs of wild animals (not too much of a sacrifice for most of us).
5 Buy 'environment friendly' products, such as recycled toilet paper.
6 Consider eating less meat.
7 If you have a garden, encourage native species to establish themselves and use fewer pesticides.
8 Help set up or maintain a conservation area at your school or local churchyard.
9 Don't drop litter, particularly of the non-biodegradable type.
10 Don't damage the countryside and in particular don't remove birds' eggs or uproot plants.

Nine hundred kiwis and a dog

Until recently, the Waitangi State Forest supported the largest-known population of the brown kiwi, a large flightless bird found only in (i.e. endemic to) New Zealand (see illustration).

On 24 August 1987, a large female kiwi was found recently killed. During the next six weeks more and more fresh carcasses were found, usually buried in the soil. Tooth marks and footprints showed that all the dead kiwis had been killed by a dog which had buried but not eaten them. Frantic searches for the predator finally resulted in success. On 30 September a German shepherd dog was found in the forest and shot. Thereafter no more kiwis disappeared.

During these six weeks the dog probably had killed about 500–600 of the 900 brown kiwis in the reserve. That works out at about a dozen birds a night. The trouble is that brown kiwis, being flightless, are defenceless against large predators. They are noisy birds, rather smelly

and very easy for a dog to find and kill. Kiwis evolved in the absence of mammalian predators – and German shepherd dogs are not native to New Zealand.

Brown kiwis breed very slowly. It will take an estimated 8–20 years for the population to recover from this attack, always assuming no other dogs get into the reserve. Introduced animal species, of which New Zealand has at least 34, have already driven many of the country's endemic species to extinction.

---

1 In Britain, to find the address of your Local Wildlife Trust, contact the Royal Society for Nature Conservation, The Green, Nettleham, Lincoln LN2 2NR. Telephone Lincoln (0522) 752326.

Summary

1 **Pollution** is the damaging release by humans of materials or energy into the environment. The materials or energy released are referred to as **pollutants**.

2 **Biodegradable** pollutants, such as waste paper, are fairly quickly broken down to harmless substances by micro-organisms. However, **non-biodegradable** pollutants cannot be so readily broken down.

3 The **greenhouse effect** takes its name from the fact that carbon dioxide and certain other atmospheric gases help to warm the Earth in much the same way that glass helps to warm a greenhouse.

4 Atmospheric carbon dioxide levels have risen at a steadily increasing rate over the last hundred years. This is due to the accelerating combustion of fossil fuels and destruction of the world's forests.

5 **CFCs** (chlorofluorocarbons) are responsible for damaging the ozone layer high in the Earth's atmosphere, thereby increasing the amount of ultraviolet radiation that reaches the Earth's surface.

6 Substances deliberately introduced into the environment to kill pests are called **pesticides**. They include **herbicides, insecticides** and **fungicides**.

7 The burning of coal, petrol and oil leads to the release into the atmosphere of sulphur dioxide and various oxides of nitrogen. When these gases dissolve in rain water, the rain acquires an unnaturally low pH and is known as **acid rain**. Acid rain probably contributes to the acidification of certain lakes and rivers and to the damage of many European and North American forests.

8 The release of untreated sewage or agricultural fertilisers into rivers or lakes may lead to **eutrophication** as the levels of nutrients and organic matter rise. This generally results in a fall in oxygen levels and to the loss of oxygen-demanding species.

9 **Conservation** involves managing the Earth's resources so as to restore and maintain a balance between the requirements of humans and of other species.

10 There are ethical and pragmatic arguments in favour of conservation.

11 Conservation can take place at international, national, local and individual levels.

12 Despite the efforts of the **International Whaling Commission,** the future of whales is still uncertain.

13 The continued loss of the remaining tropical rain forests may have serious local, regional and global consequences. Yet such loss continues apace.

14 **Captive breeding** programmes may help to save some endangered animals.

15 Effective conservation often requires careful legislation, but ultimately it relies on individual efforts.

Review questions

1 How could you investigate the extent to which different plastic bags are biodegradable?

2 It has proved easier to get international agreement to reduce CFC levels than to cut down CO_2 production. Why do you think this is?

3 List the advantages and disadvantages of using pesticides.

4 Describe the possible consequences following the discharge of a large amount of sugar into a stream.

5 Given the dangers of thermal pollution, suggest how the hot water produced by industry might be used more profitably.

6 What are the arguments for and against nuclear power?

7 What is the difference between conservation and preservation?

8 Do you think conservation measures should be targetted at endangered species or threatened habitats? Explain your answer.

9 What conservation measures would you like to see taken which are generally regarded as impractical?

10 How would a knowledge of the principles of biology be useful if you wanted to devise a conservation plan for a pond?

Further reading

The Human Impact on the Natural Environment by Andrew Goudie (Basil Blackwell, 1984), is an excellent book which goes into pollution and related topics in far more detail than this chapter can.

Another more recent book is *Biological Conservation* by I.F Spellerberg and S.R. Hardes (Cambridge University Press, 1992).

Rachel Carson's *Silent Spring* is a classic text published in 1962 but still well worth looking at. It was this book, more than any other, that gave rise to the green movement.

Probably the best regular guide to conservation matters is provided by the journal *Oryx* published four times a year by the Fauna & Flora Preservation Society, 1 Kensington Gore, London SW7 2AR, UK.

Populations and the niche concept

In the last three chapters we have seen how different species interact within communities, and how a community with its physical environment makes up an ecosystem. In this chapter we will look at the ecology of individuals within species. This is because we need to appreciate the problems faced by individual organisms in order to understand the ecology of an area. After all, natural selection operates on individuals rather than on whole species.

Populations

The word 'population' is used in everyday speech simply to mean the number of individuals of an organism. For ecologists, however, the word has a more precise definition. For one thing, the organisms in a population must belong to only one species. An ecologist would not talk about a population of songbirds, but of a population of great tits or blackbirds. Secondly, the individuals that make up a population must have the potential to breed with one another. Blackbirds in Paris do not belong to the same population as blackbirds in London (figure 5.1). Indeed, there are no doubt several populations of blackbirds in Paris, even though it may be difficult for a scientist to say where one ends and another begins.

In ecology, therefore, the word **population** refers to a group of individuals within a species that have the potential to breed with each other. The *number* of individuals in a population is called the **population size**.

CHAPTER 5

Figure 5.1 A blackbird. Just by looking at it, you can't tell whether it's a French or an English blackbird. However, different populations of blackbirds have subtle differences in their songs.

Estimating population size

There are many different ways of estimating population sizes depending on the species concerned. Perhaps the easiest technique is simply to count all the individuals in the population. However, this only really works for large sessile individuals that are reasonably spread out.

A useful technique which can be used for motile species is the **capture–recapture** method, also known as the **mark–release–recapture** method. The principle is straightforward. First a sample of individuals is caught, counted and marked in some way. Then these individuals are released. After being allowed to mix with the rest of the unmarked population, a second sample is caught and counted and the number of marked individuals noted. An estimate of the population size can then be made.

Suppose you catch 50 wood mice, mark and release them. Then a couple of days later you come back and catch 40 wood mice, four of which bear the mark you put on the 50 wood mice. In that case one in ten of the mice you caught the second time (four out of forty) had already been caught. The chances are, therefore, that when you caught and marked your original 50 wood mice, you only managed to mark one in ten of the population. In that case the best estimate you can make of the total population size is 500.

The formula for working out the population size by this method is as follows:

$$\text{Population size} = \frac{n_1 \times n_2}{n_m}$$

where n_1 is the number of individuals marked and released (1 standing for the first sample); n_2 is the number of individuals caught in the second sample (2 standing for the second sample); n_m is the number of marked individuals caught in the second sample (m standing for marked).

This formula (sometimes called the **Lincoln index**) can be used to estimate population sizes in different localities or to study changes in the population in a given locality over a period of time.

Different methods of capture and marking may be needed for different species. For instance, small mammals can be trapped in **Longworth traps** and marked by clipping off a small piece of their fur; ground beetles can be caught in **pitfall traps** and marked by placing a minute drop of waterproof paint on one of their hardened front wings (elytra).

The capture–recapture method is quite easy to apply, and can be the basis of some fascinating investigations. However, if quantitative conclusions are to be drawn you should realise that the method makes a number of major assumptions.

Can you think of five assumptions made by the capture–recapture method of estimating population size?

Figure 5.2 Generalised graph of population growth.

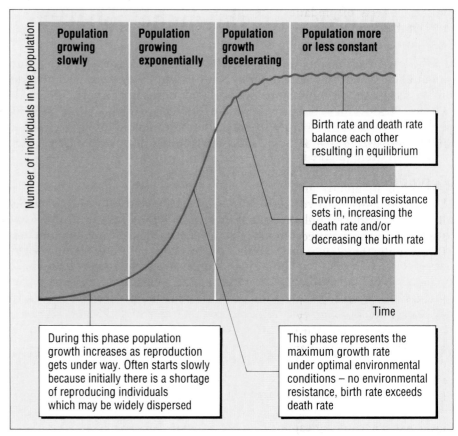

Number of individuals in the population

Population growing slowly | **Population growing exponentially** | **Population growth decelerating** | **Population more or less constant**

Birth rate and death rate balance each other resulting in equilibrium

Environmental resistance sets in, increasing the death rate and/or decreasing the birth rate

Time

During this phase population growth increases as reproduction gets under way. Often starts slowly because initially there is a shortage of reproducing individuals which may be widely dispersed

This phase represents the maximum growth rate under optimal environmental conditions – no environmental resistance, birth rate exceeds death rate

You might think that this definition of population is rather fussy. However, whether or not the individuals in an area have the potential to breed with one another has important consequences for evolution. Suppose that on an island a species of insect is divided into two separate populations. This means that over time these two populations might give rise to two distinct species. However, this is much less likely to be the case if the insects on the island all belong to one population.

We will consider speciation in more detail towards the end of this book; now we will look at the way populations increase in size.

Population growth

Consider what happens if a few individuals enter an unoccupied area. Assuming there is enough food and that predation and disease are not too severe, reproduction will occur and the number of individuals will increase as shown in figure 5.2.

At first, there may be a **lag phase** as the individuals settle into their new environment. As reproduction gets under way, the population shows **exponential growth**. Suppose that over a unit of time the population doubles from 20 to 40 individuals. Then over the next unit of time, the population will increase from 40 to 80 individuals; over the next unit of time from 80 to 160 individuals, and so on. During this exponential growth phase the population is said to grow **geometrically**. This is because the population sizes at successive time intervals form a geometric series (e.g. 20, 40, 80, 160 for our hypothetical example).

The exponential part of the growth curve represents a high growth rate under environmental conditions that permit rapid population growth. During this phase there is relatively little competition for food and space and the effects of predation and disease are relatively slight. We can sum this up by saying that there is little **environmental resistance**. Under these circumstances the struggle for existence is not too severe, survival is high and the species realises its full reproductive potential.

Figure 5.3 shows exponential growth in a species of tree over 9000 years ago. The abundance of the pine *Pinus sylvestris* is plotted as the density of pollen grains in peat samples of different ages. You can see that over the 500 years from 9500BP (years before the present) to 9000BP, the pollen density of the pine in peat samples taken from the bottom of Hockham Mere (a lake in Norfolk) increases exponentially.

Exponential growth cannot go on forever, otherwise we would soon be knee-deep in aphids and the sea would be full of jellyfish! The great Swedish botanist Carl von Linné (Linnaeus) calculated what would happen if a plant produced only two seeds a year and then died, and these two seeds in turn matured and each produced two seeds, and so on. (Incidentally, no plant is as unproductive as this.) Linnaeus found that in 20 years there would be over a million plants. You can check his calculation. He assumed that every plant could produce seeds. What would happen if instead each individual plant was either male or female, and the females produced two seeds every year and then died?

Even organisms that take a long time to reach maturity would eventually overpopulate the Earth if their numbers continued to grow exponentially. Charles Darwin calculated that a single pair of elephants would give rise to a total of 15 million descendants after five centuries. In reality, exponential growth ceases as environmental resistance builds up. Eventually, as you can see in figure 5.2, the population reaches its maximum size. This is known as the **carrying capacity** for the particular environment in which the population occurs.

The curve in figure 5.2 is idealised. In reality, populations rarely increase in such a regular manner. However, the curve shown in figure 5.2 has been very important in the history of our understanding of how populations change over time. It is referred to as a **sigmoid growth curve** because its shape looks rather like an 's', the Greek for which is *sigma*.

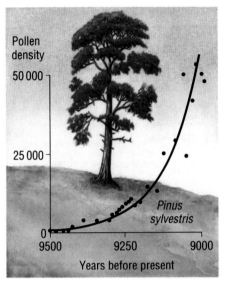

Figure 5.3 Exponential increase of pine trees in Norfolk, England over 9000 years ago. The density of pollen grains in peat samples gives a measure of the population size of the tree.

r and K selection

If a few individuals of a species colonise a new habitat, the population generally grows in size as is shown in figure 5.2. However, species differ in the rate at which their populations increase in numbers. As an extreme example, populations of bacteria increase in size rapidly, while populations of elephants increase in size much more slowly.

Population ecologists have identified two main strategies shown by organisms. Small organisms, such as bacteria, reproduce rapidly and therefore use up the available resources of a habitat before other, competing species can exploit them.

Because of their high rate of reproduction, such species have a high value of r, the intrinsic rate of increase, and are said to be **r-selected**.

Other species reproduce slowly and have much lower values of r. They spend much of their time in quite stable habitats and at population levels near to the carrying capacity (K). Accordingly, they are said to be **K-selected**. K-selected species show adaptations that enable them to survive even when their population sizes are close to the maximum.

Consider what happens when an area of soil becomes cleared of vegetation, perhaps as a result of a fire. Within a short time plants start

to grow as a result of seeds that arrive and germinate. Such seeds tend to have good means of dispersal and are often produced by annual weeds. These plants are r-selected and are efficient at exploiting new habitats. However, eventually they lose out to more K-selected plants. These species take longer to colonise the area but are better adapted to it, competing more effectively for light and nutrients.

By means of a table, list as many differences as you can between r-selected and K-selected species. Here are some of the features which you could consider: size, life span, colonising ability, number of offspring and care of the young.

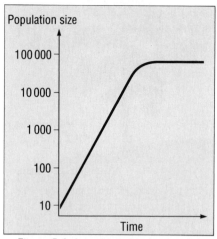

Figure 5.4 A semi-logarithmic plot of the logistic equation. Time is plotted linearly (normally) along the horizontal axis, but population size is plotted logarithmically up the vertical axis. The result is that during the exponential phase of population increase the data fall on a straight line. As the population size approaches the carrying capacity of the environment, it begins to level off. A semi-logarithmic plot is therefore a useful way of seeing whether a population is increasing exponentially or not.

The mathematics of population increase

The sigmoid growth curve can be represented mathematically by the logistic equation:

$$\frac{dN}{dt} = rN\left(1 - \frac{N}{K}\right)$$

In this equation:

N is the population size;
t is time;
dN/dt is the rate at which the population is increasing;
K is the carrying capacity;
r is the intrinsic rate of increase.

The **intrinsic rate of increase** (r) equals the number of offspring born to each individual over a unit period of time when the population is growing exponentially. Suppose a pair of organisms can produce four offspring per year; then $r = 2$ yr^{-1} and the population will double in size each year if individuals die after reproducing.

To get to grips with this logistic equation, consider what happens when the population size is very small, relative to the carrying capacity of the environment. This means that N/K is very small. Consequently $1 - N/K$ almost equals 1 and the equation for population growth reduces to:

$$\frac{dN}{dt} \approx rN$$

This is an equation for exponential growth, as we expect. Now, as the population builds up, N/K gets bigger. Eventually N almost equals K, so that N/K almost equals 1. Consequently $1 - N/K$ is very close to zero and the equation for population growth reduces to:

$$\frac{dN}{dt} \approx 0$$

In other words, the population no longer increases in size but simply maintains itself. As we expect, the population levels off.

If time is plotted linearly along the horizontal axis, but population size is plotted logarithmically up the vertical axis, the exponential phase of population growth now falls on a straight line (figure 5.4). This is called a semi-logarithmic plot, and it is a useful way of identifying the period over which population growth is exponential (figure 5.5).

Births, deaths, immigration and emigration

So far we have only considered births as a factor affecting population size. But the number of individuals in a population is affected by four factors: **births, deaths, immigration** and **emigration**. The change in the size of any population over a period of time can be summed by the equation:

Change in population size = $B + I - D - E$

where B = births, I = immigrations, D = deaths and E = emigrations.

It is easy to overlook immigrations and emigrations. However, they may be very important in reality. During the Irish potato famine from 1845 to 1849 the potato harvest was devastated by potato blight. As a result, the population fell from almost 9 000 000 to about 6 500 000. About one million people died in the famine and about one and a half million emigrated, mostly to the USA.

Throughout this period Irish farmers continued successfully to produce cereals, cattle, pigs, eggs and butter. All in all, enough food was produced to ensure that no one need have starved. However, farmers had to export these crops to England to get the money they needed to pay the rents they owed their English landowners. Farmers who failed to export their produce were evicted from their farms and had their cottages razed to the ground.

Environmental resistance

The pattern of population growth shown by different species is much the same irrespective of the species. In fact the sigmoid growth curve in figure 5.2 is shown equally by bacteria on an agar plate, yeast cells in a flask of cider and rabbits when they first entered Australia. However, the form that the environmental resistance takes depends on the species in question.

Here are the main factors that limit the sizes of populations:

- **Lack of food or water.** Probably all species have populations whose size is limited by insufficient food or water. Possible exceptions include some species of insects whose numbers may never build up to the point where food becomes limiting.

- **Lack of light.** This is particularly important for the growth of plant populations both on land and in water. Even in the calmest and cleanest waters, enough light for photosynthesis cannot penetrate more than about 50 m.

- **Lack of oxygen.** Insufficient oxygen may limit the population size of some aquatic species. This is because oxygen diffuses much more slowly through water than through air. In most home aquaria the level of oxygen saturation of the water is well below 100 per cent even with an aerator pumping away continuously.

- **Predators and parasites.** The presence of organisms that prey on or parasitise a particular species may play a crucial role in keeping down the population of that species. Parasites are often more important than predators in this respect because, being small, they have high rates of natural increase and can respond quickly to changes in the numbers of their host. On the other hand, many parasites do not kill their host, whereas predators do.

- **Disease.** This can be one of the most potent forces in checking the uncontrolled growth of populations. Diseases can spread more rapidly where large numbers of individuals of one species are crowded together. This is why so much pesticide is used in intensive agriculture. A field of wheat is a paradise for mildews and rusts.

- **Lack of shelter.** This may be shelter from predators or shelter from physical factors of the environment such as excessive heat.

- **Accumulation of toxic waste.** The build-up of a high concentration of, for example, carbon dioxide and nitrogenous waste can be an important factor limiting the population growth of certain organisms, for example insect pests of stored grain.

- **Stress.** In some cases overcrowding may cause excessive stress leading to abnormal behaviour. Female rats kept in captivity at a high population density show a breakdown in normal maternal behaviour, failing to build adequate nests and abandoning their young. It has even been argued by some biologists that, in the wild, the males of some species of

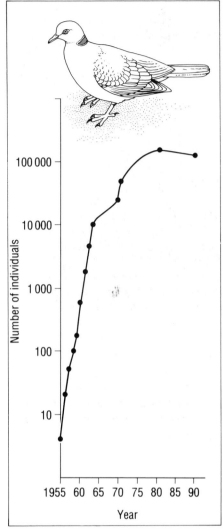

Figure 5.5 A semi-logarithmic plot showing the population size of the collared dove in Great Britain since 1955. You can see how from 1955 till about 1963 the increase was exponential. Nobody knows why the collared dove has increased in numbers so tremendously. Until about 1930, the birds were restricted in Europe to Turkey and parts of Albania, Bulgaria and Yugoslavia. Then they reached Hungary in 1932, Czechoslovakia in 1936, Austria in 1938, Germany in 1943, the Netherlands in 1947, Denmark in 1948, Sweden and Switzerland in 1949, France in 1950 and Belgium and Norway in 1952. By the mid 1970s the birds had even reached the Faeroe Islands and Iceland.

Figure 5.6 European heron eating a fish.

small mammals die prematurely as a result of excessive stress. Stress leads to very high levels of certain hormones, notably adrenaline and adrenocorticotrophic hormone (ACTH), which may cause the animals to collapse and die.

- **Weather and other catastrophies.** Weather conditions, and climate generally, may drastically reduce populations. The effects are perhaps most severe for small organisms, but in a particularly bad winter even large species may show significant declines in population size. The European heron relies on open water so that it can catch fish (figure 5.6). In bad winters, herons may starve to death. Figure 5.7 shows the effects of bad winters on the numbers of herons breeding the following year in England and Wales. As you can see, it may take several years for heron numbers to recover from a severe winter. Other catastrophic effects include fire in dry scrub and grasslands, and landslides in mountainous rain forests.

Some of the factors in the above list are **density independent**: their effectiveness is unrelated to the density of the population, i.e. to the number of individuals per unit of space. Others are **density dependent**: their effectiveness depends on the number of individuals in the population. Density dependence means that the more individuals there are in the population, the greater the proportion of the population that dies or fails to reproduce.

Population regulation

Populations do not remain constant in size; rather they fluctuate. Figure 5.7 shows how heron numbers fall after bad winters but then recover. You can see, however, that although heron numbers vary, they do so between limits: from 1928 to 1970 there were always about 2500 to 5000 breeding pairs of herons in England and Wales.

Careful field work has shown that the numbers of most species do not fluctuate widely and erratically. Instead they seem to lie near an equilibrium point which we can call the **norm** or **set point**. For a given species in a particular environment there is a certain equilibrium population which the environment can support. If the population rises above the set point, competition, predation or some other density-dependent factor reduces

Figure 5.7 Bad winters significantly reduce the numbers of herons. The most severe winters are arrowed.

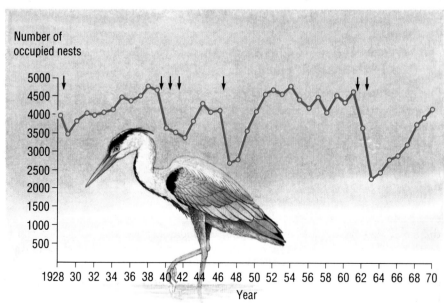

Number of occupied nests

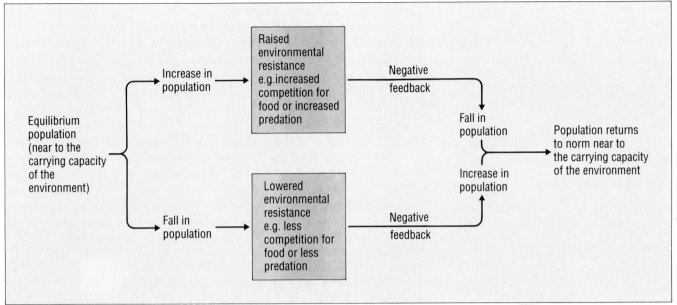

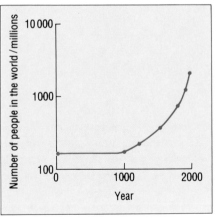

breeding or increases mortality to such an extent that the population falls. If the population falls below the set point, environmental resistance is temporarily relieved so that the population rises again (figure 5.8).

In the normal course of events populations fluctuate on either side of the set point, but the regulatory processes described above prevent the fluctuations being excessively large. We have here an example of **homeostasis**, the general principles of which are explained in Chapter 21. An increase or decrease in population sets in motion processes which keep the population on an even keel. This is an example of **negative feedback**, so called because an increase in the population above the norm leads to a decrease, while a decrease in the population leads to an increase.

Growth of the human population

Figures for early human populations are difficult to come by, but archaeological and historical evidence suggest that there may have been three major population explosions, each corresponding to a 'cultural revolution' which allowed more people to survive.

The first population explosion took place over 20 000 years ago and was probably associated with the use of tools which allowed improvements in hunting and food-gathering techniques (**tool-making revolution**). The second, some 10 000 to 6000 years ago, was brought about by improvements in farming and the widespread domestication of animals and plants (**agricultural revolution**). The third, which got underway about 300 years ago and is still in progress, has been caused by improvements in food production, industry and medicine (**scientific–industrial revolution**). Each of these bursts was associated with a substantial rise in the population set point; the birth rate rose, the death rate fell and the population surged upwards towards a new level.

Nowadays the world's population increases by some 250 000 people every day. Figure 5.9 shows how the world's population has increased over the last 2000 years. The increase is huge! The data have been plotted on a semi-logarithmic plot, so an exponential growth in population would be shown by a straight line. In fact, the curve bends upwards. That means that during the last 2000 years the human population has been increasing *faster* than exponentially.

Figure 5.8 Scheme summarising the homeostatic control of populations. The equilibrium population (norm) is the set point in a negative feedback process by which the population is kept more or less constant. Can you predict what effect a permanent change in the environmental resistance would have?

Figure 5.9 The world's population has increased hugely over the last 2000 years. Notice that this is a semi-logarithmic plot. The number of people has therefore been increasing faster than exponentially.

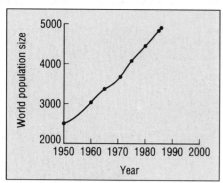

Figure 5.10 Growth in size of world human population since 1950.

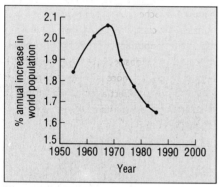

Figure 5.11 The annual percentage increase in the world's population. Since the late 1960s the rate at which the world's population is increasing has begun to slow down. However, an annual increase of 1.65 per cent still means that the world's population doubles every 42 years.

Figure 5.12 World population distribution. Each dot stands for 100 000 people. Note that it is not simply the case that developing countries are more densely populated than developed countries. The ten most densely populated countries of the world (figures are people per km²) are Hong Kong (4174), Singapore (3825), Malta (950), Bangladesh (533), Mauritius (448), Taiwan (431), Puerto Rico (361), South Korea (345), Netherlands (339) and Belgium (319).

Another way of putting this is to say that the time taken for the world's population to double has been decreasing. It took until the start of the seventeenth century for the world's population to double from what it was in New Testament times, approximately 250 million, to 500 million. However, it then doubled to 1000 million in under 250 years. It then doubled to 2000 million in about a hundred years, and then to 4000 million in about 50 years.

Figure 5.10 shows in more detail how the world's population has increased since 1950. Here the data are not plotted on a semi-logarithmic graph. A good way of seeing whether the population is growing exponentially over a relatively short period like this is to look at the annual percentage increase in population. These data are shown in figure 5.11. You can see that until the late 1960s the world's population was increasing more rapidly than exponentially. However, since then the annual percentage increase has begun to fall, so that the population growth is now slower than exponential. It is too soon to be sure at what level the world's population is likely to stabilise. United Nations' projections suggest that by the year 2020 the world's population will be approximately 8000 million (eight billion), almost twice what it currently is.

At the moment those countries in which the population is still growing most rapidly tend to be those in which the average income per person is low. Countries such as Britain, Japan and the USA have populations which are increasing less rapidly. These countries also have a high standard of living. Some people argue that the way to stabilise the world's population is to ensure that contraceptive methods are more widely available. Others maintain that a country does not stabilise its population until its economy has improved. Only then will its sanitation and medical services reduce child mortality sufficiently for people to be willing to have small families.

It is all too easy for developed countries to blame less developed countries for the problem of the world's population increase. In fact, developed countries often have more people per unit area of land than less developed countries (figure 5.12). The United Kingdom, for instance, has a population density of 230 people per square kilometre while Uganda has 68, Kenya 37 and Brazil 16. It can be argued that the less developed countries are nowadays going through the population growth which countries in the West have already experienced.

Most people feel that human populations should be left to stabilise of their own accord, without too much outside interference. However, in some countries there are considerable economic and social pressures against

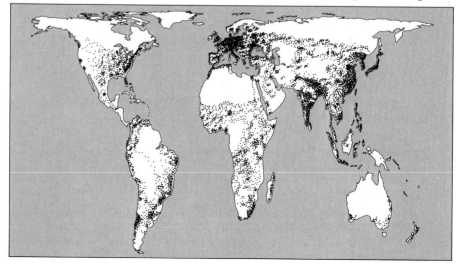

couples who have more than one or two children. But where other species are concerned, no qualms exist. Humans have devised some ingenious methods of controlling pests using other organisms as the means of population regulation, as we shall now see.

Biological control

Attempts to control pest numbers using chemicals often have unfortunate consequences, as we saw in the previous chapter (see page 44). An alternative is to use one species to control the numbers of another species. This is called **biological control**. The earliest recorded instance of this was around 2000 BC when the Chinese used ants to kill leaf-eating insects, thus protecting valuable crops. Here are some recent examples.

Control of the prickly pear cactus in Australia

The prickly pear cactus (*Opuntia*) is not native to Australia. As with so many of Australia's animals and plants, it was introduced into the country after the arrival of Europeans. In 1840 a certain Dr Carlyle brought some specimens from America and planted them in his garden. They quickly ran wild and by the turn of the century had spread over more than four million hectares of land, rendering it unsuitable for agricultural use. By 1910 the cactus was spreading at a rate of nearly 400 000 hectares per year.

The Australian government responded by setting up a research programme to find an animal that would eat the prickly pear cactus. Studies were made of the species that attacked the plant in its native America, and in 1925 eggs of the moth *Cactoblastis cactorum* were introduced to Australia from Argentina (figure 5.13). Fortunately this was a great success. The caterpillars ate the cactus and within a few years almost all the prickly pear cacti had been destroyed (figure 5.14). Today the cactus and the moth coexist at low densities. Every now and again the population of the prickly pear flares up, only to crash again as the moth's numbers increase in response.

Myxomatosis and the control of rabbits

The rabbit is not a native animal to Britain. It was introduced by the Romans, who liked eating it, but it then died out. It was then reintroduced by the Normans, and this time it stayed. For centuries the rabbit was thought beneficial: it provided valuable meat and its fur was widely used. However, by the 1950s its numbers had increased to between 60 and 100 million – more than one for every person in Britain. By then it was considered a pest, as it ate large quantities of wheat and other crops.

Myxomatosis is a disease caused by a virus that attacks a certain species of South American rabbit. The European rabbit belongs to a different genus from the South American rabbit but the myxomatosis virus can attack it with devastating results. The disease was first recorded in Britain in Kent on 13 October 1953. It is not known for certain how it got here, but there is more than a suspicion that it was deliberately introduced by a farmer to reduce his crop losses. The consequences were remarkable. The disease spread like wild-fire. Within a couple of years 99 per cent of all British rabbits were dead.

To an ecologist what is particularly interesting is the effect that the introduction of the myxomatosis virus had on the rest of the flora and fauna. It soon became clear that rabbits were responsible for maintaining much of the beautiful chalk grassland in lowland Britain. In the absence of

Figure 5.13 Caterpillars of the cactus moth (*Cactoblastis cactorum*) eating the prickly pear cactus.

Figure 5.14 The introduction of the cactus moth (*Cactoblastis cactorum*) devastated the prickly pear cactus in Australia.

Top Dense prickly pear in the Chinchilla area, Queensland, in 1926.

Bottom The same area three years later after biological control of the cactus by the moth.

Figure 5.15 A rabbit sitting outside its burrow. Although rabbits may look sweet, they can devastate a farmer's crops.

Figure 5.16 *Top* Rabbits keep grassland vegetation short and prevent colonisation by shrubs and trees.

Bottom An area with few rabbits. Notice the presence of trees and shrubs.

Figure 5.17

A Adult female Large Blue butterfly on wild thyme.

B Larva of the Large Blue butterfly being carried by *Myrmica* ants. In the absence of these ants, the butterfly dies out.

rabbits, the grass, hitherto kept short by grazing, grew rampant, ousting many of the wild flowers. Shrubs and trees began to invade these areas as there were no rabbits to eat the young seedlings (figure 5.16).

The myxomatosis epidemic also had consequences for many species of animals. Hares increased in numbers, presumably because rabbits had previously competed with them for food. One might have expected predators such as foxes and buzzards to have crashed in numbers. However, for a few years after the introduction of the virus the numbers of such predators actually increased. It is possible that this was because they fed on the large numbers of dead and dying rabbits available. Studies show that later on foxes changed their diet, shifting to small animals such as voles. Voles may have increased in numbers because of the growth of grass caused by the disappearance of the rabbit. Buzzards, however, were adversely affected in the long term: their numbers decreased by around 30 to 40 per cent.

The crash in rabbit numbers in 1953 also lead to the extinction in Britain some 30 years later of the Large Blue butterfly (figure 5.17). The habitat for the Large Blue is south-facing slopes with short turf. The butterfly relies on wild thyme and the larvae of certain *Myrmica* ants to complete its life cycle. Both the wild thyme and the ants are restricted to short grassland, and the reduction in the number of rabbits thus led eventually to the extinction of the butterfly. Attempts are now being made to restore the habitat and reintroduce the butterfly.

One thing we can learn from the myxomatosis story is how difficult it is to predict the effects of introducing a biological control agent into a new area. Indeed, there have been many disastrous instances when attempts at biological control have gone wrong and an introduced species has wiped out a harmless native species.

Fluctuating populations

The reason rabbit and prickly pear cactus numbers crashed was that in each case an organism was introduced to control their populations. However, there are some species which regularly decline in numbers without the introduction of a new predator or parasite.

A classic example of a species which shows tremendous fluctuations in its population size is the Canadian lynx. This beautiful animal has long been trapped for its fur which is then turned into coats. Annual records of the numbers trapped were kept by the Hudson Bay Company from 1821 to 1934 and these numbers are shown graphically in figure 5.18.

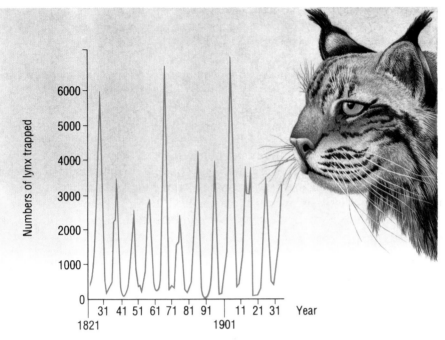

Figure 5.18 Number of lynx trapped for the Hudson Bay Company from 1821 to 1931. Notice how the numbers cycle, showing peaks every ten years or so.

Much to the surprise of the trappers they found that however hard they worked there were some years when lynx were almost never trapped. In other years, though, huge numbers of lynx were trapped. You can see from figure 5.18 that the numbers of lynx peak every ten years or so. What could cause these large fluctuations in populations?

In northern Canada, lynx depend for their food mainly on snowshoe hares (figure 5.19). When you look at what is happening to the numbers of hares as well as the numbers of lynx, you find that the hares also go through a ten-year **cycle** (figure 5.20). At first it was thought that the cycles might be caused by the following sequence of events:

1 When lynx numbers are low, few hares are eaten and so the number of hares increases greatly.
2 The large number of hares allows lots of lynx to survive and reproduce, leading to a great increase in the number of lynx.
3 There are now so many lynx that they eat most of the hares, causing the hare population to crash.
4 The lack of hares leads to many lynx starving and being unable to reproduce, leading to a crash in the number of lynx.
5 Finally, the very low number of lynx allows the hare population to recover, causing the cycle to start up again.

Figure 5.19 Predator and prey.
Top Snowshoe hare.
Bottom Canadian lynx.

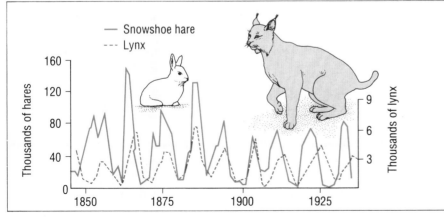

Figure 5.20 The connection between the number of snowshoe hares and the number of lynx from 1845 to 1935 as shown by the number of pelts taken by the Hudson Bay Company.

67

Unfortunately there is one thing wrong with this explanation. There are islands off the east coast of Canada that have hares but no lynx. On these islands the hares go through exactly the same sort of cycles that they do on the mainland of Canada, again with a periodicity of about ten years! So the hare cycle is clearly not dependent on the number of lynx, at least not on the islands.

Scientists are still unsure why snowshoe hare numbers fluctuate in the way they do. It is known that when there are large numbers of hares, the plants they normally eat respond by producing shoots with high levels of toxins. These toxins make the shoots unpalatable to the hares. Maybe it is the plants that cause the hares to cycle. It certainly seems that changes in the numbers of hares cause the lynx cycles, even if the lynx are not responsible for the hare cycles.

Survivorship curves

Ignoring for the moment immigration and emigration, birth and death are the two processes which affect population size. However, these processes depend on the age of individuals and on their sex. The crucial factor is the chance an individual has of surviving to a given age. This can be shown by means of a **survivorship curve**. To understand a survivorship curve, imagine a population of 100 individuals born at the same time. The curve shows how many of them are likely to be alive at any particular age.

There are three main types of survivorship curves and these are shown in figure 5.21.

- The upper curve is typical of organisms, such as ourselves, that have few young. After an initial period of relatively low juvenile mortality, mortality is very low until late in life.

- The middle curve is found in many small birds. Notice that as the vertical axis is logarithmic, the curve actually shows an exponential decline in the number of individuals surviving over time. Individuals do not die of old age, that is, there is no **senescence**.

- The lower curve is typical of many plants and fish. Thousands or millions of young are produced, few of which mature into adults. The vast majority die as juveniles.

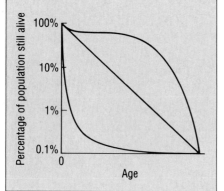

Figure 5.21 The three main types of survivorship curves found in organisms. Which type of survivorship curve do you think the following organisms have: oak tree, elephant, robin?

Population pyramids and life expectancy

Any population consists of individuals that differ in age and sex. A **population pyramid** is a convenient way of showing this.

Figure 5.22 shows a population pyramid for humans in France in 1966. (You can tell that it must be 1966 from the pyramid itself because the people born in 1866 are shown as being 100 years old and those born in 1966 as being 0.) From the pyramid you should be able to work out the total population of France in 1966, though this involves a rather tedious calculation.

More interestingly, you should be able to relate the letters (a) to (e) on the pyramid to the following events (not in order): military losses in the First World War, military losses in the Second World War, fewer births during the First World War, fewer births during the Second World War, more births immediately after the end of the Second World War.

You can see in figure 5.22 that the two halves of the pyramid are not quite symmetrical. In most countries women live longer than men (figure 5.23). In general, **life expectancy** is the further number of years a person of

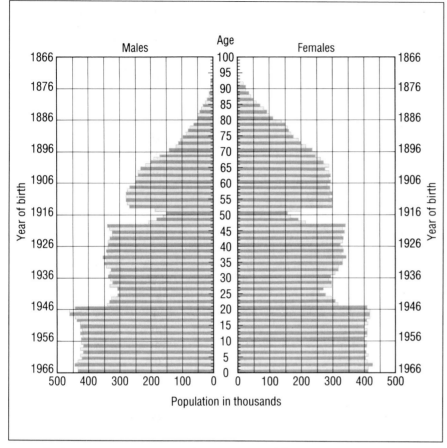

Figure 5.22 Population pyramid for France as at December 31, 1966. The width of each horizontal bar represents the population size for that particular age.

a particular age can expect to live. Average life expectancies are used by insurance companies to calculate the premiums they charge on life insurance policies so that they can be confident of making a profit. Some insurance companies take into account their clients' life styles. You may have to pay more than the average if you smoke or have a history of heart disease, for instance.

The shape of a population pyramid can be used to make predictions about how the population size of a country is changing. Figure 5.24 shows population pyramids for India and the USA in 1978. The broad base to the Indian population pyramid suggests that the population size will increase rapidly with more and more babies born each year. In fact the population size of India has increased since 1978. However, another possible explanation for the broad-based pyramid seen for India is that mortality is high.

The population pyramid observed for the USA in figure 5.24 is typical of a country with a relatively stable, even decreasing, number of people. One might have predicted in 1978 that the population would decrease. In fact it has not. The population size of the USA has actually increased substantially since then. This is partly the result of a high birth rate, partly the result of a low death rate and partly because of a high immigration rate.

The niche concept

In 1934 a biologist called G.F. Gause published a book called *The Struggle for Existence*. In it he included the results of careful experiments he had carried out on two species of *Paramecium*, a unicellular ciliate (see page 106). Gause found that he could easily keep *Paramecium caudatum* and *P. aurelia* in separate containers in his laboratory. However, when he tried to

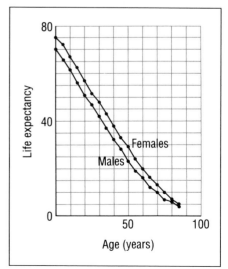

Figure 5.23 Life expectancy in the United Kingdom in 1977. It is apparent that women tend to live longer than men.

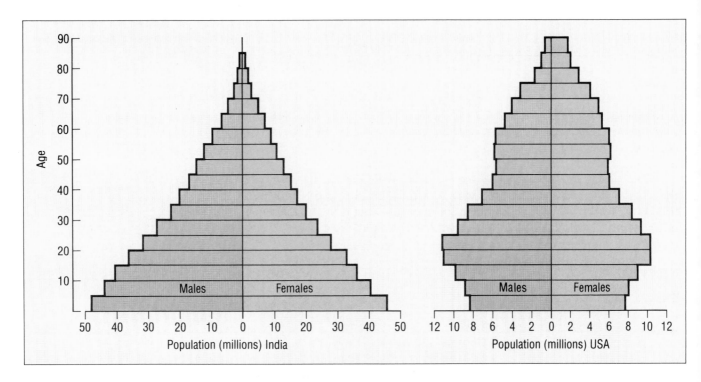

Figure 5.24 Population pyramids for India (left) and the USA (right) in 1978. Notice that a far greater proportion of the population are children in India than in the USA.

keep the two species in the same container, *P. caudatum* always died out after a few days.

The importance of Gause's experiments was not realised at the time. However, some ten years later his results were seen in a new light by ecologists looking at the question of what allows different species to coexist in a habitat. Gause's results were put into a general statement called the **competitive exclusion principle**. This states that two species cannot coexist unless there are significant differences in their ecologies. In the case of Gause's two species of *Paramecium*, their ecologies were too similar. This meant that only one species could survive when they were kept together.

Nowadays Gause's competitive exclusion principle is sometimes stated as follows: 'Each species has its own unique niche.' To understand this law, which is one of the few laws of biology, you need to understand what is meant by the term **niche**. The niche of an organism tells you what the organism *does* in its community. Niches are sometimes distinguished from habitats by saying that the habitat of an organism is its address, while its niche is its role in the community.

Describing the role of an organism is no easy task. For an animal, the most important aspect of its niche is usually its food. Describing the niche of a leopard, for instance, involves discovering, amongst other things, the sorts of prey on which leopards feed. This is called its **feeding niche**. However, the feeding niche of a leopard is only one aspect or *dimension* of its total niche.

Testing Gause's competitive exclusion principle

How can this idea be tested? What ecologists have often done is to look at similar species that coexist and see whether differences can be found between their niches. For instance, many woods contain birds that seem to have very similar ecologies. However, if you study them carefully, you nearly always find that they feed on slightly different foods or build slightly different sorts of nests or have different parasites.

Some ecologists argue that these differences support Gause's competitive exclusion principle. Others are more suspicious. After all, if you look hard enough you are bound to find some differences between the ecologies of any two species. The important question is just how different do the niches of two species have to be to allow coexistence? There is considerable uncertainty about the answer to this question.

The American zoologist G.E. Hutchinson introduced the notion of the fundamental niche of an organism as opposed to its realised niche. The **fundamental niche** is the niche a species would occupy in the absence of any competitors, predators or parasites. The niche that the species actually occupies, on the other hand, is called its **realised niche**.

For almost all species the realised niche is smaller and more restricted than the fundamental niche. One way of visualising this is to think of a fried egg: the yolk is the realised niche and the whole egg is the fundamental niche. The distinction between fundamental and realised niches can be illustrated by red and grey squirrels in Britain.

The niches of red and grey squirrels

The red squirrel is native to Britain. Until the end of the nineteenth century it was found throughout the British Isles in both deciduous and coniferous woods. Nowadays it is largely confined to coniferous woods (figure 5.25).

The reason for the red squirrel's decline is the introduction of the larger grey squirrel (figure 5.26). During the nineteenth century, many attempts were made to introduce the grey squirrel to Britain from North America where it is native to deciduous forests. Exactly why people were keen to try to establish the grey squirrel in Britain is not entirely clear. One introduction was made by an American who released over 100 individuals in Richmond Park, Surrey. Perhaps he was homesick for them.

By the beginning of the twentieth century grey squirrels were firmly established in Britain. As they increased their range, the red squirrel became rarer. Today red squirrels are only found in coniferous woods, mixed woods dominated by conifers and some islands which have never been colonised by the grey squirrel. The red squirrel's realised niche is therefore far less extensive than its fundamental niche.

The exact reasons why the red squirrel has declined in numbers are still uncertain. However, it is not because the grey squirrels attack their red relatives. Rather, the decline in the red squirrel may be an instance of Gause's competitive exclusion principle in action. It seems that the niches of the two squirrels are so similar that only one can survive in any one habitat.

Having considered the importance of an organism's niche, we are now in a position to look at the total ecology of individual species. The ecology of a single species is known as its **autecology**.

Autecology

An autecological investigation is one which sets out to identify all the important aspects of the ecology of a single species. In an oak woodland you might choose, for instance, to study the autecology of the oak trees. This would involve answering a host of ecological questions such as:

- What proportion of acorns germinate?
- What happens to the acorns that do not germinate?
- What sort of soil do the acorns need in order to germinate, grow into seedlings and eventually become young trees?
- What are the climatic factors that limit the distribution of oaks?

Figure 5.25 Red squirrel feeding in a pine forest.

Figure 5.26 Grey squirrel feeding in an oak wood.

- What are the light requirements of oaks?
- Which organisms feed on oaks?
- What proportion of oak seedlings go on to reproduce?
- What is the generation time of oaks?
- What factors affect the flowering of oak trees?
- How is pollination achieved?
- What factors affect the size and numbers of acorns produced?

It is clear that a thorough autecological study may involve more than a life's work! When you think that there are probably between 5 and 30 million different species of organism alive today, it is apparent that ecologists will never be able to study them all in such detail.

For this reason synecological studies are more practicable (see Chapter 3). A synecological study focuses on a whole community rather than on just one of the species in it. Although the overall picture obtained is bound to be more superficial, at least it allows you to see the interrelationships between the species and there is less danger of failing to see the wood for the trees.

Calculating maximum sustainable yields

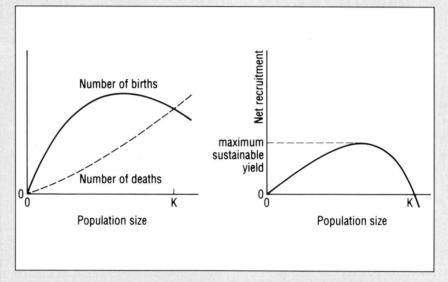

Farmers cannot allow all their produce to be eaten. If they did, they would not be able to produce any food the next year. Some of the produce has to be kept back to 'seed' the next generation. This is true whether we are talking of arable farming such as wheat and rice or pastoral farming such as sheep or cows.

The same principle holds when obtaining food from the wild. Too often humans have overhunted or overfished species to extinction or near extinction. So what, then, is the optimal harvest or catch? How can we decide how many fish or oysters or deer to catch so as to maximise the harvest without jeopardising the continuity of the population? Obviously this is an important figure to know. It is called the **maximum sustainable yield**.

Look at the left-hand graph in the illustration. It shows that the number of births and deaths in a population depends on the population size. When the population size is very small, the number of births and deaths will also be very small, though obviously there will be more births than deaths as the population grows. As the population increases, the difference between the number of births and the number of deaths also increases. However, as the population size approaches the carrying capacity (K) the number of deaths starts to catch up with the number of births.

The right-hand graph in the illustration shows the same information in a different form. The difference between the number of births and the number of deaths is called the **net recruitment** to the population. This is plotted as a function of the population size. You can see that at a population size somewhere between 0 and K, the net recruitment reaches a maximum.

This population size is the optimum if you wish to maximise the sustainable yield of the population.

So much for the theory. Unfortunately, the political difficulties in setting quotas in line with scientific predictions are immense. Each year scientists advise the European Community on the fishing quotas that should be set for the following year. Almost invariably the actual quotas set exceed the levels recommended by scientists for a sustainable harvest.

Why do you think the governments of the European Community rarely accept the scientific advice on fishing quotas?

Too much swamp stonecrop

Swamp stonecrop (*Crassula helmsii*) is native to south eastern Australia and Tasmania where it is usually found in the shallow fresh waters of swamps or by the edges of streams. It is a succulent perennial herb and in Britain can be bought from many of the larger suppliers of aquatic plants. People with garden ponds use it as an oxygenating plant since it keeps its leaves throughout the year.

It was first found naturalised in Britain in a pond at Greenstead in Essex in 1956. Since then it has spread throughout much of England and is now known from over 100 sites ranging from shallow acidic seasonal ponds to nutrient-rich lakes (see illustration). Currently it is increasing its range, and the number of sites it occupies is doubling about once every four years.

Although swamp stonecrop is quite an attractive plant, it can have a disastrous effect on the native aquatic flora. The trouble is that it forms dense swards which smother other plants. It can also colonise new sites very easily, being able to reproduce vegetatively from small fragments.

Attempts to remove the plant from affected areas have not proved

Swamp stonecrop heavily infesting an English lake.

successful, probably because it can regenerate so readily from small pieces. Control with herbicides is a possibility, though this is likely to have serious consequences for native species. A third possibility is biological control. Some fish are known to eat the plant, but introducing such species may cause more problems than it solves. Time alone will tell whether this introduced alien will cause some native British plants to become extinct.

Suppose you were asked to investigate the feasibility of introducing a species of fish to control swamp stonecrop in Britain. Outline how you would set about this task. What sort of considerations would influence your choice of fish? The writer of the box says that introducing fish to control stonecrop may cause more problems than it solves. What might these problems be?

Two views about the human population

In 1948 an international congress was held at Cheltenham on world resources in relation to the family. Here are two views about the human population which were expressed at the meeting.

Sir John Boyd Orr

When Darwin came forward with the theory of the survival of the fittest, that seemed to prove that the best thing to do was to let these people die out. That argument has been used to me – 'Why reduce mortality?

You only further overcrowd an already over crowded planet'. I think you can take it, however, that if modern science is applied and Governments are willing to do it, we can feed and clothe and house as large a population as is likely to come in the next fifty or hundred years, and that is as far as we can see.

P.K. Whelpton

It seems to me that even in countries like the USA, the population is above the economic optimum; that is, we have more people even there than is

most desirable from the standpoint of the natural resources which we possess. That does not mean that a rapid decrease in population would be desirable, but I think it does mean that if we would choose between a stationary population of say, 100 000 000 and 150 000 000 or 200 000 000 we should without question be better off with the former.

Discuss these two views in the light of events which have happened since 1948. (The population of the USA in 1992 was 256 000 000.)

Summary

1 A **population** consists of individuals of one species with the ability to interbreed.

2 After a **lag phase** a population may grow **exponentially** before reaching a **norm** or **set point** about which it then fluctuates.

3 Populations tend to grow as represented by the logistic equation, $dN/dt = rN(1 - N/K)$, where r is the **intrinsic rate of increase** and K is the **carrying capacity** of the environment.

4 Populations may change in size as a result of **births, deaths, immigrations** and **emigrations.**

5 Populations are prevented from growing indefinitely by **environmental resistance** which may take many forms.

6 There are over 5000 million people alive today – more than at any previous time in our history. Each day the world's population increases by about 250 000 people.

7 Until recently the world's human population was growing faster than exponentially. However, since the late 1960s the rate of increase has declined, giving some hope that the world's population may eventually level off at a sustainable number.

8 **Biological control** is achieved when humans use individuals of one species to keep down the numbers of another species.

9 Two successful instances of biological control are the use of the moth *Cactoblastis cactorum* to control the numbers of prickly pear cactus in Australia, and the use of the myxomatosis virus to control the numbers of rabbits both in Australia and in Britain.

10 Some populations show large **cyclical** increases and decreases in size. Ecologists still do not understand why.

11 A **survivorship curve** shows the chances an individual has of reaching a given age.

12 **Population pyramids** show the age composition of a population. They can help to indicate whether the population has been increasing or decreasing in size and what is likely to happen in the future.

13 Gause's **competitive exclusion principle** states that two species cannot coexist unless there are significant differences in their ecologies.

14 The **niche** of a species describes the role of that species in its community.

15 The **fundamental niche** of an organism is the niche it would occupy in the absence of any predators, competitors or parasites. The niche an organism actually occupies is called its **realised niche.**

16 An **autecological study** is one which sets out to identify all the important aspects of the ecology of a single species.

Review questions

1 Which of the factors that can limit the sizes of populations listed on pages 61 – 62 are density dependent and which ones are density independent?

2 List the various factors that you suspect might affect the population size of daisies on a lawn.

3 Explain precisely what is meant by the term 'population regulation'.

4 Using figures 5.9, 5.10 and 5.11 to help you, try to decide at what size the world's population may stabilise, assuming no global catastrophe. Can you predict when the population size is likely to stabilise?

5 Do you think a government has the right to impose birth control on its people, or should individuals always have the right to choose for themselves how many children they will have?

6 What circumstances might lead to the failure of an attempt at biological control?

7 Population fluctuations seem to be far more extreme in the Arctic than in tropical or temperate regions. Can you suggest why this is?

8 How would you go about constructing a survivorship curve for robins in a small wood?

9 Many islands contain fewer species than occur in the same area on nearby mainland. In view of this, would you expect island and mainland species to have the same realised niches? Explain your answer.

10 Choose any animal or plant (except the oak tree!) and outline how you might investigate its autecology.

Further reading

Jonathan Silvertown's *Introduction to Plant Population Ecology* (Longman, 1987) is probably the best introduction to population ecology available, even if it is restricted to plants.

Charles Krebs' *The Message of Ecology* (Harper & Row, 1988) is written by the person who has probably spent more time than anyone else studying population cycles. It is particularly strong on population biology.

Associations between species

There are many situations in which individual organisms form close associations with one another. Such associations may occur within the same species (**intraspecific associations**) or between different species (**interspecific associations**). Either way, the environment of each individual is profoundly influenced by the presence of the other.

Intraspecific associations, such as communication, mating behaviour, aggression and parent–offspring behaviour, form the basis of social organisation. They are dealt with in the chapter on behaviour (see Chapter 30). In this chapter we will look at interspecific associations, concentrating on how the ecology of one species shapes the ecology of the other.

First, though, we must define what is meant by the biotic environment because an organism's interspecific associations form part of its biotic environment.

Biotic environment

In Chapter 2 the physical environment of an organism was defined as the sum of the non-living factors that influence that organism – factors such as climate, soil and topography. The **biotic environment** of an organism, on the other hand, is the sum of the *living* factors that influence the organism.

Consider a female red deer (figure 6.1). Her biotic environment includes other red deer with which she interacts, such as her offspring, any males with which she mates, and other red deer with which she spends her time. These individuals are all members of her species. However, her biotic environment also includes the plants on which she feeds, the mites, ticks, flies and other parasites that bother her, the golden eagles that may carry off her young, and the soil organisms that will decompose her body when she dies.

Intimate associations

Intimate associations are found when the body of one organism (called the **host**) acts as the habitat for another organism. The host may be the only habitat in or on which the organism can survive or reproduce, in which case the association is described as **obligatory**. If the host is not essential, the association is described as **facultative**.

In these intimate associations we can see with particular clarity the workings of natural selection. No one looking at how a tapeworm is adapted to the intestine of its host can fail both to be fascinated and horrified by the manner in which all aspects of its anatomy and ecology are geared to its way of life.

The general term used to describe intimate associations between pairs of species is **symbiosis** which, loosely translated from the Greek, means 'living together'. Some older books restrict the term symbiosis to cases where the association benefits both species. However, most ecologists nowadays use symbiosis in its wider sense and divide the term into three categories distinguished by the consequences of the association to each party.

- **Parasitism.** Here one organism, the **parasite**, lives in or on the other organism, the **host** (figure 6.2). The parasite, which is smaller than its host, benefits from the relationship at the expense of the host.

CHAPTER 6

Figure 6.1 Red deer hind with calf. How many features of the hind's biotic environment can you see in this picture?

Figure 6.2 Hedgehog with two parasitic ticks. Ticks have specially adapted mouthparts which enable them to feed on the host's blood.

- **Commensalism**. In this case, one of the two organisms, the **commensal**, benefits from the association, while the other organism, usually the larger partner, neither loses nor gains.

- **Mutualism**. Here the association benefits both participants, i.e. the gain is mutual.

The dividing line between these three kinds of symbiosis is not as clear cut as might first appear. In every case one partner gains. However, it is sometimes difficult to determine whether the relationship benefits the other organism or not.

Other associations between organisms may be less intimate, but of great significance for the organisms concerned. In **predation** the relationship is such that one organism lives and the other one dies instantly. We will consider predation later in this chapter. First, though, let us look at more intimate associations, beginning with parasitism.

Intimate associations between species

How do we decide if a particular association is a case of mutualism, parasitism, predation or herbivory? Guest author Geoffrey Harper reflects on these four terms.

Assuming that in an intimate association one species always benefits, we can see that the four terms tell us something about the other species. They tell us whether it also benefits (mutualism) or is harmed (parasitism) or given the chop (predation). You might think that these terms are easy to use, but consider a horse grazing on grass (herbivory): the grass plant has its leaves eaten, presumably making it worse off than if they were not, yet the horse may at the same time be killing off the grass plant's competitors, by grazing or trampling, so benefiting the grass. A tree may have mycorrhizal fungi associated with its roots which can benefit the tree in poor soil, while the same fungi may be parasitic where the soil is more fertile. *Individual* micro-organisms in a cow may be killed and digested, but the micro-organism *population* continues to thrive. Even if we were clear what 'harm' and 'benefit' mean in biological terms, it is often difficult to measure them. In the case of many lichens, for example, it is not obvious whether the relationship is mutualistic or whether the fungus is instead parasitic on the alga.

The four terms we have been discussing are arranged along the horizontal harm/benefit axis of the illustration. Vertically, the examples are distributed according to the intimacy of the relationship, ranging from permanent intracellular contact at the top to no physical contact at all at the bottom. In the illustration, just a few examples have been plotted, and in each pair of species the larger organism always benefits.

Which of the two axes is more 'important' to the organisms themselves? The question is vague, but can be improved by adding 'as seen in the organisms' adaptations to the association'. Grass leaves are adapted to grazing by growing continuously at the base, and the plants are strongly rooted. Bees' mouthparts are adapted for obtaining nectar from flowers, and there are pollen baskets on their legs. Figwasps can recognise fig trees. All these adaptations are directly related to the kind of contact between the associated species, and probably would be little different if the grass, flowers and figs did not benefit. If this seems to be a general rule – and you can check it by thinking about other adaptations in intimate associations – it would suggest that whether an association is mutualistic, parasitic or whatever is less important than the intimacy.

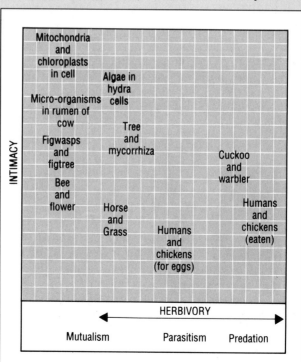

Parasitism

The association between a parasite and its host can be of two types.

- A parasite which lives on the surface of its host is called an **ectoparasite**. An example would be the tick on the hedgehog in figure 6.2.

- A parasite which lives inside its host is called an **endoparasite**. An example is the parasite that causes sleeping sickness (figure 6.3).

Parasitism is of tremendous importance. Most species, including humans, harbour parasites. Parasites may have a major impact on their hosts, reducing their health and in some cases causing their death. We will look at several parasites and then draw some general conclusions about how parasites are adapted to their way of life and how their hosts respond to their presence.

Potato blight

Potato blight is caused by the oomycete *Phytophthora infestans* whose life cycle is shown in figure 6.4. The oomycete overwinters as a system of slender branched threads called a **mycelium** in infected potato tubers. The individual threads are called **hyphae**. In the spring the hyphae grow through the infected tubers and, on reaching the air, they branch into tree-like **aerial hyphae** which bear asexual reproductive structures called **sporangia** at their tips. The sporangia are small pear-shaped bodies and – being light – they

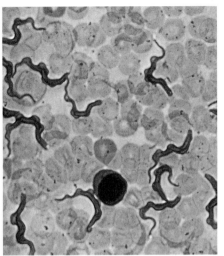

Figure 6.3 Light micrograph of a trypanosome in a human blood smear. This particular form is *Trypanosoma brucei* which causes acute sleeping sickness in humans, cattle and antelopes. Trypanosomes are flagellated unicells that live in the bloodstream. Precisely why they are so dangerous is still not known for certain. It is possible that the immune system over-reacts to the infection. At any rate, sleeping sickness is frequently fatal if untreated, though it may take several years to kill its victim.

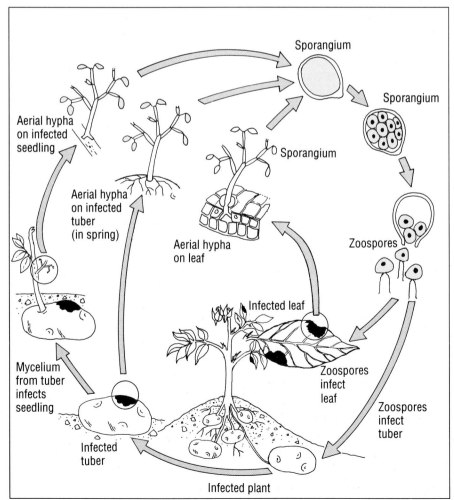

Figure 6.4 Life cycle of the organism that causes potato blight, *Phytophthora infestans*. The disease is transmitted by sporangia which produce motile zoospores. These can infect either the leaves or the tubers of potato plants, sending out hyphae which grow through the host's tissues. Sporangia are formed at the tips of the hyphae which grow out of the tubers, seedlings and adult potato plants.

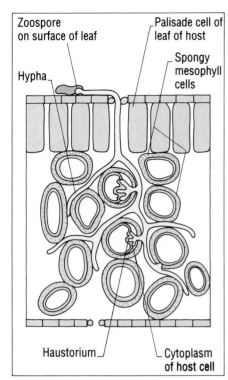

Figure 6.5 *Phytophthora infestans* is partly intercellular and partly intracellular. Specialised haustoria allow the organism to obtain its nutrients from the cells of its host, the potato plant. Haustoria are here seen attacking the spongy mesophyll cells in the leaf. They penetrate the cell walls (yellow) and then absorb nutrients from the cytoplasm (blue).

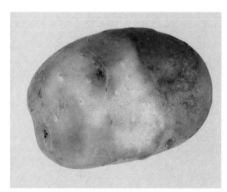

Figure 6.6 Potato tuber with a mild attack of potato blight.

are readily dispersed by wind or rain. When a sporangium lands on a wet potato leaf it may burst open, releasing about six motile **zoospores**. Equipped with a pair of flagella, the zoospores swim through the water on the surface of the leaf. They then settle down and send out hyphae which may penetrate the leaf cuticle or enter through a stoma.

Once inside the potato plant, the hyphae spread rapidly through the plant. They grow between the cells of the host, but obtain nourishment by sending out short side branches which penetrate the cellulose walls of the host cells (figure 6.5). They gain entrance by secreting cellulase at their tips. Once the cell wall has been breached, finger-like **haustoria** are produced. These secrete enzymes which cause the plasma membrane to leak. Substances leaked from the host cell are absorbed by the haustoria and passed back to the rest of the mycelium, allowing further growth to take place.

The success of this parasite is due to its combination of rapid inter-cellular growth coupled with intracellular feeding and mass production of sporangia. Infection can rapidly turn a healthy potato plant into a black putrid mass (figure 6.6). Eventually sporangia are produced and new plants become infected. In most countries reproduction is almost always asexual. In some countries, however, separate plus and minus strains are found and sexual reproduction can take place between these strains.

Potato blight is found in nearly all parts of the world where potatoes are grown. When the weather is warm (16–22°C) and moist (80–100 per cent relative humidity) the disease can cause the total destruction of an entire potato crop within as little as a week. As was discussed in Chapter 5, the disease was responsible for the death of about one-sixth of the population of Ireland during the late 1840s. Thankfully the disease is now relatively easy to control.

A combination of sanitary measures and well-timed chemical spraying can help to control potato blight. Any infected potatoes should be burnt and only disease-free potatoes should be used for 'seed'. Chemical sprays can play an important role. Traditionally these were based on copper, for oomycetes are especially sensitive to copper. Nowadays a variety of non-copper chemicals is available and in many countries farmers receive advice from meteorological stations so that they can spray in advance of warm, moist weather.

Finally, plant breeding has helped to produce resistant varieties of potato plant which are less susceptible to the parasite than older traditional varieties. However, no variety is completely immune to potato blight. *Phytophthora* has a short generation time and produces enormous numbers of offspring. As a result, despite the frequent absence of sexual reproduction, natural selection is working to produce new strains better able to infect their hosts.

Potato blight is caused by a multicellular organism that attacks a plant. As a parasite, it has many similarities to the distantly related unicellular organism that causes one of the most common human diseases, malaria.

Malaria

Malaria is probably the world's most important disease. Approximately 250 million people suffer from it, of whom about two million die each year. Most deaths occur in children under the age of six, though even in adults the disease can be fatal. Usually, however, adults survive, though commonly they continue to suffer periodic attacks for a number of years.

Description of the disease is complicated by the fact that no fewer than four different species can cause it. All are members of the genus

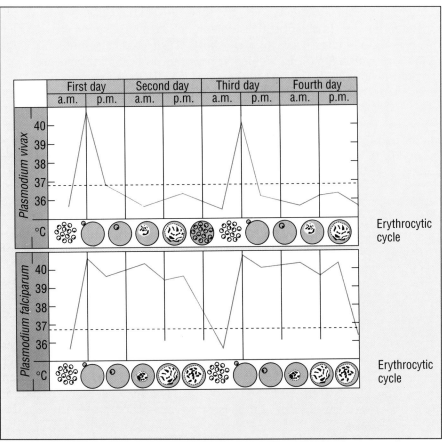

Figure 6.7 Malaria is characterised by recurrent bouts of fever at regular intervals. Notice how the course of the fever differs for the two species of *Plasmodium*. For both species, though, the host's body temperature is at its highest soon after the merozoites have been released from the red blood cells in the erythrocytic cycle. The erythrocytic cycle is explained on page 81.

Plasmodium, sporozoans in the kingdom Protoctista. The most common is *P. vivax* which thankfully is less dangerous than the next most widespread species, *P. falciparum*. The other two species are *P. malariae* and *P. ovale*.

Although the four different species have fundamentally the same life cycle, the diseases they produce differ significantly. The characteristic temperatures of people suffering from the two most common types of malaria are shown in figure 6.7. You can see that the fever produced by *P. falciparum* is worse than that produced by *P. vivax*.

For the parasite to complete its life cycle, two hosts are required: a human and a mosquito in the genus *Anopheles*. Only female mosquitoes bite humans, and so spread malaria. She uses the protein in human blood for manufacturing her eggs. When an infected female mosquito pierces the skin with her proboscis, she is searching for a capillary. At the same time saliva from her salivary glands is injected into the bloodstream. The saliva

Malaria in history

Malaria has been recognised as an important disease for over 2000 years. During the time of the Roman Empire, the swamps around Rome were a source of anopheline mosquitoes and the *mal aria* (Italian for bad air) was thought to be responsible for the disease. This gave malaria its name. It has been suggested that as the Roman Empire went into decline, the available breeding areas for the mosquitoes increased, hastening the Empire's decline and fall.

Malaria used to occur in England but a change in agricultural practice in the eighteenth century probably led to a marked decline in the disease. At about this time the number of cattle kept in England increased greatly. They provided malaria-carrying mosquitoes with a preferred source of blood. However, *Plasmodium* cannot reproduce in cattle. Accordingly malaria became rarer as the parasite was unable to complete its life cycle. It is even possible that this so improved the health of people in England that it contributed to the rapid growth of the population and subsequent Industrial Revolution.

contains an anti-coagulant which stops the blood clotting until the mosquito has finished her meal. Unfortunately, from our perspective, when the mosquito injects her saliva she will, if infected, also inject a large number of malarial parasites which at this stage are called **sporozoites**.

Within about 30 minutes these slender cells make their way via the bloodstream to the liver (figure 6.8). Here **schizogony** occurs (see page 568), a remarkable process in which a single sporozoite can give rise asexually to over 1000 **merozoites** (figure 6.9). These merozoites are released from the liver cell and may then attack red blood cells. (In certain *Plasmodium* species, but not in *P. vivax*, some of these merozoites may also attack other liver cells.)

Figure 6.8 Life cycle of the malarial parasite showing the four stages where reproduction occurs (numbered 1 to 4).

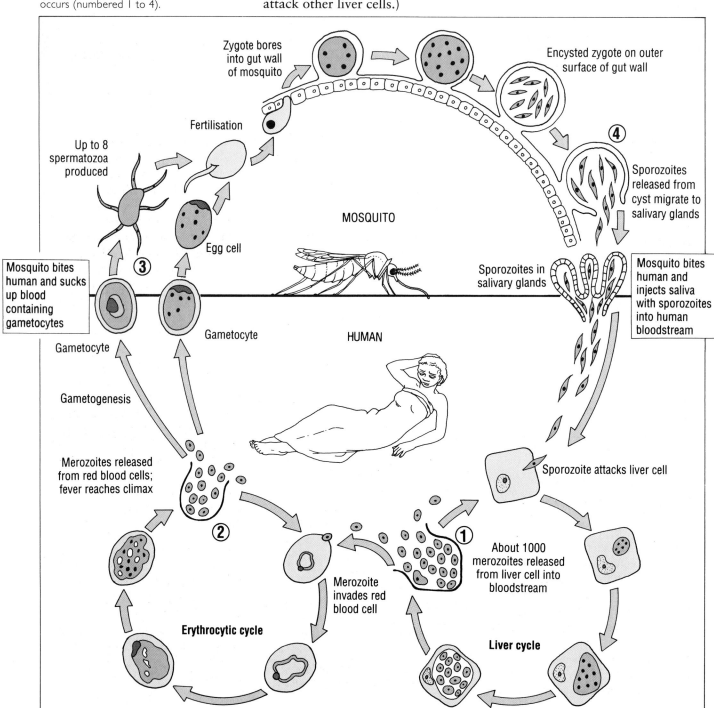

Once in a red blood cell, further asexual reproduction takes place. As the infection progresses, the asexual stages in the red blood cells become synchronised so that a blood sample taken at any one time shows most of the parasites at the same stage of development. Because of the synchronous release of merozoites from countless red blood cells, the person suffering from malaria goes through a characteristic cycle of symptoms which correspond to different stages in this so-called **erythrocytic cycle**.

After several generations some of the merozoites develop into sexual forms (**gametocytes**). These develop no further until taken up by an *Anopheles* mosquito. In the mosquito's gut, the male gametocyte produces up to eight sperm while the female gametocyte develops into a single egg. Fertilisation then takes place and diploid zygotes are formed. These burrow into the wall of the mosquito's gut where they form wart-like cysts. Within these cysts, meiosis takes place, followed by asexual reproduction. The result is that typically 10 000 haploid sporozoites are released from each cyst. Many of these sporozoites then migrate to the mosquito's salivary glands, ready to be injected into the next human she bites.

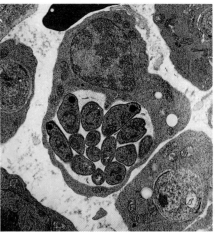

Figure 6.9 Electron micrograph showing merozoites of the malarial parasite *Plasmodium* in a human liver cell. Magnification × 1200.

Combatting malaria

To control any parasite, the life cycle must be broken. Malaria has traditionally been combatted in three ways: by attacking the parasite itself; by eliminating its **vector**, the mosquito; and by preventing the vector from biting humans.

The third of these options, protection from the vector, is the most straightforward. Mosquito nets can be used or, even more simply, the risks of infection may be reduced by keeping away from places with standing water and by staying indoors at dawn and dusk, when most species of anopheline mosquito are most active.

The mosquito may be attacked in a number of ways. Traditionally, draining of possible breeding grounds has been used. This technique was extensively employed in historical times throughout much of Europe. The expense and difficulties involved are an indication of the harm done by the disease.

More recently, a variety of insecticides have been used, most notably DDT. Two problems have been found with the widespread use of insecticides. One is that the mosquitoes evolve resistance, requiring ever higher doses, or the application of new pesticides, to kill them. The second is that many insecticides do more harm than good, either killing insects beneficial to humans or becoming concentrated in food chains and harming carnivores (see Chapter 4).

Another technique used to attack the mosquito has been to spray the breeding grounds with diesel oil – the oil is taken into the breathing tubes of the larvae and kills them. There have also been attempts at biological control and some success has been achieved by the introduction of guppies which eat the larvae. However, biological control has not proved as effective as was hoped.

For over 300 years it has been widely known that the drug **quinine**, obtained from the bark of the cinchona tree (*Cinchona ledgeriana*) can cure malaria. The tree gets its name from the Countess of Chinchon. The story is told of how the Countess caught malaria while in Peru in about 1640. She was given the bark of a local tree by her physician and experienced a miraculous cure. As a result some of the tree bark was carried back to Spain and used to cure others of malaria. Unfortunately for the story, recent historical research has shown that while the Countess was in Peru she was in remarkably good health and never suffered from malaria.

Whatever the origins behind its discovery, quinine remained the only drug against malaria until the interruption of transatlantic shipping by the Germans during the First World War prompted North American research into alternatives. By now a number of other drugs have been developed, though quinine is still widely used.

It is hoped that an effective vaccine against malaria can be developed. So far this has proved extremely difficult. Among the problems are the fact that, as we have seen, four different species of *Plasmodium* can cause the disease, and the sporozoites take only 30 minutes to infect a liver cell once they have entered their host. Further, it seems that the parasite has a high rate of mutation and new strains are always evolving.

1 *Which would you expect to be more effective and why: a vaccine that acted on the merozoites or one that acted on the sporozoites?*
2 *Do you think it would be better to combat malaria by eradicating the mosquito, eliminating the parasite or treating those who develop the disease? Explain your answer.*

Figure 6.10 Adult female cuckoo.

Figure 6.11 Nestling cuckoo ejecting the egg of a reed warbler from its nest.

The organisms responsible for malaria may not appear to have much in common with cuckoos. Yet cuckoos, to which we now turn, share one important feature with *Plasmodium*: they are unable to reproduce without their hosts.

Cuckoos

The European cuckoo is the most widespread member of the cuckoo family. It is found throughout Europe and while the males are noted for their distinctive call, it is the females and young who have been famous since time immemorial for their unusual behaviour (figure 6.10). Some 2300 years ago Aristotle recorded how the female lays her eggs in the nest of smaller birds and in 1788 Edward Jenner, who did so much to develop the technique of smallpox vaccination, provided the first detailed description of how the young cuckoo ejects the host's eggs and young from the nest (figure 6.11).

Female cuckoos never build their own nests. Instead they lay their eggs in the nests of other birds. Egg laying is carried out with a great deal of care. The female cuckoo often watches her intended victim for several days beforehand and then lays her eggs in the host's nest when neither parent is present. Less than ten seconds are required for her to glide down to the nest, lay a single egg and depart. This compares with the 20 minutes or longer normally spent by female birds laying eggs in their own nests. Not only that but the female cuckoo often removes one or more of the host's eggs in order to help her own survive.

In Britain, cuckoos exploit five main host species: meadow pipits, reed warblers, dunnocks, robins and pied wagtails. With the exception of the dunnock, cuckoo eggs closely resemble those of their hosts (figure 6.12). This must mean that there are several races of cuckoo in Britain, each adapted to a different host species. Careful experiments conducted by Nick Davies and his co-workers at the University of Cambridge since 1985 have shown that the match between the cuckoo's egg and the host's egg reduces the chance that the host will reject the cuckoo's egg.

Cuckoos lay unusually small eggs for their size. As smaller eggs take less time to hatch than larger ones, the cuckoo egg usually hatches before the host's eggs. The young cuckoo subsequently waits until the host birds are absent from the nest and then pushes their eggs (or young chicks if the eggs have already hatched) out of the nest.

You can see how impressively the cuckoo is adapted to its parasitic way of life. The benefits to the cuckoo are enormous, as the costs of rearing the offspring are transferred to another species.

Figure 6.12 Host eggs and cuckoo eggs. The bottom row shows eggs of the five species of bird most commonly parasitised by the cuckoo. From left to right these are: robin, pied wagtail, dunnock, reed warbler and meadow pipit. The top row shows a typical example of a cuckoo egg laid in the corresponding host nest.

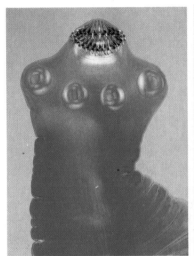 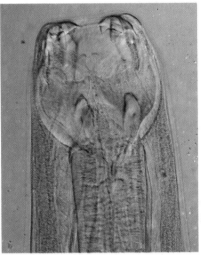 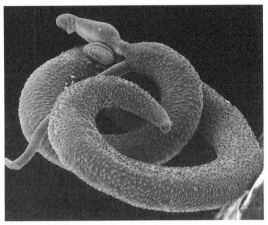

Figure 6.13 Attachment devices of three parasites.

Left Taenia solium, the pork tapeworm, inhabits the human small intestine: the head (scolex) is buried in the gut wall which it grips by means of its hooks and suckers.

Middle Ancylostoma caninum, the dog hook worm, has hooks by which it clings to and rasps at the wall of the small intestine.

Right The blood fluke *Schistosoma*. The slender flukes inhabit the blood vessels of the intestine and/or urinary system. Notice the mouth and ventral sucker.

Having looked in detail at three different parasites, we are now in a position to look at the range of adaptations that parasites show to their distinctive way of life.

Parasitic adaptations

The parasitic way of life is a precarious one. For example, a parasite needs to have a way of locating its host, must be able to prevent rejection by its host, and must be able to spread to new hosts. Parasites show many different ways of overcoming these problems, depending on whether they are ectoparasites or endoparasites.

- Many endoparasites show **degeneration**, or even total loss, of certain organs. They may lack sense organs, particularly eyes, and frequently have a reduced nervous system. Gut parasites like the tapeworm lack an alimentary canal, though their free-living relatives have one. Endoparasites that wallow in their host's body fluids often lack osmo-regulatory devices.

- Many parasites, especially ectoparasites, have **attachment devices** enabling them to cling to the host. For instance, many species of trematode inhabit the gill passages of fishes. The constant flow of water over the gills would sweep them away were it not for **suckers, hooks** or **anchors** which enable them to cling to the epithelium. Hooks and suckers are also responsible for attachment of the scolex of the tapeworm *Taenia solium* to the wall of the human gut. Some of these devices are illustrated in figure 6.13.

- Some parasites have **penetrative devices** for gaining entrance into the host and its cells. The miracidium larva of the liver fluke, for example, has a slender tip on to which open a group of glands which secrete tissue-digesting enzymes (figure 6.14). By softening the tissues, these enzymes enable the larva to bore into the foot of a freshwater snail, the interme-diate host.

We have already seen how *Phytophthora*, the organism that causes potato blight, secretes cellulase at the tips of its hyphae thereby enabling it to penetrate the cell walls of its host. Many parasitic fungi also produce cellulase, while related enzymes are produced by a number of parasitic bacteria.

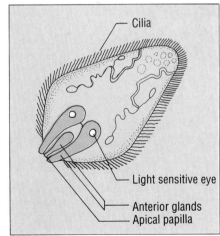

Figure 6.14 Miracidium larva of the liver fluke *Fasciola hepatica*. The cilia enable the larva to swim through water to the intermediate host, a snail. The protrusible apical papilla adheres to the snail's foot and a secretion from the anterior glands dissolves the flesh, thereby permitting the larva to penetrate. The larva then wriggles through the snail's tissues by contraction of circular and longitudinal muscles in its body wall.

Labels: Cilia, Light sensitive eye, Anterior glands, Apical papilla

- Gut parasites live in a particularly hazardous environment. They typically have **protective devices** which prevent their being harmed by the host's digestive processes. These devices include the possession of a thick protective **cuticle**, the secretion of large quantities of **mucus** and the production of **inhibitory substances** which locally inactivate the host's digestive enzymes.

- It is not only gut parasites that must protect themselves against the host's defences. The blood fluke *Schistosoma*, responsible for the human disease bilharzia, synthesises chemicals which switch off the host's immune system: the parasite coats itself with molecules which the host recognises as 'self'.

- One of the greatest problems facing any parasite is getting from one host to another. As parasites are often specific to only one species of host, a possible strategy for an animal parasite is to wait until its host mates. The various organisms responsible for sexually transmitted diseases in humans spread in this manner.

    A related strategy is to pass from mother to offspring. Again, the organisms responsible for a number of sexually transmitted diseases in humans can spread in this way, including those that cause gonorrhoea and AIDS. In the case of gonorrhoea, the bacterium can pass from mother to offspring during birth. In the case of AIDS, the causative organism, HIV, can cross the placenta and may be found in breast milk.

- Many parasites employ a **secondary** or **intermediate host** which conveys the parasite from one **primary host** to another. Thus the *Anopheles* mosquito transfers the malarial parasite *Plasmodium* from one person to another. (Of course, from the mosquito's point of view, it might be argued that we are the secondary hosts and they the primary ones!) An organism, such as the mosquito, which carries a parasite from one primary host to another is called a **vector**.

- Infection of new hosts is a hazardous business for a parasite. To raise the probability of success vast numbers of offspring are produced. The reproductive powers of many parasites are phenomenal. Countless millions of tiny wind-dispersed spores may be produced by a single parasitic fungus, and figure 6.8 on page 80 gives some idea of the reproductive powers of the malarial parasite. You can see that reproduction occurs at no less than four stages in the life cycle, two of them in the human host and two in the mosquito. In the type of malaria caused by *Plasmodium vivax*, the number of parasites in the blood may exceed 30 000 per mm^3.

- Endoparasites with a primary and secondary host may have a number of structurally distinct larval stages, each allowing rapid asexual multiplication in a different environment. This is illustrated by the liver fluke *Fasciola hepatica* whose life cycle is summarised in figure 6.15.

    The liver fluke illustrates another important principle, namely the advantage of having a **dormant resistant stage** in the life cycle. Provided they are immersed in water, the encysted cercariae of the liver fluke remain viable for up to a year, though they can only survive for a few weeks if exposed to the air. Many other parasites have stages that remain in a dormant, yet viable, state until a suitable host is found.

- Some parasites are so closely linked with their host that their tissues are actually interconnected. For example, certain plant parasites plug into other plants and tap off nutrients from the host's vascular tissues.

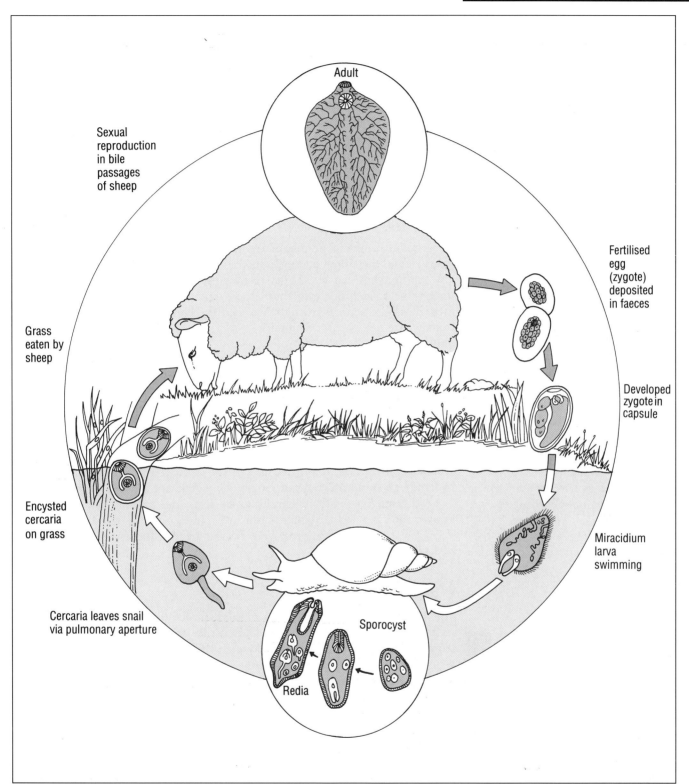

Figure 6.15 Life cycle of the liver fluke *Fasciola hepatica*. The adult fluke lives in the bile passages of sheep where it reproduces sexually producing numerous encapsulated zygotes. The ciliated miracidium larva emerges from the capsule and, swimming through water on the ground, penetrates the fleshy foot of the snail *Limnaea truncatula* where it turns into a sporocyst. Inside the sporocyst special propagatory cells divide to form rediae larvae which burrow into the liver of the snail, feeding on the tissues. Inside each redia, propagatory cells give rise to either more rediae or numerous cercariae larvae. The latter usually work their way to the mantle cavity and leave the snail via its pulmonary aperture, encysting on blades of grass. If and when it is eaten by a sheep, the cyst bursts open releasing a small immature fluke which migrates from the host's gut to its liver. Here it feeds and grows to maturity, thus completing the cycle.

Figure 6.16 Dodder (*Cuscuta*) on a host plant. The genus *Cuscuta* contains about 100 species, all of which parasitise other plants. All dodders have thin stems which wind around the shoot of the host. At intervals short side-branches, known as suckers, are given off and these penetrate the host's stem. The suckers contain vascular tissues which link up with those of the host. As a result the parasite can obtain all its water, minerals and soluble organic substances from the host. In consequence dodder has leaves that are small and scale-like and once the plant is established the roots wither away.

Figure 6.17 Hermit crab with colonial hydroids. This relationship seems to benefit only the hydroids.

One such plant is dodder (*Cuscuta*). Dodder is shown in figure 6.16 and its appearance suggests that it harms its host. However, many parasites seem to cause surprisingly little harm to their hosts. In part this may be because, over time, hosts have evolved defences against the worst effects of their parasites.

However, there may be another reason. When you think about it, it is not in the interests of a parasite to cause too much damage to its host. Suppose that a parasite killed its host within a short time. In that case the parasite would either perish with the host or be forced to begin again the hazardous business of finding a new host. This is an instance of the parasite and host evolving together – a point to which we will return later.

Commensalism

For a relationship to be commensalitic it must be shown that one partner gains, while the other neither gains nor loses. In practice, it is doubtful if any relationship can be shown to be truly commensalitic, for it is almost impossible to demonstrate that a host fails either to benefit a little or to incur a minute penalty from the association. Nevertheless, there are associations where one partner benefits substantially, while the other *appears* to be unaffected.

One such instance is the association between the colonial hydroid *Hydractinia echinata* and the hermit crab *Pagurus bernhardus* (figure 6.17). The hermit crab is a curious creature whose asymmetrical abdomen fits snugly into the coils of an empty whelk shell. *Hydractinia* is one of several organisms commonly found attached to shells occupied by hermit crabs.

In this particular association the hydroid obtains food particles from the crab and, more importantly, is taken into regions which otherwise would be unsuitable for it because of the softness of the substratum – the hydroid can stand on rocks or empty shells, but not on soft mud.

Although the hydroid clearly gains from the association, as far as is known the crab neither benefits nor loses. Indeed, when selecting an empty shell, the crab's choice seems unaffected by the presence or absence of hydroids on it.

Mutualism

For an association to qualify as mutualistic it must be demonstrated that both partners benefit. There are all possible grades of mutualism, ranging from rather loose associations in which the two organisms gain relatively little from each other, to associations so intimate that the two partners may be regarded as a single organism.

Intimate associations include cases when one partner lives inside the other. One instance is the complex community of micro-organisms that occur in the rumen of cows, sheep and other ruminants. The host benefits from the enzymes of the micro-organisms which, unlike those of the host, can break down cellulose. In return the micro-organisms are guaranteed a safe and constant environment. However, we should hesitate before assuming that the relationship is harmoniously balanced. The micro-organisms eventually pass out of the rumen and are digested by the host (see page 283).

The ultimate in intimacy is achieved when one of the partners lives inside the cells of the other. An example of this is provided by the green hydra *Chlorohydra viridissima* which harbours large numbers of the green protoctist *Chlorella* (in this case referred to as zoochlorella) in its endodermal cells.

Mistletoes that hide

Mistletoes are perennial flowering plants which grow as parasites attached to the branches of trees and shrubs. Throughout most of Europe only one species is found, but worldwide there are about 1300 species of mistletoe.

A feature of many mistletoes, especially those found in Australia, is that they mimic their hosts. Mistletoe vegetation is very similar to that of the host species. This is true for many different genera of mistletoes growing on many different genera of trees. Surely the resemblance must be advantageous to the mistletoe, rather than simply being the result of chance. But what is the advantage?

One possibility is that mistletoes that resemble their hosts are less likely to be eaten by mammalian herbivores. Mistletoes are generally palatable, and have even been used as fodder for farm animals. Evidence for this theory comes from the observation that exterminations of possums in some areas have been correlated with increased growth of mistletoes.

A second possibility is based on the fact that birds are responsible for the dispersal of mistletoe seeds. It has been argued that the resemblance of the mistletoe to its host results in birds flying to uninfected trees, expecting to find mistletoe seeds there as food. In the process, the birds may disperse mistletoe seeds to uninfected hosts.

Various lines of evidence indicate that this association is mutually beneficial. For instance, even when *Chlorohydra* is kept in the dark, the zoochlorellae survive. This suggests that, although unable to photosynthesise, they derive essential nutrients from their host. Conversely, specimens of *Chlorohydra* kept in the light but prevented from feeding heterotrophically, survive for longer than closely related species of hydra that lack zoochlorellae.

What then do these two organisms obtain from each other? The protoctist is afforded shelter, protection, nitrogenous compounds from its host's excretory waste and possibly a significant supply of carbon dioxide from its host's respiration. In return the hydra obtains carbohydrates made by the protoctist's photosynthesis and possibly a significant supply of oxygen, again from photosynthesis.

A similar metabolic relationship is found in those extraordinary organisms, **lichens** (figure 6.18). A lichen is the result of a union between a fungus and a unicellular organism. The fungus partner is usually an ascomycete or a basidiomycete (see page 109). The unicellular organism is either a green alga (a protoctist belonging to the phylum Chlorophyta) or a blue-green bacterium belonging to the kingdom Prokaryotae.

In a lichen, the fungus is nearly always the dominant organism forming most of the lichen (figure 6.19). However, the fungus is not free living and can apparently survive only when in partnership with its algal or bacterial

Figure 6.18 Two species of lichen growing on a rock on the sea shore. The grey, tufted lichen is *Ramalina siliquosa*. The yellow, crustose one is *Xanthoria parietina*.

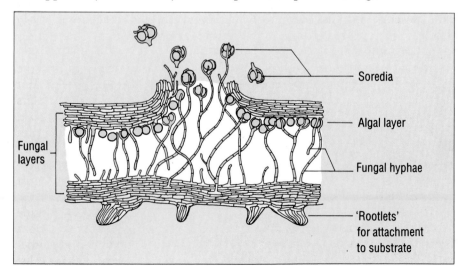

Soredia

Algal layer

Fungal hyphae

Fungal layers

'Rootlets' for attachment to substrate

Figure 6.19 Section through a lichen showing the fungal hyphae among the algal cells. Soredia are the units by which lichens reproduce. They contain both algal cells and fungal hyphae.

Figure 6.20 Greater horseshoe bat. Bats are nocturnal and can locate objects in their flight path by sensing the delay between the emission of an ultrasonic squeak and the return of its echo. The sound is produced by the larynx and emitted through the mouth or nose – in the case of the horseshoe bat through the nose. The echo is detected by the ears with their large pinnae.

Figure 6.21 Sonogram showing the search, approach and capture phases of the hunt of the north American big brown bat. When searching, the bat emits five to six pulses per second, each lasting about 10 msec and descending in frequency from about 70 to 30 kHz. Once a potential prey is located, the pulse rate increases dramatically. At the point of capture (or near miss) the bat is producing about 200 pulses per second and receives the same number of pieces of information on its prey's whereabouts.

companion. However, many (though probably not all) lichen algae can survive on their own. The complications of this relationship make it difficult to know where to classify lichens. Usually they are put in the Fungi, but they could also be in a group of their own, with the Prokaryotae or with the Protoctista.

Lichens are astonishingly hardy organisms and can thrive in the most unlikely places, for example on exposed rocks at high altitudes and in the Arctic and Antarctic. Often they flourish in places where no other organisms can survive through lack of water. Frequently they are the first species to colonise exposed rock.

Both partners clearly gain from an increase in the range of habitats they can occupy. The green algae or cyanobacteria are protected from desiccation and in turn they give the fungus carbohydrates from their photosynthesis. Lichens containing cyanobacteria have the added bonus of receiving organic nitrogen from the bacteria as these possess the enzyme nitrogenase, which enables them to fix atmospheric nitrogen.

Predation

Predators differ from parasites in that they are usually larger than their 'hosts'. More importantly, they kill their prey before eating it.

There are so many examples of predators being adapted so as to catch their prey, and of prey being adapted so as to avoid their predators, that it is difficult to know where to begin. We will concentrate on just one example: that of bats catching moths.

Nowadays we are so used to the idea that bats use **echolocation** that it is hard to imagine the incredulity with which the idea was first received. When the zoologist Robert Galambos first reported his evidence for bat echolocation to a conference in 1940, one distinguished scientist was so indignant that he seized Galambos by the shoulder and shook him, complaining that he could not possibly make such an outrageous suggestion! Today we know that not only bats, but cetaceans and even some cave-dwelling birds can echolocate.

There are 951 species of bats and they occur throughout the world except in the Arctic, the Antarctic and on the highest mountains. Echolocation is probably the key to their evolutionary success, for this allows them to forage for insects at night when many other predators are disqualified by darkness. Sounds are emitted by the bat through the open mouth or nostrils, depending on the species. Bats with elaborate noses, such as horseshoes and false vampires, emit sounds through their noses (figure 6.20).

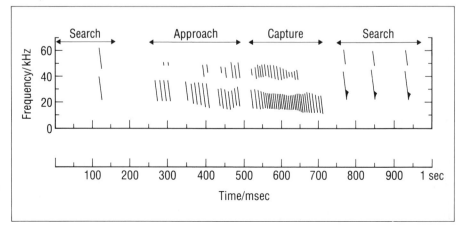

Whether a bat emits sounds through its mouth or its nose, the pattern with which the sounds are produced depends on precisely what the bat is doing. For example, the rate and frequency with which sounds are produced by the North American big brown bat depend on whether the bat is searching, approaching or attempting to capture prey (figure 6.21).

The contest between a bat and its prey is not as one sided as you might imagine. True, the bat can measure the delay between sending out a pulse of sound and hearing it return, thus pinpointing the position and movement of its prey. However, certain insects have evolved counter-adaptations. Some moths have listening membranes that detect the bat's sonar pulses, giving the moth the chance of escape. Other moths can even produce their own ultrasound, thus confusing the bats.

Coevolution

Our survey of parasitism, commensalism and mutualism raises the intriguing question of which came first. Can we assume that commensalism is the most primitive association and that parasitism and mutualism followed later, or could the order be different?

It is easy to imagine that an organism which has been living commensally (or even mutualistically) might start to exploit its host in some way, thus becoming a parasite. Equally, a parasitic association might gradually become so well balanced that no harm at all is inflicted on the host, thus turning it into a commensalitic relationship. It is likely that many different sequences have occurred in evolution.

In any event, symbiotic organisms and their hosts seem to have evolved in response to each other, a process called **coevolution**. The English biologists John Krebs and Richard Dawkins have argued that coevolution is essentially an arms race between two organisms in selfish competition. Even when the relationship is mutualistic, natural selection still favours traits that benefit whichever organism bears them. Only if this is the case can natural selection allow mutually beneficial traits to evolve.

We will consider pollination in more detail in Chapter 34, but it is clear that in insect-pollination the insect and the plant have evolved together. From the plant's point of view the insect serves only to pollinate it. Gaudy petals, quantities of nectar and seductive scents are simply necessary advertisement and bribery. From the insect's perspective, getting covered in sticky pollen is just one of the hazards of the job. The benefit comes from eating nectar or pollen.

With these thoughts in mind, we will now turn to some examples of how organisms in association have evolved in response to each other – that is, how they have coevolved.

Grasses and large herbivores

Everyone likes to chew on a piece of grass on a nice summer's day while contemplating the meaning of life, but few of us would choose to try to live on it. Indeed, we can't. Grass simply doesn't contain enough protein for us. Not only that, but it contains a surprisingly large amount of silica (SiO_2), an abrasive mineral which would soon damage our teeth.

It is thought that grasses have evolved the ability to deposit silica in their leaves and stems to reduce their risks of being grazed. In turn, large herbivores have evolved complex molars with enamel ridges for grinding up grass (see page 270). In other words, grasses and large herbivores have coevolved. Even so, elderly red deer sometimes die of starvation through having had their teeth worn down by the silica in their food.

Carnivores, herbivores and the Red Queen effect

The presence of large herbivores leads to the coevolution of large carnivores. Much of the evolution of large mammalian herbivores and carnivores over the last 60 million years has centred on both getting faster. Evidence for this comes from fossils over this period which show elongation of limb bones, a sure sign that the animals were running faster.

Not only did the limbs of the herbivores and carnivores evolve for greater speed, but their brains became larger too. Looking today at the way large carnivores such as wolves, lions and jaguars hunt their prey, it is clear that intelligence favours both the hunter and the hunted. Survival is a battle of wits. It could be that coevolution has forced both herbivores and carnivores to be more intelligent.

If coevolution has led to greater speed and intelligence in large carnivores and their prey, we would expect the hunting success of a modern cheetah or lion to be no better than that of its evolutionary counterpart 60 million years ago. The American evolutionary biologist Leigh Van Valen calls this the **Red Queen effect**. The Red Queen, you will remember from Lewis Caroll's *Through the Looking Glass*, described how her country was one where you had to run ever so fast just to remain in the same place.

Figure 6.22 Two examples of crypsis.
A Cryptic katydid (a cricket) among leaves, photographed in Tinalandia, Ecuador.
B Ringed plover nest with cryptic eggs on shingle. Photographed in Sussex, England.

Colour, patterns and mimicry

If an organism is to avoid being eaten, an obvious strategy is to blend into the background and be inconspicuous. This is known as **crypsis** and is common throughout the animal kingdom.

If you have ever seen certain stick insects and crickets you will know how impressive crypsis can be, for these animals can look remarkably like the plants on which they feed in both colour and shape (figure 6.22A). Many ground-nesting birds provide examples of crypsis for they make nests that are exceptionally difficult to find (figure 6.22B).

A quite different strategy is to be distasteful and to advertise the fact by looking especially conspicuous! This is known as **warning coloration**, and an example is provided by the monarch butterfly (*Danaus plexippus*) (figure 6.23). This colourful North and Central American butterfly lays its eggs on milkweeds in the genus *Asclepias*. The milkweeds produce a number of poisonous chemicals (cardiac glycosides) which deter most herbivores. However, the larvae of the monarch butterfly feed on milkweeds and store the poisons in their body. When the caterpillars metamorphose into adults, they fly away still with the stores of poisonous cardiac glycosides.

Monarch butterflies are sometimes caught by birds called blue jays. Within half an hour of eating a monarch butterfly the bird is violently sick. The advantage of this to the butterfly is that when the bird *next* sees a monarch butterfly, it refuses to eat it. As will be discussed further in Chapter 30, it seems that the blue jay learns to associate the butterfly's distinctive coloration with the traumatic consequences of eating it. In this way the bright colouring may reduce the chance of a butterfly being eaten.

Mimicry

There are a number of other butterfly species that look very similar to the monarch butterfly yet are completely palatable. This is an example of **Batesian mimicry**, named after the Victorian explorer, H.W. Bates, who first suggested it. In all cases of Batesian mimicry there is a distasteful species, the **model**, and one or more palatable species which resemble the model. The latter are called **mimics** (figure 6.24). The mimic obviously benefits because the risks of its being eaten are reduced.

Figure 6.23 Monarch butterflies resting during their migration in California, USA.

Figure 6.24 Hoverfly on golden rod. Hoverflies probably benefit from their resemblance to many bees and wasps.

What are the costs and benefits of the relationship from the model's point of view? If the mimic becomes too abundant, the model will suffer. This is because once the mimic is more common than the model, the chances are that a predator will eat a mimic before it first takes a model. If this is the case, it will learn to associate the distinctive patterning of the model and the mimic with a safe and tasty meal! This will be to the disadvantage of both the model and the mimic.

There is another sort of mimicry, known as **Müllerian mimicry** after the German zoologist, Fritz Müller. In this case both the model and the mimic are unpalatable or dangerous (figure 6.25). Here both partners benefit so the relationship is mutualistic.

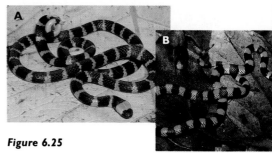

Figure 6.25

A A poisonous coral snake.

B Another poisonous coral snake, but in a different genus to the one in **A**.

Summary

1 The **biotic environment** of an organism is the sum of the living factors that influence that organism.

2 The general term used to describe intimate associations between pairs of species is **symbiosis**.

3 Parasitism is an association between two organisms in which the smaller, the **parasite**, lives either temporarily or permanently in or on the larger, the **host**. The host is harmed by the parasite, but is usually not killed by it.

4 **Commensalism** is an association in which one of the two organisms benefits, while the other neither loses nor gains.

5 **Mutualism** is an association which benefits both participants. A lichen, for instance, is the result of a mutualistic association between a fungus and either a green alga or a blue-green bacterium.

6 **Potato blight** is a disease of potato plants caused by a parasitic oomycete.

7 **Malaria** is a disease of humans caused by parasitic micro-organisms belonging to the genus *Plasmodium*. The parasites require the presence of a **vector**, a mosquito in the genus *Anopheles*, to complete their life cycles.

8 Parasites show many adaptations to their way of life, depending on whether they are **endoparasites** or **ectoparasites**.

9 **Predators** differ from parasites in that they kill their prey before eating it.

10 Over evolutionary time each organism in an association evolves in response to how the other organism has evolved. This is called **coevolution**.

11 Many organisms reduce the risk of predation by blending into the background, that is, by being **cryptic**. However, if poisonous or dangerous, it may pay an organism to advertise the fact by, for example, **warning coloration**.

12 **Batesian mimicry** occurs when a palatable mimic resembles a distasteful model.

13 **Müllerian mimicry** occurs when a distasteful mimic resembles a distasteful model.

Review questions

1 What organisms make up *your* biotic environment?

2 A naturalist observes that the black rhinoceros often has birds on its back that remove ticks from the rhinoceros's skin. How might the naturalist try to determine whether the relationship is mutualistic, commensalitic or parasitic?

3 Why has malaria proved so hard to eradicate?

4 How could you test the hypothesis that the closer the match between the egg of a cuckoo and its host, the less likely the host is to reject the cuckoo's egg?

5 List ways in which ectoparasites and endoparasites differ in their ecology.

6 Do you feel that the relationship between humans and dairy cows can be described as mutualistic?

7 Do you think lichens should be classified with algae, with fungi or on their own?

8 Suggest why stick insects are cryptic rather than warningly coloured.

9 Explain why, in Müllerian mimicry, it is advantageous for both the model *and* the mimic to be unpalatable.

10 How might you explain the 'Red Queen effect' to someone who had never heard of Lewis Caroll's characters?

Further reading

This is the last of the five chapters specifically devoted to ecology. Each of the following three books is suitable for students working at this level but goes into the subject in more detail than space permits here.

J.L. Chapman and M.J. Reiss, *Ecology: Principles and Applications* (Cambridge University Press, 1992).

T.J. King, *Ecology* (Nelson, 1989).

C.J. Krebs, *The Message of Ecology* (Harper & Row, 1988).

CHAPTER 7 | Systematics and taxonomy

The Pinatubu people who live in the remote tropical forests of the Philippines can name and describe a large number of the many different organisms growing there. They have names for at least 500 plants, about a hundred birds, many of the mammals, snakes and insects and nearly 50 different fungi. They distinguish the different types of animals and plants on the basis of similarities and differences, and they can describe the habits of the animals and the plants with which they are associated.

Take the forest bats for instance: the Pinatubu people will tell you that the bat called litlit is found in bamboo clumps whereas titidin is found on dry palm leaves, dikidik on the underside of wild banana leaves, and so on. These people have devised a system of classifying plants and animals in their surroundings which everyone agrees on and can use. There is an obvious practical use for this knowledge. These people depend on the natural environment for their food. In order to avoid mishaps they need to be able to tell each other which plants are edible and which are poisonous, and what to expect to find on each plant and behind each tree.

It is estimated that there are at least three million, perhaps as many as ten million, different kinds of organisms living on the Earth today and an even greater number have become extinct. This great diversity has given rise to the branch of biology called **systematics**.

Systematics involves looking at the diversity of living organisms and the relationships between them. It embraces **taxonomy** which is the study of the principles, rules and methods of classification, and although the two terms often are used synonymously it should be recognised that they have different meanings.

The Pinatubu people are not alone in devising a system of classifying the living things in their environment. Every culture has developed a taxonomy by which they can communicate to others about the organisms in their locality. Classifying things is a natural human activity which we acquire in early childhood, and indeed as the shelves of a supermarket demonstrate, it allows order to be brought out of chaos.

The taxonomic hierarchy

The basic unit of biological classification is the **species**. A species is a group of organisms which have numerous physical features in common and which are normally capable of interbreeding and producing viable offspring. Nowadays, biochemical, ecological and life cycle features are included with other physical characteristics in helping to classify species.

Figure 7.1 Two ways of representing the taxonomic hierarchy **A** box-in-box **B** dendrogram. Can you see how the 'box-in-box' relates to the dendrogram?

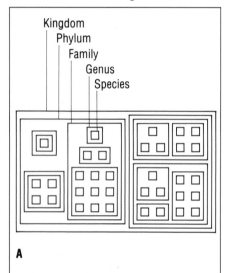

A

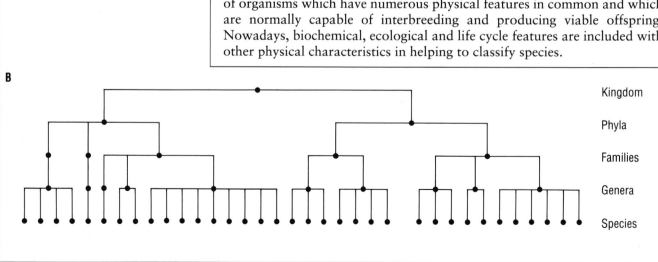

B

92

Closely related species are grouped together into **genera** (singular: **genus**). Genera are grouped into **families**, families into **orders**, orders into **classes**, classes into **phyla** (singular: **phylum**) and phyla into **kingdoms**. (When classifying plants and bacteria the term 'division' is sometimes used instead of phylum.) Intermediate categories are sometimes used: for example, a sub-phylum may be inserted between phylum and class, and sub-classes between class and order.

This ascending series of successively larger, more inclusive, groups makes up the **taxonomic hierarchy**. Each grouping of organisms within the hierarchy is called a **taxon** (plural: **taxa**) and each taxon has a rank and a name, for example class Mammalia or genus *Homo*.

Figure 7.1 shows two ways of illustrating how the hierarchical arrangement of the taxa can be represented: a 'box-in-box' arrangement or a 'tree-like' arrangement (dendrogram).

Table 7.1 shows how three well-known organisms fit into the system. The lowest three taxa (family, genus and species) are named according to strict internationally agreed rules. The names of the four highest taxa (kingdom, phylum, class and order) are often matters of opinion and are subject to the whims and fancies of individual taxonomists.

Taxonomic rank	Plant example	Animal examples	
Kingdom	Plantae	Animalia	Animalia
Phylum	Angiospermaphyta	Annelida	Chordata
Class	Dicotyledoneae	Oligochaeta	Mammalia
Order	Ranales	Terricolae	Primates
Family	Ranunculacae	Lumbricidae	Hominidae
Genus	*Ranunculus*	*Lumbricus*	*Homo*
Species	*acris*	*terrestris*	*sapiens*
Common name	meadow buttercup	earthworm	human

Table 7.1 In this table you can see how three well-known organisms are classified, one from the plant kingdom and two from the animal kingdom.

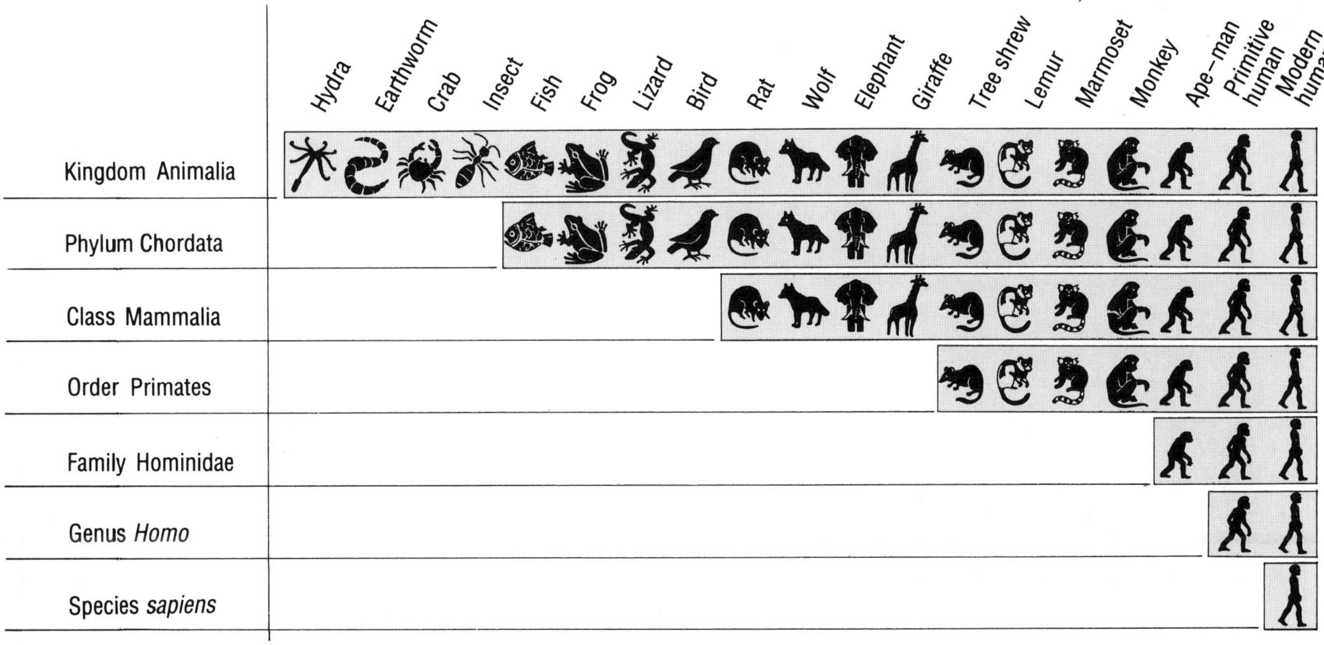

Figure 7.2 This illustration shows how humans are classified. As one proceeds down the taxonomic hierarchy from kingdom to species, the number of animals in each group decreases and the similarities between them increase. 'Ape-man' and 'primitive human' are popular terms covering a number of extinct forms known only from their fossil remains.

Figure 7.3 Two species of the same genus, *Lysandra*, which are difficult to distinguish. *Top* L. bellargus (Adonis blue butterfly) and *bottom* L. cordon (chalk blue butterfly).

Figure 7.4 *Top* The British robin (*Erithacus rubecula*). *Bottom* The American robin (*Turdus migratorius*).

As you go down the hierarchy, the number of different organisms in each taxon decreases and the similarities between them increase (figure 7.2). Thus a phylum contains a large number of organisms which share several fundamental features but display quite a wide range of form. At the bottom of the hierarchy the differences within taxa are far less pronounced. This is particularly true of the species rank; indeed the various species in a genus may be so similar that only an expert can tell them apart. This is illustrated in figure 7.3.

Naming organisms

It is customary to name an organism by its genus and species. This is known as the **binomial system** and was first introduced in 1753 by the Swedish naturalist Carolus Linnaeus. The **generic name** is written first and begins with a capital letter, followed by the **specific name** which begins with a small letter. Both names are written in italics or underlined. Closely related organisms, lion and tiger for example, have the same generic name (in this case *Panthera*) but different specific names. The lion is *Panthera leo* and the tiger is *Panthera tigris*.

If the organism belongs to a sub-species or variety, a further name is added. The British herring gull, for example, is *Larus argentatus argentatus*, and the American herring gull is *Larus argentatus smithsonianus*: both are sub-species of the same species.

When an organism's name has been referred to once in full it is acceptable to abbreviate the genus to its capital letter in all later references, for example the lion can now be referred to as *P. leo* and the tiger as *P. tigris*.

These **scientific names** are essential whenever precise identification is required, and they enable scientists to communicate accurately with each other. They are used the world over and have the merit that everyone knows exactly which organism is being referred to. However, in everyday language people generally use **common names**, such as the ones given at the foot of table 7.1.

The trouble with common names is that a particular organism may be known by several different common names, and sometimes the same common name is used for two quite different organisms. For example, *Caltha palustris*, a flowering plant in the family Ranunculaceae, is known by at least 90 different names in Britain alone, including marsh marigold, king cup, golden cup, brave celandine, horse blob, butter-flower, mare blob, May blob, May bubbles, Mary-bud, grandfather's button, policeman's button, soldier's button, and when it grows alongside other buttercups, the mixture is called publicans and sinners. In parts of America it is called a cowslip, a name which in Europe is applied to *Primula veris*, a member of a completely different family, the Primulaceae.

Similarly, the British robin, *Erithacus rubecula* belongs to a totally different family from the American robin, *Turdus migratorius* (figure 7.4). The latter's scientific name tells us that it is more closely related to the British blackbird whose scientific name is *Turdus merula*.

Nowhere are precise names more important than in agriculture and medicine. For example, attempts have been made to develop new improved varieties of wheat by crossing wild forms. In plant breeding programmes of this kind it is essential to know the exact identity of the parent varieties. Similarly, if pests are to be controlled, whether by chemical or biological means, it is necessary to know precisely the organisms involved. And in medicine it is no use developing drugs and antibiotics unless you know which particular pathogenic organisms they are intended to destroy.

Different types of taxonomy

Suppose you are faced with a group of organisms. How do you classify them into groups and sub-groups? There are several approaches.

Orthodox taxonomy

In an orthodox classification organisms are put into groups according to the presence or absence of certain fundamental characteristics. Thus all land-living vertebrates are grouped together because they have a pentadactyl limb (see page 769); they are subdivided into amphibians, reptiles, birds and mammals because each has certain features which are not found in any of the other groups.

The aim of such a classification is to show the evolutionary relationships between groups. This evolutionary (**phylogenetic**) approach to classification is discussed in Chapter 42. The important point to note at this moment is that in making the classification, particular weight is usually given to those features which are believed to be of evolutionary significance. In recent years, disenchantment with this idea has led to the growth of alternative approaches to taxonomy.

Numerical taxonomy

The purpose of **numerical taxonomy** is to construct precise, unambiguous classifications. It is often thought of as a modern method of classification. In fact, it was first tried over 200 years ago. A French taxonomist called Adanson, working in Senegal, could not fit all the species of plants he found into existing classifications, so he tried constructing his own. He did this by comparing as many characteristics as possible and considering them all to be of equal importance. Adanson's method of classification proved impractical because it involved comparing more characteristics than the human mind could cope with. Imagine classifying just a few species on the basis of, say, a hundred different characteristics. However, since the advent of computers this method of classification has developed considerably.

The principles of modern numerical taxonomy were set out by R.R. Sokal and P.H.A. Sneath in 1963. We can summarise the principles as follows:

- As many characteristics as possible are used and they all carry equal weight. The greater the number of characteristics, the more valid the classification is considered to be.

- Any observable characteristics may be used and these may be morphological, physiological, biochemical or behavioural.

Because such a classification is based only on observable characteristics it is called a **phenetic classification** ('*phen*' comes from the Greek root meaning something that is seen). This is very different from orthodox taxonomy where the characteristics used are often specially selected because they are considered to be important phylogenetically.

Now let's take an example. We will consider ten hypothetical organisms, A to J. These could be species, genera or any other taxonomic group. First we draw up a list of as many observable characteristics as possible, and then construct a grid in which we record whether or not each characteristic is present in each organism. This gives us a **data matrix** (figure 7.5).

The similarities are then quantified by comparing each organism with every other organism for all the characteristics. The similarity is expressed

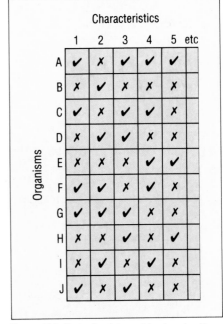

Figure 7.5 Part of a data matrix showing the presence and absence of different characteristics in ten hypothetical organisms, A to J. A characteristic is ticked if it is present and crossed if it is absent. Only five characteristics are shown here, but in practice many more would be included and they should represent as many different observable aspects of the organisms' biology as possible.

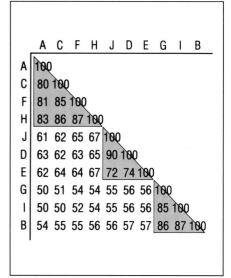

	A	B	C	D	E	F	G	H	I	J
A	100	54	80	63	62	81	50	83	50	61
B	54	100	55	57	57	55	86	56	87	56
C	80	55	100	62	64	85	51	86	50	62
D	63	57	62	100	74	63	56	65	56	96
E	62	57	64	74	100	64	56	67	56	72
F	81	55	85	63	64	100	54	67	52	65
G	50	86	51	56	56	54	100	87	85	55
H	83	56	86	65	67	87	54	100	54	67
I	50	87	50	56	56	52	85	54	100	55
J	61	56	62	90	72	65	55	67	55	100

Figure 7.6 A similarity matrix for ten hypothetical organisms, A to J. Notice that the shaded half is a mirror image of the unshaded half. It is customary only to show the unshaded half.

	A	C	F	H	J	D	E	G	I	B
A	100									
C	80	100								
F	81	85	100							
H	83	86	87	100						
J	61	62	65	67	100					
D	63	62	63	65	90	100				
E	62	64	64	67	72	74	100			
G	50	51	54	54	55	56	56	100		
I	50	50	52	54	55	56	56	85	100	
B	54	55	55	56	56	57	57	86	87	100

Figure 7.7 The matrix in figure 7.6 rearranged so that the groups showing the closest similarity are clustered together.

as the number of characteristics which the two organisms have in common divided by the total number of characteristics being considered. So if two organisms share 21 characteristics out of a total of 50, the similarity between them is $^{21}\!/_{50}$ (42 per cent). Obviously 100 per cent means that the two groups are identical with respect to the characteristics chosen, and 0 per cent means that they are completely different. The percentages are displayed as a **similarity matrix** (figure 7.6).

The next step is to rearrange the similarity matrix so that the groups which show the closest similarity are visually clustered together (figure 7.7). In simple situations this can be done by just looking at the figures, but when numerous organisms and characteristics are being considered a computer is used.

Finally, the various organisms are linked together according to the similarities between them. This gives a tree-like diagram called a **dendrogram** (figure 7.8) from which a classification can be constructed.

A dendrogram such as the one in figure 7.8 should not be regarded as an evolutionary tree. This is because it is based on observable similarities between organisms and does not necessarily reflect their evolutionary relationships. Closely related groups which have become dissimilar will be widely separated in such a dendrogram, while unrelated groups which happen to resemble each other as a result of convergence will be placed close together. (Convergence is explained on page 771.)

Only in rare cases does a phenetic classification correspond to a phylogenetic one, and there are no logical grounds for expecting it to do so. Any phylogenetic conclusions which are drawn from a phenetic classification are purely subjective.

Although numerical classification may not tell us much about evolution, it is far from being a purely academic exercise. It has been used to clarify a number of problem areas in taxonomy. For example, classification of bacteria at the species level used to be uncertain, and numerical taxonomy has been used to improve their classification. This has had consequences for medicine and biotechnology.

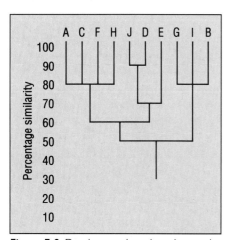

Figure 7.8 Dendrogram based on the matrix in figure 7.6. On the basis of this dendrogram we can say that A, C, F and H should be grouped together, J, D and E together, and G, I and B together. At a similarity level of 70 to 90 per cent these might represent three different genera.

Characteristics used in classification

When classifying a group of organisms, we have to choose certain features on which to base the classification. In doing this it is essential to select characteristics which are clear-cut and consistent. It is not much use selecting the characteristic 'short or long antennae' if individual specimens have antennae with all sorts of intermediate lengths. It is better to use the presence or absence of a particular structure, though even then problems can arise if in the course of evolution the structure has been severely reduced in some members of the group. Countable characteristics are often useful, particularly at the species level – for example, the number of spots on the wings of a butterfly or the number of stamens in a flower. However, one must avoid using features which are affected by the environment and may vary according to local conditions.

Nowadays all sorts of characteristics are used in classifying organisms. The main ones are as follows:

- **Gross structure**. By gross structure we mean features that can be seen without the aid of a microscope. For example, chordates are classified into fish, amphibians, reptiles, birds and mammals on the basis of their skin and various other external and internal features, and deciduous trees can be classified according to the shapes of their leaves.

- **Microscopic structure**. Although gross structure is a convenient basis for classification, sometimes microscopic features have to be used. For example, studies with the transmission electron microscope have revealed that bacteria and what used to be called blue-green algae have a unique type of cell structure, for which reason they are now put in a kingdom of their own. In this case microscopic observation of cell structure has been used to make a fundamental split in the classification of living things between prokaryotes and eukaryotes.

Microscopic structure can be useful at the generic and species levels too. For example, the number of chromosomes can enable entomologists to classify locusts and grasshoppers, and the surface features of seeds and pollen grains as revealed by the scanning electron microscope can be used in classifying flowering plants (see illustration). Indeed, this sort of technique can show up differences between species or sub-species which are identical in every other respect.

- **Chemical constitution**. Sometimes it is impossible to classify organisms using structural criteria, even cellular ones, so one resorts to comparing the chemical substances which they contain. This is particularly useful when classifying organisms like bacteria which may all look alike and have an identical cellular structure. Using techniques such as chromatography and electrophoresis, it is possible to compare the amino acid sequence in the proteins of different organisms, or in the order of bases in their DNA. This is useful not only in classifying organisms, but is indispensible when trying to establish evolutionary relationships (see page 774).

- **Other characteristics** used in classifying organisms include their immunological reactions, the types of symbionts with which

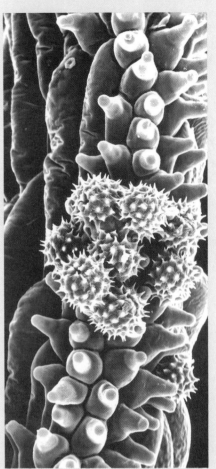

Pollen grains adhering to the stigma of a daisy seen in the scanning electron microscope magnified approximately 2000 times. Notice the elaborate features of both the pollen grains and the stigma. Features like these help in the classification and identification of flowering plants at the species and sub-species level.

they may associate, and various behavioural features such as responses to stimuli, nest-building or courtship.

Obviously characteristics which are used in classification can also be used for identification. If, for example, an animal is found to have a notochord, we know it must be a chordate, and the surface features of pollen grains can tell us the precise species or sub-species that a plant belongs to.

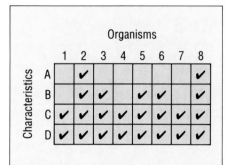

Figure 7.9 The first stage in a cladistic classification is the construction of a table. In this example, the presence of eight different characteristics in four hypothetical organisms is indicated by ticks.

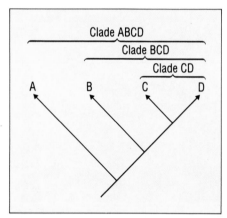

Figure 7.10 A cladogram based on the information in figure 7.9. The clades are bracketed.

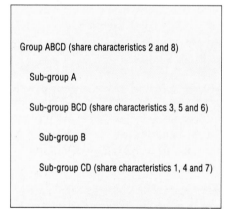

Group ABCD (share characteristics 2 and 8)

Sub-group A

Sub-group BCD (share characteristics 3, 5 and 6)

Sub-group B

Sub-group CD (share characteristics 1, 4 and 7)

Figure 7.11 A classification based on the cladogram in figure 7.10. Further explanation · in the text.

Figure 7.12 A cladogram of the amniotes. Cladistics can result in unorthodox classifications. Compare this with the orthodox classification in figure 7.13.

Cladistics

Phenetic classification uses equally weighted observable features and is not based on any preconceived ideas about ancestry. However, some biologists feel that classification *should* be based on ancestry, and in particular on the points at which different groups have diverged from each other. This type of taxonomy is called **cladistics**, which is derived from the Greek word for branch. Because branching of groups from a common ancestor to form distinct species is a central feature of evolutionary theory, cladists argue that this type of classification reflects evolutionary relationships and is therefore a *natural* classification.

To decipher the sequence of branching, a cladist looks for features which different groups of organisms have in common. Consider, for example, four hypothetical groups A, B, C and D. If you look at figure 7.9 you will see that C and D share certain characteristics which are absent in A and B; and B, C and D share certain characteristics which are absent in A. From a consideration of these shared characteristics a branching diagram called a **cladogram** may be constructed (figure 7.10).

In figure 7.10 the four groups are shown diverging in the sequence A, B, C and D. The products of each divergence, i.e. the groups with shared features, constitute a **clade**. The clades are bracketed in figure 7.10 and are identified because of characteristics they share. Thus C and D uniquely share characteristics 1, 4 and 7; B, C and D share characteristics 3, 5 and 6; and A, B, C and D share characteristics 2 and 8. The branches in the cladogram merely show how organisms are grouped together on the basis of characteristics shared by included members. They are not intended to be a phylogenetic tree.

If a cladogram is to represent what may have happened in evolution, it should be based on as many shared characteristics as possible. It is argued that groups with numerous characteristics in common are unlikely to be similar as a result of convergence (see page 771). In other words, convergence is assumed to be the exception rather than the rule. Cladists have all sorts of criteria for selecting shared characteristics, and groups are put into the same clade only when there is close agreement between them with respect to these characteristics.

The next step is to turn the cladogram into a classification. The clades form the divisions in the classification and successive clades are sub-groups within larger clades. Thus clade C D is a sub-group of clade B C D which in turn is a sub-group of clade A B C D. The result is the cladistic classification shown in figure 7.11.

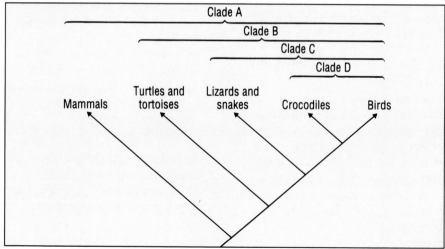

Now let's turn this into a real situation. Figure 7.12 shows a cladogram for the amniotes, vertebrate animals whose embryos are surrounded by an amniotic membrane.

From Figure 7.12 a cladistic classification would be:

Group A   Amniotes Clade A
  Sub-group A_1 Mammals
  Sub-group A_2 Clade B
    Sub-group $A_{2.1}$ Turtles and tortoises
    Sub-group $A_{2.2}$ Clade C
      Sub-group $A_{2.2.1}$ Lizards and snakes
      Sub-group $A_{2.2.2}$ Clade D
        Sub-group $A_{2.2.2.1}$ Crocodiles
        Sub-group $A_{2.2.2.2}$ Birds

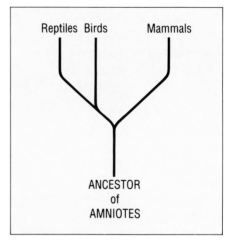

Figure 7.13 An orthodox classification of the amniotes.

This differs radically from the orthodox classification of amniotes which splits them into three groups of equal status: reptiles, birds and mammals (figure 7.13). In a cladistic classification turtles are evolutionarily closer to mammals, and crocodiles are closer to birds. The term 'reptile' does not appear at all.

Cladistics is a highly controversial aspect of taxonomy: indeed there are few areas of biology where more heated exchanges of views have taken place. Cladists claim that their classifications reflect the organisms' evolutionary relationships more accurately, while orthodox taxonomists argue that cladists ignore the varying extent to which different groups have changed since they diverged from a common ancestor. They consider that to classify crocodiles closer to birds than to other 'reptiles' is impractical as well as unsound. On the other hand, birds have been described even by orthodox taxonomists as 'feathered reptiles'.

How many kingdoms?

One of the most difficult decisions to make in systematics is how to divide living organisms into kingdoms.

Until quite recently organisms were divided into two kingdoms: the **animal kingdom**, which contained mainly motile organisms which fed heterotrophically, and the **plant kingdom** which contained mainly static organisms which fed autotrophically by photosynthesis. Unicellular heterotrophs (protozoa) were put in the animal kingdom, and unicellular autotrophs were put in the plant kingdom with the algae. Fungi and bacteria were attached to the plant kingdom mainly on the grounds that, like plants, they possessed a rigid cell wall.

There are a number of problems with having only two kingdoms. The first concerns unicellular flagellates like *Euglena* and its relatives (figure 7.14). These were put with the protozoa in the animal kingdom. However, some euglenoids, including *Euglena* itself, contain chlorophyll, feed autotrophically by photosynthesis and also swim and move in relation to light stimuli. Moreover, some flagellates can feed either autotrophically or heterotrophically depending on the conditions. With only two kingdoms, we have to contend with the fact that these organisms can, in effect, hop from one kingdom to the other!

Another problem concerns the fungi. Fungi are really very different from green plants. They lack chlorophyll and feed heterotrophically by an absorptive method and their cellular structure differs from that of plants in several ways.

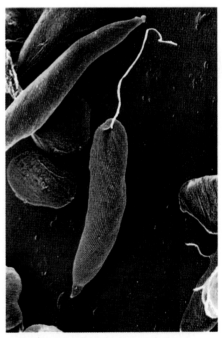

Figure 7.14 A spectacular scanning electron micrograph of *Euglena* showing the flagellum by which this unicellular organism swims through the water in which it lives. Magnification × 600.

The differences between prokaryotic and eukaryotic cell structure are explained on page 153.

A third problem concerns bacteria. The electron microscope has revealed that bacteria and cyanobacteria (formerly called blue-green algae) have a simple **prokaryotic** cell structure. So the bacteria and cyanobacteria appear to be similar to each other, and markedly different from all other organisms which are **eukaryotic**. Indeed, if living organisms have to be divided into just two kingdoms a division into prokaryotes and eukaryotes would probably be best. However, although it may be satisfactory for all the prokaryotes to be in one kingdom, the rest would form a very large and unwieldy group.

The five kingdom system

To solve the problems outlined above, a number of different schemes of classification have been proposed. All have more than two kingdoms, and one has eighteen! The scheme that has gained most support was proposed in 1959 by an American biologist, Robert H. Whittaker. He based his classification on two main criteria: the level of organisation of the organisms, and their methods of nutrition. He recognised three levels of organisation: prokaryotes, unicellular eukaryotes and multicellular eukaryotes. The methods of nutrition were: heterotrophic (which could be subdivided into ingestive and absorptive) and photosynthetic.

On this basis, Whittaker proposed the following five kingdoms:

- **Animal kingdom**: multicellular eukaryotes which feed heterotrophically by ingestion.
- **Plant kingdom**: multicellular eukaryotes which feed by photosynthesis.
- **Fungus kingdom**: multicellular eukaryotes which feed heterotrophically by absorption.
- **Protist kingdom**: unicellular eukaryotes which feed by a variety of different methods.
- **Prokaryote kingdom**: prokaryotes which feed by a variety of different methods.

Although Whittaker's scheme received widespread approval, it had one major snag. This relates to the protist kingdom which contained all unicellular organisms, including those that formerly had been regarded as animals (protozoans) and those that had been regarded as plants (unicellular algae). This in itself was no bad thing – indeed it solved the problem of awkward customers like *Euglena*. The problem was that it meant putting the unicellular algae into two separate kingdoms. This was unfortunate because they share many common features. Indeed, some of the simpler multicellular

The problem of viruses

Viruses are not included in the five kingdoms. The reason centres on the controversy, which has been going on ever since they were discovered, as to whether or not they should be regarded as living. A virus consists simply of nucleic acid surrounded by a protein coat, and it can only survive and reproduce inside a living cell. For these reasons most biologists regard viruses, not as living organisms, but as aggregations of molecules similar to those normally found in living cells.

That having been said, some viruses, such as the bacteriophage described on page 725, are surprisingly elaborate. This, together with the way they behave and reproduce, makes it difficult not to think of them as living.

Is this yet another impossible conundrum? Not really. Just as there are awkward organisms that sit on the borderline between different kingdoms, so viruses appear to be on the borderline between the living and non-living worlds. They could probably form another kingdom if scientists felt like creating one. Certainly a great deal of time and effort has been spent classifying them. This is based on their physical and chemical properties and the way they reproduce, and is essential in diagnosing the many diseases which they cause.

algae are little more than aggregates of the unicellular forms. To this may be added the fact that the algae as a whole have rather little in common with the rest of the plant kingdom.

This led two other American biologists, Lynn Margulis and Karlene Schwartz, to put forward a modification of Whittaker's scheme. They suggested that the multicellular algae should be removed from the plant kingdom and placed, along with all unicellular organisms, in a new kingdom called the **protoctist kingdom** which would replace Whittaker's protist kingdom. This makes the plant kingdom a more natural group, and it brings the multicellular algae close to their unicellular relatives. However, it results in the protoctist kingdom being something of a 'ragbag' containing a wide range of unicellular and multicellular organisms. Indeed, it has been described as the kingdom that contains all those organisms which cannot be fitted into any of the other kingdoms!

In grouping organisms into kingdoms there are bound to be anomalies. The important thing is that the anomalies should be as few as possible and the classification consistent. Margulis and Schwartz's five kingdom scheme offers this, and is therefore commended until a more rational system is proposed. It is summarised in figure 7.15 and covered in detail in the next chapter.

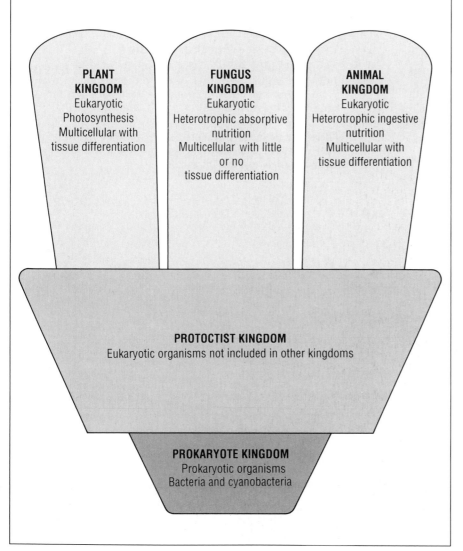

PLANT KINGDOM
Eukaryotic
Photosynthesis
Multicellular with tissue differentiation

FUNGUS KINGDOM
Eukaryotic
Heterotrophic absorptive nutrition
Multicellular with little or no tissue differentiation

ANIMAL KINGDOM
Eukaryotic
Heterotrophic ingestive nutrition
Multicellular with tissue differentiation

PROTOCTIST KINGDOM
Eukaryotic organisms not included in other kingdoms

PROKARYOTE KINGDOM
Prokaryotic organisms
Bacteria and cyanobacteria

Figure 7.15 The five kingdom system of Margulis and Schwartz.

Summary

1 The number of species of living organisms which have been discovered runs into millions, so a system of classification is essential.

2 **Systematics** is the study of biological classification. **Taxonomy** is the study of the principles of organising groups (taxa) into hierarchies.

3 A **species** is the smallest group in the taxonomic hierarchy and is defined as a group of organisms which have numerous physical features in common and are normally capable of interbreeding to produce fertile offspring.

4 Species are grouped together into **genera**, genera into **families**, families into **orders**, orders into **classes**, classes into **phyla**, and phyla into **kingdoms**.

5 As one progresses up the hierarchy the range of organisms within each group increases and the similarities between them decrease.

6 An organism's scientific name is composed of the name of the **genus** followed by the name of the species, e.g. *Homo sapiens*. This is called the **binomial system**.

7 Scientific names are essential where precise identification is required, e.g. in agriculture and medicine.

8 Three main types of taxonomy are used: **orthodox taxonomy** is based on supposed evolutionary affinities, **numerical taxonomy** is based on numerous observable characteristics, and **cladistics** is based on a consideration of ancestry and the points at which different groups have diverged from each other.

9 A **five kingdom system** is now used for the classification of living organisms. The kingdoms are **Prokaryota**, **Protoctista**, **Fungi**, **Plantae** and **Animalia**.

10 Viruses are not included in the five kingdom system since many biologists consider them to be non-living. They could form a sixth kingdom.

Review questions

1 Why do biologists classify organisms?

2 What is the importance of having an agreed scientific system for naming animals?

3 Classify any one plant and animal with which you are familiar into phylum, class, genus, and species.

4 What does a phylogenetic classification aim to show?

5 What principles form the basis of numerical classification?

6 How does a phenetic classification differ from a phylogenetic classification?

7 What makes cladistics a controversial method of classification?

8 What are the merits of having five kingdoms rather than only two?

9 What anomalies, if any, are there in the five kingdom system and how might they be solved?

10 What arguments would you use in favour of, or against, viruses forming a sixth kingdom?

Further reading

A more detailed account of the methods used in systematics and their application to modern biology can be found in *Systematics and Classification* by Grace Monger and Mary Sangster (Longman, 1988).

The controversy over cladistics and the arguments in favour of the five kingdom system are discussed further in *Biology, Advanced Topics*.

Classification of organisms

In the last chapter the scene was set for classifying living organisms into five kingdoms. In this chapter the general features of each kingdom are described. Only the major phyla within each kingdom are considered, and in most cases the classification does not go below the rank of class in the taxonomic hierarchy. Representative genera are used to illustrate the characteristics of each group, especially those that have an impact on human life.

Kingdom Prokaryotae

This is the bacterial kingdom. The members of this group have a **simple cell structure** typical of prokaryotic cells. Yet it is a very diverse group with varied methods of nutrition: autotrophic by photosynthesis and chemosynthesis, and heterotrophic by absorption. They all reproduce asexually but many reproduce sexually as well.

It is generally agreed that there are two major divisions of the kingdom Prokaryotae which here will be given phylum rank: **Cyanobacteria** and **Bacteria**.

Phylum Cyanobacteria

Until the 1960s the cyanobacteria were called blue-green algae and were included in the plant kingdom. This was because, like plants, they contain chlorophyll and carry out photosynthesis. However, it was then discovered that they have a prokaryotic cell structure, so they are now included in the same kingdom as other prokaryotes, namely bacteria. They differ from plants in other ways too. For example, they possess chlorophyll *a* only and although they carry out both photosynthesis and respiration they cannot do both at the same time, so they only respire in the dark.

The 'cyano-' refers to the characteristic blue-green appearance of many members of this group, which is caused by the presence of a blue pigment called **phycocyanin**. They may also contain a red pigment called **phycoerythrin**. They are responsible for the blue-green 'bloom' seen on the surface of ponds. **Gas vacuoles**, which they often contain, help them float on the surface of the water.

Many cyanobacteria are able to fix atmospheric nitrogen, and this together with their ability to photosynthesise means that their nutritional requirements are simple (mainly carbon dioxide and nitrogen from the air plus some minerals). For this reason they are often the first colonisers of moist soils.

There are two forms of cyanobacteria: those with **round cells** which reproduce by binary fission, and the **filamentous** ones which reproduce by fragmentation (see Chapter 32).

Cyanobacteria are widespread, occurring in warm moist soils, and in marine and freshwater environments. Because of their ability to photosynthesise, they often form the basis of food chains and this, together with their nitrogen-fixing activity, means they fill an important role in many natural communities.

Phylum Bacteria

This is a very diverse group which many modern classifications divide into at least 15 phyla. Bacteria are classified on the basis of criteria which do not

Figure 8.1 Cyanobacteria forming a 'bloom' on the surface of a lake giving the water the appearance of pea soup.

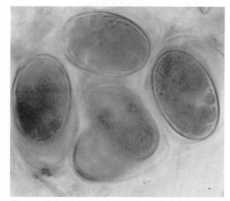

Figure 8.2 Light micrograph of the coccoid cyanobacterium *Chroococcus* showing the cells still stuck together after cell division. Magnification × 2000.

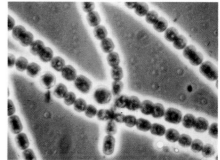

Figure 8.3 Light micrograph of *Anabaena*, a filamentous cyanobacterium, showing the arrangement of single cells into filaments surrounded by a gelatinous sheath (× 500).

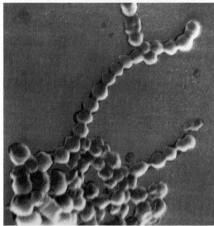

Figure 8.4 Scanning electron micrograph (SEM) of *Streptococcus*, a spherical bacterium. In this species the cocci are forming a chain. Magnification × 500.

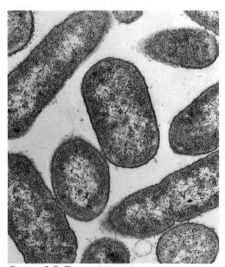

Figure 8.5 Transmission electron micrograph (TEM) of the rod-shaped bacterium *Escherichia coli*. This is a gram negative bacterium always found in the human gut. Magnification × 30 000.

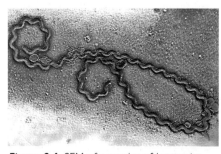

Figure 8.6 SEM of a species of *Leptospira*. This is one of a group of bacteria which are in the form of long thin spirals. They are called spirochaetes and include serious pathogens such as the bacteria which cause syphilis.

necessarily reveal evolutionary relationships. The technique of DNA sequencing may eventually provide a classification which reflects their true relationships. Until then the classification tends to be one of convenience.

The characteristics used are both structural and metabolic. The main ones are as follows.

Classification by shape

The most obvious structural feature of bacteria is that of **cell shape**. There are two basic shapes:

- **Spherical.** These are called cocci. Cocci occur singly or in pairs or they may form chains or be in clusters.
- **Rod-shaped.** These too occur singly or in chains. They may be curved or spiral and may or may not have flagella. When flagella are present they lack the 9+2 structure.

Classification by staining reaction

The terms **Gram negative** or **Gram positive** are often used to describe bacteria. These terms refer to Gram's stain, named after a Danish doctor, Hans Christian Gram. Gram's stain is used universally to distinguish between different types of bacterial cell wall. Those which stain purple are called Gram positive while those which stain pink are Gram negative.

Classification by methods of nutrition

One of the most useful ways of classifying bacteria is based on their methods of nutrition, some of which are unique to bacteria.

- **Autotrophic bacteria** build up their own organic food by photosynthesis or chemosynthesis.

    Photosynthetic bacteria use the energy of sunlight to convert carbon dioxide to carbohydrate. The process is basically similar to photosynthesis of plants but the details are different. Sulphur bacteria are an example.

    Chemosynthetic bacteria do not require sunlight and use simple energy sources such as methane, ammonia or hydrogen sulphide. Nitrifying bacteria in the soil belong to this group.

- **Heterotrophic bacteria** feed like animals and fungi on ready-made organic food. Some are parasites, others are saprobionts (see page 30). The remarkable feature of the latter is the variety of organic compounds they can use as food. This is why they play such an important role in decomposition, and why only a few organic materials such as certain plastics are non-biodegradable.

Classification by methods of respiration

Another aspect of metabolism which can be used in the classification of bacteria is their need for oxygen in respiration.

- **Aerobes** require oxygen for respiration.
- **Anaerobes** respire without oxygen.

Some bacteria are killed in the presence of oxygen – they are called **obligate anaerobes**. Others use oxygen but can respire without it – they are called **facultative anaerobes**. Bacteria which can only survive with oxygen present are **obligate aerobes**.

Classification by biochemical characteristics

Use of any one of the characteristics just described does not result in a satisfactory classification of bacteria. If cell shape alone is used, each group will be made up of bacteria which look alike but exhibit very varied metabolic characteristics. If metabolic characteristics are used, all the different shapes may occur in one group.

The only way to achieve a more definitive classification of this group is to use biochemical characteristics, and already this approach is beginning to have some interesting results. Work carried out in the USA has revealed that some bacteria (called **Archebacteria**) are fundamentally different from the rest (**Eubacteria**). These two groups are so different that some authorities feel that each should be given the rank of kingdom or at least sub-kingdom.

The Archebacteria include forms which produce methane from hydrogen and carbon dioxide in the guts of ruminants, causing them to belch. On one spectacular occasion a farm in Holland was severely damaged by fire when a vet tested the gas from the anus of an uncomfortable cow with a lighted match. The cow was unhurt!

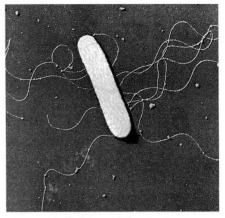

Figure 8.7 TEM of a flagellated bacterium, *Listeria monocytogenes*, which causes the disease listeria. Magnification × 15 000.

Bacteria and human life

Whatever the uncertainties of the classification of this diverse group, their impact in natural communities and on our lives is not in question. Bacteria are abundant everywhere, occurring in extremes of temperature from hot springs to freezing lakes. They are found in vast numbers in the soil and in our bodies. They are responsible for a great many processes which humans have exploited for many years and which form the basis of biotechnology.

Far too often, bacteria are given a negative image as trouble makers. But their positive value on this planet far outweighs the harm they do. The negative image arises from the fact that many bacteria cause diseases of humans and other eukaryotes. These diseases include pneumonia, tetanus, cholera and syphilis in humans, anthrax in sheep, and plant diseases such as peach blight and carrot rot. Several bacteria are associated with food poisoning. Certain species of *Salmonella* cause mild food poisoning while *Clostridium botulinum* causes a sometimes fatal form of food poisoning known as botulism. This can happen if sterilisation is not adequate when foods are canned and heat-resistant

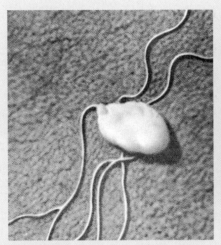

Illustration 1 A species of *Salmonella*, a common cause of food poisoning, magnified × 20 000.

spores of the bacteria survive. *C. botulinum* produces the most toxic substance known.

Against this must be balanced the fact that many bacteria are the means of curing diseases. Antibiotics such as streptomycin and chloromycetin, to name but two of the fifty or so available, are produced by bacteria (although the best-known antibiotic – penicillin – comes from a fungus). Bacteria also play a vital part in agriculture because of their role in decomposition (decay) and recycling nutrients. It has been suggested that without nitrogen-fixing bacteria we would starve as a

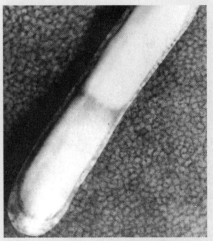

Illustration 2 *Bacillus anthracis*, the cause of anthrax, magnified × 20 000.

result of protein deficiency. Sulphur bacteria are responsible for the huge deposits of sulphur found in some parts of the world. Bacteria are also essential in sewage treatment. The food industry depends on bacteria to produce certain cheeses, yoghurts and other fermented foods such as sauerkraut. Although other organisms may be involved in decomposition, if a substance is biodegradable it is almost certainly because there is a bacterium which can use it as a source of energy. More recently bacteria have come to play an important role in recombinant DNA research and genetic engineering (see page 742).

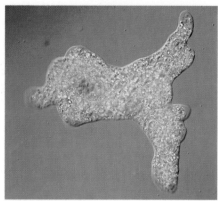

Figure 8.8 Light micrograph of a rhizopod, *Chaos carolinense*, just after ingesting a colonial flagellate, *Pandorina*, the green oval on the left. Magnification × 50.

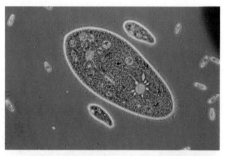

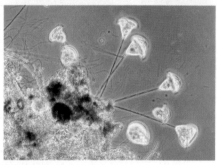

Figure 8.9 *Top* Light micrograph of the free swimming ciliate *Paramecium caudatum*. Magnification × 100
Bottom Light micrograph, in phase contrast illumination, of several *Vorticella*, a sedentary stalked ciliate, shown here attached to a green alga. Magnification × 100

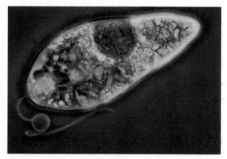

Figure 8.10 Light micrograph of the flagellate *Euglena*. Magnification × 600.

Kingdom Protoctista

This kingdom contains all the eukaryotic organisms which are not fungi, plants or animals. It is rather a 'ragbag' of a kingdom, containing organisms which do not fit elsewhere. Their cellular structure is **eukaryotic** and they may be **unicellular** or **multicellular**. They are divided into about 30 phyla but only nine are listed here. These are the ones that you are most likely to encounter during your biology course.

Phylum Rhizopoda (rhizopods)

These are unicellular and have **pseudopodia** ('false feet') which are extensions of the flexible plasma membrane produced by flowing of the cytoplasm. Pseudopodia are used both for movement and to engulf food particles. Their nutrition is heterotrophic and they reproduce asexually.

The most famous member of this group is *Amoeba proteus* but there are about 16 000 species showing great variety of form. Some are parasitic, for example *Entamoeba hystolytica* which causes amoebic dysentery.

Phylum Zoomastigina (flagellates)

These are unicellular, heterotrophic organisms which have one or more **flagella** for locomotion. The flagella, in keeping with those of all the eukaryotes, has a characteristic **9+2 structure** (see page 165). They reproduce asexually or sexually. They may be free-living or parasitic. This group includes the genus *Trypanosoma* which causes African sleeping sickness and is transmitted by the tsetse fly.

Phylum Apicomplexa (sporozoans)

All the members of this group are **spore-forming parasites** of animals. They are unicellular and heterotrophic and have **no locomotory structures**. They frequently have **complex life cycles** which involve several animal hosts, both invertebrate and vertebrate. They reproduce sexually and asexually.

The most familiar examples of this phylum are the malarial parasites (*Plasmodium spp*) which are transmitted by the female anopheline mosquito (see page 79).

Phylum Ciliophora (ciliates)

Ciliates are unicellular, heterotrophic organisms which move by the beating of numerous **cilia** which have the 9+2 structure. The cilia are also used for collecting food. Nearly all ciliates possess two nuclei, a large **macronucleus** and a smaller **micronucleus**. The micronucleus is used in a sexual process called **conjugation**. The group also reproduces asexually by binary fission.

Ciliates are very numerous in freshwater and marine environments. *Paramecium* is probably the most familiar example but the group shows a wide range of form which includes sedentary stalked species.

Phylum Euglenophyta

Most of this group are unicellular and many are photosynthetic with chloroplasts containing chlorophylls *a* and *b*. Some are heterotrophic, lacking chloroplasts, and even the autotrophic ones can be heterotrophic at times. They move by using one of two large conspicuous **flagella**, but they can also change their shape because their outer covering, called the **pellicle**, is made of a flexible protein. They reproduce asexually. They are very common in aquatic environments and the group includes colonial and parasitic forms. *Euglena* is a common genus in this group.

Phylum Oomycota (oomycetes)

The oomycetes are fungus-like protoctists and may be parasites or sapro-bionts. Traditionally they have been classified with the Fungi and they resemble fungi in their mode of nutrition. Thread-like **hyphae** which secrete enzymes grow into their host's tissues which are digested and the soluble nutrients absorbed. Unlike fungi, the hyphae have **cellulose walls**, and sexual reproduction is by fertilisation between male and female gamete-like structures (gametangia) which never bear flagella. They also reproduce asexually by spores which, unlike fungal spores, have flagella.

The phylum includes *Pythium*, which causes 'damping off' of seedlings and *Peronospora*, a mildew which grows on grapes and various other plants. The most famous example is *Phytophthora infestans* which causes late blight of potatoes. As explained in Chapter 6, this was responsible for the Irish potato famine in the nineteenth century.

Figure 8.11 Mildew, caused by an oomycete, on the surface of oak leaves.

Phylum Chlorophyta (green algae)

Green algae have many features in common with plants. They are **photosynthetic** and contain chlorophylls *a* and *b* as well as carotenes and xanthophylls. They have cellulose cell walls and store starch. They are mostly aquatic and include unicellular, colonial, filamentous and multicellular forms. They usually reproduce sexually and exhibit a wide variety of life cycles. Their spores and gametes usually have two **flagella**, though some like *Spirogyra* reproduce by conjugation and do not have flagella.

Other examples of this large and diverse group are the unicellular *Chlorella*, *Chlamydomonas* and *Acetabularia*, the colonial *Volvox*, and the multicellular green seaweed *Ulva* (sea lettuce).

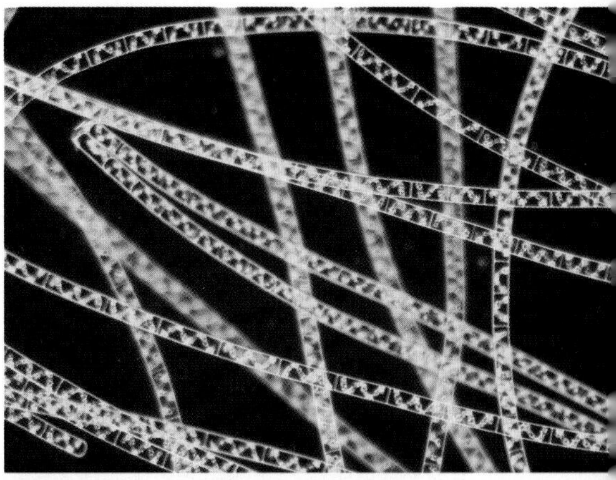

Figure 8.12 The filamentous green alga, *Spirogyra* showing the spiral chloroplast. Magnification × 30.

Phylum Rhodophyta (red algae)

The red algae are **multicellular** and mostly marine, being common inhabitants of rocky shores. They contain chlorophyll *a* and carry out **photosynthesis**. They also contain the red pigment **phycoerythrin** and the blue pigment **phycocyanin** of which the red predominates – hence their red colour. Reproduction is sexual, and their life cycles are complex although at no stage are flagella present.

They may be branched filaments or flattened sheets of cells. Sometimes they are encrusted with deposits of calcium carbonate. Agar, the jelly-like substance on which micro-organisms are grown in the laboratory, is extracted from members of this group and some, called dulse, are eaten whole.

Phylum Phaeophyta (brown algae)

The brown seaweeds are the largest protoctists. They are obvious on inter-tidal rocky shores and include all the wracks and kelps. They are all multi-cellular and show considerable cell differentiation. They reproduce sexually and many show **alternation of haploid** and **diploid generations** in their life cycles (see page 575). They carry out photosynthesis and contain chlorophyll pigments *a* and *c* (but never *b*). In addition they contain the brown pigment **fucoxanthin** which is responsible for their brown colour.

Various extracts from brown seaweeds are used in the manufacture of creams and ice cream. The wracks are also a source of iodine.

Figure 8.13 Red and brown algae growing on a sea shore, showing mainly the brown serrated wrack, *Fucus serratus*.

Sponges – a side issue

Sponges have been around for at least 570 million years. They, or rather their skeletons, were used by the ancient Greeks for scrubbing tables and floors and for padding their armour. The Romans made them into paintbrushes, tied them onto wooden poles to make mops and on occasions used them as substitutes for drinking cups. Not so long ago they were found in most' bathrooms but they have now been superseded by plastic varieties.

Some sponges are as small as a fingernail while others are large enough for a diver to sit in. They may be flat and sprawling or compact and vase-like.

These extraordinary organisms are placed in a sub-kingdom of the animal kingdom called Parazoa which means 'beside the animals'. This is because they lack tissues and organs and have no special shape. They interest taxonomists because they are thought to have had ancestors very similar to certain flagellated members of the Protoctist kingdom.

Whatever their form, the sponge body is organised in the same manner. It is made up of a collection of several distinct cell types which are organised into a system of pores, canals and chambers through which water circulates (see illustration).

This cellular differentiation is a characteristic of sponges and allows different functions to be carried out within the organism. **Epithelial cells** cover the body and **porocytes** line the pores, but the **collar cells**, which line the inner chamber, are the most characteristic feature of these animals. They bear flagella whose beating creates a current of water flowing through the body from which food particles are collected.

There is a layer of jelly-like material between the epithelial cells and collar cells which is secreted by another type of cell called an **amoebocyte**. These cells wander through the jelly and carry food particles to the non-feeding cells. Amoebocytes also carry out sexual reproduction in suitable conditions by becoming eggs or sperm. The sperm are released in the outgoing current and may be collected by another sponge. If the latter contains eggs, these may be fertilised and then develop into a ciliated larva which swims away and develops into a sponge elsewhere.

The so-called skeleton is also deposited in the jelly layer. The skeleton may be made of a protein called spongin or of **spicules** of silica or calcium carbonate which often form delicate patterns.

We cannot leave the sponges without mentioning a demonstration carried out by Tom Humphreys and Aron Moscona in the 1960s. They took red and yellow coloured sponges and forced them through a fine sieve, producing single cells or tiny clumps of cells. They then swirled them about in a suitable nutrient medium and as they collided red cells only stuck to red cells and yellow ones to yellow cells. The clusters grew and the cells arranged themselves into the characteristic body plan of the sponge. This experiment showed that a sponge is more than just a loose assemblage of cells. The cells are able to recognise each other and organise themselves in an orderly way.

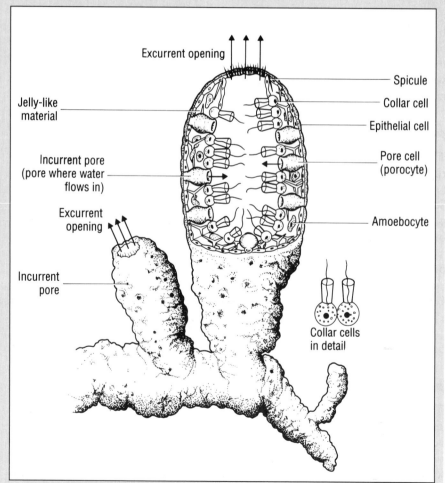

Body plan of a typical sponge, showing the different types of cell. The flagellated collar cells are similar to a group of single-celled protoctists called collar flagellates It is possible that sponges have evolved from such collar flagellates.

Kingdom Fungi

Fungi are **multicellular eukaryotes**. They are usually organised into a network (**mycelium**) of thread-like, multinucleate **hyphae** which sometimes have cross walls (septa). Their cell walls are not made of cellulose but usually contain **chitin**. There are no plastids and they **do not possess chlorophyll**. Their nutrition is **heterotrophic by absorption**. Some, including so-called 'moulds', are saprobionts; others are parasites. They reproduce by means of **spores** although most have a sexual method of reproduction (**conjugation**) as well. There are **no flagella** at any stage of the life cycle.

Many fungi cause diseases, especially of plants, and some produce substances which are powerful poisons. Some species form close associations with the roots of certain plants, particularly trees, where they seem to be essential for the absorption of nutrients. These are called **mycorrhizae** and are important in the forestry industry. The well-known antibiotic, penicillin, is obtained from the fungus *Penicillium chrysogenum*. Yeasts are used in the brewing and baking industries.

Figure 8.14 The bread mould *Mucor* showing its thread-like hyphae and several zygospores. Magnification × 100.

Phylum Zygomycota (zygomycetes)

This phylum takes its name from the **zygospore** which is produced when sexual reproduction by conjugation takes place. Certain hyphae called **gametangia** grow towards each other until they touch and join. Nuclei from both threads mingle and a thick-walled zygospore forms, inside which the nuclei fuse. Asexual reproduction also occurs by means of spores which develop inside **sporangia**. The hyphae do not have cross walls – in other words they are non-septate. Examples of this group are the common bread moulds, *Mucor* and *Rhizopus*.

Phylum Ascomycota (ascomycetes)

This group takes its name from the sac-like **ascus** formed during sexual reproduction. Sexual conjugation and fusion of nuclei of two mating types (+ and –) results in the formation of eight **ascospores** inside an ascus. Sometimes, as in the mould *Sordaria*, the asci are grouped in a cup-shaped **perithecium**. Ascomycetes also reproduce asexually by fission, spores or budding.

The hyphae in this group have cross walls although there are pores present which allow continuity of the cytoplasm. Another well-known example in this group is the bread mould *Neurospora* which was used by George Beadle and Edward Tatum in their work on the one gene-one enzyme hypothesis (see page 717).

Yeasts also belong to this phylum but differ from others in normally being unicellular.

Figure 8.15 Asci of *Neurospora*. Each ascus contains eight ascospores. Magnification × 200.

Phylum Basidiomycota (basidiomycetes)

This group includes mushrooms, toadstools, puffballs and bracket fungi. They take their name from the **basidium**, a microscopic structure which bears sexually produced spores called **basidiospores**. The familiar mushrooms or toadstools are the fruiting bodies (called **basidiocarps**) on which the basidia are formed. The hyphae have cross walls, and many members of this group form associations with roots (mycorrhizae) which were mentioned earlier.

This phylum also includes rusts, parasitic fungi belonging to the genus *Puccinia* which attack cereal crops.

Figure 8.16 Sulphur tuft toadstools, *Hypholoma fasciculare*, growing on a rotting tree stump. The toadstools are the fruiting bodies on which the basidia are formed.

Figure 8.17 The liverwort *Pellia epiphylla,* showing the flat thallus and spore capsules.

Figure 8.18 Photograph of moss showing leaves and spore capsules.

Figure 8.19 The fern, *Dryopteris borreri.* At this stage, when the fronds are just uncurling, they are often called 'fiddleheads'; the sori develop later on the underside of the fronds.

Kingdom Plantae (plants)

All plants are **multicellular eukaryotes** with **photosynthetic nutrition.** Their cell walls contain **cellulose.** The cells have green plastids called **chloroplasts** which contain chlorophyll and other pigments. They reproduce by sexual and asexual means and have **alternating haploid** and **diploid generations** in their life cycle. The haploid generation is called the **gametophyte** and produces sex cells (gametes). The diploid generation is called the **sporophyte** and produces spores in special bodies called **sporangia.**

Phylum Bryophyta (bryophytes)

Bryophytes which include mosses and liverworts are mostly restricted to moist habitats. This is partly because the sperm, which bear flagella, must swim in water to fertilise the eggs. The gametophyte is the most prominent phase in the life cycle. Bryophytes are without xylem and phloem and have no roots. They are anchored by thin filamentous structures called **rhizoids.** The sporophyte generation is small and derives nourishment from the gametophyte to which it is attached. Its most obvious feature is the sporangium which takes the form of a **spore capsule** carried at the end of a slender stalk above the gametophyte.

Class Hepaticae (liverworts)

The gametophyte is either flat and undifferentiated, called a **thallus,** or has a simple stem with **leaves in three ranks,** a so-called leafy liverwort. The rhizoids are unicellular and the short-lived spore capsules split into four valves when they open.

Class Musci (mosses)

The gametophyte has a stem and **spirally arranged leaves.** The rhizoids are multicellular and the spore capsules have an elaborate dispersal mechanism.

The remaining plant phyla are collectively called **tracheophytes** and differ from the previous plant phyla in having a **conspicuous sporophyte generation.** They show differentiation into tissues including **vascular tissues** – xylem and phloem. For this reason they are collectively described as **vascular plants.** They also have complex leaves with a waterproof cuticle.

Phylum Lycopodophyta (club mosses)

Club mosses bear a superficial resemblance to mosses. They have small **spirally arranged leaves** with the sporangia usually borne in cones.

Phylum Sphenophyta (horsetails)

Horsetails have their **leaves arranged in whorls** and their sporangia in cones. There is only one living genus, *Equisetum.*

The previous two phyla are derived from ancestors which once dominated the forests. They were, together with the tree ferns, the chief coal-forming plants of the Carboniferous period.

Phylum Filicinophyta (ferns)

Ferns have **large prominent leaves (fronds)** with sporangia in clusters (sori) on the undersides. The dominant phase is the sporophyte. There is a free-living gametophyte stage which is much reduced and dependent on water. From it the sporophyte grows.

Phylum Coniferophyta (conifers)

These are **cone-bearing plants** which lack flowers or fruits. The seed is therefore 'naked' in that it is not protected by an ovary. The leaves are usually needle-like with a thick waxy cuticle.

Coniferous trees are economically important because they are the source of 'soft wood' for the timber industry. Certain conifers such as firs and spruces provide Christmas trees, and pine nuts are increasingly used in cooking.

Phylum Angiospermophyta (angiosperms, flowering plants)

These are the familiar **flowering plants** and they are the predominant plant group of the modern world. They include all our major food plants and many of the flowers are valued for aesthetic reasons. As well as having flowers they have seeds which are enclosed in a **fruit** formed from the ovary wall. The flowers exhibit an infinite variety of mechanisms which ensure pollination, and the seeds and fruits have features which are connected with the dispersal of seeds.

Angiosperms are divided into two classes depending on the number of **seed leaves (cotyledons)** which they have in their seeds.

Class Monocotyledoneae (monocotyledons)

As the name suggests the embryo has **one seed leaf**. The leaves usually have **parallel veins**. The group includes all the grasses (and therefore all the cereals) and with the exception of palms they do not grow to a very large size. This is because cambium tissue is absent and so secondary growth cannot occur (see page 640).

Class Dicotyledoneae (dicotyledons)

In this group the embryo has **two seed leaves** and the leaves are usually **net-veined**. They often grow to a large size because cambium is present in the stem and secondary growth can occur. The group includes many familiar trees (oak, horse chestnut, beech and birch) as well as shrubs like roses and familiar meadow and garden plants such as buttercups, daisies, dandelions, nettles, peas, cabbages and wallflowers.

Figure 8.20 The Douglas fir, *Pseudotsuga taxifolia*, showing cones and needle-like leaves.

Figure 8.21 Two examples of monocotyledons.
Top Pampas grass growing wild in the Andes of Ecuador.
Bottom Pyrenean lily, *Lilium pyrenaicum*.

Figure 8.22 Some examples of dicotyledons. *Left* Many garden plants are dicotyledons. Here, shrub roses and herbaceous plants are growing together. *Right* Most trees are dicotyledons. This is a horse chestnut tree, *Aesculus hippocastanum*, in flower.

111

Figure 8.23 The two body forms of cnidarians. *Top* The sea anemone, *Tealia sp.* illustrates the polyp form. *Bottom* The medusoid form illustrated by the jelly fish *Chrysaora hyocella.*

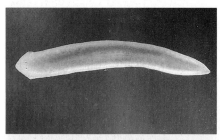

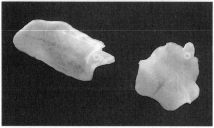

Figure 8.24 *Top* The free-living flatworm *Dugesia gonocephala. Bottom* The liver fluke, *Fasciola hepatica* showing the ventral suckers.

Figure 8.25 These roundworms, *Trichuris trichuria*, were taken from a human caecum.

Kingdom Animalia (animals)

Animals are **multicellular eukaryotes** with **nervous coordination**. They do not possess photosynthetic pigments or plastids and their nutrition is **heterotrophic**. Their cells do not have cell walls or a vacuole, and they have a high level of tissue differentiation, often with specialised **organs** as well. Reproduction is mainly sexual, with the only haploid stage of the life cycle being the eggs or sperm.

Phylum Cnidaria (cnidarians)

These animals have two cell layers to their body (**diploblastic**): an outer **ectoderm** and an inner **endoderm**. These two layers are separated by a jelly-like **mesogloea** in which lies a network of nerve cells. Two body forms exist – **polyp** and **medusa**, both of which exhibit **radial symmetry** and possess **tentacles**. The tentacles bear stinging cells called **nematoblasts** some of which can pierce and poison prey. Examples of this group are the freshwater *Hydra*, and the marine jellyfish, sea anemones and corals.

> The remaining animal groups mentioned in this chapter have three layers of cells to their bodies: an inner endoderm, outer ectoderm and – between them – a mesoderm. They are also **bilaterally symmetrical** with distinct anterior and posterior ends. They also have a dorsal ('back') and a ventral ('belly') side. Usually the anterior end forms a **head**.

Phylum Platyhelminthes (flatworms)

These are flat unsegmented animals, with a **mouth but no anus** (tapeworms are an exception). They have a rudimentary head. They are usually **hermaphrodite** and have a **complex reproductive system**. There are three classes.

Class Turbellaria (turbellarians)

These are free-living aquatic flatworms. Their outer surface is covered with cilia with which they glide over the surface of leaves and stones etc. They are scavengers and carnivores.

Class Trematoda (trematodes or flukes)

The flukes do not have cilia on their outer surface. They are ecto- or endoparasites and have one or more suckers for attachment to their hosts. The life cycle typically involves two hosts. Examples include the blood fluke *Schistosoma* and the liver fluke *Fasciola.*

Class Cestoda (cestodes or tapeworms)

Tapeworms are endoparasites. They have a flattened elongated body with a distinct head or **scolex** which bears hooks and suckers for attachment to the host. The body is usually divided into a chain of sexually reproducing parts, called **proglottids**. There is no mouth or gut, the host's digested food being absorbed directly through the integument. As with trematodes the life cycle typically involves two hosts.

Phylum Nematoda (nematodes or roundworms)

Roundworms have a slender, cylindrical body with tapering ends. In contrast to flatworms they are rounded in cross-section. They have a mouth and anus, and the sexes are separate. They are abundant in water and soil and are common parasites of plants and animals.

The threadworms of cats, dogs and children belong to this group.

Elephantiasis is a distressing condition caused by a parasitic roundworm: the lymph system becomes blocked causing expansion of the limbs so that they look like an elephant's legs.

> Members of the remaining animal groups outlined in this chapter possess a **coelom** which is a fluid-containing body cavity surrounded by mesoderm (see page 626).

Phylum Annelida (annelids or segmented worms)

The body of the segmented worms is divided into a series of units (**segments**) which are separated from each other internally by partitions called **septa**. They have a circulatory system with distinct blood vessels in which blood, often containing an oxygen-carrying pigment, circulates. Typically, annelids possess bristles called **chaetae** and excretory organs called **nephridia** in each segment. This serial repetition of structures is called **metameric segmentation**.

Figure 8.26 The free swimming ragworm, *Nereis*.

Class Polychaeta (polychaetes or marine worms)

This is an entirely marine group. Their name means 'many bristles' and refers to the numerous **chaetae** which project from the body wall. The chaetae are borne on flap-like extensions of the body wall called **parapodia**. There is a distinct head. The sexes are separate and some members of the group show remarkable synchronisation in the release of eggs and sperm thus increasing the chances of fertilisation.

The free-swimming ragworms and burrowing lugworms familiar to fishermen are examples, as are the beautiful fan and peacock worms which live a sedentary life in tubes.

Class Oligochaeta (oligochaetes)

Although commonly called earthworms, some members of this group are found in freshwater. They have relatively **few chaetae**, no parapodia and a less distinct head than members of the previous group. They are hermaphrodites and during copulation an exchange of sperm takes place. Fertilisation and development take place in a cocoon which is produced by the **clitellum** ('saddle'), a characteristic feature of earthworms.

Figure 8.27 The sedentary peacock worm, *Sabella pavonina*, showing the tube attached to a rock on the sea bed.

Class Hirudinea (leeches)

The leeches have **no chaetae** or parapodia, and no distinct head. Their distinguishing feature is a **sucker** at each end of the body. Many are free living and carnivorous, and some are ectoparasites. The most famous, though not the most numerous, are probably those which suck the blood of animals including that of humans.

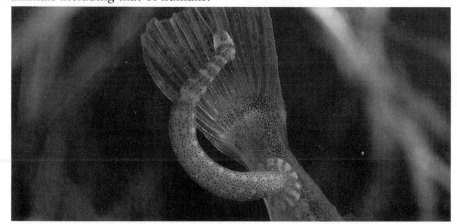

Figure 8.28 The earthworm, *Lumbricus sp.* starting to burrow into soil. Note the clitellum.

Figure 8.29 The leech, *Pisciola geometrica*, showing its suckers. It is attached to the tail of a three-spined stickleback.

Figure 8.30 The garden snail, *Helix aspersa*, crawling along a branch and showing most of the typical features of gastropods.

Figure 8.31 The spiny cockle, *Acanthocardia echinata*, showing the muscular foot protuding from the hinged shell as it burrows into the sand.

Figure 8.32 The common octopus, *Octopus vulgaris*, showing its beak and the suckers on its tentacles.

Figure 8.33 The lobster, *Homarus vulgaris*, showing most of the features typical of crustaceans.

Phylum Mollusca (molluscs)

Members of this group have a soft, flexible body with little trace of segmentation. A head, **muscular foot** and **visceral hump** are often distinguishable. The principal body cavity is represented by a blood-filled **haemocoel**. Many of them have a **shell**. **Gills** are often present and are located in a chamber called the **mantle cavity**.

The phylum is divided into a number of classes but the most common representatives belong to just three of them:

Class Gastropoda (gastropods)

The members of this group have a head, which bears eyes and sensory tentacles, and a large flat muscular foot. The shell, into which the animal can withdraw, is single and often coiled (in slugs the shell is reduced to a trace). A rasping tongue-like structure, the **radula**, is used for feeding. Snails, slugs, limpets and whelks are members of this class.

Class Pelycopoda (formerly bivalves)

In this group the head is reduced and there are no tentacles. The shell consists of two halves which are hinged. They burrow in sand and mud with the muscular foot, or attach themselves to rock or driftwood. The gills are used in food-collecting (filter-feeding) as well as for gaseous exchange. Cockles, mussels, clams and oysters belong to this class.

Class Cephalopoda (cephalopods)

Cephalopods are the largest and most complex molluscs. They have a conspicuous head into which the foot is incorporated with large **sucker-bearing tentacles** for catching prey. The shell may be absent but if present it is reduced and internal. (The exception is *Nautilus* which is the only living species with a fully developed shell.) They have a beak and radula which are used in feeding. They are active, fast-swimming animals and have well developed sense organs and nervous system. The octopus, squid and cuttlefish belong to this class.

Phylum Arthropoda (arthropods)

Arthropods are segmented animals with a hard chitinous **exoskeleton** (cuticle) and **jointed limbs**. The coelom is much reduced, and the body cavity is a blood-filled **haemocoel**.

Arthropods are a very successful group and contain most of the world's species of organisms. There are five main groups:

Superclass Crustacea (crustaceans)

There is such a wide variety of form among crustaceans that they are now usually given the rank of superclass and then subdivided further into classes the details of which need not concern us here.

Crustaceans are mainly aquatic and although the head is not clearly defined, they are distinguished by possessing two pairs of antennae and many have compound eyes. They include *Daphnia*, a free-swimming water flea; barnacles which are sessile and attached to rocks by the head; crabs, lobsters, crayfish and woodlice, the only fully terrestrial crustaceans.

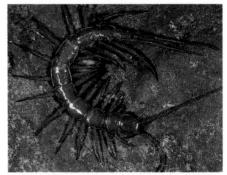

Figure 8.34 *Lithobius*, a centipede common in garden soil. Note the one pair of legs per segment.

Class Chilopoda (centipedes)

Centipedes are terrestrial and have a distinct head with a pair of jaws. The legs are similar along the length of the body, and each segment bears one pair. They are mainly carnivorous, feeding on insects and other small animals.

Class Diplopoda (millipedes)

Millipedes are also terrestrial but they have two pairs of legs on each apparent segment of the body. They are herbivorous and some species damage plant roots.

Figure 8.35 The orb web spider, *Araneus alsine*, hanging in its web and showing its four pairs of legs.

Class Arachnida (arachnids)

This is a terrestrial group. They have **four pairs of legs** which are attached to what appears to be a combined head and thorax (**cephalothorax**). The latter is separated from the abdomen by a waist-like constriction. They do not have compound eyes. Spiders, scorpions, mites and ticks are all arachnids.

Class Insecta (insects)

Insects are a terrestrial group although some of them have an aquatic larval stage in their life cycle. The body is divided into **head, thorax** and **abdomen**. Compound eyes are usually found on the head, and **three pairs of legs** and one or two pairs of wings are attached to the thorax.

Figure 8.36 The desert locust, *Schistocerca gregaria*, showing three pairs of jointed legs and two pairs of wings attached to the thorax.

Insects are a very large and diverse group. Many have complex life cycles involving **metamorphosis** (see page 634). They have a great impact on humans as ectoparasites such as bugs and lice and as carriers of diseases such as malaria. Some are serious pests of food crops and stored food. Others are valuable pollinators of crop plants. Examples include mosquitoes, fleas, locusts, bees, butterflies and stick insects.

Phylum Echinodermata (echinoderms)

This is an exclusively marine group. The skin has **spines** and they show five-way radial symmetry, although the larvae are bilaterally symmetrical. They have a **water vascular system** with **tube feet** which are primarily for locomotion but are also used for feeding.

Starfish, brittle stars, sea urchins, sea cucumbers and sea lilies are examples of echinoderms.

Figure 8.37 The common starfish, *Asterias rubens*, showing its tube feet. The five-way symmetry is clearly visible.

Figure 8.38 The bony fish commonly called a dace, *Leuciscus lecusus*, showing the scales on the skin and the fins.

Figure 8.39 The glass frog, *Centrolenella buckleyi*, which lives in the Andes. It sticks its eggs to the underside of leaves which overhang water. The tadpoles then drop into water when they hatch.

Figure 8.40 A lizard lying on a rock and showing the scales on its dry skin.

Figure 8.41 An avocet, *Recurvirostra avosetta*, wading in water.

Phylum Chordata (chordates)

Chordates are united by the possession of certain internal and developmental characteristics which are present at some stage of their development. These are the presence of a **notochord**; a **hollow dorsal nerve cord**; **visceral clefts** (which usually take the form of gill slits) and a **post-anal tail**.

Most of the chordates have a **vertebral column** and are therefore referred to as **vertebrates**. However, some lack a vertebral column: they, and all the other animal groups which we have covered so far, are described as **invertebrates**. The vertebrate chordates are divided into the following classes:

Class Chondrichthyes (cartilaginous fish)

This class includes sharks, skates and rays. They have a skeleton which is made of **cartilage**, and two pairs of fleshy fins. The mouth is in a ventral position, and the gill slits open separately to the exterior.

Class Osteichthyes (bony fish)

Most fish belong to this group which includes coelacanths and lungfish as well as the more familiar herrings, cod, mackerel and trout. Their skeleton is made of **bone** and the paired fins are supported by **bony rays**. The mouth is terminal and the gills are covered by a bony flap called the **operculum**.

Class Amphibia (amphibians)

Adult amphibians are usually terrestrial and have simple lungs ventilated by the throat muscles, while the larval tadpoles are aquatic and have gills. They have a **soft moist skin** which is used for gaseous exchange to supplement the lungs. The eggs are fertilised externally in water where they also develop. Adult amphibians suffer readily from desiccation if deprived of water for a long period. Newts, salamanders, frogs and toads make up the amphibian group.

Class Reptilia (reptiles)

Reptiles are a mainly terrestrial group and have a **dry skin with scales**. They have lungs for gaseous exchange, and these are ventilated by ribs (**costal ventilation**). The eggs are fertilised internally, covered in a leathery shell and laid on land. Lizards, snakes, crocodiles and alligators, turtles and tortoises are present-day reptiles, and extinct forms include the dinosaurs.

Class Aves (birds)

Birds are similar to reptiles in many ways. Differences between them are mainly associated with the birds' power of flight: **skin with feathers** and fore-limbs developed as **wings**. Birds, unlike any group mentioned so far, are **endothermic** which means they can generate heat energy and maintain their body temperature by physiological means. Lungs are used for gaseous exchange and extensions called **air sacs** penetrate into the long bones. Birds develop from eggs which have a hard shell.

Class Mammalia (mammals)

Mammals have **skin with hair**, the hair growing in follicles. They are mostly viviparous and the young are fed on milk. They are endothermic and have lungs for gaseous exchange with costal ventilation supplemented by a diaphragm. There are two generations of teeth in most mammals and the wide variety of dentition reflects their varied diets. There are two subclasses of mammals.

Figure 8.42 *Left to right* The egg-laying duck-billed platypus, *Ornithorhynchus anatinus*, diving under water; a kangaroo with joey hanging out of the pouch; a lioness, *Panthera leo*, suckling her cubs. *Below* A British show pony with newly born foal

- **Prototheria** are the egg-laying mammals of Australia: the spiny anteater (*Echidna*) and the duck-billed platypus (*Ornithorhynchus*). They lay large-yolked eggs but like other mammals they suckle their young.

- **Theria** are non-egg laying mammals and are further divided into the **Metatheria (marsupials)** and **Eutheria (placental mammals)**.

  Metatheria are those mammals such as kangaroos, wallabies and koala bears which have pouches in which the young are suckled for most of their development, having been born in a very immature state.

  Eutheria are all other mammals, including humans. Their young undergo considerable development inside the mother's uterus, receiving nourishment via the **placenta** before they are born. After birth they are nourished by suckling from the mother.

Summary

1 The **Prokaryote kingdom** contains two major phyla: Cyanobacteria and Bacteria.

2 The **Protoctist kingdom** contains all the eukaryotic organisms which do not fit elsewhere. They may be unicellular or multicellular and are divided into about 30 phyla which include the algae.

3 The **Fungus kingdom** contains multicellular eukaryotes which have heterotrophic nutrition. Some are parasites and are important commercially.

4 The **Plant kingdom** contains multicellular eukaryotes which are usually sedentary and have autotrophic nutrition by photosynthesis. Phyla include mosses, ferns, conifers and flowering plant.

5 The **Animal kingdom** contains multicellular eukaryotes which are usually motile and feed heterotrophically. Phyla include various types of worms, molluscs, arthropods and chordates.

Review questions

1 What feature of bacteria causes us to classify them as prokaryotes?

2 Give one example of a unicellular protoctist, and one example of a multicellular protoctist.

3 Why is a mushroom regarded as a fungus rather than a plant?

4 Give one example of a phylum whose members are triploblastic, have a coelom and are metamerically segmented.

5 Name a class of the phylum Annelida. Describe one feature which this class shares with other annelids and *one* which is unique to it.

6 Write down, in the accepted scientific manner, the name of one species from the class Mammalia and explain why it is included in this class.

7 State two characteristics that enable you to classify a buttercup as an angiosperm.

8 State one *diagnostic* characteristic of insects. What phylum do insects belong to and what are its principal features?

Further reading

A useful summary of the five Kingdom classification is given in *Biological Nomenclature, Recommendations on Terms, Units and Symbols* (Institute of Biology, 1989).

Ralph Buchsbaum's *Animals without Backbones* (Penguin, and University of Chicago Press, 1987) contains an entertaining and very readable account of the invertebrates.

A.S. Romer's *Man and the Vertebrates* (Penguin, 1975) is an equivalent book on the vertebrates.

Part II

CELLS, ORGANISATION AND BASIC LIFE PROCESSES

In this part of the book we see how living things are organised structurally and how they carry out fundamental processes that are common to all forms of life.

First we look at the main chemical substances found in organisms. We then turn to the structure of typical cells and review the functions carried out by their component parts.

Cells do not normally exist in isolation but are massed together into tissues and organs. The construction of tissues and organs, and how they are arranged, is explained.

To carry out their vital functions cells must interact with their surroundings. An important aspect of this is how materials get in and out of cells and this is discussed in some detail.

We then consider the chemical reactions that occur inside organisms. This paves the way to a detailed treatment of respiration, the process by which energy is released in cells.

Photograph: Photomicrograph of a section of compact bone.

CHAPTER 9

The chemicals of life

Cells, tissues and organs are composed of chemicals, many of which are identical with those found in non-living matter. Others are unique to living organisms. The study of chemical compounds found in living systems, and the reactions in which they take part, is known as **biochemistry**. Studies on the structure and behaviour of individual molecules constitute **molecular biology**. This is a subject in which spectacular advances have been made in recent years.

Chemical compounds are conventionally divided into two groups: **organic** and **inorganic**. Under the organic heading are included all the complex compounds of carbon. All other compounds are classified as inorganic. Both are found in living things.

In 1828 the German chemist Friedrich Wöhler synthesised the organic compound urea in the laboratory. Until then it was almost universally believed that organic compounds could only be formed in living organisms. In fact organic matter was thought to be unique to living systems, synonymous with life itself.

The principal organic compounds found in organisms are **carbohydrates**, **fats**, **proteins** and **nucleic acids**. Of the inorganic constituents, **minerals** and **water** are among the most important. Their proportions in the human body are summarised in table 9.1.

All these chemical substances, or the raw materials for making them, come from the environment. They must be obtained as **nutrients** in sufficient amounts if the organism is to function efficiently and lead a healthy life. In humans they form the constituents of a **balanced diet**, with the exception that we can make nucleic acids from other simpler chemicals and therefore do not need them in our diet.

In this chapter we shall review the structure and function of these cell constituents, apart from nucleic acids. Because of their special role in transmitting genetic information, nucleic acids will be dealt with in a later chapter (see Chapter 39).

In the present chapter we shall see that the function of a particular compound in the cell is often directly related to its structure.

Water

Water is by far the most abundant component of organisms. Most human cells are approximately 80 per cent water, and 60 per cent of the whole body is made up of it. As J.B.S. Haldane used to say, even the Archbishop of Canterbury is 60 per cent water. Life probably originated in water, and today numerous organisms make their home in it. Water provides the medium in which all biochemical reactions take place, and it has played a major role in the evolution of biological systems.

The importance of water as a medium for life springs from its abundance on the surface of the Earth and from five of its properties: its **solvent properties, heat capacity, surface tension, freezing properties** and **transparency**. Let us look at each of these in turn.

Water as a solvent

At atmospheric pressure water is a liquid between 0 and 100°C. The distance of the Earth from the sun is such that over much of the Earth's surface water exists as a liquid. Were the Earth either a little nearer to the sun, as Venus is, or a little further from it, as is Mars, life would almost

	Percentage of body mass	
Substance	Woman	Man
Water	57	64
Fat	23	15
Protein	16	17
Carbohydrate	2	2
Other organic	1	1
Inorganic	1	1

Table 9.1 The approximate percentage composition by mass of the human body shown separately for males and females. There is much variation between individuals in the relative amounts of the different chemical constituents, particularly fat.

certainly never have evolved here because water would exist either as a solid or as a gas, rather than as a liquid.

Water's properties as a solvent depend on the fact that it is a **polar molecule**. This means that the distribution of electrical charge is such that the centres of positive and negative charge are separated by a short distance. The reason is to do with the configuration of the water molecule: instead of being in a straight line, the angle between the two hydrogen atoms is only 105°, thus:

$$2\delta^-$$
$$O$$
$$H \quad 105° \quad H$$
$$\delta^+ \qquad \delta^+$$

Because of this unequal distribution of charge, water is said to have **polarity**.

Now consider what happens if a crystal of sodium chloride is placed in water. The sodium and chloride ions part company and go into solution. Water effectively weakens the attraction between ions of opposite charge because, having net positive and negative charges itself, it attracts both.

Water is therefore a good solvent for many substances. Ionic solids, like salt, and polar molecules, such as sugars and amino acids, readily dissolve in it. The only small biological molecules that do not dissolve in water are lipids, whose lack of polarity renders them insoluble. The fact that most small biological molecules dissolve in water is of great significance because all the chemical reactions that take place in cells do so in aqueous solution.

Water is unusual among small molecules in being a liquid at ordinary temperatures. The positively charged hydrogen atoms of one molecule are attracted to the negatively charged oxygen atoms of nearby water molecules, leading to the formation of small clusters of water molecules. The hydrogen–oxygen attraction that holds water molecules together is known as **hydrogen bonding**. We shall see later that, although it is not strong compared with some other types of bonding, the hydrogen bond plays an important part in holding certain organic molecules together.

Water's thermal properties

Water's thermal properties relate to its **heat capacity**. A substance's heat capacity is the amount of energy (in joules) required to raise the temperature of 1 gram of that substance by 1°C. Water has a very high heat capacity compared with other liquids. In other words, a large increase in energy results in a comparatively small rise in temperature of the water. This means that water is good at maintaining its temperature at a steady level irrespective of fluctuations in the temperature of the surrounding environment.

The importance of this from the biological point of view is that the range of temperatures in which biochemical processes can proceed is quite narrow, and most organisms cannot tolerate wide variations in temperature. The high thermal capacity of water helps to keep the temperature of organisms from varying too much.

Surface tension of water

Surface tension is the force that causes the surface of a liquid to contract so that it occupies the least possible area. It is caused by the attractive forces that hold the molecules of the liquid together. At ordinary temperatures, water has the highest surface tension of any known liquid except mercury, and this is of considerable biological significance.

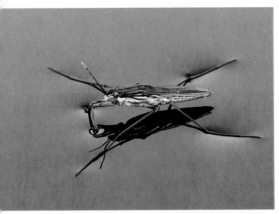

Figure 9.1 Pond skater supported on water by the force of surface tension.

Figure 9.2 Harp seal nursing her pup on sea ice in the Gulf of St Lawrence, Canada.

Figure 9.3 Giant kelp photsynthesising several metres under water off Catalina Island, California.

The strong cohesive forces which exist between water molecules play an important part in the movement of water up the vessels and tracheids in the stems of plants. Were these forces much weaker, trees could not be so tall. Surface tension also allows the surface film of standing water to support – and provide a habitat for – certain aquatic organisms (figure 9.1).

Water's freezing properties

Most liquids increase in density, and so decrease in volume, on solidifying. Water is most unusual in that the reverse is the case. Ice floats on liquid water. Water has its greatest density at 4°C. This means that in winter the warmest water is often at the bottom of a lake. As a result, lakes more than a metre or two in depth rarely freeze right through.

Even in the harshest winters organisms, including large fish, may survive at the bottom of lakes. It has been calculated that if it were not for ice floating on water, the oceans would all be frozen solid except for a thin layer of liquid water near the surface. As it is, even the coldest oceans are liquid except at certain times of the year when they may freeze at their surface (figure 9.2).

Water's transparency

This obvious feature of water is very important biologically. Were water opaque very few organisms could live in it, for the absence of light would prevent primary producers from photosynthesising (figure 9.3). That water is transparent is also of great significance to animals living in water for it allows them to see. Indeed, eyes *depend* on water's transparency.

Minerals (inorganic ions)

The term **mineral** was used in the nineteenth century to describe the inorganic nutrients (at first thought to be a single chemical) left in ash after plant or animal matter was burned. Nowadays we know that minerals are really **inorganic ions** needed for life. In biology the terms minerals and inorganic ions are used interchangeably. A **mineral salt** is a substance such as sodium sulphate that is made up of oppositely charged inorganic ions.

Some minerals are needed in relatively large amounts. This is the case for the cations calcium (Ca^{2+}), iron (Fe^{2+} or Fe^{3+}), magnesium (Mg^{2+}), potassium (K^+) and sodium (Na^+), and the anions chloride (Cl^-), nitrate (NO_3^-), phosphate ($H_2PO_4^-$) and sulphate (SO_4^{2-}) . These ions are referred to as **major mineral elements**.

Minerals needed in smaller amounts are called **trace elements** or **micronutrients**. They include cobalt (Co^{2+}), copper (Cu^{2+}), manganese (Mn^{2+}), molybdenum (generally found as MoO_4^{2-}) and zinc (Zn^{2+}). However, there is no hard and fast dividing line between major mineral elements and trace elements. Further, some trace elements needed by animals are not required by plants, and vice versa. For instance, iodide (I^-) is an essential trace element for many animals, including ourselves, but does not seem to be required by plants.

Evidence for the importance of minerals

Just because a mineral is found in an animal or a plant, it does not mean that it is necessarily essential. It is quite difficult to show which minerals really are essential for animals. In some cases farm animals or pets have been found to recover from mysterious ailments when given minute supplements of a mineral previously lacking from their diets. This provides good evidence that the mineral is an essential one.

Recently it has been shown that some highly toxic elements, such as arsenic, are required by humans in the most minute amounts. The evidence for this comes from people unfortunate enough to be unconscious for several years. During this time they are kept alive by intravenous drip feeds containing a balanced diet. Sometimes such people develop strange skin disorders after a number of years. It has been found that the addition of tiny quantities of arsenic or vanadium is enough to cure their skin complaint. You will be relieved to know that normally each of us gets enough, but not *too* much, arsenic in our diet for good health.

It is rather easier to find out which minerals are needed by plants. Plants can be grown in deionised water or purified sand to which are added in turn various minerals. In this way, a mineral that is needed can be identified, for its exclusion leads to stunted growth or even death (figure 9.4).

Some soils have very low levels of certain minerals needed by most plants. For instance, in parts of Eastern Australia, molybdenum is the limiting nutrient. The addition of just 50 g ha^{-1} has greatly increased the productivity of the land. The effectiveness of such small amounts suggests that the mineral has a catalytic role.

Functions of minerals

The more important minerals, with details of their functions, deficiency symptoms and main sources for humans are listed in table 9.2 overleaf. You will see that their functions are many and varied. However, we can summarise their roles thus:

- **As constituents of large organic molecules.** Proteins contain nitrogen and often sulphur as well. Enzymes, which are nearly always proteins, often contain metal ions such as copper, iron or zinc which function as activators. Phospholipids, as their name suggests, contain phosphorus. Nucleic acids contain phosphorus and nitrogen.

- **As constituents of smaller molecules.** Adenosine triphosphate (ATP) contains phosphorus. Phosphorus is also often required for the activation of small organic molecules. For instance, glucose is phosphorylated (has phosphorus added to it) before it is broken down in respiration. The hormone thyroxine contains iodine.

- **As constituents of certain pigments.** The two best-known biological pigments are haemoglobin and chlorophyll, which contain iron and magnesium respectively. Iron is also found in the cytochromes, a group of pigments of great importance in energy transfer.

- **As constituents of structures.** Calcium and phosphorus are found in bones. Calcium is found in plant cell walls.

- **As determinants of the anion–cation balance in cells.** Sodium, potassium and chloride ions are particularly important in this regard, especially in nerves, muscles and sensory cells where they are involved in the transmission of impulses.

- **As determinants of water potential.** Mineral salts, together with other solutes, determine the water potential, and therefore osmotic pressure, of cells and body fluids. In most organisms the water potential is not allowed to fluctuate outside quite narrow limits.

Figure 9.4 The importance of mineral elements in plants.

A The effect of deficiencies of three separate major minerals on the growth of barley. The plant on the left, the control, is growing in a solution with all the required minerals. The others are, from left to right: nitrogen-free, iron-free and sulphur-free.

B The effect of molybdenum deprivation on the growth of tomato plants. Molybdenum is a trace element required in extremely small amounts. The plant on the right has been grown in a water culture which lacks molybdenum but otherwise contains all the required minerals. The plant on the left is a control. It has been grown in a water culture which contains all the required minerals, including molybdenum.

Element	Obtained as	Functions	Deficiency symptoms in humans and flowering plants	Main sources for humans
Calcium	Ca^{2+}	Involved in selective permeability of plasma membranes and intracellular communication; activates certain enzymes; constituent of bones, teeth and plant cell walls	Poor growth of skeleton, soft bones (rickets), muscular spasms, delayed clotting; stunted growth in plants	Milk, cheese, fish, drinking water if hard
Chlorine	Cl^- by plants $NaCl$ by animals	With Na^+ and K^+, helps determine solute concentration and anion-cation balance in cells	Shortage of $NaCl$ causes muscular cramp	See sodium
Cobalt	Co^{2+}	Constituent of vitamin B_{12}; involved in nitrogen fixation	Pernicious anaemia	Most foods
Copper	Cu^{2+}	Activates certain enzymes; required for formation of haemoglobin	Certain metabolic disorders; young leaves permanently wilted	Most foods
Fluorine	F^-	Found in bones and teeth; prevents dental caries	Weak teeth, especially in children	Drinking water
Iodine	I^-	Constituent of thyroxine	Goitre	Sea fish, shellfish, drinking water and vegetables if soil contains iodine
Iron	Fe^{3+}	Constituent of haemoglobin and myoglobin, also ferredoxin and cytochromes involved in electron transfer; activates certain enzymes including catalase	Anaemia; young leaves chlorotic (yellow)	Liver, kidneys, beef, eggs, cocoa powder, apricots, drinking water if soil contains iron
Magnesium	Mg^{2+}	Activates many enzymes; constituent of chlorophyll and bones	Older leaves chlorotic	Nearly all foods
Manganese	Mn^{2+}	Activates certain enzymes; involved in photosynthesis	Malformation of skeleton; young leaves chlorotic with dead spots	Most foods
Molybdenum	MO_4^{2-}	Activates certain enzymes in nitrogen metabolism	Slight retardation of growth in plants	Most foods
Nitrogen	NO_3^- or NH_4^+ by plants; protein etc. by animals	Constituent of proteins, nucleic acids, porphyrins etc.	Protein deficiency disease (kwashiorkor); chlorosis and stunted growth in plants	Protein foods e.g. milk, meat, eggs, soya beans
Phosphorus	$H_2PO_4^-$ by plants; protein etc. by animals	Constituent of plasma membrane (as phospholipid), certain proteins, all nucleic acids and nucleotides; required for phosphorylation; also found in bones and teeth	Poor growth in plants; leaves dark green to red	Most foods
Potassium	K^+	Helps determine anion-cation balance in cells. Activates many enzymes; involved in stomatal opening.	Yellow edges and tips to plant leaves	Prunes, potatoes, brussels sprouts, mushrooms, cauliflower, beef, liver, fish
Sodium	Na^+	Helps determine solute concentration and anion-cation balance particularly in excitable tissues such as nerve and muscle	Muscular cramp	As $NaCl$ in table and cooking salt, bacon, salty fish, cheese
Sulphur	SO_4^{2-} by plants; protein by animals	Constituent of certain proteins and vitamins	Chlorosis in young leaves	Sulphur-containing protein foods
Zinc	Zn^{2+}	Activates various enzymes	Thick malformed leaves with dead spots	Most foods

Table 9.2 Summary of the principal mineral elements required by organisms.

Organic compounds

Many of the molecules in organisms contain hundreds or even thousands of atoms. Such large molecules are characteristic of life. Surprising as it may seem, few molecules containing more than about six atoms exist naturally unless made by living organisms. Organic compounds are therefore immensely important in living things.

The construction of organic molecules

An organic compound always contains at least two, and often many more, atoms of carbon. Organic compounds owe their complexity to the **carbon atom**. Carbon has a valency of four which means that in its compounds every carbon atom forms four covalent bonds. This accounts for the variety and complexity of organic molecules.

To make this clearer, think of the way an organic molecule is built up. Starting with a single carbon atom one can visualise adding on further carbon atoms (or other atoms for that matter) in any of four different directions. In this way elaborate three-dimensional molecules can be constructed, the carbon atoms forming a skeleton to which other atoms (hydrogen, oxygen, nitrogen and so on) are attached.

The carbon atom is shown in figure 9.5. The variety, complexity and sheer size of organic molecules are caused by the bonding behaviour of the carbon atom. It is doubtful if life as we know it could ever have evolved without it.

The other principal elements found in organic molecules are **oxygen** and **hydrogen**. Oxygen has a valency of two which means that it may link carbon atoms together or form side chains. Hydrogen, with its valency of one, can only occupy terminal positions in a molecule. Nitrogen is found in many organic compounds – proteins, nucleic acids and porphyrins for instance. It usually has a valency of three.

Many important organic compounds are formed by relatively small organic molecules (**monomers**) linking together to form larger, more complex molecules (**polymers**). This process of **polymerisation** contributes to the structural versatility of biological substances.

With these general considerations in mind, let us look at the main groups of organic compounds found in organisms.

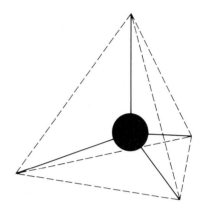

Figure 9.5 The carbon atom can make four bonds with other atoms. These bonds are arranged symmetrically so that if their ends were joined up (dotted lines) the resulting shape would be a tetrahedron. The tetrahedral shape of the carbon atom means that organic chains are not straight but 'crinkled', having a zig-zag shape.

Carbohydrates

Carbohydrates contain only the elements carbon, hydrogen and oxygen. The ratio of hydrogen to oxygen is the same as in water: two hydrogen atoms for every oxygen atom. Carbohydrates are the most abundant class of biomolecules. In animals their main function is to act as an easily accessible source of energy. They carry out this role in plants too, but here they also serve an important structural function.

Carbohydrates include **sugars**, **starch**, **cellulose** and **glycogen**. As a group, carbohydrates are most conveniently classified on the basis of their size, and this is the approach adopted here. We will start with the smallest and simplest carbohydrates, the monosaccharides.

Monosaccharides

The word **monosaccharide** literally means 'single sugar'. Monosaccharides have the general formula $(CH_2O)_n$. The letter n equals the number of carbon atoms in the molecule and its value may lie between 3 and 7 (table 9.3). Six is the most common number, giving 6-carbon sugars or **hexoses**.

Number of carbon atoms in a monosaccharide	Name
3	Triose sugar
4	Tetrose sugar
5	Pentose sugar
6	Hexose sugar
7	Heptose sugar

Table 9.3 Naturally occurring single sugars (monosaccharides) have between three and seven carbon atoms.

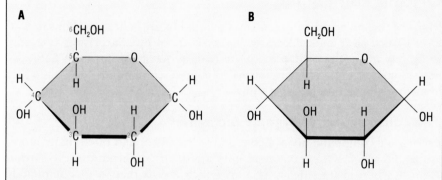

Figure 9.6 The structural formula of α glucose: **A** in full **B** slightly simplified. The molecule consists of five carbon atoms arranged in a ring with the sixth carbon atom projecting from the side. An oxygen atom links carbon atoms 1 and 5. The ring lies at right angles to the plane of the paper, the thick bonds lying in front of the thinner ones behind. The various side groups stick up and down.

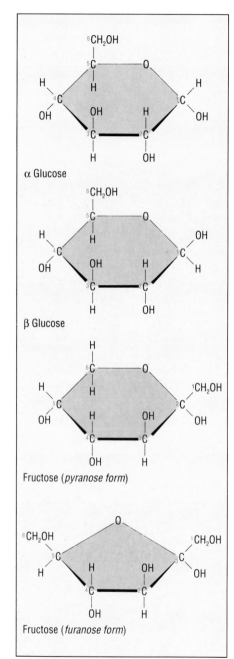

Figure 9.7 Hexose sugars generally share the same basic ring structure; they differ from each other in the arrangement of the various side groups as can be seen above by comparing α glucose, β glucose and fructose. Hexose sugars, such as these three, which have a 6-sided ring are described as pyranoses. Glucose is always found in the pyranose form, but fructose also exists as a less stable 5-sided ring (furanose form).

The hexose sugars

The best-known and most abundant hexose is glucose. Glucose, like all hexose sugars, has the formula $C_6H_{12}O_6$, but this does not convey much about its structure. It tells us that there are six carbon, twelve hydrogen and six oxygen atoms in each molecule, but it gives no information as to how these are arranged in three dimensions. This information is better shown by the structural formula given in figure 9.6.

Understanding the three-dimensional structure of glucose is important for understanding the properties of carbohydrates in general. Look at figure 9.6. First, notice the shape of the molecule: it is a ring whose sides are formed by five carbon atoms and one oxygen atom. Secondly, notice the side branches. Some of these end in hydrogen atoms, others in OH (hydroxyl) groups and one of them in a CH_2OH (alcohol) group. Each group occupies a particular position with respect to the carbon atoms of the ring. This is made clear in the structural formula by numbering the carbon atoms 1 to 6 in a clockwise direction, starting with the one at the extreme right – the only carbon atom in glucose that is bonded to two oxygen atoms.

It is the specific relationship between the carbon atoms and the side groups which determines the nature of the sugar and its properties. The type of glucose whose structural formula is shown in figure 9.6 is called α **glucose**. If, however, the H and OH groups attached to the first carbon atom are interchanged, another sugar with slightly different properties results: β **glucose** (figure 9.7). Another sugar is formed by swapping the CH_2OH group at position 6 with the H at position 1, and at the same time swapping the H and OH groups at positions 2 and 3: this is **fructose**.

All these sugars share the formula $C_6H_{12}O_6$ but they differ in their molecular structure: in the language of the chemists they are **isomers**. There is little point in multiplying examples; the important point is that the type of sugar is determined by the positioning of the atoms in the molecule. The implications of this for the properties of more complex carbohydrates will become clear later.

Monosaccharides are soluble, taste sweet and form crystals. They share these properties with their slightly larger relatives, the disaccharides, which are built up from monosaccharides.

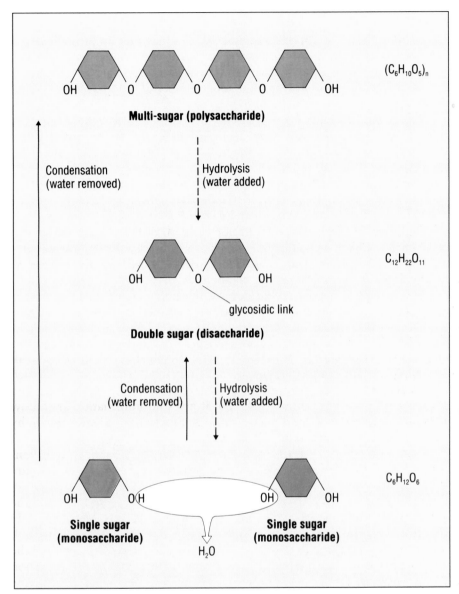

$(C_6H_{10}O_5)_n$

Multi-sugar (polysaccharide)

Condensation
(water removed)

Hydrolysis
(water added)

$C_{12}H_{22}O_{11}$

glycosidic link

Double sugar (disaccharide)

Condensation
(water removed)

Hydrolysis
(water added)

$C_6H_{12}O_6$

**Single sugar
(monosaccharide)**

**Single sugar
(monosaccharide)**

H_2O

Figure 9.8 Removal of water from monosaccharide molecules results in the formation of disaccharides and polysaccharides. Addition of water reverses this process.

Figure 9.9

Top Sugar beet being harvested. Sugar beet is a biennial plant of temperate regions. It stores sugar in swollen roots during the first year prior to producing flowers and seeds in the second year.

Bottom Sugar cane being harvested. Sugar cane is a perennial grass of the tropics and subtropics. Sugar is stored in its long thick stems.

Disaccharides

Two monosaccharide molecules may combine to form a **disaccharide** or 'double sugar'. The process is one of condensation involving the loss of water. A single molecule of water is removed from a pair of monosaccharide molecules, as shown at the bottom of figure 9.8. As a result, a covalent bond (resulting in the formation of a **glycosidic link**) is established, joining the two monosaccharide molecules together. The general formula of a disaccharide formed from two hexose sugars is $C_{12}H_{22}O_{11}$.

When a bond is formed between the carbon atom 1 of one glucose and carbon atom 4 of another, the result is a 1-4 linked compound called **maltose**. Large concentrations of maltose are found in some germinating seeds – barley, for example. Other disaccharides formed from hexose sugars include sucrose and lactose. **Sucrose** results from the union of glucose and fructose; it is the main form in which carbohydrate is transported in plants and is particularly abundant in the stems of sugar cane and the roots of sugar beet which are the sources of commercial sugar (figure 9.9).

Lactose results from the union of glucose and galactose, another hexose sugar. Lactose is the sugar found in milk.

How sweet is sugar?

The sugar that people buy for use in cooking is almost pure sucrose. Other sugars taste either sweeter or less sweet than sucrose. If we call the sweetness of sucrose 1 (for reference), then the sweetnesses of other common sugars are as follows:

Lactose	0.2
Maltose	0.3
Galactose	0.3
Glucose	0.7
Sucrose	1
Fructose	1.7

Because fructose is sweeter than sucrose, it is often used in the manufacture of sweets and diet foods as the same sweetness can be obtained for fewer calories.

However, sugars are not the only compounds that are sweet. Saccharin is 500 times sweeter than sucrose, although chemically it is quite distinct from sugars:

Certain proteins taste even sweeter than saccharin. One such protein is obtained from serendipity berries, the fruit of a West African plant. This protein is 2500 times as sweet as sucrose.

New low-calorie sweetners are being developed by the food industry. One is a dipeptide called aspartame. This compound is about 200 times sweeter than sucrose and lacks the slightly bitter aftertaste often found with saccharin.

Polysaccharides

Under appropriate conditions monosaccharides may link up through glycosidic bonds to form a **polysaccharide** or 'multi-sugar' as shown in figure 9.8. In its final form a polysaccharide consists of a long chain which may be folded or branched and in which the total number of monosaccharide units is variable.

The general formula for polysaccharides formed from hexose sugars is $(C_6H_{10}O_5)_n$. Here n may vary from as little as 40 to over 1000. Polysaccharides are insoluble in water, do not taste sweet and cannot be crystallised.

The compact structure of a polysaccharide makes it ideal as a storage carbohydrate. By building up free monosaccharide molecules into an insoluble polysaccharide, sugars can be stored in a compact form in which they will not diffuse out of the cell nor exert an osmotic effect within the cell. When occasion demands, free sugars can be obtained from the polysaccharide by hydrolysis. These sugars may then be used for the release of energy or for the synthesis of new compounds.

The best-known polysaccharides are the polymers of glucose: **starch, glycogen** and **cellulose**. Starch and cellulose are found in plants, glycogen in animals. Starch consists of a mixture of two sorts of molecule: **amylose** and **amylopectin**. The chemical characteristics of amylose, amylopectin, glycogen and cellulose are listed in table 9.4, to which we shall refer in the following account of these polymers.

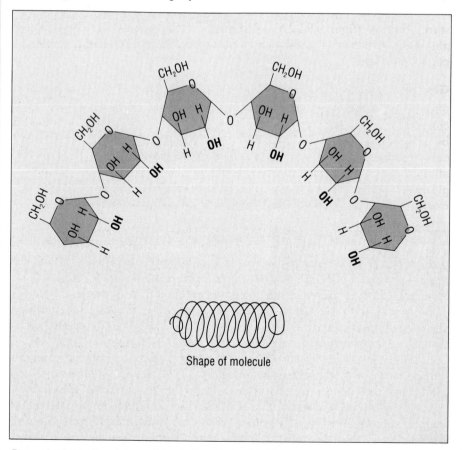

Shape of molecule

Figure 9.10 Starch mainly consists of a long chain of 1-4 linked α glucose units of which six are shown here. The chain is coiled into a helix forming, in effect, a cylinder in which most of the OH groups capable of forming cross-linkages project into the interior. These OH groups are shown in bold. There are six glucose units for every complete turn of the helix.

Polysaccharide	Basic monomer	Glycosidic bond	Branching	Relative molecular mass
Amylose	α glucose	1 – 4	None	$4 \times 10^3 - 1.5 \times 10^5$
Amylopectin	α glucose	1 – 4 and 1 – 6	≈ 4%	$5 \times 10^4 - 1 \times 10^6$
Glycogen	α glucose	1 – 4 and 1 – 6	≈ 9%	$\approx 5 \times 10^6$
Cellulose	β glucose	1 – 4	None	$2 \times 10^5 - 2 \times 10^6$

Table 9.4 Biochemical characteristics of the four most abundant polysaccharides.

Starch

Most starches consist of about 20–30 per cent **amylose** and 70–80 per cent **amylopectin**. Amylose only has bonds between the carbon 1 of one monomer and the carbon 4 of its neighbour, so it is an unbranched polysaccharide. However, although unbranched, it is not a long straight molecule. Instead it spirals, resulting in the formation of a **helix** (figure 9.10).

Amylopectin, like amylose, mainly consists of glucoses joined by 1–4 bonds. However, it has branches at roughly 4 per cent of its monomers. These branches occur between the carbon 6 of the glucose in the main chain and the carbon 1 of the first glucose in the branch chain. The two-dimensional shape of amylopectin is shown diagrammatically in figure 9.11. Its three-dimensional shape is difficult to represent on paper. Essentially it consists of a spiral with other spirals coming off it at irregular intervals.

In both amylose and amylopectin, the bonding between adjacent α glucoses means that in the resulting helix most of the OH groups capable of forming hydrogen bonds project into the interior. The significance of this will become clear in a moment when we compare starch with cellulose.

Amylose and amylopectin are usually found together, packed into starch grains (figure 9.12A). Although starch grains are particularly abundant in storage organs such as potato tubers, they are found in most parts of a plant.

Glycogen

Glycogen is the storage carbohydrate of animals. As indicated in table 9.4 it consists of long, profusely branched chains of α glucose molecules linked by 1–4 or 1–6 glycosidic links. Glycogen is more soluble than starch and exists in the cytoplasm as tiny granules (figure 9.12B). It is particularly abundant in the liver and muscles. Each of us has approximately 500 g of glycogen in our bodies, only enough for about 90 minutes of flat-out exercise. If we use it all up, we have to rely on our fat reserves.

Figure 9.11 Amylopectin is a branched polysaccharide which is found in starch. This diagram shows its two-dimensional structure.

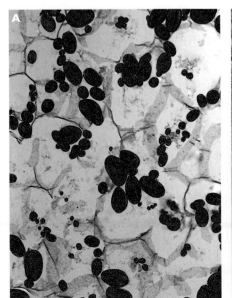
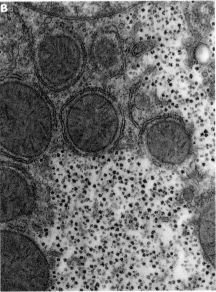

Figure 9.12 Starch and glycogen as they appear in cells.
A Photomicrograph of potato cells showing starch grains, the black oval bodies. Magnification × 200.
B Electron micrograph of a section through part of a liver cell showing glycogen granules (small black dots) in the cytoplasm. The large bodies in the cytoplasm are mitochondria. Magnification × 15 000.

Cellulose

We have seen how polysaccharides can be built up for storage. This process of linking sugar molecules can be taken further with the formation of a material of great structural importance, cellulose. Cellulose is found in plant cell walls, and we shall see later that the efficient functioning of plants is very much bound up with the properties of their cellulose cell walls.

Cellulose is a polysaccharide consisting of long chains of β glucose molecules linked by 1–4 glycosidic bonds. The way the sugar molecules are orientated means that OH groups stick outwards from the chain in opposite directions. These can form hydrogen bonds with neighbouring chains, thereby establishing a kind of lattice (figure 9.13).

This is in marked contrast to the way starch molecules arrange themselves. Like cellulose, starch consists of a long chain of glucose molecules, but the fact that cellulose is built up from β glucose means that cellulose is a long straight molecule. Starch, on the other hand, is built up from α glucose and forms a helix. The only difference between α and β glucose is in the positions of the H and OH groups on carbon 1 (see figure 9.7 on page 126). However, this difference is enough to ensure that there are no cross-linkages in starch, and is one reason why it lacks the structural properties possessed by cellulose.

A single cellulose chain may contain as many as 10 000 sugar units with a total length of 5 μm. The strength of the glycosidic bonds, together with the cross-links between adjacent chains, makes it tough like rubber. In the cell wall, groups of about 60 to 70 cellulose chains are massed together to form ribbon-like **microfibrils** each about 3.5 nm in diameter. Under the

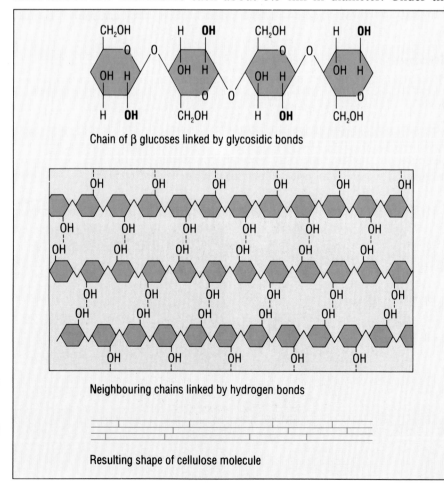

Chain of β glucoses linked by glycosidic bonds

Neighbouring chains linked by hydrogen bonds

Resulting shape of cellulose molecule

Figure 9.13 Cellulose consists of a straight chain of β glucose units joined together in such a way that the OH groups capable of forming cross-linkages project from both sides of the chain. These OH groups are shown in bold. They are capable of forming hydrogen bonds with neighbouring OH groups, resulting in the formation of bundles of cross-linked parallel chains as indicated. Compare with figure 9.10.

electron microscope it can be seen that these are laid down in layers, the microfibrils of each layer running roughly parallel with each other but at an angle to those in other layers. The microfibrils of successive layers are frequently laid down at right angles and are interwoven as can be seen in figure 9.14.

In the cell wall the cellulose microfibrils are embedded in a gel-like organic matrix containing **hemicelluloses** and **pectins**. Hemicelluloses are short polysaccharides that bind tightly but non-covalently to the surface of the cellulose microfibrils and to each other, thus holding the microfibrils in a complex three-dimensional network. There are many different sorts of hemicelluloses, each containing a variety of sugars such as glucose, xylose, galactose and fructose.

Pectins are another group of polysaccharides found in cell walls. They are characterised by the presence of many acidic, negatively charged residues. Because of their negative charge, pectins bind tightly to cations, and in the cell wall calcium ions (Ca^{2+}) are found associated with pectins, forming **calcium pectates**. Calcium pectates are particularly abundant in the **middle lamella**, the region that serves to cement together the cellulose walls of adjacent cells (see page 152).

The various chemical components of a plant cell wall are shown in figure 9.15. The result of the association between cellulose microfibrils, hemicelluloses and pectins is a material of great strength and structural complexity. The cell wall of a plant can be likened to reinforced concrete: the matrix of hemicelluloses, pectins and the occasional glycoprotein is equivalent to the concrete, the cellulose microfibrils to the metal framework within the concrete.

Despite its strength, the plant cell wall is fully permeable to water and solutes. This is because the matrix is riddled with minute water-filled channels through which salts, sugars and other small polar molecules can readily diffuse. Moreover the molecules of the matrix are strongly hydrophilic ('water-loving') with the result that in normal circumstances the cell wall is saturated with water like a sponge.

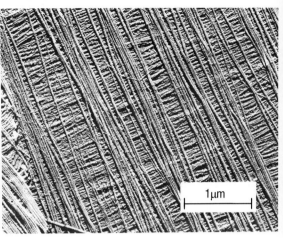

Figure 9.14 Electron micrograph of cellulose microfibrils (shadowed) showing how the microfibrils of successive layers in a cell wall are often laid down at right angles to one another.

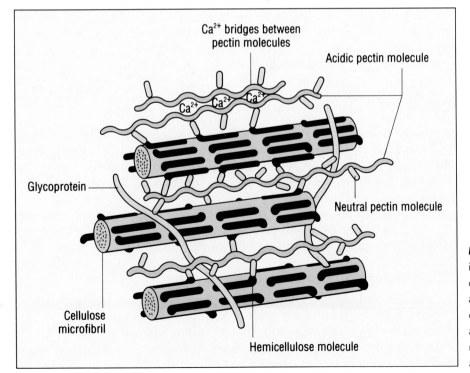

Figure 9.15 Cellulose microfibrils are found in plant cell walls held in a matrix made up of other polysaccharides, notably hemicelluloses and pectins. Acidic pectin molecules bind with calcium ions (Ca^{2+}) to form calcium pectate, and neutral pectin molecules bind with regularly arranged hemicellulose molecules and occasional glycoproteins.

Lignification

Certain plant cells, notably those concerned with providing strength and conducting water, become **lignified** during their development, and this is an important step in the formation of **wood**. In this process **lignin**, a complex polymer of various aromatic alcohols and amino acid-like substances, is deposited in the spaces between the cellulose molecules, making the cell wall much more rigid, and rendering it less permeable.

Once lignification is complete the cell can no longer absorb materials and so dies. Hence, fully lignified tissue is always dead. Its function of providing mechanical strength is entirely due to its ligno-cellulose composition. Its ability to transport water and minerals is due to the fact that lignification involves loss of the cell contents, resulting in the formation of hollow waterproof tubes.

Other sugar compounds

Simple sugars such as pentoses and hexoses can easily link up with other molecules to form more elaborate compounds. One of the most important associations is that between sugar and phosphoric acid (H_3PO_4).

Phosphorylation of hexose sugar is a necessary first step in the breakdown of sugar in respiration. Phosphorylation is also involved in the formation of **nucleotides**: in this case a pentose sugar links up with an organic base at position 1 and a phosphoric acid molecule at position 5. The details of this reaction will be considered in a later chapter on the nature of the gene as nucleotides are the building blocks of **nucleic acids** such as deoxyribonucleic acid (DNA) (see page 710). Nucleotides also have other important functions. In Chapter 14 we shall see that they play an important part in respiration.

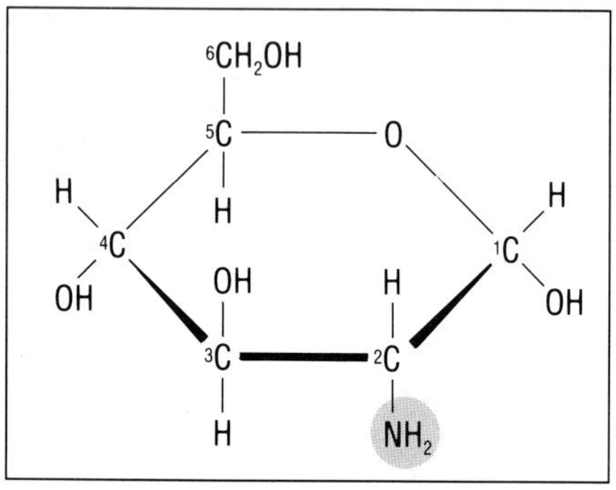

Some sugars contain nitrogen: they are called **amino sugars**. An example is given in figure 9.16. A polysaccharide that contains amino sugars is called a **mucopolysaccharide**. Mucopolysaccharides are found in the basement membranes of epithelia, the matrix of connective tissue, the synovial fluid in vertebrate joints and in the cell walls of prokaryotes. They also occur in **chitin**, a compound found in the walls of fungal hyphae and the exoskeletons of arthropods. The importance of chitin as a biological material should not be underestimated. It is widespread in nature and combines strength with durability.

Figure 9.16 Glucosamine, one of the simplest amino sugars. The hydroxyl (OH) group at position 2 of α glucose is replaced by an amino group (NH_2). In other amino sugars the nitrogen-containing side group may be more complex. Amino sugars can form long chains just as ordinary sugars can. Chitin, for example, is a polymer of acetylglucosamine.

Lipids

Lipids are biomolecules that are insoluble in water but soluble in organic solvents. Like carbohydrates, lipids contain carbon, hydrogen and oxygen. However, a lipid contains much less oxygen than a carbohydrate of the same size. Lipids, as we shall see, may also contain small amounts of other elements, such as phosphorus.

Lipids may conveniently be divided into two groups. The first consists of **fats** and **oils**. The second includes **steroids** and **terpenes** together with fat-soluble vitamins and some other compounds.

The structure of fats and oils

Natural fats and oils are compounds of **glycerol** (whose systematic name is propane-1,2,3-triol) and **fatty acids**. The only difference between a fat and an oil is that at room temperature fats are solids and oils are liquid. This is because the fatty acids in oils are smaller than those in fats, or because of the presence of one or more double bonds in some oils.

Glycerol is a small molecule with the formula $C_3H_8O_3$. The arrangement of the carbon, hydrogen and oxygen atoms is shown in the following structural formula:

$$
\begin{array}{c}
\text{H} \\
| \\
\text{H—C—O—H} \\
| \\
\text{H—C—O—H} \\
| \\
\text{H—C—O—H} \\
| \\
\text{H}
\end{array}
$$

There is only one sort of glycerol, but fatty acids show considerable structural variation. Indeed, the physical and chemical properties of a particular lipid depend on the fatty acids which it contains.

The general formula of a saturated fatty acid is $C_nH_{2n}O_2$. A more informative way of writing this is $CH_3(CH_2)_n COOH$ where n varies but is generally an even number between 14 and 22. To take an example: in **stearic acid**, a common constituent of body fat, there are 16 CH_2 groups. The formula of stearic acid is therefore $CH_3(CH_2)_{16}COOH$.

The full structure of stearic acid is shown in figure 9.17. You can see that for the most part it consists of a single chain of carbon atoms to which are joined hydrogen atoms, giving rise to a **hydrocarbon chain**. The molecule terminates in an acid carboxyl (COOH) group. This end of the molecule can therefore form hydrogen bonds with water, but overall the molecule is insoluble in water due to the presence of so many CH_2 groups.

A glance at figure 9.17 tells us that this particular hydrocarbon chain contains the maximum possible number of hydrogen atoms: all the bonds between neighbouring carbon atoms are single bonds, so no more hydrogen atoms could be added to the molecule. Such fatty acids are said to be **saturated**. Some fatty acids, however, have one or more double bonds connecting neighbouring carbon atoms. They therefore have fewer hydrogen atoms than they might, and are said to be **unsaturated**. For instance, **oleic acid**, found in both animal and plant fats, has a double bond between its two central carbons:

$$
CH_3\,(CH_2)_7 - \overset{\overset{\displaystyle H}{|}}{C} = \overset{\overset{\displaystyle H}{|}}{C} - (CH_2)_7 - COOH
$$

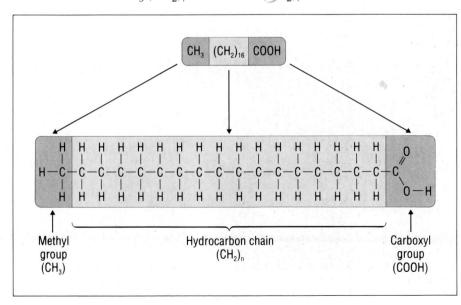

Methyl group (CH_3) Hydrocarbon chain (CH_2)$_n$ Carboxyl group (COOH)

Figure 9.17 The general formula of a saturated fatty acid is $CH_3(CH_2)_n COOH$. The fatty acid depicted on the left is stearic acid with a total of 18 carbon atoms. The systematic name of stearic acid is octadecanoic acid.

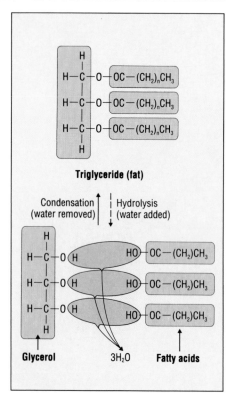

Figure 9.18 The removal of three molecules of water from a molecule of glycerol and three fatty acid molecules results in the formation of a triglyceride. The diagram shows the simplest sort of triglyceride in which three identical saturated fatty acids react with glycerol.

Saturated and unsaturated fatty acids are very important in relation to the human diet, for the amounts that we take in can help to determine our health (see box on the opposite page).

The synthesis of fats and oils

Fatty acids and glycerol are the sub-units of fats and oils. In the synthesis of a fat or oil, three fatty acid molecules combine with one glycerol molecule to form a **triglyceride**.

As with the construction of disaccharides and polysaccharides from monosaccharides, this process involves a condensation reaction in which water is lost. As you can see in figure 9.18, each of the OH (hydroxyl) groups in the glycerol molecule reacts with the COOH (carboxyl) group of a fatty acid. In this reaction water is removed and an oxygen bond (known in this case as an **ester bond**) is established between the glycerol and the fatty acid. As glycerol possesses three hydroxyl groups, three fatty acids attach themselves to the glycerol and three molecules of water are removed.

The functions of fats and oils

Although carbohydrates provide the most important direct source of energy in organisms, fats too supply energy. In fact, mass for mass they yield approximately twice as much energy on combustion as do carbohydrates. This follows from the fact that they contain relatively little oxygen. When a carbohydrate molecule is respired, much of the necessary oxygen comes from the carbohydrate itself. When, however, a fat is respired, almost all the oxygen needed is obtained from the atmosphere.

Because a given mass of fat stores considerably more energy than the same mass of carbohydrate (or protein), animals usually carry around much more fat than carbohydrate. Fat deposits beneath the skin and elsewhere represent potential sources of energy which can be drawn upon when required (figure 9.19). Fats and oils are also used as food stores in some plant seeds.

Another property of fat is that it conducts heat energy only very slowly, making it a good insulator. Animals which live in cold climates therefore have extensive fat stores. In polar bears and other Arctic and Antarctic animals, large deposits of **sub-cutaneous fat** occur beneath the skin (figure 9.20). In whales and seals this fat is known as **blubber**.

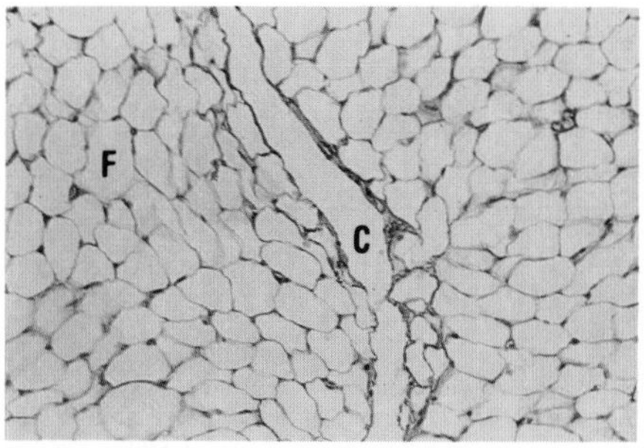

Figure 9.19 Section of fatty tissue showing a blood capillary (**C**) amongst the fat cells (**F**). In times of need the fat may be hydrolysed and the products removed in the bloodstream and used for energy transfer. Magnification × 100.

Figure 9.20 Polar bear with cubs at Cape Churchill, Canada. Polar bears have large subcutaneous fat deposits. These serve both as fuel reserves and as insulation.

Fats play a major role in the structure of the plasma membrane. Here they are combined with phosphoric acid to form **phospholipids**. In the formation of a phospholipid the phosphoric acid reacts with one of the three hydroxyl groups of glycerol. The other two hydroxyl groups of glycerol react with fatty acid chains in the usual way (figure 9.21). The part played by phospholipids in the functioning of the plasma membrane is explained on page 168.

Lipids may also act as a source of metabolic water. When respired they yield water and carbon dioxide. Some desert animals are so efficient in their conservation of water that they never need to drink water. Instead they obtain their water either from fat metabolism or directly from the foods they eat.

The structure and functions of steroids

Apart from fats and oils, **steroids** are the most important lipids in animals and plants. The general structure of a steroid is shown in figure 9.22. You can see that it consists of four interlinked rings of carbon atoms. Vitamin D is a steroid, but probably the best-known steroid, on account of the publicity it has received as a constituent of the diet, is **cholesterol**.

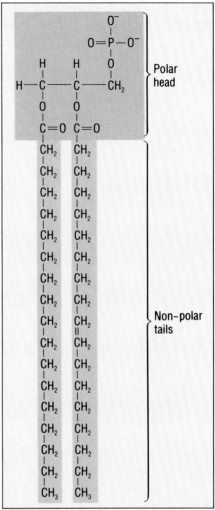

Figure 9.21 A typical phospholipid of the sort found in the plasma membrane. Notice the small polar head and the two non-polar tails. This molecule results from the reaction of one molecule of glycerol with two fatty acid molecules and a molecule of phosphoric acid.

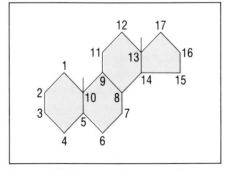

Figure 9.22 The general structure of a steroid. Four rings of carbon atoms are linked together. The carbon atoms are conventionally numbered 1 to 17 in the order shown. The various steroids differ in the side groups attached to the carbon atoms.

Coronary heart disease and diet

Coronary heart disease arises when the blood supply to the heart muscle is reduced by obstruction in the coronary arteries. This obstruction is usually the result of a mass of connective tissue and fat deposits building up in the wall of the artery. This is called an **atherosclerotic plaque**. It slows the flow of blood along the artery and may eventually cause the blood to clot, blocking the artery. Such a blockage in one of the coronary arteries will prevent blood reaching part of the heart. If the plaque is fairly small, only a small portion of the heart will lose its blood supply. If, though, one of the larger coronary arteries is blocked, the result will be a heart attack, technically known as a **myocardial infarction**.

Careful medical research has shown that many factors increase a person's chance of suffering a heart attack. These **risk factors** include being male, getting old, having close relatives who have had heart attacks, smoking, being overweight, taking too little exercise, having high blood pressure and eating too much saturated fat. We cannot do much about our gender, age or relatives. However, the other risk factors are more under our control.

The relationship between fat intake and the risk of coronary heart disease is a complicated one which has still not been fully sorted out. It does seem clear though that a high level of saturated fats and cholesterol in the diet is associated with an increase in the risk of coronary heart disease. Fats which have just one double bond per fatty acid do not seem much better for us than saturated fats. Fats with two or more double bonds per fatty acid (**polyunsaturated fats**) seem to reduce the risks.

Foods that are high in saturated fats include animal fats such as butter, cream and lard. However, switching to a low-fat diet does not guarantee that you will not get a heart attack, while some people, such as the Masai people of East Africa, have a diet that is very high in animal fats, yet have a very low rate of heart disease. But then they do not smoke, are not overweight and take a lot of exercise.

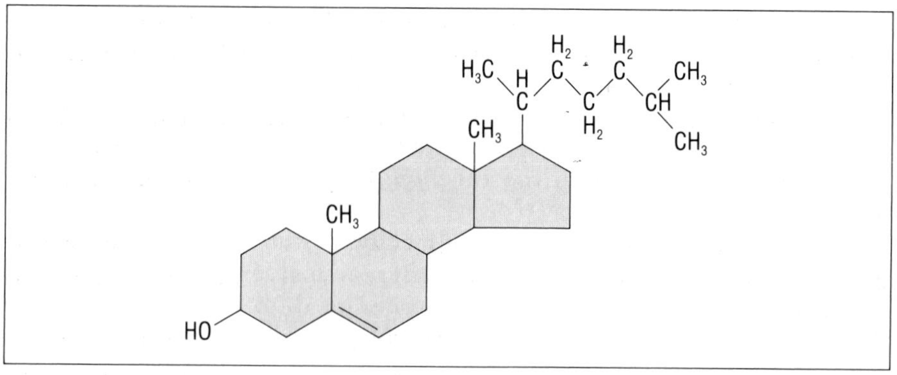

Figure 9.23 The structure of cholesterol, a steroid.

The structure of cholesterol is shown in figure 9.23. Cholesterol is found in the membranes of animal cells where it helps to keep the membranes fluid (see page 170). Other important steroids are derived from cholesterol. They include the sex hormones **progesterone** and **testosterone,** and the hormone **aldosterone** secreted by the adrenal cortex. Bile salts, such as **glycocholate** and **taurocholate,** are polar metabolic products of cholesterol needed for the normal digestion of lipids.

Cholesterol is not found in plants, but plants contain other steroids collectively known as **phytosterols.**

Other lipids

A number of other important biological molecules are also lipids. Vitamins A, E and K are **terpenes**, compounds similar to steroids but somewhat smaller. Other terpenes include turpentine and rubber and the plant growth regulators gibberellic acid and abscisic acid.

Because they are insoluble in water, lipids often reduce the loss of water by evaporation from organisms. Plant cuticles contain various **waxes** and a mixture of compounds collectively called **cutins.** Cutins and waxes are synthesised by the epidermis and then secreted on to the surface of the plant. A related lipid, **suberin,** is found in tree bark, and in the Casparian strip in roots where its function depends on its impermeability to water

In animals waxes again serve in water conservation and are found in arthropod cuticles, vertebrate skin, bird feathers and mammalian fur.

Proteins

Proteins play a number of vital roles in all organisms. They differ from carbohydrates and lipids in that they always contain nitrogen as well as carbon, hydrogen and oxygen. In addition, sulphur is often present and sometimes phosphorus and other elements.

The structure of proteins

Proteins are built up from **amino acids**. These are the sub-units of proteins in the same way that monosaccharide sugars are the sub-units of polysaccharides. There are over 100 naturally occurring amino acids and they all have an NH_2 (amino) and a COOH (carboxyl) group, as shown below:

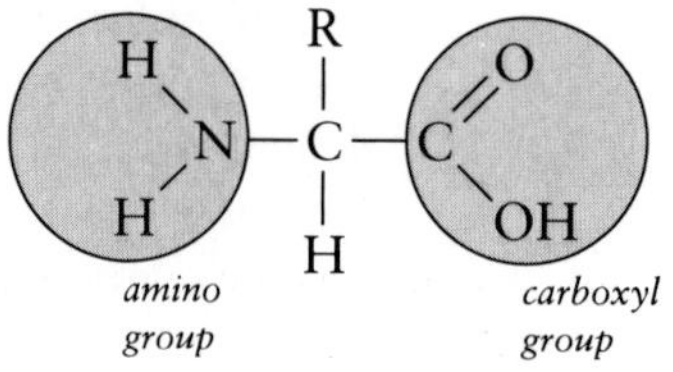

Colloids

A particle which remains dispersed in solution, rather than dissolving, settling out or floating, is called a **colloid**. Many of the larger biological molecules such as proteins and certain lipids are colloids.

Colloids are too small to settle out under gravity but too large to dissolve. The biological significance of this is that colloids exist dispersed in solution as individual molecules and so present an enormous surface area. This makes them readily available for chemical reactions, a feature of particular significance for enzymes which can therefore operate at great speeds.

They differ in the nature of the R group. The simplest amino acid is **glycine** in which R is a hydrogen atom. In **alanine** it is CH₃, in **cysteine** it is CH₂SH, and so on.

Although there are over 100 naturally occurring amino acids, only 20 are used in the biosynthesis of proteins. The names of these 20 amino acids are listed in table 9.5, together with the R groups of six representative examples.

Amino acids unite to form proteins in much the same manner that monosaccharides combine to form polysaccharides, and fatty acids and glycerol combine to form fats and oils. The first step in this process involves the union of two amino acids (figure 9.24). A reaction occurs between the amino group of one amino acid and the carboxyl group of another: a molecule of water is removed in a condensation reaction and the two amino acids become joined by a **peptide link** to form a **dipeptide**.

Continued condensation reactions lead to the addition of further amino acids resulting in the formation of a long chain called a polypeptide. Polypeptides may be composed of up to around 400 amino acids.

Names of the twenty amino acids	
Non-essential	**Essential**
Alanine	Isoleucine
Arginine*	Leucine
Asparagine	Lysine
Aspartic acid	Methionine
Cysteine	Phenylalanine
Glutamic acid	Threonine
Glutamine	Tryptophan
Glycine	Valine
Histidine*	
Proline	
Serine	*essential
Tyrosine	in children

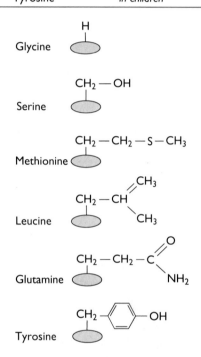

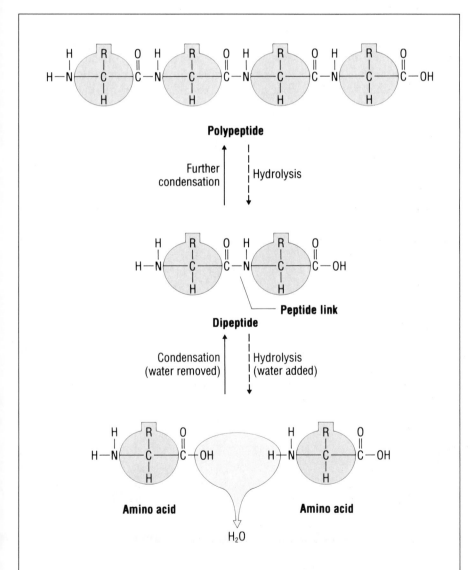

Figure 9.24 The removal of a molecule of water from two amino acid molecules results in the formation of a dipeptide. Further condensation leads to the formation of a polypeptide.

Table 9.5 *At the top* is a list of the naturally occurring amino acids involved in protein synthesis. Non-essential amino acids are so-called because they can be synthesised in the body and are therefore not needed in the human diet. Essential amino acids cannot be synthesised and are therefore needed in our diet (see page 142). Arginine and histidine, both required for growth, are non-essential in adults but essential in children.
Below are shown the R groups of six amino acids to illustrate the range of variation in their chemical structure. The R group is variable; the remainder of the molecule, i.e. the part responsible for forming peptide linkages, is common to all the amino acids. In each case only the R group is shown in full; the rest of the molecule is represented by the shaded oval. Notice that nitrogen and sulphur are present in the R groups of some amino acids.

Looked upon as a chain of amino acids, the structure of proteins is simple enough. Although only 20 amino acids are used in the natural synthesis of proteins, the number of possible ways in which they can be combined is almost infinite. The individuality of a particular protein is determined by the sequence of amino acids comprising its polypeptide chains, together with the pattern of folding and cross-linkages. Some proteins contain only a few of the 20 amino acids; others contain all of them. The total number of amino acids in a protein molecule may be as few as 40 or as many as several thousand.

The primary and secondary structure of proteins

The **primary structure** of a protein is the order of the amino acids of which its polypeptides are composed. The only bonds recognised at this level of protein structure are the covalent bonds between successive amino acids.

The **secondary structure** refers to the way the chain of amino acids folds or turns upon itself as a result of hydrogen bonding (see page 121). The first elucidation of the secondary structure of a protein was achieved in 1951 by Linus Pauling of the California Institute of Technology.

The alpha-helix

Pauling worked on **keratin**, the structural protein found in hair. He was able to demonstrate that the keratin molecule consists of a greatly elongated polypeptide chain twisted into a helix, the so-called **alpha-helix**, rather like

Figure 9.25 The alpha-helix is the most common secondary structure of proteins. The linked amino acids form a three-dimensional helix.

A An alpha-helix in outline. **R** represents the R groups which project from the chain of amino acids.

B An alpha-helix in more detail showing the individual atoms in the chain of amino acids. Carbon, black; hydrogen, white; oxygen, red; nitrogen, blue; R groups, green.

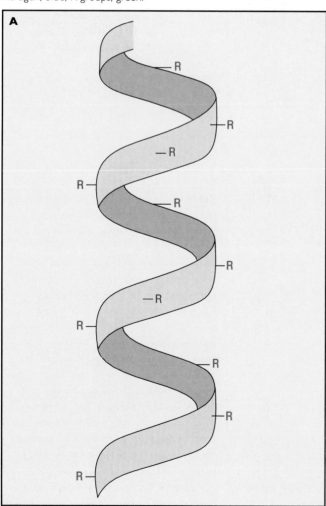

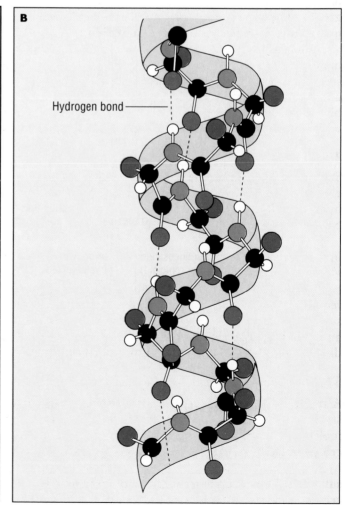

Hydrogen bond

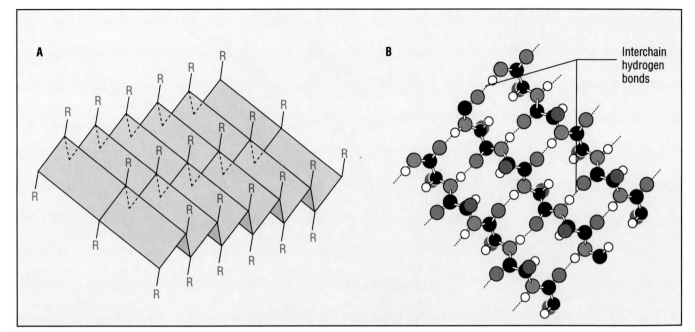

an extensible telephone cord (figure 9.25). Successive turns of the helix are linked together by weak hydrogen bonds situated between the amino groups of one turn and the carboxyl groups of the next. We now know that many other proteins besides keratin are built on a helical plan.

What is the function of the alpha-helix? Undoubtedly it helps to maintain the shape of the molecule. The alpha-helix, with its links between successive twists, is a much more stable and robust structure than a straight untwisted polypeptide chain would be. This is of great importance in the biological functioning of proteins, particularly enzymes and antibodies whose efficiency depends on their maintaining a particular shape.

Figure 9.26 The beta-pleated sheet is the other secondary structure found in proteins. Here the linked amino acids form flat sheets. **A** A beta-pleated sheet in outline, showing the R groups (**R**) projecting from the sheet. **B** A beta-pleated sheet in more detail, viewed from above. The colours of the atoms are as in figure 9.25B.

The beta-pleated sheet

Subsequently Linus Pauling, in collaboration with Robert Corey, discovered another type of secondary structure, called the **beta-pleated sheet**: hydrogen bonding between parallel chains results in a flat structure which becomes folded, as shown in figure 9.26.

Beta-pleated sheets occur less often than alpha-helices. They are found in a number of structural proteins, for instance silk, and also in some globular proteins, for instance the enzyme lysozyme.

By and large beta-pleated sheets are found in proteins whose function requires strength. Silk, for example, is for its thickness one of the strongest substances known. Alpha-helices are found in proteins such as enzymes and antibodies where the important feature of the molecule is its precise three-dimensional shape and surface contours.

The tertiary and quaternary structure of proteins

A typical protein consists of one or more polypeptide chains. The **tertiary structure** refers to the way a polypeptide folds and coils to form a complex molecular shape (figure 9.27). The polypeptide may be folded and cross-linked at intervals. The cross-links may be of several sorts including hydrogen bonds, ionic bonds and sulphur bridges (figure 9.28). The sulphur bridges are the strongest and contribute to the great toughness of certain proteins.

Figure 9.27 The tertiary structure of a hypothetical polypeptide.

Figure 9.28 Some of the different sorts of bonds that can hold the polypeptide chains of a protein together and so help maintain the tertiary structure. The strongest of these bonds are those of the sulphur bridges, as these are covalent bonds. The bonds that link the amino acids together within each chain are also covalent bonds.

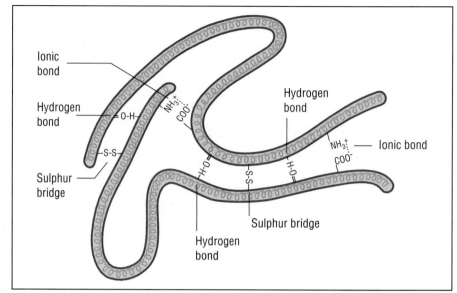

The **quaternary structure** is only present when a protein consists of two or more polypeptides. It refers to the way in which these polypeptides are arranged to form the biologically active protein. For instance, the pigment haemoglobin, found in red blood cells, contains four tightly packed polypeptide chains whose spatial arrangement is vital for the efficient functioning of the molecule (see page 311).

Many structures in organisms consist of a protein combined with another molecule to form a **conjugated protein**. The non-protein component to which the protein is attached is called the **prosthetic group**. Egg yolk, haemoglobin and other pigments are all examples of conjugated proteins. In egg yolk the prosthetic group is phosphoric acid; in haemoglobin it is an iron-containing pigment called haem.

If a protein is combined with a carbohydrate the resulting compound is called a **glycoprotein**. Usually the protein forms the core of the molecule and the carbohydrate consists of a branched polysaccharide chain projecting from it. Mucus and synovial fluid contain glycoproteins with lubricative properties. Glycoproteins also occur in the matrix of connective tissue and in the eukaryotic plasma membrane (see page 170).

Proteins as buffers

A feature of proteins is that they have both acidic and basic properties: to use the language of the chemist, they are **amphoteric**. This is due to the presence of amino (basic) and carboxyl (acidic) ions at the free ends of the polypeptide chains.

The reason why polypeptide chains are like this is that the amino acids of which they are composed have both positively and negatively charged regions: the amino group carries the positive charge and the carboxyl group the negative charge:

$$NH_3^+ - RCH - COO^-$$

An ion which has both positively and negatively charged regions is called a **zwitterion** (German for 'double ion'). All amino acids are zwitterions, and this makes it possible for proteins to combine with both basic and acidic substances. As a result, proteins can function as **buffers**, compounds which resist changes in pH on addition of moderate amounts of acid or alkali.

In acidic conditions, hydrogen ions are taken up by the carboxyl group of the amino acid, thus decreasing the acidity of the surroundings:

$$NH_3^+ - RCH - COOH$$

In alkaline conditions, hydrogen ions are released from the amino group, thus increasing the acidity of the surroundings:

$$NH_2 - RCH - COO^-$$

In their capacity as buffers, proteins play an important role within cells and in the blood and tissue fluids. They help to keep the pH at a steady level, an important aspect of homeostasis.

The functions of proteins

The function of a protein is directly related to its shape. In general proteins fall into two groups: globular and fibrous. In **globular proteins**, such as globulin itself, the polypeptide chains are tightly folded to form a more-or-less spherical shape such as that shown in figure 9.27 on page 139. One of the most important classes of globular proteins are **enzymes**, organic catalysts whose function is to speed up chemical reactions in organisms. Enzymes are nearly always proteins and the functioning of an enzyme is directly related to its shape (see page 219).

Globular proteins are also used in the construction of microfilaments and microtubules. Microfilaments are polymers of the protein **actin**, and microtubules are polymers of the protein **tubulin** (figure 9.29).

Globular proteins are also important in buffering, as explained in the box on page 140. Globular proteins are water soluble, though on account of their large size they do not go into true solution but form **colloidal suspensions**. Collectively such colloids have a very large surface area and, since they have a strong capacity to absorb water and other substances, they are important in holding molecules in position within the cell.

Among the many other classes of globular proteins, special mention should be made of **antibodies**. Each of us can make hundreds of thousands of different antibodies, which bind to particular disease-causing agents and toxins (see page 417). Other globular proteins are found in membranes where they are mainly involved in the transport of substances into and out of the cell and its membrane-bound organelles.

Fibrous proteins are insoluble and consist of long parallel polypeptide chains cross-linked at many points along their length. They are essential constituents of many structures in the body. The fibrous protein **keratin**, for instance, is found in hairs, feathers, nails, hooves and horns (figure 9.30).

Collagen is another fibrous protein. It is the most abundant protein in vertebrates, making up a third of their total protein mass. We are largely held together by collagen as it is found in bones, cartilage, tendons, ligaments, connective tissue and skin. Collagen is also found in the cornea of the eye. Collagen fibres have a tensile strength greater than that of steel. Under the electron microscope they show a characteristic banding pattern (figure 9.31). Careful analysis has shown that they consist of three polypep-

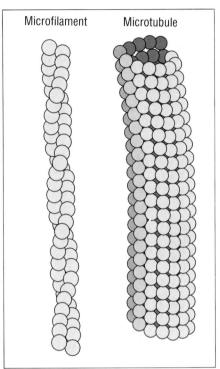

Figure 9.29 Microfilaments and microtubules are composed of globular proteins (represented by the spheres above). In the microfilament the globular protein molecules are in chains twisted round each other. In the microtubule they are arranged helically around a hollow space. Molecules can be added, or removed, at the ends, which explains the transitory nature of these structures (see page 163).

Figure 9.30 Waterbuck in the Awash Park, Ethiopia. The hair, hooves and horns of this animal are almost pure keratin.

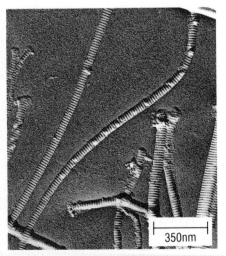

350nm

Figure 9.31 Shadowed collagen fibres from the neck tendon of a bird seen under the electron microscope. The banding pattern is characteristic of collagen.

Figure 9.32 Computer-generated model of the structure of collagen. In collagen, three helices are intertwined to form the protein. To help distinguish them here, one helix is shown in green. In the other two polypeptide chains, nitrogen atoms are blue, oxygen atoms are red and carbon atoms are silver.

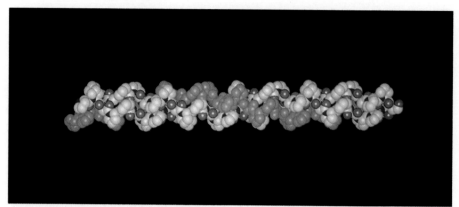

tide chains coiled round each other in a **triple helix** (figure 9.32). The resulting structure is like a plaited rope and has great strength.

Other fibrous proteins include **myosin** which is found in muscle, and **elastin** found associated with collagen in connective tissue.

Like carbohydrate and fat, protein can be broken down with the transfer of energy. However, protein is normally only used as a substantial source of energy when eaten in excess or when an animal is starving. For humans, the possibility that tissue protein may be used as a source of energy is one of the dangers of going on so-called 'starvation diets'. Under such conditions, though, the body tends to utilise less essential tissues such as the skeletal muscles first. Vital organs such as the heart and brain normally remain unaffected.

Proteins and the diet

It is clear from the preceding section that proteins are important constituents of the diet. In an animal's cells the various proteins are assembled from the necessary amino acids and it is therefore imperative that all the amino acids should be available in sufficient quantities. As indicated in table 9.5 on page 137, adult humans can synthesise twelve amino acids in sufficient quantities for them not to be required in the diet. They are therefore known as **non-essential amino acids**.

The remaining eight amino acids cannot be synthesised by the body itself, at any rate not fast enough, so they have to be supplied in the diet. Consequently they are known as **essential amino acids**. A further two amino acids are essential for growth and cannot be made in sufficient amounts by children. Children therefore have ten essential amino acids.

Figure 9.33 How the body makes non-essential amino acids by transamination. Under the influence of a transaminase enzyme, the amino acid group of the dietary amino acid changes place with the keto group of the carbohydrate derivative which in this example is pyruvic acid. This results in the formation of a new amino acid, in this case alanine.

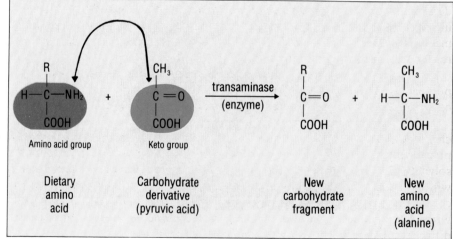

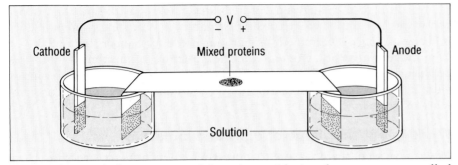

Figure 9.34 Separation of proteins by electrophoresis. A strip of absorptive paper, to which the mixture of proteins is applied, is placed between two dishes containing a suitable conducting solution. When a potential difference is applied, the proteins migrate towards one of the electrodes. If positively charged, they migrate towards the negative electrode (cathode); if negatively charged, they migrate towards the positive electrode (anode). The rate at which the proteins move depends on their size and charge.

Synthesis of the non-essential amino acids involves a process called **transamination**: the amino acid group of one of the dietary amino acids changes places with the keto group of a carbohydrate derivative which is thereby converted into a new amino acid (figure 9.33).

Most plant proteins contain fewer essential amino acids than most animal proteins. Vegetarians therefore take care to eat a wide range of plant proteins so as to be sure they get all the necessary amino acids. Some plant products, such as soya beans, provide a particularly rich source of the various essential amino acids, at least compared with other plants.

Lack of one or more of the essential amino acids can result in retarded growth and various other symptoms depending on which particular amino acids are in short supply.

The analysis of proteins

Proteins are key compounds in the working of the body. Often it is an error in the body's synthesis of a particular protein that leads to genetic diseases. This is the case, for instance, with sickle cell anaemia and cystic fibrosis. The first step in understanding such diseases generally involves identifying the proteins responsible. For this and other reasons, protein identification is important in biology.

The first step in identifying a protein is usually to separate it from others collected with it. A blood sample, for instance, contains many different proteins. A commonly used technique for the separation of proteins is **electrophoresis**. The technique relies on the fact that large charged molecules such as proteins migrate in an electric field. The rate of migration varies from one protein to another, depending on the size, shape and charge of the molecule, so they become separated from one another (figure 9.34).

The next step is to determine the sequence of amino acids in the protein, that is, its primary structure. The precise methods used to determine the primary sequence of a protein are complex and have changed in recent years as a result of automated approaches. Nevertheless, two techniques are central: **progressive hydrolysis** of the protein and **chromatography** of the resulting amino acids.

Progressive hydrolysis involves removing the amino acids from the polypeptide one at a time by the use of hydrolysing enzymes. The mixture of amino acids is then subjected to chromatography (figure 9.35).

There are various sorts of chromatography, but the simplest is **paper chromatography**. In this technique a concentrated spot of the amino acid is placed on a sheet of absorptive paper which is then dipped in a suitable solvent. The solvent rises up the paper and carries the amino acid at a speed which depends on that amino acid's physical and chemical properties. By comparing how far the amino acid has travelled after a given length of time with a reference collection showing the distance travelled by the 20 different amino acids, the amino acid can be identified.

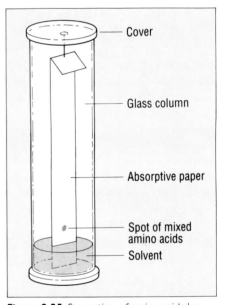

Figure 9.35 Separation of amino acids by paper chromatography. A small amount of solvent is put into a glass column. A strip of absorptive paper, containing a concentrated spot of the mixture of amino acids near its lower end, is hung in the glass column so that its end dips into the solvent. The solvent moves slowly up the strip carrying the amino acids with it. These travel at different speeds and so become separated. The strip is dried and treated so that the positions of the amino acids show up clearly.

Figure 9.36 Frederick Sanger, discoverer of the sequence of amino acids in the hormone insulin, an achievement for which he was awarded a Nobel Prize in 1958. When Sanger announced that he wanted to find out the structure of a naturally occurring protein, his professor told him he was mad! In 1980 he was awarded a second Nobel Prize, this time for his work on the chemical structure of genes. He is the first British scientist to have been awarded two Nobel Prizes.

Needless to say, analysing protein structure is easier said than done, and it was not until 1953 that the first naturally occurring protein had its primary sequence determined. In that year Frederick Sanger (figure 9.36) of Cambridge University worked out the structure of **insulin**, a hormone produced by the pancreas and involved in blood sugar regulation. Insulin is quite a small protein, containing only 51 amino acids. Since then many other proteins have had their primary structures determined.

Working out the shape of a protein molecule

As we have seen, there is more to a protein than its primary structure. How can the three-dimensional shape of the molecule be ascertained? Here again spectacular progress has been made. The approach adopted makes use of a technique developed early in the twentieth century by the physicist Sir Lawrence Bragg. In 1913 Bragg determined the precise atomic structure of sodium chloride by bombarding crystals of this salt with X-rays and analysing the way the X-rays were scattered. Since then this technique of **X-ray crystallography** has been used in the analysis of many different molecules, including proteins.

The technical problems of X-ray analysis are formidable but the principle is simple enough. A beam of X-rays is fired at the protein crystal. The X-rays are deflected by the atoms in the protein molecules and the way in which they are scattered, the **X-ray diffraction pattern**, is recorded on a photographic plate located behind the crystal. Between each firing the crystal is rotated slightly so that the X-rays hit all sides of it, thus enabling a complete analysis to be made.

Difficulties arise not so much in obtaining the X-ray pictures as in interpreting them. We have already seen that proteins are large molecules composed of thousands of atoms. Their X-ray diffraction patterns are correspondingly complex, and this makes analysis of the data a difficult and laborious business. However, with the aid of computers, it is now possible to derive from X-ray diffraction patterns the precise positioning of the atoms and the shape of the whole molecule.

X-ray crystallography allowed the elucidation of the alpha-helix and beta-pleated sheet in the 1950s. By the 1960s the same techniques had been refined to the point where the Cambridge biologists John Kendrew and Max Perutz were able to announce the complete structures of, respectively, myoglobin and haemoglobin, both oxygen-carrying proteins. For this Kendrew and Perutz shared a Nobel Prize in 1962. Once the structures of myoglobin and haemoglobin had been discovered it became possible to understand how they functioned.

Figure 9.37 Three-dimensional analysis of a protein is here illustrated by myoglobin.
A X-ray diffraction pattern of a crystal of myoglobin.
B Three-dimensional contour map showing positions of the various atoms in part of the myoglobin molecule, derived from analysis of numerous X-ray photographs like the one shown in **A**.

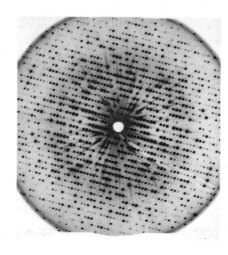

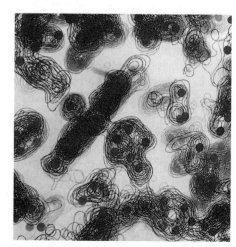

Myoglobin is the simpler of the two (figures 9.37 and 9.38). It has a relative molecular mass of 17 600 and contains over 2500 atoms which show up as groups of spots on X-ray photographs. On analysis it turns out that the molecule consists of a single polypeptide chain made up of 153 amino acids. The polypeptide chain is coiled to form an alpha-helix, and this in turn is folded on itself into a roughly spherical shape. Various kinds of chemical bond, together with electrostatic attraction, keep the folds of the chain together and help to maintain the shape of the molecule.

Myoglobin is an example of a conjugated protein: attached to the polypeptide chain is a flat group of atoms, the prosthetic group, consisting of a central iron atom surrounded by rings of carbon and nitrogen atoms. This prosthetic group is **haem** and it is to the iron atom in the middle that the oxygen molecule becomes attached. Haem belongs to a class of organic compounds known as **porphyrins** (figure 9.39).

Haemoglobin is a larger and more complex molecule than myoglobin. It contains 574 amino acids in all, almost four times as many as in myoglobin. The molecule is composed of four polypeptide chains arranged around four haem groups. Each polypeptide chain has stretches of the alpha-helix and this is folded and held together in much the same way as the single polypeptide chain is in myoglobin.

In terms of their abundance in the body, carbohydrates, lipids and proteins, along with nucleic acids, account for the overwhelming mass of organic molecules. However, even though they may not be present in large quantities, there is one more class of organic compounds which, on account of their importance, we need to discuss before leaving our survey of the chemicals of life, namely vitamins.

Vitamins

Vitamins are a mixed assortment of organic compounds grouped together not because of any chemical affinity between them but because they are all needed in the diet in small amounts. The formula of a representative vitamin is given in figure 9.40. The importance of vitamins can be appreciated from the ill-effects which follow if an organism is deprived of one of them. Indeed this was how they were discovered (see page 147).

Let us now look briefly at the various vitamins needed by humans. It isn't important to remember all the details, and you certainly should not learn by heart their chemical formulae. Rather, you should get a general feeling for vitamins: what sorts of roles they play in the body, why they are only needed in small amounts and what sorts of foods they occur in.

At first vitamins were simply given letters (vitamin A, B, etc). Later some of them were given names and some were found to consist of more than one vitamin. We will classify vitamins into fat-soluble and water-soluble. The details are summarised in table 9.6 overleaf.

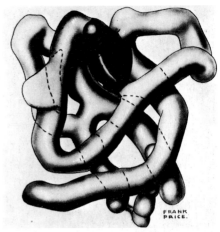

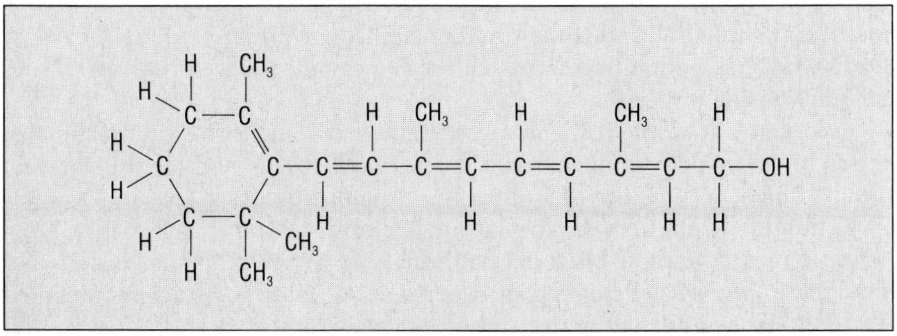

Figure 9.38 Three-dimensional model of myoglobin, constructed using data of the sort illustrated in figure 9.37. The black disc is the haem group, and the spherical object attached to it represents an oxygen molecule.

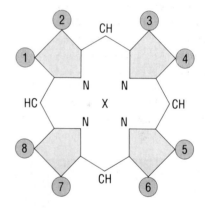

Figure 9.39 The general structure of a porphyrin. A variety of side groups can exist at positions 1 to 8, so that many different porphyrins occur. Various metal ions may be found at X. In chlorophyll the element is magnesium, in haemoglobin it is iron. Porphyrins are also found in cytochromes, coenzymes required in respiration. Porphyrins are one of the many different types of molecule with which proteins may be conjugated.

Figure 9.40 Vitamins vary greatly in their structure. This shows the chemical structure of retinol (vitamin A).

Name	Function	Principal sources	Deficiency diseases
Fat soluble			
A (retinol)	Enters into photochemical reaction in rods in retina of eye	Meat, fish, carotenoid pigments in vegetables, particularly carrots	Xerophthalmia (drying and degeneration of cornea) leading to blindness
D (calciferol)	Absorption and utilisation of Ca^{2+} for bone formation	Fish liver oil and the action of sunlight	Rickets (softening of bones)
E (tocopherol)	Not known	Most foods	Sterility in rats
K	Required for synthesis of certain blood-clotting factors	Synthesised by intestinal bacteria	Prolonged clotting time
Water soluble			
B_1 (thiamine)	Required as coenzyme in respiration	Many foods, especially husks of wheat grains and brown rice	Beri beri: wasting of muscles, circulatory failure and paralysis
B_2 (riboflavine)	Forms flavine coenzyme FAD required in respiration	Leafy vegetables, fish, eggs	Sore mouth, eyes and skin
Nicotinamide	Forms coenzymes NAD and NADP required in respiration and photosynthesis respectively	Meat, fish, milk, eggs	Pellagra: diarrhoea, dermatitis and mental disorder
B_5 (pantothenic acid)	Forms coenzyme A required in respiration	Most foods	Fatigue, poor motor coordination, sleep disturbance
B_6	Forms coenzyme required for synthesis of amino acids by transamination	Most foods	Convulsions, kidney stones
B_{12} (cobalamin)	Coenzyme in carbon transfer in nucleic acid metabolism.	Meat, eggs, dairy products	Pernicious anaemia neurological disorders
Folic acid	Coenzyme in carbon transfer in nucleic acid metabolism	Green vegetables, legumes, whole wheat products	Anaemia, gastrointestinal disorders
Biotin	Required as coenzyme for fat synthesis, amino acid metabolism and glycogen formation	Legumes, vegetables, meat	Under experimental conditions dermatitis, muscle pains and depression
C (ascorbic acid)	Required for formation of intercellular material; biochemical role unknown	Citrus fruits and green vegetables	Scurvy

Table 9.6 Vitamins required by humans.

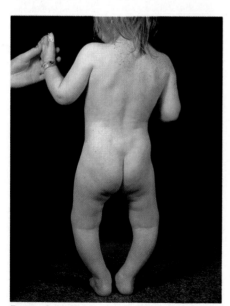

Figure 9.41 Three year-old girl suffering from rickets which has resulted in severely bowed legs.

Fat-soluble vitamins

Vitamin A (retinol) is required for the photochemical reactions involved in light perception by the rod cells in the eye (see page 477). Although it occurs in many foods, it is particularly abundant in liver, especially polar bear liver. Indeed, Arctic explorers have been poisoned by excessive amounts of vitamin A as a result of eating too many polar bear livers.

Vitamin D is present in few natural foods except fish liver oil. However, one form in which it occurs, **cholecalciferol (vitamin D_3)** is synthesised by the action of sunlight on a natural precursor found in the skin. Because of this, vitamin D deficiency is rare except in climates where there is very little sunlight or in cultures where people spend very little time in natural sunlight. Under these circumstances, vitamin D deficiency may lead to **rickets,** a condition in which the bones fail to develop properly and remain soft (figure 9.41).

Vitamin E (tocopherol) is known to prevent some forms of infertility in rats. However, no human has ever been found to be short of this vitamin and its biochemical function in humans remains obscure.

Vitamin K is needed for normal blood clotting (see page 321). Interestingly, intestinal bacteria synthesise the vitamin for us. Because of this, the only way deficiency can occur is if we lose most of our intestinal bacteria, for example by taking antibiotics for months on end.

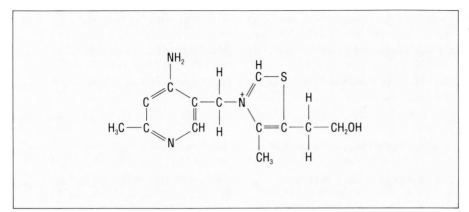

Figure 9.42 The chemical structure of thiamine (vitamin B$_1$).

Water-soluble vitamins

The **B-vitamins** form a group of eight water-soluble substances which for historical reasons are named as follows:

B$_1$ (thiamine), B$_2$ (riboflavine), nicotinamide, B$_5$ (pantothenic acid), B$_6$, B$_{12}$ (cobalamin), folic acid, biotin.

These eight vitamins are essential for the functioning of certain enzymes and are known as **coenzymes** (see page 224). For example, **thiamine (vitamin B$_1$)** serves as the coenzyme in several important reactions in carbohydrate metabolism involving the removal or transfer of aldehyde groups. Its chemical structure is shown in figure 9.42.

The discovery of vitamins

Because vitamins are required in such small amounts, they were not discovered until early in the twentieth century. In 1912 the English biochemist Frederick Gowland Hopkins showed that rats fed on a diet containing only proteins, fats, carbohydrates, minerals and water eventually became unhealthy. However, the daily addition of a small amount of milk soon restored their health.

In the same year a Polish scientist, Casimir Funk, obtained from rice husks a concentrate of an amine that alleviated the symptoms of the disease beri beri. This disease was rife amongst Japanese sailors living on little else but white (unhusked) rice.

Plainly an additional food factor besides proteins, fats, carbohydrates and minerals was required for health, and it looked like being an

amine. The term *vitamine* (meaning 'vital amine') was coined to cover the additional food factor or factors required.

Soon after, E.V. McCollum of the USA showed that young rats needed both water-soluble and fat-soluble vitamins. It therefore became clear that more than one vitamin was

Frederick Gowland Hopkins was born at Eastbourne in Sussex in 1861. After a lonely and unhappy childhood, he got a job as an assistant at Guy's Hospital and at the same time took a part-time degree in Chemistry. After graduating he took another degree, this time in medicine, and eventually qualified as a doctor. The work for which he is remembered required painstaking accuracy and many of his early experiments failed, as a result of which he suffered a nervous breakdown. However, he persevered and eventually showed that proteins, fats, carbohydrates, minerals and water on their own are insufficient for good health. Hopkins was knighted in 1925 and at the age of 68 was awarded the Nobel Prize for medicine.

required. It also became apparent that not all vitamins were amines. In fact the only vitamin that is an amine is vitamin B$_1$ (thiamine), the one discovered by Casimir Funk. Despite this, the word vitamin has been retained, though the 'e' has been dropped.

Scurvy and the discovery of vitamin C

If famine is excluded, scurvy is probably the nutritional deficiency disease that has caused the most suffering in recorded history. Some of the earliest descriptions of what is now known as scurvy come from the diaries kept by Europeans, such as the great Portuguese explorer Vasco da Gama, while on board ship in the late 1490s. Before that time, scurvy occurred only rarely among sailors. However, as voyages became longer, the problem of scurvy became more serious. During the eighteenth century, the British navy lost more sailors through scurvy than through enemy action.

During the seventeenth and early eighteenth centuries, many cures for scurvy were suggested and there was some evidence that fresh fruit could help. Unfortunately, none of the experiments had what would nowadays be considered adequate controls. Because of this, the results were generally inconclusive. In 1746, however, James Lind, a Scottish ship's surgeon, kept a group of 12 sailors all with scurvy 'as similar as I could have them' in the same quarters. He then divided the men into six pairs and fed them different diets. After six days the men whose diet included two oranges and a lemon a day were greatly improved, the men who drank just over a litre of cider a day were somewhat improved, and the others were no better. Lind concluded 'that oranges and lemons were the most effectual remedies for this distemper at sea'.

Unfortunately this trial seems to have made very little impression among the writers on scurvy over the next 50 years, and it is only quite recently that Lind's work has been praised as an exemplary example of biological experimentation. At the beginning of the twentieth century some leading scientists still thought that insanitary surroundings, overwork, mental depression, bad meat, sterilisation of milk and exposure to damp and cold could all contribute to the disease. However, in 1907 two Norwegians, Axel Holst and Theodor Frölich, showed that scurvy could be produced by diet and cured by diet. They worked on guinea pigs and found that fresh cabbage, lemon juice and apples could all alleviate the symptoms of scurvy. It is because of their work that the term 'guinea pig' is used for an experimental subject.

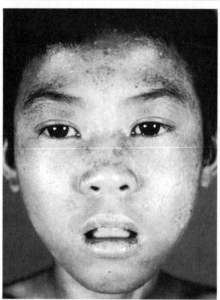

Figure 9.43 Lack of the B-vitamin nicotinamide results in the deficiency disease pellagra, one of whose symptoms is coarsening of skin exposed to sunlight. Other symptoms include abdominal pains and diarrhoea. Acute deficiency results in mental disorder and delirium.

Another important B-vitamin is nicotinamide. Insufficient quantities of this leads to **pellagra** (figure 9.43). The history of how the cause of pellagra was discovered is most interesting. Until the First World War it was generally thought that pellagra was caused by infectious micro-organisms. However, Joseph Goldberger, an Austrian-American doctor, thought it might be due to an inadequate diet. So he persuaded volunteers in a Mississippi prison to eat a diet lacking meats and milk. Sure enough, pellagra developed. Goldberger then attempted to contract the disease by exposing himself to the clothing, bedding and excreta of the prisoners. However, he did not get the disease. His failure to develop pellagra suggested that the disease was due, not to an infectious agent *present* in the prisoners, but to something *absent* from the prisoners' diet. Goldberger called the missing nutrient the P-P (pellagra-preventing) factor and after his death it was sometimes called vitamin G in his honour.

Vitamin C or **ascorbic acid** is perhaps the best-known vitamin. It is ironic therefore that its precise biochemical function is still unknown, despite the fact that lack of it has long been known to cause **scurvy**.

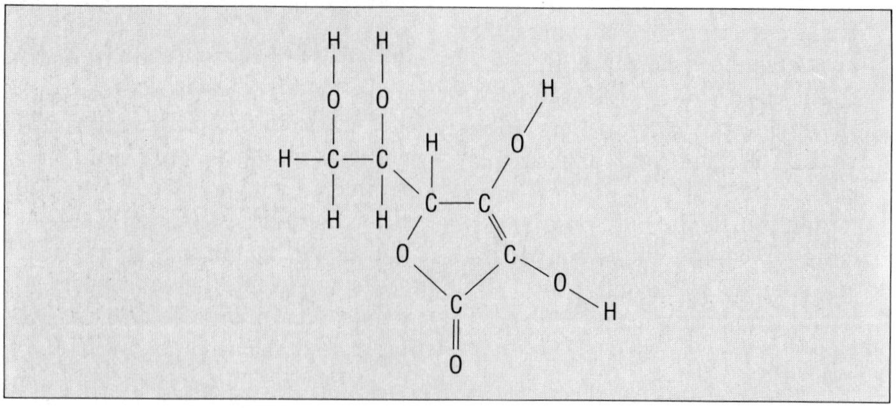

Figure 9.44 The chemical structure of ascorbic acid (vitamin C).

If you are ever asked what humans share in common with guinea pigs, red-vented bulbuls, Indian fruit bats and certain species of fish and monkeys, the answer is that they are the only animals known to require vitamin C in their diet. Other organisms can synthesise it from glucose. As you would expect, therefore, its structure is similar to that of glucose (figure 9.44).

The relationship between vitamins and coenzymes

Coenzymes are complex non-protein compounds that help the action of enzymes (see page 224). Many of them are derived from vitamins in the diet.

Take the vitamin pantothenic acid, for example. This is a necessary precursor of coenzyme A which we shall meet again in Chapter 14 in connection with respiration. If you look at the illustration you will see where the vitamin is in relation to the coenzyme molecule.

Technically, coenzyme A is a mononucleotide phosphate ester of pantothenic acid. If you are a chemist, you will know what this means. If you are not a chemist, do not worry. The important point is that the vitamin is part of the coenzyme. Without the vitamin the body is unable to make the coenzyme, and that would be bad news for us because coenzyme A

plays a vital role in a number of metabolic pathways including the Krebs cycle, the central pathway in respiration.

Structure of coenzyme A showing the position of the vitamin pantothenic acid in the molecule. Adenine, ribose and phosphate together make up the nucleotide part of the molecule. Nucleotides are explained on page 710. The addition of the two-carbon group shown at the top left results in the formation of acetylcoenzyme A whose role in metabolism is explained on page 233.

Dorothy Hodgkin

One of the most notable contributors to our knowledge of biochemistry, including vitamins, has been Dorothy Hodgkin.

Dorothy Hodgkin was born in 1910 in Cairo and her early education was in the Middle East and Africa. As a teenager she was attracted by archaeology as well as chemistry, but decided to study the latter at Oxford. After taking her doctorate at Cambridge she returned to Oxford. In the 1930s she was one of the first people to use and develop the

technique of X-ray crystallography. Her major research triumphs included the determination of the three-dimensional structures of penicillin, vitamin B_{12} and insulin. Her work has led to a better understanding of the functioning of these compounds, and has been of considerable medical importance. In 1964 she received the Nobel Prize and the year after became the first woman to receive the Order of Merit since Florence Nightingale. She has been Chancellor of Bristol University since 1970.

Summary

1 The main organic constituents of organisms are carbohydrates, lipids, proteins and nucleic acids. Inorganic constituents include minerals and water.

2 The importance of **water** as a medium for life derives from its **solvent properties, heat capacity, surface tension, freezing properties** and **transparency**.

3 **Minerals (inorganic ions)** perform a wide range of functions in organisms.

4 **Carbohydrates** contain only carbon, hydrogen and oxygen, with a ratio of two hydrogen atoms to one oxygen atom in each molecule. They provide easily accessible stores of energy, and in plants they also play an important structural role (cellulose). They are classified into **monosaccharides, disaccharides** and **polysaccharides**.

5 Monosaccharides such as glucose can be built up into polysaccharides such as starch or glycogen by condensation, and the latter can be broken down by hydrolysis.

6 Starch and cellulose differ in the way the α glucoses of which they are composed are joined together. Cellulose may become impregnated with **lignin** to form **wood**.

7 **Lipids** include fats, oils and related substances. They contain little oxygen and do not dissolve in water. Fats and oils are compounds of **glycerol** and **fatty acids** which can be united by condensation and split by hydrolysis. They are important sources of energy.

8 Plasma membranes contain **phospholipids**, which contain phosphoric acid in addition to glycerol and fatty acids. Animal membranes also contain cholesterol, a steroid. A number of hormones are also steroids.

9 **Proteins** are composed of numerous **amino acids**. Amino acids join by a condensation reaction to form **polypeptide chains**. The order of amino acids constitutes the **primary structure** of the protein.

10 The chain of amino acids may be coiled into an **alpha-helix** or **beta-pleated sheet** to give the protein its **secondary structure**. Further coiling or folding gives the protein its **tertiary structure**. Finally, several polypeptide chains may combine with one another or join with a non-protein **prosthetic group** to give the protein its **quaternary structure**.

11 Proteins may be **globular** or **fibrous**. The former are usually soluble and perform many regulatory functions (e.g. as enzymes), while the latter fulfil structural roles (e.g. collagen).

12 An important function of globular proteins is **buffering**. They owe this function to the presence of both positively and negatively charged groups in amino acids.

13 Humans can synthesise about half of the 20 naturally occurring amino acids involved in protein synthesis. The remainder, known as **essential amino acids**, are required in our diet. Most animal and some plant proteins contain a high proportion of the essential amino acids. Non-essential amino acids can be made from essential amino acids by **transamination**.

14 A mixture of proteins can be separated by **electrophoresis**. Progressive hydrolysis followed by **chromatography** enables the amino acid sequence of a protein to be established. **X-ray crystallography** can be used to work out the three-dimensional shape of the protein.

15 **Vitamins**, a mixed collection of organic compounds, are required by organisms for various metabolic purposes. Some of them function as coenzymes.

16 The chemical substances listed above are needed in a **balanced diet**. Shortage of any one of them can lead to various **deficiency diseases** and even death. Nucleic acids are also important chemicals of life, but can be made from other precursors, and so are not essential constituents of a balanced diet.

Review questions

1 Which of the following two possibilities do you think would have the more significant consequences for life on Earth and why: water having a freezing point of 10°C, or ice having a density slightly greater than that of liquid water?

2 Why are some minerals needed by organisms in much greater amounts than others?

3 Why do you think carbon is the element on which all life depends?

4 Explain why starch and cellulose differ so greatly in their properties even though both are polymers of glucose.

5 List the functions of lipids and relate these to their structure.

6 Plants contain more carbohydrate but less fat than animals. Why do you think this is?

7 Can you suggest two reasons why camels have large fat reserves in their humps?

8 Distinguish between the primary, secondary, tertiary and quaternary structure of proteins.

9 Why might taking antibiotics for a long period of time lead to vitamin K deficiency?

10 Suggest how the requirement for vitamin E in the human diet might be investigated.

Further reading

A readable account of the history of vitamin C is provided in Joan Solomon's *Discovering the Cure for Scurvy* (Association for Science Education, 1989). If you fancy a more detailed account, try Kenneth J. Carpenter's *The History of Scurvy and Vitamin C* (Cambridge University Press, 1986).

If you want to read more about biochemistry, a readable account is Steven Rose's *The Chemistry of Life* (Penguin, 1991).

The technique of protein sequencing and the structure of collagen and elastin are described in detail in *Biology, Advanced Topics*.

The cell as a basic unit

Cells carry out the essential processes that make the organism a living entity. There is really no such thing as a *typical* cell but, as we shall see, cells share certain structural and functional features and they are of almost universal occurrence in living organisms.

The cell is the basic structural and functional unit of an organism, and so it is not surprising that biologists have devoted a great deal of attention to its structure and the processes which go on inside it. The study of cells continues to be an exciting area of research as more sophisticated techniques become available for studying them.

In this chapter we shall look mainly at the *structure* of cells and their component parts. We shall not say much about the functional aspects at this stage for they will be dealt with much more fully in later chapters.

Cells as revealed by the light microscope

You will probably examine your first cells with the **light** (or **optical**) **microscope** and it is therefore best to start by considering the structure of cells as seen with this instrument. It was with a simple light microscope that cells were first discovered (see box on page 154).

An animal cell as seen with a light microscope

The structure of a typical animal cell as seen with a light microscope is illustrated in figure 10.1. The whole cell has a diameter of about one fiftieth of a millimetre (20 μm). It is bounded by a thin **plasma membrane** (also called the **cell surface membrane**). This encloses the **cytoplasm** which surrounds the **nucleus**.

On first examination the cytoplasm appears to be a uniformly homogeneous substance, but closer inspection of cells stained with special dyes shows it to contain numerous granules and inclusions. Food materials, for example **glycogen** (a polysaccharide), are stored in the cytoplasm and it is here that complex chemical reactions take place, building up materials and supplying energy for the cell's activities.

The nucleus is bounded by a **nuclear envelope** and contains a dense body called the **nucleolus** together with a material called **chromatin** which condenses into distinct bodies called **chromosomes** when the cell undergoes division. The chromosomes carry hereditary material in the form of DNA which determines the organism's characteristics and transmits these to subsequent generations.

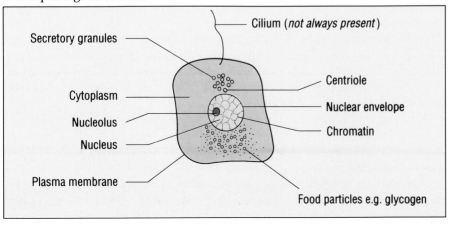

Figure 10.1 The structure of a generalised animal cell as seen under the light microscope. In suitable circumstances certain other structures can just be detected in the cytoplasm. These include mitochondria and the Golgi apparatus, both of which are described in detail later.

Figure 10.2 A typical plant cell with the nucleus near the side of the cell.

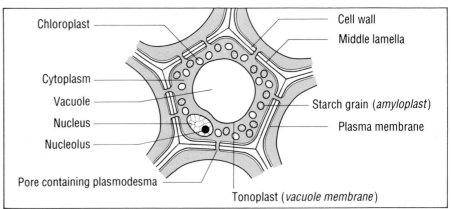

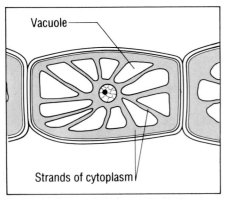

Figure 10.3 A typical plant cell with the nucleus in the centre.

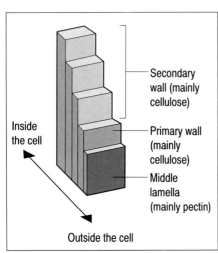

Figure 10.4 The various layers which make up the cell wall of a typical plant cell. Pectin is explained on page 131. The middle lamella and primary wall have considerable 'give' and are stretched as the cell grows and expands. The secondary wall consists of several layers of cellulose which are laid down in succession after growth has ceased. In some cells the secondary wall is hardened by impregnation with lignin to give wood or with suberin to give cork.

Later we shall have much to say about the functions of the nucleus. For the moment you should appreciate that it is vital for the continued life of the cell. This has been shown by removing it. Certain cells are large enough to permit this sort of operation to be carried out. For example, using special instruments it is possible to extract the nucleus from the single-celled protoctist *Amoeba*, which may be as large as a pinhead. When this is done the enucleated cell eventually dies. If, however, the nucleus is replaced sufficiently soon, the cell revives and will continue to live indefinitely. We now know that, although important chemical reactions take place in the cytoplasm, the nucleus is essential for directing activities.

The **centriole**, found just outside the nuclear envelope, plays an important part in the formation of **cilia** and **flagella**, slender motile 'hairs' that project from the surface of certain cells. The behaviour of the centriole is also related to the way cells divide when they multiply.

A plant cell as seen with a light microscope

As you can see in figure 10.2, most of the structures found in an animal cell also occur in plant cells. A typical plant cell, however, has certain additional features. The centre of the cell is taken up by a large **vacuole** filled with a solution containing sugars and salts, the **cell sap**. The cell is bounded by a plasma membrane beyond which is a comparatively thick **cell wall** made of the polysaccharide carbohydrate **cellulose**. This is tough but slightly elastic. The vacuole and cell wall play a major part in maintaining the shape and form of the cell, as we shall see in Chapter 12.

The central position of the vacuole means that the cytoplasm is concentrated at the sides of the cell. In most plant cells the nucleus is located somewhere in this peripheral cytoplasm, but not uncommonly it is suspended in the middle of the vacuole by slender strands of cytoplasm (figure 10.3).

Another consequence of the vacuole is that the cell has *two* membranes. In addition to the plasma membrane lining the outer surface of the cytoplasm (in contact with the cellulose wall), there is a membrane lining the inner surface bordering the vacuole. This membrane is called the **vacuole membrane** or **tonoplast**.

The cell wall is laid down during the development of the cell, and starts as a thin layer of **pectin** beneath which cellulose, secreted by the outer part of the cytoplasm, is laid down. This constitutes the **primary wall**. Further layers of cellulose make up the **secondary wall** (figure 10.4). The cellulose is strengthened by another polysaccharide called **hemicellulose** (see page 131). The point of demarcation between one cell and the next, known as the **middle lamella**, represents the fused pectate walls of the two adjoining cells.

Although each cell appears to be enclosed in a box of cellulose it is by no means isolated from its neighbours. The cellulose cell wall is interrupted at intervals by narrow pores carrying fine strands of cytoplasm which join the living cells to one another. These are called **plasmodesmata** and they facilitate the movement of materials between cells. We shall return to them presently.

Granules and inclusions found in the cytoplasm include hollow ovoid or spherical bodies called **plastids**. These are of two main types. **Leucoplasts** are usually colourless and contain starch: **starch grains** (amyloplasts) are found very widely in plant cells and they represent the major form of storage carbohydrate, equivalent to glycogen in animal cells. The other main type of plastid, **chloroplasts**, contains the green pigment **chlorophyll**. This plays a crucial role in photosynthesis, the process by which plants manufacture food materials.

Two levels of cellular organisation

Biologists today recognise a major distinction between two types of cell. The type which we have just been describing is called a **eukaryotic cell**. This means 'good or true nucleus' and reflects the fact that these cells have a clearly discernible nucleus. This is typical of the great majority of organisms including all animals and plants.

The other type of cell is called a **prokaryotic cell**, meaning 'before the nucleus'. Such cells do not have a nucleus, though they do have a long compacted strand of DNA in the middle of the cell. This type of cell is found in the Prokaryote kingdom which includes bacteria.

The distinction between eukaryotic and prokaryotic cells is one of the most fundamental dividing lines between living organisms. It is far more significant than the difference between animal and plant cells, which are both eukaryotic.

The definitions above are based only on the presence or absence of a nucleus. However, there are many other differences between eukaryotic and prokaryotic cells. In particular, eukaryotic cells have a full complement of membrane-bound **organelles** in their cytoplasm, whereas prokaryotes have a much simpler type of cell which lacks such organelles.

Fine structure of prokaryotic cells

A bacterium can be taken to illustrate the main features of a prokaryotic cell (figure 10.5). The cell is filled with **cytoplasm** but there is no membrane-bound nucleus. Instead there is a long strand of DNA with the ends joined to form a ring. This is sometimes referred to as the bacterial chromosome, though the term is misleading because it is much simpler than eukaryotic chromosomes. The ring of DNA is concentrated in certain areas of the cell and is called the **nucleoid**. In addition there may be smaller rings of DNA called **plasmids** which serve as additional chromosomes. In many disease-causing bacteria these plasmids are associated with resistance to antibiotics.

The cytoplasm contains **food storage particles**, **enzymes** and tiny granules called **ribosomes** where proteins are synthesised. The **mesosome**, formed by an intucking of the plasma membrane, is the site of respiration. Other smaller intuckings of the plasma membrane perform a similar function and may be involved in the formation of the cell wall.

Some bacteria are photosynthetic. They possess small membrane-lined **chromatophores** containing a pigment called **bacteriochlorophyll** which is similar to, but chemically simpler than, the chlorophyll of plants. The

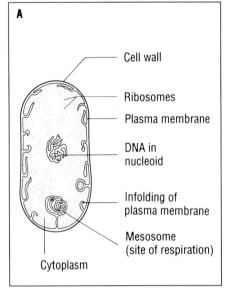

A

Cell wall

Ribosomes

Plasma membrane

DNA in nucleoid

Infolding of plasma membrane

Mesosome (site of respiration)

Cytoplasm

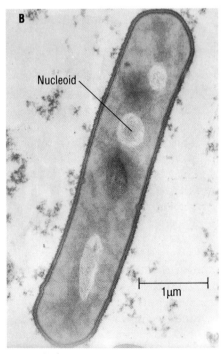

B

Nucleoid

1μm

Figure 10.5

A Diagram of a generalised bacterium to illustrate the structure of a prokaryotic cell.
B Electron micrograph of a longitudinal section of *Bacillus subtilis*.

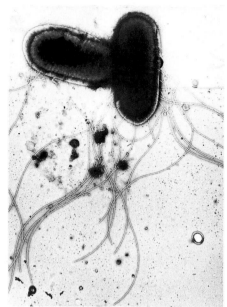

Figure 10.6 Electron micrograph of *Acetobacter*, a motile bacterium with flagella. Two cells are visible here. The flagella, revealed here by staining with phosphotungstate, are simple cylindrical threads which lack the elaborate internal structure typical of eukaryotic flagella. Because the bacterial flagellum is so different from the eukaryotic flagellum, it is sometimes given a different name: undulipodium.

chromatophore is a simple spherical body and lacks the complex internal structure typical of plant chloroplasts.

Other bacteria feed on organic substances: they secrete digestive enzymes across the cell surface and absorb the soluble products of digestion back into the cell.

Bacterial cells are lined with a **plasma membrane** which is similar to that of eukaryotic cells except that there are fewer types of phospholipid present. Outside the plasma membrane is a **cell wall** of variable thickness which is made of a substance unique to bacteria called **peptidoglycan**. This consists of a mucopolysaccharide and a polypeptide combined together and is quite different from the cellulose cell wall of plants. The cell wall helps to support the cell and maintain its shape.

Some bacteria possess, in addition to the cell wall, a slimy **capsule** which gives them extra protection against ingestion by phagocytes and may prevent them from drying out.

Certain bacteria such as the one shown in figure 10.6 have **flagella** for movement. However, they lack the internal structure typical of the flagella of eukaryotes. The bacterial flagellum is a hollow cylindrical thread equivalent to one of the microtubules inside a eukaryotic flagellum. It is shaped like a corkscrew and propels the cell, not by waving as does a eukaryotic flagellum, but by rotating about its axis like a propeller. It is one of the few rotating devices found in living organisms and its mode of attachment to the cell is surprisingly elaborate.

When a prokaryotic cell divides, the DNA replicates and the two strands move into the new cells without the aid of the elaborate spindle apparatus found in eukaryotes.

So the prokaryotic cell differs structurally from the eukaryotic cell in all sorts of ways. However, both have DNA, ATP and much the same range of enzymes and coenzymes. At the chemical level they are fundamentally similar.

The cell theory

Cells were first described in 1665 by Robert Hooke, a scientist of great talent and versatility who was an accomplished technician as well as a biologist. He designed one of the earliest optical microscopes with which he examined, amongst other things, thin sections of cork. He discovered that cork is composed of numerous box-like structures which we now know to be dead cells. Though Hooke coined the word cell for these structures, he did not realise their significance.

As more and more material was examined under the microscope, it gradually became apparent that the great majority of organisms are composed of cells. This idea is embodied in the cell theory. First proposed by M.J. Schleiden and

Theodore Schwann in 1839, the cell theory states that *cells are of universal occurrence and are the basic units of an organism.*

In 1849 cell division was described for the first time, and this led to a further facet being added to the cell theory. In 1859 Rudolf Virchow proposed that all cells come from pre-existing cells. This had not been appreciated before: Schwann thought that new cells arose from tiny particles in the fluid between cells.

During the twentieth century biologists have used increasingly powerful microscopes to study the structure of cells. At the same time various biochemical techniques have been used to unravel the metabolic pathways and molecular structures that are fundamental to the processes of life.

From your current knowledge of biology, do you think that the cell really is the 'basic unit of an organism? Can you suggest a possible alternative?

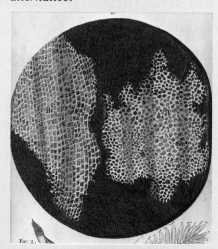

Robert Hooke's drawing of cork cells from his famous *Micrographia*, published in 1665.

Fine structure of eukaryotic cells

Eukaryotic cells are characterised by the possession of membrane-bound organelles. In a sense organelles stand in relation to the cell as organs do to the whole organism. For example, some organelles have a digestive function, breaking down complex molecules inside the cell. They are analogous to the gut of an animal, although they have an entirely different structure.

Figure 10.7 is an electron micrograph of an animal cell and figure 10.8 is a diagram of an animal cell based on detailed examination of numerous

Figure 10.7 Electron micrograph of a very thin section of a pancreas cell.

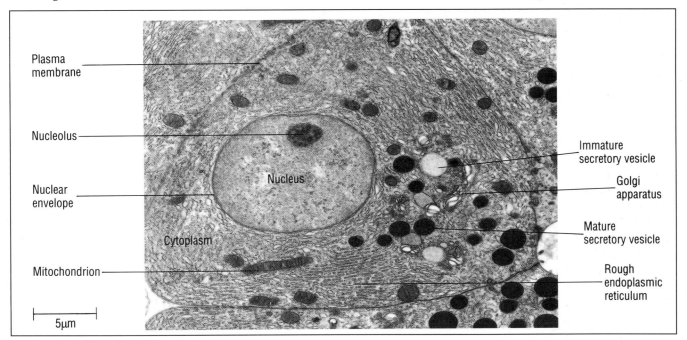

Figure 10.8 Fine structure of a generalised animal cell based on studies with the electron microscope.

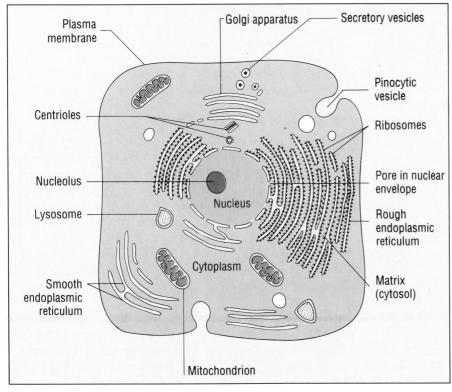

Figure 10.9 Fine structure of a generalised plant cell based on studies with the electron microscope.

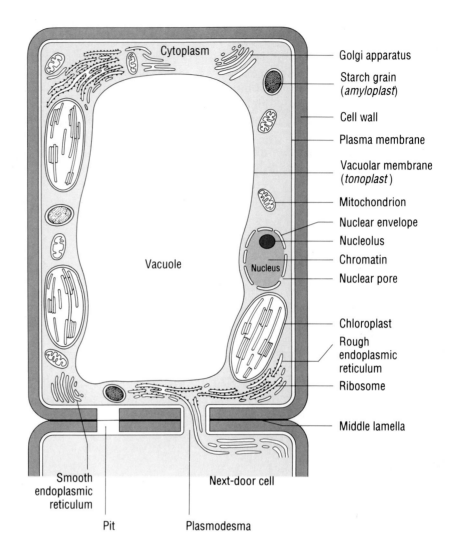

Figure 10.10 The endoplasmic reticulum consists of a series of parallel membranes, encrusted with ribosomes, enclosing a system of interconnected flattened cavities.

A Diagram of part of the endoplasmic reticulum.

B Electron micrograph of endoplasmic reticulum in a pancreas cell.

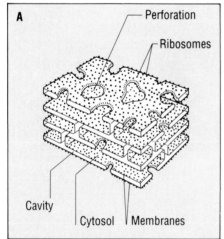

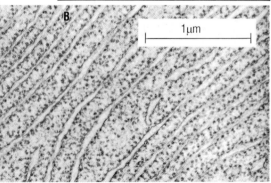

electron micrographs. Figure 10.9 is a similar diagram of a plant cell. We suggest that you refer to these illustrations as you read the following description of the various components of the eukaryotic cell.

The cytosol and endoplasmic reticulum

You will see immediately that the cytoplasm is a highly organised material. It consists of a soluble ground substance called the **cytosol** containing a system of parallel flattened cavities lined with a thin membrane about 4 nm thick (nm is the symbol for nanometre, a thousandth of a micrometre).

This system is known as the **endoplasmic reticulum**, or **ER** for short. The cavities are interconnected as shown in figure 10.10 and the lining membranes are continuous with the nuclear envelope. Attached to the cytosol side of the membranes are numerous **ribosomes**. Manufactured in the nucleolus, these are the sites where proteins are synthesised in the cell. In places the ribosomes are clustered together in small groups called **polyribosomes**.

The bulk of the endoplasmic reticulum in most cells is studded with ribosomes and accordingly is known as **rough endoplasmic reticulum**. Its general function is to isolate and transport the proteins which have been synthesised by the ribosomes. Many of these proteins are not required by the cell in which they are made but are for export, i.e. they are secreted by the cell. Such proteins include enzymes and hormones. Inside the cell these secretions may take the form of membrane-bound **zymogen granules**.

The endoplasmic reticulum is thus a kind of intracellular transport system helping to move materials from one part of the cell to another. In this connection it is interesting that the nuclear envelope is pierced by tiny pores, thus providing a route by which materials might move from the nucleus to the cytoplasm and vice versa. These pores can be seen in figure 10.11.

In certain parts of some cells the endoplasmic reticulum is not studded with ribosomes and accordingly is known as **smooth endoplasmic reticulum**. This is not continuous with the rough endoplasmic reticulum and its cavities are tubular rather than flattened sacs. It is seen particularly in cells of the liver, gut and certain glands, and is concerned with the synthesis and transport of lipids and steroids.

The cytoskeleton

Until recently the cytosol was thought to be little more than a fluid. However, it has now been shown to contain a three-dimensional network of extremely fine protein filaments, a mere 5 or 6 nm wide, rather like a spider's web. These filaments connect the various organelles such as the mitochondria with the endoplasmic reticulum, holding them in place.

This **cytoskeleton**, as it is called, was discovered by examining very thick sections with an extremely powerful transmission electron microscope. Why do you think thick sections were used, and why did the electron microscope have to be so powerful? Other components of the cytoskeleton are described on page 163.

Golgi apparatus

With special staining techniques the **Golgi apparatus** can be detected under the optical microscope as a particularly dense part of the cytoplasm, and as such it has exercised the minds of biologists ever since it was discovered by the Italian physician Camillo Golgi at the end of the nineteenth century.

Secretory vesicles are closely associated with the Golgi apparatus, suggesting that it may be concerned with the production of substances by the cell.

Figure 10.11 Pores (**P**) in the nuclear envelope as seen under the electron microscope, **A** in section and **B** in surface view.

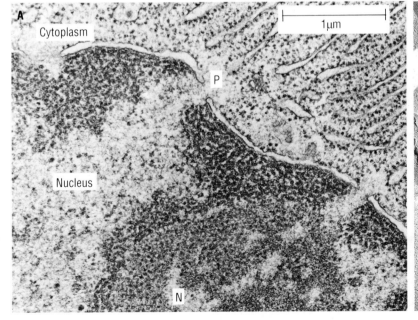

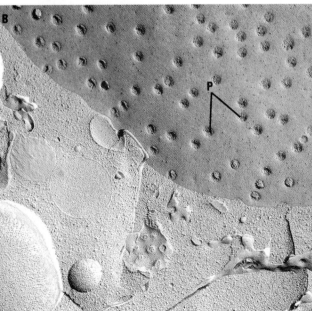

Different kinds of microscopes and microscopy

The **light (optical) microscope** was invented in the seventeenth century, and although it has been refined in many ways it is essentially the same now as it was then. A modern light microscope is shown in illustration 1. Light rays from a light source beneath the stage are transmitted through two glass lenses in series, the objective and ocular (eyepiece) lenses. Depending on their strength, these two lenses together routinely provide magnifications of up to 400 times.

The light microscope has had a profound influence on biology, but there is a limit to the amount of detail which it can show. This limit is set by its **resolving power**.

The resolving power is the minimum distance by which two points must be separated in order for them to be perceived as two separate points rather than as a single fused image. For the light microscope this distance is approximately 0.2 μm. In theory it might seem possible to magnify an object indefinitely by means of glass lenses in series, but

Illustration 1 A modern light microscope. Light rays from a source beneath the stage are transmitted through a glass condenser lens, through the specimen and then through two glass lenses, the objective and eye-piece lenses.

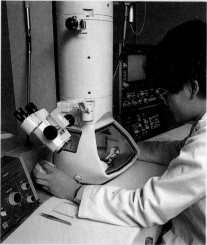

Illustration 2 A high resolution electron microscope currently used in biological research. Such an instrument has a resolving power of about 0.2 nm and achieves magnifications of about 240 000 times. The operator inserts into the microscope a tiny copper grid on which an ultra-thin section of the specimen has been placed. The section is made by embedding the tissue, suitably fixed and dehydrated, in plastic, then slicing it with an ultramicrotome which cuts very thin sections less than 100 nm thick. After mounting the section on the grid it is treated with heavy metal stains which scatter the electrons in such a way that individual structures can be distinguished..

in practice this only produces a larger, fuzzier picture; the resolution is not improved and no more detail is visible.

The limited resolution of the light microscope is imposed by the wavelength of visible light, and it means that little can be gained by magnifying an object more than 1500 times. This puts a limit on the amount of structural detail that can be detected within a cell. Higher magnifications with good resolution can be achieved by using a special objective lens with a fluid situated between the lens and the objective (**oil immersion**). But even then it is not possible to achieve effective magnifications of more than 2000 times.

Since the 1950s microscopic studies have been revolutionised by the development of the **electron microscope**. This instrument uses an electron beam instead of light, and electromagnets instead of glass lenses. The electrons are recorded on a photographic plate, which then forms a viewable image on a screen.

The electron beam has a much shorter wavelength than light, with the result that a modern electron microscope has a resolving power a thousand times greater than an optical microscope. This means that objects can be magnified much more without loss of clarity.

As we have seen, a good light microscope can only magnify an object effectively about 1500 times. The electron microscope can give clear pictures that are magnified 500 000 times. It is important to appreciate what this means in practice: with the electron microscope an object the size of a pinhead can be enlarged to the point at which it has a diameter of well over a kilometre; a cell with a diameter of 10 micrometres finishes up with a diameter of five metres.

It is difficult to exaggerate the impact which this instrument has had on biology. Materials which were formerly described as structureless have been shown to have an elaborate internal organisation, and so-called homogeneous fluids are now known to contain a variety of complex structures. The electron microscope has opened up a new world whose existence was barely realised fifty years ago.

But there are problems. One snag is that the material for examination has to be mounted in a vacuum, and is therefore dead, before it can be viewed. This, coupled with the preliminary treatment to which the material has to be subjected, may distort the delicate structures inside cells and create images that are not

A
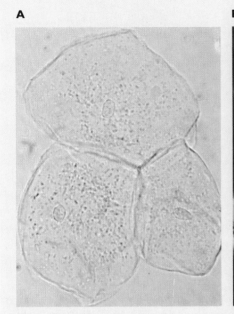

B
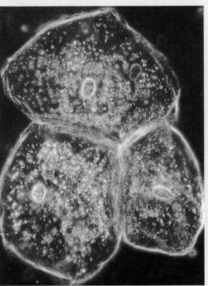

C
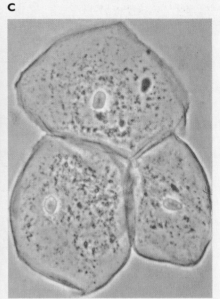

Illustration 3 Three kinds of light microscopy were used to photograph the same cheek cells:
A conventional light microscope with bright ground illumination
B dark ground illumination
C phase contrast.
Magnification × 1500.

'real'. These are called **artefacts** (literally 'of artificial making'). The electron microscopist is always on the look-out for such artefacts and uses every means to prevent them occurring.

To some extent these problems can be overcome by using other types of microscopy in addition to the electron microscope. The **phase-contrast microscope**, for example, enables transparent objects to be seen, and is ideal for studying unstained living cells. Special illumination techniques can also be employed for increasing the contrast between the object and its background; for example, **dark-ground illumination**, in which the object is illuminated from above against a dark background, enables tiny structures inside cells to be seen clearly. Another technique is to examine the object in polarised light:

the **polarising microscope** is useful for differentiating between different types of material embedded in another substance.

The kind of electron microscope shown in illustration 2 is called a **transmission electron microscope** because the electrons pass through the specimen. In the more recently developed **scanning electron microscope** solid specimens are bombarded with a beam of electrons which causes

secondary electrons to be emitted from the surface layers of the specimen. These electrons are recorded on a photographic plate and the image is viewed on a screen, as with the transmission electron microscope. The scanning electron microscope enables details of the surface to be seen very clearly as, for example, in illustration 4. However, it can only magnify up to about 80 000 times.

Illustration 4 A scanning electronmicrograph of a tick. Notice the pittings on the surface of its cuticle. Magnification × 80.

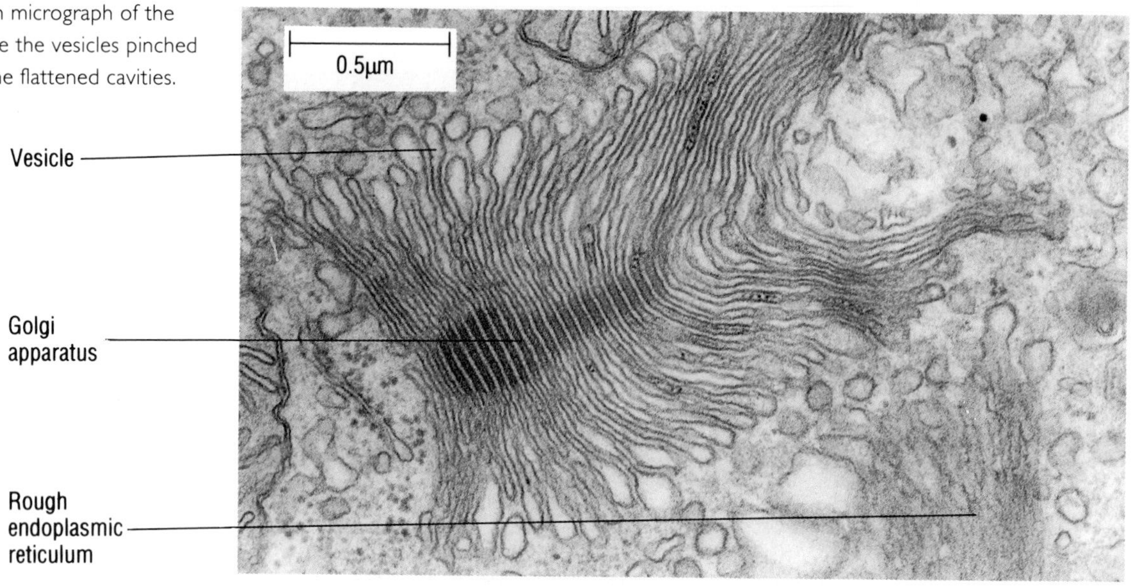

Figure 10.12 Electron micrograph of the Golgi apparatus. Notice the vesicles pinched off from the ends of the flattened cavities.

Vesicle ——

Golgi apparatus ——

Rough endoplasmic reticulum ——

0.5μm

Figure 10.12 shows what the Golgi apparatus looks like in the electron microscope. It consists of a stack of flattened cavities lined with smooth ER close to which are numerous secretory vesicles. Figure 10.13 summarises what is thought to happen. The Golgi cavities are formed by the fusion of vesicles which are pinched off the rough ER. Vesicles containing the secretory molecules then get pinched off the cavities of the Golgi apparatus. These vesicles move to the surface of the cell and discharge their contents to the exterior. So the Golgi apparatus is an assembly point through which raw materials for secretion are funnelled before being shed from the cell.

This hypothesis has received support from experiments in which the distribution of radioactively labelled substances taken up by the cell is followed by autoradiography (see page 210). Nearly all cell secretions are glycoproteins, i.e. proteins conjugated with a carbohydrate. Newly synthe-

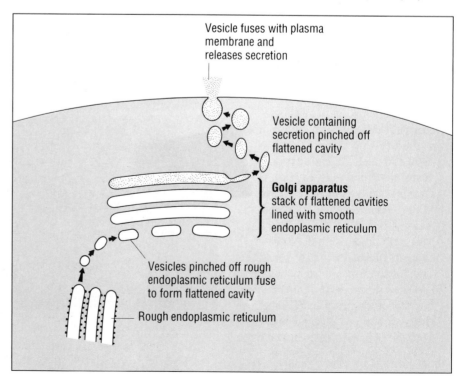

Vesicle fuses with plasma membrane and releases secretion

Vesicle containing secretion pinched off flattened cavity

Golgi apparatus stack of flattened cavities lined with smooth endoplasmic reticulum

Vesicles pinched off rough endoplasmic reticulum fuse to form flattened cavity

Rough endoplasmic reticulum

Figure 10.13 Schematic diagram illustrating the formation and function of the Golgi apparatus. Protein and carbohydrate derived from the channels of the rough endoplasmic reticulum are combined in the Golgi apparatus to form a glycoprotein secretion which is discharged from the cell as shown.

sised proteins are found in the channels of the rough ER. From here they move to the Golgi apparatus where the carbohydrate is added to them. They then leave the cell. Thus, the function of the Golgi apparatus is to add the carbohydrate component to the protein and package the finished product before it leaves the cell.

An example of a glycoprotein produced by the Golgi apparatus is mucus, the slimy substance which serves as a lubricant in animals. The Golgi apparatus also produces materials for making plant cell walls and the cuticles of insects. It also performs the incidental function of replenishing the plasma membrane: when one of its vesicles empties its contents to the exterior, the membrane lining the vesicle fuses with, and thus becomes part of, the plasma membrane. In addition certain Golgi vesicles contain digestive enzymes and become lysosomes.

Mitochondria

Embedded in the cytosol are variable numbers of **mitochondria**. Under the phase-contrast microscope, or light microscope with dark-ground illumination, they appear as minute rods, but under the electron microscope their internal structure becomes apparent. A typical cell contains about a thousand mitochondria, though some have many more than this. Their

Investigating the functions of cell organelles

To some extent the functions of organelles such as mitochondria may be tentatively surmised from their appearance in the electron microscope and from their reactions to various stains and so on. But to obtain reliable information it is necessary to isolate the individual organelles and test their properties separately.

The organelles can be isolated by **differential centrifugation**. First the cells are broken open, and their contents released, by homogenising a tissue such as liver in a suitable isotonic solution that does not adversely affect the cells' contents. The solution is ice-cold so as to prevent the action of enzymes which might damage the organelles. The homogenisation may be carried out in a blender of the type commonly used in the kitchen. The resulting suspension is then poured into a tube which is spun in a centrifuge at a speed of rotation that causes the heaviest organelles to be thrown to the bottom, forming a **sediment**. The other lighter organelles remain floating in the clear **supernatant**

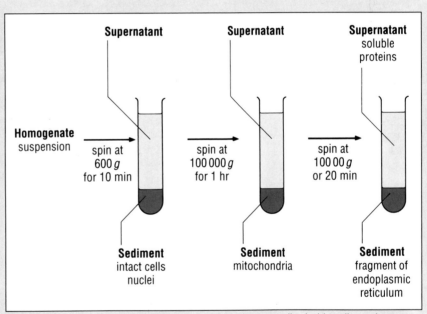

Differential centrifugation, the technique by which the organelles inside cells can be isolated. g is the unit of gravitational force: spinning at 600g means that the homogenate is subjected to a centrifugal force 600 times the force of gravity.

fluid above the sediment.

The supernatant fluid is then removed from the tube, leaving the sediment behind. The particular organelles in the sediment can then be investigated. Meanwhile the supernatant fluid is spun again at a higher speed so that another organelle is thrown down to form a new sediment. The supernatant fluid can then be re-spun at an even higher speed. In this way the different organelles can be collected and investigated separately. The supernatant fluid finally contains only soluble proteins which may be analysed by techniques of the kind described on page 143. The whole procedure is summarised in the illustration.

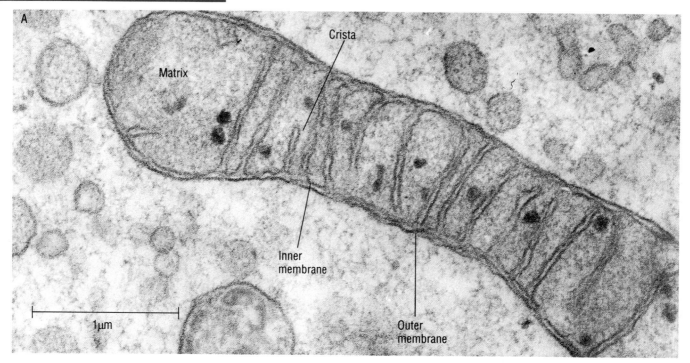

A

Crista

Matrix

Inner membrane

Outer membrane

1µm

Figure 10.14 Structure of a mitochondrion.
A Electron micrograph of a large mitochondrion in longitudinal section from the oocyte of a bird. Notice the cristae projecting into the hollow interior.
B Cutaway view showing the inside of a mitochondrion. Many of the chemical reactions involved in the transfer of energy (respiration) take place in the matrix and on the cristae. Tiny stalked particles attached to the surface of the cristae, of diameter approximately 8 nm, are the site of ATP synthesis. They are shown in **C**.

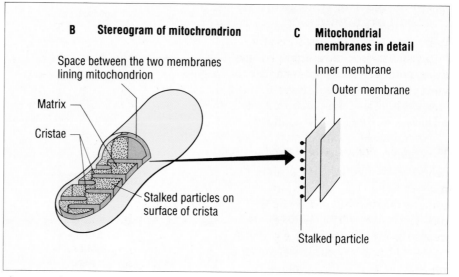

B   **Stereogram of mitochrondrion**

Space between the two membranes lining mitochondrion

Matrix

Cristae

Stalked particles on surface of crista

C   **Mitochondrial membranes in detail**

Inner membrane

Outer membrane

Stalked particle

shape and size vary, but generally they are sausage shaped with a diameter of approximately 1.0 µm and a length of about 2.5 µm.

The wall of the mitochondrion consists of two thin membranes separated by an extremely narrow fluid-filled space. The inner membrane is highly folded, giving rise to an irregular series of partitions, or **cristae**, which project into the interior (figure 10.14). The interior contains an organic **matrix** containing numerous chemical compounds.

The mitochondrion is one of the cell's most important organelles: it is here that most of the chemical reactions of aerobic respiration take place. During respiration energy is transferred to ATP, and this energy is then available for a variety of cellular functions. Some of these reactions take place in the matrix of the mitochondrion, while others occur on the inner membrane and in the cytosol. The cristae have the effect of increasing the surface area so that more ATP can be produced.

Cells whose function requires them to expend particularly large amounts of energy contain unusually large numbers of mitochondria. These are often packed close together in the part of the cell where the energy is required. This is seen dramatically in spermatozoa where the mitochondria are tightly packed at the base of the motile tail (see page 587). Mitochondria are also found alongside the contractile fibrils in muscle, and at the surface of cells where active transport occurs. In some cases the cristae may be very close together thus further increasing the surface area *within* each mitochondrion (figure 10.15).

Lysosomes

Also prominent in the cytoplasm of most cells are dark-staining spherical bodies called **lysosomes**. The word 'lysis' means to break apart, and lysosomes contain digestive enzymes responsible for splitting complex chemical compounds into simpler ones. Digestion is carried out in a membrane-lined vacuole into which several lysosomes may discharge their contents. This is discussed in more detail on page 205.

Another important function of lysosomes is to destroy worn-out organelles within the cell (figure 10.16). The unwanted structures, whether mitochondria, part of the endoplasmic reticulum or some other organelles, become enclosed in a membrane which forms a bag around them. Into this bag several lysosomes discharge their contents. The organelles are broken down by the lysosome enzymes, and the soluble products are absorbed into the surrounding cytoplasm where they may be used in the construction of new organelles.

Sometimes lysosomes may destroy the entire cell. In this case the lysosome membrane ruptures, liberating the enzymes. These proceed to digest the contents of the cell, killing it in the process. This may seem rather disastrous but in certain instances it may be advantageous, as for example when old damaged cells have to be replaced by new ones or when certain embryonic tissues are discarded during development. For example, tadpole tails are destroyed this way during metamorphosis.

Microtubules and microfilaments

Tube-like structures with a diameter of about 20 nm have been found in many cells. These are called **microtubules** and they are made of the protein **tubulin**. Microtubules are widely distributed in the cytoplasm where they may occur singly or in bundles. The spindle fibres involved in cell division are also made of tubulin (see page 555).

Microtubules seem to be associated with cellular movements and with transport inside cells. One of their more remarkable properties is the apparent ease with which they dissociate and reassemble.

Microtubules can be assembled in one part of the cell where they are needed, then taken apart and reassembled later in another part of the cell. In dividing root tip cells, for example, microtubules assemble to form the spindle. They then disintegrate and reassemble in the vicinity of the developing cell plate, and later still they are seen immediately beneath the cell wall, where they are involved in the deposition of cellulose.

Another place where we find microtubules is in cilia and flagella which will be discussed shortly.

Microfilaments are about a quarter of the diameter of microtubules (5 nm) and are solid, not tubular. Like microtubules, they are made of protein and can be readily assembled and disassembled. They occur in bundles in the cytoplasm where they are associated with cell motility such as cytoplasmic streaming and muscle contraction.

Microfilaments and microtubules are part of the **cytoskeleton** referred to on page 157. However, because of their ability to disassemble and

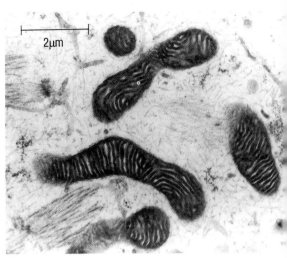

Figure 10.15 Electron micrograph of mitochondria in the heart muscle of a bird. Notice the numerous cristae packed close together inside the mitochondria, reflecting the high energy requirement of the muscle tissue.

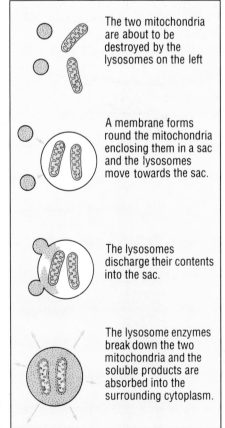

The two mitochondria are about to be destroyed by the lysosomes on the left

A membrane forms round the mitochondria enclosing them in a sac and the lysosomes move towards the sac.

The lysosomes discharge their contents into the sac.

The lysosome enzymes break down the two mitochondria and the soluble products are absorbed into the surrounding cytoplasm.

Figure 10.16 Diagrams to show how lysosomes destroy unwanted organelles in a cell. In this case two mitochondria are being broken down.

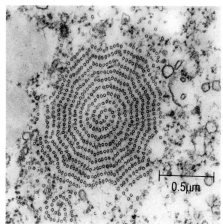

Figure 10.17 Electron micrograph of microtubules in *Actinosphaerium*, a single-celled protoctist related to *Amoeba*. Projecting from the cell body are numerous rigid pseudopodia called axopods, each stiffened internally by a spiral array of longitudinally arranged microtubules. The microtubules, each about 20 nm in diameter, are here seen in a cross-section of one of the axopods. The axopods are for feeding: food particles caught by an axopod are drawn to the cell body by retraction of the axopod. Retraction is achieved by dissolution of the microtubules from the tip inwards by disassembly of their constituent protein chains.

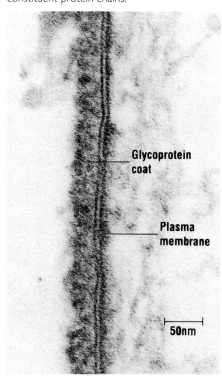

Glycoprotein coat

Plasma membrane

Figure 10.18 Electron micrograph of the plasma membrane and associated structures of *Amoeba proteus*.

reassemble so rapidly, they form a dynamic system of moving parts which is much more than just a skeleton. This is illustrated by the tiny 'sun animalicule' *Actinosphaerium* whose microtubules are shown in figure 10.17. The chemistry of microtubules and microfilaments is explained on page 141.

The cell surface

The thin plasma membrane (figure 10.18) seen under the light microscope turns out to be rather more complex when viewed in the electron microscope. When viewed in section, as in figure 10.18, it appears to be made up of three layers: two dark layers, separated by a lighter region. The total thickness of the membrane is approximately 7.0 nm (see page 168 for a detailed description).

It used to be thought that the two dark layers were protein and the light region in between was lipid. The plasma membrane was therefore seen as a thin sandwich of lipid contained between two layers of protein. However, we now know that the two dark lines are caused by the deposition of heavy metal on both sides of the membrane during the staining of the sections. This is a good example of an artefact (see page 159).

Beyond the plasma membrane is a **glycoprotein coat** of variable thickness. Cells touching each other are separated by this intercellular material. Through it materials pass as they flow in and out of cells.

Pinocytic and phagocytic vesicles

Various structures are associated with the surface of the cell. Of these the most universal are **pinocytic vesicles**, flask-like invaginations of the plasma membrane. The neck of the flask eventually closes up so that the vesicle becomes sealed off from the outside and becomes entirely enclosed within the cell. An animal cell may contain numerous small vesicles which are constantly being formed by pinocytosis at the cell surface. As we shall see later, this provides a means by which large molecules may be taken into the cell. It is thought that the large sap-filled **vacuole** characteristic of mature plant cells is formed by the fusion of numerous small vesicles derived from pinocytosis.

In some cells, much larger flask-like invaginations are formed. These are called **phagocytic vesicles** and they provide a way of drawing food particles into the cell. The cells of certain animals and protoctists also contain **food vacuoles** which are derived from the plasma membrane by phagocytosis. This is how, for example, *Amoeba* feeds (see page 205).

Microvilli

It has already been mentioned that one function of the plasma membrane is to permit the entry of materials into the cell. Plainly, the greater the surface area of the plasma membrane the greater will be the exchange of materials across it. To this end, the plasma membrane of many cells is folded to form numerous minute projections called **microvilli**.

Each microvillus is a very thin, finger-like process about 1.0 μm long and 0.08 μm wide. It is lined with plasma membrane and filled with cytoplasm which is continuous with that in the main body of the cell. Microvilli are only visible in the electron microscope though the larger ones, if densely packed, may show up under the light microscope as a fuzzy line at the cell surface, the so-called **brush border** (figure 10.19).

Two places where microvilli abound are the epithelial lining of the convoluted tubules in the kidney and the lining of the small intestine. In both cases they increase the surface area of the epithelium, thereby aiding

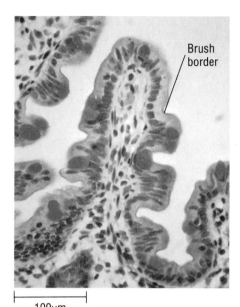

Brush
border

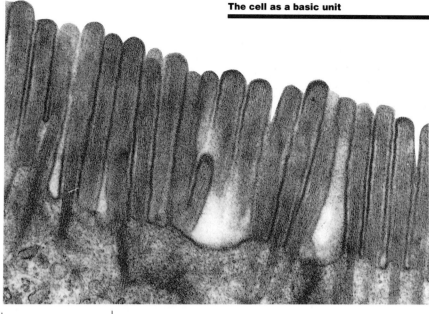

100μm

2μm

absorption of materials from the enclosed cavity. It has been estimated that a single epithelial cell may have 3000 microvilli and that in one square millimetre of intestinal lining there may be as many as 200 000 000, giving a twenty-fold increase to the surface area. Some of these microvilli contain microfilaments and undergo squeezing, worm-like movements, thereby creating a pumping effect which may aid absorption.

Cilia and flagella

The surface of certain cells is drawn out to form elongated **cilia** or **flagella**. Cilia and flagella are fundamentally similar but the former are usually shorter and more numerous than flagella (an average flagellum has a length of about 100 μm, a cilium 5 to 10 μm). Both have the ability to undulate or lash back and forth, and their functions depend on this.

Many unicellular organisms move by means of cilia or flagella. The surface of the freshwater protoctist *Paramecium*, for example, is covered with cilia which beat in a coordinated fashion, driving the organism through the water. Another freshwater protoctist *Euglena* has a single flagellum, which propels the organism by means of rapid undulations passing from the base to the tip. Many aquatic larvae have cilia for movement (figure 10.20).

Sometimes cilia occur on the underside of quite large animals such as flatworms and marine snails. Here their rapid beating, aided by muscular contractions of the body wall, enables the animal to glide on smooth surfaces.

Flagella are nearly always associated with locomotion, but cilia, which are found more widely, perform other functions as well. For example, they are often found lining ducts and tubules and other specialised surfaces, along which materials are wafted by means of their rapid and rhythmical beatings.

Until the advent of the electron microscope very little was known about the internal structure of cilia and flagella. The reason for this was that they are extremely fine, being less than 0.3 μm in diameter. They are therefore barely visible under the light microscope. However, the electron microscope has enabled cell biologists to analyse their detailed structure.

Cross-sections of a cilium show that it contains a bundle of micro-tubules which run longitudinally along its length. These are arranged in a

Figure 10.19

Left The brush border on the epithelial cells of the small intestine seen with a light microscope.

Right Electron micrograph of a small part of the brush border showing it to consist of microvilli. Notice the microfilaments inside each microvillus.

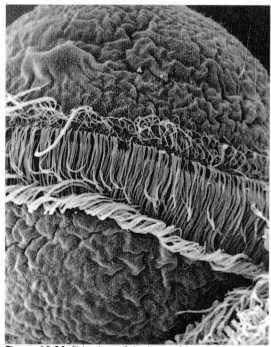

Figure 10.20 Side view of the larva of a mollusc showing the girdle of cilia by which it moves through the water. This is a scanning electron micrograph. Magnification × 1000.

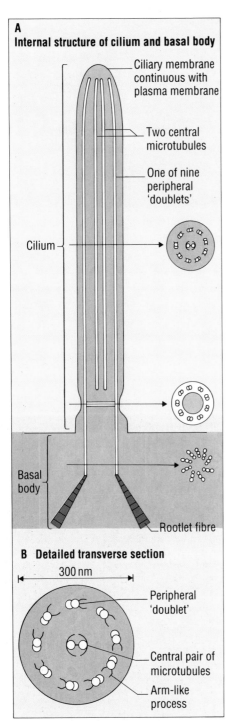

A
Internal structure of cilium and basal body

Ciliary membrane continuous with plasma membrane

Two central microtubules

One of nine peripheral 'doublets'

Cilium

Basal body

Rootlet fibre

B Detailed transverse section

300 nm

Peripheral 'doublet'

Central pair of microtubules

Arm-like process

Figure 10.21 The detailed structure of cilia and flagella based on electron micrographs. Note that the peripheral microtubules penetrate into the basal body where they may be attached to collagen rootlet fibres (not always present).

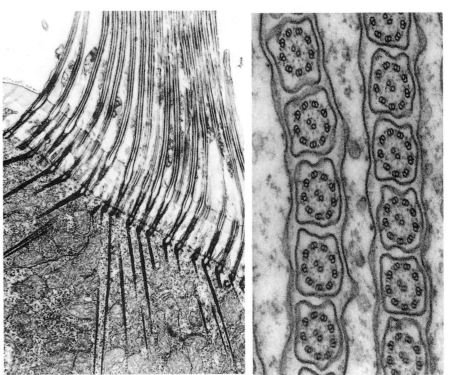

Figure 10.21 (*continued*) Fine structure of cilia and flagella as seen in the electron microscope. *Left* Longitudinal section of a tuft of cilia from the larva of the marine annelid *Harmothöe*. *Right* Transverse section through the flagella of the protoctist *Trichonympha*. Notice the 9+2 arrangement of microtubules within each flagellum.

precise way: there are two in the centre surrounded by a ring of nine paired ones, called **doublets**. This arrangement is described as the **9+2 pattern**. This assemblage of microtubules is enclosed within a membrane which is continuous with the plasma membrane (figure 10.21).

At the base of the cilium is an elaborate attachment apparatus consisting of a basal body from which rootlet fibres may be seen to penetrate into the deeper layers of the cytoplasm. The basal body is composed of a ring of microtubules continuous with those in the cilium itself. However, the two central microtubules are absent, and the peripheral ones are in threes (**triplets**). Little arm-like processes project from the peripheral doublets. These are thought to be the site of ATP hydrolysis where energy is transferred for bending of the flagellum or cilium.

How do cilia and flagella move? The current theory suggests that bending is brought about by the peripheral microtubules sliding relative to one another, each doublet sliding past its next door neighbour.

Other structures with the same organisation as cilia

As you can see in figure 10.8 on page 155, an animal cell has two rod-like **centrioles** situated at right angles to each other. Under the light microscope these appear as a single unit. Their behaviour in cell division is discussed in Chapter 31 and for the moment we will concern ourselves only with their structure.

A discovery of great interest was that the centrioles have an internal structure similar to that of the basal body of cilia and flagella, each rod containing a ring of nine triplets, but no central microtubules. This is no coincidence, for centrioles are responsible for the formation of cilia and

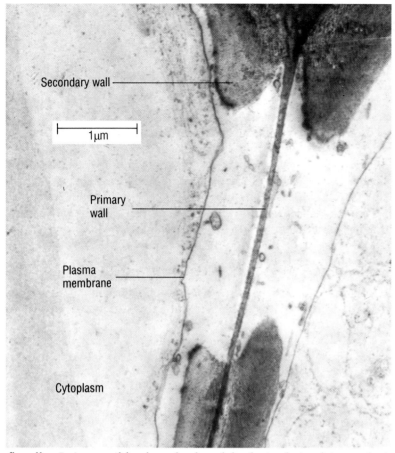

Secondary wall

1μm

Primary wall

Plasma membrane

Cytoplasm

Figure 10.22 Electron micrograph of a pit between two cortical cells in the root of the pea plant *Pisum*. Notice the complete absence of the secondary cell wall, only the primary wall being present.

flagella. It is possible that the basal body is derived in evolution from a centriole which migrated towards the edge of the cell and became associated with the plasma membrane. It is now known that the centriole is the organising centre for all the microtubules in animal cells, including those inside the cilia and flagella.

Another surprising place where the ciliary structure appears is in the eye of vertebrates. The light-sensitive cells in the retina have been shown to contain nine peripheral microtubules. Moreover they also possess basal bodies and rootlet fibres just like ordinary cilia. These cells are certainly not concerned with movement but their tell-tale internal structure suggests that they may have evolved from ciliated cells which lost their motility and became adapted for the reception of light stimuli. It seems that the 9+2 pattern of microtubules arose at an early stage in evolution and, despite much modification, is now a basic feature of many eukaryotic cells.

Chloroplasts and cell wall

These two features are unique to plants and certain other autotrophs. The fine structure of the **chloroplast** is discussed in Chapter 17. With regard to the **cell wall**, the electron microscope has confirmed earlier light microscope studies that it is not a uniform structure but is composed of **primary** and **secondary walls** as described on page 152.

In places the cell wall is absent altogether, giving rise to a **pit**. Where pits occur, two adjacent cells may be separated only by the primary wall (figure 10.22). Presumably the thinness of the wall in these regions facilitates movement of materials between adjoining cells. This function also applies to the **plasmodesmata**. The electron microscope has shown that the plasmodesmata contain endoplasmic reticulum which is therefore continuous from cell to cell (figure 10.23).

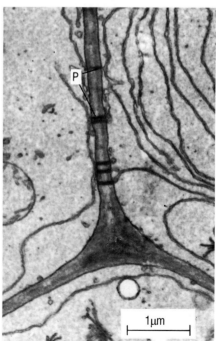

P

1μm

Figure 10.23 Plasmodesmata (**P**) linking adjacent cells in a root cap cell of maize. Notice that the plasmodesmata are connected to the endoplasmic reticulum and pass through the wall of the cell.

A

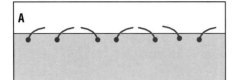

A polar lipid spreads out over the surface of water. The polar ends of the molecules, being soluble in water, enter the water while the insoluble hydrocarbon chains stay outside. If there is a large surface and comparatively few lipid molecules, the latter lie parallel to the surface as shown.

B

But if a large number of lipid molecules are packed together on a restricted surface, the hydrocarbon chains project from the water at right angles to the surface. This gives a monolayer of lipid at the air-water interface.

C

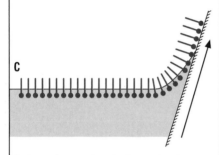

A clean glass surface is drawn slowly out through the lipid monolayer. The lipid molecules adhere to the glass as shown.

D

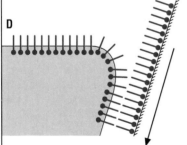

If the glass surface, after drying, is then pushed back through the lipid monolayer, the two layers of lipid molecules arrange themselves as shown, forming a lipid bilayer. This has a number of properties in common with the plasma membrane.

Figure 10.24 Diagrams illustrating the formation of a lipid bilayer. The polar ends of the lipid molecules are shown as solid dots, the hydrocarbon chains as bold lines.

Molecular structure of the plasma membrane

It is possible to make certain predictions about the structure of the plasma membrane from its physico-chemical properties. For example, substances that dissolve in oil penetrate it particularly rapidly, suggesting that it contains lipid. This is supported by the observation that its permeability properties are greatly influenced by treatment with lipid solvents.

How, then, are the lipid molecules arranged in the plasma membrane? A clue is provided by the properties of lipids. In certain lipids (phospho-lipids, for example) the long hydrocarbon chains which project from the glycerol part of the molecule are insoluble in water whereas the glycerol end of the molecule is water soluble, because it contains polar groups (see page 135). Now when such a lipid is allowed to spread over the surface of pure water, the water-soluble ends of the lipid molecules are drawn into the water and the insoluble hydrocarbon chains, if the molecules are sufficiently tightly packed, point directly away from the surface of the water. Thus we get a single layer of lipid molecules with their hydrocarbon chains orientated at right angles to the surface, a so-called **monolayer**.

The lipid component of the plasma membrane cannot in fact be a monolayer for this is only formed where there is a water surface in contact with air, and the plasma membrane generally has water in contact with both sides. However, when the non-polar sides of two monolayers are brought into contact, the non-polar ends of the lipid molecules are attracted to each other to form a **lipid bilayer** (figure 10.24). Might the plasma membrane be similarly constructed?

Research has shown that the plasma membrane is indeed a lipid bilayer, but it is more than that for it also contains protein.

The fluid-mosaic model

At one time it was thought that protein formed a continuous layer covering both sides of the membrane. However, it is now known that it takes the form of globules dotted about here and there in a mosaic pattern (figure 10.25). Some of the globules are attached to the surface of the membrane, while others penetrate into it to varying extents – indeed, some of them extend right through it and stick out on the other side.

The membrane is thought to be far less rigid than was originally supposed. Experiments on its viscosity suggest that it is of a fluid consistency rather like oil, and that there is considerable sideways movement of the lipid and protein molecules within it. On account of its fluidity and the mosaic arrangement of the protein molecules, this is known as the **fluid-mosaic model**.

The fluid-mosaic model was put forward in the early 1970s by S.J. Singer of the University of California and G.L. Nicholson of the Salk Institute. There is now sufficient evidence for us to feel confident that it is correct. For example, pieces of plasma membrane have been treated from one side with chemicals which react with the proteins but cannot pass through the membrane. In some cases the reactions are confined to the side of the membrane to which the chemicals are applied, whereas in other cases they occur on both sides, suggesting that these particular proteins span the entire membrane.

Another piece of evidence comes from the technique of **freeze fracture**. In this process a piece of plasma membrane is frozen, then split down the middle longitudinally. If the inner surface is then viewed in the electron microscope, globular structures the same size as the membrane proteins can be seen scattered about as shown in figure 10.26.

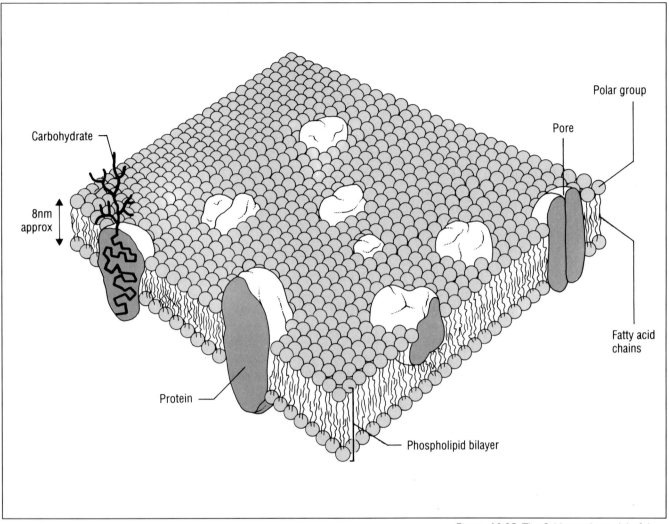

Carbohydrate

8nm approx

Protein

Phospholipid bilayer

Polar group

Pore

Fatty acid chains

Figure 10.25 The fluid-mosaic model of the plasma membrane proposed by Singer and Nicholson. The proteins exist in globular form and are either embedded in the lipid layer or extend right across it creating a mosaic pattern.

The fluid-mosaic model is thought to apply not just to the plasma membrane but to all biological membranes, and it is seen as a dynamic, ever-changing structure. The proteins serve as enzymes catalysing chemical reactions within the membrane and as pumps moving ions and molecules across it. We shall return to this in Chapter 12.

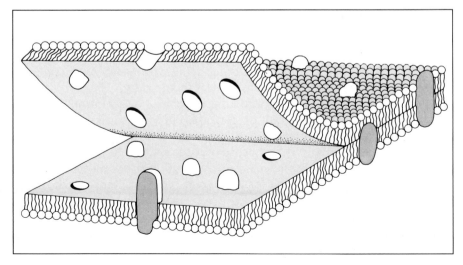

Figure 10.26 The three-dimensional structure of the membrane as deduced from the freeze-fracture technique. The membrane is split down the middle, exposing the globular proteins.

Cholesterol and the plasma membrane

Cholesterol has had a bad press: it is claimed to be a major cause of heart disease (see page 135). But in relatively small quantities it is essential because it helps to maintain the fluidity of the plasma membrane. It interacts with the hydrocarbon chains of the phospholipid molecules just behind the polar heads. This enhances the mechanical stability and flexibility of the membrane.

Evidence that cholesterol strengthens the plasma membrane comes from studying cultured mutant cells that cannot synthesise cholesterol. Such cells readily break open and release their contents. However, if cholesterol is added to the culture medium, the cells remain intact.

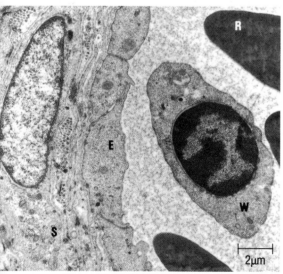

Figure 10.27 Electron micrograph of a section through a small artery. The artery is lined by epithelial cells (**E**) to the left of which is a smooth muscle cell (**S**) which, when it contracts, makes the artery constrict. Inside the artery you can see parts of three red blood cells (**R**) which carry oxygen, and a white blood cell (**W**) which destroys pathogenic micro-organisms and so helps to fight diseases. .

Pores in the plasma membrane

That the plasma membrane is perforated by pores was predicted many years ago on the grounds that certain molecules, insoluble in lipid and therefore unable to get in between the lipid molecules, are still capable of penetrating the membrane. The pores are thought to be surrounded by protein and lined with hydrophilic groups (the polar groups of the protein molecules); this would make them readily penetrated by water-soluble substances.

By measuring the resistance of the membrane to the passage of such molecules, together with other methods of determining the diameter of small pores, it has been established that the pores must be less than 1.0 nm wide. As such they are too small to be seen even with the electron microscope. In Chapter 12 we shall see how they control the passage of molecules and ions in and out of cells.

Surface carbohydrates

An interesting discovery is that the plasma membrane contains not only lipid and protein but also carbohydrate. The carbohydrate component takes the form of short polysaccharide chains which project from the outer side of the membrane. Some of the polysaccharides are attached to the phospholipids but the vast majority are attached to the proteins (to form glycoproteins). Together they make up the **glycoprotein coat** referred to on page 164.

The composition and branching pattern of these surface polysaccharides vary from one type of cell to another. This gives us a clue as to their function. When an organism is developing or a wound is healing, it is necessary that a given cell should 'know' whether it is in contact with another cell of the same type or with a cell of a different type. The surface carbohydrates enable cells to recognise each other in this way. They may also play a part in the way cells adhere together and interact, and in the mechanism by which specific hormones and foreign substances recognise, and in consequence associate with, particular types of cell. We shall return to this important topic in later chapters.

The diversity of cells

In this chapter we have considered the basic features of cells in general. But this should not be taken simply to imply that all cells are identical. Structures like chromosomes, mitochondria, endoplasmic reticulum and ribosomes are common to virtually all cells, but the shape, form and contents of individual cells show much variation. The structural characteristics of a particular cell are closely related to its functions. This will be amply illustrated in later chapters, but it is as well to appreciate from the start the striking diversity of cells among living organisms. As an example figure 10.27 shows some of the cells present in an artery.

The reason for this diversity is that in the course of evolution cells have become structurally specialised to perform particular tasks. In extreme cases specialisation may entail loss of the nucleus or cytoplasm, but in the majority of cases it involves modification of the shape and form of the cell, its basic features remaining unchanged. An epithelial cell and a nerve cell may look very different, and perform different functions, but in their fundamental structure and chemistry they are remarkably alike. This is not surprising when we bear in mind that both are living entities and, whatever else they do, they must perform those functions which are necessary for the maintenance of life.

Summary

1 The cell may be regarded as the basic unit of an organism.

2 There are two types of cell. **Prokaryotic**, meaning 'before a nucleus', and **eukaryotic**, meaning 'good or true nucleus'. Prokaryotic cells have a simpler internal structure than eukaryotic cells.

3 A typical prokaryotic cell has a **plasma membrane, cell wall, nucleoid, plasmids, ribosomes, mesosome** and sometimes **chromatophores, capsule** and **flagella**. The prokaryotic flagellum is simpler than the eukaryotic flagellum and moves by rotating rather than bending.

4 The main parts of a typical eukaryotic cell are the **plasma membrane, cytoplasm** and **nucleus**. The nucleus contains the **nucleolus** and **chromosomes**, the latter carrying hereditary material. The cytoplasm is composed of the **cytosol** and **endoplasmic reticulum** and contains various membrane-bound organelles.

5 Organelles and inclusions in the cytoplasm of eukaryotic cells include: **glycogen granules** or **starch grains**, **ribosomes** and/or **polyribosomes**, **Golgi apparatus**, **secretory vesicles (zymogen granules)**, **mitochondria, lysosomes, centrioles, pinocytic** and **phagocytic vesicles**, **microfilaments** and **microtubules** (cytoskeleton), **chloroplasts** and – at the surface – **microvilli**.

6 Some eukaryotic cells possess **flagella** or **cilia** which contain microtubules in a **9+2 arrangement**. They move by bending.

7 Typical plant cells differ from animal cells in lacking centrioles and in possessing **chloroplasts, starch grains** instead of glycogen, a central **vacuole** and a **cellulose cell wall**.

8 In plant cells a **primary wall** of cellulose is laid down on the inside of the **middle lamella**. After the cell has expanded, a further **secondary wall** may be laid down inside the primary wall. The secondary wall may be absent locally giving rise to a **pit**, and **plasmodesmata** may link adjacent cells.

9 According to the **fluid-mosaic model**, the plasma membrane consists of a **lipid bilayer** with globular protein molecules in or on it. Some of the protein molecules are **glycoproteins** with carbohydrate chains projecting from them.

10 Though basically similar, cells show considerable diversity in their contents, shape and functions. In all cases, there is a close relationship between cell structure and function.

Review questions

1 List the similarities and differences between plant and animal cells as seen under a light microscope. What additional differences, if any, are revealed by the electron microscope?

2 What features are common to all cells, and what features are unique to (a) prokaryotic cells and (b) eukaryotic cells?

3 Why do you think it is an advantage to a eukaryotic cell to possess different types of organelles?

4 If space and nutrients were available, one bacterium could produce in less than two days offspring whose total bulk was greater than that of the Earth. Why do you think bacteria can reproduce with such remarkable rapidity?

5 Distinguish between:
rough and smooth endoplasmic reticulum,
ribosome and polyribosome,
plasma membrane and cell wall,
chromatin and chromosome,
leucoplast and chloroplast.

6 Certain cells have densely packed mitochondria and the cristae are very close together. What would you predict about the function of such cells? Explain your reasoning.

7 If living organisms were found on another planet, do you think their bodies would be composed of cells like those possessed by organisms on Earth? What alternatives might be possible?

8 Summarise the fluid-mosaic theory for the structure of the plasma membrane.

9 Describe the main function or functions carried out by two contrasting eukaryotic cells. What special characteristics does each cell have in addition to those possessed by all eukaryotic cells?

10 Do you think it is right to regard the cell as the basic unit of life?

Further reading

Stephen Hurry's slim volume, *The Microstructure of Cells* (John Murray, 1980), was compiled specially for A-level students and is amply illustrated with electron micrographs. The principal organelles are dealt with in turn and the text is brief and to the point.

From Cells to Atoms by A.R. Rees and M.J.E. Sternberg, 3rd edn (Blackwell, 1993) is packed full of useful illustrated information in only 100 pages or so.

The book that everyone rushes to if they want to look something up is *The Molecular Biology of the Cell* by B. Alberts *et al* (Garland, 1989). Over 1200 pages long, this best-selling compendium is ideal for reference and is updated regularly.

Biology, Advanced Topics includes further detail on microfilaments and microtubules, the movement of cilia and flagella, the problem of artefacts and the fluid-mosaic model of the plasma membrane.

CHAPTER 11 Tissues, organs and individuals

In the last chapter we talked about cells as if they exist in isolation without any kind of functional contact with each other. This may well be true of single-celled organisms. But the vast majority of organisms are **multi-cellular**, consisting of numerous cells. In such organisms cells of one or more types are generally grouped together to form **tissues**.

The function of a tissue depends on what kind, or kinds, of cell it is composed of. Furthermore, in more complex organisms different tissues are combined to form **organs**. The study of tissues and the way they are arranged in organs is called **histology**. In this chapter we shall look at a range of tissues and organs, and discuss the part they play in the organisation of individual organisms.

Types of tissues

There are various ways of classifying tissues. We shall adopt a functional classification based on the jobs which the tissues do in the body. On this basis animal tissues may be divided into **epithelial tissue (epithelium)**, **connective tissue, skeletal tissue, blood tissue, nerve tissue, muscle tissue** and **reproductive tissue**. Plant tissues may be divided into **meristematic tissue, epidermal tissue (epidermis), parenchyma, collenchyma, sclerenchyma, vascular tissue** and **cork**.

Our purpose in this chapter is not to describe all these tissues in detail, but to look at the principles underlying their construction. Specialised tissues such as nerve tissue and plant vascular tissue are described in detail in the chapters where they belong. Here we shall be concerned with the more basic tissues, starting with animals and then going on to plants.

Animal tissues

The following description is based mainly on the mammal. The tissues to be described also occur in other animal groups though the details of their construction may be different in certain respects. We shall start with epithelial tissue – also known as epithelium – because this demonstrates how cells can be built up into multicellular structures of varying complexity.

Epithelium

Epithelium is *lining* tissue. In its simplest form it consists of a sheet of cells which fit closely together, rather like crazy paving (figure 11.1). This kind of tissue covers the surface of an animal or the organs, cavities and tubes within it. The cells rest on a **basement membrane** and have a **free surface** on the other side. The basement membrane is produced by the epithelial cells themselves and consists of a meshwork of fine protein fibres (collagen) embedded in a jelly-like matrix. It supports the epithelium and exercises some control over what passes through it.

The epithelium on the outer surface of an animal is known as the **epidermis**. In some groups, for example arthropods, the epidermis secretes a protective cuticle of varying thickness and hardness. The epithelium lining the inside of the heart, blood vessels and lymph vessels is referred to as **endothelium**.

There are several ways of classifying epithelial tissues. None of them is entirely satisfactory because the demarcation between the different types is often blurred. However, a fundamental distinction may be made between

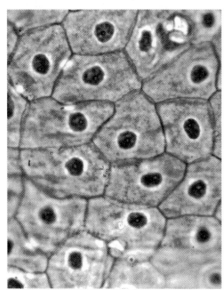

Figure 11.1 Squamous epithelium, one of the simplest tissues. Notice how the cells fit together. The nuclei of the cells are clearly seen. Magnification × 700.

epithelia that consist of only one layer of cells, and those that consist of many layers.

Epithelia consisting of one layer of cells

This kind of epithelium can be divided into five main types mainly on the basis of the shape of the constituent cells (figure 11.2).

In **squamous epithelium**, also known as pavement epithelium, the cells are flattened like paving stones. The resulting sheet of cells is thin and delicate, often less than 2.0 μm thick. It is found in places where the protective covering needs to be readily permeable to molecules or ions in solution, for example the walls of blood capillaries and alveoli in the lungs.

In **cuboidal epithelium** the height of each cell is approximately equal to its width, so when viewed in vertical section the cells appear square. The free surface is polygonal in shape and the cells fit together like a honey comb. Many glands, and the ducts leading from them, are lined with cuboidal epithelium, as are the tubules in the kidney. One of the best places to see this kind of epithelium is in the thyroid gland where it forms the lining of the cavities in which the secretion is stored.

Cuboidal epithelium may bear numerous **microvilli** on the free surface. Such is the case with certain of the kidney tubules. The microvilli increase the surface area for the reabsorption of substances.

Columnar epithelium consists of cells elongated at right angles to the basement membrane, so they appear to be column shaped when viewed in section. This kind of epithelium is found lining the small intestine. Like cuboidal epithelium, columnar epithelial cells may bear microvilli on the free surface. In the small intestine the microvilli increase the surface area for absorbing the products of digestion.

Cuboidal and columnar epithelia sometimes have cilia on the free surface, in which case we can call it **ciliated epithelium**. The cilia are capable of beating rapidly. In certain animals, free-living flatworms for example, ciliated epithelium is found on the underside of the body. The beating cilia drive the animal along, enabling it to glide over the surface of stones and weeds.

Ciliated epithelium is also found lining tubes and cavities in which materials are moved. For example, in the human and other mammals it lines the trachea and bronchial tubes. Amongst the ciliated epithelial cells are cells that secrete **mucus** (figure 11.3). Mucus is slimy, and particles which are inadvertently inhaled get caught up in it. The mucus and particles are then driven by the beating cilia towards the throat.

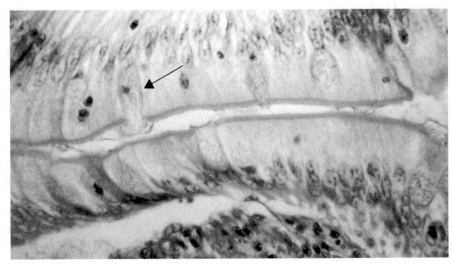

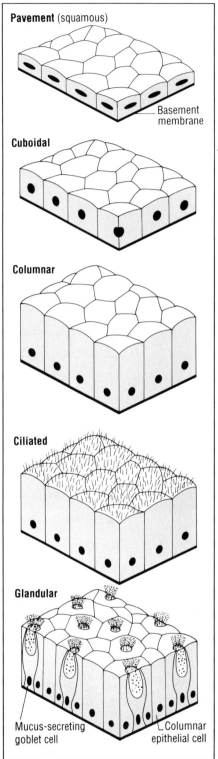

Figure 11.2 Five types of simple epithelium showing the way the cells fit together.

Figure 11.3 Mucus-secreting goblet cells in the epithelial lining of the small intestine. One of the cells is arrowed. The section has been specially stained to show up the secretory region in each cell. Magnification × 250.

173

Sometimes epithelial tissue contains so many secretory cells that we call it **glandular epithelium**. A good example is seen in the lining of the rectum. Here, there are so many mucus-secreting cells that the epithelium consists of little else. The rectal epithelium is greatly folded, thus increasing the surface area from which secretion takes place. Being slimy, mucus has a lubricating action. This facilitates the movement of faeces along the rectum and prevents the delicate epithelial surface from being damaged by abrasion.

Mucus-secreting cells usually have a wide top and a constricted base, like a wine glass. On account of their shape they are called **goblet cells**. Goblet cells are of widespread occurrence in animals. A layer of moist epithelium containing goblet cells, together with the underlying connective tissue, is referred to as **mucous membrane** or **mucosa**. Mucous membranes are often found lining cavities that are connected to the exterior, such as the gut and breathing tract. In some cases, including the breathing tract, the mucous membrane is ciliated.

Glands

Sometimes a patch of epithelium is folded inwards, forming an invagination. The cells lining the bottom of the invagination become secretory and develop into a gland.

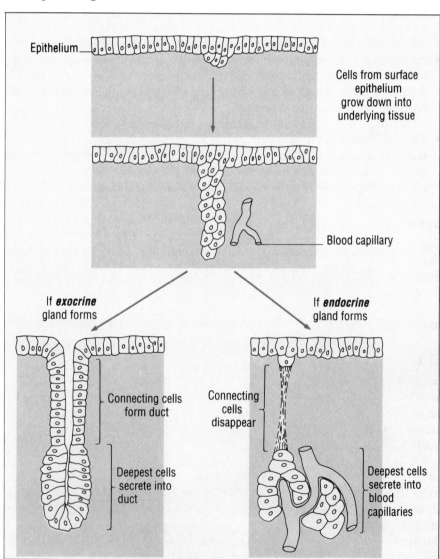

Figure 11.4 Diagram comparing the formation of an exocrine and endocrine gland. Notice that the endocrine gland loses its connection with the surface epithelium and develops a close association with blood capillaries into which it releases its secretion.

Two types of gland are recognised (figure 11.4).

- In an **exocrine gland** the epithelial connection between the gland and the surface epithelium remains as a tube or **duct** which carries the gland's secretion to wherever it has to go. The salivary glands are an example: they secrete saliva into the mouth cavity.

- In an **endocrine gland** the epithelial connection between the gland and the surface epithelium disappears, and the gland itself forms a close association with blood capillaries. Its secretion, instead of flowing down a duct, passes into the bloodstream. Endocrine glands secrete **hormones** about which we shall have much to say later in the book.

The secretory part of an exocrine gland may be like a little sack or a tube, and it may show various degrees of branching. Branching has the effect of increasing the area of the secretory surface.

Glandular epithelia release their secretions in three different ways (figure 11.5).

- The secretion may be discharged from the free surface of the cells by exocytosis (see page 204). Hormones are secreted like this, as are mucus and sweat.

- The top part of the cell, loaded with the secretion, breaks away from the lower part and releases its secretion. Meanwhile the lower part of the cell develops a new top which becomes recharged with secretion. This happens in the milk-secreting mammary glands.

- The entire gland cell may be shed from the epithelium after which it disintegrates and releases its secretion. The lost cell is then replaced by cell division in the epithelium. The sebaceous glands in the skin secrete oil in this way.

Syncytia

Sometimes the membranes between adjacent epithelial cells break down, though the cytoplasm and nuclei remain. The result is the formation of a multinucleate sheet of tissue. This is known as a **syncytium** and is found, for example, in the lining of the villi in the placenta.

Syncytia are not confined to epithelia – they are found in other tissues too. For example, skeletal muscle fibres are syncytia (see page 594).

Tubules

In most animals, ourselves included, narrow tubes such as blood capillaries are created by a layer of epithelial tissue becoming folded into a cylinder – rather like making a tube out of a sheet of paper. However, in some animals we find tubules which are constructed in a different way. They are made from **drainpipe cells**.

A drainpipe cell is a hollow cylinder, open at each end, with the nucleus situated in the 'wall' of the cylinder on one side (figure 11.6). The tubule is formed by a row of such cells joining up end to end. Because its lumen is created from the cavities within the cells, a tubule of this sort is described as **intracellular** (*intra* means 'within', *inter* means 'between' – an important distinction in biology). The fine breathing tubes (tracheoles) of insects and the excretory ducts of flatworms are examples.

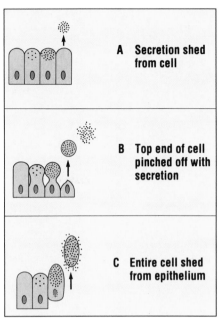

Figure 11.5 Three different ways in which glandular epithelial cells may release their secretion.

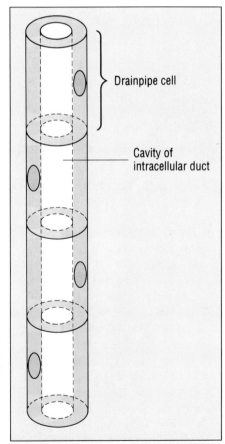

Figure 11.6 Drainpipe cells are hollow, like little cylinders. A narrow tube may be formed from a row of such cells placed end to end as shown here.

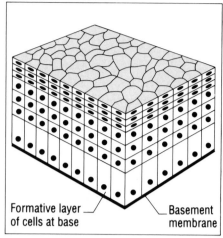

Formative layer of cells at base — Basement membrane

Figure 11.7 Stratified epithelium consists of layers of epithelial cells on top of each other. The cells are formed by cell divisions in the bottom layer.

Epithelia consisting of many layers of cells

An epithelium which consists of many layers of cells is called **stratified epithelium**. Only the bottom layer of cells rests on the basement membrane (figure 11.7). Obviously this type of epithelium is thicker than single-layered epithelia and more effective as a protective covering. It comprises the **epidermis** of the skin and the lining of certain cavities and tubes inside the body, for example the vagina and oesophagus.

The multi-layered nature of stratified epithelium derives from the fact that the cells of the bottom layer divide repeatedly in a plane parallel to the basement membrane, with the result that new cells are constantly being formed on top of the bottom layer of cells. As cell divisions continue, the older cells get pushed outwards as new cells are formed beneath them. As the cells move away from the dividing layer, they become flatter and eventually flake off, to be replaced by new ones from beneath.

In human skin, the cells at the surface of the epidermis become transformed into a tough, non-living layer composed largely of the protein keratin. This greatly enhances the skin's efficiency as a protective covering. The epidermis lining internal organs such as the vagina and oesophagus does not normally become keratinised, at least not to anything like the same extent as the skin.

There are several variants of stratified epithelium. For example, the lining of the trachea appears to be composed of several layers of cells but careful observation shows that all the cells rest on, or at least touch, the basement membrane. This is known as **pseudo-stratified epithelium**.

Another arrangement is found in the lining of the bladder. Here the cells are all approximately the same size, do not flake off, and can change their shape when the bladder wall is stretched as it fills up with urine. This is called **transitional epithelium**.

The problem of classifying tissues

In classifying tissues it is difficult to devise a simple system which is both useful and logical.

This is well illustrated by connective tissue. We can classify connective tissue in three different ways, each based on a different definition of connective tissue. In this book connective tissue is defined *functionally* as a tissue which fills spaces and connects structures together. As such, it embraces areolar, collagen and elastic tissue.

However, we could equally well define connective tissue *structurally* as a tissue consisting of cells and other inclusions in some kind of matrix. Thus defined, connective tissue would include blood, lymph, cartilage and bone, as well as areolar, collagen and elastic tissue. Structurally all these tissues are fundamentally similar – they all consist of cells and other inclusions in a matrix. They differ in the types of cells and inclusions, and in the nature of the matrix. For example, in cartilage and bone the matrix is solid, whereas in blood it is fluid.

These particular tissues have something else in common too: they are all derived from the same cells in the embryo. These cells constitute an embryonic tissue called the **mesoderm**. From a *developmental* standpoint, connective tissue may therefore be regarded as any tissue derived from the mesoderm.

Difficulties arise in classifying plant tissues too. For example, in this book we have classified collenchyma and sclerenchyma separately on the basis of their quite different cell walls: collenchyma cells have cellulose walls whereas sclerenchyma cells have lignified walls.

However, we could have classified them together *functionally* as **mechanical tissue** because both are involved in providing plants with mechanical strength and support.

Some tissues belong to two categories. For example, one of the major contributors to the mechanical strength of plants is xylem tissue. Xylem tissue should therefore be included as mechanical tissue. However, it also transports water and mineral salts, so it qualifies as vascular tissue as well.

Connective tissue

The tissues and organs in an animal's body must be held in the right positions. This function is performed by connective tissue which binds organs and tissues together and fills the spaces between them. From this function we would expect connective tissue to be strong, and this indeed is often the case. It consists of a jelly-like ground substance or **matrix** in which several types of cell and protein fibres are embedded. The matrix is similar in chemical composition to the basement membrane of epithelial tissue (see page 172).

There are four main kinds of connective tissue, and their toughness and other physical properties are determined by the type and number of protein fibres which they contain.

The most basic type is **areolar tissue**. This is found all over the body: beneath the skin, connecting organs together, and filling spaces between other tissues. The matrix contains four main types of cell and two types of protein fibre (figure 11.8). The main cell types are:

- Large flat **fibroblasts** which produce the ground substance and fibres.
- A variable number of **fat** cells.
- Amoeboid **macrophages**.
- Small oval **mast cells**.

The macrophages and mast cells both help to defend the body against disease (see Chapter 24).

Areolar tissue is quite easily torn and broken. What little strength it has is due to its fibres. These are of two types.

- **Collagen fibres** (white fibres) which are unbranched and run parallel to each other in bundles.
- **Elastic fibres** (yellow fibres) which are branched and form a network criss-crossing the matrix.

The other types of connective tissue are basically like areolar tissue but differ from it in the structures present in the matrix. In **collagen tissue** (also known as white fibrous tissue) the ground substance contains mainly collagen fibres and the fibroblasts which produce them. This tissue is flexible but relatively unstretchable, and it has great tensile strength.

When does a '-blast' become a '-cyte'?

If you read about connective and skeletal tissue in histology books, you will find that sometimes the name given to the main type of cell in the tissue ends with the suffix *-blast* and sometimes with the suffix *-cyte*.

Why are these two endings used? The answer is that they both refer to the same type of cell but at different stages of its development. *Blast* is used when the cell is not fully developed and is still manufacturing its product – for example the matrix of cartilage or bone. *Cyte* is used when the cell is mature and has finished manufacturing its product.

Thus, a cartilage cell which is still dividing and secreting chondrin is called a chondro*blast*, but once the cell stops dividing and secreting it becomes known as a chondro*cyte*. Similarly, a bone cell which is still actively laying down bone is called an osteo*blast*, but once the cell stops laying down any more bone it becomes an osteo*cyte*. And a connective tissue cell which is actively producing collagen or elastic fibres is called a fibro*blast*, whereas the inactive cell in fully formed connective tissue is more properly called a fibro*cyte*.

It is unlikely that anyone will get fussed if you use *blast* when you should really use *cyte*, or vice versa. Besides, it is often difficult to decide what stage of development a cell has reached. Names are invented by people not nature and can sometimes be confusing.

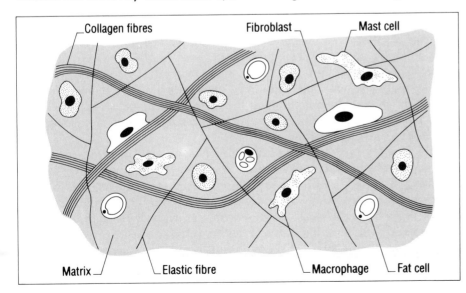

Figure 11.8 Areolar tissue as it appears in a microscopic section, showing the different types of cells and inclusions.

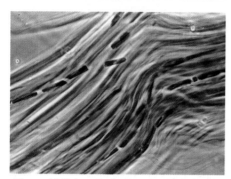

Figure 11.9 Longitudinal section of a tendon showing densely packed collagen fibres. The dark cigar-shaped objects are fibroblasts which tend to occur in rows. Magnification × 500.

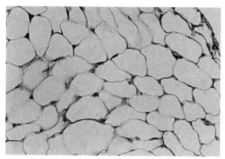

Figure 11.10 Section of adipose tissue showing closely packed fat cells. The clear region inside each cell is fat. These cells are so full of fat that the nuclei (darkly stained) have got pushed against the plasma membranes. Magnification × 200.

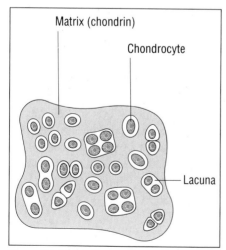

Figure 11.11 Hyaline cartilage as it appears in a microscopic section. Notice the chondroblasts scattered about singly and in small groups.

Tendons, attaching muscles to bones, are composed of collagen tissue. Collagen tissue is far tougher than areolar tissue: the areolar tissue connecting organs together is easily broken, but it is difficult to break a tendon with its densely packed collagen fibres (figure 11.9).

Although collagen is relatively unstretchable, it does have a certain amount of elasticity. In fact considerable energy can be stored in stretched tendons, which is useful in locomotion.

In **elastic tissue** (also called yellow elastic tissue) the matrix contains mainly elastic fibres and the fibroblasts which produce them. This tissue is flexible like collagen tissue, but it is not as strong and is more stretchable. It is found in ligaments, the tough strands which bind bones together across the joints. It is also found in the wall of the bladder, allowing it to stretch as it fills up with urine.

Collagen and elastic fibres are both fibrous proteins (see page 141). X-ray analysis of collagen has shown it to consist of three polypeptide chains coiled round each other to form a triple helix. The chains are inter-linked by hydrogen bonds and the whole structure is tough and inextensible, like a plaited rope. Elastin, about which less is known, is characterised by numerous cross-links which are thought to enable elastic fibres to return to their original length after being stretched.

Finally **adipose tissue** contains large numbers of closely packed **fat cells** with a network of collagen and elastic fibres in between (figure 11.10). Normally the fat cells are full of fat, making adipose tissue an important energy store. In the skin it fulfils the additional function of insulation.

Skeletal tissue

Skeletal tissue is responsible for supporting the body and providing it with a strong framework whose rigid components can move relative to each other at smoothly articulating joints. Like connective tissue it consists of cells embedded in a matrix, but in this case the matrix is hard.

Two kinds of skeletal tissue occur in vertebrates: **cartilage** and **bone**. The skeleton of cartilaginous fishes, such as the dogfish, sharks and rays, is composed entirely of cartilage. The mammal, on the other hand, has a predominantly bony skeleton with cartilage at the joints and in the discs between the vertebrae.

Cartilage

Cartilage is softer than bone and you can slice through it quite easily with a sharp knife or scalpel. When pressed it 'gives' slightly, rather like hard rubber. This makes it useful as a cushioning material.

The matrix of cartilage, **chondrin**, consists mainly of a mucopolysaccharide called **chondroitin sulphate** in which are embedded spherical cells called **chondrocytes**. Bundles of collagen fibres and elastic fibres may also be present in varying amounts.

The simplest type of cartilage is called **hyaline cartilage**. Under the light microscope the matrix appears homogeneous, with chondrocytes dotted about here and there (figure 11.11). The cells tend to occur singly or in small groups. This is because of the way cartilage develops. The cells secrete the matrix. Known at this stage as **chondroblasts**, they divide repeatedly first into two and then into four. As the daughter cells secrete the matrix, they get pushed apart (figure 11.12). The cells finish up imprisoned in little spaces called **lacunae** within the matrix which they themselves have produced. When this stage is reached the cells become known as chondrocytes.

Hyaline cartilage is found in the wall of the trachea (windpipe) where its function is to prevent the wall caving in. It is also found in the ends

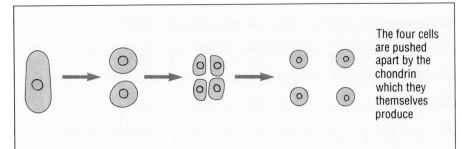

The four cells are pushed apart by the chondrin which they themselves produce

Figure 11.12 This diagram shows how the chondroblasts divide in hyaline cartilage tissue. After a cell divides the daughter cells get pushed apart by the matrix which they themselves produce.

(epiphyses) of the limb bones where it is associated with the formation of bone tissue (ossification), and at the joints where it performs a cushioning function and provides a smooth articulating surface.

Cartilage may be strengthened by the presence of collagen or elastic fibres. In some cases the fibres are so abundant that the matrix is almost squeezed out of existence. Cartilage containing collagen fibres (**fibro-cartilage**) is found in the intervertebral discs of the vertebral column. Cartilage containing elastic fibres (**yellow elastic cartilage**) is found in the nose and the pinna of the ear. Elastic cartilage is tough but bendable, as you will know from wiggling your ear.

Bone tissue

Bone consists of an organic matrix impregnated with mineral salts containing calcium and phosphate. The main salt is calcium hydroxyapatite, $Ca_{10}(PO_4)_6(OH)_2$. These salts are in the form of tiny sub-microscopic crystals and they confer upon bone its property of extreme hardness. The organic matrix contains densely packed collagen fibres which help to give bone its tensile strength, enabling it to bear heavy loads and withstand severe stresses without breaking.

Both the organic matrix and the mineral salts are produced by cells called **osteoblasts**. Projecting from these cells are slender processes which link up to form a network as shown in figure 11.13. In the development of

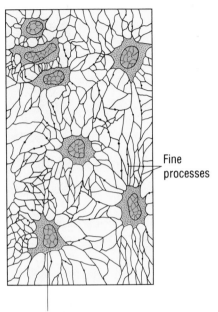

Fine processes

Main body of cell (*osteoblast*)

Figure 11.13 Osteoblasts (bone cells) as they appear during the formation of bone tissue. The cells produce the matrix and the mineral salts with which it is hardened.

Bones and ionising radiation

It is well known that ionising radiation is dangerous. Bones are particularly susceptible to its effects. Why is this?

It is characteristic of bone tissue that it very readily takes up foreign ions which replace the calcium or phosphate ions in the hydroxyapatite crystals. For example, lead (Pb^{2+}), radium (^{226}Ra) and strontium (Sr^{2+}) will all replace calcium if they happen to get into the body.

Large numbers of radioactive elements are released by atomic fission in nuclear reactors and when nuclear weapons are detonated. Some of these radioactive elements,

if they get into the body, become concentrated in the bones where they either replace calcium in the mineral part of the bone tissue or become incorporated into the organic matrix. The harm they do is through the ionising radiation which they emit. This may damage the osteoblasts and cause cancer of the bone. It may also damage the marrow, increasing the mutation rate in the blood-forming cells and causing leukaemia, a type of cancer of the blood.

One of the most hazardous radioactive elements, with a very high affinity for bone tissue, is strontium-90 (^{90}Sr). Massive amounts of this element were released by the atomic bombs that

were dropped on Japan towards the end of the Second World War. The incidence of bone cancer and leukaemia was very high amongst the survivors of this terrible event.

The harmful effects of these radioactive elements are made worse by the fact that they persist for so long: the half-life of strontium-90 is 28 years, and that of plutonium-239 is 24 300 years. Moreover, once these elements get into the environment they may enter food chains, becoming more and more concentrated as they pass from one trophic level to the next (see page 34). Strontium-90 behaves just like calcium: it becomes concentrated in teeth and bones and gets into the milk produced by mothers.

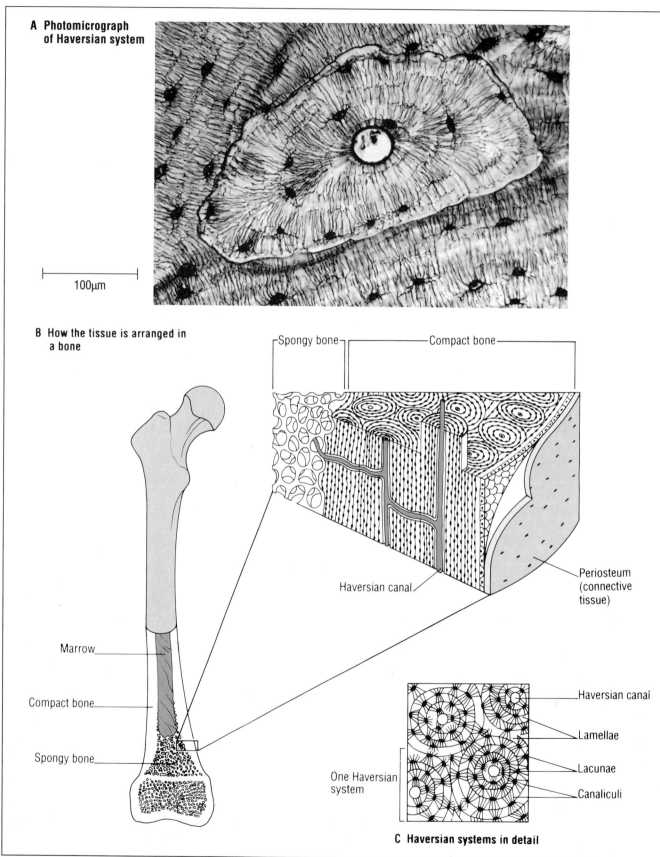

A Photomicrograph of Haversian system

100μm

B How the tissue is arranged in a bone

Spongy bone — Compact bone —

Haversian canal

Periosteum (connective tissue)

Marrow

Compact bone

Spongy bone

One Haversian system

Haversian canal

Lamellae

Lacunae

Canaliculi

C Haversian systems in detail

Figure 11.14 Photomicrograph of a section of compact bone showing Haversian systems in transverse section, with explanatory diagrams below.

a limb bone such as the femur, numerous osteoblasts arrange themselves in concentric rings around a series of **Haversian canals**, each of which contains an artery and a vein. Because of the concentric arrangement of the osteoblasts, the matrix is laid down in a series of layers or **lamellae** encircling the Haversian canals (figure 11.14). Each osteoblast finishes up in a space (lacuna) from which narrow channels called **canaliculi** traverse the lamellae. The canaliculi contain the fine processes of the osteoblasts during the development of the bone. Once imprisoned in the lacunae, the osteoblasts stop secreting matrix material and are known as **osteocytes**.

In **compact bone** the Haversian canals and their surrounding lamellae are packed tightly together, giving a very dense material. Another type of bone, called **spongy bone**, is of looser construction and forms a three-dimensional network of interconnected strands with spaces in between. In a limb bone such as the femur, the shaft contains compact bone with the Haversian canals running longitudinally. In contrast, the two ends (epiphyses) contain spongy bone. The functional reason for this difference is explained on page 510.

The centre of the femur and many other bones is filled with marrow. There are two types of marrow: red and yellow. **Red marrow** contains developing blood cells (hence its colour), whereas **yellow marrow** is predominantly fatty tissue. In an embryo only red marrow is found, but in the course of development some of it becomes replaced by yellow marrow. In the adult, red marrow is found mainly in the vertebrae, ribs, sternum, scapula, pelvis and the upper epiphyses of the femur and humerus – in other words mainly in the axial skeleton (see page 508). Here, inside the bones, blood cells – both red and white – are manufactured.

Although surrounded by skeletal tissue, red bone marrow is a tissue in its own right. It is known as **haemopoietic tissue** from the Greek words *haema*, 'blood' and *poieo*, 'to make'. Haemopoietic tissue is not restricted to the bone marrow; it is also found in the lymphatic system which is involved in the manufacture of certain types of white blood cell.

Muscle tissue

Muscle tissue is unique in being able to **contract**, which allows it to change in length or develop tension. This feature is the basis of its main function which is to enable the body, or parts of it, to move.

There are three types of muscle tissue.

- **Cardiac muscle** is found in the wall of the heart.
- **Skeletal muscle** is attached to the skeleton.
- **Smooth muscle** occurs in the walls of the gut, blood vessels, bladder and other tubes and cavities in the body.

Cardiac and skeletal muscle are dealt with in later chapters, but smooth muscle will be described here because it illustrates the basic structure of muscle tissue and is widely distributed in the body.

Smooth muscle tissue is made up of numerous slender **muscle fibres** (figure 11.15). Each fibre is a single cell with a nucleus and cytoplasm. It is spindle shaped, typically about 0.2 mm long, and the cytoplasm contains thread-like **myofibrils** which are responsible for contraction.

In certain places, the skin for example, smooth muscle fibres occur singly or in small groups, mixed up with connective tissue. In other situations the smooth muscle fibres are concentrated into sheets with all the fibres running in the same direction. We find such an arrangement in the wall of the small intestine where the sheets are arranged in two layers. In the inner layer the muscle fibres encircle the intestine (**circular muscle**); in

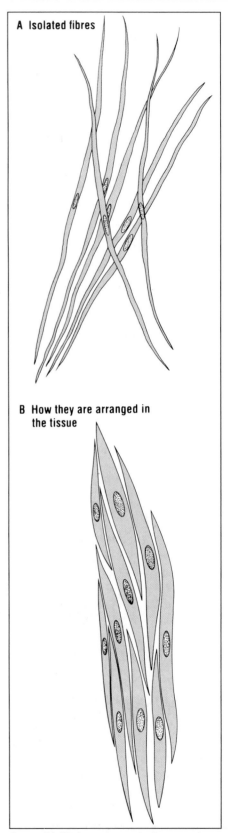

A Isolated fibres

B How they are arranged in the tissue

Figure 11.15 Smooth muscle tissue consists of elongated muscle fibres, shown singly in **A**, which may be massed together into a sheet or bundle as shown in **B**.

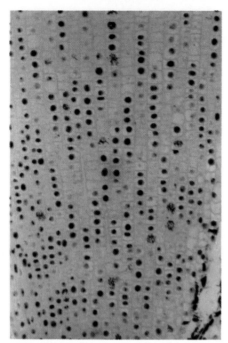

Figure 11.16 Photomicrograph of meristematic tissue as seen in a longitudinal section through the tip of an onion root. Notice how simple the cells are and how regularly they are arranged in the tissue. Many of them are in the process of dividing. Magnification × 200.

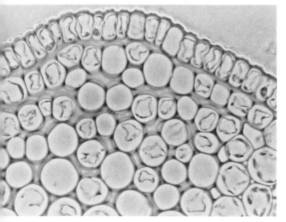

Figure 11.17 Photomicrograph of a transverse section of the stem of a deadnettle. Epidermal tissue can be seen lining the outer side of the stem (the topmost layer of cells in the photomicrograph). Notice the cuticle on the outer surface of the epidermis. Beneath the epidermis is a wad of collenchyma tissue which strengthens the stem. Collenchyma tissue is described on the opposite page. Magnification × 200.

the outer layer the muscle fibres run along the length of the intestine (**longitudinal muscle**). These two sets of muscle tissue produce opposite effects; in other words they are **antagonistic** in their actions. When the circular muscle contracts and the longitudinal muscle relaxes, the intestine narrows (constricts); but when the longitudinal muscle contracts and the circular muscle relaxes, the intestine widens (dilates).

Other tubes and hollow organs work in a similar way – arteries, for example. The same principle also applies to the locomotion of certain soft-bodied animals such as the earthworm (see page 526).

In some places smooth muscle fibres are packed together to form a ring of muscle surrounding a tubular organ. The muscular ring is called a **sphincter**, and by relaxing or contracting it can open or close the tube. Examples are the **anal sphincter** which controls the opening and closing of the anus, and the **pyloric sphincter** which controls the passage of food from the stomach to the duodenum (see Chapter 16).

Plant tissues

Some of the animal tissues which we have been looking at have their counterparts in plants, but plants also have certain unique tissues which may be related to their way of life. Here we shall concentrate on the tissues found in flowering plants.

Meristematic tissue

From a plant's **meristematic tissue** all the other tissues are derived. It is found wherever growth occurs, for example in the tip of the stem and root. Meristematic cells are small and immature, with thin walls. The walls are thin because at this stage very little cellulose has been laid down. The cells lack chloroplasts and the large vacuole characteristic of mature plant cells, but they contain other organelles including undifferentiated plastids which are destined to give rise to leucoplasts and chloroplasts (see page 153). Their important feature is their ability to divide and subsequently differentiate into other types of cell. They are shown in figure 11.16.

Epidermal tissue

A plant's equivalent to epithelium is its **epidermis** which is located at the surface of, for example, stems and leaves (figure 11.17). Its cells are usually somewhat flattened, and often irregular when looked at in surface view. They fit together like a jigsaw, forming a protective layer covering the more delicate tissues beneath. With the exception of the stomatal guard cells, plant epidermal cells lack chloroplasts. Their outer walls are frequently thick and covered with a layer of waxy material which constitutes the **cuticle**. The cuticle is impermeable to water and prevents excessive evaporation in dry conditions.

Cork

Cork is the hard tissue covering the surface of shrubs and trees. The cells are small and more or less spherical and, as they develop, their walls become impregnated with a fatty substance called **suberin** which renders them impervious to water and gases. Consequently the cells die and lose their contents. Cork is therefore a dead tissue. However the tissues underneath are very much alive. The function of cork is to protect these living tissues from cold, insect attack and physical damage. The detailed structure of cork and how it is formed are explained on page 644.

Parenchyma, collenchyma and sclerenchyma

Parenchyma is packing tissue, and its main function is to fill the spaces between other tissues. The cells are roughly spherical in shape, with flattened faces where they press against each other (figure 11.18). If the cells are fully turgid and tightly packed, as they normally are, parenchyma helps to maintain the shape and firmness of the plant.

In certain regions of a plant, the parenchyma tissue may fulfil other more specialised functions. For example, in roots the cells frequently contain starch grains and thus serve a storage function. In leaves they contain chloroplasts and can therefore photosynthesise; this kind of tissue is known as **chlorenchyma**. Some aquatic plants contain parenchyma tissue with large air-filled spaces between the cells; this is called **aerenchyma tissue** and it helps to make the plant buoyant.

In a typical herbaceous plant much of the stem is filled with parenchyma and this helps to keep it erect (figure 11.19A). Two other tissues also help with this: collenchyma and sclerenchyma.

Collenchyma is composed of living cells whose cellulose walls are thickened at the corners. Where several such cells lie in contact with each other, a tough rib of cellulose is created (figure 11.19B). Typically, collenchyma is found in the outer part of stems and in the midrib of leaves. Its function is to provide strength with flexibility.

Sclerenchyma is much stronger and more rigid than collenchyma and plays a major part in support. It occurs in stems and in the midribs of leaves where it mainly takes the form of elongated **sclerenchyma fibres** (figure 11.7C). The cells start off as living cells with cellulose walls. However, as the cells develop the cellulose becomes impregnated with **lignin**, a complex aromatic compound which makes the wall not only strong and rigid but

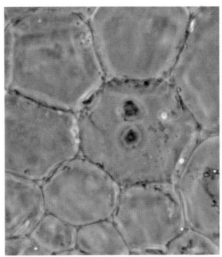

Figure 11.18 Photomicrograph of parenchyma tissue as seen in a section of the central region of a sunflower stem. Magnification × 400.

Figure 11.19 The structure of parenchyma, collenchyma and sclerenchyma. Only the cell walls are shown. The transverse section shows where these tissues occur in a typical dicotyledonous stem. Collenchyma and sclerenchyma are also found in the midrib and veins of leaves where their function, as in the stem, is to provide strength and support.

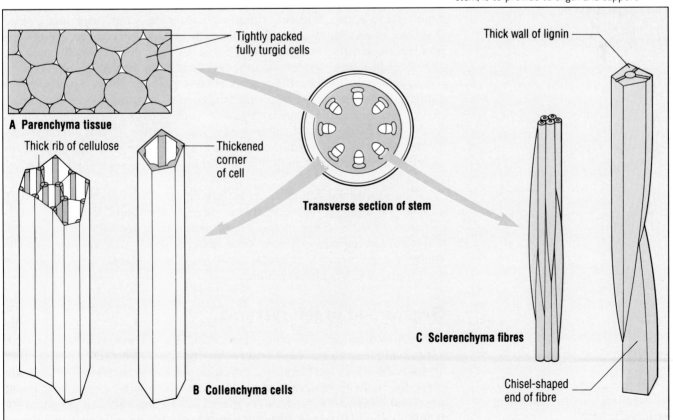

Tightly packed fully turgid cells

A Parenchyma tissue

Thick rib of cellulose

Thickened corner of cell

Transverse section of stem

B Collenchyma cells

Thick wall of lignin

C Sclerenchyma fibres

Chisel-shaped end of fibre

also impervious to water, gases and solutes. Deprived of oxygen and nutrients, the cell contents die and degenerate, leaving a hollow fibre of lignin with tapering ends. Mature sclerenchyma tissue consists of tightly packed bundles of such fibres.

Vascular tissue

Vascular tissue is concerned with transport, and is functionally equivalent to the circulatory system of animals. However, that is where the similarity ends, for the two systems could not be more different. There are two sorts of vascular tissue: xylem and phloem.

- **Xylem tissue** consists of elongated, lignified tubes called **vessels** and **tracheids**. The way vessels and tracheids differ is explained on page 339, but they are fundamentally similar. Like sclerenchyma fibres, they begin as living cells but with the lignification of their walls they die and lose their cell contents. They finish up as hollow tubes whose function is to transport water and mineral salts from the roots to the leaves.

  Being lignified, vessels and tracheids also contribute to support. Together with sclerenchyma, they make up the **wood** of shrubs and trees. Typically there is a lot of wood in the trunk and branches but less in the roots, except in specialised roots providing support such as the ones in figure 11.20.

- **Phloem tissue** consists mainly of unlignified living cells called **sieve tubes** whose function is to transport soluble food substances from one part of the plant to another. Although they are alive, they derive much of their energy from adjacent **companion cells**.

Animal and plant tissues compared

Animals and plants lead very different lives, so it is not surprising to find that their tissues show many differences. If we get down to the core of the problem these differences stem from one basic distinction, namely nutrition. Plants, unlike animals, can synthesise their own organic food. This of course relates to the fact that plants possess photosynthetic tissue whereas animals do not. But it explains other things too. For example, since animals cannot synthesise their own organic food, they have to obtain it in ready-made form, and this often means searching for it. This explains why animals possess muscle and nerve tissue, as well as specialised epithelia for digesting and absorbing food. Photosynthesis renders such tissues unnecessary in plants.

All this can be summed up by saying that their method of feeding imposes on animals the necessity to move and respond rapidly, and this demands a greater range of specialised tissues than are necessary in plants. It is a curious paradox that the root cause of this is that animals *lack* the ability to perform a chemical process which plants are capable of performing, namely photosynthesis.

Organs and organ systems

A further indication of the complexity of animals is seen in the fact that all but the simplest ones possess **organs**. An organ is a structurally distinct part of the body which performs one or more particular functions. Organs are generally made up of several types of tissue which have a highly organised structural relationship with each other. Take the mammalian stomach, for example. The wall of the stomach consists of smooth muscle, nerve tissue,

Figure 11.20 A giant Banyan tree in Rajasthan, India. In the course of its growth large aerial roots have been let down from the larger branches. Well endowed with strengthening tissue, these prop roots form, in effect, secondary trunks, providing extra support and enabling the tree to spread over a considerable area. It is said that Alexander the Great sheltered the whole of his army under a single Banyan tree.

connective tissue, blood and several different types of epithelia, all organised into a complex system of interrelated structures whose combined function is the storage and processing of food before it passes on to the small intestine.

In most animals different organs are interrelated to form **organ systems**. An organ system is made up of several organs which together perform a specific function. For example, the stomach is part of the digestive system which also includes the rest of the gut (alimentary canal), along with various accessory organs such as the pancreas and liver. Sometimes an organ belongs to more than one system. The pancreas, for example, secretes hormones in addition to digestive enzymes, and therefore belongs to the endocrine as well as the digestive system.

In the development of organs animals are unsurpassed in the world of living things. However, plants have organs too though they are generally less elaborate and fewer in number than in animals. One of the most obvious plant organs is the leaf whose principal function is photosynthesis. The flower is a reproductive organ, and structures such as bulbs and corms are organs of perennation and vegetative reproduction.

Whole organisms

So far in this chapter we have been talking about parts of organisms: cells, tissues, organs and organ systems. Now we turn our attention to the whole organism – the *individual*.

A distinction may be made between organisms which consist of only one cell (**unicellular organisms**) and those that consist of more than one cell (**multicellular organisms**). Some multicellular organisms are constructed mainly of tissues and have few, if any, organs. Others possess organs as the basis of their construction.

Because unicellular organisms consist of only one cell, it is tempting to think of them as simple. Nothing could be further from the truth. They can be highly complex. The reason is that they have to carry out within a single cell all the functions which a multicellular organism can divide between many different types of cell. This is well illustrated by *Paramecium* which is described in the box on page 186.

Most organisms are single entities and there is no difficulty in recognising an individual. Some organisms, however, are made up of numerous similar parts or **modules**. A rose bush, for instance, consists of lots of branches each bearing leaves and buds, and the cnidarian *Obelia* is composed of numerous hydra-like individuals. Organisms which are constructed on this sort of plan are described as **modular organisms**.

Certain modular organisms are regarded as colonies rather than single individuals. Such is the case with *Obelia* and its relative the Portuguese man of war (figure 11.21). The Portuguese man of war is a floating colony consisting of several types of individual, each specialising in a particular activity. The colony behaves as a single unit – a sort of 'super-organism' whose individuals are equivalent to the organs of other multicellular organisms. The phylum to which these animals belong, the cnidarians, is important ecologically: it includes the corals whose vast colonies, encrusted with calcium carbonate, make up coral reefs.

The advantages of being multicellular

A single cell cannot grow indefinitely. When it reaches a certain size it either stops growing or divides into two smaller cells which then grow. Indefinite

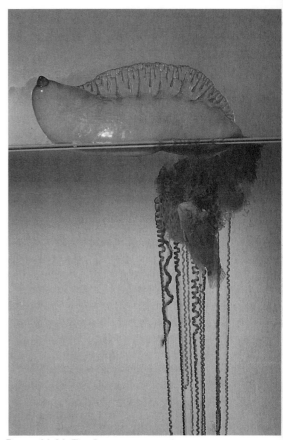

Figure 11.21 The Portugese man of war, *Physalia*, a complex floating colony. Different types of individual hang down from the underside of the gas-filled float. Some have long retractable tentacles armed with sting cells. The tentacles may be over 7 m long and are used for defence and catching prey such as the fish seen here. Other individuals have mouths and are for feeding. And some produce gametes and serve a reproductive function.

Paramecium, a complex unicell

Paramecium is a comparatively large freshwater protoctist whose internal structure can be observed under the light microscope. In addition to the usual organelles which one would expect to find in any cell (mitochondria, endoplasmic reticulum and so on), it has a number of special features (illustration 1). The cell is bounded by a protective **pellicle** from which protrude large numbers of **cilia**. By beating backwards and forwards the cilia 'row' the organism through the water. Just beneath the pellicle are numerous **trichocysts**: each is a tiny sac from which a needle-like thread can be discharged. Some species use these for defence.

There are two nuclei: the **macronucleus** controls metabolic functions, including growth, while the **micronucleus** is necessary for reproduction. Two **contractile vacuoles**, one at each end, get rid of excess water (osmoregulation). The water drains through the collecting channels into the contractile vacuole which, when full, discharges its contents to the outside through a hole in the pellicle. Small particles of food, swept into the **oral vestibule** by ciliary action, are taken up into **food vacuoles** at the base of the **cytopharynx**. The food vacuoles circulate through the cytoplasm while the food is being digested, and any undigestible material is discharged through an opening in the pellicle called the **cytoproct**.

Perhaps the most intriguing aspect of *Paramecium* is the pellicle and associated structures. The electron microscope has shown this part of the organism to be surprisingly elaborate. The **basal bodies** of the cilia are interconnected by a system of threads (microtubules) situated immediately beneath the pellicle which itself is elaborately sculptured (illustration 2).

The cilia beat in a beautifully

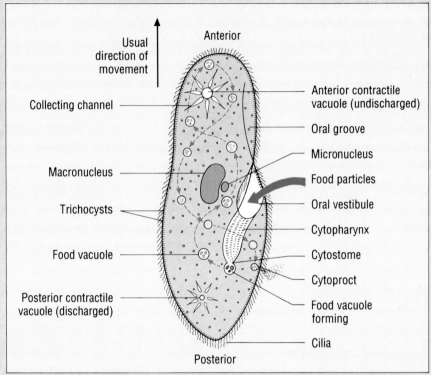

Illustration 1 Diagram of *Paramecium* showing structures visible under the light microscope. The arrows show the course taken by food particles which have been taken into the cell.

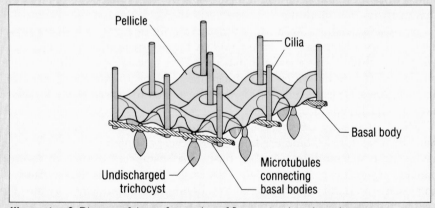

Illustration 2 Diagram of the surface region of *Paramecium* based on electron micrographs. The basal bodies of the cilia are interconnected by a system of threads immediately beneath the elaborately sculptured pellicle.

coordinated manner in which each performs its backstroke slightly before the one in front, a so-called **metachronal rhythm** (see page 527). This ensures that the organism swims smoothly, rather than jerkily. If the organism bumps into an obstacle or swims into an unfavourable region, the cilia go into reverse and the organism backs away.

It then alters its direction slightly, and swims forward again. By means of this avoiding reaction noxious stimuli are avoided.

So *Paramecium*, though unicellular, is by no means simple. This is true not only of its structure but also of the way it works. The cilia, for example are as coordinated as the legs of a multicellular organism.

growth seems to be limited by the nucleus. It appears that a single nucleus can only exert control over a certain volume of cytoplasm. This means that for an organism to increase in size beyond a certain point it must become multicellular.

Becoming multicellular, then, allows an increase in size. With this comes the possibility of specialisation: instead of every cell carrying out all tasks, certain cells become specialised for one function, others for a different function. This **division of labour** permits greater efficiency and enables the organism to exploit environments that are denied to simpler forms. But, although it is an advantage to the whole organism, it means that individual cells are unable to exist on their own: the cells lose their independence and have to rely on one another's specialised activities.

With increased size and cell specialisation come all sorts of other advantages. For example, in animals better muscles and a skeleton can be developed. These give the animal greater strength and allow it to tackle larger prey, while at the same time enabling it to move faster towards prey or away from predators. Having specialised cells also means that more sophisticated physiological mechanisms can be developed which allow, for example, a constant body temperature to be maintained.

Although the multicellular state permits greater specialisation, the increased size that accompanies it can create difficulties. One of these difficulties concerns the acquisition of oxygen and food materials and their distribution to the cells. How this difficulty has been overcome is the subject of the next chapter.

Symmetry

If you examine an animal such as the toad in figure 11.22A, you will find that its external and internal structures are arranged symmetrically on either side of the midline. Now imagine bisecting the animal in two so as to produce two halves which are mirror images of each other. There is only one plane through which this is possible, and that is vertically down the middle. Such an animal is described as **bilaterally symmetrical**. Most animals, including the human, are bilaterally symmetrical at least in their external features.

Now think of an animal like the sea anemone (figure 11.22B). In this case the various structures are arranged round a central point like the spokes of a wheel. To get two mirror image halves, this animal could be bisected in more or less any plane that passes through the centre. Such an animal is described as **radially symmetrical**. Radial symmetry is seen in a number of invertebrate animals.

There is no sharp dividing line between these two types of symmetry. For instance, sea anemones are radially symmetrical externally but bilaterally symmetrical inside. Higher plants have radially symmetrical stems and roots, but bilaterally symmetrical leaves – and flowers may be either radially or bilaterally symmetrical depending on the particular group the plant belongs to. For example, the rose and buttercup families have radially symmetrical flowers, whereas the orchid and pea families have bilaterally symmetrical flowers. Animals such as mammals and birds are bilaterally symmetrical externally but show some degree of asymmetry internally.

Radial symmetry is found mainly in sedentary or slow-moving organisms. Bilateral symmetry, on the other hand, is associated with locomotion in a particular direction. A bilaterally symmetrical animal has a definite front and back end, and a top side and bottom side. These are known as **anterior, posterior, dorsal** and **ventral** respectively.

Figure 11.22 The two main types of symmetry found amongst organisms.

Top Bilateral symmetry displayed here by the Oriental fire-bellied toad *Bombina orientalis* with respect to its limbs.

Bottom Radial symmetry as seen in the Dahlia sea anemone *Tealia felina* with respect to its tentacles.

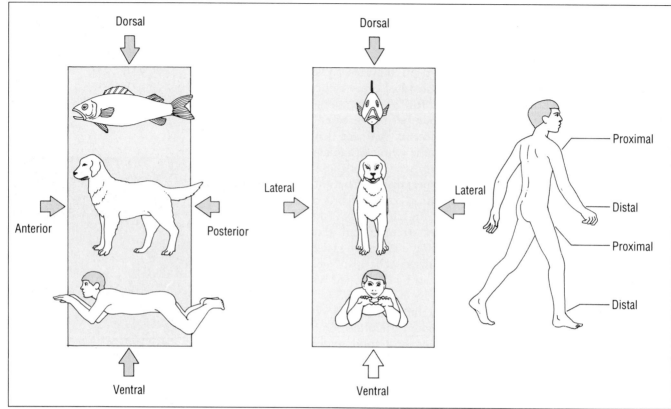

Figure 11.23 The principal terms used to describe the topography of animals.

Directional locomotion is associated with the development of a **head** at the leading end, with all the elaborations which that involves (see page 453). Typically such animals have appendages of one sort or another projecting from both sides of the body. Some or all of the appendages may be used as **limbs** for locomotion. The near end of an appendage, i.e. the end nearest to the centre of the body, is described as the **proximal end**, the other end as the **distal end** (figure 11.23).

Sub-cellular organisation: viruses

Viruses are the smallest objects to display fundamental properties of life. Although they have no powers of active movement, they can reproduce, transmit characteristics to the next generation, and evolve by natural selection. However, they can only reproduce inside the cell of a living organism. In so doing they destroy the cell. For this reason viruses are usually associated with disease. Smallpox, measles, poliomyelitis, AIDS and numerous plant diseases are all caused by viruses.

Viruses are so small that they can only be seen with the electron microscope (figure 11.24). However, they were discovered before the electron microscope was invented by an ingenious experiment which is explained in the box on page 189. Now, thanks to the electron microscope, many types of virus have been described, and chemical analyses of them have told us what they consist of. In fact a virus is nothing more than a coiled up strand of nucleic acid surrounded by a protein coat (see page 725). It reproduces by entering, or injecting its nucleic acid into, a living cell of its host. The host cell may then make numerous copies of the virus, and the cell is destroyed in the process.

Viruses are on the borderline between life and non-life: as someone has put it, you don't know whether to call them 'organules' or 'molecisms'.

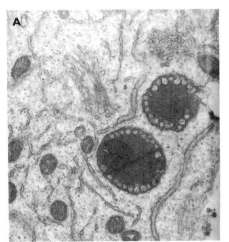

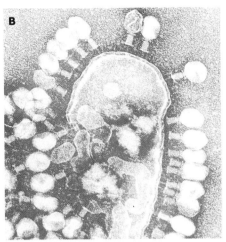

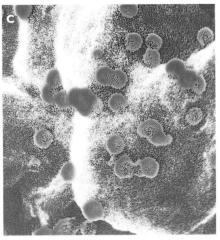

They are like living organisms in possessing replicable nucleic acid, but non-living in being unable to transfer energy and assimilate new materials without the participation of a living cell. Sir Peter Medawar has described a virus as 'simply a piece of bad news wrapped up in protein'. Certainly the damage they cause is out of all proportion to their apparent simplicity.

You will find much more about viruses in other parts of the book, but in the meantime consider this problem. Viruses are generally considered to be non-living entities and as such they are not put into a kingdom or classified in the same way that organisms are. Do you think this is justified?

Figure 11.24 Electron micrographs of three types of virus greatly magnified.
A Semliki Forest viruses, the cause of human encephalitis, replicating inside two vacuoles (the black bodies) in a brain cell.
B Bacteriophage viruses surrounding and destroying a colon bacillus, *Escherichia coli*.
C Human immunodeficiency viruses (HIV), the causative agent of AIDS, on the surface of a T-lymphocyte.

How viruses were discovered

Professor M.W. Beijerinck of Delft University, Holland, was a tyrannical head of department. He said that scientists should not get married, sacked an assistant for becoming engaged and began his lectures with 'gentlemen and ladies'. But he was a superb research worker.

Beijerinck suspected that there might be disease-causing agents smaller than bacteria. So he extracted some juice from a tobacco plant that was suffering from tobacco mosaic disease. He then passed the juice through a filter made of porous clay whose pores were too small to let through any known bacteria. Finally he applied the filtrate to a leaf of a healthy tobacco plant and found that the plant quickly developed tobacco mosaic disease.

Of course the filtrate might have been infective simply because it contained a toxic fluid produced by the bacteria. So Beijerinck extracted and filtered some juice from the second plant – the one he had infected – and applied it to a leaf of a third plant. This, too, developed the disease. Moreover, the filtered juice extracted from the third plant induced the disease in a fourth plant, and so on indefinitely. This suggested that the infective agent was multiplying, for otherwise it would have been rendered ineffective by progressive dilution.

This was the first indication that disease-causing particles of sub-microscopic dimensions existed. Beijerinck himself thought that he had obtained some kind of infectious fluid. He called it 'virus' which simply means poison.

That was at the beginning of the twentieth century. It was not until the early 1930s that viruses were actually seen. Wendell Stanley, a young American scientist working at the Rockefeller Institute in New York, extracted, purified and crystallised the juice obtained from diseased tobacco plants. The crystals proved to be highly infective when applied in solution to healthy tobacco plants. When the crystals were viewed in the then newly invented electron microscope, objects like the ones in the illustration were seen. These are tobacco mosaic viruses (TMV), the first type of virus to be isolated and characterised.

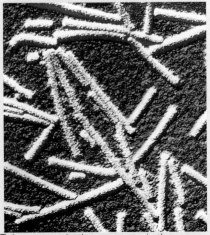

Tobacco mosaic viruses as seen in the electron microscope, magnified approximately 50 000 times.

Summary

1 Cells are massed together to form **tissues**, and different tissues are massed together to form **organs**. Different organs may be structurally and/or functionally united to form **organ systems**.

2 **Animal tissues** include:

- **Epithelium** which is subdivided into squamous, cuboidal, columnar, ciliated, glandular and stratified.
- **Connective** tissue which is subdivided into areolar, collagen (white fibrous), elastic (yellow elastic) and adipose (fatty) tissue.
- **Skeletal tissue** which is subdivided into cartilage and bone.
- **Blood.**
- **Nerve tissue.**
- **Muscle tissue** which is subdivided into smooth, cardiac (heart) and skeletal muscle.
- **Reproductive tissue.**

3 Some classifications of tissues include skeletal tissue and blood as types of connective tissue. All these tissues originate from the same type of embryonic cell, and all consist of cells surrounded by some kind of matrix.

4 Plant tissues include:

- **Meristematic tissue.**
- **Epidermis.**
- **Parenchyma** (packing tissue) of which there are several specialised types including **chlorenchyma** (photosynthetic tissue).
- **Collenchyma.**
- **Sclerenchyma.**
- **Vascular tissue** which is subdivided into xylem and phloem.
- **Cork.**

5 The chief differences between animal and plant tissues (and between animals and plants in general) can be related to their different methods of nutrition.

6 In **unicellular organisms** all functions have to be carried out within one cell.

7 Most organisms are **multicellular**, and this carries with it certain advantages and disadvantages.

8 Some organisms, e.g. colonial animals and many types of flowering plants, are **modular organisms** composed of numerous similar parts (**modules**).

9 Organisms show various types of symmetry, the most common being **radial symmetry** and **bilateral symmetry**.

10 Terms commonly used to describe the topography of animals include **anterior, posterior, dorsal, ventral** and **lateral**.

11 **Viruses** are sub-cellular particles of protein and nucleic acid, generally considered to be non-living.

Review questions

1 Make a list of all the functions of epithelia you can think of, and give one example of each.

2 What are the main structural and functional differences between collagen and elastic tissue? Why do you think tendons are made of collagen tissue whereas ligaments are made of elastic tissue?

3 What is adipose tissue, where is it found and what are its main functions?

4 Give reasons for regarding skeletal tissue and blood as types of connective tissue.

5 Sclerenchyma tissue is functionally equivalent to bone. Suggest similarities between them which might help to explain their ability to support heavy loads.

6 Make a list of five organ systems of the human body, and say which organs belong to each system.

7 By means of a table, compare the tissues of a mammal and a flowering plant.

8 Which structures in *Paramecium* are equivalent to these structures in the human: legs, mouth, anus, kidneys and skin. In each case say in what sense the structures are equivalent.

9 How would you define a virus? Do you think viruses should be regarded as living organisms?

10 Explain, without the use of diagrams, the difference between radial and bilateral symmetry. Which organs or organ systems in the human body are *asymmetrical*. Can you think of cases where the entire organism is asymmetrical?

Further reading

For a survey of animal tissues, see *An Advanced Atlas of Histology* by W.H. Freeman and Brian Bracegirdle (Heinemann, 1976). For plant tissues see *Anatomy and Activities of Plants* by C.J. Clegg and Gene Cox (Murray, 1978). The latter book has the added merit of looking at tissues from a functional point of view.

You will find a good account of *Paramecium* and other unicellular organisms in Ralph Buchsbaum's *Animals without Backbones* (Penguin, 1975). This is a wonderfully readable book which makes invertebrate zoology fun! The latest edition, written with three co-authors and published by Chicago University Press in 1987, is particularly useful.

In *Biology, Advanced Topics* there is a discussion of cell size in relation to the development of the multicellular state, and slime moulds as organisms which are both unicellular and multicellular.

Movement in and out of cells

In Chapter 10 we saw that the plasma membrane is composed of a double layer of phospholipid molecules, the **lipid bilayer**. You will recall that the interior of the membrane is hydrophobic – that is, it repels water molecules. This enables the membrane to hold in the water-soluble contents of the cell and prevent them leaking out. However, this very property makes it difficult for water-soluble substances to pass in and out of cells. At least it *would* be difficult were it not for special mechanisms which make such movements possible. In this chapter we shall look at these mechanisms and see how they enable substances to get in and out of cells.

In general, substances pass in and out of cells by four main processes:

- **Diffusion.**
- **Active transport.**
- **Osmosis.**
- **Endocytosis** and **exocytosis.**

We shall consider these four processes in turn, and discuss their consequences on the functioning of cells.

Diffusion

If you drop a crystal of potassium permanganate into a beaker of water it dissolves. Gradually the purple colour of the permanganate spreads through the water until eventually it is uniformly distributed. The reason for this is that, as the crystal dissolves, the permanganate ions move away from the crystal through the water.

What causes the ions to behave in this way? The answer depends on the fact that they are in a state of continual random motion. They can move in any direction, but the fact that initially there are far more of them in the vicinity of the crystal increases the probability that they will move *away* from the crystal. In other words, there is a *net* movement of ions away from the crystal. This process is called **diffusion**.

Diffusion is defined as the net movement of particles (molecules or ions as the case may be) from a region where they are at a relatively high concentration to a region where they are at a lower concentration. The difference in concentration between the two regions is called the **concentration gradient** or **diffusion gradient**. Diffusion will always take place wherever such a gradient exists, and it will continue until eventually the particles are uniformly distributed throughout the system. When that happens **equilibrium** is said to be reached.

Diffusion is a passive process which takes place by random thermal motion. It does not require energy from metabolism, and it will take place equally readily in non-living and living systems.

Why is diffusion important in biology?

Think of a cell in your own body. To stay alive the cell takes up oxygen. Because the oxygen is continually being used up in respiration, its concentration inside the cell is lower than in the blood and tissue fluids. This concentration gradient results in oxygen molecules diffusing into the cell from outside. The same thing applies to carbon dioxide but in the other direction: its concentration is higher inside the cell, where it is continually being formed, than outside. This causes the carbon dioxide molecules to diffuse out of the cell.

CHAPTER 12

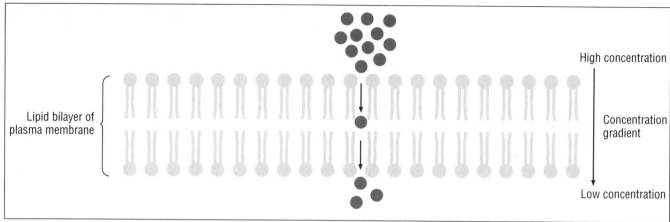

Figure 12.1 Simple diffusion through the plasma membrane of a cell. Small uncharged particles pass between the lipid molecules down a concentration gradient.

Anything that increases the concentration gradient, i.e. makes it *steeper*, will speed up diffusion. This is one function of a **circulatory system**. By quickly carrying away the diffused substance, the circulation helps to maintain a steep concentration gradient, thus encouraging further diffusion. Similarly, the conversion of the diffused substance into another substance will help to maintain a concentration gradient, favouring continued diffusion. For example, when glucose enters a cell it is rapidly converted into glucose 6-phosphate (see page 232), thus sustaining the gradient and encouraging more glucose to diffuse into the cell.

If diffusion is to take place, any membranes or partitions in the system must be readily permeated by the molecules or ions in question. Such is the case with the plasma membrane in relation to oxygen and carbon dioxide: the membrane is permeable to both these gases, as indeed it is to any small, uncharged particles. They pass between the lipid molecules as shown in figure 12.1.

Facilitated diffusion

Charged particles (ions), and relatively large molecules such as glucose, do not readily pass through the plasma membrane because they are relatively insoluble in lipid. In the plasma membrane certain proteins assist such particles to diffuse in or out of the cell. This process is called **facilitated diffusion**. The protein molecules span the membrane from one side to the other. There are two types: **channel proteins** and **carrier proteins**.

Channel proteins

Figure 12.2 illustrates a channel protein. The configuration of the protein molecule is such that it forms a water-filled pore in the membrane. You can

Figure 12.2 Facilitated diffusion through a channel protein in the plasma membrane of a cell. As with simple diffusion, the diffusing particles move down a concentration gradient.

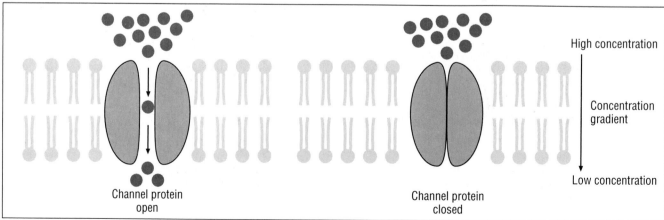

see one in figure 10.25 on page 168. Unlike the interior of the lipid bilayer, the lining of the channel is hydrophilic ('water-loving'), so water-soluble substances pass through it relatively easily.

Channel proteins are particularly concerned with transporting ions in and out of cells. The channels are selective, allowing certain ions to pass through but not others. Some of the channels can open and close rather like gates. These **gated channels** open only when they receive an appropriate signal. The signal may be a mechanical disturbance of the membrane, a change in the voltage across the membrane, or the binding of another molecule or ion with the protein.

We shall come across examples of these three types of signal in later parts of the book. In the meantime, can you predict in general terms why these gated channels are important in the lives of organisms?

Channel proteins speed up the rate at which ions diffuse across the plasma membrane. However, like simple diffusion, the movement is passive and does not involve the transfer of metabolic energy. Consequently it can only take place *down* a concentration gradient.

Carrier proteins

In this case the diffusing molecule or ion combines with the protein and is then carried across the membrane and deposited on the other side. It is not known exactly how this happens, but figure 12.3 shows a model which is consistent with the known facts. As with channel proteins, the movement is entirely passive.

Carrier proteins have been likened to enzymes. The relationship between the protein and the transported molecule is specific, and the mode of attachment is similar to that between the active site of an enzyme and its substrate (see page 219). Carrier proteins are susceptible to poisons, just as enzymes are, and several different molecules may compete for transport by the same carrier.

Active transport

There are certain biological situations where molecules or ions appear to break the laws of physics and move *against* a concentration gradient – that is, from a region of low concentration to a region of higher concentration. A spectacular example is provided by certain seaweeds which take up iodide ions so vigorously that they are more than two million times more

Figure 12.3 Facilitated diffusion via a carrier protein in the plasma membrane of a cell. The carrier protein picks up the particles on one side of the membrane and releases them on the other side. Again, notice that the particles move down a concentration gradient.

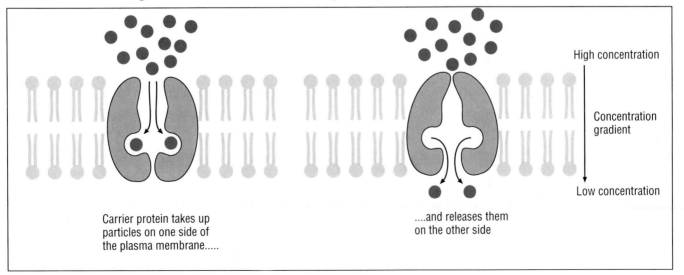

Carrier protein takes up particles on one side of the plasma membrane.....

....and releases them on the other side

High concentration

Concentration gradient

Low concentration

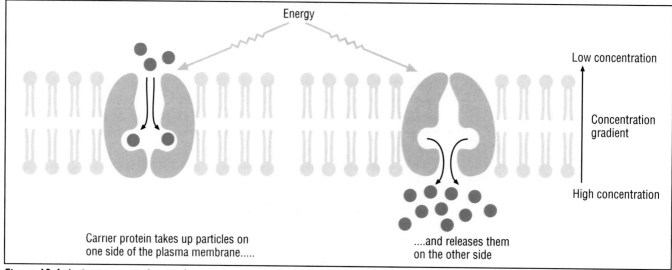

Energy

Low concentration

Concentration gradient

High concentration

Carrier protein takes up particles on one side of the plasma membrane.....

....and releases them on the other side

Figure 12.4 Active transport via a carrier protein in the plasma membrane of a cell. Energy is transferred to the carrier protein from the hydrolysis of ATP. This enables the protein to move the particles *against* a concentration gradient.

concentrated inside the cells than in the surrounding water. This movement of molecules or ions against a concentration gradient is called **active transport.**

Active transport can only take place in a living system which transfers energy by respiration. Respiration involves the hydrolysis of ATP (see page 230). Anything that inhibits the formation of ATP, or prevents it being used, stops active transport. Cyanide, for example, prevents ATP being synthesised and therefore inhibits active transport. Another interesting observation is that cells which are known to engage in active transport on a large scale have exceptionally large numbers of mitochondria, the site of respiration.

How does active transport take place? The current view is that it involves carrier proteins similar to those responsible for facilitated diffusion. However, in active transport the carrier protein is coupled with a source of energy which enables it to transport molecules or ions against a concentration gradient (figure 12.4). The energy source is ATP and the carrier protein is ATPase, the enzyme which catalyses the hydrolsis of ATP. Ion gradients created by active transport can in turn be used to provide energy for the transport of other ions and molecules.

Active transport is extremely important. It allows cells to take up nutrients even when their concentration outside the cell is very low. It also enables cells to get rid of unwanted substances when their concentration is much greater outside the cell. We shall meet examples later in the book. The carrier proteins work in only one direction so, although there may be some leakage in the other direction, they effectively act as one-way valves.

Active transport is responsible for the well established observation that animal cells contain high concentrations of potassium ions but low concentrations of sodium ions. The mechanism responsible for this is the **sodium–potassium pump** which moves these two ions in opposite directions across the plasma membrane. The sodium–potassium pump has a particular significance for **excitable cells**, such as nerve cells, which respond to stimuli (see Chapter 25).

Is this two-way movement of potassium and sodium ions performed by the same carrier or by two different ones? This was investigated by following the passage of radioactively labelled ions across the plasma membrane of certain cells. It was found that the concentrations of sodium and potassium ions on the two sides of the membrane are interdependent, suggesting that the same carrier transports both ions. More recent work has

How the sodium–potassium pump was discovered

The discovery of the sodium-potassium pump is a classic example of how scientific progress is made. Guest author Peter Kohn explains.

In 1989 a major scientific journal celebrated the publication of its one thousandth volume by publishing some of the most important papers from its earlier volumes together with comments from the original authors on how the papers came to be written. One author, Jens Skou, gives a fascinating insight into the discovery of the sodium – potassium pump. His comments reveal how a clear-thinking and careful scientist may make a major breakthrough in a completely unexpected direction.

Skou was a Danish medical doctor who had taken a few years away from his clinical training in the early 1950s to study the action of local anaesthetics. He had discovered that a substance's anaesthetic action was related to its ability to dissolve in a layer of lipid spread on the surface of water. He believed that by dissolving in the lipid part of the plasma membrane, the anaesthetic molecules affected the opening of sodium channels which he assumed to be protein. This, he argued, would affect the movement of sodium ions and make nerve cells inexcitable, thus causing anaesthesia.

Skou thought that other types of membrane protein might also be affected by local anaesthetics dissolving in the lipid part of the membrane. He therefore had the idea of looking at an enzyme which was embedded in the membrane and finding out if its properties were affected by local anaesthetics. He had heard about an ATPase which had recently been found in the sheath surrounding the giant nerve fibres (axons) of the squid, and he reasoned that it might be a suitable candidate for his studies. As he had

no access to squid giant axons, he decided to look for the enzyme in crab nerves.

The enzyme was there, but unfortunately its activity was very variable and he needed a highly active enzyme for his studies. Eventually he managed to discover that ATPase was most active when exposed to the right combination of sodium, potassium and magnesium ions. Only then did he realise that this enzyme might have something to do with the active movement of sodium and potassium across the plasma membrane. This idea had been postulated many years before – in fact the term 'sodium–potassium pump' was already in use. However, the mechanism was quite unknown.

Skou published his findings. However, in his paper he was wary of identifying the enzyme with the active ion movement, so he left out the term 'sodium–potassium pump' from the title of his paper. Indeed, he seems only gradually to have realised the importance of his discovery, and he continued his studies on local anaesthetics with a different enzyme – cholinesterase – which was more active than ATPase and could be obtained more easily.

In 1958 Skou went to a conference in Vienna to describe his work on cholinesterase. There he met a former colleague, Robert Post, who had been studying the pumping of sodium and potassium in red blood cells. Post had recently discovered that three sodium ions were pumped out of the cell for every two potassium ions pumped in, and in his research he had made use of a substance called ouabain which had recently been shown to inhibit the pump.

Post had not read Skou's paper but was excited when Skou told him about his work with ATPase. Post asked whether the enzyme was inhibited by ouabain. At this stage Skou was unaware that ouabain

Jens Skou, who discovered the sodium-potassium pump.

inhibited the pump, but he immediately telephoned to his laboratory in Denmark and arranged for the experiment to be done. Ouabain did indeed inhibit the enzyme, thus establishing a link between the enzyme and the sodium–potassium pump.

Later it became clear that the enzyme is the complete pump, not merely part of it. This was shown by reincorporating highly purified enzyme into a phospholipid bilayer and reconstituting the pump. Although the identity of the pump and the enzyme is now completely established, the structural changes which allow the enzyme to perform the transport process are only gradually being revealed.

Jens Skou never returned to his medical training. Instead he has spent a lifetime studying the enzyme responsible for the sodium-potassium pump. Although now retired, he still continues his research in the Institute of Biophysics at the University of Aarhus in Denmark.

confirmed this idea and has provided some of the details of how it may happen.

Active transport of sodium and potassium ions and other chemicals provides a mechanism for transporting water across membranes. The active pumping of the chemicals across the membrane creates a concentration gradient and the water molecules then follow passively. The mechanism responsible for the passive movement of the water molecules is **osmosis** which is the subject of the next section.

Osmosis

Look at the experiment in figure 12.5. The mouth of a thistle funnel is covered with a membrane such as cellophane. The funnel is then filled with a concentrated solution of sucrose and immersed in a beaker of pure water. What happens? Quite quickly the level of the solution in the tube begins to rise. This is because water is passing into it from the surrounding beaker.

To explain why this happens it is necessary to appreciate that the membrane is permeable to the water molecules but impermeable (or relatively so) to the much larger sucrose molecules. In other words the membrane is **partially permeable**.

Now consider the situation on either side of this partially permeable membrane. In the beaker there is nothing but water molecules; in the funnel there are water molecules plus sucrose molecules. The presence of the sucrose molecules means that the concentration of water molecules in the funnel is less than in the beaker. The result is that in a given period of time more water molecules diffuse from the beaker to the funnel than from the funnel to the beaker. In other words there is a net movement of water molecules from the beaker into the funnel. The movement of water molecules across a partially permeable membrane is known as **osmosis**.

Osmosis is really a special case of diffusion. It involves the diffusion of water molecules from a region where they are highly concentrated (the beaker) to a region where they are less concentrated (the funnel) across a partially permeable membrane.

The fluid in the funnel is, of course, a **solution**. A solution consists of the molecules of one substance (the **solute**, in this case sucrose) dissolved in another (the **solvent**, in this case water). In the experiment the beaker contains pure water. However, osmosis would still occur from the beaker to the funnel if the beaker contained another sucrose solution, provided that the concentration of water molecules was greater than in the funnel.

If the concentration of water molecules is the same in the beaker and the funnel, there will be no net movement of water into or out of the funnel; and if the concentration of water molecules is greater in the funnel than in the beaker, there will be a net movement of water from funnel to beaker. In general terms, *osmosis will occur whenever two solutions containing different concentrations of water molecules are separated by a partially permeable membrane.*

The membrane does not have to be *completely* impermeable to the solute molecules. Many naturally occurring membranes allow the passage of solute as well as solvent, though not at the same rate. All that is necessary for osmosis to occur is that the solvent molecules move more rapidly than the solute molecules.

Water potential

We can explain the movement of water molecules in terms of thermodynamics. Look at figure 12.6. You will appreciate that there will be a net

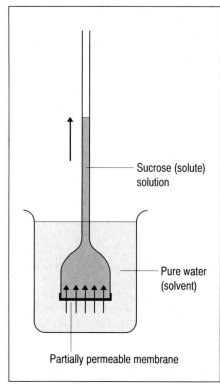

Figure 12.5 A simple demonstration of osmosis. The apparatus is called an osmometer. The solid arrows indicate the net flow of water (solvent) into the sucrose (solute) solution. The membrane, being partially permeable, allows water molecules to pass into the thistle funnel from the beaker but prevents sucrose molecules passing from the thistle funnel into the beaker. As a result of the net flow of water into the funnel, the solution rises up the tube as indicated by the broken arrow.

Sucrose (solute) solution

Pure water (solvent)

Partially permeable membrane

movement of water molecules from the left of the partially permeable membrane to the right. The reason, in thermodynamic terms, is that the potential energy of the water molecules on the left is greater than the potential energy of the water molecules on the right. The potential energy of the water molecules is called the **water potential**. Water will diffuse from a region of high water potential to a region of lower water potential, and the steeper the water potential gradient the greater will be the tendency for water to diffuse in this direction. For practical purposes we can therefore define water potential as the capacity of a system to *lose* water.

At a standard temperature and pressure (in this case 25°C and 100 kPa) pure water is given a water potential of zero. Adding solute molecules to the water *lowers* the water potential, making it negative. This is because the presence of the solute molecules lowers the concentration of the water molecules, thus reducing the number of water molecules that can diffuse out of it (remember, water potential is the capacity of a system to *lose* water). If you go on adding solute, the water potential gets lower and lower, i.e. more and more negative.

The symbol used for the water potential and other energy potentials in cells is ψ (the Greek letter psi). It is customary to express ψ in kilopascals (kPa) or megapascals (MPa). When water flows down a water potential gradient, the net movement of water molecules is always from a less negative value (e.g. –500 kPa) to a more negative value (e.g. –600 kPa). If you find these negatives confusing, you might find it helpful to read the box at the foot of the page.

Osmotic pressure and water potential, two alternative terms

Look again at figure 12.5. As more and more water flows across the partially permeable membrane, a hydrostatic pressure builds up in the funnel. This is called **osmotic pressure**. A solution with a low water potential has a high osmotic pressure.

One can use either water potential or osmotic pressure to express the concentration of a solution i.e. the relative amounts of water and solute. Animal and medical physiologists generally use osmotic pressure, whereas plant biologists tend to use water potential. This is rather unfortunate, but until agreement is reached we have to get used to both systems. The various terms are summarised at the bottom of figure 12.6.

In the current edition of this book we shall use osmotic pressure mainly in animal contexts and water potential for plants. The terms are not incompatible or mutually exclusive – they are simply different ways of looking at the same thing. One of the advantages of the water potential concept, particularly in botany, is that it need not be restricted to osmotic situations. It can be applied to any situation where water is present, including soil and air.

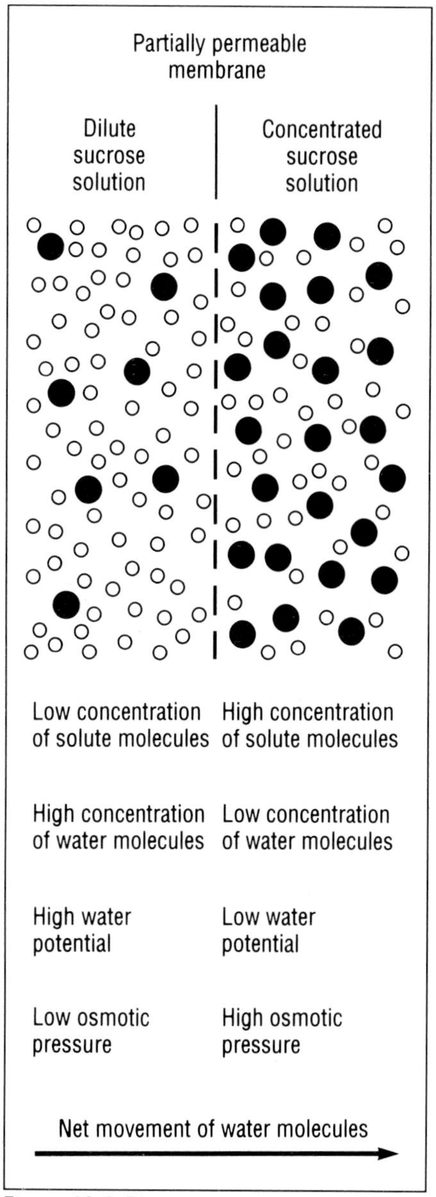

Partially permeable membrane

| Dilute sucrose solution | Concentrated sucrose solution |

Low concentration of solute molecules — High concentration of solute molecules

High concentration of water molecules — Low concentration of water molecules

High water potential — Low water potential

Low osmotic pressure — High osmotic pressure

Net movement of water molecules →

Figure 12.6 Diagram summarising the conditions on the two sides of a partially permeable membrane, and the terms used to describe them. The large black blobs represent sucrose molecules, the smaller white circles represent water molecules. The terms 'high' and 'low' are relative.

Trouble with negatives?

In plant water relations some people (including the author of this chapter) have difficulty with the semantic problem of 'high' and 'low' with respect to negative values of the water potential. Thus a water potential of –600 kPa is lower than a water potential of –500 kPa, though 600 is the larger figure.

If you have difficulty deciding whether a more negative value is higher or lower, you might find it useful to make a mental comparison with below zero temperatures. You probably have no difficulty knowing that a temperature of –15°C is lower than –10°C. Exactly the same principle applies to water potential values.

This analogy was suggested by Professor Sutcliffe who found it to be helpful with his students.

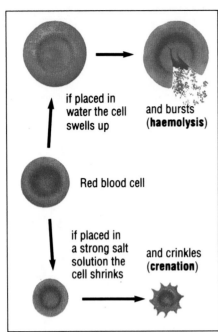

if placed in
water the cell
swells up

and bursts
(**haemolysis**)

Red blood cell

if placed in
a strong salt
solution the
cell shrinks

and crinkles
(**crenation**)

Figure 12.7 The effect of immersing a red blood cell in **A** pure water or a hypotonic solution, and **B** a hypertonic solution. The cell only bursts if the hypotonic solution is very dilute.

Osmosis and cells

Cells owe many of their properties to the fact that the plasma membrane is partially permeable. If a cell is surrounded by pure water, or a solution whose solute concentration is lower than that of the cell's contents, water flows into the cell by osmosis and the cell swells up. In this case the water potential of the external solution is higher, and the osmotic pressure lower, than the solution inside the cell. The external solution is said to be **hypotonic** to the cell (*hypo* means 'lower than').

On the other hand, if the cell is surrounded by a solution whose solute concentration is greater than that of the cell's contents, water flows out of the cell and the cell shrinks. In this case the water potential of the external solution is lower, and the osmotic pressure higher, than the solution inside the cell. The external solution is said to be **hypertonic** to the cell (*hyper* means 'higher than').

Finally, if the cell has the same solute concentration as the surrounding solution, there will be no net flow of water into or out of the cell. In this case the external solution is said to be **isotonic** with the cell (*iso* means 'the same as').

The terms hypotonic, hypertonic and isotonic refer, of course, to osmotic pressure and are therefore not normally used in plant studies. However, they are used in animal studies and human physiology.

How osmosis affects animal cells

Let us take red blood cells to illustrate how osmosis can affect animal cells. A solution of 0.9 per cent sodium chloride is isotonic with human cells, and if red blood cells are immersed in such a solution they will neither swell nor shrink. However, if they are placed in a hypotonic solution, they swell and may even burst (figure 12.7A). The bursting of red blood cells is called **haemolysis** (meaning literally 'blood splitting').

On the other hand, if red blood cells are immersed in a hypertonic salt solution (say 1.2 per cent) they shrink and the plasma membrane crinkles as shown in figure 12.7B. This is known as **crenation**.

It follows that if a cell is to maintain its normal size and shape it must exist permanently in an isotonic environment or, failing that, it must have special mechanisms enabling it to survive in a hypertonic or hypotonic medium. These special mechanisms are the business of **osmoregulation** which is immensely important in the lives of organisms. This is discussed in detail in Chapter 22, but one example will be mentioned at this stage to clarify the principle involved. The example is the unicellular organism *Amoeba*. (This of course is a protoctist not an animal, but we will let that pass!)

Amoeba has both marine and freshwater species. The marine species are isotonic with sea water with the result that there is no net loss or gain of water by the cell. The freshwater species, on the other hand, are markedly hypertonic to their surrounding medium. The result is that water continually flows into the cell across its partially permeable plasma membrane. The organism would undoubtedly swell up and burst, just like a red blood cell in water, were it not for the **contractile vacuole**, a spherical sac which collects water as fast as it enters and periodically discharges it to the outside. By this means the cell is prevented from swelling, and its osmotic pressure is kept constant.

There is of course another way of solving the problem, and that is to adjust the solute concentration inside the organism so that it equals the solute concentration of the external medium. Organisms do in fact do this, as is explained in Chapter 22.

Diffusion and the structure of organisms

Organisms rely on diffusion to fulfil many of their needs, and this has a profound effect on their structure. For example, the way an organism undergoes gaseous exchange is related to its size. An organism's oxygen requirements (its needs) are approximately proportional to its volume, i.e. the bulk of respiring tissue which it possesses. Its exchanges, however, are proportional to the surface area over which diffusion of oxygen takes place.

In any organism the surface area over which diffusion takes place must be sufficient to fulfil the needs of the respiring tissues. Now it is a simple mathematical rule that as an object increases in volume, the ratio of its total surface area to its volume decreases. In other words, the larger the object, the smaller is its **surface–volume ratio** (see illustration).

The significance of this principle is as follows. In a small organism like *Amoeba*, or even an earthworm, the surface–volume ratio is large enough for diffusion across the general body surface to satisfy its respiratory needs. But in larger organisms the surface–volume ratio is too small for this to be the case. Such organisms have developed special surfaces for gaseous exchange. These surfaces are usually greatly folded, thus increasing the surface area for diffusion. Lungs and gills are examples. The general strategy of increasing the surface area for diffusion is also shown by individual cells in the development of microvilli.

Lungs and gills have a good blood supply, and this illustrates another general principle. If there is no circulatory system the organism has to depend on passive diffusion for getting oxygen from the respiratory surface to the innermost tissues. In this case the size and shape of the

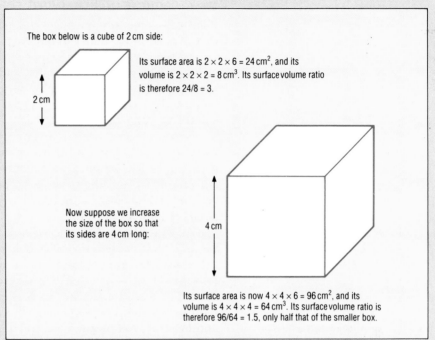

The box below is a cube of 2 cm side:

2 cm

Its surface area is $2 \times 2 \times 6 = 24\,cm^2$, and its volume is $2 \times 2 \times 2 = 8\,cm^3$. Its surface volume ratio is therefore $24/8 = 3$.

Now suppose we increase the size of the box so that its sides are 4 cm long:

4 cm

Its surface area is now $4 \times 4 \times 6 = 96\,cm^2$, and its volume is $4 \times 4 \times 4 = 64\,cm^3$. Its surface volume ratio is therefore $96/64 = 1.5$, only half that of the smaller box.

The surface-volume ratios of two different sized cubes

organism are limited by the **diffusion law** which states that the rate of diffusion is inversely proportional to the distance over which it has to take place. In practical terms this means that the bulkier the tissue, the slower is the rate at which oxygen reaches the cells furthest from the surface. In small organisms the diffusion distance is short and there is no problem. However, in larger organisms like ourselves the distance is far too great for diffusion – and if the organism is active with a high demand for oxygen, diffusion is even less likely to suffice. In many organisms this problem is overcome by a circulatory system with an oxygen-carrying pigment such as haemoglobin.

However, not all organisms solve the problem by having a circulatory system with an oxygen-carrying pigment. Some get round it by *reducing* the diffusion distance so that none of the cells is far away from the surface. Some of the ways this is achieved are considered in Chapter 18.

In addition to respiration, diffusion affects another important life process, namely the distribution of food substances. In the majority of animals the circulatory system takes on the job of transporting food materials as well as oxygen. However, some animals lack a circulatory system, and in them diffusion may be the only way of distributing soluble food substances through the body. The same applies to bacteria and protoctists.

In the preface of one of his books, the zoologist David Newth exhorts his readers to adopt a critical attitude towards his book. He says: 'treat even the most plausible statements with a little suspicion, and reserve particular mistrust for general assertions expressed with unqualified confidence.

The discussion presented in this box is exactly the sort of thing David Newth had in mind when he made his remark. Are there any statements here which cause you to feel uneasy? Can you detect any flaws in the argument? Have any important points been omitted?

How osmosis affects plant cells

Plant cells generally have a water potential which is markedly lower than that of their immediate surroundings. Their lower water potential is mainly due to the presence of various solutes in the fluid within the vacuole (the cell sap). The plasma membrane, and the tonoplast membrane surrounding the vacuole, are both partially permeable, letting water through but not solutes. The cell wall, however, is fully permeable to both water and solutes.

Now consider what happens when such a cell is immersed in pure water or a solution whose water potential is higher than that inside the vacuole. As you might expect, water flows through the plasma membrane and tonoplast into the vacuole by osmosis (figure 12.8A). As a result the cell swells. However, it does not burst. This is because the cellulose cell wall stretches and develops tension, resisting further expansion of the cell.

As water flows into the vacuole by osmosis, the tension developed by the cell wall causes an internal hydrostatic pressure to develop. This is called the **pressure potential**, and it opposes the continued uptake of water into the cell by osmosis. The pressure potential reaches its maximum when the cell wall is stretched as much as it can be and the cell cannot take in any more water. At this point the cell is described as **fully turgid**, or, to put it another way, **full turgor** is achieved.

Now consider what happens if the cell is immersed in a solution whose water potential is lower than that inside the cell. The effects of this may be observed by mounting a small piece of plant epidermis in a concentrated sucrose solution and watching one of the cells under a microscope (figure 12.8B). First the volume of the cell decreases as water flows out of the

Figure 12.8 The effect of immersing a partially turgid plant cell in **A** pure water and **B** a solution whose solute concentration exceeds that of the cell sap in the vacuole. Because the cell wall is fully permeable to both water and solutes, the external solution passes through the cell wall and fills the space between the cell wall and the cytoplasm.

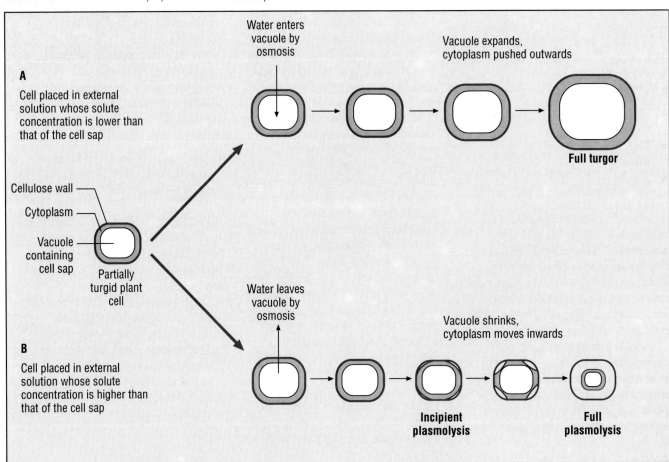

vacuole by osmosis. Within a matter of minutes the cytoplasm starts to pull away from the cell wall, leaving a perceptible gap between the wall and the plasma membrane. This withdrawal of the cytoplasm from the cell wall is called **plasmolysis** (figure 12.9). The point when the cytoplasm *just* starts pulling away from the cell wall is called *incipient* plasmolysis; full plasmolysis is reached when the cytoplasm has completely withdrawn from the cell wall.

Plasmolysis rarely occurs in nature. However, when induced by experiment it can help us to understand the water relations of plant cells, as we shall see in a moment.

Turgor and plant cells

Provided there is plenty of water in the environment, a plant's cells are usually surrounded by a watery solution whose solute concentration is lower than that inside the cells – indeed, the cell walls will be saturated with such a solution. Water therefore tends to enter the cells by osmosis, making them turgid.

Turgor plays a very important part in plants. It supports them and maintains their shape and form. The stems of herbaceous plants are kept erect by being filled with turgid cells packed tightly together. Turgor is also responsible for holding leaves in a flat, opened-out position.

Certain plant cells are able to undergo quite rapid changes in their solute concentration with consequent changes in turgor. This allows such cells to change their shape. Stomatal guard cells behave this way, as do the cells responsible for the leaf movements of insectivorous plants.

The water relations of plant cells

This is an important topic because it explains many aspects of how plants work. In considering the water relations of a plant cell we need to take into account the following three pressures.

- The net water potential of the whole cell: we shall refer to this simply as the **water potential**.
- The water potential of the solution in the vacuole: we shall call this the **solute potential**.
- The hydrostatic pressure caused by the cell wall pressing inwards against the cytoplasm: this is the **pressure potential**.

Let us imagine that we have just plasmolysed a plant cell by placing it in a concentrated sucrose solution. We then take the cell out of the solution and immerse it in pure water. What happens? Water immediately flows into the vacuole by osmosis, and the cell starts to expand. At this stage the cell wall is not pressing against the cytoplasm, so the pressure potential is zero and the water potential equals the solute potential. To begin with the water and solute potentials have a low value (i.e. very negative), but as water enters the cell the value gradually increases (i.e. becomes less negative).

As the influx of water continues, the cell goes on expanding until the cytoplasm starts pushing against the cell wall. At this point a pressure potential starts to develop. This raises the water potential, making it even less negative. This is understandable when you think about it: the water potential is the cell's capacity to lose water, and the pressure of the cell wall against the cytoplasm tends to force water out of the cell, rather like a hand squeezing a wet sponge. The water potential now exceeds the solute potential by the amount of the pressure potential.

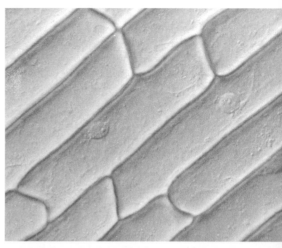

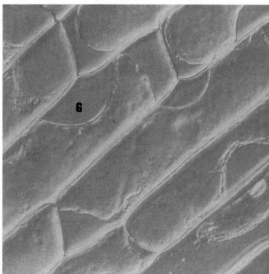

Figure 12.9 Plasmolysis in epidermal cells of an onion bulb. The top photomicrograph shows a group of cells in a fully turgid state. The bottom photomicrograph shows the cells after being immersed in a hypertonic solution. Notice that in the plasmolysed cells, gaps have developed between the cytoplasm and the cell wall. One such gap is labelled G.

Figure 12.10 Graph showing the relationship between the water potential (ψ), solute potential (ψ_s) and pressure potential (ψ_p) of a plant cell at different stages of turgor and plasmolysis.

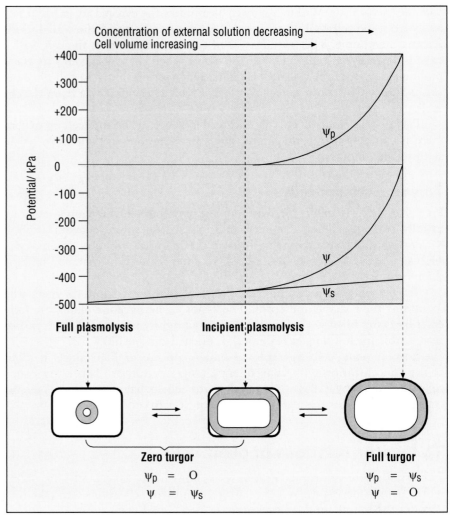

As the cell continues to expand, the pressure potential gets steadily greater. At the same time the water potential increases, becoming less and less negative. Eventually full turgor is reached: the cell can expand no more and the water potential reaches zero. When this point is reached the solute potential and pressure potential become equal in value, exactly counter-balancing each other.

We can summarise the water relations of a plant cell by the following equation:

water potential   =   solute potential   +   pressure potential
(usually negative)   (always negative)   (usually positive)

or in symbols:

$$\psi \quad = \quad \psi_p \quad + \quad \psi_p$$

In a plasmolysed cell ψ_p is zero and $\psi = \psi_s$. At full turgor ψ_p is equal and opposite to ψ_s, so $\psi = 0$. These relationships are summarised in figure 12.10.

Measuring the water and solute potentials of plant cells

We can compare the water and solute potentials of a plant tissue by means of an experiment. To measure the water potential, pieces of tissue of known mass or volume are placed in a series of solutions of different solute concentrations. The solution which produces no change in mass or volume of the

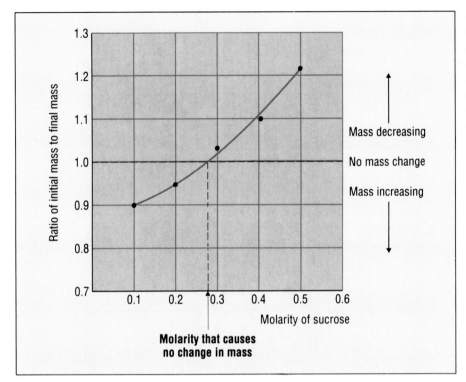

Figure 12.11 Results of an experiment to determine the water potential of potato tuber cells. Samples of tissue are placed in a series of sucrose solutions of different molarities, and the change in mass is measured. The concentration of sucrose causing no change in mass has a molarity of 0.27M. If this is converted to the corresponding pressure reading using a suitable table, the value of the water potential of the potato tissue can be found.

tissue has a water potential equal to that of the tissue. Some class results are shown in figure 12.11.

Measuring the solute potential is slightly more difficult because one has to eliminate effects caused by the pressure potential. One method is to find the concentration of an external solution which causes the cells to *just* begin to plasmolyse (incipient plasmolysis). With the cell walls no longer pressing in on the cells' contents, we may assume that the water potential of the external solution is equal to the solute potential of the sap. In practice, the individual cells tend to plasmolyse at different rates, and for practical purposes incipient plasmolysis is taken as the point when 50 per cent of the cells are visibly plasmolysed.

Wilting

We have seen that water can be removed from plant cells by osmosis. It can also be removed by evaporation. If the cells in the stem and leaves of a plant lose more water as a result of evaporation than they can absorb, turgor is reduced and the plant droops. This is called **wilting**.

Of course water does not evaporate from *all* the cells of the plant, only from those that are exposed to the atmosphere, namely the ones in the immediate vicinity of the stomata. As water evaporates from these cells, the water potential gradient steepens and water passes from the cells in the centre of the plant into the peripheral cells from which water is evaporating. Some plants respond to water stress by closing their stomata, so wilting is prevented or at least slowed down.

Wilting can sometimes be observed in garden plants on hot dry days, or in indoor plants kept by absent-minded owners. Such plants usually recover quite quickly when they are given water (figure 12.12). However, if the roots are kept unwatered for too long permanent wilting may occur and the plant will die.

Although wilting is generally disadvantageous to plants, it can be useful in removing leaves from the direct rays of the sun.

Figure 12.12 A small herbaceous plant which is so wilted that all its leaves and branches are lying on the ground can be upright again within half an hour of being watered. The photograph shows a blanket flower, *Gaillardia aristata* in wilted and normal conditions.

Figure 12.13 Exocytosis and endocytosis are ways of releasing particles from, and taking particles into, a cell. In exocytosis the membrane surrounding the vesicle fuses with, and becomes part of, the plasma membrane with which it has an identical molecular structure. In endocytosis the membrane surrounding the vesicle is derived from the plasma membrane.

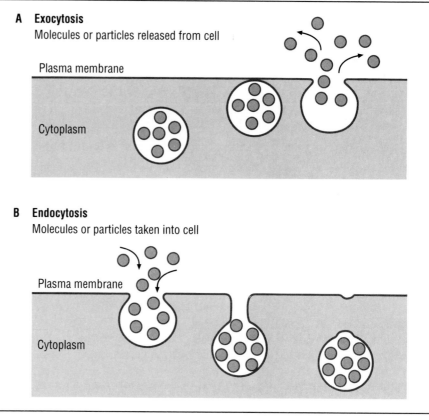

A **Exocytosis**
Molecules or particles released from cell

Plasma membrane

Cytoplasm

B **Endocytosis**
Molecules or particles taken into cell

Plasma membrane

Cytoplasm

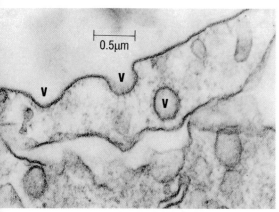

Figure 12.14 Electron micrograph of a cell showing vesicles (**V**) in the process of being formed by endocytosis. Three vesicles are visible in different stages of formation. The one on the left has just started to be formed by invagination of the surface membrane; in the middle one the invagination has pushed further into the cytoplasm, and the one on the right has become sealed off.

Endocytosis and exocytosis

So far we have discussed how small things get in and out of cells by traversing the plasma membrane. But sometimes larger objects are taken into, or expelled from, cells by a process which relies on the versatility of the plasma membrane mentioned in Chapter 10.

First consider how such materials get out of the cell. A vesicle containing the material moves towards the surface of the cell and fuses with the plasma membrane. The vesicle then opens to the exterior and its contents leave the cell. This process is called **exocytosis**, and it is shown in figure 12.13A.

Exocytosis provides a means by which enzymes, hormones, antibodies and cell wall precursors are released from cells. The vesicles are often derived from the Golgi apparatus.

Certain materials get into cells by the reverse of exocytosis. First the plasma membrane invaginates to form a flask-shaped depression which envelops the material. The 'neck' of the flask then closes, and the invagination becomes sealed off to form a **vesicle** which moves into the body of the cell. This process is called **endocytosis**, and is shown in figure 12.13 and 12.14.

The membrane lining the vesicle, derived from the plasma membrane, remains intact. Any substances absorbed into the cytoplasm from the vesicle must traverse the lining membrane first before they can be regarded as being fully inside the cell. Endocytosis is therefore not a substitute for transport across the plasma membrane, but a supplementary process facilitating it. How the contents of the vesicle are absorbed into the cytoplasm will become clear in a moment.

There are two types of endocytosis, which differ according to the size of the vesicles. We shall look at each in turn.

Pinocytosis

Pinocytosis literally means 'cell drinking'. It was first observed in *Amoeba*. In this organism tiny channels are continually being formed at the cell surface by invagination of the plasma membrane. From the inner ends of the channels small vesicles are pinched off, and they move towards the centre of the cell. Smaller vesicles may then be pinched off the larger ones, and these migrate to different parts of the cell. These **pinocytic vesicles** provide a means by which liquids can be brought into the body of the cell, and their breaking up into numerous smaller vesicles aids distribution and increases the surface area across which absorption can take place.

Pinocytosis, as described above, can be seen under the light microscope. However, much smaller invaginations of the plasma membrane are visible in the electron microscope. The ones in figure 12.14 are an example. About 3 µm in diameter, these invaginations become sealed off from the outside of the cell, forming minute vesicles. Invagination can be induced by the attachment of certain materials to the cell surface, and it provides a means by which molecules may be selectively taken up into cells. The process is highly specific, involving the binding of the molecules with corresponding receptor molecules in the plasma membrane. In this way the cell can take up substances it needs and ignore others.

Judging from electron micrographs, pinocytic vesicles appear to be of widespread occurrence in cells. Once the vesicles have become sealed off from the exterior, they may fuse with neighbouring lysosomes. Alternatively the membrane surrounding the vesicle may break down, releasing the enclosed molecules which are then incorporated into the cytoplasm.

Phagocytosis

Certain cells can take in relatively large particles by a process known as **phagocytosis** which literally means 'cell eating'. The plasma membrane invaginates and forms a vesicle enclosing the particles. The particles are then digested by enzymes shed into the vesicle from neighbouring lysosomes (figure 12.15). The soluble products of digestion (glucose, amino acids and the like) are then absorbed across the lining of the vesicle into the surrounding cytoplasm. Any indigestible material may be got rid of by the vesicle moving to the surface of the cell and fusing with the plasma membrane (exocytosis).

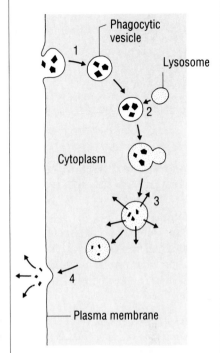

1 Small particles are taken up by phagocytosis to form a phagocytic vesicle.

2 A lysosome fuses with the vesicle and discharges its contents into it.

3 The lysosome enzymes digest the particles. and the products of digestion are absorbed into the surrounding cytoplasm.

4 The vesicle membrane fuses with the plasma membrane, and any indigestible matter is voided.

Figure 12.15 Diagram showing the phagocytic digestion of food particles inside a cell. Because the particles are digested *within* the cell, this is called intracellular digestion.

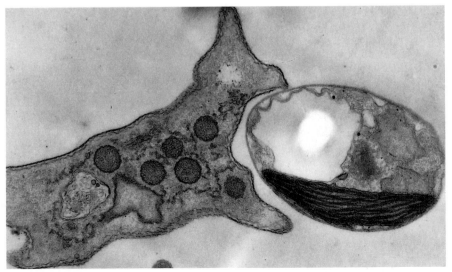

Figure 12.16 In this remarkable electron micrograph, an amoeba (*left*) appears to be ingesting a unicellular alga by phagocytosis. Magnification × 330.

Phagocytosis occurs in white blood cells which ingest bacteria and other foreign bodies, thus helping to defend the body against disease. It also occurs in *Amoeba* which feeds on a variety of small organisms (figure 12.16).

Phagocytosis, like pinocytosis, can be selective, the cell discriminating between different kinds of particle. *Amoeba*, for example, ingests particles of nutritional value but usually fails to take up particles that are of no food value. Similarly phagocytic white blood cells will only attack certain types of bacteria.

Worked examples of the water potential concept

Example 1

A plant cell with a water potential of –700 kPa is immersed in a sucrose solution whose water potential is –350 kPa. In which direction will water flow?

Water will flow from the sucrose solution into the cell. This is because the water potential of the cell is lower than (i.e. more negative than) the sucrose solution, and there is always a net flow of water from a region of high water potential to a region of lower water potential, i.e. down the water potential gradient.

Example 2

A plant cell has a solute potential of –1240 kPa and a pressure potential of 350 kPa. What is the water potential of the cell?

The water potential of the cell is –890 kPa. This is calculated from the relationship between the water potential of the cell (ψ), the solute potential (ψ_s) and the pressure potential (ψ_p):

$$\psi = \psi_s + \psi_p$$
$$\psi = -1240 + 350$$
$$= -890 \ kPa$$

Example 3

A plasmolysed cell is found to have a solute potential of –960 kPa. What is the water potential of the cell?

The water potential of the cell is –960 kPa. This is because in a plasmolysed cell ψ_p is zero, so $\psi = \psi_s$.

Example 4

A plant cell, after being immersed in pure water for several hours, has a solute potential of –800 kPa. What is the water potential of the cell, and what is its pressure potential?

The water potential of the cell is zero. This is because, after several hours in pure water, the cell will be fully turgid and in this condition ψ is zero. The pressure potential is 800 kPa. This is because in a fully turgid cell ψ_p is equal and opposite to ψ_s. (Note that ψ_s is negative and ψ_p positive.)

Example 5

Two plant cells, A and B, are next to each other in a tissue. The water potential of cell A is –700 kPa, and the water potential of cell B is –550 kPa. In which direction will water flow, from A to B or from B to A?

Water will flow from B to A. This is because water flows down a water potential gradient, just as in Example 1.

What effect will the flow of water have on the solute and pressure potentials of cells A and B?

The solute and pressure potentials of cell A will increase because the cell has gained water. The solute and pressure potentials of cell B will decrease because it has lost water. Eventually an equilibrium will be reached and there will be no net flow of water from one cell to the other.

Example 6

Two cells, C and D, are next to each other in a tissue. Their solute and pressure potentials are as follows:

	Cell C	Cell D
ψ_s	–630	–540
ψ_p	380	320

In which direction will water flow, from C to D or from D to C?

To arrive at the answer to this question we have to calculate the water potential of each cell from the relationship

$$\psi = \psi_s + \psi_p$$

For cell C:

$$\psi = -630 + 380$$
$$= -250 \ kPa$$

For cell D:

$$\psi = -540 + 320$$
$$= -330 \ kPa$$

Water flows down a water potential gradient, so there will be a net flow of water from cell C to cell D.

Summary

1. Materials move in and out of cells by diffusion, active transport, osmosis, endocytosis and exocytosis.

2. **Diffusion** is the net movement of particles down a concentration gradient, i.e. from a region of higher concentration to a region of lower concentration.

3. In **facilitated diffusion** particles are helped to move rapidly down a concentration gradient by **channel proteins** or **carrier proteins** in the plasma membrane.

4. In **active transport** particles are moved *against* a concentration gradient by carrier proteins in the plasma membrane. This process requires energy from respiration.

5. **Osmosis** is the net movement of water molecules across a **partially permeable membrane**. The plasma membrane is partially permeable and osmosis may occur across it.

6. Osmotic influx of water into a red blood cell may burst the cell (**haemolysis**). Osmotic loss of water from the cell makes the cell shrink and crinkle (**crenation**).

7. Osmotic influx of water into a plant cell causes the cell to become **turgid**. Osmotic loss of water from the cell may induce **plasmolysis**.

8. The behaviour of water molecules in organisms may be expressed in terms of **osmotic pressure** or **water potential**. Osmotic pressure is generally used for animals and related organisms, water potential for plants.

9. The water relations of a plant cell can be summarised as follows:

$$\psi = \psi_s + \psi_p$$

where ψ is the water potential, ψ_s the solute potential and ψ_p the pressure potential.

10. The water potential of a plant tissue can be determined by balancing it with an external solution which does not produce a mass or volume change in the tissue. The solute potential can be determined by balancing it with an external solution that produces incipient plasmolysis.

11. Particles which cannot pass through the plasma membrane may be taken into cells by **endocytosis** or released from them by **exocytosis**.

12. There are two types of **endocytosis**: **pinocytosis** (uptake of small particles) and **phagocytosis** (uptake of large particles).

Review questions

1. What part do carrier proteins play in diffusion? In what ways is a carrier protein similar to an enzyme?

2. By means of diagrams suggest a mechanism by which sodium and potassium ions might be transported across a plasma membrane in opposite directions by the same protein molecule.

3. The concentration of a solution may be expressed in terms of the water potential or osmotic pressure. Explain.

4. Justify the statement that osmosis is simply a special case of diffusion.

5. What happens to the appearance of (a) a red blood cell and (b) a plant epidermal cell when placed in a solution whose solute concentration is much higher than that of the cell contents.

6. Why is turgor important to plants?

7. Under what *natural* circumstances might the cells of a plant become plasmolysed?

8. The method for measuring the solute potential of plant cells described on page 202 involves measuring the solute potential when the cells are incipiently plasmolysed. Can we assume that this is the same as the solute potential of *fully turgid* cells? Explain your answer.

9. 'A particle which has been drawn into a cell by phagocytosis is not truly inside the cell.' Explain this statement.

10. Suggest a mechanism which enables a cell to 'recognise' whether or not a particle is of nutritional value.

Further reading

If you want to take the water potential concept further, there is a succinct article on cell water relations by C.S. Hutchinson and J.F. Sutcliffe in the *Journal of Biological Education*, Vol 15, No 2, Summer 1983.

The late Professor Sutcliffe was an authority on plant water relations, and he wrote an excellent book in the Studies in Biology series called *Plants and Water*, which is warmly recommended (Arnold, 1979).

For information on the molecular aspects of transport across the plasma membrane, you cannot do better than consult Alberts *et al*, *The Molecular Biology of the Cell* (Garland, 1989).

The advantages of the water potential concept and the way the fluid-mosaic model fits in with current ideas about molecular and ionic movement are discussed in *Biology, Advanced Topics*.

CHAPTER 13 | Cells and chemical reactions

In previous chapters we have mentioned on numerous occasions the various chemical substances found in cells. In this chapter we shall consider the reactions in which they take part.

The chemical reactions that occur in cells constitute **metabolism**, and the participating molecules are called **metabolites**. Some of these metabolites are synthesised within the organism, while others have to be taken in from the environment.

Metabolism is a basic characteristic of all living systems – indeed it is the metabolic reactions, particularly those that transfer energy, which keep the organism alive. It is only the truly dead parts of organisms, such as the hair and nails of mammals, the shells of molluscs and the lignified fibres of plants, which do not metabolise – and it is *because* they do not metabolise that they are dead.

Types of metabolism

Two types of chemical reaction occur in cells: **synthetic** and **breakdown**. Synthetic reactions include those in which molecules are linked together by chemical bonds to form more complex compounds:

$$A \; + \; B \; \rightarrow \; AB$$

A and B are the **substrate molecules** or **reactants**. AB represents the **product**. We met this kind of reaction in Chapter 9, for example the bonding together of monosaccharide molecules to form a disaccharide, of fatty acids and glycerol to form a lipid, and of amino acids to form a dipeptide.

Breakdown reactions are those in which a complex compound is split into simpler molecules:

$$AB \; \rightarrow \; A \; + \; B$$

In this case AB is the substrate, and A and B are the products. The hydrolysis of a disaccharide into its constituent monosaccharide molecules, of a lipid into fatty acids and glycerol, or of a dipeptide into its constituent amino acids are examples.

Both kinds of reaction occur in cells at the same time. Synthetic reactions comprise **anabolism**, and breakdown reactions **catabolism**. The important difference between them is that anabolic reactions generally require (i.e. absorb) energy, whereas catabolic reactions generally release energy.

Energy-absorbing reactions are termed **endergonic**, energy-releasing reactions **exergonic**. These terms are derived from the Greek word *ergon*, meaning 'work'. The terms endothermic and exothermic are sometimes used for these two types of chemical reaction, but they are less suitable because they imply that the energy is always thermal, i.e. heat energy. Later we shall see that this is not always the case.

The relationship between these two types of biochemical reaction in a typical animal cell is shown in figure 13.1. Try to construct a similar scheme for a typical plant cell, and note the differences.

Anabolic reactions are concerned with building up structures, storage compounds and complex metabolites in the cell. Starch, glycogen, lipids and proteins are all products of anabolic pathways. Plants, and other autotrophic organisms, synthesise these complex organic molecules from simple inorganic sources such as carbon dioxide and water. They have much greater synthetic powers, and their anabolic pathways are therefore

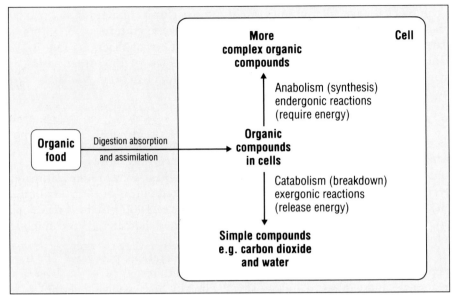

Figure 13.1 The fate of organic food substances in a generalised animal cell. The food substances may be either built up into more complex molecules (anabolism), or broken down into simpler molecules (catabolism).

more extensive, than those of animals and other heterotrophs. But even animals have to synthesise complex substances from simpler *organic* raw materials – for example, glycogen has to be synthesised from glucose molecules, and proteins from amino acids. Anabolic reactions are therefore a feature of all living organisms, but are particularly extensive in autotrophs.

Catabolic reactions are mainly concerned with mobilising food stores and making energy available in cells. Energy is required for three main purposes.

- **For synthesis** – for example, the synthesis of proteins, storage compounds, etc.
- **For work** – for example, contraction of muscles, transmission of nerve impulses and secretion of glands.
- **For maintenance** – for example, maintenance of a constant internal environment, and of the tissues and organs in a state of health and repair.

Energy is very important in living organisms. We shall consider it in more detail presently.

Small steps and gentle reactions

Metabolites are not converted into products in single, large reactions. Instead they are converted gradually, step by step, through a series of small reactions which together comprise a **metabolic pathway**. Each reaction, though small in itself, brings the raw material closer to the end product.

There are five main reasons why metabolism proceeds in small steps.

- Large catabolic reactions would create unfavourable conditions, such as very high temperatures, that would be incompatible with life.
- Energy can be derived from small catabolic reactions in a usable form. How this is achieved is explained in the next chapter.
- Substances can be *partially* broken down so as to provide raw materials for other reactions. Certain intermediate compounds in a catabolic pathway may have functions in their own right.
- It is not possible to synthesise, in one step, complex organic compounds from simple raw materials in the gentle conditions prevailing in cells.
- Having small steps in an anabolic pathway increases the cell's ability to *control* what products are made.

Figure 13.2 Metabolic maps like this one convey something of the complexity of biochemical pathways.

Living cells have the unique ability to perform numerous individual reactions in dilute aqueous solution at low temperatures and within a narrow range of pH. However, the sheer number of reactions requires a fantastic degree of organisation in the cell. Much of this organisation is achieved by **enzymes** which catalyse the individual reactions. We shall have much more to say about enzymes later.

Reconstructing metabolic pathways

Occasionally a drug company produces a map of the metabolic pathways which occur in cells (figure 13.2). You will see at once how complex it is, and the question we have to ask is: how have all these metabolic pathways been established and their individual steps worked out? The enormity of the task will be appreciated when we recall that over 1000 different reactions occur in an individual cell, an object only 20 μm in diameter. This can make a biochemist's life something of a nightmare.

So how do you set about reconstructing a metabolic pathway? The first step is to grind up the organ that you are interested in – the liver for example – and extract its juices. This is done by homogenising chunks of it in a **Waring blender**, a machine similar to the one used for liquidising food in the kitchen. This separates the cells from each other and breaks them open. The resulting suspension is then filtered to separate the juice from the solid fragments and particles. Finally, the juice is differentially **centrifuged** to separate the various fractions (see page 161). Experiments can then be performed on the individual fractions – the mitochondria, for example, or the cytoplasmic matrix.

Each step in a metabolic pathway is catalysed by a specific enzyme. If a particular enzyme is inactivated by a specific poison, the substance on which the enzyme normally acts will accumulate, and the product(s) will decline. By systematically blocking the various enzymes that are believed to participate in a particular process, metabolic pathways can be reconstructed. This approach has proved very valuable in identifying the intermediate compounds formed in respiration and many other pathways.

Isotope labelling

A technique which is often used in reconstructing metabolic pathways is **isotope labelling**. This technique depends on the fact that the atoms of a particular element are not all identical but exist in several different forms or **isotopes**. The isotopes of a particular element share the same atomic number and chemical properties but are distinguished from each other by their relative atomic masses. Moreover, some of them are unstable, emitting characteristic radiations such as alpha particles or gamma rays. Radioactive carbon, ^{14}C, is an example of such an isotope, the 14 indicating that it has a relative atomic mass of 14 as compared with the normal carbon atom ^{12}C with its relative atomic mass of 12. Radioactive isotopes can be detected, and the amount of radiation accurately measured, by means of a Geiger–Müller tube or some other monitoring device sensitive to the radiations being emitted.

The development of cyclotrons and nuclear reactors has made available to biologists an artificial source of isotopes which can be used in biochemical research. The organism is supplied with a specially prepared compound in which one of the elements is replaced with its radioactive isotope. For example, plants can be put in an atmosphere containing $^{14}CO_2$ – that is, carbon dioxide in which the normal carbon, ^{12}C, is replaced with the radioactive isotope, ^{14}C. The radioactive carbon is described as a **tracer**, and we say that the carbon dioxide has been **labelled**. Such labelled compounds, though easily detected with great sensitivity, are indistinguishable chemically from normal compounds, and are treated by the organism in exactly the same way.

Having supplied an organism with a labelled compound such as carbon dioxide, an analysis can be carried out to find out which parts of the organism have come to contain the radioactive element. To do this the relevant parts of the organism are placed on a photographic film in the dark. As radioactivity has the same effect on photographic film as light does, subsequent development of the film reveals the exact whereabouts of the radioactive material. The pictures obtained are called **autoradiographs**. The way they are made is shown in figure 13.3, and an example is given in figure 13.4.

If you want to identify the particular cells or organelles which have taken up a radioactive isotope, you have to cut sections of the organ or tissue and expose them to a photographic film. In this way photomicrographs or electron micrographs can be made, showing the precise location of the radioactivity.

You can, if you wish, take the procedure even further and find out which particular compounds the radioactive isotopes have become incorporated into. This is done by homogenising the organ or tissue and then separating the chemical constituents by **chromatography** (see page 143). If paper chromatography is used the chromatogram is exposed against a photographic film and the radioactive compounds identified in the resulting autoradiograph.

This kind of technique has been used to trace the fate of various elements in metabolism. The organism is supplied with a labelled compound, the choice of which depends on the pathway being investigated, and analysis is carried out at various times after the beginning of the experiment to determine where the radioactive isotope has got to, and which compounds contain it.

Not all isotopes are radioactive. Some are stable and do not emit radiations. The only way of distinguishing this kind of isotope from the usual one is by the fact that it has a different mass. Examples are the heavy isotope of oxygen, ^{18}O (oxygen is usually ^{16}O), and the heavy isotope of nitrogen, ^{15}N (nitrogen is usually ^{14}N). These heavy isotopes can be detected, and their amounts determined very accurately, by means of a **mass spectrometer**, an instrument which separates them according to their relative atomic masses.

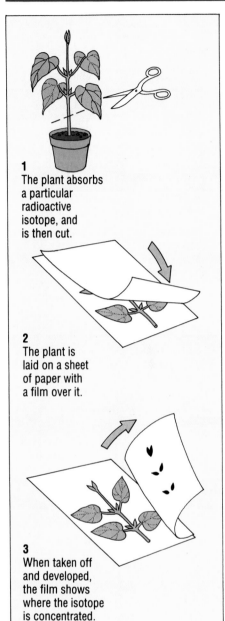

1 The plant absorbs a particular radioactive isotope, and is then cut.

2 The plant is laid on a sheet of paper with a film over it.

3 When taken off and developed, the film shows where the isotope is concentrated.

Figure 13.3 How an autoradiograph is made. This particular autoradiograph shows that the isotope has got into the buds of the plant but nowhere else.

Figure 13.4 An example of the use of radioactive isotopes and autoradiography in biological research. A tomato plant was spotted (at the arrow) with the herbicide paraquat labelled with radioactive carbon ^{14}C. The autoradiograph displayed here was taken 24 hours later and it shows that the paraquat has been transported to all the leaves.

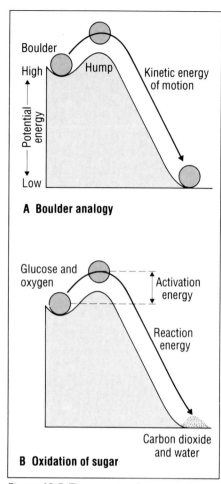

A Boulder analogy

B Oxidation of sugar

Figure 13.5 The concept of energy. Just as kinetic energy is released when the boulder rolls down the hill, so also energy is released when glucose and oxygen react to form carbon dioxide and water.

In later chapters we shall come across examples of metabolic reactions and pathways which have been worked out by painstaking research using tracers. Our present knowledge of photosynthesis and respiration is largely the result of such techniques.

Energy

One of the most important metabolic pathways yielding energy is the breakdown of glucose in **respiration**:

$$C_6H_{12}O_6 \; + \; 6O_2 \; \rightarrow \; 6CO_2 \; + \; 6H_2O \; + \; \text{Energy}$$

What this greatly over-simplified equation tells us is that the process involves the *oxidation* of glucose. The same reaction takes place if you burn a sample of sugar; in this case the sugar reacts with the oxygen and is broken down into carbon dioxide and water with the release of heat energy which causes an increase in temperature. However, in cells the process is much more complex, and the glucose never reacts with the oxygen directly. Nor is all the energy simply lost to the surroundings as heat energy; at least some of it is transferred to other molecules and used for the purposes outlined at the beginning of the chapter.

Biologists often talk about energy being made available by the breakdown of sugar, implying that the breaking of chemical bonds in the sugar molecules releases energy. And yet in chemistry we learn that energy is released not when chemical bonds are broken, but when they are formed. In fact respiration supplies energy not by the breaking of bonds in the substrate, but by the formation of strong bonds in the products. However, the overall effect of the process is to yield energy, and it is in this sense that biologists talk about the breakdown of sugar giving energy.

In fact we can look upon the glucose and oxygen molecules as containing **potential energy** which is transferred when they react together. Respiration transfers energy because the reactants (glucose and oxygen) are thermodynamically less stable than the products (carbon dioxide and water). The energy so transferred is capable of doing useful work. The energy which is released by a reaction and is capable of doing useful work is called **free energy**.

As an analogy, think of a boulder sitting in a hollow at the top of a hill (figure 13.5). While at rest the boulder contains potential energy (or, more precisely, gravitational energy). If, however, it is pushed so that it rolls down the hill, its potential energy is transferred to the energy of motion, i.e. kinetic energy.

The boulder analogy can usefully be taken a step further. When the boulder reaches the bottom of the hill and comes to rest, it contains less potential energy than it did at the top of the hill. In order to restore its potential energy it must be raised to its former position, and this requires the expenditure of energy. Similarly there is far less potential energy in the carbon dioxide and water resulting from the oxidation of glucose than there is in the more unstable glucose and oxygen molecules. The potential energy can only be restored if the carbon dioxide and water are built up again into glucose, a chemical feat which requires the input of energy and can only be performed by autotrophs such as plants.

This illustrates a further point, namely that chemical matter can be cycled. The carbon dioxide produced by respiration can be resynthesised by autotrophs into sugars and other substances. Some of these substances will in turn be consumed by animals that eat the plants – or by animals that eat the animals that eat the plants. This bears out the principle, already met in Chapter 3, that animals are dependent on plants – or, putting it more broadly, heterotrophs are dependent on autotrophs. The reason is that only autotrophs can resynthesise sugars from carbon dioxide and water.

These ideas are embodied in the **carbon cycle**. However, other elements circulate too – oxygen, nitrogen, sulphur and phosphorus, for example. In fact matter can be cycled with what may be regarded as complete efficiency: none is lost and none need be gained from outside sources. Of course a lot of carbon in dead organisms of the past has become 'locked up' in deposits within the Earth as peat, coal, oil and natural gas. However, the human species, with its unprecedented record for exploiting the Earth's natural resources, has ensured that these great reserves of carbon rejoin the cycle.

Energy too can be cycled, but not all of it can be made to do useful work. For example, only a proportion of the energy that comes from the oxidation of sugar is capable of being used to resynthesise sugar – the rest is lost as heat energy. The bulk of the energy required for the building up of sugars comes from an outside source, namely the radiant energy of the sun. The trapping of this solar energy by plants and other autotrophs requires the participation of **chlorophyll**. Chlorophyll is therefore of enormous importance in the living world. The process by which the energy of sunlight is used for building up sugars from carbon dioxide and water is, of course, **photosynthesis** and it involves energy being transferred from sunlight to organic molecules.

Energy transfer

The idea of energy being transferred is an obvious fact in our daily lives. For example, if you light a match chemical energy in the match head is transferred to heat energy and light energy. This idea is also important biologically because it means that, given the right conditions, an organism (or certain specialised cells within it) can transfer energy from one situation to another. For example, the photosynthetic cells of a plant can transfer light energy from the sun into chemical energy within the sugar molecules. Chemical energy in turn may be transferred to other things. For example, in muscle tissue chemical energy is transferred to the mechanical process of contraction, in luminescent organsism like the glow-worm it is transferred to light, and in the electric eel it is transferred to electrical pulses. Two examples are shown in figure 13.6 on the next page.

This fundamental idea is summed up in the **First Law of Thermodynamics** which states that when energy is transferred, there is no net loss or gain of energy. In other words the total amount of energy which we are left with at the end is equal to the amount we start off with. However, this does not mean that all the energy transferred manifests itself in the same way. The examples given above show clearly that this is not the case.

Let us return to our boulder for a moment. As the boulder rolls down the hill only a proportion of the potential energy is transferred to the kinetic energy of motion – the rest is used to overcome friction and is transferred to the surroundings as heat energy. This is summed up in a corollary of the **Second Law of Thermodynamics**, namely that when energy is transferred a proportion of it becomes heat energy. This too is an obvious fact of everyday life. The internal combustion engine generates energy for powering a car, but most of the energy simply heats up the engine and its surroundings. This energy plays no part in powering the car and is therefore lost.

This principle is of great importance in biology. It means that when sugar is metabolised in respiration, not all the energy can be used for

Figure 13.6 Two examples of energy transfer in organisms.

Top Weight-lifting and power-lifting are extreme examples of muscle contraction where chemical energy is transferred to the mechanical process of contraction. This process enables a trained weight-lifter to lift more than three times his body mass.
Bottom Fireflies seen as faint streaks of light over a farmyard in Iowa, USA. This is an example of bioluminescence, the ability of an organism to emit visible light as a result of chemical energy being transferred to light energy. The energy transfer in bioluminescence is exceptionally efficient, hardly any heat energy being produced in the process.

synthesising more complex molecules and driving important biological processes such as growth and movement. Most of it is transferred to heat energy and lost. Of course it does not follow that this heat energy is of no use to the organism; indeed it helps many animals to maintain a constant body temperature. But from a thermodynamic standpoint this proportion of the transferred energy has no direct metabolic use. The same applies to a car: the heat energy generated by the motor, though useless for powering the car, may help to keep the driver warm.

Activation energy

The boulder analogy illustrates another important concept. You will recall that the boulder rests in a slight hollow at the top of the hill. It is obviously necessary to push it over the hump before it can start rolling down the hill, and this *requires* energy. The hump represents an **energy barrier**, and energy is required to push the boulder over this barrier. Much the same applies to our glucose and oxygen molecules: they are not naturally reactive – indeed they are quite *un*reactive – and a small amount of energy must be applied, by heating them for example, before the process of oxidative breakdown can get underway. This is called the **activation energy**.

Clearly any factor, physical or chemical, that helps the glucose molecule over the energy barrier and reduces the activation energy necessary to get the reaction going will facilitate the process and speed up the reaction. Let us now look more closely at the factors which speed up biological reactions.

The speed of biological reactions

Consider the type of chemical reaction in which two substrate molecules, A and B, react to form a product, AB – the sort of reaction that unites two monosaccharide molecules to form a disaccharide. What kind of factors influence the speed of such a reaction?

To answer this we must remember that the substrate molecules are in a state of continual random motion. Only when they collide and come into contact can they react. Clearly any factor that increases the frequency of collision will increase the speed of the reaction. In general three factors achieve this effect.

- The concentration of the substrate molecules.
- The temperature of the reaction mixture.
- The presence of a catalyst.

The first two need little explanation. It is obvious that the more concentrated the substrate molecules, that is, the more densely packed they are, the more likely they are to collide and react. Raising the temperature speeds up the random motion of the molecules, thereby increasing the probability of their colliding. It also raises their energy level, so they are more likely to react when they do collide.

Any factor which, directly or indirectly, raises the concentration of the substrate molecules will obviously speed up the reaction. Increasing the pressure has this effect, as does removal of some of the water in which the substrate molecules are dissolved. But the most effective way of concentrating the substrate is to supply a catalyst. The substrate molecules are absorbed on to the surface of the catalyst where, having been brought into close proximity, they react. The product then leaves the surface of the catalyst, which is unchanged by the process and may be used again.

Catalysts have the effect of lowering the activation energy required to get the reaction going, and as such they are very important. Many inorganic catalysts are known – for example, iron, platinum, nickel and so on. Catalysis is also important in metabolism, but in this case the catalysts are always organic substances and operate in a slightly different way from the surface catalysts described above. The catalysts found in living systems are called **enzymes**, to which we now turn.

Enzymes

Enzymes were discovered by the German chemist, Eduard Buchner, towards the end of the nineteenth century. His discovery is an example of one of those fortuitous accidents by which advances are sometimes made in science. Buchner had been trying to obtain a fluid of medicinal use from yeast. However, his extracts kept going bad. To prevent this he tried adding sugar to one of the extracts, sugar being well known as a preservative of fruit. To his surprise the sugar was converted into alcohol – in other words it fermented.

Now there was nothing new about the discovery that yeast promotes fermentation – in fact this had already been demonstrated by Louis Pasteur some 20 years before. But Pasteur believed that fermentation was brought about by the *living* yeast cells. Buchner showed that it was not the living yeast cells that were responsible for fermentation, but the juice extracted from them.

The word **enzyme** was coined for the active ingredient in the juice that causes fermentation. *Enzyme* literally means 'in yeast', but it is now used as a collective name for the thousands of organic compounds that have since been extracted from cells and found to speed up the chemical reactions which occur in organisms.

Why are enzymes important?

Without enzymes the reactions that occur in living organisms would be so slow as hardly to proceed at all, and this would be incompatible with the maintenance of life. Of course the speed of the reactions could be increased by raising the temperature, but this would kill the organism by denaturing the proteins and disrupting the membranes, as well as being very expensive energetically. Enzymes therefore enable metabolic reactions to proceed rapidly but at low temperatures.

But enzymes do more than merely speed up the reactions. They also control them. It was mentioned earlier that over 1000 different reactions take place in an individual cell. The functional organisation which this demands is achieved by each individual reaction being catalysed by a specific enzyme in a particular place within the cell. It is this which ensures that metabolism proceeds by small, gentle steps in an orderly fashion.

In recent years enzymes have become important for a quite different reason: making products that are useful to humans. This is an aspect of **biotechnology** about which we shall have more to say at the end of the chapter.

Naming and classifying enzymes

There are as many enzymes in living organisms as there are types of chemical reactions. Obviously one cannot know all their names. It is more profitable to understand how they are classified.

Enzymes are divided into two groups: **intracellular** and **extracellular**. Intracellular enzymes occur inside cells where they speed up and control metabolism. Extracellular enzymes are produced by cells but achieve their effects outside the cell; they include **digestive enzymes** that break down food in the gut.

Some enzymes occur free in solution, while others are fixed to the plasma membrane or to various membranes inside the cell. Probably most enzymes are fixed to membranes.

Normally an enzyme is named by attaching the suffix *-ase* to the name of the substrate on which it acts. Thus **carbohydrases** act on carbohydrates, **lipases** on lipids, **proteases** on proteins and **nucleases** on nucleic acids. Within each of these major groups certain enzymes act on particular substrates. For example, carbohydrases include **maltase** which acts on maltose, and **sucrase** which acts on sucrose. The '-ase' rule does not always apply. For example, **pepsin** and **trypsin**, both found in the mammalian gut, act on proteins. They were discovered and named before the '-ase' idea was introduced.

Following the recommendation of the International Union of Biochemical Societies, enzymes are divided into six categories according to the type of chemical reaction which they catalyse. Each of these categories can be further subdivided into smaller groups. The six categories are as follows.

- **Oxidoreductases**. These enzymes are involved in biological oxidation and reduction reactions. They include **dehydrogenases** which catalyse the removal of hydrogen atoms from a substrate, and **oxidases** which catalyse the addition of oxygen to hydrogen with the formation of water. These enzymes play an important part in the final stages of respiration.

- **Transferases**. These enzymes catalyse the transfer of groups of atoms, from one substance to another. The groups transferred include, for example, amino groups (NH_2). Enzymes which specifically transfer amino groups are called **transaminases**. They enable organisms to synthesise certain amino acids (see page 142).

- **Hydrolases**. These enzymes catalyse the addition of water to, or its removal from, certain substrates. The carbohydrases, lipases, proteases and nucleases mentioned earlier are all examples of this category of enzyme. They play an important part in the building up (**condensation**) and breaking down (**hydrolysis**) of storage compounds such as starch, and other polymers.

- **Lyases**. These enzymes break chemical bonds by means *other* than hydrolysis, thus creating double bonds. They include **decarboxylases** which remove carboxyl groups (COOH) from intermediates in respiration, with the formation of carbon dioxide.

- **Isomerases**. These enzymes catalyse the transfer of atoms from one part of a molecule to another. The new molecule and the original one are isomers, i.e. they each contain the same atoms but arranged differently. That is why these enzymes are called isomerases. In an early stage of respiration an isomerase enzyme rearranges the atoms in the sugar molecules so that they can enter the metabolic pathway.

- **Ligases**. These enzymes catalyse the joining together of two molecules, coupled with the breakdown of ATP. They include **phosphokinases** which catalyse the addition of phosphate groups to, for example, glucose in respiration (see page 231), and DNA ligase which is involved in the synthesis of DNA.

From this classification you will appreciate that there is considerable variety in the types of enzyme found in living organisms, and the functions they perform. However, all enzymes have certain properties in common, as we shall now see.

The properties of enzymes

Enzymes are nearly always proteins, though as we shall see later they may contain a non-protein component. Some of their properties therefore reflect those of proteins.

The main properties of enzymes are as follows:

- They generally work very rapidly.
- They are not destroyed by the reactions which they catalyse.
- They can work in either direction.
- They are inactivated by high temperatures.
- They are sensitive to pH.
- They are usually specific to particular reactions.

Let us look at each of these properties in detail.

The speed of action of enzymes

An enzyme's speed of action is expressed as its **turnover number**. This is the number of substrate molecules which one molecule of the enzyme turns into product per minute.

The turnover numbers of different enzymes vary from about 100 to several million, though for the majority it is around several thousand. One of the fastest enzymes is **catalase**. This enzyme is found in a number of organs and tissues, including the liver, where its job is to speed up the decomposition of hydrogen peroxide (H_2O_2) into oxygen and water:

$$2H_2O_2 \rightarrow 2H_2O + O_2$$

Hydrogen peroxide is a by-product of metabolism and is toxic, and its rapid conversion to water is therefore important. Catalase has a turnover number of approximately six million, increasing the speed of the reaction by 10^{14} compared with what it would be in the absence of the enzyme. Its action can be demonstrated by dropping a small piece of liver into a beaker of hydrogen peroxide. The fizzing and bubbling that ensues as oxygen is given off is a dramatic demonstration of an enzyme in action (figure 13.7).

In their speed of action enzymes are much more efficient than inorganic catalysts. Finely divided platinum or iron filings will also speed up the decomposition of hydrogen peroxide, but nothing like as quickly as a piece of liver. The reason is that the enzyme achieves a greater lowering of the activation energy.

There is an even faster enzyme than catalase, and that is **carbonic anhydrase**. This enzyme catalyses the combination of carbon dioxide and water in red blood cells (see page 320). It has a turnover number of 36 million. Why do you think this enzyme needs to have such a high turnover number?

Enzymes can be used again

Enzymes are not altered by the reactions they catalyse, and so can be used again. The explanation of this will become clear when we discuss how enzymes work. This is not to say that a given molecule of an enzyme can be used indefinitely, for the action of an enzyme depends critically on its shape and this is readily affected by changes in temperature, acidity and so on. In this respect enzymes differ from inorganic catalysts which can be used over and over again almost indefinitely.

Because enzymes wear out, there has to be a constant replacement of old enzyme molecules by new ones. The raw materials for making them come from the organism's food.

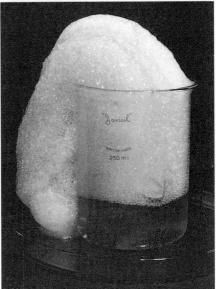

Figure 13.7 An enzyme in action.
Top A piece of liver (approximately 35 g) is dropped into a beaker of hydrogen peroxide. *Bottom* The result after three minutes. Liver contains catalase, one of the fastest acting enzymes known.

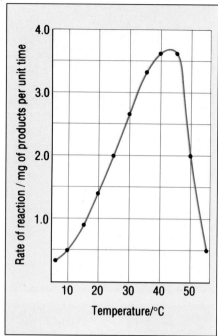

Figure 13.8 The effect of temperature on the rate of an enzyme-controlled reaction. All other variables, including the concentration of enzyme and substrate, were kept constant.

What happens when an enzyme is denatured?

Enzymes, like other proteins, consist of polypeptide chains held in a particular position by cross-links (see page 140). When an enzyme is denatured the cross-links are broken and the polypeptide chains open up and become randomly arranged. As a result the protein loses its normal shape and becomes biologically inactive.,

Denaturation is brought about by heating, extremes of pH, and certain chemicals such as urea, alcohol and detergents. It is normally irreversible.

Enzymes work in either direction

Metabolic reactions are generally reversible. For example, consider this hypothetical reaction:

$$A + B \rightleftharpoons C + D$$

The enzyme which catalyses this reaction works in such a way that the reaction can proceed from left to right or from right to left, depending on circumstances – hence the two-way arrows.

The direction in which the reaction proceeds at any given time depends on the relative amounts of substrates and products present, that is, on the equilibrium conditions. If there is a lot of A and B compared with C and D, the reaction will go from left to right until an equilibrium between substrates and products is reached. If, on the other hand, there is a lot of C and D compared with A and B, the reaction will go from right to left, again until an equilibrium is reached.

Equilibrium is reached when there is a particular ratio between the concentrations of (A + B) and (B + C). This ratio is always the same for a particular reaction but varies from one reaction to another. It is called the **equilibrium constant**. We can sum up the relationship like this:

$$K = \frac{[C]\,[D]}{[A]\,[B]}$$

where K is the equilibrium constant and [ ] means concentration. An enzyme has no effect on the value of the equilibrium constant; it merely speeds up the reaction until equilibrium is reached.

The effect of temperature on enzymes

Figure 13.8 shows the effect of temperature on the rate of an enzyme-controlled reaction. Up to about 40°C the rate increases smoothly, a ten degree rise in temperature being accompanied by an approximate doubling of the rate of the reaction. Above this temperature the rate begins to fall off and then declines rapidly, ceasing altogether at about 60°C. The reason for this is that enzymes, being proteins, are **denatured** at high temperatures (see box alongside). In fact enzymes can be denatured at any temperature – it is one of the reasons why they cannot be used over and over again indefinitely. However, the higher the temperature, the less time it takes for an enzyme to become denatured.

Because of the susceptibility of enzymes to heating, few cells can tolerate temperatures higher than approximately 45°C. Organisms that live in environments where the temperature exceeds 45°C either have heat-resistant enzymes or are able to regulate their body temperature. Some examples of heat-tolerant organisms are given on page 411.

The effect of pH on enzymes

Every enzyme has it own range of pH in which it functions best. Most intra-cellular enzymes have their optimum function round about neutral (pH 7). Excessive acidity (pH markedly less than 7.0) or alkalinity (pH markedly greater than 7.0) denatures them and renders them inactive. For this reason the pH of the cells and body fluids needs to be regulated (see page 375).

Digestive enzymes behave differently. Some of them work optimally in a distinctly acidic or alkaline environment. Thus the protease enzyme pepsin functions most effectively in an acid medium at a pH of about 2.0. It is found in the stomach where conditions are markedly acidic. Trypsin, on the other hand, functions most effectively in an alkaline medium at about pH 8.5. It is found in the duodenum where conditions are alkaline.

The specificity of enzymes

Normally a given enzyme will catalyse only one reaction, or type of reaction. The degree of specificity varies, and some enzymes are more catholic in their choice of substrates than others. Most intracellular enzymes work only on one particular substrate. Catalase, for example, acts only on hydrogen peroxide, and is ineffective on any other natural substrate. However, pancreatic lipase, an extracellular digestive enzyme in the duodenum, will digest a variety of different fats.

The specificity of intracellular enzymes helps to explain why metabolism proceeds in such an orderly way, each enzyme catalysing one particular reaction within the cell. Enzyme specificity also explains how organisms manage to digest proteins within a protein container. For example, the various proteases in the human gut digest the proteins in the food but not the proteins in the gut wall.

How enzymes work

We can explain the properties of enzymes by suggesting that when an enzyme-controlled reaction takes place the enzyme and substrate molecules become joined together for a short time. As well as being consistent with the known properties of enzymes, this hypothesis is supported by other lines of evidence. One important piece of evidence comes from studying the effect on the rate of an enzyme-controlled reaction of altering the substrate concentration.

A graph summarising the results of such studies is shown in figure 13.9. Curve A shows the effect on the reaction rate of gradually increasing the concentration of substrate, the enzyme concentration being kept constant. As you can see, the reaction rate rises with increasing substrate concentration until, at a certain substrate concentration, it reaches a maximum and levels off.

These results fit in with the idea that the substrate molecules collide with the usually much larger enzyme molecules and then join onto them. Obviously the more substrate molecules there are, the greater are the chances that the substrate and enzyme molecules will collide. The plateau in the graph can be explained by hypothesising that when the substrate concentration reaches a certain level, the system becomes saturated: all the enzyme molecules are working flat out and adding more substrate makes no difference to the rate of the reaction. When this point is reached the only way to increase the reaction rate is to raise the concentration of the enzyme, and curve B shows the results of doing just this.

The lock-and-key hypothesis

Studies of this sort, together with other lines of evidence, led scientists to propose that in an enzyme-controlled reaction the substrate molecules combine with the enzyme to form an **enzyme-substrate complex**. The substrate molecules then react together, and the product leaves the enzyme. The enzyme, unchanged by the reaction, can then be used again:

enzyme + substrate → enzyme-substrate complex → enzyme + product

It is thought that each enzyme molecule has a precise place on its surface to which the substrate molecules become attached. This is called the **active site**. In Chapter 9 we saw that every protein has a particular shape, and this applies to enzymes no less than to other proteins. We can picture the active site of an enzyme molecule as having a distinctive configuration into which only certain specific substrate molecules will fit. The shape of the active

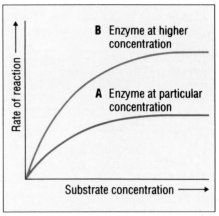

Figure 13.9 The effect of substrate concentration on the rate of an enzyme-controlled reaction at two different enzyme concentrations. The temperature was kept constant at an optimum value. Notice that when the concentration of the enzyme is increased the reaction proceeds at a faster rate and reaches a higher plateau.

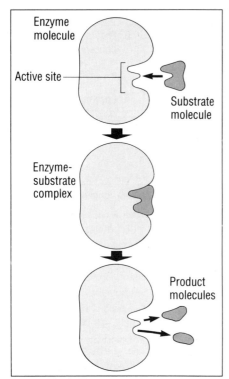

Figure 13.10 The lock and key mechanism proposes that the substrate fits into an active site on the surface of the enzyme, where the reaction takes place.

site, and the positions of the various chemical groups and bonds within it, ensure that only those substrate molecules with a complementary structure will combine with the enzyme. Thus we have an explanation of the specificity of enzymes: the enzyme and substrate molecules fit together like a lock and key. This explanation of enzyme action is known as the **lock and key mechanism**, and it is illustrated in figure 13.10.

Is the lock and key mechanism purely hypothetical or is there evidence to support it? Over the years much progress has been made in elucidating the molecular structure of enzymes and the way they interact with their substrates. One enzyme which has been particularly studied is **lysozyme**. This enzyme is found in tears and other secretions where its function is to destroy pathogenic bacteria by dissolving their cell walls. The bacterial cell wall is a polysaccharide consisting of chains of amino sugars (figure 13.11A). Lysozyme dissolves the cell wall by breaking the glycosidic bonds between certain of the amino sugars. Now lysozyme is a globular protein and X-ray diffraction studies have shown that there is a groove on one side of the molecule into which the polysaccharide chain fits (figure 13.11B). Further analysis has shown that part of the amino sugar chain (six amino sugars to be exact) fits into the groove. The chain is held in place by hydrogen bonds and ionic attraction, and becomes broken at the position indicated by the arrow in figure 13.11B. This therefore seems to be the active site.

Another discovery has emerged from the work on lysozyme. When the substrate binds to the enzyme, the substrate molecule becomes slightly distorted and this puts a strain on the bonds between the amino sugars. As a result less energy is needed to break the chain. In this way the enzyme lowers the activation energy required for the reaction.

Michaelis constant

The way the substrate concentration affects the rate of an enzyme-controlled reaction is summed up by the **Michaelis constant**. This is the concentration of substrate required to make the reaction go at half its maximum rate (see illustration).

The Michaelis constant is always the same for a particular enzyme, but varies from one enzyme to another. It tells us how readily the enzyme reacts with its substrate – in other words it is a measure of the *affinity* of the enzyme for its substrate. A low Michaelis constant means that there is a high affinity between the enzyme and substrate, the substrate molecules reacting readily with the enzyme molecules. On the other hand, a high Michaelis constant means that there is a relatively low affinity between the enzyme and substrate, the substrate molecules reacting less readily with

the enzyme molecules.

The importance of this in the cell is that some reactions proceed quickly even when there is very little substrate present, whereas others require a much higher concentration of substrate. By comparing the Michaelis constants of different enzymes we can learn much about the reactions which they catalyse and their functions in the body. Moreover, the Michaelis constant of a particular enzyme can be changed by certain types of enzyme inhibitors, and this can give us important information about how these inhibitors work.

The Michaelis constant was developed in 1913 by Leonor Michaelis and Maud Menten (it is sometimes called the Michaelis–Menten constant). They derived the constant from mathematical considerations, and it enabled them to *predict* that the

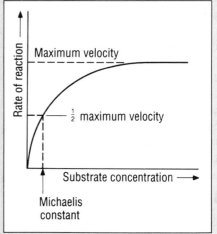

Michaelis constant is the substrate concentration which enables an enzyme-controlled reaction to proceed at half its maximum rate.

substrate combines with the enzyme. This prediction was borne out by later experimental observations, thus adding considerable weight to the theory.

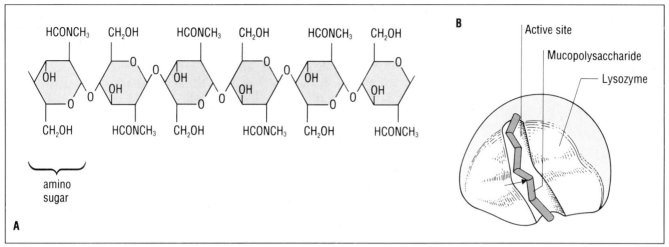

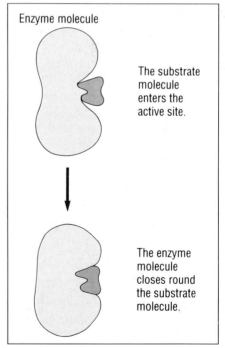

Figure 13.11

A Part of the mucopolysaccharide found in the cell wall of bacteria.

B Greatly simplified diagram, based on X-ray diffraction studies, of the lysozyme molecule showing how the amino sugar chain of the mucopolysaccharide fits into the active site. The amino sugars are held in place by hydrogen bonds and various other types of attraction. The chain becomes broken at the position indicated by the arrow.

The lock and key mechanism helps to explain why enzymes are inactivated by high temperatues and changes in pH. Heating denatures the enzyme, bringing about a change in shape that prevents the substrate fitting into the active site. Changes in pH break the bonds which maintain the three-dimensional shape of the enzyme, and alter the ionic charges on the side groups within the active site itself.

The induced fit hypothesis

The lock and key mechanism, as originally proposed, suggested that there is an exact fit between the substrate and the active site of the enzyme. However, more recent research has suggested that the active site may not necessarily be exactly the right shape to begin with. It is believed that when the substrate combines with the enzyme it causes a small change to occur in the shape of the enzyme molecule, thereby enabling the substrate to fit more snugly into the active site. This is called the **induced fit hypothesis** and it is illustrated in figure 13.12.

The induced fit hypothesis is supported, once again, by X-ray diffraction studies. Scientists have compared the detailed shape and molecular configuration of certain enzyme molecules on their own and when combined with their substrates, and have found that they are not the same. Significant changes in shape do indeed take place, both to the enzyme molecule and also to the substrate, improving the fit and helping to make the substrate more reactive.

Inhibition of enzymes

Certain substances inhibit enzymes, thereby slowing down or stopping enzyme-controlled reactions. These **enzyme inhibitors** are of special interest for three main reasons.

- They give us important information about the shapes and properties of the active sites of enzymes.
- They can be used to block particular reactions, thereby enabling biochemists to reconstruct metabolic pathways (see page 210).
- They have important medical and agricultural uses as, for example, drugs and pesticides.

Later we shall see that inhibitors also play a natural part in the way enzymes are controlled in cells. But first, let us look at the different types of enzyme inhibition that can occur.

Figure 13.12 The induced fit hypothesis. When the substrate molecule enters the active site it causes (i.e. *induces*) the enzyme molecule to change its shape so that the two molecules fit together more snugly.

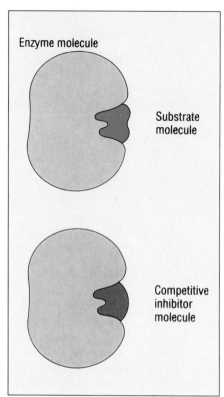

Figure 13.13 In competitive inhibition of an enzyme, an inhibitor molecule, similar in structure to the substrate molecule, competes with the substrate molecule for the active site.

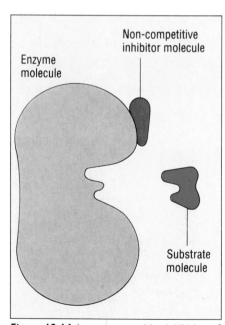

Figure 13.14 In non-competitive inhibition of an enzyme, an inhibitor molecule combines with the enzyme molecule, preventing the substrate molecule from interacting with the enzyme.

Irreversible inhibition

In this type of inhibition the inhibitor molecule combines permanently with the enzyme molecule, making it impossible for the substrate to react with it.

Some irreversible inhibitors enter the active site of the enzyme, thereby preventing the substrate molecules from taking up their normal position. In some cases the bonding is so firm that the inhibitor cannot be dislodged even if the enzyme is broken into fragments. This has provided a useful technique for identifying the active sites of enzymes. The part of the enzyme molecule which is still attached to the inhibitor after fragmentation is the part that contains the active site.

Irreversible inhibitors of this sort include organophosphate insecticides and certain types of nerve gases. Both work the same way. They combine with the enzyme cholinesterase which controls the transmission of nerve impulses across the junctions (synapses) in the nervous system (see page 449). They achieve their toxic effects by preventing nerve impulses reaching the skeletal muscles, thus paralysing the victim and preventing breathing.

Other examples of irreversible inhibitors include heavy metals such as arsenic, mercury and lead. They combine covalently with sulphydryl (–SH) groups in the enzyme molecule, usually in places other than the active site. Although the metal atoms may be removed from the enzyme by chemical treatment, the attachment is effectively irreversible.

Reversible inhibition

Reversible inhibitors form a relatively loose association with the enzyme, becoming detached if and when circumstances permit. There are two types of reversible inhibition: **competitive** and **non-competitive**.

Competitive inhibition

In this type of inhibition another molecule, similar to the substrate, competes with the substrate for the active site of the enzyme.

This is illustrated by one of the metabolic steps in respiration. The reaction involves the oxidation of succinate (see page 232). The enzyme which catalyses it is succinate dehydrogenase. Now another substance called malonate has a molecular configuration similar to that of succinate, and if it is added to the system the reaction is slowed.

The malonate molecule is so similar to the succinate molecule that it fits into the active site of the enzyme. It thus competes with the normal substrate. The enzyme has no effect on the malonate; once in position the malonate simply stays in the active site. It is like putting the wrong key in a lock: the key fits the lock but will not open it – instead it gets stuck. Competitive inhibition is illustrated diagrammatically in figure 13.13.

Sulphonamide drugs, and antibiotics such as penicillin, are competitive inhibitors. These compounds are used to destroy, or prevent the growth of, pathogenic bacteria. They exert their action by combining with enzymes essential for the metabolism of the bacteria.

Non-competitive inhibition

In this type of inhibition the inhibitor molecule does not normally enter the active site, so it does not compete with the substrate. Instead it becomes attached to some part of the enzyme outside the active site (figure 13.14). Once in position, it prevents the enzyme working.

A well-known non-competitive inhibitor is cyanide. It inactivates cytochrome oxidase which is responsible for the transfer of electrons in respiration (see page 234). Cyanide therefore prevents the organism respiring. This makes cyanide a deadly poison.

Variations on the theme

Classifying enzyme inhibitors into reversible and irreversible, and into competitive and non-competitive, can be useful. However, there is considerable variation in the way different inhibitors achieve their actions, and rigid categorisation is not always possible.

Some inhibitors combine, not with the enzyme, but with the enzyme–substrate complex. The substrate enters the active site as usual. The inhibitor then combines with the enzyme–substrate complex in such a way that the substrate gets jammed in the active site and products are not formed.

Another variation is seen in those enzymes which require a metal ion for their action (see page 224). Inhibitors of such enzymes often work by combining with the metal ion rather than with the enzyme. Cyanide works this way – it combines with a metal ion associated with the cytochrome oxidase.

Natural inhibitors

By now you may have got the impression that enzyme inhibition is always unnatural and disastrous. Far from it. Cells contain many natural inhibitors which ensure that particular enzymes do not function until they are needed. The inhibition is often removed by another enzyme which serves as an activator.

Telling the difference between competitive and non-competitive inhibition

How can you tell if an enzyme inhibitor is competitive or non-competitive? After all, you cannot *see* if the inhibitor enters the active site or attaches itself to some other part of the enzyme molecule.

To tackle this problem you have to adopt an indirect approach. First you find the effect on the rate of the reaction of increasing the substrate concentration at a particular concentration of the enzyme. You then repeat the experiment in the presence of the inhibitor. The sort of results you get are shown in illustrations 1 and 2.

Look carefully at the graphs. You will see that at low substrate concentrations both types of inhibitor slow down the reaction to the same extent. But look what happens at high substrate concentrations. If the inhibitor is competitive, the reaction rate eventually reaches almost the same maximum value that it did before. The reason is that at high substrate concentrations, the substrate molecules compete with the inhibitor so effectively that the reaction rate is almost as fast as it would be if the inhibitor was not there.

If, on the other hand, the inhibitor is *non*-competitive, the reaction rate never comes close to the maximum value that it reached before. The reason is that the inhibitor puts a certain proportion of the enzyme molecules out of action, so in effect the enzyme concentration is lowered. At this lower enzyme concentration the original maximum reaction rate can never be reached, however much you increase the substrate concentration.

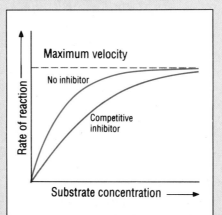

Illustration 1 Graph showing the effect of a competitive inhibitor on the relationship between the substrate concentration and the rate of an enzyme-controlled reaction.

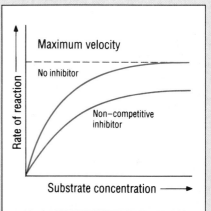

Illustration 2 Graph showing the effect of a non-competitive inhibitor on the relationship between the substrate concentration and the rate of an enzyme-controlled reaction.

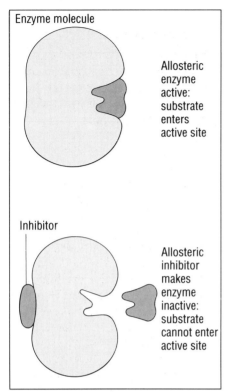

Enzyme molecule

Allosteric enzyme active: substrate enters active site

Inhibitor

Allosteric inhibitor makes enzyme inactive: substrate cannot enter active site

Figure 13.15 An allosteric enzyme and how it may be inhibited. When inactive the enzyme's shape is such that the substrate cannot enter the active site. When active the enzyme's shape changes so that the substrate molecule can fit into the active site. The inhibitor puts the enzyme into its inactive state.

Here is an example. The digestive enzyme trypsin is secreted by the pancreas as an inactive precursor, trypsinogen. The active site is masked by a polypeptide chain which is stripped off only when the enzyme reaches the small intestine. The removal of the polypeptide chain is catalysed by an enzyme called enterokinase present in the small intestine (see page 281).

Inside cells, variations in the rate of metabolism are brought about by enzyme inhibitors. For example, suppose a metabolic pathway becomes overactive and too much end product is produced. In these circumstances the end product inhibits one of the enzymes in the metabolic pathway responsible for its own production. By this means the formation of further end product is slowed down. This is called **end product inhibition**, and it is an example of negative feedback (see Chapter 21). A metabolic process involving end product inhibition is described on page 241.

Allosteric enzymes and their inhibition

The word *allosteric* means 'different shapes', and it is a characteristic of such enzymes that they exist in two different forms, one active and the other inactive. The inactive form of the enzyme is shaped in such a way that the substrate will not fit into the active site. For the enzyme to become active, its shape must be altered so that the substrate will fit into the active site.

Allosteric enzymes may be inhibited by certain chemicals which combine with them. The inhibitor alters the shape of the enzyme, changing it from the active to the inactive form (figure 13.15). Other substances function as activators, changing the enzyme from the inactive to the active form. In this way individual enzymes can be turned on or off, depending on circumstances, and metabolism as a whole can be regulated and adjusted to suit the needs of the organism.

Cofactors

Some enzymes only work in the presence of another chemical which serves as a 'helper'. Such chemicals are called **cofactors**.

In some cases the cofactor is a metal ion such as zinc (Zn^{2+}), iron (Fe^{2+} or Fe^{3+}), magnesium (Mg^{2+}) or copper (Cu^{2+}). The metal ion may help to bind the enzyme and substrate together, or it may serve as the catalytic centre of the enzyme itself. For example, iron is the catalytic centre of catalase. Indeed, iron on its own will catalyse the decomposition of hydrogen peroxide, though not as effectively as when it is associated with the enzyme.

In other cases the cofactor is a complex non-protein organic molecule known as a **coenzyme**. Often the coenzyme functions as a carrier, transferring chemical groups or atoms from the active site of one enzyme to the active site of another. A good example of a coenzyme of this kind is **nicotinamide adenine dinucleotide (NAD)**. NAD, and other similar coenzymes, work in conjunction with oxidoreductase enzymes in respiration, their function being to transfer hydrogen atoms from one enzyme to the next (see page 234).

Sometimes the function of a coenzyme is carried out, not by a separate substance, but by a non-protein group of atoms attached to the enzyme. This is called a **prosthetic group**. The function of the prosthetic group is to transfer atoms or chemical groups from the active site of the enzyme to some other substance. The prosthetic group can therefore be regarded as a kind of built-in coenzyme. For example, the enzyme **cytochrome oxidase** has a prosthetic group which transfers hydrogen atoms to oxygen with the formation of water. This too is explained on page 234.

There is no hard and fast distinction between coenzymes and prosthetic groups. They simply represent different degrees of attachment to the enzyme: coenzymes are loosely bound to the enzyme whereas prosthetic groups are tightly bound. In both cases the active centre is often a metal ion such as iron or copper. In cytochrome oxidase the metal is iron but copper is also required for the catalytic action of the enzyme.

Prosthetic groups are not confined to enzymes – they are essential components of certain other proteins as well. For example, haemoglobin and other blood pigments contain a prosthetic group (the haem part of the molecule) whose role is similar to that of enzyme prosthetic groups, namely to carry atoms or chemical groups and transfer them from one place to another. In the case of blood pigments it is oxygen that is carried.

Humans and other animals obtain cofactors, or the raw materials for making them, from their food. Metal ions come from the mineral component of the food, whereas coenzymes are derived mainly from vitamins. For example, NAD is synthesised from nicotinic acid, one of the B-vitamins.

You can see now why vitamins and minerals are so important in the diet. However, only very small amounts of them are needed because the cofactors themselves are required by cells in such tiny quantities.

Putting enzymes to use

Many of the reactions catalysed by enzymes have commercial uses, the conversion of starch to sugar being just one example. These reactions can be made to happen without enzymes, for example by heating and/or the use of strong acids. Indeed in the past this has been the main approach used in industry. However, enzymes with their fast but gentle action provide a promising alternative.

There are three main advantages of using enzymes in industrial processes, and they are directly related to the properties of enzymes.

- They are specific in their action and are therefore less likely to produce unwanted by-products.
- They are biodegradable and therefore cause less environmental pollution.
- They work in mild conditions, i.e. low temperatures, neutral pH and normal atmospheric pressure, and are therefore energy-saving.

The main disadvantage of enzymes is that they are highly sensitive to changes in the physical and chemical conditions surrounding them. Thus they may be readily denatured by even a small increase in temperature and are highly susceptible to poisons and changes in pH. This means that the conditions in which they work must be stringently controlled. In particular the enzyme–substrate mixture must be uncontaminated with other substances that might affect the reaction, and the equipment must be scrupulously clean.

To be effective in a production process the enzyme molecules must be brought into maximum contact with the substrate molecules. This is achieved in one of two ways. One way is simply to mix solutions of the enzyme and substrate in suitable concentrations. The other way is to attach the enzyme molecules to an inert surface such as plastic beads and then bring the surface into contact with a solution of the substrate. This latter method has the advantage of enabling the enzyme molecules to be used over and over again, with the result that a lot of product can be made from a relatively small amount of the enzyme.

Investigating cofactors

How can we find out if a cofactor is needed for a particular enzyme to work? One way is to put a solution of the enzyme in a sealed bag made of a partially permeable membrane such as cellophane. The bag is then suspended in distilled water.

The membrane allows small molecules and ions to pass through, but holds back the larger protein molecules. In the course of the next few hours, metal ions and coenzymes leave the enzyme molecules and diffuse through the membrane to the surrounding water. To make sure that all such cofactors diffuse through, the distilled water should be changed several times.

The bag now contains a solution of the enzyme, minus any cofactors that may have been present. The enzyme solution is now tested for its enzyme activity. If the activity is reduced, we conclude that one or more factors necessary for the working of the enzyme have been lost. If we put the missing factors back and find that the enzyme's activity is restored, our conclusion is confirmed.

How could you extend this experiment to identify the particular cofactor(s) associated with an enzyme?

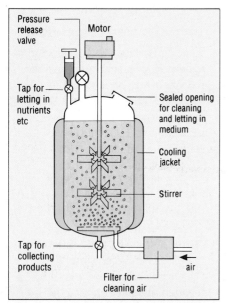

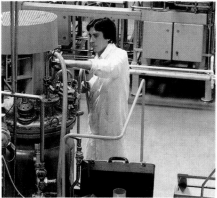

Figure 13.16 An industrial fermenter.
Top Diagram of a generalised fermenter.
Bottom A scientist at work in a commercial fermentation plant where genetically engineered strains of bacteria, yeasts and other micro-organisms are cultured for various industrial uses.

Commercial enzymes are produced by micro-organisms such as yeasts and bacteria. Sometimes naturally occurring strains of these micro-organisms are used, but increasingly nowadays special strains are developed by genetic engineering to produce particular enzymes. The micro-organisms themselves are grown in vast **fermenters** from which their enzymes are removed as and when required (figure 13.16).

Approximately 2000 enzymes have been identified, and of these over 150 are used in industrial processes. For example, amylases which convert starch to sugars are used for making syrups, fruit juices, chocolates and other food products. Cellulases, which break down cellulose, are used for softening vegetables, removing the seed coat from cereal grain, and extracting agar jelly from seaweed. And proteases are used for tenderising meat, skinning fish and removing hair from hides. But perhaps the best-known use of enzymes is in biological washing powders.

Biological washing powders

A biological washing powder contains enzymes, usually proteases, which remove 'biological' stains such as food, blood and so on. The first attempt to make such a product was carried out by Otto Rohm in Germany in 1913. He used the protease trypsin which he extracted from the pancreas of animals.

Since then biological washing powders have had a chequered history. They have been beset with manufacturing problems, and people suspected that the products were not as effective as they were trumped up to be. More important, many people turned out to be allergic to them. Today, however, they have regained their popularity. After being subjected to considerable scrutiny, the claims of the manufacturers have been found to be justified (or reasonably so), and the allergic reactions have been reduced by encapsulating the enzymes in wax from which they are released only when in the wash. The result is that biological washing powders are now manufactured on a very large scale (figure 13.17).

The advantage of these modern biological washing powders is that they are effective at relatively low temperatures, and are therefore energy saving as well as gentler on the clothes. However, as with any other new product, possible health hazards – particularly to those who are involved in their manufacture – need to be constantly considered and investigated. After all, protease enzymes break down proteins under natural conditions inside the body. There may be unknown dangers in allowing such proteins to come into contact with the skin and mucous membranes.

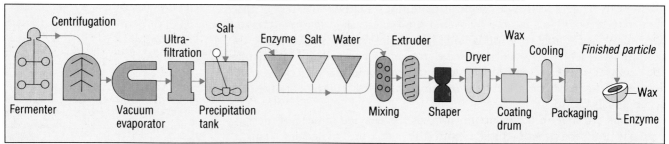

Figure 13.17 The main steps in the production of a biological washing powder. The enzyme is produced by bacteria in a fermenter. The bacterial cells are separated from the culture medium by centrifugation, and water is removed by vacuum evaporation and/or ultrafiltration. Any bacterial cells still present are filtered out. The enzyme is then separated from the liquid by precipitation with, for example, a salt. Next the enzyme is granulated with common salt which acts as a preservative, and mixed with water to form a paste. The paste is then extruded and shaped into spheres in a shaper. Finally the spheres are dried and coated with a layer of wax, then cooled. The finished particles are added to the other ingredients of the washing powder and packaged. The wax subsequently melts in the wash, releasing the enzyme.

Summary

1 Chemical reactions in cells constitute **metabolism**. Metabolic processes proceed in small steps which together constitute a **metabolic pathway**.

2 Metabolic pathways can be reconstructed by various techniques such as isotope labelling, chromatography and the use of enzyme inhibitors.

3 Metabolic reactions may build up substances (**anabolism**) or break them down (**catabolism**). The former absorb energy (**endergonic**), whereas the latter release energy (**exergonic**).

4 The energy released by catabolic reactions is required for synthesis, for work e.g. muscular contraction and active transport, and for maintaining the tissues in a state of health and repair.

5 Oxidative breakdown of sugar yields carbon dioxide, water and energy (**respiration**). The chemical products of this catabolic process can be resynthesised into sugars by plants and other autotrophs (**photosynthesis**).

6 To initiate chemical reactions such as the oxidative breakdown of sugar, a small amount of **activation energy** must be supplied.

7 Chemical reactions in living organisms are catalysed by **enzymes**. Enzymes speed up reactions by lowering the amount of activation energy required to get them going.

8 Enzyme-controlled reactions can be speeded up by raising the temperature or by increasing the concentration of the substrate.

9 Enzymes are nearly always proteins, and this is reflected in some of their properties.

- They generally work rapidly.
- They are not destroyed by the reactions they catalyse.
- They can work in either direction.
- They are inactivated if heated much above 45°C.
- They are sensitive to pH.
- They are usually specific.

10 Enzymes work by combining with substrate molecule(s) to form an **enzyme–substrate complex**. The enzyme molecule has an **active site** where the substrate molecules become temporarily attached.

11 When a substrate molecule enters the active site, it may induce the enzyme molecule to change its shape, thereby ensuring a closer fit (**induced fit hypothesis**).

12 Enzymes are prevented from working by various **inhibitors**. Enzyme inhibition may be either **irreversible** or **reversible**. Reversible inhibition may be **competitive** or **non-competitive**.

13 The product of a metabolic reaction may itself act as an inhibitor, slowing down the reaction by a negative feedback process.

14 **Allosteric enzymes** have two different shapes, one active and the other inactive. Certain chemicals inhibit such enzymes, others activate them.

15 Some enzymes are assisted in their action by non-protein **cofactors**. These include **metal ions**, **coenzymes** and **prosthetic groups**.

16 Enzymes are used commercially for speeding up various processes. One of their best-known uses is in **biological washing powders**.

Review questions

1 Why is it important for a metabolic pathway to proceed in small steps rather than one big jump?

2 Outline how one step in a metabolic pathway might be established.

3 Explain the differences between anabolism and catabolism.

4 Summarise the First Law of Thermodynamics. Why is it important in biology?

5 Explain the lock and key mechanism of enzyme action. How might it be refined in the light of modern knowledge?

6 List the main properties of enzymes. To what extent can each property be explained by the lock and key mechanism?

7 Explain the difference between competitive and non-competitive inhibition of enzymes.

8 What is meant by end product inhibition, and why is it important?

9 What is an allosteric enzyme, and how might its action be controlled?

10 How are enzymes produced for commercial use? Give five examples of how enzymes are used commercially.

Further reading

Steven Rose's *The Chemistry of Life* (Penguin, 1991) is a popular introduction to biochemistry published by Penguin. It is written for Mrs Rose who insisted that biochemistry be made intelligible, and that is certainly what this book succeeds in doing.

Introducing Biochemistry by E.J. Wood and W.R. Pickering (John Murray, 1982), sponsored by the Biochemical Society and written specifically for A-level students, is somewhat more demanding but still very readable.

If it's detail you're after, then try *Biochemistry* by L. Stryer (Freeman, 1981). This will answer most of your questions.

In *Biology, Advanced Topics* the interconversion of starch and glucose and the control of biochemical reactions are discussed.

CHAPTER 14

The release of energy

In the last chapter we saw that for cells to perform their functions energy is required. In this chapter we shall examine in more detail the process by which cells obtain energy, and its importance in organisms as a whole.

Energy is made available to cells by the metabolic breakdown of organic compounds, principally carbohydrates, with the formation of thermodynamically more stable products. The reactions involved comprise **respiration**. Oxygen is normally required, and carbon dioxide and water are produced.

Respiration occurs in all organisms and in every living cell, for it is the only way a living system can obtain usable energy. This applies no less to plants than to animals. The fact that a plant can absorb energy from sunlight does not exempt it from the necessity to respire. A plant uses the energy of sunlight to build up organic compounds which it *then* breaks down in order to transfer energy for use by the cells.

The general nature of respiration

Respiration usually involves the oxidation of glucose. The process may be summarised by the following well-known equation:

$$C_6H_{12}O_6 + 6O_2 \longrightarrow 6H_2O + 6CO_2 + \text{Energy}$$

Glucose, Oxygen, Water, Carbon dioxide

This simplified equation is misleading for a number of reasons. For example, it gives the impression that respiration occurs in a single chemical reaction, a notion which is far from the truth as we shall see later. It also suggests that some of the oxygen which is used in respiration finishes up in the carbon dioxide molecules, which we shall see later is not true. And there is also the implication that oxygen reacts directly with the glucose, which is not the case. But despite its shortcomings the equation is useful as an overall summary of the process, and its general validity can be demonstrated by various experiments.

Experiments confirming the respiration equation

That oxygen is used in respiration can be demonstrated in small organisms by means of a **respirometer** (figure 14.1). The organisms are placed in a small chamber (usually a large test tube) which is connected to a manometer. Carbon dioxide is absorbed by soda lime placed in the respiration chamber so that a movement of the manometer fluid will only be caused by the uptake of oxygen. The rate of oxygen consumption is estimated by timing how long it takes for the manometer fluid to move a certain distance towards the chamber.

In humans oxygen consumption can be studied by means of an apparatus called a **spirometer**, which can also be used to record the depth and frequency of breathing (see page 260). Spirometry enables us to compare the oxygen consumption of a human subject in different conditions, such as when the person is at rest or taking exercise.

That carbon dioxide is produced can be demonstrated in humans by breathing out through **lime water** which turns milky in the presence of carbon dioxide. For small organisms a more sensitive reagent is needed. The organism is placed in a sealed chamber containing a **hydrogencarbonate indicator solution** sensitive to small traces of carbon dioxide.

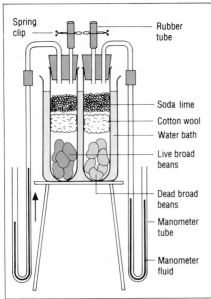

Figure 14.1 A simple respirometer for measuring the oxygen uptake by small organisms such as woodlice or germinating beans. The organisms are placed in a pair of large test tubes as shown. The test tube containing dead organisms serves as a control. As oxygen is used, the level of the fluid rises in the manometer tube, as indicated by the arrow. You can estimate the rate of respiration by timing how long it takes for the manometer fluid to rise through a certain distance. The fluid can be returned to its original level by opening the spring clip. The water bath should be kept at a constant temperature.

Labels on figure: Spring clip, Rubber tube, Soda lime, Cotton wool, Water bath, Live broad beans, Dead broad beans, Manometer tube, Manometer fluid

The oxygen and carbon dioxide content of atmospheric and exhaled air can be measured quantitatively by means of **gas analysis**. In this procedure a small sample of the air is brought into contact first with a reagent which absorbs carbon dioxide, then with a reagent which absorbs oxygen. The decrease in volume of the air sample when subjected to each reagent tells us how much carbon dioxide and oxygen are present. Details of this and other techniques are given in the Student's Manual.

Modern methods of investigating respiration involve the use of machines which measure the total volume of air expired and draw off small samples for analysis. The samples are fed into a device which makes a continuous record of the oxygen and carbon dioxide present.

These and many other experiments indicate that organisms take in oxygen and give out carbon dioxide, but how do we know that this is connected with the oxidation of glucose? This has been shown by the use of radioactive tracers. For example, mice have been fed with glucose in which the normal carbon (^{12}C) was replaced with its radioactive isotope (^{14}C). The radioactive carbon subsequently got into the carbon dioxide which the mice breathed out, confirming that the carbon dioxide comes from the breakdown of glucose.

Respiration and energy

The respiration equation suggests that living organisms release energy. That they do so can be demonstrated by means of a **calorimeter**. A calorimeter suitable for use with living organisms consists of a chamber with insulated walls which prevent heat energy being lost. The size of the chamber depends on the type of organism being investigated. For human subjects the calorimeter chamber may be the size of a small room. Energy released by the occupant is estimated by measuring the rise in temperature of a current of water circulated through the chamber.

That the release of energy is connected with respiration is suggested by the fact that it proceeds at the same rate as oxygen consumption and carbon dioxide production. This can be shown by collecting a person's expired air both at rest and during muscular activity, and comparing its oxygen and carbon dioxide content. The air is collected in a **Douglas bag**, a large expandable sac impermeable to respiratory gases. The bag is connected to the person's mouth by a flexible breathing tube fitted with a valve so that air is breathed in from the atmosphere and out into the bag. Leading from the breathing tube is a short side-tube from which samples of the expired air can be taken for gas analysis. The Douglas bag is light and can be easily attached to a person's back, enabling expired air to be collected during various forms of exercise (figure 14.2A).

The amount of energy actually expended during exercise can be estimated by pedaling a **bicycle joulometer**, the kind of bicycle that people use indoors for keeping fit. The bicycle is fixed in a stationary stand, the back wheel being replaced by a flywheel working against a frictional resistance. In this way the mechanical work done can be measured while the subject breathes in and out of a Douglas bag, spirometer or other device from which the oxygen consumption can be measured (figure 14.2B). From experiments of this sort it can be shown that oxygen consumption is directly proportional to the work done by the subject.

So respiration really does seem to be associated with energy transfer in the body. However, the energy that comes from oxidising glucose cannot make a muscle contract. The link between the oxidation of glucose and the body's energy-requiring activities is provided by another substance: **adenosine triphosphate (ATP)**. What is ATP and what does it do?

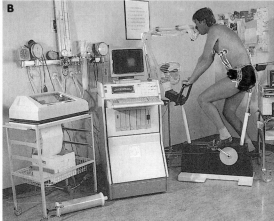

Figure 14.2 Investigating the connection between respiration and energy expenditure.
A An athlete collects his expired air in a Douglas bag for subsequent analysis in the laboratory. Knowing the total volume of air expired in a given time, the rate of oxygen consumption can be calculated.
B While pedalling the bicycle joulometer a continous record is made of this man's energy expenditure and oxygen consumption together with other variables such as heart rate and blood pressure.

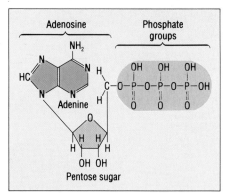

Figure 14.3 The structural formula of adenosine triphosphate (ATP), the universal supplier of energy in cells. ATP is a nucleotide, a group of substances which form the building blocks of nucleic acids.

ATP: the vital link

ATP is the universal currency of energy in all living organisms, from bacteria to humans. Chemically it is a nucleotide, a group of organic substances which form the building blocks of nucleic acids (see page 710). Its structural formula is shown in figure 14.3. Notice that it consists of an organic component called **adenosine** to which is attached a chain of three **inorganic phosphate groups**.

Now in the presence of the right enzyme ATP is readily hydrolysed. This is an exergonic reaction and a relatively large amount of free energy is released – about 34 kJ per mole altogether. Some of the energy is transferred to the surroundings as heat energy, but a proportion of it may be transferred to other molecules and systems and used directly for driving biological activities such as muscle contraction:

Catalysed by the enzyme ATPase, the hydrolysis of ATP yields adenosine diphosphate (ADP) and inorganic phosphate:

$$\text{ATP} \xrightarrow{\text{ATPase}} \text{ADP} + \text{Pi} + 34\text{kJ}$$

ATP	ADP	Pi	34kJ
Adenosine triphosphate	Adenosine diphosphate	Inorganic phosphate	Energy

In this reaction the terminal phosphate group is detached from the end of the ATP molecule. This involves breaking the bond between the last two phosphate groups and forming new bonds in the products, ADP and inorganic phosphate. The formation of these new bonds results in energy being transferred to an energy-requiring process in the cell:

$$\underset{\text{ATP}}{\text{Adenosine} - P - P - P} + \underset{\text{water}}{H_2O} \xrightarrow{\text{ATPase}} \underset{\text{ADP}}{\text{Adenosine} - P - P} + \text{Pi} + \text{Energy}$$

muscle contraction etc.

ATP was first isolated in the early 1930s, having been extracted from muscle tissue. Its function in muscles was subsequently demonstrated in America by Albert Szent-Gyorgyi (figure 14.4). He showed that isolated muscle fibres contract when ATP is placed on them but not when glucose is placed on them. This suggested that ATP rather than glucose is the *immediate* source of energy for muscle contraction.

Since then ATP has been shown to be the immediate source of energy for many other biological processes including nerve transmission, active transport, biosynthesis and luminescence. Luminescence is particularly interesting because it can be used as a quantitative test for ATP. When solutions of ATP are added to a standard preparation of luminescent tissue, the tissue glows and the degree of luminescence is a measure of the amount of ATP present.

ATP is truly remarkable. Considerable energy can be transferred from it to other molecules. And yet it is a remarkably stable compound, reacting only when circumstances permit. This makes it ideal as a supplier of energy in living cells.

Figure 14.4 Albert Szent-Gyorgyi, who discovered the energetic role of ATP in muscle. 'Genius', Szent-Gyorgyi used to say, 'is seeing what everyone else has seen, and thinking what no one else has thought.'

Providing energy for ATP synthesis

If ATP is the immediate source of energy in cells, it follows that there should always be a ready supply of it for use when required. This is where respiration comes in. The purpose of oxidising glucose is to provide a continual source of energy which can be used for synthesising ATP. The synthesis of ATP involves attaching a phosphate group (derived from phosphoric acid) to ADP, the reverse of what happens when ATP is hydrolysed. This is an endergonic reaction, and the energy for it comes from the oxidation of glucose. The oxidative breakdown of glucose is thus coupled with the synthesis of ATP:

$$\text{glucose} + \text{oxygen} \quad \diagdown \quad \text{ADP} + \text{Pi}$$
$$CO_2 + H_2O \quad \diagup \quad \text{ATP}$$

In humans and other vertebrates phosphate groups for making ATP from ADP are stored in a compound called **creatine phosphate**. (Invertebrates use a similar compound called arginine phosphate.) Creatine phosphate is found particularly in muscles where its function is to provide a ready source of phosphate groups for rephosphorylating ADP.

ATP is not stored – in fact there is barely enough ATP in a typical muscle to sustain contraction for more than a second or so. This means that ATP has to be synthesised 'on the go', the rate of synthesis keeping pace with the demand. To see how this is achieved we must look at what happens when glucose is oxidised in respiration.

The breakdown of glucose in respiration

The glucose which is broken down in respiration is derived from the hydrolysis of polysaccharides such as starch and glycogen. These storage compounds provide a continual supply of glucose molecules for use when required.

As with other biochemical processes, the breakdown of glucose does not happen in one jump but in a series of small steps. The pathway can be divided into two parts, **glycolysis** and the **Krebs cycle**. Glycolysis takes place first, its products being fed into the Krebs cycle. Each step is catalysed by a specific enzyme. The overall process is summarised in figure 14.5 on the next page to which you should refer as you read the following account.

Glycolysis

Glycolysis literally means 'sugar splitting'. As you know, glucose is a hexose sugar with six carbon atoms (see page 126). During glycolysis the hexose sugar is converted through a series of steps into **pyruvic acid** which has three carbon atoms. (Pyruvic acid, in keeping with other organic acids in the cell, usually occurs as the anion of a salt and is therefore better referred to as **pyruvate**.)

Before glycolysis can get underway the hexose sugar has to be **phosphorylated**. In this process, which takes place in several steps and is catalysed by phosphokinase enzymes, two phosphate groups are added to the sugar molecule. The reactions are endergonic and the necessary energy is provided by the hydrolysis of two molecules of ATP, which also donate their terminal phosphate groups for attachment to the sugar. This initial

Figure 14.5 The metabolic pathway in which sugar is broken down in respiration. The process starts with phosphorylation of 6-carbon sugar (glucose). In the diagram this is shown happening in one step but in fact it involves several steps. In the first a phosphate group is added to the glucose molecule, resulting in the formation of **glucose 6-phosphate**, so-called because the phosphate group is attached to the glucose molecule at position 6 (see page 126). A second phosphate group is then attached to the sugar which is subsequently split into two molecules of 3-carbon sugar. These are in equilibrium with each other and normally both are converted into pyruvic acid and fed into the Krebs cycle.

The overall function of the pathway is to produce ATP molecules. Energy is transferred to ATP mainly as a result of the removal of pairs of hydrogen atoms from intermediate compounds in the pathway. The diagram shows the stages at which hydrogen atoms are removed, together with the numbers of ATP molecules synthesised. The ATP molecules circled are produced via the hydrogen carrier system which is explained on page 234. Usually three ATP molecules are synthesised every time two hydrogen atoms pass through the carrier system. However, in the conversion of succinate to fumarate only two ATPs are produced because in this case the initial carrier (NAD) is absent.

One of the most important intermediates in the pathway is acetyl CoA because it links glycolysis with the Krebs cycle. Coenzyme A is a complex molecule derived from the vitamin pantothenic acid (see page 149). Its function is to transfer an acetyl group (CH_3CO) from pyruvate to oxaloacetate. In this way two carbon atoms are added to the oxaloacetate with the formation of citrate.

The process outlined here is called **oxidative phosphorylation**. It is oxidative in the sense that hydrogen atoms are removed from certain compounds and combined with oxygen. It is phosphorylation in that phosphate groups are added to ADP to give ATP. The process also involves **decarboxylation**, the removal of carboxyl groups with the formation of carbon dioxide.

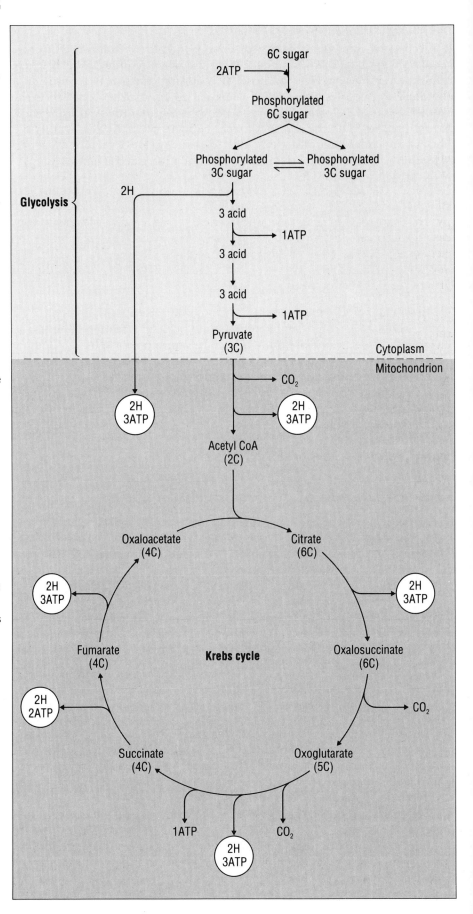

phosphorylation activates the sugar and maintains a steep concentration gradient favouring the diffusion of more glucose into the cell.

The scene is now set for the glycolytic breakdown of the sugar to occur. First, the phosphorylated 6-carbon sugar is split into two molecules of phosphorylated **3-carbon sugar**. A 3-carbon sugar is called a **triose**. These two trioses can both enter the pathway leading to pyruvate. The first step of the pathway involves dehydrogenation: two hydrogen atoms are removed from the triose by a dehydrogenase enzyme. These hydrogen atoms are taken up by a hydrogen carrier which, for reasons which will be explained later, leads to the synthesis of ATP from ADP and inorganic phosphate.

Meanwhile, the triose, now deprived of two of its hydrogen atoms but still phosphorylated, is converted via a series of 3-carbon compounds to pyruvate. Two of the steps are directly coupled with ATP synthesis: in each case the substrate is at a much higher energy level than pyruvate, and sufficient energy is transferred for the synthesis of a molecule of ATP from ADP and inorganic phosphate. The substrates also provide their phosphate groups for the ATP molecules.

The pyruvate now enters a mitochondrion where it is converted into a 2-carbon compound called **acetyl coenzyme A** (acetyl CoA for short). In this reaction carbon dioxide is given off, and the pyruvate loses a pair of hydrogen atoms which again results in the synthesis of ATP.

Acetyl CoA is a complex molecule incorporating a coenzyme (coenzyme A), a derivative of pantothenic acid (vitamin B_5). Acetyl CoA is a very important intermediate in respiration. It links glycolysis with the Krebs cycle, and – as we shall see later – it also links the oxidation of fats and proteins with the Krebs cycle.

The Krebs cycle

Acetyl CoA has two carbon atoms and it reacts with a 4-carbon organic compound called **oxaloacetate** to form **citrate** with six carbon atoms. What's really happening here is that coenzyme A transfers two carbon atoms from pyruvate to oxaloacetate, thereby converting the latter to citrate. This is a nice example of a coenzyme carrying out its function of transferring chemicals from one compound to another (see page 224).

There now follows a series of reactions in which the citrate is gradually converted back to oxaloacetate, step by step. If you look at figure 14.5 you will see that two of the steps involve decarboxylation with the formation of carbon dioxide. More importantly, four of the steps involve the removal of pairs of hydrogen atoms (dehydrogenation) leading to the synthesis of ATP from ADP and inorganic phosphate. In addition to the ATP formed as a result of dehydrogenation, one of the steps in the cycle is coupled directly with the synthesis of ATP.

Reconstructing the steps in this complex pathway was one of the early triumphs of modern biology, much of it derived from the brilliant work during the 1940s and 50s of Sir Hans Krebs, whose name is given to the cycle. An important piece of equipment which Krebs used in his work was a special kind of respirometer devised by his teacher, Otto Warburg. It is called a **Warburg manometer** and is described in the box on page 235.

Careful auditing has shown that the complete oxidation of one molecule of the 6-carbon sugar can yield a net total of 38 molecules of ATP. Of these, 30 are produced by the Krebs cycle compared with only eight by glycolysis. You can check this for yourself by adding up the ATPs in figure 14.5. Don't forget that *two* molecules of the 3-carbon sugar go through the process, and two molecules of ATP are required for the initial phosphorylation of the 6-carbon sugar.

Figure 14.6 In the hydrogen carrier system, hydrogen atoms from intermediates in the breakdown of sugar are used to reduce a succession of hydrogen carriers, eventually combining with oxygen to form water. When the hydrogen atoms are transferred from one carrier to the next, the latter becomes reduced and the former is reoxidised. This oxidation–reduction process is linked with ATP synthesis, as shown in the diagram.

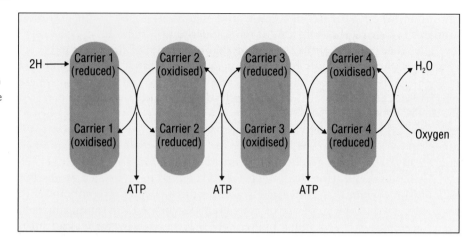

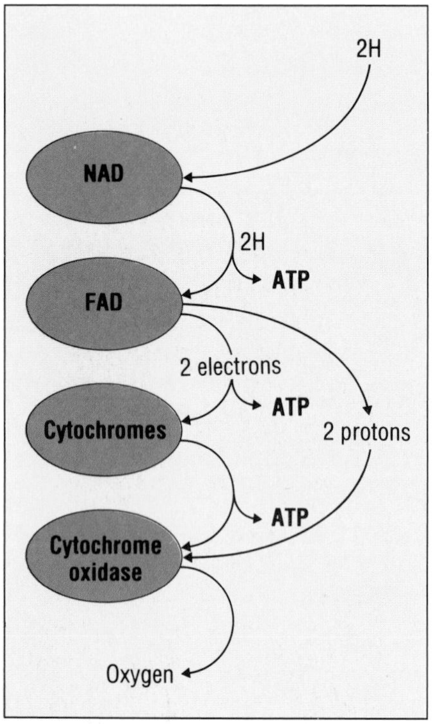

Figure 14.7 Simplified diagram illustrating what happens to the hydrogen atoms as they pass through the carrier system. NAD stands for nicotinamide adenine dinucleotide, FAD for flavine adenine dinucleotide. NAD, FAD and the cytochromes are coenzymes. They are jointly responsible for transferring hydrogen atoms from the initial dehydrogenase enzyme to cytochrome oxidase. Notice that at the FAD stage the hydrogen atoms split into protons and electrons which rejoin at the cytochrome oxidase stage. From the energy point of view it is the electrons that matter. At the beginning of the chain the electrons have a high potential energy. At each step of the chain the electrons fall to a lower energy state, and the energy released is used for ATP synthesis.

The hydrogen carrier system

In the foregoing account of glycolysis and the Krebs cycle we have talked about pairs of hydrogen atoms, removed from various intermediates, leading to the synthesis of ATP. How do these hydrogen atoms generate ATP?

The answer centres on what happens to them. Under the influence of a dehydrogenase enzyme, the two hydrogen atoms are removed from the intermediate compound and taken up by a hydrogen acceptor. The hydrogen atoms (or their electrons) are then passed along a series of **hydrogen carriers**, finally combining with oxygen to form water. This system is called the **hydrogen carrier system**. At each step energy is transferred and used for the synthesis of ATP from ADP and inorganic phosphate. Usually a total of three ATP molecules are produced for every two hydrogen atoms that enter the system. However, the number of carriers in the chain can vary, and sometimes fewer ATP molecules are produced.

The hydrogen carrier system is really a series of coupled oxidation–reduction reactions. When the first carrier accepts hydrogen atoms it becomes reduced. When the hydrogen atoms are transferred to the second carrier, the latter becomes reduced and the first carrier becomes reoxidised. At each step sufficient energy is transferred for a molecule of ATP to be produced (figure 14.6).

Although the details of the hydrogen carrier system vary, it usually follows the pattern shown in figure 14.7. The initial hydrogen carrier is usually **nicotinamide adenine dinucleotide (NAD)**, derived from the vitamin nicotinic acid. When it accepts hydrogen atoms it becomes reduced:

$$NAD^+ + 2H \rightarrow NADH + H^+$$

The next carrier is **flavine adenine dinucleotide (FAD)**, derived from vitamin B_2 (riboflavine). This accepts the hydrogen atoms from NAD, becoming reduced in the process. The hydrogen atoms now dissociate into their constituent electrons and protons. The electrons are taken up by the third carrier which consists of a complex of protein pigments called **cytochromes**. They have iron-containing prosthetic groups, rather like haemoglobin, and the iron is responsible for transferring the electrons.

When the electrons have been through the cytochrome system they rejoin the protons to form hydrogen atoms again. The hydrogen atoms are then taken up by the final carrier, **cytochrome oxidase**. This is an oxidoreductase enzyme and is the only component of the chain which is able to reduce oxygen. Having taken up the hydrogen atoms, it transfers them to oxygen with the formation of water.

The Warburg manometer and how it helped to unravel respiration

To find out what happens to sugar during respiration, it is necessary to study the rate of respiration of small pieces of tissue in different conditions. This can be done using a **Warburg manometer**. This apparatus was designed by the German chemist Otto Warburg in the 1940s and is used to measure the rate of respiration of small pieces of tissue.

A homogenised suspension of the tissue is placed in a special flask, as shown in illustration 1. The flask is connected to a U-shaped manometer tube. A compartment in the centre of the flask contains a small piece of filter paper soaked in potassium hydroxide (KOH). This absorbs any carbon dioxide produced so that movement of the fluid in the manometer tube is caused only by oxygen uptake.

The rate of oxygen uptake is determined by timing how long it takes for the fluid to rise through a certain distance in the right-hand side of the tube. The flask is kept at a constant temperature by being shaken continuously in a thermostatically controlled water bath.

Connected to the side of the flask are one or more side arms from which various reagents such as enzymes and inhibitors can be added to the tissue sample in the course of the experiment. This is done by tilting the flask so that the reagent flows in from the side arm. In this way different factors influencing the rate of respiration may be investigated.

How can this apparatus be used to establish a step in the metabolic breakdown of sugar? Suppose we suspect that the following reaction occurs (it is one of the reactions in the Krebs cycle):

$$\text{succinate} \quad \rightarrow \quad \text{fumarate}$$

and suppose we have identified the enzyme which catalyses this reaction (succinate dehydrogenase). If the proposed reaction does occur in cells, and if it is part of respiration, then inhibiting the enzyme should have certain predictable results, namely an accumulation of succinate, a decline in the amount of fumarate and a fall in the rate of oxygen uptake.

Predictions of this sort can be tested with the Warburg apparatus. Two flasks are set up, one to serve as a control. Tissue samples are placed in the flasks, and the enzyme is added. It so happens that succinate has a specific inhibitor: malonate (see page 222). This is let into one of the flasks. The effect on the rate of oxygen consumption is determined and compared with that of the control. The contents of the flasks can be analysed at the end of the experiment to find out how much substrate and product are present.

Illustration 2 shows a Warburg apparatus. Notice the two manometers. The flasks are inside the cylindrical chamber which contains the thermostatically controlled water bath. On the left is Sir Hans Krebs whose discovery of the citric acid cycle owes much to the Warburg apparatus. Krebs was educated in Germany where he was a pupil of Warburg. Later he emigrated to England and, after a brief period at Cambridge, became Professor of Biochemistry at Sheffield University and later at Oxford. In 1953 he won the Nobel Prize for Medicine for his work on carbohydrate metabolism.

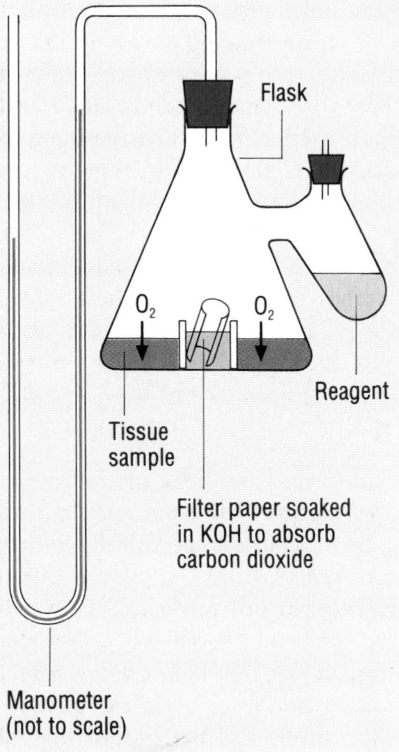

Flask

O_2 O_2

Reagent

Tissue sample

Filter paper soaked in KOH to absorb carbon dioxide

Manometer (not to scale)

Illustration 1 Warburg flask used for measuring oxygen uptake by small samples of tissues.

Illustration 2 Sir Hans Krebs with a Warburg apparatus. Notice the two manometers which are used to measure the uptake of oxygen by the tissue samples.

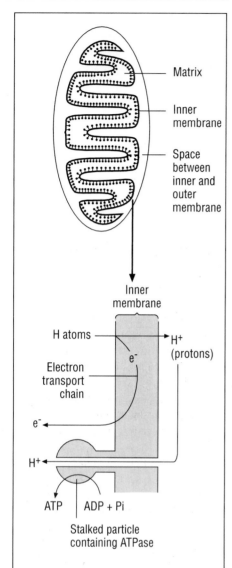

Figure 14.8 The chemiosmotic theory proposes that the energy for ATP synthesis comes from an electrochemical gradient across the inner mitochondrial membrane. The gradient arises as a result of hydrogen ions (protons), derived from hydrogen atoms obtained from intermediates in respiration, being moved outwards across the membrane. The electrons from the hydrogen atoms pass through the electron transfer chain within the membrane and are deposited back inside the mitochondrial matrix. Meanwhile the protons flow back into the mitochondrial matrix via special channels in the membrane. ATPase, associated with the stalked particles on the inner surface of the membrane, catalyses the synthesis of ATP from ADP and inorganic phosphate. What do you think happens to the protons and electrons once they are back in the mitochondrial matrix?

What happens where?

Where do all the reactions which we have been describing take place? This has been investigated by isolating the different components of cells and finding out what happens in each one. First a chunk of liver is homogenised in a Waring blender and made into a suspension by mixing it with a saline solution. The components of the suspension are then separated by **differential centrifugation** as explained on page 161.

The conclusion to be drawn is that glycolysis takes place in the cytoplasm whereas the Krebs cycle takes place in the matrix of the mitochondria. The hydrogen carrier system is associated with the mitochondrial membranes.

Recent research with radioactive tracers has pinpointed the positions of the carriers and enzymes in the mitochondrial membrane. You will recall that the mitochondrion is lined by two membranes separated by a narrow gap. From the inner membrane **stalked particles** jut into the interior of the mitochondrion. The carriers are located in the inner membrane, and ATPase, which catalyses the synthesis of ATP from ADP and inorganic phosphate, is associated with the stalked particles.

How does the carrier system result in ATP synthesis?

The discovery that the carriers are located in the inner mitochondrial membrane has led to the formulation of a theory explaining how ATP is produced (figure 14.8).

The basic idea is that the hydrogen atoms are picked up by the initial carrier (usually NAD) on the matrix side of the membrane. After the hydrogen atoms have split into electrons and protons, the electrons are taken up by the cytochromes but the protons are moved across to the other side of the membrane and deposited in the narrow gap. This results in an **electrochemical gradient** being set up across the inner membrane. It is this electrochemical gradient that provides the energy for synthesising ATP molecules. The protons rejoin the electrons by flowing through the inner mitochondrial membrane via channels corresponding in position to the stalked particles.

This explanation of how ATP is produced is called the **chemiosmotic theory**. It was put forward by the English scientist Peter Mitchell, who was awarded the Nobel Prize in 1978.

Respiration without oxygen

From the foregoing account you will realise that the bulk of useful energy yielded by metabolism comes from the transfer of hydrogen atoms or electrons. For this to work oxygen must be available to accept the hydrogen atoms from the final carrier. This kind of respiration – involving the participation of oxygen – is called **aerobic respiration**, and organisms which engage in it are described as **aerobes**.

Most organisms are aerobes. However, a small but significant minority of organisms can obtain energy by breaking down sugar in the absence of oxygen. This is known as **anaerobic respiration**, and the organisms which do it are called **anaerobes**. Many micro-organisms, including yeast and some bacteria, can respire anaerobically. So can certain species of annelids that live in oxygen-deficient mud, and gut parasites such as tapeworms. Sometimes particular tissues respire anaerobically if conditions make this necessary. For example, vertebrate skeletal muscles respire anaerobically during vigorous activity, and so do the roots of certain plants when the soil is waterlogged.

Two kinds of anaerobe are recognised.

- **Obligate anaerobes** live permanently in oxygen-deficient conditions, and have no need at all for oxygen. Indeed in some cases they may be poisoned by oxygen, even in small concentrations.
- **Facultative anaerobes** respire aerobically when oxygen is present, but if oxygen happens to be absent or in short supply they resort to anaerobic respiration. The majority of anaerobes fall into this category.

Types of anaerobic respiration

In anaerobic respiration sugar, instead of being oxidised to carbon dioxide and water, is converted into either **lactic acid** or **ethanol**. Lactic acid is the end product of anaerobic respiration in animals, ethanol in plants and yeast. The latter process is called **alcoholic fermentation**. Anaerobic bacteria can produce both end products, depending on the species. The overall equations for these two types of anaerobic respiration are as follows:

Anaerobic respiration with ethanol formation: (alcoholic fermentation):
$$C_6H_{12}O_6 \rightarrow 2CH_3CH_2OH + 2CO_2 + 210 \text{ kJ}$$
$$\text{ethanol}$$

Anaerobic respiration with lactic acid formation:
$$C_6H_{12}O_6 \rightarrow 2CH_3CH(OH)COOH + 150 \text{ kJ}$$
$$\text{lactic acid}$$

Aerobic respiration for comparison:
$$C_6H_{12}O_6 + 6O_2 \rightarrow 6H_2O + 6CO_2 + 2880 \text{ kJ}$$

Notice that in anaerobic respiration the sugar is not broken down as completely as it is in aerobic respiration. The consequence is that less energy is released than in aerobic conditions. The meagre energy yield of a couple of hundred kilojoules in anaerobic respiration contrasts sharply with the 2880 kJ produced in aerobic conditions.

What happens in anaerobic respiration?

Why is sugar not broken down completely in anaerobic respiration? The answer is that in anaerobic conditions there is no oxygen to accept hydrogen atoms as they come off the carrier system. This means that the carrier system cannot operate in anaerobic conditions. With no carrier system there can be no Krebs cycle, and accordingly it has been found that in anaerobic conditions the Krebs cycle does not take place. Glycolysis occurs in the usual way, and indeed is much speeded up, but the pyruvate, instead of being converted into acetyl CoA and fed into the Krebs cycle, is converted into lactic acid or ethanol. How this conversion takes place provides a nice example of the neatness of biological systems.

You will recall that the first step in the conversion of the 3-carbon sugar to pyruvate involves dehydrogenation: two hydrogen atoms are removed. In aerobic conditions these two hydrogen atoms are taken up by NAD after which they enter a mitochondrion and bring about the synthesis of ATP. However, in anaerobic conditions the NAD hands them to pyruvate which is thereby reduced and converted into ethanol or lactic acid. One effect of this is that it prevents hydrogen ions accumulating in the cell and raising the acidity. This would undoubtedly happen otherwise, for anaerobic respiration takes place at a very much faster rate than aerobic respiration.

Fireflies can prevent food poisoning

Testing food to see if it has become contaminated with bacteria traditionally takes several days. However, a new technique has been developed which produces the same result within minutes.

All living cells contain ATP. If ATP is mixed with two compounds extracted from fireflies – luciferin and luciferase – light is released. If a sample of food is taken, it can be treated with a substance called apyrase which breaks down any *eukaryotic* ATP, but has no action on *prokaryotic* ATP. Any ATP left over may therefore be assumed to be prokaryotic in origin. So if a sample of food, having been treated with apyrase, gives off light when mixed with luciferin and luciferase, bacteria must be present.

The food industry is extremely interested in this technique because at present it is almost impossible routinely to test foods for bacterial contamination before they leave the factory. In 1985 more than 40 cases of *Salmonella* poisoning resulted after baby food from Farley's factory in Cumbria became contaminated by bacteria. The plant had to close and the parent company, Glaxo, lost an estimated £25 million.

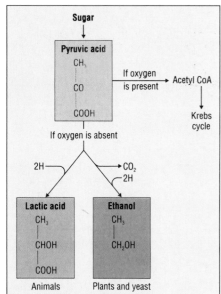

Figure 14.9 In anaerobic conditions pyruvic acid (pyruvate) is converted into either lactic acid or ethanol. The two hydrogen atoms which reduce the pyruvate come from the dehydrogenation of the 3-carbon sugar at the beginning of glycolysis. In aerobic conditions these two hydrogen atoms are taken up by NAD and shunted into a mitochondrion where they are sent through the hydrogen carrier system. But in anaerobic conditions the two hydrogen atoms are used to reduce the pyruvate. Lactic acid is formed in one step as shown here. Ethanol is formed in two steps: in the first step a molecule of carbon dioxide is removed from the pyruvate with the formation of acetaldehyde; in the second step the two hydrogen atoms are added to the acetaldehyde with the formation of ethanol.

Figure 14.10 Beer fermenting in a large vat in a brewery. The froth is caused by the evolution of carbon dioxide from the yeast.

Figure 14.9 shows how pyruvate is converted into lactic acid and ethanol. Notice the difference between the two reactions. Lactic acid is formed simply by adding the two hydrogen atoms to the pyruvate. Ethanol, however, is formed by adding the two hydrogen atoms and taking away a molecule of carbon dioxide. Alcoholic fermentation is therefore accompanied by the evolution of carbon dioxide, a fact which is made use of in baking: yeast is added to the flour and water and, when the mixture is warmed, the carbon dioxide gas causes the dough to rise.

Thus in anaerobic respiration glycolysis continues but the Krebs cycle is omitted. The omission of the Krebs cycle means that far fewer ATP molecules are produced than in aerobic conditions. In fact the anaerobic breakdown of a single molecule of the 6-carbon sugar yields only two molecules of ATP compared with the possible 38 molecules produced in aerobic conditions. Aerobic respiration is therefore much more efficient, and the ability of organisms to utilise oxygen must have been a very important step in the evolution of life.

To some extent the shortcomings of anaerobic respiration are compensated for by the fact that it can occur at a greatly accelerated rate, at least for short periods. So, although inefficient in energy terms, it can be useful as a short-term measure and undoubtedly has contributed to the survival of many species.

What happens to the products of anaerobic respiration?

In anaerobic respiration a lot of energy remains locked up in the ethanol or lactic acid molecules. In animals this energy can be released by subsequent conversion of the lactic acid back into pyruvate which is then oxidised in the usual way. This requires oxygen. In humans the lactic acid that accumulates during muscular activity can be subsequently reconverted into carbohydrate or broken down with the release of energy when oxygen becomes available. Any lactic acid not disposed of this way is excreted.

Plants, however, cannot make use of ethanol. It cannot be reconverted into carbohydrate, nor can it be broken down in the presence of oxygen. As it is toxic it must not be allowed to accumulate, and this is probably why very few plants are complete anaerobes. Many plants (or parts of plants) can respire anaerobically for a short time – germinating seeds for example, and roots living in waterlogged soil. But before the concentration of ethanol reaches a certain level they must revert to aerobic respiration, otherwise they will be poisoned by the ethanol.

This is even true of yeast. Yeast is a classic example of an anaerobe, and the brewing and wine-making industries depend on this. But in fact yeast grows much better in aerobic than in anaerobic conditions. If too little oxygen is present the ethanol concentration rises so much that the yeast cells are killed. The secret in making beer and wine is not to let conditions become too anaerobic. Of course it is useful commercially to develop new strains of yeast which are tolerant to high concentrations of ethanol. This is a major occupation of microbiologists working for brewery companies.

Energy from non-carbohydrate sources

Carbohydrates are not the only substances which give energy. Energy can also be derived from the oxidation of fats and proteins. The metabolic pathways involved are closely linked with carbohydrate metabolism, as you can see in figure 14.11. Notice that most of them lead to acetyl CoA. Acetyl CoA is thus a kind of crossroads in metabolism. It is formed during the oxidation of fats and proteins as well as carbohydrates and represents a common pathway by which the products of all three are fed into the Krebs cycle.

Most of the reactions are reversible. This is important because it means that carbohydrates can be converted into fat for storage or used for the synthesis of certain fatty acids and amino acids.

Now let us look in a bit more detail at how energy is obtained from fat and protein.

Energy from fat

Fat is used as a source of energy when carbohydrate is in short supply or when the demand for energy is particularly great. First the fat is split into **fatty acids** and **glycerol**. The latter is phosphorylated and converted into triose sugar which is then converted into pyruvate and fed into the Krebs cycle. Meanwhile each fatty acid goes through a series of reactions in which carbon atoms are split off its hydrocarbon chain, two at a time. Each 2-carbon unit is actually an acetyl group (CH_3CO). This combines with coenzyme A to form a molecule of acetyl CoA. The acetyl CoA then enters the Krebs cycle.

The process in which each 2-carbon unit is split off the fatty acid takes place in the mitochondria. It occurs in a series of steps, some of which involve the removal of hydrogen atoms. The latter pass through the carrier system with the synthesis of ATP. When eventually a molecule of acetyl CoA has been formed, the fatty acid, now containing two fewer carbon atoms in its hydrocarbon chain, goes through the same series of reactions again. This process is repeated, using the same enzymes, until the hydrocarbon chain has been completely dismantled. It is called the **fatty acid spiral** (figure 14.12). The whole sequence transfers a lot of energy for ATP synthesis. Still more ATP molecules are produced every time an acetyl CoA molecule is fed into the Krebs cycle.

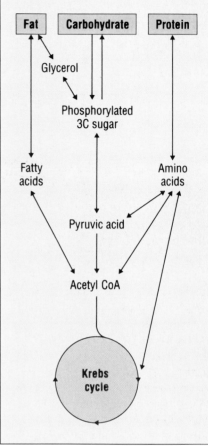

Figure 14.11 Simplified scheme showing how carbohydrate, fat and protein metabolism are interconnected. Notice that all three pathways converge on the Krebs cycle.

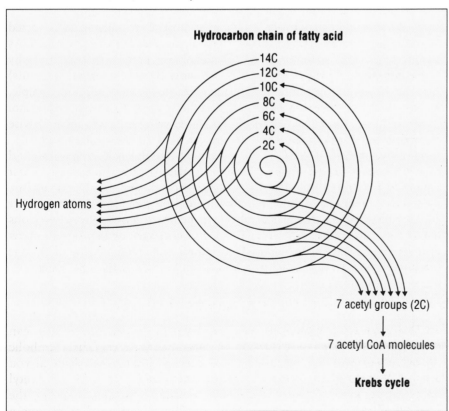

Figure 14.12 A hypothetical fatty acid with 14 carbon atoms in its hydrocarbon chain is here shown going through the fatty acid spiral. The hydrocarbon chain is broken down, two carbon units at a time. Each 2-carbon unit (an acetyl group) becomes incorporated into a molecule of acetyl CoA which is fed into the Krebs cycle. After each 2-carbon unit has been removed from the hydrocarbon chain, the rest of the chain repeats the process and loses another two carbons. The process is repeated until the hydrocarbon chain has been completely dismantled. Each turn of the spiral produces, in addition to an acetyl group, two pairs of hydrogen atoms which go through the hydrogen carrier system with the synthesis of ATP.

Exactly how many ATP molecules are produced by the complete oxidation of a fatty acid depends on the number of carbon atoms it contains. A fatty acid with a long hydrocarbon chain will obviously give more molecules of acetyl CoA, and therefore more ATP molecules, than one with a relatively short chain. The complete oxidation of a molecule of stearic acid with 16 carbon atoms in its hydrocarbon chain yields a net total of about 150 molecules of ATP. This is nearly four times as many as are given by the oxidation of a single glucose molecule.

The fatty acid spiral takes place in the liver where the necessary enzymes are located. However, so much acetyl CoA may be formed that the liver cannot use it all. The liver converts the excess acetyl CoA into acids known collectively as **ketone bodies**. These are released into the bloodstream and taken to other tissues. Once inside the cells, they are reconverted into acetyl CoA and fed into the Krebs cycle with the release of energy. In this way the rapid oxidation of fats in the liver can supply the needs of the whole body.

Energy from protein

Proteins are not stored as such so our only reserves are the tissues themselves. Only if an organism is starving is its tissue protein used as a source of energy, but a certain amount of energy is always derived from excess dietary protein. The protein is first split into its constituent **amino acids**. Each amino acid is then **deaminated**: its amino (NH_2) group is split off with the formation of ammonia. The ammonia is quickly converted into urea which is later excreted (see page 364).

Meanwhile the carbon fragment left after the removal of the amino group is fed into carbohydrate metabolism. Depending on the particular amino acid in question, it may enter the carbohydrate pathway by being converted into pyruvate, acetyl CoA or one of the Krebs cycle intermedi-

The respiratory quotient

The **respiratory quotient (RQ)** is the amount of carbon dioxide produced, divided by the amount of oxygen used, in a given time:

$$RQ = \frac{CO_2 \text{ produced}}{O_2 \text{ used}}$$

The importance of the RQ is that it can tell us what kind of substance is being oxidised, i.e. the substrate being used in respiration. Theoretical RQs for the complete oxidation of carbohydrate, fat and protein can be worked out from the appropriate chemical equations. The figures are as follows:

Substrate	RQ
Carbohydrate	1.0
Fat	0.7
Protein	0.9

In theory we might expect an organism to give one of these three RQs, or a close approximation to it, depending on the type of food being respired. However, this rarely happens in practice because many factors influence the values obtained by experiment. For example, a respiratory substrate is rarely oxidised completely, and often a mixture of substrates is used in the body. Most animals have an RQ in resting conditions of between 0.8 and 0.9. The human's is generally around 0.85. As protein is normally not used to a great extent, an RQ of slightly less than 1.0 can be taken to mean that fat and carbohydrate are being respired.

As well as giving us some indication of the type of food being used, the RQ can tell us what sort of metabolism is going on. For example, high RQs

(exceeding 1.0) are often obtained from organisms, or tissues, which are short of oxygen. Under these circumstances they resort to anaerobic respiration, with the result that the amount of carbon dioxide produced exceeds the amount of oxygen used. High RQs also result from the conversion of carbohydrate to fat, because carbon dioxide is liberated in the process. This is most noticeable in organisms that are laying down extensive food reserves – in animals preparing to hibernate, for example, and in fattening livestock.

A very low RQ, on the other hand, may mean that some (or all) of the carbon dioxide released in respiration is being put to some sort of use by the organism. In plants it may be used for photosynthesis, in animals for the construction of calcareous shells, and so on.

ates. Whatever the route, once the carbon fragment gets into the carbohydrate pathway, ATP molecules are synthesised in the usual way.

The metabolic rate

The **metabolic rate** is the amount of energy expended by an organism in a given time, and it is a measure of the speed at which the energy-yielding reactions take place. The metabolic rate depends on the amount of physical work done. But even when an organism is at rest and doing nothing, a certain amount of energy is still needed for basic functions such as breathing, beating of the heart, keeping up the body temperature and so on – in short for maintaining the life of the cells. This is the minimum amount of energy on which the body can survive, and it represents the **basal metabolic rate (BMR)**.

The BMR does not remain constant throughout life, but changes as growth, development and ageing take place. In a newborn baby the BMR is low: about 100 kJ m^{-2} h^{-1} (kilojoules per square metre of body surface per hour). It then rises rapidly, reaching a maximum of about 220 kJ m^{-2} h^{-1} by the end of the first year. This corresponds to the child's period of most rapid growth. The BMR then gradually declines as the rate of growth

How the rate of respiration is controlled

It is important that sugar should be respired and energy released at the right rate. In practice the rate is determined by the amount of ATP which has been synthesised. If ATP synthesis has been going on apace and there is a lot present in the cells, then respiration is automatically slowed down. This is achieved by **end product inhibition** (see page 224).

The key factor controlling the rate of sugar breakdown is the ratio of ATP to ADP. The mechanism is shown in the illustration. A high concentration of ATP relative to ADP *inhibits* one of the phosphokinase enzymes which catalyses the initial phosphorylation of the sugar. This enzyme is one of the first in the metabolic pathway, so it sets the pace of the whole process. Modulating the activity of the enzyme by this feedback process is therefore an effective way of controlling the overall rate of respiration.

The phosphokinase enzyme is allosteric, that is, it can exist in

different shapes (see page 224). Whether the enzyme is active or inactive depends on its shape and this in turn is determined by the concentration of ATP relative to ADP.

Because of the way it is controlled, very little ATP need be stored. Feedback control ensures that it is synthesised at the same rate as it is used. In fact the amount of ATP in the body remains remarkably constant – at about 50 g in a normal person. However, the amount synthesised in the course of a day can be as much as 100 kg. The turnover is therefore colossal. Indeed the constancy of ATP, and the fact that it is held in steady state, has led some biologists – principally Barbara Banks of University College, London – to suggest that ATP's main energy function is to serve as a phosphorylating agent which, by being held in steady state, controls the rate of metabolism.

Simplified scheme showing how respiration is controlled. An excess of ATP relative to ADP inhibits the phosphokinase enzyme, thereby slowing down the rate at which glucose is respired. This is an example of negative feedback (see Chapter 21).

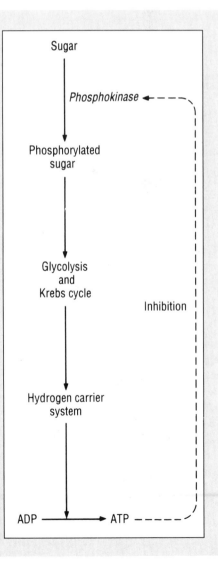

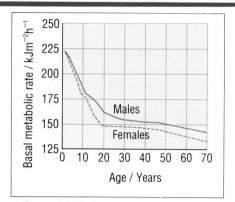

Figure 14.13 Graph showing how the basal metabolic rate of the human declines with age.

decreases, and continues to do so even after growth has ceased altogether (figure 14.13).

The BMR also varies with the sex and health of the individual. For a healthy young woman it is about 150 kilojoules per square metre of body surface per hour (kJ m^{-2} h^{-1}), and for a healthy young man it is about 167 kJ m^{-2} h^{-1}. It is customary to express the BMR per unit of body surface, but for general purposes it is sufficient to give the total energy output per day. For an average-sized woman this comes to about 5850 kJ per day, and for a man about 7500 kJ per day.

Variations in the metabolic rate

The basal metabolic rate applies to a person lying at rest. It does not even include the energy required to feed oneself, and therefore as an indication of a person's normal energy expenditure it is hardly applicable to everyday life. The moment you stand up and walk across the room, your metabolic rate increases – and if you engage in any sort of vigorous activity, such as lifting a suitcase or running for the bus, your metabolic rate increases even more. In fact the energy expended by the body may increase more than ten times during strenuous muscular activity, as table 14.1 makes clear.

Amongst animals there are considerable variations between different species. For example, the metabolic rate of a shrew or humming bird at rest is over 5000 times that of a freshwater mussel. Shrews and humming birds are two of the fastest metabolisers.

Activity	Energy expenditure (kJ min^{-1})	
	Woman	Man
Sleeping	3.8	4.2
Sitting	5.0	5.8
Light work	15.0	17.0
Sawing	34.0	38.0
Maximum work	57.0	63.0

Table 14.1 Energy expenditure in relation to different kinds of activity.

Food and energy

The energy expended by the body comes from the oxidation of food, and it is therefore useful to know the contribution made by different types of food to our energy needs. This can be found by measuring the amount of energy transferred to the surroundings when a known quantity of food is burned. The apparatus used for this is called a **food calorimeter** (figure 14.14).

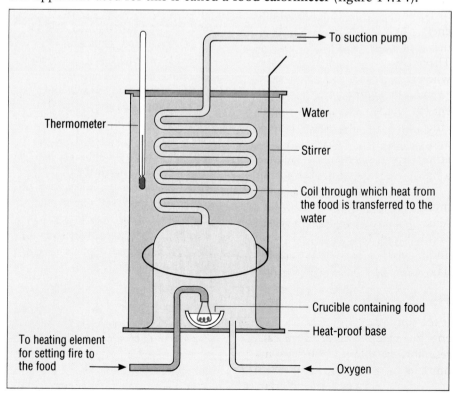

Figure 14.14 A food calorimeter. A sample of dry food of known mass is ignited, and the rise in temperature of the water is noted. The stirrer ensures that the temperature of the water is even. The energy content of the food is calculated knowing that 4.2 kJ of energy is required to raise the temperature of 1.0 g of water by 1°C. In some circles the energy value of food is expressed in an older unit, the kilocalorie (or Calorie with a capital C). One kilocalorie (or Calorie) is approximately equal to 4.2 kilojoules. The term 'calorimeter' is derived from this older unit.

The sample of food is dried so as to remove all traces of water, and then weighed. It is then placed in a strong steel chamber which is filled with oxygen and tightly sealed. The calorimeter is surrounded by a jacket containing a known volume of water whose temperature is recorded. The food is ignited by means of a small electric heating coil, and the amount of heat energy transferred to the surroundings is calculated by measuring the rise in temperature of the water.

From food calorimetry the **energy values** of the three main types of food substance have been established. They are as follows:

- Carbohydrate   17.2 kJ per gram
- Fat   38.5 kJ per gram
- Protein   22.2 kJ per gram

Predictably, these figures are more or less in proportion to the number of ATP molecules produced by the oxidation of these three types of substance in the body.

Carbohydrate and fat are the body's main sources of energy, and any excess can be stored for use later. Protein is required for growth and repair and is not a primary source of energy. However, if there is an excess of protein in the diet, as there often is in affluent countries, then the excess will be oxidised with the release of energy. If carbohydrate and fat are in short supply and the body's reserves have been used up, proteins from the tissues are used for supplying energy. This is what happens with people who are starving. The less vital organs such as the skeletal muscles are used first, which is why starving people look so thin and emaciated. The heart and brain remain unaffected.

Alcohol, as well as being socially popular, can be a supplementary source of energy. However, it cannot be stored and therefore can only be used as an immediate source of energy. Moreover, much of it is excreted, exhaled or incompletely oxidised, thus reducing its energy contribution.

If the total energy content of a person's food is estimated over a period of time, it is found to be equal to the person's energy expenditure plus the energy contained in the body's tissues and any lost in materials such as urine and faeces. This is not really surprising in view of the First Law of Thermodynamics which states that energy is neither gained nor destroyed when it is transferred.

It is obviously important to any organism that it should transfer the energy of its food to the energy of muscular contraction with maximum efficiency, i.e. with minimum loss as heat energy. Knowing the energy input and output, the organism's **efficiency** can be calculated. For humans the efficiency of the body as a whole turns out to be approximately 23 per cent, a figure that compares favourably with machines such as cars.

Although the efficiency of the human body may seem rather low, it must not be forgotten that the heat energy, though lost in the metabolic sense, is not all wasted. At least some of it may be used to warm the body and maintain a constant body temperature. This is one reason why shrews and humming birds have such high metabolic rates, and it neccessitates having a high food intake (figure 14.15).

Figure 14.15 Animals with high metabolic rates, such as shrews and humming birds, have a high food requirement to meet the demands of their metabolism much of which is concerned with keeping up their body temperature. The top photo shows a male rufus humming bird feeding on the nectar of a flower. In the bottom photo a common shrew *Sorex araneus* is about to eat an earthworm. Shrews eat almost incessantly, day and night.

Human energy requirements

It follows from what has been said that our metabolic rate is limited by the energy value of the food we eat. Unless the body is to draw heavily on its reserves, the necessary energy must be provided by the diet. What then are our energy requirements?

It goes without saying that we must receive sufficient energy-giving

Type of person	kJ per day
Newborn baby	2000
Child 1 year	3000
Child 2-3	6000
Child 5-7	7500
Girl 12-15	9500
Boy 12-15	12 000
Girl 16-18	10 000
Boy 16-18	15 000
Office worker	11 000
Factory worker	12 500
Heavy manual worker	15 000
Pregnant woman	10 000
Woman breast-feeding	11 000

Table 14.2 Approximate amounts of energy required daily by different types of people.

food to sustain the basal metabolic rate. This means that a woman must receive at least 5850 kJ, and a man 7500 kJ, per day. But in practice we need much more than this, in order to meet the requirements which our daily activities demand. For example, a woman's energy requirements increase during pregnancy, and a coalminer's are much greater than those of a high court judge.

Despite these individual variations, attempts have been made to work out the daily energy requirements of an 'average person', one who spends a normal proportion of time sleeping, sitting, standing, walking and performing the sundry activities which most people go through in their daily lives. Ignoring individual variations, this works out at about 9600 kJ per day for a young woman, and about 13 400 kJ per day for a young man.

These figures are recommended by the United Nations Food and Agriculture Organisation (FAO) and other official bodies. In view of these generally agreed figures, it is disturbing to realise that over two-thirds of the world's population receive less energy than the recommended minimum. In many parts of the world the daily energy intake is only just sufficient to maintain the basal metabolic rate. Tragically, some people receive even less than this and are in a state of starvation.

On the other hand, the daily energy intake of people living in affluent countries is often far more than they need. If you take in more energy than you use, the excess will be stored as fat. This causes an increase in body mass, a condition known as **obesity**. Obesity and its attendant problems are characteristic features of an affluent society, and they can only be countered by sensible eating habits and regular exercise.

Obesity

Obesity is the most common nutritional disease in Britain and other affluent societies. Guest author Dr James Parkyn discusses this condition.

In Britain about ten per cent of children are overweight and by adolescence the proportion has risen to between 13 and 23 per cent, the majority being adolescent girls. In the adult population some 20 to 30 per cent are above the 'desirable' weight for their height. The prevalence of obesity peaks between the ages of 40 and 50 years for men, 50 and 60 for women.

Why are so many people obese? There is no simple explanation, but factors which may play a part in causing obesity include the following:

Genetic factors

It has been sugggested that obese people are programmed to use the energy from their food more

efficiently for sustaining the resting metabolic rate and other activities, thus leaving a surplus which is converted to fat.

Behavioural factors

Habit and learned eating behaviour seem to be important in regulating food intake. Often an entire family enjoy their food and are big eaters. This can even extend to pets; it is a common observation that obese people own obese dogs!

Structural factors

An obese person has a larger number of fat cells than a thin person. The reason is that when a fat cell becomes full of fat it divides and the additional fat cells remain in the body. Hence fat children tend to grow into fat adults.

Metabolic factors

Over the years an obese person must ingest more energy than he or she expends. A person who takes in 1260

kJ (about ten per cent) more energy each day than he or she uses undergoes a net gain of 420 kJ daily after allowing for the increased energy loss caused by increased heat energy production. This amounts to 153 300 kJ in a year, leading to the deposition of about 4 kg of fat in the body tissues.

Obesity shortens lives. This fact, based on statistical investigations, is well known to insurance companies which therefore raise their premiums for clients who are overweight. Obese people are more likely to develop certain disabling diseases. These include diabetes (five times more common amongst obese people), gall stones, high blood pressure, strokes (twice as common amongst obese people) and coronary heart disease. In women obesity is associated with heavy menstrual periods and failure to ovulate (causing infertility) and complications in childbirth. An obese person is also more likely to have problems during surgical operations.

Summary

1 Energy is transferred by **respiration** which occurs in all living cells. It generally involves the oxidation of glucose with the formation of water and carbon dioxide.

2 Experiments can be carried out to demonstrate the general validity of the respiration equation. For example, oxygen consumption, measured with a **respirometer**, can be related to energy expenditure.

3 The immediate source of energy for biological functions is **adenosine triphosphate (ATP)**. In the presence of the appropriate enzyme, ATP can be hydrolysed into adenosine diphosphate (ADP) and inorganic phosphate with the transfer of free energy.

4 The purpose of breaking down glucose in respiration is to provide energy for the synthesis of ATP.

5 In **aerobic respiration** glucose is broken down in two main stages: **glycolysis** followed by the **Krebs cycle**.

6 Most of the energy for ATP synthesis is derived from the **hydrogen carrier system**, or **electron transport chain**, associated mainly with the Krebs cycle.

7 Differential centrifugation experiments indicate that glycolysis takes place in the cytoplasm, the Krebs cycle in the matrix of the mitochondria, and the electron transfer chain in the inner mitochondrial membrane.

8 According to Mitchell's **chemiosmotic theory**, the energy for ATP synthesis is derived from an electro-chemical gradient arising as a result of the distribution of the electron carriers across the inner mitochondrial membrane.

9 In **anaerobic respiration** glucose is converted into **ethanol** or **lactic acid**. Because the Krebs cycle is omitted, considerably less energy is transferred than in aerobic respiration.

10 The rate of glucose breakdown is controlled by a feedback system which enables the amount of ATP in the body to be held in steady state.

11 Fat and protein breakdown, as well as carbohydrate, feed into the Krebs cycle and provide energy for ATP synthesis as well as permitting metabolic interconversions to take place.

12 The **respiratory quotient (RQ)** is the amount of carbon dioxide produced divided by the amount of oxygen consumed in a given time. The RQ can give useful information about the nature of the food being respired, and the kind of respiration that is taking place.

13 The minimum rate of energy transfer for the maintenance of life is called the **basal metabolic rate (BMR)**. Actual metabolic rates usually exceed the BMR and depend on the activity of the individual.

14 The **energy value** of different food substances can be determined by means of a **food calorimeter** which measures the amount of energy transferred to the surroundings when a known quantity of food is burned.

15 People's daily intake of energy falls short of the recommended minimum in many poorer parts of the world, whereas in more affluent regions it is well in excess of what is needed.

Review questions

1 Explain how each of the following can be used to establish the general validity of the respiration equation:

  (a) hydrogencarbonate indicator,
  (b) respirometer,
  (c) calorimeter,
  (d) radioactive isotope of carbon.

2 An isolated muscle fibre will contract in a solution of ATP but not in a solution of glucose. Explain.

3 What has to happen to sugar before glycolysis can get underway, and why?

4 Explain the main events which occur in glycolysis in
(a) aerobic and
(b) anaerobic conditions.

5 Construct a metabolic chart of the Krebs cycle in sufficient detail to show its principal features.

6 Describe one technique which was used in the discovery of the Krebs cycle.

7 'The Krebs cycle provides *reducing power* for the *electron transport system*.' Explain the words and phrases in italics.

8 If you drive past a rice field it may smell alcoholic. Explain.

9 How, and in what circumstances, is energy made available in the human body from fat and protein?

10 What is meant by an organism's *basal metabolic rate*. How would you find the basal metabolic rate of a human subject?

Further reading

The books mentioned at the end of the last chapter are also applicable to this chapter. Steven Rose's book is particularly useful in that it gives a clear account of glycolysis and the Krebs cycle, uncluttered by unnecessary detail.

Krebs has written a delightful autobiography which contains a brief account of the cycle but is more noteworthy for the account of his life, first in Germany and then in England (Hans Krebs in collaboration with Anne Martin, *Reminiscences and Reflections*, Oxford University Press, 1981).

The connection between glycolysis and the Krebs cycle is developed further in *Biology, Advanced Topics*. There is also an integrated survey of metabolic pathways.

Part III

OBTAINING THE ESSENTIALS FOR LIFE

*R*espiration is the fundamental process that keeps organisms alive. In Part III we consider how organisms obtain the raw materials for respiration and other life processes.

For aerobic respiration to occur two things are required: food and oxygen. How organisms acquire oxygen is discussed in detail, along with other aspects of gaseous exchange.

In animals and certain other organisms food is obtained in organic form, a process called heterotrophic nutrition. In contrast, plants and certain other organisms can synthesise their own organic substances from simple inorganic sources, a process called autotrophic nutrition. Heterotrophic and autotrophic nutrition form two important chapters in this part of the book.

An organism's problems do not end after food and oxygen have been taken into the body. They must then be transported, by active or passive means, to the cells. How this is achieved in animals and plants is discussed in the final three chapters.

Photograph: A female gerenuk, *Litocranius walleri*, reaches for the leaves of an acacia tree in Samburu Game Reserve, Kenya.

CHAPTER 15 | Gaseous exchange

All living organisms exchange gases with the environment. This is necessary to allow the cells to obtain the supply of the gases needed for metabolic processes and to facilitate the removal of gaseous metabolic waste. Exchange of gases, whether it is with the atmosphere or in an aquatic medium, is therefore very important.

Most living cells require a supply of oxygen to carry out **respiration**. Carbon dioxide is a metabolic waste product of respiration. In addition plants require carbon dioxide for **photosynthesis** and produce oxygen in the process. We shall therefore concentrate on the exchange of carbon dioxide and oxygen.

Efficient gaseous exchange in all organisms depends on three conditions being met. These are:

- The maintenance of a **diffusion gradient** to sustain the exchange process.
- The provision of a **large surface area** across which the supply and removal of the gases can take place.
- The presence of a **moist surface membrane** so that the gases can go into solution.

With these three requirements in mind let us look at gaseous exchange in plants and animals.

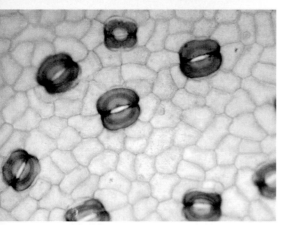

Figure 15.1 Photomicrograph of lower epidermis of privet leaf showing stomata in surface view. Magnification × 200.

Gaseous exchange in plants

The living cells in the roots, stems and leaves of plants respire aerobically most of the time and yet there is no special system within plants for the transport of oxygen or carbon dioxide. These gases move entirely by diffusion. It is therefore not surprising to find that plant tissues are either permeated by air spaces through which gases can diffuse freely or have their respiring cells close to the surface. For example, the arrangement of cells in a leaf accommodates many air spaces (see page 297). However, there is a problem. The leaves and stems of flowering plants are usually covered with a cuticularised epidermis which reduces water loss but at the same time prevents any significant exchange of gases. How then, do gases get in and out of plants? The answer is that they do so via the **stomata**.

Stomata

Stomata (singular: *stoma* = mouth) are pores in the epidermis of the leaves and stems of plants, which can open and close (figures 15.1 and 15.2). The pore itself is bordered by a pair of modified epidermal cells called **guard cells** which can draw apart or close together rather like sliding doors.

The stomata are usually most numerous in the lower epidermis of the leaf where there may be as many as 860 per mm² (sycamore) though more usually the number is around 200 per mm². In most trees and shrubs they are absent from the upper epidermis, but in water plants with floating leaves, such as water lilies, they are only present in the upper epidermis. Grasses and other monocotyledons in which the leaves are held more or less vertically, have stomata on both surfaces.

In passing it should be noted that in woody stems the epidermis is replaced by an impervious layer of densely packed corky cells. Gaseous exchange in these circumstances takes place in localised regions called **lenticels** where the corky cells are loosely packed (see page 644).

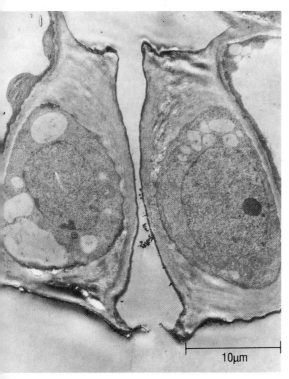

10μm

Figure 15.2 Electron micrograph of a section through a stoma of a French bean leaf. The guard cells have been sectioned transversely.

Measuring the resistance to air flow through a leaf

Whether stomata are open or closed and how effective they are at allowing the passage of gases through them can be investigated by using a simple piece of apparatus called a **porometer**.

A porometer is an instrument which measures the resistance to air flow through a leaf. There are many variations in the design of porometers but they all work on the same principle. In the one illustrated a leaf is clamped between two Perspex plates; the rubber bulb of the pipette is squeezed and the glass tube inserted into the socket. The bulb is released and the time taken for it to reinflate is a measure of the degree of openness of the stomata. The apparatus must, of course, be airtight and this can be checked by using a thin glass slide between the plates instead of a leaf.

One of many types of porometer for measuring resistance to air flow through a leaf. This apparatus can be used to estimate the degree of openness or closure of stomata over a period of time.

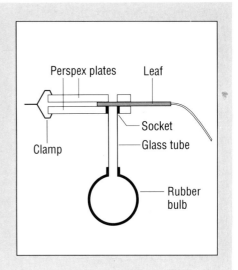

In 1900 a discovery was made by two researchers, H.T. Brown and F. Escombe, which helps to explain why stomata provide an effective way of allowing gases to move in and out of leaves. They showed that a greater volume of gas will pass through numerous small holes in a given time than through a single hole of the same total area. This is because diffusion is faster at the perimeter than in the centre of a hole, and the combined perimeter of many small holes is greater than the perimeter of a few large ones. The stomata are therefore ideal for gaseous exchange.

Allowing the exchange of carbon dioxide and oxygen between the inside of the leaf and the surrounding atmosphere is only one function of stomata; another is to allow water to evaporate from the leaf, thus cooling the plant (see page 410). However, the plant faces a conflict. If the stomata are open, carbon dioxide is available for photosynthesis but water loss may exceed water uptake. If they are closed, less water vapour is lost, but so is the cooling effect of the evaporation of water. Moreover carbon dioxide is no longer available for photosynthesis, and the plant could run short of oxygen too. The state of the stomata can therefore be crucial in the life of a plant, especially in dry conditions.

The opening and closing of stomata

In order to understand how stomata open and close we must look at their structure. In figure 15.3A you will notice that the guard cells are sausage shaped and, unlike other epidermal cells, contain chloroplasts. There is a large, sap-filled vacuole and, a point of great importance, the inner cellulose wall (i.e. the wall lining of the pore itself) is thicker and less elastic than the outer wall.

Stomatal opening and closing depends on changes in turgor of the guard cells. If water flows into the guard cells by osmosis, their turgor increases and they expand. But they do not expand uniformly in all directions. The relatively inelastic inner wall makes them bend and draw away from each other as shown in figure 15.3. The result is that the pore opens. If the guard cells lose water the reverse happens: their turgor decreases and they straighten, thus closing the pore.

We now know that the guard cells increase their turgor by actively accumulating potassium ions (K^+), thus lowering their water potential and causing the inflow of water by osmosis from the surrounding epidermal cells.

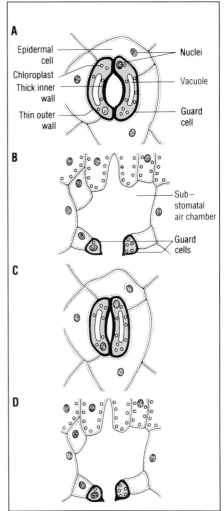

Figure 15.3 Structure and action of a stoma. **A** and **B** are a surface view and section of an open stoma. **C** and **D** are the same views of an almost closed stoma. The pore is never completely closed.

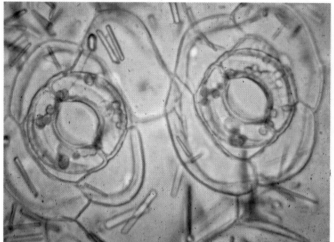
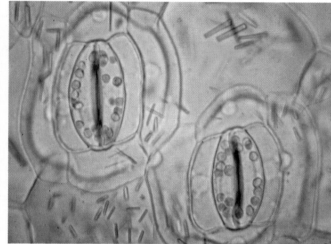

Figure 15.4 Photomicrographs of stomata of flax (*Commelina*) *left* open, *right* closed. Notice that chloroplasts are present in the guard cells but absent from the other epidermal cells. Magnification × 400.

When potassium ions are lost from the guard cells, their water potential increases. Water flows out, causing them to become flaccid and the stomata close. Table 15.1 shows the potassium ion concentration in the open and closed guard cells of some common plants.

The accumulation of potassium ions in the guard cells requires the expenditure of energy. The necessary energy is provided by the transfer of electrons during photosynthesis, which generates ATP (see page 301). This is why the guard cells contain chloroplasts.

Table 15.1 Potassium ion concentrations in open and closed stomata.

| Species | Potassium (mM) in guard cells that are | |
	open	closed
Vicia faba (broad bean)	645	138
Nicotiana tabacum (tobacco)	500	219
Commelina communis (flax)	448	95
Zea mais (maize)	400	150

When do stomata open and close?

The timing of the opening and closing of stomata depends on a number of environmental factors. Under natural conditions stomata open at daybreak and close at night, so light appears to be the main factor which initiates opening (figure 15.5).

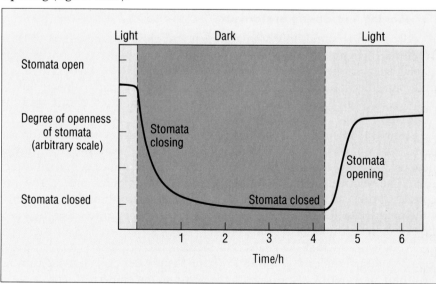

Figure 15.5 The effect of illumination on the movement of the stomata of *Pelargonium*.

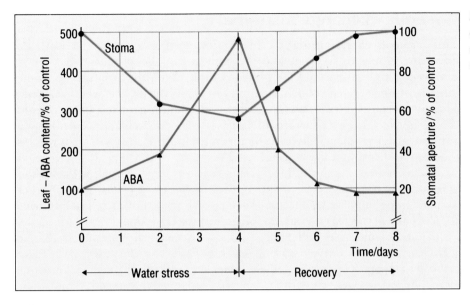

There are, however, situations in which other conditions can override the effect of light. For example, on a warm sunny day as the temperature increases, more and more water vapour is lost through the open stomata. If the water loss exceeds the uptake of water from the soil, the water content of the plant falls and the plant suffers from **water stress**. Eventually the guard cells lose their turgor and close the stomata. In such conditions, photosynthesis may also be reduced, resulting in a rise in the concentration of carbon dioxide in the leaf. This too causes the stomata to close with the result that for the moment no further carbon dioxide diffuses in. Conversely a fall in the internal concentration of carbon dioxide promotes the opening of the stomata, thus encouraging more carbon dioxide to diffuse in.

Water stress is now known to cause the concentration of the plant hormone **abscisic acid** to rise quite quickly in the leaves, and this results in closure of the stomata. When water is again available the concentration of abscisic acid falls and the stomata reopen (figure 15.6).

Diffusion inside the stoma

Once inside the leaf, the gases in the sub-stomatal air chambers diffuse through the intercellular spaces between the mesophyll cells. When the gases come into contact with the wet surfaces of the cells carbon dioxide and oxygen go into solution. In addition some carbon dioxide dissolves to form carbonic acid (H_2CO_3) which dissociates to give hydrogencarbonate ions (HCO_3^-). In either case the carbon dioxide diffuses through the plasma membrane to the chloroplasts. It is then fixed in the photosynthetic process (see page 299). As a result, the diffusion gradient of carbon dioxide from the atmosphere to the chloroplast is maintained.

Carbon dioxide and oxygen may also diffuse from the cells into the sub-stomatal air spaces and thence out through the open stomata. The direction of diffusion depends on the environmental conditions and the requirements of the plant. It is the net exchange of carbon dioxide and oxygen in relation to respiration and photosynthesis which matters.

Stomata and negative feedback

The events which control the opening and closing of stomata are an example of **negative feedback**. In the case of drought, partial closure of the stomata is maintained until turgor is restored, at which time the stomata will open again. In the case of photosynthesis, a reduction in the concentration of carbon dioxide inside the leaf opens the stomata, resulting in an *increase* in the concentration of carbon dioxide inside the leaf. Negative feedback is explained fully on page 361.

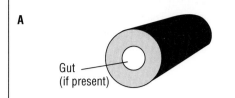

A

Gut
(if present)

Gaseous exchange takes place across the entire surface of body. Found in a wide range of small organisms from protoctists to earthworms.

B

Gaseous exchange takes place across the surface of a flattened body. Flattening increases the surface-volume ratio and also decreases the distance over which diffusion has to occur within the body, e.g. flatworms.

Figure 15.7 Organisms which undergo gaseous exchange across the entire surface of the body are either small or flattened.

Gaseous exchange in animals

Most animals carry out aerobic respiration so their cells must receive an adequate supply of oxygen, and the carbon dioxide produced has to be removed. Land animals get their oxygen direct from the atmosphere. Some aquatic animals, such as fish, use oxygen dissolved in the water. Others, such as mosquito larvae, water spiders and whales, get their oxygen from the air above the water surface. In all cases gaseous exchange depends on a concentration gradient between the medium and the sites where oxygen is required and carbon dioxide is released.

In small animals, the surface–volume ratio is large enough for diffusion across the external surface to satisfy their respiratory needs. But in larger animals, especially active ones, the surface–volume ratio is too small for this to be so and a special **gaseous-exchange surface** is needed.

Animals that use the external body surface for gaseous exchange include free-living flatworms and earthworms. For the most part these animals are small enough not to require a special surface for gaseous exchange. Moreover, some of them are comparatively inactive and their sluggishness considerably reduces their need for oxygen. The free-living flatworms are interesting in this context. They glide over stones and leaves in streams and lakes which are well aerated. The smallest species are almost cylindrical, but the larger species are flattened which has the effect of increasing the surface–volume ratio and decreasing the distance over which gases have to diffuse.

These adaptations are summarised in figure 15.7. They help to solve the problem of gaseous exchange. However, the overall size of an animal is limited if the only area available for gaseous exchange is the external body surface. This limit does not apply to animals which have special surfaces for gaseous exchange.

Specialised gaseous exchange surfaces

Most animals have special surfaces for gaseous exchange. Some are shown diagrammatically in figure 15.8. In all cases they consist of numerous flaps, sacs or tubes which provide a large area for diffusion.

The simplest devices are **external gills**, epidermal outgrowths from the body surface found in aquatic animals such as lugworms and young tadpoles. In contrast, **internal gills**, found in fish, are enclosed in cavities within the body where they are protected from damage and in which blood can be brought very close to the surrounding water.

Air-breathing vertebrates have **lungs** which are sac-like outgrowths of the pharynx in which air is brought close to the blood. A quite different arrangement is found in insects. Here, air pores at the surface open into a system of branching **tracheal tubes** which ramify through the body, coming into close association with all the tissues.

Although these various devices might seem rather different, they all have one essential feature in common: the exposure of a large surface area to whatever medium the animal happens to live in. This, we saw earlier in the chapter, is a basic requirement for efficient gaseous exchange.

We shall now look in detail at gaseous exchange systems in fishes, mammals and insects.

Gaseous exchange in fishes

If you look at table 15.2 you will see that water is denser and more viscous than air. The concentration of oxygen in water is lower, and it diffuses more slowly, than in air. As far as gaseous exchange is concerned, this

	Air	**Water**
Density	1	777
Viscosity	1	100
Oxygen content	210	8
Diffusion rate	10 000	1

Table 15.2 Comparison of a sample of fresh water and air. The oxygen content is in cm³ per litre; other figures are in arbitrary units.

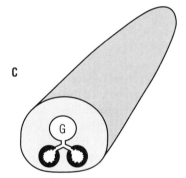

A

External gills. These increase the surface area but they are unprotected and therefore easily damaged. Gaseous exchange usually takes place across the rest of the body surface as well as the gills, e.g. lugworm.

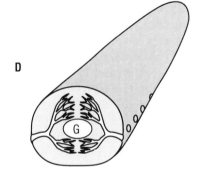

B

Internal gills. Highly vascularised. Ventilation mechanism draws water over the gill surfaces, e.g. fishes.

C

Lungs. Highly vascularised. The lungs are sacs connected to the pharynx. Air is drawn into them by a ventilation mechanism. Found in all air-breathing vertebrates.

D

Tracheal system. Gaseous exchange takes place at the terminal ends of fine **tracheal tubes** which ramify through the body and penetrate into all the tissues. Found in insects and other arthropods.

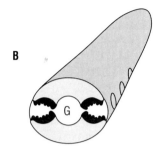

Figure 15.8 Diagrams showing different kinds of surfaces for gaseous exchange. In each case the gaseous exchange surface is shown in black and the gut is labelled G.

presents fishes with certain difficulties and it is one of the reasons why they are generally less active than mammals.

The properties of water as compared with air mean that the surface for gaseous exchange and the ventilation mechanism in fishes need to be quite different from those of mammals. The idea of a fish propelling water in and out of sac-like lungs, such as mammals have, would be quite out of the question (why?). In fishes gaseous exchange takes place across the surface of highly vascularised **gills** over which a one-way current of water is kept flowing by a specialised pumping mechanism. The density of the water prevents the gills from collapsing and lying on top of each other, which is what invariably happens when a fish is taken out of water.

In Chapter 8 we saw that there are two classes of fish – those with a skeleton made of cartilage (chondrichthyes) and those in which the skeleton is made of bone (osteichthyes). The principles of gaseous exchange are the same in both groups, though the arrangement of the gills and the way they open to the exterior are different (figure 15.9).

Gaseous exchange in bony fish

In bony fish, like cod and whiting, the entire gill region is flanked by a muscular flap of skin, the **operculum,** which can be seen in figure 15.9. This

Figure 15.9 Top The head of a white-tipped shark, *Traepodon obesus*, showing five separate gill slits typical of cartilaginous fishes.
Bottom The head of a bony fish called a bleak, *Alburnus alburnus*, showing the operculum covering the gills. An operculum is typical of bony fishes.

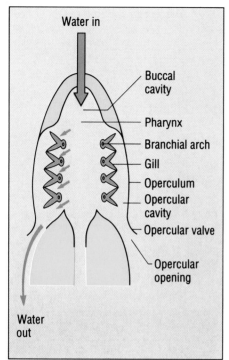

<figure>**Figure 15.10** Diagram of a horizontal section through the pharynx and gill region of a bony fish. The muscular operculum covers the entire gill region on either side of the body. The way water flows through the system is shown on the left by the blue arrows.</figure>

encloses an **opercular cavity** into which the gills project (figure 15.10). Water is drawn into, and pumped out of, the pharynx by movements of the operculum (figure 15.11). The ventilation cycle maintains a continuous stream of water over the gills at all times and this ensures their efficiency.

In figure 15.12 two adjacent gills are shown in detail. The gills are constructed in such a way that a large surface area of highly vascularised epithelium is exposed to the water as it flows through. Each gill is composed of two piles of leaf-like **lamellae** which project from a solid base strengthened by a bony **branchial arch**. On the upper and lower surfaces of the lamellae are numerous vertical **gill plates** which greatly increase the surface area of the gill.

The base of each gill contains an **afferent branchial artery** which brings deoxygenated blood to the gill from the ventral aorta beneath the floor of the pharynx. The base of the gill also contains an **efferent branchial artery** which carries oxygenated blood away from the gill to the dorsal aorta above the roof of the pharynx.

The afferent and efferent branchial arteries are interconnected within each lamella and its gill plates by an extensive system of capillaries. Gaseous exchange takes place as the blood flows through the capillaries in the plates. The barrier between the blood and the water consists of only two thin layers of epithelium with a total thickness of about 0.5μm, so diffusion readily takes place across it.

The orientation of the gaseous-exchange surfaces means that as water passes from the pharynx into the opercular chamber, it inevitably flows between the gill plates in a direction opposite to the blood flow. Moreover, the free ends of adjacent gills touch each other, and this means that no water can avoid passing between the lamellae as it flows from the pharynx to the opercular chamber. This system is certainly efficient, about 80 per cent of the oxygen being extracted from the water as it flows over the gills compared with 50 per cent in the dogfish (see box opposite).

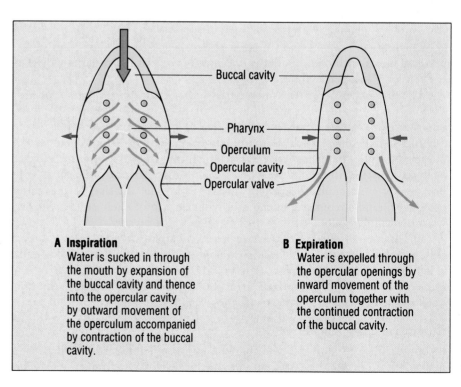

A Inspiration
Water is sucked in through the mouth by expansion of the buccal cavity and thence into the opercular cavity by outward movement of the operculum accompanied by contraction of the buccal cavity.

B Expiration
Water is expelled through the opercular openings by inward movement of the operculum together with the continued contraction of the buccal cavity.

<figure>**Figure 15.11** Diagrams summarising the ventilation of the gills of a bony fish. Direction of water flow shown by blue arrows, movements of the operculum by red arrows.</figure>

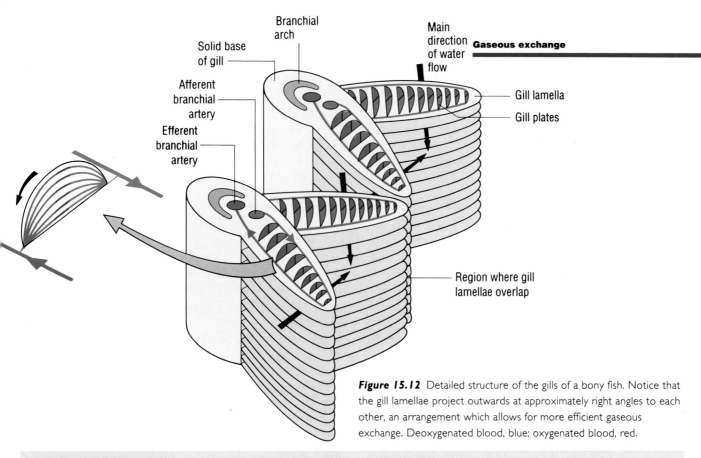

Figure 15.12 Detailed structure of the gills of a bony fish. Notice that the gill lamellae project outwards at approximately right angles to each other, an arrangement which allows for more efficient gaseous exchange. Deoxygenated blood, blue; oxygenated blood, red.

Parallel flow and counterflow

In gill systems water and blood flow close to each other and gaseous exchange takes place from one to the other. If the blood and water flow in the same direction at the same speed (**parallel flow**), the concentration difference in dissolved oxygen would be great at first, but would steadily decrease as the blood and water flowed together across the gaseous-exchange surface (illustration 1). On leaving the gaseous-exchange surface, the oxygen in the blood would be in equilibrium with the oxygen in the water at a point well below its maximum saturation with oxygen. Parallel flow is not therefore very efficient. It can, however, be improved if the flow of water is very rapid compared with that of the blood. This will ensure a higher saturation of the blood by the time it leaves the gaseous-exchange surface.

For *maximum* gaseous exchange to take place, it is best for the blood and water to flow in opposite directions

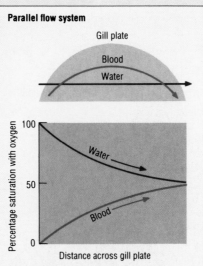

Illustration 1 Diagram illustrating parallel flow across the gills of a fish.

(**counterflow**). This ensures that as blood flows across the gaseous-exchange surface, it meets water which has had less and less oxygen extracted from it (illustration 2). By the time the blood is about to leave the gaseous-exchange surface it will have almost the same partial pressure of oxygen as the inhalent water. In other words the same steep

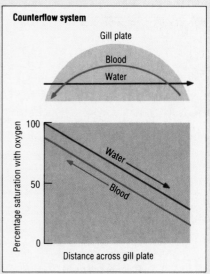

Illustration 2 Diagram illustrating counterflow across the gills of a fish. In both diagrams it is assumed that the blood and water move at the same speed and have equal oxygen capacities.

diffusion gradient is maintained throughout the gaseous-exchange surface.

In bony fishes the structural arrangement of the gills is such as to make the counterflow system more certain.

Gaseous exchange in mammals

The medium for gaseous exchange in mammals is air. Most mammals are terrestrial and need to conserve water. They are endothermic and usually active, so their demand for oxygen is high.

The mammalian lung is a remarkably efficient structure which fulfils the function of gaseous exchange with minimum water loss and heat energy transfer. To illustrate this let us look at the human system.

The human gaseous exchange system

The human lungs and associated structures are shown in figure 15.13. The **lungs** are situated in the **thorax**, the walls of which are formed by the **ribs** and **intercostal muscles**, and the floor by the **diaphragm**. The lungs are surrounded by a very narrow **pleural cavity** lined by **pleural membranes**. The pleural cavity contains a thin layer of lubricating fluid which allows the pleural membranes to slide easily over each other as the thorax expands and contracts during breathing.

Air is drawn into the lungs via the **trachea** and **bronchi**. The expansion of the thoracic cavity is brought about by the upward and outward movement of the ribs and forward movement of the sternum, accompanied by flattening of the diaphragm. The rib movements are achieved by the contraction of the external intercostal muscles, and the flattening of the diaphragm by contraction of its muscles which are arranged mainly in a radial direction. All this constitutes **inspiration** (figure 15.14A).

Figure 15.13 The human gaseous exchange and ventilation system. Expansion of the thorax draws air down the trachea and bronchi into the lungs. Incomplete rings of cartilage keep the trachea and bronchi permanently open. The right hand side of the diagram shows the ribs and intercostal muscles in position. On the left hand side the ribs and intercostal muscles have been removed and the lungs opened up to show the bronchial tubes.

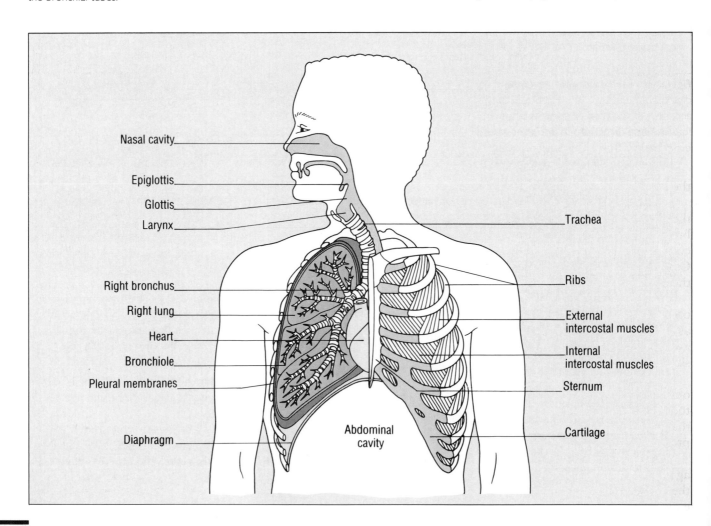

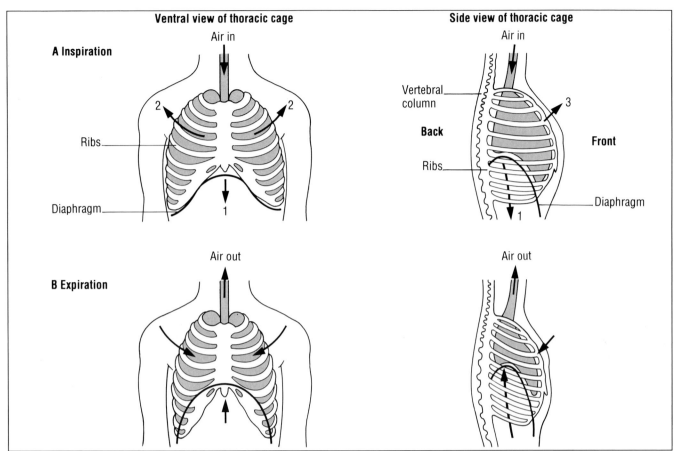

Ventral view of thoracic cage   Side view of thoracic cage

Figure 15.14 A Diagrams showing how the thorax expands. Expansion in the downwards
direction takes place by descent of the diaphragm (arrow 1), in a sideways direction by upward
and outward movement of the ribs (arrow 2), and in a back-to-front direction by upward and
forward movement of the sternum (arrow 3). **B** The reverse movements occur during
expiration.

The process then goes into reverse, air being expelled from the lungs in
the act of **expiration** (figure 15.14B).

Expiration is a mainly passive process resulting from elastic recoil of
the tissues that have been stretched during inspiration. However, in forced
breathing or when the breathing tubes are blocked, expiration is aided by
contraction of the internal intercostal muscles and **abdominal muscles**.
Contraction of the latter raises the pressure in the abdominal cavity, forcing
the diaphragm upwards.

The pressure and volume changes that occur during the ventilation
cycle are shown in figure 15.15. At rest the pressure in the lungs is the same
as atmospheric pressure, but because the lungs are elastic and tend to pull
away from the walls of the thorax, the pressure in the pleural cavity is
slightly less than atmospheric.

During inspiration, when the walls and floor of the thorax are moving
outwards and downwards respectively, the pleural pressure falls. This has
the immediate effect of lowering the lung pressure to below atmospheric, so
that air enters the lungs. This increases their volume and returns the lung
pressure to atmospheric.

On expiration the pressure of the thoracic wall and the diaphragm
against the pleural cavity raises the pleural pressure. This is transmitted to
the lungs where the pressure increases and volume decreases as air is
expelled.

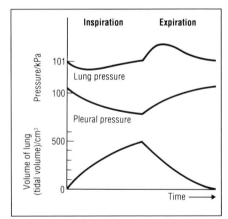

Figure 15.15 Pressure and volume changes
during the ventilation cycle of a human.
Volume changes are measured by means of a
spirometer (see box on page 260); pressures
are measured by running a fine tube from the
appropriate cavity to a suitable manometer.
For practical purposes the pleural pressure
can be estimated by measuring the pressure in
the oesophagus.

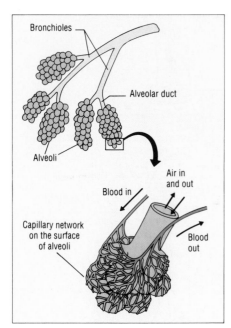

Figure 15.16 The bronchioles in the mammalian lung terminate as numerous alveoli across whose much folded and highly vascular walls gaseous exchange takes place.

Figure 15.17 The relationship between the alveoli and capillaries in a mammalian lung. **A** Photomicrograph of a section through several alveoli and capillaries, magnified × 200. The alveoli are separated from the bloodstream by a very thin alveolar barrier consisting of only two layers of pavement epithelial cells, as shown in **B**. The phagocytes are important in defence against disease.

Structure of the lungs

The lungs are spongy in texture, and consist of a tree-like system of tubes which ramify from the two **bronchi**. Each tube eventually becomes a very narrow **bronchiole** which terminates as a bunch of tiny sac-like **alveoli** (figure 15.16).

Although a certain amount of gaseous exchange can take place across the walls of the smaller bronchioles, it is the alveoli which play the leading role in this respect. The efficiency of the mammalian lung as a gaseous-exchange surface depends on the fact that a vast number of alveoli come into very close association with an extensive capillary system.

The alveolar epithelium is covered internally with a thin layer of fluid in which the oxygen dissolves before it diffuses into the cells. If this fluid had a normal surface tension it would pull the alveolar walls inwards making it difficult to expand the lungs and possibly causing the alveoli to collapse. However, the fluid contains a 'surfactant', a detergent-like lipoprotein which reduces the surface tension and prevents this happening.

In humans the two lungs contain approximately 700 million alveoli, giving a total surface area of over 70 m², if the lungs were opened out into a continuous sheet they would just about cover the surface of a tennis court! The capillary network in the lungs has a total area of about 40 m². In the lungs, therefore, an enormous surface area for gaseous exchange is packed into a comparatively small space. This general principle also applies to other terrestrial vertebrates such as amphibians and reptiles. However, in these animals the total surface area of the lungs relative to their size is nothing like so great.

The relationship between the alveoli and the capillaries is an extremely intimate one. The walls of the capillaries and alveoli both consist of a single layer of flattened epithelial cells which are extremely close to each other (figure 15.17). The resulting barrier between the alveolar cavity and the blood is a mere 0.3 μm thick in its thinnest part. As such it offers minimum resistance to the diffusion of gases from one side to the other.

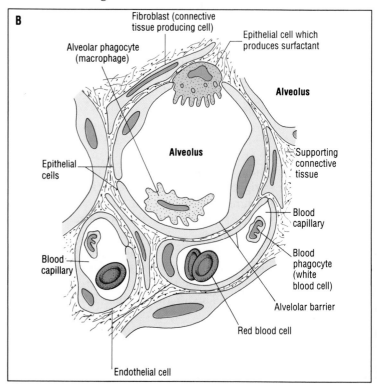

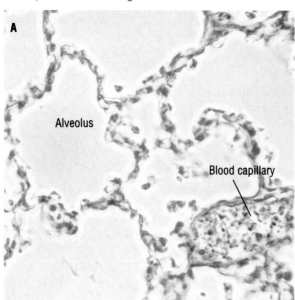

The ventilation cycle

A person breathing normally at rest takes in, and expels, approximately half a litre of air during each ventilation cycle. This is known as the **tidal volume**, and it can be recorded and measured by means of a spirometer (see box on page 260).

The rate at which a person breathes is expressed as the **ventilation rate**. This is usually expressed as the volume of air breathed per minute. Thus:

ventilation rate = tidal volume × number of breaths per minute

The ventilation rate changes according to the circumstances: in muscular exercise, for example, both the frequency and depth of breathing increase, resulting in a higher ventilation rate. We shall return to this later. The important point is that the lungs have a much greater potential volume than is ever realised in resting conditions, and this permits the ventilation rate to adapt to changing needs.

If you take a deep breath, you can take into your lungs about three litres of air over and above the tidal volume. This is called the **inspiratory reserve volume**, and is brought into use when required. If at the end of a normal expiration you expel as much air as you possibly can, the extra air expired is about one litre, and is called the **expiratory reserve volume**.

The total volume of air that can be expired after a maximum inspiration (i.e. the tidal volume plus inspiratory and expiratory reserve volumes) is known as the **vital capacity**. The vital capacity of an average person lies between 4 and 5 litres but in a fit athlete it may exceed 6 litres. Even after maximum expiration, about 1.5 litres of air remain in the lungs. This is known as the **residual volume**. The various lung volumes just described are shown in figure 15.18.

How much of the air taken in is actually used in gaseous exchange? Of the half litre or so inspired in quiet breathing, only about 350 cm^3 gets into the parts of the lung where gaseous exchange is possible. The rest remains in the trachea and bronchial tubes, collectively known as the **dead space**, where no gaseous exchange takes place. If the capacity of the lungs is about 6 litres, it is clear that in resting conditions only a small fraction of the total volume of air present in the lungs and associated tubes is actually used in gaseous exchange.

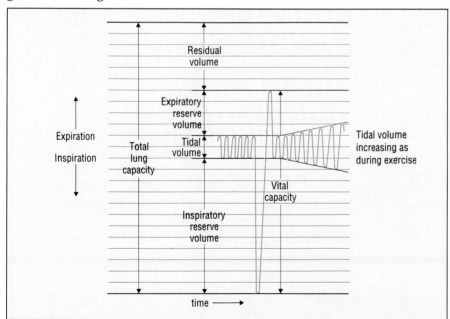

Figure 15.18 Diagram showing typical human lung volumes. The tracings are based on spirometer recordings obtained from a large number of individuals. The horizontal divisions correspond to 250 cm^3. There is considerable variation between different individuals in the tidal volumes and vital capacity. These tracings emphasise how little air is drawn into the lungs in resting conditions. The reserve volumes are brought into action only when necessary.

At each inspiration during normal quiet breathing, about 350 cm³ of inspired air mixes with some 2.5 litres of air already present in the alveoli. With so little new air mixing with so much air already present, it is probable that the composition of the air in the depth of the lungs remains relatively constant during resting conditions. Through this air, situated between the inspired air and the blood, gases diffuse to and from the alveolar surface.

Spirometry

In humans a special piece of equipment called a **spirometer** can be used to record and measure lung volumes and oxygen consumption (illustration 1).

Spirometers come in various shapes and forms but they all operate on the same principle. The person breathes in and out of an airtight chamber consisting of a light Perspex 'lid' floating in water. As the person inhales the lid goes down, and when the person exhales it goes up. These movements can be recorded by a pen writing on a revolving drum, by a chart recorder or by a computer acting via an interface device. In the one in the photograph a kymograph is being used.

To use the spirometer, the chamber is first filled with oxygen from a cylinder. The person is then connected to it by a mouthpiece at the end of a flexible tube. Between the tube and the oxygen chamber there is a canister containing a substance such as soda lime, which absorbs carbon dioxide. This ensures that all the carbon dioxide expired by the person is absorbed before the air is breathed in again. A nose clip must be worn so that the lungs, bronchi and trachea form a closed system with the spirometer.

The lung volumes and ventilation movements shown in figure 15.18 were measured with a spirometer. The apparatus can also be used to measure how much oxygen is used in a given time. As oxygen is used up, the spirometer 'lid' slowly sinks and the difference between the top and bottom of the trace represents the volume of oxygen used.

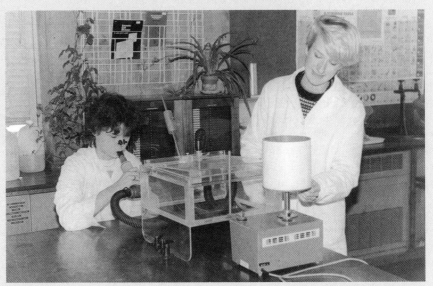

Illustration 1 A spirometer in use. The trace is being recorded on a kymograph.

In order to calculate volumes, the recording paper has to be calibrated for time and volume so that the depth and frequency of the person's inspirations and expirations can be measured. From these measurements the rate of oxygen consumption can be calculated. Illustration 2 shows a spirometer trace of human ventilation.

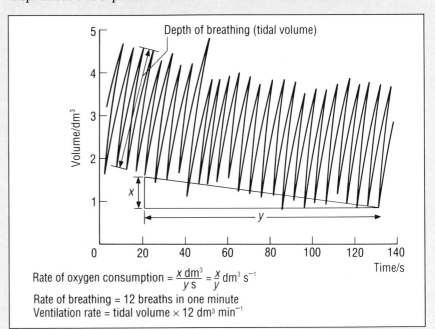

Rate of oxygen consumption = $\dfrac{x\,\text{dm}^3}{y\,\text{s}} = \dfrac{x}{y}\,\text{dm}^3\,\text{s}^{-1}$

Rate of breathing = 12 breaths in one minute
Ventilation rate = tidal volume × 12 dm³ min⁻¹

Illustration 2 A spirometer trace of human ventilation.

Exchanges across the alveolar surface

Table 15.3 compares the composition of inspired (i.e. atmospheric) and expired air. This indicates the exchanges that take place in the lungs: oxygen is taken up and carbon dioxide given out.

Analysis of the blood flowing to and from the alveoli gives us an insight into what happens at the gaseous-exchange surface itself (figure 15.19). Blood reaching the alveoli has a lower partial pressure of oxygen, and a higher partial pressure of carbon dioxide, than the alveolar air. There is thus a concentration gradient favouring the diffusion of these two gases in opposite directions.

As blood flows past an alveolus, oxygen diffuses into it and carbon dioxide out, so that by the time the blood leaves the alveolus, it has almost the same partial pressure of oxygen and carbon dioxide as the alveolar air. During this equalisation of partial pressures, the percentage saturation of the blood rises from about 70 per cent to over 90 per cent. The composition of alveolar air, however, remains relatively unchanged because of exchanges between it and the inspired air.

In fact the process is not quite as efficient as it may seem because some alveoli are inevitably under-ventilated. Moreover, a proportion of the blood which goes to the lungs does not go through any alveolar capillaries and therefore never gets oxygenated. The result is that the blood leaving the lungs is not as fully oxygenated as it might be.

	Atmospheric air (%)	Expired air (%)
Oxygen	20.95	16.4
Nitrogen	79.01	79.5
Carbon dioxide	0.04	4.1

Table 15.3 A comparison of the oxygen, carbon dioxide and nitrogen in atmospheric and inspired air in a resting human at sea level.

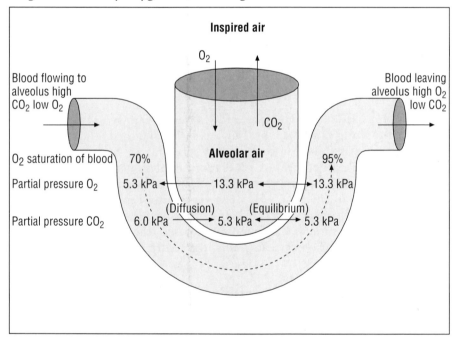

Figure 15.19 Diagram summarising the exchange of oxygen and carbon dioxide that takes place as blood flows past an alveolus in the mammalian lung. By the time the blood leaves the alveolus it has the same partial pressure of oxygen and carbon dioxide as the alveolar air, and it is almost fully saturated with oxygen.

The effects of fluctuations in oxygen and carbon dioxide

It is important to realise that conditions in the human body change all the time and yet it still manages to function adequately. This is particularly so in an active person. At the moment you are probably sitting in a chair reading this book; if you walk across the room, changes immediately occur in your body to which adjustments must be made. The changes will be even greater if you exert yourself. But even with very slight exertion, there is bound to be a momentary increase in the metabolic rate. This will result in an increase in the amount of oxygen used and carbon dioxide produced. The oxygen content of the blood will therefore fall and carbon dioxide will rise.

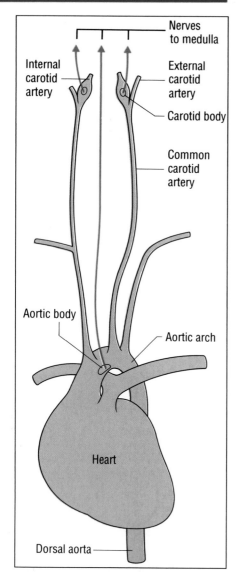

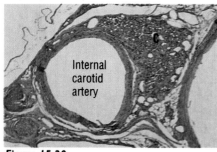

Figure 15.20

Top Diagram showing the positions of the aortic and carotid bodies, ventral view.

Bottom Photomicrograph of a section of the carotid body (**C**). The carotid body consists of a mass of epithelial-type cells and nerve fibres which are sensitive to excess carbon dioxide or insufficient oxygen in the blood. The clear areas in the carotid body are blood spaces. The nerve fibres are stimulated as the blood flows through these spaces. Magnification × 25.

The significance of these changes can best be appreciated by considering the effects that follow if these respiratory gases fluctuate badly. To take oxygen first, a deficiency of oxygen (hypoxia) deprives the tissues of a vital requirement for metabolism. The consequence is that the senses, particularly vision, are impaired, as is the brain. This results in the adoption of a slap-happy state of mind. This can happen to aircraft pilots, for example, if their oxygen apparatus breaks down, and can result in gross misjudgements of situations – something which fortunately happens more often in films than in real life! The trouble is that the person may be quite unaware that anything is wrong, and so does nothing about it. Unconsciousness occurs suddenly, followed by paralysis (caused by irreparable damage to nerve cells) and death.

What about excess oxygen? Breathing pure oxygen at atmospheric pressure presents no problems. The saturation of our arterial blood with oxygen is about 96 per cent under normal circumstances, and breathing pure oxygen will not appreciably increase the amount of oxygen delivered to our tissues. However, if breathed at pressures greater than atmospheric, as in diving, excess oxygen can be very dangerous. At first, the tissues metabolise very rapidly, to keep pace with the oxygen supply. As the oxygen builds up, however, it inhibits certain enzymes involved in the Krebs cycle, thus interfering with cell respiration.

Cells are even more susceptible to changes in the level of carbon dioxide. An accumulation of this gas increases the acidity of the blood and tissue fluids, inhibits enzymes and stops essential metabolic processes. This is why breathing air rich in carbon dioxide is so dangerous. Rebreathing one's own expired air can be fatal very quickly.

The control of breathing

As long ago as 1905, J.S. Haldane and J. Priestley showed that in humans the ventilation rate can be doubled by increasing the carbon dioxide in the air from its usual 0.04 per cent to 3.0 per cent. In humans and other mammals the overall control of ventilation involves groups of nerve cells comprising a **ventilation centre** in the posterior part of the brain called the **medulla oblongata** (see page 452). The ventilation centre responds to the level of carbon dioxide, and to a lesser extent oxygen, in the bloodstream. If the partial pressure of carbon dioxide rises, the centre responds by increasing the ventilation rate. If it falls, the centre responds by decreasing the ventilation rate.

The chemical control of breathing

We now know that a change in the level of carbon dioxide in the blood is the effective stimulus initiating a change in ventilation rate. A small change in the amount of carbon dioxide is more effective than even a large change in the amount of oxygen. For this reason, the partial pressure of oxygen in the blood may vary considerably, but the partial pressure of carbon dioxide only shows very small deviations.

How is the ventilation centre informed of the level of carbon dioxide in the blood? In the walls of certain arteries there are receptor cells which are sensitive to chemical changes in the blood flowing past them. They function as **chemoreceptors**, detecting changes in pH and the partial pressure of carbon dioxide. They are found between the internal and external carotid arteries on each side of the neck, where they form the **carotid bodies**, and in the wall of the aorta close to the heart where they form the **aortic body** (figure 15.20).

If the partial pressure of carbon dioxide rises, the chemoreceptors are stimulated and impulses are sent to the ventilation centre in the brain increasing its activity. In addition there are chemoreceptors in the brain near the ventilation centre itself. They too detect changes in the pH and partial pressure of carbon dioxide – indeed this is probably the main pathway by which the ventilation centre is stimulated.

These chemoreceptors are situated in two ideal locations. Those near the ventilation centre in the brain monitor the cerebrospinal fluid so that instant responses can be given. Those in the carotid arteries and the aorta monitor the blood flowing to the head and to all organs of the body except the lungs.

The role of the brain

It is in the ventilation centre that overall control of breathing is brought about. The ventilation centre receives impulses from three sources:

- **Stretch receptors** in the smooth muscle within the walls of the bronchial tubes.
- **Chemoreceptors** in the carotid artery and aorta.
- The higher centres in the forebrain (**cerebral cortex**) which control voluntary changes in breathing.

These three sources of nerve impulses are shown in figure 15.21. Let us look at each in turn.

Impulses from stretch receptors

Sensory branches of the vagus nerve carry impulses from the stretch receptors in the wall of the bronchial tubes to the ventilation centre. If impulses are recorded from the vagus nerve with an oscilloscope, it can be shown that as the lungs inflate, the frequency of impulses increases. The job of these stretch receptors is to signal to the ventilation centre the degree of expansion of the lungs. As inspiration proceeds the impulses eventually reach such a frequency that they *inhibit* inspiration, thereby initiating expiration which is largely a passive process.

Cessation of inspiration is therefore caused by expansion of the lungs themselves. However if the vagus nerves are cut, rhythmical breathing will still continue, though deeper and slower than before. It is therefore evident that the ventilation centre possesses an **intrinsic rhythmicity** which can bring about regular breathing. Impulses reaching the ventilation centre from the stretch receptors in the lungs keep this intrinsic mechanism under control and prevent the lungs being over-expanded.

Impulses from chemoreceptors

If the partial pressure of carbon dioxide in the blood rises, the chemoreceptors in the carotid and aortic bodies are stimulated and impulses are conveyed via sensory nerves to the ventilation centre in the brain. The latter responds by sending impulses to the external˙ intercostal muscles and diaphragm muscle, thereby bringing about an increase in the ventilation rate.

This has been confirmed by experiments. In one experiment the carotid body was perfused with blood containing different levels of carbon dioxide. It was found that increasing the carbon dioxide content of the blood had the effect of speeding up the rate of breathing. Cutting the carotid nerves abolished this response.

A further experiment was carried out but in this case the action potentials were recorded from the carotid nerves. Increasing the carbon dioxide in

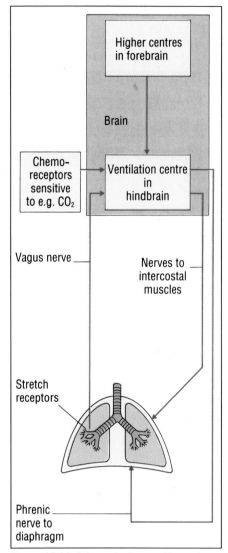

Figure 15.21 Schematic diagram illustrating the nervous control of ventilation in the mammal. The ventilation centre receives nervous impulses from various sources, while it sends out impulses to the inspiratory muscles in a rhythmical manner.

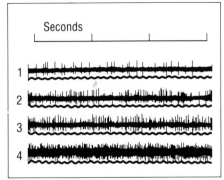

Figure 15.22 Impulses recorded from the carotid nerve in response to perfusion of the carotid body with fluid containing different concentrations of carbon dioxide and oxygen. The impulses were recorded with an oscilloscope (see page 441).

1 Low CO_2, high O_2
2 High CO_2, high O_2
3 Low CO_2, low O_2
4 High CO_2, low O_2

Notice that the highest frequency of impulses is given by a high concentration of carbon dioxide accompanied by a low concentration of oxygen.

the blood raised the frequency of impulses in these nerves. Similar responses were produced by lowering the partial pressure of oxygen. The highest frequency of impulses was obtained when an increase in carbon dioxide concentration was accompanied by a decrease in oxygen (figure 15.22).

The ventilation centre, then, is influenced by impulses from various receptors which can alter the normal pattern of breathing. In addition it is itself sensitive to carbon dioxide in the blood.

Impulses from the cerebral cortex

The ventilation centre is also under the influence of higher centres in the brain, that is, the cerebral cortex: if this were not so, voluntary changes in breathing would not be possible and the American, Robert Foster, would not have been able to hold his breath for 13.72 minutes submerged in a swimming pool!

The control of ventilation is an example of homeostasis in which a system acts to maintain a steady state (see Chapter 21). In responding to changes in the partial pressure of carbon dioxide in the blood, the body not only prevents an accumulation of this poisonous gas but also ensures that sufficient oxygen is delivered to the tissues at all times. The efficiency of this process can be tested by subjecting a person to an atmosphere containing an abnormally low partial pressure of oxygen. This is precisely what happens at high altitudes where the atmospheric pressure, and hence the partial pressure of oxygen, is considerably lower than at sea level. How does a person adjust to such conditions?

Adjustment to high altitudes

The answer depends on how high the altitude is and how quickly the person gets there. High is taken to mean above 3000 m. An aircraft pilot flying straight up to a great height without oxygen apparatus develops symptoms of **hypoxia** at about 4000 m, and becomes unconscious at about 8000 m. On the other hand a mountaineer who ascends slowly over a period of days or weeks has time to get used to the progressively rarefied atmosphere. At about 4000 m he or she begins to develop signs of oxygen lack – breathlessness, headache, nausea and fatigue (**mountain sickness**). But these unpleasant symptoms wear off as one becomes **acclimatised**.

Adjustments to high altitude occur in both the ventilation and circulatory systems as the homeostatic responses to oxygen lack get pushed to their limit. The ventilation rate increases temporarily and this, together with parallel adjustments in the circulatory system, causes the rate of oxygen delivery to the tissues to go up. The circulatory aspects of this are dealt with in Chapter 19.

In the Himalayan expedition of 1953, Edmund Hillary and Sherpa Tenzing spent three hours at a height of over 8000 metres without oxygen apparatus, levelling snow and pitching a tent (figure 15.23). It was not easy but the fact that they managed to do it at all indicates the importance of acclimatisation as a physiological process. An unacclimatised person at such a height would be unconscious within five minutes. Since then several other mountaineers have climbed Everest without the use of oxygen apparatus.

People living permanently at high altitudes have larger tidal volumes at each breath rather than an increased ventilation rate – in other words they breathe more deeply rather than faster. They also tend to be 'barrel-chested' and this may be because they have an increased lung surface area. They certainly have a larger vital capacity and residual volume than people living nearer to sea level.

Figure 15.23 Edmund Hillary and Sherpa Tenzing on the slopes of Everest, 1953. Notice that they are not using oxygen apparatus. Hillary and Tenzing were the first climbers ever to reach the summit of Everest, 8848 m above sea level.

Gaseous exchange in insects

In insects the cuticle on either side of the thorax and abdomen is perforated by a series of segmentally arranged pores or **spiracles** which open into a system of **tracheal tubes** or **tracheae** (singular trachea) (figure 15.24). The spiracles are guarded by valves or hairs to prevent excessive evaporation through them. The tracheae are arranged in a regular pattern, some of them running longitudinally, some transversely. The larger tracheae are about a millimetre in diameter, and are kept permanently open by spiral or annular thickenings of hardened chitin, the same material that makes up the cuticle.

The function of the spiracles and tracheae is to permit the passage of air to a further system of tubes, the **tracheoles**. These are very fine intracellular tubes, a mere 1 μm in diameter. They are extremely numerous and penetrate deep into all the tissues, particularly the muscles. Unlike the tracheae, they are not lined with a cuticle, gaseous exchange occurring freely across their walls.

The mechanism of gaseous exchange in insects is in marked contrast to most other animals. Instead of being picked up by blood at the gaseous-exchange surface and then conveyed to the tissues, oxygen is conveyed directly to the tissues via this system of ramifying air tubes.

How does oxygen get to the tissues along these tubes? In most insects diffusion is the answer, which may be one reason why insects are generally rather small in size. However, in some species diffusion is aided by rhythmical movements of the thorax or abdomen. Such ventilation is seen, for example, in the locust where it has been demonstrated that, by the differential opening and closing of the spiracles, air is drawn into the body through the thoracic spiracles and leaves via the abdominal spiracles. In all flying species ventilation is aided by muscular movements during flight.

Insects can control the rate at which oxygen is delivered to the tissues. The mechanism depends on the fact that the tracheoles contain varying amounts of watery fluid. In severe muscular activity (flight, for example), lactic acid accumulates in the tissues. This raises the solute concentration of the tissue fluids, with the result that water is drawn out of the tracheoles into the tissues by osmosis. This has the effect of opening up the air passages, facilitating the diffusion of oxygen to the tissues (figure 15.25).

The tracheoles are extraordinary structures whose pattern of growth can be modified according to the needs of the tissues. If a body segment is deprived of oxygen because its main trachea is damaged, the tracheoles of neighbouring segments respond by growing towards the deprived segment. In this way uniform distribution of oxygen to the tissues is ensured.

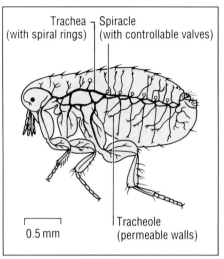

Figure 15.24 The tracheal system of a flea. The tracheal tubes convey oxygen to all tissues of the body, and carbon dioxide from the tissues to the exterior. Only the left half of the system is shown.

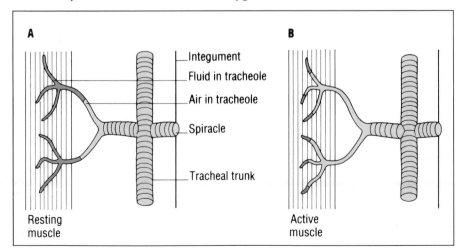

Figure 15.25

A A small part of the tracheal system of an insect. The spiracles open into a main longitudinal tracheal trunk on each side of the body. Branches of the tracheal trunks break up into numerous tracheoles which penetrate into the tissues.

B Shows withdrawal of the fluid from the tracheoles during muscular exercise. This facilitates diffusion of oxygen to the muscle tissue.

Smoking and health

Research on smoking and its link with disease is a classic example of how biology impinges on society. Guest author Ann McNeill looks at some of the issues.

There are over 4000 chemicals in cigarette smoke, including 40 known carcinogens. Smoking is the largest single preventable cause of death in Britain, killing more people than all other avoidable dangers added together including fires, drugs, alcohol and road accidents.

If cigarettes were introduced today, there is little doubt that they would be banned outright. However, back in the early sixteenth century when tobacco was first discovered by Spanish explorers in America and then brought back to Europe, the dangers were unknown. Since then, people have sniffed, chewed or smoked tobacco. At first it was smoked in pipes, and it was not until the mid-nineteenth century, when cigarettes were invented as a convenient way to smoke tobacco, that the habit really increased in popularity.

In 1936 an American doctor, Alton Ochsner, was intrigued by an outbreak of lung cancer cases, a condition so rare in those days that he had only encountered it once before – in 1919. He investigated the patients and found that all of them were cigarette smokers. This led to epidemiological studies being carried out in the UK and the USA. These studies concluded independently that smoking was correlated with lung cancer. Committees on smoking and health were set up in both countries, leading eventually to the first reports of the Royal College of Physicians in 1962 and the United States Surgeon General in 1964. These reports detailed the risks of smoking, and in the UK there was an immediate five per cent drop in cigarette sales. However, to the surprise and disappointment of the medical profession, the reports did not lead to political action to stem the epidemic.

Since then, further reports have been produced by the UK, the USA, the World Health Organisation and other international bodies. World conferences on the subject take place every two years. The medical evidence, based as it is on an unprecedented body of statistical data, is very clear: smoking kills. In addition to lung cancer, smoking causes heart disease, emphysema, gangrene (leading to amputation), reduced fertility in men and women, and a host of other diseases. Indeed, new diseases caused by smoking are still being discovered today. An example of a well established smoking-related condition, chronic lung disease, is illustrated below.

Why do people still smoke?

In 1991 approximately one in three adults were smokers. Smokers do not appear to have accepted the simple statistic that their cigarettes have a one in four chance of killing them. Why do people ignore the evidence about smoking?

One reason centres on nicotine which is contained in tobacco smoke. Nicotine is a very powerful drug which affects nearly every organ in the body. It does not itself cause lung cancer – the aromatic compounds collectively called 'tar' cause cancer. However, it is poisonous. If the nicotine contents of a single cigarette were injected into a person intravenously, it would be fatal. Obtained through smoking, it can cause heart disease as explained in illustration 2. Nicotine is addictive, but not so much so that it is impossible to give up smoking.

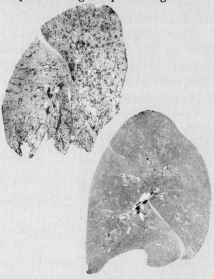

The photographs compare the appearance of the lungs of a smoker (*left*) and a non-smoker (*right*). The smoker's lung is blackened with the tar from cigarettes.

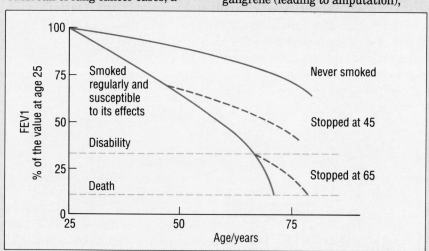

Illustration 1 In chronic lung disease, lung function declines with age as shown by this graph. Lung function is measured as the forced expiratory volume in one second (FEV1). Notice that lung function declines more rapidly in smokers than in non-smokers, but that the decline can be slowed by stopping smoking.

The second reason is that, the tobacco industry, which consists of powerful multinational companies makes money out of cigarettes. It is in their commercial interests to keep people smoking. In the United Kingdom alone the tobacco industry needs to recruit 300 new smokers every day just to replace those who die of smoking-related diseases. Those involved in promoting cigarettes know that newcomers to the habit (mainly teenagers) only need to smoke three or four cigarettes before smoking becomes a part of their image and lives.

My research has shown that young people who smoke regularly inhale as much smoke per cigarette as adults. Nicotine can therefore start to play its role from an early age. The tobacco industry largely ignores the dangers of the habit and promotes smoking as glamorous, sophisticated and healthy, associating it with positive images such as slimness, beauty, 'macho' and fitness. This is done by (for example) the simple expedient of sponsoring sporting events. In England alone, the tobacco industry spends over £100 million every year promoting its products this way. In contrast, a mere £3.5 million was spent on anti-smoking campaigns in England in 1991.

Young people have a right to grow up in a society that is free from pressures to smoke, and smokers have the right to make *informed* choices about whether or not to smoke. In fact, the majority of smokers want to stop. True, some say that they 'enjoy' smoking or that they 'need' to smoke because it helps to calm their nerves. Yet often these feelings are simply a relief from the withdrawal effects which a smoker experiences when deprived of a cigarette: anxiety, irritability and the craving for a cigarette are classic drug withdrawal symptoms. The cigarette – or rather the inhalation of nicotine – relieves these symptoms, thus appearing to have a positive effect.

Young people are often reluctant to associate the act of smoking with disease because the symptoms take years to appear. Smoking has therefore been likened to slow-motion suicide. The damage builds up slowly, almost imperceptibly, and often the warning signs are ignored. For example, the early morning cough and shortness of breath are readily written off as minor inconveniences. Death, when it comes, can be slow, drawn-out and painful. Anyone who has watched a person die of lung cancer will testify to this.

Smoking and society

Everyone should have the right to breathe smoke-free air. We now know that passive smoking, i.e. breathing other people's smoke, causes lung cancer and other respiratory diseases. It may also cause heart disease and chronic middle-ear disease, amongst other conditions. The risk of contracting lung cancer from passive smoking is some 50 to 100 times greater than the risk of getting it from exposure to asbestos. The smoke issuing from the lit end of a cigarette can contain greater amounts of the substances mentioned earlier than smoke which has been inhaled, because it has not gone through a filter.

Many people feel that the tobacco industry should be denied the right to promote their products as anything other than what they are – deadly. For example, it should not be permitted to describe as 'mild' a carcinogenic product which kills when used in the way that it is intended to be used.

The UK government requires the health warning 'smoking kills' to be displayed on every packet of cigarettes. Originally such health warnings were the result of a voluntary agreement between the government and tobacco industry, but in 1990 legislation was passed making them mandatory. Although this is a step in the right direction, much more needs to be done before the epidemic is eradicated. In international conferences on smoking we have therefore moved on from discussing the results of medical research, which are now so well established, to focusing on what steps should be taken to help smokers give up the habit and prevent young people from taking it up.

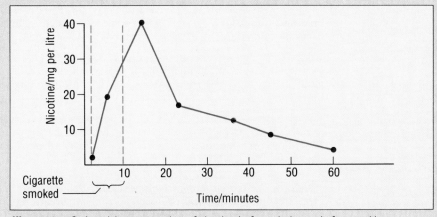

Illustration 2 Arterial concentration of nicotine before, during and after smoking a cigarette. The effects of nicotine on the body are varied and complex but it increases the heart rate, raises the blood pressure and promotes blood-clotting. Over the years these effects can combine to cause heart disease. Carbon monoxide in cigarette smoke is also a major contributor to heart disease.

Summary

1 All living organisms exchange gases with the environment. The two main gases exchanged are **oxygen** and **carbon dioxide** which participate in aerobic respiration and photosynthesis.

2 In plants carbon dioxide is taken up through **stomata** which are located on the surfaces of **leaves** and **stems**.

3 The **guard cells** bordering the stomata are controlled by an osmotic mechanism, dependent on the active transport of potassium ions, which ensures that stomata are generally open during the day and closed at night.

4 The degree of openness or closure of the stomata can be estimated by means of a **porometer** which measures resistance to air flow of a leaf.

5 In small or flattened animals the **surface–volume ratio** is large enough for gaseous exchange to take place by diffusion across the body surface. Larger animals, with a smaller surface–volume ratio, possess special **gaseous-exchange surfaces**.

6 In fishes water is pumped over much folded and vascularised **gills** which present a large surface area to the water.

7 For gaseous exchange in aquatic animals a **counterflow system** is more efficient than **parallel flow**. The gills of bony fishes achieve a counterflow.

8 In humans air is drawn by expansion of the thorax into the **lungs** where gaseous exchange occurs by diffusion across a very extensive and highly vascularised **alveolar surface**.

9 Lung volumes and oxygen consumption can be measured by means of a **spirometer**.

10 In mammals and other vertebrates rhythmical breathing movements are coordinated by the **ventilation centre** in the medulla oblongata of the brain.

11 The ventilation centre is informed of the concentration of carbon dioxide, and to a lesser extent oxygen, by **chemoreceptors** in the **aortic** and **carotid bodies**. The ventilation centre is also stimulated directly.

12 Experiments suggest that carbon dioxide is the most important stimulus initiating changes in the ventilation rate.

13 An alteration in the concentration of oxygen and carbon dioxide in the blood results in an appropriate change in the ventilation rate.

14 The effects of a slowly diminishing oxygen supply, such as occurs when ascending a mountain, are offset by **acclimatisation**, a series of responses to the low partial pressure of oxygen.

15 In insects gaseous exchange occurs in the **tracheal system**. Air reaches the tissues by diffusion, aided in some species by rhythmical movements of the thorax and abdomen.

Review questions

1 What are the main requirements for efficient gaseous exchange to take place?

2 How is a typical leaf adapted for gaseous exchange?

3 List the internal and external factors which control gaseous exchange in plants?

4 Suggest a possible reason why stomatal guard cells contain chloroplasts whereas other epidermal cells of a plant lack them.

5 Review the types of systems used for gaseous exchange in aquatic and terrestrial animals.

6 Explain how the counterflow mechanism works in the gill of a bony fish.

7 What is meant by the term *ventilation rate* and what may cause it to change in a terrestrial animal?

8 Trace the structures through which a molecule of oxygen has to pass in its journey from just outside your nose to one of your red blood cells.

9 How is the ventilation rate controlled in humans?

10 How do humans adjust to being at a high altitude?

Further reading

Knut Schmidt-Nielsen's *Animal Physiology: Adaptation and Environment* (Cambridge University Press, 1979) is a readable and informative general physiology text which includes aspects of breathing in animals.

Jonathan Miller's stimulating book, *The Body in Question* (Jonathan Cape, 1978) includes a chapter which provides a general background to breathing with the emphasis on humans.

Rather more detail, particularly on the comparative aspects, is provided by P.T. Marshall and G.M. Hughes in *The Physiology of Mammals and Other Vertebrates* (Cambridge University Press, 1980).

Biology, Advanced Topics includes a detailed account of the alveolar barrier and the way rhythmical breathing is controlled in mammals. There is also a detailed account of the physiology of diving.

Heterotrophic nutrition

All living organisms need a source of energy. In Chapter 14 we saw that for most organisms this is provided by the oxidation of food (respiration). Food and oxygen are therefore essential requirements for living organisms. In this chapter we shall look at the food requirement.

Some organisms can manufacture their own food substances from simple inorganic raw materials. Most plants and some prokaryotes are able to do this. They are said to have **autotrophic nutrition** and are called **autotrophs**. Their nutrition is the subject of the next chapter. Animals, fungi, many prokaryotes and protoctists are unable to synthesise organic compounds to use as food. They have **heterotrophic nutrition** and are called **heterotrophs**.

Heterotrophic organisms have to acquire and take in all the organic substances they need in order to survive. The examples shown in figure 16.1 illustrate how varied heterotrophic organisms are. A heterotroph feeding on organic substances in solution (such as a parasite in the human gut) can simply absorb the substances across its integument. Most animals, however, have a means of obtaining food and taking it into a **gut (alimentary canal)**. This is called **ingestion**. All heterotrophs (except gut and blood parasites) have to convert solid food into soluble compounds capable of being **absorbed**. This is the process of **digestion**.

When the soluble products of digestion are absorbed they are distributed to various parts of the organism where they are either built up into complex materials (**assimilation**) or broken down for the release of energy (**respiration**).

Different ways of feeding

A convenient way of classifying heterotrophic organisms is in terms of the type of food they eat:

- **Herbivores** feed on plants.
- **Carnivores** feed on animals.
- **Omnivores** eat food of plant *and* animal origin.
- **Liquid feeders** consume a variety of animal and plant juices.
- **Microphagous** feeders which live on small particles suspended in water.

In each case the method of feeding can be related to the type of food.

CHAPTER 16

Figure 16.1 A variety of heterotrophic organisms. *Clockwise from top.*
A A bracket fungus growing on a tree trunk.
B A zebra grazing on grass.
C A human leech sucking blood from a person's arm.
D A fish caught in the tentacles of a sea anemone.
E A frog catching an insect.

Figure 16.2 The molar tooth of an elephant. Notice the ridges of enamel alternating with cement and dentine. As a tooth wears down it moves forward in the jaw and when none of it is left another grows forward to replace it. During its lifetime an African elephant may wear down as many as 24 molar teeth, each one of which is about the size of a housebrick, although only four are in use at any one time. An elephant has only a certain number of teeth and when all of them are worn out the animal will die of starvation.

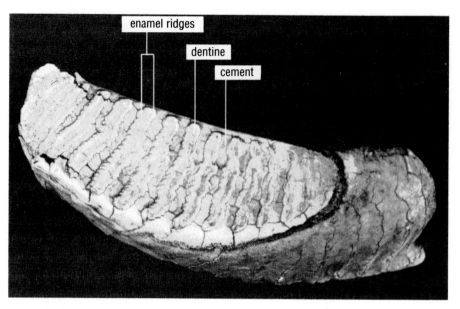

Figure 16.3 The skull of a sheep showing its long incisors for tearing grass and the gap (diastema) between the incisors and premolars.

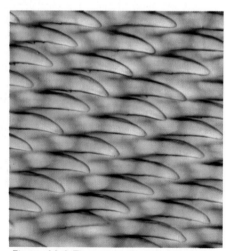

Figure 16.4 The radula of a slug. Numerous pointed teeth project forward from a sheet of tissue. Operated by muscles, the sheet moves backwards and forwards, over a hard cartilaginous pad, and is used for rasping and tearing plant food.

Herbivores

The problem facing all herbivores is that the concentration of nutrients in the food they eat is low and a large proportion of it is not digested. They therefore have to spend a great deal of time eating if their energy requirements are to be met. Cellulose in plant cell walls makes plant material tough and, as we shall see later, difficult to digest. Herbivores have to grind their food and the necessary apparatus for doing this is found mainly in three groups of animals: mammals, molluscs and insects.

Herbivorous mammals such as the horse or elephant use their **premolar** and/or **molar teeth** for grinding. These have a large surface area with ridges which are formed as the result of the uneven wear of the hard enamel and the softer dentine and cement (figure 16.2). The way in which the ridged premolars and molars in the upper and lower jaws grind against each other sharpens them. They also continue to grow throughout much of the animal's lifetime.

In addition to the ridged molars, herbivorous mammals have certain other adaptive features in their dentition. These include long **incisor teeth** for cutting or pulling grass and other such plants, and the absence of canine teeth leaving a gap called the **diastema** where food can be held (figure 16.3).

Herbivorous molluscs such as the snail possess a rasping organ, the **radula**. The radula is like a serrated conveyor belt, which, by rubbing backwards and forwards against the hardened roof of the mouth, can tear plant food (figure 16.4).

Herbivorous insects like the locust have a pair of mandibles with a jagged edge for cutting through leaves of grass and other plants (figure 16.5).

We shall consider how herbivores digest the cellulose in their plant food at the end of the chapter.

Carnivores

The problem here is not so much digesting the food as obtaining it. So we find that carnivores are adapted for catching prey. These adaptations take various forms: for example, high speed locomotion, sharp claws and dagger-like **canine** teeth in the great cats, **sucker-bearing tentacles** in octopuses and squids, and **tentacles armed with stinging cells** in sea anemones and jellyfishes.

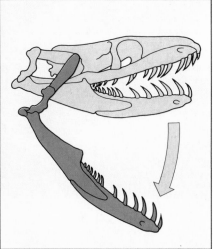

Figure 16.5 A locust eating a stalk of grass. The jaw-like mandibles are used for cutting and crushing plant food.

Figure 16.6 The skull of a python. The upper and lower jaws are loosely connected and the front bone of the lower jaw can be bent back. Both features allow the throat to be opened very wide. The position of the lower jaw after opening of the mouth is shown in red. The backwardly pointing teeth mean that prey is forced down the throat and cannot escape by slipping outwards.

Once captured, the prey is dealt with in one of three ways. It may be swallowed whole, chewed up and then swallowed, or digested externally outside the body and then ingested. Ingesting the food whole, without breaking it up first, is the method used by pythons and boa constrictors, and also by sharks, and sea anemones. The problem is that this puts a tremendous strain on the digestive system, which consequently takes a long time to break the food down into an absorbable state.

Pythons and boas can tackle animals as big as goats and antelopes. They seize the prey with their mouths, and coil themselves around it so that it cannot breathe. As a result it dies of suffocation. The snake then draws its victim into its gut using its backwardly pointing teeth and loosely connected jaw which becomes disarticulated (figure 16.6). The process of swallowing may take several hours, and the digestion of a complete antelope or goat can take weeks (figure 16.7).

The majority of carnivores chew their prey first. This is achieved by the **mouthparts** in carnivorous arthropods like crabs and crayfish. In the latter, the food, generally soft, is torn by the shredding action of manipulative structures called **maxillipeds**. Chewing is carried out by the **mandibles** (figure 16.8).

In mammals, the sharp **incisor teeth** are used for biting pieces of flesh and pulling it off the bone. In some mammals, the last pair of premolars in the upper jaw and the first pair of molars in the lower jaw are enlarged and

Figure 16.7 An anaconda having swallowed a spectacled caiman, a relative of the alligator. The bulge shows the position of the caiman inside the snake.

Figure 16.8 A crab holding its prey and using its mandibles for chewing.

271

Figure 16.9 A dog's skull showing the canine and carnassial teeth. On each side of each jaw there are three incisors, one canine and four premolars; there are two molars on each side of the upper jaw and three on each side of the lower jaw. The dental formula of a dog is therefore: i ⅔, c 1/1, pm 4/4, m ⅔.

have sharp ridges for shearing flesh. As any dog owner knows, these **carnassial teeth** are very effective at scraping flesh off bones (figure 16.9).

Animals that digest their food outside their bodies and then ingest it, do so in a variety of ways. Digestion is rarely completed outside the body, but it breaks the food up sufficiently for it to be drawn into the gut by suction or ciliary action. For example, blowflies, which feed on the carcasses of dead animals, pump saliva containing digestive enzymes onto the flesh and suck the fluid food into their stomachs (figure 16.10).

Insectivorous plants

Early reports that there were man-eating trees growing in remote parts of the world have gradually faded into legend, but there are over 400 known species of plants which can trap and digest small animals, particularly insects.

These insectivorous plants live in nitrogen-deficient soils. Only a few such plants – sundews, butterworts and bladderworts – are found in Britain and they are restricted to wet heath and moorland. Most species are tropical or sub-tropical, like the Venus fly-trap and the pitcher plants. All have green leaves and obtain their carbohydrate by photosynthesis; they obtain their nitrogen from the bodies of their victims. The insect is attracted by colour, scent or sugary bait, then trapped, killed and digested by a fluid containing **proteases** (protein-digesting enzymes). The resulting amino acids are absorbed into the plant.

The method of trapping the insect varies from one species to another: sticky leaves in butterwort, adhesive hairs in sundew and an elaborate underwater trap in bladderworts. The Venus fly-trap has infolding leaves with spikes along the free edges and a hinge-like midrib (see figure 16.13 on page 274). When an insect alights on a leaf, it stimulates certain hairs and the two halves of the leaf spring together, the spikes interlocking so that the unfortunate animal cannot escape. Pitcher plants have leaves which are modified to become flask-like containers containing digestive fluid. Insects are attracted to the lips of the pitcher by nectar secreted near the brim. In trying to reach the nectar the insect falls into the fluid where it dies and is digested.

Liquid feeders

Animals that feed on liquid food fall into two groups: **absorbers** and **suckers**. Absorbers include gut parasites such as tapeworms which live in the small intestine of mammals. They feed on the digested food of the host, absorbing it straight through the integument. They therefore need no gut or digestive enzymes of their own.

Many prokaryotes, protoctists and fungi feed on dead animals and plants. These **saprobionts** penetrate into the material, secreting a variety of enzymes, including proteases, which break down the solid components of the material into soluble products. The enzymes are secreted across the body surface and, as a result of their action, the saprobiont becomes surrounded by a solution from which it absorbs all the chemicals it requires across its surface.

Many saprobiontic micro-organisms can respire anaerobically, which enables them to penetrate deep into food material where little or no oxygen is available. The dissolving of solid organic matter by saprobiontic bacteria and fungi is the first step in the **decay** of dead bodies, as a result of which the elements present in the organic compounds are ultimately recycled.

Saprobionts are not the only organisms to digest their food outside their bodies. Many parasitic bacteria, fungi and protoctists which feed on the

Figure 16.10 A blowfly feeding on a slice of bread and honey. The expanded tip of the proboscis down which digestive enzymes flow is in contact with the food. After partial digestion outside the body, the semi-liquid food is sucked up into the stomach.

tissues of their hosts also do this. The potato blight fungus is an example (see page 77).

The sucking forms are mainly insects which feed on blood or plant juices. Their mouthparts consist of a sharp **proboscis** which can pierce the integument, and through which fluid is drawn by the sucking action of the pharynx. In the mosquito the proboscis consists of two tubes, a wide one for carrying food and a narrower one for carrying saliva, surrounded by a group of sharp **stylets** whose cutting action helps the proboscis to pierce the skin. Having gained entry, saliva flows down the salivary tube into the blood which is then sucked up the food tube into the pharynx. The saliva contains an enzyme which prevents the blood from clotting and keeps it in a fluid state.

Piercing and sucking mouthparts are also found in insects such as aphids which feed on plant juices. In contrast, butterflies have a long flexible proboscis ideally suited for probing into flowers. These three mouthparts are shown in action in figure 16.11.

Microphagous feeders

Microphagous feeders are always aquatic and feed on tiny particles suspended in water. Since their food is already 'broken up', the physical part of digestion is a relatively simple matter. The problem facing a microphagous feeder is collecting, sorting and concentrating the particles, and conveying them to the mouth. Generally speaking, water is drawn towards the body either by the movements of appendages as in various crustaceans, or by the action of cilia. The water then goes through some kind of sieve which filters off the particles. For this reason microphagous feeders are also known as **filter-feeders**.

A typical filter feeder is the freshwater mussel *Anodonta* which uses sheet-like gills for sorting and straining food particles. At the posterior end of the body are two apertures, the **inhalant** and **exhalant siphons**. Cilia on the gills draw water through the inhalant siphon, and particles suspended in the water get trapped in mucus on the surface of the gills and are wafted towards the mouth. Only small particles of nutritional value are taken into the mouth. Larger particles of sand or silt drop off the gills and are carried away in the water which passes out through the exhalant siphon (figure 16.12).

Figure 16.11
A A mosquito pierces the skin with its sharp proboscis, down which anti-clotting enzymes flow before blood is sucked into the stomach.
B Aphids pierce plants and suck up their juices.
C An elephant hawk moth hovering while drinking nectar from a flower through its long, flexible proboscis.

Figure 16.12 A freshwater mussel *Anodonta* showing the inhalant (frilled) and exhalant (smooth) siphons. Water is drawn in through the inhalent siphon, flows through the perforated gills and then leaves by the exhalant siphon. Small particles suspended in the water are collected on the gills by ciliary action and passed to the mouth.

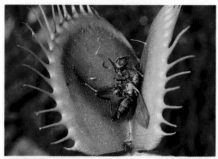

Figure 16.13 Venus flytrap *Dionaea muscipula*, a carnivorous plant native on marshlands in parts of the USA. The modified leaf snaps shut on a fly. The teeth on the edge of the leaf interlock, trapping the creature while the inner surface secretes digestive enzymes. The leaf then absorbs the soluble products of digestion.

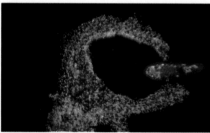

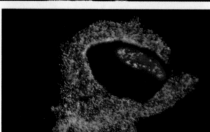

Figure 16.14 *Amoeba* ingesting a paramecium. The paramecium is taken into the cup-shaped phagocytic vesicle where it is digested.

Digestion

Consider the problem faced by the Venus flytrap in figure 16.13. Its food is solid and in the form of large complex molecules which are insoluble and relatively inert chemically. These molecules are too large to pass into the cells of the plant. **Digestion** is the process by which these molecules are turned into soluble products which can be absorbed.

Where does digestion take place?

Many animals digest their food completely before taking it into the cells. This is called **extracellular digestion** and the gut is where it usually takes place. In contrast to this, solid food particles may be taken into the cells by **phagocytosis** (see page 205) and then digested within the cells. This is called **intracellular digestion**.

One of the best-known examples of intracellular digestion is provided by the single-celled protoctist *Amoeba*. This organism has a very thin, flexible plasma membrane enabling it to change its shape as a result of cytoplasmic streaming within the cell. When the cytoplasm streams towards one particular point a projection called a **pseudopodium** is formed. When a pseudopodium comes into contact with a small particle of nutritional value, a diatom or green flagellate for example, it responds by forming a cup-shaped invagination which engulfs the food particle. Eventually the 'lips' of the cup seal, and the food becomes enclosed in a **phagocytic vesicle** (figure 16.14). Digestive enzymes are now secreted into the vesicle and the soluble products of digestion are absorbed into the surrounding cytoplasm. The entire process of digestion is therefore carried out inside the cell.

In some animals, digestion is divided into extracellular and intracellular phases. Extracellular enzymes secreted into the gut break the food down into small particles. These are then taken up by phagocytosis into the cells lining the gut (or in some cases a special digestive gland) where digestion is completed by intracellular enzymes.

In evolution the tendency has been for intracellular digestion to be replaced by extracellular digestion. It would appear that in the early stages of animal evolution the function of extracellular digestion was to break the food into particles small enough to be taken into the cells by phagocytosis. This would be particularly important to an animal like a sea anemone which has no physical means of breaking up its food.

In the subsequent evolution of digestive systems, extracellular digestion seems to have gradually replaced intracellular digestion. In humans and all other vertebrates digestion is almost entirely extracellular. However, as we shall see later, the final stages of protein and carbohydrate digestion in mammals are now known to be intracellular.

Physical and chemical digestion

The physical part of digestion in mammals is achieved by the cutting and/or crushing action of teeth, or their equivalent, followed by rhythmical contractions of the gut which pound the food into a semi-solid state. To fulfil this function the gut wall, particularly the mammalian stomach, is well endowed with muscles. These are responsible for mixing the food and pushing it along the gut.

The chemical part of digestion is achieved by the secretion of **digestive enzymes**. The physical action has an important role as it increases the surface area over which enzymes can act. Some of the enzymes are secreted by glands situated outside the gut: salivary glands and pancreas, for example. Others come from glands located in the gut wall itself. Copious quantities of mucus, secreted along with the digestive enzymes, protect the mucosa and facilitate the passage of food along the gut. Variable quantities of acid or alkali are also secreted to provide the correct pH for optimum functioning of the enzymes.

How digestive enzymes work

It is useful to look at the action of digestive enzymes in general terms before getting involved with the details. This can be illustrated by the digestion of proteins. A protein is generally attacked first by enzymes that break the peptide links in the interior of the molecule (figure 16.15). Such enzymes, called **endopeptidases**, have the effect of splitting proteins and large polypeptides into smaller polypeptides. In the human gut pepsin and trypsin are examples.

The smaller polypeptides are then attacked by enzymes which break off their terminal amino acids. These enzymes are called **exopeptidases**. Some exopeptidases, known as **aminopeptidases**, will only attack the end of a polypeptide chain which has a free amino ($-NH_2$) group. Others, known as **carboxypeptidases**, only attack the end of a polypeptide chain with a free carboxyl ($-COOH$) group. Either way, the result is the liberation of free amino acids.

The same principles apply to the digestion of carbohydrates. Certain enzymes break the glycosidic links in the interior of polysaccharide chains, forming disaccharides such as maltose. Carbohydrate digestion is completed by enzymes which attack the disaccharides, liberating free monosaccharides.

In the case of fats, triglycerides are attacked by an enzyme called **lipase** which breaks the bonds between the glycerol and hydrocarbon chains. This yields a mixture of (mainly) monoglycerides and free fatty acids. (A monoglyceride is glycerol linked to a single hydrocarbon chain.)

Digestion in humans

In the human, as in most animals, digestion takes place in the gut or **alimentary canal**. This is essentially a long tube connecting the mouth with the anus. However, the tube is not uniform all along its length: in some places it is quite narrow, being either straight or coiled. In other places it is wider and more capacious.

One of the straightest stretches of the alimentary canal is the gullet (oesophagus) which connects the pharynx with the stomach. It does not need to be coiled as its function is simply to convey food to the stomach. It runs straight through the thorax where it is located close to the trachea on the ventral side of the heart and lungs.

In the abdomen however the alimentary canal becomes highly coiled. It is here that most of digestion takes place and the products of digestion are absorbed into the bloodstream. Coiling has the effect of increasing the surface area for digestion and absorption. This part of the gut has a profuse blood supply. Blood is drained away from it by the hepatic portal vein which carries the absorbed food to the liver.

Various glands open into the alimentary canal. Some of the glands are embedded in the wall of the gut itself, others are located some way from the gut. The glands secrete digestive enzymes into the gut lumen (cavity). They also secrete sodium hydrogencarbonate (or, in the case of the stomach, hydrochloric acid) which gives the contents of the gut an optimum pH for the action of the digestive enzymes. Mucus is also secreted to ease the passage of materials along the gut and protect its inner lining.

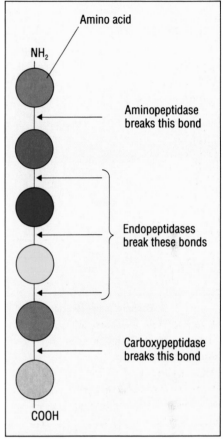

Figure 16.15 How a protein is digested. Endopeptidases break the bonds between amino acids in the interior of the molecule, and exopeptidases (aminopeptidase and carboxypeptidase) liberate the terminal amino acids.

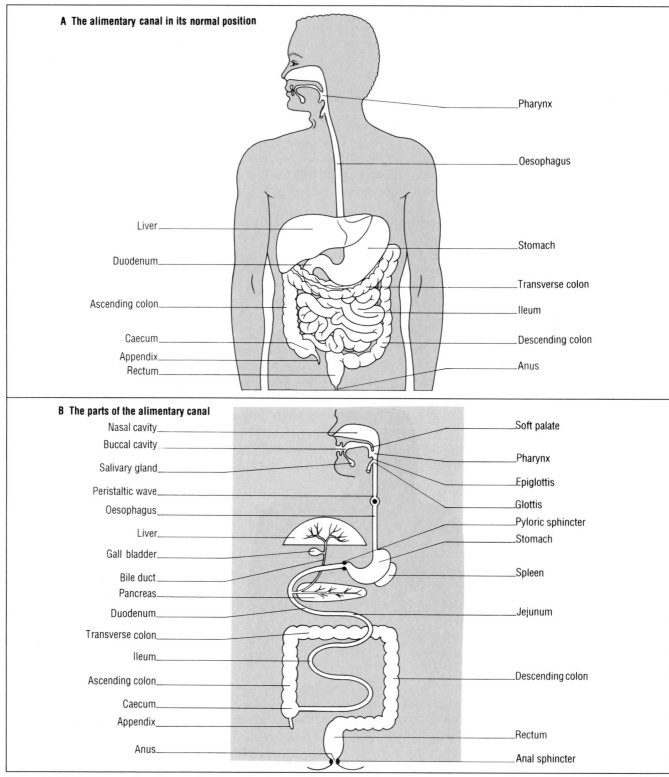

A The alimentary canal in its normal position

Pharynx

Oesophagus

Liver

Duodenum

Stomach

Transverse colon

Ascending colon

Ileum

Caecum

Descending colon

Appendix

Rectum

Anus

B The parts of the alimentary canal

Nasal cavity

Buccal cavity

Salivary gland

Peristaltic wave

Oesophagus

Liver

Gall bladder

Bile duct

Pancreas

Duodenum

Transverse colon

Ileum

Ascending colon

Caecum

Appendix

Anus

Soft palate

Pharynx

Epiglottis

Glottis

Pyloric sphincter

Stomach

Spleen

Jejunum

Descending colon

Rectum

Anal sphincter

Figure 16.16 The human alimentary canal and associated organs. The entire alimentary canal is approximately 8–9 m long. Most of its length is taken up by the small intestine (duodenum, jejunum and ileum) which is roughly 6 m long. In the course of its passage along the gut, food spends 3–5 hours in the stomach, about 4 hours travelling along the small intestine and from 6 to 20 hours in the large intestine. Digestion takes place mainly in the stomach and small intestine, the latter also being where most absorption takes place. Indigestible material (dietary fibre, roughage) passes on to the large intestine (caecum, appendix, colon and rectum). By the time it reaches the rectum much of the water has been removed. The contents of the rectum (faeces) consist mainly of indigestible cellulose, water, various salts, discarded epithelial cells and large numbers of bacteria particularly the colon bacillus *Escherichia coli*.

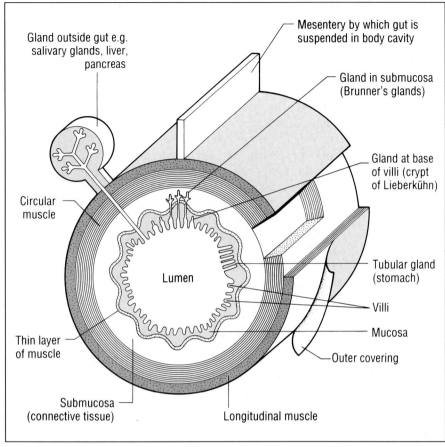

The detailed structure of the human alimentary canal is shown in figure 16.16. Its wall contains muscle tissue (mainly smooth muscle) and its inner surface is lined with **mucosa** (see page 174). The general plan is the same in all regions of the gut with a fairly constant arrangement of circular and longitudinal muscle layers. There are, however, variations in the amount of folding and the glands present in different regions (figure 16.17).

It takes about 13 hours for food to travel the length of the gut although this time varies tremendously. With a high dietary fibre intake it may take as long as 29 hours.

Let us now consider what happens to a meal as it passes along the human gut.

In the buccal cavity

The first part of the digestive process begins in the buccal cavity where the food is broken up into smaller pieces by the chewing action of the teeth (**mastication**) and moistened by **saliva** from the salivary glands.

The structure of a tooth is shown in figure 16.18. As you can see, the **crown**, which projects into the buccal cavity, is covered with **enamel**. Enamel is the hardest substance in the body. It consists of mineral salt crystals bound together by keratin. Beneath the enamel is a layer of **dentine** which is similar to bone but with a higher mineral content, thus making it harder. The dentine is perforated by fine channels called **canaliculi** which contain the cytoplasmic processes of the tooth-forming cells (**odontoblasts**). The central **pulp cavity** contains a network of blood capillaries and many sensory nerve endings. The **root** is embedded in a socket in the bone of the jaw. The root is covered with a bone-like substance called **cement** which is attached, securely but not inextricably, to the socket by tough fibres.

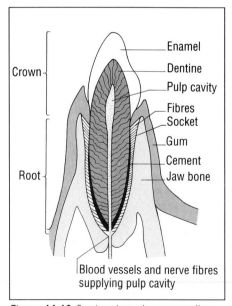

Figure 16.18 Section through a mammalian tooth, the structure of which is described in the text.

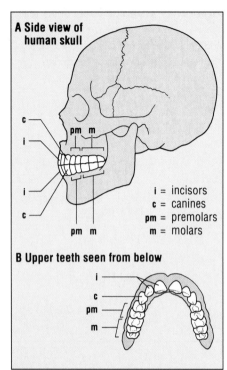

A Side view of human skull

c
i
pm m
i
c
pm m

i = incisors
c = canines
pm = premolars
m = molars

B Upper teeth seen from below

i
c
pm
m

Figure 16.19 *Top* Side view of a human skull showing the teeth. On either side of each jaw there are two incisors, one canine, two premolars and three molars. Thus the dental formula is: i ²⁄₂, c ¹⁄₁, pm ²⁄₂, m ³⁄₃. *Bottom* A plan of the upper jaw showing the shape and arrangement of the various teeth.

Teeth are well suited to their function by being differentiated into different types. Figure 16.19 shows the skull and teeth of a human. The **incisors** and **canines** are for cutting the food, the **premolars** and **molars** for crushing it. The canines are less dagger-like than in carnivores, and the distinction between premolars and molars is less clear cut than in most other mammals.

While being chewed, the food is mixed with saliva secreted by the **salivary glands**. There are three pairs of major salivary glands and numerous minor ones. The minor ones secrete continuously whereas the major ones are under the control of the parasympathetic nervous system and are stimulated by the sight, smell, taste or thought of food, though this last reflex is weakly developed in humans. Saliva is a watery mixture of mucus, mineral salts and the enzyme **salivary amylase**.

Salivary amylase is traditionally associated with the hydrolysis of the polysaccharide starch to the disaccharide maltose, but its primary role is more likely to be the removal of starch debris left around the teeth after eating a meal. Saliva is generally neutral or very faintly alkaline, this being the optimum pH for the action of the enzymes.

The watery part of saliva moistens the food as it is being chewed, and the mucus helps to bind the food together and lubricate it. The action of the tongue shapes the food into a **bolus** which is forced through the pharynx into the oesophagus in the act of swallowing. Triggered by tactile stimulation of the soft palate and the wall of the pharynx, swallowing is a reflex in which contraction of the tongue forces the bolus against the soft palate thus closing the nasal cavity. The opening into the larynx, the **glottis**, is closed by the valve-like **epiglottis**, so the bolus enters the oesophagus. While all this is happening, breathing is momentarily inhibited to prevent food entering the lungs. The nerve centre responsible for controlling this swallowing reflex is located in the posterior part of the brain.

In the stomach

The bolus is propelled from the buccal cavity down the oesophagus by a propagated contraction of the circular muscles, a process called **peristalsis**.

The stomach is a dilated part of the gut where the food remains for two hours or more. Once in the stomach the food is acted on by **gastric juice** secreted by **gastric glands** in the stomach wall (figure 16.20).

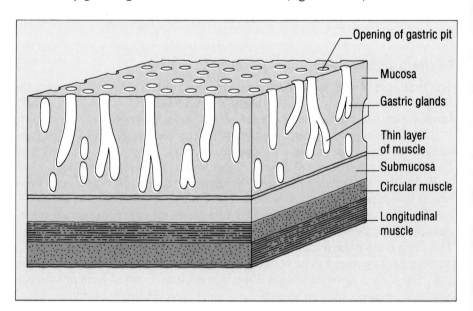

Opening of gastric pit
Mucosa
Gastric glands
Thin layer of muscle
Submucosa
Circular muscle
Longitudinal muscle

Figure 16.20 The thick wall of the stomach contains tubular gastric glands. There are about 35 million gastric glands in the human stomach.

Gastric juice is a watery secretion containing **hydrochloric acid** and the enzyme **pepsin** which breaks down proteins into short polypeptide chains. Pepsin is secreted by the peptic (or chief) cells which are clustered at the base of the gastric glands (figure 16.21).

Pepsin is secreted as an inactive precursor **pepsinogen**. Why is pepsin secreted in an inactive form? The reason is that it is a protein-digesting enzyme and this prevents the gastric gland being destroyed by its own enzyme (**autodigestion**). It remains inactive until it reaches the lumen of the stomach where it is activated by hydrochloric acid, and also by pepsin itself – in other words the reaction is **autocatalytic**. Once secreted, the active form of the enzyme is prevented from attacking the tissues by the mucus lining the stomach wall; this is secreted by cells situated towards the neck of the gastric glands.

Not only does the hydrochloric acid contribute to the activation of the pepsinogen, but it also provides the optimum pH for the functioning of the enzyme and it kills micro-organisms which may have been taken in with the food.

The acid is secreted by special **oxyntic cells** in the middle regions of the gastric glands and it gives the gastric juice a pH of less than 2.0. The production of hydrochloric acid by the oxyntic cells is a remarkable process, and bears certain similarities to the way carbon dioxide is carried in red blood cells. Inside the oxyntic cell, the enzyme **carbonic anhydrase** catalyses the formation of carbonic acid (H_2CO_3) from carbon dioxide and water. The carbonic acid dissociates into hydrogencarbonate (HCO_3^-) and hydrogen (H^+) ions. The latter then combine with chloride ions (Cl^-), derived from the dissociation of sodium chloride, to form HCl which is then secreted by the cell.

Control of gastric secretion

What brings about the secretion of gastric juice? At the beginning of the twentieth century, the Russian physiologist Ivan Pavlov (1849–1936) carried out some classic experiments on digestion in dogs (figure 16.22). He showed that gastric juice, like saliva, will flow as the result of the sight, smell, taste or expectation of food. But this reflex production is relatively slight in humans compared with the copious secretion that occurs when the food arrives in the stomach. Here mechanical and chemical stimulation of the stomach lining by the food itself causes secretion.

But there is another method by which gastric secretion is controlled. In the pyloric region of the stomach (the part just before the duodenum) enzyme-secreting cells are absent although mucus is still secreted to

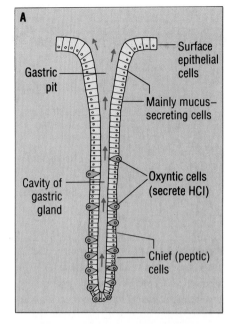

Figure 16.21 A gastric gland in detail. The gland, seen in longitudinal section in **A**, is lined with mucus, chief and oxyntic cells which secrete mucus, enzymes and hydrochloric acid respectively.

B Scanning electron micrograph of the inner lining of the stomach showing an opening into a gastric pit (**g**). Magnification × 900.

Figure 16.22 Pavlov's famous experiment carried out in 1902. An operation was performed on an anaesthetised dog in which the oesophagus was diverted so that it opened to the exterior in the neck, and a small part of the stomach ('Pavlov pouch') was separated from the main part without disturbing its innervation and then connected to the exterior by a tube so that its secretions could be collected. Gastric juice is secreted when food is eaten without getting into the stomach (arrow 1) and when food gets into the stomach without passing through the mouth (arrow 2). What conclusions would you draw from these observations?

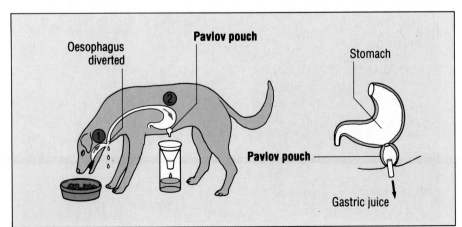

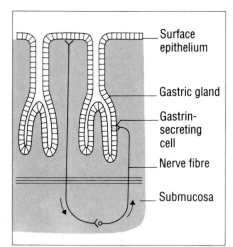

Figure 16.23 Gastrin is released into the bloodstream as a result of a local reflex in the stomach wall. Following a meal, distension of the stomach, and chemical substances in the food, stimulate nerve endings beneath the surface epithelium. Nervous impulses are then transmitted via the nerve pathway to gastrin-secreting cells in the gastric gland. It is uncertain as to which particular cells secrete the gastrin.

lubricate the pyloric sphincter at the entrance to the duodenum. Scattered amongst the mucus-secreting cells are some special cells which secrete a hormone called **gastrin** into the bloodstream. The presence of food in the stomach stimulates the secretion of gastrin. Gastrin then stimulates the secretion of pepsin and hydrochloric acid. It also stimulates the muscular movements of the stomach. So we can see that the secretion of gastric juice is controlled by the nervous system and by a hormone (figure 16.23).

While the digestive enzymes are acting, the rhythmical muscular contractions of the stomach wall pound the food into a semi-fluid state called **chyme**.

In the small intestine

The **duodenum** is the first loop of the small intestine. The passage of food into the duodenum is controlled by a ring of muscle, the **pyloric sphincter**, situated immediately between the far end of the stomach and the beginning of the duodenum. By alternately contracting and relaxing, the pyloric sphincter can hold food back or let it through. The emptying of the stomach is carefully controlled and small quantities of chyme are let through intermittently.

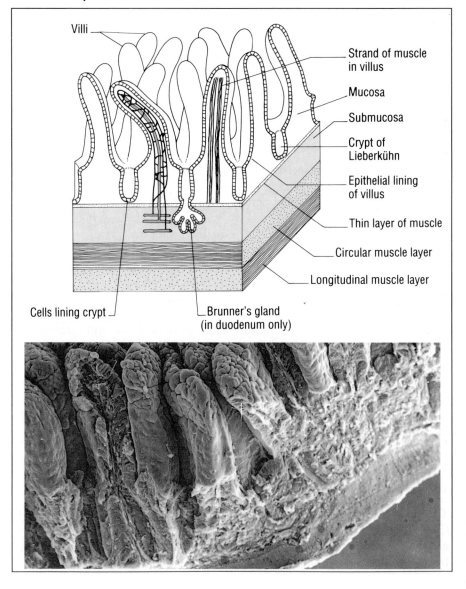

Figure 16.24 Diagram of part of the wall of the mammalian small intestine showing glands and villi. Note Brünner's glands opening into crypts of Lieberkühn. Crypts are present in all parts of the small intestine whereas Brünner's glands are restricted to the duodenum. The epithelial cells lining the villi are of two main kinds: goblet cells which secrete mucus, and columnar epithelial cells which are involved in digestion and absorption. Blood and lymph capillaries are included in the second villus from the left; they are shown in more detail in figure 16.27 on page 285. Below the diagram is a scanning electron micrograph of villi on the inner side of the wall of the small intestine. Magnification × 50.

The inner surface of the small intestine is covered with numerous finger-like projections called **villi** between which are glands called **crypts of Lieberkühn** (figures 16.24 and 16.25). A great deal of digestion takes place in the small intestine. The agents of digestion come from three sources: the **liver**, the **pancreas** and the **wall of the small intestine**.

The liver and bile

The liver produces **bile** which, after storage in the **gall bladder**, flows along the **bile duct** into the duodenum. Bile is a mixture of substances, not all of which are involved in digestion. Those which are – the **bile salts**, sodium taurocholate and sodium glycocholate – **emulsify** fats by lowering their surface tension, causing them to break up into numerous tiny droplets. In this way the total surface area of the fat is increased, thereby facilitating the digestive action of the enzyme **lipase** (see below). It must be stressed that the bile salts are not enzymes. They are not proteins and have no chemical effect on the fats, only the physical effect of emulsifying them.

Bile is also rich in sodium hydrogencarbonate ($NaHCO_3$) which, together with that from the pancreas, neutralises the acid from the stomach. The pH of the small intestine is therefore distinctly alkaline, which favours the action of the various enzymes.

Pancreatic juice

The pancreas produces **pancreatic juice** which flows into the duodenum from the pancreas via the pancreatic duct. The main pancreatic enzymes are:

- **Pancreatic amylase** which breaks down starch to the disaccharide maltose.
- **Pancreatic lipase** which breaks down triglycerides in the emulsified fat into monoglycerides and fatty acids.
- **Proteases** (protein-splitting enzymes) which include **trypsin**, **chymotrypsin, carboxypeptidase** and **elastase**.

The four proteases are secreted as inactive precursors: **trypsinogen, chymotrypsinogen, procarboxypeptidase** and **proelastase**. As with pepsin in the stomach, this prevents autodigestion. Trypsinogen is converted into trypsin by the action of the enzyme **enterokinase**, secreted by the wall of the small intestine. The trypsin then activates the other three proteases. These pancreatic proteases break down proteins and polypeptides into **tripeptides** and **dipeptides**.

Pancreatic juice also contains **nucleases** which break down nucleic acids into nucleotides, and a variety of **peptidases** which release some free amino acids from polypeptide chains.

Intestinal enzymes

Various enzymes, associated with the epithelial lining of the small intestine, complete the digestion of carbohydrates by breaking down disaccharides into monosaccharides. These enzymes include:

- **Maltase** which hydrolyses maltose to glucose, thus completing the digestion of starch.
- **Sucrase** which hydrolyses sucrose (cane sugar) to glucose and fructose.
- **Lactase** which hydrolyses lactose (milk sugar) to glucose and galactose.

The end products of carbohydrate digestion are all monosaccharides. The final stage of carbohydrate digestion is intracellular, as disaccharides are absorbed by the plasma membrane of the epithelial cells before being broken down into monosaccharides.

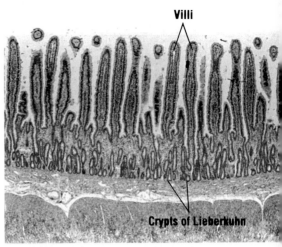

Figure 16.25 Section of the wall of the ileum showing villi and crypts of Lieberkühn. Magnification × 20.

Lactase

The enzyme **lactase** (also known as ß-**galactosidase**) hydrolyses lactose to its constituent monosaccharides. This enzyme is found in all human babies, but is only found in adults from northern Europe and a few African tribes. Most other human groups, including Orientals, Arabs, Jews, most Africans, Indians and Mediterranean peoples produce little or no lactase as adults and may even show lactose intolerance. This condition is characterised by diarrhoea and pains in the large intestine and is caused by ingesting large amounts of milk in the absence of the enzyme that would otherwise break it down.

Secretion	Source	Site of action	Flow induced by	Enzymes etc.	Substrate	Products
Saliva (neutral or slightly acid)	Salivary glands	Mouth cavity	Expectation and reflex action	Salivary amylase Lysozyme	Starch Bacteria	Maltose Dead bacteria
Gastric juice (distinctly acid)	Stomach wall (gastric glands)	Stomach (lumen)	Expectation, reflex action, contact with stomach lining, and hormone (gastrin)	Pepsin	Proteins	Polypeptides
				Rennin	Soluble casein	Insoluble casein
Bile (alkaline)	Liver	Duodenum (lumen)	Reflex action and hormones	Bile salts (not enzymes)	Fats	Fat droplets
Pancreatic juice (alkaline)	Pancreas	Duodenum (lumen)	Reflex action and hormones	Pancreatic amylase	Starch	Maltose
				Proteases (e.g. trypsin)	Proteins and Polypeptides	Tripeptides and dipeptides
				Peptidases	Polypeptides	*Amino acids*
				Pancreatic lipase	Fats	Monoglycerides and *fatty acids*
				Nucleases	Nucleic acids	Nucleotides
Intestinal enzymes (intracellular)	Plasma membranes	Small intestine (epithelial cells)	Mainly contact with intestinal lining	Maltase	Maltose	*Glucose*
				Sucrase	Sucrose	*Glucose + fructose*
				Lactase	Lactose (milk sugar)	*Glucose + galactose*
				Peptidases	Dipeptides and tripeptides	*Amino acids*
				Nucleotidases	Nucleotides	*Pentose sugars + phosphoric acid + organic base*

Table 16.1 Summary of the main enzymes associated with the mammalian gut, together with their source, site of action and functions. The products in italics are soluble. Rennin is secreted only by young ruminants such as cattle, and possibly by human babies. It has the effect of coagulating milk protein (casein), turning it into a semi-solid which is then digested by pepsin. The reason why milk is coagulated is that otherwise it would pass through the stomach too quickly for digestion to take place.

The epithelial cells also absorb tripeptides and dipeptides which are then broken down into **amino acids** by various peptidases. Thus the final stages of protein digestion are also intracellular.

Nucleotidases are also present in the epithelial cells of the small intestine. They split nucleotides into their constituent subunits.

Brunner's glands, found in the wall of the duodenum, secrete an alkaline mucus which helps to neutralise the acid from the stomach and protects the duodenal lining from autodigestion. These glands do not produce any enzymes.

The enzymes are present in the cells at the bottom of the **crypts of Lieberkühn.** These cells are constantly dividing and the daughter cells move slowly up the sides of the crypt and then the villus, until after a few days they reach the tip. They are then shed into the lumen of the intestine and are replaced by new ones which move up behind them. The entire epithelial lining is replaced every three to five days in this way. It has been shown that the enzymes in these cells catalyse the final stages of digestion as the cells move up the sides of the villus.

Control of intestinal secretion

How is the flow of secretions in the small intestine controlled? In the case of bile and pancreatic juice, control is partly by nervous reflexes triggered by the sight, smell and taste of the food, and also by hormones. The presence of acidified chyme in the duodenum stimulates certain cells scattered throughout the mucosa of the duodenum to secrete two hormones into the bloodstream. These two hormones are known as **secretin** and **cholecystokinin-pancreozymin** (CCK-PZ).

Digestion of cellulose

We mentioned earlier that the problem facing all herbivores is that the nutrient content of their food is low and a high proportion of it is difficult to digest. This is due to the large amount of cellulose in their diet. If maximum value is to be derived from plant food, cellulose must also be digested. This requires the enzyme **cellulase**, a powerful carbohydrase which breaks ß-glycosidic links and so splits cellulose into its constituent monosaccharides (see page 130).

A variety of micro-organisms, mainly bacteria and protoctists, are able to secrete cellulase; so can fungi which use it to dissolve plant cell walls so as to penetrate into the cells. But apart from this, cellulase is extremely rare, and is practically unheard of in the animal kingdom.

Mammals cannot produce cellulase themselves and yet many of the meat and milk producers such as cattle, sheep, goats and camels are herbivores and cellulose is certainly digested in their guts. Cellulose is also digested in other herbivores such as horses and rabbits. How do they do it?

Ruminants

Ruminant (cud-chewing) mammals like the cow have an enlarged 'stomach' at the lower end of the oesophagus (see illustration). This is divided into four chambers, of which the **abomasum** is the true stomach. Grass and other plant food is ground up by the molars and then passed down the oesophagus into the first chamber, the **reticulum**. Here it is formed into balls of cud which are regurgitated and chewed again when the cow is not actually feeding.

When it is swallowed for the second time, the food passes into the **rumen**, by far the largest chamber. Here it is mixed with vast numbers of cellulose-digesting bacteria and

with copious quantities of saliva which have been added from the salivary glands. A cow may produce as much as 100 to 190 litres of saliva a day! The rumen is a fermenting chamber and in anaerobic conditions the cellulose is broken down into ethanoic, propionic and butyric acids, with the evolution of carbon dioxide and methane gas. These gases are released from both ends of the digestive tract. Meanwhile the contents of the rumen pass through the **omasum** into the abomasum and thus to the duodenum where the soluble products of digestion are absorbed.

As well as cellulose-digesting bacteria other bacteria are present, which synthesise proteins from ammonia. These bacteria are ingested in the rumen by protoctists, which are therefore a rich source of protein. The protoctists pass out of the rumen into the rest of the gut where they are digested by the ruminant's own enzymes, and the protein is made available to the host. This makes a significant contribution to the protein requirements of the animal.

The reason why urea is added to cattle feed is that it is broken down to ammonia which is then used by

the protein-synthesising bacteria, further supplementing this source of protein. The other nutritional value of rumen bacteria is in the synthesis of B-vitamins. Cows obtain all the vitamin B_{12} they need from these mutualistic micro-organisms.

Non-ruminants

Non-ruminant herbivorous mammals also possess fermentation chambers where micro-organisms digest cellulose. In horses and rabbits they are the caecum and appendix, a blindly ending diverticulum of the gut situated at the point where the small intestine joins the large intestine. However, having a fermentation chamber near the end of the gut has disadvantages. Food cannot be regurgitated and the products of digestion cannot be shunted forwards into the small intestine efficiently for absorption to take place. You have only to compare the appearance of horse dung and cowpats to see which method is the most efficient.

To make up for this deficiency, rabbits and hares reingest their own faeces, a phenomenon known as **coprophagy**. If rabbits are deprived of eating their soft faeces they show signs of nutritional deficiency.

What about humans? Humans do not possess a rumen or a large caecum, and the appendix is apparently functionless. Yet we eat significant quantities of plant material in our diet and are constantly encouraged to eat more fibre. High fibre diets are known to prevent diverticulitis of the colon and are thought to reduce the incidence of bowel cancer and colitis. Bacteria are present in the human colon but until recently their fermenting activity was considered to be insignificant. However, it is now thought that the action of these bacteria on carbohydrate in the colon can contribute up to 10 per cent of our energy requirements.

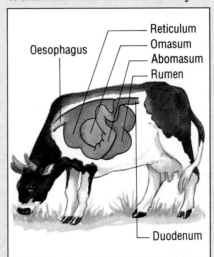

The 'stomach' of a cow showing the positions of the four chambers. The rumen makes up 80 per cent of the volume.

Oesophagus

Reticulum
Omasum
Abomasum
Rumen

Duodenum

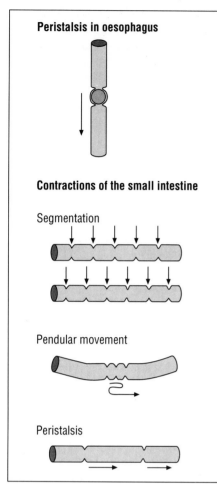

Figure 16.26 Various movements of the gut brought about by localised contractions of the circular muscle.

Secretin acts on the liver and pancreas, causing the liver to secrete bile and the pancreas to secrete the fluid (non-enzymatic) components of the pancreatic juice. CCK-PZ stimulates the pancreas to secrete its enzymes, and it also acts on the smooth muscle in the wall of the gall bladder causing it to squirt bile into the bile duct. Another hormone called **enterogastrone** inhibits any further secretion of acid by the stomach.

Movements of the small intestine

Muscular contractions of the gut wall keep the food moving along the small intestine and mix it thoroughly with the various juices secreted into it. The movements are of three main kinds (figure 16.26). The first is called **segmentation**: circular constrictions at 1 to 2 cm intervals divide the gut contents into segments. Each contraction lasts about a second and is followed by a similar constriction in a different place. This mixes the chyme with the digestive enzymes.

The second is a **pendular movement** which causes the chyme to move back and forth along 15–20 cm lengths of small intestine. This type of movement both mixes the chyme and increases the flow of blood to the intestinal lining thus aiding absorption.

Lastly **peristalsis**, which occurs over long lengths of the gut, is brought about by contraction and relaxation of the circular muscles and causes waves of contraction to push the food along towards the large intestine.

As a result of all these activities the food in the small intestine is converted into a watery emulsion called **chyle**. It is from this that the products of digestion are absorbed.

Absorption and assimilation

In humans digestion begins in the mouth and is completed in the small intestine. The small intestine is therefore the logical site for the absorption of the products of digestion. We have already seen how the digestive function of the small intestine is carried out and we shall now turn our attention to its absorptive function.

The structures in the small intestine responsible for absorption are the villi. The detailed structure of a villus is shown in figure 16.27. Villi contain smooth muscle enabling them to contract and expand, thus bringing them into contact with newly digested food. Near the periphery of each villus there is an arteriole and a venule with an interconnecting network of capillaries. Monosaccharide sugars (mainly glucose) and amino acids are absorbed by a combination of diffusion and active transport from the epithelial cells, where the final stages of digestion have been completed, into the capillaries. The blood from the venules, which contains the dissolved nutrients, eventually reaches the **hepatic portal vein** whence it flows to the liver.

Fat is dealt with rather differently. In the centre of each villus is a blindly ending lymph capillary. Fat is absorbed into the epithelial cells lining the villi as little droplets called **micelles** which contain monoglycerides, bile salts and free fatty acids. Triglyceride fat is then resynthesised and shed into the lymphatic vessels as a white emulsion of minute globules. This gives the lymphatic vessels a milky appearance, for which reason they are known as **lacteals**. As the lymphatic system ultimately opens into the veins, the fat eventually finds its way into the circulatory system which distributes it round the body. Most absorption of fat is thought to take place by this route, although some short chain fatty acids may be reabsorbed directly into the bloodstream.

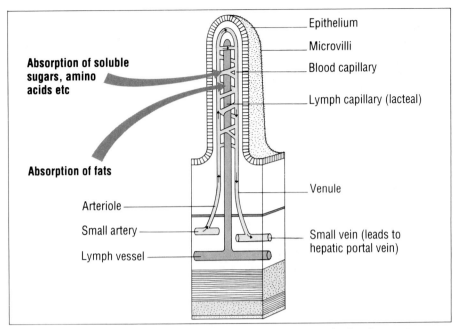

Epithelium

Microvilli

Blood capillary

Absorption of soluble sugars, amino acids etc

Lymph capillary (lacteal)

Absorption of fats

Venule

Arteriole

Small artery

Small vein (leads to hepatic portal vein)

Lymph vessel

Figure 16.27 Detailed structure of a villus showing the epithelial lining with microvilli on the outside and the blood vessels and lacteal inside.

The villi greatly increase the surface area over which absorption can occur. The surface area is further increased by the fact that the epithelial cells lining each villus bear numerous microvilli (figure 16.28).

The epithelial cells also contain large numbers of mitochondria, reflecting the high energy requirements of active absorption. Inorganic salts, vitamins and water are absorbed in the small intestine and also in the **colon** whose wall is also much folded. Thus by the time it reaches the **rectum**, indigestible food is in a semi-solid condition and ready to be egested through the anus as **faeces**. This process is called **defaecation** and is facilitated by the lubricative effect of large amounts of mucus secreted by numerous goblet cells in the lining of the rectum.

The processes of digestion and absorption are now complete. Through the bloodstream the soluble food nutrients are taken to the tissues where they are either assimilated (built up into complex materials) or used in respiration for the transfer of energy.

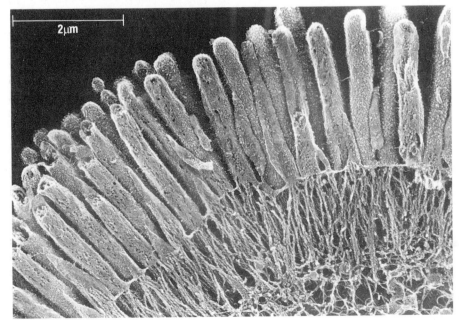

2µm

Figure 16.28 Scanning electron micrograph of part of an epithelial cell from the small intestine. This particular cell comes from the lining of a villus. Notice the closely packed microvilli. They give the cell a large surface area for absorption and also for enzyme action, at least the part which takes place on the membrane lining them. There is evidence that some intestinal microvilli may undergo worm-like movements, thereby facilitating absorption.

How much food?

Food is the source of energy for metabolic processes. The connection between food intake and metabolic rate is therefore important in appreciating the factors which determine the food requirements of an animal. Here we shall consider one of these factors, namely size.

The size of an animal obviously has some bearing on the amount of food it eats as a small animal eats far less in absolute terms than a large one. However, the relationship between food consumption and body mass is not a simple one. This is partly because the surface area is also important.

Mathematically it can be shown that, for animals of the same shape, the surface area increases as the square (power of 2) of the linear measurement, and the volume (or mass) increases as the cube (power of 3). Surface area will therefore be related to volume (or mass) by the power of $\frac{2}{3}$ or 0.67.

This can be seen in illustration 1 in which the surface areas of a range of vertebrates are plotted against their body masses. The slope of the line drawn through the scatter points is very nearly equal to 0.67 which is what we should expect.

As a result of this relationship between surface area and body mass, small animals have more surface area relative to their body mass than larger ones. Heat energy is generated as a result of metabolic activity in the cells of the body, so larger animals generate more heat energy than small ones because they have a greater mass. However, they lose comparatively less heat energy to the environment per unit of body mass because their surface area is relatively less. The consequence of this is that in order to generate enough heat energy to maintain their body temperature, small animals have a higher metabolic rate per gram of body mass and therefore require more food per gram of body mass than larger ones.

We can now look at how this applies to real animals. For example, shrews, which are the smallest mammals, have to eat almost continually in order to stay alive and will consume between one and three times their own mass of food each day. We now know that they have to do this in order to maintain their body temperature. A large animal such as a lion may only eat once every three or four days. Its metabolic rate per gram of body mass is lower than that of a shrew, but because its surface area relative to its body mass is less it is able to generate enough energy to maintain

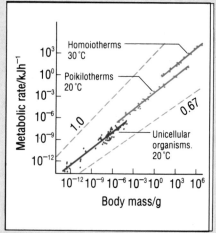

Illustration 2 The metabolic rates of various organisms in relation to their body masses. Note that each mark on the axes denotes a thousandfold increase in magnitude.

its body temperature.

From this we might conclude that food consumption will be more closely related to surface area than body mass. In illustration 2 the metabolic rate (and therefore food consumption) is plotted against body mass. If metabolic rates were directly related to body mass the points would lie along a line of slope 1.0, and if they were related directly to surface area they would lie along a line of slope 0.67. We can see from the graph that they actually fall somewhere in between the two, at a line of slope about 0.75. This means that the food requirements for animals should be calculated using the body mass raised to the power of 0.75.

Exactly why this should be is not fully understood although it is obvious that there are other factors affecting the quantity of food eaten. For example, the animal's shape, whether it lives in air or water, how active it is and the insulating properties of its outer covering and whether it is ectothermic or endothermic will all have some effect on food consumption. Furthermore the energy value of the food eaten also has to be taken into account.

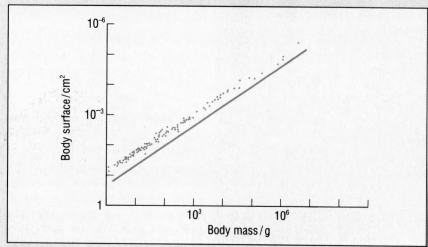

Illustration 1 A scattergram showing the surface areas of vertebrates in relation to their body masses. The line shows the data for spheres with a specific gravity of 1.0.

Summary

1 Organisms which feed on organic food are said to have **heterotrophic nutrition** and are called **heterotrophs**.

2 The problem facing any heterotroph is how to acquire and take in organic food and then break it down into soluble products capable of being absorbed.

3 In most heterotrophs food is successively **ingested, digested, absorbed, distributed** and **assimilated**. The functions of digestion and absorption are carried out in a **gut** (**alimentary canal**). Indigestible remains are egested.

4 Heterotrophic organisms can be classified in terms of the type of food they eat as **herbivores, carnivores, omnivores, liquid feeders** and **microphagous feeders**.

5 Herbivores have special adaptations for ingesting and digesting plants, e.g. the ridged **molar teeth** of horses and elephants, the **mandibles** of locusts and the **radula** of snails.

6 Carnivores have adaptations for catching and killing prey (e.g. **claws, canine teeth, tentacles**) and for crushing and slicing their food (e.g. **carnassial teeth**).

7 Insectivorous plants have adaptations for trapping and digesting small animals, particularly insects. In this way the nitrogen requirements of these plants are supplemented by heterotrophic means.

8 **Liquid feeders** include absorbers (e.g. tapeworm) and suckers (e.g. mosquito). The mouthparts of sucking insects are adapted in different ways to form various types of proboscis.

9 **Microphagous feeders** feed on small particles suspended in water which are collected and filtered. They are hence also known as **filter feeders** (e.g. bivalve molluscs).

10 **Digestion**, the breaking down of food into soluble substances, is either **extracellular** or **intracellular**. It may be entirely intracellular as in *Amoeba*, or extracellular and intracellular as in humans.

11 Digestion takes place by physical and chemical means. In mammals physical digestion is achieved by teeth, gut muscles, and the action of bile on fats. Chemical breakdown is the result of the action of **digestive enzymes**.

12 Digestive enzymes work by splitting specific chemical bonds in the molecules of the food substances.

13 The mammalian gut is differentiated into a series of specialised regions, each showing a close relationship between structure and function.

14 Chemical digestion is achieved by enzymes secreted by the stomach wall, the pancreas and the wall of the small intestine. The final stages of digestion of carbohydrates and proteins is intracellular.

15 Secretion of digestive enzymes is initiated by expectation, reflex stimulation, hormones or direct mechanical stimulation, depending on the gland in question.

16 The digestion of cellulose requires the enzyme **cellulase** which very few animals secrete. Herbivores harbour cellulase-secreting micro-organisms in special parts of their gut.

17 To aid absorption, the surface area of the absorptive epithelium is increased by the presence of **villi** and **microvilli**.

Review questions

1 Explain the meanings of the terms ingestion, digestion, absorption and assimilation.

2 What are the main characteristics of the teeth of a named herbivore and a named carnivore?

3 Summarise the functions of the human stomach.

4 Which enzymes in the human digestive system are involved in the breakdown of (a) polysaccharides, (b) proteins and (c) fats?

5 How is the secretion of pancreatic juice controlled?

6 Explain how the structure of the wall of the small intestine is related to its functions.

7 How are food materials mixed and moved along the gut?

8 Outline the special features of the gut of a named herbivore which enable it to digest its food.

9 What contribution did Ivan Pavlov make to our understanding of digestion? Do you think his experiments would be ethically acceptable today?

10 Trace what happens to the components of a ham sandwich after it has been ingested.

Further reading

Knut Schmidt-Nielsen's *Animal Physiology* (Cambridge University Press, 1990) is a readable and informative general physiology text and contains plenty of information on the comparative aspects of feeding and digestion.

At one time it was thought that the wall of the small intestine secreted its enzymes into the cavity of the intestine. Henry Leese explains what really happens in an article entitled *The digestion and absorption of carbohydrate and protein: the role of the small intestine* (*Journal of Biological Education*, Vol 18, No 4, 1984).

In *Biology, Advanced Topics* there is an account of protein digestion at the molecular level and cellulose digestion in ruminants and other mammals

CHAPTER 17 | Autotrophic nutrition

The type of feeding employed by plants and other non-heterotrophic organisms involves the synthesis of organic compounds from inorganic raw materials. It is called **autotrophic nutrition** and is the subject of this chapter.

Different types of autotrophic nutrition

There are two types of autotrophic organisms.

- **Photoautotrophs.** These organisms (green plants, some protoctists and bacteria) are able to trap the energy of sunlight and use it to convert simple inorganic substances into the complex organic compounds required for living. The process usually involves the synthesis of sugars from carbon dioxide and water using sunlight as the source of energy and the green pigment **chlorophyll** for trapping the light energy. This is known as **photosynthesis**.

- **Chemoautotrophs.** Certain bacteria synthesise organic compounds from carbon dioxide and water but the energy is supplied by special methods of respiration involving the oxidation of various inorganic materials such as hydrogen sulphide, ammonia and iron(II). This method of synthesis, which does not require sunlight, is called **chemosynthesis**.

The importance of photosynthesis

As a means of manufacturing sugar the contribution of photosynthesis is astounding. A hectare (2.47 acres) of corn can convert as much as 10 000 kg of carbon from carbon dioxide into the carbon of sugar in a year, giving a total yield of 25 000 kg of sugar per year.

Although it is difficult to arrive at a total world figure for photosynthesis, one biologist has calculated that 35×10^{15} kg of carbon are fixed by plants per year. Our ability to solve the world's food problem will depend, at least in part, on agriculturalists increasing these figures still further. A knowledge of photosynthesis, as revealed by the most recent research, can only help in this direction.

But there is another reason why photosynthesis is important. It created the Earth's oxygen-containing atmosphere in the geological past and regulates the concentration of carbon dioxide in it. The concentration of carbon dioxide in the atmosphere remains almost constant in spite of the

Photosynthesis and the energy crisis

Hardly a day passes without our attention being drawn to the fact that people in many parts of the world do not have enough to eat. Shortage of food is essentially an energy problem. All living organisms require energy in order to grow, maintain themselves and reproduce. Plants, some protoctists and certain bacteria can manufacture their own food by trapping energy from sunlight. These same organisms – producers as they are called – are subsequently consumed by heterotrophs, including ourselves. They are therefore the basis of food chains. The world's food problem arises from the fact that in global terms the producers cannot manufacture food fast enough to keep pace with the demands of an ever-increasing human population. It is a matter of supply and demand.

We can extend the idea of supply and demand to fossil fuels. Coal, natural gas and oil were formed from land plants and marine organisms millions of years ago. These organisms captured energy from the sun and subsequently became the fossil fuels which we so relentlessly remove from the Earth's crust today. You could say that when we burn these fuels we are using 'fossil sunshine'. Regrettably, this invaluable source of energy is being used up far faster than it could ever be replaced by natural means.

fact that it is continually being removed during photosynthesis. This is because plants and animals produce carbon dioxide when they respire.

Oxygen which is added to the atmosphere as a result of photosynthesis is removed during respiration and the carbon dioxide is replenished. These two processes – photosynthesis and respiration – create a cycling of carbon dioxide and oxygen in the atmosphere which is summarised in figure 17.1. The ecological significance of the carbon cycle is discussed on pages 31 and 41.

Demonstrating photosynthesis

The main product of photosynthesis is **monosaccharide sugar**, although this is often built up into **starch** for storage. The other product of photosynthesis is **oxygen**. To show that photosynthesis has taken place you need to demonstrate the presence of these end products. Techniques for doing this and for measuring the rate of photosynthesis are described in the Students' Manual.

The conditions required for photosynthesis

For photosynthesis to take place a plant requires **carbon dioxide, water, light, chlorophyll** and a **suitable temperature**. The necessity for these factors can be demonstrated by simple experiments either on whole plants or single leaves. As an indication of whether or not photosynthesis has been taking place, the leaves are tested for starch with dilute iodine solution. The practical details are explained in the Students' Manual.

Carbon dioxide

The necessity for carbon dioxide can be demonstrated by the arrangement shown in figure 17.2. A plant such as *Pelargonium* is well watered and then destarched by putting it in the dark for 48 hours. One of the green leaves is then deprived of carbon dioxide by enclosing it in a flask containing a small volume of potassium hydroxide (caustic potash), which absorbs the carbon dioxide from the air in the flask. A second leaf is enclosed in a separate flask containing water, to serve as a control. The flasks must be made completely airtight.

The plant is placed in a well-lit place for several hours, after which the two leaves are removed and tested for starch. The control leaf is usually found to have formed a significant quantity of starch, the other leaf little or none.

Before reading on, consider this question. Do you think it would be better to use two plants in this experiment rather than two leaves from the same plant? (You should always be as critical as possible of other people's experiments, and try to think of better ones yourself!)

Water

The necessity for water is difficult to demonstrate by a simple experiment. Depriving a plant of water will certainly kill it but this might be due to any number of reasons, not necessarily connected with photosynthesis. The only way of showing unequivocally that water is required for photosynthesis is to trace what happens to it after it has been taken into the plant. Such an experiment is described on page 298 and it shows that water is required for photosynthesis.

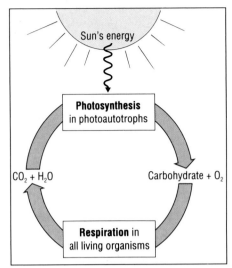

Figure 17.1 Photosynthesis plays an important part in the cycling of carbon dioxide and oxygen in the atmosphere.

Figure 17.2 One way of demonstrating that carbon dioxide is required for photosynthesis. Explanation in text.

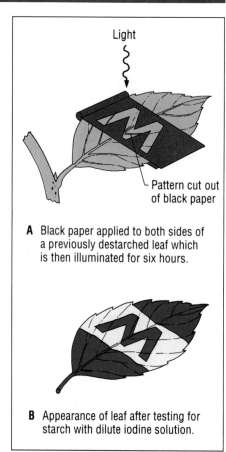

Light

A Black paper applied to both sides of a previously destarched leaf which is then illuminated for six hours.

B Appearance of leaf after testing for starch with dilute iodine solution.

Figure 17.3 A simple demonstration to show the necessity for light in photosynthesis. No starch is formed in the covered part of the leaf. Although this is a striking demonstration of the importance of light in photosynthesis, it is not an ideal scientific experiment. What are its shortcomings? Can you think of a better way of finding out if light is needed for starch formation?

Figure 17.5 Comparison of absorption and action spectra of a plant shows a close correspondence between the two, indicating that most of the wavelengths of light absorbed by chlorophyll are used in photosynthesis. The graphs are based on data obtained from the sea lettuce *Ulva taeniata*. In this particular alga efficiency in blue light is unusually high. The marked non-correspondence of the two curves at X is because of absorption of this wavelength by carotenes which are not used in photosynthesis.

Light

The importance of light can be demonstrated by covering part of both surfaces of a previously destarched leaf with opaque paper and then exposing the leaf to light for several hours.

On testing the leaf with dilute iodine solution it is found that the dark blue colour, signifying the presence of starch, is confined to the illuminated parts of the leaf. The covered part does not turn dark blue, indicating the failure of this part of the leaf to form starch. The completed test gives a **starch print** (figure 17.3).

Not all the wavelengths of light (i.e. colours) are absorbed by chlorophyll. This can be shown by projecting a beam of light through a solution of extracted chlorophyll and then a prism which separates it into its different wavelengths. After passing through the prism the light is projected on to a screen and any colours absent from the normal spectrum are those that have been absorbed by the chlorophyll. This gives us an **absorption spectrum** for chlorophyll (figure 17.4). It turns out that the red and blue ends of the spectrum are much reduced in intensity, showing that light of these colours is absorbed to varying extents by the chlorophyll. However, the middle part of the spectrum, green light, is hardly absorbed at all: most of it is reflected, which is why chlorophyll looks green.

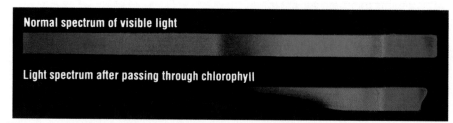

Normal spectrum of visible light

Light spectrum after passing through chlorophyll

Figure 17.4 *Top* The visible spectrum obtained by passing white light through a prism so that it is split into its different colours. *Bottom* The absorption spectrum of chlorophyll obtained by passing light through a chlorophyll extract and a prism.

But are the wavelengths absorbed actually used in photosynthesis? That they are can be shown by exposing leaves to different coloured lights and then determining the amount of carbohydrate or oxygen formed in each case. This gives us an **action spectrum** for photosynthesis. Red and blue light turn out to be the most effective wavelengths in photosynthesis; green is only used to a slight extent. There is thus a close correlation between the absorption and action spectra, as can be seen in figure 17.5.

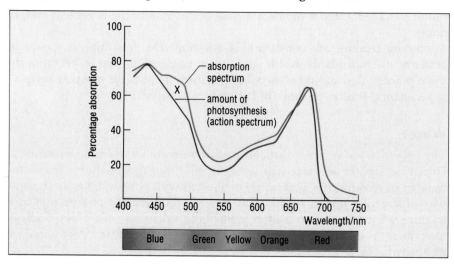

Chlorophyll

That chlorophyll is required for photosynthesis can be shown by studying the distribution of starch in a **variegated leaf**. A variegated leaf is one which lacks chlorophyll in some parts, giving it a cream appearance wherever the green pigment is absent. This is quite common in geranium and ivy plants.

If a variegated geranium plant, previously destarched, is exposed to light and one of its leaves is then tested for starch, the dark blue colour develops only in those parts of the leaf that were green. In fact the distribution of the dark blue colour corresponds exactly to the distribution of chlorophyll (figure 17.6).

In the case of variegated ivy this experiment may be taken a step further. Some varieties of this plant have four different shades of colour in their leaves: dark green towards the centre, then two zones of progressively paler green, and at the edge a yellow rim. If after a period of illumination,

Figure 17.6 A variegated geranium leaf before and after testing for starch with dilute iodine solution. Notice that the dark colour indicating starch corresponds to the green areas where chlorophyll is located.

Detecting the site of photosynthesis

The German botanist T.W. Engelmann realised that it was no use trying to detect the site of photosynthesis in an ordinary cell filled with densely packed chloroplasts. It was necessary to find a large cell containing a localised chloroplast. It so happens that the filamentous alga *Spirogyra* fills the bill very nicely. The filaments of *Spirogyra* are composed of comparatively large cylindrical cells placed end to end. Each contains a ribbon-like chloroplast which describes a spiral round the edge.

Engelmann chose *Spirogyra* for his experiments and used the evolution of oxygen as an indication that photosynthesis was proceeding. His method of detecting oxygen illustrates the ingenuity of this remarkable biologist. He had previously discovered that certain bacteria (*Pseudomonas*) move vigorously in the presence of oxygen, clustering together where the oxygen concentration is highest. A filament of *Spirogyra* was mounted on a microscope slide in a drop of water containing numerous bacteria. The slide was first put in darkness which prevented photosynthesis, stopped the evolution of oxygen and immobilised

the bacteria. The slide was then exposed to light and viewed under a microscope. Motile bacteria were seen to cluster round the edge of the cells adjacent to the chloroplast, indicating the evolution of oxygen at that point (see illustration).

Engelmann's experiment was carried out in 1883. It illustrates an important general point, namely the use that can be made of one organism to demonstrate a biochemical process in another.

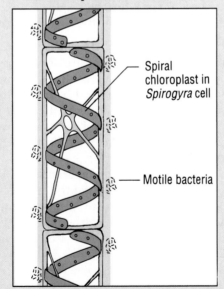

In his classical experiment, Engelmann used bacteria of the genus *Pseudomonas* to demonstrate that oxygen is given off during photosynthesis by the filamentous alga *Spirogyra*. After oxygen deprivation motile bacteria are seen only in the immediate vicinity of the chloroplast.

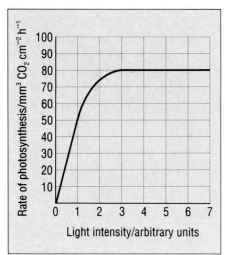

Figure 17.7 The result of an experiment showing the effect of different light intensities on the rate of photosynthesis of cucumber plants. The temperature was kept at 20°C and the carbon dioxide concentration at 0.03 per cent. The rate of photosynthesis was determined by measuring the volume of carbon dioxide taken up per square centimetre of leaf per hour.

one of these leaves is tested for starch, the intensity of the blue colour follows exactly the same pattern as the chlorophyll.

Temperature

Photosynthesis proceeds by a series of chemical reactions controlled by enzymes which are sensitive to temperature. It can be shown by comparing a plant's rate of photosynthesis at different temperatures that the optimum temperature for photosynthesis in most plants growing in temperate regions is around 30°C. At lower temperatures the rate is slowed. If the temperature exceeds about 40°C the process stops altogether because the enzymes become denatured.

Interaction of factors controlling photosynthesis

Consider the following experiment. A plant is subjected to a series of increasing light intensities. The rate of photosynthesis is determined at each intensity, and the results plotted on a graph (figure 17.7). The temperature and carbon dioxide concentration are kept constant, the temperature at 20°C, the carbon dioxide concentration at 0.03 per cent – its normal value in the atmosphere. The experimental details need not concern us; let us concentrate on what happens and why.

As you can see from figure 17.7, the rate of photosynthesis rises steadily as the light intensity increases, and then levels off as the process reaches its maximum rate. What causes the rate of photosynthesis to stop increasing?

Here are three possible answers (you may think of others):

- The photosynthetic process is going at the fastest possible rate and no amount of additional light will make it go any faster whatever the circumstances.
- There is insufficient carbon dioxide available to allow the process to speed up any further.
- The temperature is too low for the chemical reactions to go any faster.

How can we decide between these three possibilities? The simplest way is to raise either the temperature or carbon dioxide concentration and repeat the experiment. The result of doing this is shown in figure 17.8. Curve A is the same one as we obtained before. If the experiment is now repeated at the same carbon dioxide concentration but at a higher temperature (30°C instead of 20°C), curve B is obtained which is virtually identical to curve A. This shows that it cannot be temperature that is preventing the process going any faster.

However, if the temperature is kept the same and the carbon dioxide concentration is increased to 0.13 per cent, curve C is obtained: the rate of photosynthesis rises to a maximum which is more than double that achieved at the lower carbon dioxide concentration.

This shows that our second hypothesis is the correct one, carbon dioxide is limiting the rate of photosynthesis in the first experiment. What is limiting the process where curve C flattens out? Curve D shows that in this case the rate of photosynthesis is increased by raising the temperature, thus indicating that temperature is the limiting factor where curve (C) flattens out.

The facts demonstrated by this experiment can be put into a general statement, called the **law of limiting factors**. *When a chemical process depends on more than one essential condition being favourable, its rate is limited by that factor which is nearest its minimum value.* In figure 17.8 light is the limiting factor where the curves are rising. When the curves flatten out we know that some other factor is limiting the process.

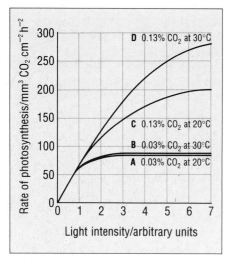

Figure 17.8 The results of an experiment investigating the effect of different light intensities on the rate of photosynthesis of cucumber plants at two temperatures and two carbon dioxide concentrations.

Photosynthesis and the environment

Limiting factors are important to plants in their natural surroundings. On a warm summer day, light and temperature are generally well above their minimum value for plants living in the open, and carbon dioxide is the factor limiting photosynthesis. But in the cool of the early morning or evening, light or temperature may become limiting factors as they do in winter.

Habitat is also important: for plants living in shady places such as the floor of a forest or wood, light will be the limiting factor most, if not all, the time.

Plants often compete for light. Tall plants will get plenty of light while those growing beneath them may not always get enough. Tallness is most clearly seen in trees although herbaceous plants like nettles and willowherbs also have sturdy, erect stems with leaves in a well-lit position for photosynthesis. Their great height makes taller trees like beech and oak the dominant plants of a temperate woodland community, though for sheer size the jackpot must go to the California redwoods which can reach heights of over 100 metres.

Plants which live in the shadow of taller trees and shrubs exhibit various strategies for obtaining sufficient light. Climbing plants like *Clematis* and honeysuckle have twining stems and others, like white bryony, have tendrils enabling them to 'scramble' towards light. Certain woodland plants grow to maturity and flower in early spring before the leaves come out on the trees, a good example being dog's mercury. Other woodland plants, such as violets, can photosynthesise in conditions of very low illumination and thus survive in relatively dark places (figure 17.9).

In large plants the leaves may cast shade on each other. You will often find that the leaves of such plants fit together in a sort of mosaic pattern, leaving few gaps between one leaf and the next, a condition called **leaf mosaic**. This is seen, for example, in beech trees and is the reason why they cast so much shade. Next time you are lying in a beech wood, look up at the canopy and notice how dense it is. Leaf mosaic makes beech woods very dark and the ground flora is sparse as a result (figure 17.10).

Compensation point

In order to survive, a plant must receive sufficiently intense light for sufficiently long to replenish its supplies of carbohydrates which have been lost by respiration. When photosynthesis and respiration proceed at the same rate so that there is no net loss or gain of carbohydrate, the plant is said to be at its **compensation point**.

The time taken for a plant to reach its compensation point, having been in darkness, is called the **compensation period**. The length of this period varies with different plants and conditions. Plants with the ability to utilise dim light are called **shade plants** and they generally reach their compensation point earlier in the day than those requiring bright light which are called **sun plants**.

The site of photosynthesis

The distribution of starch in a variegated leaf demonstrates that photosynthesis can only take place in the green parts of a plant, and this suggests that the process is closely associated with **chlorophyll**. Chlorophyll is contained within **chloroplasts** so it is logical to conclude that photosynthesis takes place in or close to the chloroplasts.

Figure 17.9 Adaptations shown by three different plants for obtaining light in dimly lit places.
A Black bryony showing twining stems and leaves presented towards light.
B Dog's mercury growing under trees in early spring before the tree leaves have formed a canopy.
C Primroses flowering in a wood under trees.

Figure 17.10 Leaf mosaic formed by the leaves of a beech tree. Notice that the leaves are arranged in such a way that they do not cast shade on each other.

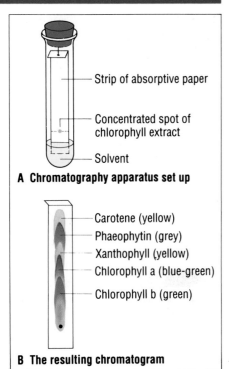

A Chromatography apparatus set up

- Strip of absorptive paper
- Concentrated spot of chlorophyll extract
- Solvent

- Carotene (yellow)
- Phaeophytin (grey)
- Xanthophyll (yellow)
- Chlorophyll a (blue-green)
- Chlorophyll b (green)

B The resulting chromatogram

Figure 17.11 Different pigments in a leaf can be separated by paper chromatography.
A A strip of absorptive paper carrying a concentrated spot of the leaf extract is dipped into a suitable solvent, for example a mixture of propanone and petroleum ether. The solvent rises up the paper sweeping the pigments with it. The pigments travel at different speeds, thus becoming separated as shown in **B**.

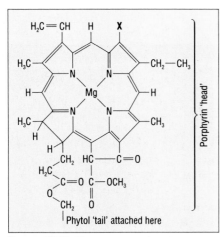

Figure 17.13 The structure of chlorophyll. In chlorophyll *a*, X is CH_3 and in *b* it is –CHO. The arrangement of the porphyrin 'head' and phytol 'tail' is important in determining the orientation of the molecules in the chloroplast membranes.

The chloroplast pigments

What we have been calling chlorophyll is in fact a mixture of various pigments. These pigments can be extracted from leaves with propanone and separated by chromatography (figure 17.11). At least five pigments can be identified: **chlorophyll *a*** (blue-green), **chlorophyll *b*** (yellow-green), **xanthophyll** (yellow) and **carotene** (yellow). The fifth pigment, **phaeophytin** (grey), is a breakdown product of chlorophyll.

By making separate solutions of each pigment and determining the absorption spectrum of each, it can be shown that chlorophyll *a* and *b* absorb light from both the red and blue/violet parts of the spectrum, whereas xanthophyll and carotene absorb light only from the blue/violet part (figure 17.12).

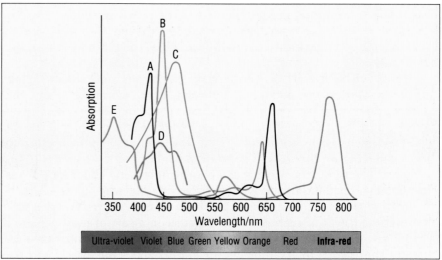

Figure 17.12 Absorption spectra of various photosynthetic pigments: **A** chlorophyll *a*; **B** chlorophyll *b*; **C** xanthophyll; **D** carotene; **E** bacteriochlorophyll of purple sulphur bacteria. Note the differing abilities of the various pigments to absorb different wavelengths. Chlorophyll *a* absorbs at longer and shorter wavelengths than either chlorophyll *b* or xanthophyll, and bacteriochlorophyll can absorb in the infra-red and ultraviolet parts of the spectrum.

Chlorophyll *a* is the most abundant pigment and is of universal occurrence in all photosynthesising plants. Its function is to absorb light and use it in the manufacture of carbohydrate. The other pigments do this too and then hand on the energy to chlorophyll *a*.

Why are these accessory pigments necessary? Would not chlorophyll *a* alone be sufficient? To answer this look again at figure 17.12. Chlorophyll *a* utilises light from only limited parts of the spectrum. The other pigments utilise light from other parts of the spectrum, so they effectively increase the range of wavelengths from which the plant can obtain energy.

The amount of energy which the pigment can absorb from the light depends on two things: its **intensity** and its **wavelength**. The greater the intensity of the light, the greater will be the amount of energy that falls on, and is absorbed by, the pigment in a given time. The wavelength is important because it determines the frequency with which the light waves strike the pigment. The shorter the wavelength of the light, the more energy it contains. Thus there is more energy in blue light at 450 nm wavelength than there is in red light of the same intensity at 750 nm. So perhaps it is not surprising that the pigments illustrated in figure 17.12 absorb more light at the blue end of the spectrum.

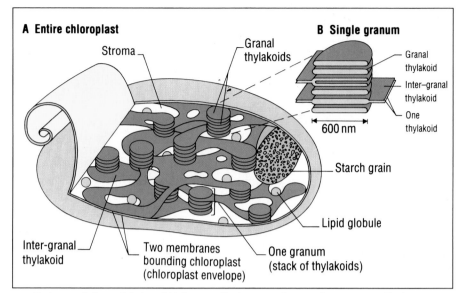

A Entire chloroplast

Stroma

Granal thylakoids

B Single granum

Granal thylakoid

Inter–granal thylakoid

One thylakoid

600 nm

Starch grain

Lipid globule

Inter-granal thylakoid

Two membranes bounding chloroplast (chloroplast envelope)

One granum (stack of thylakoids)

Figure 17.14 The structure of a chloroplast. **A** Stereogram showing the internal structure of the whole chloroplast. **B** Section of a single granum, showing that it consists of a stack of thylakoids.

It is useful to think of light as distinct packets of energy called **quanta**. The energy contained in a single quantum of light is called a **photon**. When a photon strikes a molecule of a pigment such as chlorophyll it may bounce off (i.e. be reflected), which is what happens in the green part of the spectrum. Alternatively it may be absorbed by the chlorophyll molecule. What happens to this light energy will be explained presently.

Chlorophyll belongs to a group of organic compounds known as **porphyrins** which also include haemoglobin and other respiratory pigments (see page 309). A characteristic feature of porphyrins is that they form complexes with metal ions. In the case of chlorophyll the metal is magnesium, located at the centre of the molecule (figure 17.13). A long chain alcohol called phytol is attached to the porphyrin head. It is only after the phytol 'tail' has been added to the porphyrin that photosynthesis can take place.

Structure of the chloroplast

With very few exceptions chlorophyll is contained within chloroplasts. A chloroplast of a higher plant is biconvex in shape, about 5 μm across at the widest part. Studies with the electron microscope show it to have an elaborate internal structure which can be related to its function.

The structure of the chloroplast is shown in figures 17.14 and 17.15. As you can see, it is bounded by a double membrane within which are numerous structures called **thylakoids**. Each thylakoid consists of a pair of membranes close to each other with a narrow space between. In places the thylakoids are arranged in neat stacks, rather like a pile of coins. Each stack is called a **granum** (plural grana). Its diameter is about 600 nm. The grana are connected to each other by a less regular arrangement of **inter-granal thylakoids**. All the thylakoid membranes within a chloroplast are continuous and enclose an interconnecting space.

The function of the thylakoid membranes is to hold the chlorophyll molecules in a suitable position for trapping the maximum amount of light energy. In its internal organisation the chloroplast appears to achieve this admirably. A typical chloroplast contains approximately 60 grana, each consisting of about 50 thylakoids. The chlorophyll molecules are, as it were, laid out on shelves stacked on top of each other with considerable economy of space. This provides a large surface area without taking up too much room.

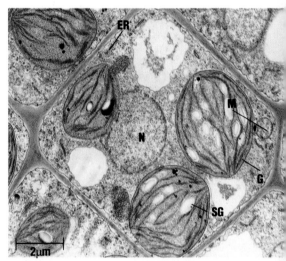

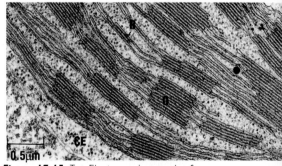

Figure 17.15 *Top* Electron micrograph of chloroplasts in leaf cells of the moss, *Tortula muralis*. These chloroplasts contain numerous starch grains (**SG**) and have two to six thylakoids per granum (**G**). You can also see the nucleus (**N**), a mitochondrion (**M**) and endoplasmic reticulum (**ER**). *Bottom* Electron micrograph of part of a chloroplast in a mesophyll cell of *Zea mays* (maize). The chloroplast envelope (**CE**), grana (**G**) and ribsomes (**R**) can all be distinguished.

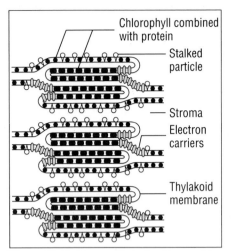

Figure 17.16 Diagram illustrating the possible arrangement of chlorophyll and related molecules within the thylakoid membranes, based on studies of isolated grana.

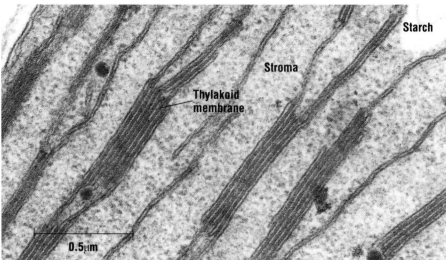

Figure 17.17 High magnification electron micrograph of the thylakoids and stroma in a chloroplast of the grass *Agrostis*. The dots in the stroma are ribosomes where the chloroplast proteins are synthesised.

Figure 17.16 shows how the chlorophyll molecules and related structures are arranged in the thylakoid membrane. Notice the **stalked particles** attached to the thylakoid membranes. They contain enzymes for catalysing the synthesis of ATP.

The thylakoids are surrounded by a protein-rich matrix, the **stroma**. This contains the enzymes responsible for the reduction of carbon dioxide, together with starch grains and numerous ribosomes (figure 17.17).

Next, we have to consider where the chloroplasts are in relation to the whole plant and how light, carbon dioxide and water get to them. In some organisms like the alga *Spirogyra* all the cells contain chloroplasts and carry out photosynthesis. But in most plants, organs specialised for photosynthesis have been developed. These are the **leaves**.

Figure 17.18 The leaf is a complex organ for photosynthesis. The photosynthetic cells are held in the best position for gaining maximum light. Strengthening tissue maintains the shape of the leaf. Stomata allow the entry of carbon dioxide whilst the cuticularised epidermis prevents excessive water loss. Vascular tissues in the midrib and veins bring water and mineral salts to the leaf, and remove the products of photosynthesis from it.

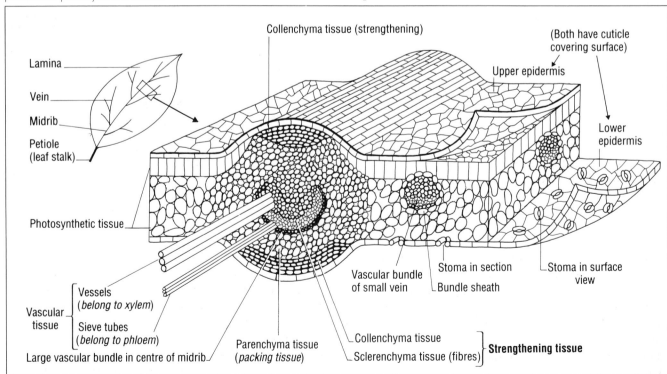

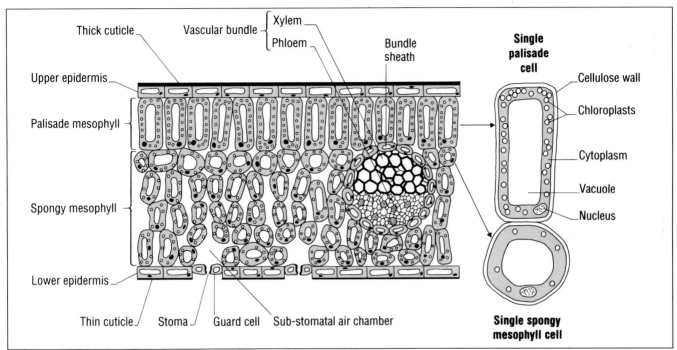

Xylem
Phloem

Thick cuticle — Vascular bundle

Bundle sheath

Single palisade cell

Upper epidermis

Cellulose wall

Chloroplasts

Palisade mesophyll

Cytoplasm

Vacuole

Spongy mesophyll

Nucleus

Lower epidermis

Thin cuticle — Stoma — Guard cell — Sub-stomatal air chamber

Single spongy mesophyll cell

Structure of the leaf

Leaves are generally thin and flat and collectively present a large surface area to the light. Their thinness minimises the distance over which the diffusion of carbon dioxide has to take place. Of course being thin and flat makes them liable to sag, but their shape is maintained by the turgor of the living cells inside them, and by the **midrib** and **veins** which are well endowed with strengthening tissue. Their large surface area, while allowing maximum gaseous diffusion, increases evaporative water loss but this is reduced by the impermeable **cuticle** on the leaf surface.

Most of the salient features of a flowering plant leaf (dicotyledonous type) are shown in figures 17.18, 17.19 and 17.20. You will see that the leaf is covered on both sides by a layer of **epidermal cells**, on the outer surface of which is the cuticle. The cuticle is generally thicker on the upper surface of the leaf than on the lower surface.

The inside of the leaf is filled with cells containing chloroplasts. These cells are of two types. Those immediately beneath the upper epidermis, called the **palisade cells**, are elongated with their long axes perpendicular to the surface. They are separated from each other by narrow air spaces and are densely packed with chloroplasts. The chloroplasts tend to arrange themselves in the part of the cell which receives maximum illumination, usually the upper part. The palisade cells collectively form the **palisade mesophyll** which may be one or several cells in thickness.

Filling the leaf between the palisade layer and the lower epidermis is the **spongy mesophyll**. Its cells are irregular in shape and arrangement; they also contain chloroplasts but fewer than the palisade cells, which is why the lower side of a leaf usually looks paler than the upper side. Assuming that the plant is well supplied with water, the thin cellulose walls of the spongy mesophyll cells are permanently saturated with moisture. Between the spongy mesophyll cells are large **air spaces** which communicate with each other and with the much narrower air spaces between the palisade cells. This system of air spaces allows gases to diffuse freely between the cells within the leaf.

Figure 17.19 Photosynthetic cells in a leaf as seen in a diagrammatic transverse section. Note the intercellular air spaces allowing free diffusion of carbon dioxide, and the close proximity of the photosynthetic cells to the vascular tissues.

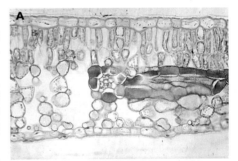

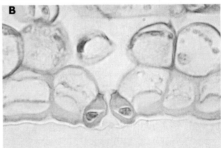

Figure 17.20 Photomicrographs of a dicotyledonous leaf in transverse section.

A The whole leaf from upper to lower epidermis including a small vein, × 70.

B A stoma and sub-stomatal air chamber on the lower side of the leaf, × 500.

Use figure 17.19 to help you identify the structures in these photomicrographs.

Figure 17.21 Plants can be kept indefinitely in an illuminated sealed container ('bottle garden'). The carbon dioxide from respiration is used for photosynthesis, and the oxygen from photosynthesis is used for respiration.

The source of oxygen in photosynthesis

S. Ruben and M. Kamen and their co-workers established that the oxygen evolved in photosynthesis comes from the water and not from carbon dioxide. In an experiment carried out in 1941 they placed the green protoctist *Chlorella* in water in which the oxygen atom had been replaced by the heavy isotope of oxygen, ^{18}O. By using a mass spectrometer they found that ^{18}O was present in the oxygen given off by the organism. If, however, the protoctist was given normal water but the carbon dioxide was labelled with ^{18}O, the oxygen given off contained no ^{18}O, thus confirming that the oxygen formed in photosynthesis comes only from the water.

The lower epidermis is pierced by numerous pores called **stomata** (singular **stoma**). The upper epidermis may have some too but they are usually fewer than in the lower epidermis. Each stoma opens into a **sub-stomatal air chamber** which connects with the intercellular air spaces described above. Bordered by **guard cells** which can open or close the pore, the stomata regulate the passage of carbon dioxide and water vapour across the surface of the leaf. How they open and close is explained on page 249.

The midrib and veins

The diagram in figure 17.18 includes the central midrib as well as two smaller veins. The veins consist of conducting tissue specialised for transporting materials to and from the leaf. The **xylem** brings water and mineral salts from the roots in elongated conducting tubes called **vessels** and **tracheids**. The **phloem** carries soluble food materials from the leaf in specialised rows of cells called **sieve tubes**. The xylem and phloem together constitute a **vascular bundle**. The xylem elements, being lignified (woody), also provide the flexible leaf with mechanical strength.

The midrib is basically similar to the smaller veins except that there is a greater abundance of conducting tissue and, in addition, much specialised strengthening tissue (**sclerenchyma** and **collenchyma**) for supporting the leaf.

The leaf as an organ of photosynthesis

How does the leaf work as a photosynthetic organ? Carbon dioxide from the atmosphere diffuses through the stomata into the sub-stomatal air chambers and thence via the intercellular air spaces to the chloroplasts in the spongy mesophyll and palisade cells.

Water, drawn up from the soil via the conducting tissues of the roots and stem, passes out of the xylem elements in the veins to the surrounding cells. Maintenance of this flow is discussed in Chapter 20. Its importance in the present context is that it supplies water for photosynthesis. With the water come mineral salts (including nitrates, sulphates and phosphates) required for the synthesis of proteins and other compounds. Oxygen and excess water vapour diffuse out of the leaf via the intercellular air spaces and stomata. Sugar and other products of photosynthesis are moved to other parts of the plant in the sieve tubes.

The importance of the stomata

It is clear from what has been said that the stomata play a vital part in photosynthesis. When they are open the rate of photosynthesis may be ten or twenty times as fast as the rate of respiration. Under these circumstances the plant will use the carbon dioxide from its respiration for photosynthesis. However, the bulk of its carbon dioxide must be brought in from the atmosphere. If the stomata are closed photosynthesis can still continue, using the carbon dioxide from respiration.

In fact an equilibrium can be reached between photosynthesis and respiration, photosynthesis using carbon dioxide from respiration, and respiration using oxygen from photosynthesis (figure 17.21). However, the rate of photosynthesis under these circumstances will be much slower than when an external source of carbon dioxide is available.

Of course the stomata cannot remain closed indefinitely because open stomata are necessary to maintain the flow of water from the roots to the leaves.

The chemistry of photosynthesis

In the process of photosynthesis energy from sunlight is trapped by chlorophyll and used for the manufacture of carbohydrate from carbon dioxide and water. The process can be summarised by the following equation:

$$CO_2 \xrightarrow{} + H_2O \xrightarrow[\text{Chlorophyll}]{\text{Energy of sunlight}} CH_2O + O_2$$

Carbon dioxide + Water → Carbohydrate + Oxygen

Though useful as an overall summary of the process, this simplified equation is misleading because it gives the impression that the oxygen evolved comes from the carbon dioxide, which we know is not true (see box on the opposite page). It also suggests that photosynthesis takes place in a single photochemical reaction, whereas it occurs in many steps, not all of which require light.

If photosynthesis consisted only of photochemical reactions one would not expect the process to be influenced by temperature since photochemical reactions are temperature insensitive. But in fact the rate of photosynthesis is strongly influenced by temperature, provided of course that other factors are not limiting it. A 10°C rise in temperature approximately doubles the rate. This is typical of ordinary chemical reactions, and it would therefore seem that photosynthesis proceeds in more than one stage, each with different light and temperature requirements.

We can see these two factors, light and temperature, operating in curve C in figure 17.8 (see page 292). Over the first part of the curve, when it is rising steeply, light is influencing the rate of photosynthesis and temperature has no effect on it, i.e. a light-requiring reaction is setting the pace. However, when the curve flattens out temperature controls the rate. This suggests that at least some of the reactions are not limited by light.

Photosynthesis as a three-stage process

Photosynthesis takes place in three main stages:

- Light harvesting.
- Electron transport.
- Reduction of carbon dioxide.

The first two stages require light and take place in the thylakoids of the chloroplast. The third stage does not require light and takes place in the stroma.

The three stages are summarised in figure 17.22. Although they take place simultaneously it is convenient to study them separately, and as the primary event of photosynthesis is the capture – or harvesting – of light, this is where we shall begin.

Stage 1 Light harvesting

Pigment molecules, arranged in specific association with protein and lipid molecules in the thylakoid membranes of the chloroplasts, form the light harvesting system. It acts rather like a funnel, collecting photons of light and transferring the energy to special molecules of chlorophyll *a* in a **reaction centre** (figure 17.23).

The transfer of the energy to a reaction centre is achieved in the following way. When a chlorophyll molecule absorbs light, the energy is passed to an electron and this raises its energy level. The chlorophyll

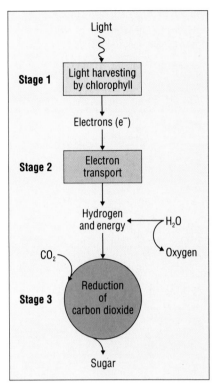

Figure 17.22 In photosynthesis, light energy is absorbed (harvested) by chlorophyll (stage 1). As a result, electrons are released from the chlorophyll and transferred through an electron transport system (stage 2). This process, which is associated with the splitting of water, provides hydrogen and the necessary energy for reducing carbon dioxide with the formation of sugar (stage 3).

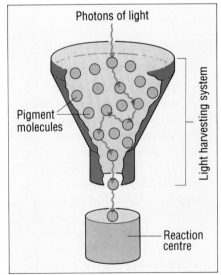

Figure 17.23 The light harvesting system is here likened to a funnel. Photons of light are collected and passed in a random manner from pigment molecule to pigment molecule until they reach the reaction centre.

Figure 17.24 The path taken by electrons which leads to the formation of reduced NADP (i.e. NADPH).

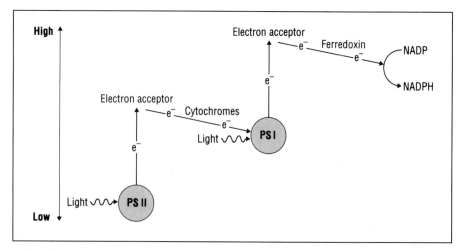

molecule goes from the 'ground' state to an 'excited' state. An 'excited' chlorophyll molecule can immediately pass its energy to a neighbouring chlorophyll molecule which itself becomes 'excited', while the original one returns to the 'ground' state. In this way energy can be transferred very rapidly from one chlorophyll molecule to another in a manner which has been described as a 'random walk'. This is indicated by the arrows in figure 17.23. The other pigments act rather like 'antennae', collecting energy and transferring it to chlorophyll *a*.

An 'excited' chlorophyll *a* molecule is very unstable and will dissipate its energy as fluorescent light and return to its ground state in 10^{-9} second. However, the transfer of energy from an excited molecule of chlorophyll *a* to a special molecule of chlorophyll *a* in a reaction centre probably takes place within 10^{-12} second, which is a thousand times faster than when the energy is lost through fluorescence.

There are two kinds of reaction centre in plants called **Photosystem I (PS I)** and **Photosystem II (PS II)**. While many chlorophyll molecules are involved in the capture of light energy, only a very few make up the reaction centres. PS I absorbs light at 700 nm and PS II at 690 nm. These two centres differ not only in the structure of their chlorophylls but also in their functions, as we shall see. The transport of electrons through these two centres comprises the second stage of photosynthesis, which we must now consider.

Stage 2 Electron transport

Two products are formed as a result of the transfer of electrons. They are **reduced nicotinamide adenine dinucleotide phosphate, (NADPH)**, and ATP. NADPH is a reducing agent whose role will become clear later. For the moment, let us concentrate on how it is produced. The events to be described are shown in figure 17.24. We shall start with PS I.

When light is absorbed by a chlorophyll molecule in PS I an electron is displaced and transferred to an electron acceptor which in turn donates it to a protein called **ferredoxin**. The latter then passes the electron to **nicotinamide adenine dinucleotide phosphate (NADP)** which is thereby reduced to NADPH.

Obviously for this process to continue the electron displaced from PS I must be replaced. This is where PS II comes in. When PS II absorbs light, an electron is displaced from it and passed along a chain of electron carriers, which include the cytochromes. Eventually the electron replaces the electron displaced from PS I which is thus returned to its ground state.

In order for this process to continue the PS II molecule must be restored

The Hill reaction

In 1938 Robert Hill demonstrated that isolated chloroplasts, when illuminated in the presence of an electron acceptor produced oxygen and acquired reducing properties. He used the coloured dye called dichlorophenol-indophenol (DCPIP) as the electron acceptor. This is blue in the oxidised state but becomes colourless when reduced. As carbon dioxide was not involved in this reaction, Hill concluded that water had been split into hydrogen and oxygen – what is now known as the **Hill reaction**.

to its ground state. This is brought about by a process in which water is split and an electron donated to PS II. As light is associated with this reaction, it is called **photolysis of water** and it results in the release of molecular oxygen. This is the oxygen which is given off during photosynthesis. The photolytic splitting of water is called the **Hill reaction** after the scientist who discovered it, and it is one of the principal events of photosynthesis.

Now we must turn to the other function of electron transport, the synthesis of ATP. How is the ATP produced? You will recall from your study of respiration that for ATP to be synthesised, ADP and inorganic phosphate must be present. As a result of electron flow from PS II to PS I in the thylakoid membranes, there is an accumulation of hydrogen ions (H⁺) inside the thylakoid, creating a gradient. The passage of H⁺ out of the thylakoids provides the energy for ATP to be synthesised in the presence of ATPase. This is called **non-cyclic photophosphorylation** (figure 17.25).

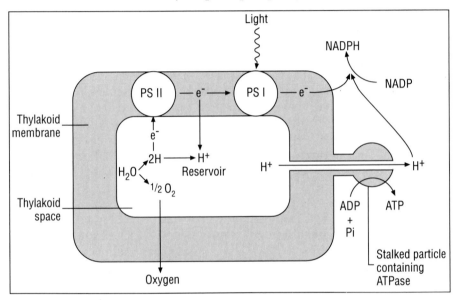

Figure 17.25 How ATP and NADPH are formed in photosynthesis. As a result of the splitting of water and the flow of electrons in the thylakoid membrane, hydrogen ions accumulate in the thylakoid space. As a result the hydrogen ion concentration is about a thousand times greater in the thylakoid space than in the stroma, creating a steep electrochemical gradient. The diffusion of the hydrogen ions (H⁺) out of the thylakoid provides the energy for the synthesis of ATP in the presence of ATPase. It also provides the hydrogen for reducing NADP with the formation of NADPH. The passage of electrons from PS II to NADP via PS I occurs in the manner shown in figure 17.24. The whole process is called non-cyclic photophosphorylation.

Sometimes the electrons follow a different route. In this case PS I is both the donor and acceptor of electrons. There is again an accumulation of H⁺ and ATP is synthesised as before. Because there is a cyclical flow of electrons in this pathway, it is called **cyclic photophosphorylation** (figure 17.26). NADPH is not formed by this method.

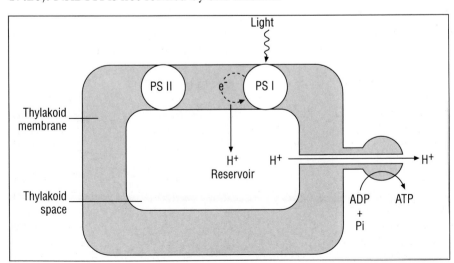

Figure 17.26 If ATP rather than NADPH is needed, the plant automatically switches to cyclic photophosphorylation, as shown here. Electrons from PS I, instead of being passed to NADP, return to PS I. This cyclical transfer of electrons results in hydrogen ions accumulating in the thylakoid space with the consequent synthesis of ATP.

Insofar as energy is derived from an electrochemical gradient resulting from the movement of hydrogen ions (i.e. protons) across the thylakoid membrane, cyclic and non-cyclic photophosphorylation are applications of the chemiosmotic theory explained on page 236 in connection with mitochondria. There are, in fact, many similarities between what happens in the thylakoids and what happens in mitochondria. However, one *difference* is that, whereas in mitochondria protons are moved outwards, in the thylakoids they are moved inwards.

It is of interest that some herbicides, such as paraquat and diquat, work by interfering with electron transport during photosynthesis.

We now turn to the third stage of photosynthesis, namely the reduction of carbon dioxide to form carbohydrate.

Stage 3 Reduction of carbon dioxide

The events we have been concerned with so far have taken place in the thylakoids. The scene now shifts to the stroma of the chloroplast. Here the NADPH and ATP formed in the previous stages provide the reducing power and the energy for synthesising sugars from carbon dioxide.

The reduction of carbon dioxide and subsequent synthesis of carbohydrate takes place in a series of small steps, each controlled by a specific enzyme. The individual steps were analysed by Melvin Calvin and his associates at the University of California. They did this by illuminating the unicellular green alga *Chlorella* in the presence of carbon dioxide labelled with the radioactive isotope of carbon, ^{14}C (figure 17.27). The algae were allowed to photosynthesise for a certain period of time after being given the labelled carbon dioxide. They were then quickly killed with boiling ethanol which inactivated all their enzymes and stopped the reactions instantaneously. The radioactive compounds which had been formed were then extracted from the organisms and separated by paper chromatography. Autoradiographs were made and the amount of radioactivity in the different compounds was determined. The algae were killed at intervals after initial fixation of the carbon dioxide, from a few seconds to a few minutes. By identifying the intermediates formed after different periods of time and determining the amount of radioactivity in each one, the pathway through which carbon compounds are built up was established.

Figure 17.27

Left Melvin Calvin who discovered how carbohydrates are made in photosythesis. *Right* Calvin's 'lollipop' apparatus. The 'lollipop' refers to the thin transparent vessel containing a suspension of *Chlorella*. Carbon dioxide labelled with radioactive ^{14}C is bubbled through the suspension, and subsequent analysis of the radioactive compounds formed enables the path taken by carbon in photosynthesis to be traced.

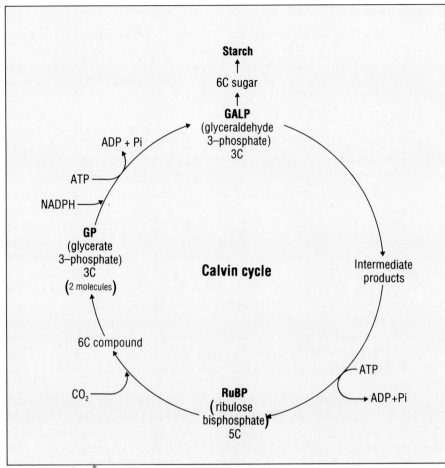

Figure 17.28 The main steps in the Calvin cycle. The details of how the 3-carbon sugar (GALP) leads to the regeneration of ribulose bisphosphate as well as giving the 6-carbon sugar are complicated, but basically what happens is this. Say we have 12 molecules of 3-carbon sugar. Two of these combine with each other to give one molecule of 6-carbon sugar. The remaining 10 molecules of 3-carbon sugar go through a complex series of reactions from which 6 molecules of 5-carbon ribulose bisphosphate eventually emerge. These then react with 6 molecules of carbon dioxide giving a total of 12 molecules of 3-carbon glycerate 3-phosphate which in turn yield 12 molecules of 3-carbon sugar. This brings us back to where we started. Note that no carbon atoms are 'lost' in this process.

From these investigations it emerged that the chain of reactions is cyclical, now known as the **Calvin cycle** (figure 17.28). In the first step the carbon dioxide combines with a 5-carbon organic compound called **ribulose bisphosphate** (abbreviated to **RuBP**). This serves as a carbon dioxide acceptor and fixes the carbon dioxide, i.e. incorporates it into the photosynthetic machinery of the plant. The enzyme needed for this is called **RuBP carboxylase**.

The combination of carbon dioxide with ribulose bisphosphate gives an unstable 6-carbon compound which splits immediately into two molecules of a 3-carbon compound, **glycerate 3-phosphate (GP)**.

The next step is crucial: the GP is reduced to form a 3-carbon sugar, **glyceraldehyde 3-phosphate (GALP)**. The hydrogen for the reduction comes from NADPH which also supplies most of the energy, the rest coming from ATP. The 3-carbon sugar is now built up to a 6-carbon sugar which can be converted into starch for storage.

Not all the 3-carbon sugar is converted into 6-carbon sugar. Some of it (the majority in fact) enters a series of reactions, driven by ATP, which results in the regeneration of ribulose bisphosphate. This is very important because only by ensuring a supply of ribulose bisphosphate can the continued fixation of carbon dioxide take place.

Starch is not the only end product of photosynthesis. This is shown by the fact that in Calvin's experiments radioactive carbon was eventually identified in other compounds, including amino acids. For amino acids to be formed nitrates are required. These are converted to ammonium ions which are used for the formation of glutamine. From this other amino acids are made by transamination (see page 142).

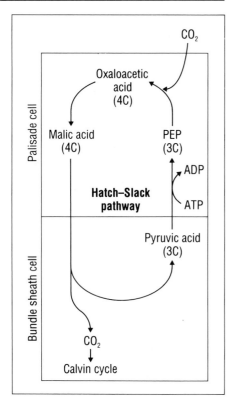

Figure 17.29 Summary of the pathway by which carbon dioxide is fixed in C_4 plants such as maize.

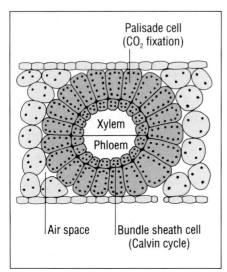

Figure 17.30 Diagrammatic transverse section of part of the leaf of a C_4 plant showing the close relationship between the palisade cells, which here form a circle round the vascular bundle, and the bundle sheath cells. The palisade cells are well placed for absorbing carbon dioxide from the adjacent intercellular air spaces, and the phloem is ideally situated for carrying away the abundant products of photosynthesis.

The C_4 system

We have seen that the substrate for fixation of carbon dioxide is ribulose bisphophate. However, some plants – particularly cane-type plants such as sugar cane and maize – use another compound as the substrate for carbon dioxide fixation in certain of their cells. This compound is known as **phosphoenol pyruvate (PEP)**.

Experiments in which the leaves of such plants are supplied with radioactive $^{14}CO_2$ have shown that the immediate product of carbon dioxide fixation is not 3-carbon GP but the 4-carbon compound oxaloacetic acid. Because of this, such plants are called C_4 **plants** in contrast to those that only produce 3-carbon GP which are known as C_3 plants.

The oxaloacetic acid formed in C_4 plants is subsequently converted into malic acid, from which carbon dioxide is fed into the Calvin cycle to from carbohydrate. Meanwhile, so long as light is available, the PEP can be resynthesised. This series of reactions was unravelled by two Australian scientists, Hal Hatch and Roger Slack, and is called the **Hatch–Slack pathway** (figure 17.29).

What is the point of this? The answer lies in the observation that the carboxylation of PEP is a very rapid reaction. This is because the enzyme **PEP carboxylase**, which catalyses this reaction, has an exceptionally high affinity for carbon dioxide even when the latter is in low concentration. This process therefore provides the plant with a means of building up a store of fixed carbon dioxide which can subsequently be converted into carbohydrate.

Because of its high yield of photosynthetic products, the C_4 system is an important property of crop plants such as maize and sugar cane. It operates particularly efficiently at high temperatures and light intensities. This is because the rapid fixation and storage of carbon dioxide means that carbon dioxide no longer limits the process, as it may in C_3 plants. The C_4 system is therefore specially suitable for tropical plants.

More recent research has shown whereabouts in the leaves of C_4 plants the reactions take place. The initial fixing of the carbon dioxide by PEP is carried out in the palisade cells, which in C_4 plants are arranged round the vascular bundles as shown in figure 17.30. The malic acid then passes into the bundle sheath cells next door. The bundle sheath cells of C_4 plants are unusual because they contain chloroplasts, and it is here that the carbon dioxide is released from malic acid and fed into the Calvin cycle. Meanwhile the pyruvic acid resulting from the decarboxylation of malic acid passes back into the palisade cells where it is reconverted into PEP.

CAM plants

The C_4 pathway is not confined to cane-type plants in the tropics. It also occurs in certain plants that live in arid environments such as the desert. These plants run the risk of severe water loss resulting from evaporation through their open stomata. However, certain species get round this problem by opening the stomata at night and closing them by day. As a means of preventing excessive water loss this would seem an admirable idea, but what happens about photosynthesis? Such plants take up carbon dioxide at night when the stomata are open and fix it into malic acid. When daybreak comes the stomata close and the carbon dioxide is released for photosynthesis. This ingenious 'trick' was first discovered in the Crassulaceae, a family of succulents which include a number of desert species. For this reason it is called **crassulacean acid metabolism**, and plants which can do it are known as **CAM plants**.

It is important to appreciate the difference between CAM plants and other C_4 plants. In CAM plants the initial fixation of carbon dioxide by PEP and the conventional Calvin cycle are separated in *time*. The stomata are generally closed during the day so there is little water loss, and the carbon dioxide is fixed during the night when the stomata are open. In C_4 plants like sugar cane and maize the fixation of carbon dioxide and the Calvin cycle take place in different parts of the leaf – they are separated in *space*. The initial fixing of the carbon dioxide by PEP is carried out in the palisade cells whereas the Calvin cycle occurs in the bundle sheath cells.

Autotrophic bacteria

Autotrophic bacteria are divided into two groups: **photosynthetic** and **chemosynthetic**. Both can build up organic compounds from simple inorganic raw materials. They differ in the way they obtain the necessary energy. Let us look at each in turn.

Photosynthetic bacteria

Like green plants, these bacteria are able to build up carbon dioxide and water into organic compounds using energy from sunlight. The energy is trapped by a pigment called **bacteriochlorophyll** which is similar to, though somewhat simpler than, chlorophyll. They differ from green plants in their source of hydrogen for reducing the carbon dioxide. Instead of obtaining it from water they get it from hydrogen sulphide, for which reason they are known as **sulphur bacteria**.

Sulphur bacteria live at the bottom of lakes, ponds and rock pools where hydrogen sulphide is supplied by the metabolism of anaerobic decay bacteria. The residual sulphur resulting from the splitting of hydrogen sulphide is deposited in the bacterial cells.

$$CO_2 + 2H_2S \xrightarrow[\text{Bacteriochlorophyll}]{\text{Light}} CH_2O + 2S + H_2O$$

This process is essentially the same as plant photosynthesis except that hydrogen sulphide, rather than water, provides the hydrogen for reducing the carbon dioxide.

Bacteriochlorophyll comes in two closely related forms, green and purple, giving the so-called **green** and **purple sulphur bacteria** respectively. The absorption spectrum of the purple form is included in figure 17.12, from which it will be seen that it absorbs light of wavelengths on either side of those absorbed by chlorophyll and related pigments. This enables sulphur bacteria to survive underneath green seaweeds in rock pools on the seashore. Much of the light that can be used by the bacteria passes straight through the algae and is then absorbed by the bacteria.

Chemosynthetic bacteria

The chemosynthetic bacteria can also synthesise organic from inorganic materials but instead of using sunlight they obtain the necessary energy from special chemical processes which generally involve the oxidation of compounds other than sugar. Thus **iron bacteria**, living in streams that run over iron-containing rocks, oxidise divalent iron salts. The **colourless sulphur bacteria** (not to be confused with green and purple bacteria discussed in the last section) live in decaying organic matter and oxidise hydrogen sulphide to water and sulphur. There are even **hydrogen bacteria** which can oxidise hydrogen with the formation of water.

Photorespiration

We have seen that C_4 plants are particularly efficient at fixing carbon dioxide. C_3 plants are less efficient, at least at high temperatures and light intensities. Why is this? The answer is partly because of a process called **photorespiration**.

In photorespiration oxygen competes with carbon dioxide for the enzyme RuBP carboxylase. Instead of combining with the carbon in carbon dioxide and forming two molecules of GP, the ribulose bisphosphate splits into one molecule of GP and a 2-carbon compound called glycollate which is broken down into carbon dioxide again. This is an oxidative process similar to respiration, but no ATP is formed from it and so from the energy point of view it is useless and wasteful.

The net effect of photorespiration is that atmospheric oxygen depresses the rate of photosynthesis in C_3 plants. Photorespiration also occurs in C_4 plants but its effect is not noticeable because the rapid fixing of carbon dioxide by PEP has the effect of building up a very high concentration of carbon dioxide in the bundle sheath cells. With such an advantage it is not surprising that C_4 plants grow so well in conditions of high temperatures and light intensity.

Ecologically, the different mechanisms have their advantages and disadvantages. CAM plants grow slowly but compete well with C_3 and other C_4 plants in arid conditions because they are able to conserve water. C_4 plants are more productive than C_3 plants at high temperatures, but at lower temperatures C_4 plants lose out to C_3 species presumably because the activity of their enzymes is depressed by photorespiration.

A particularly important group of chemosynthetic organisms are the **nitrifying bacteria** found in the soil. Through their metabolic activities they enrich the soil in available nitrogen, i.e. nitrogen in a form obtainable by plants. Some of these bacteria, specifically *Nitrosomonas* and *Nitrococcus*, obtain energy by oxidising ammonia (formed by the breakdown of animal and plant proteins during decay) to nitrite. The conversion involves several steps. As soon as it is liberated into the soil, the ammonia combines with carbon dioxide to form ammonium carbonate. This is then converted to nitrous acid under the influence of the bacteria.

$$(NH_4)_2CO_3 + 3O_2 \rightarrow 2HNO_2 + CO_2 + 3H_2O + \text{Energy}$$

The nitrous acid immediately combines with, for example, calcium or magnesium salts to form the appropriate nitrite.

Another nitrifying bacterium, *Nitrobacter*, oxidises nitrites to nitrates:

$$Ca(NO_2)_2 + O_2 \rightarrow Ca(NO_3)_2 + \text{Energy}$$

In all these cases the energy released is used for the synthesis of organic compounds.

These nitrifying bacteria do not exist in isolation but form part of a natural system in which nitrogen compounds are converted from one form to another step by step. Thus the ammonia released from the dead bodies and faeces of animals and plants by the activities of saprobiontic bacteria and fungi is converted by *Nitrosomonas* and *Nitrococcus* into nitrites. *Nitrobacter* then converts the nitrites into nitrates which are subsequently absorbed by plants.

The full sequence of conversions constitutes the **nitrogen cycle** summarised in figure 17.31. It shows how nitrogen compounds circulate in nature and demonstrates the interdependence of animals, plants and bacteria.

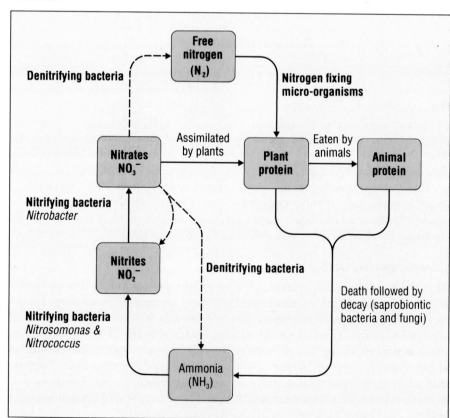

Figure 17.31 Scheme summarising the cycling of nitrogen in nature. The broken arrows signify denitrification. Explanation in text.

Denitrification

Looking at figure 17.31, you will notice that certain bacteria convert nitrates, the main form of nitrogen which is directly available to plants, into nitrites, ammonia or even nitrogen. Although many plants can absorb ammonium compounds, nitrites and nitrogen cannot be used – in fact nitrites are toxic to most plants. As these bacteria deprive the soil of available nitrogen compounds they are known as **denitrifying bacteria.**

Why do denitrifying bacteria deprive the soil of nitrates? The reason why they do this is that they tend to live in conditions of oxygen shortage, and they use oxygen from nitrate (NO_3^-) as the final acceptor in the hydrogen carrier system (see page 234). This yields ATP whose subsequent hydrolysis releases energy for the synthesis of organic compounds.

The significance of the nitrogen cycle in the environment is discussed in more detail in Chapter 3 where you will also find a more detailed diagram of the cycle (see page 33).

Fixation of nitrogen

Certain prokaryotes are able to absorb atmospheric nitrogen and build it up into amino acids, a synthetic feat that commands our admiration. How they fit into the nitrogen cycle is shown in figure 17.31

The best known **nitrogen-fixing organisms** are bacteria that live in the roots of leguminous plants such as peas, beans and clover. It has long been known that such plants are able to thrive in soils deficient in nitrates, and we now know that they owe this ability to the nitrogen-fixing bacteria in their roots.

The bacteria enter the young plant through its root hairs, and they cause the cortical cells of the root to proliferate, forming a swelling called a **root nodule** (figure 17.32). A vascular strand connects the nodule with the vascular tissues in the main root. In the cells of the nodule the bacteria multiply rapidly, fixing atmospheric nitrogen which is then built up into amino acids and proteins.

The importance of nitrogen fixation

It has been shown that the association between the bacteria and their host is mutually beneficial, both partners gaining from the relationship. Some of the products of the bacteria's nitrogen fixation pass into the host plant and are utilised by it. This has been confirmed by supplying an infected plant with the heavy isotope of nitrogen, ^{15}N. Eventually the ^{15}N gets into the whole of the plant, not just the part containing the bacteria. The beneficial effect of the bacteria on the host is clearly illustrated in figure 17.33.

What do the bacteria gain from the host apart from protection? From the host's photosynthesis they obtain carbohydrates. The latter provide a source of carbon for the synthesis of protein as well as energy for driving the endergonic reactions involved. An association of this sort, in which both partners benefit, is called **mutualism** and is discussed in detail in Chapter 36. However, not all nitrogen-fixers live inside the tissues of other organisms. Many free-living examples are also known.

If nitrogen fixation could be carried out in other crop plants such as wheat and maize it would reduce the need for applying expensive fertilisers to crops as well as increasing the production of plant protein. Plant breeders and genetic engineers are working together to try to achieve this (see page 744).

Figure 17.32 Nodules in the root system of a three-month old tree. The seeds were inoculated with an effective strain of nitrogen-fixing bacteria.

Figure 17.33 The beneficial effects of nitrogen-fixing bacteria can be seen by comparing these two clover plants. The seed from which the right-hand plant was grown was inoculated with an effective strain of nitrogen-fixing bacteria, whereas the one on the left received no such treatment. Both plants were planted at the same time and maintained under the same conditions.

Summary

1 Autotrophic nutrition, the synthesis of organic compounds from inorganic sources, takes place by **photosynthesis** and **chemosynthesis** both of which play an important part in the **carbon cycle**.

2 The raw materials of photosynthesis are carbon dioxide and water; the major products are carbohydrate and oxygen. Sunlight is the source of energy which is trapped by **chlorophyll**.

3 The external conditions required for photosynthesis are carbon dioxide, water, light and a suitable temperature.

4 Photosynthesis is subject to the **law of limiting factors**, i.e. its rate is limited by that factor which is nearest its minimum value.

5 When photosynthesis and respiration proceed at the same rate so that there is no net loss or gain of carbohydrate, the plant is said to be at its **compensation point**.

6 The photosynthetic pigments in a green leaf are **chlorophyll *a*** and **chlorophyll *b*** plus the accessory pigments **xanthophyll** and **carotene**. The function of the accessory pigments is to increase the range of wavelengths from which energy can be harvested.

7 The **absorption spectrum** of chlorophyll indicates that red and blue light are absorbed most, and the **action spectrum** for photosynthesis shows that these are the most effective wavelengths in photosynthesis.

8 Photosynthesis occurs in the **chloroplasts**. Inside the chloroplasts chlorophyll is located on pairs of parallel membranes called **thylakoids**.

9 The chloroplasts are mainly in the **leaves** whose anatomy shows a close relationship between structure and function.

10 Photosynthesis is a three-stage process, the first of which involves the **harvesting of light** energy by specialised pigments such as chlorophyll.

11 In the second stage, electrons are transferred through electron carriers as a result of which ATP and reduced NADP (i.e. NADPH) are formed.

12 In the third stage, carbon dioxide is reduced to form sugars in the **Calvin cycle**. Hydrogen for the reduction, and energy to drive the process, come from the second stage.

13 C_3 **plants** fix carbon dioxide into a 3-carbon compound (glycerate 3-phosphate). C_4 **plants** fix carbon dioxide into a 4-carbon compound (oxaloacetic acid) which is then converted to malic acid.

14 Some C_4 plants living in arid conditions take up carbon dioxide at night and fix it into malic acid. During the day the stomata close and the carbon dioxide is released for photosynthesis. These are known as **CAM plants**. (CAM stands for crassulacean acid metabolism.)

15 In C_3 plants the substrate for carbon dioxide fixation (ribulose bisphosphate) sometimes combines with oxygen instead of carbon dioxide resulting in **photorespiration**.

16 In chemosynthesis organic compounds are synthesised from inorganic raw materials, the necessary energy coming from the oxidation of e.g. iron salts, nitrates and nitrites.

17 Chemosynthetic bacteria are important in the **nitrogen cycle** which involves nitrifying, dentrifying and nitrogen-fixing bacteria.

Review questions

1 Briefly explain the difference between autotrophic and heterotrophic nutrition.

2 Summarise the importance of photosynthesis to humans.

3 What are the ideal conditions for photosynthesis? Choose *one* condition and describe how you would show that it is needed for photosynthesis.

4 Explain the law of limiting factors as applied to photosynthesis.

5 The atmosphere of glasshouses in which commercial crops are grown is often enriched with carbon dioxide. Why is this a good idea, and what should be borne in mind when carrying it out?

6 Explain how the external and internal structure of leaves and the structure of chloroplasts are adapted for photosynthesis.

7 If a photosynthesising plant was exposed to radioactively labelled carbon dioxide (^{14}C) in which order would the labelled carbon appear in the following compounds: (a) GALP (b) GP (c) pyruvate? Explain your answer.

8 How many molecules of carbon dioxide must enter the Calvin cycle to produce one sugar molecule?

9 What are the differences in the way C_3 and C_4 plants fix carbon dioxide? Outline the advantages of the C_4 system.

10 Why is it not surprising that sugar cane is a tropical crop whereas wheat is a temperate one?

Further reading

If you want to find out more about photosynthesis a useful account in little more than 100 pages is provided by D.O. Hall and K.K Rao in *Photosynthesis* (Cambridge University Press, 1992.)

In *Biology, Advanced Topics* there is an account of chemiosmosis in chloroplasts and mitochondria, the synthesis of amino acids and nitrogen fixation.

The principles of transport

In the previous three chapters we have seen that gases are exchanged between organisms and the environment, that soluble food substances are absorbed through the gut wall of animals and that plants require water and mineral salts as well as carbon dioxide in order to manufacture food. Waste products are also produced as a result of metabolic processes.

It follows that the raw materials for processes like respiration and photosynthesis must be transported to the cells which need them, and that waste products must be carried away. Soluble food absorbed by the gut wall of animals must be transported around the body, and the products of photosynthesis must be taken to all parts of the plant. So there is a need for the distribution of raw materials and useful products and for the removal of waste substances in all organisms. Although small organisms do not need a special system for this to take place, all larger ones have special **transport systems**.

Transport inside plants and animals

In small organisms all transport needs can be met by **diffusion**, a purely physical process which is discussed in detail in Chapter 12. Another way in which particles can move is by **active transport** which is also described in Chapter 12. This enables substances to move against a concentration gradient and of course it requires energy from respiration.

Although diffusion provides a means by which substances can be transported, it can only meet the requirements of small organisms. All larger organisms have some kind of transport system involving **mass flow**. Mass flow occurs when all the particles in a liquid or gaseous medium move in the same direction at the same speed.

Transport in animals

One of the simplest mass flow transport systems is seen in aquatic animals which use the surrounding water as the medium. This is the case in sponges and jellyfish (figure 18.1). However, in most animals the mass flow system has become enclosed in tubes or vessels which have no connection with the exterior and contain their own distinctive fluid. In such systems the fluid usually circulates round the body and is known as the **circulatory system**.

Most circulatory systems have the following features:

- A transport medium, usually called **blood**, capable of carrying dissolved materials such as food, oxygen and carbon dioxide.
- **Vessels** to carry the medium to all parts of the body.
- Some kind of **pump**, to propel the medium in the vessels.
- One-way **valves** to keep the medium flowing in one direction.
- A close association between the tissues and the medium so that the cells can obtain the required substances from the medium and deliver their waste products to it.

First, let us look at the transport medium. A few animals have a type of blood which is more or less like sea water. One of the substances to be transported is oxygen. Now, 100 cm³ of sea water can carry about 0.5 cm³ of oxygen, which is not very much, and such animals are therefore sedentary or slow-moving. Animals which are more active usually have a **pigment** in their blood, the function of which is to increase its oxygen-carrying capacity. In most species the pigment is contained in special **blood**

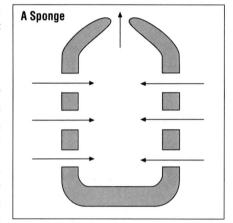

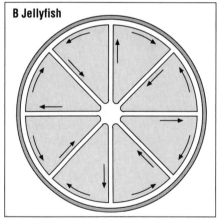

Figure 18.1 Schematic representations of two simple transport systems found in animals.
A In a sponge the body is perforated by many pores. A current of sea water is drawn in through the pores by the concerted action of numerous flagellated cells. The cells collect food particles from the water which then leaves through a hole at the top.
B In a jellyfish a series of canals link the gut cavity to a peripheral circular canal. Cilia lining the canals cause the fluid to circulate, distributing digested food to all parts of the body.

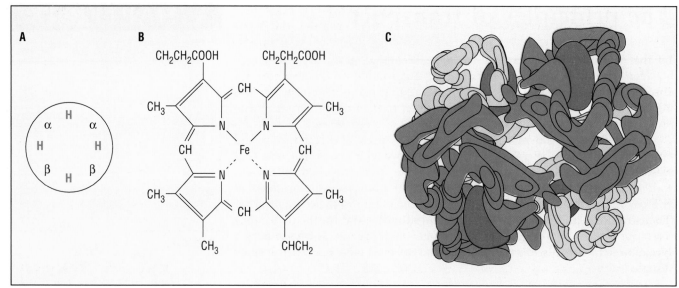

Figure 18.2 The chemical nature of haemoglobin.

A A simple representation of adult human haemoglobin. The Hs stand for four haem groups each of which contains an iron atom, and the α and β stand for two types of polypeptide chain. Each chain is associated with one of the four haem groups.

B The structure of haem, the prosthetic group of haemoglobin. Haem, a porphyrin, is the part of the haemoglobin molecule that combines with oxygen. Note that the iron at the centre of the haem is in the divalent (iron (II)) state. It remains in this state while oxygen is being transported.

C A model of the haemoglobin molecule as deduced from X-ray diffraction studies. In this model the α globin chains are brown and the β chains are grey. The haem groups are represented by the red discs.

cells but in some species it is free in the fluid part of the blood – the **plasma**.

Haemoglobins are the most common oxygen-carrying pigments. They are made up of two parts: a **prosthetic group** and a **protein**. The protein part consists of four polypeptide chains known as **globin**, each associated with a complex iron-containing prosthetic group called **haem** (figure 18.2). It is with the haem group that the association with oxygen takes place.

Haemoglobins are found in all vertebrates and some invertebrates, and each species has its own distinct form. There are several other groups of pigments and they differ from each other mainly in the nature of the prosthetic group. **Chlorocruorin** and **haemoerythrin** both contain iron, and **haemocyanin** contains copper. These three pigments are confined to invertebrate groups, particularly annelids and molluscs. Blood pigments are compared in table 18.1.

From table 18.1 you can see that the pigments differ in their oxygen-carrying capacities and that in some cases they are dissolved in the plasma rather than contained inside cells. We shall discuss the carriage of gases by the blood in Chapter 19.

Other materials are also transported in the blood. For example, soluble food materials, waste products and hormones are all conveyed from one place to another in the plasma. Cells are constantly shedding things into the blood which flows past them, and removing things from it. Blood provides the medium through which this continual exchange takes place.

If the transport medium is to be efficient at moving substances around

	Haemoglobin	Chlorocruorin	Haemocyanin	Haemoerythrin
Colour of pigment	red	green	blue	red
Metal in prosthetic group	iron	iron	copper	iron
Molecule of oxygen carried per atom of metal	1:1	1:1	1:2	1:3
Location in blood	cells or plasma	plasma	plasma	cells or plasma

Table 18.1 A comparison of some of the features of oxygen-carrying pigments.

the body, some kind of pump is required. Certain animals, nematodes for example, depend on contractions of the body wall to move the blood around. However, such contractions will not keep the blood moving in a particular direction, so this is not very efficient.

If, however, the blood is enclosed in a tubular vessel, contraction of the muscle in the wall of that vessel may produce a directional flow which is what is needed if the blood is to circulate. In annelids such as the earthworm, the dorsal vessel contracts: waves of contraction pass from the posterior end of the vessel towards the anterior end, sweeping the blood forward. However, in most animals above a certain size there is a specialised pumping device – the **heart**.

Open and closed circulations

There are two kinds of circulatory systems in animals: **open** and **closed**. They both allow the transported materials to be exchanged between the blood and the cells, but there is a different relationship between the blood and the surrounding tissue in each case (figure 18.3).

In open systems the blood circulates in large open spaces. The cells are in contact with the blood and materials are exchanged by direct diffusion through the plasma membranes. Arthropods and most molluscs have this kind of circulatory system. In insects, for example, the body cavity is filled with blood, and is called a **haemocoel**. Here the blood seeps around amongst the organs which are literally bathed in blood.

In closed systems the blood is entirely enclosed within tubular vessels. Gaseous exchange occurs across the wall of **blood capillaries** which ramify through the organs and come into close association with all the cells. This sort of system is typical of vertebrates, including humans, and of annelids and cephalopod molluscs.

The haemoglobin molecule as a carrier

Research by Max Perutz at Cambridge helps us to understand haemoglobin's affinity for oxygen. When one of the four polypeptide chains in the haemoglobin molecule receives an oxygen molecule in the lungs its structure is altered in such a way that the remaining three polypeptide chains accept oxygen more readily. In the tissues the reverse occurs: one of the polypeptide chains loses its oxygen molecule and this causes the others to give up their oxygen more readily. In other words haemoglobin takes up oxygen more rapidly if it already possesses one or more oxygen molecules, and conversely it releases oxygen more rapidly if it has already released one or more oxygen molecules.

The chemical explanation of this depends on the fact that each of the four polypeptide chains is associated with an iron-containing haem group (figure 18.2). It is thought that when an oxygen molecule joins on to the iron atom in the first haem group, the position of the polypeptide chains is altered slightly. This has the effect of exposing the iron atoms of the remaining haem groups to oxygen molecules, which are then readily taken up. Thus, although the oxygen is actually carried by the haem, its ability to do so is influenced by the associated polypeptide chains.

It is thought that hydrogen ions, derived from the carriage of carbon dioxide, lower haemoglobin's affinity for oxygen by binding to the polypeptide chains, thereby influencing the haem groups and reducing their tendency to take up oxygen.

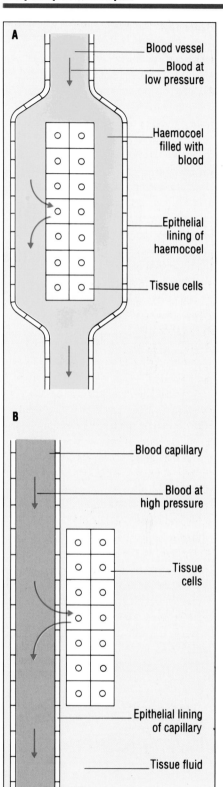

Figure 18.3

A An open circulation. **B** A closed circulation. Notice the close relationship between the blood and the tissue cells. The green arrows signify exchanges between the tissue cells and the blood.

The principles of transport

Figure 18.4 The insect heart and how it works. The heart is essentially a tube, subdivided into a series of chambers each of which has a valved opening on either side. **A** During diastole, the pericardial muscles pull the walls of the heart chambers outwards, causing blood to be sucked in through the open valves. During systole, the heart wall contracts in a wave which starts at the rear and works its way forward. As a result the valves close and the blood is swept forward. **B** In this transverse section of the thorax notice that the heart is situated towards the dorsal side of the body and is attached to the cuticle and pericardial membrane by ligaments. The disposition of the ligaments is such that when the pericardial muscle contracts it pulls the heart wall outwards as illustrated in the previous diagram. In all the diagrams the arrows show the direction in which the blood flows.

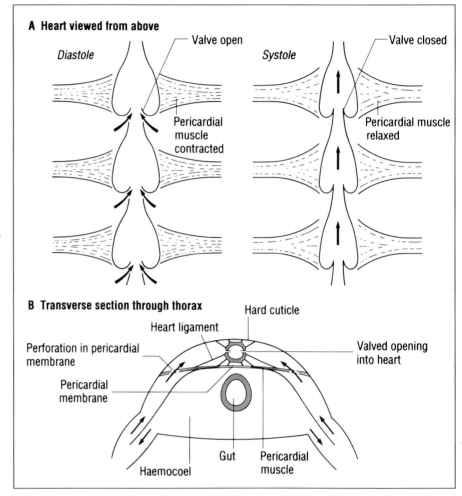

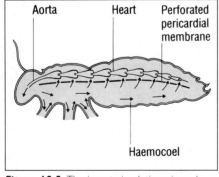

Figure 18.5 The insect circulation viewed from the side. Blood flows forward in the tubular heart whence it enters the haemocoel and circulates amongst the tissues and organs, as indicated by the arrows. It then returns to the heart via the valved openings.

Figures 18.4 and 18.5 show the open circulation of an insect. A dorsally situated heart pumps blood into the haemocoel in which the organs lie. The heart contains valves which ensure that blood enters the heart when it relaxes and leaves it when it contracts. Because the blood is in large spaces and the heart is only weakly muscular, the blood pressure can never be very high. This limits the efficiency of the open system. Open blood systems are therefore not found in large animals.

In Chapter 15 we saw how gaseous exchange in insects takes place through the tracheal system. The insect circulatory system is not therefore concerned with transporting oxygen and carbon dioxide. Accordingly, it lacks an oxygen-carrying pigment. However, it does play an important part in distributing food substances and eliminating nitrogenous waste matter.

In animals with a closed system the heart is more muscular and higher blood pressures can be developed, which makes closed systems much more efficient than open ones. Animals with closed systems are generally larger, and often more active, than those with open systems. We shall look in detail at the closed system of the mammal in Chapter 19.

A disadvantage of a closed circulatory system is that the blood is in vessels and their walls form a barrier between the blood and the surrounding tissue cells. Oxygen and other substances have to cross this barrier. This happens in the tissues where substances diffuse through the thin walls of narrow **blood capillaries** into the surrounding tissue fluid and thence into the cells. At the same time, waste products diffuse from the cells into the tissue fluid and so to the blood capillaries.

From this you can see that simple diffusion is the main way of getting substances into and out of the cells even in animals with closed circulatory systems. The circulation simply moves the transport medium (blood) as near to the tissue cells as possible. So diffusion, which is the only method of transport in small organisms, is also important in large animals even though they have a transport system to move materials over long distances.

Single and double circulations

Animals with closed circulations have two fundamentally different systems which are illustrated in figure 18.6. The simpler of the two is seen in fishes.

In fishes deoxygenated blood is pumped by the heart to the gills, whence it flows to various parts of the body and then returns to the heart. The blood flows only once through the heart for every complete circuit of the body; this is called a **single circulation** (figure 18.6A).

The problem with this arrangement is that blood has to pass through two capillary systems, the capillaries of the gills and then those of the body, before returning to the heart. Capillaries offer considerable resistance to the flow of blood, and this means that in fishes there is a marked drop in blood pressure before the blood completes a circuit. For this reason the blood flow tends to be sluggish as the venous blood returns from the tissues to the heart. This is overcome to some extent by the fact that fishes have large **sinuses**, which offer minimum resistance to blood flow, in place of veins. Nevertheless the problem of getting blood back to the heart is an acute one and probably imposes severe limitations on the activities of many species of fish.

In mammals this problem has been overcome by the development of a **double circulation** in which the blood flows twice through the heart for every complete circuit of the body (figure 18.6B). Blood is pumped to the lungs at a much lower pressure than that at which it is pumped to the rest of the body. In humans the pressure in the pulmonary artery is about one-sixth of that in the aorta.

Returning to fishes, sharks seem to be able to swim very fast in spite of the fact that the amount of oxygen which can be delivered to the tissues is limited by the relatively low blood pressure – less than 2 kPa in the dorsal

Figure 18.6 The arrangement of the heart and blood vessels

A in the single circulation of a fish,

B in the double circulation of a mammal. The arrows indicate the direction of the blood flow. Oxygenated blood, light grey; deoxygenated blood, dark grey.

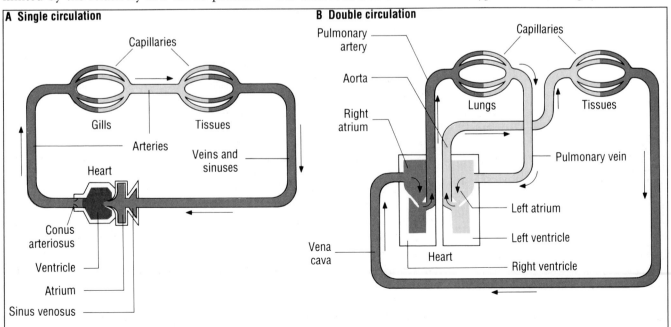

A Single circulation

Capillaries

Gills

Tissues

Arteries

Veins and sinuses

Heart

Conus arteriosus

Ventricle

Atrium

Sinus venosus

B Double circulation

Pulmonary artery

Capillaries

Aorta

Lungs

Tissues

Right atrium

Pulmonary vein

Left atrium

Left ventricle

Vena cava

Heart

Right ventricle

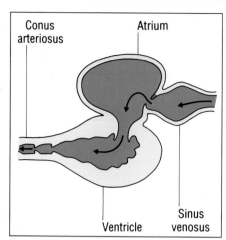

Figure 18.7 The two-chambered heart of a fish viewed from the side. The blue tint represents deoxygenated blood.

aorta. The explanation lies partly in the fact that fish are ectotherms and their metabolic rate is sufficiently low for the limited oxygen supply to satisfy their needs.

A higher metabolic rate demands a higher oxygen supply and this is only possible if the pressure in the vessels carrying the oxygenated blood to the tissues is also higher. Birds and mammals, being endotherms, have a higher metabolic rate than fishes. An increased oxygen supply could in theory be achieved by having a higher pressure in a single circulation, but in animals with lungs the necessary pressure would be so high that it would drive fluid through the capillaries of the lungs causing them to become waterlogged.

Separation of oxygenated and deoxygenated blood

In the single circulation of a fish only deoxygenated blood flows through the heart. The heart has two main chambers, the **atrium** and the **ventricle**, the ventricle being more muscular than the atrium. It is an S-shaped structure and there is a chamber before the atrium called the **sinus venosus** from which the heart beat originates (figure 18.7).

In mammals, with a double circulation, the heart is divided into right and left sides with two atria and two ventricles. This division of the heart prevents the oxygenated blood on the left side from mixing with the deoxygenated blood on the right side. The structure of the mammalian heart is dealt with in detail in the next chapter so there is no need to elaborate on it further here except to emphasise that oxygenated and deoxygenated blood are kept completely separate.

The frog shows an interesting intermediate condition (figure 18.8). It has a double circulation in that blood is returned to the heart from the lungs before being pumped to the rest of the body, and the atrium is divided into right and left sides which receive deoxygenated and oxygenated blood respectively. However the ventricle is completely undivided! So it would seem that deoxygenated and oxygenated blood would become mixed in the single ventricle. There is, however, far less mixing of the blood than one

Figure 18.8 The heart of a frog showing the two atria and single ventricle, viewed from the ventral side. The broken lines outline the sinus venosus on the other side of the heart. The sinus venosus opens into the right atrium via the sino-atrial opening. The two atria open into the single ventricle from which blood is pumped into the arteries. Oxygenated blood, red; deoxygenated blood, blue; mixed oxygenated and deoxygenated blood, purple. The extent to which oxygenated and deoxygenated blood get mixed in the ventricle is discussed in the text.

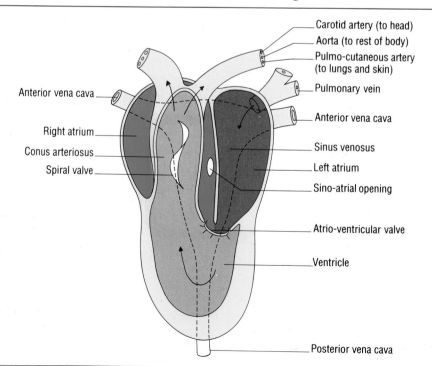

would expect, and separation of the two bloodstreams is surprisingly complete. Largely deoxygenated blood is sent to the lungs while the most highly oxygenated blood is delivered to the head and brain. The rest of the body gets blood which is quite well oxygenated.

Over the years there has been much speculation and contention about how this separation of the blood is achieved. From the ventricle the blood is pumped into a chamber called the **conus arteriosus** before it enters the three major arteries carrying blood to the lungs, the head and the rest of the body. The conus arteriosus contains a **spiral valve**, an S-shaped flap of tissue attached to its wall. It is possible that various folds in the ventricle wall together with the spiral valve in the conus control which of the three major arteries the blood enters as it leaves the heart.

The general principle illustrated here is that if a double circulation is to be developed, it must be coupled with some kind of mechanism for keeping the deoxygenated and oxygenated bloodstreams apart. The mammalian heart, being divided into completely separate right and left sides, achieves this admirably. It is really two pumps joined together which work simultaneously and send out blood at different pressures to different places.

Having a double circulation is only one way of overcoming the pressure problem. An alternative solution would be to have two separate hearts, one for pumping blood to the body, the other for pumping blood to the gaseous-exchange surface. This is precisely what happens in squids and octopuses. Blood is pumped from the **main heart** to various parts of the body. It then flows through a system of sinuses to a pair of **branchial hearts** which pump it to the gills (figure 18.9).

Octopuses are on a quite different evolutionary line from vertebrates. But like vertebrates they are active creatures. Comparing their circulations shows us how the same physiological problem can be solved in two quite different ways.

Transport in plants

Vascular plants have two distinct transport systems both of which consist of tubes. One system is concerned with the movement of **water** and **mineral salts** which are obtained from the soil. The other system is concerned with transporting **sugars** and other soluble products of photosynthesis, from the leaves where they are made to other parts of the plant.

Plants are relatively inactive and their metabolic needs are such that they do not need the dynamic type of transport system characteristic of animals. However, the distances over which substances need to be moved in the tallest plants are far greater than in animals – think of the size of a redwood tree for example – and as plants have no pump, like the heart, the question we have to ask is: how are the contents of their transport system moved?

We shall look at the detailed structure and functioning of the transport system of plants in Chapter 20. It is sufficient here to note that the system of tubes in which water and mineral salts are transported is the **xylem**, while the system of tubes conducting dissolved food substances is the **phloem**.

The fascinating thing is that the two systems employ quite different principles. Xylem transport is essentially a passive process, depending mainly on water potential gradients within the plant. Indeed, the xylem tissue in which it takes place is composed of dead cells. Phloem transport, on the other hand, is an active energy-requiring process which takes place in living tissue.

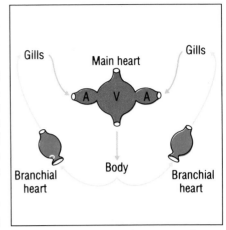

Figure 18.9 The octopus has separate hearts serving the gills and body. **A**, atrium; **V**, ventricle. Oxygenated blood, red; deoxygenated blood, blue.

Do plants have a circulatory system?

The xylem transports water and mineral salts from the roots to the leaves, and the phloem transports sugars and other products of photosynthesis from the leaves to the roots. These photosynthetic products are in solution, the water having come from the xylem. At the root end of the system sugars are removed by the cells for use in metabolic processes, and water flows out by osmosis into the intercellular spaces.

Some of the water which flows out in the roots is taken up into the xylem, and is transported up to the leaves again where it may be used in photosynthesis, lost by evaporation through the stomata or drawn into the phloem whence it may return to the roots again. So although there are two distinct transport systems, xylem and phloem, it is possible for water to be transported between leaves and roots in a closed loop, travelling up in the xylem and down in the phloem. Plants, therefore, may be said to have a circulatory system.

Summary

1 There is a need for the distribution of raw materials and the removal of metabolic waste in all organisms.

2 In small organisms the transport of materials takes place by **diffusion** or **active transport**. However, larger organisms generally require special **transport systems**.

3 Transport systems usually involve **mass flow**, which is the movement of particles in a gaseous or liquid medium in the same direction and at the same speed.

4 Animals possess a range of transport systems from water-filled canals to blood-filled **circulatory systems**.

5 Essential features of most circulatory systems include a transport medium (**blood**), **vessels** to carry the medium, a **pump** to propel the medium, a system of **valves** for keeping the medium flowing in one direction, and a close association between the medium and the tissue cells.

6 In many animals the oxygen-carrying capacity of the blood is increased by the presence of a **pigment**. Haemoglobin is the most common pigment but there are others. The pigments may be in the plasma or in **blood cells**.

7 There are two kinds of circulatory systems in animals, **open** and **closed**. Open systems are typical of arthropods and molluscs, closed systems are typical of vertebrates.

8 In open systems the organs are surrounded by the blood in a **haemocoel**. In closed systems the blood is enclosed within vessels which separate it from the tissues; exchange of materials takes place via **tissue fluid**.

9 A circulation in which blood flows only once through the heart for every complete circuit of the body is called a **single circulation**. A **double circulation** is one in which the blood flows through the heart twice for every complete circuit of the body.

10 Fishes have a single circulation with an undivided heart. A double circulation requires that oxygenated and deoxygenated blood is kept separate, so in mammals the heart is completely divided into right and left sides. Amphibians are intermediate, having a double circulation with a partially divided heart.

11 Plants have two transport systems, both consisting of tubes: the **xylem** transports water and mineral salts, and the **phloem** transports the products of photosynthesis.

12 Xylem and phloem transport involve quite different principles: xylem transport is essentially passive whereas phloem transport is active.

13 Because of the closed system that seems to exist between the xylem and phloem, plants may be said to have a circulatory system.

Review questions

1 What are the main features of a circulatory system in animals?

2 How can the oxygen-carrying capacity of blood be increased?

3 What are the fundamental differences between an open and a closed circulatory system?

4 With reference to insects, explain how blood is kept moving in an open circulation.

5 What is a single circulation and what are its disadvantages?

6 Why must a double circulation require a mechanism for keeping oxygenated and deoxygenated blood separate?

7 The movement of water and dissolved food substances in plants is based on different principles. What are they?

8 What is the argument for claiming that plants have a circulatory system? Do you consider that the argument is valid?

9 In what respects is the transport of substances in plants (a) easier and (b) more difficult than in animals?

10 To what extent are the activities of an animal limited by its circulatory system?

Transport in the mammal

In the previous chapter the need for a transport system was considered, together with some of the general features of transport systems in animals and plants. In this chapter we shall be mainly concerned with transport in the mammal, considering first the composition and functions of blood and then the structure of the circulatory system and the mechanism by which blood is conveyed through it.

Blood

Blood is a specialised tissue consisting of several types of cell suspended in a fluid medium called **plasma** (figure 19.1). The cellular constituents consist of:

- **Red blood cells** (**erythrocytes**), which carry oxygen.
- **White blood cells** (**leucocytes**), which have an important role in the immune system (see Chapter 24).
- **Blood platelets**, cell fragments involved in blood-clotting (see page 321).

So blood has a varied structure and performs a wide range of functions. As far as transport is concerned, its two important components are the red blood cells and plasma.

Plasma

Plasma is mainly water containing a variety of dissolved substances which are transported from one part of the body to another. Thus food materials (such as glucose and amino acids) are conveyed from the small intestine to the liver, urea from the liver to the kidneys, hormones from various endocrine glands to their target organs, and so on. Cells are constantly shedding substances into the blood which flows past them, and removing other substances from it. Plasma provides the medium through which this continued exchange takes place.

Figure 19.1 Chart summarising the constituents of mammalian blood. The two components responsible for transport are the red blood cells and the plasma. The white blood cells are responsible for defence against disease and are considered in Chapter 24. The red cells are manufactured in the red bone marrow in the centre of certain bones, from which they pass into the general circulation. The numbers of the different types of cells in the blood are approximate.

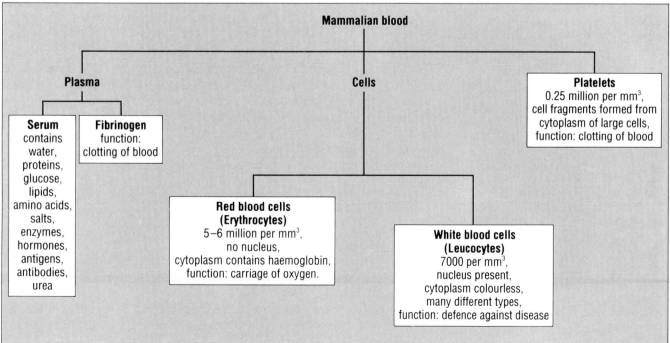

Mammalian blood

Plasma

Serum
contains water, proteins, glucose, lipids, amino acids, salts, enzymes, hormones, antigens, antibodies, urea

Fibrinogen
function: clotting of blood

Cells

Red blood cells (Erythrocytes)
5–6 million per mm³, no nucleus, cytoplasm contains haemoglobin, function: carriage of oxygen.

White blood cells (Leucocytes)
7000 per mm³, nucleus present, cytoplasm colourless, many different types, function: defence against disease

Platelets
0.25 million per mm³, cell fragments formed from cytoplasm of large cells, function: clotting of blood

Figure 19.2 Scanning electron micrograph of red blood cells showing their biconcave surfaces. Magnification × 2000.

Red blood cells

The prime function of the red blood cells is to carry oxygen from the lungs to the tissues, and their structure is modified accordingly; they also play a part in transporting carbon dioxide. If you look at a smear of human blood on a slide under a microscope, you will see that the red blood cells are small and numerous. There are approximately five million per cubic millimetre, each about 8 μm across at its widest part.

The red blood cell has a unique structure. There is no nucleus, and other organelles are degenerate. The cell is sunk in on each side giving it the shape of a **biconcave disc** (figure 19.2). Surrounded by a thin, flexible plasma membrane, the whole of the interior of the cell is filled with the red pigment **haemoglobin** (see page 310). The lack of a nucleus permits more haemoglobin to be packed into the cell.

The red blood cell has a limited life span of about 120 days. The red bone marrow manufactures new ones at the rate of about 1½ million per second to replace those destroyed. A single red blood cell contains 250 million molecules of haemoglobin, each of which can carry four molecules of oxygen. It is therefore possible for 1000 million molecules of oxygen to be carried by a single cell. The biconcave disc provides a large surface–volume ratio for the absorption of oxygen.

Carriage of oxygen

Oxygen diffuses into the red blood cell across its plasma membrane and combines with the haemoglobin to form **oxyhaemoglobin**. In Chapter 18 it was explained that each of the four haem groups in the haemoglobin molecule can combine with a molecule of oxygen, so a single haemoglobin molecule carries a total of four oxygen molecules. The attachment of the oxygen does not involve chemical oxidation of the iron which remains in the iron(II) state throughout the process. The union is a loose one, the oxygen molecules being attached to the haemoglobin in the lungs and equally readily detached in the tissues:

$$\underset{\text{Haemoglobin}}{\text{Hb}} \quad + \quad 4O_2 \quad \underset{\text{tissues}}{\overset{\text{lungs}}{\rightleftharpoons}} \quad \underset{\text{Oxyhaemoglobin}}{\text{HbO}_8}$$

Oxygen dissociation curve

The ability of the blood to transport enough oxygen to meet the needs of the body is largely attributable to the affinity of haemoglobin for oxygen. This can be demonstrated experimentally by subjecting samples of blood to different partial pressures of oxygen, and then determining the percentage saturation of the blood with oxygen in each case (partial pressures are explained in the box alongside).

In practice the blood samples are placed in a series of cylindrical glass containers into which air mixtures of known oxygen partial pressure are introduced. Each sample of blood is given time to come to equilibrium with the air mixture, and then its percentage saturation is determined. If the percentage saturation is then plotted against the oxygen partial pressure, an **oxygen dissociation curve** is obtained.

You will notice in figure 19.3 that the curve is S-shaped (sigmoid). This is very appropriate for a blood pigment. Over the steeply rising part of the curve, a small increase in the partial pressure of oxygen achieves a relatively high percentage saturation of the blood. The flat part of the curve at the top corresponds to the situation in the lungs: over this range a high saturation is maintained even if the partial pressure of oxygen in the alveoli falls. So the

What is partial pressure?

The partial pressure of a gas is a measure of its concentration and is expressed in kilopascals (kPa). For example, at sea level the total atmospheric pressure is 101.3 kPa and because the atmosphere contains approximately 21 per cent oxygen, this gas contributes 21 per cent of the total pressure, which is 21.2 kPa. In other words, the partial pressure of oxygen in the atmosphere is a measure of how much of the whole atmospheric pressure is due to the oxygen present in it. (The partial pressure of oxygen is written pO_2).

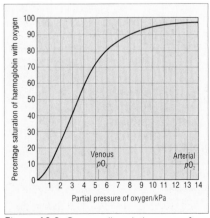

Figure 19.3 Oxygen dissociation curve for human haemoglobin. The sigmoid shape indicates haemoglobin's affinity for oxygen.

oxygen dissociation curve favours the loading of haemoglobin with oxygen in the lungs.

The oxygen dissociation curve, as well as facilitating the loading of haemoglobin with oxygen in the luı gs, also facilitates unloading in the tissues. The steep part of the curve corresponds to the range of oxygen partial pressures found in the tissues. Over this part of the curve, a small drop in oxygen partial pressure will bring about a comparatively large fall in the percentage saturation of the blood. So if the partial pressure of oxygen falls as a result of the tissues utilising oxygen at a faster rate, the haemoglobin gives up more of its oxygen. The shape of the oxygen dissociation curve ensures that the red blood cells take up oxygen in the lungs and release it in the tissues. The points where loading and unloading of oxygen typically occur are indicated in figure 19.3 as the arterial and venous pO_2 respectively.

The effect of carbon dioxide on the oxygen dissociation curve

In the experiment just described all factors apart from the partial pressure of oxygen were kept constant. Consider now what happens if the experiment is repeated at three different partial pressures of carbon dioxide. The results are shown in figure 19.4. You will notice that increasing the partial pressure of carbon dioxide has the effect of shifting the oxygen dissociation curve to the right. This is called the **Bohr effect** after the man who first discovered it, Christian Bohr. (He was the father of the eminent Danish physicist, Niels Bohr, who proposed a structure for the hydrogen atom in 1913.)

When the Bohr effect is operating, the haemoglobin must be exposed to a higher partial pressure of oxygen in order to become fully saturated. But equally it will *release* its oxygen at higher partial pressures of oxygen. In other words carbon dioxide makes the haemoglobin less efficient at taking up oxygen, but more efficient at releasing it.

The release of oxygen is therefore favoured in the tissues where the partial pressure of carbon dioxide tends naturally to be high as a result of its continual release from the respiring cells. On the other hand in the lungs the partial pressure of carbon dioxide is lower owing to its continual escape into the atmosphere, and this favours oxygen uptake.

Oxygen dissociation curves of myoglobin and other blood pigments

From the discussion so far the fact emerges that the further an oxygen dissociation curve is to the left the more firmly the pigment absorbs and holds on to its oxygen. There are certain types of blood pigment which readily take up oxygen even when the partial pressure of oxygen is very low. Such is the case with **myoglobin**, which has an oxygen dissociation curve situated well to the left of haemoglobin (figure 19.5).

Closely related to haemoglobin chemically, myoglobin is found in muscles where it remains fully saturated with oxygen at partial pressures well below that required for haemoglobin to give up its oxygen. Myoglobin stores oxygen, releasing it when the partial pressure of oxygen falls very low, as in severe muscular exertion. Myoglobin is responsible for the colour of 'red muscles', and is particularly abundant in active animals which are liable to suffer from oxygen shortage such as seals and other diving mammals.

Interestingly, the haemoglobin of animals like the lugworm, which burrow in oxygen-deficient mud, is functionally similar to myoglobin. The oxygen dissociation curve of lugworm haemoglobin is situated well to the left of human haemoglobin and reflects its unusually high affinity for

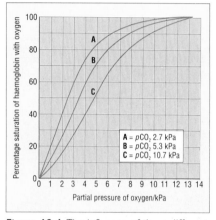

Figure 19.4 The influence of three different concentrations of carbon dioxide on the oxygen dissociation curve for human haemoglobin. Notice that the effect of a high concentration of carbon dioxide is to shift the curve to the right, i.e. it lowers the affinity of haemoglobin for oxygen.

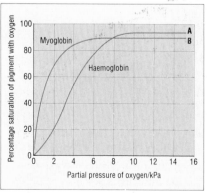

Figure 19.5 Oxygen dissociation curves for myoglobin and haemoglobin. Notice that the myoglobin curve is well to the left of the haemoglobin curve, indicating its much higher affinity for oxygen.

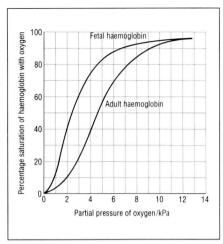

Figure 19.6 The oxygen dissociation curves for adult and fetal human haemoglobin.

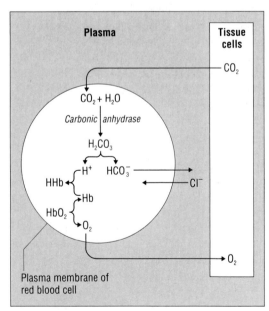

Figure 19.7 Summary of the main chemical events that take place in a red blood cell on reaching the tissues. The uptake of carbon dioxide results in the formation of hydrogen ions whose presence aids the dissociation of oxyhaemoglobin (HbO_2). The haemoglobin combines with the hydrogen ions, forming haemoglobinic acid (HHb). This promotes oxygen dissociation.

oxygen at low partial pressures.

Not only do the haemoglobins of different species vary widely in their affinities for oxygen, but they may even vary during the life cycle of a single individual. For instance, the haemoglobin of the human fetus (**fetal haemoglobin**) has an oxygen dissociation curve situated to the left of adult haemoglobin. The reason for this is that fetal blood has to pick up oxygen from the mother's blood across the placenta, and this can only take place if the fetal haemoglobin has a higher affinity for oxygen than the mother's haemoglobin (figure 19.6).

An unfortunate property of haemoglobin is that it combines even more readily with carbon monoxide than with oxygen. The result of this union is carboxyhaemoglobin. The carbon monoxide combines with the haemoglobin at the sites normally occupied by the oxygen molecules, thus preventing the latter from taking up their normal position. This makes carbon monoxide a powerful 'respiratory poison'. Carbon monoxide is a constituent gas of vehicle exhaust and indeed is formed whenever combustion is incomplete such as in gas-fired central heating boilers.

The explanation of the Bohr effect, the shifting of the oxygen dissociation curves by carbon dioxide, is to be found in the mechanism by which carbon dioxide is transported by the blood.

Carriage of carbon dioxide

Carbon dioxide diffuses from the tissues into the red blood cells where it combines with water to form carbonic acid, H_2CO_3. This is normally a very slow reaction, but in the red blood cell it is greatly accelerated by the presence of the enzyme **carbonic anhydrase** (see page 217). Because of this enzyme, most of the carbon dioxide enters the red blood cells rather than remaining in the plasma. The carbonic acid then dissociates into hydrogencarbonate and hydrogen ions.

If the hydrogen ions were allowed to accumulate they would increase the acidity of the cell and kill it. However, they are **buffered** by the haemoglobin itself. Their presence encourages the oxyhaemoglobin to dissociate into haemoglobin and oxygen. The latter diffuses out of the cell to the tissues, and the haemoglobin takes up the hydrogen ions forming a very weak acid, **haemoglobinic acid**, HHb. It is therefore clear that the Bohr effect is due not to carbon dioxide as such, but to the hydrogen ions resulting from its presence. These chemical events are summarised in figure 19.7.

The carriage of carbon dioxide as just explained results in an accumulation of hydrogencarbonate ions in the red blood cell, but the plasma membrane is highly permeable to these negative ions, which therefore readily diffuse out into the plasma. However, the membrane is relatively impermeable to positive ions, so the inside of the cell tends to develop a net positive charge. Electroneutrality is maintained by an inward movement of chloride ions from the plasma, the so-called **chloride shift**.

Although most of the carbon dioxide is carried in this way, some of it combines with amino groups in the haemoglobin molecule, forming **carbaminohaemoglobin**, $HbCO_2$. A very small amount of carbon dioxide, probably not more than 5 per cent, never gets into the red blood cells at all but dissolves in the plasma and is carried in solution.

When the red blood cells reach the lungs, the partial pressure of oxygen is high and the partial pressure of carbon dioxide is low. With this sudden change in the equilibrium conditions, all the reactions described above go into reverse. As a result oxygen is taken up by the red blood cells and carbon dioxide is released.

Blood clotting

We are all familiar with the way our blood congeals when we cut ourselves. This is called **blood clotting**.

When a blood vessel is damaged, speed is vital in order to prevent loss of blood so the clotting system has to come into action quickly. Within the first few seconds small bodies in the bloodstream called **platelets** stick to the damaged tissue and send out chemical messages which trigger a series of changes terminating in the formation of a gel-like **clot**.

Platelets are fragments of cells, shaped like flattened discs, which arise in the bone marrow. During their short life of five to seven days they circulate in the blood until they detect damage to a blood vessel, which may be a puncture from outside or damage to the inner side of the wall. Very quickly they become sticky and change from flattened discs to spheres with long thin projections (illustration 1). They then adhere to the damaged surface of the blood vessel.

These activated platelets attract **clotting factors** from the plasma and also release certain clotting factors themselves. In addition they release ADP which causes more platelets to become sticky, with the result that a large number of platelets clump together at the site

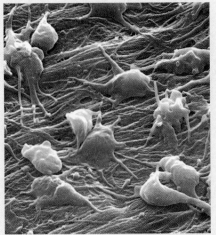

Illustration 1 Scanning electron micrograph of activated platelets showing their thin extensions. Magnification × 3500.

of the damage.

Most of the clotting factors are plasma proteins. They exist in a soluble and inactive state in the blood and are activated by the breaking of one or more of their peptide bonds. They are mostly given Roman numerals (up to XII), and when one factor acts on the next it turns it into its active state. Some of them are enzymes. However factor V and factor VIII (lack of which causes the inherited blood clotting deficiency disease, haemophilia) are not enzymes but are concerned with binding enzyme and substrate molecules together. The way the factors act one on another is summarised in illustration 2.

Calcium ions, phospholipids and vitamin K also play a part in the clotting process. The phospholipids are associated with the membrane surrounding the platelets. Many of the factors are dependent for their formation or action on vitamin K, a group of quinone compounds found in abundance in vegetables.

To the question 'What activates the first clotting factor?' there is, as yet, no certain answer, though contact of the platelets with an unfamiliar surface seems to be an important stimulus triggering the process. Also important in initiating clotting is a protein called **thromboplastin** which is released from damaged tissues.

This cascade of factors acting on each other ends with the formation of factor X. This causes a protein called **prothrombin** to form **thrombin**. Thrombin then acts on the soluble plasma protein **fibrinogen**, causing it to turn into solid threads of **fibrin**. The fibrin threads tangle together and trap protein and water molecules, forming the clot itself. When this happens, the long arms of the platelets shorten and draw back into the centre of the platelet. This has the effect of pulling together the edges of the cut and reducing the loss of blood and entry of micro-organisms. At the same time the platelets secrete a

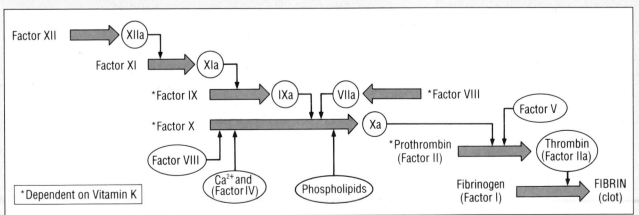

Illustration 2 Diagram of the cascade of factors required for blood clotting. Each factor, which has a Roman numeral, is converted to its activated form, e.g. factor XI → XIa, which then activates the next factor down the pathway.

substance which causes the local capillaries to constrict, further reducing blood loss.

Why should the clotting process be controlled by such a complex succession of factors? There are two main reasons. First, it allows an initially small stimulus to generate a relatively large response – in other words, it amplifies the response. Secondly, by controlling the individual steps in the cascade, the final response can be finely tuned so as to meet precisely the requirements at the place where the clot occurs.

Of course it is imperative that clotting should *not* occur inside normal healthy blood vessels. An anticoagulent called **heparin** is secreted by mast cells in the walls of the blood vessels, and this may help to prevent clotting occurring inside the blood vessels. Heparin has the effect of inhibiting thrombin, so fibrinogen cannot be converted into fibrin. In addition, mechanisms exist which quickly remove any fibrin that may be formed in the blood. In this way the blood is maintained in a fluid state. The building up of plaque in the walls of the vessels can disrupt these mechanisms and cause clotting to occur inside a vessel. This is what happens in a heart attack (see page 135).

Haemophilia, factor VIII and HIV

One of the most common blood clotting disorders is haemophilia A which is caused by a deficiency or complete absence of factor VIII. Haemophilia A is a sex-linked disorder which affects approximately 4000 males in the United Kingdom.

During the 1960s it became possible to concentrate factor VIII from donated blood and give it to males suffering from haemophilia A. As a result the quality of life for many haemophiliacs improved greatly. To a large extent haemophilia ceased to be a life threatening condition.

A single donor never gives more than a pint (500 dm³) at any one time, and this contains only a minute amount of factor VIII. As a result each haemophiliac receives factor VIII from thousands of different donors. It had long been realised that this put haemophiliacs at a significant risk of developing viral hepatitis, as only one of these thousands of donations needed to come from someone infected with viral hepatitis for the recipient to risk becoming infected too. In 1985 it became apparent that HIV (Human Immunodeficiency Virus) was spreading among haemophiliacs in the same way. By then a total of 1200 of the 5000 haemophiliacs in the UK had become infected with HIV. By January 1990 over 100 of them had died from AIDS.

Since 1985 donated factor VIII has been heat-treated so as to destroy the virus. Infection with HIV by this route is therefore no longer a risk for haemophiliacs. In the long-term, genetically engineered microorganisms may be used to produce factor VIII, so eliminating altogether the need for its donation.

The mammalian circulation

The general layout of the mammalian circulatory system is shown in figure 19.8. Basically the muscular **heart** pumps the blood into a system of **arteries** which branch into **arterioles**. Within the tissues the arterioles branch into **capillaries** where exchange of materials between blood and cells takes place. From the capillaries blood is collected up into a series of **venules** which join up to form **veins** which the blood returns to the heart.

The heart is divided into four chambers: **right** and **left atria**, and **right** and **left ventricles**. Blood returning to the heart from all parts of the body, except the lungs, enters the right atrium, whence it passes into the right ventricle, and then via the **pulmonary artery** to the lungs. This is relatively deoxygenated blood, oxygen having been removed from it and carbon dioxide added to it during its passage through the tissues. As this blood flows through the capillaries in the lungs it unloads its carbon dioxide and takes up oxygen.

The oxygenated blood now returns via the **pulmonary veins** to the heart, entering the left atrium. From this chamber it passes into the left ventricle, and thence to the **aorta**, the main artery of the body. From this numerous arteries, some single and some paired, convey blood to the capillary systems in the organs and tissues, where gaseous exchange takes place. Corresponding veins convey the deoxygenated blood to the **venae cavae** (great veins) by which it is returned, once again, to the right atrium.

The walls of the arteries and veins are elastic, and the heart and veins are equipped with **valves** which prevent blood flowing in the wrong direction.

From a functional point of view the two most important parts of the circulatory system are the heart and the capillaries. As the organ responsible for pumping the blood, the heart is of the utmost importance in maintaining the tissues in a state of health and efficiency. The capillaries represent the place where exchange of materials takes place, and as such provide the *raison d'être* for the circulatory system. We will deal with these two parts of the circulatory system in turn.

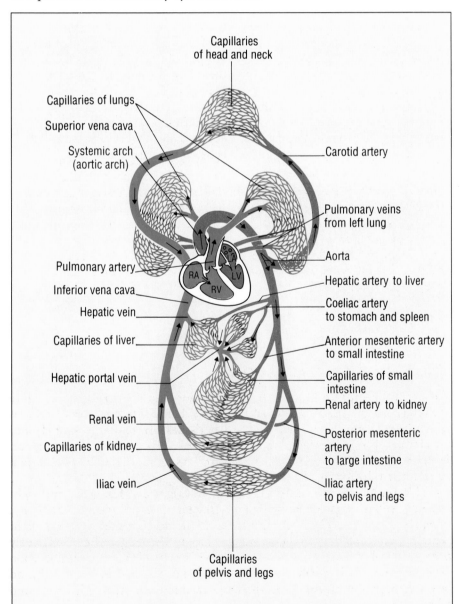

Figure 19.8 General plan of the mammalian circulation. Arteries to the arms are not shown: they arise from the systemic arch shortly after it leaves the heart. Bilaterally disposed organs such as the arms, legs and kidneys have paired arteries and veins, i.e. one on each side of the body. Median organs such as the gut have unpaired arteries and veins. Most of the veins carry blood straight back to the heart, but the hepatic portal vein is an exception: it carries blood from the gut to the liver and is unique in having capillaries at both ends. **RA**, right atrium; **LA**, left atrium; **RV**, right ventricle; **LV**, left ventricle. Oxygenated blood, red; deoxygenated blood, blue.

William Harvey – an English physician

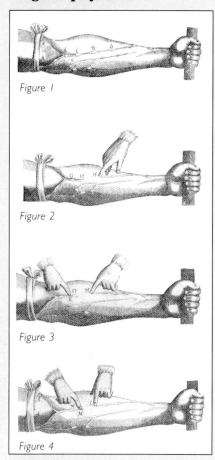

Figure 1

Figure 2

Figure 3

Figure 4

Illustration 1 *Harvey's original drawings demonstrating that blood flows towards the heart in the cutaneous vein of the arm.*

Figure 1 On tying a ligature around the upper arm, the veins in the arm show up as small swellings at B, C, D etc.

Figure 2 If blood is pushed down with the finger from O to H blood does not flow back through valve O.

Figure 3 If an attempt is made to push the blood through valve O, the valve becomes swollen but the part of the vein between O and H remains empty.

Figure 4 If a finger is put at L and another finger M pushes the blood towards and beyond the valve N, the part of the vein from N to L remains empty because the blood cannot pass back through the valve at N. When the finger at L is removed, the vein fills with blood again.

At one time it was thought that blood was pumped from the heart and subsequently drawn back into it via the same vessels, a sort of ebb-and-flow system. This kind of thing does actually happen in certain invertebrate animals, but not in vertebrates. That the blood circulates was first discovered by the seventeenth century physician, William Harvey (1578–1657). By meticulous dissection and ingenious experiments, Harvey showed beyond all reasonable doubt that blood flows away from the heart in certain vessels (arteries), and returns to it in different vessels (veins).

In 1628 William Harvey published an account of his experiments in *Anatomica de mortu cordis et sanguinis in animalibus* (On the anatomy and motions of the heart and blood in animals) – a book which has been described as the most important publication in the history of medicine. It is remarkable to find a book published so long ago in which the anatomical detail is so accurate.

One of Harvey's experiments is shown in illustration 1 – a simple experiment to be sure, but a masterpiece of deductive reasoning. The painting in illustration 2 shows Harvey demonstrating his technique to a group of physicians in London. The conclusion to be drawn is that blood flows in only one direction in the arm vein, and is prevented from flowing in the other direction by the valves.

Although Harvey discovered that the blood circulates in mammals, he was unable to demonstrate the existence of vessels connecting the arteries and veins. This was left to the Italian physiologist, Marcello Malpighi, who, towards the end of the seventeenth century, saw and described capillaries and demonstrated that they form the link between the arteries and veins.

Illustration 2 Harvey demonstrates his famous experiment on the circulation in the arm to a group of physicians in London.

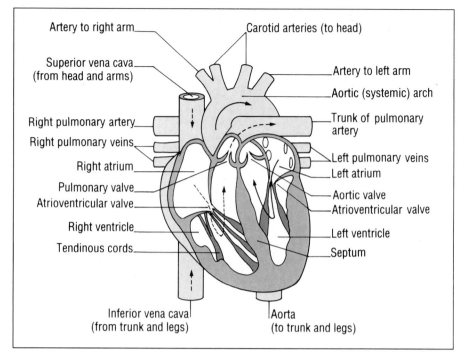

Figure 19.9 Ventral view of the mammalian heart and the blood vessels connected to it. Oxygenated blood, solid arrows; deoxygenated blood, broken arrows. The atrioventricular valve on the right side of the heart consists of three flaps or cusps (tricuspid valve); the atrioventricular valve on the left side of the heart consists of two flaps (bicuspid valve or mitral valve). The pulmonary valve guarding the entrance to the pulmonary artery, and the aortic valve at the entrance to the aortic arch, both consist of pocket-like flaps which catch the blood if it tries to flow back into the heart.

The heart

The heart undergoes contraction (**systole**) and relaxation (**diastole**) rhythmically throughout the animal's life. Its performance is prodigious: in the course of a normal human life span it beats over 2.5×10^9 times, pumping a total of more than 1.5×10^6 litres of blood from each ventricle.

Figure 19.9 shows the mammalian heart, and the passage of blood through it. As we have already seen, blood returning via the venae cavae enters the right atrium. The resulting pressure in this chamber forces open the flaps of the **atrioventricular valve** (also known as the **tricuspid valve** because it consists of three flaps). The result is that blood flows through the atrioventricular opening into the right ventricle.

When the atrium and ventricle are full of blood the atrium suddenly contracts, propelling the remaining blood into the ventricle. The contraction spreads from the right atrium over the rest of the heart. Atrial systole is relatively weak but the ventricles, whose thick walls are particularly well endowed with muscle, contract more powerfully. As a result, blood is forced from the right ventricle into the pulmonary artery.

The blood is prevented from flowing back into the atrium by the flaps of the atrioventricular valve, which closes tightly over the atrioventricular opening. The atrioventricular valve is prevented from turning inside out by tough strands of connective tissue, the **tendinous cords** or 'heart strings' which run from the underside of each flap to the wall of the ventricle (figure 19.10).

Once in the pulmonary artery, blood is prevented from flowing back into the ventricle by pocket-like **semilunar valves** guarding the opening of the pulmonary artery.

From the lungs oxygenated blood returns to the left atrium via the pulmonary veins. It is then conveyed to the left ventricle and so into the **systemic arch** which leads to the **aorta**. This flow of blood takes place in the same way as on the right side of the heart. A minor difference is that the atrioventricular valve consists of two flaps rather than three, for which reason it is called the **bicuspid valve**. It is also known as the **mitral valve** because its two flaps are rather like a bishop's mitre.

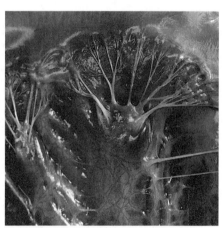

Figure 19.10 Atrioventricular valves and tendinous cords in a sheep's heart. The tendinous cords prevent the flaps of the valve being pushed inside out by the pressure of blood when the ventricle contracts.

Figure 19.11 Flow of blood through the heart during diastole and systole and the action of the valves.
Ventricles relaxed: atrioventricular valves open, pulmonary and aortic valves closed.
Ventricles contracted: atrioventricular valves closed, pulmonary and aortic valves open.
Oxygenated blood, red; deoxygenated blood, blue.

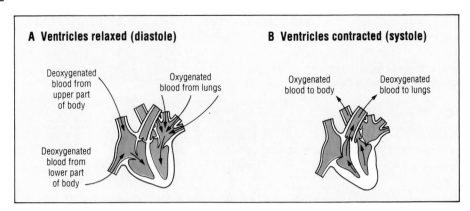

Although systole starts at the right atrium, it quickly spreads to the left so that the whole heart appears to contract synchronously. Thus deoxygenated blood is pumped from the right ventricle into the pulmonary artery at the same time as oxygenated blood is pumped from the left ventricle into the aortic arch. Figure 19.11 shows the flow of blood through the heart and the actions of the valves.

Figure 19.12 Graphs illustrating the pressure and volume changes that occur during the mammalian cardiac cycle (dog). Pressure changes were measured in the left atrium and ventricle, and the aorta. Volume changes were measured for both ventricles. The electrical activity in the heart wall (electrocardiogram) and heart sounds (phonocardiogram) as recorded in a human subject are also shown. The actions at different points on the graphs are as follows:

A Atrium contracting: blood flows into ventricle.
B Ventricle starts to contract: ventricular pressure exceeds atrial pressure so atrioventricular valve closes.
C Ventricular pressure exceeds aortic pressure, forcing aortic valve open: blood therefore flows from ventricle into aorta, and ventricular volume falls.
D Ventricular pressure falls below aortic pressure resulting in closure of aortic valve.
E Ventricular pressure falls below atrial pressure so blood flows from atrium to ventricle; ventricular volume rises rapidly.
F Atrium continuing to fill with blood from pulmonary vein: atrial pressure exceeds ventricular pressure so blood flows from atrium to ventricle.
Electrocardiogram (ECG): P wave corresponds to wave of excitation spreading over atrium; QRS and T waves correspond to wave of excitation spreading over ventricle.
Phonocardiogram: the first and second heart sounds (labelled 1 and 2 in the diagram) are due to sudden closure of atrioventricular and aortic valves respectively.

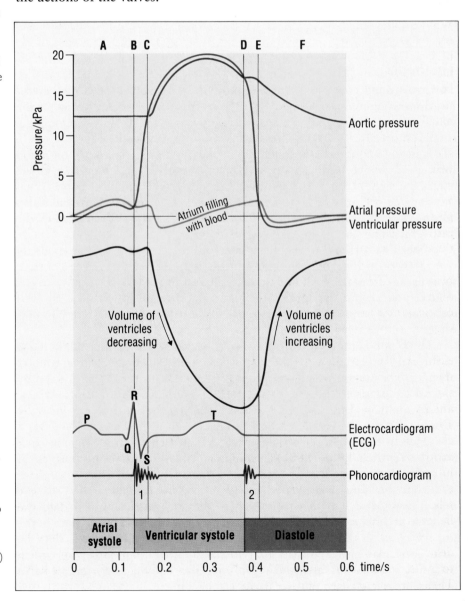

Systole is followed by diastole during which the heart refills with blood again. The entire sequence of events is known as the **cardiac cycle**, and is accompanied by electrical activity in the wall of the heart and by 'sounds' corresponding to the closing of the various valves. The mammalian cardiac cycle is summarised in figure 19.12.

Cardiac muscle

One of the most remarkable features of the heart is its ability to contract rhythmically without fatigue. It owes this property to its muscle. Known as **cardiac muscle**, it consists of a network of interconnected muscle fibres (figure 19.13)

The fibres are divided up into uninucleate cells containing fine contractile **myofibrils**. The muscle fibres show the same kind of cross-banding as skeletal muscle, and the mechanism of contraction is believed to be substantially the same (see Chapter 28). The interconnections between the fibres ensure a rapid and uniform spread of excitation throughout the wall of the heart, which in turn ensures a uniform contraction.

The beating of the heart

What initiates the beating of the heart? Most muscles contract as the result of impulses reaching them from nerves. This is not, however, true of the heart, which will continue beating rhythmically even after its nerve supply has been cut. Indeed the heart will go on beating for a short time after it has been entirely removed from the body, a fact which is of importance in heart transplant operations. Cardiac muscle is, therefore, **myogenic**: its rhythmical contractions arise from within the muscle tissue itself.

What then initiates this rhythm? The mammalian heart has a specialised plexus (network) of fine cardiac muscle fibres embedded in the wall of the right atrium close to where the venae cavae enter it. This is called the **sinoatrial node (SAN)**, and experiments have shown that it serves as a **pacemaker**. If cut out, it will continue to beat at the normal rate. Other pieces of excised atrium will also beat on their own, but at a slightly slower rate. Pieces of excised ventricle contract very much more slowly – at about a third of the normal rate.

Experiments indicate that different parts of the heart are capable of beating at their own intrinsic rate. However, in the intact heart the beating of the ventricles is dependent on the atria, and the atria on the SAN. In other words the SAN, the region of the heart with the fastest intrinsic rhythm, sets the rate at which the rest of the heart beats.

Confirmation that the SAN is the pacemaker has come from recording electrical activity from various parts of the heart wall. It has been found that contraction of the heart is preceded by a wave of electrical excitation, similar to the nerve impulse discussed in Chapter 25. This starts at the SAN and then spreads over the two atria, accompanied by contraction (figure 19.14). When the wave reaches the junction between the atria and ventricles, it excites another specialised group of cardiac muscle fibres called the **atrioventricular node (AVN)**. Continuous with the AVN is a strand of modified cardiac muscle fibres, called the **bundle of His**. This runs down the interventricular septum and fans out over the walls of the ventricles where it breaks up into a network of fibres called **Purkinje tissue** just beneath the endothelial lining.

When the AVN receives excitation from the atria, it sends impulses down the bundle of His to the Purkinje tissue. The impulses then spread out to the cardiac muscle tissue in the walls of the ventricles, making it contract. Thus the pacemaker sends out rhythmical waves of electrical excitation

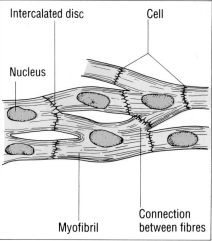

Figure 19.13 Network of cardiac muscle fibres as seen under the light microscope. Notice the connections between adjacent fibres. These facilitate the spread of excitation over the heart and cause synchronous contraction of the muscle. The intercalated discs are reinforced plasma membranes and serve as tough junctions between the myofibrils of successive cells.

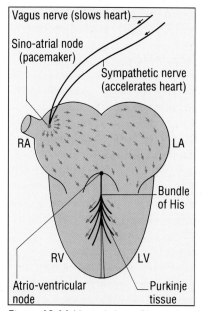

Figure 19.14 Ventral view of heart showing the spread of electrical exicitation that causes contraction. The rhythmical beating of the heart is initiated by the pacemaker, the nerves merely serving to speed up or slow down its rate. The Purkinje tissue transmits impulses relatively slowly, so as to ensure that the ventricles contract after the atria. The Purkinje tissue is named after a Czechoslovakian physiologist whose name in the Czech language is spelt Purkyne but pronounced *Purkinjee*.

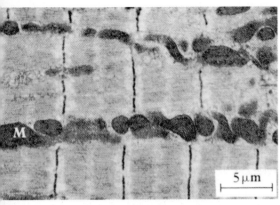

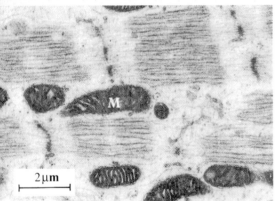

which are transmitted first over the atria and then – via the AVN, bundle of His and Purkinje tissue – to the ventricles. The role of the Purkinje tissue is not to contract but simply to transmit excitation over the ventricles (figure 19.15). The most remarkable aspect of the whole performance is that the rhythmical initiation of the excitatory waves by the pacemaker is quite independent of nervous control.

Not only is the rhythmical beating of the heart independent of nervous control, but the heart automatically pumps into the arteries the same amount of blood as it receives from the veins, even when the latter varies. This is because the extent to which the cardiac muscle contracts is proportional to the initial length of the muscle fibres. In other words, the more the muscle is stretched during diastole, the greater is the subsequent systolic contraction.

Innervation of the heart

The fact that the pacemaker initiates the rhythmical beating of the heart does not mean it has no nerve supply. On the contrary, it receives two nerves, a **sympathetic nerve** which is part of the sympathetic nervous system, and a branch of the **vagus nerve** which belongs to the parasympathetic nervous system (see page 458). These do not initiate the beating of the heart, but can modify the activity of the pacemaker, speeding up or slowing down the rate at which the heart beats.

The roles of the two nerves have been demonstrated in animals like frogs and turtles by attaching the heart to a lever that writes on a slowly revolving drum. The sympathetic and vagus nerves are hooked on to fine electrodes through which weak electrical stimuli can be delivered. In this way impulses can be generated in one or other of the two nerves. The results of such an experiment are shown in figure 19.16. If the sympathetic nerve is stimulated, the heart speeds up; if the vagus is stimulated, it slows down.

The vagus and sympathetic nerves are therefore antagonistic in their effects. This double innervation makes an animal's transport system much more versatile than would otherwise be the case. It means that the volume of blood expelled from the heart per unit time – the **cardiac output** – can be modified to suit the needs of the animal as occasion demands. We shall return to this later in the chapter.

Figure 19.15 Microscopic structure of the heart wall.

Top Electron micrograph of part of a cardiac muscle cell. The cell contains numerous myofibrils of which several can be seen here in longitudinal section. Note the densely packed mitochondria (**M**) between the fibrils for providing energy. The banding pattern in the fibrils has the same basis as in skeletal muscle (see page 498).

Bottom Conducting tissue in the wall of the ventricle. This consists of modified cardiac muscle fibres which, instead of contracting, conduct electrical impulses like nerves. Compare this electron micrograph with the appearance of cardiac muscle seen in the top picture. Notice that the conducting tissue has fewer myofibrils and mitochondria.

Figure 19.16 The effect on the turtle heart of stimulating **A** the vagus nerve and **B** the sympathetic nerve with high frequency stimuli. In each case the period of stimulation was from a to b. The recordings were made by attaching the heart to a lever which wrote on a revolving drum (kymograph). Note that impulses in the sympathetic nerve accelerate the heart rate, whereas impulses in the vagus slow it down.

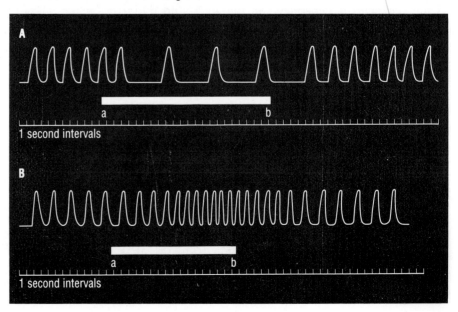

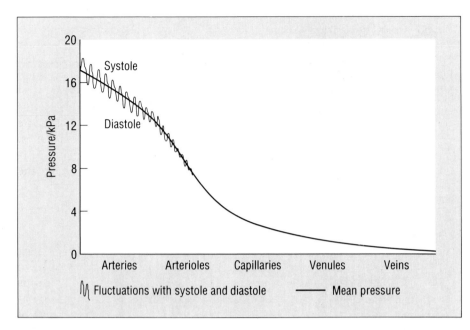

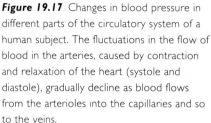

Figure 19.17 Changes in blood pressure in different parts of the circulatory system of a human subject. The fluctuations in the flow of blood in the arteries, caused by contraction and relaxation of the heart (systole and diastole), gradually decline as blood flows from the arterioles into the capillaries and so to the veins.

Figure 19.18 The structure of an artery and a vein. Their walls contain elastic and collagen fibres and smooth muscle. They are therefore tough but stretchable and can constrict or dilate. The vein has a thinner wall and wider lumen than the artery as you can see clearly in the photomicrograph below. The diagrams show the arrangement of the different types of tissue in the walls.

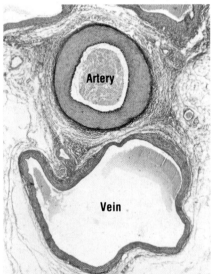

Arteries and veins

Blood is expelled from the heart only when it contracts. Blood flow through the arteries is therefore intermittent, the blood flowing rapidly during systole and slowly during diastole. However, by the time the blood reaches the capillaries it is flowing evenly (figure 19.17). The gradual change from intermittent to even flow is made possible by the elasticity of the arterial walls which contain much elastic tissue and smooth muscle (figure 19.18).

When blood is pumped into the aorta, the valves at the entrance prevent the back-flow of blood to the heart and the wall of the first part of the artery is distended. As the heart relaxes, the distended section of the artery recoils, which distends the next section – and so on. Thus a wave of distension followed by recoil (the **pulse wave**) progresses along the artery. The blood itself flows more slowly than the pulse wave, falling to 1 mm per

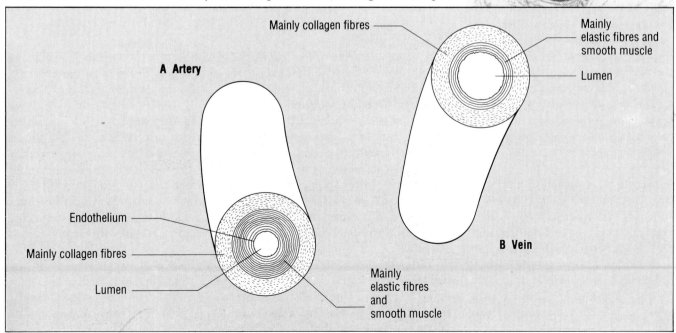

Figure 19.19 The contraction of skeletal muscles in conjunction with valves in the veins helps to return blood to the heart. If blood flows backwards it is caught in the pocket-like valves as indicated by the downward-pointing arrows.

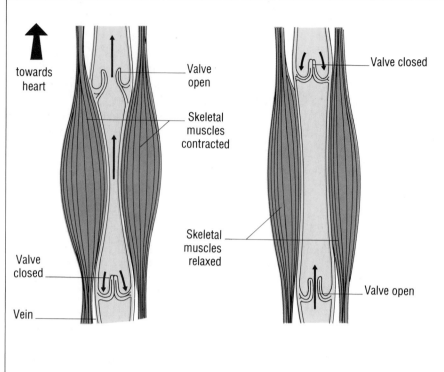

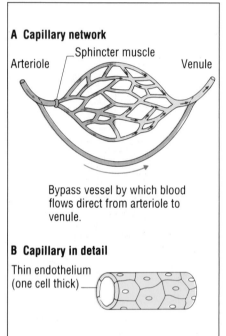

Figure 19.20 Diagram of a capillary network. The capillaries provide a vast irrigation system which supplies the cells with their needs. It is said that if all the body's capillaries were placed end to end they would extend for over 80 000 km! The bore of the capillaries averages about 10 μm, just wide enough to permit the passage of red blood cells in single file. The single layer of lining epithelial cells is, at its thinnest, less than 0.1 μm thick, thus facilitating rapid exchange of materials between the blood and tissue cells. No cell is more than 25 μm from the nearest capillary. The capillaries have no muscle layer and are incapable of changing their diameter to any extent. Blood flow through them is controlled by constriction or dilation of the arterioles, whose walls contain smooth muscle, and of the sphincter muscles at the ends of the arterioles. Oxygenated blood, red; deoxygenated blood, blue.

second by the time it reaches the capillaries. To some extent the blood is kept flowing by wave-like contractions of the smooth muscle in the walls of the smaller arteries.

Veins have thinner walls and a larger lumen than arteries. Blood flow through them is assisted by contraction of the skeletal muscles which squeezes the blood along (figure 19.19). Back-flow is prevented by valves, and by the large diameter of the veins which minimises the resistance to flow. Also the negative pressure developed in the thorax during inspiration will tend to draw blood back to the heart. Contraction of the smooth muscle in the walls of the veins can also increase the return of blood to the heart.

The capillaries

As a transport system, the job of the circulation is to take up materials in one part of the body and deliver them to another. There must therefore be an intimate relationship between the circulatory system and the tissues. This is achieved by the **capillaries**.

Figure 19.20 shows a small part of a capillary network. In contrast to arteries and veins, the capillaries are narrow (an average of 10 μm in diameter) and thin walled. The wall consists of a single layer of very thin **pavement epithelium** which allows rapid diffusion of dissolved substances into or out of the capillary. The cells are bathed in tissue fluid derived from the blood plasma which provides a medium through which diffusion can take place. The close proximity between the capillaries and the tissue cells, and the thinness of the barrier between them, facilitates this exchange of materials.

The flow of blood through the capillaries can be regulated. Rings of muscle surround the ends of the arterioles at the points where they break up into capillaries. Under the influence of nerves, hormones or local conditions, these **sphincter muscles** contract or relax, thereby decreasing or increasing the flow of blood through them.

In some parts of the body larger vessels form a direct connection between arteries and veins, thereby bypassing the capillaries. By constricting or dilating, these **shunt vessels** can regulate the amount of blood which flows through a particular set of capillaries at any given time. This occurs in parts of the body where the blood flow needs to be adjusted from time to time. An example is the skin whose blood supply varies according to the external temperature (see page 400).

The capillaries are like a vast irrigation system, different parts of which can be opened or closed according to local needs and conditions. This, coupled with the fact that the heart can vary its rate of beating, makes the mammalian circulation a highly adaptable transport system

Blood pressure

Blood pressure is the term used to describe the pressure in the aorta. It is highest when the ventricles contract (**systolic pressure**) and lowest when the ventricles relax (**diastolic pressure**). You might expect it to be measured in kilopascals but it is medical practice to measure it in millimetres of mercury, the normal values being 120 mm Hg for systolic pressure and 80 mm Hg for diastolic pressure.

A rise in blood pressure means that the heart is overworking and this can put a strain on the circulatory system. A fall in blood pressure can affect the functioning of organs such as the kidneys. It is therefore important that blood pressure should be maintained within normal limits.

How is the blood pressure controlled? At the base of the internal carotid artery, on each side of the neck, is a small bulbous swelling called the **carotid sinus**. In its walls are sensory cells sensitive to stretching. If the arterial pressure rises, the walls of the carotid sinus are distended and the stretch receptors stimulated. Impulses are then transmitted via sensory nerves to a group of nerve cells in the medulla of the brain called the **cardiovascular centre**. This responds by sending out impulses in the appropriate effector nerves which reduce the cardiac output and dilate the peripheral blood vessels, thereby lowering the arterial pressure.

If the arterial pressure falls too much the stretch receptors will stop being stimulated; the cardiac output will then increase and the peripheral blood vessels will constrict, resulting in a rise in arterial pressure. The carotid sinus is thus a sensitive pressure gauge, detecting changes in arterial pressure and signalling these to the cardiovascular centre. The latter then brings about appropriate adjustments. This is an example of a homeostatic system whose principles are discussed in Chapter 21.

Figure 19.21 summarises the way the heart rate is controlled by changes in blood pressure.

Control of the circulation

In Chapter 15 we saw that the ventilation centre in the medulla of the brain controls the rate of breathing. In a similar kind of way the cardiovascular centre controls the rate at which the heart beats. A number of reflexes are involved including the carotid sinus reflex already described. Depending on circumstances, the cardiovascular centre sends impulses down the sympathetic nerve to the heart, increasing its rate of beating; or down the vagus nerve, decreasing its rate of beating.

As with the ventilation centre, the cardiovascular centre is connected by nervous pathways to higher centres in the brain. It can therefore be influenced by impulses reaching it from the cerebral cortex. However, although we can exercise voluntary control over our rate of breathing, we cannot change the rate of our heart beat at will.

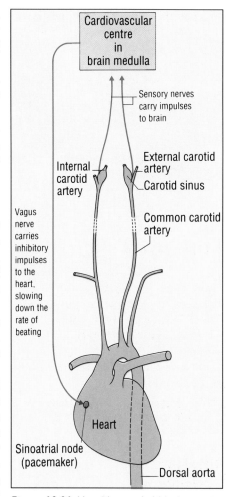

Figure 19.21 How changes in blood pressure bring about changes in the heart rate. An increase in arterial pressure stimulates stretch receptors in the walls of the carotid sinuses which leads reflexly to slowing of the heart.

Figure 19.22 The Weddell seal can remain submerged for an hour or more while diving. During the dive the blood flow to all parts of the body except the central nervous system and heart is restricted. The heart rate and output are reduced, but sufficient to maintain the blood pressure.

Most people have experienced the increased pulse rate that accompanies excitement, shock and various other emotions. In this case impulses are conveyed from the higher centres to the sympathetic nervous system and thence to the **adrenal glands**. The latter respond by secreting the hormone **adrenaline** into the bloodstream. The effects of adrenaline are almost the same as those produced by the sympathetic nervous system, and their joint function is to prepare the body for coping with demands that may be made on the circulatory system before they actually happen. This is achieved by increasing the cardiac output and causing general constriction of arterioles except for those serving vital structures such as the skeletal muscle and heart itself. As a result there is a general rise in blood pressure, and blood is diverted to those places where it is needed most. This diversion of blood is enhanced by various local responses. For example, carbon dioxide tends to accumulate in the active muscles. This causes the arterioles serving the muscles to dilate, thereby increasing the bloodflow through them.

Response to oxygen deprivation

What happens if an animal is suddenly deprived of oxygen? For most species the result is disastrous, death occurring within a matter of minutes. But certain animals, notably those capable of diving, can survive for much longer. For example, a seal can remain under water for over 20 minutes and certain species of whales for an hour or more (figure 19.22). How is this achieved?

By recording the heart beat, blood pressure and other variables in a variety of diving mammals, it has been found that very soon after the dive commences the cardiac frequency decreases dramatically. This is called **bradycardia** ('brady' is derived from the Greek word *brados*, meaning slowness). At the same time the arterioles of all but the vital organs constrict. This rapid reflex response results in the body's oxygen store, derived from its haemoglobin and myoglobin, being sent to those organs that are least able to endure oxygen deprivation, namely the heart and brain. The lowered cardiac frequency is just enough to keep the tissues ticking over.

It is now known that this response is not restricted to diving mammals like seals and whales but is shown by many other animals, diving ducks for example, when confronted with sudden oxygen deprivation. It also occurs in humans – a human diver will develop bradycardia within 30 seconds after the beginning of a dive – and in fishes it occurs when they are taken *out* of water. It therefore seems to be a life-saving response of general importance.

Adjustments during exercise

In this box we see how the circulatory and other systems enable the body to adjust during a sprint.

A number of processes occur before, during and after the sprint. Here they are, in roughly the order in which they occur.

1 Before and during the early stages of the sprint the sympathetic nervous system is alerted and adrenaline is secreted into the bloodstream. Triggered by impulses received from the brain in anticipation of the race, there is an increase in the cardiac output and general constriction of arterioles except for those serving vital organs, so that blood under high pressure is diverted to the active muscles. Anticipation of the race also brings about an increase in the ventilation rate.

2 During the sprint the metabolic rate increases. This is caused by shortage of ATP. We only have enough ATP in our muscles at any one time to provide for several seconds maximal exertion. It is therefore manufactured on the go. A decrease in the amount of ATP relative to ADP activates the enzyme which initiates the further breakdown of glucose or muscle glycogen.

3 The increased metabolic rate results in carbon dioxide building up in the skeletal muscle tissues. This causes local dilatation of the arterioles, leading to an increased blood flow through the muscles. It has been found that the increase in body temperature (which may be up to 2°C after a game of squash and up to 4°C in a marathon) renders the tissues more sensitive to carbon dioxide, thereby accentuating this mechanism.

4 Rapid movement of the limbs stimulates stretch receptors in the skeletal muscles and tendons. These transmit impulses to the cardiovascular centre leading to a further increase in the cardiac output.

5 Any fluctuations in the level of carbon dioxide in the bloodstream are monitored by the chemoreceptors in the carotid and aortic bodies and medullary centre, leading to appropriate adjustments in the ventilation rate.

6 During the race the metabolic rate of the active muscles increases greatly and the demand for oxygen rises accordingly. Despite the mechanisms described above, insufficient oxygen is delivered to the muscles to keep pace with their demands. As a result the muscles start respiring anaerobically with the formation of lactic acid. This accumulates during the race, but afterwards it is oxidised via the Krebs cycle or circulated to the liver where it is converted back to glycogen (see illustration). For this to happen oxygen is required. Constituting the so-called **oxygen debt**, it accounts for the heavy panting that ensues after the race.

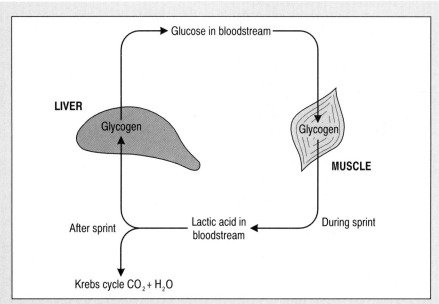

Scheme summarising carbohydrate metabolism during and after a sprint. As a result of the conversions shown here, energy is made available for the race, and the glycogen store in the muscle is replenished afterwards.

7 The lactic acid which accumulates during the sprint has the same effect on the arterioles as carbon dioxide, i.e. it causes local vasodilatation. It also stimulates the aortic and carotid bodies, thereby accentuating the ventilation responses initiated by the carbon dioxide.

8 Carbon dioxide itself will continue to increase, partly because of the oxidation of lactic acid in the Krebs cycle, but also because of the way lactic acid is buffered in the bloodstream. In this process lactic acid dissociates into lactate and hydrogen ions:

$$\text{lactic acid} \rightarrow \text{lactate} + \text{H}^+$$

The hydrogen ions then combine with hydrogencarbonate ions to form carbonic acid, which splits into carbon dioxide and water:

$$\text{H}^+ + \text{HCO}_3^- \rightarrow \text{H}_2\text{CO}_3$$

9 While all this has been happening, the greatly increased metabolic rate results in a rise in body temperature. This is offset by the body's cooling processes described in Chapter 23.

The same kind of adjustments occur in longer races. One difference, however, is that the oxygen debt may be paid on the run, an equilibrium being established between oxygen supply and oxygen usage. When this point is reached **second wind** is said to be acquired.

For the short period involved in a sprint, the muscles can function perfectly efficiently under anaerobic conditions, provided of course that the oxygen debt is paid immediately afterwards. This enables an athlete to hold his or her breath during a sprint, the hundred metres for example. Under these circumstances circulatory and metabolic adjustments occur as described above, but changes in breathing are temporarily suspended until after the race.

Many complex physiological changes occur during muscular activity. What this brief and simplified account shows is that several different systems cooperate in bringing about appropriate adjustments, which together maintain the continued efficiency of the body.

Summary

1 Mammalian blood is composed of **red** and **white blood cells** (**erythrocytes** and **leucocytes** respectively) and **platelets** suspended in **plasma**. Dissolved food substances are transported in the plasma, oxygen by the red blood cells.

2 Mammalian red blood cells are non-nucleated, biconcave discs. They contain haemoglobin whose affinity for oxygen is shown by its **oxygen dissociation curve**.

3 Haemoglobin's affinity for oxygen is lowered by the presence of carbon dioxide. Thus loading of haemoglobin with oxygen is favoured in the lungs, whereas unloading is favoured in the tissues.

4 **Myoglobin** and **fetal haemoglobin** have a higher affinity for oxygen than adult haemoglobin, and this is related to their functions.

5 The carriage of carbon dioxide in the blood depends on the presence of the enzyme **carbonic anhydrase** in the red blood cells.

6 The mammalian circulation with its **heart, arteries, capillaries** and **veins** is well adapted for delivering oxygen at high speed to the tissues.

7 The heart is divided into four chambers: two **atria** and two **ventricles**. Blood is propelled through the heart by a series of events which constitute the **cardiac cycle**. The ventricles have thick muscular walls, and **valves** prevent blood flowing in the wrong direction.

8 The heart beat is initiated by the **sinoatrial node** (**pacemaker**) which, though it has an innate rhythm, is influenced by its nerve supply. The sympathetic nerve accelerates the beating of the heart and the vagus nerve slows it.

9 Despite variations in the frequency with which it beats, the heart automatically pumps into the arteries the same amount of blood as it receives from the veins.

10 **Cardiac muscle** has a similar microscopic structure to that of skeletal (striated) muscle but adjacent fibres are interconnected. It contracts repeatedly without fatigue.

11 **Arteries** and **veins** are adapted in their structure and properties for carrying blood away from, and back to, the heart respectively.

12 **Capillaries** are narrow and thin-walled and come into intimate association with the tissue cells. Exchanges take place between the capillary blood and the neighbouring tissues.

13 The circulation is controlled by the **cardiovascular centre** in the medulla oblongata in the hindbrain. It responds to, amongst other things, changes in blood pressure as monitored by stretch receptors in the walls of the **carotid sinuses**.

14 The higher centres in the brain, a variety of reflexes and the hormone adrenaline are also involved in the initiation of cardiovascular responses.

15 When facing total oxygen deprivation many animals, particularly diving mammals and birds, undergo **bradycardia**: the cardiac frequency falls and blood is redistributed to the vital organs.

16 Rapid responses to changing conditions are also seen during and after a bout of heavy exercise. The ventilation, circulatory, nervous and endocrine systems all cooperate to bring about appropriate adjustments.

Review questions

1 List the components of blood and summarise their functions.

2 How does the presence of haemoglobin in the blood of a mammal contribute to efficient oxygen transport?

3 Explain the significance of the S-shaped oxygen dissociation curve.

4 It has been found that the oxygen dissociation curve is displaced to the right by high temperatures as well as by high carbon dioxide concentrations. Why is this useful?

5 How is carbon dioxide carried in the blood, and how does this help to explain the Bohr effect?

6 Give a step-by-step account of the cardiac cycle of the mammal.

7 Describe how the rhythm of the heart beat is initiated and maintained. How is the rate of the heart beat altered in natural circumstances?

8 What are the main functions of blood capillaries and how is their structure and organisation suited to carry out these functions?

9 How does the blood pressure change as blood flows round the circulatory system?

10 What adjustments are made to the circulation as a result of exercise, and how are these achieved?

Further reading

Jonathan Miller gives an interesting historical review of our understanding of the heart and blood in *The Body in Question* (Jonathan Cape, 1978)

If you are thinking of a medical career you will be fascinated by a short and readable book called *Heart Disease, What it is and How it's treated* by John Wallwork and Rob Stepney (Blackwell, 1987).

Biology, Advanced Topics includes an account of how haemoglobin works and the biological basis of coronary heart disease.

Transport in the flowering plant

In Chapter 18 the systems by which substances are transported in plants were introduced briefly. In this chapter we shall take a closer look at the uptake of water and mineral salts from the soil, their transport in the xylem and the loss of water vapour from the leaves. We shall also discuss the transport of organic compounds in the phloem.

Uptake and transport of water

Plants and animals require water for essentially the same reasons. It is the medium in which all metabolic reactions take place and it is needed for the transport of solutes around the organism. In plants it performs the additional function of generating a pressure potential in the cells which helps to support the plant.

Uptake of water by roots

As well as anchoring the plant, the roots provide the surface through which water is taken up. The surface area is greatly increased by the presence, just behind the tip of the root, of thousands of tiny **root hairs** (figure 20.1). A plant's roots may present an enormous surface for the absorption of water. For instance, at four months the root system of a single rye plant, including the root hairs, was found to have a total surface area of 639 m², which is about 130 times greater than the surface area of its shoot system.

In order to follow what happens to the water that is taken up by the roots, we must examine the internal structure of the root.

Internal structure of the root

Figure 20.2 shows the arrangement of the tissues in the root of a typical dicotyledon. The root hairs belong to the outer layer of cells, the **epidermis** – each root hair is a slender extension of a single epidermal cell.

CHAPTER 20

Figure 20.1 Scanning electron micrograph of root hairs on a root of a wheat seedling. The root hairs greatly increase the surface area over which water and mineral salts can be absorbed.

Figure 20.2 Internal structure of a young dicotyledonous root.
A Stereogram of the root showing the positions of the various tissues.
B A root hair in detail, showing its close association with the soil from which it absorbs water and mineral salts. Notice that the root hair is an extension of a single epidermal cell.

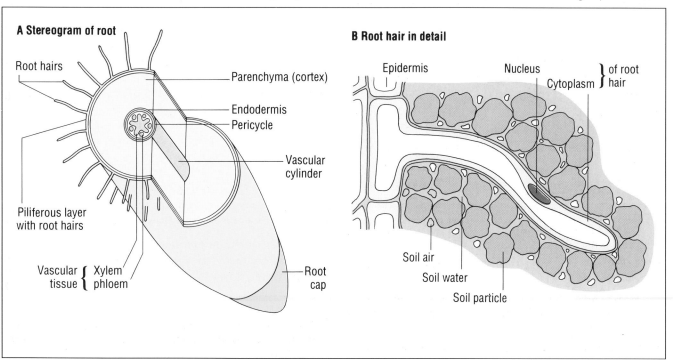

A Stereogram of root

Root hairs
Parenchyma (cortex)
Endodermis
Pericycle
Vascular cylinder
Piliferous layer with root hairs
Vascular tissue { Xylem / phloem
Root cap

B Root hair in detail

Epidermis
Nucleus
Cytoplasm } of root hair
Soil air
Soil water
Soil particle

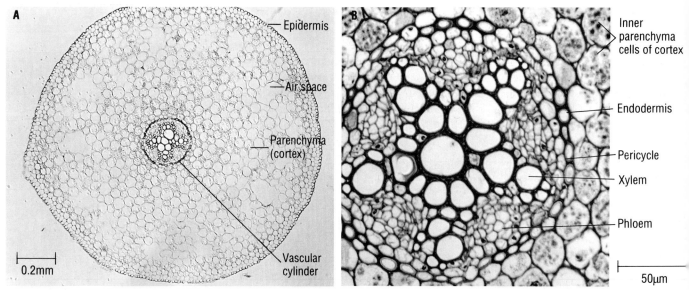

Figure 20.3 Photomicrographs of a buttercup root.

A Transverse section of the root. Starch grains are visible in some of the parenchyma cells of the cortex.

B The vascular cylinder at higher magnification.

The root hairs are confined to the part of the epidermis immediately behind the tip where they comprise the so-called **piliferous layer**. Further back, in the older part of the root, the piliferous layer sloughs off and is replaced by the layer of cells immediately underneath. This becomes the functional epidermis.

The root hairs penetrate between the soil particles and are in close contact with the soil water. It has been found that the cells towards the tip of the root, including the root hairs, take up water as much as six times faster than the cells in the older regions of the root further back.

Beneath the epidermis, large thin-walled **parenchyma cells** make up the **cortex** which constitutes the main body of the root. In the centre there is a core of vascular tissues, referred to as the **vascular cylinder**. The vascular cylinder of a young root consists of several groups of lignified **xylem cells** between which are distinct groups of **phloem cells**.

The centre of the vascular cylinder consists of parenchyma tissue to begin with, but as the root develops this changes into xylem. So, when viewed in transverse section, the xylem finishes up looking like a star with several 'spokes'. A typical pattern can be seen in figure 20.3.

The vascular cylinder is bounded by a layer of parenchyma cells called the **pericycle** which becomes lignified in older roots. Outside the pericycle is a layer of cells called the **endodermis**.

The roots of monocotyledons are much the same as dicotyledons except that the xylem has many more 'spokes' and surrounds a core of parenchyma cells.

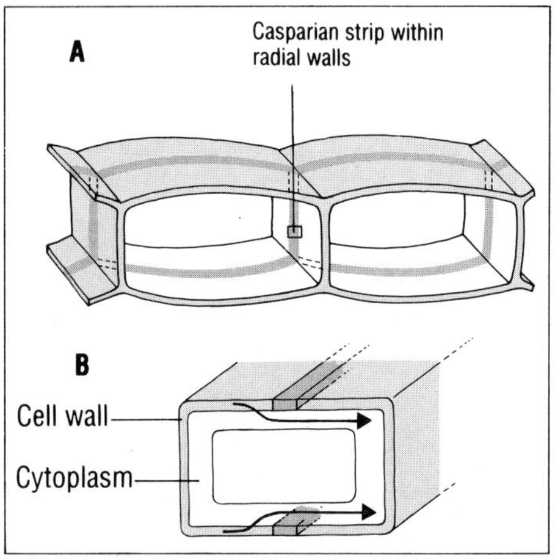

The route taken by water

Most of the water probably enters the root, from the soil, down a gradient of water potential. Inside the root the water follows two main pathways:

- The **apoplast**. This consists of the interconnected cellulose cell walls of adjacent cells which are in contact with each other and therefore form a continuous system. The water flows in the spaces between the cellulose microfibrils (see page 131).
- The **symplast**. This consists of the cytoplasm which is continuous from cell to cell via the **plasmodesmata** (see page 153). To get into the symplast, water has to cross the partially permeable plasma membrane by osmosis.

Figure 20.4

A Endodermal cells of the root showing the suberised Casparian strip in the radial walls.

B Diagram showing how the Casparian strip diverts the water from the cellulose wall (apoplast pathway) to the cytoplasm (symplast pathway).

Both pathways are used, but most of the water probably follows the apoplast pathway as this is the faster of the two. Once the water reaches the endodermis, its flow is barred by an impermeable thickening of suberin called the **Casparian strip** in the radial walls of the endodermal cells. The Casparian strip diverts the water, forcing it to take the symplast pathway through the endodermal cells (figure 20.4).

What is the significance of this diversion? It is thought that the endodermal cells actively transfer salts from the cortex to the pericycle. The resulting high concentration of salts in the pericycle cells creates a low water potential which causes water to move into them by osmosis. Once in the pericycle, the water flows into the xylem down a water potential gradient in both the symplast and apoplast pathways.

Figure 20.5 summarises the passage of water from the soil to the xylem in the root.

From root to leaf

Water is transported from the roots to the leaves via the stem. In order to understand how this happens we must first look at the internal structure of the stem, in particular the vascular tissues (figure 20.6).

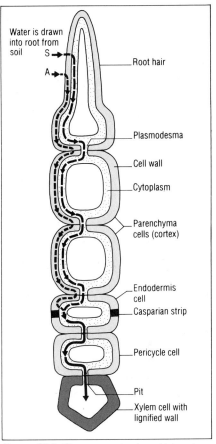

Figure 20.5 The two routes by which water may pass from the soil to the xylem in the centre of the root. The apoplast pathway (**A**) consists of the cell walls, the symplast pathway (**S**) consists of the cytoplasm.

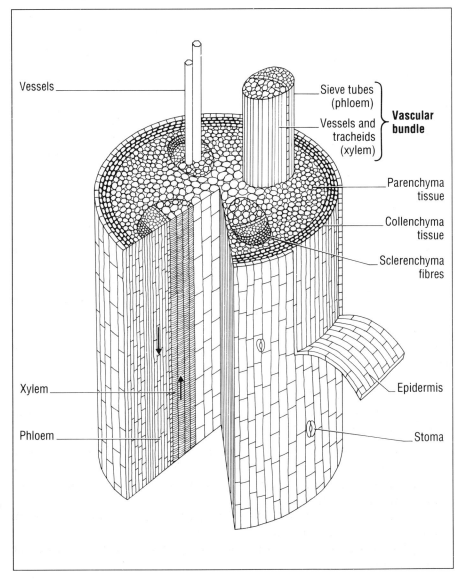

Figure 20.6 Internal structure of a dicotyledonous stem. The peripheral part of the parenchyma (outside the ring of vascular bundles), together with the collenchyma, make up the cortex; the central parenchyma (inside the ring of vascular bundles) comprises the medulla; and the parenchyma between the vascular bundles comprises the medullary rays. The terms cortex, medulla, medullary ray and vascular bundle are topographical terms, signifying different *regions* of the stem. The terms collenchyma, parenchyma, xylem and phloem refer to the different types of *tissue* in the stem. The arrows signify the upward flow of water and mineral salts in the xylem and the downward flow of soluble food substances in the phloem.

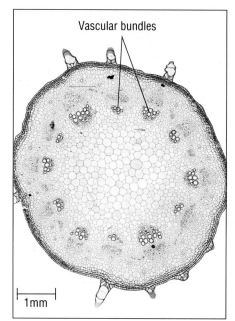

Figure 20.7 Photomicrograph of a transverse section of a buttercup stem showing the structure of the stem of a typical dicotyledon. Notice that the vascular bundles are arranged in a regular ring towards the outside of the stem.

Internal structure of the stem

In the stem the vascular tissue is organised into a series of **vascular bundles**. In dicotyledons the vascular bundles are arranged in a ring (figure 20.7), but in monocotyledons they are scattered throughout the stem in a random manner (figure 20.8). In both cases the individual bundles run the entire length of the stem, connecting with the vascular cylinders in the roots and with the vascular bundles in the midrib and veins of the leaves.

The vascular bundles are embedded in **parenchyma tissue** which forms the bulk of a young stem. This is surrounded by a layer of **collenchyma tissue** whose thickened cellulose walls provide the stem with strength while allowing it to be flexible. The outermost collenchyma cells may contain chloroplasts, giving the stem a green colour and enabling it to photosynthesise.

The surface of the stem is covered with a layer of **epidermis** which usually has a cuticle like that of leaves and may be pierced by a number of stomata. The parenchyma cells, when fully turgid, press against each other and against the surrounding collenchyma and epidermis. This contributes to the mechanical strength of the stem, helping to maintain its erect form and preventing it from drooping.

Also important in providing mechanical strength is the **pericycle** which is located on the immediate outside of the vascular bundles. It consists of **sclerenchyma tissue** which is made up of tightly packed lignified **fibres**. This lignified tissue, along with that of the xylem, helps to make the stem rigid.

If we examine vascular bundles more closely, as in figure 20.9, we see that there is a clear demarcation between the xylem and phloem. The xylem is towards the inner side of the vascular bundle, the phloem towards the outside. This applies to both dicotyledons and monocotyledons.

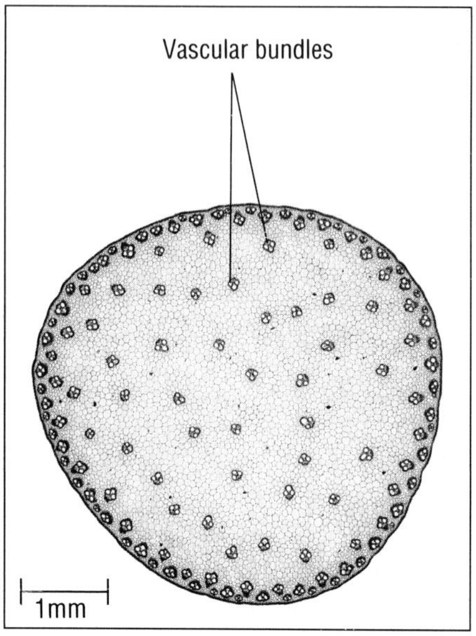

Figure 20.8 Photomicrograph of a transverse section of a maize stem showing the vascular bundles scattered throughout the stem. This arrangement is typical of monocotyledons.

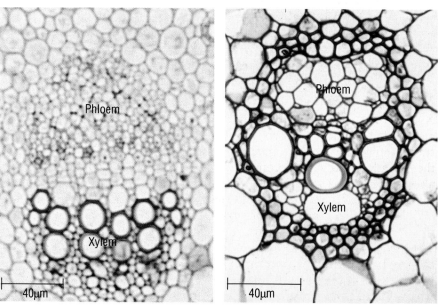

Figure 20.9

Left Photomicrograph of a single vascular bundle in a buttercup stem showing the large thick-walled xylem cells and the thinner walled phloem cells.

Right Photomicrograph of a single vascular bundle of maize. This shows the typical arrangement of xylem and phloem cells in cereals which is often likened to a monkey's face!

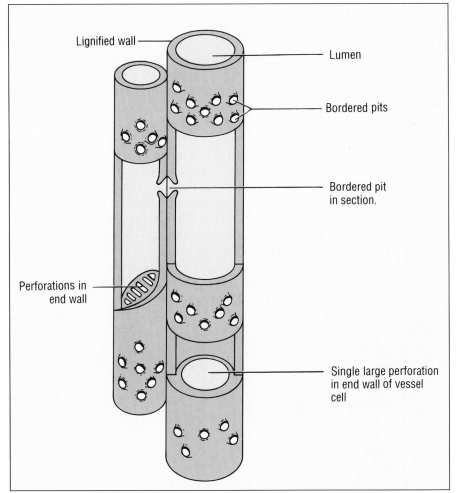

Figure 20.10 Diagram showing the detailed structure of vessels. Each vessel is a long tube with a lignified wall. It starts off as a chain of cylindrical cells whose end walls become perforated by a single large opening or by a number of parallel slit-like openings. With the lignification of the walls, the cells die and lose their contents so the tubes become empty except for the water and mineral salts which they transport from the roots to the leaves.

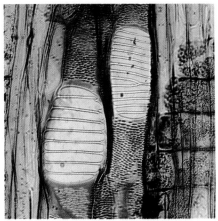

Figure 20.11 Electron micrograph showing the perforations in the end wall of a vessel cell of birch. Magnification × 150.

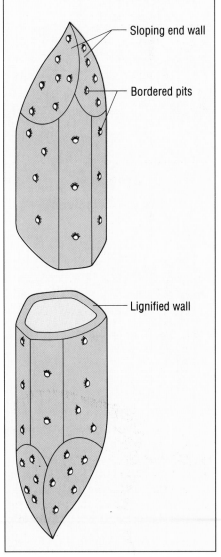

Figure 20.12 Diagram of a tracheid showing the tapered ends and pits.

Xylem tissue

Xylem contains two types of conducting cells: **tracheids** and **vessels**. These are dead cells and they form a system of pipes through which water can travel. The cells are dead because once they have reached their full size, their cellulose cell walls become impregnated with **lignin** which is imperme-able to water and solutes. The living contents of the cells die, leaving just the cell walls to form a system of empty pipes.

Vessels are characteristic of angiosperms and are absent from the xylem tissue of conifers. Tracheids occur in a few angiosperms and all conifers. The detailed structure of vessels is shown in figure 20.10. Water moving up the plant encounters little resistance as it moves along the vessels. This is because vessels are formed from a chain of cylindrical cells the end walls of which break down so that the cells are in open communication with each other. Alternatively, there may be ladder-like bars extending across the end, forming a perforation plate (figure 20.11). In tracheids, on the other hand, the end walls remain intact, and are perforated only by small holes called **pits** (figure 20.12). Water moves up a plant ten times faster in vessels than in tracheids.

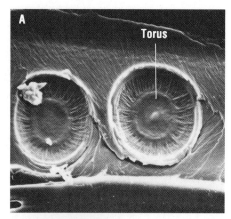

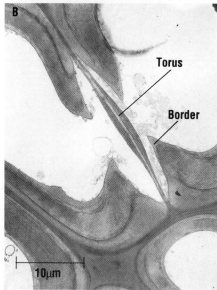

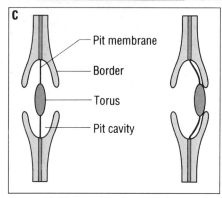

Pits occur in the walls of both tracheids and vessels. Where a pit occurs lignin fails to be deposited and only the cellulose cell wall remains. The pits match up with the pits of neighbouring cells, so the cell cavities are connected to adjacent cell cavities on either side and, in the case of tracheids, above and below as well. This permits the passage of water. The pits are frequently bordered by a lignified rim. These **bordered pits** sometimes have a central 'plug' or **torus** (figure 20.13). The torus may act as a control valve safeguarding the system as a whole if the water column in one of the xylem tubes should collapse.

As xylem cells develop, lignified thickenings of various kinds, often rings or spirals, are laid down on the immediate inside of the walls (figure 20.14). **Annular** and **spiral** thickening can be seen in longitudinal stem sections which have been treated with acidified phloroglucinol, which stains lignin red. Wood is mainly composed of tracheids and vessels, which gives some idea of the strength of these water-conducting cells and the role they also have in support (see Chapter 35).

Xylem tissue is found in all mature parts of the plant. The vessels and tracheids of the roots, stems and leaves connect to form a continuous system of water-conducting channels serving all parts of the plant.

Figure 20.13 Scanning electron micrograph of a bordered pit, **A** in surface view and **B** in section. Bordered pits are found in both flowering plants and conifers. The torus is common in conifers but comparatively rare in flowering plants. When there is an unequal pressure in two adjacent tracheids, the torus may be pushed over to one side, thus acting as a valve as shown in **C**.

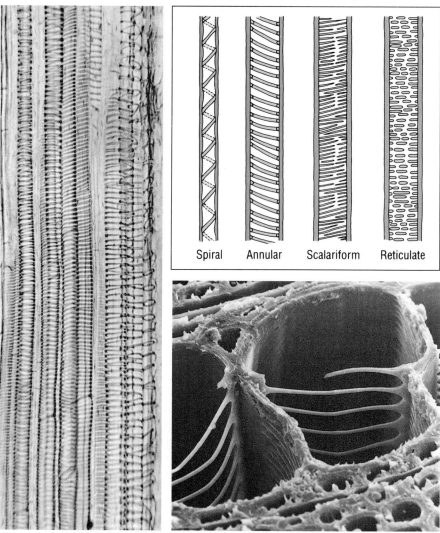

Figure 20.14 Different kinds of thickening found in xylem vessels. The photomicrograph (*above left*) is a longitudinal section of xylem magnified 300 times. The scanning electron micrograph (*right*) shows two vessels magnified 5000 times.

The ascent of water up the stem

Measurements have shown that there is a gradient of **water potential** through the whole plant, highest in the soil surrounding the roots and lowest in the atmosphere surrounding the leaves. This creates a flow of water through the plant as shown in figure 20.15. Moreover, the evaporation of water from the leaf cells would lower their pressure potential, further facilitating the flow of water.

Although this water potential gradient provides the basic mechanism by which water flows through plants, it cannot explain everything. In particular it cannot, on its own, explain how water rises to the top of very tall trees. To explain how this happens we need to examine some other forces that exist in plants.

Root pressure

If the stem of a plant is severed the cut end will exude copious quantities of water for a considerable time, suggesting that there is a force pushing water up the stem from the roots. This force is known as **root pressure**, and it was discovered by Stephen Hales in 1727. Hales found that it could be responsible for raising water to a height of over 6.4 m in a vine. He noticed, however, that it only occurred at certain times of the year.

Root pressure can be measured by attaching a suitable mercury manometer to the cut end of the stem (figure 20.16). In this way it has been found that sizeable pressures can be set up by the roots of some plants: a stump of *Fuchsia*, for example, can develop a pressure of over 90 kPa. We now know that root pressure is partly the result of osmotic inflow across the partially permeable membranes of the endodermis. However, metabolic inhibitors, low temperatures and shortage of oxygen cause a reduction of root pressure which suggests it is an active process involving the expenditure of energy. This explains why Hales found that it did not occur at all times of the year. Root pressure alone, therefore, does not account for the rise of water to the tops of tall trees. To complete the story we need to turn to what happens when water reaches the leaves.

Forces generated by the leaves

Water evaporates from the leaves by a process called **transpiration** which is discussed in detail later. The water lost this way is replaced by water drawn up through the xylem tubes in what is called the **transpiration stream**. Continuous columns of water therefore hang from the top of the plant. The force which holds them there is generated by the evaporation of water from the leaf to the atmosphere, and by surface tension forces in the walls of the leaf cells.

A column of water rises to a maximum height of 10 m in a tube which has a vacuum at its upper end under atmospheric pressure at sea level. How, then, can a continuous flow be maintained through the 20 m trunk of an average oak tree, or the 100 m of a redwood? If neither a vacuum nor root pressure can raise water to these heights there must be other mechanisms involved.

Water tends to adhere to the walls of any container. This is because there are forces of **adhesion** between the water molecules and the molecules comprising the material lining the container. Adhesion is defined as the force of attraction between unlike molecules. Now the narrower the container the greater will be the proportion of water molecules in contact with its walls. This results from the fact that the smaller the container the greater the area of its wall in comparison with the volume of water enclosed, i.e. the surface–volume ratio is greater. Being very narrow,

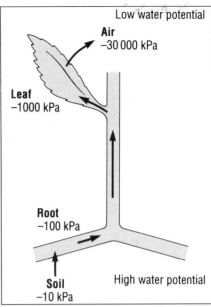

Figure 20.15 Estimated water potentials of soil water, root, leaf and air. There is much variation. These figures are based on a typical mesophyte growing in good soil. The steepest gradient is between the leaf and the air. Why do you think this is? The arrows indicate the flow of water through the plant.

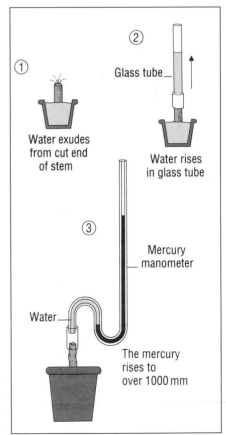

Figure 20.16 Three ways of demonstrating root pressure in a potted plant.

considerable adhesive forces will be expected to develop in the tracheids and vessels of the xylem, and these forces must be sufficient to support a considerable mass of water.

But the problem is not only to hold up the column of water but also to prevent it breaking in the middle. What is responsible for this? The answer is the force of **cohesion**. Cohesion is defined as the force of attraction between like molecules, in this case the water molecules. Experiments carried out by Josef Böhm in 1893 and by Dixon and Joly in 1895 provided evidence for the physical properties of water we have just discussed, i.e. adhesion and cohesion. These experiments are described in the box below.

The **cohesion–tension theory**, as it is called, offers an explanation of the rise of water in the xylem of all plants including tall trees. Cohesive forces between water molecules hold the continuous columns of water together, and when water transpires from the leaf the whole of the water column moves up the xylem.

However, there's a problem. If you suck water up a straw the walls collapse if you suck too hard, and the column of water breaks. In the xylem the thickened walls normally prevent this happening. The tension in the xylem of a very tall redwood tree must be colossal, but the tensile strength of the water columns must be sufficient or such trees could not exist.

Further evidence that the water is under tension in the xylem comes from taking measurements of the diameter of tree trunks over 24 hours with an instrument called a dendrograph. The measurements show that the diameter of a tree trunk decreases during the day. It reaches the minimum size in the afternoon after which the diameter increases again to reach a maximum in the early morning (figure 20.17).

In dry weather, however, when there is a shortage of water in the soil

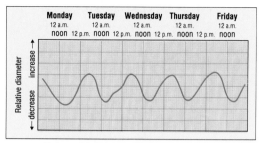

Figure 20.17 Daily variations in the diameter of the trunk of the Monterey pine, *Pinus radiata*.

Experimental evidence for the tensile strength of water

The tensile strength of water was demonstrated by the Austrian botanist Josef Böhm in 1893 using the apparatus shown in the illustration. The porous vessel and tube were filled with water and the end of the tube inserted into a bottle of mercury. The evaporation of water vapour through the porous vessel caused water to move up the capillary tubing, pulling the mercury behind it to a height of one metre.

This was a physical model of the movement of water up the xylem. If a bubble had got into the water column in Böhm's apparatus the mercury would have fallen back to 760 mm, the normal barometric height of mercury. This is because the water column, being broken, would no longer have the same tensile strength as it had before.

Just two years later in 1895 the Irish botanist H.H. Dixon and his co-worker J. Joly modified Böhm's experiment, using a pine twig instead of a porous pot. Transpiration from the pine needles also lifted a column of mercury, again demonstrating the tensile strength of a column of water. As a result of this experiment Dixon and Joly proposed what is now known as the cohesion theory of the rise of water in the xylem.

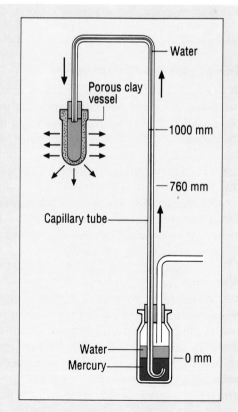

Böhm's apparatus for demonstrating the tensile strength of water.

the tension gets so high that the water columns do break and are said to make a distinct cracking sound as they do so. This is called **cavitation** and it results in a 'bubble' of gas forming in the tracheid or vessel. The bordered pits mentioned earlier act as valves ensuring that only a few vessels or tracheids are affected, thus safeguarding the system as a whole. The pits also allow the transpiration stream to find a way round an air bubble by moving into an adjacent vessel, past the bubble and then back into the original vessel chain. Also the 60 or so additional xylem vessels which are produced each year in secondary growth help to compensate for the vessels blocked by air bubbles.

From leaf to air

The stomata, as well as permitting the entry of carbon dioxide, allow the evaporation of water from the plant, the phenomenon known as transpiration which was referred to earlier. Transpiration is by no means restricted to the leaves for there are generally a number of stomata in the stem epidermis as well. However, the leaves with their large surface area and abundant stomata are the main source of water loss. To a small extent evaporation also takes place through the cuticle of the epidermal cells (**cuticular transpiration**) but this rarely exceeds 15 per cent of the total water loss.

The rate at which water is transpired from a plant may be considerable, particularly if the atmosphere is warm and dry. In one hour during a hot summer day a leaf may lose more water than it contains at any one moment. An oak tree may transpire as much as 680 litres of water in a day. It has been estimated that a sunflower plant may transpire over 200 litres of water during its life of six months. These figures give some idea of the scale of transpiration. They also emphasise how essential it is for a plant to have an adequate system of water uptake, for the water which is lost must be replaced.

How transpiration can be measured and the factors which affect the rate of transpiration are discussed in the box on page 344.

The evaporating surface

In figure 17.19 on page 297 you can see that each stoma opens into a small **sub-stomatal air chamber** which is lined with **spongy mesophyll cells**. The effective evaporating surface of a leaf consists of the saturated walls of these spongy mesophyll cells. The water evaporates from the walls and moves down a gradient of water potential from the plant to the atmosphere. As evaporation proceeds, water vapour accumulates in the sub-stomatal chambers from which it escapes through the open stomata. Provided that the plant has an adequate supply of water, the water which evaporates from the spongy mesophyll cells is replaced by water from the xylem vessels in the leaf. The water flows mainly in the apoplast pathway (figure 20.18).

Water stress

When a plant loses more water through transpiration than it can take up into its roots, it wilts and is said to suffer from **water stress**. The loss of water from the leaves raises the tension of the water columns in the xylem, and the water potential gradient from the soil to the xylem increases. As a result, the roots remove more and more water from the soil. Once the flow of water to the roots slows down, the stomata close rapidly thereby reducing water loss to a minimum. There is evidence that this rapid stomatal response is brought about by the hormone abscisic acid (ABA) secreted by the cells in the wilted leaves (see page 654).

The structure of leaves is dealt with on pages 296-298 in the context of photosynthesis.

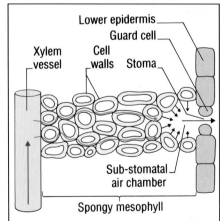

Figure 20.18 Water movement in a leaf. Continual evaporation through the open stoma (black arrows) encourages the further movement of water from the xylem towards the surface of the leaf (red arrows). The water moves mainly through the apoplast (cellulose walls), here coloured yellow. Water moves up the xylem vessel (blue arrow) to replace the water lost from the leaf.

Factors affecting the rate of transpiration

The rate of transpiration of a plant can be measured in various ways. A commonly used method is to measure the rate at which the plant takes up water, the assumption being that this is the same rate at which water evaporates from the leaves and other exposed surfaces. The apparatus for doing this is called a **potometer**.

There are various types of potometer but they all work on the same principle. The cut end of the stem of a leafy shoot is attached to a capillary tube full of water. There must be no air locks in the system: the water in the stem and the capillary tube should form a continuous system. The rate of water uptake is measured by introducing an air bubble into the capillary tube and timing how long it takes for the bubble to travel a certain distance along the tube.

Futher details of potometry are given in the Student's Manual.

What factors, then, affect the rate of transpiration? For convenience we can divide them into internal and external factors.

The most important internal condition affecting transpiration is the state of the stomata: their number, distribution, structural features and how open they happen to be. Any factor that influences the opening and closing of the stomata will obviously affect transpiration. In some plants the stomata and other features are modified to prevent excessive water loss.

External conditions affecting transpiration include:

- **Temperature**. A high temperature provides latent heat of vaporisation and therefore encourages evaporation from the mesophyll cells.

- **Relative humidity**, the degree to which the atmosphere is saturated with water vapour, is important because it determines the **saturation deficit**, i.e. the humidity difference between the inside and outside of the leaf. Normally the relative humidity in the sub-stomatal chambers is very high. (Why should this be so?) The lower the relative humidity of the surrounding atmosphere the greater will be the saturation deficit, and the faster will water vapour escape through the stomata.

- **Air movements**. Water vapour tends to build up on the underside of the leaf as it diffuses out of the stomata. Obviously the atmosphere will be most highly saturated immediately outside each stoma and become progressively less saturated as water vapour diffuses away. Water vapour molecules are deflected by the perimeter of a stoma, and the closer they are to the perimeter the greater is the deflection. The diffusion paths of the water vapour molecules therefore describe a hemisphere around the stoma, called a **diffusion shell** (see illustration). If the air is still, diffusion shells build up around the stomata and the rate of evaporation from the mesophyll cells inevitably decreases. Air movements blow away these diffusion shells thereby increasing the rate of evaporation from the leaf.

- **Atmospheric pressure**. The lower the atmospheric pressure, the greater is the rate of evaporation. (Why is this?) For this reason alpine plants, which live at high altitudes where the atmospheric pressure is lower than at sea level, are liable to have a high rate of transpiration, and many of them therefore have adaptations which prevent excessive loss of water.

- **Light**. If the light intensity is increased the rate of evaporation from a plant increases. The reason is not that light affects evaporation as such, but that it causes the stomata to open, thereby increasing water loss from the plant.

- **Water supply**. Transpiration depends on the walls of the mesophyll cells being thoroughly wet. For this to be so the plant must have an adequate water supply from the soil. If for some reason the plant cannot take up water from the soil (for example if it is too dry) sooner or later the stomata close, thus reducing the rate of transpiration.

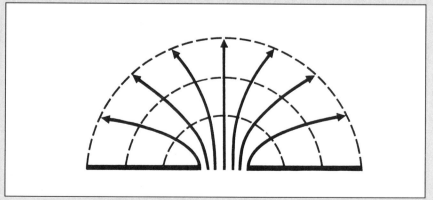

Diagram of a diffusion shell. Points of equal water potential (joined by broken lines) form a series of hemispheres over the pore. As a result, the paths of diffusion of molecules along the water potential gradient are curved (shown by arrowed lines). This means that the molecules near the edge of the pore escape more readily than those in the centre.

The closing of the stomata reduces the rate of photosynthesis. This is one of the most noticeable side-effects of water stress. However, it is brought about not by the shortage of water as such but by the closing of stomata which then reduces the uptake of carbon dioxide.

The functions of transpiration

Transpiration is the inevitable result of the necessity for the inside of the leaf to be open to the atmosphere for the uptake of carbon dioxide. As such it might be regarded as more of a nuisance than a help. But it does have a positive function, namely that it cools the leaves, an important effect particularly in hot conditions (see page 410). In addition, the transpiration stream provides the pathway through which mineral salts are transported in the plant. To that topic we now turn.

Uptake of mineral salts

In addition to carbon dioxide and water, plants require a variety of mineral elements (see page 124). These are absorbed as the appropriate ions from the surrounding water in the case of aquatic plants, and from the soil water in the case of terrestrial plants.

The concentration of certain ions may be many times greater in the cells of aquatic plants than in the surrounding water (figure 20.19). This indicates that they enter the plant against a concentration gradient. Moreover certain ions are more concentrated than others. These observations suggest that ions are selectively absorbed by active transport, involving the expenditure of energy.

There are good reasons to believe that in terrestrial plants, mineral ions are absorbed by similar means. It has been found, for instance, that the uptake of certain ions by young barley roots is increased by raising the temperature, and decreased by oxygen deprivation or treatment with a metabolic poison, all strong indications that active transport is involved (figure 20.20).

Like water, mineral ions are taken up into the root hairs and other surface cells in the young parts of the root. Active transport occurs across the plasma membranes of the root hairs, and the ions move from cell to cell via the symplast through plasmodesmata. There is some evidence that the endodermis may actively secrete salts into the vascular tissues (see page 337).

Once inside the vessels and tracheids, the ions are carried up the stem along with the water in the transpiration stream. This has been shown by **ringing experiments**. All the living tissues are removed in a ring from around the central core of vessels and tracheids in a woody stem, and the plant is then placed in a solution containing radioactive phosphate, $^{32}PO_4{}^{3-}$. Removal of the living cells in no way impedes the upward movement of the radioactive phosphate which can subsequently be detected in the leaves by means of a Geiger–Müller tube.

From the xylem vessels the ions are conveyed, probably by a combination of diffusion and active transport, to their two main destinations: the photosynthetic cells of the leaf and the various growing points in the plant. Here they are put to their sundry uses, for example the building up of amino acids and proteins.

Special methods of obtaining nutrients

Some soils are deficient in mineral salts, and plants living in them have special means of obtaining nitrogen and other essential elements. For

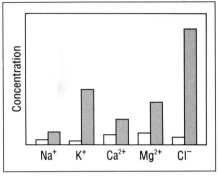

Figure 20.19 Bar chart showing the relative concentrations of different ions in pond water (clear boxes) and in the cell sap of the green alga *Nitella* (shaded boxes). The much greater concentration of ions in the cells suggest that their absorption involves active transport.

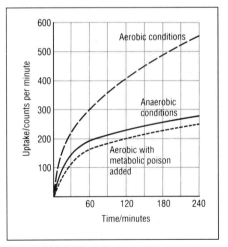

Figure 20.20 The influence of oxygen deprivation and metabolic poison on the uptake of sulphate ions by intact barley plants. The plants were provided with sulphate labelled with radioactive ^{35}S and the amount taken up by the plants was measured by means of a Geiger–Müller tube. The much reduced uptake in anaerobic conditions and with addition of a metabolic poison suggests that active transport is involved. (Data kindly supplied by Dr Richard Gliddon, Queen Elizabeth School, Bristol)

Figure 20.21 The bird's nest orchid, *Neottia nidus-avis*. It has no chlorophyll so cannot photosynthesise and depends on its mychorrhiza for carbohydrates and proteins. It lives under beech trees where little light penetrates and where few other plants are found.

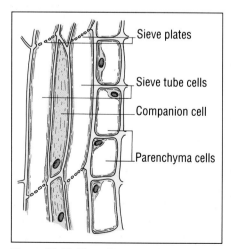

Sieve plates

Sieve tube cells

Companion cell

Parenchyma cells

Figure 20.22 The cells present in the phloem as seen in a longitudinal section of phloem tissue under the light microscope.

example, the roots of many plants, which live in soil rich in humus but deficient in mineral salts, possess a **mycorrhiza**, an association between their roots and a fungus. Birch and beech trees are examples of plants which have such an association. The fungus has the effect of increasing the absorbing area of the root. In some cases the fungus is located on the surface of the root, in others it is internal; either way, it has the ability to break down the humus into soluble nutrients, some of which are absorbed and utilised by the host.

The majority of plants with mycorrhizal roots only obtain phosphorus, and perhaps nitrogen, compounds from the fungus. They can photosynthesise normally and can therefore manufacture their own carbohydrates, some of which are absorbed by the fungus. The association is therefore one in which both partners benefit, an example of **mutualism**.

Although most plants with mycorrhizal roots can photosynthesise, there are some that lack chlorophyll and cannot do so. A good example is the bird's nest orchid, *Neottia nidus-avis*, an unusual inhabitant of beech woods (figure 20.21). Because it has no chlorophyll it is a pale brown colour. Such plants depend upon their mycorrhiza for carbohydrates as well as protein.

Another special adaptation is seen in leguminous plants such as peas, beans, gorse and clover which harbour **nitrogen-fixing bacteria** in their roots.

Plants living in nitrogen-deficient soil sometimes resort to feeding on animals as a means of obtaining nitrogen. These **insectivorous plants** trap small animals, mainly insects, in a modified leaf where they are subjected to the action of protease enzymes and digested. The products of digestion are absorbed into the leaf and transported to wherever they are needed.

Transport of organic substances

So far we have considered the uptake and transport of water and mineral ions in plants. They are needed as raw materials for various metabolic processes. Now we must consider how the products of metabolism are transported. In particular, the products of photosynthesis (sugars, amino acids and the like) have to be moved from the leaves where they are formed to the parts of the plant where they are needed. All the cells that are unable to photosynthesise need a share of these materials, especially those in the apices of the roots, stem and branches where cell division and growth are taking place.

Transport of food materials to these **growing points** is greatest in the spring and summer when growth is most prolific. Later in the year many plants form **perennating organs** (such as tubers, bulbs and corms) to which food materials are transported for storage until the following season. When the next season arrives the stored food is transported in soluble form to the growing points of the new plant.

Transport of the soluble products of photosynthesis in a plant is called **translocation**, and a number of experiments have been done showing that it occurs in the part of the vascular tissue known as the **phloem**. We must start by looking in detail at this tissue.

Phloem tissue

When the phloem tissue of a flowering plant is observed under a microscope three main types of cell may be seen: **sieve cells, companion cells** and **parenchyma cells** (figure 20.22).

Sieve cells lack nuclei, which disintegrate during development. The cells are placed end to end to form long **sieve tubes** running parallel with the long axis of the plant. It is the sieve tubes which form the channels for translocation. Sieve tubes are only found in angiosperms; conifers have less specialised sieve cells which are not aligned in a vertical manner.

Each sieve cell has perforated end walls known as **sieve plates**. The perforations between one cell and the next are perfectly matched and allow the passage of materials from one to another (figure 20.23).

Slender **cytoplasmic filaments** extend from one sieve cell to the next through the pores in the sieve plate. The cytoplasm of these filaments is structurally very simple: it contains no endoplasmic reticulum, mitochondria, plastids or other organelles. All these disintegrate during development. A few such organelles persist immediately adjacent to the cellulose wall, but elsewhere they are absent.

Closely applied to the side of each sieve cell are one or more companion cells, which possess a nucleus, dense endoplasmic reticulum, ribosomes and numerous mitochondria. Plasmodesmata connect each sieve cell with its adjacent companion cell or cells (figure 20.24). The latter are the site of intense metabolic activity. On purely structural grounds we might predict that translocation of food materials takes place along the sieve tubes, with the adjacent companion cells providing the necessary energy for some part of the process.

The sieve tubes with their perforated sieve plates seem to be well suited for transport. However, the perforations are often blocked with protein and, during dormancy, with carbohydrate. This gives the plant some protection from leakage of the phloem contents during grazing by herbivores.

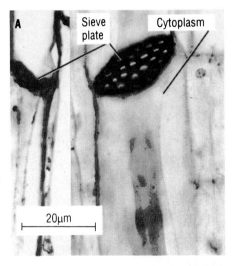

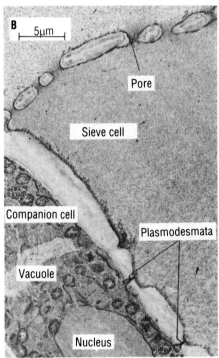

Figure 20.23

A Photomicrograph of sieve cells from the phloem of a flowering plant, showing the sieve plate.

B Electron micrograph of part of a sieve tube and neighbouring companion cell showing the pores in the sieve plate The micrograph also shows plasmodesmata piercing the cellulose wall between the sieve tube and companion cell.

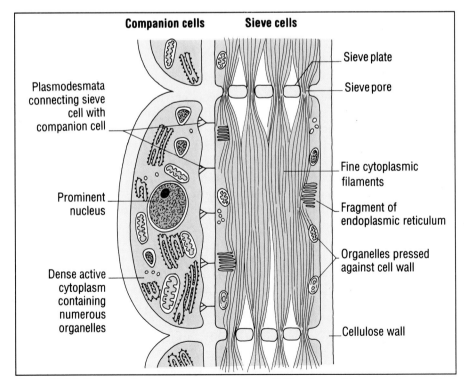

Figure 20.24 Diagram of a sieve cell and companion cell. The sieve cell has no nucleus and not many organelles, what few there are being pushed to one side. In contrast the companion cell has a prominent nucleus and dense cytoplasm containing numerous mitochondria, abundant endoplasmic reticulum and ribosomes.

Figure 20.25 An experiment to test the hypothesis that translocation of food substances occurs in the phloem. Two privet shoots were prepared. One of them (the experimental shoot) was ringed – that is, the outer part of the stem including the phloem tissue (but not the xylem) was removed. The other shoot (the control) was left intact. A drop of sucrose solution containing radioactive carbon dioxide (^{14}C) was applied to one leaf of each shoot (fed leaf). Both shoots were given water and left in the light for 24 hours. They were then dried and placed flat on a piece of photographic film and left for four to five days in the dark. The radiation from the plants was recorded on the film and the resulting autoradiographs showed the distribution of the ^{14}C. Notice that in the control shoot the ^{14}C has spread to the leaves at the top of the shoot, but in the experimental shoot the ^{14}C has been blocked at the ringing site where the phloem was removed.

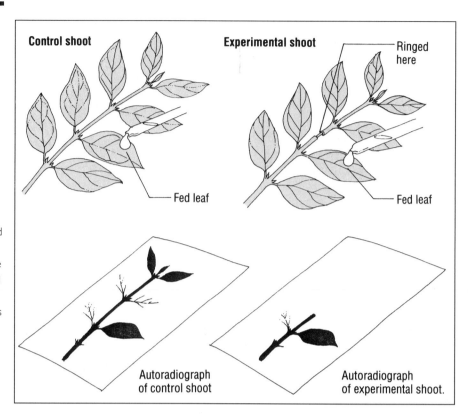

Figure 20.26 The toothwort *Lathraea squamaria* is a parasite on the roots of hazel, elm and poplar. It has no chlorophyll and obtains its food from the phloem of the host plant.

Establishing the site of translocation

How do we know that translocation occurs in the phloem? Some of the earliest investigations involved **ringing experiments** of the type described on page 345. It so happens that in a mature tree trunk the phloem is confined to the inner part of the bark. Now if a ring of bark is stripped off a tree trunk it can be shown that the sugar concentration increases immediately above the ring and decreases below it, indicating that the downward movement of sugars is blocked at that point.

More critical investigations have been carried out with **radioactive tracers**. If a plant is exposed to carbon dioxide labelled with radioactive ^{14}C, the ^{14}C becomes incorporated into the products of photosynthesis which are subsequently detected in the part of the stem that contains the phloem (figure 20.25). That these substances are confined to the phloem can be shown by cutting sections of the stem, placing the sections in contact with photographic film and making **autoradiographs**. It is found that the sites of radioactivity correspond precisely to the positions of the phloem. These experiments indicate that organic food materials are transported in the phloem. In fact one can imagine that the sieve tubes carry a constant stream of materials from the leaves to the rest of the plant.

A number of **parasitic organisms** make use of this and tap into the phloem of certain plants in order to gain nourishment. Thus several parasitic plants send out sucker-like processes which pierce the roots or stem of the host plant and link up with the sieve tubes. Dodder, a climbing plant belonging to the convolvulus family, attaches itself to the stems of various host plants in this way. Broomrapes and toothwort go for the roots (figure 20.26). In all these cases the fact that the parasite acquires ready-made organic food means that it does not require chlorophyll. Accordingly it lacks the green colour characteristic of most plants and may be either yellow in appearance or more highly coloured as a result of the presence of other pigments.

A striking example of an animal parasite that feeds on the contents of the phloem is that enemy of every gardener – the aphid. Aphids include green flies, white flies and black flies. They suck plant juices by means of a sharp proboscis rather like a hypodermic needle which is inserted into the stem or one of the leaf veins. The plant juices then pass up the proboscis to the aphid's gut.

Use has been made of this by Tom Mittler of the University of California to study translocation. His method is beautiful for its simplicity and ingenuity. An aphid alights on a stem or leaf and inserts its proboscis into the tissue (figure 20.27). A stream of carbon dioxide is then passed over the animal to immobilise it. The proboscis is then cut as close to the head as possible, and left sticking into the plant. It is found that fluid exudes from the cut end of the proboscis and may continue to do so for days, providing a perfect technique for tapping the contents of the phloem with minimum injury to the plant (figure 20.28). The fluid is collected with a micropipette, and chemical analysis shows that it contains sucrose and a wide range of amino acids (table 20.1).

That these substances really come from the phloem can be confirmed by cutting thin sections of the part of the stem or leaf which has the proboscis in it. In this way it has been demonstrated that the tip of the proboscis pierces a single sieve tube.

The rate at which fluid exudes from a sieve tube through an aphid proboscis may exceed 5 mm^3 per hour, which must delight the average aphid as it means that it does not even have to suck in order to get a plentiful supply of food – the pressures in the plant are sufficient to force out the fluid. For a botanist this provides a means of calculating the speed of translocation. An exudation rate of 5 mm^3 per hour means that an individual sieve tube cell must be emptied and refilled between three and ten times per second. From this it can be calculated that the speed of translocation in an individual sieve tube is of the order of 1000 mm^3 per hour, a figure which is about twice that obtained from work with radioactive tracers. (Why do you think the difference occurs?)

Loading and unloading the sieve tubes

We come now to the way sugars and other soluble products of photosynthesis are fed into the sieve tubes in the leaf and removed from them in the roots and other parts of the plant where they are needed. In some flowering

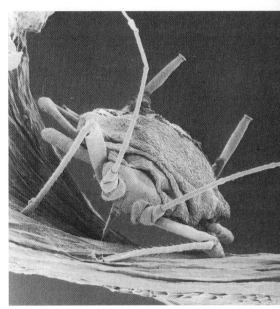

Figure 20.27 This photograph shows an aphid with its proboscis inserted into the phloem tissue of a leaf.

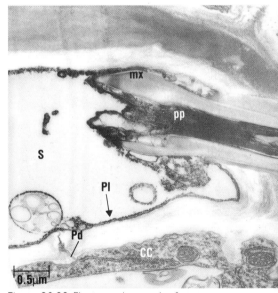

Figure 20.28 Electron micrograph of a section through a leaf vein showing the proboscis of an aphid inserted into a sieve cell (**S**) in the phloem. The food canal of the proboscis is full of material, presumably phloem protein (**pp**). Above the food canal is one of the sharp maxillary stylets (**mx**) which enables the proboscis to pierce the plant tissue. The plasma membrane (**Pl**) surrounding the sieve cell is clearly visible. Below the sieve cell you can see part of an adjacent companion cell (**CC**) and one of the plasmodesmata (**Pd**) which connect it to the sieve cell.

Amino acid	Concentration	
	mol m^{-3}	%
Glutamic acid	13.0	34.76
Aspartic acid	8.8	23.53
Threonine	5.4	14.44
Glycine	2.4	6.42
Alanine	2.0	5.35
Serine	1.6	4.28
Valine	1.6	4.28
Isoleucine	1.0	2.67
Phenylalanine	0.6	1.60
Histidine	0.4	1.07
Leucine	0.4	1.07
Lysine	0.2	0.53
Arginine	Trace	Trace
Methionine	Trace	Trace
Total amino acids	35.2	100

Table 20.1 The amino acid composition of phloem exudate obtained from Castor oil (*Ricinus*) plants.

plants the cells which surround the sieve tubes in the phloem include, in addition to the companion cells, specialised parenchyma cells called **transfer cells**.

Transfer cells differ from ordinary parenchyma cells in possessing irregular intuckings of the primary cell wall and plasma membrane. These intuckings increase the surface area and bring the plasma membrane into close association with the cytoplasm of adjacent cells. In the leaf the transfer cells are responsible for moving the products of photosynthesis from the mesophyll cells to the sieve tubes. They also carry water and salts from the xylem vessels to the mesophyll cells and indeed to the sieve tubes too.

The transfer cells are metabolically active and, together with the companion cells, they supply the necessary energy for loading the sieve tubes. In the roots, storage organs and growing points, similar cells are responsible for retrieving solutes from the sieve tubes and moving them to the cells that need them. However, not all species possess transfer cells, and in those that lack them the energy comes from the other cells.

Transfer cells are not confined to the phloem. They are found in a number of places where active transport is thought to occur, for example in the secretory tissues inside nectaries and in the hydathodes at the edges of certain leaves (see page 392). They also occur in salt-secreting glands in the leaves of the saltbush *Atriplex*, a halophyte which lives in dry, saline soil in the Australian and Californian deserts.

The mechanism of translocation

We have seen that the sieve tubes are loaded with sugars by active transport, but what maintains the flow of the sugars once they have entered the sieve tubes? Of course it would be possible for sugars and other substances in the sieve tubes to move by diffusion along concentration gradients, but the speed at which they travel rules this method out. The truth is that there is, as yet, no complete answer to this question.

The mass flow hypothesis

Among the many mechanisms proposed over the years, one which has gained some support from experimental work is the **mass flow hypothesis** put forward in 1927 by Ernst Münch. The way mass flow is believed to occur in the sieve tubes may be illustrated by the model in figure 20.29. Münch himself used such a model for demonstrating his hypothesis. If set

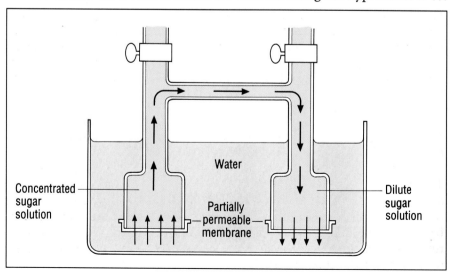

Figure 20.29 Ernst Münch's demonstration of how mass flow might occur in the phloem. Water flows through the system from left to right, carrying the sugar molecules with it. Full explanation in the text.

up correctly, water passes into the left-hand funnel by osmosis through the partially permeable membrane. The hydrostatic pressure so developed causes the sugar solution to flow into the right-hand funnel and forces water out through the partially permeable membrane on that side. There is therefore a flow of solution from left to right which will cease when the concentrations in the two funnels are equal.

Of course in the living plant the flow must be *continuous*. In order to maintain a continuous flow, sugars would have to be loaded into the sieve tubes at one end (the **source**) and off-loaded at their destination (the **sink**). The loading of sugars into the phloem is achieved in the leaf by active transport, as we have seen. This creates a high sugar concentration at the source which draws water into the sieve tubes by osmosis.

At the root end of the system, sugars are removed for use in metabolic processes, and water flows out into the intercellular spaces. The continual input of sugars and water at the top of the system and their removal at the bottom creates a pressure gradient which maintains the downward flow of fluid in the sieve tubes.

If the mass flow hypothesis is correct, we would expect there to be a pressure in the sieve tubes. That such a pressure exists is supported by the aphid experiment mentioned earlier and by the simple experiment described in figure 20.30.

Electro-osmosis

There is, however, a problem with mass flow. If it occurs we would expect different substances to move at the same speed, but it is known from tracer experiments that sugars and amino acids can move at different speeds, and even in opposite directions within the same group of sieve tubes.

There is another objection to the mass flow hypothesis. Calculations indicate that the pressure gradients which actually exist would be insufficient to overcome the considerable resistance imposed by the sieve pores, particularly as the pores are bunged up with the filaments mentioned earlier. This has led to the suggestion that mass flow might be aided at the sieve plates by **electro-osmosis**. Electro-osmosis is the passage of water across a charged membrane. It is argued that an electrical potential might be maintained across the sieve plate, the lower side being negative relative to the upper side. Such a potential could be maintained by an active pumping of positive ions in an upward direction. A charged solution in a sieve element would be expected to flow through the sieve plate towards the negative side in a manner similar to that which occurs in electrophoresis (see page 143). The mechanism is summarised in figure 20.31. Although theoretically possible, there is little experimental evidence that it actually happens, though in certain plants potential differences of the right order of magnitude are claimed to have been detected.

Surface spreading

Another mechanism which has been put forward is **surface spreading**. The idea here is that solute molecules might spread over the interface between two different cytoplasmic materials, as oil spreads at a water–air interface. The molecular film so formed could be kept moving by molecules being added at one end and removed at the other. A major objection here is that the films would be so thin that a very large number of them would need to be formed to account for the known rates of translocation. However, sieve tubes do contain numerous membranes and filaments which collectively might provide the necessary surface.

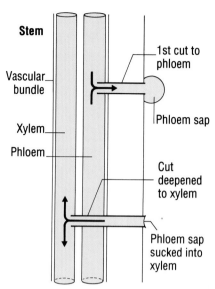

Figure 20.30 A demonstration of the pressures in a stem. When a cut is made into the phloem, a drop of fluid oozes out, indicating that the pressure in the phloem is greater than atmospheric. In contrast, when the cut is made deeper so that it penetrates the xylem, the fluid moves in again, indicating that in the xylem the pressure is less than atmospheric.

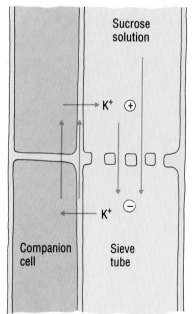

Figure 20.31 Possible mechanism for the electro-osmotic flow of water and sugars through the pores of the phloem sieve plates. The potassium ions (K^+) create a gradient of electrical potential, as a result of which water molecules flow through the sieve plate dragging the sucrose molecules with them.

Active transport

Independent movement of different substances strongly suggests that translocation involves some sort of active mechanism. This is supported by other lines of evidence. For example, phloem tissue has a high rate of respiration, and there is a close correlation between the speed of translocation and the metabolic rate. Again, lowering the temperature and treatment with metabolic poisons both reduce the rate of translocation, suggesting that it is an active energy-requiring process which cannot be explained by physical forces alone.

Streaming

In their search for a mechanism of translocation, botanists nowadays attach increasing significance to the fine **protein filaments** which span the sieve cells from end to end. As shown in figure 20.24A (on page 347), these filaments are continuous from one sieve cell to the next via the pores in the sieve plates. High magnification electron micrographs suggest that in the vicinity of the sieve plate the protein filaments take the form of microtubules of approximately 20 nm diameter, but as they traverse the sieve cell they break up into finer strands. It has been suggested that solutes might be transported by **streaming** along these protein filaments, the necessary energy coming from the sieve tubes themselves or the companion cells. It is envisaged that some strands convey solutes downwards, while others convey them upwards, thus accounting for the bi-directional flow of materials that is known to occur in the sieve tubes. Some botanists claim to have seen cytoplasmic streaming in sieve tubes.

How exactly this streaming occurs is unknown, but one suggestion is that the protein is contractile, rather like that found in muscle, and material is swept along by some kind of wave-like movement of the filaments. But this is highly speculative and the reader is advised to consult recent articles on the subject for the latest views.

Whatever the details of the mechanism, streaming of the cytoplasm has been observed in many different plant cells. You have probably observed it yourself in the cells of Canadian pondweed *Elodea* where sometimes the chloroplasts circulate round and round the cells (cyclosis). It is possible that a similar kind of cytoplasmic streaming occurs in sieve cells, at least in young ones which still contain active cytoplasm (figure 20.32).

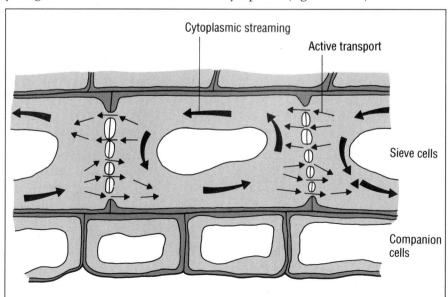

Fig 20.32 Diagram showing how cyclosis (cytoplasmic streaming) might occur in young sieve cells. Coupled with active transport through the sieve pores, it could account for bi-directional transport of food substances in the sieve tubes. Cytoplasmic streaming (cyclosis), thick arrows; active transport, thin arrows.

Summary

1 Roots are adapted for the uptake of water by the possession of a permeable epidermis with **root hairs**.

2 Water moves through the living tissues of the root via either the **apoplast** (cellulose cell walls) or the **symplast** (cytoplasm). The **Casparian strip** in the radial walls of the **endodermal cells** diverts the water through the symplast pathway into the xylem.

3 The **stem** is adapted for carrying water and mineral salts from roots to leaves. The water and salts are transported in lignified **xylem elements** (**tracheids** and **vessels**) within **vascular bundles** which are continuous with the vascular tissues in the roots and leaves. Lateral movement is possible through **bordered pits** which in certain species contain a **torus**.

4 **Root pressure** is a phenomenon which contributes to the rise of water up the stem but it cannot account for the rise of water to the tops of tall trees.

5 Water evaporates from leaves by **transpiration** which is an integral part of the mechanism by which water is taken into the plant from the soil.

6 The water moves down a water potential gradient from the soil, through the plant to the air.

7 The rise of water in tall stems is thought to be helped by two physical properties of water: **adhesion** and **cohesion**. These forces hold the water columns up in the xylem and prevent them breaking (**cavitation**).

8 In the leaves water evaporates from the surfaces of the spongy mesophyll cells into the sub-stomatal chambers, whence it diffuses through the stomata to the outside.

9 The rate of transpiration can be estimated indirectly by measuring the rate of water uptake by a cut leafy shoot using a **potometer**.

10 The rate of transpiration depends on temperature, relative humidity, air movements, atmospheric pressure, light and water supply.

11 Mineral salts are taken up as ions by active transport and are carried in the transpiration stream through the xylem to the leaves.

12 Some plants have special methods of obtaining essential elements, particularly nitrogen: they may harbour mutualistic **mycorrhizal fungi** or nitrogen-fixing bacteria in their roots, or they may adopt a parasitic or insectivorous habit.

13 Organic compounds manufactured in the leaves are **translocated** to the rest of the plant in **sieve tubes** in the **phloem** within the vascular tissues. The structure of the sieve tubes shows adaptations for this function.

14 The mechanism of translocation is not fully understood although mass flow, active transport or streaming in strands of cytoplasm have all been suggested. Considerable controversy still surrounds this aspect of plant physiology.

Review questions

1 What features enable land plants to absorb water from the soil?

2 Describe the pathways water may take to reach the xylem, once the water has entered the root.

3 What evidence suggests that root pressure alone cannot account for the rise of water to the tops of tall trees?

4 Combine all the evidence available to you in this chapter to put forward a general theory to explain the rise of water in a plant.

5 What role do stomata play in controlling the loss of water by transpiration, particularly during a period of water stress?

6 How does the uptake of mineral ions differ from the uptake of water from the soil?

7 When transplanting plants from one place to another it is important to take some of the natural soil still clinging to its roots. Suggest reasons for this.

8 Summarise the way the soluble products of photosynthesis are believed to be transported from the leaves to other parts of the plant.

9 Why do you think the mechanism by which substances are transported in the phloem is still so uncertain?

10 What part have aphids played in research on the phloem?

Further reading

C.J. Clegg and Gene Cox (who originated many of the micrographs in this book) have written an excellent book entitled *Anatomy and Activities of Plants* (John Murray, 1978) which contains numerous photomicrographs accompanied by a brief explanatory text.

On the functional side, *Transport Phenomena in Plants* by D.A. Baker (Chapman and Hall, 1978) is only 80 pages long but deals with certain aspects of xylem and phloem transport in more detail than is possible in this book.

J.F. Sutcliffe's book, *Plants and Water*, mentioned on page 207 in connection with plant water relations, is also useful for this chapter.

These topics are discussed further in *Biology, Advanced Topics*: stomatal opening and closure, water movement in terms of the water potential concept and the uptake of nutrient ions

Part IV

CONTROL OF THE INTERNAL ENVIRONMENT

*T*he conditions in which life processes can take place are quite narrow, and fluctuations in the conditions surrounding the cells of a multicellular organism – the internal environment – can profoundly affect their normal functioning. This part of the book is concerned with how organisms adjust to changing conditions.

First the principles underlying the body's adjustment mechanisms are outlined, the control of blood sugar being taken by way of illustration. There is a detailed account of the liver, one of the most important organs in controlling the internal conditions in the mammalian body.

In subsequent chapters two other aspects of control are discussed: first the elimination of nitrogenous waste matter and regulation of water balance, then the control of the body temperature. The control mechanisms involved in both these processes have been of paramount importance in the evolution of living things.

The human body must respond quickly to the invasion of harmful microorganisms. This important aspect of control of the internal environment is discussed in the final chapter.

Photograph: Edward H. White floats in space during the Gemini–Titan 4 space flight.

CHAPTER 21   The principles of homeostasis

One of the generalisations to emerge from physiological studies carried out over the last century or so is that the conditions in which cells can function properly are narrow. Even quite small fluctuations in osmotic pressure, temperature or the amounts of certain chemical substances can disrupt biochemical processes and in extreme cases may kill the cells.

This basic idea was first recognised by the French physiologist Claude Bernard (figure 21.1). In 1857 he wrote *La fixite du milieu interieur est la condition de la vie libre* ('The constancy of the internal environment is the condition for free life').

Claude Bernard's famous statement will form the theme of this chapter. First we shall examine the term 'internal environment'. Then we shall look at the principles underlying the mechanisms by which 'constancy' is maintained. And finally, we shall see what Claude Bernard meant by 'free life'.

Figure 21.1 Claude Bernard, 1813–1878, has been described as the father of modern experimental physiology. He was the first person to appreciate the importance of the 'internal environment' in the functioning of organisms. Born in Villefranche in the Rhone Valley, France, Bernard studied medicine. However, he abandoned the idea of medical practice in favour of scientific research and eventually became Professor of General Physiology at the Sorbonne. From all accounts he was a harsh man who worked relentlessly in his laboratory and expected the same of others. 'One must live in the laboratory', he once said.

What and where is the internal environment?

In mammalian tissues the cells are surrounded by tiny spaces filled with **tissue fluid**. The tissue fluid provides the cells with the medium in which they have to live, and represents the organism's internal environment. It is this that must be kept constant, or at least held within narrow limits, if the cells are to continue their vital functions. To see how this is achieved we must first understand how tissue fluid is formed.

The formation of tissue fluid

Tissue fluid is formed from the blood by a process of ultra-filtration in which small molecules and ions are separated from the larger molecules and cells. Analysis of tissue fluid shows that it consists of blood plasma, minus the proteins. The walls of the capillaries act as a filter holding back the comparatively large plasma protein molecules together with the cellular components of the blood, but allowing water and other constituents of the plasma to pass through. Research has shown that the actual filter is not the capillary endothelial cells themselves but the **basement membrane** on which they rest (figure 21.2).

How does this process of ultra-filtration take place? When blood reaches the arterial end of a capillary it is under pressure because of the pumping action of the heart and the resistance to the blood flow offered by the narrow capillaries. The hydrostatic pressure forces the fluid part of the blood through the capillary walls into the intercellular spaces. This outward flow is opposed by the osmotic pressure of the blood, created by the presence of the plasma proteins. However, the hydrostatic pressure of the blood is greater than the osmotic pressure, so there is a net flow of fluid out of the capillaries.

Once formed, the tissue fluid circulates amongst the cells and eventually returns to the blood system. At the venous end of the capillary system the hydrostatic pressure of the blood is relatively low and is here exceeded by the osmotic pressure. The hydrostatic pressure has decreased mainly because the capillaries open into the much wider venules which offer less resistance to the blood flow. The osmotic pressure has increased because the loss of water from the blood has concentrated the plasma proteins. With the osmotic pressure now exceeding the hydrostatic pressure, tissue fluid flows back into the capillaries and is thus returned to the circulation. The pressure causing this flow is relatively small, so not all the tissue fluid

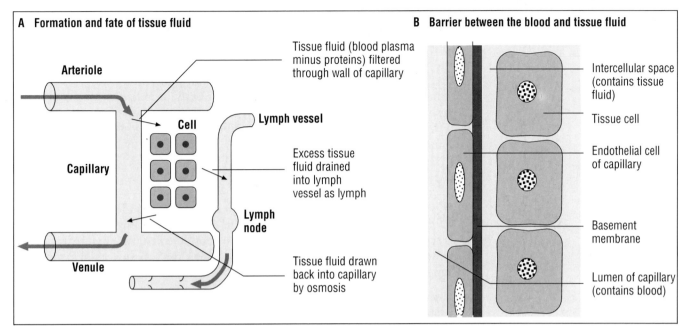

A Formation and fate of tissue fluid

Arteriole

Cell

Capillary

Venule

Tissue fluid (blood plasma minus proteins) filtered through wall of capillary

Lymph vessel

Excess tissue fluid drained into lymph vessel as lymph

Lymph node

Tissue fluid drawn back into capillary by osmosis

B Barrier between the blood and tissue fluid

Intercellular space (contains tissue fluid)

Tissue cell

Endothelial cell of capillary

Basement membrane

Lumen of capillary (contains blood)

follows this route. The residual tissue fluid is drained into the **lymph vessels**, where it becomes **lymph** which eventually passes into the veins.

It is important that tissue fluid should be returned to the blood system at the same rate as it is formed. If for some reason tissue fluid is formed faster than it can be removed, it accumulates in the tissues. As a result the tissues swell up, a condition called **oedema** (figure 21.3).

Tissue fluid is the medium in which the cells are bathed. From it the cells receive all the substances they need, and into it they release unwanted substances. This is Claude Bernard's *milieu interieur*, and since it is formed from the blood it is the blood which must be kept constant. Much of an animal's physiology is concerned with doing just this.

What factors must be kept constant?

The most important features of the internal environment that must be kept constant are:

- The concentration of glucose.
- The concentration of various ions, e.g. sodium and potassium.
- The concentration of carbon dioxide.
- The osmotic pressure, determined by the relative concentrations of water and solutes (**osmoregulation**).
- The temperature (**thermoregulation**).
- The pH (acid-base balance).

In addition certain toxic substances must be got rid of altogether or at least kept at very low concentration. These include nitrogenous waste products arising from protein metabolism.

If tissues are removed from an animal and subjected to conditions markedly different from those prevailing in the body, they will die; but if maintained under the correct conditions, they will survive. This was appreciated by the nineteenth century physiologist Sidney Ringer who perfected the art of keeping tissues and organs alive outside the body. He found, for example, that the heart of a frog or mammal would continue to beat for a long time outside the body if kept in a mixture of sodium, potassium and calcium salts, provided of course that it was adequately oxygenated.

It is now known that virtually all tissues can be kept alive in a suitable

Figure 21.2 The formation and fate of tissue fluid.

A shows very diagrammatically how tissue fluid is formed, and what happens to it subsequently. The lymph node contains numerous cells which are important in defence against disease (see page 416).

B Greatly magnified view of the wall of the capillary showing the basement membrane through which tissue fluid is filtered from the blood.

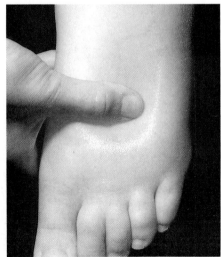

Figure 21.3 A case of oedema in the foot. Oedema tends to occur if the mean blood pressure in the capillaries is consistently too high, or if the concentration of plasma proteins in the blood is too low. A common cause medically is a high pressure at the venous end of the capillaries due to heart failure.

mixture of ions similar to the tissue fluids. Such solutions, which vary according to the species, are known as **physiological salines** or **Ringer's solution.**

Maintenance of a constant internal environment is called **homeostasis**, a Greek word meaning 'staying the same'. Many physiological processes are homeostatic in that they are responsible, directly or indirectly, for regulating the internal environment. It is impossible to exaggerate their importance. Without them life would be impossible. As an example let us take the control of glucose in the human body.

The homeostatic control of glucose

The normal concentration of glucose in human blood is approximately 90 mg per 100 cm^3, and even after the heaviest carbohydrate meal rarely exceeds 150 mg per 100 cm^3. What keeps it constant? Before trying to answer this question let us briefly consider the various things that can happen to glucose in the body.

- It is broken down into carbon dioxide and water (respiration), particularly in active tissues such as the muscles.
- It may be built up into glycogen and stored.
- It may be converted into fat and stored in the body's fat depots.
- If glucose is in short supply, glycogen may be broken down into glucose.

The concentration of glucose in the blood and tissue fluids at any given moment is determined by the relative extent to which these different processes occur in the body. For example, if there is too much glucose, as for example after a large meal rich in carbohydrate, the cells convert the surplus glucose into glycogen. If there is a deficiency of glucose, the cells convert glycogen into glucose, thereby raising the glucose concentration in the body.

In prolonged deficiency, glucose may be formed from non-carbohydrate sources, including fat and protein. This is called **gluconeogenesis.**

The role of the pancreas

The cells cannot regulate the concentration of glucose unaided. They have to receive instructions telling them what to do. The instructions are provided by the hormone **insulin**, which is secreted into the bloodstream by special cells in the **pancreas**. In Chapter 16 we discussed one function of the pancreas, namely the production of digestive enzymes. We see now that it also functions as an **endocrine gland**, secreting a hormone into the bloodstream.

Insulin increases the uptake of glucose by the cells, and facilitates the conversion of glucose to glycogen and fat. At the same time it inhibits the formation of glucose from glycogen and non-carbohydrate sources. The overall effect of insulin is therefore to lower the concentration of glucose in the bloodstream (figure 21.4). In the *absence* of insulin, the reverse happens and the glucose concentration rises.

Clearly insulin plays a crucial role in the regulation of blood glucose. Its importance can be illustrated by considering what happens if the pancreas is surgically removed from an animal. The result is a drastic increase in the general level of glucose in the blood, accompanied by a decrease in the glycogen content of the liver and muscles. The blood glucose concentration exceeds its normal value (a condition known as **hyperglycaemia**). When it reaches a critical concentration, glucose starts to be excreted in the urine, a condition called **glycosuria**. These changes can be quickly reversed if insulin

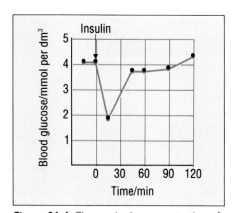

Figure 21.4 Changes in the concentration of blood glucose following the injection of a small quantity of insulin into the bloodstream of a human subject. The moment when the insulin was injected is indicated by the arrow. Notice the sharp fall in the glucose concentration immediately afterwards.

is injected into the bloodstream.

Which particular tissues respond to insulin? The main ones are the liver, skeletal muscles and adipose tissue. The liver is particularly important in the control of blood glucose, as indeed it is in other aspects of homeostasis. We shall look at it more closely in a moment.

Diabetes

In certain individuals the pancreas is unable to produce as much insulin as it should. The result is a condition known as **diabetes mellitus**. The symptoms are similar to those seen in an animal deprived of its pancreas. There is an increase in the blood glucose concentration (**hyperglycaemia**), and glucose appears in the urine (**glycosuria**). The production of urine increases and the patient may suffer from intense thirst. Later symptoms include severe loss of body mass, muscular waste and skin lesions. If untreated, the patient goes into a **diabetic coma** and dies.

Diabetes, causes and treatment

Guest author Patricia Kohn discusses the causes of diabetes mellitus and what can be done about this condition.

Diabetes mellitus – usually just called diabetes – is not a single disease with a single cause. There are two distinct types: early onset and late onset.

Early onset diabetes is the more severe form of the disease and usually starts early in life, often quite suddenly. It is characterised by a deficiency in the pancreatic secretion of insulin, caused by destruction of the insulin-secreting cells in the pancreas. In some people this may be due to an inherited vulnerability to the effects of a virus infection. In others the immune system may mistakenly attack the pancreas cells, treating them as foreign tissue.

Late onset diabetes does not usually manifest itself before middle age and it tends to come on gradually. In some patients insulin secretion is deficient. In others the concentration of insulin in the blood is normal or even above normal, but the target cells fail to respond to it.

Very often these older diabetics have been overweight for many years before the disease develops, and this observation gives us a clue to the cause of their insulin resistance. Insulin is secreted in response to an increase in the blood glucose concentration. Chronic overeating of sugary foods causes repeated stimulation of the pancreas which responds by secreting large quantities of insulin. Now it has been shown that repeated exposure of target cells (the cells on which hormones act) to high concentrations of a hormone diminishes the cells' responsiveness to the hormone. In the case of insulin, this may result eventually in the target cells failing to dispose of glucose in the usual way, and a state of diabetes is induced.

Treatment in such cases can often be by diet alone. Simply cutting down carbohydrate intake will ease the stimulation of the pancreas, reducing insulin secretion and allowing the target cells to recover. For patients with insulin deficiency, certain drugs can be taken by mouth which stimulate the secretion of insulin. Such drugs are useful in cases of mild insulin deficiency where there is still a certain amount of pancreatic function left. These older patients do not usually need insulin injections.

Unfortunately juvenile onset diabetes cannot be treated by adjusting the diet alone. Patients with this type of diabetes require regular injections of insulin. People differ in the speed with which the hormone is absorbed from the injection site. The amount, timing and type of insulin given must be tailored to the needs of the individual. As diabetes is for life, patients must learn to manage much of their treatment themselves without constant recourse to doctors. They must learn how to juggle diet and insulin dosage to keep their blood glucose reasonably normal, and they must learn to recognise the signs of both hyper- and hypoglycaemia.

However, continuous monitoring of blood glucose has shown that even apparently well-controlled diabetics are hyperglycaemic for too much of the time. New approaches to treatment are therefore being researched. These include pancreas transplants and the administration of insulin by sub-cutaneous infusion from a portable pump. Such pumps deliver a low dosage continuously and are programmed to increase the dose at meal times. In addition, the idea of an artificial pancreas is being explored. Such a device would be implanted semi-permanently. It would monitor the blood glucose concentration continuously and relay the readings to a microprocessor controlling the dosage of insulin. The technology to achieve this is available, and research into the necessary miniaturisation is underway.

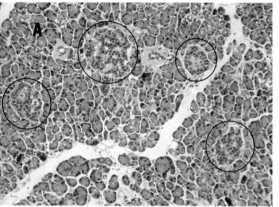

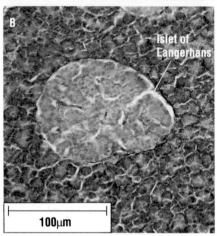

Islet of
Langerhans

100μm

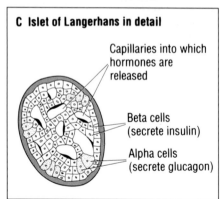

C Islet of Langerhans in detail

Capillaries into which
hormones are
released

Beta cells
(secrete insulin)

Alpha cells
(secrete glucagon)

Figure 21.5 Insulin and glucagon are secreted by the islets of Langerhans in the pancreas.

A Section of the pancreas as seen under the low power of the light microscope showing islets of Langerhans scattered amongst the tissue that secretes digestive enzymes. The islets are ringed.

B A single islet of Langerhans at greater magnification. The spaces which you can see amongst the cells are blood capillaries.

C Diagram of an islet of Langerhans showing the insulin- and glucagon-secreting cells and their close proximity to the capillaries into which they release their secretions.

Diabetes can be controlled by regular injections of insulin. Unfortunately the hormone cannot be taken by mouth as it is a protein and is digested in the gut. Diabetics must therefore inject themselves with insulin at regular intervals, though milder cases can be controlled by other chemical agents taken orally.

Insulin, and its role in regulating glucose and preventing diabetes, were discovered in the early 1920s by two Canadian physiologists, Frederick Banting and Charles Best. They removed the pancreas from dogs, thereby inducing diabetes with the inevitable rise in the blood glucose concentration. At the same time they extracted substances from the pancreases of other dogs. They then injected the pancreatic extracts into the bloodstream of the depancreatised dogs. Although their research was beset with difficulties, they eventually found that an extract of the pancreas, suitably prepared, reduced the high blood glucose levels of diabetic dogs. This extract contained the substance that we now call insulin.

By 1922 insulin was being produced commercially and used to treat human diabetics. The results were dramatic and patients who had suffered misery for years suddenly had their lives transformed (see box on page 363). Banting and Best's discovery stands as a landmark in the history of physiology and clinical medicine.

There are enough diabetics in the world to make insulin production an extremely important part of the pharmaceutical industry. A premium is placed on the mass production of pure and cheap insulin. Traditionally insulin has been obtained from the pancreases of slaughtered animals, but now human insulin can be produced by genetic engineering.

Glucagon, a second pancreatic hormone

In the 1950s a second pancreatic hormone was discovered. It is called **glucagon**. Like insulin, glucagon is involved in the control of blood glucose, but whereas insulin lowers the blood glucose concentration, glucagon raises it. Glucagon therefore opposes insulin in its action. Moreover, each hormone inhibits the other's release from the pancreas.

Glucagon prevents the blood glucose level falling too low following the secretion of insulin. A sub-normal blood glucose concentration is called **hypoglycaemia** and, if uncorrected, it can cause a person to go into a coma. Hypoglycaemia is particularly liable to occur during fasting, and one of glucagon's main functions is to counteract this.

Glucagon raises the blood glucose level mainly by stimulating the liver to convert glycogen into glucose. It also promotes the formation of glucose from non-carbohydrate sources.

Which cells secrete insulin and glucagon?

Insulin and glucagon are secreted by special groups of cells in the pancreas called **islets of Langerhans** after a German medical student, Paul Langerhans, who discovered them in 1869. No one knew what their function was. They were called 'islets' because they looked like little islands in a sea of otherwise uniform tissue. If you look at a section of the pancreas under the light microscope, you can see the islets dotted about here and there, embedded in the tissue that secretes the digestive enzymes (figure 21.5A).

By suitable staining techniques two types of secretory cells can be distinguished in the islets: **alpha cells** and **beta cells** (figure 21.5B). The alpha cells, located in the peripheral part of the islet, secrete glucagon, whereas the more centrally placed beta cells secrete insulin. Both hormones

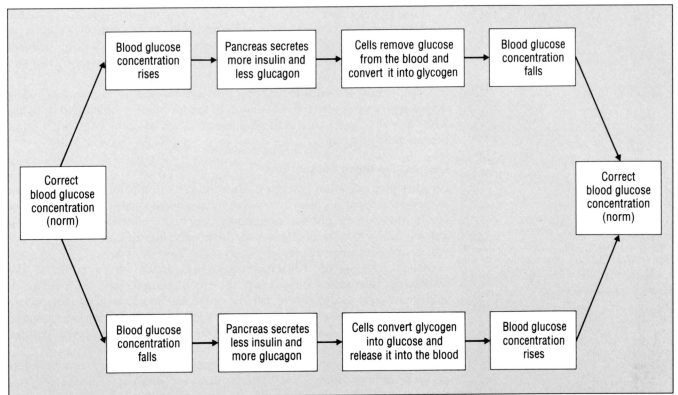

Figure 21.6 Homeostatic scheme for the control of the blood glucose concentration in the human body. The way the cells remove glucose from, or add it to, the blood is explained in the text.

are secreted into blood capillaries within the islet, from which they pass into the general circulation.

How are the islet cells controlled?

How do the islet cells know when to secrete insulin and glucagon? The effective control agent is the concentration of glucose in the blood. If the blood glucose concentration rises above a certain value (the norm), this stimulates the islet cells to produce correspondingly more insulin and less glucagon. As a result, the glucose concentration falls. Conversely, if the blood glucose concentration falls below the norm, the islet cells secrete less insulin and more glucagon and the glucose concentration rises.

We have here a control system in which the glucose itself switches on the mechanism by which it is itself regulated. The sequence of events is summarised in figure 21.6.

Some generalisations about homeostasis

The glucose story illustrates an important principle of homeostasis: **negative feedback**. Negative feedback means that when something changes, the *opposite* effect is produced. In the case of glucose regulation, an increase in the concentration of glucose sets into motion the processes which decrease it. Conversely a decrease in the glucose concentration sets into motion the processes which increase it. The result is that, whatever the direction of the change, the concentration of glucose automatically returns to the optimum value. This optimum value represents the **norm** or **set point** in the homeostatic process.

To counteract a change in the concentration of blood glucose, some kind of **corrective mechanism** must be involved. The corrective mechanism is triggered by the very entity which is to be regulated. In other words the system is *self-adjusting*. This is true of homeostatic systems in general.

For the corrective mechanism to work there must be **receptors** capable of detecting the change, and **effectors** that carry out the corrective measures. We may also predict that there must be some kind of **control centre** for coordinating the overall response. In many homeostatic processes the control centre is in the brain.

The principles outlined above are summarised in figure 21.7. The diagram is really a generalised version of the mechanism illustrated in figure 21.6. We shall meet this kind of diagram again in connection with other homeostatic processes.

Dampening down fluctuations

Another generalisation emerging from the control of blood glucose is that homeostasis must necessarily involve fluctuations, small though these may be. In the case of glucose regulation, when the concentration of blood glucose falls it overshoots the norm, thus triggering the corrective processes which cause it to rise again.

The secret of an efficient homeostatic system is to minimise the overshoot, thus dampening down the fluctuations (figure 21.8). This is achieved by gradually cutting off the corrective mechanism as the glucose concentration approaches the norm, by secreting an antagonistic hormone (glucagon) and by having a system whose components (receptors, control centre and effectors) respond quickly with the minimum delay.

The way homeostasis works means that it is impossible for anything to be *absolutely* constant. Fluctuations, however small, are inevitable. It is therefore more accurate to talk about things being held in *steady state* rather than constant.

The scope of homeostasis

We have seen how homeostasis works in the regulation of glucose. Later we shall apply it to the regulation of osmotic pressure and body temperature. However, it is by no means confined to physiological situations. The size of a population of animals or plants is kept under control by homeostatic means, and essentially the same mechanism maintains the constancy of species over long periods of time.

Nor are homeostatic processes restricted to biology. To take an everyday example, the **thermostat** in an oven or central heating system operates on a homeostatic basis, switching itself on or off according to the temperature. Many machines involve similar principles, as do industrial processes and economic systems. For example, in the car industry the production of spare parts is regulated by the demand.

Positive feedback

Sometimes a deviation from the norm is not corrected. Instead it leads to a further deviation. The result is a 'runaway' situation in which a change triggers more change in the same direction. This is known as **positive feedback**.

At first sight positive feedback would appear to be damaging, even destructive. Think, for example, how harmful it would be if an increase in body temperature led not to a decrease but to a further increase in temperature. This is in fact what happens in heat stroke (see page 404). However, in certain circumstances positive feedback is useful.

An example of useful positive feedback is seen in amphibians such as frogs and toads. Their development is controlled (as ours is) by the thyroid hormone, thyroxine. In the tadpole the secretion of thyroxine is kept in steady state by negative feedback. However, just before the tadpole is due

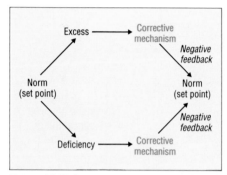

Figure 21.7 Generalised scheme summarising any homeostatic control process. A deviation from the norm (set point) sets into motion the appropriate corrective mechanism which restores the norm. In other words the deviation triggers the *opposite* effect (negative feedback).

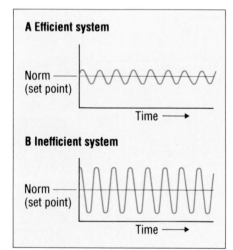

Figure 21.8 Graphs comparing an efficient homeostatic system with an inefficient one. In both graphs the vertical axis represents the magnitude of the particular feature under consideration, for example the concentration of blood glucose, salt concentration or body temperature. Notice the much larger fluctuations in the inefficient system. In reality the fluctuations would be less regular than in these theoretical graphs.

to undergo metamorphosis into the adult, negative feedback is replaced by positive feedback. In consequence the concentration of thyroxine rises, and this triggers metamorphosis.

What is happening here is that a homeostatic system is jumping into a new gear. A new set point is established and thereafter negative feedback takes place around the new set point. We shall come across other examples of this in later chapters.

The meaning of Claude Bernard's 'free life'

Consider two animals, A and B. Animal A has no homeostatic mechanisms and therefore cannot maintain a constant internal environment. For example, if the surrounding temperature rises, its body temperature rises too. The result is that it can only live in places where the external environment is itself pretty constant.

Animal B, on the other hand, has evolved an impressive repertoire of homeostatic mechanisms which enable it to maintain a constant internal environment even when the external environment varies. So, instead of being restricted to a specific external environment, animal B can move with ease from one environment to another.

There are many animal species like B – for example, mammals whose

The effect of insulin

Dr Frederick Banting, co-discoverer of insulin, describes the effect of insulin on one of his patients.

Early in June 1922, I was in my office and a man carried his wife into the office under his arm. He was a very handsome man of 30 and he deposited in the easy chair 76 lbs of the worst looking specimen of a wife that I have ever seen. She snarled and growled and ordered him about. I felt sorry for him. I placed her in hospital more in pity for him than in regard for her.

She was one of the most uncooperative patients with which I have ever dealt. It was in those early days when insulin was very scarce and precious and we endeavoured to get as much experimental knowledge as possible from each dose. She would steal candy or any kind of food she could lay hands on. She demanded that her poor husband come to the hospital early in the morning and every night he must not leave until she was asleep, yet she scolded him, cursed him and treated him like nothing all day long. I could

never understand why he took it all patiently, unruffled and even cheerfully. She was a terrible looking specimen of humanity with eyes almost closed with oedema, a pale and pasty skin, red hair that was so thin that it showed her scalp, and what there was was straight and straggling. Her ankles were thicker than the calves of her legs and her body had sores where the skin was stretched thin over the bones. Above all she had the foulest disposition that I have ever known. I could not understand and I marvelled at and sympathised with the poor husband.

She was in hospital some weeks and improved considerably and then he took her home. I was frankly glad to see the last of her. For his sake I had been kind. As a case to follow she seemed hopeless. I did not write to them nor did I hear from them.

A year later I was at my desk early one morning when the phone rang. A cheerful chuckling voice asked if I would be there for ten minutes. I said I would. The receiver was hung up. I went on with my correspondence.

In a few minutes I heard the outer

door open and a moment later my office door was thrown wide open and in rushed one of the most beautiful women I have ever seen. She was a stranger. I had never seen her before yet she threw her arms around my neck and kissed me before I could move from where I stood. Over her beautiful head I saw the laughing face of the patient husband. I stood back. The three of us stood hand in hand. I looked at them. The husband said 'Doctor I wanted you to see her now. This is the girl I married – before she had diabetes.' We laughed and talked. She was a devoted wife. He was no longer the slave but did most of the talking. I asked them many questions. As they went out he whispered 'I'll have to take some insulin myself doctor.'

Months later I received a tiny envelope with the name and a pink ribbon. A daughter. And I wondered if the little one had red hair, and I prayed she would never have diabetes.

(Reproduced from *The Discovery of Insulin* by Michael Bliss, Faber and Faber 1988)

powers of temperature regulation allow them to be equally at home in temperate or tropical regions, and fishes whose efficiency at controlling their internal osmotic pressure allows them to migrate from sea to fresh-water or vice versa.

This ability to exploit widely differing external environments is what Claude Bernard meant by 'free life'. It has been made possible by the development of homeostatic mechanisms of the kind we shall be looking at in the next few chapters.

The mammalian liver

Earlier it was said that the liver plays an important part in the regulation of glucose. This is only one of several homeostatic functions performed by this vital organ. The rest of this chapter will be devoted to looking at the liver with its homeostatic role in mind.

In studying the liver we see a close relationship between structure and function. We will therefore start by reviewing its functions, and then relate these to its structure.

Functions of the liver

It has been estimated that the liver performs over 500 functions. For our purposes these can be conveniently reduced to ten.

1 **Metabolism of carbohydrates, lipids and proteins.** Along with certain other tissues, the liver controls the concentration of glucose in the bloodstream, and it is the main organ supplying glucose in times of shortage. The liver removes lipids from the blood and either oxidises them with the transfer of energy, or modifies them chemically before they are sent to the body's fat depots for storage. The liver's main contribution to protein metabolism is to synthesise the non-essential amino acids by transamination (see page 142). It also gets rid of excess protein, as we shall see in the next point.

2 **Excretion of nitrogenous waste.** The body is unable to store proteins or amino acids, and any surplus is destroyed in the liver. The amino acids are first **deaminated** by the liver cells: the amino (NH_2) group is removed from the amino acid molecule, with the formation of ammonia. The rest of the amino acid is then fed into carbohydrate metabolism and respired.

Meanwhile the ammonia, which is highly toxic and must not be allowed to accumulate, enters a series of reactions called the **ornithine cycle** in which it reacts with carbon dioxide to form the less toxic nitrogenous compound **urea** (figure 21.9). The urea is then released from the liver cells into the bloodstream, and taken up by the **kidney** which eliminates it from the body. How this is done is explained in Chapter 22.

3 **Detoxification.** The liver renders harmless (detoxifies) many drugs and poisons by changing them chemically. For example, hydrogen peroxide, a highly toxic by-product of certain metabolic pathways, is rapidly split into water and oxygen by the enzyme catalase which occurs in high concentration in the liver (see page 217).

An important detoxification function of the liver is the disposal of ethanol (alcohol). The ethanol is first converted into acetaldehyde which is then oxidised. There is, however, a limit to the capacity of the liver to cope with this highly toxic substance. If taken in excess, ethanol may kill

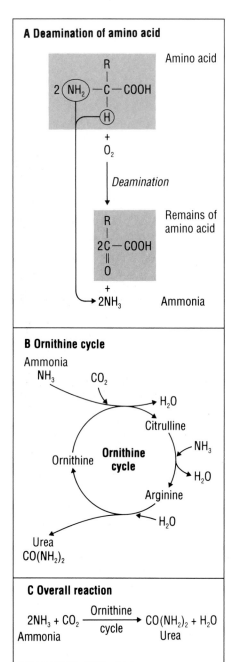

Figure 21.9 The fate of surplus amino acids in the body.

A The amino group is removed from the amino acid with the formation of ammonia (deamination).

B The highly toxic ammonia then reacts with carbon dioxide from respiration to form urea (ornithine cycle).

C The overall reaction for the ornithine cycle.

the liver cells which become replaced with useless fibrous tissue. This condition is called **cirrhosis of the liver** and is a contributing cause of death in alcoholics.

4 **Inactivation of certain hormones** after they have achieved their effects. Insulin, glucagon, thyroxine and various steroid hormones (including the sex hormones) are dealt with in this way.

5 **Thermoregulation.** Its consistently high metabolic rate, coupled with its large size and excellent blood supply, make the liver ideal for the steady transfer of heat energy. Of course other organs transfer heat energy too – the skeletal muscles for example – but the liver does this even when the body is resting and the general metabolic rate is low. This helps to maintain the body temperature.

6 **Production of bile.** Bile is synthesised by the liver and stored in the gall bladder. From the latter it passes down the bile duct to the duodenum. The **bile salts** play an important part in digestion by emulsifying fats in the small intestine (see page 281).

In addition the bile contains **bile pigments**, the principal one being a brown pigment called **bilirubin**. The bile pigments are the breakdown products of haemoglobin, resulting from the destruction of used red blood cells by phagocytes in the liver, spleen and bone marrow. Once in the gut, bilirubin is converted into another closely related pigment which is responsible for giving the faeces their brown colour.

7 **Formation of cholesterol.** Cholesterol is an important constituent of plasma membranes (see page 169) and the liver is the main site of its synthesis. Excess cholesterol is excreted in the bile. If there is a surplus, it may precipitate in the gall bladder or bile duct as **gall stones** (figure 21.10). These sometimes block the bile duct, leading to obstructive jaundice in which the skin acquires a characteristic yellow appearance due to retention of bilirubin in the blood.

The amount of cholesterol in the blood is largely determined by dietary intake in conjunction with the activities of the liver. If there is a considerable excess in the blood, some of it may be deposited in the walls of certain arteries, obstructing the smooth passage of blood and often leading eventually to an intravascular clot. If this occurs in one of the coronary arteries serving the heart, a **coronary thrombosis** or 'heart attack' may result. The elimination of excess cholesterol is therefore an important function of the liver.

8 **Formation of red blood cells.** In the fetus the liver is responsible for the formation of red blood cells, but gradually this function is taken over by the bone marrow. However, the adult liver still plays an important part in the production of red blood cells for it stores **vitamin B$_{12}$**, a porphyrin with cobalt in the centre, which is required for the formation of red blood cells in the bone marrow.

If vitamin B$_{12}$ is lacking the result is **pernicious anaemia**, characterised by a drastic reduction in the number of red cells and therefore in the amount of haemoglobin in the blood. If untreated, pernicious anaemia is fatal.

9 **Synthesis of plasma proteins.** These include fibrinogen, responsible for the clotting of blood. In fact most of the factors needed for blood clotting are made by the liver. The other plasma proteins have a number of functions connected with homeostasis, some of which are discussed in Chapter 24.

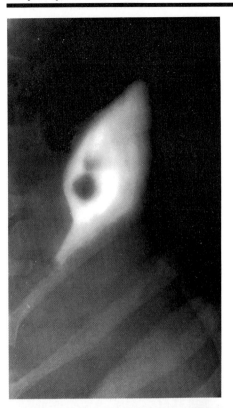

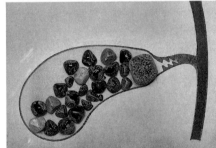

Figure 21.10 The top picture is an X-ray image of a gall bladder containing two gall stones (the dark circular areas). The picture was obtained by cholecystography. In this procedure the patient swallows a radio-opaque iodine compound which is absorbed in the gut and expelled from the liver in bile after which it becomes concentrated in the gall bladder. Subsequent X-ray examination shows the outline of the gall bladder and the presence of any stones. The bottom picture is a model of a gall bladder which is almost full of gall stones.

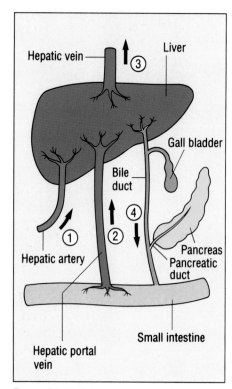

Figure 21.11 Schematic diagram showing the connections of the liver. Arrow 1 represents oxygenated blood, arrow 2 blood rich in soluble food substances, arrow 3 blood containing all the products of the liver except bile, arrow 4 bile.

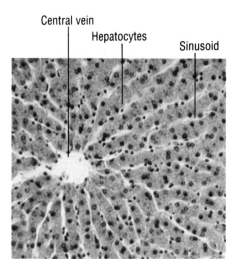

Figure 21.12 Photomicrograph of a transverse section of a lobule of the liver. Notice the rows of hepatocytes (liver cells) radiating out from the central vein, and the blood capillaries (sinusoids) between them.

10 **Storage of certain vitamins and minerals.** We have already seen that the liver stores vitamin B_{12}. Most of the other B-vitamins are also stored by the liver, as are vitamins A and D. Minerals stored by the liver include iron and copper.

Reviewing these functions of the liver, one is struck by the extent to which it controls the physical and chemical composition of the internal environment. Each of the functions listed above is in some way connected with homeostasis. We can summarise the role of the liver by saying that it synthesises certain vital substances required by the body, stores compounds which are of no immediate use, ensures that the blood has the right glucose concentration and generally regulates the internal environment

Structure of the liver

The structure of the liver is directly related to its functions. It is the largest organ in the body, weighing in the human adult about 1.5 kg, 3–4 per cent of the total body mass. It has an excellent blood supply, receiving more blood per unit time than any other organ. In fact it has been calculated that the blood flow through the liver is well over a litre per minute, which is marginally greater than that of the kidneys.

The liver has been described as the body's metabolic centre. As such, it must have a good blood supply from which it can draw its raw materials, and into which it can shed its products. The connections of the liver are summarised in figure 21.11. Its blood supply is derived from two sources.

- The **hepatic artery** which brings oxygenated blood from the heart via the dorsal aorta.
- The **hepatic portal vein** which brings blood rich in food materials from the gut. As much as three-quarters of the blood reaching the liver does so via the hepatic portal vein.

The liver releases its products into the **hepatic vein**: glucose, amino acids, lipids, plasma proteins, urea, cholesterol and of course carbon dioxide from the respiration of its cells. Bile is secreted into the **bile duct**.

The liver's microscopic structure

Examination of the liver with the light microscope shows it to be composed of numerous **lobules,** roughly cylindrical in shape and approximately one millimetre in diameter. Each lobule is filled with a large number of small polygonal cells called **hepatocytes** ('liver cells') which are arranged in rows radiating outwards from the centre. You can see the arrangement of these cells in the photomicrograph in figure 21.12.

The lobules may be regarded as the basic units of the liver. Figure 21.13A shows how they relate to the bile system and blood vessels. Running alongside each lobule are branches of the hepatic artery, hepatic portal vein and bile duct. The first two are referred to as **interlobular vessels** since they lie *between* adjacent lobules. In the centre of each lobule is a branch of the hepatic vein, referred to as the **intralobular** or **central vein**.

The interlobular vessels are connected with the central vein by a system of blood capillaries, here called **sinusoids,** which run between the chains of liver cells and follow the same radiating pattern. They can be seen clearly in figure 21.12. The sinusoids, like all capillaries, have a flattened endothelial lining. Across this endothelial lining substances pass to and from the liver cells.

Also running alongside the chains of liver cells are fine channels called **canaliculi** which connect up with the branches of the bile duct at the edge of the lobule. The canaliculi have no endothelial lining – they are simply intercellular spaces. So the liver cells bear an intimate relationship both with the sinusoids and with the canaliculi. This is made clear in figure 21.13.

Blood reaches each lobule via the interlobular vessels: oxygenated blood arrives in the branches of the hepatic artery, blood rich in food materials in the branches of the hepatic portal vein. The blood then flows along the sinusoids towards the central vein. As it does so, the hepatocytes take up from the blood what they require, and shed their products into it. The only exception is the bile which is secreted, not into the sinusoids, but into the canaliculi whence it trickles to the bile duct.

Attached to the walls of the sinusoids are specialized **Kupffer cells**, large phagocytic macrophages which destroy old red blood cells and remove bacteria and foreign particles from the blood flowing through the liver. All other functions of the liver are carried out by the hepatocytes.

The fine structure of the hepatocytes

Figure 21.14 shows an electron micrograph of two adjacent hepatocytes. The cells have a prominent Golgi apparatus, abundant mitochondria and numerous glycogen granules. These are features we would expect to find in any cell whose principal activities are secretion and the storage and transfer of energy.

The only really noteworthy organelles are the **peroxisomes**. Peroxisomes are found in most mammalian cells but they are exceptionally large in the liver. They contain catalase and other enzymes responsible for detoxification. Much of the ethanol that a person drinks is disposed of by the peroxisomes.

Otherwise the hepatocytes show no special features. This is not really surprising when one bears in mind that the liver's numerous functions are essentially metabolic, requiring complex chemical pathways rather than specialised organelles. For sheer metabolic versatility, this unremarkable looking cell is probably unrivalled anywhere else in the body.

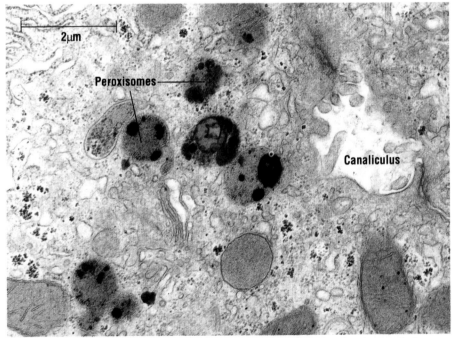

Figure 21.14 Electron micrograph of two adjacent hepatocytes. Notice that the canaliculus between the two cells has no endothelial lining; it is simply an intercellular space lined by the plasma membranes of the two adjoining cells. Notice also the peroxisomes.

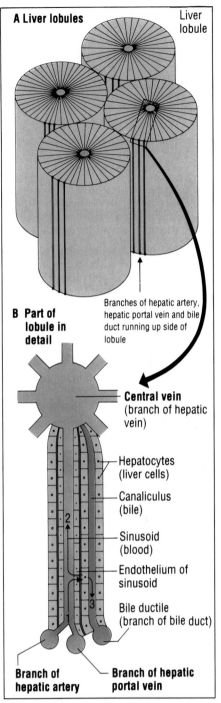

Figure 21.13 A Schematic diagram of a liver lobule. Each lobule is roughly cylindrical in shape and approximately 1 mm in diameter. There is an intimate relationship between the hepatocytes, sinusoids and canaliculi. In **B** arrow 1 represents substances which are taken up into the hepatocytes from the arterial and hepatic portal blood; arrow 2 represents substances which pass from the hepatocytes into the blood; and arrow 3 represents the components of bile which the hepatocytes release into the canaliculus.

Summary

1 'The constancy of the internal environment is the condition for free life.' This principle was first put forward by Claude Bernard in 1857. Maintenance of a constant internal environment is called **homeostasis**.

2 By 'free life' is meant the ability of a species to inhabit a wide range of environments.

3 The 'internal environment' is the immediate surroundings of the cells. In animals this consists of **tissue fluid** which bathes the cells.

4 Tissue fluid consists of plasma minus proteins and is formed by ultra-filtration from the blood capillaries. Excess tissue fluid passes into the **lymphatic vessels** where it constitutes **lymph**.

5 The main features of an animal's internal environment which need to be controlled are its chemical composition, osmotic pressure, pH and temperature. In addition nitrogenous waste products and other toxic substances are either eliminated altogether or at least kept to a minimum.

6 The principles of homeostasis can be illustrated by the control of blood glucose in the mammal. A rise in the glucose level results in the secretion of **insulin** from the **islets of Langerhans** in the **pancreas** and this brings about the metabolic disposal of excess blood sugar in the liver and certain other organs.

7 Insulin's effects are opposed by another hormone, **glucagon**, also secreted by the islets of Langerhans.

8 Failure of the pancreas to secrete sufficient insulin results in **diabetes mellitus**.

9 In general, homeostatic control processes work as follows: any deviation from the norm (**set point**) sets into motion the appropriate **corrective mechanism** which restores the norm (**negative feedback**).

10 Various mechanisms help to minimise deviations from the set point, thereby dampening down fluctuations and improving the efficiency of the homeostatic system.

11 In certain circumstances a deviation from the norm may result in a further deviation (**positive feedback**).

12 One of the most important homeostatic organs in the body is the **liver**. Its homeostatic functions include the regulation of carbohydrates, lipids and amino acids, elimination of haemoglobin from used red blood cells and the transfer of heat energy.

13 The structure of the liver, showing an intimate association between the liver cells, blood vessels and bile channels, is admirably adapted to perform its numerous functions.

Review questions

1 What would be the effect on the body's homeostatic processes of removing the pancreas? Explain your answer.

2 At one time doctors tested a patient's urine for sugar by tasting it. Nowadays more hygienic methods are used.
   (a) How would a patient's urine be tested for sugar now?
   (b) Suppose sugar was found in the urine. How would you explain its presence?

3 There is usually a net breakdown of glycogen stores in the early morning. Why does this happen and how is it brought about?

4 Interaction between organs is fundamental to the homeostatic mechanisms of complex animals. Explain this statement with particular reference to the control of blood glucose.

5 Explain, with an example, the meaning of the term negative feedback.

6 All homeostatic systems involve fluctuations. How are the fluctuations kept as small as possible?

7 A physiologist who is a world authority on the control of blood sugar is employed as a consultant to an airline. In what ways might the consultant be able to help the airline?

8 How is the structure of a liver lobule suited for the rapid exchange of materials between the liver cells and the blood?

9 Which substances pass
   (a) from the hepatic artery to the liver cells,
   (b) from the hepatic portal vein to the liver cells,
   (c) from the liver cells to the hepatic vein,
   (d) from the liver cells to the bile duct?

10 State five functions of the liver. To what extent is each function related to homeostasis?

Further reading

Two short books, written by specialists, are well worth reading: *Homeostasis* by Richard Hardy (Arnold, 1976) and *Homeostasis, Origins of the Concept* by L.L. Langley (Van Nostrand Reinhold, 1965). Both books, though introductory, deal in depth with different aspects of this topic.

For more detail on the liver you should consult an advanced textbook of human physiology. Few such books deal with the liver all in one section. You will probably have to look up specific aspects in the index.

The Discovery of Insulin by Michael Bliss (Faber and Faber, 1988) reads like a detective story and is a most interesting account of how science progresses.

In *Biology, Advanced Topics* the factors that contribute to the efficiency of homeostatic mechanisms and some of the complexities involved in the control of blood sugar are discussed.

Excretion and water balance

Excretion is defined as the removal from the body of the waste products of metabolism. The term is generally taken to mean **nitrogenous** waste such as urea and ammonia, but other materials like carbon dioxide and the bile pigments are also waste products of metabolism, and their removal is as much a part of excretion as the elimination of urea. The term is also extended to include toxic substances such as drugs, though these are not products of metabolism. In the broad sense excretion is therefore a large subject. However, in this chapter we shall be concerned mainly with **nitrogenous excretion**.

You will recall that the blood and tissue fluid contain a variety of solutes (glucose, salts and the like) dissolved in water. The concentrations, relative and absolute, of these solutes has to be regulated, as does their total concentration relative to water. The latter gives the blood and tissue fluids a particular osmotic pressure, and this too must be kept constant. Maintaining the correct balance between the water and solutes in the body is achieved by **osmoregulation**.

These two processes, excretion and osmoregulation, are both aspects of homeostasis, and the physiological mechanisms involved are bound up with each other. Indeed, in the mammal the same system performs both functions. This is the **urinary system** to which we must now direct our attention.

The mammalian urinary system

The mammalian urinary system is shown in figure 22.1. Its principal organs are the **kidneys** of which there are two, one on each side of the abdomen. If you put your hands on your hips, your kidneys are just under your thumbs. The essential job of the kidneys is to control the composition of the body fluids by selectively removing unwanted substances from the blood. To this end the kidneys have an exceptionally good blood supply – the blood flow per unit mass of tissue is far greater than for any other organ except the liver which comes a close second.

Blood is conveyed to each kidney by the **renal artery**, a branch of the dorsal aorta. After flowing through the kidney, the blood is collected into the **renal vein** from which it flows to the posterior vena cava. Meanwhile, substances which have been removed from the blood in the kidneys pass down the two **ureters** to the **bladder**. The fluid which enters the bladder is called **urine**, and every now and again it is expelled to the exterior via the **urethra** in the process of **urination**. We shall see how urination takes place later, but in the meantime let us look in detail at the kidney.

The kidney

Each of our kidneys contains between one and two million microscopic structures called **nephrons**. The nephron can be regarded as the basic unit of the kidney, performing all its regulatory functions. It is the nephron that produces urine.

Figure 22.1B shows how a typical nephron is positioned in relation to the kidney as a whole. The kidney consists of two main regions: an outer **cortex** and inner **medulla**. Part of the nephron lies in the cortex, and part of it in the medulla.

To understand how the nephron works, we must first examine its structure.

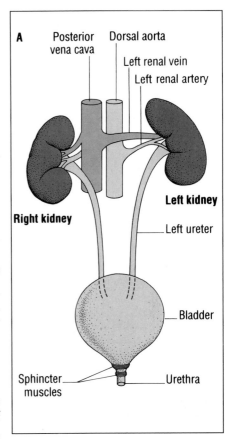

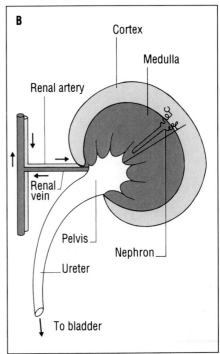

Figure 22.1 The mammalian urinary system,
A Ventral view of the whole system
B Section through kidney.

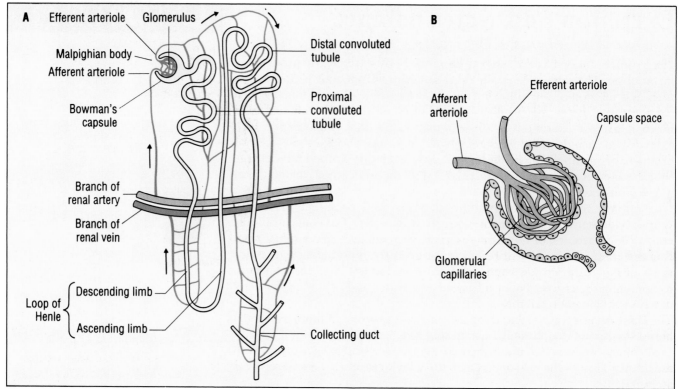

Figure 22.2 Microscopic structure of the mammalian kidney.

A Single nephron with its blood supply.

B Malpighian body enlarged to show its internal structure.

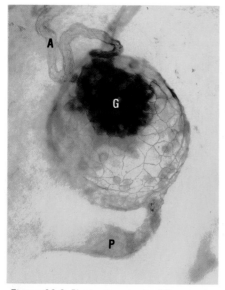

Figure 22.3 Photomicrograph of Bowman's capsule and associated structures. **A**, arteriole; **G**, glomerulus; **P**, proximal convoluted tubule.

Structure of a nephron

Figure 22.2 shows the detailed structure of the nephron. At its inner (proximal) end there is a spherical structure called the **Malpighian body**. This is about 200 μm in diameter, and is located in the cortex of the kidney. The Malpighian body consists of a cup-shaped **Bowman's capsule** which is like a hollow rubber ball that has been pressed in on one side. The invagination contains a dense network of capillaries called a **glomerulus**. The inside of the capsule, the **capsule space**, is separated from the lumen of the capillaries by only two layers of cells: the epithelium of the capsule and the endothelium of the capillaries. These two layers of cells are highly specialised. Their significance will become clear presently.

Leading from the Bowman's capsule is a tubule, about 60 μm in outer diameter, whose lumen is continuous with the capsule space. The first part of the tubule is located in the cortex of the kidney and is coiled: it is called the **proximal convoluted tubule** (*proximal* because it is the first part, *convoluted* because it is coiled). You can see the beginning of it in figure 22.3.

The proximal convoluted tubule leads to a U-shaped **loop of Henle**, named after the German microscopist, F.G.J. Henle, who discovered it in the nineteenth century. It consists of a straight **descending limb** which plunges down into the medulla, where it does a hair-pin bend and returns to the cortex as the **ascending limb**. The ascending limb of the loop of Henle leads on to the final part of the nephron, the **distal convoluted tubule**. This, as the name implies, is coiled and it opens into a **collecting duct**. Several nephrons share the same collecting duct.

The collecting ducts converge at the **pelvis** of the kidney, emptying their contents into the ureter which conveys them to the bladder as urine. The tubules and collecting ducts are lined with a single layer of epithelial cells, mainly of the cuboidal type.

Each nephron has its own blood supply. Blood from the renal artery is carried to the glomerulus by an **afferent arteriole** and leaves it by an **efferent** arteriole. The latter splits up into a capillary network which envelops the tubule of that particular nephron. Blood from the capillaries drains into the renal vein. So blood flows first to the glomerulus and then to the capillaries surrounding the tubules before leaving the kidney.

The kidney accomplishes its regulatory functions by three separate but related processes: filtration, reabsorption and secretion. The fluid part of the blood is *filtered* from the glomerulus into the capsule space. As the resulting fluid flows along the tubules, useful substances are *reabsorbed* back into the bloodstream in the amounts required by the body. In addition certain unwanted substances in the blood are actively *secreted* into the tubules. Let us examine each of these processes in turn.

Filtration in Bowman's capsule

Our knowledge of what happens in the Bowman's capsule, and indeed the entire nephron, is based on **micropuncture experiments** pioneered by A.N. Richards at the University of Pennsylvania in the 1930s and repeated since then with ever-increasing sophistication by other research workers. The technique involves inserting a micropipette into an individual capsule and drawing off a small quantity of fluid from the capsule space (figure 22.4). The fluid is then analysed and its composition compared with that of the blood.

It turns out that the fluid in the capsule space has the same composition as blood plasma *minus the plasma proteins*. It seems that the capsule fluid is formed by a process of filtration from the glomerular capillaries. The filtrate (called **glomerular filtrate**) contains all the constituents of blood except the blood cells and plasma proteins. These are held back because they are too large to pass through the barrier between the glomerular capillaries and the capsule space. This barrier therefore performs the function of a **dialysing membrane**, separating the plasma proteins from the other components of the plasma. This is filtration at the molecular level, and it is called **ultra-filtration**.

For ultra-filtration to occur, two things are necessary.

- There must be sufficient pressure to force fluid through the filter.
- The barrier must be constructed in such a way as to retain molecules above a certain size while allowing smaller molecules (and ions) to pass through.

Research on the kidney has shown that both these conditions are satisfied in the Bowman's capsule.

The filtration pressure

It has long been known that the blood pressure in the glomerular capillaries is considerably higher than in the capillaries of other organs. The reason is that the efferent arteriole in which blood leaves the glomerulus is markedly narrower than the afferent vessel (see figure 22.2B). The resulting high pressure in the glomerular capillaries tends to force the fluid constituents of the blood into the capsule space.

This hydrostatic pressure in the glomerular capillaries is opposed by the hydrostatic pressure of the fluid in the capsule space and by the osmotic pressure of the plasma proteins in the glomerular blood. These two pressures will tend to *prevent* fluid passing through into the capsule space. However, if you look at the figures in table 22.1 you will see that when added together they are less than the hydrostatic pressure of the blood in the glomerular capillaries. There is therefore a net pressure favouring the formation of glomerular filtrate.

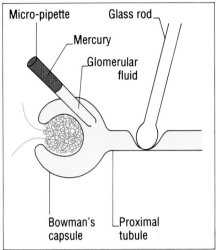

Figure 22.4 Diagram showing micropuncture technique for removing a sample of fluid from a Bowman's capsule. The proximal tubule is blocked by pressing on it with a fine glass rod. A micropipette, filled with mercury, is inserted through the wall of the capsule into the capsule space beneath. The mercury is then slowly withdrawn from the pipette, and as a result fluid is withdrawn from the capsule. The fluid is then analysed and compared with the composition of the blood. The glass rod and pipette are operated by micromanipulators, mechanical devices which scale down the movements of the experimenter. When the experimenter's hand moves through a distance of, say, one centimetre, the pipette moves only a fraction of a millimetre.

Pressure	Value
Hydrostatic pressure of blood in glomerulus	8.0 kPa
Hydrostatic pressure of fluid in capsule	2.4 kPa
Osmotic pressure of blood in glomerulus	4.3 kPa
Net filtration pressure	1.3 kPa

Table 22.1 Values for the pressures in the Malpighian body (glomerulus and Bowman's capsule) which affect filtration.

The structure of the filter

The electron microscope has provided information on the structure of the filter (figure 22.5). It is made up of two cell layers: the epithelium of the capsule and the endothelium of the glomerular capillaries. Between these two cell layers is the basement membrane.

The capsule epithelial cells are quite unlike ordinary epithelial cells (figure 22.5A). Instead of fitting together to form a continuous sheet, they are arranged in an irregular network rather like a net curtain. The cells are called **podocytes**, which literally means 'footed cells'. Each podocyte has about six arm-like **major processes** from which much finer **minor processes** project. The minor processes – the 'feet' of the podocyte – lie between similar processes of neighbouring podocytes and extend to the basement membrane. Between adjacent minor processes are narrow spaces, about 0.1 μm wide. These **filtration slits**, as they are called, are large enough to allow the passage of all the constituents of blood plasma, including the proteins, but not the blood cells.

Figure 22.5 Structure of the glomerular barrier through which ultra-filtration occurs in the Bowman's capsule.

A Diagram showing how the epithelial cells (podocytes) of the capsule fit together to form a perforated covering over a glomerular capillary.

B Schematic diagram of a single podocyte showing the way it relates to the endothelium of the capillary.

C Electron micrograph of a section through the wall of a glomerular capillary and adjoining podocytes. Can you say in what plane the section has been cut relative to the diagram in **B**?

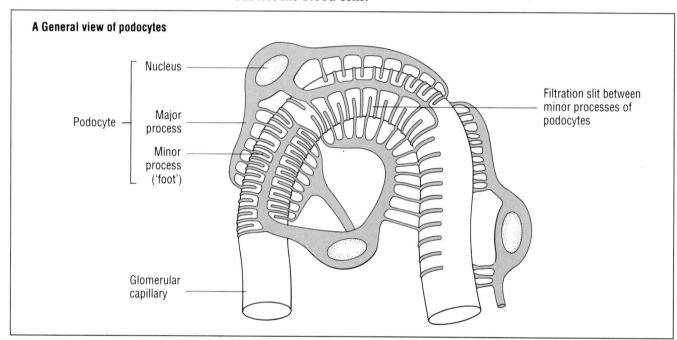

A General view of podocytes

Nucleus

Podocyte { Major process

Minor process ('foot')

Filtration slit between minor processes of podocytes

Glomerular capillary

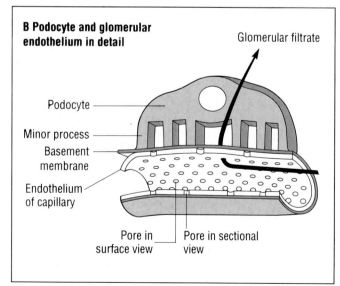

B Podocyte and glomerular endothelium in detail

Glomerular filtrate

Podocyte

Minor process

Basement membrane

Endothelium of capillary

Pore in surface view

Pore in sectional view

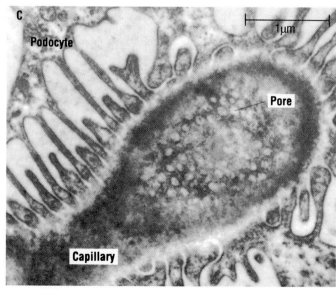

C

Podocyte

1 μm

Pore

Capillary

On the other side of the basement membrane are the endothelial cells of the glomerular capillaries. The electron microscope has shown these cells to be perforated by numerous **pores**. These pores, like the filtration slits, are large enough to allow the passage of blood plasma (figures 22.5B and C).

If the pores and slits let through all the constituents of blood plasma, which component of the barrier serves as the dialysing membrane holding back the plasma proteins? There is only one answer: the basement membrane. This is the only *continuous* structure between the blood and the capsule space, the only part of the barrier which has not got holes in it large enough to let through the plasma proteins. So the basement membrane must be the dialysing membrane responsible for ultra-filtration – as indeed it is in the formation of tissue fluid (see page 356).

Reabsorption from the tubules

After the glomerular filtrate has been formed, it flows along the tubule of the nephron and eventually emerges from a collecting duct as urine. Researchers have compared the volumes and composition of glomerular filtrate and urine, and have found that for most substances the amount excreted is considerably less than the amount filtered (table 22.2). It is therefore clear that these substances are reabsorbed back into the bloodstream as they flow along the tubule.

Whereabouts in the nephron does reabsorption take place? This, too, has been investigated by micropuncture experiments. For example, small quantities of fluid have been extracted from various parts of the tubule and analysed (figure 22.6A). This is an exceedingly difficult task, bearing in mind the narrowness of the tubule, and it can only be done by using extremely fine micropipettes mounted on micromanipulators. Another approach is to inject a fluid of known composition into one end of an isolated stretch of tubule and withdraw it from the other end (figure 21.6B). The fluid is then analysed.

These studies have shown that all the glucose and most of the water and salt (sodium and chloride ions) are reabsorbed in the proximal convoluted tubule. Small amounts of water and salt are reabsorbed in the distal tubule. Most of the remaining water is reabsorbed in the collecting duct by a mechanism which depends on the loop of Henle – more about that in a moment. In general, most reabsorption is completed in the proximal tubule, the distal tubule being mainly for fine adjustment.

Reabsorption of glucose and salts takes place by **active transport**. Transfer of these substances from the tubule to the blood can occur against a concentration gradient. That the process involves the expenditure of energy comes from the observation that it can be slowed down or stopped by treating the tubules with a metabolic poison such as cyanide or dinitrophenol. In the case of salts, sodium ions are reabsorbed actively and the chloride ions then follow passively. Water is also reabsorbed passively by osmosis following the active reabsorption of sodium ions.

You will notice in table 22.2 that *all* the glucose which is filtered is reabsorbed. The concentration of glucose in the blood is controlled, not by

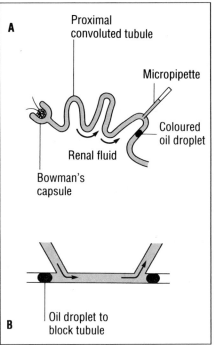

Figure 22.6 Two ways of investigating the functions of the kidney tubules by micropuncture techniques.

A A tiny drop of coloured oil is injected into a tubule. A fine micropipette is inserted into the tubule in front of the oil droplet. Fluid is then withdrawn from the tubule at a rate that keeps the oil droplet stationary. The fluid is then analysed and compared with glomerular filtrate.

B An artificial fluid of known composition is injected into one end of an isolated length of tubule and withdrawn from the other end. It is then analysed to find out if any changes have occurred in its composition.

Substance	Filtered	Reabsorbed	Excreted
Na^+	26000	25850	150
Cl^-	19000	18800	200
Urea	870	460	410
Glucose	800	800	nil
Amino acids	400	400	nil
Water	180000	179000	1000

Table 22.2 The amounts of various substances filtered, reabsorbed and excreted by the kidney of an adult human on a normal diet.

the kidney, but by other homeostatic processes, principally the insulin–glucagon mechanism described in Chapter 21. In normal circumstances the concentration of blood glucose is kept low enough for the kidney to reabsorb all the glucose that passes through it. However, if the blood glucose concentration exceeds a certain critical value, the kidney cannot reabsorb it all and glucose starts appearing in the urine. This is what happens in people who have diabetes.

Glucose is not the only substance to be completely reabsorbed by the kidney. Amino acids are too. As with glucose, the reabsorption of amino acids takes place by active transport in the proximal convoluted tubule.

Secretion into the tubules

Certain substances are actively transferred into the tubules from the surrounding blood capillaries. The word **secretion** is used for this. You are probably more familiar with secretion as the process by which glands produce substances. However, in the context of the kidney the word is used for the active expulsion of unwanted substances. This process happens in both the proximal and distal convoluted tubules.

There is evidence that in some mammals a certain amount of urea is actively secreted in this way. Ammonia and uric acid are certainly secreted, as are hydrogen ions (see page 375). Potassium ions are secreted *and* reabsorbed: their final concentration in the bloodstream depends on the balance between these two opposing processes.

The fact that these substances are secreted into the tubules does not mean that they are not filtered. They are able to pass through the glomerular filter, and are therefore present in the glomerular filtrate. Secretion allows additional amounts to be removed from the blood and added to the tubule fluid, thus speeding up their elimination from the body.

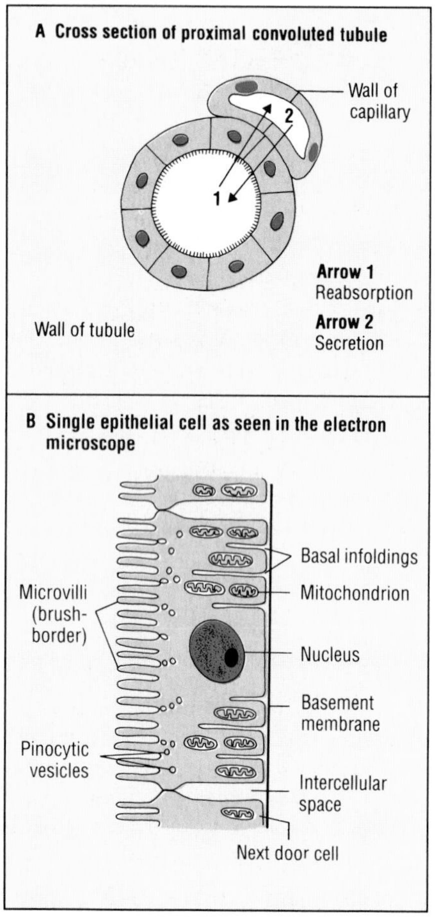

Structure of the tubule cells

The tubules that make up the nephron are lined with a single layer of mainly cuboidal epithelium which lies close to the endothelium of adjacent blood capillaries. There is therefore a close relationship between the tubules and the surrounding blood vessels, which correlates well with their functions of reabsorption and secretion.

The structure of the individual epithelial cells lining the tubules can also be related to their functions. To illustrate this let us consider the structure of one of the epithelial cells lining the proximal convoluted tubule where, as we have seen, most of the reabsorption and secretion take place. The structure of one such cell is shown in figure 22.7). Its free surface (i.e. the surface bordering the lumen of the tubule) bears numerous **microvilli** about 1 μm in length. There are so many microvilli that in humans the total surface area achieved by the proximal convoluted tubules of the two kidneys is of the order of 50 m². Between the microvilli, numerous pinocytic vesicles can be seen.

The surface area of the other side of the epithelial cell (i.e. the surface bordering the capillary) is increased by infoldings of the plasma membrane. Between these **basal infoldings** lie numerous mitochondria which presumably supply energy for active transport.

Another interesting feature of these tubule epithelial cells are the large **intercellular spaces** between adjacent cells. Only towards the free surface are the cells in contact. You can imagine how intrigued research workers must have been when they first discovered this feature. It is seen in other absorptive cells too, such as those lining the small intestine. Can you suggest a hypothesis explaining their function?

Figure 22.7 Microscopic structure of the proximal convoluted tubule.

A In this low-magnification view notice how the epithelial lining is closely associated with an adjacent capillary.

B Detail of an individual epithelial cell based on electron micrographs. The inner side of the epithelial cell bears numerous microvilli between which pinocytic vesicles can be seen. The outer side is greatly folded, with mitochondria between the folds.

How the pH is controlled

The blood and tissue fluid normally have a pH of about 7.4. The pH does not alter very much, which is just as well because even quite small deviations in pH can be fatal. This constancy is maintained despite the fact that excess hydrogen ions, which increase the acidity (lower the pH), are constantly being formed as by-products of metabolism.

Keeping the pH constant depends on controlling the relative concentrations of acid and base, the **acid–base balance**. This is achieved in three main ways.

- The lungs expel carbon dioxide which would otherwise accumulate and combine with water to form carbonic acid.
- The buffering mechanisms in the blood lower the hydrogen ion concentration (see page 320).
- The kidneys create hydrogencarbonate ions and get rid of the hydrogen ions.

The kidney mechanism is summarised in the illustration. In the cells lining the proximal and distal convoluted tubules carbon

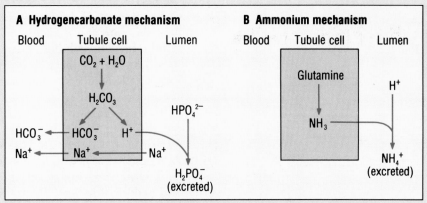

A Hydrogencarbonate mechanism

Blood   Tubule cell   Lumen

$CO_2 + H_2O$

H_2CO_3

HCO_3^- HCO_3^- H^+ HPO_4^{2-}

Na^+ Na^+ Na^+

$H_2PO_4^-$
(excreted)

B Ammonium mechanism

Blood   Tubule cell   Lumen

Glutamine

H^+

NH_3

NH_4^+
(excreted)

Two ways in which the hydrogen ion concentration is reduced by the kidney.

dioxide reacts with water to form carbonic acid, just as it does in the blood. The carbonic acid then dissociates into hydrogen ions and hydrogencarbonate ions. The hydrogencarbonate ions are reabsorbed into the blood whose pH is raised in consequence. Meanwhile the unwanted hydrogen ions are pumped into the lumen of the tubule.

Once in the lumen, the hydrogen ions are buffered by (mainly) hydrogenphosphate ions (HPO_4^{2-}) which take up hydrogen ions, forming dihydrogenphosphate ions ($H_2PO_4^-$). The latter are excreted in the urine. Meanwhile, sodium ions are reabsorbed in exchange for the

hydrogen ions. Once in the bloodstream the sodium ions maintain electrical neutrality with the hydrogencarbonate ions.

If the fluid in the kidney tubules is more than usually acidic, an additional mechanism comes into play. Excess hydrogen ions combine with ammonia in the distal convoluted tubules to form ammonium ions (NH_4^+). These too are excreted in the urine. The epithelial cells lining the distal tubules contain an enzyme which enables them to produce ammonia from the amino acid glutamine when circumstances make this necessary.

How calcium ions are controlled

The concentration of calcium ions in the blood is controlled by a hormone called **parathormone** secreted by the parathyroid glands (see page 462).

Parathormone increases the uptake of calcium ions by the gut and their reabsorption in the kidneys. It also encourages the release of calcium ions from the bones. The overall effect of this hormone is therefore to raise the concentration of calcium ions in the blood.

The secretion of parathormone by the parathyroids is regulated by the concentration of calcium ions in the blood. As you might expect, an excess

of calcium ions inhibits the secretion of the hormone. The actions of parathormone are opposed by another hormone called **calcitonin** which is secreted by the thyroid gland. However, its role in calcium ion regulation is minor compared with that of parathormone.

Also instrumental in regulating calcium ions is **vitamin D** (calciferol) which we obtain from such foods as eggs, butter and liver – fish liver oil is a particularly rich source. Calciferol is converted in the body into an active form which is responsible for the mineralisation and hardening of bones. In addition to its dietary source, calciferol can be synthesised in the skin under the influence of ultraviolet rays, for

example in sunlight. A growing child can get all the calciferol needed for proper bone formation in this way. Whatever its source, the active form of calciferol promotes the absorption of calcium ions from the gut and their uptake by the bones. A growing child who has a deficiency of calciferol is liable to develop **rickets**, a condition in which the bones remain soft and tend to bend.

Although softening of bones is a bad thing, parathormone-induced demineralisation of bones constantly occurs in a healthy growing individual as old bone is replaced by new. This is an essential part of the way bones grow and of the way the calcium concentration in the blood is controlled.

The role of the loop of Henle

It is in the interests of terrestrial animals to be able to conserve water. In mammals this function depends on the loop of Henle. Mammals are the only vertebrates whose kidneys can produce a markedly hypertonic urine, that is a urine with a higher osmotic pressure than that of the blood plasma. Desert mammals, which produce a particularly concentrated urine, have an extra-long loop of Henle.

What exactly does the loop of Henle do? At one time it was thought that it reabsorbed water back into the bloodstream, but its role is now known to be more subtle than that. What it does is to concentrate salt in the medulla of the kidney. The high salt concentration then causes a vigorous osmotic flow of water out of the collecting ducts, thereby concentrating the urine and making it hypertonic to the blood.

In achieving this the loop of Henle employs the principle of a **hair-pin countercurrent multiplier** (figure 22.8). Imagine that renal fluid has just gone down the descending limb and is starting to flow up the ascending limb. As the fluid flows up the ascending limb, salt is actively removed from it and deposited in the surrounding tissue fluid. From there the salt equilibrates with the fluid in the descending limb.

This active transfer of salt takes place at all levels of the loop of Henle. At any given level, the effect is to raise the salt concentration in the descending limb above that in the adjacent ascending limb. The effect at

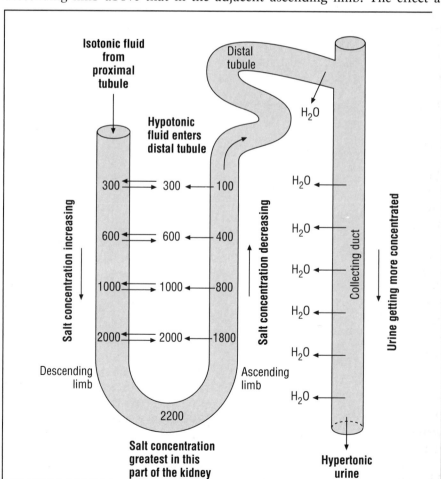

Figure 22.8 Diagram to show the role of the loop of Henle in the reabsorption of water. The numbers in the descending and ascending limbs, and in the tissue in between, represent osmolarity values in milliosmoles per kilogram of water (mOs kg^{-1}). The shunting of sodium ions from the ascending to the descending limb creates a high salt concentration in the medullary tissue of the kidney, and this results in water flowing out of the collecting duct by osmosis.

any one level is slight, but the overall effect is multiplied by the length of the hair-pin. As the renal fluid flows down the descending limb towards the apex of the loop, it becomes more and more concentrated; as it flows up the ascending limb it becomes more and more dilute.

The result of this process is to produce a region of particularly high salt concentration in the deep part of the medulla. The collecting duct passes through this region before opening into the pelvis. As fluid flows down the collecting duct, water may pass out of it by osmosis. This raises its solute concentration, resulting in the production of a markedly hypertonic urine. Meanwhile, the water which has been reabsorbed is taken away in the bloodstream.

The blood vessels play an important part in this mechanism. The capillaries in the medulla are arranged differently from those in the cortex. Known as **vasa recta** (literally 'straight vessels'), they too are U-shaped and run parallel with the loop of Henle. Only about one per cent of the blood that flows through the kidney goes through the vasa recta, so the blood flow is sluggish. Moreover, their U-shape means that they have a counter-current system similar to that which occurs in the loop of Henle itself. This helps to ensure that the high salt concentration in the medulla is not rapidly dissipated by the blood.

What we have been calling salt is in fact sodium and chloride ions. It is thought that sodium ions are actively moved, the chloride ions following passively. Interestingly, it has been found that urea, as well as salt, is retained in the medulla and this helps to build up the high solute concentration necessary for the osmotic withdrawal of water from the collecting ducts. This makes sense of the otherwise surprising fact that so much urea, a toxic waste substance, is reabsorbed by the kidney.

The kidney as an osmoregulator

In its treatment of water, the use of the kidney as an osmoregulator can be seen most clearly. The amount of water reabsorbed is geared to the body's needs, and it is upon this that the osmotic pressure of the blood and tissue fluids depends. The question is: how does the kidney know how much water to reabsorb? The answer is that the osmotic pressure of the blood itself determines the reabsorptive activities of the kidney. Briefly the mechanism is as follows.

In the brain there are groups of cells sensitive to a rise in the osmotic pressure of the blood, such as might occur if the person loses a lot of water or takes in an excessive amount of salt. These **osmoreceptors** are situated in the hypothalamus at the base of the **pituitary gland** (see page 452). When the receptors are stimulated, a hormone is released from the posterior lobe of the pituitary gland into the bloodstream. The hormone is carried to the kidney where it speeds up the rate at which water is reabsorbed. As a result, less urine is produced per unit time and it is more concentrated.

Of course the reabsorbed water was, only a short time before, removed from the blood by ultra-filtration. Reabsorbing it cannot therefore reduce the osmotic pressure of the blood; it can only slow down the rate at which the osmotic pressure increases. In fact there must always be a net loss of water from the body because urine production must continue, albeit at a reduced rate.

How, then, is the osmotic pressure of the blood returned to normal? The answer is that when the osmotic pressure of the blood increases, the person feels thirsty and drinks. **Drinking** is initiated by the osmoreceptors in the hypothalamus. It is an essential part of the homeostatic mechanism by which the osmotic pressure of the blood is controlled.

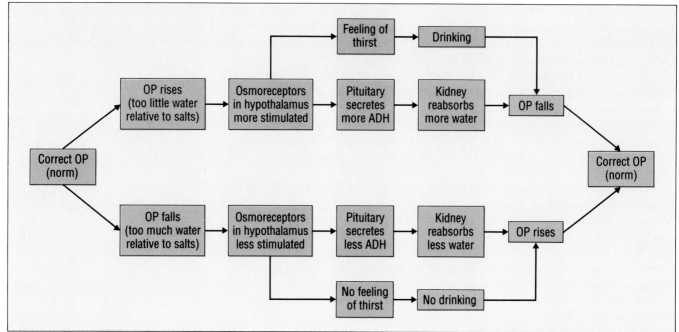

Figure 22.9 Scheme summarising the way the osmotic pressure of the blood is kept constant in a mammal. The process works in essentially the same way as other homeostatic mechanisms, deviations from the norm (set point) being corrected by negative feedback (see page 361).

Drinking, particularly if excessive, results in the osmotic pressure of the blood falling below its normal value. The osmoreceptors are now less stimulated than before. As a result less hormone is produced, less water is reabsorbed by the kidney, and a more copious and dilute urine is produced. Result? The osmotic pressure of the blood rises.

The production of a large quantity of watery urine is known as diuresis, and clearly the action of the hormone is to counteract this condition. It is therefore known as **antidiuretic hormone**, or **ADH** for short.[1] Its role in the homeostatic control of osmotic pressure is summarised in figure 22.9.

The importance of ADH may be appreciated by considering what happens to someone who has a faulty pituitary which fails to produce the hormone. The person permanently produces large quantities of dilute urine and has to make good the loss by drinking a lot of water, otherwise the body quickly becomes dehydrated. This condition is called **diabetes insipidus**. Don't confuse this with diabetes mellitus which is quite different (see page 361).

How does ADH exert its effect on the kidney? Research suggests that it makes the cells lining the collecting ducts more permeable to water, thus facilitating the osmotic movement of water into the surrounding tissues. The distal convoluted tubule is also affected, so this too reabsorbs some of the water.

The control of ions

We have seen how the kidney controls the osmotic pressure of the blood and tissue fluid by regulating the amount of water expelled in the urine. However, the osmotic pressure is determined by the relative concentrations of water and solutes, including ions. Controlling the concentration of ions is therefore an important aspect of osmoregulation. As determinants of the osmotic pressure, sodium and chloride ions are particularly important for they make up the bulk of the salt in the blood.

But there is another reason for controlling ions which was touched on in Chapter 21. Cells will function efficiently only if they are bathed in a solution with the correct ionic composition. Not only does the total

1 ADH is also known as **vasopressin** because large doses bring about constriction of blood vessels with a resulting increase in blood pressure. (The word vasopressin comes from Latin and literally means 'to press a vessel'.) At one time it was thought that vasopressin and ADH were two separate hormones, but it is now known that they are one and the same. The result is that the hormone has two names! In this book we shall call it ADH because this more accurately reflects its natural function.

How sodium ions are controlled

The concentration of sodium ions in the blood and tissue fluid is controlled by a hormone called **aldosterone** secreted by the adrenal cortex (see page 442).

Aldosterone increases the uptake of sodium ions by the gut and their reabsorption in the kidney. The result is that the concentration of sodium ions in the blood rises.

The secretion of aldosterone by the adrenal cortex is stimulated by **adrenocorticotrophic hormone (ACTH)** from the anterior lobe of the pituitary gland. The main method of control depends on the negative feedback process shown in illustration 1. If the concentration of sodium ions is too high, the adrenal cortex becomes inhibited with the result that it secretes less aldosterone. If the concentration of sodium ions is too low, the inhibitory influence is removed with the result that the adrenal cortex secretes more aldosterone.

The way the feedback control of the adrenal cortex takes place is summarised in illustration 2. A fall in the concentration of sodium ions in the blood causes an immediate fall in the blood volume because water is lost with the sodium ions. Inevitably the fall in blood volume is

accompanied by a fall in blood pressure. The decreased blood pressure causes an enzyme called **renin** to be released into the blood from special cells lining the afferent glomerular arterioles in the kidney. The renin catalyses the conversion of one of the plasma proteins into a substance called **angiotensin** which stimulates the adrenal cortex to secrete aldosterone.

A rise in the concentration of sodium ions in the blood has the reverse effect: the blood volume and pressure fall, less renin and angiotensin are produced so less aldosterone is released from the adrenal cortex.

From this brief account you will appreciate that angiotensin raises the blood pressure. This effect is enhanced by the fact that, as well as influencing the sodium ion concentration in the body, it is a powerful vasoconstrictor. It is one of a number of mechanisms which help to maintain the blood pressure.

The control of sodium ions is inextricably bound up with that of potassium ions. In the kidney, for example, the reabsorption of sodium ions is accompanied by the loss of potassium ions. This is because of the sodium–potassium pump which moves these ions in opposite directions (see page 194). The result

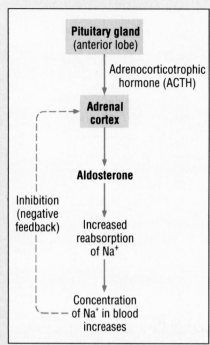

Illustration I How the sodium ion concentration in the blood and tissue fluid is controlled.

is that as the sodium ion concentration in the blood rises, the potassium ion concentration falls. The mechanisms that control the sodium ion concentration therefore also control the *relative* concentrations of sodium and potassium ions. This is called the **sodium–potassium balance**, and holding it in steady state is essential for the normal functioning of cells.

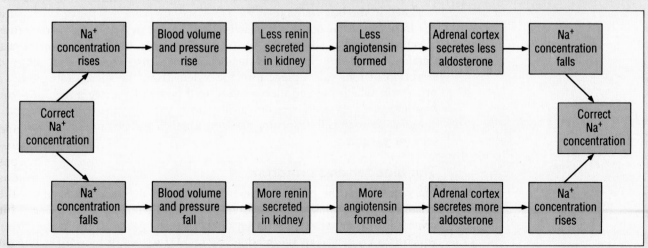

Illustration 2 The feedback pathway by which aldosterone-secretion is regulated in the control of the sodium ion concentration.

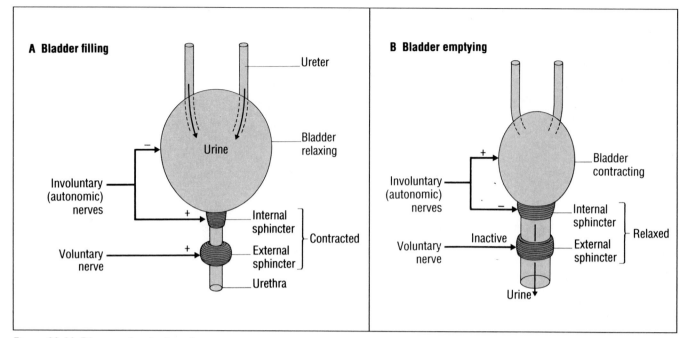

Figure 22.10 Diagrams showing how the emptying of the bladder (urination) is controlled. The arrows indicate the flow of urine. (+ nervous excitation, − nervous inhibition.)

quantity of all the ions have to be right, but their *relative* concentrations must be right too.

Ionic regulation in animals is complex, but the principles are quite simple. In general terms, the concentration of a particular type of ion − sodium for example − in the blood and tissue fluid is regulated by a hormone which affects three things.

- The uptake of the particular ions into the bloodstream from the gut.
- Their removal from the blood by the kidneys and elimination in the urine.
- Their release into the bloodstream from organs (if any) which contain them in high concentrations.

By adjusting the balance between these three processes, the concentrations of ions in the blood and tissue fluid are held in steady state. The result is that the cells are bathed in a fluid whose ionic composition is suited to their needs.

To illustrate these principles, the control of sodium ions (Na^+) is explored in the box on page 379.

In plants, ionic control is based on a different principle. Some degree of selection is exercised by the roots. For example, there is a preferential uptake of potassium ions from the soil. There is also evidence that selective secretion of ions takes place into the xylem from the surrounding cells, a process in which the endodermis may well be involved (see page 336). But for the most part ionic regulation in plants occurs at the level of the individual cells, each cell absorbing the ions it needs and passing unwanted ions into the vacuole.

The bladder and urination

The result of all the processes described so far is the production of a fluid, urine, which contains all the substances which the body does not want. The urine trickles out of the collecting ducts into the pelvis of the kidney from which it is conveyed to the bladder by regular waves of muscular contraction which pass down the ureters. The urine therefore enters the bladder in a series of squirts.

The bladder and its associated structures are shown in figure 22.1 (on page 369). As the bladder fills up with urine it expands and presses against the ureters, closing them and preventing urine flowing back into them from the bladder. The wall of the bladder is lined on the inside by **transitional epithelium** (see page 176). This type of epithelium is stretchable and is therefore ideally suited to lining the bladder. Outside the epithelium is a layer of **smooth muscle** which relaxes as the bladder expands. Because the bladder muscle relaxes, the pressure in the bladder does not increase greatly until the bladder is almost full. The urethra is kept closed by two rings of muscle, the **internal** and **external sphincters**. The expulsion of urine from the bladder is called **urination**. For urination to occur, the two sphincters open and the bladder muscle contracts.

The bladder muscle and internal sphincter have a nerve supply which belongs to the autonomic (involuntary) nervous system. The external sphincter, however, is innervated by the voluntary nervous system. When the bladder is filling up with urine, impulses in the involuntary system make the bladder muscle relax and internal sphincter contract. When urination occurs impulses in the involuntary system make the bladder muscle contract and internal sphincter open. At the same time the external sphincter opens voluntarily, so urine flows through. The mechanism is summarised in figure 22.10.

Urination is a reflex which is triggered by the filling of the bladder itself. Impulses reaching the brain from the bladder wall create an awareness of the presence of urine in the bladder which later gives way to a feeling of urgency. Eventually urination becomes inevitable.

Excretion and osmoregulation in other organisms

In South Devon there is a freshwater lake, Slapton Ley, which is separated from the sea by a narrow causeway. In 1976 a severe storm, coupled with an exceptionally high tide, resulted in sea water flowing over the causeway into the lake. As a result most of the fish in the lake died. What had happened to them?

Sea water contains about twice as much salt as the blood of a fish, so it has a considerably higher osmotic pressure. Although the fish's scaly skin is relatively impermeable, the lining of the mouth cavity and gills acts as a partially permeable membrane. So when a freshwater fish is immersed in sea water, water flows out of its body by osmosis.

The Slapton Ley episode illustrates an important generalisation, namely that most aquatic animals cannot tolerate appreciable fluctuations in the salinity of their external medium. This is not to say that the osmotic pressure of their body fluids, the internal OP, is necessarily the same as the external OP. On the contrary, many animals can maintain a difference between the internal and external OP, but their ability to do so breaks down if the OP of the external medium deviates too far from its normal value.

From the point of view of osmoregulation animals fall into two groups: those that cannot regulate their internal osmotic pressure at all, and those that can – at least to some degree. The former are all marine invertebrates, and as they are thought to represent the starting point in an evolutionary sequence we shall consider them first.

Renal dialysis

People with kidney failure can be treated by renal dialysis. Guest author Patricia Kohn explains what this is and how it has developed.

The kidney performs its functions of excretion and osmoregulation by ultra-filtration followed by selective reabsorption and secretion. Renal dialysis relies solely on passive diffusion to carry out these functions.

Renal dialysis is commonly carried out by a **kidney machine** of the sort shown in illustration 1. The patient's blood is passed along numerous narrow tubes made of a partially permeable **dialysing membrane**. The tube is immersed in a specially prepared **dialysis fluid** which contains the desirable components of blood plasma at the same concentration as in the blood itself. These chemicals include sodium ions and glucose. Unwanted substances such as urea are absent from the dialysis fluid.

The lining of the tubes holds back the blood cells and plasma proteins but allows all the other chemicals to diffuse through freely (illustration 2). As the desirable substances are present in equal concentrations on both sides of the membrane, no net change in their concentrations will occur. However, there will be a net loss from the blood of unwanted substances such as urea because they are not present in the dialysis fluid, and any excess of normal plasma constituents such as potassium or phosphate will also be lost. Frequent replacement of the dialysis fluid ensures that a steep concentration gradient is maintained, favouring the continued diffusion of these unwanted substances.

The osmoregulatory function of the kidney is also performed during renal dialysis. Net water loss from the blood can be induced by raising the solute concentration of the

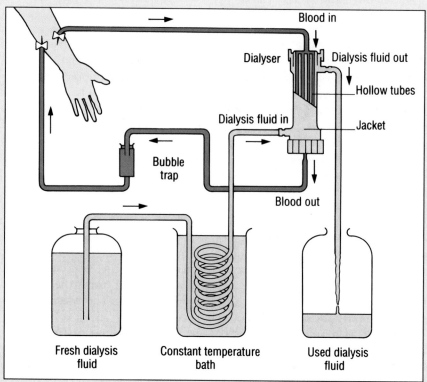

Illustration 1 A modern kidney machine.

dialysis fluid by the addition of a solute such as dextran to which the dialysing membrane is impermeable. Water will then flow out of the blood by osmosis.

Finding the right membrane

The key piece of technology which makes renal dialysis possible is the dialysing membrane. The principle of dialysis was discovered in the 1860s,

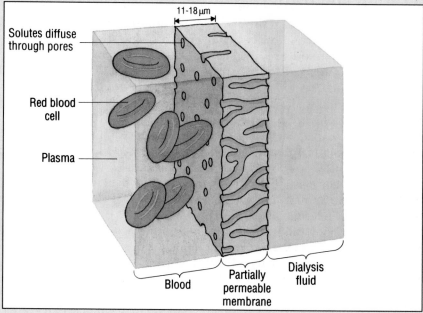

Illustration 2 Diagram of the dialysing membrane used in an artificial kidney. The membrane is partially permeable, allowing the passage of all the components of blood except for the blood cells and plasma proteins.

but it was not until 1924 that it was applied to the removal of unwanted substances from human blood. The dialysing membrane used then was celloidin, a cellulose-based synthetic material. However, the celloidin membrane was very fragile and few patients were treated.

Then in the 1930s a breakthrough occurred. Seamless cellophane tubing was developed for the sausage industry and became available in large quantities. Cellophane is much tougher than celloidin, and the sausage skins provided a source of ready-made dialysis tubing. In Holland, a young physician called Willem Kolff. Kolff found that sausage skin cellophane was an efficient dialysing membrane for separating urea from blood.

In 1945, using a machine with such a membrane, he succeeded in saving the life of an elderly woman with acute renal failure.

After the war, modern methods of renal dialysis were developed. Today it is a routine procedure. The cellophane membrane was used for many years but has now been replaced by membranes based on other cellulose esters and different polymers. The membranes take the form of a coiled tube, parallel sheets or hollow fibres depending on the type of machine.

The problem of pressure

A problem that faced the early pioneers was that efficient dialysis requires a very high rate of blood flow through the machine – between 200 and 300 cm³ per minute. The only blood vessels that will deliver blood at this pressure are arteries, so every time treatment was given an artery had to be pierced. Arteries are narrower and deeper down than veins, so this procedure was difficult and not without risk. Clearly, if treatment was to be lifelong, some easier form of access to the

circulation had to be developed so that dialysis could be carried out at home.

The modern solution to this problem, first used in 1966, is to join an artery to a nearby vein, creating a so-called **arteriovenous fistula** (illustration 3). The blood passes from the artery to the vein at a high flow rate, and is then drawn off from the vein by means of a needle inserted through the skin. Two puncture sites are needed, one to take the blood to the machine, the other to return it to the patient.

A machine that filters the blood

Modern dialysing membranes are sufficiently strong to withstand pressures high enough to separate particles of different sizes by an ultra-filtration process analogous to that used by the kidney itself. In fact it has become possible to treat patients by a system which relies solely on ultra-filtration to remove toxic solutes. The water and desirable solutes filtered are not reabsorbed as in the kidney, but are replaced by the correct volume of a specially prepared substitution fluid which is added to the blood as it returns to the patient's body. This technique has certain advantages over conventional dialysis. In the future it may offer an improved quality of life for people with renal failure.

Peritoneal dialysis

As an alternative to being put on a kidney machine, a person may be given **peritoneal dialysis** in hospital. Between one and two litres of sterile dialysis fluid are let into the abdominal cavity via a tube inserted through the body wall. The fluid is left in the abdominal cavity for several hours and then siphoned out and replaced by a fresh lot.

The principle underlying peritoneal dialysis is very simple. The

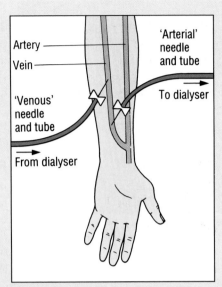

Illustration 3 The arteriovenous fistula provides a convenient and easy way of attaching a person to a kidney machine.

abdominal cavity and all the organs in it are lined with a **peritoneal membrane**. This membrane covers a total area of about 2 m² and it has its own extensive blood supply. While the dialysis fluid is in the abdominal cavity, equilibration takes place between the fluid and the surrounding blood. Since the dialysis fluid is changed regularly, toxic substances such as urea are lost from the blood just as they are in a kidney machine.

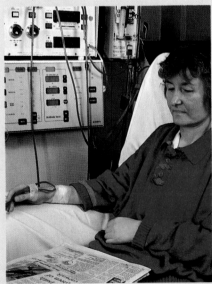

Illustration 4 A kidney machine in use.

Figure 22.11 Marine invertebrates such as the sea anemones and starfish in this picture have body fluids which are isotonic with sea water.

Marine invertebrates

There is good reason to suppose that life began in the sea. Many animals, notably marine invertebrates such as sea anemones, jellyfish, spider crabs and starfish, have remained in the sea throughout their evolutionary history (figure 22.11). Their body fluids are isotonic with sea water – indeed in animals like the starfish the tissues are perfused with sea water itself.

Since their internal osmotic pressure (OPi) is equal to the external osmotic pressure (OPe), there is no need for these animals to osmoregulate, so long as they remain in the open sea.

From sea to fresh water

In the evolutionary history of animals, migration from sea to fresh water has happened on more than one occasion. To be able to undergo such a migration, an animal must be able to maintain an osmotic pressure independent of that of the surrounding water. To illustrate this, compare the results of immersing three different species of crab in diluted sea water (figure 22.12).

The fully marine spider crab *Maia* cannot osmoregulate at all with the result that its environment is restricted to the sea. On the other hand, the shore crab *Carcinus* is capable of some degree of osmoregulation, enabling it to live in the brackish water of estuaries. However, its powers of osmoregulation break down if the external medium becomes too dilute, so it cannot migrate very far up rivers. The third species, the mitten crab *Eriocheir*, can osmoregulate much more efficiently than *Carcinus*, enabling it to penetrate upstream into completely fresh water.

Although osmoregulation is necessary for permanent migration from sea to fresh water, it is not the only means by which a marine animal can withstand dilution of its surrounding medium. There are two other ways:

- The animal may possess tissues that can tolerate a wide range of salinities. This is true, for example, of the lugworm *Arenicola* which survives in the comparatively dilute waters of the Baltic Sea, and the ragworm *Nereis* which flourishes in the Gulf of Finland.
- The animal may avoid the effects of dilution by behavioural means. This is the method used by the estuarine snail *Hydrobia*, which burrows into the mud when the tide is going out, thus escaping the twice-daily dilution of its external medium with fresh river water.

Animals thus adapted can penetrate for variable distances upstream, but for full exploitation of freshwater the ability to osmoregulate is essential.

The problem facing freshwater animals

The problem facing a freshwater animal is that OPi is greater than OPe. The danger here is dilution of the tissues resulting from the osmotic influx of water across the exposed partially permeable surfaces of the body.

There are two possible solutions to this problem:

- Water might be eliminated as fast as it enters by means of a kidney or some equivalent device, salts being reabsorbed from the water before it leaves the body.
- Salts might be actively taken up from the external medium, thereby counteracting the diluting effect of the inflowing water.

Both these solutions would involve the movement of ions against a concentration gradient (active transport), so they would require the expenditure of energy. With these general principles in mind, let us take a brief look at the osmoregulatory devices of two different fresh water organisms.

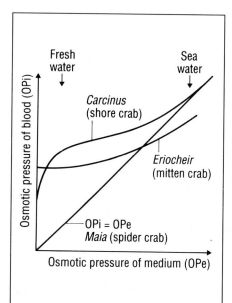

Figure 22.12 Graph showing the effect of changing the osmotic pressure of the external medium (OPe) on the internal osmotic pressure (OPi) of three genera of crabs. Note that *Maia* cannot osmoregulate at all, *Carcinus* can do so provided that the external medium is not too dilute, and *Eriocheir* can osmoregulate even in freshwater.

The contractile vacuole

This device is found in *Amoeba* and other unicellular protoctists that live in freshwater. It is a small membrane-lined sac located in the cytoplasm.

The plasma membrane surrounding the organism is partially permeable, and since OPi is greater than OPe water flows into the cell by osmosis. To counter this, water is collected up into the contractile vacuole as fast as it enters the cell. The contractile vacuole gradually expands as it fills up with water, and eventually discharges its contents to the exterior through a small pore in the plasma membrane. The cycle is then repeated (figure 22.14).

To be effective as an osmoregulatory device, the contractile vacuole must eliminate water but not salts. The electron microscope shows the contractile vacuole of *Amoeba* to be surrounded by mitochondria and tiny vesicles. It is thought that the vesicles collect fluid from the cytoplasm and then pump salts back into the cytoplasm by active transport, energy being provided by the mitochondria. The vesicles, now containing water, fuse with the contractile vacuole which gradually expands. Treating *Amoeba* with a metabolic poison puts the contractile vacuole out of action: the cell can no longer get rid of surplus water so it swells up and dies.

Fresh water bony fish

Fresh water bony fish such as carp, trout and stickleback are liable to osmotic influx of water across the gills and the lining of the mouth cavity and pharynx. So the fresh water bony fish must get rid of water and save salts. This is achieved in three main ways (figure 22.15):

- The rate of filtration in the kidney (**glomerular filtration rate**) is very high, much more so than in marine fish. The cortex of the fish kidney is structurally similar to that of the mammal. The high filtration rate is achieved by the glomeruli being exceptionally large and numerous.

- As the renal fluid flows along the kidney tubules, salts (i.e. sodium and chloride ions) are extensively reabsorbed back into the bloodstream with the result that the urine is markedly hypotonic to the blood.

- **Chloride secretory cells** in the gills take up sodium and chloride ions from the water and move them against the concentration gradient into the bloodstream. The result is that chloride is some 800 times more concentrated in the animal's blood than it is in the surrounding fresh-water. This active transport of salts requires energy.

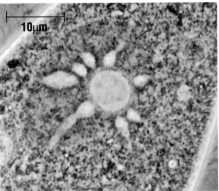

Figure 22.13 Photomicrograph of a contractile vacuole of the unicellular protoctist *Paramecium*. The spherical contractile vacuole is surrounded by radiating collecting channels. Water passes from the cytoplasm into the collecting channels and thence into the contractile vacuole.

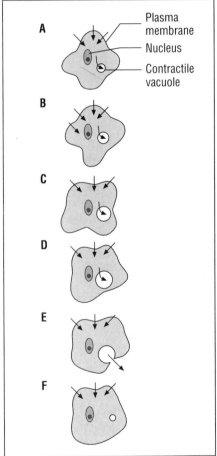

Figure 22.14 Osmoregulation in *Amoeba*. The arrows indicate the flow of water. Water which enters the cell by osmosis is collected up into the contractile vacuole and discharged to the exterior.

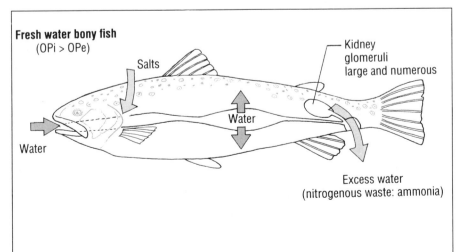

Figure 22.15 Summary of osmoregulation in a freshwater bony fish such as a trout.

Why do turtles cry and penguins have runny noses?

Marine birds and reptiles face the same osmotic problem that confronts marine bony fishes, namely a surplus of salt. How do they get rid of it?

Marine reptiles have salt-secreting glands in the head. In a turtle the glands are located behind the eyes, and the salty fluid emerges from the posterior corner of the orbit – hence the turtle 'shedding tears'. In the marine iguana lizards of the Galapagos Islands the glands open into the nasal cavity. Every now and again the lizard gives a powerful exhalation and the salty fluid is expelled as a fine spray.

Salt-secreting nasal glands are also found in marine birds such as penguins, gulls and cormorants. The fluid trickles out of the nasal openings, giving the impression that these birds have runny noses.

The activity of the salt glands can be related to feeding habits and diet. For example, the petrel, a bird of the open sea that feeds on plankton, takes in a lot of salt with its food and produces a highly concentrated fluid from its salt glands. In contrast, the cormorant, a coastal fish-eater, takes in less salt and produces a relatively dilute fluid from its salt glands.

Comparing marine bony fishes with these other vertebrates is interesting because it shows how the same physiological problem is solved by different groups of animals in essentially the same way. We can even extend the comparison to plants. A land plant living in salty water may excrete surplus salt from salt glands (see page 391).

Figure 22.16 Summary of osmoregulation in a marine bony fish such as a mackerel.

Thus, to summarise, freshwater bony fish solve their osmotic problem by combining the expulsion of water with the active uptake of salts.

Marine vertebrates

Unlike marine invertebrates, whose body fluids are isotonic with sea water, marine vertebrates have body fluids which are hypotonic to their surroundings; in other words OPi is less than OPe. The result is that water is liable to leave the body by osmosis, leading to dehydration of the tissues. So the animal must save water and get rid of salts.

How this is done is well shown by marine bony fish such as mackerel and cod. It is achieved by a combination of three processes (figure 22.16):

- The glomerular filtration rate in the kidney is relatively low. The glomeruli are small and few in number compared with freshwater species.

- Salts are actively extruded by chloride secretory cells in the gills. In freshwater species these cells move salts inwards. In marine forms they move them outwards.

- Nitrogenous waste is excreted in a form which requires relatively little water for its elimination. Freshwater species excrete their nitrogenous waste as ammonia, a highly soluble toxic substance which has to be diluted by a large volume of water. This is no hardship for a freshwater fish which has more water than it knows what to do with. However, marine species, facing potential water shortage, cannot afford such a loss. For this reason ammonia is replaced by other nitrogenous substances which are less soluble and less toxic than ammonia. This means that they can be excreted in a more concentrated form, with less water-loss from the body.

The two main nitrogenous waste substances produced by these fish are **urea** which is considerably less toxic than ammonia, and a compound called **trimethylamine oxide** which is totally non-toxic.

So marine bony fish solve their osmotic problem by saving water and getting rid of salts. Marine cartilaginous fish such as sharks and rays get round the same problem in a quite different way. These fish retain urea in the body with the result that their internal osmotic pressure is very slightly *higher* than that of the surrounding sea water. The result is a slight influx of water which is readily expelled by the kidney.

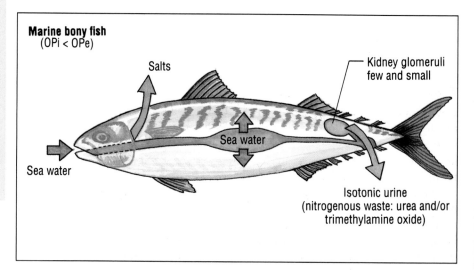

Marine bony fish
(OPi < OPe)

Salts

Kidney glomeruli few and small

Sea water

Sea water

Isotonic urine (nitrogenous waste: urea and/or trimethylamine oxide)

Terrestrial animals

Like marine bony fish, terrestrial animals are liable to lose water, but whereas in a fish this is caused by osmosis, in a terrestrial animal it is caused by evaporation from permeable surfaces exposed to the atmosphere. Terrestrial animals have a number of features which help them to overcome this problem. These features are outlined below.

They have a waterproof integument

This obvious way of reducing water loss is particularly evident in reptiles, birds and mammals. In these three vertebrate groups the surface of the body is protected by structures which contain the protein **keratin**. The scales of reptiles, feathers of birds and hair of mammals all contain keratin, as does the upper part of the epidermis (see page 397). Keratin makes these structures hard, thus providing protection from physical damage. It also makes them waterproof, a property which is enhanced in birds and mammals by the presence of oil on the surface of the skin.

The impermeability of the skin is one reason why these animals can live successfully in hot, dry places such as the desert. Of all terrestrial vertebrates the least well adapted in this respect are amphibians. The skin of most amphibians is thin and moist, with the result that water readily evaporates from it. This is one reason why amphibians are generally restricted to damp places.

Amongst invertebrates, insects have developed waterproofing to a remarkable degree. Insects have a hard cuticle whose surface is covered with a microscopically thin layer of **wax**. The wax, in common with lipids generally, is impermeable to water and confers on the cuticle its water-proofing properties (figure 22.17).

An animal cannot insulate itself entirely from the outside world. It must be able to breathe, and a certain amount of water will always evaporate from the gaseous-exchange surfaces. Insects breathe through small holes in the cuticle called **spiracles**. These are guarded by hairs or, in some species, by valves which can open and close. In this way evaporative water loss is reduced to a minimum.

They have a low glomerular filtration rate

You will recall that marine bony fish have a low filtration rate because the glomeruli in their kidneys are small and few. The same adaptation is found in many terrestrial vertebrates, particularly those that inhabit hot, dry habitats. For example, the desert frog *Chiroleptes*, one of the few amphibians to flourish in hot deserts, has fewer and smaller glomeruli than frogs living in moist temperate regions (figure 22.18).

They produce a non-toxic nitrogenous waste

It was mentioned earlier that marine bony fish excrete nitrogenous waste in the form of urea or trimethylamine oxide, an adaptation for conserving water. Similar trends are found in terrestrial animals. For example, amphibians and mammals excrete **urea** which, being less toxic than ammonia, requires less water for its removal.

Reptiles, birds and insects have taken this a step further and excrete nitrogenous waste as **uric acid**. Uric acid is insoluble in water. This means that water can be removed from it before it leaves the body, the uric acid being excreted in a semi-solid form. In insects the uric acid is produced by the **Malpighian tubules**, a bunch of narrow tubes leading off the gut.

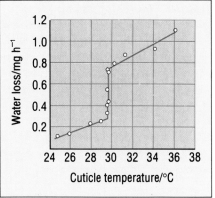

Figure 22.17 The results of an experiment designed to test the hypothesis that the wax on the surface of an insect cuticle makes the cuticle waterproof. A cockroach nymph was gradually warmed up and the rate of water loss from its body was measured at a series of temperatures. Below about 30°C there was very little increase in water loss as the temperature was raised, but as the temperature approached 30°C the rate of water loss suddenly increased dramatically. It was found that at this temperature the arrangement of the wax molecules changed and the cuticle became permeable to water.

Figure 22.18 The Australian desert frog *Chiroleptes* has a very low filtration rate in its kidneys and retains urine in its bladder for use during the dry season. So much urine may be retained that the animal swells up like a ball, as shown in this picture. The Aborigines use these frogs as a source of water. Desert frogs in general show many interesting adaptations for living in hot, dry places. For example, some of them have a waterproof skin and excrete uric acid instead of urea.

Figure 22.19 The internal anatomy of an insect with the gut unravelled and deflected to one side. Notice the Malpighian tubules. Each tubule opens into the gut at its inner end, while its closed outer end floats freely in the blood-filled body cavity. Soluble nitrogenous waste in the blood is absorbed by the tubules and converted into uric acid which passes along the tubules into the gut and out with the faeces. Water is reabsorbed back into the blood in the colon and rectum, particularly the rectum.

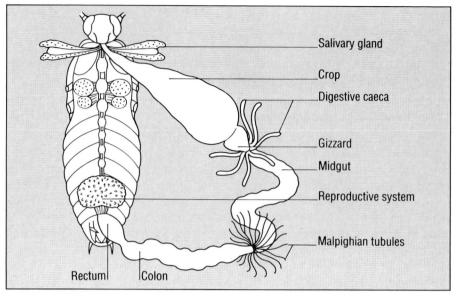

Salivary gland

Crop

Digestive caeca

Gizzard

Midgut

Reproductive system

Malpighian tubules

Rectum   Colon

Figure 22.20 The kangaroo rat *Dipodomys*, a desert rodent which lives in the North American desert, shows many adaptations to life in a hot, dry environment. It is amazingly good at conserving water. This is achieved by not sweating, by producing a highly concentrated urine and very dry faeces and by staying in its burrow during the heat of the day thereby reducing evaporation from the lungs.

The pocket mouse

Although a correlation between water conservation and a long loop of Henle makes sense, it is not the whole story. The most 'powerful' kidney known is that of the pocket mouse *Perognathus*, a nocturnal rodent found in the south-western desert of North America. Its urine is six times as concentrated as that of humans, but its loops of Henle are much shorter. It seems that the pocket mouse can maintain exceptionally steep gradients across its loops of Henle, possibly by producing a much higher concentration of ATP to power the active transport involved.

They reabsorb water

Insects reabsorb water mainly in the rectum (figure 22.19). Uric acid, produced by the Malpighian tubules, moves into the rectum where water is reabsorbed so vigorously that, in some species, the material which finally passes out of the anus is solid.

We saw earlier that the **loop of Henle**, present in birds and mammals, plays an important part in the reabsorption of water by the kidney. Desert mammals have an extra-long loop of Henle and produce a more concentrated urine in consequence. Take the kangaroo rat, for example, an animal that shows all sorts of adaptations for living in the desert (figure 22.20). The kangaroo rat produces urine four times as concentrated as the human's, a feat which is made possible at least partly by its long loop of Henle.

In birds, as in many other vertebrates, the ureters and rectum open into a common cavity called the cloaca. *Cloaca* is the Latin word for sewer, which is apt because it receives excretory waste and faeces. Water is extensively reabsorbed from the faeces and excretory waste by the wall of the cloaca. What passes out is a semi-solid mixture of faeces (black or brown) and uric acid (white) which birds, with singular disregard for anti-litter laws, deposit on pavements and buildings.

They avoid exposing themselves to the atmosphere

Many terrestrial animals behave in such a way as to avoid, or at least reduce, the problem of water loss. Earthworms, for example, burrow deeper when the surface soil is dry. Some species of earthworm respond to very dry conditions by going into a state of dormancy, a phenomenon called **aestivation**. The worm coils up into a tight ball in a pocket of air and surrounds itself with mucus which then dries. The metabolic rate falls and the worm goes into a state of suspended animation from which it is aroused when conditions become wet again. Another animal that aestivates is the garden snail *Helix*. In dry conditions it retreats into its shell, the opening of which becomes covered by a tough membrane secreted by the foot.

Aestivation can also be useful to aquatic animals in drought conditions.

For example, the African and South American lungfishes can survive even if the water dries up completely. The fish burrows into the soft mud which later dries and hardens into a 'cocoon' with the fish inside. Here the fish remains until the arrival of the next rainy season six or seven months later.

They make use of metabolic water

As you know, one of the products of respiration is water (see page 228). Some desert animals rely on this **metabolic water** as a source of water. The amount of water yielded by respiration depends on the food substance being metabolised. For example, one gram of carbohydrate yields approximately 0.56 grams of water, but almost twice as much water is produced by one gram of fat. For this reason a desert animal such as the kangaroo rat tends to metabolise fat rather than carbohydrate. The kangaroo rat's water-conservation powers are so good that it produces more water by metabolism than it loses through evaporation and excretion.

They have tissues tolerant to water loss

The camel is another animal which thrives in the desert (figure 22.21). Amongst its many adaptations is an ability to go for long periods without drinking. It is popularly believed that water is stored in the hump, but in fact fat is stored here and water is obtained from its metabolism just as in the kangaroo rat. However, the camel cannot produce more metabolic water than it loses by evaporation. How then does it survive without drinking?

The answer was discovered by the American physiologist, Knut Schmidt-Nielsen. He found that the camel's tissues are exceptionally tolerant to dehydration. As the days go by, more and more water is lost and the body fluids become more and more concentrated, and yet the camel survives. In fact it will survive water loss that reduces its body mass by as much as 30 per cent, ten per cent more than would be fatal to a human. Little wonder that when it does drink, it does so with great gusto. Schmidt-Nielsen reports that a camel which was given water after 16 days without it, drank 40 litres in ten minutes! Apparently this record has now been broken by another camel which managed 60 litres!

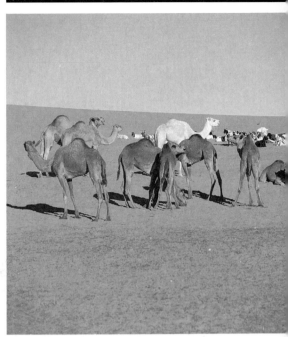

Figure 22.21 The camel is well adapted to living in the hot, dry desert. Some of its adaptations are discussed in the text.

Water regulation in plants

Plants can be classified into three groups according to how much water is available to them in their natural environment.

- **Hydrophytes** are plants which live partially or completely submerged in freshwater. Examples are water lilies and the Canadian pondweed *Elodea*. Obviously such plants have no difficulty getting enough water.
- **Mesophytes** grow in normal, well-watered soil. Most land plants in temperate regions belong to this category. Usually the water which they lose by transpiration is readily replaced by uptake from the soil, so they require no special means of conserving water.
- **Xerophytes** live in dry places such as the hot desert where the water potentials in the soil and air are very low. These plants face the possibility of drastic dehydration and have ways of preventing this.

How plants survive drought

In general plants are better than animals at tolerating fluctuations in the water content of their tissues. Those that live in dry places are particularly

Figure 22.22 The desert in bloom, the result of a shower of rain.

Figure 22.23 Two desert succulents. The Saguaro cactus (*left and rear*) grows in the desert of Arizona and Northern Mexico. The prickly pear (*right foreground*), though native to the North American desert, is now found in desert regions all over the world. In both these plants water is stored in the thick stems and branches. Excessive transpiration is prevented by having an epidermis with a thick cuticle and very few stomata. A superficial root system ensures that after a shower of rain, water is quickly absorbed before it has time to evaporate.

tolerant to desiccation. Indeed, some species are so adaptable that their tissues can, to all intents and purposes, be completely dried out and yet resume normal functioning later when water becomes available. This is seen in certain desert species and also in many mosses and ferns.

Life cycle adaptations

Most species can survive dry periods as **seeds** or **spores**. The living contents of seeds and spores are generally in a highly dehydrated state and protected within a hard case. Metabolism proceeds at a very slow rate. In this condition a seed or spore may remain viable for a considerable time, germinating into a new plant when water becomes available and other conditions are suitable.

The use of seeds for surviving dry conditions is well illustrated by small desert ephemerals. Germination, growth and flowering – the entire life cycle in fact – takes place during the few weeks following a burst of rain. Suddenly the arid desert landscape is turned into a spectacular carpet of colour (figure 22.22). After the seeds have been dispersed, the parent plants die and the seeds remain dormant in the dry soil until the next rains come.

Adaptations relating to transpiration and water uptake

The main problem facing a land plant is that the rate of transpiration may exceed the rate of water uptake from the soil. Factors affecting the rate of transpiration are discussed on page 344. Many species have adaptations which minimise transpiration and/or maximise water uptake.

For example, some plants that live in dry places have extremely long **vertical roots** which absorb water from deep down in the soil. Many Mediterranean trees and shrubs such as *Acacia* and *Oleander* do this. Other plants, including most cacti, have **superficial** roots which grow out horizontally just beneath the surface. This puts them in the best position to absorb water quickly before it has a chance to evaporate.

The mesquite tree, which grows in the arid regions of the south-western United States, has a deep taproot *and* numerous horizontal fibrous roots. The taproot may grow down as far as 20 metres below the surface, reaching the water table, and the fibrous roots extend over a wide area.

Another method used by some plants is to **store water** in large parenchyma cells contained within swollen stems or leaves. This makes the tissues wet and juicy, for which reason these kinds of plants are called **succulents**. Two well-known succulents are the giant Saguaro cactus of the North American desert and the prickly pear cactus (figure 22.23). In both these plants water is stored in the thick stem and branches, and the leaves are modified into sharp spines which may deter thirsty animals that might otherwise tap the valuable juices.

There is no point in being a succulent without having ways of preventing the stored water being lost. One method is to **reduce the number of stomata**, an adaptation seen in many desert plants including the prickly pear. The stomata of some plants, for example the evergreen shrub *Hakea* of the Australian desert, are sunk down into **pits** in which humid air tends to accumulate, thus reducing the rate of transpiration from the leaves. Some plants achieve the same thing by having a **hairy epidermis** which holds humid air against the leaf surface. These devices are accompanied in some plants by **folding of the leaves**, an adaptation seen in marram grass, which thrives on dry coastal sand dunes (figure 22.24).

In mesophytic plants transpiration is not confined to the stomata; a certain amount of water evaporates through the cuticle as well. In xerophytes this cuticular transpiration is reduced by having **small leaves** with a low surface area, and by having a **thick cuticle** which is impermeable to water. This is particularly well seen in desert plants, but it is also shown by many evergreen trees and shrubs in temperate regions – pine trees for example.

Some plants may suffer from water shortage in the winter because the freezing of the soil water decreases its availability from the soil, causing what is called **physiological drought**. One way of circumventing this problem is to **shed the leaves** before winter sets in, thereby reducing the leaf surface to nil. This is what deciduous trees do. Although there are many other reasons for leaf-fall, there is no doubt that it is a very effective way of cutting down transpiration. One of the most spectacular examples of it is shown by *Ocotillo*, the 'vine cactus' of the North American desert (figure 22.25). This shrub comes out in leaf every time it rains and sheds its leaves immediately afterwards.

Crassulacean acid metabolism: a physiological adaptation

The adaptations mentioned so far are essentially structural ones, but some plants solve their water problems physiologically. For example, certain succulents **reverse the normal stomatal rhythm**. Instead of the stomata opening by day and closing at night, they open at night and close by day.

As a means of preventing excessive water loss reversing the stomatal rhythm seems an excellent idea, but what happens about photosynthesis? Such plants take up carbon dioxide at night, when the stomata are open, and fix it into malic acid. When daybreak comes, the stomata close and the carbon dioxide is released for photosynthesis. This is called **crassulacean acid metabolism** after the group of plants, the Crassulaceae, in which it was first observed. It is explained more fully on page 304.

Halophytes

You will recall that a marine bony fish faces the problem of water loss because the surrounding sea water has a higher salt concentration than its tissue fluids. Much the same applies to plants that live on mud flats and salt marshes by the edge of the sea. They are faced with the problem of having to take up water from an external medium which has a higher salt concentration, and therefore lower water potential, than ordinary soil water. Nevertheless, certain species of plants appear to thrive in these conditions. They are called **halophytes**, meaning 'salt plants'.

How do halophytes prevent osmotic loss of water? They do so by actively absorbing salts into their roots, with the result that the solute concentration of their tissues is higher than that of the surrounding water. They can then take up water by osmosis in the usual way. But there is a problem: the plants may absorb salt so vigorously that it becomes toxic to them. They get round this by isolating the surplus salt and storing it in their cells, or by secreting it from **salt glands** on the leaves.

Getting rid of surplus water

Excessive uptake of water, potentially so dangerous for animals, is not a problem for most plants because the cellulose cell walls impose a natural limit on the amount of water that can be taken in. However, in certain conditions more water may be taken up by a land plant than is removed by evaporation (transpiration). Pressure builds up and water may exude from the leaves, either through open stomata or from special structures called **hydathodes**. This process is called **guttation**.

Guttation is particularly common in tropical rain forests where, because of the high rainfall and humid atmosphere, plants have a plentiful

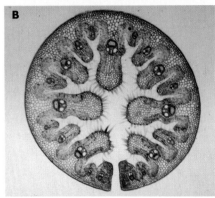

Figure 22.24

A Marram grass, *Ammophila arenaria*, growing on a sand dune.

B The photomicrograph shows a cross-section of one of the leaves in the folded position. Stomata occur only in the furrows on the inner side of the leaf where the photosynthetic tissue is located. Large thin-walled epidermal cells at the bases of the furrows shrink when they lose water from excessive transpiration. This causes the leaf to fold. The stiff, interlocking hairs help to hold in water vapour. The epidermis on the outer side of the leaf has a thick cuticle and lacks stomata. Magnification × 20.

Figure 22.25 *Ocotillo*, a North American desert shrub, produces leaves every time it rains. This may happen five or six times a year.

Figure 22.26 Guttation occurring at the edges of a leaf of lady's mantle, *Alchemilla vulgaris*. This plant is found around streams and in moist pastureland, particularly in hilly situations where at times the rate of water uptake exceeds the rate of transpiration.

water supply but a low rate of transpiration. One botanist remarked that standing under a guttating tree in the rain forest is like being out in a gentle drizzle! Even in a temperate country like Britain, water may sometimes drip from the leaves of trees on humid evenings in summer, especially in damp places such as close to a river or stream (figure 22.26).

Guttation is useful to plants because it maintains the transpiration stream and ensures a continued supply of nutrients in very humid conditions when normal transpiration cannot take place.

Other substances produced by plants

Plants provide a wide variety of substances which at first sight seem to be excretory products. However, many of them have been found to have a function, for example in defence against herbivores and parasites (see page 431). Even the salt secreted by halophytes may have a function. It has been shown that in some species the salt crystals trap water vapour from the surrounding air, which may then be absorbed by the leaf cells as liquid water. Thus what seems at first to be excretion may in fact be an ingenious mechanism enabling the plant to obtain water.

Trees produce various gums, resins and latexes. Whether we regard these compounds as excretory or not, once collected they have wide-ranging industrial applications. From them we get such products as turpentine, paints, varnishes, soaps, cosmetics, surgical goods, foods, golf balls, bubble gum and rubber. The story of rubber is told in the box on the opposite page.

Rubber

Tim King explains where natural rubber comes from and how it is obtained.

Rubber comes from the rubber tree, *Hevea brasiliensis*, which belongs to the spurge family of flowering plants, the Euphorbiaceae. Most members of this group produce **latex**, a white fluid of complex chemical composition which occurs in elongated cells called **laticifers**. The laticifers grow rapidly through the phloem tissue, branching profusely. The end walls between successive cells are often absent, so the tissue appears multinucleate. Modified chloroplasts containing liquid latex, together with droplets of various other substances, accumulate in the cytoplasm. When the bark is breached, the liquid flows out as a watery alkaline suspension. This is collected in cups attached to the bark, a process called **tapping** (see illustration 1). It is then poured into buckets and coagulated with acid to separate out the rubber. The rubber is then pressed into sheets for export.

Commercial rubber trees yield over two metric tonnes of latex per hectare per year, far more than a wild tree produces. Modern rubber plantations have clones of trees which have been selected for rapid rubber production (illustration 2). A high-yielding trunk is often grafted onto a robust root system below and onto a rapidly photosynthesising, disease-resistant canopy above. The latex produced by such a plant is standardised for a specific purpose.

Rubber is the only non-conducting compound which absorbs vibration and is waterproof, flexible and elastic. These properties stem from its molecular structure which has been likened to a bundle of wiggling snakes in constant motion. The 'snakes' are long chain polymers of an unsaturated hydrocarbon called **isoprene**. There are about 5000 isoprene units in each chain. The chains are cross-linked, and the number of cross-linkages increases when the rubber is **vulcanised** by being treated with sulphur compounds at high temperature. When a rubber sheet is stretched some of the chains become parallel to one another.

The production of natural rubber is cheaper than making synthetic rubber which requires expensive petroleum. About six million metric

Illustration 1 Latex being tapped from a rubber tree in Liberia, West Africa.

tonnes of natural rubber are extracted from rubber trees every year, mainly in South-East Asia. Two-thirds of this is used for manufacturing tyres. Aircraft and bulldozer tyres consist almost entirely of natural rubber, but car radial tyres contain only about 40 per cent, the rest being synthetic. In tyre manufacture, the liquid rubber solidifies in layers on a cord base, in a mould, and is then vulcanised when its final shape is formed. Other rubber products include waterproof clothes (the original use for rubber, conceived in 1823 by Mr Macintosh), cushioning, gloves, wellingtons, wire insulation, washers, stoppers, elastic bands, fan belts, shoe soles and heels, balls and condoms.

Conservationists use the story of rubber to illustrate the potential value of natural tropical products. In the rain forests there are thousands of plant species whose products have not yet been investigated for their possible value to humans.

Illustration 2 A rubber plantation in Indonesia.

Summary

1 **Excretion** is the elimination from the body of the waste products of metabolism. **Osmoregulation** is the process by which the osmotic pressure of the blood and tissue fluid is kept constant.

2 In mammals, excretion and osmoregulation are carried out by the **urinary system** whose principal organ is the **kidney**.

3 Each kidney contains approximately 1.5 million **nephrons** which perform the functions of excretion and osmoregulation by a combination of **ultra-filtration**, **reabsorption** and **secretion**.

4 The dialysing membrane responsible for ultra-filtration is the basement membrane in the part of the nephron known as **Bowman's capsule**.

5 In the tubules of the nephrons water is reabsorbed by osmosis, and glucose and salts by diffusion and active transport. Ammonia and water are secreted into the tubules.

6 Further water is reabsorbed osmotically from the collecting ducts as the result of a special part of the nephron known as the **loop of Henle** conserving salts on the principle of a **hair-pin countercurrent multiplier**.

7 Reabsorption of water by the kidney is controlled by **antidiuretic hormone** (**ADH**) from the posterior lobe of the pituitary gland.

8 **Ionic regulation** in animals is achieved by hormones which regulate the uptake of ions in the gut and their elimination by the kidneys.

9 In animals the **acid–base balance**, and hence **pH**, is controlled by the lungs, blood and kidneys.

10 Freshwater animals, including freshwater fish, eliminate excess water by means of a kidney or comparable device. In some cases salts are taken up actively by the gills from the surrounding water.

11 Marine vertebrates, including most marine fish, eliminate excess salts and retain as much water as possible. Their nitrogenous excretory waste tends to be relatively insoluble and non-toxic.

12 Terrestrial animals are liable to lose water by evaporation from exposed surfaces. They possess a variety of adaptations for preventing excessive water loss.

13 Depending on the availability of water, plants may be classified into **hydrophytes**, **mesophytes** and **xerophytes**. A wide range of water-conserving devices are seen in land plants, particularly xerophytes.

14 Land plants which live in places where the water is salty are called **halophytes**. They have adaptations for getting rid of excess salt.

20 Land plants living in humid conditions may gain more water than they can lose by transpiration. The surplus water is lost by **guttation**.

Review questions

1 Name the parts of a nephron starting at the proximal end and finishing with the distal end.

2 A person with very low blood pressure is in danger of kidney failure. Why?

3 Explain the effect on the quantity and composition of a person's urine of:
 (a) drinking a large amount of water,
 (b) eating a very salty meal.

4 A kidney with short loops of Henle produces a more dilute urine than a kidney with long loops of Henle. Explain the reason.

5 The main organ in the human body responsible for excretion and osmoregulation is the kidney. What other organs are involved and what part do they play?

6 What can you say about the environment of a fish whose kidneys have few glomeruli and whose nitrogenous waste is trimethylamine oxide? Explain your answer.

7 During its life cycle a salmon migrates from the sea to freshwater. What changes would you expect to take place in its kidneys as it undergoes this journey?

8 To what extent are the methods used by terrestrial animals to conserve water comparable with those seen in plants?

9 Many halophytes are succulents. Why do you think this is?

10 What are *hydathodes*? What sort of plants have them, and why?

Further reading

All standard textbooks of human physiology contain a detailed treatment of the kidney. As clear as any is the account in *Textbook of Physiology* by Emslie-Smith *et al.* ('BDS') (Churchill Livingstone, 1988).

Comparative aspects of excretion and osmoregulation are very well covered by Knut Schmidt-Nielsen in *Animal Physiology: Adaptation and Environment,* 4th edn. (Cambridge University Press, 1990). This book covers invertebrates as well as vertebrates and is full of interesting information.

If you can beg, borrow or otherwise acquire a copy of *Comparative Biochemistry* by the late Earnest Baldwin, you will be amply rewarded. This little book, now sadly now out of print but still around in some libraries, contains a beautifully succinct account of osmoregulation in different animals.

On the plant side, *Plant Physiology* by F.B. Salisbury and C.W. Ross, 4th edn. (Wadsworth, 1992) is written in a pleasant style and has numerous diagrams, graphs and photographs.

Biology, Advanced Topics looks in detail at three contrasting osmoregulatory devices: the proximal convoluted tubule of the kidney, the contractile vacuole of protoctists and the salt glands of halophytes.

Temperature regulation

It is well known that irrespective of fluctuations in the temperature of the environment, the temperature of the human body remains at about 36.9°C. Many of the body's organs and physiological processes contribute towards the maintenance of this **constant body temperature**.

In this chapter we shall see how a constant body temperature is maintained in the human, and we shall look briefly at how other organisms manage in this respect. But first we must ask why our body temperature needs to be kept constant.

Why is a constant body temperature necessary?

A constant body temperature of about 36.9°C is the optimum temperature for the action of enzymes, upon which the organised functioning of our cells depends. At this temperature the enzymes work at close to their maximum rate. However, if the temperature rises much above 40°C, enzyme action goes into a sharp decline (see page 218). This is because enzymes are proteins, and become denatured. One of the first organs to be affected is the brain. Since the brain controls breathing and the circulation, the rise in body temperature disrupts the normal functioning of these important systems.

An abnormally low body temperature (hypothermia) can be equally serious: it has the effect of slowing metabolic activities and impairing brain function.

Types of temperature regulation

Organisms can be divided into two groups: those that can maintain a constant body temperature irrespective of changes in the environmental temperature, and those that cannot do so (figure 23.1). For many years the terms **homoiothermic** and **poikilothermic** have been given to these two groups respectively. Homoiothermic is a Greek word meaning *having the same temperature*. Homoiothermic animals are popularly described as 'warm blooded': their body temperature is independent of the environmental temperature, so that in cold conditions their blood is at a higher temperature than that of their surroundings. Mammals and birds are homoiothermic, and their success is often attributed at least in part to this important feature.

Poikilothermic means *having a variable temperature*. Poikilothermic animals are described as 'cold blooded': their body temperature changes with fluctuations in the environmental temperature. If the environment is cold, so are they. All organisms apart from mammals and birds fall into this category.

Unfortunately the terms homoiothermic and poikilothermic are not very useful. It is true that homoiothermic animals maintain a constant body temperature independent of the environment. However, it is not true that the temperature of a poikilotherm is necessarily variable, nor is it true that its blood is always cold. Many so-called cold-blooded animals maintain a surprisingly constant body temperature, well above (or below) that of the environment.

More useful terms are **endothermic** and **ectothermic**. Endothermic organisms generate heat energy within the body, and keep it there. Ectothermic organisms absorb heat energy from their surroundings, i.e. from outside the body by, for example, basking in the sun. Both can

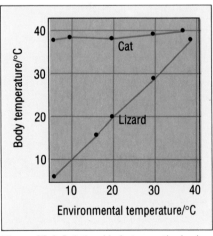

Figure 23.1 Relationship between the body temperature and environmental temperature for a cat and a lizard. The environmental temperature is the air temperature immediately outside the body. Notice that the cat maintains a more or less constant body temperature irrespective of changes in the environmental temperature. However, the lizard's body temperature is the same as the environmental temperature.

Figure 23.2 Physical mechanisms by which heat energy may be lost from a naked person. The percentages show how much heat energy may be lost by each mechanism when the room temperature is 21°C.

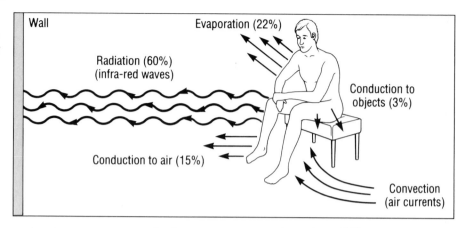

maintain a constant body temperature, but by different means – endotherms by physiological means, ectotherms by behavioural means.

Even these terms can be misleading because the distinction between endotherm and ectotherm is not always clear cut. For example, most endotherms (including the human) supplement their physiological mechanisms by absorbing heat energy from, or losing it to, their surroundings.

How heat energy is lost and gained

An organism whose body temperature exceeds the temperature of its surroundings may lose heat energy by four physical processes (figure 23.2).

- **Conduction** is the transfer of heat energy from the hotter to the cooler of two objects in contact with each other. A person sitting on a cold chair will lose heat energy to the chair. Heat energy can also be conducted to the surrounding medium, air or water as the case may be.

- **Radiation** is the transfer of heat energy from a body to colder objects that are not in contact with it. The heat energy is transferred by infra-red waves. As much as 60 per cent of the total heat energy lost by a person sitting in a room at 21°C may be caused by radiation.

- **Evaporation** is the change of a liquid to a vapour, and it is accompanied by cooling. As much as 25 per cent of the total heat energy lost by a person at 21°C can be caused by evaporation of water from the surface of the skin, and it explains the cooling effect of sweating.

- **Convection** is the movement of air resulting from local pockets of warm air being replaced by cooler air, and vice versa. These air movements can help to spread heat energy through the environment, and they speed up the loss of heat energy from objects by conduction and evaporation. Convection can be aided by devices such as electric fans which create air movements artificially ('forced convection').

Of course conduction, radiation and convection can work both ways. If the environmental temperature is higher than the body temperature, heat energy will be gained by these processes. However, a body cannot gain heat energy by evaporation – it can only lose it.

We also gain heat energy from metabolism, and as metabolism goes on all the time we never fail to gain heat energy this way.

To sum up, the body is continually gaining and losing heat energy. When these two processes proceed at exactly the same rate, the person is said to be in **heat balance**. The purpose of temperature regulation is to keep the body in heat balance. In endothermic animals the key structure involved in this is the skin.

The structure of the skin

The structure of mammalian skin is shown in figure 23.3. Nearly all the structures seen in these pictures play some part in temperature regulation.

The skin is divided into two main layers, the **epidermis** at the surface, and the **dermis** beneath. Below the dermis is another layer, not strictly part of the skin, called the **hypodermis**.

The epidermis is made up of **stratified epithelium** (see page 176). The bottom-most layer of cells, the **Malpighian layer**, contains variable amounts of the black pigment **melanin** which protects the body from the harmful effects of ultraviolet rays from the sun.

The cells of the Malpighian layer divide repeatedly in a plane horizontal to the surface of the body. As new cells are formed, the older ones get pushed outwards towards the surface, flattening as they do so. After a time, the cytoplasm becomes full of granules and the cells die. Finally they become converted into scales of **keratin**, giving rise to the **keratinised layer** at the surface of the epidermis. You will recall that keratin is a tough, fibrous protein (see page 141). The keratinised layer gives the skin its protective properties and makes it waterproof. This dead tissue constantly flakes off or is worn away. In parts of the body where the skin is subjected to constant pressure, such as the soles of the feet, the keratinised layer becomes very thick.

Oil is secreted on to the surface of the epidermis by **sebaceous glands** which open into the **hair follicles**, the deep pits from which the **hairs** project. The oil makes the hair supple and enhances the skin's water-proofing properties.

The roots of the hairs are embedded in the dermis or hypodermis. Running from the side of each hair follicle to the base of the epidermis is an **erector pili muscle**. When this muscle contracts, the hair is pulled into a more vertical position.

Figure 23.3 Structure of mammalian skin.
A Photomicrograph of a vertical section of human skin. Magnification × 15.
B Diagram of a small part of the skin. Nearly all the structures shown are involved directly or indirectly with temperature regulation. Broken arrows, blood flow. Solid arrows, nerve impulses.

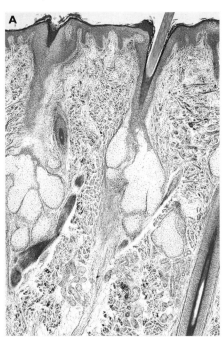

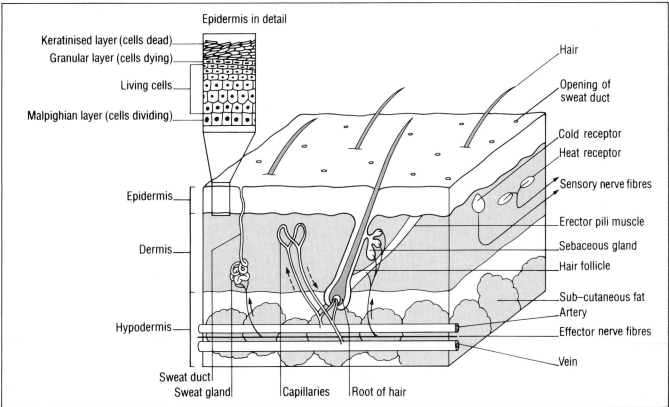

The dermis contains **sweat glands** which secrete a salty solution, **sweat**. The sweat passes down the **sweat ducts** to the surface of the epidermis, and its subsequent evaporation cools the skin and the blood flowing through it.

The hypodermis is permeated by arteries and veins. Blood flows from the arteries towards the surface of the skin in arterioles which split into capillaries below the epidermis. The blood is drained from the capillaries in venules which lead on to the veins. There is thus a continuous flow of blood towards the surface of the skin and then away again. The way this flow can be modified is important in temperature regulation.

In the dermis are receptors sensitive to touch, pressure, pain and temperature. Evidence suggests that the temperature receptors (**thermo-receptors**) are of two types, one sensitive to warmth and the other to cold. They enable us to detect changes in the temperature of our surroundings. Sensory nerve fibres lead from the receptors, and effector nerve fibres supply the erector pili muscles and sweat glands.

The structures described above are embedded in a loose connective tissue made mainly of collagen fibres but containing some elastic fibres too. This makes the skin soft and pliant. The hypodermis consists mainly of fat cells. This **sub-cutaneous fat** serves as an insulator and helps to prevent heat energy being lost from the body. However, this is a purely structural adaptation and endotherms have more dynamic means of keeping warm, as we shall now see.

Hypothermia

Hypothermia is the condition in which the body temperature falls dangerously below normal. It happens if heat energy is lost from the body more rapidly than it can be produced, for example when a person wearing inadequate clothing is subjected to prolonged cold.

As the body temperature falls, one of the first organs to be affected is the brain. This results in the person becoming clumsy and mentally sluggish. Since brain function is impaired, the victim may not realise that anything is wrong and so does nothing about it such as putting on more clothes. Indeed, there are cases of people in this condition taking *off* some of their clothes!

As the body temperature falls, the metabolic rate falls too and that makes the body temperature fall even further – a case of positive feedback. Death usually occurs when the body temperature drops to about 25°C, though people have been known to survive lower body temperatures than this. The cause of death is usually ventricular fibrillation, a condition in which the normal beating of the heart is replaced by uncoordinated tremors.

The people most at risk from hypothermia are babies and the elderly: babies because of their small size (high surface–volume ratio) and undeveloped temperature regulation mechanisms, the elderly because their thermoregulatory mechanisms may have deteriorated through old age. Of these two groups the elderly are the more susceptible. Human babies are remarkably resilient and have been known to survive body temperatures as low as 9°C.

Hypothermia is exacerbated by inadequate clothing, lack of heating in the home and poor diet. It is therefore a social problem, afflicting in particular people on low incomes. The elderly are particularly at risk especially if they live on their own.

Healthy young adults are prone to hypothermia if, for one reason or another, they are exposed to the cold for a long time. Most at risk are hikers, climbers and pot-holers, particularly if their clothes get damp. Matters are made worse if mental impairment causes them to make mistakes or lose their bearings. Fatal accidents have been caused this way.

Artificial hypothermia is sometimes used in surgical operations on the heart. By cooling the patient the metabolic rate is reduced and the demand for oxygen by the brain and other vital tissues is lowered. This allows the heart to be stopped while the operation is performed without the risk of the patient suffering brain damage through lack of oxygen. But the patient must not be cooled for too long or the tissues may be permanently damaged. Lowering the body temperature to 25°C allows about ten minutes for the operation. The patient is cooled either by circulating the blood through a cooling machine or by placing ice packs or some equivalent device in contact with the body.

How do endotherms respond to cold conditions?

Consider what happens when a mammal is subjected to severe cold. Heat energy is liable to be lost from the body by the physical processes mentioned earlier, but this is counteracted by the following responses:

- The hairs are raised into a more vertical position by contraction of the erector pili muscles. Air gets trapped in the spaces between the hairs and, being a poor conductor of heat, it serves as an insulatory layer round the animal (figure 23.4). This response is involuntary, and is brought about by the automatic nervous system (see page 458).

    In humans the body hair is much reduced, its place being taken by clothes. Even so the erector pili muscles contract just the same, resulting in 'goose pimples'. In birds the feathers serve the same function as the hair of mammals, being raised in cold weather.

- The arterioles leading to the superficial capillaries constrict. As a result the blood flow to the surface of the skin is reduced, thereby cutting down the loss of heat energy from the blood to the surroundings (figure 23.5). This vasoconstriction is brought about by the sympathetic nervous system and is particularly powerful in exposed structures such as the ears which have a large surface–volume ratio and are therefore particularly susceptible to cold.

- The metabolic rate increases, heating the inside of the body. A general increase in the metabolic rate is brought about by the hormones adrenaline and thyroxine which are produced in extra large amounts in cold conditions. The main organ to respond to these hormones is the liver, but the muscles – activated by the nervous system – also play a part. There is a general increase in muscle tone, and this may be followed by spasmodic contractions (shivering).

    In winter as much as 40 per cent of the food we eat may be used for generating heat energy in resting conditions. However, we may augment these automatic responses by voluntary actions, such as rubbing our hands together or stamping our feet.

Figure 23.4 In the top photograph the cat Septimus is out in the snow on a very cold day and his hair is standing on end. The bottom photograph shows Septimus on a warm day in summer with his hair lying flat against his body.

How do endotherms respond to hot conditions?

The responses to high temperatures involve the reverse of the above processes.

- The hairs are lowered by relaxation of the erector pili muscles, so they lie flat against the surface of the skin. Less air is trapped between the hairs, insulation is therefore reduced, and heat energy can be lost more readily by conduction, radiation and convection.

    However, heat energy will be lost only if the external temperature is lower than the body temperature. If the external temperature is *higher* than the body temperature, the hair becomes important in insulating the body against overheating from outside. This is of special significance to large animals like the camel which, in the open desert, cannot escape the heat of the sun.

- The arterioles leading to the superficial capillaries dilate. As a result the blood flow to the surface is increased and more heat energy can be lost to the surroundings. In exposed extremities such as the ears, special **shunt vessels** bypass the superficial capillaries, adding another level of control to heat energy loss from the skin.

- Sweating occurs, and the evaporation of water from the moist skin cools the blood as it flows through the superficial capillaries. As a means of

Figure 23.5 The blood supply to the skin of exposed structures such as the ears, nose, fingers and toes shows special features which help to lose heat energy in warm conditions and retain heat energy in cold conditions. The diagram shows a small part of the skin of, for example, an ear. In warm conditions vessel 1 dilates. Being much wider than the capillaries, it offers less resistance to the flow of blood and allows the blood to flow rapidly into the venous plexus, a network of thin-walled venules from which heat energy can readily be lost to the surroundings. In cold conditions vessel 1 constricts, and vessel 2 dilates, thereby holding back the blood from the surface and reducing the loss of heat energy to the surroundings.

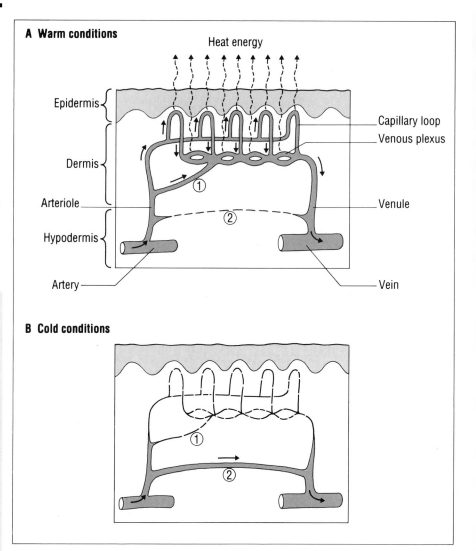

The cooling effect of sweating

The cooling effect of sweating depends not only on the temperature of the surrounding air but also on its relative humidity, i.e. the degree to which the atmosphere is saturated with moisture. When the relative humidity is low, evaporation and hence cooling are rapid. When the relative humidity is high, evaporation and cooling are slow. This is why a temperature of 35°C in the desert with a relative humidity of only 20 per cent is more comfortable than a temperature of 25°C in a tropical swamp with a relative humidity of 90 per cent. At very high humidities a large proportion of the sweat does not evaporate at all but drips from the skin or sinks into the clothes, creating conditions which many people find intolerable.

The evaporating power of the atmosphere is greatly increased by air movements. A gentle breeze will disperse the layer of humidity that builds up round the body after a long period of sweating. As well as cooling the body this encourages further evaporation to take place. The use of electric fans in hot weather is based on this principle.

cooling the human body, sweating is extremely important. Indeed when the external temperature exceeds the body temperature there is no other way of doing it. Sweating is an involuntary response brought about by the sympathetic nervous system.

- Panting occurs. In dogs and cats there are no sweat glands except in the pads of the paws. These animals make up for this deficiency by panting. This speeds up evaporation from the lungs, pharynx and other moist surfaces, helping to cool the blood.

- The metabolic rate decreases, so less heat energy is generated by the body. This fits in with the well-known observation that animals are generally less active, and require less food, in hot weather than in cooler weather. However, it is important to bear in mind that there is a limit to how far the metabolic rate can fall. In normal circumstances metabolism must continue at least at the basal rate, and some heat energy will always be generated as a result.

So we see that when the temperature of the environment changes, the body responds in such a way as to maintain its temperature at a constant level. But how does the body know when to 'switch on' its heating or cooling devices? The answer is that the brain tells it to do so. How this happens is the subject of the next section.

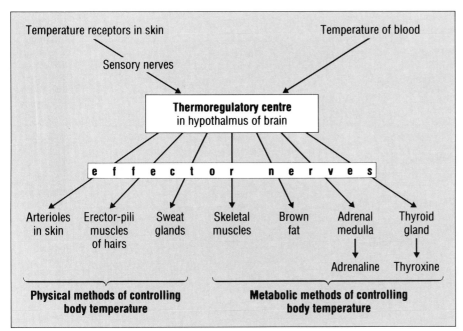

The role of the brain in temperature regulation

For a long time, since about 1912 in fact, it was suspected that the brain was responsible for controlling the body temperature, and experiments have narrowed down the site of this control to the **hypothalamus** (see page 454). Electrical stimulation of a specific part of the hypothalamus brings about thermoregulatory responses, and nerve impulses can be recorded from this region when the environmental temperature is changed. It seems therefore that the hypothalamus contains a **thermoregulatory centre**.

In addition, the skin contains millions of thermoreceptors which are connected to the central nervous system by sensory nerves. Through these nerves the thermoreceptors signal changes in the skin temperature to the brain.

The information which passes into and out of the brain in temperature regulation is summarised in figure 23.6.

You will recall from Chapter 21 that for any homeostatic process to work, there must be a receptor, a control mechanism and an effector. We must now ask whether the thermoregulatory centre in the hypothalamus serves only as a control device, or whether it functions as a receptor as well. In other words, does it simply relay information which it has received from the thermoreceptors to the appropriate effectors, or is the centre itself sensitive to changes in body temperature?

To answer this question, an ingenious experiment was carried out by T.H. Benzinger and his team at the Naval Medical Research Institute in Maryland, USA. Their technique involved putting a volunteer in a special form of calorimeter which enabled simultaneous measurements to be made of the temperatures of the hypothalamus and the skin, together with the loss of heat energy from the body by radiation, convection and sweating (figure 23.7). The temperature of the hypothalamus was recorded by placing a thermocouple in the outer ear close to the ear drum. Previous tests had shown that the temperature measured at this point was the same as that of the hypothalamus itself.

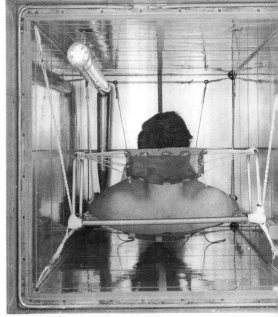

Figure 23.7 Benzinger's experiment on the role of the hypothalamus in temperature regulation. The calorimeter with a volunteer inside. The lining of the chamber is interlaced with thousands of thermoelectric junctions which measure heat energy loss from the skin.

Figure 23.8 The results of Benzinger's experiment are shown in these recordings.

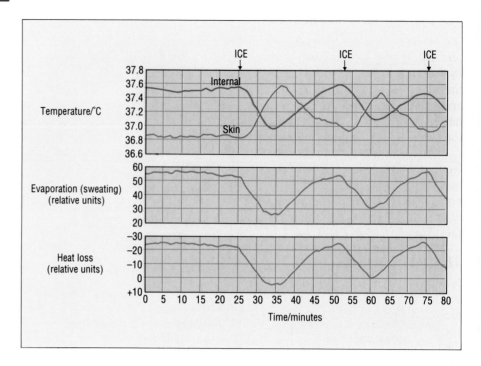

The subject, lying in the calorimeter at a constant temperature well above that of his body, was asked to consume a large quantity of iced sherbet at 30 minute intervals. The results are shown in figure 23.8. On each occasion, immediately after taking the iced sherbet, three changes occurred:

1 The temperature of the hypothalamus fell, owing to the cooling of the blood by the ice in the gut.
2 Less heat energy was lost from the skin because of decreased sweating.
3 The skin temperature rose due to reduced heat energy loss from it.

The important thing to emerge was a perfect correlation between the fall in temperature of the hypothalamus and the decrease in the rate of sweating. The inescapable conclusion is that the decreased temperature of the blood is in some way detected by the hypothalamus, which then causes a decrease in the rate of sweating. That the skin receptors play little or no part in the response is indicated by the fact that the skin temperature *rose* during this period. If the temperature changes were detected by the receptors in the skin, a rise in the skin temperature would switch on the body's cooling processes – exactly the reverse of what actually happened.

Figure 23.9 The homeostatic control of body temperature in a mammal. As a result of its being controlled by negative feedback, the body temperature constantly fluctuates very slightly on either side of the norm (set point).

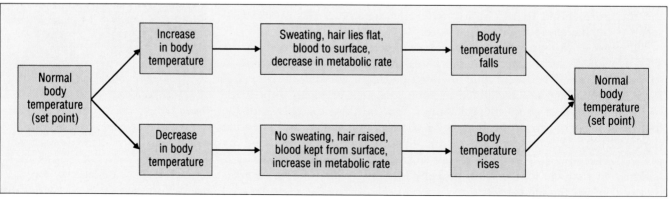

The hypothalamus as a thermostat

It seems, then, that the hypothalamic centre functions as a **thermostat**. It is sensitive to the temperature of the blood flowing through it, and responds by sending nerve impulses to the appropriate effectors. If the temperature of the blood is higher than normal, the thermoregulatory centre detects this and sets into motion the various processes that cool the body. On the other hand, if the temperature of the blood is below normal, the centre initiates the processes that warm the body.

We have here yet another homeostatic system involving **negative feedback** (figure 23.9). Because it is controlled by negative feedback, the body temperature constantly fluctuates very slightly on either side of the norm or set point (figure 23.10). When the body temperature increases in disease it is probable that the set point of the hypothalamic thermostat is raised to a new level.

The role of the thermoreceptors in the skin

We have seen that the hypothalamus *detects* changes in temperature as well as initiating appropriate responses. Does this mean that the thermo-receptors in the skin play no part in temperature regulation? On the contrary, while the hypothalamus detects temperature fluctuations inside the body, the skin receptors detect temperature changes at the surface. They enable you to *feel* whether the external environment immediately outside your body is hot or cold. This information, acting via the thermoregulatory centre, initiates voluntary activities such as taking exercise in severe cold, or moving into the shade if conditions are very hot.

The effect of changing the environmental temperature

We saw earlier that in cold conditions the body temperature of an endotherm is kept higher than the environmental temperature partly by generating extra heat energy inside the body, and partly by preventing heat energy being lost. We can refer to these as metabolic and physical mechanisms respectively. To what extent does an animal depend on each of these mechanisms in its life?

To answer this, consider what happens to a naked person if the air temperature is gradually lowered from a pleasant 29°C to freezing point.

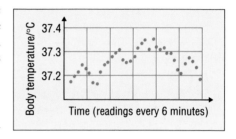

Figure 23.10 The body temperature of a human subject taken at six minute intervals over a period of several hours. The temperature was taken with a very sensitive thermometer inserted into the rectum. The rectal temperature is slightly higher than the oral temperature. Notice the fluctuations resulting from the fact that the body temperature is controlled by negative feedback. The fluctuations are extremely slight and, although they are going on in our bodies all the time, they are far too small for us to notice them.

How does the camel survive in the hot desert?

A camel can survive for days without water and be active in the full heat of the sun. How does it manage it? Part of the answer is that it saves water by not sweating, at least not until its body temperature reaches about 40°C.

The trouble is that by not sweating the camel is deprived of its most effective means of keeping cool. The result is that during the day its body temperature gradually increases, rising as high as 40°C by sundown. In the cool of the desert night, heat energy is lost from the body to such

an extent that the body temperature falls as low as 34°C. This is important because it means that during the following day the temperature climbs from an abnormally low starting point. This prevents the body temperature reaching the lethal level by the end of the day.

In the last chapter we saw that the camel's tissues are exceptionally tolerant to dehydration. Now we find that they are also tolerant to daily fluctuations in temperature. The camel is reputed to be a bad-tempered animal – perhaps that's why.

The camel illustrates an important principle, namely the close relationship between an animal's physiology and its environment. The camel's daily temperature rhythm fits snugly into the 24 hour cycle, sundown coming just before the body temperature reaches a dangerous level.

What would happen if the days were longer or hotter, or the camel larger? Use this information about the camel's body temperature to suggest what may have caused the extinction of the larger dinosaurs.

Heat stroke

Once the upper critical temperature has been reached, the cells are no longer adequately protected by the body's cooling processes. As a result, metabolism becomes subject to the temperature rule, more than doubling its rate every time the temperature increases by 10°C. Moreover, once the temperature-regulating mechanisms fail, the metabolic rate goes on rising even if the environmental temperature stays the same. The reason is that every time the metabolic rate increases, it generates more heat energy which raises the metabolic rate a bit more, and so on. This is an example of **positive feedback** (see page 362).

Prolonged exposure to an excessively high environmental temperature can result in heat stroke. This is a complex condition which takes a number of different forms depending on its severity. The brain is the main organ to be affected. The person feels giddy and develops flu-like symptoms which may lead on to convulsions and unconsciousness. If nothing is done about it, death occurs.

To begin with the physical mechanisms – insulation and so on – keep the body temperature at its normal level, and the metabolic rate remains unchanged. However, at about 27°C (the exact temperature varies from person to person) the physical mechanisms are no longer able to keep the body temperature constant, and the metabolic rate starts rising. The environmental temperature at which this happens is called the **lower critical temperature**.

As the environmental temperature is lowered further, the metabolic rate continues to rise until eventually it can no longer generate enough heat energy to maintain the body temperature. When this point is reached, the body temperature and metabolic rate fall, and the subject is liable to die. Of course the experiment is not normally taken to this extreme! However, it is important to realise that this is essentially what happens when people suffer from **hypothermia** (see box on page 398).

Now consider the result of *increasing* the air temperature from about 29°C. To begin with, the body's physical mechanisms – sweating and so on – keep the body temperature at its normal level. However, there comes a point when the physical mechanisms can no longer cope, and the body temperature starts rising with the environmental temperature. The environmental temperature at which this happens is called the **upper critical temperature**.

The upper critical temperature depends on the humidity of the atmosphere and it varies from person to person. It is particularly high in people who have become acclimatised to high environmental temperatures, such as in the tropics. This reflects the efficiency of their cooling mechanisms, particularly sweating.

It is impossible to give an exact figure for the environmental temperature at which death occurs because it depends on so many things. However, the *body* temperature at which death occurs is about 42°C for most humans, though some people have endured higher body temperatures than this and lived to tell the tale. The record is held by a man with heat stroke whose body temperature rose to 46.5°C!

To summarise, between the upper and lower critical temperatures the metabolic rate remains unchanged and physical mechanisms keep the body temperature constant. Above the upper critical temperature and below the lower critical temperature the metabolic rate increases. These observations are shown graphically for a generalised mammal in figure 23.11.

Figure 23.11 The effect of environmental temperature on the metabolic rate of a generalised mammal. Between the upper and lower critical temperatures physical mechanisms keep the body temperature constant and the metabolic rate remains unchanged. Above the upper critical temperature the body's cooling mechanisms fail to keep the body temperature constant with the result that the metabolic rate increases as the environmental temperature rises. Below the lower critical temperature physical mechanisms fail to hold heat energy in the body, so the metabolic rate rises and generates extra heat energy.

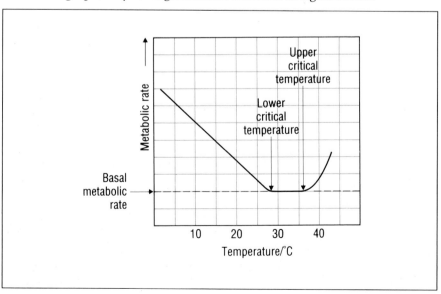

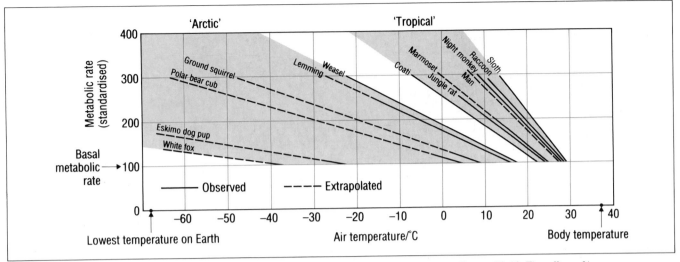

Figure 23.12 The effect of low environmental temperatures on the metabolic rates of various mammals. The metabolic rates are standardised by giving the resting metabolic rate for each animal a value of 100 per cent and expressing any increase in the metabolic rate in relation to this value. This makes it possible to compare widely differing species on the same scale. Notice that the lower critical temperature at which the metabolic rate starts to rise is much lower for 'arctic' animals than for 'tropical' animals.

The lower critical temperature and the environment

We have seen that in the human the lower critical temperature is about 27°C. Compared with other mammals this is quite high and it supports the view that the human is essentially a tropical species whose origins are to be found in the warmer parts of the world.

The lower critical temperature has been determined for different mammals, and it has been found to be lower for species living in cold places than for those which live in warm places. For example, the desert kangaroo rat *Dipodomys* has a lower critical temperature of about 30°C, whereas for the Arctic fox it may be as low as –40°C. Moreover, below the lower critical temperature the metabolic rate rises more slowly in cold-dwellers than in warm-dwellers (figure 23.12).

These findings reflect the fact that animals living in cold environments have special adaptations for keeping warm. Let us look briefly at some of these adaptations.

Adaptations for living in cold environments

The most obvious adaptation is in the insulation efficiency of the hair. In cold-dwellers the hair is usually thicker and better at holding air round the body than it is in warm-dwellers. In many mammalian species the hair thickens as winter approaches and becomes sparser in summer (figure 23.13A).

Another adaptation is in the thickness of the sub-cutaneous fat. Animals living in cold climates, polar bears and seals for example, have a particularly thick layer of sub-cutaneous fat. In the seal and other marine mammals such as whales, the fat is called the **blubber** (figure 23.13B).

Figure 23.13 Two-well known animals with special adaptations for preventing loss of heat energy.

A The polar bear has a thick layer of sub-cutaneous fat and a dense coat of hair, both of which insulate it efficiently against heat energy loss. The polar bear inhabits some of the coldest places on Earth and it does not hibernate.

B The Cape seal, a marine mammal whose distribution extends to the Antarctic, has an exceptionally thick layer of sub-cutaneous fat (blubber) which helps to insulate it against heat energy loss.

A The Arctic fox of the northern tundra has small ears.

B The red fox of temperate regions has medium-sized ears.

C Blanford's fox of the Middle East desert has large ears.

Figure 23.14 Allen's rule is here illustrated by comparing the ears of closely related foxes in different parts of the world.

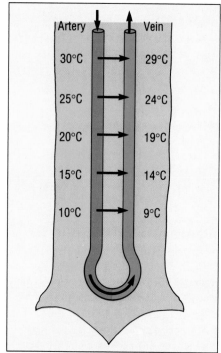

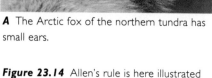

Figure 23.15 Diagram showing the countercurrent heat exchange system in a limb. The artery and vein run parallel with each other. At each level, heat energy is transferred from the artery to the vein, so that by the time the venous blood leaves the limb it is almost as warm as the arterial blood. In some cases the veins may be wrapped round the arteries in a most intimate way.

Because of its relatively large surface–volume ratio, a small animal loses more heat energy per gram of body mass than a larger animal. This means that a small animal must generate more heat energy per gram to maintain the same temperature as a larger animal. For this reason it was suggested many years ago that closely related animals tend to be larger in cold regions than in warmer regions. This is called **Bergmann's rule**. Although it seems to make good sense, this long-cherished principle has recently been challenged by some biologists.

Less contentious is the observation that extremities such as the ears tend to be smaller in animals that live in cold regions than in their relatives living in warm regions. This is called **Allen's rule** and an example is given in figure 23.14. The small ears of the Arctic fox minimise heat energy loss from the exposed surface. On the other hand, the large ears of the desert fox, richly supplied with blood vessels, serve as cooling devices like the radiator of a car.

It has been found that certain mammals, including humans, possess patches of a special kind of fat tissue, called **brown fat**, in various parts of the body, particularly between the shoulder blades. Brown fat has an exceptionally high metabolic rate and generates a large amount of heat energy very quickly. This is particularly important in newborn animals whose temperature control mechanisms have not yet developed, and in animals coming out of hibernation where rapid warming of the tissues is essential. Brown fat is discussed in more detail in the box on the opposite page.

Another interesting adaptation is seen in the flippers of dolphins and the legs of ducks, both of which are highly susceptible to loss of heat energy particularly if they happen to be in cold water. In the limbs the arteries and veins are very close to each other (figure 23.15). As blood flows down the artery, heat energy passes from it to the much cooler blood which is returning in the opposite direction in the vein. This achieves two things. Firstly it means that the arterial blood has already been cooled by the time it reaches the end of the limb, so that relatively little heat energy is lost to the surroundings. Secondly it has the effect of warming the venous blood before it gets back to the main part of the body.

This is called a **contercurrent heat exchange system**. It is a very efficient way of conserving heat energy, and its occurrence is now thought to be widespread amongst animals. It even occurs in the legs of humans to a certain extent, and the same principle is used by heating engineers.

As an endotherm, the human is in a rather embarrassing position. Our low critical temperature of about 27°C is not much below that of the desert

Brown fat

Guest author Patricia Kohn explains what brown fat is and why it is useful to humans.

The existence of a special form of adipose tissue, **brown fat** has been known for many years. Like the cells of normal fat, brown fat cells contain large lipid-filled droplets in the cytoplasm. Unlike normal fat cells, however, the cytoplasm contains enormous numbers of specialised mitochondria and the tissue is highly vascularised. These features give brown fat its characteristic brownish appearance.

The function of this tissue is to generate heat energy (thermogenesis), in animals coming out of hibernation and in newborn animals, including human babies. The possession of such a tissue is useful to babies for two main reasons. First, their surface–volume ratio is much greater than that of adults, so they lose a greater proportion of their metabolic heat energy. Second, they cannot shiver and warm themselves up as adults can.

Instead of shivering, babies generate heat energy from their brown fat, a process called **non-shivering thermogenesis**. The mechanism is activated by stimulation of the sympathetic nerves with which brown fat tissue is supplied. This causes the brown fat to be broken down into fatty acids and glycerol which, instead of being exported for use by other tissues, are oxidised 'at home' with the release of much heat energy.

The capacity of brown fat to generate heat energy is vastly greater than that of any other tissue. Its maximum rate of oxygen consumption is ten times that of skeletal muscle, but all the energy released appears as heat energy, none as ATP. This 'uncoupling' of the

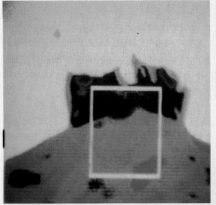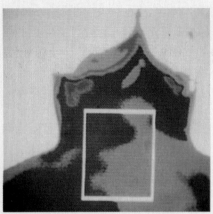

Thermograms of a person's back before and after being treated with a drug which mimics the sympathetic nervous system. The dark patches show those parts of the skin whose temperature reached 34.1°C. These 'hot spots' correspond closely to the distribution of brown fat in the human body.

energy-releasing pathway from the synthesis of ATP enables a mere 50 g of brown fat to increase the total heat energy production of the body by 20 per cent. This function is a special property of the numerous mitochondria. The many blood vessels which pervade the tissue allow the blood to be warmed as it passes through.

Until recently it was believed that the only stimulus activating brown fat was a fall in body temperature, so the sole function of this tissue seemed to be to generate heat energy. However, a second role for it has been proposed. We all know people who eat well and don't take much exercise, and yet stay thin. It has been suggested that these thin people dispose of some of their excess energy intake by activating their brown fat and simply 'burning it off'.

The exact mechanism of this **diet-induced thermogenesis** is unknown, and the concept is still somewhat controversial. Most of the experimental evidence has been obtained from rats. In one experiment rats were induced to overeat by have their normal rather boring diet of rat pellets supplemented with a variety of tasty 'junk foods' gleaned from supermarket shelves – crisps,

chocolate biscuits and so forth. Surprisingly their body mass did not increase as much as was expected. What did increase was their oxygen uptake, though there had been no increase in physical activity. Clearly extra kilojoules were being disposed of in response to the increased intake of food, and brown fat seemed to be the most likely tissue responsible.

The possible role of brown fat in controlling body mass was long overlooked partly because the amount present in adult humans is proportionately much less than in babies, and it was thought to be thermogenically inactive. However, in experiments on human volunteers, administration of a drug which mimics the sympathetic system resulted in increases in skin temperature of between 0.5 and 0.8°C over the sites of the main brown fat deposits, namely the nape of the neck and upper part of the back. The presence of these 'hot spots' suggests that brown fat can be thermogenically active in adults.

It remains to be seen whether the thermogenic response can be elicited by overeating, but if brown fat is found to have a role in keeping certain fortunate people slim, it will help to explain one of life's minor injustices!

Figure 23.16 A lizard basking on a rock gains heat energy from the sun and from the rock itself.

Figure 23.17 Heat gains and losses by an ectotherm such as a lizard. The body is warmed by radiation from the sun, convection currents in the air, reflection from nearby surfaces, and conduction from the ground. The body is cooled by comparable processes working the other way round, together with evaporation from the lungs and mouth cavity. As a result the animal maintains a near-constant body temperature of approximately 36°C.

kangaroo rat, and equips us for little else than running around naked in the tropics. We owe this to the scantiness of our hair, a deficiency for which we compensate by wearing clothes. Had we not developed the ability to make and wear warm clothes, humans would never have been able to exploit the temperate regions of the world, let alone the poles. The wearing of clothes is an example of **behavioural control** of body temperature, to which we now turn.

Behavioural control of body temperature

When an animal finds itself in a particularly hot environment, it may adjust its behaviour in such a way as to cool itself. When cold it behaves so as to warm itself up. Such adaptive behaviour is seen in our own species when we put on extra clothes or stamp our feet to keep warm.

Behavioural control is particularly important for ectothermic organisms, in which it is the only effective method of temperature regulation. Even unicellular organisms such as *Paramecium* will actively seek out a region in their environment (freshwater) which provides the optimum temperature. Similar responses are shown by ectothermic animals such as insects and fish. However, it is in reptiles that the behavioural control of temperature is most fully developed.

Many lizards and snakes gain heat energy by lying in the sun, or absorbing it from rocks and sand (figure 23.16). By absorbing heat energy from, or losing it to, the surroundings, the animal maintains its body at a constant temperature of about 36°C. The physical processes involved are shown in figure 23.17. Behavioural thermoregulation is particularly evident in desert ectotherms, which could suffer lethal rises in the body temperature if they stayed out in the midday sun. Desert lizards tend to be most active in the early morning and evening when it is neither too cold nor too hot. These are the times when one sees them scurrying about for food. In the heat of the day they retire to a shady place such as under a rock, or burrow into the sand.

Some reptiles have special ways of keeping cool. For example, alligators cool themselves by opening their mouths and letting water evaporate from the moist surfaces in the buccal cavity (figure 23.18). Approximately 65 per cent of metabolic heat energy can be lost by this **thermal gaping**. Iguana lizards enhance the cooling effect of thermal gaping by breathing rapidly and protruding the tongue, which has a rich blood supply. Tortoises employ a different strategy: they **salivate** over their neck and front legs, and the evaporation of the water cools the body.

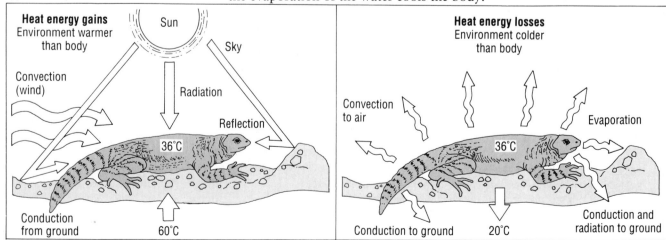

At night, when it can be extremely cold, a desert lizard may burrow or seek out a crevice in which to build up a warm atmosphere from the heat energy generated by its metabolism. These animals are not insulated as a mammal is, but by shifting from one place to another they do the next best thing, which is to make sure that the temperature of their immediate surroundings is always agreeable.

Although we tend to associate behavioural thermoregulation with ectotherms, endotherms show similar responses and can use them to augment their physiological mechanisms. My dog used to lie in front of the fire until he became unbearably hot, then he would move behind the settee to cool off.

The same principle is seen in **migration**. Triggered by the seasonal changes of autumn, many species of birds that spend the summer months in northern regions, migrate southwards to warmer latitudes in winter. Thus swallows migrate from Northern Europe to South Africa, golden plovers from Canada to the southernmost tip of South America, and so on. By leaving their summer territories, such birds avoid the harsh northern winter.

Temperature and hibernation

We have seen that below the low critical temperature, the metabolic rate increases. This involves the expenditure of energy and requires a plentiful supply of food to provide the fuel. In winter, when the environmental temperature is low and food is scarce, this can be difficult so the animal may **hibernate**.

Hibernation occurs in many temperate and arctic animals, and is usually stimulated by cold. The animal responds by going into a deep sleep: the metabolic rate falls to the minimum required to keep life ticking over. The body temperature also falls, and is maintained at a much lower level than normal, often about 18°C but as low as 2°C in the hamster. Generally, temperature regulation does not stop altogether but operates at a lowered set point (figure 23.19). It is comparable to saving fuel in a central heating system by turning the thermostat down to a lower setting.

Figure 23.18 At temperatures above about 38°C, alligators open their mouths and evaporation of moisture from the buccal cavity cools their blood.

Figure 23.19 Metabolic rate (as a percentage of the basal metabolic rate) and body temperature of a ground squirrel before, during and after hibernation. During hibernation the set point in the homeostatic control of body temperature falls from its normal 38°C to 8°C.

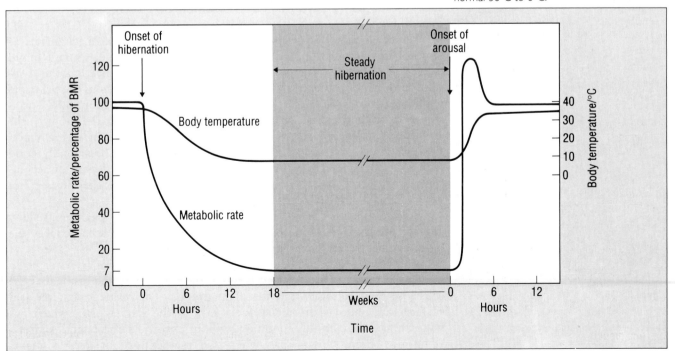

Figure 23.20 The California palm tree, *Washingtonia fillifera*, thrives in the hot desert so long as it has a reasonable water supply.

Figure 23.21 The California monkey flower, *Mimulus cardinalis*, responds to high environmental temperatures by opening its stomata and transpiring rapidly.

There is of course another way of saving fuel, and that is by switching the thermostat off altogether. Bats do this, their body temperature following that of the environment during hibernation. The danger here is that if the environmental temperature falls *too* low, the animal may die of cold. However, some bats are remarkably resilient. A horseshoe bat can become frozen almost solid and yet remain alive.

We saw earlier that because of its larger surface–volume ratio, the rate of heat energy loss per unit mass is greater for a small animal than for a large one. If this loss of heat energy is to be made good by metabolism, a very high metabolic rate may be required. In winter a small animal simply cannot eat sufficient food quickly enough to supply the fuel for maintaining such a high metabolic rate. For this reason it is mainly small animals that go in for hibernation.

There is one type of animal which is so small, and loses heat energy so quickly, that it cannot maintain its body temperature at a constant level even overnight. This is the humming bird, which gets round the problem in a very interesting way. At night its metabolic rate falls, and its body temperature drops to that of the environment. In other words it switches off its thermostat and goes into a state of 'hibernation'. As this happens every 24 hours, it is called **diurnal hibernation**. This is a very useful adaptation in such a small animal. Its only alternative would be to feed actively (and fairly continuously) at night, a task which it is incapable of performing as it cannot see in the dark.

Temperature control in plants

Plants can tolerate fairly wide fluctuations in temperature. This is what one would expect of ectothermic organisms that are rooted to the ground and incapable of getting out of the sun's rays. Plants of different regions are adapted to different temperature ranges. Thus species in temperate parts of the world thrive best between about 25 and 30°C, whereas the optimum temperature for arctic and alpine plants may be as low as 15°C. However, there are limits to the range which each group can tolerate, and experiments suggest that plants may be better at controlling their temperature than was once thought.

Plants gain or lose heat energy by the same physical mechanisms as animals do: conduction, radiation and convection – and, as you might expect, they lose heat energy by evaporation. In fact **transpiration**, the evaporation of water through (mainly) the stomata of the leaves, is the principal way that plants keep cool. If the air temperature exceeds about 30°C, transpiration keeps the plant at a temperature which is lower than that of the air, often considerably lower, even when the leaves are in full sunlight. Obviously for this to be possible the plant must have a reasonably good water supply. The California palm tree, *Washingtonia fillifera*, an accomplished temperature regulator by plant standards, flourishes in the hot desert but is restricted to oases (figure 23.20).

Plants have other ways of preventing overheating. For example, a **shiny cuticle** reflects heat radiation, and having a **small leaf area** reduces the uptake of heat energy from the sun.

Wilting can also be important. Wilting is caused by more water being transpired than can be replaced through the roots, with the result that the cells lose their turgidity and the plant droops. The result is that the leaf surfaces are removed from the direct rays of the sun. A plant which has wilted may remain in this condition without untoward effects until sunset.

It has been shown that when the temperature of certain plants approaches danger-point, a sudden increase in transpiration cools the plant sufficiently to save it from disaster. Such is the case with the California monkey flower, *Mimulus cardinalis* (figure 23.21). When the leaf temperature reaches 41.5°C, the stomata suddenly open right up and the transpiration rate increases by four times. The cooling effect of this is enough to keep the leaf temperature at 42°C even when the air temperature exceeds 60°C!

Surviving extremes of temperature

Organisms which cannot control their body temperature may have to withstand freezing temperatures, at least at certain times of the year. How do they do it? In general there are three ways.

- **By supercooling.** Supercooling is the lowering of the temperature of a fluid to below its freezing point without the formation of ice. Ice crystals can damage tissues, and supercooling provides a way of avoiding this. Experiments have shown that certain reptiles can be supercooled to as low as −8°C without freezing. Plants and fishes also go in for supercooling.

- **By freezing tolerance.** Some organisms, notably plants and insects, can tolerate the formation of ice in their tissues. Certain insect larvae can recover after as much as 90 per cent of the body has been frozen. In these organisms ice crystals form between, rather than inside, the cells. The cells themselves shrink and recover later when the ice melts. In some species of fish, ice damage is lessened by the presence of glycerol in the tissues. Glycerol is used in human blood banks and sperm banks to prevent injury to the cells when they are frozen for storage.

- **By using an antifreeze.** The antifreeze in the radiator of a car lowers the freezing point so that the water does not freeze in

Green algae flourishing in hot water in Waimangu Thermal Valley, New Zealand.

winter. A similar substance has been found in the blood of certain Antarctic fish. Of course the presence of solutes in the blood means that the freezing point of any animal's blood will be slightly lower than that of pure water. However, in these fish a special antifreeze is present which lowers the freezing point even further. The substance has been found to be a glycoprotein, and it keeps the blood in an unfrozen state even when the surrounding sea water is at a temperature of −1.8°C.

What about high temperatures? The main adaptation here is tolerance. This enables certain types of algae to flourish in hot springs at temperatures of 55 to 60°C (see illustration). However, it is prokaryotes that show the greatest tolerance. There are many reports of

bacteria growing in boiling hot springs in North America and New Zealand, but the jackpot must go to certain bacteria which have been discovered in the hot water rising from sulphide-encrusted vents in the deep ocean floor. Some of these bacteria were living at temperatures of 350°C. It is claimed that in the laboratory they reproduced enthusiastically in sea water at 250°C, doubling in number every 40 minutes!

Heat-tolerant bacteria possess membranes which are more heat-stable than those of other prokaryotes, and their enzymes work optimally at temperatures well above those that would denature the enzymes of other organisms. For example, *Thermophilus*, a bacterium which lives in hot springs, possesses enzymes that work best at 80°C.

Summary

1 Organisms cannot withstand fluctuations in body temperature beyond that which is compatible with the functioning of their enzymes.

2 On the basis of their ability to regulate their body temperature animals are classified into **homoiothermic** and **poikilothermic** or, more usefully, **endothermic** and **ectothermic**.

3 Heat energy is lost or gained by **conduction, radiation, evaporation** and **convection**. The problem in temperature regulation is to overcome, control or make use of these physical processes.

4 Endothermic animals (e.g. mammals) have various structural and physiological ways of coping with excessive low or high environmental temperatures, many of them involving the **skin**.

5 Structures in mammalian skin important in temperature regulation include the **blood supply, hairs, sweat glands, thermoreceptors** and **sub-cutaneous fat**.

6 Thermoregulatory responses are controlled by a **thermoregulatory centre** in the **hypothalamus** of the brain which responds to changes in the temperature of the blood.

7 In endotherms physical (non-metabolic) mechanisms maintain a constant body temperature when the environmental temperature ranges between a **higher** and a **lower critical temperature**. Above the higher critical temperature and below the lower critical temperature, the metabolic rate rises.

8 The lower critical temperature is significantly lower for 'arctic' than for 'tropical' animals.

9 Some endothermic animals reduce excessive loss of heat energy from exposed structures by means of a **counter-current heat exchange system**.

10 Many animals regulate their body temperature by **behavioural means**. In ectothermic animals this is the only method. **Migration** and **hibernation** are ways of avoiding unfavourable environmental temperatures.

11 Some organisms are **temperature tolerant**. They are able to survive even when subjected to wide temperature fluctuations.

12 Plants have a number of structural features which help them to withstand high temperatures. To some extent plants are cooled by **transpiration**, in some cases markedly so.

Review questions

1 What is meant by the term *heat balance*? Under what circumstances is a person likely to be out of heat balance?

2 Make a list of all the structures in mammalian skin which play a part in temperature regulation. Briefly give the function of each.

3 In cold conditions blood is diverted from the surface of the skin and the skin goes pale, and yet people get rosy cheeks in cold weather. Explain this apparent contradiction.

4 Two expeditions are being organised, one to the South Pole, the other to the Sahara Desert. Design the clothes for each expedition and explain why they would be suitable.

5 During a fever, a body temperature of less than about 40°C is treated by covering the patient with extra blankets, but if the body temperature exceeds this value ice packs are placed in contact with the patient. Suggest a reason for each treatment.

6 Our body temperature is kept *near*-constant rather than absolutely constant. Why is this?

7 Provided that the atmosphere is unsaturated, it is possible for a person to spend 30 minutes in a sauna at 130°C.
(a) Why must the atmosphere be unsaturated?
(b) Suggest how a person can survive at such a high temperature?
(c) How could you find out if this temperature is higher than the upper critical temperature?

8 It has been suggested that the lack of insulation provided by human hair is not due to the low numbers of hair follicles, but to the poor quality of our hair. How might this suggestion be investigated?

9 In this chapter some examples are given of how animals keep cool by *behavioural* means. Suggest some other examples, either from your own observations or by predicting possible mechanisms.

10 On a still sunny day the roof of a car may get too hot to touch but the leaves of a nearby plant remain within 12°C of the air temperature, even in full sunlight. Explain.

Further reading

You will find an excellent general account of temperature regulation in Knut Schmidt-Nielsen's two books *How Animals Work* (Cambridge University Press, 1972) and *Animal Physiology: Adaptation and Environment,* 4th edn. (Cambridge University Press, 1990). The former is simple and easy to read, the latter more detailed.

Benzinger's own account of his famous experiment with the human calorimeter can be found in *Scientific American, The Human Thermostat,* January 1961, and is well worth reading.

A detailed survey of temperature regulation in animals is given in Richard Hardy's small monograph *Temperature and Animal Life* (Edward Arnold, 1979).

Biology, Advanced Topics explores the role of the hypothalamus in the physiological and behavioural control of body temperature.

Defence against disease

The body of an animal is constantly being invaded by **micro-organisms**, particularly **bacteria** and **viruses** but also some **protoctists** and **fungi**. They enter the body through one of its openings, particularly the nose and mouth, and thus gain entry to the lungs or stomach. They also enter the reproductive system during sexual intercourse – indeed, some *only* get into the body this way. Another mode of entry is via the skin when it is broken as a result of a cut or bite.

Many of these micro-organisms either feed on the tissues or liberate poisonous substances (**toxins**) into the bloodstream, thereby bringing about disease. Diseases caused by viruses include influenza, poliomyelitis and the common cold; bacteria cause typhoid, diphtheria and tuberculosis, while malaria and amoebic dysentery are caused by unicellular protoctists. The activities of these disease-causing micro-organisms – or **pathogens** as they are called – are not, of course, confined to humans. All animals and plants are susceptible, though the particular micro-organisms that infect them may be different.

In destroying the tissues and liberating toxic substances, these pathogenic micro-organisms change the internal environment and upset the smooth running of the body. Their control by the body's natural defence mechanisms is thus an aspect of homeostasis. Since we know more about these defence mechanisms in mammals than in other organisms our discussion will be mainly confined to them.

The body's defences against disease can be divided into those which prevent the entry of micro-organisms, and those which destroy them once they manage to get in. We will deal with each in turn.

Preventing entry

The skin with its hard, keratinised outer layer serves as an effective barrier to most micro-organisms. However, much as an animal might like to envelop itself in an impenetrable barrier, this is patently impossible. Thus the alimentary tract and gaseous-exchange surfaces are major pathways through which micro-organisms can get into the body. To some extent access to the gaseous-exchange surface is prevented by **cilia** lining the trachea and bronchi. Micro-organisms and undesirable particles get caught up in **mucus** secreted by numerous goblet cells and are carried by the beating cilia towards the glottis and thence to the throat where they are swallowed.

Coughing and **sneezing** help to expel foreign bodies from the breathing tract as figure 24.1 makes only too clear. The acid in the stomach kills many of the bacteria that come in with the food and from the breathing tract; in more extreme cases **vomiting** and **diarrhoea** expel undesirable bacteria from the gut.

Areas of the body not covered by skin such as the eyes, nose and mouth are particularly vulnerable to invasion by bacteria. An enzyme has been discovered in tears, nasal secretions, saliva, urine and other body fluids which is capable of destroying certain bacteria. Because it bursts (lyses) the bacteria, this enzyme is called **lysozyme**. It works by splitting molecules in the bacterial cell walls. It is a powerful enzyme, effective even in low concentrations, and undoubtedly plays some part in keeping bacteria out of the body.

In the vagina a carbohydrate is secreted which mutualistic bacteria

Figure 24.1 Short-duration flash photograph of a sneeze. Notice the vast number of droplets emitted from the mouth and nose. This is one way in which pathogenic micro-organisms are transferred from one person to another.

Figure 24.2 The body's barriers to invasion by pathogenic micro-organisms. The bacteria in the large intestine occur naturally and by competing with other bacteria they help to prevent pathogens from gaining a foothold if they manage to get into the gut. One disadvantage of antibiotics is that they tend to kill off the useful bacteria as well as the pathogenic ones.

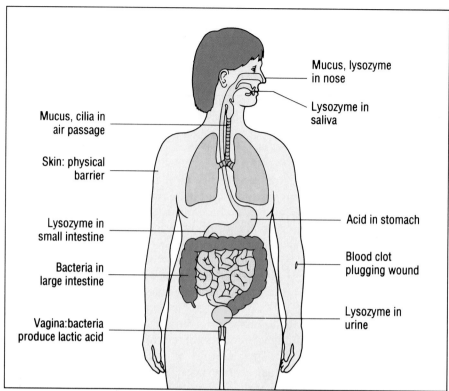

Figure 24.3 The crude conditions in which surgical operations were carried out a hundred years ago contrast sharply with the modern operating theatre. The picture shows the use made in the nineteenth century of the Lister carbolic spray for creating antiseptic conditions in the immediate vicinity of the wound.

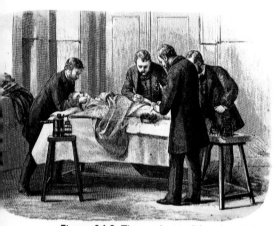

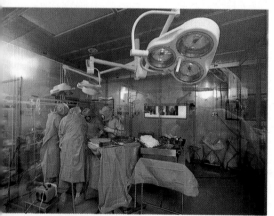

Figure 24.4 Today hospitals attempt to create a totally germ-free atmosphere in their operating theatres.

metabolise, producing lactic acid. This makes the vagina acidic, creating an unfavourable environment for many pathogenic yeasts, bacteria and viruses.

The entry of micro-organisms through wounds is, as everyone knows, a major cause of infection. To some extent this is prevented, or at least cut down, by the **clotting of blood**. A necessary prerequisite for the healing of wounds, blood clotting not only prevents excessive bleeding but also blocks the entry of micro-organisms.

Figure 24.2 summarises the body's barriers to infection.

Antisepsis and asepsis

In considering temperature regulation we saw that humans are unique amongst animals in supplementing the body's natural homeostatic mechanisms with artificial devices. This is also true of disease control. **Environmental health** and **hygiene** are aimed at preventing the entry of micro-organisms into the body.

The foundations of these preventive measures were laid more than a century ago by the French microbiologist Louis Pasteur, who established the germ theory of disease and showed that micro-organisms come from pre-existing micro-organisms. He discovered that micro-organisms could be destroyed by heat treatment, thus providing the basis of **sterilisation** and preservation of foods. Treatment of milk by heating is still known as **pasteurisation.**

Pasteur's work on micro-organisms and sterilisation inspired the English surgeon Joseph Lister to look for other means of destroying bacteria: Lister's use of carbolic acid in the operating theatre marked the beginning of **antiseptics** (figure 24.3). Today antisepsis has been largely supplanted by **aseptic techniques**, which aim to eliminate germs from the environment altogether. It would be unrealistic to think that this can ever be achieved in the general environment, but it is certainly aimed at in modern operating theatres and intensive care units (figure 24.4).

The immune system

Micro-organisms are much more difficult to deal with once they get into the body. They multiply prodigiously, attack cells and/or release **toxins** into the bloodstream. The body must somehow distinguish them from its own cells and destroy them in a way that limits damage to its own tissues. This task is carried out by the **immune system**.

All animals have to defend themselves against micro-organisms. During the evolution of the immune system different cells, mostly **white blood cells** (**leucocytes**), have emerged to produce a complex defence system. This is especially so in mammals.

The simplest components of the immune system are cells which engulf and digest foreign material in the blood and tissues in the same way as *Amoeba* engulfs and digests its food – by **phagocytosis**.

Phagocytosis

Phagocytosis is carried out by white blood cells called **phagocytes**. There are two main types of phagocyte:

- **Neutrophils** which are cells with an irregular many-lobed nucleus and a granular cytoplasm.
- **Macrophages** which are larger cells with a regular horseshoe-shaped nucleus and a non-granular cytoplasm.

Neutrophils are the commonest type of immune cell and make up about 60 per cent of all white blood cells in the bloodstream. The bone marrow produces 80 million of these cells every minute and their number increases during an infection. They move about in contact with the endothelium of the blood vessels where they ingest bacteria (figure 24.5). Once taken up, the bacteria are digested by lysosomes as described on page 205.

The neutrophils can squeeze between the cells lining the capillaries and migrate into the tissues. They wander through the tissues to the site of an infection, attracted by chemicals released by the micro-organisms and the local tissue cells (chemotaxis). Neutrophils are rather short-lived, surviving for no more than a few days.

Macrophages develop from another type of white cell in the blood called **monocytes** which make up only 6 per cent of the white blood cells. Monocytes are made in the bone marrow and, after circulating in the blood for one or two days, they squeeze through the cells lining the capillaries and migrate into the tissues where they become macrophages (figure 24.6).

The macrophages wander around the tissues collecting up 'rubbish', which may be micro-organisms or other foreign bodies (in the lungs dust as well as micro-organisms are collected in this manner). They are particularly numerous in the lungs, liver, kidney, spleen and lymph nodes. Although the neutrophils are the first cells to arrive at a site of infection, the longer-lived macrophages take over at any major site.

One result of phagocytosis at the site of a local infection, which we have all experienced, is **inflammation**. This is caused by **mast cells** releasing inflammatory substances such as **histamine** which dilate the blood vessels and make them leaky, so that plasma and white blood cells flow out into the infected area. Hot, red, swollen and painful, the inflamed area contains numerous bacteria and phagocytes, many of which die and form pus. Sometimes the inflamed area forms a boil. The host's cells form scar tissue around the boil whose head may eventually burst open as a result of the pressure of pus inside it.

Phagocytes are a very efficient means of defence but to be successful they must identify correctly which cells to engulf. They could do untold

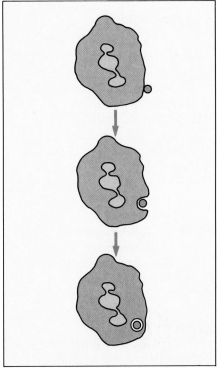

Figure 24.5 A neutrophil ingests a bacterium. When the bacterium (red blob)comes into contact with the surface of the phagocyte, a cup-shaped indentation is formed and the bacterium is taken into a vesicle where it is digested. Fully engorged, a single neutrophil may contain as many as 20 visible bacteria, many of them still alive and moving.

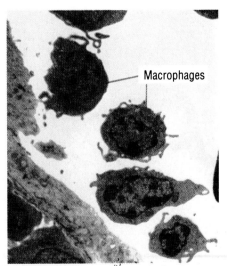

Macrophages

Figure 24.6 Electron micrograph showing phagocytic macrophages in a capillary. Notice the amoeboid shape of the cells and phagocytic vesicles in the cytoplasm.

Lymph nodes

The lymph nodes are our so-called 'glands' which sometimes swell up when we are suffering from an infection. They are widely distributed in the body, particulary the groin and armpits. Each lymph node consists of a network of delicate fibres through which lymph percolates. Lymph is a colourless fluid, derived from the blood by a mechanism which is explained on page 357 It is brought to the node by a lymph vessel and drained away from it by another lymph vessel. The latter leads ultimately to a vein in the neck where the lymph rejoins the bloodstream.

The lymph nodes contain phagocytic macrophages which remove pathogens and foreign particles from the lymph. These phagocytes are mainly fixed to the fibrous network though they can move out of the lymph node to nearby tissues.

The lymph nodes also contain large numbers of lymphocytes. These are explained on the next page.

Lymphoid tissue is found in other place besides the lymph nodes – the spleen and tonsils for example.

damage to the body if they engulfed the body's own cells. So how do phagocytes recognise which cells to engulf? Certain chemicals are common to the cell walls of all bacteria but do not occur on mammalian cells. A simple method of recognition could be that these chemicals stimulate the phagocytes – probably by sticking to them – to engulf and digest the bacteria. Other cells in the immune system produce molecules which bind to the bacteria and 'label' them as targets for the phagocytes.

Phagocytosis, however, has distinct limitations: it does not act against certain bacteria and is not very effective against viruses because they reproduce inside the body's own cells where they are protected from attack.

Complement

One way in which phagocytes are helped is by a group of proteins present in the blood called **complement**. Complement proteins are made by macrophages, monocytes and other cells in the body, particularly in the liver. Complement proteins are normally inactive in the blood, but in certain circumstances they interact to produce activated proteins. Some stick to invading micro-organisms, particularly yeasts and bacteria, identifying them to phagocytes as foreign material. Some destroy the bacterial membranes, while others attract phagocytes and stimulate them to become more active.

Larger invaders

Not all invaders of the mammalian body are as small as bacteria and viruses. Some parasites are multicellular and are too large to be engulfed by phagocytes. Examples are nematode worms, flukes and tapeworms. Special cells exist to deal with these larger invaders. These include a type of white blood cell called **eosinophils** which produce a powerful enzyme capable of breaking down the body wall of flukes and other such parasites. At the same time **basophils** (another type of white blood cell) and mast cells produce chemical substances which stimulate the immune system to mount an attack against these invaders at the site of infection.

Natural immunity

The type of resistance to infection described so far provides what is called **natural immunity**. Its key features are:

- It is **non-specific**, that is, the cells responsible for it (i.e. phagocytes, eosinophils, mast cells and the rest) cannot distinguish between one type of micro-organism and another. Phagocytes, for example, will engulf any foreign cell that they encounter provided that it is 'labelled' for them.
- It is **non-adaptive**, that is, the response is the same no matter how many times a person is infected with the same type of micro-organism. Natural immunity does not improve if the same micro-organisms get into the body a second time or more.

Adaptive immunity

If natural immunity fails, the body has a second line of defence called **adaptive** or **acquired** immunity which is fundamentally different from natural immunity. The special features of adaptive immunity are:

- It is **specific**, that is, different types of the cells responsible for it can distinguish between different types of micro-organism.
- It has a **memory**, which enables its cells to produce an enhanced response to repeated infection by the same type of micro-organism.

It is the task of another kind of white blood cell, called **lymphocytes**, to bring about this type of response to infection. Lymphocytes make up about 24 per cent of the white blood cells. They are called lymphocytes because they are abundant in the **lymphatic system**, particularly the **lymph nodes** (see box on page 416).

There are two types of lymphocytes in the blood and lymph: **B lymphocytes** and **T lymphocytes** (also called B cells and T cells for short). Each is responsible for a different kind of **immune response**. These are truly remarkable cells and we shall look at them in turn.

B lymphocytes

The B lymphocytes originate in the bone marrow (B stands for *bone-marrow* derived). Any substance that initiates an adaptive immune response is called an **antigen** – it may be a pathogen or its toxic products, or various non-harmful molecules and cells such as pollen and penicillin. When a B lymphocyte encounters an antigen it produces an **antibody**, a specialised protein molecule called immunoglobulin. The antibody combines with the antigen and helps to eliminate it from the body.

What makes B lymphocytes so remarkable is that they can produce highly specific antibodies against a vast number of different types of antigen. To understand how this comes about we must consider what happens to the B cells in the bone marrow.

During embryonic development large numbers of B lymphocytes are formed in the bone marrow. Each one undergoes rapid cell division to form a clone of identical B cells. (A clone is a population of identical cells formed by mitotic cell division – see page 553.) At birth, each clone consists of a small number of identical B lymphocytes programmed to recognise just one type of antigen and to respond to it by secreting antibodies which bind to that antigen alone. The immune system contains at least ten million different clones of B cells, so that between them they can recognise any antigen that is likely to get into the body.

How does each B lymphocyte recognise its unique antigen? The way it does so is rather neat. The B cell carries on its surface the same kind of antibodies that it is capable of producing. These surface antibodies act as receptors. When an appropriate antigen comes along, it combines with one of the receptors. This activates the B cell, causing it to start making the antibodies which are then released into the blood and lymph.

Although each B cell has the ability to produce large quantities of its own specific antibody, it does so only if it is needed – that is, if it encounters the right kind of antigen. The particular type of antibody that each B cell produces binds only to one specific type of antigen – or, at the most, several closely related antigens such as the smallpox and cowpox antigens. When a particular antigen gets into the body, it is recognised by the matching clone, which then divides rapidly to make thousands more identical B cells, all secreting antibodies that bind to that antigen.

This process is called **clonal selection** because the antigen 'selects' the appropriate clone of B cells from among the millions in the body. The clonal selection theory was first put forward in the 1950s by the Australian scientist Sir Macfarlane Burnet who was subsequently awarded a Nobel Prize for his work. Since then much evidence has been obtained to support it.

A micro-organism is complex chemically and is likely to possess not just one but several different types of antigens. These will activate several different clones of B cells to produce appropriate antibodies. This is known as **polyclonal activation** and it produces a mixture of different antibodies,

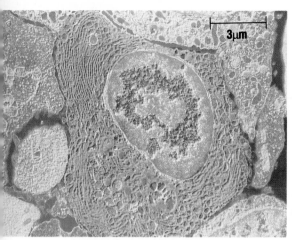

Figure 24.7 Electron micrograph of an antibody-producing plasma cell. Notice the dense endoplasmic reticulum (yellow). This bears numerous ribosomes characteristic of a cell which is engaged in rapid protein synthesis.

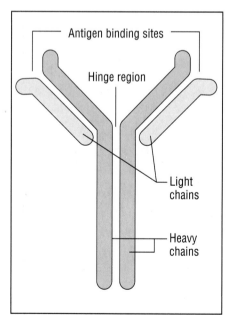

Figure 24.8 Diagram showing the structure of an antibody molecule. Each antibody has four polypeptide chains, two heavy and two light. There are two antigen-binding sites. The hinge region allows flexibility when the antibody binds to the antigen, enabling *both* binding sites to make contact with a matching area of the antigen.

each of which binds to a different type of antigen on the same micro-organism.

The clones are, in effect, 'antibody factories' and the cells show a number of features which fit in with this idea. For example, they are particularly rich in ribosomes, indicative of the high rate of protein synthesis necessary for producing large numbers of antibodies. These mature antibody-producing cells are sometimes called **plasma cells** and one of them is illustrated in figure 24.7.

It is now possible to make large quantities of antibodies in the laboratory and this has provided scientists with a source of antibodies for research into their structure and properties (see box on page 419). Sequence analysis and X-ray diffraction studies have shown that each antibody molecule consists of four polypeptide chains, two heavy and two light (figure 24.8). The antibody molecule has two binding sites, each of which links up with an antigen molecule. The regions of the antigen and antibody molecules which bind together have matching shapes, like jigsaw puzzle pieces fitting together.

The type of immunity provided by B lymphocytes and their antibodies is called **humoral immunity** – *humoral* refers to the blood and lymph in which the antibodies circulate. The strength of this system lies in its ability to respond to specific antigens which were previously unknown to the body. Its weakness is that if challenged by a massive dose of antigen – the measles virus for example – antibodies cannot be produced quickly enough to prevent illness. This is because, with so many B cells needed, only a few of each type can be present at the outset, and the body needs time for these to proliferate into enough antibody-producing cells to fight the disease.

Fortunately, as a result of infection special **memory cells** develop from the clone which produces the antibodies, and these memory cells may survive for months or even years. If the body is subjected to another attack by the same antigen – the measles virus for example – it is quickly recognised by the memory cells which transform at once into antibody-producing cells. As a result, the level of antibody is built up very quickly and the pathogens are destroyed so rapidly that no symptoms appear. This is how we become **immune** to diseases.

We have seen that the B lymphocytes work by producing specific antibodies when the appropriate antigens get into the body. However, the B lymphocytes respond in this way only if they receive the right signals. These signals come from the T lymphocytes which we must now consider.

T lymphocytes

The T lymphocytes also originate in the bone marrow but they have to pass through the **thymus gland** during their maturation (T stands for *thymus-derived*). In the thymus gland they undergo a complex 'education' process without which they cannot take part in the immune response.

Evidence for the involvement of the thymus gland in the immune response comes from experiments on mice. If the thymus is removed from newborn mice, the animals develop a wasting disease characterised by retarded growth: the lymph nodes are much reduced in size and there is a reduction in the number of lymphocytes in the blood; the immune response does not develop and antibodies fail to be produced.

T lymphocytes look exactly like B lymphocytes but they do not produce antibodies. They are responsible for what is called **cell-mediated immunity**. T lymphocytes are more varied in their action than B lymphocytes, but, like B lymphocytes, they have to make contact with their matching antigen before they can start work. There are special receptors on their surface which enable them to recognise the correct antigen.

The main types of T lymphocyte, and their functions, are as follows:

- **T helper cells** help other cells in the immune system. For example, they stimulate B lymphocytes to divide into antibody-producing cells. If these helper cells are not present, the B lymphocytes cannot go into action. They also enhance the action of phagocytes. It is the T helper cells which are invaded by HIV (human immunodeficiency virus) and this explains why other infections are associated with AIDS (see box on page 420).

- **T suppressor cells** suppress other cells in the immune system. For example, they inhibit the production of antibodies by the B lymphocytes, and they also suppress the action of phagocytes. They act as brakes in the immune system, dampening it down and preventing it from over-reacting.

- **T killer cells** destroy body cells infected with viruses before the viruses have time to proliferate. They also attack cells from other individuals if they get into the body, and in doing so they cause the rejection problems associated with skin grafts and transplant surgery (see pages 426–7). The T killer cells are regulated in the same way as B cells, by the T helper and T suppressor cells.

The symptoms of AIDS

It is characteristic of AIDS that symptoms may not develop for many years. When symptoms do occur, the most common sign is swelling of the lymph nodes. Subsequently the person may display fever, persistent diarrhoea, severe fatigue and drenching sweats. These are symptoms of **AIDS-related complex (ARC)**. Usually this progresses to AIDS itself, characterised by a wide range of illnesses attributable to a collaspe of the immune system. There is more about this in the box on page 420.

Monoclonal antibodies

When a micro-organism gets into the body, or when a vaccine is administered, antibodies are always produced. For certain sorts of laboratory research it is useful to have a pure preparation of antibodies with single specificity.

Until comparatively recently it was impossible to obtain such pure cultures. However, in 1975 Cesar Milstein and Georges Kohler at Cambridge succeeded in fusing antibody-secreting cells with tumour cells. The resulting cells, called **hybridomas**, secrete antibodies, and are immortal – a property of tumour cells.

These hybridoma cells can be cultured as a pure clone, and their antibodies collected. Antibodies produced this way are, like the cells that produce them, all identical and they are called **monoclonal antibodies**.

Milstein and Kohler were awarded a Nobel Prize for their work in 1984. Their technique is summarised in the illustration.

For what specific purposes do you think monoclonal antibodies are required?

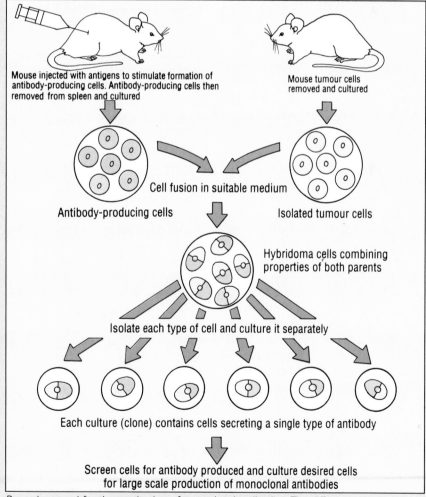

Mouse injected with antigens to stimulate formation of antibody-producing cells. Antibody-producing cells then removed from spleen and cultured

Mouse tumour cells removed and cultured

Cell fusion in suitable medium

Antibody-producing cells

Isolated tumour cells

Hybridoma cells combining properties of both parents

Isolate each type of cell and culture it separately

Each culture (clone) contains cells secreting a single type of antibody

Screen cells for antibody produced and culture desired cells for large scale production of monoclonal antibodies

Procedure used for the production of monoclonal antibodies. The different colours represent the different kinds of antibodies which the cells produce.

AIDS: how HIV damages the immune system

Research on AIDS and its causative agent, HIV, has shed light on other conditions and on how the immune system works. Guest author Anthony Pinching explains.

In the early 1980s some astute doctors noticed that they were starting to see patients with evidence of severe **immunodeficiency** for no previously recognised reason. Immunodeficiency is a state where part of the body's immune defence against disease becomes defective, leading to an increased susceptibility to certain infections. These infections are described as opportunistic because they take advantage of the host's impaired defences, causing problems that would not normally arise. The pattern of infection in these new cases indicated that this particular defect mainly affected the cell-mediated part of the immune system.

Previously, immunodeficiency had been confined to relatively uncommon congenital disorders where a person was born without a part of the immune system, and to situations where a previously normal immune system had become damaged or suppressed by disease or drug therapy, such as that used to prevent rejection of transplanted organs. The new cases were occurring in people whose immune system had shown no previous signs of damage and where there was no recognisable cause of immunosuppression. The condition became known as **AIDS (acquired immune deficiency syndrome)** and the cause turned out to be a virus, now known as **human immunodeficiency virus, HIV**.

HIV is a small virus consisting of RNA genes surrounded by a protein coat. The RNA codes for its own specific proteins, one of which is an enzyme called reverse transcriptase.

This enzyme reverses the usual process of gene transcription so that a DNA copy of the virus can be made from its RNA (see page 728). This DNA copy is then spliced into the gene of the infected human cell, causing persistent infection and making the host cell become a factory for HIV replication.

One of the virus proteins that the DNA codes for is a glycoprotein in the viral coat, called **gp120**. This is vital in targeting the virus to cells of the immune system which thus become infected and damaged.

An early finding in people with AIDS was that they have a greatly reduced number of **T helper lymphocytes**. These cells are characterised by a molecule on their surface membrane called **CD4** which is central to communication between cells of the immune system. The viral gp120 molecule has a region that binds to a part of the lymphocyte CD4 molecule, rather like a key fitting into a lock. In this way the virus is able to recognise the lymphocyte and attach itself to it. After such attachment, the membrane surrounding the virus fuses with the membrane of the lymphocyte, allowing the viral RNA to enter the host cell.

Other cells of the immune system, notably macrophages and related cells, also carry CD4 and can become infected in the same way, though they may be infected by other routes as well. Such cells are important because they seem to act as a reservoir of HIV infection.

CD4 lymphocytes and their interactions with macrophages are at the very heart of cell-mediated immunity, so their role as HIV targets fits well with the susceptibility of AIDS patients to infections that affect this part of the defence mechanism. Tests on people with AIDS have shown that they have many defects in their immune system, but most striking and

consistent is a reduction in the number and functioning of their CD4 lymphocytes.

Infection of the CD4 lymphocytes by HIV leads to their premature death. This may be caused by the virus itself, or by killer T cells attempting to eliminate the virus-infected cells, or both. Virus-induced damage includes lysis and – more importantly – the fusion of numerous CD4 cells, uninfected as well as infected, to form giant syncytial cells. CD4 cells that are not infected by HIV show defects in their functioning, probably caused by gp120.

The loss of CD4 lymphocytes and their functional impairment has knock-on effects on many other cells. For example, macrophages cannot be properly activated to kill certain organisms, B lymphocytes are unable to develop new antibody responses, and killer T cells show impaired function. Some of these effects are the result of reduced lymphokine signals which normally come from CD4 lymphocytes.

All this leads to progressive impairment of the cell-mediated immune system and, to a lesser extent, the humoral system. The net result is the development of increasing susceptibility to certain bacteria, fungi, protoctists and viruses and to some rather unusual virus-induced tumours such as Kaposi's sarcoma, a type of skin or internal tumour which was very rare before the advent of AIDS.

In parallel with immunodeficiency, HIV can damage the nervous system. This too appears to result from both a loss of cells and defective function in those that remain. The main cells in the nervous system that harbour HIV are the macrophages. It seems that HIV infection of these cells causes the release of virus proteins or macrophage products which in turn damage or alter the function of neighbouring nerve cells.

Together the T helper cells and T suppressor cells regulate and control the production of antibodies by the B cells, and enhance or suppress the action of phagocytes. T cells also secrete short-lived messenger proteins called **lymphokines** which activate or suppress every aspect of the immune response. One of their functions is to stimulate macrophages to engulf other cells much more readily. This enables the macrophages to attack bacteria which have invaded the immune system and to fight fungal infections and tumours.

One group of lymphokines are called **interferons**. These are effective against a wide range of viruses and they work by inhibiting the protein-making machinery of the infected cell so that the virus cannot proliferate. They also stimulate changes in uninfected cells which makes them resistant to the virus.

Summary of the cells in the immune system

In the course of the last few pages we have encountered no less than ten different types of immune cell, and you have every reason to feel confused! It would therefore be helpful at this point to pause for a moment and draw the threads together. To help you, two illustrations are provided.

Figure 24.9 summarises the origin and fate of the B and T lymphocytes. Although this is a useful diagram, it does not show the complex interactions that occur between the different types of cell. The arrows suggest that the B and T lymphocytes are completely separate, whereas we have seen that they are functionally interconnected.

Figure 24.10 shows the cells of the whole immune system. You will see that all the cells come from a common **stem cell** in the bone marrow. This divides repeatedly and the daughter cells then differentiate into all the kinds of immune cell which we have been considering.

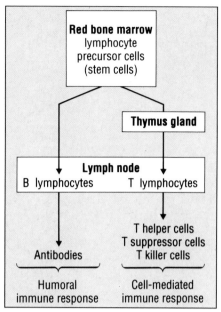

Figure 24.9 Simplified summary of the origin and fate of B and T lymphocytes.
T lymphocytes perform many functions, and the way they interact with one another and with the B lymphocytes is highly complex. Both types of lymphocyte can produce memory cells which recognise and respond to later doses of antigen which they have previously encountered.

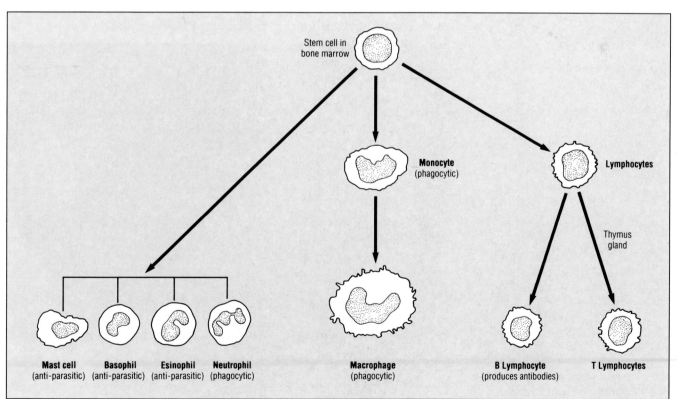

Figure 24.10 Diagram summarising the cells of the immune system and showing how they originate from a common type of stem cell in the bone marrow.

Immunity and immunisation

The type of immunity provided by antibody production is called **active immunity** because the body makes its own antibodies in response to the arrival of an antigen.

During the development of a mammal, a certain number of antibodies pass from the mother to the fetus via the placenta or, after birth, via the milk. This confers **passive immunity** on the young animal, at any rate for a short time after birth. The human infant, for example, may be protected from diseases such as measles and poliomyelitis as a result of passive immunity, and this is undoubtedly one of the advantages of breast-feeding. However the number of antibodies conferred in this way is limited, and such immunity is short-lived.

Active artificial immunity

In immunity, as in so many other aspects of homeostasis, we have augmented nature's methods with our own. **Active artificial immunity** can be established by introducing a small quantity of antigen, the **vaccine**, into the body (**immunisation**). This activates the appropriate antibody-producing cells which are then at the ready if and when that particular micro-organism gets into the body. For example, protection against poliomyelitis may be secured this way (figure 24.11).

Immunisation techniques were first developed in the eighteenth century by the Gloucestershire physician Edward Jenner. He observed that people who contracted the mild disease cowpox seemed to have a defence against the much more serious disease, smallpox. He carried out what today would be considered a highly unethical experiment. He introduced the pus from a cowpox vesicle which he obtained from a dairy-maid into an eight-year-old boy. This had the effect of protecting the boy against smallpox. The cowpox virus itself did not harm the boy but stimulated his body to manufacture antibodies against the much more virulent smallpox virus.

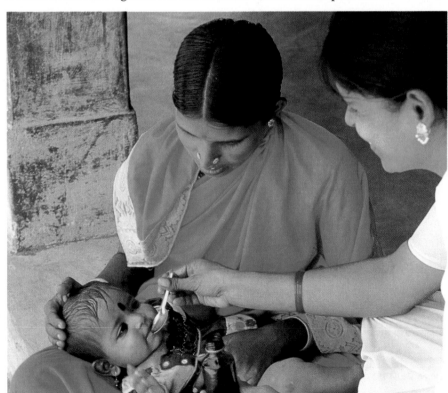

Figure 24.11 A nurse administering an oral vaccine against polio to a child in India. The oral vaccine is of a live attenuated type: the virus is cultured under special conditions so that it loses its virulence but retains its ability to stimulate antibody production.

We now know that the cowpox virus triggers production of the same antibodies as the smallpox virus. Jenner's was a momentous discovery in the history of medical science, from which great advances have been made. He used a thorn for his inoculation whereas nowadays a sterile needle is used, but it was Jenner's initial discovery that led to the eventual eradication of smallpox.

Vaccines used today usually involve the use of weakened (**attenuated**) forms of the virus or bacterium. An attenuated micro-organism will not cause the disease but it stimulates the immune system to produce antibodies against it. The BCG vaccine, which gives protection against tuberculosis, is an example. It is named after two French scientists, Calmette and Guérin. In 1908 they discovered, by accident, that after 13 years in a special culture medium the bacillus causing tuberculosis had become attenuated.

Many vaccines are now prepared by growing and treating pathogenic micro-organisms in such a way that they lose their capacity to cause the disease but not their ability to stimulate the production of the appropriate antibodies. Generally it is necessary for two successive doses of the vaccine to be given. The reason for this is explained in figure 24.13. In some cases it is necessary to provide continued immunity by giving 'booster' doses of the vaccine at regular intervals.

Passive artificial immunity

A quite different technique is to give a person antibodies from another individual. In this **passive artificial immunity** the recipient is not induced to produce his or her own antibodies but is supplied with them, ready-made as it were, from an outside source. The antibodies are usually prepared by injecting antigens responsible for the disease into a suitable animal, or by extracting the antibodies from the bloodstream of a person who is already making them.

The drawback with this procedure is that the protection, though immediate, is relatively short-lived, lasting only as long as the antibodies persist. As antibodies are proteins, and proteins are continually being broken down and replaced, they may last for only several weeks. On the other hand, active immunity, where the individual is induced to manufacture his or her own antibodies, can last a lifetime.

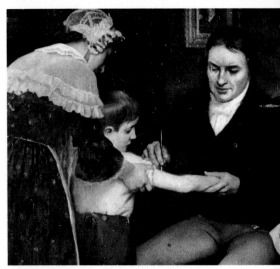

Figure 24.12 Edward Jenner innoculating a child against smallpox. Using a thorn mounted on a holder, he scratched the boy's skin and introduced the pus from a cowpox vesicle into his bloodstream.

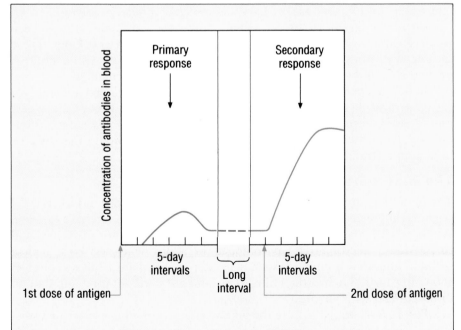

Figure 24.13 The effect of immunisation on antibody production. The first dose of antigen triggers the production of a relatively small number of antibodies (primary response). The second dose results in a larger, more rapid and sustained production of antibodies (secondary response). Immunity against some diseases (e.g. measles and poliomyelitis) can last a lifetime; but for other diseases (e.g. typhoid, cholera and tetanus) further doses of antigen ('boosters') need to be given from time to time. The enhanced response to a second dose of antigen is due to the presence of memory cells. These are explained on page 418.

Chemotheraphy and antibiotics

If disease-causing micro-organisms succeed in avoiding the body's defence mechanisms, both natural and artificial, further efforts to combat the disease can be employed. Our endeavours in this area include the use of **chemotherapy**. This is the administration of chemical substances, natural or synthetic, that kill or prevent the reproduction of micro-organisms. The term is now extended to include the inhibition of dividing malignant cells in cancer. The chemical substances used are called **chemotherapeutic agents**. Some of these substances are secreted by micro-organisms and are selectively toxic to other micro-organisms, in which case they are called **antibiotics**.

One of the best-known antibiotics is **penicillin** which was discovered by the British bacteriologist Alexander Fleming in 1928 as a result of a fortuitous accident. Fleming had been working on the bacterium *Staphylococcus aureus,* and it happened that one of his plates became contaminated with some spores of a mould which are believed to have floated into his laboratory through an open window. Fleming noticed that the bacteria were absent in the vicinity of the mould (figure 24.14).

Fleming reasoned that the mould had secreted a chemical which was toxic to the bacteria. The mould was subsequently identified as *Penicillium notatum*, for which reason the active substance was named penicillin.

The discovery was not widely noticed at the time and Fleming himself was unable to isolate pure penicillin. It was the need for better anti-bacterial drugs during the Second World War that led to renewed interest in penicillin. In 1940 two Oxford scientists, Howard Florey and Ernst Chain, succeeded in isolating and purifying the active substance, thereby enabling it to be injected into patients. A programme of research was carried out in the USA and large-scale production of penicillin commenced within three years, using *Penicillium chrysogenum* which gave a higher yield than the original *P. notatum*.

Since the 1940s penicillin has saved countless millions of lives. It proved to be effective against numerous bacterial infections including pneumonia, meningitis, gangrene, gonorrhoea, syphilis and anthrax. Penicillin kills bacteria by preventing the synthesis of peptidoglycan, a constituent of the cell wall; this has the effect of making them 'burst' (lysis). However, it is not effective against viruses as they have a completely different structure.

Since the discovery of penicillin many more antibiotics have been isolated from a range of micro-organisms, both bacteria and fungi. These include erythromycin, streptomycin and chloramphenicol. Also a number of synthetic antibiotics have been developed, including penicillins.

Although chemotherapeutic agents have had an enormous influence on the control of disease, they have one serious drawback. Every time a new one is used, resistant strains of micro-organisms arise (see page 798). Further drugs then have to be developed. New drugs should therefore be used with restraint and discrimination.

The importance of the immune system

The immune system is essential for survival. Even with the aid of medical science, the longest time anyone has survived without an effective immune system is 12 years. In order to achieve this doctors in Houston, Texas, had to provide a microbe-free environment for a boy who was born with a severely impaired immune system. He was enclosed in a 'plastic bubble' soon after birth. He breathed filtered air and ate sterilised food and had no direct contact with anyone.

The doctors hoped to cure the boy by giving him a bone-marrow trans-

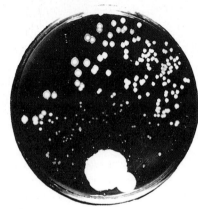

Figure 24.14 The top picture shows Fleming examining the petri dish which led to his discovery of pencillin. Below is a photograph of the contaminated petri dish (culture plate). Notice the absence of staphylococcal (bacterial) colonies (small white blobs) in the vicinity of the *Penicillium* colony (large white blob). Fleming, a Scotsman, worked at St Mary's Hospital in London. In 1945 he, together with Howard Florey and Ernst Chain, were awarded the Nobel Prize for medicine.

plant but the operation was unsuccessful. This illustrates how much we need an immune system and one that works – which thankfully it does most of the time. The plight of people with AIDS has also made this abundantly clear, for the symptoms which they develop are entirely attributable to a collapse of the immune response. This is explained in the box on page 420.

Problems arising from the immune system

Occasionally, the immune system over-reacts to a harmless foreign substance that enters the body, and sometimes it responds when we don't want it to, such as when foreign tissue is introduced into the body in transplant surgery. Let us look at these situations in detail.

Allergy

Every year millions of people suffer bouts of sneezing, running noses and itchy eyes during the pollen season – all of which are symptoms of hay fever. These unpleasant symptoms are the result of an excessive immune response or **hypersensitivity** and they constitute an **allergy**. Allergies can be induced by a variety of agents such as grass pollen, cat fur, fungal spores and certain drugs, or as a result of an insect bite. What happens is that antigens from one of these sources bind with the mast cells and are then attacked by antibodies. This causes the mast cells to produce potent chemical substances such as **histamine** which are responsible for the unpleasant symptoms.

Histamine causes dilation of the capillaries, flushing of the skin, itching, and constriction of the bronchi. It also increases the permeability of the capillaries, which results in an increase in the rate of formation of tissue fluid, causing swelling of the organs and tissues. Many of the symptoms of allergies can be attributed to histamine. One method of treating such allergies is to give the patient **anti-histamine drugs**. The normal function of histamine in the body, if it has one, is obscure.

Transplantation surgery

Transplantation surgery is an important field of medical endeavour in which great advances have been made in recent years. Indeed, **organ transplantation** is now a common operation in some hospitals.

The problem is that, despite the increasing skills of the surgeons and the use of the most up-to-date surgical techniques, many organs are **rejected**. This is because the recipient's immune system attacks and kills the foreign cells. For success the tissues of the donor and recipient must be as genetically similar as possible, which is why rejection is never seen between identical twins.

How compatible the cells of the recipient and donor are can be determined beforehand by **tissue matching**. However closely the tissues match, all patients who have transplantation surgery also receive controlled doses of various **immunosuppressive drugs**. These drugs suppress the body's normal immune response by inhibiting cell division of lymphocytes and so increasing the chances of the graft being accepted.

However, it is as well to remember that organ transplantation is a highly unnatural event which never occurs in nature. The fact that transplanted organs are rejected is merely the result of individual diversity, a reflection of the fact that every individual is genetically unique. Rejection is part and parcel of the body's normal defence against invading micro-organisms. The immune system cannot distinguish between pathogenic micro-organisms and useful tissue introduced by a well-meaning surgeon.

Figure 24.15 These two people have defective immune systems, the little boy in the top picture because he has an immune deficiency disease and the man in the bottom picture because he has been treated with immunosuppressive drugs after receiving a bone marrow transplant. Both need to be protected from possible infection while their immune systems are impaired, This is achieved by enclosing them in a sterile, germ-free atmosphere. The boy has a plastic head cover and is wearing a protective suit which keeps out pathogens but allows him to move freely and lead a more or less normal life. The man is in a sterile plastic tent, and the doctor who is examining him is wearing special clothes to pevent cross-infection.

Organ transplantation

Sir Roy Calne, a leading transplant surgeon, explains some of the problems and achievements in transplantation surgery

Since the first transplant operations were carried out in the 1960s, organ grafting has emerged from being a perilous final attempt at saving life to become the standard treatment for many major diseases of vital organs. More than 200 000 organ grafts have been performed worldwide, and results continue to improve.

The problem of rejection

The greatest problem facing the transplant surgeon is rejection of the transplanted organ. Unless special treatment is given to suppress the patient's immune system, a graft between members of the same species is rejected after 5 to 14 days. The body destroys the foreign tissue as it would a bacterium or virus. The speed of rejection depends on how closely matched the tissues of the donor and recipient are. Thus, grafts between identical twins are accepted permanently, since identical twins have the same genes and are perfectly matched. In grafts between siblings, there is a one in four chance that the main tissue types will match each other. In grafts between unrelated people, the chance of the tissues matching is remote.

The chief factors that determine rejection are the ABO blood groups and the tissue typing of the white blood cells. However, even if these are matched, rejection may still occur because there are minor tissue groups that we cannot yet identify. Therefore, in all cases except identical twins, drug treatment to prevent rejection is necessary after a transplant operation. The drugs prevent the recipient's lymphocytes attacking the graft. Their dosage needs to be carefully watched: too low a dose results in the graft being

rejected; too high a dose suppresses the immune system to such an extent that the patient readily succumbs to infection.

The surgical procedure

We can now transplant all vital organs except the brain – and even if it were possible to transplant the brain so that it functioned, the outcome would be a body grafted to the brain rather than the other way around.

Of course, the grafted organ must continue to function properly after the transplantation operation. It is therefore necessary to join up the arteries and veins of the donor organ to those of the recipient, and if the organ has a duct this must also be dealt with. Speed is essential, for the circulation to the organ must be re-established before the cells die.

Donors

For paired organs such as the kidneys, a volunteer – usually a close relative – can be a donor, provided the blood group and tissue match are satisfactory. The donor can manage with the one remaining organ. In the same way, a lobe of the liver can be removed for grafting without jeopardising the donor's health. It is even possible for a donor who happens to be receiving a combined heart-lung transplant to give his or her own heart to another patient – the so-called 'domino' operation.

However, most human transplants are taken from recently dead donors. Organs from patients dying of cancer or an infectious disease cannot be used for fear of transmitting the disease to the recipient. In practice, most donors have died from brain injury caused by trauma or haemorrhage following a ruptured brain artery. In such patients the heart can be kept beating only by ventilating the lungs with a machine. When tests make it absolutely certain that the donor's brain is irreversibly damaged, the

ventilator should be stopped since to continue resuscitation in these circumstances would be fruitless and very distressing for the relatives. If permission has been given, organs may then be removed for transplantation.

Which organs are transplanted?

Vital organs commonly grafted to replace those that have become diseased are the following:

- **Kidney**. This was the first organ to be transplanted. The donor kidney is usually placed on one side of the lower abdomen. The current success rate is encouragingly high: in cases where the donor and recipient are unrelated 80 per cent of transplanted kidneys are functioning after one year; and in cases where the kidney comes from a matched sibling, the figure is over 90 per cent. The longest survivor with graft function is over 25 years. Should a kidney graft fail, the patient can be kept in a reasonable state of health by repeated dialysis until another kidney becomes available for transplantation. Some patients have had as many as five or six kidney transplants.

- **Heart and lungs**. These are grafted in their normal positions after removal of the diseased organs. They may be grafted together or separately. Heart transplants are more successful than lung transplants since the latter are more prone to infection and rejection. Approximately 70 per cent of heart grafts, and 60 per cent of lung grafts, are functioning after one year whether they are grafted separately or together.

- **Liver**. This is the most difficult organ to transplant because of its multiple connections and complex blood supply. Moreover, in liver disease, blood clotting is impaired and serious bleeding can occur, making surgery difficult. However, the procedure has improved and 70 per cent of liver grafts are now functioning after one year. The longest survivor had the operation 23 years ago.

Suppressing the immune system

In principle, all recipients of organ grafts receive the same drugs to inhibit rejection, whatever the transplanted organ. Each drug has particular advantages and disadvantages. Their combined action is to inhibit the production or action of lymphocytes.

Patients generally receive small doses of azathioprine, corticosteroids and cyclosporin. This 'triple therapy' combines the effectiveness of all three drugs but avoids most of the more serious side effects. If rejection starts to occur, extra doses of corticosteroids or anti-lymphocyte proteins usually reverse the rejection.

For the majority of patients who respond well, their quality of life can be virtually normal. They can participate in active sports and have children, but they need to continue taking immunosuppressive drugs in low doses indefinitely. As a result, they are more susceptible to infection and cancer than normal people are.

The future

Most transplant failures are caused by the graft being rejected, or from infection resulting from excessive immunosuppression. No doubt safer and more effective drugs will be developed. As the results of organ grafting within the human species improve, efforts may be made to use organs taken from other animal species. This will introduce new moral dilemmas.

Another development will be the grafting of non-vital organs. Already, more than 2000 pancreas grafts have been performed to combat diabetes,

Illustration 1 A human liver being transported before being used in a transplant operation.

but there is controversy over whether this treatment is better than insulin-injection. The first successful bowel grafts have been reported. Grafts of testes and ovaries will raise new ethical debates!

But whatever the ethical problems, organ grafting is now an established and preferred treatment for many previously fatal diseases and its continued development will form one of the main branches of surgery.

1 *What do you think Sir Roy Calne means when he says that a brain transplant would be 'a body grafted to the brain rather than the other way round'?*

2 *Consider the ethical issues that might arise from:*
   (a) *transplanting organs from humans to other animals,*
   (b) *transplanting ovaries and testes from one human to another.*

Illustration 2 Four years after receiving a new heart, Alex Walker completes an eight-mile post round twice a day and trains at his local athletics club three times a week.

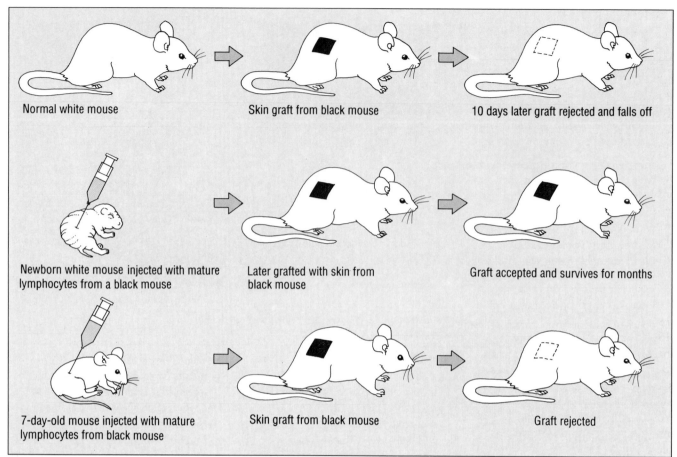

Figure 24.16 An experiment demonstrating
Sir Peter Medawar's discovery that a mouse
will accept a skin graft if it is given a dose of
the donor's cells before birth.

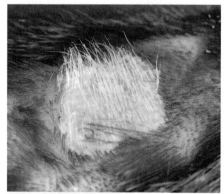

Figure 24.17 Photograph of a successful graft
of rat tail skin (white hairs) about four months
after transplantation to an adult mouse.
Normally such a graft would be rejected but in
this case the adult mouse was rendered
immunologically tolerant by means of anti-
lymphocytic serum.

Immunological tolerance

Will the body not accept foreign tissue under any circumstances? The answer is that it will, provided that the formation of antibodies against it is first prevented. One way of achieving this is to introduce some of the foreign tissue into the recipient before, or very soon after, birth.

This was first discovered by Sir Peter Medawar who injected cells obtained from an adult mouse into a fetus. He found that, after birth, the recipient accepted, permanently, grafts of skin and other tissues from the donor. The recipient had been made **immunologically tolerant** to the donor's tissues by receiving a prenatal injection of the donor's cells. For this achievement Medawar, together with Burnet (the originator of the clonal selection theory), was awarded a Nobel Prize for medicine in 1960. Figure 24.16 summarises Medawar's discovery.

Since then a number of agents capable of inducing immunological tolerance have been developed. These include a preparation made by inducing lymphocytes into a horse and collecting, then purifying, the antibodies produced. The resulting **anti-lymphocytic serum** is capable of destroying the original lymphocytes to such an extent that an animal treated with the serum will subsequently accept grafts from another individual (figure 24.17).

Blood groups

We have seen that living material introduced deliberately into the body may be treated by the recipient as 'foreign' and rejected by the immune system. The same sort of thing occurs when blood is transferred from one person to another.

The ABO system

The entire human population can be divided into four groups on the basis of the reaction between the blood of different individuals when mixed together. These groups are called **A, B, AB** and **O** and they are known collectively as the **ABO system**. The capital letters stand for different types of glycoproteins present on the surface of the person's red cells. These glycoproteins are antigens, similar to those found on the surface of bacteria. We all make antibodies against foreign antigens, but not of course against those on our own red cells.

The antibodies are called **anti-A** and **anti-B**. If an individual has a particular antigen on the red cells, the corresponding antibody is not present in the plasma. Thus a person belonging to blood group **A** has red cells with **A** antigens on them; the plasma does not then contain **anti-A** antibodies, but it does contain **anti-B** antibodies. A person belonging to blood group **B** has **B** antigens on the red cells and the plasma contains **anti-A** antibodies only. In blood group **AB** the red cells carry both antigens **A** and **B** and neither antibodies are present in the plasma. Group **O** blood has neither antigens but both antibodies.

Figure 24.18 summarises what happens when blood of different groups are mixed together in a transfusion. All is well provided that the recipient's blood does not contain antibodies that will bind to the donor's red cell antigens. If it does, the donor's red cells are linked together by the antibodies, forming clumps which may block the recipient's blood vessels. This is called **agglutination**. For example, if blood of group A is given to a patient of blood group B, the anti-A antibodies in the patient's blood will cause agglutination of the donor's red cells because they carry the A antigen. It does not matter that the donor's antibodies (anti-B) are incompatible with the recipient's antigens (B) because the recipient receives relatively little blood and the dilution effect minimises agglutination.

The Rhesus system

In addition to the ABO system there are many other antigens on human red blood cells. One of these is the **Rhesus antigen**, so-called because it was first discovered by injecting rabbits with red blood cells obtained from the Rhesus monkey. The majority of people possess red blood cells with the Rhesus antigen present, and they are known as **Rhesus-positive (Rh+)**. The remainder lack the rhesus antigen and are called **Rhesus-negative (Rh-)**.

Unlike the ABO system, Rhesus-negative blood does not already contain anti-Rhesus antibodies. However, if Rhesus-positive blood finds its way into a Rhesus-negative recipient, the latter responds by producing the corresponding anti-Rhesus antibodies.

Fortunately it takes about a week for the antibodies to appear in the bloodstream, by which time all the donated red cells will have died – so no harm results. But if a Rhesus-negative recipient subsequently receives another dose of Rhesus-positive blood, the anti-Rhesus antibodies already present will bring about a much faster and more intense response causing agglutination of the donor's red cells, often with fatal results. This can occur during pregnancy. The trouble starts when a Rhesus-negative mother bears a Rhesus-positive child. Sometimes during labour, fragments of the fetus's red blood cells, containing the Rhesus antigen, pass across the placenta into the mother's bloodstream. The mother responds by producing anti-Rhesus antibodies which pass back across the placenta into the fetal circulation. Generally the antibodies are not formed sufficiently quickly or in sufficient amounts to affect the first child, but a subsequent Rhesus-positive child will suffer from massive destruction of red blood cells.

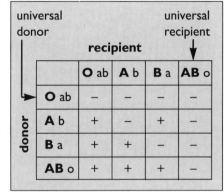

	recipient			
	O ab	**A** b	**B** a	**AB** o
O ab	−	−	−	−
A b	+	−	+	−
B a	+	+	−	−
AB o	+	+	+	−

Figure 24.18 Summary of reactions that occur when bloods of different groups are mixed. + agglutination; − no agglutination. The capital letters refer to antigens on the red blood cells, small letters to antibodies in the plasma. A universal donor (group O) can give blood to a recipient of any group without causing agglutination. A universal recipient (group AB) can receive blood from a donor of any group without agglutination. In practice blood transfusions are normally carried out using blood which belongs to the same group as that of the recipient. The group to which a sample of blood belongs is determined by a compatibility test.

Preventing haemolytic disease

One way of preventing haemolytic disease would be to stop the mother producing anti-Rhesus antibodies in response to the Rhesus antigens which she has received from the fetus. Immunologists have now developed a way of doing this. When the first Rhesus-positive child is born the Rhesus negative mother is injected with anti-Rhesus antibodies. These coat the fetal cells and destroy them before the mother's immune system has time to resond. The injected anti-Rhesus antibodies only last in the mother's blood for a few weeks, so they do not affect subsequent pregnancies.

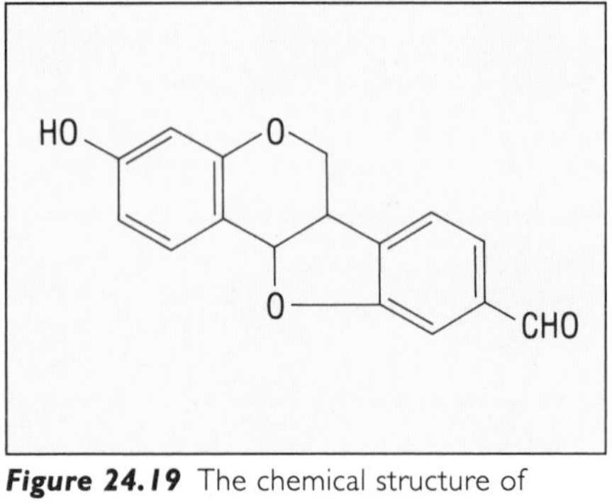

Figure 24.19 The chemical structure of medicarpin, a phytoalexin produced by the broad bean and other leguminous plants in response to infection by fungi. About 20 phytoalexins have been identified and most of them are phenolic ring compounds of the kind shown here. Each species of plant produces one or two particular phytoalexins which, unlike antibodies, are not specific and will attack a wide range of fungal infections.

Figure 24.20 A cell of French bean following attempted infection by a pathogenic fungus. The growth of the fungus has been totally inhibited by phytoloalexins produced by the cell. Magnification × 900.

This condition is known as **haemolytic disease of the newborn**. As a result, the newborn baby suffers from acute anaemia and is very breathless as a result of shortage of oxygen; the baby also appears yellow as a result of the breakdown of its haemoglobin into other pigments.

Haemolytic disease used to be a major cause of death in newborn infants and was treated by replacing the child's blood with a complete transfusion of Rhesus negative blood. A more modern method of prevention is explained in the box alongside.

Plant defences against disease

Plants do not possess phagocytes or an immune system. However, that does not mean that they have no means of protection against disease. Just like animals they have all sorts of protective devices (thick cuticle, hairs, thick bark and the like) which make it difficult for micro-organisms to get in. If a vascular plant is damaged the wound becomes plugged by a mass of undifferentiated parenchyma cells called **callus tissue** and/or by protective chemicals such as resins which prevent the entry of micro-organisms. In fact plants produce a bewildering array of chemicals. At one time they were thought to be excretory products but many of them are now known to have defence functions

Diseases such as rust in wheat and potato blight are the cause of serious losses in yield. One way of overcoming these diseases is to produce strains of the crop which are resistant to the disease. This is the job of plant breeders and considerable success has been achieved in this area.

Many plants, however, seem to possess a natural resistance to fungal infection and this may be connected with the presence of protective chemicals within their cells. One of these natural fungicides has been identified and given the name **wyerone** as its structure was established at Wye College in Kent. Many other such substances occur naturally and may play a part in disease resistance in plants.

In the 1940s the first evidence for an active defence mechanism in plants was found. Substances were discovered which were produced in response to fungal attack, and they were given the name **phytoalexins**. In recent years the structure of many phytoalexins has been established. The formula of one of them is given in figure 24.19.

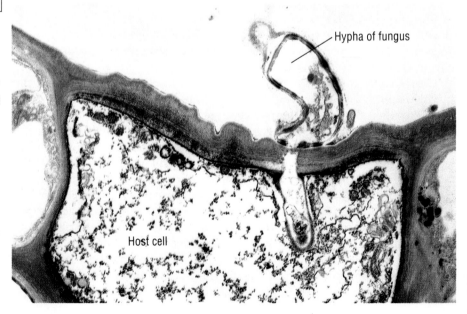

Hypha of fungus

Host cell

One of the first phytoalexins to be characterised was called **pisatin** as it was extracted from peas (*Pisum sp*). Healthy pea tissues do not contain pisatin. However, when inoculated with a spore suspension of a fungus and incubated, pisatin was found to be present in the pea tissues. Phytoalexins are certainly produced in response to infection and the indications are that they are an important aspect of defence in plants. Figure 24.20 shows the effect of one of them.

Phytoalexins are not the only way in which plants are protected against disease, but they do suggest that there is a system, analogous to antibody production in animals, in which chemicals are produced in response to infection. Disease resistance in plants is a complex subject in which much research is being undertaken at the present time.

Excretion or defence?

Plant substances which were once regarded as excretory products are now known to have defence functions. Tim King explains.

The vacuole in a plant cell serves as a toxic waste dump. Poisonous compounds are extracted from the delicate metabolic reactions in the cytoplasm and isolated in the vacuole. These compounds include various hydrocarbons and also tannins, abundant in oak leaves and tea leaves. Less complex compounds are also found, such as the calcium oxalate crystals shown in the illustration.

It might be tempting to regard these chemicals as excretory products. However, they are energetically expensive to produce – the seedlings of a tropical tree may devote as much as ten per cent of its energy expenditure to their manufacture. It therefore seems sensible to propose that they have a function of some kind.

We now know that these substances provide a defence against attack by herbivores and parasites. It has recently been demonstrated that plant cells increase the production of such compounds when the surrounding tissues are attacked. Moreover, wounding triggers the release of gaseous ethene which increases the production of defence substances not only by that plant but

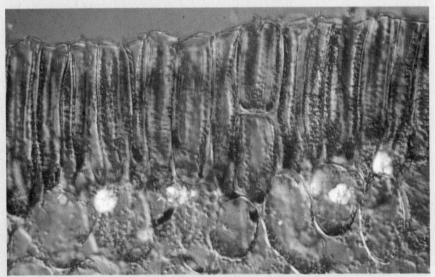

Calcium oxalate crystals in the leaf cells of *Begonia*. The leaf has been sectioned transversely and crystals can be seen in both the palisade and spongy mesophyll cells as translucent dots. Such crystals are found in a number of plant species and they may help to defend the plant against micro-organisms and/or herbivores. Magnification × 300.

by neighbouring plants too.

Leaf fall may also be important in defence against disease. There are many reasons for leaf fall, but one is that it disposes of old leaves that may have become infected.

Imagine you are a parasite about to attack a tree. Which parts of the tree would you go for? Mature leaves may be protected by some of the compounds already mentioned. The obvious targets are the young leaves and buds, and the secondary phloem just beneath the bark. Trees secrete a wide range of gums, resins and latexes when the bark is breached.

These seal the wound, prevent the loss of valuable compounds and reduce the chance of infection or attack by parasites and herbivores.

Once collected, these compounds have wide-ranging industrial applications. From them we get such products as turpentine, paints and varnishes, soaps and cosmetics, surgical goods, foods, golf balls, bubble gum and rubber. The story of rubber is told on page 393.

How would you test the hypothesis that the calcium oxalate crystals in the illustration have a defence function?

Smallpox: the rise and fall of a disease

Smallpox has been known for thousands of years. It is described in the earliest literature and occurred, often in epidemic proportions, throughout the world. First recorded in Britain in the 13th century, there were particulary severe outbreaks in Britain and her North American colonies during the 18th century. In 1796 a breakthrough in the control and prevention of the disease was achieved by Edward Jenner with his discovery of a vaccine (see page 422). At first his ideas were derided by the medical establishment, but Jenner persisted and vaccination was eventually adopted first in Britain and soon afterwards in other countries. Napoleon had all his troops vaccinated, the Empress of Russia decreed that her subjects should receive universal vaccination and Thomas Jefferson, President of the United States, had his family vaccinated.

The disease is caused by a virus called *Variola*, of which the most virulent type, *Variola major*, was responsible for killing up to 25 per cent of sufferers before vaccination

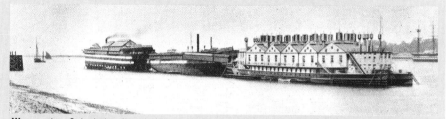

Illustration 2 Isolation hospitals were built well away from the general population. The picture shows a floating hospital on the River Thames around 1900. Buildings were erected on barges to house the sick.

got underway. The symptoms were rather like those of influenza: high temperature, headache and muscle pains. This was accompanied by an outbreak of pus-filled blisters on the skin (illustration 1). These pustules erupted, discharged and then scabbed over within about three weeks. Survivors of smallpox were often left with permanent disfiguring pock marks.

A highly infectious disease, smallpox was spread in a number of ways, not all of them fully understood. The virus was present in the patient's urine and faeces as well as in the skin pustules and throat, and one of the main routes of infection was through inhalation. Without vaccination everyone was vulnerable. If a case of smallpox was diagnosed the area medical officer of health had to be notified and the patient confined in an isolation hospital (illustration 2). Anyone in contact with a smallpox case had to be quarantined and vaccinated.

Babies were particulary susceptible to the disease and in Britain compulsory vaccination of all children under the age of three years was instituted in 1853 and continued until 1948. This certainly produced results: in 1901 there were 356 deaths from smallpox in Britain, in 1956 there were none.

During the 1950s a worldwide vaccination programme was established by the World Health Organisation, its aim being to provide everyone with lifelong immunity from smallpox. This led to a dramatic fall in the incidence of the disease. In May 1980 the World Health Organisation announced officially that smallpox had been eradicated from the world.

The conquering of smallpox is a success story in medicine. It is ironical that only a year after it was declared extinct, the first case of AIDS, a *new* disease, was reported. The struggle to combat disease, in all its formidable complexity, continues.

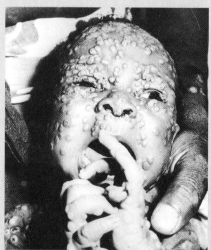

Illustration 1 A baby with smallpox, showing the pustules typical of this disease. The head and limbs were particulary affected by the pustular rash which also spread into the mouth and throat.

Illustration 3 The public were kept away from areas where there were cases of smallpox. The picture shows a public road in England during an outbreak of the disease in the early 1950s.

Summary

1 The destruction of pathogens and/or the neutralisation of toxic substances produced by them is an important aspect of homeostasis.

2 The body of an organism is defended from infection by preventing the entry of pathogenic organisms and/or destroying them after they have entered.

3 Preventing entry is achieved by means of **barriers**, e.g. skin and clotting of blood; **rejection**, e.g. coughing; and **destruction**, e.g. lysozyme in external secretions. Artificial methods include **antisepsis** and **asepsis**.

4 Destruction of micro-organisms, once they are inside the body, is the responsibility of the **immune system**.

5 Phagocytosis is carried out by white blood cells called phagocytes and contributes, with **complement**, to **natural (non-specific) immunity**.

6 The other type of immunity is **adaptive** or **acquired immunity** and this is the function of white blood cells called **lymphocytes**.

7 There are two kinds of lymphocyte. **B lymphocytes** give rise to humoral immunity and this involves the production of **antibodies** in response to antigens.

8 B lymphocytes divide to form clones. Each clone produces one type of antibody which recognises, and attacks, a specific antigen.

9 Large quantities of **monoclonal antibodies** can now be made in the laboratory.

10 **T lymphocytes** give rise to **cell-mediated immunity**. There are several types of T lymphocytes with different functions. They acquire their immune function in the thymus gland.

11 Artificial immunity may be conferred on an animal by active or passive means depending on whether the animal is stimulated to produce its own antibodies or receives ready-made antibodies from an external source.

12 An enhanced immunological response occurs if the body receives a second dose of antigen soon after the first.

13 Sometimes an excessive immune response occurs to a harmless antigen, causing damage to the tissues. This is called an **allergy**.

14 An unfortunate aspect of the cell-mediated immune response is that foreign tissue introduced into a recipient in a transplantation operation is usually rejected. The use of **immunosuppressive drugs** increases the chance of a transplant being accepted.

15 A graft is accepted by the recipient if cells from the donor are introduced into the recipient before, or soon after, birth. The recipient then becomes **immuno-logically tolerant** to the donor's cells.

16 An immune reaction occurs when blood belonging to two incompatible groups in the ABO system is mixed.

17 An immune response is also seen when **Rhesus-positive** and **Rhesus-negative** bloods come into contact. In certain situations this occurs during pregnancy, resulting in **haemolytic disease of the newborn**.

18 Other efforts to combat disease include the use of **chemotherapeutic agents** such as antibiotic drugs.

19 Plant defences against disease-causing micro-organisms include various **protective devices** (e.g. cuticle), the formation of **callus tissue** and the production of **phytoalexins**.

Review questions

1 Summarise the physical and chemical barriers which the human body has against invading pathogens.

2 Describe phagocytosis. What are its limitations?

3 Explain the difference between natural and adaptive immunity.

4 Explain what is meant by the terms *specificity* and *memory* in relation to the immune system.

5 Explain the role of B and T lymphocytes in the body's defence against disease.

6 Using information given in this chapter, suggest why we do not launch an immune attack against our own organs and tissues.

7 Explain how immunisation prevents disease.

8 Why is transplantation surgery beset with so many difficulties?

9 What barriers do flowering plants possess to combat infection?

10 What are phytoalexins? How might they act in preventing infection in plants.

Further reading

Of all the topics in biology, immunology is probably the most rapidly advancing. To keep abreast of developments you should look at current issues of periodicals such as *Biological Sciences Review* and *Scientific American*.

An extremely useful summary of the immune system is to be found in the booklet *Immunology* by Basiro Davey, published by the Biochemical Society in 1990.

Monclonal antibodies and the generation of antibody diversity are discussed in detail in *Biology, Advanced Topics*.

Part V

RESPONSE AND COORDINATION

To survive, an organism must react to changes in its external environment. This necessitates having mechanisms for detecting such changes and bringing about appropriate responses. Since the structures that detect changes may be a long way from those that respond, a means of rapid communication within the body is required.

In animals rapid internal communication is achieved by means of a nervous system, and the first chapter in this part of the book contains a detailed account of the nervous system and how it coordinates our responses. An alternative means of communication is provided by hormones which are discussed in the next chapter.

How environmental stimuli are monitored and the information fed into the nervous system is then explained with particular reference to the mammalian ear and eye. The way animals respond to information transmitted through the nervous system is discussed with reference mainly to the contraction of muscle.

An animal's response to stimuli may involve complex locomotory movements and behaviour patterns. These are explained and illustrated in the final two chapters.

Photograph: A competitor dives off the high board in the Olympic Games, Barcelona, 1992.

CHAPTER 25 Nervous communication

It is important that in a complex animal like the human changes in the external environment should be instantly detected and appropriate signals sent quickly to the relevant parts of the body. It is also important that within the body different organs should be able to communicate with each other rapidly. This rapid communication is achieved by the **nervous system**.

The nervous system is composed of **nerve cells (neurones)** which transmit messages, or **impulses** as they are called, from **receptors** to **effectors**. In general terms, the receptors detect changes in the environment (**stimuli**), and the effectors – usually muscles – produce a **response**.

Receptors and effectors are dealt with in Chapters 27 and 28. In this chapter we shall look at the nervous system and how it works.

General organisation of the nervous system

The main parts of the human nervous system are shown in figure 25.1 and summarised in table 25.1. In keeping with the nervous system of other vertebrates, the system is subdivided into two main parts, the **central nervous system (CNS)** and the **peripheral nervous system**. The CNS is made up of the **brain** and **spinal cord**.

The peripheral nervous system consists of the numerous **nerves** which link the CNS with the receptors and effectors. They are subdivided into two groups: **spinal nerves** connected to the spinal cord, and **cranial nerves** connected to the brain. The spinal nerves are associated with receptors and effectors in the trunk, including the arms and legs, whereas all but one of the cranial nerves are associated with receptors and effectors in the head and neck.

Peripherally each nerve splits into branches which serve the receptors and effectors in that region of the body. In the trunk the spinal nerves are gathered together to form large compound nerves which go to the limbs – the **brachial nerves** to the arms, and the **sciatic nerves** to the legs.

The cranial nerves are fewer in number than the spinal nerves; humans, in keeping with other mammals, have twelve on each side. Those supplying the mouth and jaws are like the spinal nerves in that they serve receptors *and* effectors. The other cranial nerves serve either receptors or effectors, but not both. For example, the **optic nerves** are connected only to the eyes, and the **auditory nerves** to the ears.

The only cranial nerve that serves structures outside the head and neck is the **vagus**, the 'wandering' nerve. This nerve emerges from the posterior part of the brain and passes down the neck to the thorax and abdomen, giving off branches to various receptors and effectors. The vagus is part of the **autonomic nervous system** which we shall discuss at the end of this chapter. For the moment we shall concentrate on how the nervous system enables us to respond to stimuli.

Reflex action

A reflex action is an immediate, short-lived response to a stimulus, brought about by the nervous system. In humans the withdrawal of the hand from a hot object is an example. Another example is the rapid straightening of the leg when the tendon just below the knee is tapped. This familiar **knee jerk** is important clinically; abnormalities of it are used for diagnosing certain disorders of the nervous system.

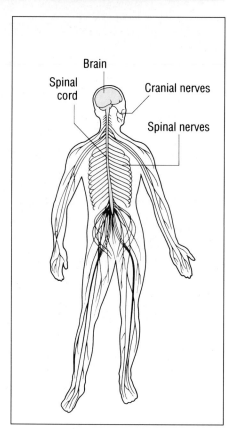

Figure 25.1 General plan of the human nervous system. In reality the brain is encased within the cranium (part of the skull) and the spinal cord is surrounded by the vertebral column. In this diagram the skeletal structures are not shown, so the central nervous system is exposed to view.

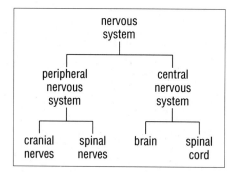

Table 25.1 Structural subdivisions of the nervous system of a vertabrate

The structural basis of reflex action is the **reflex arc**. This is the series of structures along which impulses travel when they bring about a reflex response.

The structure of a generalised reflex arc

A generalised reflex arc is shown in figure 25.2. It starts with a **receptor** which leads to a **sensory neurone** in a peripheral nerve. Inside the CNS the sensory neurone is linked to a **connector neurone**. This in turn is linked to an **effector neurone**. The effector neurone extends into a peripheral nerve and goes to an **effector**. The point where one neurone links up with the next one is called a **synapse**.

To bring about a reflex action, impulses have to travel through the reflex arc from the receptor to the effector via the structures in between, including the synapses. There is always a very slight delay between the moment that a receptor is stimulated and the onset of the response. This is due to the time that it takes for impulses to through the reflex arc.

This general description of a reflex arc applies to any animal with a CNS. It applies to worms, insects and fish just as it does to humans. Of course there are variations on the theme. For example, there may be several connector neurones, one after the other. And in the human knee jerk there is no connector neurone at all: the sensory neurone is linked directly to the motor neurone.

A human reflex arc

Suppose you tread on a nail. You respond by quickly pulling your leg away. The reflex arc involved in this response is illustrated in figure 25.3. The neurones are located in one of the spinal nerves serving the leg. This nerve, in common with other spinal nerves, splits into two just outside the spinal cord to which it is therefore attached by two connections, a **dorsal root** and a **ventral root**.

The receptors in this reflex are free nerve endings in the skin of the foot, just under the epidermis, and they give rise to the sensation of pain. They are usually referred to simply as pain receptors. The main effector is the

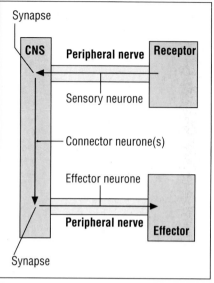

Figure 25.2 Schematic diagram showing the basic components of a typical reflex arc. There is much variation in the number of neurones between the receptor and effector. In the simplet reflexes a sensory neurone connects directly with an effector neurone, but in most cases sensory and effector neurones are linked by at least one connector neurone.

Figure 25.3 Diagrammatic cross section of the spinal cord to illustrate the main reflex arc involved in the response to treading on a nail. The arrows indicate the direction in which impulses are transmitted through the nervous system.

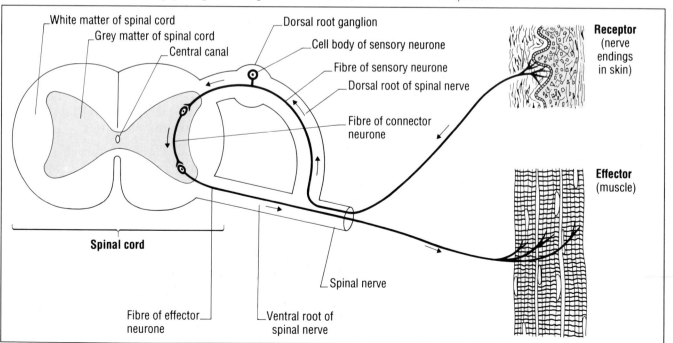

flexor muscle at the back of the leg – when it contracts the leg bends (flexes) at the knee. The neurones in this reflex arc possess a **cell body** and an elongated **nerve fibre** which transmits the impulses. We shall look at the detailed structure of these neurones in a moment – here we are simply concerned with the course they take in the reflex arc.

The fibre of the sensory neurone enters the spinal cord via the dorsal root. The cell body of this neurone is located in the **dorsal root ganglion**, a swelling of the dorsal root. The ganglion contains the cell bodies of many other sensory neurones besides this one, which is why it is swollen. In the **grey matter** of the spinal cord the sensory neurone makes synaptic connection with the connector neurone. This in turn makes synaptic connection with the effector neurone which passes out of the spinal cord in the ventral root and supplies the flexor muscle.

With this anatomical picture in mind let us trace how the response is brought about. Stimulation of the pain receptors in the skin fires off impulses in the sensory neurone. The impulses enter the spinal cord, travel along the connector neurone, and leave the cord in the effector neurone. Very quickly the impulses reach the flexor muscle which then contracts.

Some complications

Think about this response for a moment. There are several things about it which give us important information about reflex action.

- First, the response involves the contraction of other muscles in the leg besides the flexor already mentioned. For example, certain muscles bend the leg at the hip, and others flex the foot. These muscles augment the action of the knee flexor and make the overall response more effective. Obviously impulses must be sent to these muscles at the same time as they are sent to the knee flexor.

- Second, most of the muscles in the leg, as in other parts of the body, are in pairs and the action of one opposes the action of the other (see page 515). Thus the flexor muscle which bends the leg is opposed by an **extensor muscle** which stretches the leg. Plainly when the flexor contracts, the extensor must relax. So when impulses are sent to the flexor they must *stop* being sent to the extensor.

- Third, the response may involve muscles in other parts of the body besides the leg. For example, you might jump back and let out a cry. This would involve the muscles of the back, arms and larynx, necessitating the spread of impulses to reflex arcs other than those that deal with the leg. More importantly, various muscles will adjust your posture so that you do not fall over when your leg is withdrawn from the ground.

From these observations we may conclude that different reflex arcs are connected with each other. Careful examination of the nerve pathways in the spinal cord show that this is indeed the case. Different reflex arcs are interconnected by neurones whose fibres run longitudinally in the **white matter** of the spinal cord. These neurones form nerve tracts which not only connect different reflex arcs together but also connect them with the brain. Some of the tracts carry impulses up the spinal cord to the brain. Others carry impulses down the cord from the brain.

In bringing about a full response the synapses play a crucial part, for they determine which particular muscles will contract. For example, when you flex your leg, a synapse in the pathway leading to the extensor muscle is automatically inhibited. This ensures that when the flexor muscle contracts the extensor relaxes (figure 25.4).

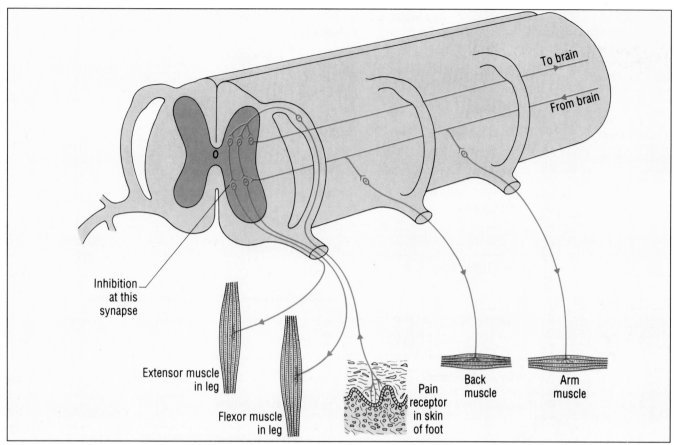

Inhibition at this synapse

Extensor muscle in leg

Flexor muscle in leg

Pain receptor in skin of foot

Back muscle

Arm muscle

The brain ensures that the correct muscles contract or relax at the right moment. This process is called **coordination**. If a simple reflex like withdrawing your foot from a nail requires coordination, think how much more is needed for activities like walking and running – or ballet dancing (figure 25.5). We shall have more to say about the coordinating role of the brain later. But first we must turn our attention to the basic units of the nervous system, namely the neurones.

Figure 25.4 Simplified diagram of part of the spinal cord showing the pathways through which impulses are transmitted in bringing about a full response to treading on a nail. The arrows indicate the direction of transmission of impulses. Transmission occurs across all the synapses shown except for the one in the pathway leading to the extensor muscle. This synapse is temporarily blocked (inhibited) while the reflex is in progress.

Figure 25.5 A very high level of nervous coordination is needed by these ballet dancers.

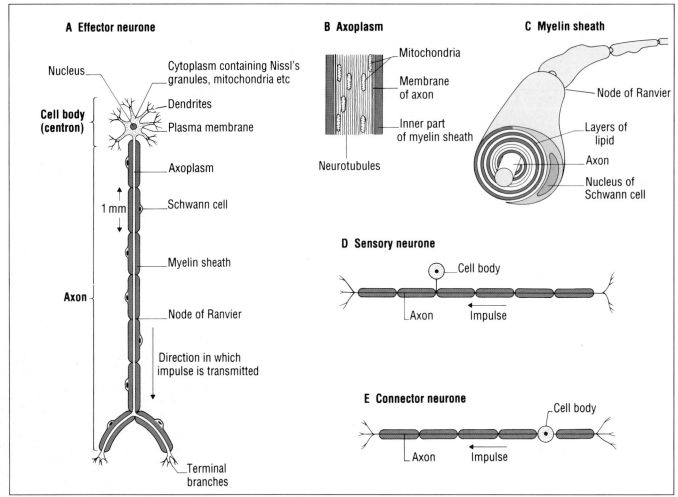

Figure 25.6 The structure of neurones (nerve cells).

A Effector neurone. The dendrites make contact with other neurones in the spinal cord. The terminal branches at the far end of the axon are connected to an effector.

B Detail of the axoplasm as seen in the electron microscope. Proteins synthesised in the cell body are transported along slender microtubules, here called neurotubules.

C Detail of the myelin sheath. The electron microscope shows the sheath to consist of layers of lipid, formed by an extension of the plasma membrane of the Schwann cell which wraps itself round the axon.

D Sensory neurone. The cell body is at the end of a short stalk to one side of the main conducting fibre. The branches at the right hand end are connected to the receptor.

E Connector neurone. The branches at both ends are connected to other neurones.

The structure of neurones

An effector neurone can be taken to illustrate the structure of a typical neurone (figure 25.6A). The **cell body** contains the nucleus and cytoplasm. Slender processes called **dendrites** extend from the cell body, like the branches of a tree, and make synaptic contact with other neurones. Also extending from the cell body is a long **nerve fibre** which transmits impulses to the effector. A nerve fibre which transmits impulses away from the cell body, as this one does, is called an **axon**.

Despite its specialised shape, the neurone possesses the same basic features as other animal cells. The cell body is enclosed within a plasma membrane, and the cytoplasm contains the usual range of organelles. Ribosomes are particularly prominent and, as in other cells, they are the site of protein synthesis. The cell body has a high rate of protein synthesis because it has to supply proteins to the axon. A human axon can be over a metre long, so the axon adds greatly to the total volume of the cell.

The axon's job is to transmit impulses to the effector. It is filled with cytoplasm, here called **axoplasm**, which is continuous with the cytoplasm in the cell body. The axoplasm lacks ribosomes, so it cannot make its own proteins; instead, the cell body makes the proteins which are then transported along the axon to where they are needed. The axoplasm contains numerous microtubules which are involved in this transport process (figure 25.6B).

The axon is bounded by a plasma membrane continuous with that of the cell body. Outside the plasma membrane there is usually a fatty **myelin sheath**. This is not part of the nerve cell itself, but is formed by a series of accessory cells called **Schwann cells**. Each Schwann cell wraps itself round the axon like a Swiss roll (figure 25.6C). Where one Schwann cell ends and the next one begins, the myelin sheath is absent. These points occur at regular intervals along the axon and are called **nodes of Ranvier**. They are approximately one millimetre apart. The function of the myelin sheath is to insulate the axon and speed up the transmission of impulses along it. Later we shall see how this is done.

Many other types of neurone are found in the nervous system. They vary in shape and the number of dendrites, but their basic structure is similar to the effector neurone just described. Figure 25.6 includes a sensory and connector neurone from the spinal cord for comparison with the effector neurone.

In addition to the Schwann cells already mentioned, various other accessory cells are found in the nervous system. The collective name for these is **glia**. Some, like the Schwann cells, form myelin sheaths around the axons. Others support and protect the neurones, or form scar tissue following damage.

From a functional point of view, the most important part of the neurone is the nerve fibre, for it is this that carries the impulses upon which the functioning of the nervous system depends. What exactly is a nerve impulse and how is it transmitted?

The nature of the nerve impulse

It gradually became clear many years ago that the impulse transmitted by an axon is an electrical phenomenon and that in certain respects an axon is like an electric cable. In fact nerve impulses can be recorded and measured using an apparatus which is sensitive to small electrical changes. Such an instrument is the **cathode ray oscilloscope** illustrated in figure 25.7. Impulses are picked up from the nerve through a pair of electrodes and fed into an oscilloscope on whose screen they appear as 'spikes'. The oscilloscope incorporates an amplifier which enlarges the signals. This is necessary because the electrical change associated with a typical nerve impulse is very small – a mere 50 millivolts or so.

The oscilloscope has been used extensively by neurophysiologists to measure the magnitude and speed of transmission of impulses, and to analyse the pattern of impulses generated in different parts of the nervous system. But useful though this information is, it tells us little about the fundamental nature of the nerve impulse.

What we really need to know is what happens to an axon when an impulse passes along it. This has proved a difficult question to answer mainly because most axons are very fine, rarely exceeding 20 μm in diameter. This makes them too small to see, let alone do experiments on. But fortunately certain animals possess axons which are exceptionally large – so large in fact that they are called **giant axons**. One such animal is the squid. The largest of its giant axons is about a millimetre in diameter – still small, but big enough for a neurophysiologist to do something with.

The last fifty years have seen major advances in our understanding of the nerve impulse. These advances have been due in large part to some remarkable experiments on the giant axons of the squid, pioneered by Alan Hodgkin and Andrew Huxley at Cambridge. Sir Andrew tells the story himself in the box on page 444. Basically what they did was to insert a very

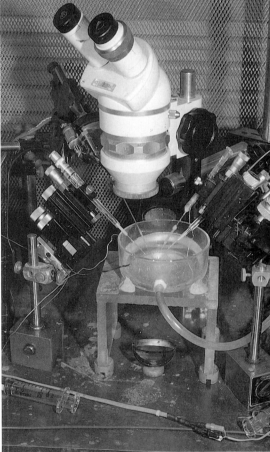

Figure 25.7 Dr Peter Skorupski prepares to record nerve impulses from nerve tissue. In the top picture two oscilloscopes and an amplifier can be seen on Peter's right, and the preparation dish containing the nerve tissue is on the bench behind him. Below is a close-up view of the preparation dish and recording electrodes. The metal cage shields the electrodes from mains interference.

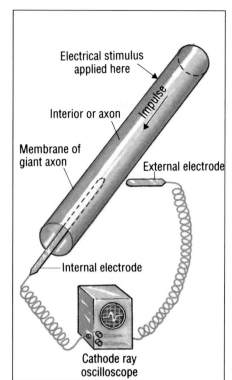

Electrical stimulus
applied here

Interior or axon

Impulse

Membrane of
giant axon

External electrode

Internal electrode

Cathode ray
oscilloscope

Figure 25.8 How the nerve impulse was investigated by Hodgkin and Huxley. One microelectrode is inserted into the interior of the giant axon of a squid. The other microelectrode is placed outside the membrane surrounding the axon. The electrodes are connected to a cathode ray oscilloscope. Electrical activity is recorded when the axon is resting and also when it transmits impulses generated by applying an electrical stimulus to the right hand end.

Figure 25.9 Summary of the events that occur in the giant axon at rest and during passage of an impulse. The top part of the picture shows the resting and action potentials as they appear on the screen of an oscilloscope. The lower part shows the electrical charges inside and outside the membrane, together with the movement of sodium and potassium ions across the membrane at rest and during passage of the action potential (the red area). Notice that the entry into the axon of sodium ions, which initiates the action potential, is followed by a loss of potassium ions. This causes the resting potential to be restored. Depolarisation of the membrane corresponds to the rising phase of the action potential, repolarisation to the falling phase.

fine **microelectrode** into the axon, and place another one outside the axon close to the membrane (figure 25.8). This enabled them to record differences in electrical potential *across* the membrane. The electrodes were connected to an oscilloscope for recording the potentials. The following account of the nerve impulse is based on Hodgkin and Huxley's discoveries.

The electrical nature of the nerve impulse

When the axon is at rest, that is when it is *not* transmitting an impulse, a potential difference of approximately 70 mV exists between the inside and the outside of the axon, the inside being negative relative to the outside. As this is the situation when the axon is at rest, it is called the **resting potential**. It shows that the membrane is *polarised* – that is, it is able to maintain a potential difference between its two sides.

When an impulse passes the electrodes, the resting potential is momentarily reversed and the inside becomes positive relative to the outside. This sudden reversal of the resting potential is called the **action potential**. The term used for the electrical change which occurs during the passage of the action potential is **depolarisation**, and we say that the membrane has been *depolarised*.

The resting and action potentials, as recorded with an oscilloscope, are shown in the top part of figure 25.9. As you can see from the time scale, the action potential is extremely short-lived. It lasts about a millisecond (one thousandth of a second), after which the resting potential is restored.

The ionic basis of the impulse

Later experiments provided an ionic explanation of the electrical events described in the last section. Several approaches have been used. For example, the axoplasm has been extracted from giant axons and analysed chemically. Another technique is to replace some of the ions in the axon with their radioactive isotopes, and then trace their movements across the axon membrane in resting conditions and during transmission of impulses. Here too, it is the large size of the giant axons which makes this sort of experiment possible.

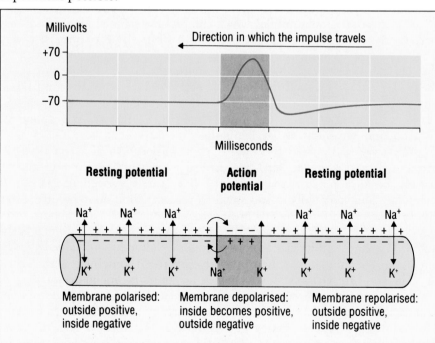

The results of these investigations are summarised in the lower part of figure 25.9. When the axon is at rest, the concentrations of ions on the two sides of the membrane are different. There is an excess of potassium ions inside the axon and of sodium ions outside. This difference is maintained by the active pumping of sodium ions out of the axon and potassium ions into it. We have met this process before – it is called the **sodium-potassium pump** and is what happens in other animal cells (see page 194).

The sodium-potassium pump works in such a way that three sodium ions are expelled for every two potassium ions admitted. Moreover, some of the potassium ions leak back out agin. The result is that there is a slight surplus of negative ions inside the axon, making the inside of the axon negative relative to the outside: this is the resting potential. Only a very slight excess of negative ions inside the axon is required to create the resting potential, though in practice it may be enhanced by the presence inside the axon of negative organic ions to which the membrane is impermeable.

When an impulse passes along the axon the membrane suddenly becomes permeable to sodium ions which, being about ten times more concentrated outside the membrane, begin to diffuse into the axon. This depolarises the membrane and reverses the resting potential. The inside of the axon now becomes positive and the outside negative: this is the action potential.

As sodium ions enter the axon, potassium ions begin to leave. This marks the beginning of the recovery process in which the inside of the axon regains its negative charge. However, we now have some sodium ions inside the axon which must be got rid of sooner or later or the system will run down. This is achieved by the sodium-potassium pump which expels the sodium ions and brings in potassium ions, thus restoring the distribution of ions which normally exists when the axon is at rest.

So we see how an action potential develops in an axon, but what causes it to pass along the axon from one end to the other? The answer lies in the distribution of ions at the leading end of the action potential (figure 25.10). On each side of the membrane positive and negative ions lie alongside each other. This creates local electrical currents which depolarise the next section of the membrane. In this way the action potential passes along the axon rather like fire spreads along a trail of gunpowder.

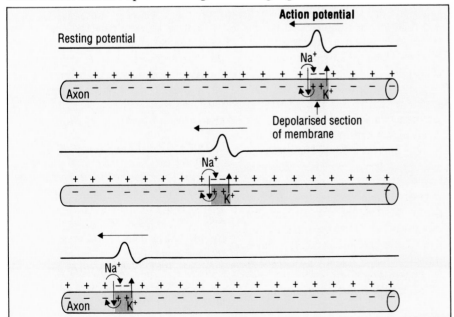

Figure 25.10 This diagram shows three stages in the transmission of an impulse along an axon. The action potential (the red area) is transmitted as a wave of depolarisation which spreads rapidly along the axon. Local currents at the leading end of the action potential (curved arrows) cause depolarisation of the next section of the membrane, so the action potential propagates itself along the axon.

Unravelling the nature of the nerve impulse

Guest author Sir Andrew Huxley describes how he and Sir Alan Hodgkin discovered the nature of the nerve impulse.

Alan Hodgkin is four years older than I am, and was already a well-known figure in nerve research by the time I completed my undergraduate work in the summer of 1939. We had met at Trinity College, Cambridge, where both of us were living in college, he as a Fellow and I as an undergraduate. He invited me to join him in August 1939 at the Marine Biological Laboratory, Plymouth, where he was planning some experiments on the giant nerve fibres of the squid. We had to leave Plymouth earlier than we had intended because of the imminent prospect of war, but we did succeed in recording both the resting and action potentials with internal electrodes pushed down inside these giant nerve fibres. Thus, for the first time, it was possible to measure directly the actual values of the potential difference across the surface membrane of a nerve fibre.

The striking and unexpected thing we found was that the amplitude of the potential change during the passage of the impulse was greater than the resting potential. In fact the inside of the fibre, which was electrically negative to the external solution in the resting state, became electrically positive for about a millisecond during the action potential. This was an important discovery because up till then it had been thought that during the action potential the membrane became highly permeable to all ions, so that the potential difference across it would be abolished and approach zero. What we found was that the potential was reversed.

The cause of the reversal was established in further experiments with internal electrodes in squid giant fibres carried out, again at Plymouth,

in the summer of 1947 by Hodgkin in collaboration with Bernard Katz. They showed that the increase in permeability of the membrane during the action potential does not allow all kinds of ions to cross but is specific to sodium ions. The concentration of sodium ions is many times higher in the external fluid than in the inside of the nerve fibre, so that they diffuse inwards during this period of high permeability, carrying their positive charge and thus raising the internal potential.

For most of the war Hodgkin was engaged in the development of short-wave airborne radar, and I was engaged in operational research in gunnery, at first for Anti-Aircraft Command and later for the Navy. We met a good many times and discussed plans for collaborating again when the war ended. I had been elected to a Research Fellowship at Trinity College during the war, so we both returned to Cambridge when released from our war duties, and got down to experiments again.

Some of our work was done at Cambridge using isolated nerve fibres from crabs and lobsters. These, although fairly large, are not large enough for putting electrodes inside. Analysis of the permeability changes could only be done with internal electrodes, which meant using squids – and the only laboratory in Britain where they were available was the Marine Biological Laboratory at Plymouth.

So back we went to Plymouth in the summers of 1948 and 1949, Katz joining us for the earlier experiments. Almost all our research was done at night. This was because the squids were caught in a trawl during the day, and we used them as soon as they were brought in because they did not survive well in captivity. A successful experiment would go on into the small hours of the morning, and often dawn was breaking by the time we returned to our boarding house.

We hoped to correlate the action

potential with permeability changes in the membrane. First we applied changes of membrane potential to the giant fibre and analysed the time course of the permeability changes. The next stage was to see whether these would account for the time course of the potential change that occurred when an action potential was propagated spontaneously along the nerve fibre. This involved some heavy computation requiring the repeated solving of four simultaneous differential equations, three of them non-linear. For each solution a value for the transmission velocity had to be guessed and, depending on the outcome, an improved value chosen for the next solution.

The first electronic computer in Cambridge (EDSAC I) was not yet running, so I spent the best part of a year in 1950–51 doing the computation with a hand calculating machine. Later, I ran the equations on EDSAC I (programmed entirely in machine language) and then on EDSAC II and other computers. Fortunately they confirmed the hand calculations. This came as a great relief because the first solutions on an electronic computer, carried out in the United States, had shown a serious discrepancy from our results. This was later traced to a programming error.

Our findings were published in 1952. Hodgkin and I then turned to other problems. In the meantime new methods became available which led to an understanding of the molecular mechanism by which permeability changes occur in the nerve membrane.

In 1963 Sir Alan Hodgkin and Sir Andrew Huxley were awarded a Nobel Prize for their work on the nerve impulse. Subsequently, each became Master of Trinity, Hodgkin from 1978 to 84, Huxley from 1984 to 90. Bernard Katz, who collaborated with them in some of the experiments, received a Nobel Prize in 1970 for showing how nerve impulses make muscle fibres contract.

How do the ion movements take place?

The ability of a nerve to transmit impulses depends ultimately on the sodium-potassium pump. How does it work? Basically the process is the same as that which occurs in other animal cells: a single **carrier protein** in the membrane transports sodium ions out of the axon and potassium ions into it.

As the sodium ions are being moved against an electrochemical gradient, the process must involve the expenditure of energy. Treating an axon with a metabolic poison such as dinitrophenol abolishes the sodium-potassium pump and prevents the expulsion of sodium ions. Their expulsion will, however, start up again if the poison is washed away. This confirms that the pump requires energy. When treated with a poison which prevents ATP-formation, the axon loses ATP at about the same rate as the sodium-potassium pump runs down, suggesting that the two are connected. When the poisoned axon is given some ATP, the sodium-potassium pump starts up again and the resting potential is at least partly restored.

What causes sodium ions to enter the axon during the passage of an impulse? In the membrane there are specific **channel proteins** which open up and allow the sodium ions to pass through. The opening of these channels is triggered by the change in potential across the membrane resulting from the local currents at the leading end of the action potential. Once depolarisation is complete, the channels close and the influx of sodium ions ceases. This mechanism is in accord with what we know about membrane transport in general.

Properties of nerves and impulses

Having discussed the nature of the nerve impulse, we can go on to consider some of the more important properties of nerves and the impulses which they transmit.

Stimulation

What sort of stimuli generate nerve impulses? In natural circumstances impulses are generated as a result of the stimulation of receptors. But impulses can be set up in nerves by directly applying any stimulus which opens the sodium channels and causes local depolarisation of the membrane. For example, a nerve can be stimulated by being pinched.

In the laboratory nerves are usually stimulated with weak electrical shocks. Such stimuli are particularly useful experimentally because their strength, duration and frequency can be controlled and they do not damage the nerve fibres.

The all-or-nothing law

Suppose you stimulate one end of an axon with a series of electrical stimuli of gradually increasing intensity, and record action potentials from the other end. Figure 25.11 shows what happens. You will notice that if the strength of the stimulus us below a certain **threshold intensity**, no action potential is evoked. However, if the intensity of the stimulus exceeds this value, a full-sized action potential is given and any further increase in the intensity of the stimulus, however great, does not give a larger potential.

This is called the **all-or-nothing law** which states that the response of an excitable unit (in this case an axon) is independent of the intensity of the stimulus. In other words, the size of the impulse is independent of the size of the stimulus. All that is necessary for a full-sized action potential to be produced is that the stimulus is above the threshold.

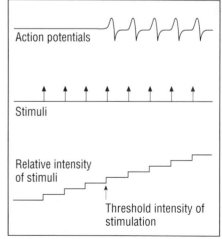

Figure 25.11 The all-or-nothing law. One end of an axon is stimulated with eight electrical shocks of gradually increasing intensity, and action potentials are recorded from the other end. The results, shown above, indicate that a stimulus either evokes a full-sized action potential or no action potential at all.

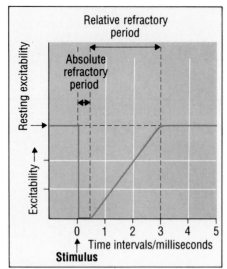

Figure 25.12 The graph shows how the excitability of an axon changes following the application of an above-threshold stimulus. The excitability is the ease with which the axon can be stimulated: the greater the excitability, the lower the intensity of stimulation required to generate an action potential. Notice that, following the transmission of an action potential, the excitability of the axon falls to zero (absolute refractory period) after which it gradually returns to normal (relative refractory period)

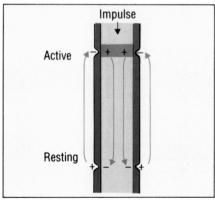

Figure 25.13 Diagram showing how an impulse is transmitted along a myelinated axon. The sheath insulates the axon, preventing currents crossing the membrane, so action potentials only develop at the nodes where the sheath is absent. Suppose an action potential develops at the node shaded red. When this node becomes depolarised, currents flow along the inside and outside of the axon as shown by the red arrows. These currents depolarise the next node. The same thing then happens at successive nodes all along the axon, so the impulse leaps from node to node.

The all-or-nothing law is an important concept on which much of the functioning of the nervous system depends. It means that the 'quantity' of information sent through the nervous system is determined not by the size of the impulses but by their number and frequency.

Refractory period

After an axon has transmitted an impulse, it cannot transmit another one straight away. The axon has to recover first. The membrane has to be repolarised and the resting distribution of ions restored before another action potential can be transmitted.

The period of inexcitability following the transmission of an impulse is called the **refractory period**, and typically it lasts about 3 milliseconds. It can be divided into an **absolute refractory period** during which the axon is totally incapable of transmitting an impulse, followed by a somewhat longer **relative refractory period** during which it is possible to generate an impulse in the axon provided that the stimulus is stronger than usual (figure 25.12).

The importance of the refractory period is that, together with transmission speed, it determines the maximum frequency at which an axon can transmit impulses. For most axons the maximum frequency is about 500 per second, though some neurones can reach 1000 per second.

Transmission speed

If the nervous system is to be efficient as a means of communication, its neurones must transmit impulses quickly. In fact **transmission speeds** vary enormously, depending on the type of neurone and the animal in question. The slowest neurones transmit at speeds of about 0.5 metres per second, the fastest ones at over 100 metres per second.

What enables neurones to transmit impulses at such high speeds? In vertebrates like ourselves the **myelin sheath** is responsible. You will recall that the myelin sheath is composed of fatty material interrupted at approximately one millimetre intervals by nodes of Ranvier. At the nodes the sheath is absent and the nerve fibre is surrounded only by its plasma membrane.

Experiments have shown that when a myelinated axon transmits an impulse, depolarisation occurs only at the nodes. Between one node and the next the myelin sheath insulates the axon, so currents cannot flow across the axon membrane in these regions. But when a node becomes depolarised, the juxtaposition of positive and negative ions between that node and the next creates local currents which depolarise the next node (figure 25.13). These currents are equivalent to the local currents at the leading end of the action potential in figure 26.10. The difference is that here, in the myelinated axon, the currents occur over a longer distance. The result is that the impulse leaps from node to node, thereby increasing the overall transmission speed.

The majority of vertebrate nerve fibres are myelinated, and there is little doubt that this has increased the efficiency of the vertebrate nervous system in the course of evolution. Interestingly, certain invertebrates have achieved the same thing but by different means. Instead of having myelin sheaths they have very thick axons which transmit impulses exceptionally rapidly. We have already met these **giant axons** in the squid, but other invertebrates have them too, for example earthworms, fanworms and lobsters. These animals are all sessile or slow moving, but they have rapid **escape responses** which enable them to draw quickly away from danger. The impulses that bring about the escape responses are transmitted at high speed along the giant axons.

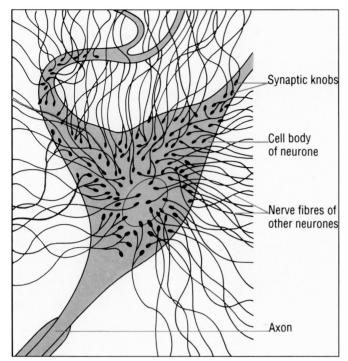

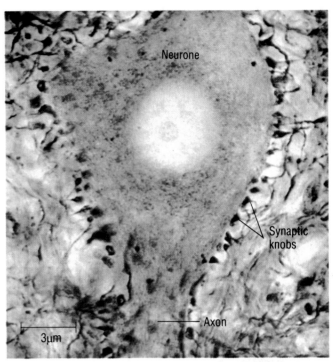

Figure 25.14 Neurones connect with one another via synapses.
A Diagram showing synaptic knobs on the surface of a motor neurone. A single neurone may have on it as many as 50 000 synaptic knobs derived from many different neighbouring neurones.

B Photomicrograph of a section through a neurone in the spinal cord of a cat showing synaptic knobs on the surface of the cell body. The section was specially stained to show up the synaptic knobs.

The synapse

The cell body and dendrites of a typical neurone in the brain or spinal cord are covered with numerous **synaptic knobs** derived from other nerve cells (figure 25.14). Each knob is the swollen end of a dendrite, and as many as 50 000 of them may be in contact with a single neurone. The computing facility of the nervous system depends on the complex interconnections which these synapses permit.

It has long been known that transmission across synapses occurs not by electrical but by chemical means. One of the earliest experiments supporting this notion was performed in 1921 by an Austrian scientist, Otto Loewi (see box on page 450). At that time nothing was known about the detailed structure of the synapse. However, physiological studies suggested that there must be a gap between the neurones at that point. It was thought that, on arrival of an impulse, a chemical substance might cross the gap and set up an impulse in the adjoining neurone. In more recent years this idea has received support from the electron microscope which has been used to study the fine structure of synapses.

The fine structure of the synapse and how it works

The synaptic knob contains numerous **mitochondria** and **vesicles**. Between the knob and the adjoining neurone there is a small but definite gap, the **synaptic cleft**. The membrane on the near side of the cleft (which belongs to the knob) is called the **presynaptic membrane**, and the membrane on the far side (belonging to the adjoining neurone) is called the **postsynaptic membrane**. The space between the two membranes is approximately 20 nm across.

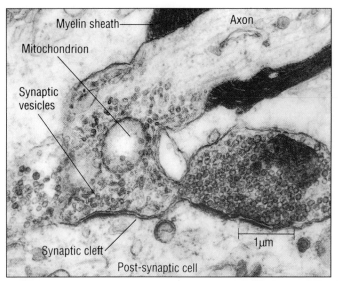

Figure 25.15 Structure of the synapse.
Left Electron micrograph of a section through a synaptic knob in the spinal cord of a fish. *Right* Diagram of a synaptic knob. The synaptic cleft separating the presynaptic and postsynaptic membranes is approximately 20 nm wide.

Figure 25.16 This diagram shows how transmission across a synapse is thought to occur.

The synaptic cleft and other features of the synapse are shown in figure 25.15. Notice that the synaptic cleft forms a definite gap between the presynaptic and postsynaptic membranes. Research on synapses has shown how this gap is bridged when an impulse comes along.

When an impulse arrives at a synaptic knob it causes **calcium ions** to diffuse in from the surrounding tissue fluid. These ions cause some of the synaptic vesicles to move to the presynaptic membrane and discharge a **neurotransmitter substance** into the cleft. This is an example of exocytosis (see page 204). The neurotransmitter substance then diffuses across the cleft to the postsynaptic membrane which consequently becomes partially depolarised (figure 25.16).

How does this partial depolarisation occur? The postsynaptic membrane contains specific protein receptors with which the transmitter molecules combine. Once combined, protein channels open up in the membrane, allowing sodium ions to diffuse from the cleft into the postsynaptic neurone. If the membrane becomes sufficiently depolarised, an action potential is initiated in the axon of the postsynaptic neurone.

Inevitably this method of transmission results in a slight delay – usually about one millisecond – so synapses have the cumulative effect of slowing

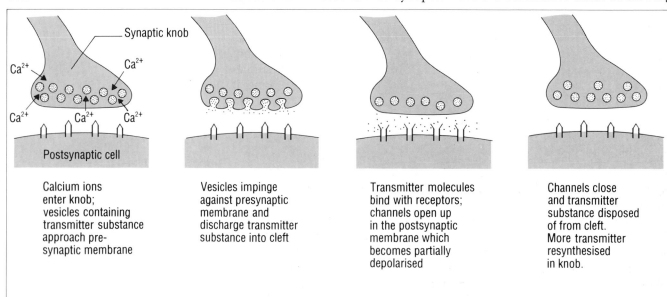

Calcium ions enter knob; vesicles containing transmitter substance approach pre-synaptic membrane

Vesicles impinge against presynaptic membrane and discharge transmitter substance into cleft

Transmitter molecules bind with receptors; channels open up in the postsynaptic membrane which becomes partially depolarised

Channels close and transmitter substance disposed of from cleft. More transmitter resynthesised in knob.

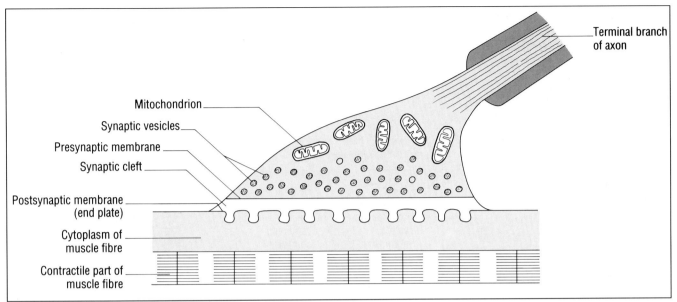

Mitochondrion

Synaptic vesicles

Presynaptic membrane

Synaptic cleft

Postsynaptic membrane
(end plate)

Cytoplasm of
muscle fibre

Contractile part of
muscle fibre

Terminal branch
of axon

Figure 25.17 Diagram of a neuromuscular junction. The postsynaptic membrane, formed from the plasma membrane (sarcolemma) surrounding the muscle fibre, is folded to form the muscle end plate. Notice that the neuromuscular junction is essentially the same as the interneural synapse in figure 25.15.

down transmission in the nervous system. However, the effect is negligible. An undoubted advantage of synapses is that they prevent impulses going in the wrong direction. An impulse can pass along an axon in either direction, but it can cross a synapse in only one direction. This is because synaptic vesicles are found only on the presynaptic side of the cleft, and protein receptors only on the postsynaptic side.

The neuromuscular junction

The point where a motor neurone makes contact with a muscle fibre is called the **neuromuscular junction**. The electron microscope has shown its internal structure to be very similar to that of a synaptic knob, so we can regard it as a special kind of synapse (figure 25.17). The main difference relates to the postsynaptic membrane. In the neuromuscular junction this is greatly folded to form a **muscle end plate**.

Transmission at the neuromuscular junction takes place in the same way as at synapses between neurones. Indeed much of our knowledge of what happens at synapses comes from work on neuromuscular junctions, which are relatively large and easy to get at. When an impulse arrives at the neuromuscular junction, a neurotransmitter substance is released from synaptic vesicles into the synaptic cleft. The neurotransmitter substance diffuses across the cleft and depolarises the muscle end plate. An **end plate potential** develops and, once it has built up sufficiently, an action potential is generated in the muscle fibre.

Neurotransmitter substances

One of the most widespread neurotransmitter substances is an ammonium base called **acetylcholine**. It occurs at synapses and neuromuscular junctions in the voluntary nervous system and in certain parts of the involuntary system (see page 460). If you move your arm or leg, it is acetylcholine which activates the muscles.

Acetylcholine must not be allowed to remain in the synaptic cleft after it has depolarised the postsynaptic membrane. If it did, the postsynaptic neurone would go on firing off impulses indefinitely. This is prevented by an enzyme called **cholinesterase** present in the cleft. As soon as acetylcholine has done its job, it is hydrolysed by cholinesterase and rendered inactive. The products of the hydrolysis pass back into the synaptic knob

Otto Loewi and the discovery of chemical transmission

Guest author Patricia Kohn explains how chemical transmission in the nervous system was discovered.

In the mid-nineteenth century it was well established that nerve and muscle action both involved electrical phenomena. The mechanism of neuromuscular transmission was also assumed to be electrical, though proponents of this idea were a bit vague about whether or not there was a gap between nerve and muscle cells.

Some dissenting voices, however, were heard. With the experimental demonstration of the first hormones, the concept of chemical transmission began to emerge. The similarity of the effects of the hormone adrenaline and stimulation of the sympathetic nervous system led to the suggestion that adrenaline might be released at the sympathetic nerve endings. However, established opinion is always difficult to overturn, and the advocates of electrical transmission were well dug in.

Then along came Otto Loewi. In 1921 he carried out an experiment which was so simple in conception and so easy to perform that one wonders why no-one had done it before. It involved using a frog's heart. The heart has a dual nerve supply: impulses in the **sympathetic nerve** speed up the rate at which it beats, whereas impulses in the vagus nerve slow it down. Loewi removed the heart from the body, with the **vagus nerve**

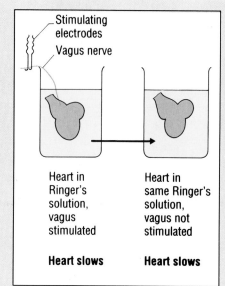

Otto Loewi's experiment which put the idea of chemical transmission on a firm footing. Many variations of this experiment have been carried out and they all confirm Loewi's original findings.

intact, and filled it with Ringer's solution. He then stimulated the vagus nerve repetitively for fifteen minutes. As expected, the heart rate slowed. He then transferred the Ringer's solution to a second heart from which the vagus nerve had been removed. To his delight, the second heart slowed.

Loewi concluded that vagal stimulation of the first heart had released a substance, some of which had found its way into the Ringer's solution. The effect of vagal stimulation was then mimicked when the Ringer's solution was applied to the second heart. The experiment is summarised in the illustration.

The inspiration for this experiment came to Loewi in a dream.

Apparently he woke up in the middle of the night and wrote it down, but in the morning he could not read what he had written. Fortunately the next night he had the same dream again. He decided to take no risks this time, so he got up and did the experiment in the middle of the night!

Of course Loewi did not know what the released substance was, so he simply called it **vagusstoff** – 'vagus stuff'. Over the next few years he was able to demonstrate that it was in fact **acetylcholine**. This did not come as too much of a surprise to the scientific ommunity. Acetylcholine was already known to mimic the activity of the parasympathetic division of the autonomic nervous system of which the vagus is an important part. During the early 1930s several other physiologists extended Loewi's work and showed that chemical transmission also occurs in the autonomic ganglia.

Although Loewi demonstrated that chemical transmission occurs, the evidence was still confined to the junctions in the autonomic nervous system. What about the voluntary system? This problem was eventually resolved in 1936 by Sir Henry Dale who managed to detect the minute amounts of acetylcholine that are released at the skeletal neuromuscular junctions. Loewi and Dale shared a Nobel Prize in 1936.

The discovery of chemical transmission was of enormous significance, not only for pure research but also because it led to an understanding of how drugs affect the nervous system.

where they are resynthesised into acetylcholine, using energy from ATP. One of the functions of the mitochondria in the synaptic knob is to provide energy for the synthesis of acetylcholine.

Another widespread transmitter substance is **noradrenaline**. This occurs, along with acetylcholine, in the involuntary nervous system. It works in the same way as acetylcholine but is inactivated differently. After it has depolarised the postsynaptic membrane it is taken up into the synaptic knob where its action is terminated.

Helping synapses

The local potential which develops in a postsynaptic neurone when the neurotransmitter substance impinges upon it is known as an **excitatory postsynaptic potential (EPSP)**. If enough neurotransmitter substance is released, the EPSP may get large enough to generate an action potential in the neurone.

Usually neurones only fire when excited through several synapses simultaneously. A single synapse fails to produce enough transmitter subtance for an action potential to be generated in the postsynaptic neurone. However, sufficient transmitter is produced by several synapses acting together. The EPSPs produced by the different synapses add together, generating an action potential. This is called **spatial summation**.

A neurone may fail to generate an action potential when only one impulse arrives at the synapse, but does so when two or more impulses arrive in quick succession. In this case the EPSPs created by successive impulses add together sufficiently for an action potential to be fired off in the neurone. This is called **temporal summation** and it involves a process called **facilitation**. The first impulse fails to cross the synapse but it leaves an effect which makes it easier for the next one to get across. How would you explain this in terms of the neurotransmitter substance?

Hindering synapses

Certain synapses inhibit postsynaptic neurones, making it more difficult for excitatory impulses to get across. The transmitter released at the inhibitory synapse causes the inside of the postsynaptic neurone to become more negative than usual. This increased negativity, which can be recorded with an oscilloscope, is called an **inhibitory postsynaptic potential (IPSP)**. It makes it harder for the postsynaptic membrane to become depolarised, so action potentials are not fired in the neurone.

If an excitatory synapse is continually bombarded with impulses at high frequency there comes a time when the postsynaptic neurone stops responding and action potentials are no longer generated in it. It is as if the synapse gets tired. What actually happens is that the transmitter substance runs out, and its resynthesis cannot keep pace with the rate at which impulses reach the synapse. The synapse has become **fatigued**.

Synapses vary in how quickly they fatigue. Some do not fatigue at all, whereas others do so after transmitting only a few impulses. A fatigued synapse must be given time to regenerate a new supply of transmitter substance before it can transmit again. Rapidly fatiguing synapses are a feature of relatively inactive animals such as sea anemones. The synapses of more active animals such as ourselves are generally slow to fatigue.

The role of synapses in the nervous system

We have seen that synapses can influence the ease with which impulses are transmitted through the nervous system. An impulse reaching a synapse may facilitate the passage of other impulses or it may inhibit them. Sometimes an impulse may cross the synapse unimpeded, at other times it may be blocked. The pattern of facilitation and inhibition of the synapses therefore determines the flow of impulses within the nervous system as a whole.

What *decides* whether a particular synapse should be open or closed? One of the most important deciding factors is the brain, to which we now turn.

Drugs and synapses

Any substance that prevents the action of a neurotransmitter substance will stop transmission at synapses which use that particular transmitter. On the other hand, any substance that prevents the transmitter being disposed of after it has done its job will prolong the action of the transmitter.

A substance that prevents the action of acetylcholine is curare, a poison which can be extracted from certain tropical trees. Curare blocks neuromuscular junctions in the voluntary system, so it stops the skeletal muscles contracting. At high enough concentrations it causes paralysis and death. South American Indians put it on their arrowheads, and some snakes have a similar compound in their venom. Controlled doses of such substances are used by surgeons to make the patient's muscles relax during operations.

Another acetylcholine inhibitor is atropine which occurs in the juice of the deadly nightshade, *Atropa belladonna*. Atropine blocks certain synapses in the involuntary nervous system by preventing acetylcholine depolarising the postsynaptic membrane. Its effect on the eye is explained on page 477.

The opposite effect is produced by organophosphate insecticides and nerve gases. They inhibit cholinesterase. Without cholinesterase, acetylcholine remains in the synaptic cleft and causes repeated firing of the postsynaptic neurone or, if it is a neuromuscular junction, repeated contractions of the muscle. The result is that the nervous system becomes overactive and muscles contract uncontrollably, in some case with fatal results.

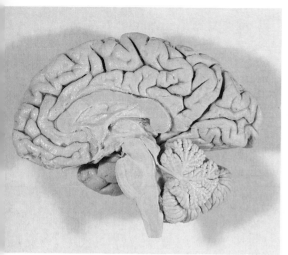

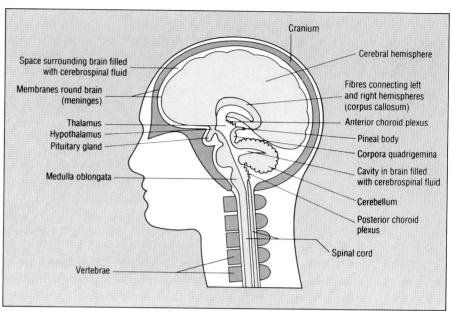

Figure 25.18 Structure of the human brain.
Left Photograph of a brain sectioned vertically along the midline.
Right Diagram, based on the photograph, showing the different parts of the brain.

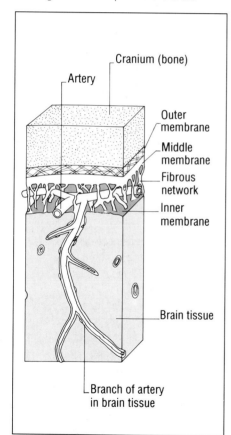

Figure 25.19 The brain is protected by the cranium and meninges which are shown here in three-dimensional view. The meninges consist of the inner, middle and outer membrane. The space between the inner and middle membranes is traversed by the fibrous network and filled with cerebrospinal fluid.

The brain

In all vertebrates the central nervous system develops as a longitudinal tube of nerve tissue towards the dorsal side of the embryo (see page 627). The anterior end of the tube, situated in the head, expands to form the brain. The rest of the tube becomes the spinal cord.

When fully formed, the human brain consists of two main parts, a pair of **cerebral hemispheres** at the anterior end and, immediately behind, a narrow brain stem. Associated with the brain stem are various structures which are shown in figure 25.18.

Having been formed from a tube originally, the brain is hollow. The cavities of the brain, called **ventricles**, are continuous with one another and with the central canal of the spinal cord. The cavities are filled with **cerebrospinal fluid** whose origin is explained below.

The brain tissue is composed of neurones – at least 10^{10} (ten billion) of them – together with supporting glia cells (see page 440). Each neurone may be connected by synapses to as many as 25 000 others. The total number of synapses is therefore vast. However, the number is not fixed and static – new synapses can be formed by learning and repetition, and the pattern of connections can change. This structural versatility may help to explain how we acquire special skills like riding a bicycle. It may also be the basis of memory.

Protection and nourishment of the brain

Brain tissue is soft with a consistency that has been likened to that of a ripe avocado pear. It therefore needs protection. The brain is enveloped by three connective tissue membranes called **meninges** (figure 25.19):

- The **inner membrane** adheres to the brain tissue itself and is very delicate.
- The **middle membrane**, also delicate, encloses a space which is traversed by a network of fine fibres rather like a spider's web. The space is filled with **cerebrospinal fluid** which cushions the brain and prevents it jarring. Amongst the fibres are arteries which penetrate into the brain tissue and supply it with oxygen and nutrients.
- The **outer membrane** is much tougher and merges with the bony tissue of the cranium.

The cerebrospinal fluid is produced by two **choroid plexuses** in the roof of the brain stem. The brain tissue here is very thin, with the result that the meninges lie very close to the ventricles. The blood capillaries in these areas are particularly numerous. Cerebrospinal fluid is formed from these capillaries by active transport possibly aided by ultrafiltration.

The whole of the brain and its meninges are enclosed within the **cranium**, which is part of the skull – in fact the hard outer meninge is firmly attached to the bone tissue of the cranium. Small holes (foramina) in the cranium allow for the entry and exit of blood vessels and nerves. Posteriorly the meninges envelop the spinal cord which is enclosed within the vertebral column.

The overall role of the brain

The overall role of the brain is **coordination**. To accomplish this there are special **centres** in different parts of the brain for dealing with specific functions such as locomotion, breathing and so on. Neurones and synapses are particularly concentrated in these centres, and they are connected with the spinal cord and peripheral nerves by tracts of nerve fibres.

Collectively the brain centres carry out three separate but related functions:

- They receive impulses from receptors.
- They integrate these impulses.
- They sent out new impulses to the appropriate effectors.

By integration we mean that if impulses arrive simultaneously from several different receptors, the centre interprets and correlates the incoming information before sending impulses to the effectors. In addition certain parts of the brain, particularly the cerebral hemispheres, are responsible for higher functions such as memory and intelligence.

Investigating brain function

Various techniques can be used to find out the functions of particular regions of the brain. One method is to study the behaviour of people suffering from wounds or lesions in which certain identifiable regions of the brain have been damaged.

Another approach is to stimulate different regions of the brain with carefully controlled electrical stimuli, and observe the results. Alternatively, one can stimulate individual receptors such as the eye, and record electrical activity from various parts of the brain.

The above techniques involve experimenting on the brain itself. A quite different approach is to study the responses and behaviour of human subjects, and then attempt to explain them in terms of brain function. This is the approach used by psychologists.

Functions of the main parts of the human brain

Let us start at the back and work forward. The most posterior part of the brain is the **medulla oblongata,** or medulla for short. Suppose the whole of a person's brain in front of the medulla is destroyed in a car accident. All voluntary movement ceases. However, breathing and the control of the circulation continue. This is because the medulla contains centres controlling these basic functions (see pages 262 and 331).

Other actions controlled by the medulla include swallowing, salivation and movements of the gut. They all fall within the province of the autonomic nervous system which presides over the body's involuntary responses – more about that shortly.

Cephalisation

The brain is an integral part of the **head**, which itself is a fundamental feature of most animals. The development of a head in evolution is known as **cephalisation**. Why have heads developed in animals, and why is the head always associated with some kind of brain?

The head appears to have developed as a result of **directional locomotion**. move in a definite direction with the anterior end in the lead. Since this is the end to come into contact with new environmental situations first, it is not surprising to find that in the course of evolution it has become equipped with highly sensitive receptors for receiving stimuli and monitoring the environment. In some animals these receptors take the form of elaborate **sense organs** such as eyes, nose and ears.

With the development of the head as the main region of stimulus-reception, the flow of impulses into the anterior end of the nervous system increases. The brain develops primarily as a centre for receiving all this 'sensory information' and relaying the appropriate signals to the rest of the body. In more complex animals such as insects and vertebrates the brain is also important as an integrating centre for coordinating movement and more advanced types of behaviour.

The complexity of the head results partly from its neuro-sensory function but also from the fact that it contains the mouth and associated feeding structures. It is logical that these should be at the leading end of the body. The necessity for them to be properly coordinated results in further elaboration of the nervous system in the head region.

Just above the medulla is the **cerebellum,** a greatly folded expansion of the roof of the brain stem. A person with a badly damaged cerebellum finds it difficult to make precise movements. If, for example, the person tries to pour cream into a cup of coffee, most of the cream is likely to go into the saucer. These kinds of observations indicate that the cerebellum is responsible for the fine adjustment of intentional movements, particularly those that have to be learned.

The cerebellum is particularly important in the performance of complicated physical actions. For example, suppose you want to jump over a gate. The cerebellum integrates the motor impulses required to bring about the muscular response with sensory information from the eyes, balancing organs and muscle spindles, so that the enterprise is carried out successfully in a fully coordinated manner.

Immediately in front of the cerebellum are four small bumps called the **corpora quadrigemina.** In vertebrates such as fishes they take the form of much larger **optic lobes** which play an important part in vision. In the human they help to control eye movements and certain auditory reflexes, but otherwise they have little function.

More important is a dense mass of nerve cells and fibres on the ventral side of this part of the brain. This is called the **reticular formation.** It helps to integrate the information travelling up and down the brain so that fully coordinated responses are given. The reticular formation extends back into the medulla where it contains the ventilation and cardiovascular centres.

The thalamus and associated structures

The next part of the brain, as we move forward, contains the **thalamus** on the dorsal side and the **hypothalamus** below. The thalamus integrates sensory information and relays it to the higher centres of the brain. The **hypothalamus** contains centres controlling such functions as sleep, aggression, feeding, drinking, osmoregulation, temperature regulation and sexual activity. There is a fairly precise localisation of function in this part of the brain. Electrical stimulation applied to the appropriate regions will induce specific responses such as sleep or drinking.

Projecting downwards from the hypothalamus is the **pituitary gland.** This is an **endocrine gland** and secretes a wide range of hormones which are discussed in the next chapter. Some of the functions of the hypothalamus are brought about by these hormones, so there is a close connection – functionally as well as structurally – between the pituitary gland and the brain.

Immediately in front of the pituitary is the **optic chiasma.** At this point the two optic nerves, one from each eye, cross each other on their way into the brain. The routes taken by the nerve fibres in the optic chiasma are such that impulses from each eye go to both sides of the brain.

The dorsal side of this part of the brain bears a slender stalk called the **pineal body.** There is evidence that this functioned as a third eye in certain extinct vertebrates. The only existing animal to have such a third eye is the Tuatara lizard, *Sphenodon,* which is found on the offshore islands of New Zealand. In this intriguing reptile the pineal body – situated on top of the head – has a lens, pigmented retina and optic nerve which passes through a hole in the cranium. Although covered with skin, there is evidence that the tuatara's pineal body is sensitive to light.

In other vertebrates the pineal body has an endocrine function. It produces a hormone called **melatonin** which causes constriction of the pigment cells in the skin of frogs (see page 463). In mammals the same hormone helps to control the reproductive state of seasonal breeders such as sheep. In humans it may be involved in the onset of puberty.

The cerebral hemispheres

In the human, and indeed all mammals, the **cerebral hemispheres** are the largest and most prominent part of the brain. The two hemispheres are separated by a deep cleft down the middle, but they are linked together at their base by a transverse band of nerve fibres called the **corpus callosum**.

The superficial part of the cerebral hemispheres consists mainly of a special tissue, the **neopallium**, which is present in amphibians and reptiles but is enormously expanded in mammals particularly the human. Its outer layers constitute the **cerebral cortex** which contains millions of densely-packed neurones interconnected in a most complex manner. The cerebral cortex is greatly folded, rather like a crumpled piece of paper. This enables a large number of neurones to be packed into a relatively small space (figure 25.20).

So far as understanding how it works, the cerebral cortex is the most elusive part of the brain. However, its importance is in no doubt. An individual with a badly damaged cerebral cortex cannot see, hear, think or speak properly and is unable to move in a coordinated fashion. In severe cases the individual is unconscious and does not respond to stimuli. This leads to the general conclusion that the cerebral cortex is needed for all voluntary responses.

Localisation in the cortex

Experiments have been carried out to discover which regions of the cortex are responsible for particular functions. These investigations suggest that the cortex can be divided into **sensory, motor** and **association areas** (figure 25.21):

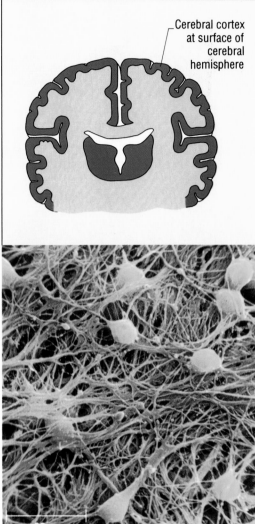

Figure 25.20 The diagram is a vertical section through the cerebral hemispheres, cut transversely, showing the folded cerebral cortex. Below is a scanning electron micrograph of a very small part of the human cerebral cortex. The human brain contains approximately 10 000 million neurones of which over 9000 million are in the cerebral cortex.

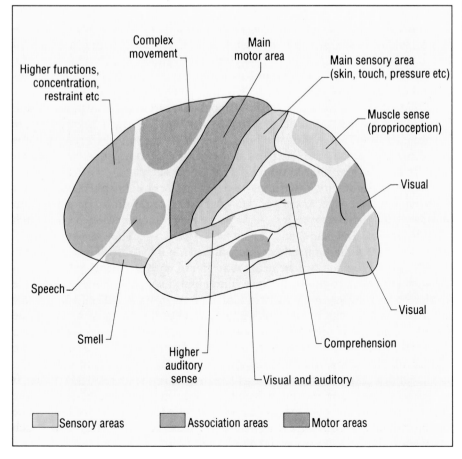

Figure 25.21 Side view of the left cerebral hemisphere showing the main sensory, association and motor areas of the cerebral cortex. The front of the brain is to the left.

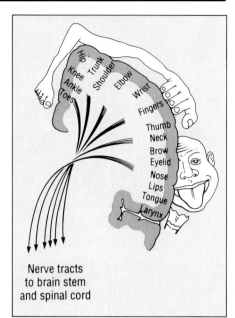

Nerve tracts
to brain stem
and spinal cord

Figure 25.22 This diagram shows which areas of the motor cortex are responsible for particular functions. The sizes of the different parts of the human figure indicate the extent of each motor area. From the motor areas nerve tracts pass down to the lower parts of the brain and thence to the spinal cord.

Restoring brain function

The functional versatility of the brain is truly remarkable. In one case a boy's brain was damaged by a pitch fork which went through his head. The result was that he could no longer read. However, he was re-taught how to read as though he was a child all over again.

Not everyone is as lucky as this and many people with brain damage never regain the skills they have lost, at least not fully. But brain research proceeds apace and new forms of treatment are constantly being developed. A promising recent discovery is that a certain protein, called **nerve growth factor**, can stimulate neurones to form new connections. This offers hope to people with degenerative brain disorders such as Parkinson's disease.

- The sensory areas receive impulses from receptors via nerve fibres in the spinal cord and/or brain, and particular sensory areas are associated with specific senses – sight, hearing and so on. Stimulation of a receptor such as the eye results in electrical activity in the appropriate sensory region of the cortex. Damage to the region abolishes that sense.

- The motor areas send out impulses to the voluntary muscles via nerve fibres which pass down the brain stem into the spinal cord. There is considerable localisation of function. Electrical stimulation of a particular area will initiate a precise response such as flexing of the little finger or movement of the lips (figure 25.22).

- The association areas sort out, integrate and, where appropriate, store information before sending it to the relevant motor areas. For example, when a person sees an object and says what it is, the association areas translate the visual experience into a spoken word.

The higher functions of the brain

The largest and most complex association area is in the anterior part of the cerebral hemispheres – the **frontal lobes**. This part of the brain is particularly well developed in humans and appears to be responsible for those subtle and highly individual aspects of behaviour which we usually label personality. People whose frontal lobes have been badly damaged are unable to think in an organised way, to concentrate and to correlate different pieces of information. Abstract thought is particularly difficult. At one time surgical cutting of nerve fibres in the anterior part of the frontal lobes was done to relieve extreme mental anxiety. Sometimes, this operation led to a lowering of the patient's mental state and finer judgements.

One might be tempted to conclude that the frontal lobes are the seat of all our higher functions such as memory, imagination, thought and intelligence. However, it is not as simple as that. Although the frontal lobes are undoubtedly involved in these processes, other parts of the cerebral hemispheres also play a part.

Most of the nerve tracts leading from the cerebral hemispheres cross over in the lower parts of the brain, so that the right hemisphere is connected to the left side of the body, and the left hemisphere to the right side. This means that the left hand, for example, is controlled by the right hemisphere, and the right hand by the left hemisphere.

Experiments have shown that the two cerebral hemispheres supervise different skills. The right hemisphere is primarily responsible for spatial and musical sense, whereas the left hemisphere is more concerned with mathematical ability, language and deductive reasoning. Thus artists depend mainly on the right hemisphere, accountants on the left. This applies to right-handed people – it is the other way round with left-handers!

Although we can make a broad functional distinction between the two hemispheres, they do not work in isolation from each other. The corpus callosum, which links them together, allows impulses to cross from one to the other and ensures that they cooperate in carrying out their functions.

In fact, localisation in the cerebral cortex generally is not as sharp as it may seem. There are many cases of people with head injuries losing a particular function of the brain and then regaining it later. Brain tissue is notoriously reluctant to repair itself, so we must assume that the lost function is taken over by neighbouring regions of the brain. Some parts of the cortex have no obvious role, and it is possible that they take over the functions of other areas if and when necessary.

Electrical activity in the brain

Guest author Patricia Kohn discusses the electrical activity that goes on in the brain and relates it to sleep.

In 1875 an English physician, Richard Caton, showed for the first time that the brain possesses its own electrical activity. He recorded what he called 'feeble currents of varying direction' from the cerebral cortex. Today the recording of these 'feeble currents' is a routine procedure. Electrodes are placed on the scalp, and the electrical signals are fed into a recording device. The trace so obtained in this way is called an **electroencephalogram** or **EEG**.

The EEG in activity and at rest

The EEG trace appears as an irregular wavy line. The frequency, amplitude and pattern of the waves vary with the type of activity going on in the brain. For example, if you are alert and struggling with a difficult mental problem, your EEG will be irregular with small, high frequency waves. On the other hand, if you are relaxed with your eyes closed, your EEG will be more regular with larger waves of lower frequency. This latter pattern is called the **alpha rhythm** and it changes as soon as you open your eyes.

What causes the EEG and how is it related to brain function? The EEG is recorded as the potential difference between two electrodes placed on the scalp. Beneath the electrodes are millions of neurones. Each neurone is covered with thousands of synapses derived from other neurones. As the incoming signals induce postsynaptic potentials, the cell becomes positively charged at one end and negatively charged at the other end. If this happens to sufficient neurones at the same time, the electrical field generated is large enough to be detected by the electrode. The more in synchrony the neurones are the larger and more regular will be the waves in the EEG. The more unsynchronised the neurones, the smaller and more irregular will be the waves. Mental activity therefore seems to be associated with the cortical cells becoming less synchronised.

The EEG during sleep

At one time it was thought that during sleep the brain shuts down and becomes inactive. The EEG shows that this is not the case. As we pass from being awake to being fully asleep (as judged by how difficult it is to wake the person up) the EEG passes through several distinct patterns (see illustration). In deep sleep the EEG is highly synchronised and the waves are large and slow.

This deep **slow-wave sleep** lasts for an hour or so, and then we are on our way back to lighter sleep. At this point the EEG pattern becomes highly unsynchronised and an observer would notice that, under closed lids, our eyes are moving. For this reason, it is called **rapid eye movement sleep (REM sleep)**. There may be other signs of activity too: for example, the fingers may twitch and the teeth grind, and in males the penis may become erect. If woken during this stage, we are likely to report that we have been dreaming. Despite the active-looking EEG, we are still profoundly asleep and most of our skeletal muscles are totally relaxed.

After a period of this REM sleep the EEG changes again, indicating that we are on the way down to deep slow-wave sleep once more. This cycle may be repeated four or five times during a full night's sleep.

As well as telling us how active the brain is, EEGs are useful for diagnosing certain types of brain disorders. For example, doctors can distinguish between different types of epilepsy from EEG patterns, and the EEG can also be used to locate brain tumours.

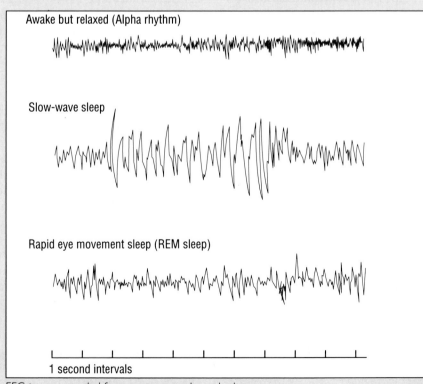

EEG traces recorded from a person awake and asleep.

Brain chemistry

Parkinson's disease is characterised by uncontrolled contractions of the voluntary muscles: the limbs tend to become rigid and a characteristic tremor develops in the hands particularly when the person intends to do something with them. Research has shown that these symptoms are caused by degeneration of particular neurones in the brain which have a substance called **dopamine** as their transmitter substance. These dopamine synapses are part of an extremely subtle and only partly understood mechanism whereby the brain translates our desire to make a particular movement into the necessary instructions to be transmitted to the muscles.

Dopamine is just one of a number of neurotransmitter substances which have been discovered in the brain. Some have an excitatory effect on synapses, others an inhibitory effect. More and more evidence is coming to hand which suggests that the state of the brain synapses, as determined by these transmitter substances, plays an important part in determining a person's mental state and behaviour. For example, an excess of dopamine synapses seems to be associated with schizophrenia. This mental disorder is characterised by personality changes which can give rise to periodic episodes of abnormal behaviour.

Certain psychoactive drugs affect brain function by interfering with synapses. They bind with the receptors in the postsynaptic membranes, preventing the transmitter substance depolarising the membrane. Hallucinatory drugs such as LSD do this, as do tranquillisers such as valium. It has been suggested that the brain may produce chemicals of its own which have a tranquillising effect, calming the person down.

Certain substances have been discovered in the brain which inhibit the sensation of pain. These are small polypeptides and are similar in their action to the pain-killing drug morphine, for which reason they are called **endorphins**. (Endorphin is short for 'endogenous morphine-like substance'.)

Endorphins have other generally suppressive effects on the body – for example, they reduce the cardiac frequency and the metabolic rate. This suggests that they may be functioning not just as neurotransmitters but as hormones, exerting their effects a long way from where they are produced.

The autonomic nervous system

This part of the nervous system is concerned with controlling the body's involuntary responses, such as the beating of the heart, movements of the gut and secretion of sweat.

The autonomic nervous system is divided into two distinct parts: the **sympathetic** and **parasympathetic systems**. Both contain nerve fibres serving structures over which the body normally has no voluntary control, and which are not innervated by the voluntary part of the nervous system. In both cases nerve fibres emerge from the brain and spinal cord and pass to the organs concerned. Both systems have many such pathways. At certain points in the pathways there are ganglia containing synapses.

The basic plan of the autonomic system is shown in figure 25.23. The sympathetic system consists of a **sympathetic chain** which runs down the body on each side of the vertebral column just below the spinal nerves. The chain consists of a series of ganglia strung together like a string of beads. The ganglia are linked to the ventral roots of the spinal nerves by slender connections; and from each ganglion nerves pass to the various organs, either directly or via further ganglia. The synaptic connections inside the ganglia ensure the rapid spread of excitation to all the appropriate effectors. For example, in the main ganglion in the neck (the most anterior ganglion

Effector	Parasympathetic system	Sympathetic system
Heart	slows down	speeds up
Arterioles	–	constrict
Bronchioles	constrict	dilate
Iris	constricts	dilates
Tear glands	secrete	–
Salivary glands	secrete	–
Gut movements	speed up	slow down
Anal sphincter	relaxes	contracts
Bladder sphincter	relaxes	contracts
Bladder wall	contracts	relaxes
Erector pili muscle	–	contracts
Sweat glands	–	secrete

Table 25.2 Summary of the main responses produced by the two parts of the mammalian autonomic nervous system. Note that the effects produced by the sympathetic generally oppose those produced by the parasympathetic. It should also be noted that the sympathetic system, while causing general vasoconstriction, dilates those arterioles serving vital organs such as skeletal muscle. In addition to the functions listed, the sympathetic system causes secretion of adrenaline from the adrenal medulla (see page 463). The actions of this hormone are similar to those initiated by the sympathetic nervous system.

in figure 25.23) there are about ten thousand incoming nerve fibres and a million outgoing fibres.

The parasympathetic system consists of the whole of the **vagus nerve** and its branches, together with certain other cranial and spinal nerves. In this case the ganglia are located in the walls of the effectors, and there are no ganglia in the course of the nerves themselves.

The functions of the sympathetic and parasympathetic systems are summarised in table 25.2. Notice that, in the main, their effects oppose each other. The overall function of the sympathetic system is to prepare the body for an emergency – for example, widening of the pupils, acceleration of the heart, tightening of the anal and bladder sphincters, contraction of the erector pili muscles and secretion of sweat. These are all responses which we associate with a sudden shock. The parasympathetic system on the other hand tends to calm the body down. This part of the nervous system is probably at its most active in a person snoozing after Sunday lunch.

Bearing in mind that the autonomic system is in charge of *involuntary* responses, it may surprise you to see that it controls the emptying of the bladder and the opening of the anal sphincter. After all, these are actions over which humans have very definite voluntary control. However, other

Figure 25.23 Schematic diagram summarising the main features of the human autonomic nervous system. The parasympathetic system is shown on the left, the sympathetic system on the right. In reality both systems are on each side of the body. The yellow areas show the ganglia where synapses occur. Preganglionic nerve fibres are represented by blue arrows, postganglionic fibres by red arrows. The two systems differ in the positions of the ganglia. In the parasympathetic system the ganglia are in the walls of the effectors, so the preganglionic nerve fibres are long and the postganglionic fibres short. In the sympathetic system the ganglia are close to the spinal cord, so the preganglionic fibres are short and the postganglionic fibres long.

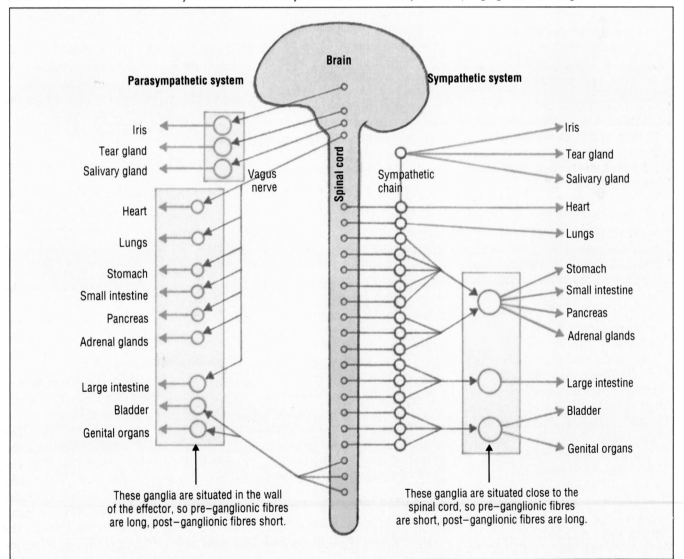

animals do not normally control these functions voluntarily, at least not without training, and even we have to learn to do so. The interconnections in the nervous system as a whole are such that voluntary control *can* be imposed on the autonomic system but only through conditioning (see page 535).

Neurotransmitters in the autonomic nervous system

Two neurotransmitters occur in the autonomic nervous system. The ends of the parasympathetic nerves produce acetylcholine, the same transmitter that is found in the voluntary part of the nervous system. The sympathetic nerves, on the other hand, produce mainly noradrenaline. Noradrenaline is almost identical chemically with the hormone adrenaline, and many of the responses produced by the sympathetic system are also produced by this hormone. This demonstrates the close connection between nerves and hormones. Hormones are the subject of the next chapter.

Electrical transmission in plants

It is usually said that plants do not have a nervous system. But is this really true? Guest author Tim King describes some interesting discoveries in plants.

Touch a leaf of the sensitive plant, *Mimosa pudica*, and within a few seconds the leaflets close up along the midrib and the leaf stalk bends downwards (see illustration). Dramatic responses such as this and the rapid closure of the leaves of the Venus fly-trap suggest that plants may be able to transmit impulses in much the same way as animals can.

In *Mimosa* the impulse takes about ten seconds to travel from the tip of a leaflet to the base of the leaf stalk, a distance of about 20 cm. The response is brought about by an organ at the base of the leaf stalk called the **pulvinus**. The cells of the pulvinus have thin walls and are capable of rapid changes in volume, which enables them to change their shape when they receive an impulse.

Electrodes placed 15 mm apart along the petiole, connected to reference electrodes in the soil, confirm that a wave of electrical activity – an impulse – passes along it at a speed of about 2 cm per

second. This transmission speed can treble with a 10°C increase in temperature, suggesting the involvement of chemical reactions. In the Venus fly-trap the impulse travels five times faster. In both species the plasma membrane of phloem cells seems to be involved in the transmission of the impulse.

There are a number of similarities between electrical transmission in plants and animals. Phloem cells are particularly rich in potassium ions, just as neurones are. In *Mimosa* some of the phloem cells are excitable, that is, they can trigger an impulse when activated by appropriate stimuli. When the impulse reaches a pulvinus cell, a large number of potassium ions are released as the cell changes shape, just as a stomatal guard cell releases potassium ions just before the pore closes or an axon releases potassium as an impulse flows along it.

In guard cells, the release of potassium ions is accompanied by a movement of calcium ions from the plasma membrane into the cytoplasm. This probably opens gated channels in the membrane, allowing the potassium ions to flow out. It has recently been shown that merely touching a tobacco plant causes calcium ions to be released

The touch response of the sensitive plant, *Mimosa pudica*.

from the membranes into the cytoplasm of the cells. Perhaps this is how, in the sensitive plant, a tactile stimulus generates an impulse.

These discoveries suggest that excitable plant and animal cells may be rather similar in the way they generate and transmit impulses. Perhaps plants have a nervous system after all and merely react more slowly than animals.

Summary

1. In most animals the nervous system consists of a **central nervous system (CNS)** (subdivided into the **brain** and **spinal cord**), and **peripheral nervous system** (subdivided into **cranial** and **spinal** nerves).

2. The simplest response produced by the nervous system is a **reflex action**. The structural basis of reflex action is the **reflex arc** which consists of a **receptor**, a chain of **neurones**, and an **effector**.

3. An effector neurone possesses a **cell body** from which arise a variable number of **dendrites** and a long **axon**. The axon generally has a **myelin sheath**.

4. At rest the inside of an axon is negative with respect to the outside (**resting potential**) but during the passage of an impulse this situation is momentarily reversed to give an **action potential**.

5. The resting potential is maintained by the **sodium-potassium pump** which expels sodium ions and takes in potassium ions. During the passage of an action potential, sodium ions enter the axon whose membrane thus becomes depolarised.

6. The size of an action potential is independent of the strength of stimulation. This is the **all-or-nothing law**.

7. For a brief period after it has transmitted an impulse, an axon is totally inexcitable (**absolute refractory period**). This is followed by a slightly longer period during which the axon is partially excitable (**relative refractory period**).

8. High speeds of transmission are achieved by having a myelin sheath with **nodes of Ranvier** (vertebrates) or by having **giant axons** (certain invertebrates).

9. Neurones are interconnected by **synapses**. Transmission across a synapse is achieved by a **neurotransmitter substance** which diffuses across the gap and depolarises the membrane of the next neurone. **Neuromuscular junctions** work in the same kind of way.

10. Important properties of synapses include **summation**, **inhibition** and **fatigue**.

11. Synapses ensure that impulses travel through the nervous system in only one direction. They also account for the actions of many drugs and poisons and they play a major part in **coordination**.

12. Coordination is a particularly important function of the brain. The **medulla oblongata** and **hypothalamus** coordinate various automatic functions, the **cerebellum** coordinates fine movement, and the **cerebral hemispheres** supervise all voluntary responses as well as being responsible for memory, intelligence and other higher functions.

13. Involuntary responses are dealt with by the **autonomic nervous system**. This is subdivided into the **sympathetic** and **parasympathetic systems**. The overall role of the sympathetic system is to prepare the body for an emergency, an effect which is generally opposed by the parasympathetic system.

14. The brain is an integral part of the **head** which in the course of evolution has become progressively more and more elaborate, a process known as **cephalisation**.

Review questions

1. Outline the sequence of events that takes place in the nervous system during a *named* human reflex.

2. What structural features does an effector neurone possess which are (a) the same as and (b) different from those of a simple cuboidal epithelial cell?

3. What are *giant axons* and where are they found? What part did they play in elucidating the nerve impulse?

4. Why is *depolarisation* not an ideal word for describing what happens during the passage of an action potential?

5. Summarise what happens to sodium and potassium ions during the rising and falling phases of an action potential.

6. State the all-or-nothing law. In view of this law, how does the nervous system manage to produce *graded* responses?

7. If you stimulate a nerve with repetitive stimuli at low frequency, every stimulus generates an action potential. But if you stimulate the nerve at a very high frequency, an action potential may be generated only by every other stimulus. Explain.

8. Explain the following in terms of how synapses work:
   (a) Impulses travel through a reflex arc in only one direction.
   (b) When a surgeon uses curare to relax a patient's muscles, the drug does not slow or stop the heart.

9. Outline the course taken by impulses in the nervous system when you hear a joke and laugh.

10. Speculate on what may be happening in your nervous system (a) just before an important tennis match and (b) immediately after Sunday lunch.

Further reading

R. D. Keynes, in a Scientific American article entitled 'The Nerve Impulse and the Squid', describes some of the experimental evidence underpinning Hodgkin and Huxley's work on the nerve impulse. (*Scientific American*, December 1958, Offprint No. 58.)

If you are particularly interested in the brain you might browse through *The Mitchell Beazley Atlas of the Human Body* or read Colin Blakemore's stimulating book *The Mind Machine* (BBC Books, 1988) based on his BBC/WNET television series.

Biology, Advanced Topics contains further information on the membrane potential of nerves, the sodium-potassium pump and the visual cortex as an aspect of brain function.

CHAPTER 26

Hormonal communication

A hormone is a chemical substance produced in one part of the body, from which it is transported – usually in the bloodstream – to another part where it evokes a response. A minute quantity of a hormone may have a profound effect on the organism's development, structure or behaviour. Hormones are always organic compounds, some of which have a rather complex structure.

In the human and other vertebrates, hormones are secreted into the bloodstream by **endocrine glands**. The word endocrine means 'internal secretion'. Since endocrine glands shed their secretions directly into the bloodstream, they have no ducts. This contrasts with **exocrine glands**, such as the salivary glands, whose secretions are carried by ducts to specific destinations (see page 174). The pancreas is an example of an organ which is an exocrine *and* endocrine gland. Its exocrine function is to secrete digestive enzymes, its endocrine function is to secrete insulin.

Once in the bloodstream, hormones are carried round the body and bring about responses in specific **target organs**. A hormone's target organs may be situated a long way from the gland that secretes the hormone.

The main endocrine glands of the human body are shown in figure 26.1. Though they may be widely separated from one another spatially, they do not necessarily work in isolation. Some of them cooperate with, or are influenced by, other hormones as we shall see presently.

Functions of mammalian endocrine glands

The functions of the main endocrine glands of a mammal and the hormones they secrete are summarised in table 26.1. Some of the individual hormones are discussed in appropriate contexts in other parts of the book. For example, insulin is dealt with in Chapter 21, sex hormones in Chapter 33 and growth hormone in Chapter 36. You will find detailed page references for these and other hormones in the index.

The table is confined almost entirely to the mammal, but of course hormones occur in other animals too, and comparable substances occur in plants, as explained in Chapter 36.

In the present chapter we shall be more concerned with the *principles* of hormonal communication and its role in controlling various processes that go on inside the human body – metabolism, growth, sexual development and so on. In regulating these activities hormones are serving a coordinating role. As such they bear certain resemblances to the nervous system, and it is instructive to compare the two systems from a functional point of view.

Hormonal and nervous communication compared

Hormones and nerves both involve transmission of messages which are triggered by stimuli and produce responses. The target organs of a hormone are equivalent to a nerve's effectors. The main difference between the two systems is in the nature of the message. In the endocrine system the message is a chemical substance (a **chemical messenger** as it is sometimes called) which is conveyed through the circulatory system. In the nervous system the message is a discrete, all-or-nothing **action potential** which is transmitted along a nerve fibre.

Despite this difference, there is one fundamental similarity between the nervous and endocrine systems: both involve **chemical transmission**. In the last chapter we saw that transmission at synapses and neuromuscular

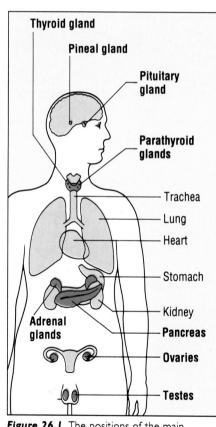

Figure 26.1 The positions of the main endocrine glands in the human body. The endocrine glands are coloured red. The adrenal glands consist of two parts: the adrenal medulla in the centre, and the adrenal cortex round the edge. Each secretes its own hormone or hormones.

Thyroid gland

Pineal gland

Pituitary gland

Parathyroid glands

Trachea

Lung

Heart

Stomach

Kidney

Adrenal glands

Pancreas

Ovaries

Testes

Gland	Hormone	Chemical structure	Main functions
Thyroid	Thyroxine	Amino acid (tyrosine) with iodine-containing group attached	Raises basal metabolic rate
	Calcitonin	Polypeptide	Opposes action of parathormone (see below)
Parathyroids	Parathormone	Polypeptide	Controls concentration of calcium and phosphate ions in blood
Pancreas	Insulin	Protein	Lowers blood sugar concentration
	Glucagon	Polypeptide	Raises blood sugar concentration
Adrenal medulla	Adrenaline	Ring compound with short side chain	Prepares body for emergency: metabolic rate increases, blood diverted to vital organs, etc.
Adrenal cortex *adrenal cortical hormones*	Aldosterone	Steroid	Controls concentration of sodium and potassium ions in blood
	Cortisol	Steroid	Prevents excessive immune response (anti-stress)
	Androgens	Steroid	Promote development of testes and secondary sexual characters of male
Pineal body	Melatonin	Hydroxy-indol	Causes concentration of melanin in frog's skin; promotes sexual development in mammals
Testes	Androgens	Steroids	Promote development of testes and secondary sexual characters of male
Ovaries	Oestrogens	Steroids	Promote development of ovaries and secondary sexual characters of female; control menstrual cycle and pregnancy
	Progesterone	Steroid	Controls menstrual cycle and pregnancy
Pituitary (anterior lobe)	Thyroid-stimulating hormone (TSH)	Polypeptide	Causes thyroid gland to secrete thyroxine
	Adreno-corticotrophic hormone (ACTH)	Protein	Causes adrenal cortex to secrete adrenal cortical hormones
	Growth hormone	Protein	Stimulates growth
	Prolactin	Protein	Causes mammary glands to secrete milk
gonado-trophic hormones	Follicle-stimulating hormone (FSH)	Glycoprotein	Controls testes and ovaries
	Luteinising hormone (LH)	Glycoprotein	Controls testes and ovaries
Pituitary (posterior lobe)	Antidiuretic hormone (ADH)	Polypeptide	Causes reabsorption of water in kidneys
	Oxytocin	Polypeptide	Causes contraction of uterus at birth

Table 26.1 The principal endocrine glands of mammals, together with their hormones and main functions. The hormones secreted by the gut are not included – they are explained in Chapter 16. You will find full references to these and other hormones in the index. The pancreas is both an endocrine and exocrine gland: the endocrine part consists of the islets of Langerhans whose structure and function are explained in Chapter 21.

junctions is achieved by a chemical substance – a neurotransmitter. The latter is equivalent to a hormone in the endocrine system. The main difference between them is that the neurotransmitter substance has to travel a mere fraction of a micrometre to reach its destination, whereas a hormone may have to travel the full length of the body.

An analogy

In comparing the nervous and endocrine systems as means of communication, you may find an analogy helpful. You are stranded on a desert island. How do you communicate with the outside world? Fortunately there are two hundred empty beer bottles on the island. So you write letters, put them in the bottles and float them out to sea, confident that sooner or later at least one of them will be washed up on the mainland. This is equivalent to the endocrine system. But there is another possibility. It so happens that there is a telephone box on the island. So you ring home. This is equivalent to the nervous system.

Can you see any flaws in this analogy? If so what are they?

Other differences flow from this. There are four main ones:

- The nervous system produces responses more quickly than the endocrine system. This is because it takes less time for a nerve impulse to reach its destination and produce a response than it does for a hormone. The hormone is limited by the speed at which blood travels through the arteries.

- Since it is shed into the bloodstream, there is nothing to stop a hormone being carried to every part of the body. A nerve impulse, however, is transmitted by a particular nerve fibre to a specific destination.

- Because hormones are carried all over the body, the responses produced by them are often widespread. A single hormone may act on target organs far removed from each other. In contrast, nervous responses may be very localised, involving the contraction of only one muscle in a particular part of the body.

- Hormonal responses frequently continue for a long time. The reason is that hormones tend to be secreted continuously in a steady 'trickle'. Examples of such long-term responses are growth and metabolism. Nervous responses, however, are usually brought about by sporadic bursts of nerve impulses and are therefore short-lived, such as the contraction of a muscle in reflex action.

Despite these differences the endocrine and nervous systems are closely connected. This is best illustrated by the **adrenal glands**. The middle part of these glands, the **adrenal medulla**, secretes the hormone **adrenaline**. This is almost identical chemically to the neurotransmitter substance **noradrenaline** which is produced at the ends of the sympathetic nerves. The hormone adrenaline evokes many of the same responses as impulses in the sympathetic nerves: acceleration of the heart, redistribution of the blood etc. The combined effect of the adrenal medulla and sympathetic nervous system is to prepare the body for emergency. The nervous system produces an instant response with no delay. The response is then sustained by the slower action of the hormone.

We see, then, that there is a close connection between the endocrine and nervous systems. In the case of the adrenal medulla and sympathetic nervous system, the connection is so close that one cannot help suspecting that the two share a common evolutionary origin. Innervated by the sympathetic nervous system, the adrenal medulla can be looked upon as a conglomeration of modified neurones which, far removed from the effectors, shed their transmitter substance into the bloodstream. During embryonic development the secretory cells of the medulla are derived from the same group of cells that elsewhere give rise to sympathetic ganglion cells, but as they differentiate they become rounded and thoroughly unlike nerve cells in their appearance, so their final form belies their origin.

An endocrine gland in detail: the thyroid

The **thyroid** may be taken to illustrate some of the features of an endocrine gland. This gland is situated in the neck close to the Adam's apple which is part of the larynx. It secretes **thyroxine**, a complex organic compound containing iodine. The iodine required for its synthesis is obtained from the diet.

The microscopic structure of the thyroid gland is shown in figure 26.2. It demonstrates the essential requirement of any endocrine organ, namely a close association between the hormone-producing cells and the blood-stream. The secretory cells are arranged round a series of hollow **follicles** in which an inactive form of the hormone is stored before being released into the bloodstream. Numerous capillaries lie between the follicles, their thin walls in close contact with the follicle cells.

From the blood flowing through the capillaries the follicle cells take up the raw materials they need for synthesising thyroxine, and into it they release the hormone. The details are summarised in figure 26.3. The raw materials are amino acids, sugars and iodide. Having been absorbed into the follicle cell, they are converted into a complex glycoprotein called **thyroglobulin**. The iodide is taken up by active transport. This process is so efficient that the iodide is several hundred times more concentrated in the follicle cells than in the blood. Once in the cell, the iodide is oxidised to iodine and incorporated into the thyroglobulin.

Thyroglobulin consists of thyroxine conjugated with a protein. It is an inactive precursor of the hormone and is transferred by exocytosis into the follicle where it is stored. When needed it is taken up by endocytosis into the follicle cell where a protease enzyme separates the thyroxine from the protein. The free hormone is then secreted from the follicle cell into the bloodstream.

The whole process is rather like a production line: the product is manufactured in a factory (the thyroid cell), stored in a warehouse (the follicle) and then dispatched by a transport system (the blood). Actually the thyroid gland is unusual in storing its hormone before releasing it into the bloodstream; most endocrine glands secrete their hormones straight into the blood.

The function of thyroxine

Thyroxine is responsible for controlling the **basal metabolic rate**, and is therefore important in growth. Under-secretion of it during development (**hypothyroidism**) causes arrested physical and mental development, a condition called **cretinism**. At the age of 14 or 15 years cretins are stunted and pot-bellied, and so mentally retarded that they may not even be able to feed themselves. In adults hypothyroidism is not so serious since by this time growth is complete. The condition is called **myxoedema**. The symptoms are a decreased metabolic rate, increase in the amount of subcutaneous fat, coarsening of the skin and general physical and mental sluggishness.

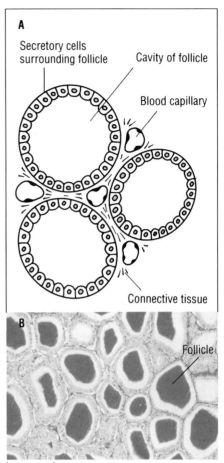

Figure 26.2 The microscopic structure of the thyroid gland.

A Diagram showing the close relationship between the follicles and blood capillaries.

B Photomicrograph of a thin section through part of the thyroid gland. Notice the follicles in which thyroxine is stored before being shed into the bloodstream.

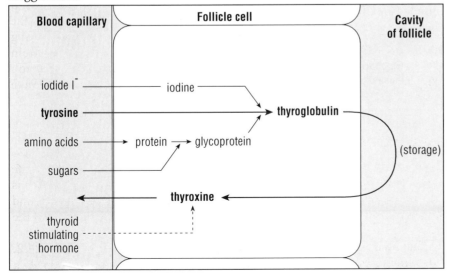

Figure 26.3 How thyroxine is made in a thyroid cell. The cell takes up the amino acid tyrosine and all other necessary raw materials from the blood in the adjacent capillary, stores the inactive thyroglobulin in the follicle, and sheds the hormone into the capillary blood as instructed by thyroid-stimulating hormone from the anterior lobe of the pituitary gland.

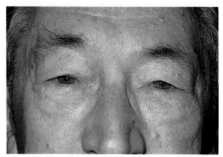

Figure 26.4 This photograph shows puffiness round the eyes and coarsening of the skin which can happen when the thyroid gland of an adult persistently produces too little thyroxine (hypothyroidism).

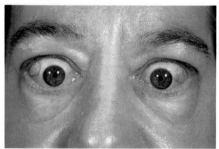

Figure 26.5 This photograph shows the protrusion of the eyeballs (exophthalmia) which can happen when a person's thyroid gland persistently produces too much thyroxine (hyperthyroidism).

Over-production (**hyperthyroidism**) leads to **exophthalmic goitre**, so called because of the characteristic protrusion of the eyeballs (exophthalmia) and swelling of the thyroid gland in the neck (goitre). Other symptoms include a greatly increased metabolic rate, loss of body mass and an accelerated heartbeat, all this being accompanied by a general physical and mental restlessness. Plainly the thyroid is important in determining its owner's general mental and physical state. It is interesting to speculate on the extent to which our own personalities may be altered by minor fluctuations in thyroid activity.

A deficiency of thyroxine in the body may be caused either by the thyroid gland failing to work properly, or to a shortage of iodine in the diet. Dietary shortage of iodine used to be common in certain iodine-deficient regions of the world – for example, parts of Switzerland, the Great Lakes in North America and Derbyshire in England where goitre cases were referred to as 'Derbyshire neck'. In such areas the problem can be overcome by adding iodine to the drinking water or by supplying the inhabitants with iodised salt. The remedy for myxoedema used to be to take thyroid orally – the old prescription was one fried sheep's thyroid weekly with redcurrant jelly. Nowadays carefully regulated quantities of thyroxine are administered to the patient.

An over-abundance of thyroxine is generally caused by an overactive, often excessively large thyroid gland. In the old days, the remedy was for a surgeon to remove part of the thyroid and hope for the best. If severe myxoedema resulted, small pieces of the thyroid were grafted back. Nowadays surgical removal of thyroid tissue is carried out with much greater precision. Sometimes surgery is avoided altogether by injecting controlled doses of radioactive iodine into the patient's bloodstream. This is taken up by the thyroid cells, killing those in which it accumulates above a certain concentration.

Control of thyroxine production

There are two problems here, and they apply to most endocrine glands. First, at any given time it is important that thyroxine should be secreted at a steady level so that its concentration in the bloodstream is held more or less constant. Second, it must be possible to vary the amount secreted at certain times to fit in with the changing needs of the body.

Keeping the concentration of thyroxine constant is an example of homeostasis and is achieved by a negative feedback process of the kind outlined in Chapter 21. The mechanism is summarised in figure 26.6. The

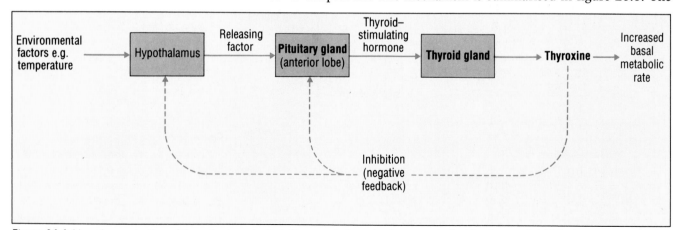

Figure 26.6 How the production of thyroxine is controlled. If too much thyroxine is present in the bloodstream, it inhibits its own production by the negative feedback mechanism shown here.

secretion of thyroxine into the bloodstream is triggered by a hormone produced by the anterior lobe of the pituitary gland. This is called **thyroid stimulating hormone (TSH)**. Now the production of TSH is regulated by thyroxine itself. A slight excess of thyroxine inhibits the anterior lobe of the pituitary which responds by secreting less TSH. This in turn reduces the activity of the thyroid gland, leading to a drop in the amount of thyroxine produced. This in turn reduces the activity of the thyroid gland, leading to a drop in the amount of thyroxine produced. This then removes the inhibitory influence on the pituitary so that more TSH will be produced – and so on.

The second problem – changing the amount of thyroxine secreted – is dealt with by the brain. The production of TSH by the pituitary gland is controlled by the hypothalamus – we shall see how in a moment. The hypothalamus itself is subject to environmental influences such as temperature so that in some animals the secretion of thyroxine – and hence metabolism and growth – can be geared to the seasons. The hypothalamus is subject to feedback inhibition by thyroxine so that excessive secretion is prevented.

How hormones were discovered

Guest author Patricia Kohn puts hormones into historical perspective.

When, long ago, people started to control the behaviour and development of domestic animals by castration, they were unwittingly performing the first experiments in endocrinology. However, the notion that organs like the testes produce their effects by releasing chemical substances into the blood only became clear in the 19th century. The more obvious endocrine glands like the thyroid and pituitary were well known to anatomists, and some of them had been described as long ago as the second century AD Diseases which we now know to be caused by endocrine abnormalities were also described by the ancient physicians, and their accounts make it clear that they were familiar with diabetes mellitus, goitre, cretinism and several other endocrine disorders.

Many functions were ascribed to these mysterious organs. Some of them seem, with the benefit of hindsight, most peculiar. For example, the pituitary was once thought to act as a drain through which excess mucus from the brain could pass into the back of the nose; and the thyroid was thought to protect the brain from sudden increases in blood-flow by acting as a sort of sponge.

The idea that substances necessary for the well-being of the whole body might be secreted into the blood grew up in the mid–18th century, but at that time it was believed that *all* cells produced such secretions. It was not until the 19th century that Claude Bernard, famous for his insight into the importance of homeostasis, put forward the idea that 'internal secretions' were responsible for regulating bodily functions.

In the latter half of the 19th century experiments were carried out on animals in which endocrine glands were removed and the effects compared with the symptoms of known diseases. This was followed by attempts to treat patients with extracts of various glands, even though in many cases the functions of the glands were not understood. On occasions this kind of therapy got out of hand. One of the pioneers of endocrinology, Charles Edouard Brown-Sequard, nearly got this emerging subject a bad name by claiming that testicular extracts produced amazing rejuvenating effects on elderly men – including himself! Such notions were without foundation and were vigorously rejected by the rest of the scientific community.

During the early part of the 20th century a more systematic approach was applied to establishing the functions of the various endocrine glands. The principle was to remove the gland from an experimental animal, study the effects and then remedy them by treating the animal with extracts of the gland. This eventually led to the identification of the functions of most of the endocrine glands.

Once the extracts were shown to be biologically active, the chemists moved in. They purified the extract down to a single chemical which still showed the same properties. This was the actual hormone. With the hormone available in a pure form, chemical analysis could be carried out to reveal its structure. In some cases it then became possible to synthesise the substance artificially and use it to treat people with hormone deficiency diseases.

All this painstaking work laid down the foundations for the modern molecular approach which is showing how hormones bring about their effects on individual target cells by interacting with receptors inside the cell or on its surface.

Figure 26.7 Diagram of the pituitary gland, viewed from the side, showing its blood and nerve connections with the hypothalamus. The three black blobs in the hypothalamus are nerve centres.

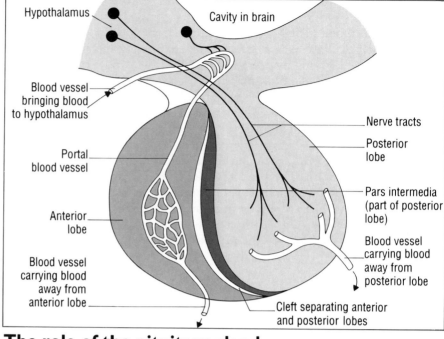

The role of the pituitary gland

The production of thyroid stimulating hormone illustrates one of the most important functions of the pituitary gland, namely to regulate the activity of other endocrine glands. The pituitary secretes other stimulating hormones (known collectively as **trophic hormones**) which activate such endocrine glands as the adrenal cortex and gonads. The pituitary is in turn inhibited by the hormones secreted by these target organs (negative feedback).

The pituitary gland is closely influenced by the brain and, through the brain, by the receptors. In this way environmental changes, as well as the animal's general mental state, can influence hormonal activity. We saw this a moment ago in the way the brain controls the thyroid gland. The same sort of mechanism ensures that certain mammals breed in the spring. They are brought into season by **gonad stimulating hormones** which are secreted by the anterior lobe of the pituitary gland. With the approach of spring the brain senses, through the eyes, that the amount of daily light is increasing. As a result, the hypothalamus sends messages to the pituitary gland instructing it to secrete these hormones.

The brain and the pituitary gland

Figure 26.7 shows the close relationship between the pituitary gland and the brain. The gland projects down from the floor of the brain and is divided into an **anterior** and a **posterior lobe**, each of which secretes certain hormones. In the hypothalamus there are two groups of nerve centres. One is connected to the anterior lobe, the other to the posterior lobe. These centres send instructions to their respective lobes telling them whether or not to release their hormones into the bloodstream. The two groups of centres communicate with the pituitary in different ways – by hormones called **releasing factors** in the case of the anterior lobe, and by nerve impulses in the case of the posterior lobe.

Let us take the anterior lobe first (figure 26.8). The nerve centres in the hypothalamus are connected to the anterior lobe by a **portal blood vessel.** (A portal blood vessel is one with capillaries at both ends.) When the hypothalamic centres are stimulated either naturally or by experimental means,

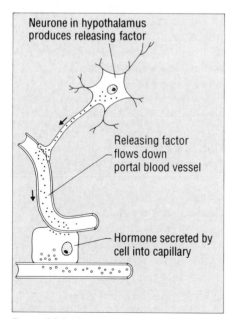

Figure 26.8 How the anterior lobe of the pituitary gland produces its hormones. The anterior lobe receives releasing factors (dots) which reach it from the hypothalamus via the portal blood vessels. The releasing factors then cause the cells in the anterior lobe to secrete their hormones (circles) into the bloodstream.

releasing factors are secreted into the portal vessel by the nerve cells. The releasing factors are then carried by the blood in the portal vessel to the anterior lobe where they regulate the secretion of its various hormones. There are specific releasing factors for each hormone: some of the releasing factors stimulate release of the hormone, others inhibit it.

Now the posterior lobe (figure 26.9). In this case the nerve centres in the hypothalamus are connected to the lobe, not by blood vessels, but by neurones. The axons of these neurones perform two functions:

- They carry hormones from the nerve centre to the posterior lobe where they are stored in the nerve terminals.

- When appropriate, they transmit impulses from the nerve centre to the posterior lobe, causing the hormones to be released into the blood.

An example of a hormone which is secreted this way is **antidiuretic hormone (ADH)** (see page 378). In this case the stimulus which causes impulses to be sent to the posterior lobe is a rise in the osmotic pressure of the blood. The stimulus is detected by osmoreceptors in the hypothalamus, and in consequence ADH is released from the posterior lobe into the bloodstream.

It may surprise you to find axons producing hormones in this way. But in fact it is quite common and is yet another indication of the close connection between the nervous and endocrine systems. The process is known as **neurosecretion**, and the cells that do it are called **neurosecretory cells**. The production of ADH is a good example of this in mammals, but we also find it in other animals such as crustaceans and insects.

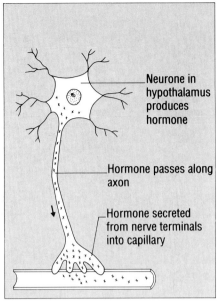

Figure 26.9 The posterior lobe receives its hormones (crosses) from the hypothalamus via axons (neurosecretion). The hormones are stored in the expanded nerve terminals until the arrival of nerve impulses from the hypothalamus triggers their release into the bloodstream.

Prostaglandins

Prostaglandins provide another means of communication in the body. Guest author Patricia Kohn explains.

Until relatively recently it was thought to be characteristic of hormones that they travel via the circulation to distant target organs.

It gradually became apparent, however, that such a sharp definition is an oversimplification. One reason was the discovery that some chemical messengers, also act locally. **Prostaglandins** are an example of these 'local hormones'.

Prostaglandins are fatty acids containing twenty carbon atoms, five of which form a ring. Unlike other chemical messengers, they are not synthesised and then stored in specialised cells until some kind of signal causes them to be released. Instead they are continually being synthesised and released from virtually all types of cell. The precursor is one of the membrane phospholipids: the fatty acid component of the phospholipid is split off by a phospholipase enzyme and, after various modifications, is secreted as the prostaglandin. As quickly as the prostaglandin molecules are released they are degraded by enzymes in the tissue fluid and the whole process ticks over continuously.

When the need arises, however, the activity of the phospholipase is greatly increased, with the result that prostaglandin synthesis is speeded up. The effects of prostaglandins are very varied. However, they produce one effect which is common to all tissues and organs: they help to initiate the **inflammatory response**.

Inflammation occurs when a tissue is injured or infected (see page 415). One of the main features of inflammation is vasodilatation with resultant increase in blood flow through the capillaries. The prostaglandins bring about vasodilatation by direct action on the arterioles. Other features of inflammation, such as increased permeability of the capillaries and the migration of white blood cells, are brought about by other agents, but prostaglandins increase their effectiveness. The pain which accompanies inflammation is caused by the stimulating effect of the prostaglandins on these other agents.

Sometimes the immune system mistakenly identifies certain of the body's own tissue antigens as foreign ones. In these cases the inflammatory response does not cease quickly, as happens when an acute infection is defeated. Instead it gives rise to chronic and sometimes painful diseases such as rheumatoid arthritis. Treatment of these conditions is based on the use of **anti-inflammatory drugs**. One of the most useful is the familiar aspirin which suppresses the production of prostaglandin molecules and so reduces inflammation.

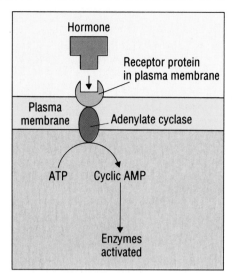

Figure 26.10 Schematic diagram showing how a hormone such as adrenaline affects its target cell. The hormone molecule binds to a receptor site on the plasma membrane. This activates adenylate cyclase which catalyses the conversion of ATP to cyclic AMP. The latter then activates specific enzymes in the cytoplasm.

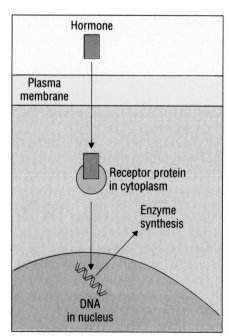

Figure 26.11 Schematic diagram showing how a steroid hormone such as progesterone is believed to affect its target cell. The hormone molecule enters the cell and binds with a specific protein which carries it to the nucleus where it switches on the appropriate genes in the DNA.

How hormones control cells

Let us suppose that a hormone has reached its target organ. How does it cause the cells to respond? Some light has been thrown on this question by the discovery that many animal cells contain a compound called **cyclic adenosine monophosphate (cyclic AMP)**. Cyclic AMP is similar to ATP, which we have already met in connection with energy transfer, except that it contains only one phosphate group instead of three and this phosphate group is attached to the adenosine part of the molecule in the form of a ring. Cyclic AMP is formed from ATP by the enzyme **adenylate cyclase** which is found in the plasma membrane.

Cyclic AMP occurs in extremely low concentration inside the cell (approximately one part per million), but it has been found that its concentration increases if the cell is brought into contact with the appropriate hormone. This has led to the suggestion that cyclic AMP may serve as a **second messenger** linking the hormone with the cell's response.

Research in recent years supports the kind of model shown in figure 26.10. When a hormone molecule reaches the target cell, it binds to the plasma membrane at a specific **receptor site**. The receptor site is located on the outer surface of the membrane and is associated with a molecule of adenylate cyclase. The binding of the hormone to the membrane increases the activity of adenylate cyclase, causing ATP on the immediate inside of the membrane to be converted into cyclic AMP. The cyclic AMP then activates specific enzymes which bring about the appropriate response within the cell. The extent of the particular response is determined by the concentration of cyclic AMP, which in turn depends on a delicate balance between adenylate cyclase, responsible for its synthesis, and another enzyme – a phosphodiesterase – which destroys it.

Although cyclic AMP was the first second messenger to be discovered, others are now known. A common feature of them is that the enzymatic changes which occur on the inner side of the plasma membrane lead to a rise in the concentration of the second messenger inside the cell. In other words the second messenger amplifies the response, a very small amount of hormone producing a disproportionately large effect.

Hormones which involve a second messenger include adrenaline and ADH. In these two cases the second messenger is cyclic AMP. However, not all hormones employ a second messenger. For example, thyroxine and steroid hormones such as progesterone work in a different way (figure 26.11). In this case the hormone molecule is fat-soluble and can diffuse through the plasma membrane into the cell. In the cytoplasm it binds to a specific receptor protein which carries it into the nucleus. It then activates the appropriate genes in the DNA. The genes direct the synthesis of enzymes which bring about the response.

There are variations on the two models outlined above but one feature is common to them all, namely that the hormone molecules have to bind to specific receptor proteins, either on the cell surface or inside the cell, before they can produce an effect. There is a complimentary configuration between the hormone molecule and its receptor, just as there is between an enzyme and its substrate. This explains why a given hormone acts only on certain target organs. A cell will respond to a hormone only if it possesses the 'right' receptors.

What these receptors are really doing is to enable the cell to *recognise* signals from other cells. This is the basis of how cells communicate with each other, not only through hormones but in other types of interaction as well.

Summary

1 A **hormone** is a chemical substance which is secreted into the bloodstream by an **endocrine gland** and which produces a response in specific **target organs**.

2 The **endocrine system** may be compared with the **nervous system**. Both provide means of communication within the body, but they work in different ways.

3 The close connection between the endocrine and nervous systems is illustrated by the **adrenal medulla** whose principal hormone, **adrenaline**, is similar to the neurotransmitter substance (noradrenaline) produced by the sympathetic nervous system.

4 The basic requirement of any endocrine gland is a close association between the secretory cells and blood capillaries. This is demonstrated by the **thyroid gland** whose cells absorb the raw materials for making the hormone from the bloodstream and shed the hormone into it.

5 The thyroid gland also illustrates how the production of a hormone may be controlled by **negative feedback**, in which process the **pituitary gland** plays an important part.

6 Failure of the control mechanism may result in an excess or deficiency of the hormone, and this may have profound consequences on the functioning of the body.

7 The pituitary gland provides another example of the close connection between the endocrine and nervous systems. The pituitary gland is attached to the **hypothalamus** of the brain.

8 The hypothalamus communicates with the anterior lobe of the pituitary by means of **releasing factors** which are carried in **portal blood vessels**.

9 The hypothalamus communicates with the posterior lobe of the pituitary by means of neurones. The neurones secrete hormones as well as transmitting impulses.

10 The secretion of hormones by neurones is quite common in animals and is called **neurosecretion**.

11 Some hormones affect their target cells by activating the appropriate enzymes via **cyclic AMP**. Others work by influencing the cells' genes (DNA). In both cases the hormone binds to a specific receptor before it can exert its effects.

Review questions

1 What is an *endocrine gland* and how does it differ from an *exocrine gland*? Illustrate your answer by reference to the pancreas.

2 Suggest two features which you would expect any mammalian endocrine gland to possess. Give reasons for your answer.

3 Name an endocrine gland which controls (a) the metabolic rate, (b) blood sugar concentration, (c) growth rate, (d) the osmotic pressure of the blood, (e) sexual development.

4 In this chapter it is stated that hormonal responses are generally slow, prolonged and widespread whereas nervous responses are rapid, localised and short-lived. Do you think this is a valid generalisation?

5 'The endocrine system is more than just a collection of independent, hormone-secreting glands.' Discuss.

6 In the early part of the 20th century numerous thyroid transplantation operations were carried out with remarkable success by the late Albert Kocher M.D. of Berne, Switzerland. In the operation, thyroid tissue was taken from patients with hyperthyroidism and grafted onto the thyroids of patients with hypothyroidism. Of 204 transplantations, 86 per cent were successful and the transplanted tissue was active for at least several years. Comment.

7 Use the thyroid gland to illustrate the part played by negative feedback in hormonal control.

8 In low concentrations adrenaline causes the bladder and anal sphincters to constrict, but in high concentrations the same hormone makes these sphincters dilate. Speculate on the possible significance of this.

9 The pituitary is often described as the 'master gland' of the endocrine system. Justify this title.

10 Hormones which affect their target cells via cytoplasmic receptors produce responses more slowly than those acting via membrane receptors but the responses are usually more prolonged. Suggest a reason for this.

Further reading

You will find a useful general account of hormones in 'Animal Hormones' by J.W. Buckle (Arnold, 1983).

More detail is given by R.N. Hardy in *Endocrine Physiology*, 2nd edn. (Arnold, 1993) and there is a clear account of the second messenger theory in *The Molecular Biology of the Cell* by Alberts et al (Garland, 1989).

How hormones act on their target cells is discussed further in *Biology, Advanced Topics*.

CHAPTER 27

Reception of stimuli

It is obviously important to an organism, particularly an active one, that it should be aware of conditions around it so as to respond appropriately to any changes that may occur. These changes, or **stimuli**, may be local, such as a prick with a pin, or more general, such as the intensity of illumination.

Whatever the nature of the change, the stimulus is registered by **receptors** from which impulses are relayed to the CNS. The receptors consist of **receptor cells** (also called **sensory cells**) which may be single, scattered more or less uniformly over the whole body, or concentrated to form a **sense organ**. In some animals the sense organs reach a high degree of elaboration – the mammalian eye and ear for example.

Classification of receptors

Receptors can be classified according to the type of stimulation they respond to:

- **Chemoreceptors** are stimulated by chemicals, for example receptors mediating the senses of smell and taste, and receptors that detect changes in the concentration of carbon dioxide or oxygen in the blood.
- **Mechanoreceptors** are sensitive to mechanical deformation, for example receptors sensitive to touch, pressure, tension (stretch), sounds (ear) and displacement of the body (balance).
- **Photoreceptors** are stimulated by light, for example the eyes of verte-brates and the scattered light-sensitive cells of invertebrates such as the earthworm.
- **Thermoreceptors** are stimulated by temperature, for example receptors located in the mammalian skin, sensitive to warmth and cold.

Although receptors are commonly associated with the integument where they detect changes in the external environment, receptors also occur inside the body where they register internal changes such as the concentration of carbon dioxide in the blood, the degree of tension in the muscles, or the position of the head relative to gravity. These two types of receptor, distin-guished by whether they are stimulated by external or internal stimuli, are known as **exteroceptors** and **interoceptors** respectively.

Interoceptors specifically concerned with giving details of position and movement are termed **proprioceptors**, and they are important in achieving equilibrium and coordinated locomotion.

In this chapter we shall start by considering the structure and func-tioning of individual receptor cells, and then explore how these are inte-grated to form complex sense organs.

Receptor cells

The essential job of receptor cells is to transfer the energy associated with the stimulus to an electrical change in the nerve, i.e. the **nerve impulse**. For example, photoreceptors transfer energy from light to nerve impulses, and thermoreceptors transfer heat energy to nerve impulses.

Receptor cells possess the characteristics of cells in general plus certain unique features of their own depending on the kind of stimulation they are adapted to receive. Commonly the distal end of the cell is drawn out into one or more slender processes which are adapted to receive a specific stimulus (figure 27.1). The cell responds by generating an action potential in the nerve fibre to which it is attached.

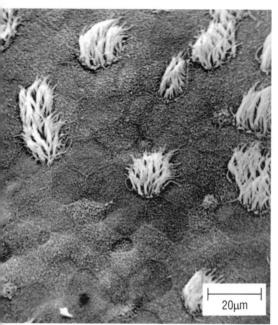

Figure 27.1 Scanning electron micrograph of sensory processes (confusingly called 'cilia') projecting from the olfactory epithelium in the nose. Each bunch of processes projects from the free surface of a single receptor cell. These particular receptor cells are chemoreceptors responsible for our sense of smell. Their processes are stimulated by odorous airborne molecules that impinge upon them. The receptor cells are interspersed amongst ordinary (non-sensitive) epithelial cells whose outlines can just be seen in this picture.

20μm

Each type of receptor cell is specialised in position and structure to respond to one kind of stimulus. For example, the photoreceptor cells of a vertebrate are located in the retina at the back of the eye. Other parts of the eye collect and focus light on the receptor cells. Inside the eye the receptor cells are protected from other forms of stimulation. In addition they possess special features which enable them to absorb energy from the light and transfer it to nerve impulses. The same principle applies to other receptors such as the ear, balance organs and so on.

Types of receptor cell

Structurally a distinction may be made between two kinds of receptor cell (figure 27.2). In the simpler case the sensitive device consists of the end of a sensory neurone which is adapted to receive stimuli. It is continued inwards as a nerve fibre which makes synaptic connection with a connector neurone in the CNS (see page 437). This type of sensory unit is typical of olfactory receptors in the nose and free nerve endings sensitive to pain in the skin.

In the second kind of receptor a separate cell is modified to receive the stimulus and to transmit the response to an associated sensory neurone with which it is in synaptic contact. This is typical of the receptor cells in the eye and ear.

The main difference between these two types of receptor is that in the first type there is no synapse between the sensory device and the nerve fibre, whereas in the second type there is.

Functioning of receptor cells

The job of a receptor cell is to respond to a specific stimulus by sending off an action potential in the sensory nerve fibre. This has been demonstrated in a wide range of animals by exposing sensory nerve fibres and placing them in contact with recording electrodes connected to an oscilloscope (see page 441). When the receptor cells are stimulated by appropriate stimuli, action potentials appear on the screen of the oscilloscope.

The sensitivity of some receptors is astonishing. For example, the hair-like mechanoreceptors of certain insects will respond to a deflection of as little as 3.6 nm, a property which makes them highly sensitive to airborne sounds. And the chemoreceptors on the antennae of certain moths are stimulated by a single molecule of scent. So sensitive are these chemoreceptors that males of the Chinese saturnid moth *Arctias selene* can locate females as much as 10 km away.

It is easier to demonstrate what a receptor does than to show how it does it. Small and often inaccessible, most receptor cells defy investigation by standard physiological techniques. There are no large receptor cells equivalent to the giant axons of the squid. Nevertheless, certain receptor cells are sufficiently large and accessible for physiologists to carry out experiments on them. These include muscle spindles, olfactory and taste receptors, and various types of skin receptor. Physiologists have inserted microelectrodes into such receptors and have recorded the electrical changes which take place when they are stimulated.

How receptor cells work

On receiving a stimulus, the sensitive part of the receptor cell develops a local non-conducted positive charge called the **generator potential**. The generator potential is caused by depolarisation of the membrane surrounding this part of the cell, brought about by movement of ions similar to that which takes place in the transmission of nerve impulses (see page 442).

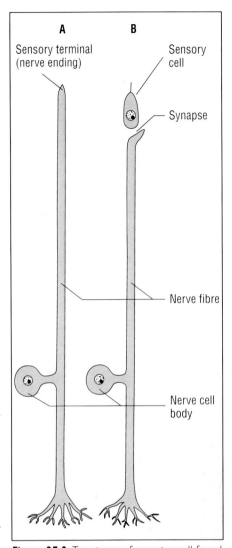

Figure 27.2 Two types of receptor cell found in humans and other vertebrates. In **A** the terminal end of a sensory neurone is modified to receive stimuli. In **B** an epithlelial cell is modified to receive stimuli and makes synaptic connection with a sensory neurone.

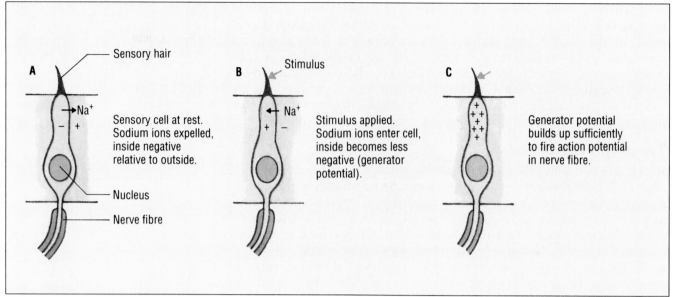

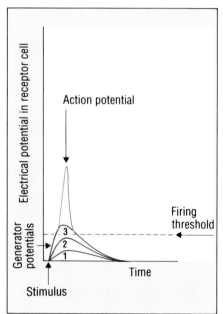

Figure 27.3 These schematic diagrams show the development of a generator potential and firing of an action potential (impulse) when a receptor cell is stimulated. In the hypothetical receptor cell shown here, stimulation is achieved by a slight deflection of the sensory hair which projects from the end of the cell.

Figure 27.4 The electrical changes which develop in a receptor cell when stimulated with three separate stimuli of increasing intensity. The generator potentials produced by the first two stimuli are too small to reach the firing threshold, so they fail to initiate action potentials. However, the third stimulus produces a generator potential which reaches the firing threshold and causes an action potential to be discharged.

The size of the generator potential depends on the intensity of the stimulus. If the stimulus is weak, only a slight potential develops. However, if the stimulis is strong enough, the generator potential may build up to such an extent that it reaches the necessary level, or **threshold**, to fire off an **action potential** in the adjacent nerve fibre (figures 27.3 and 27.4). If the generator potential is maintained after an action potential has been conducted away, a second one will be fired off. Generally action potentials will continue to be discharged as long as the generator potential remains above the threshold.

Frequency of discharge

The ability of a receptor cell to generate impulses in a sensory nerve fibre is thus dependent on the development of a local potential change. Since this discovery a number of interesting facts about the generator potential have emerged.

In the first place it has been found that the larger the generator potential, the shorter is the interval between successive action potentials. In other words the size of the generator potential (which itself depends on the intensity of stimulation) determines the frequency of action potentials discharged from the receptor. Thus a weak stimulus brings about a comparatively small generator potential and a low-frequency discharge of impulses in the nerve fibre; a stronger stimulus produces a larger generator potential and a higher-frequency discharge of impulses.

And there is a further point. The larger the generator potential the longer it takes to fall below the firing threshold after stimulation has ceased. This means that the total number of impulses fired off in the axon is greater with stronger stimuli.

These facts provide an explanation of the everyday experience that weak stimuli generally produce small, short-lived responses whereas strong stimuli produce larger, more prolonged responses. For example, you would respond more violently if you were hit by a cricket ball than if a fly landed on you. We shall have more to say about these **graded responses** in the next chapter.

Adaptation

If a steady stimulus is maintained, the generator potential gradually declines and the frequency of action potentials decreases. Eventually the generator potential may fall below the firing threshold and no further action potentials are discharged (figure 27.5). When this state is reached the receptor is said to be **adapted**.

The speed at which a receptor adapts depends on the size and duration of its generator potential in relation to the firing threshold. These in turn depend on the properties of its membrane. Some receptors adapt rapidly, others slowly or not at all. The one in figure 27.5 is a rapidly adapting receptor and only five action potentials are discharged.

The importance of adaptation is that it protects the organism from excessive discharge of impulses in its sensory nerves. To illustrate the point of this, think what happens if you put on a coarse shirt. At first the tickling sensation is almost intolerable, but within half an hour or so the unpleasant sensation disappears and there is no further discomfort. This is because the tactile receptors in the skin stop firing impulses. Of course it is not only receptors that adapt in this way. Synapses do so too (see page 451), and it is sometimes difficult to decide whether an animal's failure to respond to repeated stimulation is due to adaptation of its receptors or failure of synapses in the nervous system.

Fusion of stimuli

If a receptor cell is stimulated repetitively the stimuli can be detected separately only if the frequency is not too great. If the stimuli exceed a certain frequency, they appear to fuse into one continuous stimulus. To be detectable the frequency must be sufficiently low for the generator potential produced by each stimulus to die down before the next stimulus is received. If the frequency of stimulation is increased, there comes a point when the generator potentials fuse, resulting in a continual stream of action potentials being discharged from the receptor. When this point is reached the separate stimuli can no longer be detected.

The initial events in the reception of a stimulus

We have seen that sensory cells do their job by developing a generator potential which fires off action potentials. But how does a stimulus create a generator potential in the first place? In the case of mechanoreceptors, physical disturbance of the cell opens up ion channels in the plasma membrane which depolarises the membrane locally, just as happens in nerve cells. For example, bending of the hair in the hypothetical tactile receptor cell in figure 27.3 depolarises the membrane in that region of the cell.

In other receptors the mechanism may be less direct. In the photoreceptors in the eye, for example, the stimulus sets into motion a chain of chemical reactions which depolarise the plasma membrane.

But whether the mechanism is direct or indirect, the generator potential provides the link between the stimulus and the impulse which is fired off in the nerve. In other words the generator potential transduces the stimulus into a propagated electrical signal.

To carry out this transduction efficiently, receptor cells are often massed together to form localised sense organs. A typical sense organ includes many supplementary structures in addition to the receptor cells themselves. The function of these supplementary structures is to protect the receptor cells and ensure that they receive the kind of stimuli to which they are adapted to respond. To illustrate this let us look briefly at two of our sense organs, the eye and ear.

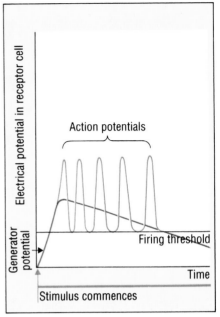

Figure 27.5 When a receptor cell is stimulated with a prolonged stimulus, action potentials continue to be discharged for as long as the generator potential remains above the firing threshold.

The human eye

The structure of the human eye is shown diagrammatically in figure 27.6. The eyes of other mammals conform to this general plan.

The photoreceptor cells are concentrated in the **retina** which lines most of the interior of the eye ball. The spherical shape of the eye ball is maintained by the jelly-like **vitreous humour** which fills the **posterior chamber**. The retina is nourished by the vascular **choroid layer** and protected by the thick connective tissue **sclera**. Heavy pigmentation in the choroid layer shields the retina and prevents light being reflected within the eye.

The front of the eye is protected by the thick transparent **cornea** which is continuous with the sclera. The cornea, surrounding sclera and inner surface of the eyelids are covered by the delicate and highly sensitive **conjunctiva**. Behind the cornea is the **anterior chamber** which is filled with a watery **aqueous humour**. Projecting into the anterior chamber is the **iris**, a circular structure just in front of the **ciliary body**.

The anterior part of the eye is mainly concerned with refracting (i.e. bending) light rays and bringing them to focus on the retina. The structures which do the refracting are the cornea and the lens. The cornea does most of the refracting, but the lens makes a significant contribution which is related to its structure.

The lens

The lens is rather like a transparent rubber balloon filled with fluid. It is held in position by slender fibres which make up the **suspensory ligament**. The fibres are attached to the **ciliary body** which encircles the lens. The ciliary body contains smooth muscle fibres disposed mainly in a circular direction and controlled by the autonomic nervous system.

When the ciliary muscle relaxes, the perimeter of the lens is pulled outwards giving it a flattened shape; when the ciliary muscle contracts, the tension on the lens is released so that it returns to a more spherical shape. By changing its shape the lens can alter its refractive power and thus **accom-**

Figure 27.6 Diagrammatic section of the human eye. The light-sensitive photoreceptor cells are located entirely in the retina which covers most of the inside of the eyeball. All the other parts of the eye (lens, cornea, iris etc) are ancillary structures which, collectively, protect the retina and ensure that it receives the right kind of stimulation.

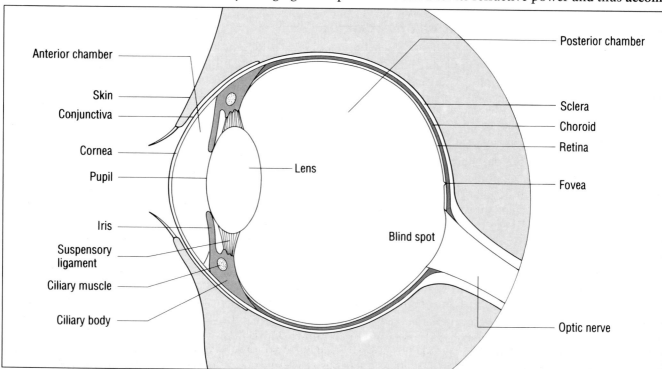

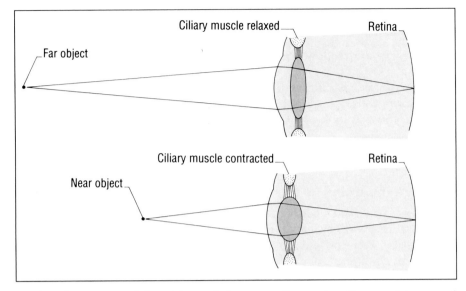

modate for near and far objects. It becomes flatter for distant objects and rounder for closer objects. In this way an object can be kept in focus irrespective of its distance from the eye (figure 27.7).

The iris

The iris surrounds the aperture, or **pupil** of the eye. It contains two sets of smooth muscle fibres, one circular and the other radial. Differential contraction of these two sets of muscles has the effect of varying the size of the pupil, like the opening and closing of the iris diaphragm in a microscope or camera. Closure of the pupil is triggered reflexly by light. In this way excessive light is prevented from falling on the retina (figure 27.8).

The iris muscles, like those of the ciliary body, are controlled by the autonomic nervous system. Atropine, which stops the action of acetylcholine, prevents the circular muscles of the iris from contracting. To dilate the pupils opticians sometimes put a few drops of atropine into their patients' eyes before examining the retina with an opthalmoscope. Film stars sometimes do the same thing to keep their pupils open in bright light.

The retina

The retina contains two types of photoreceptor cells: **rods** and **cones**.

The cones are found over most of the retina but are particularly concentrated in the centre directly behind the lens. This is called the **fovea**, and it is the part of the retina that we use when we look directly at an object. The rods on the other hand lie outside the foveal region in the more peripheral part of the retina. We use this part of the retina when we look at an object out of the corner of our eyes.

The cones enable us to perceive the environment in conditions of good illumination. In other words they are responsible for **daylight vision**. They enable us to see things clearly and sharply, and in colour. However, they are relatively insensitive to low light intensities, and this is why they will only work in good light.

The rods enable us to perceive the environment in conditions of low illumination. In other words they are responsible for **night vision**. They are sensitive to very small intensities of light, which is why they can operate at low levels of illumination. However, they do not register things as clearly and sharply as the cones, and they cannot respond to different colours so they only allow us to see things in black, white and various shades of grey.

Figure 27.7 These diagrams show how the shape of the lens is changed according to whether a distant object or a near object is being viewed. This is called accommodation. When a near object is viewed, the curvature of the lens is increased so that it bends (refracts) the light rays more strongly. This is brought about by contraction of the ciliary muscle, which releases the tension on the lens allowing it to adopt a more spherical shape. For far objects the lens is flattened by relaxation of the ciliary muscle which springs outwards, increasing the tension on the lens. The cornea, as well as the lens, refracts light rays; in fact most of the eye's refraction takes place at the air-cornea interface, as this is where the largest change in refractive index occurs. That is why you cannot see very clearly under water without goggles. However, the cornea cannot vary its refractive power and therefore plays no part in accommodation.

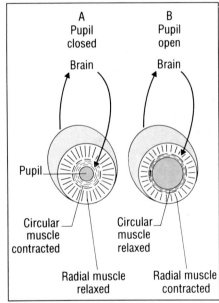

Figure 27.8 The opening and closing of the pupil is controlled by a reflex.

A If the illumination is increased, nerve impulses are transmitted from the retina to the brain and thence to the iris, making the circular muscle contract and the radial muscle relax; so the pupil constricts.

B If the illumination is decreased, the opposite occurs: the radial muscle contracts and the circular muscle relaxes, so the pupil dilates. The iris muscles are controlled by the autonomic nervous system, the radial muscle by the sympathetic and the circular muscle by the parasympathetic (see page 458).

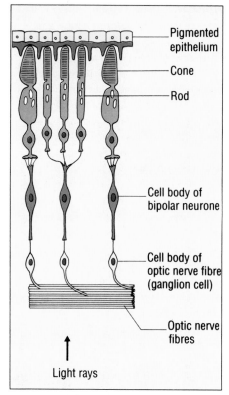

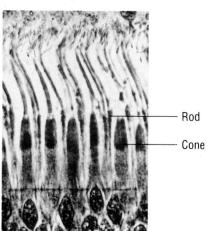

Figure 27.9

Top Simplified diagram of a small part of the retina. Rods and cones make synaptic connection with bipolar neurones which in turn synapse with nerve fibres that converge to form the optic nerve. Notice that the photoreceptor cells lie towards the outer part of the retina, and the bipolar neurones and optic nerve fibres lie towards the inside where the light rays come from. This means that light rays have to traverse a thin layer of nerve fibres and cell bodies before they reach the light-sensitive cells.

Bottom Rods and cones as seen in a vertical section of a small part of the retina. Magnification × 400.

When do we use our rods, and when do we use our cones? Here is a rough rule of thumb:

- When you are reading comfortably in a good light you are using your cones.
- When you are reading with difficulty in a poor light you are using your cones *and* rods.
- When you are looking at the countryside on a moonlit night you are using your rods.

Image inversion

Suppose you look at a person. The illustration shows how light rays reflected from the person, are transmitted through your eye. Notice that the light rays from the head cross the light rays from the feet. The result is that the image is upside down on the retina. The same thing happens when light rays pass through a camera.

Why then don't we see everything upside down? The answer lies with the brain. The brain analyses and interprets information which it receives from the retina in such a way that we see things the right way up.

The remarkable thing is that the brain can modify its interpretation of the retinal image according to circumstances. This was demonstrated some years ago by a rather spectacular experiment. A human subject was given a pair of specially made spectacles fitted with prisms which caused him to see everything upside down. However, after a few hours the brain started to make the necessary adjustment and he began to see things the right way up again.

The brain did not make the adjustment all at once. The subject saw things the right way up for a short while, and then upside down again. It was a week or more before the adjustment was complete and things appeared the right way up all the time. Apparently some visual anomalies still occurred and individual objects still tended to look peculiar. However, the adjustment was sufficiently good for the subject to do such things as catching balls and riding a bicycle.

There was an interesting corollary to this experiment. When the subject eventually took the spectacles off, everything went upside down again and the process of adjustment had to be repeated.

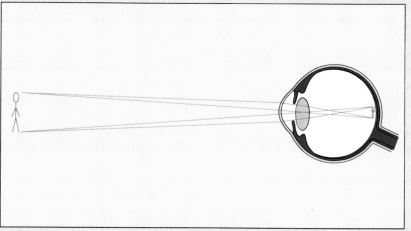

Light rays from the person are transmitted through the eye in such a way that the image formed on the retina is upside down.

Interactions between the photoreceptors

The way the rods and cones are arranged in the retina is shown in figure 27.9. Each one makes synaptic connection with a **bipolar neurone**, so called because two dendrites extend from its cell body. The bipolar neurones make synaptic connection with nerve fibres which run over the surface of the retina and converge at the blind spot where they pass through the back of the eye as the **optic nerve**.

Figure 27.9 is a simplified representation of the retina. In actual fact the photoreceptor cells are interconnected by horizontal neurones, as are the bipolar neurones and ganglion cells. This allows considerable interaction to take place between neighbouring photoreceptors. For example, when you look at a view the photoreceptor cells in one region of the retina may inhibit the photoreceptor cells in an adjacent region. Indeed the photoreceptor cells in the two regions may inhibit each other, but to different degrees. This is called **mutual** or **lateral inhibition**.

The importance of this from the visual point of view is that it can heighten the contrast at light-dark boundaries and therefore enhance contours, an effect which is often accentuated by artists in their drawings and paintings. A similar process occurs in other receptors. For example, in the human ear it may lead to a sharpening of the sense of pitch.

How does light stimulate the rods and cones?

For a generator potential to develop in a rod or cone, the light must first be absorbed by a **photochemical pigment**. Rods contain a reddish photochemical pigment called **phodopsin** (old name: **visual purple**). Briefly, when light strikes a rod the photochemical pigment is broken down, and this leads to the development of a generator potential. The pigment is then rapidly resynthesised and can be used again.

This resynthesis is experienced when we enter a dimly lit room from bright light. At first nothing can be seen, but gradually we begin to make out our surroundings. Vision becomes possible when the photochemical pigment, previously broken down by the bright light, has been regenerated. This is known as **dark adaptation**.

Rhodopsin itself is a complex protein (**opsin**) conjugated with a comparatively simple light-absorbing component called **retinene**. Retinene, an aldehyde of **vitamin A (retinol)**, can exist in two different isomeric forms known as 'cis' and 'trans' isomers. When a quantum of light strikes a molecule of rhodopsin, the retinene changes from the 'cis' form to the 'trans' form. This initiates the splitting of the rhodopsin into opsin and retinene, which in turn triggers a chain of further reactions leading to the excitation of the rod. The resynthesis of rhodopsin from opsin and retinene takes place by a series of energy-requiring reactions.

The rod is structurally adapted to carry out its functions, as you can see in figure 27.10. Numerous **mitochondria**, situated close to the receptive part of the cell, furnish the necessary energy, and stacks of sheet-like **lamellae** increase the surface area for holding the pigment molecules.

Though the details are different, cones operate on the same principle as the rods. The initial process in the receptor mechanism involves the splitting of a photochemical pigment similar to rhodopsin. There are several forms of this pigment, known collectively as **iodopsin**. The cone pigment is less readily broken down than rhodopsin and it regenerates more slowly. This is why the cones only function in conditions of good illumination.

Having discussed the way rods and cones work, we can use this information to explain three important properties of the eye: its sensitivity,

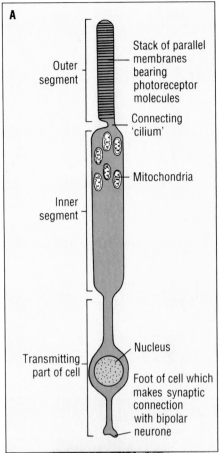

A

Outer segment — Stack of parallel membranes bearing photoreceptor molecules

Connecting 'cilium'

Mitochondria

Inner segment

Transmitting part of cell — Nucleus

Foot of cell which makes synaptic connection with bipolar neurone

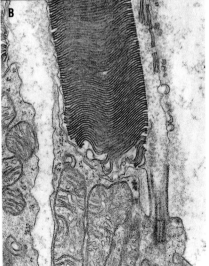

B

Figure 27.10 The detailed structure of a rod.
A Diagram of a rod from the human retina. The molecules of the photochemical pigment, rhodopsin, are located on the membranes in the outer segment. The connecting 'cilium' is so called because it contains an internal array of microtubules similar to that found in cilia.
B Electron micrograph of the upper part of a rod, showing some of the structures seen in the diagram. Magnification × 2500.

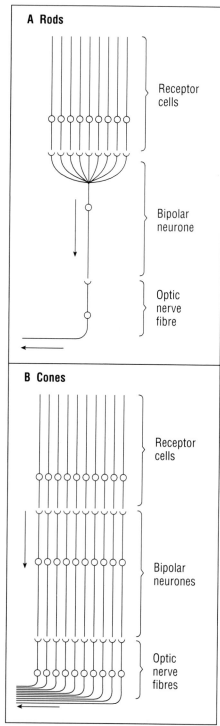

Figure 27.11 The greater sensitivity of rods, compared with cones, can be explained by their connections in the retina.

A shows how a group of rods converge onto a single optic nerve fibre. This allows summation to occur and increases overall sensitivity.

B shows how the cones are arranged. In the central part of the fovea each cone has its own optic nerve fibre.

precision and colour discrimination. Let us take each in turn.

Sensitivity

High sensitivity is a property of the rods. This is what makes the eye capable of seeing in low illumination. The sensitivity of the rods is achieved partly by the chemical and electrical events within a single sensory cell being triggered by the minutest of stimuli. However, there is more to it than this. In the human eye there are about 150 million sensory cells (about 7 million cones, the rest being rods) but only one million fibres in the optic nerve. This means that a large group of rods must share, or converge onto, a single optic nerve fibre. Microscopic examination of the retina shows that this is indeed the case (figure 27.11A). Numerous rods make synaptic contact with a single bipolar neurone which in turn connects with the cell body of a single optic nerve fibre. This is known as **retinal convergence**.

The importance of retinal convergence is that it enables the eye to be more sensitive than it would otherwise be. Look at it this way. A quantum of light hitting a single rod may be sufficient to excite that rod but insufficient to generate an action potential in the bipolar neurone attached to it. However, several rods, stimulated simultaneously, might be able to excite the bipolar neurone. On the basis of extremely careful experiments it has been estimated that six rods stimulated simultaneously are enough to fire an impulse in an optic nerve fibre. We have met this process of **summation** before in connection with synaptic transmission (see page 451), and now we see how it can effectively increase the sensitivity of a receptor. It is interesting that the cones, which are considerably less sensitive than the rods, show far less convergence. Indeed, in the centre of the fovea each cone has its own optic nerve fibre (figure 27.11B).

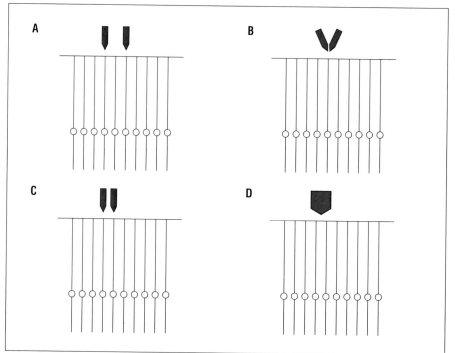

Figure 27.12 The principle of visual acuity. For two dots to be distinguished (resolved) their images must activate two cones separated by at least one in between (**A**). If the images fall on a single cone, the dots cannot be distinguished and will appear as a single dot (**B**). Nor can the dots be distinguished if their images fall on next-door cones (**C**), for this is no different from a single image falling on the two cones (**D**).

Precision

Imagine yourself looking at two black dots on a piece of paper which is gradually moved further and further away. There comes a point when the two dots can no longer be distinguished or *resolved*, as separate entities, and they appear as one. The ability of the eye to resolve two or more stimuli separated spatially is known as its **visual acuity**. In comparison with lower animals the vertebrate eye has particularly high visual acuity, a property that it owes to the cones. What is it about the cones that makes this possible?

To answer this question consider what must happen if two dots are to be distinguished (figure 27.12). If their images fall on the same cone they will obviously not be perceived separately. Even if they fall on next-door cones they cannot be distinguished, for the result will be the same as a single image falling on both cones. To be seen as two separate dots their images must fall on two different cones separated by at least one between. From this it follows that the closer together the cones, the higher will be the

Common defects of the eye

Probably the most common defects of the eye are short-sightedness (myopia) and long-sightedness (hypermetropia).

- A **short-sighted** person can focus on objects close to, but not far away from, the eye. This is caused by the eyeball being too long (or the lens too strong) with the result that the point where the light rays converge is in front of the retina. The condition can be corrected by wearing spectacles with concave lenses which bend the light rays outwards before they reach the eye (illustration 1).

- A **long-sighted** person can focus on objects far away from, but not close to, the eye. This is caused by the eyeball being too short (or the lens too weak) with the result that the point where the light rays converge is behind the retina. The condition can be corrected by wearing spectacles with convex lenses which bend the light rays inwards before they reach the eye (illustration 2).

In elderly people the lens tends to harden, so its shape cannot be changed. Accommodation for near objects becomes difficult, so the person becomes long-sighted. This is

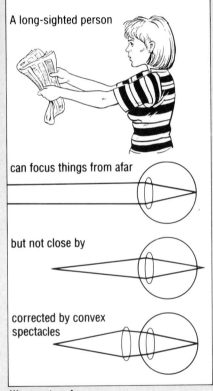

Illustration I
Long-sightedness (hypermetropia)

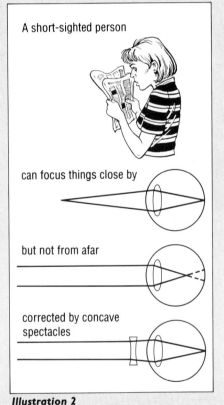

Illustration 2
Short-sightedness (myopia)

why elderly people sometimes hold the book which they are reading a long way away. Again, the remedy is to wear spectacles with convex lenses.

Some people have a defect of the eye called an **astigmatism**. This is

caused by the cornea or lens (or both) being unevenly curved, with the result that the light rays converge at a certain point in one plane but at a different point in another plane. Astigmatism can be corrected by wearing spectacles with specially made lenses.

acuity of the eye. The structure of the retina fits in exactly with this idea. Most of the 7 million cones are concentrated in or around the fovea in the centre of the retina. The fovea is not much more than a millimetre across and the cones in it are thinner than elsewhere, enabling more of them to be packed into this small area.

If the cones are to signal two separate signals to the CNS, they must obviously connect with different optic nerve fibres. Plainly they would lose their identity if they were to share the same sensory pathway. For this reason cones show little or no convergence. In the central part of the fovea each cone has its own bipolar neurone which connects with a single optic nerve fibre. This, coupled with the close proximity of the cones to each other, enables the eye to discriminate between objects very close together. In other words it increases the **resolving power** of the eye. The same principle applies to the sense of touch.

Colour vision

The now generally accepted theory of colour vision, the **trichromatic theory**, depends on the principle that all colours can be produced by mixing the primary colours-blue, green, and red-in various proportions.

The theory proposes that in the retina there are three functionally distinct types of cone, each sensitive to one of these three wavelengths. It is thought that a particular colour is perceived by its wavelengths stimulating one, two, or all three cone types to a varying degree. In other words the sensation, the colour 'seen', is determined by the relative excitation of the three types of receptor cells.

Can it be shown that there are in fact three types of cone in the retina? The answer is yes. To mention one experiment, the particular wavelengths of light absorbed by single cones have been determined by projecting very fine beams of light of known wavelength through an isolated retina placed on a slide on a microscope stage. After passing through the eyepiece the intensity of light is measured by means of an extremely sensitive photomultiplier. The results are compared with light passing through a control tissue lacking photoreceptors. These experiments, carried out by George Wald and his collaborators at Harvard University, have shown that in the retina of humans and monkeys there are three types of cone each containing a different pigment with maximum absorption in, respectively, the blue, green and red parts of the spectrum (figure 27.13). The three pigments are different forms of iodopsin which was mentioned earlier.

Colour vision is therefore the result of differential stimulation of three different types of cone. The intensity of colour is thought to be determined by the absolute frequency at which impulses are discharged from the three receptors; the type of colour by the relative frequency of discharge from each. The brain also plays a vital part because it has to interpret the pattern of incoming signals.

Although there are three types of cone in the retina, there is no sharp distinction between them in their colour sensitivities. The parts of the spectrum to which each is sensitive overlap, as you can see from the absorption spectra in figure 27.13. This too is important in determining the range of colours that we can see.

Some people have red and green absorption curves that are so close together that they cannot distinguish between these two colours. They are **red-green colour blind**, a sex-linked inherited condition (see page 694). In another type of colour blindness one of the three types of cone may be missing altogether. A person with this defect can only see colours formed by mixing two primary colours – the ones whose cones are present.

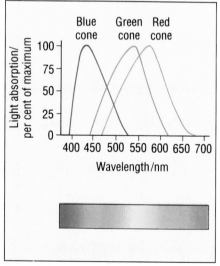

Figure 27.13 Absorption spectra of the three cone pigments in the human retina. Notice that the range of wavelengths sensed by each pigment is broad and overlaps with that of the other pigments. The red-sensitive pigment has its peak in the yellow part of the spectrum but it extends into the long wavelengths far enough to be sensitive to red.

Visual sensation and the brain

Our eyes monitor the environment and send signals to the brain. The brain integrates the signals and produces the appropriate visual image. The actual visual sensation which we experience is not always an exact representation of what is registered by our eyes. This is because the brain, susceptible to all sorts of influences past and present, modifies the image so that we see what our brain is conditioned to see.

The brain affects what we see in five main ways:

- It interprets retinal images and in so doing may prejudice us to see objects in a particular way. A well known example of this is shown in illustration 1.
- It fills in gaps, enabling us to recognise objects which would otherwise be unrecognisable. It is remarkable how imprecise an object can be for us to recognise it.
- It creates images which may mislead us into thinking that we have seen something when we have not. Sometimes a visual experience may arise entirely within the brain and have no basis in reality at all.
- It filters out unnecessary images so that much of what we see is barely registered by the conscious brain. A driver, concentrating on what is in front of the car, is aware of only a tiny fraction of what he or she actually sees.
- It distorts things, giving rise to optical illusions and other visual aberrations. Some examples are given in illustration 2. Optical illusions are fun, but they have a serious side to them. For example, they are used by stage designers and advertisers to create visual effects, and by architects to overcome restrictions in the scale and dimensions of their buildings.

Illustration 1 Do you see a young girl or an old woman? Can you switch from one to the other? What sort of influences determine what you see?

Illustration 2 This picture of a living room contains four well-known optical illusions. The guitar at the front looks smaller than the one behind; the rear edge of the carpet looks much shorter than its front-to-back dimension; the front edge of the carpet looks shorter than the bottom width of the back wall; and the vertical lines on the wallpaper above the fireplace don't look parallel.

The insect eye

Insects have a type of eye that contrasts interestingly with the vertebrate eye. There are some basic similarities – for example, there are photoreceptor cells which work in much the same way as ours. However, the way the photoreceptor cells are arranged is quite different.

The insect eye, in common with other arthropods, is composed of numerous 'mini-eyes', for which reason it is called a **compound eye**. The 'mini-eyes' are called **ommatidia**. Each ommatidium contains a group of photoreceptor cells which functions as a single unit (illustration 1).

Arthropods have a much lower visual acuity than vertebrates. The honey bee, for example, has an acuity about a hundredth that of the human, and most arthropods are worse off than that. It is said that an insect's view of the world is rather like looking at a newspaper photograph through a magnifying glass – dotty.

On the other hand, the ommatidia are extremely sensitive and the time taken to receive a stimulus, fire an impulse and recover, is considerably shorter than for a rod in the human eye. The result is that successive stimuli (flashes of light, for example) merge together and fuse at higher frequencies in insects than in humans. In the honey bee stimulus fusion occurs at approximately 200 per second, whereas in the human the figure is more like 50 per second. This, coupled with the fact that the compound eyes cover a substantial area of the head, means that the insect eye is very good at detecting movement over a wide field (illustration 2). This, aided by rapid transmission of impulses in the nervous system, means that reaction times are much reduced – as is well known to anyone who has tried to swat a fly.

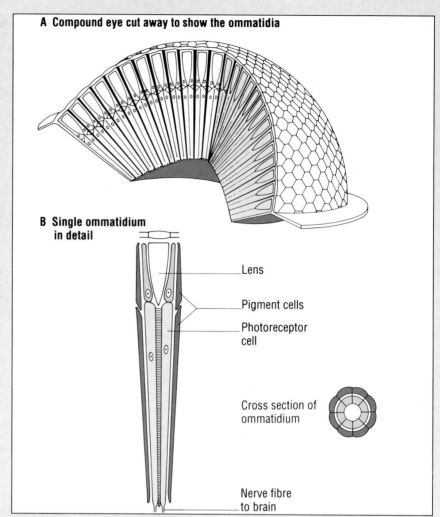

A Compound eye cut away to show the ommatidia

B Single ommatidium in detail

Lens

Pigment cells

Photoreceptor cell

Cross section of ommatidium

Nerve fibre to brain

Illustration 1 The compound eye of a honey bee.

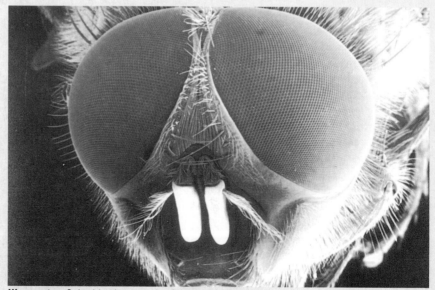

Illustration 2 In this photograph of the head of a blowfly notice how much of the head is covered by the compound eyes.

The human ear

Figure 27.14 shows the main parts of the human ear. It consists of three chambers surrounded by bone:

- An air-filled **outer ear**.
- An air-filled **middle ear**.
- A fluid-filled **inner ear**.

The middle ear is separated from the outer ear by the **tympanic membrane**, or **ear drum**. It is separated from the inner ear cavity by an **oval window (fenestra ovalis)** and **round window (fenestra rotunda)**, both of which are covered by membranes.

Spanning the middle ear chamber from the tympanic membrane to the oval window are three tiny bones called **ear ossicles** (the **malleus, incus** and **stapes**) which are held in position by slender ligaments and muscles. The **Eustachian tube**, which connects the middle ear with the pharynx, ensures that the air pressures on the two side of the tympanic membrane are equal.

The inner ear is made up of two main parts, the **vestibular apparatus** and **cochlea**. These two parts of the inner ear are continuous with each other though they carry out separate functions. The entire inner ear is filled with a fluid called **endolymph** and is separated from the wall of the skull by another fluid called **perilymph**. The endolymph is therefore on the inside of the perilymph (*endo* means 'inner' and *peri* means 'outer').

The vestibular apparatus is responsible for our sense of balance, the cochlea for hearing. Let us start with the cochlea.

Figure 27.14 The human ear consists of three main parts: the outer, middle and inner ears. The middle ear contains the three ear ossicles: the malleus, incus and stapes. On account of their shapes they are also called the hammer, anvil and stirrup respectively. The foot of the stapes fits neatly into the oval window. The inner ear, embedded in the side of the cranium, is divided into two main parts which, though connected, perform quite different functions: the cochlea is for hearing and the vestibular apparatus for balance.

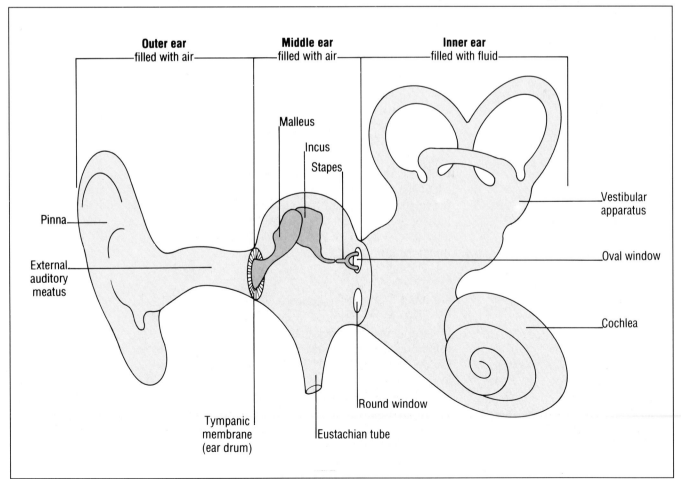

Outer ear — filled with air
Middle ear — filled with air
Inner ear — filled with fluid

Malleus
Incus
Stapes

Vestibular apparatus

Oval window

Cochlea

Pinna

External auditory meatus

Tympanic membrane (ear drum)

Eustachian tube

Round window

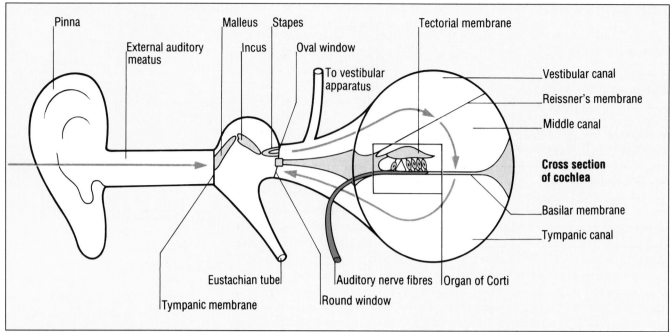

Figure 27.15 This highly schematic diagram illustrates the basic structure and mode of action of the auditory part of the human ear. In this diagram the cochlea has been sectioned transversely close to its base so that its internal structure can be seen. The receptor cells are located in the organ of Corti which runs along the length of the cochlea. As with the eye, the purpose of the other structures is to protect the receptor cells and ensure that they receive the right kind of stimulation which in this case is mechanical disturbance resulting from sound waves hitting the tympanic membrane. The arrows indicate the path taken by the sound waves through the ear.

The cochlea

The cochlea consists of a coiled tube which is divided longitudinally into three parallel canals: the **vestibular canal** (connecting with the oval window), the **middle canal**, and the **tympanic canal** (connecting with the round window). The three canals are separated from each other by membranes: **Reissner's membrane** between the vestibular and middle canals, and the **basilar membrane** between the middle and tympanic canals. All three canals are filled with fluid: endolymph in the middle canal and perilymph in the other two canals.

The relationship between the canals and membranes is shown in the cross-sectional view on the right hand side of figure 27.15.

The cross section also shows the receptor cells that respond to sound. Into the middle canal projects a shelf, the **tectorial membrane**, which runs parallel with the basilar membrane for the full length of the cochlea. Receptor cells span the gap between the basilar and tectorial membranes. Their bases are rooted in the basilar membrane where they are connected to nerve fibres that join the **auditory nerve**. At the other end they bear fine hairs which just reach the tectorial membrane. This part of the cochlea, the part that actually responds to sound, is called the **organ of Corti** and it is illustrated in figure 27.16.

Hearing

So much for the structure. How does it work? In simple terms what happens is this. Sound waves enter the outer ear and impinge on the tympanic membrane which vibrates accordingly. The movements of the tympanic membrane are transmitted by the three ear ossicles to the oval window. This results in displacement of fluid in the vestibular canal, which in turn causes movement of Reissner's membrane. This displaces fluid in the middle canal which moves the basilar membrane, thereby displacing fluid in the tympanic canal. Displacement of this latter fluid is taken up by stretching of the membrane covering the round window.

Thus vibrations of the tympanic membrane, set up by sound waves hitting it, are transmitted via a series of ossicles, membranes and fluid-filled canals, to the basilar membrane. Here, deep in the inner ear, sensory stimulation takes place. Movement of the basilar membrane distorts the sensory cells of the organ of Corti, resulting in impulses being fired in the auditory nerve.

There is still controversy over many aspects of how the cochlea responds to sound. For instance, what is the precise nature of the stimulus that excites the receptor cells? Are they pulled, pushed, or what? The hairs that project from these cells are stiff, and current opinion is that the longest ones just reach the tectorial membrane (figure 27.16). It is believed that movement of the basilar membrane subjects them to shearing forces, possibly accentuated by the **pillar cells** that run from the basilar membrane towards the tectorial membrane. The mechanical disturbance is then registered by the sensitive part of the cell whose membrane becomes depolarised, resulting in the development of a generator potential.

Intensity and pitch

A complete account of hearing must of course explain how the ear discriminates between sounds of different **intensity** and **pitch**. The intensity of a sound is related to the amplitude of the sound waves impinging upon the tympanic membrane. This in turn determines the amplitude with which the basilar membrane vibrates. Loud sounds, that is sound waves of large amplitude, bring about greater displacement of the basilar membrane than softer sounds. The result is that the receptor cells are stimulated more strongly, and larger volleys of impulses are discharged in the auditory nerve.

What about pitch? The pitch of a sound is set by the frequency of the sound waves. High notes are caused by sound waves of high frequency, low notes by sound waves of lower frequency. The pitch of a sound determines the frequency at which the basilar membrane vibrates. Careful experiments on the inner ear have shown that the receptor cells in different regions of the cochlea respond to different frequencies. Those towards the apex respond to low notes while those towards the base respond to high notes.

How is this localisation of response in the cochlea accomplished? The mechanism depends on the fact that the basilar membrane gradually decreases in stiffness from the base of the cochlea to the apex. It is thought that movement of the ear ossicles sets up a travelling wave which passes along the basilar membrane for a certain distance, and then dies out. How far it gets depends on the frequency. High frequency waves travel only a short distance, low frequency waves much further. This, coupled with differential sensitivity of the receptor cells, could result in different parts of

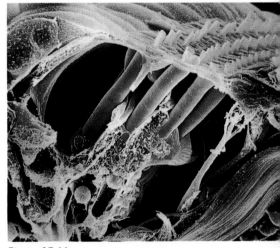

Figure 27.16

Left Detail of the organ of Corti as seen in a transverse section of the cochlea. The receptor cells are shown in red, their sensory hairs extending to the tectorial membrane. It is possible that the pillar cells augment the stimulation process in some way.

Right Scanning electron micrograph of a small part of an organ of Corti. The tectorial membrane has been removed, exposing the tufts of sensory hairs underneath. The sensory hairs project from the upper ends of the receptor cells which are arranged in three rows. Each receptor cell possesses up to 100 sensory hairs. Magnification × 700.

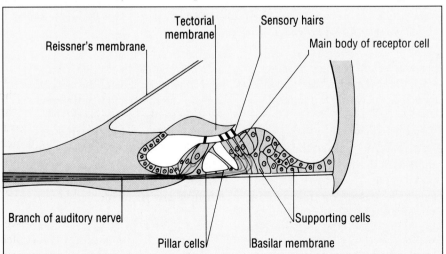

the cochlea responding to different frequencies. The sensation produced in the brain is determined by the pattern of impulses generated in the many fibres of the auditory nerve.

In real life pure notes consisting of only one frequency are rare. Most sounds consist of a fundamental frequency (the lowest one) together with a number of higher frequencies (overtones). Our ears can detect these different frequencies simultaneously.

The audible range

The human ear is only capable of detecting sounds within a certain range of frequency and intensity. Let us take frequency first. The frequency of a sound, i.e. the pitch or note, is measured in sound wave cycles per second. One cycle per second is a Hertz (Hz). At its best, the human ear can detect sounds ranging in frequency from about 20 to 20 000 Hz. Within this range the average person can distinguish between approximately 2000 different pitches (notes), though trained musicians can do much better than this. Pitch discrimination is best between 1000 and 3000 Hz, which corresponds

What do the ear ossicles do?

The ear ossicles are the smallest bones in the body. When pressure changes associated with sound waves reach the tympanic membrane, the latter vibrates in sympathy with the sound waves. The movements of the tympanic membrane are transmitted to the ear ossicles which vibrate in sympathy. The consequence is that the foot of the stapes moves backwards and forwards in the oval window at the same frequency as the movements of the tympanic membrane. In this way movements of the tympanic membrane are faithfully transmitted to the fluid in the inner ear.

But the ear ossicles do more than just transmit the movements – they also increase their force. This is necessary because the pressure changes created by the sound waves have to pass from air to water, and water is a much denser medium than air. The three ossicles articulate with each other in such a way as to form a lever system which increases the force sufficiently to move the fluid in the inner ear (see illustration). The foot of the stapes fits neatly into the oval window, and when it moves forward it displaces the fluid in the inner ear. The fluid is, of course,

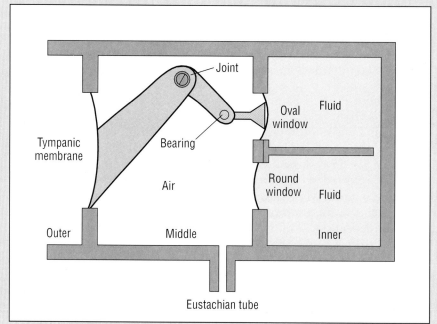

A mechanical model of the ear showing the lever system formed by the three ear ossicles in the middle ear. The ossicles transmit pressure changes associated with airborne sound waves from the outer ear to the fluid in the inner ear.

incompressible and the pressure wave thus created is taken up by the membrane covering the round window.

Muscles are attached to the ossicles. They run from the malleus and stapes to the wall of the middle ear chamber. When there is a loud sound the muscles contract and the movements of the ossicles are dampened down. This is a protective reflex, triggered by the sound itself, and it helps to prevent the receptor cells in the cochlea being damaged by excessive noise. However, the time-lag of this reflex is rather long, and it cannot cope with sudden loud sounds, which rarely occur in nature but are all too common in our artificial environment.

to the range encompassed by normal human speech. Within this range our pitch sensitivity is sufficient to enable us to tell one voice from another by the varying pattern of overtones.

Some animals have a much wider frequency range than we do. For example, dogs and cats can hear high-pitched sounds which are inaudible to humans, and bats can hear the ultrasonic squeaks which they make in order to locate objects in their surroundings. Changes occur with age. For example, a young child can hear sounds at the top of the human range (about 20 000 Hz), but this ability is progressively lost as one gets older.

What about intensity? This is measured in decibels (dB). By agreement, the quietest sound which can just be heard by an average young person is given a decibel value of zero. This is the **threshold of hearing**. Figure 27.17 shows the range of sound intensities from the threshold to the loudest sound that a human being can tolerate. This is a logarithmic scale – the loudest tolerable sound (120 dB) is actually one million million times as loud as the threshold sound. Sounds above 120 dB can be painful and may cause immediate damage to the cochlea receptors. Long-term exposure to sounds over 85 dB can also damage the receptors, leading to partial loss of hearing.

The vestibular apparatus and balance

The vestibular component of the inner ear consists of an assemblage of interconnected sacs and canals which are continuous with the middle canal of the cochlea. Like the middle canal, they are filled with endolymph and they contain receptor cells. However, instead of being sensitive to sound, the receptor cells are proprioceptors which give us our sense of balance (figure 27.18).

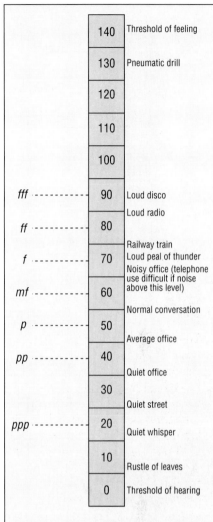

Figure 27.17 The audible range of the human ear expressed in Hertz (Hz) above the threshold of hearing. On the left are the approximate values for the markings on musical scores made by the conductor Leopold Stokowski: *p* (piano), quiet; *pp* (pianissimo), very quiet; *ppp*, extremely quiet; *f* (forte), loud; *mf* (mezzo forte), moderately loud; *ff*, (fortissimo) very loud; *fff*, extremely loud.

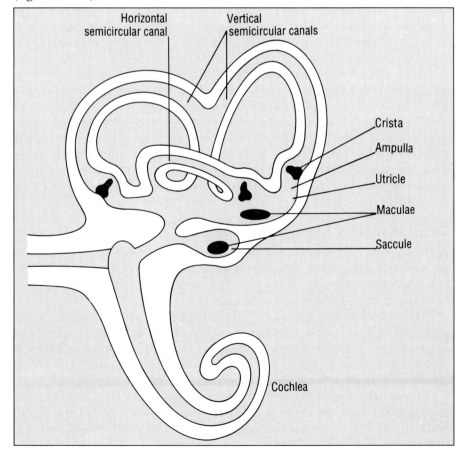

Figure 27.18 The vestibular apparatus in the inner ear, showing the location of the two main types of receptor (black blobs) responsible for our sense of balance.

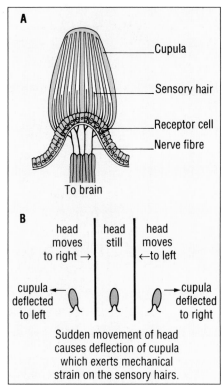

Figure 27.19 The ampulla organ is stimulated by movements of the head.

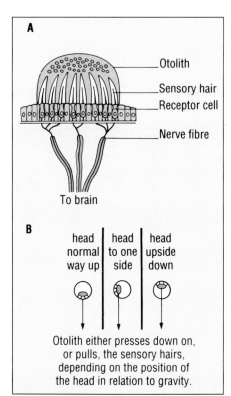

Figure 27.20 The utricle organ is stimulated according to its position relative to the force of gravity.

The semicircular canals

The vestibular apparatus includes three **semicircular canals** in planes at right angles to each other. At one end of each semicircular canal is a swelling (**ampulla**) which contains a receptor called a **crista**. The semicircular canals open into the **utricle** which in turn connects with the **saccule**. The utricle and saccule both contain receptors called **maculae**.

The ampulla receptors (cristae) consist of groups of receptor cells with hairs rather like those in the cochlea. However, in this case the hairs are embedded in a dome-shaped gelatinous cap, the **cupula** (figure 27.19A). The ampulla receptors are sensitive to movements of the head, and the fact that the three semicircular canals are in different planes ensures sensitivity to movement in any plane. Thus if you shake your head the horizontal canal is activated; if you nod your head one of the vertical canals is brought into play, and so on. Because of the inertia of the fluid in the semicircular canals, the cupula gets deflected in a direction opposite to that in which the head is moving (figure 27.19B). This puts a mechanical strain on the receptor cells, causing them to fire impulses in the sensory nerve fibres.

Not all the receptor cells are stimulated equally. Which particular ones are stimulated most depends on the direction in which the cupula is deflected, and this in turn determines the pattern of impulses discharged in the sensory nerve fibres. This pattern is interpreted by the brain which therefore enables you to know the direction in which your head has been moving. An increase in the speed of movement increases the frequency of the impulses. So the overall function of the semicircular canals is to register **directional acceleration**.

The utricle and saccule

The utricle and saccule give information on the *position* of the head. The receptors (**maculae**) consist of a group of receptor cells, the free ends of which are embedded in a gelatinous substance containing a concretion of densely packed particles of calcium carbonate called an **otolith** (figure 27.20A). According to the position of the head, the pull of gravity on the otolith will vary. Thus when your head is the normal way up, in the vertical position, the otolith will press down on the sensory hairs. With the head tilted sideways the otolith will exert an oblique pull on the hairs, and if the head is upside down the otolith will pull the hairs directly downwards (figure 27.20B). The differential distortion of the receptor cells resulting from the head being in different positions determines the pattern of impulses discharged in the sensory nerve fibres. This is interpreted by the brain which thus makes you aware of the position of your head.

Other receptors important in balance

The vestibular apparatus is not the only structure in the body sensitive to position and movement. Other proprioceptors such as muscle spindles are also important (see page 516). So, of course, are the eyes and pressure receptors in the skin on the soles of the feet.

The importance of these other receptors can be seen in simple experiments which you can do on yourself. For example, stand up straight with your eyes open. Then raise one foot off the ground and note your ability to keep balance. Now repeat with your eyes closed. Do you find it less easy to keep your balance with your eyes closed?

Or try this experiment. Stand up straight with your feet close together, arms at your sides and eyes open. Notice the way the body sways slightly from side to side (postural swaying). Now slowly lean forward and note how your feet respond in helping you to retain your balance.

Hearing loss – how technology can help

Guest author Geoffrey Curtis describes some recent advances in hearing aid technology.

There are two main causes of hearing loss: conductive and sensorineural. Conductive loss is caused by a defect in the hearing process up to, but excluding, the receptor cells and sensory nerve. Sensorineural loss, as the name implies, is caused by a defect in the receptor cells and/or sensory nerve.

Nearly four million people in the United Kingdom have a degree of hearing loss which is, or could be, helped by a suitable hearing aid, and over ninety per cent of these cases have a sensorineural cause brought on by wear and tear within the cochlea as a natural part of the ageing process. The problem is most severe at the high frequency end of the auditory range. The reason for this is understandable when you think how the cochlea works. According to the travelling wave theory (see page 488), all sound signals enter the cochlea at the high frequency end, irrespective of their own frequencies, and then travel along it to their own points of

Illustration 1 An acoustic chair designed and built for a Central European ruler around 1819 by an English firm which supplied hearing aids to six royal families.

registration. Imagine a pianist picking out a tune with one finger but doing so by dragging the finger across every note, depressing but not sounding it, from the top end of the keyboard down to the specific note required. Plainly there would be excessive wear and tear in the top range, but relatively little at the lower end.

It was originally thought that hearing aids could only help people with conductive loss. However, modern advances in hearing aid technology have meant that the majority of sensorineural cases can now be greatly helped. But before getting involved with the modern technology, let us take a quick look at some of the older devices.

Acoustic chair to miniature aids

Early attempts at overcoming hearing problems consisted of ear trumpets and speaking tubes. One ingenious example is shown in illustration 1: an acoustic chair. The hollow arms, shaped like ear trumpets, housed concealed resonators which led to an outlet on the back of the chair, close to the occupant's ears.

In 1876 Alexander Graham Bell filed for patent on a device which was originally designed to help his wife's hearing problem but was later modified into the early telephone. Crude electronic devices appeared in the early years of the twentieth century. The earliest ones were barely portable, but with improved miniaturisation, especially in batteries, they soon became wearable and were extensively worn until the 1950s. This type of hearing aid originally consisted of a small box, about the size of a pencil case, containing the microphone and power source, which was pinned to the clothes in the chest area. An electrical cord transmitted sound signals to a miniature receiver which was attached to an ear fitting. The

latter was moulded to fit the ear and placed in the pinna.

Smaller modern versions of these devices are still used today by people with very severe hearing loss. However, thanks to miniaturisation, most hearing aids can now be worn either behind the pinna (post-aural) or, more recently, within the pinna (intra-aural).

The post-aural aid

A compact unit containing a power source and one or two microphones is placed immediately behind the pinna so as to pick up sound as close as possible to its normal reception point (illustration 2). The sound signals are then amplified by the instrument and passed down a plastic tube held inside the pinna by an individually moulded ear fitting. Advanced

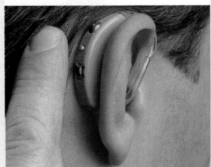

Illustration 2 A post-aural hearing aid. Volume and tone controls are at the back of the unit.

instruments have controls which enable the hearing aid technician to tune the performance to the maximum benefit of the user. This is achieved by varying three main parameters:

- The acoustic gain, i.e. the amount by which the sound signals are amplified. For example, an amplification from 60 dB input to 85 dB output means that the gain is 25 dB.
- The maximum output, i.e. the loudest sound that the instrument can produce. A person with impaired hearing may be more sensitive to loud sounds than a normal person, and it is important that the total sound output does not exceed the person's tolerance level.
- The acoustic response, i.e. the amplification characteristics expressed in terms of the acoustic gain at each frequency (illustration 3).

Further variations in the response can be made by modifying the ear mould so that maximum assistance is gained from the natural resonance of the ear canal.

The only size restriction on a post-aural aid is that it should fit comfortably behind the ear. Extra size allows the inclusion of more components which in turn permits greater sophistication and, if needed, more power. Moreover, the relatively long distance between the microphone behind the ear and the point of possible sound leakage around the ear mould helps to reduce acoustic feedback. Acoustic feedback occurs – as it does in any amplified sound system – when the amplified sound escapes and is picked up by the microphone and re-amplified. In a hearing aid this can cause a high-pitched whistle which can be annoying for users and disconcerting for their friends.

The intra-aural aid

The intra-aural hearing aid places a microphone within the pinna close to the opening into the ear canal (illustration 4). Indeed, the latest microchip and transistor technology enables very effective instruments to be worn entirely inside the ear canal with the microphone where the natural ear opening is located. Both positions ensure that sound signals are collected by the natural pinna shape.

These instruments are prescription-built to fit the exact

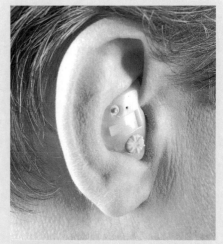

Illustation 4 An intra-aural hearing aid in position within the ear.

contours of the person's ear, and they contain circuits which have been individually designed to give a response which makes maximum use of the user's residual hearing. Although the smaller size of the instrument imposes restrictions on the number of components, modern technology allows miniaturisation to such an extent that even the smallest intra-aural aids have additional controls to allow fine tuning by the technician.

A great advantage of the canal-type of instrument is that it leaves the inside of the pinna virtually empty. Recent research has shown that considerable amplification (particularly in the frequency range 3000 to 5000 Hz) is achieved by the pinna before the sound arrives at the microphone. This natural amplification has been found to be between 8 and 20 dB, depending on the exact configuration of the pinna, and it is therefore clear that this part of the ear acts as an effective pre-amplifier. This boost at the beginning of the hearing process means that the hearing aid does not have to produce so much gain, thus reducing distortion.

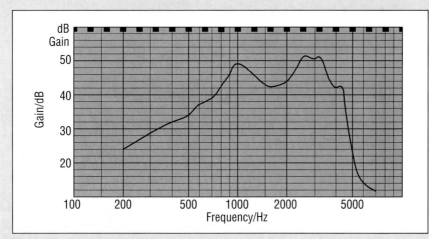

Illustration 3 Graph showing the gain achieved at different frequencies by a high performance post-aural hearing aid in its normal position behind the ear with the volume control turned right up. Gains of between 42 and 52 dB are achieved at frequencies over the normal speech range (1000 to 3000 Hz).

Summary

1 Receptors may consist of isolated **receptor cells** or multicellular **sense organs**. They can be classified, into **chemoreceptors, mechanoreceptors, photoreceptors** and **thermoreceptors.**

2 The function of receptors is to transfer the energy associated with the stimulus to nerve impulses.

3 In general sensory cells, when stimulated, develop a local **generator potential** which, if it builds up sufficiently, elicits **action potentials** in a sensory neurone.

4 If a stimulus is maintained, the generator potential usually declines and the action potentials decrease in frequency until they cease altogether (**adaptation**).

5 For repetitive stimuli to be detected separately, the generator potential produced by each stimulus must fall below the firing threshold before the next stimulus is delivered.

6 The mammalian eye and ear illustrate the structure and functioning of two specialised **sense organs.**

7 In the case of the eye the receptor cells, **rods** and **cones,** are located in the **retina** on which light rays are brought to a focus by the **cornea** and an adjustable **lens.**

8 The cones, which are particularly concentrated in the fovea, are responsible for high acuity colour vision in conditions of good illumination (**daylight vision**), the rods for black-and-white vision at low levels of illumination (**night vision**).

9 The efficiency of the rods in night vision is due to their sensitivity and rapid resynthesis of photochemical pigment, and to the fact that they show **retinal convergence.**

10 The acuity of the cones is due to their high density in the fovea, and to their one-to-one relationship with the optic nerve fibres.

11 According to the **trichromatic theory**, colour vision is achieved by differential stimulation of three types of cone, each of which contains a different photochemical pigment.

12 The mammalian ear performs two functions: hearing and balance. **Hearing** is dealt with by receptor cells in the **organ of Corti** in the **cochlea**, to which sound waves are transmitted via a series of membranes, ossicles, and fluid-filled canals.

13 The properties of the cochlea permit the ear to discriminate between sounds of different intensity and pitch.

14 **Balance** is dealt with by the **vestibular apparatus**. Receptor cells associated with the **semi-circular canals** are sensitive to directional acceleration of the head. Receptor cells in the utricle and saccule are sensitive to the position of the head relative to gravity.

Review questions

1 Summarise the sequence of events which occurs when a receptor cell is stimulated sufficiently strongly for an impulse to be discharged in the adjoining nerve fibre.

2 What is sensory adaptation, how would you explain it, and what use is it?

3 Use your knowledge of the eye to explain the following everyday experiences:
  (a) When reading a book the words you look at directly are clear and sharp, whereas surrounding words are blurred.
  (b) If you try to make out a particularly faint star in the sky, it is better not to look directly at it but slightly to one side of it.
  (c) The flicker on a cinema screen can be seen when you look at the screen out of the corner of your eye, but not when you look directly at it.
  (d) In dim illumination brightly coloured objects appear to be black, white or various shades of grey.
  (e) When you enter a dimly lit room from bright sunlight, the room seems pitch dark to begin with, but gradually objects become visible.

4 What is it about the arrangement of the cells in the retina that enables a person to:
  (a) see the individual dots in a newspaper photograph,
  (b) read a newspaper even when the light is poor?

5 Explain how we are able to see colours.

6 Summarise the sequence of events which takes place from the moment a note is played on a piano to the moment the sound is heard.

7 Which structures in the eye and ear:
  (a) protect the receptors,
  (b) ensure that the receptors receive appropriate stimuli,
  (c) transfer the energy of the stimuli to nerve impulses?

8 Our sense of hearing is really a sense of touch. Explain.

9 Account for the following:
  (a) A person who is continually subjected to a very loud sound of a particular pitch may eventually become deaf to sounds of that pitch.
  (b) After you have been on a fast roundabout in a fairground, you feel dizzy.

10 How do we keep our balance?

Further reading

Sensation and Perception by Stanley Coren and Lawrence Ward (Harcourt, Brace, Jovanovich, 1989) gives an excellent up to date account of human receptors and is full of intriguing demonstrations which you can do yourself.

If you are interested in the experimental basis of perception, you might look at some of the *Scientific American* articles in *The Perceptual World*, edited by Irvin Rock (Freeman, 1990).

Biology, Advanced Topics looks in more detail at the retina and the organ of Corti with particular reference to the events occuring in the receptor cells.

CHAPTER 28 · Muscles and other effectors

An **effector** is a structure which responds, directly or indirectly, to a stimulus by performing some kind of action. Most effectors are controlled by the nervous system and respond when they receive impulses from nerves. However, certain effectors have no nerves going to them and respond to direct stimulation.

The most common effectors are **muscles** and **glands**. Less widespread, but no less important to the animals possessing them, are **pigment cells**, **light-producing organs** and **electric organs**.

In this chapter we shall concentrate mainly on muscles, since more is known about them than most effectors.

Different types of muscle

All types of muscle have one thing in common: they are composed of numerous contractile **muscle fibres** which together make up **muscle tissue** (see page 181). The muscle fibres are usually orientated in a particular direction and when they contract the whole muscle shortens or develops tension

It is customary to divide vertebrate muscle tissues into three types according to their location in the body:

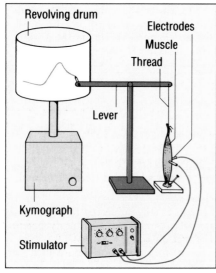

Figure 28.1 Investigating the properties of skeletal muscle by means of a gastrocnemius muscle preparation. One of the tendons is attached to a fixed piece of cork, the other to a recording lever. The muscle is kept permanently moist by pipetting Ringer's solution onto it. A pair of electrodes is placed in contact with the muscle. When the experimenter activates the stimulator an electrical stimulus is sent into the muscle through the electrodes, and the muscle responds by contracting. When the muscle contracts it pulls the lever which makes a tracing on the revolving drum (kymograph). The stimulator can deliver single stimuli or repetitive stimuli at a range of frequencies.

- **Skeletal muscle.** This is attached to the skeleton and is therefore involved in locomotion. As it is innervated by the voluntary part of the nervous system, it is also known as **voluntary muscle**. When viewed under the microscope its fibres are seen to have stripes running across them, for which reason it is called **striated muscle**. Characteristically it contracts, and fatigues, rapidly.

- **Smooth muscle.** This is found lining the gut, blood vessels and various cavities, and is innervated by the automatic (involuntary) part of the nervous system, for which reason it is also known as **involuntary muscle**. It is called smooth muscle because its fibres do not have stripes running across them – in other words it is unstriated. In contrast to skeletal muscle, it contracts, and fatigues, slowly. The structure of smooth muscle is described on page 181.

- **Cardiac muscle.** Situated in the wall of the heart, its fibres are striated and joined by cross-connections to form a network. Like smooth muscle, it is innervated by the autonomic nervous system. It contracts over and over again rhythmically, without fatigue. The structure of cardiac muscle is described on page 328.

All three types of muscle are supplied by nerves. Skeletal muscle will normally only contract if it receives impulses from its nerves. However, cardiac muscle and some smooth muscle can contract on their own without the contractions being initiated by the nervous system. In other words the contractions are **myogenic**, i.e. generated from within the muscle tissue itself. In these cases the function of the nerves is to speed up or slow down the frequency of the contractions.

The fundamental question is: how do muscles contract? In attempting to answer this we shall focus our attention, as physiologists have done, on skeletal muscle. But first let us look briefly at what skeletal muscle is capable of doing.

Properties of skeletal muscle

When a muscle is activated it either shortens or, if it is attached to a rigid skeleton, develops tension. Its properties can be investigated by attaching it to a movable lever that writes on a revolving drum (**kymograph**).

A preparation which has often been used in this kind of work is the **calf (gastrocnemius) muscle** of the frog. The muscle, removed from the leg, is set up as shown in figure 28.1. The muscle is stimulated with single or repetitive stimuli, either directly or through its nerve, and the resulting contractions are recorded on the drum.

Let us now look at some recordings, and discover the properties of skeletal muscle from them (figure 28.2)

The simple twitch

If a single stimulus of sufficient strength is applied to the muscle, the latter responds by giving a quick contraction or **twitch** (figure 28.2A). It takes about 0.1 seconds for the contraction to reach its height, and a further 0.2 seconds for relaxation to be complete. The entire response is therefore over in approximately 0.3 seconds. These figures are typical of a frog gastrocnemius muscle, but in animals as a whole there is much variation between different muscles.

There is a short delay between the application of the stimulus and the onset of the muscular contraction. This is called the **latent period**. It is caused partly by the inertia of the apparatus but also by the time taken for the electrical response to be translated into a contraction. Typically the latent period lasts about 0.02 seconds.

Summation

Now consider what happens if two stimuli are delivered in succession (figure 28.2B and C). If the interval between the stimuli is sufficiently long, two separate twitches are given by the muscle, one after the other. However, if the interval is gradually shortened there comes a point when the two twitches fuse, or **summate**, to give a single smooth contraction. Each impulse initiates a contraction, but the second contraction starts before the muscle begins to relax, so that the summated response is larger and lasts longer than the simple twitch.

Tetanus

We can take the above experiment a stage further. Instead of stimulating the muscle with only two stimuli, we send a train of stimuli into the muscle. If the frequency of stimulation is not too great, separate twitches can be discerned (figure 28.2D). If the frequency is great enough, the muscle goes into a maintained contraction or **tetanus**, relaxing only when the stimuli are switched off (figure 28.2E). Numerous twitches have fused, as it were, to give a single prolonged response. To produce a smooth tetanus in a frog gastrocnemius muscle a minimum frequency of approximately 20 stimuli per second is required.

What is the significance of this? When the muscles of an animal contract under natural conditions they do so tetanically and not in simple twitches. For example, if you bend your arm, the flexor muscle undergoes a tetanic contraction as a result of a train of high-frequency impulses reaching it from the brachial nerve. How long the contraction goes on for depends on the duration of the train of impulses, and that depends on you. Just as an experimenter can stop tetanising a muscle by switching off the stimuli, so you (using your brain) can voluntarily stop your flexor muscle contracting by 'turning off' the impulses streaming down to it.

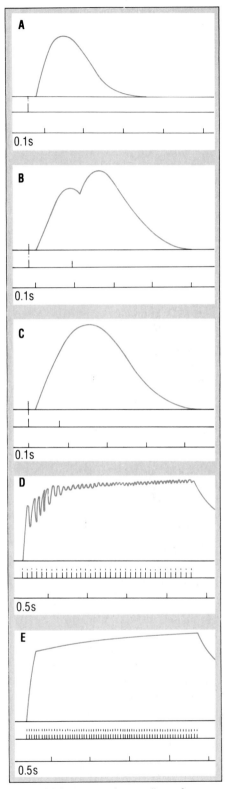

Figure 28.2 Kymograph recordings of responses obtained by stimulating a muscle with electrical stimuli. In all cases the stimuli are dotted and a time scale is shown below each recording.

Fatigue

A tetanic contraction cannot go on indefinitely, and if stimulation is continued the muscular responses gradually decline and eventually disappear altogether. This **fatigue** is brought about by various factors operating within the muscle. Can you think what they might be? If, instead of being stimulated directly, the muscle is excited through its nerve, the responses decline even more quickly. This is due to exhaustion of the transmitter substance (acetylcholine) at the neuromuscular junctions.

Graded contractions

We have already seen that a contraction can be sustained by sending a train of stimuli into the muscle, i.e. by producing a tetanus. By varying the frequency of the stimuli (the number per unit time), contractions of different strength can be produced. Low frequencies produce relatively weak contractions whereas high frequencies produce more powerful contractions. Such **graded contractions** are very important in the normal functioning of our muscles. A high-frequency tetanic contraction may be twenty times more powerful than a single individual contraction.

There is another way of grading contractions, and that is by varying the number of fibres within the muscle that contract. The motor nerve that supplies a particular muscle contains numerous axons each of which supplies a group of fibres within the muscle. The group of muscle fibres supplied by a single axon is called a **motor unit**. Graded contractions can be produced by varying the number of motor units which are brought into play. If only a few motor units are activated, a weak contraction is given. If all the motor units are activated, a much more powerful contraction is given.

Muscles differ in the size of their motor units. In some muscles the motor units consist of only a few fibres, whereas in other muscles the motor units may consist of several hundred fibres. Predictably, muscles with small motor units give rise to more delicate movements than muscles with large motor units. Where would you expect to find muscles with small motor units, and why?

Electrical activity in muscle

The experiments described above involve using a whole muscle. More detailed investigations may be carried out on single muscle fibres which are teased out of the whole muscle, isolated and experimented on individually. Micro-electrodes can be inserted into the muscle fibre so that its electrical as well as mechanical properties may be studied.

What emerges from these experiments is that the membranes of muscle fibres are basically similar to those of nerve cells. When not active they have a **resting potential**, and when activated this is momentarily reversed to give an **action potential**. This generally lasts longer, and is transmitted more slowly, than that of a nerve cell, but otherwise the two are similar and have essentially the same ionic basis.

Like nerves, muscle fibres obey an **all-or-nothing law**. By stimulating an isolated muscle fibre with shocks of gradually increasing intensity, it can be shown that the size of the action potential, and the resulting contraction, are independent of the intensity of stimulation. If the strength of a stimulus is below the threshold required to excite the fibre, no action potential and no contraction are given. If the stimulus is above this threshold an action potential and contraction are given, and further increase in the intensity of the stimulus will not enhance this response.

Muscles also have a **refractory period**. After contraction there is a brief period of complete, followed by partial, inexcitability. These are the **absolute** and **relative refractory periods** respectively. They are generally slightly longer than for a nerve.

From an electrical standpoint nerves and muscles are therefore very similar. The main difference is that in a muscle the action potential is accompanied by a contraction. How the electrical and mechanical events are coupled together will be discussed later.

Fast and slow twitch muscle fibres

Guest author Patricia Kohn explains these two kinds of muscle fibre and discusses their significance in athletic events.

There are two main types of fibre in human skeletal muscles. they are known as **slow twitch fibres** and **fast twitch fibres**, where 'slow' and 'fast' refer to the time taken to reach peak tension following a single stimulus. The contractions in figure 28.2 are fast twitches.

Slow twitch fibres are adapted to perform in conditions where the oxygen supply can keep pace with the demand for ATP, and respiration is therefore aerobic (see page 236). The fuel molecules (glucose and/or fatty acids) are broken down into carbon dioxide and water via the Krebs cycle. This takes place in the mitochondria which are particularly plentiful in slow twitch fibres. These fibres have a good blood supply, and they contain much myoglobin to serve as an oxygen store (see page 319). The high myoglobin and blood content give muscles with a lot of slow twitch fibres a characteristically brownish red colour ('red muscles').

Slow twitch fibres predominate in those muscles involved in sustained but relatively low levels of activity, such as the maintenance of posture. They also occur in the major muscle groups of the limbs where they are the main source of power in long distance running. In these activities the pace is such that aerobic respiration can provide the necessary energy and anaerobic respiration is not needed.

Fast twitch fibres are the exact opposite. They are adapted for sudden bursts of maximum activity, such as occur in sprinting, throwing, jumping and lifting. These activities may consume ATP at such a rate that the supply of oxygen for aerobic respiration cannot keep up with demand. The energy need is therefore met by very high rates of anaerobic respiration in which, you will recall, glycolysis occurs but not the Krebs cycle. This is reflected in the 'metabolic profile' of this kind of muscle: enzymes of the glycolysis pathway are plentiful but there are relatively few mitochondria, the myoglobin content is low and the blood supply unexceptional. Muscles with a high proportion of fast twitch fibres are therefore 'white muscles'.

The maximum work rate of muscles rich in fast twitch fibres cannot be sustained for long. The 400 metres sprint is notoriously difficult, and great fatigue is felt if anaerobic respiration continues at a high rate for long. This is probably due to a fall in pH which occurs in the muscle fibres as lactic acid, the end product of anaerobic glycolysis, accumulates. In contrast, fatigue in slow twitch fibres is probably caused by a switch to fatty acids as the main fuel when glygogen runs out. This occurs towards the end of the marathon and is known in the trade as 'the bonk' or 'hitting the wall'.

All human muscles contain both types of fibre though in differing proportions. However, the muscles of some other animals are composed almost exclusively of one or other type. For example, a trout has predominantly fast twitch fibres with only a narrow band of slow twitch muscle on either side of the body. The slow twitch fibres are sufficient to propel the fish while it is cruising along slowly, but if the need for swift escape arises, the fast twitch muscle is activated and the fish darts to safety.

Humans do not have such sharply differentiated muscles, but there are interesting differences between different kinds of athletes. Trained sprinters have a high proportion of fast twitch fibres, whereas marathon runners have a high proportion of slow twitch fibres. Is this difference inborn or the result of the very different training which these two kinds of athlete undergo? Studies on those long-suffering experimental subjects, identical twins, suggest that basically the fibre composition of our muscles is genetically determined. Studies on horses bred for short sprints or long distance events confirm this idea. However, there is evidence that training can bring about changes in the proportions of the different types of fibre. This may be due to conversion of one type to the other, but it is also possible that there is a population of unspecialised fibres which can form either type given the appropriate stimulus.

Structure of skeletal muscle

A whole muscle is made up of many hundreds of **muscle fibres** varying in length from 1 to 40 millimetres (figure 28.3A). If an individual fibre is sectioned longitudinally, stained and examined under the microscope, the structures shown in figure 28.3B can be seen.

The fibre is filled with a specialised cytoplasm called **sarcoplasm** in which about 100 nuclei are spaced out evenly just beneath the bounding membrane or **sarcolemma**. The nuclei are not separated from each other by plasma membranes – in other words they are not in separate cells – so the fibre is a syncytium (see page 175). Numerous parallel **striations** traverse the fibre from one side to the other. Little else can be seen, though in good sections it is sometimes possible to make out slender threads running along the length of the fibre (figure 28.3C). These are called **myofibrils**.

Until the early 1950s this was all that was known about the structure of muscle, and a frustrating picture it was for it gave no clue as to how contraction takes place. However, since then the electron microscope has revealed a wealth of information about muscle that goes a long way towards explaining how it works.

The fine structure of muscle

Under the light microscope the striations cannot be seen in detail, and the myofibrils appear as extremely thin lines. However, in the electron microscope the internal structure of individual myofibrils shows up clearly, and the reason for the striations becomes apparent. This is shown in figure 28.4. Notice that each myofibril is divided up into alternating **light** and **dark bands**. As the light and dark bands of adjacent myofibrils lie alongside each other, one gets the impression of continuous striations running right across the entire fibre.

Figure 28.5 will help you to interpret the electron micrograph in figure 28.4. You can see that each dark band has a relatively light region in the middle. This is called the **H zone**, and it has darker regions on either side. Running across the middle of the H zone is a dark line (the **M line**), and traversing the middle of the light band is an even darker line, the **Z line**. The region of a myofibril from one Z line to the next is called a **sarcomere**. For

Figure 28.3 Structure of skeletal muscle.

A A whole muscle sliced transversely to show its internal stucture. The muscle is composed of numerous muscle fibres bound together by connective tissue.

B Several muscle fibres as seen in longitudinal section under the low power of a light microscope. Notice the striations. Muscle fibres vary in diameter from about 10 to 100 µm depending on the type of animal they come from. They get thicker with age and also with exercise.

C A single muscle fibre as seen under the high power of a light microscope in ideal conditions. Myofibrils can just be seen, as can detail of the striations, but note that no clue is given as to the possible mechanism of contraction.

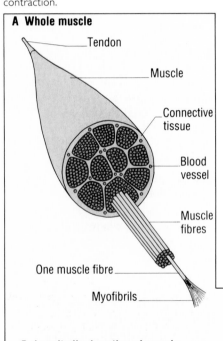

A Whole muscle

- Tendon
- Muscle
- Connective tissue
- Blood vessel
- Muscle fibres
- One muscle fibre
- Myofibrils

B Longitudinal section of muscle fibres as seen under the light microscope

- Nuclei
- Muscle fibres

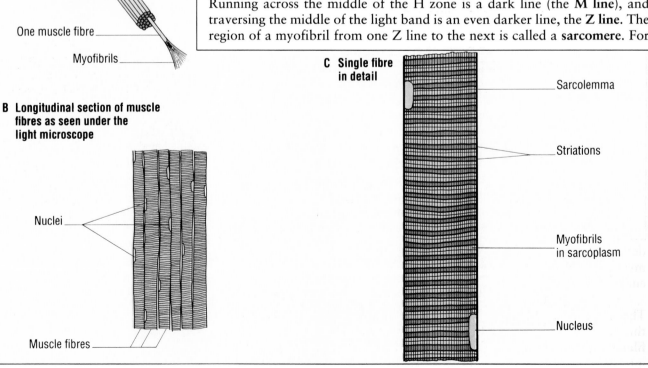

C Single fibre in detail

- Sarcolemma
- Striations
- Myofibrils in sarcoplasm
- Nucleus

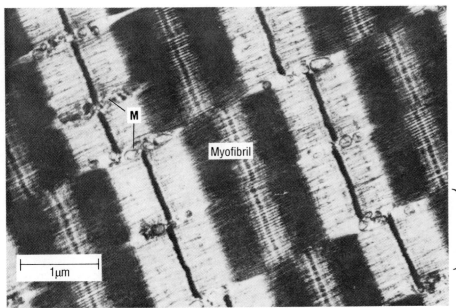

Myofibril

1μm

one myofibril
(width)

Figure 28.4 Low magnification electron micrograph of part of a skeletal muscle fibre in longitudinal section. Parts of seven myofibrils can be seen with their characteristic pattern of alternating dark and light bands. Notice the mitochondria (**M**) between adjacent myofibrils.

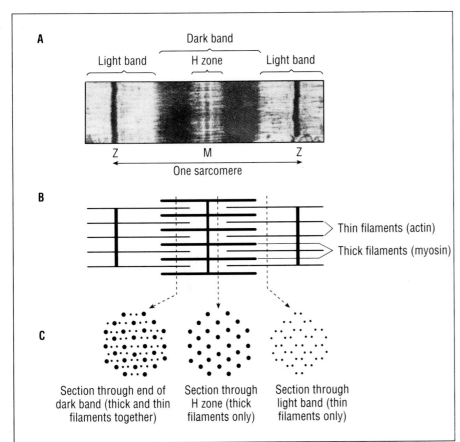

Figure 28.5 The detailed structure of individual myofibrils has been worked out with the electron microscope. The light and dark bands seen in low magnification electron micrographs (**A**) are due to the presence of alternating groups of thick and thin filaments which interdigitate between each other, as shown in **B**. The groups of filaments are held in alignment at the Z and M lines. The arrangement of the filaments has been confirmed by examining cross sections of myofibrils in the electron microscope as shown in **C**.

descriptive purposes the sarcomere can be regarded as the basic unit of the myofibril; the whole myofibril consists of a long chain of such units placed end to end.

The explanation of the banding pattern is made clear in figure 28.5B. The myofibril is composed of numerous longitudinal filaments of two types: thick and thin. The **thick filaments** are confined to the dark band. The **thin filaments** occur in the light band, but extend in between the thick filaments into the dark band. The areas on either side of the H zone are therefore

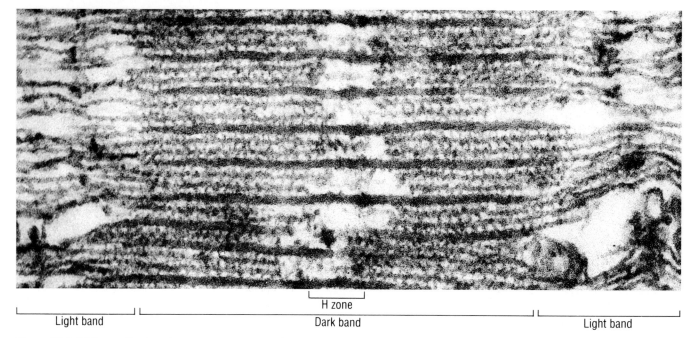

| H zone |
| Light band | Dark band | Light band |

Figure 28.6 High magnification electron micrograph of one complete sarcomere in a myofibril. Notice the thick and thin filaments in between each other.

particularly dark because they contain both thick and thin filaments. The H zone consists of thick filaments only, which is why it is slightly lighter than the two ends of the dark band. Cross sections through individual myofibrils give the appearance shown in figure 28.5C. This interpretation of the banding pattern is not just speculation. It is confirmed by high resolution electron micrographs such as the one shown in figure 28.6.

The chemistry of muscle

So far this description has been purely structural. But while electron-microscopists were busy describing the fine structure of muscle, biochemists were investigating its chemistry. It had been found some years before that the contractile apparatus of muscle contains two proteins: **actin** and **myosin**. When these proteins are extracted from muscle fibres and placed in a solution of ATP, contraction occurs. This means that from a purely biochemical standpoint all that is required for contraction is a mixture of actin, myosin and ATP.

Where is the actin and myosin in relation to the fine structure of the myofibril? The answer has been found by treating muscle with chemicals that selectively dissolve one or other of these proteins, and then examining the myofibrils under a phase-contrast microscope. If a muscle is treated with a solution that selectively dissolves myosin, all the dark bands disappear. If, however, it is treated with a solution that removes actin, all the light bands disappear. The conclusion is that the thick filaments are composed by myosin, the thin filaments of actin.

So myofibrils consist of alternating sets of thick myosin and thin actin filaments which overlap in the dark band. What then happens when the muscle contracts?

How muscle contracts

The theory of how skeletal muscle contracts was deduced from its fine structure. It is a classic example of how studies with the electron microscope not only provide information on the structure of an organ, but also throw light on how it works.

The sliding filament hypothesis

From the structure of the myofibril it would seem a reasonable proposition that contraction occurs by the thick and thin filaments sliding between each other. The thin filaments in each light band are held together at the Z line, and the thick filaments are held together at the M line, so each set of filaments would be expected to slide as a unit. The orderly arrangement of the filaments would therefore be maintained during the contraction process.

This sliding hypothesis was first put forward by Hugh Huxley and Jean Hanson of London University. By a combination of different kinds of microscopy and logical deduction, they secured good evidence to support it. They argued as follows. If it is true that the filaments slide, the banding pattern in the myofibril should change as contraction occurs. When the muscle is fully relaxed (or stretched) the light bands, and H zones, should be comparatively long. The dark ends of the dark band, however, should be relatively short. When contracted, the light bands, and the H zones, would be expected to get much shorter, and the dark ends of the dark bands longer. All this should be accompanied by a change in the overall length of the sarcomeres; from being long in the relaxed muscle they should become comparatively short.

This is precisely what Huxley and Hanson found. They studied the banding pattern of isolated myofibrils contracting in a solution of ATP and found the change in the banding pattern to be exactly as they predicted.

Convincing confirmation of the sliding hypothesis was obtained by comparing the electron microscopic appearance of stretched myofibrils with those at normal resting length. As living materials cannot be viewed in the electron microscope it is impossible to see the sliding process actually taking place, but examining electron micrographs of muscle in different states of contraction is the next best thing (figure 28.7).

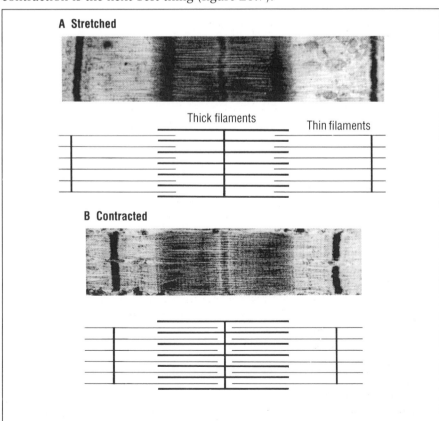

Figure 28.7 The sliding filament hypothesis proposes that when a myofibril shortens the thick and thin filaments slide between each other, as shown here. The hypothesis predicts that when contraction takes place the banding pattern should change, and the sarcomere should shorten. This does in fact happen, as you can see in the two electron micrographs.

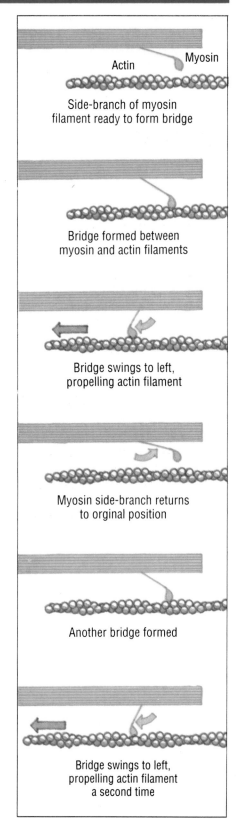

Figure 28.8 These diagrams summarise the ratchet mechanism by which the thick (myosin) and thin (actin) filaments are pulled towards each other.

In severely contracted muscles new bands appear at the positions occupied by the M and Z lines. These new bands can be interpreted by postulating that when a muscle contracts to this extent the filaments meet and then crumple or overlap. In the case of the thin filaments, this has been confirmed by the discovery that, in transverse sections of myofibrils cut through this region, there are twice the normal number of thin filaments. When a muscle is contracted to this extent the light bands and H zones disappear altogether, both types of filaments occurring together throughout the length of the fibril.

What propels the filaments?

We are now faced with the question: how do the two sets of filaments move in between each other? Here again the electron microscope comes to the rescue. In high-magnification electron micrographs, such as the one shown in figure 28.6 on page 500, **bridges** can be seen connecting the thick and thin filaments where they overlap. These bridges project from the thick filaments at roughly 6.0 nm intervals, describing a spiral pathway round the filament. In the region of overlap each thick filament is surrounded by a hexagonal array of six thin filaments (see figure 28.5C on page 499). Successive bridges projecting from the thick filament are attached to each of these thin filaments in turn so the spiral pattern of bridges repeats itself once every six bridges, a distance of about 40 nm.

The ratchet mechanism

Research on muscle has shown that these bridges bring about contraction. Evidence suggests that during shortening of the muscle each bridge attaches itself to a thin filament. The bridge then swings through an arc. The concerted movement of many bridges has the effect of pulling the thin filaments past the thick ones. After it has completed its movement, each bridge detaches itself from the thin filament, swings back to its original position and re-attaches itself at another site further along. The cycle is then repeated. Shortening of the muscle is thus brought about by the bridges going through a kind of **ratchet mechanism**.

To account for the known rate at which muscles contract, it has been estimated that each bridge goes through its cycle between 50 and 100 times per second. This figure, together with measurements of the rate of respiration of contracting muscle, indicate that for each bridge to go through a complete cycle the hydrolysis of one molecule of ATP is required. The ATP consumption of contracting muscle is therefore considerable, which explains why the gaps between adjacent fibrils contain numerous mitochondria. You can see them in figure 28.4 on page 499.

Evidence for the ratchet mechanism

The ratchet hypothesis is supported by various lines of evidence. Special techniques in electron microscopy have shown the detailed structure of actin and myosin, and X-ray analysis supports the view that the bridges undergo substantial movement during contraction. The ratchet idea also explains many facts about muscle which have been known for a long time, and is consistent with recent research on the molecular structure of the muscle filaments. Figure 28.8 shows parts of a thick and a thin filament in detail and summarises how the ratchet mechanism is believed to work.

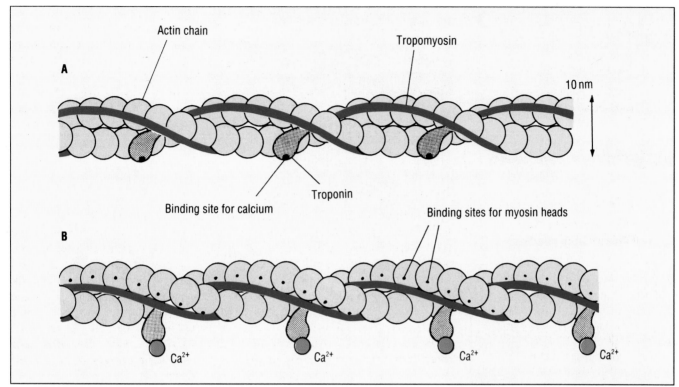

What controls the formation of the bridges?

It is obviously important that the bridges should work only when the muscle is required to contract. How, then, are they controlled?

The answer to this question comes from experiments on the molecular structure of the actin filaments. In addition to the actin itself, the filaments contain two other proteins known as **tropomyosin** and **troponin**. The way these two proteins relate to the actin is shown in figure 28.9. When the muscle is at rest, the tropomyosin is disposed in such a way that it covers the sites on the actin molecule where the myosin bridges become attached. When the muscle is required to contract, calcium ions become attached to the troponin molecules. The calcium ions activate the troponin molecules, causing them to move slightly. This has the effect of displacing the tropomyosin and exposing the binding sites. Once the tip of the myosin bridge has become attached to the actin filament, ATP is hydrolysed and the bridge goes through its cycle.

From the above account you will appreciate that ATP is needed to *break* the link between the myosin bridge and the actin. After death the amount of ATP in the body falls. Under these circumstances the bridges cannot be broken and so they remain firmly bound. This results in the body becoming stiff, a condition known as *rigor mortis*.

The sarcoplasmic reticulum

When a muscle is activated through its nerve, action potentials are set up in the individual muscle fibres. A wave of depolarisation sweeps along the membrane (sarcolemma) surrounding each muscle fibre, and this is quickly followed by a contraction. How is the electrical activity in the muscle fibre linked to the mechanical process of contraction?

The link is provided by calcium ions and it depends on the endoplasmic reticulum in the muscle fibre. This is more specialised than in other cells, and is called the **sarcoplasmic reticulum**. It consists of a system of

Figure 28.9 How the ratchet mechanism is thought to be controlled.

A When the muscle is relaxed tropomyosin covers the sites where the myosin bridges will bind with the actin filament.

B When contraction is about to take place calcium ions combine with troponin which displaces the tropomyosin and uncovers the binding sites.

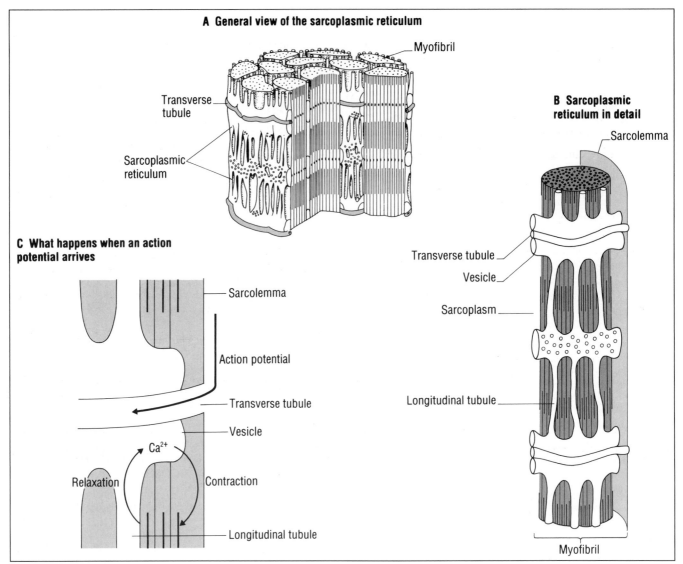

A General view of the sarcoplasmic reticulum

Myofibril

Transverse tubule

Sarcoplasmic reticulum

B Sarcoplasmic reticulum in detail

Sarcolemma

Transverse tubule

Vesicle

Sarcoplasm

Longitudinal tubule

Myofibril

C What happens when an action potential arrives

Sarcolemma

Action potential

Transverse tubule

Vesicle

Ca²⁺

Relaxation   Contraction

Longitudinal tubule

Figure 28.10 The sarcoplasmic reticulum of skeletal muscle.

A General view of part of the sarcoplasmic reticulum showing how it envelops the myofibrils.

B The components of the sarcoplasmic reticulum and how they relate to the actin and myosin filaments in the myofibril.

C An action potential sweeping along the sarcolemma is transmitted inwards by the transverse tubules. Calcium ions are then released from the adjacent vesicles into the sarcoplasm where they initiate the contraction process. After contraction the ions are taken up by the longitudinal tubules and returned to the vesicles.

membrane-lined cavities which envelop the myofibrils as shown in figure 28.10A. The cavities are attached to a series of **transverse tubules**, which are invaginations of the sarcolemma corresponding in position to the Z lines. Relatively large cavities in the immediate vicinity of the transverse tubules, called **vesicles**, are interconnected by narrow **longitudinal tubules**. The way these structures relate to an individual myofibril and its filaments is shown in figure 28.10B.

How does the sarcoplasmic reticulum work? The vesicles contain a high concentration of calcium ions. As an action potential sweeps along the sarcolemma, electrical signals are transmitted to the interior of the muscle fibre via the transverse tubules. When the signals reach the vesicles, the membrane becomes permeable to calcium ions which diffuse down the steep concentration gradient from the vesicles into the surrounding sarcoplasm. The calcium ions then activate the troponin and the muscle contracts.

Immediately after contraction, the calcium ions are actively removed into the longitudinal tubules. This lowers their concentration in the sarcoplasm and allows the muscle to relax. Meanwhile the calcium ions diffuse back to the vesicle where they may be used again. The mechanism is summarised in figure 28.10C.

Summary

1 **Effectors** are structures which respond directly or indirectly to stimuli. The body's principal effectors are **muscles** and **glands**.

2 Vertebrate muscles are classified into **skeletal** (voluntary, striated), **smooth** (involuntary, non-striated), and **cardiac** (heart) muscle. Each possesses certain characteristic properties.

3 Generally muscles contract when impulses reach them through the nervous system but sometimes, as in the case of cardiac muscle, contractions are **myogenic**.

4 Vertebrates have two kinds of skeletal muscle: **fast twitch** and **slow twitch**. The former is for short bursts of activity, the latter for more prolonged activity.

5 When a skeletal muscle receives a single electrical stimulus or a single impulse through the nerve that innervates it, it responds by giving a simple **twitch**.

6 With repetitive stimuli at a sufficiently high frequency, muscle twitches **summate** to produce a **tetanus** whose duration depends on how long the stimulation is continued.

7 A skeletal muscle is made up of groups of fibres, each group being innervated by a single axon: this comprises a **motor unit**. By varying the number of motor units activated, weak or stronger contractions can be produced.

8 Contraction of a muscle fibre is initiated by an impulse (**action potential**) whose ionic basis is similar to that of a nerve impulse. The muscle action potential obeys the **all-or-nothing law** and is followed by an **absolute** and **relative refractory period**.

9 Muscle fibres contain numerous **myofibrils** which are made up of alternating sets of thick myosin and thin actin **filaments**. The way the filaments are aligned gives skeletal muscle its striated appearance.

10 Studies on the fine structure of skeletal muscle indicate that when a muscle contracts the thick and thin filaments slide between one another, propelled by **cross bridges** acting as ratchets.

11 The ratchet mechanism depends on two other proteins, **troponin** and **tropomyosin**, which are associated with the actin filaments. Slight movement of these protein molecules, initiated by calcium ions, exposes the binding sites on the actin molecules to which the bridges become attached.

12 The calcium ions which initiate the above mechanism are released from the **sarcoplasmic reticulum** on the arrival of a muscle action potential.

13 Other effectors, besides muscles and glands, include **chromatophores** (pigment cells), **electric organs** and **light-producing organs**.

Review questions

1 Give four examples of effectors other than muscle.

2 Make a table summarising the differences, structural and functional, between smooth, cardiac and skeletal muscle.

3 What are *myogenic contractions* and where do they occur?

4 In what respects are muscle fibres functionally similar to nerve fibres, and in what ways are they different?

5 How are muscular contractions in the human body varied in (a) duration and (b) strength?

6 Which parts of a skeletal muscle fibre are visible (a) under a good light microscope and (b) in the electron microscope?

7 When a myofibril contracts what happens to the light bands, dark bands and H zone?

8 What happens to the banding pattern if a myofibril is treated with (a) a solution that dissolves actin, and (b) a solution that dissolves myosin?

9 What is a sarcomere? Draw one sarcomere showing the positions of the thick and thin filaments before and after contraction.

10 Explain, without the use of diagrams, the role of calcium ions in the contraction process. Your account should include the following words: *sarcolemma, sarcoplasmic reticulum, troponin* and *tropomyosin*.

Further reading

Muscle by D.R. Wilkie (*Studies in Biology* No 11, Arnold, 1976) is a short book which deals in detail with many aspects of muscle physiology that are touched on in this chapter.

For an account of the sliding filament theory by one of its discoverers, read *The contraction of muscle* by H.E. Huxley (*Scientific American*, November 1958). A later article by Professor Huxley deals with the more biochemical aspects of muscle contraction (*Scientific American*, December 1965).

Factors affecting muscle performance and the molecular basis of muscular contraction are dealt with more fully in *Biology, Advanced Topics*.

Other effectors

Although muscles and glands are the most widespread effectors, they are not the only ones. Here we look briefly at three other effectors.

Pigment cells

Pigment cells (**chromatophores**) are found in the skin of many animals including amphibians, reptiles, octopuses and squids. These cells are important in adaptive coloration. The predominantly greeny-brown colour of the common frog, for example, enables it to blend with its natural background.

Some animals can change their colour by concentrating or dispersing the pigment in the chromatophores. In most species this is achieved by migration of the pigment within the cell.

In octopuses and squids the same thing is achieved in a different way. Here the pigment is dispersed by muscle fibres pulling the plasma membrane of the chromatophore outwards.

To be able to change colour is a great advantage. Camouflage is more varied and effective, and a sudden colour change may serve as a

Illustration 1 Chromatophores in the skin of a vertebrate. Note the arm-like extensions of the cells into which the pigment can migrate.

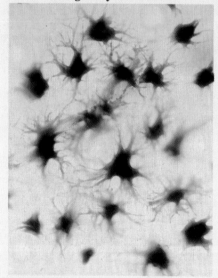

Illustration 2 The elephant fish, *Gnathenemus petersi*, emits low voltage electrical pulses. It is used by Thames Water to monitor the quality of river water. The rate of emission of pulses changes when the water contains chemical pollutants.

warning signal. In the chameleon the chromatophores contain a wide range of pigments including green, yellow, red and black. By varying the relative concentrations of these different pigments, the animal can adopt a wide variety of colours depending on its background.

Electric organs

Found in certain species of fish, notably the South American electric eel and the Mediterranean electric ray, these organs consist of stacks of sheet-like **electroplates**. They are modified muscle fibres innervated by the autonomic nervous system. Instead of contracting when they receive impulses from their nerves, they send out electric pulses. The total discharge from all the plates simultaneously can exceed 700 volts, which is more than enough to immobilise quite sizeable prey.

Many fish produce much lower voltages, emitting a pattern of electric pulses which are used not for killling prey but for locating objects in their immediate vicinity. The fish is sensitive to the disturbances of the electric field surrounding it – a kind of radar system in fact. Such a system is particularly useful to species living in the murky waters of tropical rivers where visibility is low.

Light-producing organs

Light-production by organisms (**bioluminescence**) is common in marine animals, particularly deep sea fishes, and in certain terrestrial animals such as the firefly and glow worm. Such animals have light-producing cells which are under nervous control. In most species light is produced by the oxidation of an organic compound, **luciferin**, catalysed by the enzyme **luciferase**. For this reaction ATP is required.

Light-producing organs are sometimes quite elaborate. For example, certain species of shrimp possess a reflecting layer behind the light-producing cells together with a special lens for concentrating the light and making it brighter.

The function of luminescence is not always clear. In many species it brings the sexes together for spawning, and in some cases sudden flashes of light may serve as warning signals. Can you think of any other possible functions of luminescence?

Illustration 3 The squid *Liocranchia* has luminescent spots on its head. Notice also the chromatophores in the skin.

Movement and locomotion

In the last chapter we saw how muscle contracts. There we were looking at muscle on its own, in isolation from the rest of the body. In this chapter we shall see how muscles move the body. To achieve this muscles work in conjunction with the **skeleton**. Indeed the muscles and skeleton are so inextricably bound up with each other that it is customary to regard them as a single functional system: the **musculo-skeletal system**.

The aim of this chapter is to analyse movement and locomotion in terms of the musculo-skeletal system. But of course muscles cannot work without nerves and receptors, so we shall have occasion to refer to them too. We begin with the skeleton.

The human skeleton

The skeleton is composed of numerous incompressible **bones**. In some places adjacent bones are firmly connected, but usually they articulate with each other at well lubricated **joints**. The bones are held together by **ligaments** and **muscles**. The muscles are attached to the bones by **tendons**.

Bones are constantly subjected to severe compression, tension and shearing forces, and they are adapted in their composition and structure to withstand these forces.

The human skeleton, in common with that of most other vertebrates, is constructed of two main types of tissue: **bone** and **cartilage** (see page 178). Cartilage is softer than bone tissue and is found mainly between the bones where it serves as a shock absorber, preventing jarring. The cartilage discs between successive vertebrae are particularly important in this respect, and they also give the vertebral column a certain degree of flexibility.

In cartilaginous fish (Chondrichthyes), which include sharks and rays, the skeleton is made entirely of cartilage. Their skeleton is much softer than that of bony fish (Osteichthyes) which is made of bone, like ours is.

Although a large bone like the femur is extremely hard and strong, it does have a certain amount of flexibility. When you jump from a height, the various bones in the leg bend slightly and then spring back to their usual shape.

Structure of a limb bone

A typical limb bone is shown in figure 29.1. The slender middle part of the bone is called the **shaft**, and the two swollen ends are called the **epiphyses**. The entire bone is covered with a layer of connective tissue called the **periosteum**. Beneath the periosteum is a layer of extremely hard **compact bone**. This is particularly thick in the shaft region where it consists of tightly packed Haversian systems disposed longitudinally (see page 181). Compact bone is located here because this is where the greatest stress occurs. The centre of the shaft contains soft **bone marrow**.

The epiphyses contain a network of bony fibres called **spongy bone**. This makes the ends of the bone very strong and enables them to withstand forces imposed upon them in a variety of different directions. For example, the head of the femur, which sticks out sideways from the main axis of the bone, is able to bear the weight of the body acting downwards. The spongy bone inside it is comparable to the criss-cross fret in a crane (figure 29.2).

Although we may think of bones as inert structures, they are really very much alive. They have a blood and nerve supply and contain living tissues with metabolic needs just like those of other tissues.

CHAPTER 29

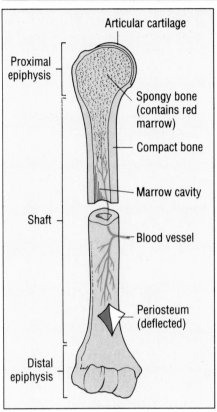

Figure 29.1 The humerus, a typical limb bone. The top half has been sectioned longitudinally to show the inside.

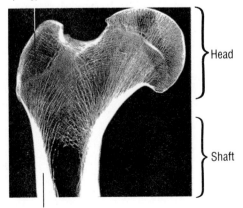

Figure 29.2 X-ray photograph of the top part of the femur showing the network of bony fibres that makes up the spongy bone in the epiphysis.

Functions of the human skeleton

The skeleton performs four basic functions:

- In conjunction with the muscles, it brings about movement, and is therefore the basis of locomotion.
- Again in conjunction with the muscles, it supports the body, holding it up and maintaining its shape and form.
- It protects the soft organs, particularly the brain, spinal cord, heart and lungs.
- It manufactures blood cells, which are produced by cell division in the bone marrow in the centre of certain bones.

Figure 29.3 The human skeleton showing its constituent parts in their normal positions.

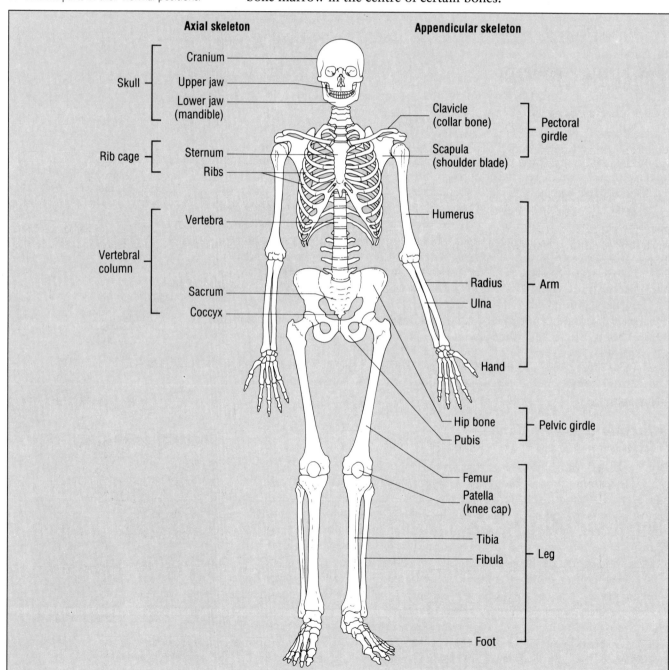

Structure of the human skeleton

The human skeleton is shown in figure 29.3. For convenience it can be divided into two parts: the **axial skeleton** and the **appendicular skeleton**.

The axial skeleton

This comprises those components of the skeleton which lie along the main axis of the body, namely the **skull, vertebral column** and **rib cage**. The vertebral column is composed of a chain of **vertebrae** (singular: **vertebra**). The **ribs** run from the vertebrae to the **sternum** which guards the front of the chest.

The vertebral column is shown in detail in figure 29.4. Its function is to carry the weight of the body, and this is reflected in the structure of the component vertebrae. The main body of the vertebra is stout and strong, the mode of articulation with its neighbours is firm and secure, and from the upper part various processes project for the attachment of ligaments and tendons.

The appendicular skeleton

Appendicular comes from the Latin word 'to hang', and it refers to those components of the skeleton which are attached to, or articulate with, the axial skeleton. They include the bones of the arms and legs (**limb bones**) together with the **pectoral** and **pelvic girdles** with which they articulate.

The pectoral girdle is made up of two main bones, the shoulder blades (scapulae), one on either side of the rib cage. In contrast, the two sides of the pelvic girdle are fused with each other and with the sacral region of the vertebral column. This provides a firm base for the articulation of the thigh bone (femur).

Figure 29.4 The vertebral column of the human.

A The whole vertebral column viewed from the side.

B A typical vertebra from the middle part of the vertebral column, viewed from the front.

C Three lumbar vertebrae showing how they fit together.

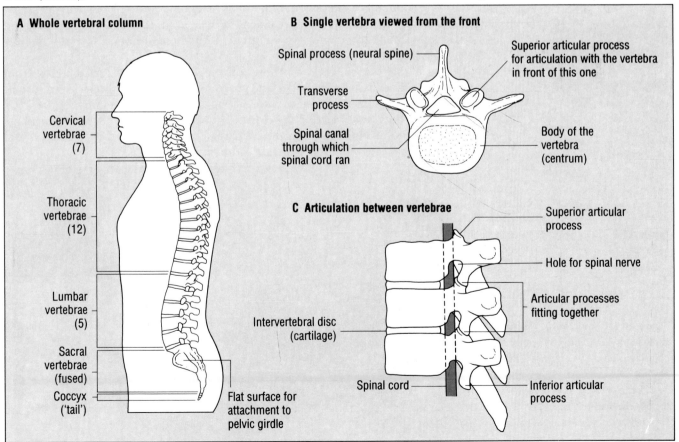

A Whole vertebral column

- Cervical vertebrae (7)
- Thoracic vertebrae (12)
- Lumbar vertebrae (5)
- Sacral vertebrae (fused)
- Coccyx ('tail')
- Flat surface for attachment to pelvic girdle

B Single vertebra viewed from the front

- Spinal process (neural spine)
- Transverse process
- Spinal canal through which spinal cord ran
- Superior articular process for articulation with the vertebra in front of this one
- Body of the vertebra (centrum)

C Articulation between vertebrae

- Superior articular process
- Hole for spinal nerve
- Articular processes fitting together
- Inferior articular process
- Intervertebral disc (cartilage)
- Spinal cord

The bones of the hands and feet are shown in detail in figure 29.5. For the variety of movements which they can make, the hands are particularly versatile and this is reflected in the large number of bones which they contain. The feet are similar. They have a potential dexterity comparable to that of the hands, though this is rarely developed except by those who are unable to use their hands (figure 29.6).

Types of bones

As you can see, the bones in the body are many and varied. It is therefore helpful to classify them, and the most useful way to do this is according to their shapes. On this basis bones fall into four groups:

- **Long bones** have a greater length than width and are found mainly in the limbs. Their ends are specially adapted to articulate with each other.
- **Short bones** are shaped like small cylinders and are found, for example, in the wrists and ankles where they allow considerable freedom of movement.
- **Flat bones** have a large surface area for the attachment of muscles or for protecting underlying structures. Examples are the pelvis, scapula and cranium.
- **Irregular bones** have complex shapes related to particular specialised functions. They include the vertebrae and jaw bones.

How do bones develop?

The skeleton of a human embryo is composed of cartilage. As the embryo develops, the cartilage is gradually replaced by bone in a process called **ossification**. The developing bone tissue hardens by becoming impregnated with minerals. The main mineral is calcium, and this is why growing children need plenty of this element in their food. If you remove the calcium from a bone by treating it with an acid, the bone becomes soft and flexible like rubber.

Some bones, such as those of the cranium, develop directly from connective tissue just under the skin. However, most bones start off as cartilage. Such is the case with a long bone like the femur. Figure 29.7 shows how such a bone develops. The cartilage is produced by cartilage cells (**chondroblasts**). Soon the cartilage becomes invaded by blood vessels, and bone cells (**osteoblasts**) start producing bone tissue.

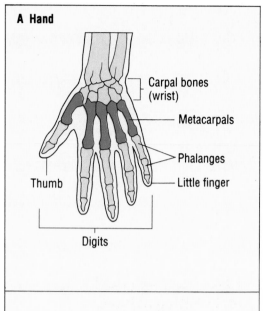

A Hand

Carpal bones (wrist)

Metacarpals

Phalanges

Thumb

Little finger

Digits

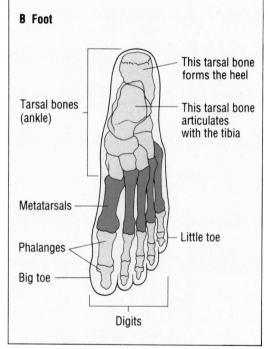

B Foot

This tarsal bone forms the heel

Tarsal bones (ankle)

This tarsal bone articulates with the tibia

Metatarsals

Phalanges

Little toe

Big toe

Digits

Figure 29.5 The bones of the human hand and foot.

Figure 29.6 Christy Brown was born with severe paralysis of many of his muscles, particulary those of his arms and right leg. However, he overcame his disability with remarkable determination. Here he is seen at the age of nineteen writing with his left foot. He went on to become an accomplished artist and author.

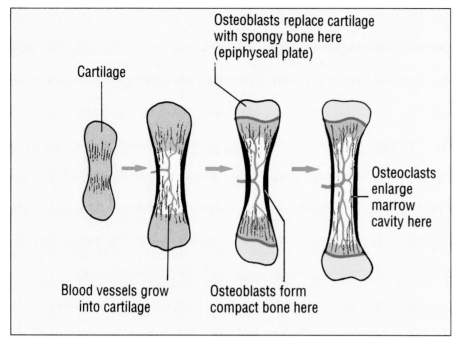

Cartilage

Osteoblasts replace cartilage with spongy bone here (epiphyseal plate)

Osteoclasts enlarge marrow cavity here

Blood vessels grow into cartilage

Osteoblasts form compact bone here

Figure 29.7 How a developing limb bone grows in length and girth.

A transverse **epiphyseal plate** appears at the base of the epiphysis at each end of the bone. Here chondroblasts divide repeatedly to form cartilage tissue towards the epiphysis, and at the same time osteoblasts destroy the chondroblasts from below and replace them with spongy bone. In this way the bone increases in length. Meanwhile osteoblasts gather beneath the periosteum in the shaft and lay down compact bone there. Eventually the osteoblasts stop forming bone and become trapped in the bone tissue which they themselves have produced. They are then known as **osteocytes** (see page 181).

As new bone tissue is laid down, old bone tissue is resorbed at the centre. This is achieved by **osteoclasts**, large multinucleate cells formed from the bone marrow. Consequently the marrow cavity in the centre of the bone gradually expands.

Ligaments and tendons

The bones that make up the skeleton are connected to each other by tough connective tissue **ligaments** which, being elastic, are well suited to bear sudden stresses. They are composed of tightly packed bundles of **elastic fibres** (see page 178).

The bones are moved relative to one another by an elaborate system of **skeletal muscles**. The muscles are attached to the bones by **tendons**, tough connective tissue strands consisting almost entirely of **collagen fibres** (see page 177).

Tendons, being composed of collagen, are less elastic than ligaments. This makes sense when you think about it. If tendons were highly elastic, they would simply stretch when the muscle contracted. However, they do have a certain degree of elasticity and this allows them to store energy during locomotion.

Skeletal muscles have their **origin** on one bone and their **insertion** on another. In other words, the muscles span the joints. Ligaments too span the joints. The stresses and strains to which the ligaments and tendons are subjected can be considerable, so they need to be firmly attached to the bones: their collagen and elastic fibres run into the periosteum surrounding the bone, securing a firm attachment which is difficult to break.

Osteoclasts and the remodelling of bone

Osteoclasts are important throughout the time the bone is developing. Their eroding activities enable the bone to be continually changed and remodelled to meet the stresses and strains to which the limb is subjected. They are also responsible for cutting channels in the bone, thereby enabling blood vessels to grow into it. These channels become the Haversian canals of mature bone.

The process of remodelling continues even after the bone reaches its full size. Its crystalline structure results in piezo electrical currents flowing through it. These currents stimulate the formation of bone tissue in the lines of load bearing, so that bone tissue is formed where it is needed and resorbed where it is not. In other words, *bone tissue is laid down or resorbed in response to the mechanical demands made upon it*. This makes the skeleton an incredibly efficient material. By minimising the amount of material necessary to carry out its mechanical functions, its mass and metabolic costs are kept to a minimum.

Fractures

Guest author Glyn Evans explains how different kinds of fractures can be treated.

When someone is suspected of having fractured a bone, the first thing we need to know is where exactly the fracture is, and that means taking an **X-ray**.

Although X-rays are immensely useful, they have their limitations for they only give us a two-dimensional image of the skeleton. However, with the aid of a computer we can build up a three-dimensional image using a more modern X-ray technique called **computed tomography scanning**.

The trouble is, though, that bombarding the body with X-rays can be a health hazard, and in recent years it has become possible to obtain an image of the skeleton without the use of X-rays. The technique is called **magnetic resonance imaging** (**MRI**) and it can produce images of 'slices' of the skeleton as well as the surrounding soft tissues. In this way abnormalities of the skeleton and any accompanying damage to the surrounding soft tissues can be identified.

If an animal in the wild, or a person living in an isolated community, breaks a bone, the fracture heals by a natural process without the assistance of an orthopaedic surgeon. The first thing that happens is that the cut surfaces of the bone bleed. Soon the blood clots and solidifies. Blood vessels grow into the clot and a repair tissue develops which holds the bone ends together. This tissue then slowly hardens and eventually calcium salts are deposited in it, converting it into bone tissue which joins the two parts of the bone together.

Nature is superbly equipped to heal fractures. However, fractures which are allowed to heal naturally nearly always heal with the bone in a crooked position. This may be due to the pull of the muscles, or to the deformity caused by the injury itself. The role of the orthopaedic surgeon is not normally to bring about healing, which would happen anyway, but to keep the bone in the correct alignment while healing takes place.

Illustration 1 shows the main kinds of fractures that can occur in a long bone. Obviously fractures can occur in many other places, the wrist and fingers for example. In many cases all that is required to hold the bone in the right position is a Plaster of Paris cast. This acts as a splint while the fracture heals. However, this

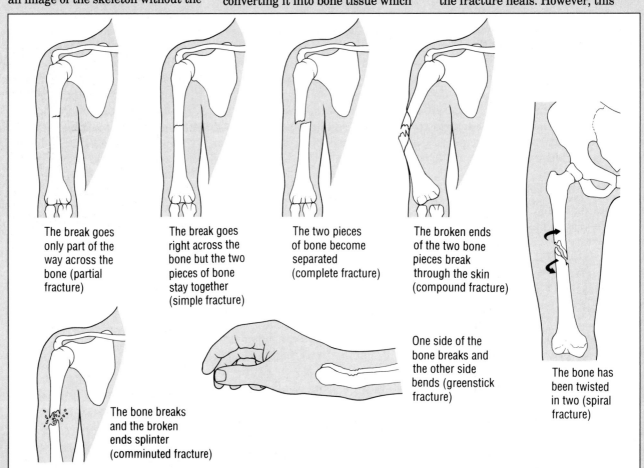

The break goes only part of the way across the bone (partial fracture)

The break goes right across the bone but the two pieces of bone stay together (simple fracture)

The two pieces of bone become separated (complete fracture)

The broken ends of the two bone pieces break through the skin (compound fracture)

The bone breaks and the broken ends splinter (comminuted fracture)

One side of the bone breaks and the other side bends (greenstick fracture)

The bone has been twisted in two (spiral fracture)

Illustration 1 Different kinds of fracture that may occur to a long bone.

does not always work, and it may be necessary to fix the broken pieces of bone together in some way. In some cases we make use of the fact that the long bones have a marrow cavity and insert a stainless steel rod in the cavity to act as an internal splint. If this is not possible, we can attach a plate to the surface of the bone with stainless steel screws.

If the skin over the fracture site is broken, some kind of external fixation may be necessary: pins are inserted through the skin into the bone and then linked together by a rod outside the skin. A system which we have developed is shown in illustration 2. This particular 'fixator' is used for small bones such as those of the hand. Larger versions are used for bigger bones such as the femur.

On rare occasions the natural process of healing fails and the pieces of bone do not knit together. When this happens it is possible to take a piece of bone from another part of the

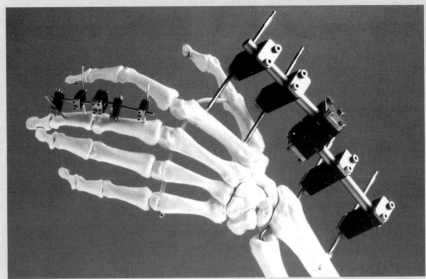

Illustration 2 A fixator may be used for holding small bones in place following a fracture of the wrist or fingers. The pins can be inserted using a power tool with wire-driving attachment.

body, usually the pelvis, and insert it into the fracture site. Such a **bone graft** helps the fracture to heal. Another way of promoting healing is to use electromagnetic induction: a flexible electric coil is wrapped round

the fracture and this induces an electric field at the fracture site. No-one knows exactly how this works but it certainly helps fractures to heal.

Replacement surgery

Replacing parts of the skeleton with artificial substitutes is now a common procedure. Glyn Evans explains what happens.

Like any mechanical device, the joints in the skeleton undergo wear. Unlike the hinges of a door, however, the joints in our skeleton are normally able to repair any damage that occurs. But if the joint surfaces wear faster than they can be repaired, the joint as a whole wears out. This results in **osteoarthritis**. Another thing that may happen is that the joint surfaces get destroyed by disease, giving rise to conditions such as **rheumatoid arthritis**.

In severe cases of arthritis a **joint replacement** may be necessary. The commonest joint which requires replacing is the hip joint. We remove the head of the femur (the ball) and

replace it with a stainless steel ball attached to a rod inserted into the marrow cavity. Usually a small plastic cup is placed in the acetabulum, the natural socket in the pelvis (see illustration).

In most cases the plastic cup and the metal rod are held in place by an acrylic cement. However, in younger patients hip replacements can be carried out without the use of a cement. For this to be possible the components have to be exceptionally well engineered so that they lock into place in their respective bones.

At one time **bone cancer** generally required amputation of the affected limb. These days, if a person has a tumour involving the femur, the entire femur is removed and replaced with a custom-made metal one. This is inserted into the leg with a hip replacement at the top and a knee replacement at the bottom.

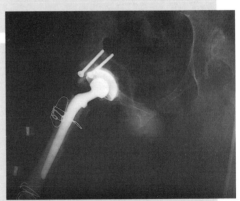

X-ray image of the pelvic area following surgery to replace a patient's right hip joint which had been severely damaged by rheumatoid arthritis.

Technology has enabled great advances to be made in treating disorders of the skeleton but of course problems do occur. The biggest enemy is infection. We also have to contend with the fact that metal components tend to work loose after a time, and metal fatigue sometimes occurs. However, the development of new materials may prevent these problems arising.

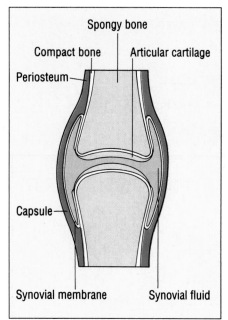

Figure 29.8 The structure of a typical synovial joint.

Figure 29.9 Ball and socket and hinge joints illustrated by the hip joint and knee joint respectively. In both diagrams the fibrous capsule has been removed and the articular cartilage is coloured blue.

Joints

Joints vary in the amount of movement they permit. Some joints, such as those between the vertebrae, permit very little movement; whereas others, such as those between the different limb bones, allow considerable movement.

The latter type of joint is called a **synovial joint**. The structure of a synovial joint is shown in figure 29.8. The joint is enclosed within a **capsule** made of connective tissue. The inside of the capsule is lined with a **synovial membrane** which secretes **synovial fluid**. The synovial fluid fills the cavity inside the joint and serves as a lubricant. The articulating surfaces are covered with a layer of **articular cartilage** which, being relatively soft, serves as a cushion preventing jarring. The articular cartilage and synovial fluid provide an exceptionally smooth surface against which the bones move with the minimum of friction.

Ligaments run between the two bones both inside the joint (i.e. inside the capsule) and outside it. Together with the capsule itself, they hold the joint together and prevent the bones coming apart. The muscles and tendons also help to strengthen the joint.

All synovial joints have the same basic structure, but they differ in the shape of the articulating surfaces. This has important consequences, for it determines the freedom of movement at the joint. Synovial joints are of two main kinds: **ball and socket joints** and **hinge joints** (figure 29.9). Ball and socket joints permit extensive movement in any plane, including rotation. Examples are the shoulder and hip joints. Hinge joints, on the other hand, permit extensive movement in only one plane. Examples are the elbow and knee joints. You can test this for yourself by moving your arms and legs and seeing what sort of movement is possible at the various joints.

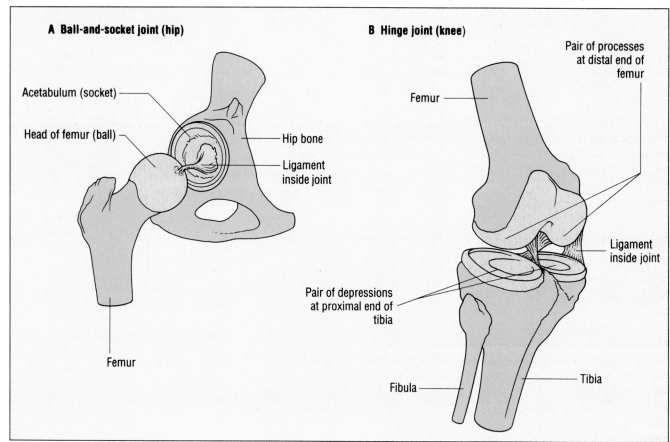

Muscles and the skeleton

To fulfil its function of supporting the body and permitting movement, the skeleton works in conjunction with muscles. To gain an insight into how they work together let us look at the arm.

The lower arm bones (the radius and ulna) are moved by two muscles, the **biceps** and **triceps**. Figure 29.10 shows the origin and insertion of these muscles and what happens when they contract. Notice that they produce opposite effects: the biceps bends the arm at the elbow, and the triceps straightens it. A muscle such as the biceps which pulls two limb bones towards each other, i.e. closes the joint, is called a **flexor**; a muscle such as the triceps which pulls two limb bones away from each other, i.e. opens the joint, is called an **extensor**. The biceps and triceps are the main flexor and extensor muscles in the arm.

The bones which are pulled by the muscles act as **levers**. A lever is a solid bar which is turned about a fixed point or **pivot**. Levers are common in everyday life: you are using a lever when you prize open the lid of a box, or when you propel someone up and down on a seesaw. In any lever system two opposing forces operate on one or other side of the pivot: a **load** and an **effort**. Different kinds of lever are recognised depending on the positions of the load and the effort relative to the pivot. Figure 29.10 shows the lever systems which operate when the arm is flexed by contraction of the biceps and extended by contraction of the triceps.

Antagonistic muscle action

Plainly the biceps and triceps (indeed all flexors and extensors) oppose each other in their actions. Such muscles are described as **antagonistic**. It is obviously necessary that when the biceps contracts the triceps should relax, and *vice versa*. This is achieved by the coordinating action of the central nervous system, operating via the synapses in the spinal cord (see page 438). This principle applies to any pair of antagonistic muscles, not only in the human but in the other animals as well.

In practice a contracting muscle's antagonist does not relax completely: it maintains sufficient tension to give the other muscle a firm base to work against. This is important in the control of movement and the maintenance of **posture**. When your body is in a fixed position, as for example when you are standing still, all your postural muscles are in a state of slight contraction, a phenomenon known as **muscle tone**. The maintenance of muscle tone is largely due to the presence in our muscles of special receptors called **muscle spindles**.

Muscle spindles and tendon organs

Muscle spindles and tendon organs are examples of **proprioceptors**, receptors which are sensitive to position and movement. Together with other proprioceptors, such as those in the vestibular apparatus in the inner ear, they play an important part in the maintenance of posture and control of movement. In fulfilling this function they work in conjunction with the brain, particularly the **cerebellum** (see page 454).

It is helpful to understand what these receptors achieve before considering how they do it. If a muscle is stretched (for example by its antagonist) the muscle spindle initiates a reflex which causes that muscle to contract. In other words *when a muscle is stretched it responds by contracting*. This is called a **stretch reflex** and, insofar as the stimulus evokes a corrective response, it is an example of negative feedback.

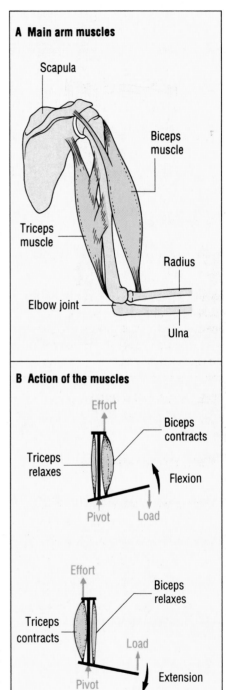

A Main arm muscles

Scapula

Biceps muscle

Triceps muscle

Radius

Elbow joint

Ulna

B Action of the muscles

Effort

Biceps contracts

Triceps relaxes

Flexion

Pivot

Load

Effort

Biceps relaxes

Triceps contracts

Load

Pivot

Extension

Figure 29.10 The main muscles which flex and extend the arm at the elbow joint, and their actions.

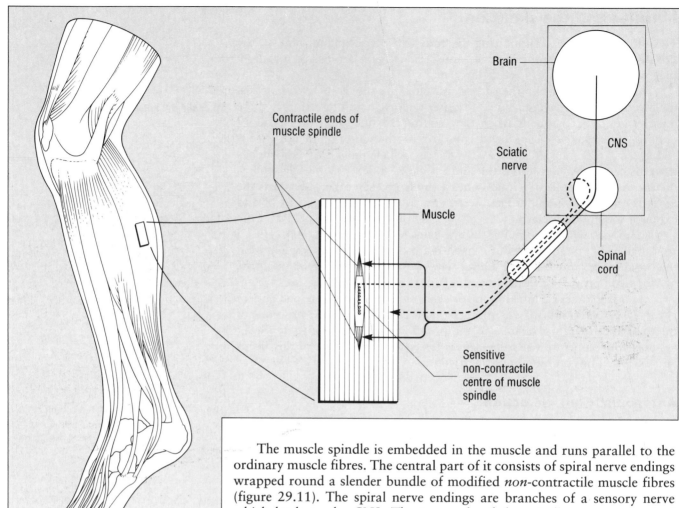

Contractile ends of
muscle spindle

Brain

Sciatic
nerve

CNS

Muscle

Spinal
cord

Sensitive
non-contractile
centre of muscle
spindle

Figure 29.11 Diagram of a muscle spindle.
Stretching the muscle (in this case the calf
muscle) stimulates the sensitive centre of the
spindle, leading reflexly to the contraction of
the muscle. Contraction of the contractile
ends of the spindle sets the tone of the
spindle.

The muscle spindle is embedded in the muscle and runs parallel to the
ordinary muscle fibres. The central part of it consists of spiral nerve endings
wrapped round a slender bundle of modified *non*-contractile muscle fibres
(figure 29.11). The spiral nerve endings are branches of a sensory nerve
which leads to the CNS. The two ends of the spindle are composed of
contractile muscle fibres which receive effector nerves from the CNS.

Muscle spindles work as follows. As soon as the muscle is stretched,
nerve impulses are discharged from the spiral nerve endings to the CNS.
This results in impulses being transmitted via the appropriate effector
nerves to the muscle, making it contract. The nerve pathway in this stretch
reflex is shown by the broken arrow in figure 29.11. It has been found that
the more the spindle is stretched, the greater is the frequency of impulses
discharged in the nerve and the harder the muscle contracts.

The contractile ends of the spindle set the tone of the receptor so that it
is not slack when the muscle is stretched. This is particularly important
when the muscle is liable to considerable stretching, such as when a heavy
load is lifted or during the maintenance of posture. Under these circumstances contraction of its two ends increases the stretch on the spindle and
so augments the response. The nerve pathways through which this is
achieved are shown by the solid arrows in figure 29.11.

Stretch receptors are not confined to muscles; they are also found in
tendons where they are referred to as **tendon organs**. A tendon organ
consists of branched nerve endings which, when stretched, discharge
impulses to the CNS. Experiments show that the tendon organ only
responds when the tension is extreme. This is because it has a high
threshold, much higher than the muscle spindle. Excitation of the tendon
organ reflexly *inhibits* the muscle, thereby preventing it from contracting so
powerfully that it might get damaged.

Locomotion

In considering the locomotion of any animal three things must be taken into account:

- **Propulsion**: the animal must be propelled with sufficient force in the appropriate direction.
- **Support**: the animal must be supported by its body acting against the particular medium in which it lives.
- **Stability**: the animal may become temporarily unstable while moving, but eventually stability must be restored.

How animals cope with these three problems depends on whether they move on land, in water or in air. Here we shall be mainly concerned with locomotion on land. Humans, of course, are **bipedal**, using only their hind limbs for locomotion. Most land-living vertebrates are **tetrapods**, using all four limbs for locomotion. This difference does not affect propulsion, at least not in any fundamental sense, but it does affect support and stability, as we shall see.

Propulsion on land

The legs of land-living vertebrates contain numerous muscles most of which are directly or indirectly involved in propulsion. The muscles can be divided into seven groups according to their actions (figure 29.12).

- **Protractors** pull the limb forward.
- **Retractors** pull the limb backwards.
- **Adductors (depressors)** pull the limb inwards.
- **Abductors (levators)** pull the limb outwards.
- **Flexors** pull two parts of the limb towards each other.
- **Extensors** pull two parts of the limb away from each other.
- **Rotators** swivel the whole, or part, of the limb.

Protraction / Retraction

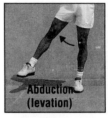

Abduction (levation) / Adduction (depression)

Flexion / Extension

Rotation

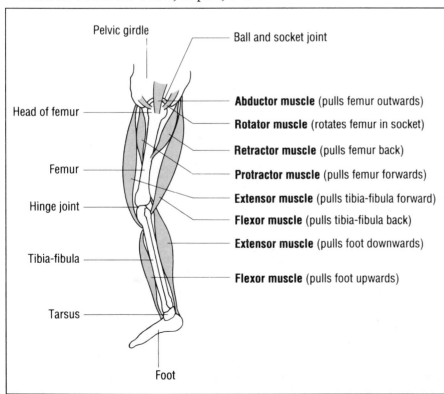

Pelvic girdle — Ball and socket joint

Head of femur

Femur

Hinge joint

Tibia-fibula

Tarsus

Foot

Abductor muscle (pulls femur outwards)

Rotator muscle (rotates femur in socket)

Retractor muscle (pulls femur back)

Protractor muscle (pulls femur forwards)

Extensor muscle (pulls tibia-fibula forward)

Flexor muscle (pulls tibia-fibula back)

Extensor muscle (pulls foot downwards)

Flexor muscle (pulls foot upwards)

Figure 29.12

Left A small selection of the more important muscles found in the hind leg of a typical tetrapod, looking from the outside. Adductor muscles are found on the inner side of the leg and are therefore invisible in this diagram. They pull the femur inwards.

Right The various actions produced by the muscles illustrated by the human leg illustrated here by a young boxer.

Some of these muscles are **extrinsic**, that is they have their origin outside the limb itself, i.e. on the limb girdles. The rest are **intrinsic**, having both their origin and insertion within the limb.

Clearly the different sets of muscles oppose each other. Thus protractors are **antagonistic** to retractors, adductors to abductors, and flexors to extensors. The different muscles are supplied by axons from the main nerve serving the limb, the brachial nerve in the case of the forelimb and the sciatic nerve in the case of the hindlimb. By directing impulses down the appropriate axons, the CNS ensures that each set of muscles contracts at the right time.

Propulsive action of the muscles

In propelling the body forward the most important muscles are the retractors and extensors. When they contract the limb acts as a lever. The foot presses downwards and backwards against the ground, resulting in an equal and opposite force which is transmitted along the length of the limb against the body (figure 29.14A). This force can be resolved into a vertical component and a horizontal component. The former lifts the body off the ground, the latter propels it forward.

The relative magnitude of these two forces will depend on the angle between the ground and the main axis of the limb (the angle **a** in figure 29.14A). If this angle is 90° and the point of contact of the foot with the ground is directly below the centre of gravity, there will be a lift force but no forward force, with the result that the body is thrust vertically upwards. This is what high-jumpers try to achieve then they leave the ground (figure 29.14B).

On the other hand, if the angle is small and the foot is a long way behind the centre of gravity, the forward force will be considerable but the upward force relatively small. This is what sprinters aim to achieve when they take their positions at the starting blocks (figure 29.14C).

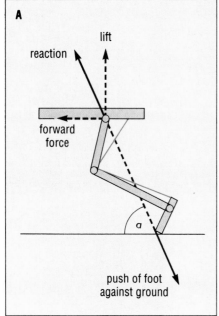

Figure 29.14 These diagrams illustrate the action of the limb in propelling the body forward.

A Model of a limb, showing the retractor and extensor muscles (red). The extent to which the body is propelled forwards rather than upwards depends on the size of the angle **a**.
B For a high jumper the angle **a** should approach 90° so as to gain maximum lift.
C For a sprinter the angle **a** should be small so as to gain maximum forward thrust.

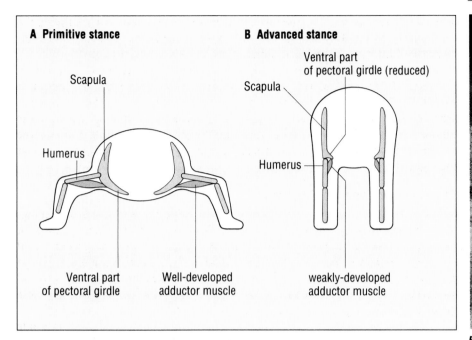

A Primitive stance

Scapula

Humerus

Ventral part
of pectoral girdle

Well-developed
adductor muscle

B Advanced stance

Ventral part
of pectoral girdle (reduced)

Scapula

Humerus

weakly-developed
adductor muscle

Figure 29.15

Left Diagrammatic end-on views of a primitive and an advanced tetrapod to show their respective stances. Note that the primitive condition requires the development of powerful adductor muscles to hold the body off the ground.

Right Photograph of a rock lizard, *Pseudocordylus subviridis*, showing the primitive splayed-out position of the limbs.

Support on land

The limbs must hold the body off the ground both when the animal is in motion and also when it is standing still. For maximum efficiency the limbs should be directly beneath the body.

To appreciate this, we have only to compare the forelimbs of mammals and reptiles (figure 29.15). In a lizard, for example, the limbs splay out from the body, giving the animal a bow-legged appearance. Holding the body off the ground necessitates the contraction of powerful adductor muscles running from the ventral side of the pectoral girdle to the humerus. One cannot help thinking that walking for a heavy reptile like a crocodile must be a great strain, like push-ups for a human. No wonder such animals spend much of their time lying on their bellies.

In mammals this problem has been overcome by bringing the limbs into a straight line immediately beneath the body. The result is that the load is transmitted along what are essentially straight struts. Predictably, the adductor muscles are considerably reduced and the ventral part of the pectoral girdle is absent altogether.

In most tetrapods it is necessary for the **vertebral column** to bridge the gap between the forelimbs and hindlimbs (figure 29.16). The tetrapod skeleton can, in fact, be regarded as a bridge in which the limbs represent the piers and the vertebral column the span. What kind of bridge is it? This question was investigated many years ago by the great zoologist D'Arcy Thompson. On the basis of mathematical considerations, he came to the conclusion that the vertebral column is comparable to a **cantilever bridge** like the Forth railway bridge in Scotland.

Though extravagant in its use of materials, the cantilever is a very strong construction and there is no risk of it breaking in the middle. This is important when you think of the weight it has to bear. In a horse, for example, the entire weight of the abdomen acts downwards at right angles to the vertebral column.

In the human, being bipedal, the vertebral column is more like a tower than a bridge. The weight of the body is transmitted down the main axis of the vertebral column, each vertebra pressing against the one below. Here the problem is not so much breaking in the middle, as withstanding the

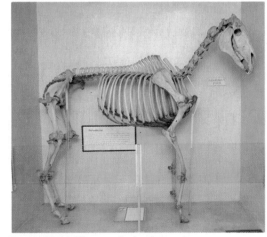

Figure 29.16 The vertebral column of a tetrapod is like the span of a bridge, and it has to carry the weight of the abdomen, which may be considerable in a herbivore such as the horse, whose skeleton is shown here. Herbivores are particularly heavy because of the long length of the gut.

519

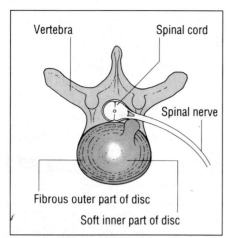

Figure 29.17 Diagram of a 'slipped disc'. The inside of the intervertebral disc contains hyaline cartilage and is soft and rubbery at the centre. The outer part of the disc consists of fibrocartilage and is relatively hard and tough. In a 'slipped disc' the outer fibrous layer splits, and the inner material bulges out. Great pain may be caused if the extruded material presses on a nerve.

downward pressure. The intervertebral discs, being made of cartilage are particularly vulnerable in this respect. If the pressure suddenly becomes unevenly distributed, one of the discs may burst on one side, giving what is misleadingly called a **slipped disc** (figure 29.17).

Stability on land

For a tetrapod at rest, with its four legs planted fairly and squarely on the ground, stability is not a major problem. The animal is like a four-legged table with the centre of gravity falling inside the area delineated by its four legs (figure 29.18A). However, when the animal is in motion, problems arise because periodically at least one leg must be taken off the ground. When this happens, the tetrapod changes to being a tripod. If the animal is to remain stable when it takes a foot off the ground, it must first shift its centre of gravity into the triangle delineated by the three legs that are still in contact with the ground. If it fails to do this, it will topple over.

The sequence of events that occurs during tetrapod locomotion is based on this simple fact of mechanics. Imagine a slow-moving tetrapod with its legs in the positions shown in figure 29.18B-1. In order to progress, the first thing it must do is to move its weight forward so that its centre of gravity falls within the triangle delineated by the right fore, right hind and left forelimbs (figure 29.18B-2). It then lifts the left hindlimb and brings it up behind the left forelimb (figure 29.18B-3). It then lifts its left forelimb and places it out in front (figure 29.18B-4). The centre of gravity is now shifted into the new triangle delineated by the left fore, left hind and right forelimbs (figure 29.18B-5). The right hindlimb can now be raised and brought up behind the right forelimb. The animal thus progresses in a **diagonal pattern** in which the order of leg-raising is: left hind, left fore, right hind, right fore – and so on.

The diagonal pattern is clearly seen in slow-moving tetrapods like newts and salamanders. In mammals mechanical stability is augmented by reflexes arising from proprioceptors such as the muscle spindles and vestibular apparatus in the inner ear, from pressure receptors in the soles of the feet, and of course from the eyes. This enables such animals to maintain equilib-

Figure 29.18 The problem of stability in a tetrapod.

A A stationary tetrapod is like a table. If all four legs are in contact with the ground, the table will remain stable if the centre of gravity is anywhere within the area delineated by the four legs. If one leg is taken off the ground the table will fall over unless the centre of gravity is shifted into the triangle delineated by the three legs that remain in contact with the ground.

B Successive stages in the diagonal locomotory pattern of a walking tetrapod. The order in which the feet are raised off the ground is: left hind, left fore, right hind, right fore. Note that a foot can be raised only if the centre of gravity (represented by the circle) is first shifted into the triangle delineated by the three feet that remain in contact with the ground.

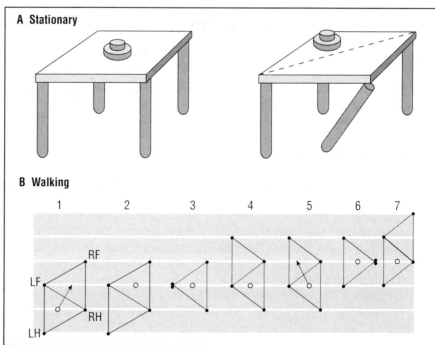

rium when two, three or even all four legs are taken off the ground at the same time. But even in a galloping horse, as slow-motion films show, the diagonal pattern can still be detected, the legs being slightly out of phase with each other during the locomotory cycle (figure 29.19).

The importance of the centre of gravity

Plainly the position of the centre of gravity plays an important part in an animal's life. In an animal like a horse the centre of gravity lies towards the front of the body, so the animal can raise one of its hindlimbs with no risk of instability. But if it is to raise one of its forelimbs, it must first move its weight back so that its centre of gravity is nearer the hind legs.

In squirrels, bears and kangaroos the centre of gravity lies towards the rear, so the forelimbs can be lifted off the ground without loss of stability. This enables such animals to sit on their haunches, a useful thing to be able to do for it enables the animal to survey its environment from an elevated vantage point. In the kangaroo the centre of gravity is so far back that it would fall over backwards were it not for the strong muscular tail acting as a support. In this way the kangaroo can rest on a tripod whilst surveying its surroundings (figure 29.20). The ability to stand permanently on the hindlimbs (bipedalism) has been an important development in the evolution of the human species (see page 826).

Locomotion in water

Water, being denser than air, offers more resistance to the movement of objects through it. In larger aquatic animals such as fish and porpoises this disadvantage has been overcome by streamlining. On the credit side, water provides more support than air and provides a relatively thick medium on which propulsive devices can gain a purchase. Let us start by considering how fishes gain support from the water in which they live.

Support in fishes

Bony fish such as trout are made buoyant by a gas-filled **swim bladder** situated towards the dorsal side of the body. There are two types of swim bladder: open and closed. The **open swim bladder** is connected to the pharynx by a duct, and air is taken into it, or expelled from it, through the mouth. So by 'blowing bubbles' a goldfish can make itself heavier and sink to a lower level in the water. On the other hand, to occupy a higher level in the water it must first swim to the surface and gulp air into its swim bladder.

The **closed swim bladder** is more sophisticated. Gas, mainly oxygen, is secreted into it, or withdrawn from it, by vascular 'gas glands' in its lining. By this means the density of the fish can be adjusted with minimum inconvenience to the animal, enabling it to stay at the required depth without having to swim up to the surface. The majority of bony fish have swim bladders of this type.

Cartilaginous fish such as sharks do not possess a swim bladder of any kind. They sink if they stop swimming, and support comes from the process of swimming itself. Anteriorly support is derived from a pair of large pectoral fins, and to a lesser extent from a somewhat smaller pair of pelvic fins further back. By being held at a slight angle to the body, these horizontal fins provide a lift force as well as a forward propulsive force. How the side to side movements of the tail are produced and how they propel the fish forward will be explained next.

Figure 29.19 Three stages in the locomotory cycle of a galloping horse.

Figure 29.20 The great grey kangaroo (*Macropus giganteus*) uses its strong muscular tail to provide support when in the upright position. In doing so it becomes a tripod.

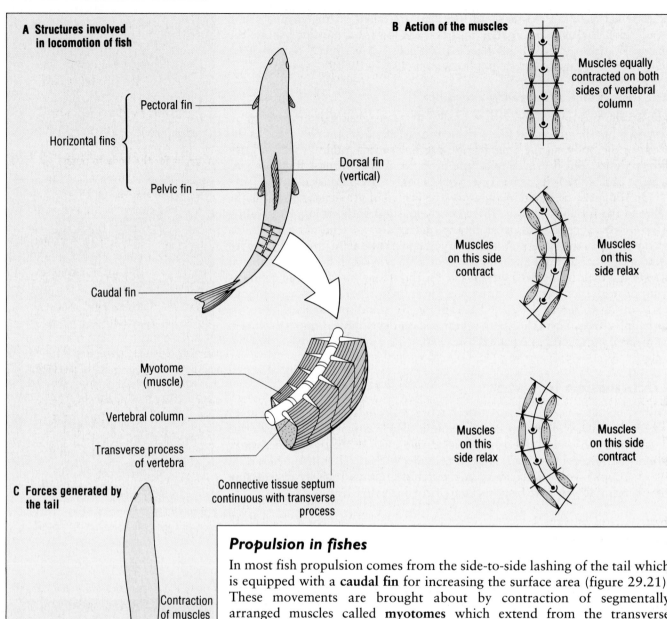

A Structures involved in locomotion of fish

Horizontal fins
Pectoral fin
Pelvic fin
Dorsal fin (vertical)
Caudal fin
Myotome (muscle)
Vertebral column
Transverse process of vertebra
Connective tissue septum continuous with transverse process

B Action of the muscles

Muscles equally contracted on both sides of vertebral column

Muscles on this side contract
Muscles on this side relax

Muscles on this side relax
Muscles on this side contract

C Forces generated by the tail

Contraction of muscles on this side pulls tail towards right
Forward force
Reaction
Lateral drag
Direction of movement of tail
Push of tail against water

Figure 29.21 Locomotion in a fish.

A The powerful myotome muscles on either side of the vertebral column swing the tail from side to side.

B The muscles contract alternately on either side, bending the vertebral column as shown.

C The forces set up as the tail moves through the water.

Propulsion in fishes

In most fish propulsion comes from the side-to-side lashing of the tail which is equipped with a **caudal fin** for increasing the surface area (figure 29.21). These movements are brought about by contraction of segmentally arranged muscles called **myotomes** which extend from the transverse processes of one vertebra, and the connective tissue septum continuous with it, to the next. The tail sweeps from side to side by alternate contractions of the myotomes on each side of the body. The myotomes on the left and right sides are, of course, antagonistic and their contractions are coordinated by the CNS.

When the fish is swimming, forces are set up as shown in figure 29.21C. As the tail sweeps across towards the right it pushes against the water, as a result of which it experiences a force which can be resolved into forward and sideways components. The forward component drives the fish through the water. The sideways component tends to swing the tail towards the left and the head towards the right. This **lateral drag** is counteracted by the pressure of water against the head and dorsal fin. The result is that the fish moves forward without the body swinging from side to side too much.

In the type of fish just described propulsion is achieved by the tail lashing from side to side. Most other fish use the same basic method of propulsion though different amounts of the body may be involved. In eels, for example, the entire body is thrown into lateral undulations which, progressing from front to rear, exert forces similar to those exerted by the tail of other fish.

In bony fish, the pectoral and pelvic fins are small fan-like appendages on either side of the body. They can be pulled into the side or stuck out at will, and are used for steering and braking. In some species the pectoral and pelvic fins are very mobile, making these fishes astonishingly agile.

Stability in fish

A fish is liable to the same kinds of instability that affect boats: yawing, pitching and rolling.

- **Yawing**, the side-to-side oscillations of the front part of the body resulting from the propulsive action of the tail, is counteracted by the general massiveness and inertia of the head and by the pressure of water against the side of the body and the vertical fins. In many bony fishes the stabilising effect of these features is enhanced by lateral flattening of the body.
- **Pitching**, the tendency of the front end to plunge vertically downwards, is counteracted by the flap-like horizontal fins. The larger the surface area these fins have, the more effective they are as stabilisers.
- **Rolling**, the rotation of the body about the longitudinal axis, is counter-acted by both the vertical and horizontal fins rather like the feathers at the back of an arrow.

Locomotion in air

The technical problems connected with movement in air are considerable. This is due to the rarity of the medium which provides little support and no purchase for the propulsive devices. For these reasons the principles involved with movement through air are rather different from those involved in aquatic locomotion.

Flight has been successfully developed in three groups of animals: birds, bats and insects. In all three cases the flight mechanism depends on the possession of **wings**.

Flight in birds

The bird wing consists of a row of feathers projecting from the forelimb (figure 29.22). The number of digits is reduced compared with the human,

Swimming on land

The eel-like method of locomotion is not confined to aquatic animals. Snakes move by lateral undulations which pass along the body from front to rear, as in eels. So long as there are firm objects like stones or tufts of grass for the body to push against, the animal can glide forward. A striking demonstration of this is seen in eels. An eel placed on a flat slippery surface makes little or no progress, but if placed on a peg-board it progresses quickly and efficiently by gaining a purchase on the pegs. In effect, the animal is swimming on land. This enables eels to move overland if necessary as they migrate up rivers to fresh water. It also means that, from a locomotory point of view, an animal like a grass snake is as adept in water as it is on land – grass snakes are in fact excellent swimmers.

Figure 29.22 The wing of a bird showing the main feathers involved in flight.

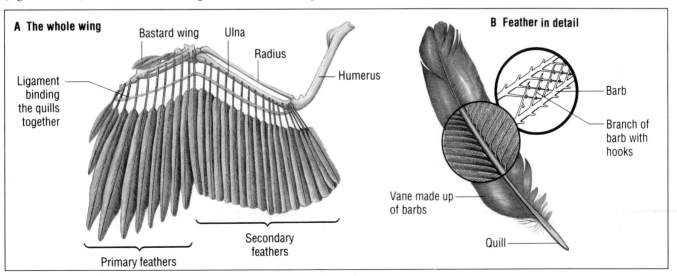

A The whole wing

Bastard wing
Ulna
Radius
Humerus
Ligament binding the quills together
Primary feathers
Secondary feathers

B Feather in detail

Barb
Branch of barb with hooks
Vane made up of barbs
Quill

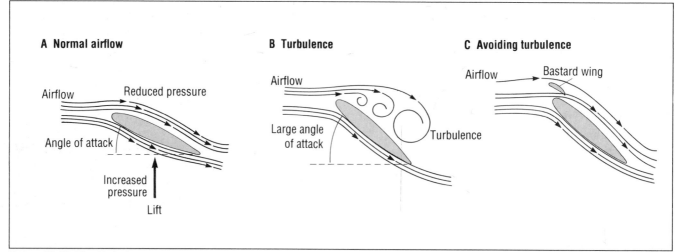

A Normal airflow

Airflow
Reduced pressure
Angle of attack
Increased pressure
Lift

B Turbulence

Airflow
Large angle of attack
Turbulence

C Avoiding turbulence

Airflow
Bastard wing

Figure 29.23 The bird wing as an aerofoil.
A The air flows faster over the upper surface of the wing than the lower surface. This creates a reduced pressure above the wing and an increased pressure below it, thereby providing the bird with lift. The lift force can be increased by holding the wing at a greater angle to the airstream, i.e. by increasing the angle of attack.
B If the angle of attack is too large, turbulence may occur above the wing.
C Turbulence is normally prevented by the bastard wing and by the end-feathers which serve as slots, smoothing the flow of air over the upper surface of the wing.

and the feathers give the wing a large surface area. The feathers themselves are extremely light and are arranged rather like the slats of a Venetian blind with the result that air can pass between them as the wing goes up but not when the wing goes down.

A bird can fly either passively by gliding or actively by flapping its wings.

Passive flight

When a bird **glides,** the wings act as **aerofoils.** An aerofoil is any smooth surface which moves through the air at an angle to the airstream. The main properties of an aerofoil, as applied to the wing of a bird, are summarised in figure 29.23. The air flows over the wing in such a way that the bird is given lift, the amount of lift depending on the angle at which the wing is held relative to the airstream, that is the 'angle of attack'. Turbulence, which could cause the bird to lose height, is prevented by the bastard wing and by the feathers at the end of the wing which separate from each other: they smooth the flow of air over the wing.

Now let us consider the various forces acting on the wing. Think of a bird such as a gull which has been actively flying in still air, and then glides. The forward motion of the bird creates a flow of air over the wings, setting up the forces shown in figure 29.24. As a consequence of these forces, the

Figure 29.24 Diagram illustrating the forces operating on a bird gliding in still air. The weight of the bird acting downwards can be resolved into two components: a **sinking force** and, at right angles to this, a **driving force** propelling the body obliquely downwards. Assuming that the bird is moving at constant speed, these two forces are opposed by equal forces acting in the opposite direction. The sinking force is opposed by a **lift force** acting obliquely upwards, and the driving force by a **drag force**. The resultant of these two forces is the **aerodynamic force**, and is equal and opposite to the weight.

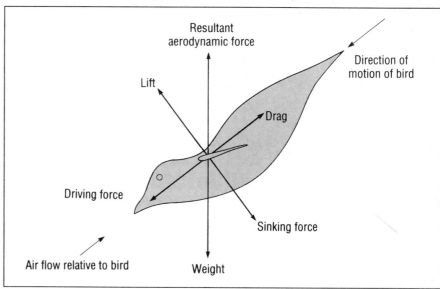

Resultant aerodynamic force

Lift

Direction of motion of bird

Drag

Driving force

Sinking force

Air flow relative to bird

Weight

bird does not drop like a stone but glides along an inclined path.

The speed of gliding depends on the bird's weight and the size and shape of the wings. A heavy bird with small wings obviously glides faster than a light bird with large wings. The distance a bird can glide in still air depends on the height it starts gliding from and the angle between its downward path and the horizontal. For an expert glider such as an albatross this angle is small and the bird can glide almost horizontally (figure 29.25). This is achieved by holding the wings at an angle of attack that ensures that drag is minimised and maximum lift is obtained.

Even the best gliders cannot maintain an absolutely horizontal path in still air, but if the air is rising the bird can maintain its level or even climb. Birds are constantly using upward air currents for gaining height. These upcurrents arise in several ways – for example when air, warmed by the earth's surface, rises and is replaced by cooler air (**thermal upcurrents**) or when horizontal wind hits a vertical obstruction such as a cliff (**obstructional upcurrents**). When you see gulls gliding on the windward side of a cliff they are making use of such obstructional upcurrents.

Active flight

When little or no support can be gained from upward air currents, the same effect can be achieved by flapping the wings (**active flight**). The flapping of the wings creates an airflow over them which produces much the same system of forces as in gliding flight. At the completion of the downstroke, the wings are returned to their original position, front edge first so as to minimise downward drag.

The wings are operated by powerful depressor and levator muscles rich in myoglobin (see page 319). The way these **flight muscles** are attached to the skeleton is shown in figure 29.26. The depressor muscle is responsible for the powerful downstroke: it runs from the underside of the humerus to the sternum. The levator muscle is arranged in a way which is unique to birds. The tendon at the distal end of the muscle has its insertion on the upper side of the humerus whence it passes through a small hole bounded by the scapula, coracoid and clavicle. The proximal end of the muscle is attached to the sternum. In order to provide an adequate surface for the attachment of these two very large muscles, the sternum of birds is greatly expanded and has a deep **keel** to increase its surface area.

Figure 29.25 In this photo of a gliding albatross notice the enormous wing span compared with the size of the body. The wing span of the wandering albatross, *Diomedea exulans*, may exceed three metres.

Figure 29.26 The musculo-skeletal basis of flight in birds.

A The skeleton of a pigeon showing the deep keel on the lower side of the sternum for the attachment of the flight muscles.

B Diagrammatic front view of the skeleton showing the origin and insertion of the flight muscles. The large and powerful depressor muscle pulls the wing downwards and gives the bird lift during active flight. The tendon of the levator muscle passes through the foramen triosseum and has its insertion on the top side of the humerus. When it contracts it pulls the wing upwards, like a pulley (**C**).

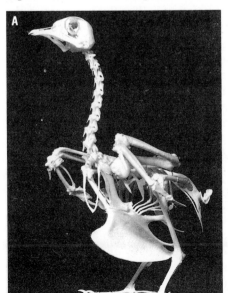

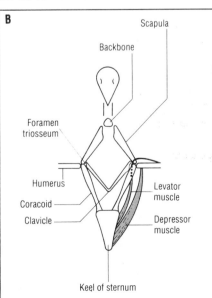

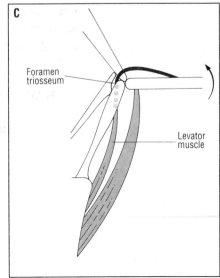

Figure 29.27 The distal part of the leg of an arthropod showing the extensor and flexor muscles. Notice that the muscles are internal to the skeleton, which is therefore called an exoskeleton.

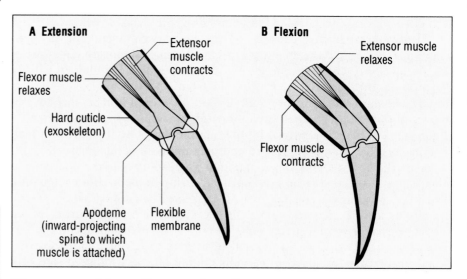

A Extension

Extensor muscle contracts

Flexor muscle relaxes

Hard cuticle (exoskeleton)

Apodeme (inward-projecting spine to which muscle is attached)

Flexible membrane

B Flexion

Extensor muscle relaxes

Flexor muscle contracts

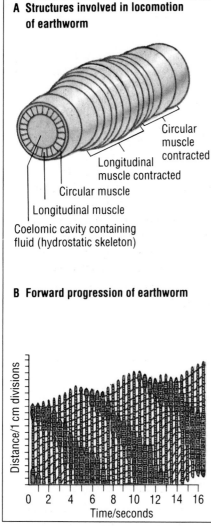

A Structures involved in locomotion of earthworm

Circular muscle contracted

Longitudinal muscle contracted

Circular muscle

Longitudinal muscle

Coelomic cavity containing fluid (hydrostatic skeleton)

B Forward progression of earthworm

Distance/1 cm divisions

0 2 4 6 8 10 12 14 16
Time/seconds

Figure 29.28 In the earthworm the body wall muscles contract against the fluid in the body cavity which acts as a hydrostatic skeleton.

A A bulge is formed by localised contraction of the longitudinal muscle.

B The worm progresses forward by bulges being propagated slowly from the anterior to the posterior end of the body. In the diagram the wavy lines link the same relative points on the worm.

Movement in other animals

The type of skeleton which we and other vertebrates possess is called an **endoskeleton**. This name derives from the fact that the skeletal elements, bone or cartilage as the case may be, are internal to the muscles which are attached to them. Thus in our own limbs the bones are ensheathed by the muscles that move them. For example, in the arm the biceps and triceps muscles are external to the arm bones (see figure 29.10 on page 515).

A rather different arrangement is found in arthropods such as insects and lobsters. Here the hard cuticle performs the function of a skeleton. As the muscles are inside the cuticle, it is called an **exoskeleton**. For example, the flexor and extensor muscles of an insect's leg are enclosed within the box-like exoskeleton to which they are attached (figure 29.27). Bending occurs at the joint, where the hard exoskeleton is replaced by a flexible membrane like the concertina connection between the coaches of a train. The muscles are attached to inward projections of the exoskeleton called **apodemes**. The muscles are antagonistic, the flexor bending the leg and the extensor straightening it.

A totally different system is found in soft-bodied invertebrates such as sea anemones and earthworms. In these animals there is no hard skeleton at all, its place being taken by a fluid under pressure. The fluid is surrounded by muscles which press against it, for which reason it is called a **hydrostatic skeleton**.

The earthworm is a classic example of an animal with a hydrostatic skeleton. The body wall contains muscles which contract against the fluid in the coelomic body cavity, creating a pressure which maintains the animal's shape in much the same way as a balloon's shape is maintained when full of air. There are two antagonistic sets of muscle tissue in the body wall: circular and longitudinal. When the **circular muscle** contracts and the longitudinal relaxes, the body becomes long and thin; when the **longitudinal muscle** contracts and the circular relaxes, the body becomes short and fat.

Transverse **septa** divide the body cavity into a series of watertight compartments (**segments**). This means that a change in pressure in one part of the body does not immediately spread to other parts, so localised bulges can occur (figure 29.28). Locomotion is achieved by these bulges being propagated along the body. This is an effective means of propulsion for a burrowing animal like the earthworm. Where the bulges occur, bristle-like **chaetae** protrude from the body wall and gain a purchase on the soil.

Flight in insects

Insect flight obeys much the same aerodynamic principles as bird flight, but its musculo-skeletal basis is quite different. Instead of being attached to the wings, the flight muscles are attached to the hard cuticle surrounding the **thorax**. When the muscles contract they alter the shape of the thorax in such a way that the wings go up and down.

The mechanism is summarised in the illustration. It depends on the ingenious way the wings are attached to the thorax. The base of each wing is attached to both the roof and the walls (i.e. sides) of the thorax, the roof attachment being median to (i.e. slightly further in than) the wall attachment.

The thorax contains two sets of flight muscles: a pair of **dorsoventral muscles** run from the roof to the floor of the thorax, and a pair of **longitudinal muscles** run from the anterior surface of the dome-like roof to the posterior surface. When the dorsoventral muscles contract, the roof attachment of the wing is pulled downwards relative to the wall

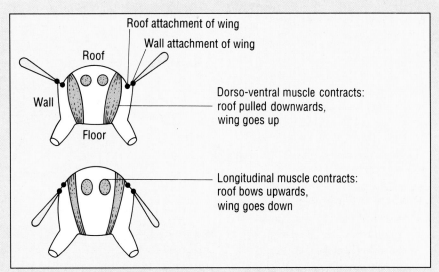

Diagrams of the thorax of an insect in cross-section showing how flight takes place.

attachment, with the result that the wing goes up. When the longitudinal muscles contract, the top of the dome-like roof rises slightly and the roof attachment of the wing is pulled upwards relative to the wall attachment, with the result that the wing goes down.

Since the muscles responsible for the wing movements are not actually attached to the wings, they are known as **indirect flight muscles**. There are, in addition, some muscles attached to the base of the wing itself. These **direct flight muscles** are responsible for making adjustments to the wing stroke and folding the wings at rest.

Although the indirect flight muscles appear to be working at a considerable mechanical disadvantage, a tiny contraction is sufficient to produce a sizeable movement of the wing tip. In the wasp, for example, a miniscule contraction moves the wings through an angle of 150°.

Cilia and flagella

Many small organisms swim by means of cilia or flagella. Flagella, and flagella-like structures such as sperm tails, achieve their propulsive action using principles similar to (but not identical with) those involved in the swimming of fishes such as eels. Undulations pass along the flagellum from base to tip, driving the organism in the opposite direction.

Cilia, such as those of *Paramecium*, employ a different principle. Each cilium, held out straight from the body, swings back through an arc of about 180°, propelling the organism forward like the oars of a rowing

boat (see illustration). On completing its movement, the cilium returns to its original position, bending as it does so. Then, held out straight once more, it repeats its backstroke.

The numerous cilia projecting from the surface of an organism like *Paramecium* beat in relays, giving an effect like waves passing over a cornfield in a gust of wind. This is called a **metachronal rhythm**. The combined effect of all the cilia of *Paramecium* is to propel the organism through the water at a speed of about 3 mm per second.

How do cilia and flagella bend? The mechanism depends on the 9+2 array of microtubules found in these organelles (see page 166). You will

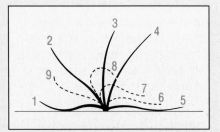

Action of a cilium. Cilia are rigid when they beat backwards (stages 1–5 in the diagram), but bend when they return to their original position (stages 6 to 9).

recall that the peripheral microtubules have little arms projecting from them. These arms are believed to serve as ratchets, causing the microtubules to slide relative to one another in the same kind of way as muscle.

Amoeboid movement

Amoeboid cells such as *Amoeba* itself and phagocytic white blood cells can change their shape, and this is the basis of how they move. The mechanism has been studied in *Amoeba*, but the principles probably apply to other amoeboid cells too.

The plasma membrane, in keeping with cells generally, is flexible. Inside the cell, the cytoplasm consists of a fluid **endoplasm** in the centre surrounded by a stiffer **ectoplasm** towards the periphery.

When the cell moves, the fluid endoplasm flows inside the 'wall' of ectoplasm to form a temporary projection called a **pseudopodium** (illustration 1). When it reaches the leading end of the advancing pseudopodium, the endoplasm everts, rather like a cuff being folded back, and is converted into the stiffer ectoplasm. At the other end of the cell the reverse happens: the ectoplasm *inverts* and is converted into fluid endoplasm. So the cell moves by a fluid core flowing forward through a tube of its own making (illustration 2).

How does this process take place? Much research has been done on this over the years, and a number of theories have been suggested. They all depend on the idea that there are protein filaments in the cytoplasm. This is now well established, and in fact **actin filaments** are known to be present. Here are four theories:

- The endoplasm is squeezed forward from the rear, rather like toothpaste being squeezed out of a tube. This is achieved by the protein filaments folding up in the endoplasm and opening out in the ectoplasm. The folding process at the rear could provide the pressure forcing the endoplasm forward.
- The endoplasm is pulled forward from the front. This is achieved by the protein filaments opening out in the endoplasm and folding up in the ectoplasm, the reverse of the situation envisaged by the previous theory.
- The endoplasm moves forward by the protein filaments in the cytoplasm sliding against each other, rather as in muscle. Cross-bridges from the ectoplasm filaments might propel the endoplasm filaments forward.
- The endoplasm flows forward by the protein filaments disintegrating into their component molecules at the front, and reassembling at the rear. Having been released at the front, the protein molecules pass back to the rear in the ectoplasm.

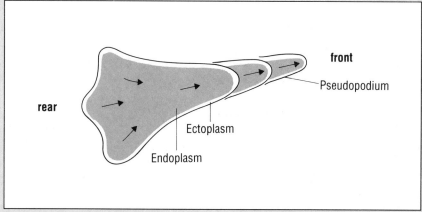

Illustration 1 This diagram shows a pseudopodium being formed by an amoeba. The arrows indicate the direction in which the fluid endoplasm flows. The photomicrograph shows an amoeba in the process of forming a pseudopodium.

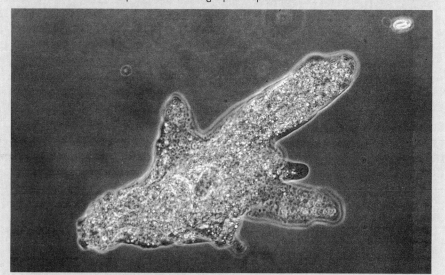

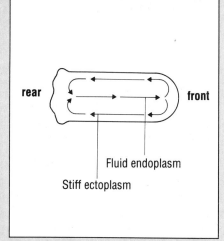

Illustration 2 In amoeboid movement the fluid endoplasm moves forward to the leading end where it is converted into a more solid ectoplasm.

Summary

1 Movement is brought about by muscles working in conjunction with a **skeleton**.

2 The human skeleton, as well as bringing about movement, supports the body, protects the soft structures and produces blood cells.

3 The skeleton can be divided into the **axial** and **appendicular skeletons**, both of which are composed by numerous **bones**.

4 The bones articulate with each other at **joints** and are held together by **ligaments** and **muscles**. Muscles are attached to the bones by **tendons**.

5 A limb bone such as the femur is composed of **compact bone** and **spongy bone** whose distribution can be related to the stresses and strains which the bone has to bear.

6 Most bones start off as cartilage which is then replaced by bone. Bone is laid down by bone-forming **osteoblasts** and remodelled by bone-destroying **osteoclasts**.

7 **Synovial joints**, such as exist between successive limb bones, allow the bones to move against each other with minimum friction.

8 There are two main types of synovial joint: the **ball and socket joint** and the **hinge joint**. Their shapes dictate their freedom of movement.

9 Bones are susceptible to various types of **fracture**. For a fracture to heal satisfactorily the parts of the broken bone must be held in correct alignment.

10 The skeleton is operated by sets of **antagonistic muscles** whose actions, coordinated by the nervous system, bring about movement and maintain posture.

11 **Muscle spindles** ensure that antagonistic muscles contract to just the right extent.

12 In maintaining posture and producing movement, the skeleton provides a system of **levers** which are worked by the muscles.

13 In considering the locomotion of an animal three things should be taken into account: **propulsion, support** and **stability,** and these can be applied to animals that move on land, in water or in the air.

14 The type of skeleton possessed by vertebrates is called an **endoskeleton**. Invertebrates have an **exoskeleton** (e.g. insects) and a **hydrostatic skeleton** (e.g. the earthworm).

15 **Cilia** and **flagella** are associated with the locomotion of certain small aquatic organisms, particularly unicellular forms. **Amoeboid movement** occurs in *Amoeba* itself and also in phagocytes and white blood cells.

Review questions

1 Name two parts of the human skeleton which
(a) carry particularly heavy loads,
(b) protect soft organs,
(c) make blood cells,
(d) move continuously, even when we are asleep.

2 Whereabouts in a fully developed limb bone are
(a) compact bone,
(b) spongy bone,
(c) cartilage,
(d) marrow?

What is the *functional* significance of their distribution?

3 Explain the flexing of your arm at the elbow in terms of antagonistic muscles, bones, nerves and proprioceptors.

4 It is important that a muscle spindle should have a low threshold and should not adapt quickly. Why?

5 What are tendon organs and what is their function?

6 What is a synovial joint? How does the shape of a synovial joint determine its freedom of movement?

7 How does the position of the centre of gravity affect the stability of (a) a horse, and (b) a human?

8 What are the principal propulsive devices of a trout and a pigeon? Explain how they work in terms of their muscles and skeleton.

9 Explain the meaning of the terms endoskeleton and exoskeleton and give one example of each.

10 What is a hydrostatic skeleton? Where in an earthworm are the muscles and skeleton responsible for changing the shape of the body?

Further reading

As a starter there is Sir James Gray's, *How Animals Move* (Cambridge University Press, 1953). Based on the author's Royal Institution Christmas Lectures, this short book is a classic of its kind.

Still short but much more mathematical in its approach is *Locomotion of Animals* by R McNeill Alexander (Blackie, 1982). Many of the topics in this book are developed further in *Animal Mechanics* by the same author (Blackwell, 1983).

Christy Brown tells the story of his battle against cerebral palsy in *My Left Foot* (Minerva, 1954).

Why don't organisms use wheels for locomotion? This question is discussed in *Biology Advanced Topics*. So is the use of aerofoils in flight, and the mode of action of cilia and flagella.

CHAPTER 30 Behaviour

In nature, those animals that respond appropriately to changes in their environment are more likely to survive and reproduce. The responses that animals make to the stimuli they receive we call **behaviour**. The stimuli may come from other organisms or from the physical environment. An animal's behaviour will help it to locate food, avoid predators and, in sexual species, find a mate with which to reproduce (figure 30.1).

Although this chapter confines itself to animal behaviour, some botanists have suggested that plants can be thought of as behaving too. Ground ivy sends out runners as it grows. The number of runners the plant produces, and the direction in which they grow, depend on the abundance of nutrients in the soil. Such behaviour is comparable to the foraging behaviour of certain animals.

The study of animal behaviour is known as **ethology**, and a person who studies behaviour is called an **ethologist**. In this chapter we shall look at various aspects of animal behaviour and discuss to what extent studies of animal behaviour tell us anything about human behaviour.

Figure 30.1 Three male ruffs on a lek in South Sweden. Females (called reeves) come to such leks and choose a male with which to mate. A lek is an area where the birds congregate before mating.

Studying behaviour

One of the attractions of ethology is that many of its techniques are still relatively simple. Ethologists may spend months or years carefully observing the behaviour of the species they are studying, just jotting down observations in a notebook, making measurements or taking photographs.

The golden rules for studying behaviour are as follows:

- Study the *natural* behaviour of your animals. Ensure that their behaviour is not affected by your presence. This means that you must either acclimatise the animals to your presence, or keep out of their sight, hearing and smell.
- Try to keep an open mind. Don't, for example, assume that males are more aggressive than females. They are in some species, but not in others.
- Don't anthropomorphise. That is, don't interpret what you observe in terms of human experience. What you think is a monkey grinning may be a sign not of amusement, but of fear (figure 30.2).
- Make precise observations and when possible be quantitative. It may appear difficult at first to say much about the behaviour of a field full of grazing sheep. However, if you concentrate on certain recognisable individuals and determine how much time they spend feeding and how much time ruminating, or how many mouthfuls they take and how far they move each minute they are feeding, you will have collected some useful data.
- Once you have collected some data, try to think up hypotheses about your animals. If you were studying the grazing behaviour of sheep, you might hypothesise that they feed for longer bouts as they get older. Or you might consider the idea that they spend more time looking up if they are on their own than if they are in a group.
- Whenever feasible try to test your hypothesis by further observations and measurements. Sometimes experimentation will be necessary. Certain questions about the feeding behaviour of birds, for example, can be answered by providing different types of food at winter bird-tables.

Figure 30.2 The fear response of the rhesus monkey, *Macaca mulatta*. It is usually accompanied by a tendency to flee. The expression is best described as a 'bared-teeth display', as this describes what the display is, not what we think it means.

Tools and techniques

The precise techniques used in investigating animal behaviour will depend on the species studied and the questions being asked. Many famous and important studies have used nothing more than a pencil, notepad, camera and stopwatch. **Video cameras** may be useful for studying rapid behaviours, for example the pollinating behaviour of bees. Similarly **tape-recordings** provide a permanent record of bird-song or deer roars.

Sometimes specialised equipment is required to compensate for limitations in human senses. Although most humans have excellent eyesight in the visible spectrum, nobody can see in the ultraviolet and infrared parts of the spectrum. Most people have a good sense of hearing, except for very high pitched sounds (**ultrasound**). **Bat detectors** enable the ultrasonic noises of bats to be monitored and may also be used to reveal the high pitched squeaks made by juvenile rodents. **Sound spectrograms** enable a visual record to be kept of sounds such as bird song (figure 30.3).

Humans have a poor sense of smell, and sophisticated pieces of apparatus are available for the chemical analysis of animal scents. Scents are far more important to many species than most people realise. They may be used in territorial advertisement and for individual recognition. To one mouse, for example, the smell of another mouse tells it how closely related they are to each other, how dominant it is and, if it is a female, whether or not she is sexually mature, and, if sexually mature, whether in oestrus or pregnant.

The development of behaviour

How are animals able to behave in such adaptive ways? How do lions become skilful hunters, terns agile fliers and otters graceful swimmers? To almost every behaviour there are two components, one **instinctive** and one **learned**. Otters instinctively swim when they first take to water. Instincts are genetically inherited from parents and handed down in evolution. In most cases they are common to all the members of a species. Like structural features, such as eyes and limbs, instincts are subject to natural selection. However much we try, we can never swim like an otter. However, otters must also learn to swim effectively. When young they practise swimming and become more skilful at it.

Interaction between genetic and environmental influences

Although the distinction between instinct and learning is a useful one, it is rarely possible to say whether a particular behaviour is learned or instinctive. Take human speech, for example. At first one might think it is instinctive; after all, we all speak don't we? But in fact not everyone can speak. People who are born deaf have to be taught very patiently and skilfully to speak, otherwise they grow up deaf and dumb. Normally we learn to speak only by hearing others speak. This is why children in France speak French, while children in Germany speak German.

Clearly, the capacity for speech is genetic. Some people have wasted years trying to teach chimpanzees or gorillas to speak out loud. Usually the animals manage about two or three words after several years of training for several hours each day! These animals simply have not got the muscles nor the speech areas of the brain to enable them to speak true words. However, the chimpanzee Sarah learned over a period of six years to associate some 130 differently shaped and coloured blocks of plastic with words which she had been taught (figure 30.4).

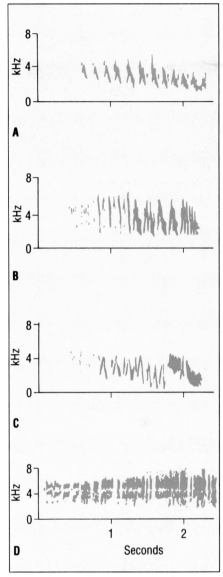

Figure 30.3 Sound spectrograms of chaffinches, *Fringilla coelebs*. A sound spectrogram is a means of showing sounds on paper. Time is presented along the horizontal axis and the frequency of the sound along the vertical axis.

A The song of a chaffinch reared in isolation.
B The song of a chaffinch reared in a group but without adults.
C The song of a normal chaffinch, allowed to hear adult song.
D The song of a deaf chaffinch.
What conclusions can be drawn from these sound spectrograms?

Figure 30.4 Chimpanzees can be trained to use symbols to stand for words, demonstrating their very considerable intelligence. From top to bottom, the six blocks on the magnetic board stand for: 'Sarah', 'insert', 'apple', 'pail', 'banana', 'dish'. After seeing this combination of symbols, Sarah would nearly always put the apple in the pail and the banana in the dish.

Instinctive behaviour is sometimes referred to as **innate behaviour**, meaning that it is inborn and does not have to be learned. However, the distinction between innate and learned behaviour is by no means a sharp one. Laughing gulls peck at their parents' bills for food from the first day of hatching. This behaviour happens very soon after hatching and in a stereotyped fashion, in the sense that all laughing gull chicks peck in a similar manner. This suggests that the pecking is innate. However, the American ethologist Jack Hailman published a paper on the pecking of laughing gull chicks with the paradoxical title 'How an instinct is learned'. Hailman found that during the days after hatching the chicks learn to peck more accurately and become better at judging the distance between themselves and their parents' beaks.

Some ethologists have compared behaviour to a cake. A cake is the result of ingredients, a recipe and the cooking. No useful purpose is served by arguing about how much of the cake is due to the recipe or to the ingredients or to the cooking. In the same way it is impossible to classify some parts of a behaviour pattern as innate and other parts as learned. However, for purposes of analysis, it is convenient to consider instinct and learning separately, as we shall do in the account that follows.

Instinct

Defined formally, instinctive behaviour is an innate, usually stereotyped response to one or more environmental stimuli. Thus defined, it ranges from simple reflexes to complex behaviour patterns. Let us start at the simple end of the range with reflexes.

Reflex

A **reflex** is a simple act of behaviour in which a stimulus produces a specific short-lived response. The physiological basis of reflexes is discussed in Chapter 25. Here we are more concerned with their functions.

Escape response of the earthworm

A familiar example of a reflex action is the escape response of an earthworm. On warm, wet nights lots of earthworms may be observed lying on the surface of the ground (figure 30.5). If you walk towards them, they quickly disappear into their burrows. The function of this behaviour is probably to reduce the chance of the earthworm being eaten by a badger or fox or other predator.

The escape response of an earthworm is a fairly simple behaviour and its physiological mechanism is well understood. Normally the posterior end of the worm remains in the burrow. On the detection of vibrations by touch receptors in the skin, the powerful longitudinal muscles contract, shortening the body. Meanwhile the bristle-like **chaetae** are protracted, enabling the posterior part of the worm to grip the sides of the burrow.

The key to a successful escape is speed, and the nerve impulses which elicit the earthworm's escape response are carried very rapidly by **giant axons** (see page 446). A large **median giant axon** transmits impulses from receptors at the front of the worm to its rear. If it is attacked at its rear end, for instance by a subterranean mole, the worm may also escape. In this case a pair of **lateral giant axons**, each slightly narrower than the median giant axon, transmits nerve impulses from receptors at the rear end of the animal to its front. Chaetae at the front end grip tightly to the soil and the worm rapidly contracts in length, as its rear is pulled forwards.

Figure 30.5 An earthworm at night with its posterior end still in its burrow. If disturbed, it grips the wall of the burrow with its posterior end and jerks quickly back.

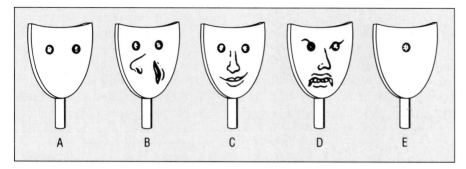

Kinesis

A **kinesis** is a behaviour pattern in which an animal responds to an alteration in stimulus intensity by changing its activity level. A classic example is the response of woodlice to humidity. The lower the humidity, the more the woodlice move about. As woodlice normally inhabit damp habitats, this behaviour is clearly adaptive.

It is important to emphasise that the woodlice do not move up a gradient of humidity. They simply move *more* in a non-humid environment. Eventually by sheer chance they are likely to reach a more humid environment, and then they move less. The result of this behaviour is that woodlice spend most of their time in moist habitats.

There are two types of kinesis. In **orthokinesis** the *speed of movement* depends on the stimulus intensity. In **klinokinesis** the *rate of turning* depends on the stimulus intensity. The two types differ in mechanism but have much the same effect.

Taxis

A **taxis** is a movement that is oriented in relation to the direction of a stimulus. *Euglena* swims towards light (provided the light is not too intense). *Euglena* is therefore said to be **positively phototactic**. Earthworms move away from light and are therefore **negatively phototactic**. Many animals are **chemotactic**, moving towards certain chemicals and away from others.

Sign stimuli

Animals typically respond to only some of the many stimuli detected by their sensory receptors. A **sign stimulus** produces a selective stereotyped response. Such selective behaviour is adaptive because it allows an animal to respond immediately in an appropriate way to *relevant* aspects of its environment, and to ignore others.

Everyone knows that babies smile at people. But what triggers the baby's smile? When a baby is about one to two months old, a pair of eyes is all that is necessary to trigger smiling (figure 30.6). The two eyes constitute the sign stimulus which causes the baby to smile.

We shall now look in detail at two examples of behaviour in which sign stimuli play an important part.

Herring gull pecking

Shortly after it emerges from its egg, a herring gull chick begins to peck at the tip of its parent's beak. This causes the adult gull to regurgitate a mass of half-digested food which the chick eats. On close inspection it can be seen that the chick directs its pecks at the red spot on its parent's yellow beak (figure 30.7). In 1937 the German ornithologist F. Goethe discovered that newly hatched herring gull chicks would peck at the red spot on the

Figure 30.7 Herring gull chick pecking at the red spot on the beak of one of its parents. This causes the parent to regurgitate food for the chick.

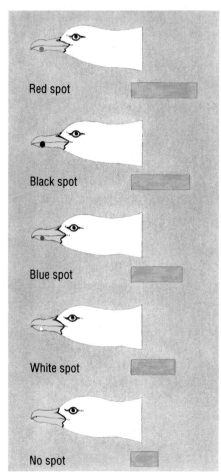

Figure 30.8 Results of experiments showing that the red spot on the beak is the most effective stimulus eliciting the begging response of herring gull chicks. The strength of the response was measured as the number of pecks directed at the model over a 30 second period. The length of the bar beneath each model indicates the strength of the response.

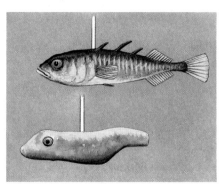

Figure 30.9 Two models of female three-spined sticklebacks. A detailed model (above) but lacking a swollen abdomen fails to elicit courtship from a territorial male with a nest. A crude model (below) which has a swollen abdomen is vigorously courted.

beak of a dead herring gull held in his hand. When he painted over the red spot with yellow paint, the baby birds pecked less frequently.

Inspired by this initial result, Goethe reared some herring gull eggs in an incubator. When the chicks hatched they were presented with two types of beaks. Yellow beaks with a red spot received more than three times as many pecks as did uniformly yellow beaks. These isolated hand-reared birds would also sometimes peck at cherries or the red undersoles of tennis shoes if given the opportunity. Goethe's experiments suggested that the birds had an innate and selective response to the contrast of red on yellow.

Subsequent work by the Dutch ethologist Niko Tinbergen showed that a red spot elicited more pecks than spots of other colours (figure 30.8).

Stickleback courtship and reproduction

Sticklebacks are small freshwater fish. In a series of experiments dating from the 1930s, Tinbergen and others investigated the reproductive behaviour of the three-spined stickleback.

In the spring, male sticklebacks set up territories from which they chase away other sticklebacks. They then build nests out of weeds and stop chasing away females swollen with eggs. When a female appears, the territorial male moves towards her in a curious zig-zag fashion (the zig-zag dance). When she sees him, the female responds by swimming towards the male and presenting her swollen abdomen to him. The swollen abdomen acts as a sign stimulus. Tinbergen showed that realistic model females lacking a swollen belly are not courted, while crude model females provided with a swollen lower surface are (figure 30.9).

Having displayed her swollen abdomen to the male, the female follows the male to the nest entrance which the male pokes with his snout. The female enters the nest and the male gives her rump several prods with a trembling motion. This stimulates the female to lay her eggs. After releasing the eggs, she leaves the nest and the male enters it and ejaculates over the eggs. He then chases the female away.

In order for stickleback courtship to proceed to fertilisation, a whole chain of behaviours needs to be completed (figure 30.10). If any stage of the courtship fails to produce the appropriate sign stimuli, courtship ceases and the two fish separate.

A male may mate with as many as five females. Then he begins regular ventilation of the eggs by fanning with his pectoral fins. The time spent in fanning increases daily until the eggs hatch, when it stops. Fanning serves to aerate the eggs. Evidence for this is provided by the observation that artificial lowering of the oxygen concentration leads to increased fanning.

Learning

It is surprisingly difficult to produce an acceptable definition of **learning**. One which has been suggested is that 'learning refers to a more or less permanent change in behaviour which occurs as a result of experience'. Animals vary in how much they are capable of learning. In general the larger an animal's brain, the more it can learn, though it must be remembered that much of the brain has nothing at all to do with learning. The tremendous capacity humans have for learning is due to our large cerebral hemispheres with their extensive cortical folding and organisation (see page 455).

Let us now look at the different types of learning. There is no universally accepted classification of learning, though the one used here is the most widely adopted.

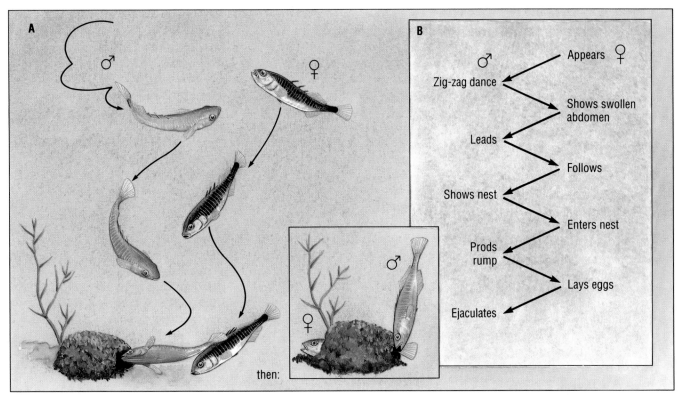

Figure 30.10
A Courtship and mating in the three-spined stickleback. The inset shows the female in the nest and the male is prodding her rump.
B The chain of stimuli which guide the sequence of events in courtship and mating of three-spined sticklebacks. If at any stage either sex fails to produce the appropriate stimulus, the chain of stimuli is broken and fertilisation is not achieved.

Habituation

If an animal is repeatedly given a stimulus which is associated neither with benefit nor with harm, it soon learns not to respond. This is called **habituation**. It differs from other forms of learning in that it involves the *loss* of a response. Birds soon ignore the scarecrow which prevented them from landing when it was first placed in a field. They have become habituated to it.

It is easy to see the function of habituation. An animal needs to respond to changes in its environment only when it is appropriate to do so. The rabbit that disappears down its burrow every time it hears the wind will have no time to feed. On the other hand, the rabbit that fails to disappear quickly when it hears an *unfamiliar* noise risks being caught by a predator. We usually continue to sleep when there are familiar, sometimes quite loud, noises around us, but wake up at a quieter but strange sound.

Classical conditioning

At the turn of the century the Russian physiologist Ivan Pavlov studied the production of saliva by dogs in response to food. As we saw in Chapter 16, the smell, sight and taste of food induce the flow of saliva. Pavlov mounted his dogs in a harness and collected their saliva by means of a tube leading from the salivary duct. When the dogs had got used to the apparatus, Pavlov rang a bell before each portion of food was presented. At first this stimulus caused no response, except that the dog pricked up its ears momentarily. However, after about five or six such tests, the dog began to salivate after the bell rang but *before* the food appeared.

In Pavlov's experiments the dogs had become **conditioned** to the ringing of the bell. This type of learning is called **classical conditioning**. The dogs had learnt to respond to a previously neutral stimulus, namely the ringing of a bell. The salivation response to this stimulus is a **conditioned reflex**. Prior to learning, only the presence of food produced salivation.

Stickleback courtship and reproduction: a modern interpretation

Tinbergen's classic account of stickleback behaviour is still the one found in textbooks. Recently, however, several investigators have questioned either his observations or the details of his experimental procedure.

Perhaps the most remarkable challenge to the classic account is provided by Rowland. Rowland carefully repeated Tinbergen's experiments on the importance of stickleback colouration in territorial encounters between males. He found exactly the opposite of what Tinbergen had reported! Adding colour to a model stickleback male made it *less* likely to be attacked by a territorial male.

We can see the importance of proper experimental design. Rowland carefully replicated his experiments and tested his hypothesis using appropriate statistical tests. Tinbergen merely described his observations. It may be unfair to criticise Tinbergen with the benefit of hindsight. Certainly he wasn't alone in not using statistics. Lorenz, with whom Tinbergen and von Frisch shared the Nobel Prize, boasted that none of his publications contained any tables or graphs!

Rowland also claimed that his findings made more sense than Tinbergen's. He argued that it is difficult to imagine how the red colouration could have evolved if its effect was to release aggression from opponents.

Rowland's results contradict the classic stickleback story. A study by Li and Owings supplements it. Li and Owings considered the behaviour of the *female* sticklebacks. The earlier work by Tinbergen had concentrated on the male's behaviour to the extent that females were viewed merely as passive recipients of the males' attentions.

Unlike previous researchers, Li and Owings watched female sticklebacks for as long as they watched males. First of all Li and Owings compared the behaviour of six females in one tank with the behaviour of six males in another tank of the same size and shape. They found that some females defended territories and there were more aggressive encounters in the all-female groups than in the all-male groups.

What is the function of this female aggression? Aggression by dominant females helps them to reproduce successfully at the expense of subordinate females. On at least two occasions a dominant female poked or squashed a subordinate female, and repeated attacks led to the subordinate females prematurely shedding their eggs. Li and Owings also studied tanks containing six females and six males.

Female-female interactions were again important. On three occasions a subordinate female accepted a courting male before the dominant female. Each time this happened the dominant female disrupted courtship. On two other occasions a subordinate female attempted to disrupt the courtship of a dominant female, but the attempts failed.

To produce a conditioned reflex, the ringing of the bell must precede the appearance of the food by not more than a certain period of time. Otherwise the animal cannot learn to associate the two stimuli with each other. Usually a time gap of only a few seconds is most effective in producing a conditioned response. However, rats and many other animals will learn to avoid a novel food that causes vomiting, even if vomiting only occurs an hour or more after eating the food.

Trial and error learning

Suppose a hungry dog is allowed to roam around a room. As soon as it jumps onto a particular chair we give it some food. The dog soon learns to associate jumping onto that chair with a **reward**. If hungry it will go straight to the chair as soon as it enters the room. As with classical conditioning, this is a form of associative learning. However, the dog has learned to associate a reward not with a particular stimulus, but with its own behaviour. This sort of learning is known as **trial and error learning**. Plainly it is a type of conditioning, in this case referred to as **operant conditioning** in contrast to Pavlov's classical conditioning.

Animals may learn *not* to do certain things by operant conditioning. Cats can (sometimes) be trained not to scratch the furniture, and dogs not to chew table legs. In such cases the animal learns that a **punishment** rather than a reward will result if the behaviour occurs.

There are many examples of operant conditioning in humans. Children are constantly rewarded for what others consider good behaviour, and punished for bad behaviour. Experimental psychologists talk about particular behaviours being **positively reinforced**; this simply means that they are conditioned to occur.

Adults too can be conditioned. In one case the members of a class agreed, without their teacher knowing, to smile appreciatively only when he placed his hand on his chest. The professor soon became conditioned to spend the entire lecture imitating Napoleon!

Latent learning

If a rat is placed at the entrance to a maze it typically enters the maze and runs here and there, busily sniffing and exploring. If the rat is rewarded with food when it finds the exit from the maze, it gradually learns, by trial and error, the quickest way through the maze. You can see this in curve A in figure 30.11.

Now look at curve C in figure 30.11. This shows a rat which was placed in a maze once a day for 10 days but was *not* rewarded for finding its way to the exit. From day 11 it *was* rewarded on reaching the exit. A rat which has had the opportunity to explore can find its way through a maze with fewer mistakes than a rat which has had no experience of that maze.

The implication is that the rat has learned something about the maze while exploring, even though it was not rewarded for reaching the end. What is learned remains hidden or *latent*, hence the term **latent learning**. For an animal in its natural environment, the benefit of latent learning is clear. For instance, a knowledge of the precise physical details of the area in which it lives may make the difference between life and death on the sudden appearance of a predator.

Insight learning

If we are faced with a new problem, we sometimes solve it by trial and error. Often, however, we pause and try to work out a solution. **Insight learning** occurs when an animal solves a problem apparently by looking at it, assessing the situation and then arriving at a solution.

The first experiments which demonstrated this type of learning in non-humans were done on chimpanzees. Presented with a bunch of bananas too high to reach and a few boxes, some chimpanzees piled up boxes to make a stand for themselves (figure 30.12). Often they arrived at this solution quite suddenly (insight learning). However, they benefited from previous experience of playing with boxes (latent learning) and showed considerable trial and error (operant conditioning) when actually building a stable pile of boxes.

To an observer watching their behaviour, these chimpanzees displayed what in ordinary parlance we would call 'intelligence'.

Intelligence

Intelligence is notoriously difficult to define. One way of looking at it is to say that an animal is intelligent if it is good at solving problems it has not encountered before. On this understanding of the term, intelligence is closely related to insight learning.

Even if people agree on what is meant by intelligence, they may not agree on how to measure it. Considerable controversy surrounds the design and use of **IQ (Intelligence Quotient)** tests for humans. Some psychologists have even defined intelligence as that which is measured by IQ tests!

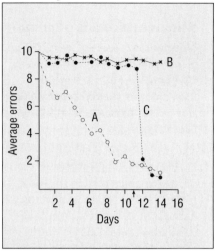

Figure 30.11 Performance of rats placed once a day in a maze in which there were fourteen T junctions at which the rats could turn either left or right.

A Rats given food at the end of the maze on each day. Note the improvement in their performance.

B Rats given no food at the end of the maze, and therefore having no motivation for improving their performance.

C Rats given food only at the end of the maze on day 11 and thereafter.

Latent learning has occurred in the rats in group **C**.

Figure 30.12 Chimpanzees may stack boxes on top of one another to reach bananas otherwise out of reach. This is an example of insight learning.

The neural basis of memory

Memory is the basis of learning and is therefore an aspect of behaviour. Guest author Patrick Bateson discusses the basis of memory and shows how behaviour can impinge on neurophysiology.

The precise ways in which environmental information is processed and stored in the brain for future use are not known for any animal. However, it is plain that there are several jobs for which learning and memory are required. For instance, some memory is required for the recognition of familiar objects and social companions. Other sorts of memory are needed to store links between causally related events. These associative memories are particularly important in predicting the occurrence of important resources, such as food, and potential danger. In view of these various functions of memory, it is likely that more than one set of neural mechanisms are involved. Whether the differences in functions have been achieved during the evolution of brains by subtle rearrangements of essentially similar mechanisms or by entirely different processes is not yet known.

Despite uncertainties about the details, storage of information is likely to involve a change in the connections between neurones, some synapses being strengthened and others weakened. The starting point for the sequence of events that brings this about is whether or not the neurone which brings an input and the neurone it addresses are electrically active at the same time. If they are, the connection becomes stronger and, if they are not, it becomes weaker. The neurone providing the input sends its signal as a chemical transmitter. The strength of the connection depends on how many receptor sites, sensitive to that transmitter, are present in the neurone receiving the input. Steps in the strengthening process involve 'marking' the membrane of the junction between the two neurones for a limited period of time, possibly by changing temporarily the ease with which calcium ions can pass through channels in the membrane. Meanwhile, new protein is synthesised to make more receptors. These receptors are moved into place so that the junction between the two neurones ends up with more receptor sites than had existed previously. Conversely, the weakening process may lead to a reduction in the number of receptor sites.

Detection of a familiar but complex visual stimulus involves putting together a combination of features present in the stimulus, such as colour, shape and size. At one time it was supposed that the familiar face of one's grandmother might be localised in a single cell. However, the requirement to synthesise a pattern from such a complex object is more likely to involve a population of cells rather than a single one. On this view, the representation is formed at the strengthened (and weakened) connections between feature detectors and the next layer of neurones.

Computer models of neural nets based on the properties of real neurones have been constructed. In such models, connections are strengthened as the result of correlated activity, or weakened through uncorrelated activity. These models are helping us to understand how animals may learn and how objects are recognised. Some models are now being constructed to see how the neural rules that govern learning have evolved. If a rule is allowed to mutate, and the computer solves a problem more quickly as a result, then the new set of rules is used in future. In this sense the models not only mimic what happens in real brains, they also simulate the process of Darwinian evolution that gave rise to brains.

Figure 30.13 Konrad Lorenz's famous experiment with newly hatched ducklings.

Imprinting

In his beautifully written and fascinating book, *King Solomon's Ring*, the Austrian zoologist and founder of ethology Konrad Lorenz describes how young geese follow the first moving object they see after they hatch. Generally, of course, the first mobile object they see is one of their parents, but Lorenz found they would **imprint** on almost anything that moved, including himself. He found, however, that newly hatched mallard ducks would not imprint on him. Until, that is, he started quacking! Lorenz describes how he crawled around his garden on his hands and knees followed by a batch of ducklings only to look up suddenly and find a group of tourists staring at him in horror, unable to see the ducklings in the tall spring grass (figure 30.13).

It is now known that there is a **sensitive period** during which imprinting occurs. A number of mammals are born, and birds hatched, sufficiently mature to be able to move around very soon after birth. In these species imprinting on a parent occurs within a few days of birth or hatching. This allows the young animal both to recognise and follow its parents from an early age. Lorenz found that birds which had imprinted on other species of bird, or on humans or even on cardboard boxes, later attempted to court and mate with them.

We now know that during early childhood, humans, in common with a number of other species, become imprinted on their brothers and sisters and subconsciously learn *not* to mate with them subsequently. Evidence for this in humans comes from studies of young adults raised on Israeli kibbutzim. Such young adults never marry within their rearing groups. The only exceptions are pairs who have been separated from one another for a large part of their childhood. The functional significance of this is that normally one grows up with one's brothers and sisters. Thanks to this learned behaviour, the risk of inbreeding is avoided (see page 804).

Displacement activity

When an animal is confronted with several alternative courses of action, it may perform what appears to be an irrelevant behaviour. For example, if a bird sitting on its eggs is suddenly confronted by a predator, it may be torn between fleeing the nest and attacking the predator. So, it does neither. Instead, it preens its feathers! This is an example of a **displacement activity**.

Displacement activities are inappropriate behaviours which are sometimes seen when an animal is in a state of internal conflict. Examples in humans include scratching an ear and unnecessarily running a hand through one's hair. Two other examples are shown in figure 30.14.

Reproductive behaviour

For organisms that reproduce sexually, reproductive success depends on finding a mate. During the course of evolution an amazing diversity of patterns of courtship and mating have arisen. Here we will focus on one particular problem which faces an organism reproducing sexually, namely choosing a mate.

Choosing a mate

It must be emphasised that the phrase 'choosing a mate' does not imply that organisms consciously try to decide with whom to mate. For the vast majority of species the 'decisions' made are almost certainly subconscious. Indeed, the extent to which humans are capable of exercising free will may be more limited than we realise.

Species-specific signals

At the most basic level, a mate must be an individual of the same species but the opposite sex. In many species what ensures that the 'right' individuals mate with each other is **courtship**, such as that which we have already seen in the stickleback (see page 534).

Courtship conveys a great deal more information than just the species and sex of the individuals performing. As females generally invest more time and energy in their offspring than do males, **mate choice** is particularly important for females. Males therefore make themselves attractive to females, advertising their fitness-enhancing characteristics such as good genes, adaptive behaviour and possession of valuable resources.

Figure 30.14 Two examples of displacement activities. Phil (top) is biting his nails while going through some accounts, and Clare is twisting her hair while revising for an examination. Humans commonly display such displacement activities in tense situations.

Figure 30.15 Sound spectrograms showing the calling songs of male crickets.
A The song of *Teleogryllus oceanicus*.
B The song of *T. commodus*. Arrows indicate the start of a single song.

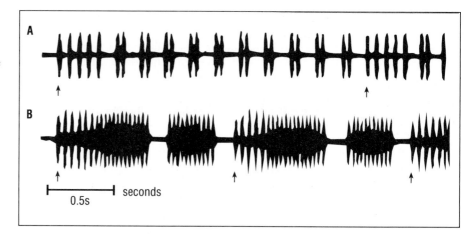

Courtship behaviour tends to be specific to each species. For example, males of the closely related cricket species *Teleogryllus oceanicus* and *T. commodus* both sing songs to attract females, but the songs are different (figure 30.15). Interestingly, the difference between the songs is due to different alleles at a single locus in the two species (alleles are explained on page 678). Hybrid females prefer the songs of hybrid males.

Courtship may provide an opportunity for individuals to prove to each other that they can reproduce successfully. In the common tern, males bring fish to the females during courtship. The greater the number of fish the male brings to the female, the more likely she is to mate with him, and the more offspring subsequently survive (figure 30.16).

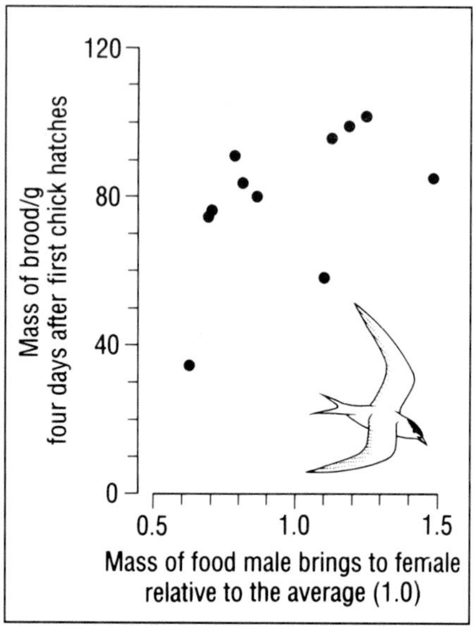

Communication

The ability of animals to **communicate** with one another is fundamental to much of animal behaviour. Communication between two individuals involves the following:

- A **signal**: the message conveyed from one individual to another.
- A **sender**: the individual who transmits the signal.
- A **context**: the setting in which the communication occurs (e.g. courtship, dominance display).
- A **channel**: the medium in which the signal is transmitted (e.g. chemical, auditory or tactile).
- A **receiver**: an individual who detects the signal.
- A **code**: the rules which enable the receiver to decipher the signal.

Communication may be either **intraspecific** (occurring between individuals of the same species) or **interspecific** (occurring between individuals of different species). Most communication is intraspecific and we will concentrate on this type. The importance of communication to animals can be illustrated by the phenomenon of **territorial defence**.

Territorial defence

A **territory** is a more or less exclusive area defended by an individual or group. Not all species have territories, but in those that do, territories have a variety of functions. They may allow exclusive access to food. Some hummingbirds, for instance, defend patches of flowers; the individual territory-owner enjoys exclusive access to the nectar produced by the flowers. In other species territories allow one sex, usually the male, to defend an area to which females are attracted for mating.

Figure 30.16 The relationship between the amount of food a male tern, *Sterna hirundo*, brings to his mate and the total mass of the brood shortly after hatching. Note that the females which have the most food brought to them subsequently produce the heaviest broods. The heavier the brood is, the greater the number of chicks likely to survive to adulthood.

Many studies have been made of territorial behaviour and territories can be advertised by their owners in a variety of ways. Here we shall confine ourselves to sticklebacks and humans.

Sticklebacks

As described earlier, in spring male sticklebacks defend territories from which they chase away intruders.

Tinbergen reported that the characteristic red patch on the belly of sexually mature males made them particularly likely to be chased away by territory holders. Tinbergen claimed that a realistically shaped but non-red model male stickleback provoked fewer attacks from a territorial male than extremely crude models painted red on their lower surfaces.

In sticklebacks the territory functions as an exclusive area within which a male may build a nest and court females in comparative safety.

Humans

The English Zoologist Desmond Morris points out that humans advertise their territories at three levels: at the level of the individual, the family and the larger group.

Figure 30.17 Personal space seen in the spacing behaviour of people in a queue. To invade people's personal space is to threaten them.

- **Individual territory**
  Each of us is surrounded by a 'portable' territory called a **personal space** (figure 30.17). If people encroach on our personal space we feel uncomfortable. When we get jammed into a lift we are forced to abandon our personal space. Our response is to ignore the other people. We keep quiet, adopt a neutral expression and avoid eye contact.

    We can advertise our personal territory even in our absence. In an experiment carried out in a library, placing a pile of journals on a table by a seat successfully reserved the place for an average of 77 minutes. When a jacket was draped over the back of the chair, the place remained unoccupied for over two hours.

- **Family territory**
  The family is the breeding unit. Morris argues that the **family territory** displays conspicuous boundary-lines such as garden fences and walls. Many families at the seaside set up a temporary territory, advertised by rugs, towels and a wind-break.

- **Group territory**
  Humans probably evolved as group-living animals with only a few dozen individuals at most in each group. Patriotism can be considered as the endpoint of the **societal territory**, manifested in national boundaries and frontier check-points. Most of us also belong to smaller groups such as games clubs, music societies or groups of friends. Often such groups have territorial signals – badges, headquarters and slogans permitted only to members of the group.

Honeybee dances

Honeybees, despite their small size, have one of the most remarkable communication systems of any species. More than 2000 years ago Aristotle found that although a source of food placed within flying distance of a hive might remain undiscovered for hours or even days, once a bee had located the food, many new bees soon appeared. In a series of classic experiments dating from the 1920s the Austrian biologist Karl von Frisch investigated how communication occurs in the honeybee.

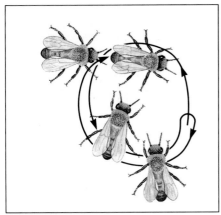

Figure 30.18 The round dance of the honeybee. The bee on the right at the top is dancing. The other three are picking up the cues she gives.

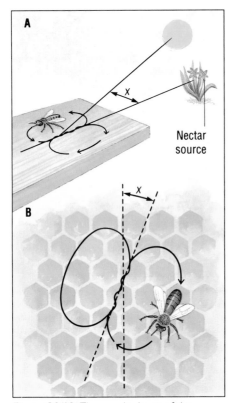

Figure 30.19 The waggle dance of the honeybee.

A The directional component of the dance is easiest to see when the dance is performed outside the hive on a horizontal surface. Here the bee repeatedly runs directly towards the food site.

B Inside the dark hive the dance is performed on a vertical comb and oriented with respect to gravity. The angle the dance makes clockwise from the vertical is the same as the angle of the food source clockwise from the sun (the angle *x* in the diagram).

When worker honeybees collect food from a rich source within about 80 metres of the hive, they perform a **round dance** on their return (figure 30.18). Inside a hive it is dark, so the other workers cannot watch the dance; instead they follow the dancing worker as she moves around on the comb. If, as a result of the round dance, workers fly out of the hive to look for the food, they search only within about 80 metres of the hive.

The round dance conveys no precise information about the distance to the food source, nor does it tell the bees in which direction to fly. Their search is helped by the fact that they pick up odour cues from the body of the dancing bee, and they may taste her regurgitated nectar. However, the round dance does convey information about the *richness* of the food source. The higher the quality of the food source, the more often the dancing bees change the direction of their dances.

If a bee finds a rich source of food more than about 80 metres from the hive, on her return she performs a **waggle dance** (figure 30.19). This conveys precise information about the distance to the food source in the range of roughly 80–1000 metres. The information seems to be conveyed in three different ways:

- The greater the speed with which the bee completes a single dance circuit, the nearer the food;
- The more abdominal waggles given during the straight-run portion of the dance, the nearer the food;
- The higher the pitch at which sound bursts are produced while dancing, the nearer the food.

It is not known for certain whether all three types of signal are used by the other bees in the hive. The most important information is probably the pitch at which the dancing bee produces sound bursts.

The waggle dance also conveys information about the direction of the food source (figure 30.19). In the dark hive, on the side of the honeycomb, the angle which the straight-run portion of the waggle dance makes to the vertical equals the angle that the food source makes clockwise to the sun.

Language

Human language is vastly richer than the communication system of any other species. It involves **true language**. This means both the use of **symbols** (e.g. words) for abstract ideas, and an appreciation of **syntax**. Syntax means that the same symbol may convey different messages depending on its position relative to other symbols. (Consider, for example, the different uses of the word 'bow' as in 'I bow down before you' and 'I shoot with a bow'.)

It was mentioned earlier that the chimp Sarah learned to use different shaped and coloured blocks as word symbols. Another chimp, Washoe, learned over 100 signs of the American sign language for the deaf. A major controversy has arisen over the extent to which chimpanzees and certain other primate species really can generate sentences and engage in true language. Whatever the outcome of this debate, humans obviously have an exceptionally rich and versatile communication system.

Charles Darwin pointed out the extent to which we have a system of **non-verbal communication**. This involves postures, gestures and facial expressions of considerable complexity and subtlety. Try moving the muscles of your face to indicate each of the following emotions: indignation, curiosity, amusement, approval, fear. Non-verbal communication may or may not be conscious. Both men and women subconsciously register approval of objects they have seen by enlarging their pupils. This is why people prefer photographs of individuals whose pupils look large.

Chimpanzee research at Gombe

Research on animal behaviour does not necessarily involve elaborate equipment and techniques. A good pair of eyes and empathy with the animals under investigation can be just as valuable, as guest author Jane Goodall explains.

In 1960 I began a study of chimpanzees in the Gombe National Park, Tanzania, that is still in progress today. At first the chimpanzees were so shy that they would run off even if I was 500 yards away. However, I discovered a wonderful vantage point from which, using binoculars, I was gradually able to learn something of the chimpanzees' behaviour. And because I always wore the same coloured clothes and never tried to get too close, they gradually got used to me. I'll never forget the day when two males, whom I had named David Greybeard and Goliath, continued to groom each other, only glancing briefly towards me, as I arrived just 20 yards away. I was accepted! Gradually the others also lost their fear and eventually I was able to follow some of them when they travelled through the forest. I remember vividly the first time I saw a chimpanzee using a tool – David Greybeard fishing for termites with a twig – and when I observed chimpanzees cooperating to hunt a colobus monkey. Anthropologists were so excited by these things that we were able to get more money for the project.

For the first few months I had to have an African helper. Once I had proved my bush sense I was able to be alone. One day David Greybeard took bananas from my camp. After this I left them out for him. He came often, and eventually others followed him – such as Goliath and Hugo, Flo and Olly. I soon learned that every chimpanzee has his or her own distinctive appearance and personality.

Next Hugo van Lawick was sent by the National Geographic Society to photograph and film the research. I still spent most of my time following chimpanzees in the forest. At first I scribbled notes which I transcribed every evening. Later I used a tape recorder. A different chimpanzee was followed each day, from dawn to dusk, and his or her behaviour was noted in detail. In 1964 the first research assistant arrived. By 1972 many American and European students had come to study chimpanzee behaviour. In 1975 four of these were kidnapped. They were eventually released, but it was not possible, for a while, for non-Tanzanians to work at Gombe. We had already trained a number of Tanzanian field staff – these men gradually became more responsible. I still spend as much time as possible at Gombe, following many adults whom I knew as infants.

Even after 30 years, we are still continually learning new things. Just recently, for example, a three year old infant, who had lost his mother, was adopted by a non-related 12 year old adolescent male. This young male, without doubt, saved the infant's life. The adoption of an infant chimpanzee by an unrelated adult is something that had never been observed before.

I would like to emphasise that it is possible to record data objectively despite feeling empathy with one's subjects. Yet implicit in much science education is the notion that a good scientist must be coldly distanced from his or her subject. This is not true – nor should it happen. Compassion must always come first.

Understanding chimpanzees helps us to understand ourselves. We are not as different from the rest of the animal kingdom as we used to think. Chimpanzees are like us not only physiologically, but behaviourally and emotionally also. And they possess many cognitive abilities we used to think unique to ourselves. They help us to cross the imagined gap between *us* and *them* and to develop a new attitude, a new respect, for all living creatures.

Social behaviour

In some species individuals are **social**, typically being found in groups; in others individuals are **solitary**, usually occurring on their own. To understand the reasons for this difference one needs to consider the advantages *and* the disadvantages of being in a group. **Sociobiology** is the branch of biology devoted to studying the biological basis of social behaviour.

Advantages and disadvantages of sociality

In some species larger groups suffer less predation. Woodpigeons benefit from being in a large group because they are less likely to be attacked successfully by hawks (figure 30.20). Even if a predator is successful in attacking a group, each individual is safer in a larger group simply because the chance of it being the unlucky one caught by the predator is smaller. If a predator takes just one prey individual at a time, the probability of an animal in a group of two being killed is 0.5; for an animal in a group of 10, the probability is only 0.1. This assumes that large groups are not attacked proportionately more often.

Predators too may benefit from living in groups. Thus some species are more successful at catching large prey when hunting in groups than when hunting on their own. Classic studies in the African Serengeti have shown that this is so for lions, spotted hyenas and wild dogs.

There are many other advantages of living in a group. Groups of woodlice huddle together and survive desiccation better. Group living may also allow individuals to do things they could never achieve on their own. Honeybees build hives with an internal air-conditioning system created by thousands of worker bees fanning with their wings. From late spring to autumn this keeps the colony between 34.5° and 35.5°C. In winter the energy released by the bees means that the temperature never falls below 17°C. Collectively honeybees are endothermic.

However, being in a group has costs too. In particular, members of a group may compete for food, simply by virtue of sharing the same area. The presence of even a few companions means that resident herbivores, such as rabbits, have to move further afield each day to feed. Moreover, living in a group gives dominant individuals, particularly males, the opportunity to monopolise the breeding. For a subordinate this is indeed a disadvantage.

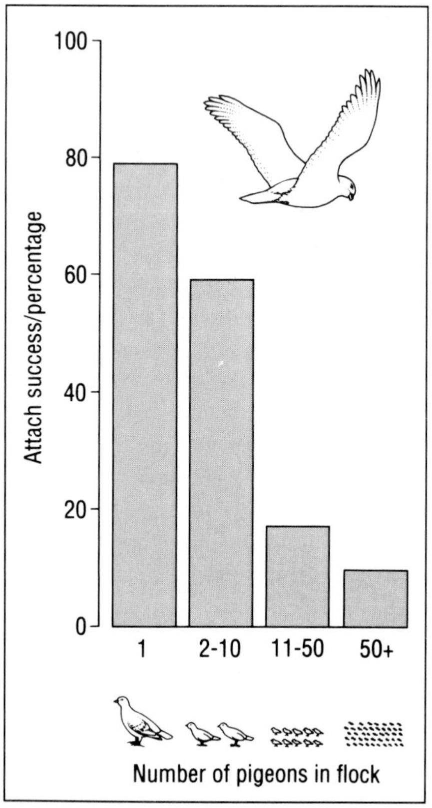

Altruism and kin selection

Whatever the size of a honeybee colony only *one* female reproduces! The workers are all sterile. Darwin realised that **worker sterility** appeared to contradict his theory of natural selection (see Chapter 43). After all, how can sterility evolve if, by definition, sterile individuals leave no offspring? Darwin suggested that the worker bees might be thought of as striving to rear sisters while the queen bee concentrates on producing offspring.

Altruism is the word given to behaviour which is *disadvantageous* for the individual performing the behaviour, but *helpful* to another individual. Worker honeybees are altruistic in that they help their mother to produce offspring rather than lay eggs themselves.

How has altruism evolved? One possible way is by **kin selection**. Kin selection is said to occur when a decrease in an individual's fitness, the number of offspring it produces, is more than compensated by an increase in the fitness of its relatives. We will look at lions for an example of this phenomenon.

Figure 30.20 Larger flocks of woodpigeons are less likely to suffer from successful attacks.

Lions

Lions live in social groups, called **prides**, which usually consist of about half a dozen adult females, their dependent offspring and some two to four adult males (figure 30.21). Daughters born into the pride commonly remain there for life, while sons leave before they reach reproductive maturity. Because of this, the females within a pride are quite closely related.

One noteworthy feature of life in the pride is that the cubs may suck from any adult female with milk. Such communal suckling is rare in mammals. In most species each female suckles only her own offspring. Because the females within a lion pride are quite closely related, kin selection has been invoked to explain the existence of communal suckling.

The adult males in a pride may be driven away by a new coalition of males. If a pride is taken over, the new adult males kill as many as possible of the young cubs. The function of this **infanticide** is more subtle than might appear at first sight. In common with many other mammals, female lions do not ovulate when they are lactating. However, once their cubs have been killed, the females come back into oestrus. Infanticide therefore allows the new males to sire their own cubs more quickly. In the African Serengeti 25 per cent of all cubs die from infanticide.

Early data suggested that the adult males in a pride were full or half-brothers. Kin selection was therefore used to explain the cooperation between the males in a pride. It now appears that some 40 per cent of breeding coalitions contain non-relatives. What then is the explanation for the cooperation between the adult males? The answer, it is thought, lies in **reciprocal altruism**, to which we now turn.

Reciprocal altruism

As the phrase suggests, this is where one animal, A, helps another, B. At some later point B **reciprocates**, that is, helps A. The expression "you scratch my back and I'll scratch yours" sums it up.

A fundamental difficulty in the evolution of reciprocal altruism is the possibility of **cheating**. Cheating occurs when B accepts help from A, but then fails to reciprocate! It seems that reciprocal altruism has evolved in those species where individuals can recognise each other. Individual recognition allows altruists to detect a cheat and ensure that they don't help it in future.

We shall now look at two examples of reciprocal altruism.

Vampire bats

Vampire bats are social animals found in Central and South America. They live in groups whose membership changes little over the course of a year or longer. As is well known, vampire bats fly out at night to find animals from which to take blood. Usually they attack horses, cattle, goats or pigs, but occasionally they attack humans or wild animals. On some nights an individual bat is unsuccessful in its search for food and returns to the group without having obtained a meal. This is potentially very serious for the unsuccessful bat as it can only survive two consecutive nights without a meal. After that the bat usually starves to death.

Fascinatingly, a bat that fails to obtain a meal during the night is usually fed by another member of the group when it returns. The altruist regurgitates blood for the hungry bat. Careful observations show that bats which have received regurgitated blood meals subsequently reciprocate. Furthermore, the probability that a bat will regurgitate blood for a hungry bat is independent of the degree of relatedness between the two bats. This rules out kin selection. If kin selection was responsible for this kind of altruism, regurgitation would be restricted to close relatives.

Figure 30.21

A The adult females in a pride of lions cooperate in hunting and suckle any of the cubs. Here we see two adult females with their dependent young.

B Adult male lions have large manes which make them obvious to prey and therefore poor hunters. The males in a pride leave the hunting to the females and sleep about 20 hours a day.

Humans

It can be argued that reciprocal altruism is the basis of human society. We are very good at remembering people we have helped. If we are honest with ourselves, don't we usually expect such people to reciprocate in the future? People who give us presents on our birthday are more likely to get presents back from us. The bank that lends us money expects us to reciprocate, with interest, and banks have effective methods of dealing with cheats!

Reciprocal altruism is more likely to persist in groups where all the individuals know each other. Once humans started living in towns and cities, rather than in small bands, the risks involved in reciprocal altruism became greater. We would therefore expect altruism to be confined to people who know each other well. How often do we do something helpful, at a cost to ourselves, to people we are sure we will never meet again?

Having discussed the advantages and disadvantages of sociality and altruism in a number of species, we can now look in detail at the social behaviour of honeybees, chimpanzees and humans.

Figure 30.22 Part of a colony of honeybees. In the upper left hand corner the queen is surrounded by workers. Some of the cells are capped. Others contain eggs and larvae in various stages of development, while some contain pollen or honey (extreme upper right). Near the centre towards the right, a worker extrudes her tongue to sip regurgitated nectar from a sister. At the lower left another worker is dragging a drone away by one of his wings. Towards the bottom right are two queen cells, one of which is shown as if cut open, so as to display the queen pupa inside.

The social life of honey bees

At the peak of its numbers in summer, a healthy colony of honeybees consists of up to sixty thousand **workers**, a few hundred males (**drones**) and a single **queen**. In addition there are a number of combs containing **eggs**, **larvae** and **pupae**, with stores of honey and pollen (figure 30.22). There is a strict division of labour: the queen lays eggs, the drones fertilise queens and the workers – sterile females – forage for food, rear the young and guard the hive.

The great majority of the eggs laid by the queen are diploid, the result of one of the haploid sperms she stores fusing with one of her haploid eggs. (Diploid and haploid are explained on page 552.) These diploid eggs develop into females. Whether these females turn out to be workers or queens depends on the way they are looked after. Eggs that will develop into queens are laid in special large queen cells which hang almost vertically (figure 30.22). For the first three days, queen larvae and worker larvae appear to be treated the same: they are fed on **royal jelly**, a highly nutritious food secreted by the hypopharyngeal and mandibular glands of the workers. After that, however, only the queen larvae continue to be fed on royal jelly. Worker larvae are switched from this to a mixture of pollen and nectar.

To produce males, the queen lays *unfertilised* eggs. Males are therefore haploid. Males do not help in the hive – all the workers are females. Rather, they attempt during the **nuptial flight** to mate with newly emerged queens from other colonies. Honeybees, in common with other bees, ants and wasps, are said to be **haplodiploid**, because males are haploid and females diploid.

The social life of chimpanzees

The chimpanzee is our closest relative. Humans and chimpanzees probably shared a common ancestor until only five to eight million years ago. Tragically chimpanzees are becoming increasingly rare in the wild as their habitat is destroyed and large numbers of them are taken for medical research. The features of their behaviour which perhaps stand out are their intelligence and the flexibility of their behaviour (figure 30.23).

Chimpanzees are found in forested areas throughout equatorial Africa. Their basic social unit is a loose association of about 30 to 80 animals that tend to remain in the same area for many years. They spend 25–50 per cent of their time on the ground and the rest in trees. Chimpanzees feed on the fruit, leaves, bark and seeds of a wide variety of plant species. They also consume termites and ants and occasionally kill and eat small baboons and other monkeys.

A considerable amount of cooperation occurs between individual chimpanzees. The species is unusual among mammals in that the females at puberty disperse from the troops in which they were born. This means that within a group, males may be closely related to each other. This may account for the frequent grooming between males, their cooperation in hunting and subsequent begging and sharing of meat.

In both sexes there is a period of several years during which the young are dependent on their mothers. This long period gives the young chimpanzee time to learn a great deal from its mother. The relative abundance of food in their environment means that time is also available for extensive and complex social interactions between the members of a group.

The pioneering work by the British ethologist Jane Goodall has shown the richness of chimpanzee culture. As with us, every animal is an individual and generalisations about their behaviour may oversimplify.

Figure 30.23 Chimpanzees make and use tools. This type of behaviour was previously thought unique to humans. Here an adult female has selected a stick, stripped it of leaves and is inserting it into a termite mound so as to extract some of the insects.

Figure 30.24 Female army recruits undergoing basic training. This is an example of secondary socialisation.

Human society

Human societies have much in common with those of monkeys and apes. Kinship is important and certain individuals are more dominant than others. However, we differ in the precision and subtlety of our communication system, our distinctive intelligence and the tremendous capacity we have for learning from others. Indeed, our knowledge and beliefs are **cultural** and differ from one society to another. Much of our behaviour is socially rather than genetically transmitted.

Socialisation

The process by which each of us learns to become a member of our society is called **socialisation**. **Primary socialisation** refers to the learning that takes place during childhood, mainly within the family. We spend longer learning from our parents than does any other species. **Secondary socialisation** refers to the learning that take place later, at school or in work, for instance (figure 30.24).

Socialisation takes place without our consciously trying to fit into society. It is only when people attempt to live in a different society that they realise the extent to which they have been moulded by the society in which they grew up. **Resocialisation** may be necessary if we move home, change our job or get married.

Norms and roles

Every society has a set of **norms**. These are unwritten patterns of behaviour which are usually accepted without question by the members of that society. Norms may change over time, and this may be one reason for the existence of a 'generation gap'. What was thought appropriate behaviour for teenagers twenty years ago may be thought by the present generation to be boring or weird.

Every day each of us occupies several **roles**. The same person might be a teacher, a mother, a wife, a friend, a neighbour and a daughter. The way we behave depends on our role at a particular time. **Role conflict** occurs when an individual's expected behaviour in one role conflicts with his or her expected behaviour in another role. Having a boyfriend or girlfriend with whom one wants to spend a lot of time may conflict with getting the examination grades one needs. In one's role as a boyfriend or girlfriend, one may be expected to spend a lot of time together in the evening. But in one's role as a diligent student one may be expected to do two or three hours homework each night!

Gender differences

One result of socialisation is that boys and girls are 'expected' to behave differently. We hear a lot about equality of opportunity nowadays, but what would be your initial reaction to a girl who wanted to become a bricklayer, or to a boy who wanted to be a midwife?

Stereotypes abound about male and female behaviour. Males are said to be more aggressive, more competitive and more prepared to take risks; girls to be more caring, more expressive and more affected by relationships. This may often be the case but these differences probably say more about the way society expects males and females to behave than about any innate differences between the sexes. One reason for studying human behaviour is that it forces us to look objectively at why we do the things we do and like the things we like. That may be the first step to deciding if we are happy with the way we are, or would like to be different.

Summary

1 An animal's **behaviour** consists of the responses it makes to the stimuli it receives.

2 The study of animal behaviour is known as **ethology**.

3 Most behaviours have two components, one **instinctive** and one **learned**; however, trying to disentangle the two is often very difficult.

4 Instinctive, or **innate**, behaviour, is inborn and does not have to be learned. It ranges from simple acts of behaviour such as **reflexes**, to complex behaviour patterns such as courtship.

5 A behaviour pattern in which an animal responds to an alteration in stimulus intensity by changing its activity level is called a **kinesis**. A movement that is orientated in relation to the direction of a stimulus is called a **taxis**.

6 Animals respond to only some of the many stimuli detected by their sensory receptors. A stimulus that produces a selective stereotyped response is known as a **sign stimulus**.

7 Learning is a more or less permanent change in behaviour which occurs as a result of experience.

8 Types of learning include **habituation, classical conditioning, trial and error learning, latent learning, insight learning** and **imprinting**.

9 **Courtship** allows animals to mate with a individual of the right sex and species. It also enables the two individuals to gather information about each other's fitness and receptivity.

10 **Communication** between individuals requires a **signal**, a **sender**, a **context**, a **channel**, a **receiver** and a **code**.

11 A **territory** is a more or less exclusive area defended by an individual or group.

12 On her return to the hive from foraging, a worker honeybee can provide information for her fellow workers about the direction, distance and value of a food source. This information is largely encoded in the **round dance** or **waggle dance** she performs.

13 **True language** involves the use of **symbols** (e.g. words) for abstract ideas, and an appreciation of **syntax**.

14 True language is found almost exclusively in humans. However, humans also use a wide repertoire of **non-verbal communication**.

15 An organism may be **solitary** or **social**. There are advantages and disadvantages to being in a group.

16 Behaviour that is disadvantageous for the individual performing it, but helpful to another individual, is said to be **altruistic**.

17 Helping behaviour can evolve as a result of **kin selection**, when help is given only to close relatives, or as a result of **reciprocal altruism**, when the altruist subsequently receives aid in return.

18 The process by which humans learn to become members of a society is called **socialisation**.

Review questions

1 Explain why the distinction between instinct and learning, though useful, should not be pressed too far.

2 Design an experiment to investigate whether woodlice reach humid areas by orthokinesis, klinokinesis or both.

3 How could you investigate the role, if any, of the male's red belly in the courtship behaviour of sticklebacks?

4 To what extent has your own behaviour been positively reinforced at school or college?

5 What is the difference between memory and intelligence?

6 List as many human displacement activities as you can.

7 Explain the difference between altruism and kin selection.

8 What are the advantages to humans of living in groups?

9 List as many communication channels as you can think of, both in humans and in other animals.

10 Do you agree that much of our behaviour is socially rather than genetically transmitted? What sort of evidence supports this idea?

Further reading

Of the many superb accounts of animal behaviour that exist, the following are particularly worth consulting. Each is written by one of the great pioneers of ethology:

Jane Goodall's classic study of chimpanzee behaviour, *In the Shadow of Man* (Collins, 1971).

King Solomon's Ring: New Light on Animal Ways by Konrad Lonrenz (Methuen, 1971), contains his work on imprinting and much more besides.

In *Curious Naturalists*, Niko Tinbergen describes his work on herring gulls, camouflage and learning in insects (Penguin Education, 1974).

The Dance Language and Orientation of Bees by Karl von Frisch (Harvard University Press, 1967) is an account of his painstaking research on communication in honeybees.

Part VI

REPRODUCTION, GROWTH AND DEVELOPMENT

To appreciate how organisms reproduce it is necessary to understand how cells divide. Cell division is the subject of the opening chapter of this part of the book. The next three chapters deal with reproduction of the whole organism, starting with the general principles and then going on to the mammal and flowering plant.

Reproduction is accompanied by growth and development. A chapter is devoted to the structural aspects of growth and development. In the next chapter we explain how growth and development are controlled by a variety of different internal and external influences.

Some of the most important research on the control of growth has been carried out on plants. The classical experiments which led to the discovery of plant growth substances are described in detail.

The results of investigations on plant growth help us to understand how plants respond to stimuli such as light and gravity, so plant responses are also treated in this part of the book.

Photograph: A lioness sleeps with her cubs in Masai Mara Game Reserve, Kenya.

CHAPTER 31

Cell division and the cell cycle

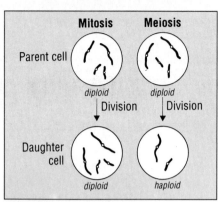

Figure 31.1 What do mitosis and meiosis achieve? A cell contains different types of chromosomes and usually there are two of each type, the diploid state (two large and two small chromosomes in the parent cells shown above). Mitosis results in daughter cells with the same chromosome complement as the parent cell. Meiosis, however, results in daughter cells with only half the number of chromosomes of the parent cell, i.e. one of each type, the haploid state.

Growth, reproduction and the replacement of old cells all involve the multiplication of cells. In order to multiply, cells undergo **cell division**: one divides into two, these two may divide into four and so on. The phrase 'cell division' is misleading in some ways because it implies that the process involves halving the cell and its contents. In fact we know that in most cases cell division is preceded by cell growth, so that when the parent cell divides, the two **daughter cells** are essentially similar to the parent cell. Understanding cell division is largely a matter of appreciating how an organism manages to ensure that this similarity is preserved.

In any description of cell division, the chromosomes are the key to understanding what is going on. As the vehicles of heredity they determine the characteristics of the cell and its progeny. It is essential that they are correctly distributed between the daughter cells.

Two types of cell division can be recognised according to the behaviour of the chromosomes (figure 31.1):

- In **mitotic cell division** (**mitosis**) the daughter cells finish up containing exactly the same number of chromosomes as the parent cell, typically two of each type (**diploid state**). Mitosis is the type of cell division which takes place when an organism grows, replaces old cells or reproduces asexually.

- In **meiotic cell division** (**meiosis**) each daughter cell ends up with exactly half the number of chromosomes as the parent cell, i.e. one of each type (**haploid state**). This type of division is associated with sexual reproduction. It generally takes place in the formation of gametes, or in some cases spores.

In this chapter we will look at mitosis and meiosis in some detail. We will also examine the causes of cancer, because cancers occur when cell division gets out of control. First, however, we will look at how cell division, particularly mitosis, fits into the life of a cell.

The cell cycle

The entire sequence of events which takes place in a cell between one cell division and the next comprises the **cell cycle**. In eukaryotes it can be divided into four phases:

- **M phase (mitotic phase).**
- **G_1 phase (first growth phase).**
- **S phase (synthesis phase).**
- **G_2 phase (second growth phase).**

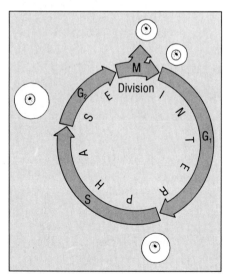

Figure 31.2 The cell cycle consists of four phases. The longest phase is nearly always the G_1 (first growth) phase in which a cell makes lots of biochemicals and increases the numbers of most of its organelles. The S (synthesis) phase is characterised by the replication of the genetic material. The short G_2 (second growth) phase is followed by the M (mitotic) phase in which nuclear and cytoplasmic division occurs, giving rise to two new cells.

The sequence of these four phases is shown in figure 31.2. The mitotic phase consists of **nuclear division** (mitosis) and **cytoplasmic division**. During this phase cells make few new chemicals, in other words they have a low rate of synthesis. After the mitotic phase, the daughter cells enter the first growth phase, during which there is a great increase in the rate at which new cell components are made. The start of DNA synthesis marks the beginning of the synthesis phase which ends once DNA synthesis is complete. The cell then enters the second growth phase during which a small amount of further growth takes place. With the completion of the second growth phase, the mitotic phase is entered once more.

Figure 31.2 shows the relative lengths of the four phases of the cell cycle for a population of cells which doubles in number every 24 hours. The period between successive cell divisions is called **interphase**. You can see that the M phase lasts only an hour or two and that interphase makes up the remaining 95 per cent of the time.

Each of us, when adult, has about 10^{13} cells, that is ten thousand thousand million of them. These cells differ greatly in the lengths of their cell cycles. Some, such as skeletal muscle cells, red blood cells and neurones never divide, while others such as liver cells normally divide only once every year or two. At the other extreme, certain epithelial cells in the gut divide every twelve hours on average (figure 31.3).

Despite this great variation in the length of the cell cycle, the time cells spend in the S, G_2 and M phases varies surprisingly little: typically, in humans, they take about 12 to 18 hours altogether. The G_1 phase, however, can last from a few hours to months or even years.

Interphase

It should be clear to you that the great majority of cells spend nearly all their time in interphase. During interphase the chromosomes are not visible as distinct bodies either under the light microscope or the electron microscope. Instead they are mostly strung out in the form of long **chromatin threads**. Not until the cell leaves interphase and enters mitosis do the chromatin threads condense to form visible chromosomes.

Interphase is sometimes described as a resting stage. This is a complete misnomer. The first growth phase is in many respects the 'normal' active stage of the cell cycle. During this phase protein synthesis, the formation of new organelles and all the countless processes which go on in an active cell take place, as a result of which the cell doubles in size. The synthesis phase is characterised by the replication of the genetic material (DNA). A cell cannot divide until its chromosomes have doubled up.

During interphase a cell builds up a sufficiently large store of energy, a kind of 'energy reservoir', to carry it through mitosis. It can be shown that this accumulation of energy takes place during interphase rather than during mitosis itself by inhibiting respiration at different stages in the cell cycle. If a cell is treated with a metabolic poison such as cyanide at any point during interphase, mitosis fails to take place. If, however, the cell is treated with the poison after mitosis has started, the cell will successfully go through to the end of mitosis and the start of the first growth phase.

Just before mitosis begins, the **centrioles** are among the most prominent organelles in the cell. Centrioles are found in the cells of all animals and most protoctists, but they are absent from cone-bearing and flowering plants. Their structure is described on page 166. Centrioles always come in pairs. Unlike other organelles, they replicate during the S phase, along with the DNA. This means that by the start of mitosis, each cell has two pairs of centrioles.

Mitosis

For purposes of description mitosis is divided into four stages: **prophase, metaphase, anaphase** and **telophase**. At each of these stages certain crucial events take place, particularly in regard to the chromosomes. However, it is important to realise that mitosis is a continuous process and there are no sharp breaks between one stage and the next. Typically the entire process takes about an hour and is followed by cytoplasmic division, during which the cytoplasms of the two daughter cells separate.

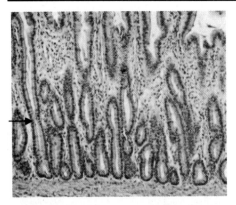

Figure 31.3 Epithelial cells lining the bottom of the crypts of Lieberkühn in the wall of the small intestine divide frequently. The arrow indicates the region where most cell divisions take place. The reason why this happens is explained on page 282. The crypts are here seen in a transverse section of the wall of the ileum. Magnification × 70.

Ultrarapid cell division

The most rapid cell cycles take place in the post-fertilisation divisions of some zygotes. For instance, the haploid egg of the frog *Xenopus* measures just over a millimetre in diameter and acts as a store of all the materials needed for the construction of the early embryo. Before fertilisation the egg waits in prophase of the first meiotic division. At ovulation hormones cause the egg to proceed as far as its second meiotic division.

Fertilisation is then followed by a remarkably rapid sequence of cell divisions in which the single diploid egg cleaves to generate an embryo consisting of 4096 cells. To all intents and purposes the cells miss out the first and second growth phases. DNA synthesis is followed almost immediately by mitosis. The first division takes about 90 minutes. The next eleven occur at about 30 minute intervals. The net result is that just seven hours after fertilisation, the single zygote has transformed itself into a mass of much smaller cells.

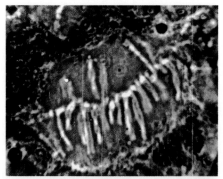

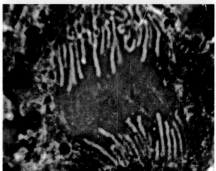

Figure 31.4 Frames from a film of mitosis made in 1957 by the American (formerly Polish) biologist, Andrew Bajer. This was the first successful film of mitosis ever made. Bajer used endosperm tissue, the nutritive tissue surrounding the embryo inside seeds. The cells divide prolifically and, being a rather soft and runny tissue, a thin smear can be made on a microscope slide without harming the individual cells. Viewed in phase-contrast the movements of the chromosomes during mitosis can be seen clearly.

Figure 31.5 Mitosis in a generalised animal cell. Two pairs of chromosomes are shown: a long pair and a short pair. Plant cells undergo mitosis in the same way except that there are no centrioles. For the sake of comparison a cell in interphase is drawn in **A**, although interphase is, strictly, not part of mitosis.

Observing mitosis

One of the easiest places to see the stages of mitosis is in the tip of a growing root. The root tip is cut off, sectioned or macerated and treated with a dye such as acetic orcein which stains the chromosomes. In good preparations the various stages of mitosis can be seen clearly. However, the trouble is that the chromosomes are locked in a fixed position and nothing can be seen of their movements. It is like looking at still photographs of an athlete in action: useful for analysis but conveying nothing of the dynamic movements involved.

In recent years films have been made of unstained living cells under the phase-contrast microscope (figure 31.4). As cell division is slow, time-lapse photography is used, successive frames being exposed at intervals of, say,

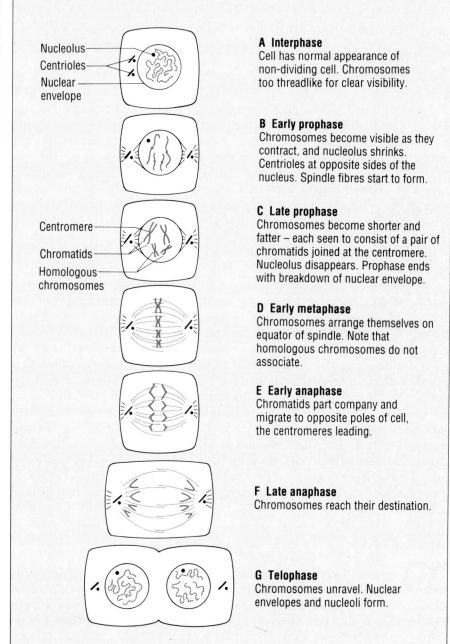

A Interphase
Cell has normal appearance of non-dividing cell. Chromosomes too threadlike for clear visibility.

B Early prophase
Chromosomes become visible as they contract, and nucleolus shrinks. Centrioles at opposite sides of the nucleus. Spindle fibres start to form.

C Late prophase
Chromosomes become shorter and fatter – each seen to consist of a pair of chromatids joined at the centromere. Nucleolus disappears. Prophase ends with breakdown of nuclear envelope.

D Early metaphase
Chromosomes arrange themselves on equator of spindle. Note that homologous chromosomes do not associate.

E Early anaphase
Chromatids part company and migrate to opposite poles of cell, the centromeres leading.

F Late anaphase
Chromosomes reach their destination.

G Telophase
Chromosomes unravel. Nuclear envelopes and nucleoli form.

two seconds. When projected, the movements of the chromosomes, speeded up many times, can be followed in detail.

Let us now follow what happens when a cell undergoes mitotic division. For convenience we will consider a cell which contains only four chromosomes: a pair of long ones and a pair of short ones. It is typical of cells that they contain two of each type of chromosome, the so-called diploid state. The events are summarised in figure 31.5

Prophase

If interphase can be thought of as preparing the cell for division, prophase (figure 31.5B and C) can be described as 'mobilisation for action'. Certain clearly visible events can be seen under the microscope. The most obvious is the condensing of the chromatin threads to form distinct chromosomes. Long and thin at first, they gradually become shorter and fatter. As the chromosomes shorten, it becomes increasingly clear that each chromosome consists of a pair of bodies lying close alongside each other. These are called **chromatids**. They tend to lie parallel along most of their length but are joined only in a specialised region called the **centromere**. The centromere holds the two chromatids together until later in mitosis. The two chromatids of one chromosome are usually referred to as **sister chromatids**.

It is essential to appreciate what these two chromatids are. After mitosis is finished, each chromosome consists of a single very long thread of DNA accompanied by special proteins which protect the DNA and help to regulate its functioning. During the replication of the genetic material, an exact copy of this single thread is made. These two threads cannot be distinguished visually until prophase when they make their appearance as the two chromatids. We will consider the molecular basis of these events in a later chapter, but for the moment it is sufficient to realise that the two chromatids making up a chromosome at the start of mitosis are identical. Except for the occasional mutation, they contain exactly the same genetic material point for point along their length.

Condensing of the chromosomes is one of the most important events in prophase. If it failed to happen it would be impossible for the chromosomes to move around the cell without getting tangled up. While the chromosomes are getting shorter and thicker, other changes are happening. The cytoplasmic microtubules that are part of the cell's cytoskeleton disassemble and reassemble to form a structure known as the **spindle** (figure 31.6).

In cells where centrioles are present, one pair is found at one end of the spindle and the other pair at the other end. This is achieved by one pair skirting the nuclear envelope so that it comes to rest at the opposite side of the nucleus. The two pairs of centrioles are now said to be at the **poles**, and the spindle fibres can be seen to go from one pole to the other. Also during prophase the nucleolus starts to disperse, so that it seems to disappear. Prophase ends, and metaphase begins, with the breakdown of the nuclear envelope.

Metaphase

As the nuclear envelope breaks down, it dissociates into vesicles which are indistinguishable from bits of endoplasmic reticulum. With certain staining techniques, these vesicles can be seen outside the spindle throughout mitosis. Later we shall see the role these vesicles play in cytoplasmic division. As the nuclear envelope disrupts, the chromosomes migrate to the central plane of the cell and arrange themselves around the middle of the

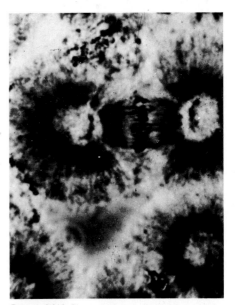

Figure 31.6 Phase-contrast photomicrograph of isolated spindle apparatuses obtained from sea urchin eggs. Note the spindle fibres. The cells are at metaphase as can be seen by the positioning of the chromosomes on the equator of the spindle.

What triggers cell division?

The start of mitosis is subject to a number of controls. In many cells mitosis only takes place when cells have reached a certain critical mass. As a result, the rate at which a cell increases in mass determines the time interval between cell divisions. In the very early stages of embryonic development, however, the period between M phases seems to be determined by a timer or oscillator, so that cell division occurs at regular time intervals. A further control in some cells couples the start of the M phase with the completion of the S phase, so that if the chromosomes are not yet fully replicated, nuclear division does not begin.

Recently it has been discovered that the onset of mitosis in all eukaryotic cells is regulated by an enzyme called p34^{cdc2} protein kinase – p standing for protein, 34 meaning that its relative molecular mass is 34 000 and *cdc2* referring to the cdc2 gene of the yeast *Schizosaccharomyces pombe* from which the protein was first purified and identified. This enzyme is activated by changes in its phosphorylation state. In turn, it is thought to phosphorylate key proteins which lead to the major events of mitosis including chromosome condensation, the formation of spindle fibres from microtubules and the breakdown of the nuclear envelope.

Of course, even if this theory turns out to be correct, it simply replaces the question 'What triggers cell division?' by the question 'What causes dephosphorylation of p34^{cdc2}?'. It is thought that another group of proteins called cyclins are involved, but it is clear that there is still a tremendous amount to be learned about the control of mitosis.

spindle, known as its **equator** (figure 31.5D). Finally, the chromosomes become attached to the spindle fibres at the centromeres.

Anaphase

For anyone who has watched a film of mitosis, this is the most spectacular part of the whole process (figure 31.5E and F). Suddenly the chromatids belonging to each chromosome part company and move towards opposite poles of the spindle.

Anaphase begins with the splitting of the centromeres down the middle. This allows each chromatid to be pulled by one of the spindle fibres towards the pole it is facing. This takes only a few minutes as the chromosomes move towards the poles at a speed of about 1μm per minute. Anaphase is said to end once the separated daughter chromatids arrive at the two poles. The spindle fibres that draw them to the poles, like the proverbial Cheshire cat, become disassembled into nothingness.

Telophase

The end of anaphase marks the beginning of telophase, the last stage of nuclear division. The reverse of the various processes that occurred in prophase now occur. The condensed chromosomes begin to unravel themselves, a new nuclear envelope forms around each group of daughter chromosomes and new nucleoli form (figure 31.5G).

How do the chromatids separate during anaphase?

In recent years there has been a great deal of research on how the chromatids separate during anaphase. It is now believed that two related but distinct processes are going on. First, the chromatids are pulled towards the poles. This is accompanied by a shortening of spindle fibres that run from the chromatids to the poles. Secondly, the poles themselves separate. This is accompanied by a lengthening of pairs of overlapping spindle fibres that run from pole to pole.

Precisely how the chromatids are pulled towards the poles is still not known. However, spindle fibres are microtubules composed of **tubulin** (see page 141). As the chromatids move towards the poles, individual tubulin molecules are subtracted from the spindle fibres that run from the chromatids to the poles, causing them to shorten and so pull the chromatids to the poles.

Lengthening of the pole-to-pole fibres, on the other hand, is caused by the *addition* of tubulin molecules.

At the same time, the microtubules that are joined to one pole *push* against the microtubules that are joined to the other pole. The result is that the two poles are forced apart possibly by a ratchet mechanism comparable to that which occurs in muscle (see page 502).

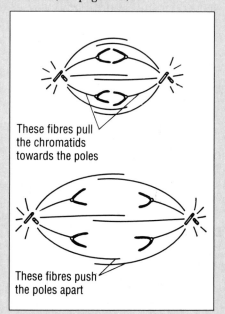

These fibres pull the chromatids towards the poles

These fibres push the poles apart

Two simultaneous processes draw the chromosomes to the poles and push the two poles apart.

Mitosis is now at an end. However, the two new nuclei are still contained within the one cell. Mitosis is therefore followed by cytoplasmic division which starts even before telophase is finished.

Cytoplasmic division

The cytoplasm divides by a process known as **cleavage**. In animal cells, the plasma membrane around the middle of the cell is drawn inwards to form a **cleavage furrow**. This gradually deepens until eventually the cell is cut in two and two cells result (figure 31.7).

Cleavage is accomplished by the contraction of a ring composed mainly of actin filaments. These filaments are bound to the cytoplasmic face of the plasma membrane (figure 31.8). The mechanism by which they contract is still unknown, though the protein myosin is thought to be involved. That myosin should play a part in this process is not surprising, given the presence of actin: as we saw in Chapter 29, the proteins actin and myosin work together to enable muscles to contract. Evidence that myosin is involved in cleavage comes from a number of sources. For instance, an injection of anti-myosin antibodies into sea urchin eggs causes the cleavage furrow to relax.

In plants, cytoplasmic division occurs in a very different way. A new cell wall, the **cell plate**, grows across the middle of the cell as a result of the Golgi apparatus depositing vesicles where the new cell wall is to be formed. These vesicles contain the pectins, hemicelluloses and cellulose which make up the primary cell wall. These cell wall precursors are deposited by the vesicles at the edge of the cell plate causing it to extend outwards (figure 31.9).

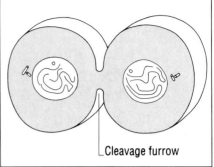

Cleavage furrow

Figure 31.7 Cytoplasmic division in a generalised animal cell. The original parent cell had two pairs of chromosomes: a long pair and a short pair as in figure 31.5.

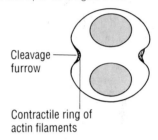

Cleavage furrow

Contractile ring of actin filaments

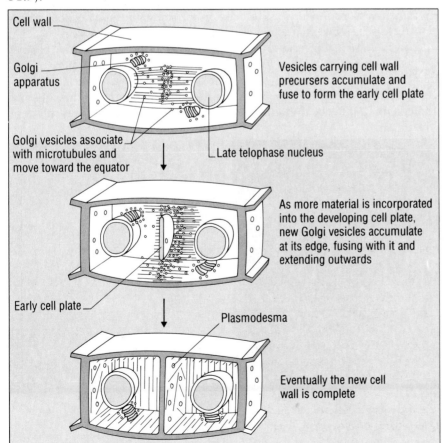

Cell wall

Golgi apparatus

Golgi vesicles associate with microtubules and move toward the equator

Late telophase nucleus

Vesicles carrying cell wall precursers accumulate and fuse to form the early cell plate

As more material is incorporated into the developing cell plate, new Golgi vesicles accumulate at its edge, fusing with it and extending outwards

Early cell plate

Plasmodesma

Eventually the new cell wall is complete

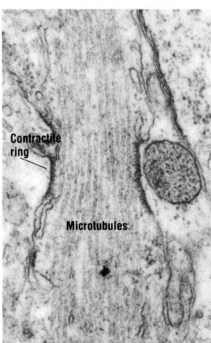

Contractile ring

Microtubules

Figure 31.8 Diagram and electron micrograph showing the contractile ring of actin filaments responsible for the cleavage furrow at cytoplasmic division in an animal cell.

Figure 31.9 Diagramatic representation of cytoplasmic division in a plant cell. As a result a new cell wall is formed between the two cells. Plasmodesmata provide a connection between the two cells.

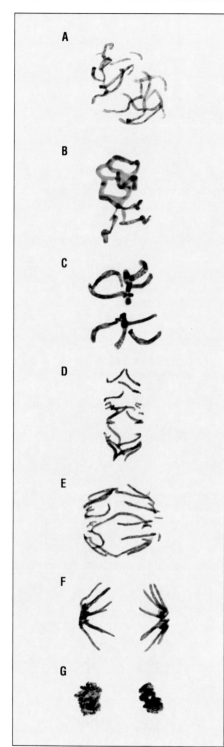

Figure 31.10 Mitosis in a plant with 8 long chromosomes and 6 much shorter ones that can only sometimes be seen. The material was prepared in such a way that only the chromosome are visible.

A Early prophase;	**E** Mid-anaphase;
B Late prophase;	**F** Late anaphase;
C Metaphase;	**G** Telophase.
D Early anaphase;	

The essential principle underlying mitosis

The really important thing about mitosis is that the daughter cells receive precisely the same number and types of chromosomes as the original parent cell: two long ones and two short ones in the case illustrated in figure 31.5. In other words, the genetic constitution is maintained from one generation to the next.

Two salient features of mitosis ensure that the chromosome constitution is preserved:

- The fact that the DNA of the parent cell has replicated before mitosis begins.
- The arrangement of the chromosomes on the spindle.

As a result of DNA replication during the cell cycle, the parent cell contains twice the genetic information it normally does. The arrangement of the chromosomes on the spindle ensures that the chromatids are distributed evenly between the two daughter cells. This even distribution of the chromatids is admirably illustrated in the photomicrographs in figure 31.10.

The role of mitosis

Mitosis is the type of cell division that takes place during the growth of an organism, for example in the development of a fertilised egg into an adult human being. The fact that these divisions are mitotic means that all the cells of the body have the same chromosome constitution, a total of 46 chromosomes (23 pairs) in our case.

Mitosis allows an organism to replace old or damaged cells. If you cut yourself, epithelial cells in the skin are stimulated to divide mitotically to cover up the cut (figure 31.11). These epithelial cells continue to divide until they are surrounded by skin cells on all sides. In this way they know when to stop dividing, that is when the cut is covered over by skin.

Mitosis is also the basis of asexual reproduction. This is the process that occurs when an *Amoeba* undergoes binary fission, when a bud develops in *Hydra* or when a new plant develops from a vegetative organ such as a corm or bulb. In each case mitosis ensures that the chromosome complement, and hence the genetic constitution, of the offspring is the same as the parent's.

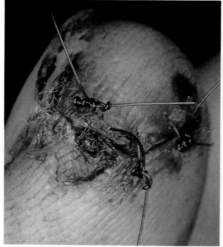
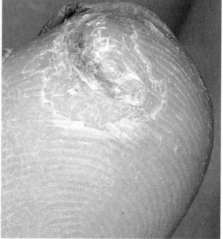

Figure 31.11 The repair of damaged tissue requires mitotic cell division, as in this cut finger where stitching has been used to speed recovery and reduce scarring.
A Index finger with stitches following an industrial accident with a bow saw.
B The same finger one week after the removal of the stitches showing fresh skin and a scab.

Meiosis

We have seen that a built-in feature of mitosis is the preservation of the parental complement of chromosomes. In meiosis, however, the number of chromosomes is halved, the daughter cells receiving only one of each type of chromosome instead of two. The daughter cells are said to be in the haploid state, haploid coming from the Greek word *haplous*, single.

The role of meiosis

In animals, meiosis occurs in the formation of **gametes** (sex cells), that is eggs and sperm, which are therefore haploid. To understand the significance of meiosis we must pause for a moment to consider the function of gametes. A gamete is a cell which usually develops no further until it fuses with another gamete. Thus a sperm and an egg have no future unless they unite to form a **zygote** which then has the potential to develop into an adult organism.

In the process of fertilisation the nuclei of the two gametes fuse to form the nucleus of the zygote. Now if the gametes were to have two, rather than one, of each type of chromosome, the zygote would have four of each type, twice the normal number. Let us assume that this zygote develops into an adult which itself produces gametes with the same number of chromosomes, that is with four of each type of chromosomes. If two of these gametes were to unite, a zygote would be formed with eight of each type of chromosome, and so on. In other words, if gametes were formed by mitosis rather than by meiosis, the chromosome number would double with each succeeding generation. By halving the chromosome number prior to fertilisation, meiosis ensures that this does not happen. When gametes with the haploid number of chromosomes unite, the normal diploid condition is restored.

In the next chapter we shall see that meiosis does not invariably happen in gamete-formation; in some organisms it occurs in the formation of spores. In one sense this does not matter: it is immaterial *when* halving of the chromosome number occurs so long as it happens at some stage in the life cycle.

The essential principle underlying meiosis

How does meiosis achieve this halving of the chromosome number? The answer lies in the behaviour of the chromosomes during the division process. Meiosis consists of two successive divisions: the parent cell splits into two (**first meiotic division**) and the products then divide again (**second meiotic division**), giving a total of four daughter cells. There is no synthesis of genetic material between these two divisions, so each daughter cell ends up being haploid.

In a haploid cell, each chromosome is unique with respect to its length and the genes it contains. In a diploid cell, each chromosome has a partner of exactly the same length and with precisely the same genes. So, in a diploid cell the chromosomes occur in **homologous pairs**. In the first meiotic division the homologous chromosomes of each pair line up together and then get separated from each other and go into different cells. The second division is concerned with separating the chromatids.

With these basic ideas in mind, let us examine in detail the events that take place in meiosis (figure 31.12). As in mitosis, the process is divided for convenience into a series of stages. These are given the same names as in mitosis, but each is followed by I or II indicating whether it belongs to the first or second meiotic division.

Figure 31.12 Meiosis in a generalised animal
cell. As in the diagrams of mitosis only two
pairs of chromosomes are shown: a long pair
and a short pair. In **C** to **E** homologous
chromosomes are shown diagrammatically
lying side by side; in reality the association is
so intimate that at first the four chromatids
cannot be distinguished from each other. For
the sake of comparison a cell in interphase is
drawn in **A**, although interphase is, strictly, not
part of meiosis.

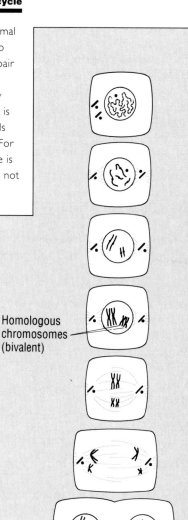

Homologous
chromosomes
(bivalent)

A Interphase
Cell in normal non-dividing condition
with chromosomes long and threadlike.

B Early prophase I
Chromosomes contract, becoming more
clearly visible. Nucleolus shrinks.

C Mid-prophase I
Homologous chromosomes come
together forming a bivalent.

D Late prophase I
Each chromosome seen to consist of a
pair of chromatids.

E Metaphase I
Chromosomes arrange themselves on
equator of spindle.

F Anaphase I
Homologous chromosomes part company
and migrate to opposite poles of the cell.

G Telophase I
Nuclear envelopes and nucleoli form.

H Prophase II
The two daughter cells prepare for the
second meiotic division: centrioles have
replicated and a new spindle is formed.

I Metaphase II
Chromosomes arrange themselves on
the spindle in the usual way.

J Anaphase II
Chromatids part company and migrate
to opposite poles of the cell.

K Telophase II
Spindle apparatus disappears and the
chromosomes begin to regain their threadlike
form. New nuclear envelopes and nucleoli
form. These four haploid cells form a tetrad (see page 562).

Prophase I

In many respects this is similar to the prophase of mitosis: the chromosomes condense, the nucleolus disappears, the centrioles, if present, arrange themselves at opposite sides of the nucleus and a spindle forms (figure 31.12B to D). However, there is one fundamental difference. In mitosis homologous chromosomes do not associate with each other in any way. But in meiosis they come to lie side by side, a proces known as **synapsis**. In this condition each pair of homologous chromosomes constitutes a **bivalent**, so that in figure 31.12D there are two bivalents.

As prophase proceeds the homologous chromosomes may become intimately coiled round each other. Later, they move slightly apart, but the chromatids remain in contact at certain points called **chiasmata** (singular **chiasma**). Extremely important genetic changes occur in association with the chiasmata, but we will deal with these genetic aspects separately.

Although chiasmata are found in most meiotically dividing cells, we shall start by considering what happens in meiosis when chiasma formation does not occur. Although such achiasmate divisions are uncommon, they are simpler to understand than divisions involving chiasmata.

Metaphase I

As in mitosis the nuclear envelope breaks down and the chromosomes move to the equator of the spindle (figure 31.12E). The important difference from mitosis is that here homologous chromosomes do this together; in other words, each bivalent behaves as a unit. They arrange themselves in such a way that the centromeres of the two homologous chromosomes making up a pair orientate towards opposite poles. The cell is now poised ready for the separation of the homologous chromosomes.

Anaphase I

The homologous chromosomes, each made up of a pair of chromatids joined at the centromere, move towards opposite poles of the spindle (figure 31.12F). The sister chromatids also separate slightly from one another along their length, except at the centromere.

Telophase I

When the chromosomes reach their respective poles the cell starts to divide across its middle, and, as in mitosis, nuclear envelopes form around the two new nuclei and the spindle breaks down (figure 31.12G).

Interphase

At the end of meiosis I, a brief interphase usually occurs. The chromosomes expand somewhat, but they soon re-condense and prophase II begins. During this interphase no DNA synthesis occurs. Indeed in some organisms the cells go straight from telophase I to prophase II.

The second meiotic division

Separation of the homologous chromosomes that make up a bivalent is achieved by the first meiotic division. The purpose of the second division is to separate the chromatids from one another.

In prophase II (figure 31.12H) a new spindle is formed at right angles to the first one. In metaphase II (figure 31.12I) the chromosomes move to the equator of the spindle, the chromatids orienting towards opposite poles as in mitosis. Anaphase II (figure 31.12J) sees the chromatids separating and moving apart from each other. The chromatids become the chromo-

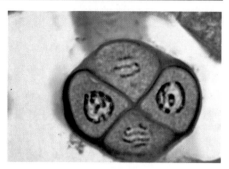

Figure 31.13 Tetrad of four haploid cells derived from a single parent diploid cell.

somes of the daughter cells. When they reach the poles, the cells enter telophase II (figure 31.12K). Characteristically of telophase, the spindle apparatus disappears, the chromosomes begin to regain their threadlike form, and new nuclear envelopes and nucleoli form.

Meiosis is now complete. Cytoplasmic division follows so that four haploid cells (sometimes referred to as a **tetrad**) have been formed from the original single diploid parent cell (figure 31.13).

The importance of meiosis in bringing about variation

We have seen that meiosis leads to a halving of the chromosome number. However, it also plays an essential part in promoting genetic variation. This is brought about partly because each of the chromosomes making up a homologous pair carries different genetic material, with the result that the daughter cells are bound to be genetically distinct. Furthermore, the different pairs of homologous chromosomes arrange themselves on the spindle, and subsequently separate, entirely independently of each other, so that the daughter cells finish up containing different combinations of chromosomes. This is explained in more detail in Chapters 37 and 43.

A further reason why meiosis promotes genetic variation is that it normally involves the formation of chiasmata, to which we must now turn.

Chiasmata

Towards the end of prophase I the intimate association between homologous chromosomes tends to weaken and the four chromatids within a bivalent move slightly apart. It may now be seen that the chromatids are in contact with each other at certain points. These are the chiasmata.

The number of chiasmata varies considerably. As many as eight may be present and most bivalents have at least one, though sometimes, as in male *Drosophila* flies, none is found. Chiasmata can be formed between any two of the non-sister chromatids (figure 31.14).

As the cell moves from prophase I to metaphase I, the homologous chromosomes in a bivalent become increasingly separated from one another except at the chiasmata. This results in the bivalents adopting characteristic shapes, which vary according to the number and positions of the chiasmata:

- A bivalent with only one chiasma assumes a cross-shaped configuration.
- The formation of two chiasmata results in a ring.
- Where three or more chiasmata are present a series of interconnected loops results. However, not all the loops need necessarily be visible because consecutive ones may be at right angles to one another like links in a chain.

Chiasmata have two functions; one genetic, the other mechanical. The less important of these is the mechanical one: chiasmata help to hold pairs of homologous chromosomes together while they manoeuvre themselves onto the spindle prior to separation.

The genetic function is discussed in more detail in Chapters 38 and 43 and will only be touched on here. The chiasmata represent places where non-sister chromatids break and rejoin, as indicated in figure 31.15. When this happens a portion of one chromatid changes places with the equivalent portion of another. This enables exchange of genetic material to occur between homologous chromosomes, a process known as **crossing over**. Since the two homologous chromosomes usually contain different genetic material, crossing over promotes genetic variety, which in turn plays an important part in the process by which evolution takes place.

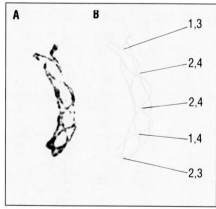

Figure 31.14 Chiasmata. **A** is a photomicrograph of a bivalent at late prophase I from the testis of a grasshopper. **B** is an interpretative diagram. Chiasmata are numbered according to which chromatids are in contact. Note that chiasmata can be formed between any two non-sister chromatids.

Observing meiosis

To observe stages in meiosis one must choose a reproductive tissue in which gametes or spores are being produced. In flowering plants meiosis can be observed in developing pollen grains or embryo sacs. This means examining the contents of anthers or ovules respectively. In animals meiosis can be observed in the testes or ovaries.

In all these cases the tissues must be stained appropriately in order to show up the chromosomes, this being achieved either by sectioning or by making squash preparations. The photomicrographs shown in figure 31.16 were obtained from the testis of a grasshopper, a convenient choice because the chromosomes are large and comparatively few in number, enabling individual chromosomes to be seen and followed clearly.

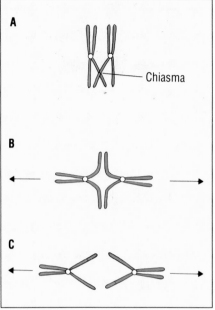

Figure 31.15 Crossing over takes place during prophase of the first meiotic division. **A** shows a chiasma at mid-prophase I: notice that two of the chromatids of homologous chromosomes have broken and changed places. **B** shows the chromosomes separating at late prophase I. **C** shows the two chromosomes, each with its exchanged portion of chromatid separating during metaphase I. Later, at anaphase I, they will move apart as shown in figure 31.16D.

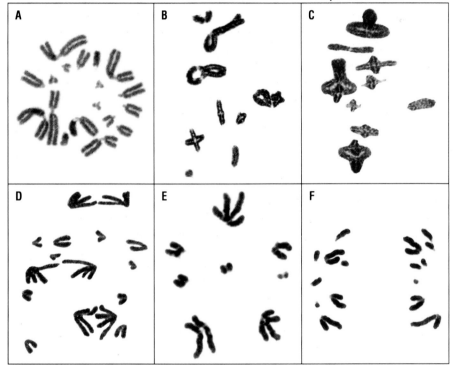

Figure 31.16 Photomicrographs of meiosis in testis of a grasshopper. **A** Early prophase I: full complement of chromosomes, each consisting of a pair of chromatids, are clearly visible.
B Mid-prophase I. Homologous chromosomes have come together and chiasmata have been formed.
C Late-prophase I. Homologous chromosomes are more condensed now and have pulled apart.
D Anaphase I: homologous chromosomes are moving to opposite poles. **E** Prophase II: the chromatids of each chromosome can be seen clearly. **F** Anaphase II: the chromatids are moving to opposite poles.

The differences between mitosis and meiosis

This brief account of cell division will have shown that there are many detailed differences between mitosis and meiosis. As we have seen, there are two central distinctions. The first is that in meiosis homologous chromosomes associate with one another, whereas in mitosis they do not. This is clearly seen in late prophase, when the chromosomes make their appearance as distinct bodies, and again at metaphase when they arrange themselves on the spindle (figure 31.17). The second is that no DNA replication occurs between the first and second meiotic divisions. If you think about it, all the other differences between these two types of nuclear division stem from these fundamental differences in the behaviour of the chromosomes.

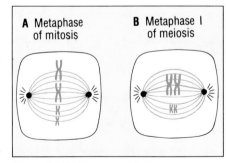

Figure 31.17 The essential difference between mitosis and meiosis lies in the behaviour of the chromosomes. This can be seen at metaphase when they arrange themselves on the spindle. In mitosis (**A**) homologous chromosomes do not associate with one another, whereas in meiosis (**B**) they come together and then segregate.

Cancers

Cancer is not a single disease. There are hundreds of different sorts, and they attack different parts of the body. Despite these differences, all cancers have in common that they involve the uncontrolled growth of cells. In a cancerous cell something goes wrong with the control of the cell cycle and the cell starts to divide more often than it should. Eventually a mass of cancerous cells results, called a **tumour,** which may spread to other parts of the body (figure 31.18).

What causes cancer?

In a cancerous cell, a specific change or **mutation** has happened in the genetic material as a result of which the controls which prevent excessive cell division fail to work. Generalisations about cancer are difficult as there are so many different types, though the chances of developing most cancers increase with age. Apart from increasing age, there are three main causes of cancer: chemicals, radiation and viruses. As well as these environmental causes, some people inherit a greater likelihood of developing cancer.

Chemicals

In 1775 a London surgeon called Percival Pott noticed that boys who swept chimneys for a living had a very high incidence of cancer of the scrotum. Pott argued that the cancer was caused by contact with soot. Percival's theory led to a law being passed in Denmark, but not in Britain, requiring chimney sweeps to wear protective clothing and wash more regularly. The occurrence of scrotal cancer subsequently fell.

A number of industrial chemicals are known to cause cancer, that is they are **carcinogenic.** Asbestos is an example. In most countries there are laws designed to reduce the risks associated with such substances. However, worldwide, the chemicals that cause the most cancers are those found in cigarettes.

Cigarette smoke is a complicated aerosol containing a suspension of millions of tiny particles. There are many different compounds in cigarette smoke but **tars** are the ones responsible for lung cancer. In Britain lung cancer kills about 40 000 people a year and over 90 per cent of these deaths are due to smoking (see page 266).

*Figure 31.18 **A** and **B*** A cancerous cell divides more often than normal cells and gives rise to a mass of cancerous cells called a tumour. *C* The tumour may be carried to other parts of the body via blood vessels or the lymphatic system. This can give rise to new (secondary) cancers some distance from the original one. A tumour which spreads in this way is described as malignant.

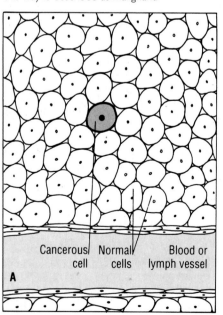

Cancerous cell Normal cells Blood or lymph vessel

A

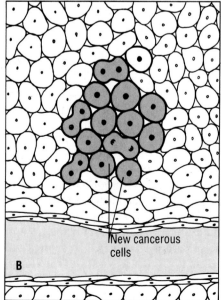

New cancerous cells

B

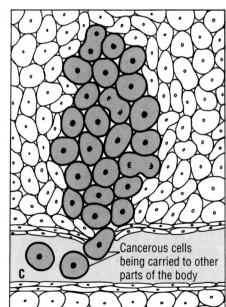

Cancerous cells being carried to other parts of the body

C

The extent to which our diet is responsible for cancer is less certain. Nevertheless, there is good evidence that a low fibre intake increases the chance of getting cancer of the bowel. It is also known that cancers of the breast and bowel are most common in countries where people eat a lot of fat. However, a causal link between these cancers and fat intake has yet to be established.

Sometimes cancer may be caused, not by external chemicals in the environment, but by an excess of naturally occurring substances inside the body – certain hormones for example. An example of this is given in the box on page 566.

Radiation

Several sorts of radiation may lead to cancer. Exposure to too much ultraviolet radiation in sunlight, especially if sunburn results, may lead to skin cancer developing, sometimes many years later. X-rays can damage the genetic material of a cell and cause cancer. The risks from X-rays are particularly great for the developing fetus, which is why pregnant women tend not to be given X-rays.

Nuclear power stations inevitably produce small amounts of radiation, just as coal mines produce coal dust. There is some evidence in Britain that the children of men who work in nuclear power stations may have a higher incidence of cancers of their white blood cells (**leukaemia**), though the evidence is still controversial. The accident at the nuclear plant in Chernobyl on 26 April 1986 contaminated millions of people in the then USSR (CIS) and northern Europe (figure 31.19). Mary Morrey, of Britain's National Radiological Protection Board, has estimated that Chernobyl will cause an extra 1000 deaths in the European Community, chiefly from cancer. The number of extra deaths in the CIS is more difficult to estimate, but will undoubtedly be many times this number.

Viruses

Some cancers are now known to be caused by viruses. It appears, for example, that **cervical cancer** (cancer of the cervix) is associated with the presence of **human papilloma viruses (HPVs)**. Some strains of these viruses may be passed on during sexual intercourse with an infected partner. In this sense cervical cancer behaves like a sexually transmitted disease. Some liver cancers are also believed to be caused by viruses.

Inherited cancers

Finally we come to the few cancers where heredity is implicated. Here no clear-cut pattern of inheritance is found. All we can say is that there is a tendency for certain cancers to run in families. This is the case, for instance, with a form of bowel cancer called familial polyposis coli.

Treating cancers

Treatments for cancer are improving all the time and many cancers can now often be cured. A number of techniques are used, but their common aim is to destroy the cancerous cells, while leaving the normal healthy cells intact.

The most direct treatment is **surgery**. Obviously surgery is most appropriate if the cancer is localised. If a cancer has spread to many regions of the body, other techniques have to be used. When surgery is used, the aim is to remove the entire tumour. Surgical techniques have now improved to the point where the cosmetic effects of the operation may hardly be noticed. For instance, surgical treatment of breast cancer nowadays rarely requires

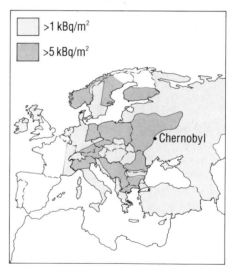

☐	>1 kBq/m²
■	>5 kBq/m²

Figure 31.19

A Aerial photograph of the Chernobyl nuclear power plant, near Kiev. Taken in May 1987, just over a year after the accident that devastated the plant and released large quantities of radioactive contaminants into the environment.

B Radioactive contamination as a result of the nuclear accident at Chernobyl on 26 April 1986. The pattern of contamination is the result of wind and rainfall. The becquerel (Bq) is a unit of radioacitve activity. 1 kBq corresponds to one thousand decays per second.

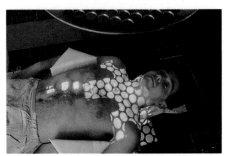

Figure 31.20 Person undergoing radiotherapy on a linear accelerator to treat Hodgkin's disease, a type of cancer. The illuminated discs over the patient's chest indicate the areas which are to receive X-rays. Other areas, such as the lungs, are protected from radiation by lead blocks.

the removal of the entire breast. Instead only the tumour itself may be removed, leading to almost no disfigurement.

A second way of treating cancers is to use high-energy ionising radiation to destroy the cancerous cells. This is called **radiotherapy** (figure 31.20). X-rays, gamma rays from a radioactive isotope such as cobalt, beams of electrons or beams of neutrons may be used depending on the type and position of the cancer.

A third technique in treating cancers is the use of drugs, i.e. **chemotherapy**. To understand how chemotherapeutic drugs work it helps to remember the details of the cell cycle. While a cell is in the first growth phase, its chromosomes are much less susceptible to these drugs than when they are in the other phases. Now cancerous cells spend less time in the first growth phase than do non-cancerous cells, simply because they spend so much of their time dividing. This means that chemotherapeutic drugs are more likely to kill cancerous cells than healthy ones. Can you now explain why chemotherapy may cause a patient's hair to fall out?

Oestrogens and breast cancer

Guest author Professor Vivian James explains how advances in biochemistry are helping to conquer breast cancer.

In the United Kingdom two women die of breast cancer every hour.

The causes of this distressing disease are not well understood, but an important clue came in the 1890s when a Glasgow surgeon, George Beatson, made a remarkable observation. He found that removing the ovaries of women with breast cancer produced, in some cases, a spectacular regression of tumour growth. Beatson had concluded from earlier veterinary studies that there was a functional relationship between the ovaries and mammary glands. We now know that the connection is provided by oestrogens, and Beatson's pioneering study pointed to the involvement of oestrogens in breast cancer.

Oestrogens are steroid hormones secreted by the ovaries which control sexual development (see page 598). We now know that a high proportion of breast tumours need oestrogens in order to grow, and that oestrogens act on the tumour cells via oestrogen receptors. These receptors, located in the tumour cells, are proteins which specifically bind with oestrogens to

form an oestrogen-receptor complex. This complex then activates a chain of events which leads to protein synthesis and growth.

This discovery led to the idea that the disease might be treated by removing the source of the oestrogens by, for example, removing the ovaries as Beatson did, or by administering drugs specifically designed to inactivate oestrogens. These anti-oestrogens are now widely used clinically.

An alternative approach is to use drugs which block oestrogen synthesis. One of the fundamental steps in the synthesis of oestrogen is the conversion of an androgen precursor to oestrogen, and this requires the participation of an enzyme called an aromatase. By using an aromatase inhibitor, it is possible to prevent the synthesis of oestrogen, thereby effectively depriving the patient of the hormone.

Only about 70 per cent of breast tumours contain oestrogen receptors, and of these only two-thirds respond to anti-oestrogen treatment, so clearly other factors are also involved. Further research has shown that tumours are dependent on polypeptides produced by the tumour cells themselves. These compounds are produced together with enzymes which break down the surrounding connective tissue, allowing the

tumour to spread locally. However, the effect of these growth factors can be counteracted by growth *inhibitory* factors which are produced by the normal healthy breast tissue. These inhibitory factors keep the tumour in check. The rate of tumour growth depends on the overall effect of these opposing factors.

The application of basic biochemical research has made it possible to recognise oestrogen-dependent tumours and thus identify patients who will respond to anti-oestrogen therapy. Anti-oestrogens, and inhibitors that block steroid synthesis, have offered an alternative method of treatment which is less traumatic than surgical removal of the ovaries.

What about the future? If we can find out more about the chemistry of the polypeptides which mediate the invasive growth of the tumour, we may be able to develop drugs that will counter their activities. And if we can characterise the growth inhibitory factors, we may be able to use them in the treatment of breast cancer.

Further advances in our understanding of the biology of tumour cell growth should pave the way to the development of better kinds of therapy, and eventually to the prevention of this distressing human disease.

Summary

1 Cell division is necessary for **growth, reproduction** and the **replacement** of old or damaged cells.

2 The sequence of events which takes place in a cell between successive cell divisions is known as the **cell cycle**. It is divided into the **M** (mitotic), G_1 (first growth), **S** (synthesis) and G_2 (second growth) phases.

3 The collective name given to the first growth phase, synthesis phase and second growth phase is **interphase**. DNA replication is confined to the synthesis phase.

4 The mitotic phase consists of **nuclear division (mitosis)** and **cytoplasmic division**.

5 Mitosis leads to the production of two **daughter cells**, each with the same number and types of chromosomes as the **parent cell**. Usually the cells contain two of each type of chromosome (**diploid state**).

6 Mitosis can be divided into four stages: **prophase** in which the chromosomes condense, **metaphase** in which they arrange themselves on the equator of the **spindle**, **anaphase** when they separate and are pulled towards the two **poles** by **spindle fibres**, and **telophase** in which two new nuclear envelopes form.

7 Nuclear division is followed by cytoplasmic division. In animal cells the membrane around the middle of the cell is drawn inwards by a ring of **actin filaments** to form a **cleavage furrow** which eventually divides the cell in two. In plant cells a new cell wall, the **cell plate**, grows across the middle of the cell as a result of deposition of substances by Golgi vesicles.

8 In **meiosis** the number of chromosomes is halved, the daughter cells receiving only one of each type of chromosome (**haploid state**).

9 Meiosis occurs in the production of **gametes** or **spores** and is necessary for sexual reproduction.

10 Meiosis consists of two successive divisions with no intervening replication of the genetic material. As a result four **haploid** cells are formed from a single **diploid** one.

11 In the first meiotic division **homologous chromosomes** separate from one another and go into different cells. In the second meiotic division the **sister** chromatids of each chromosome segregate into different cells.

12 Meiosis promotes **genetic variation** in three ways:

- the two chromsomes of each homologous pair carry different genetic material and end up in separate cells;
- the different pairs of homologous chromosomes **segregate independently**;
- **chiasmata** are usually found resulting in the exchange of genetic material (**crossing-over**) between non-sister chromatids.

13 **Cancers** are due to a breakdown in the control of the cell cycle. Cancerous cells divide more often than they should and form **tumours**.

14 Cancers may be caused by certain **chemicals**, by various sorts of **radiation**, by some **viruses** or they may even have a **hereditary component**.

15 At present cancers may be treated by **surgery**, high-energy ionising radiation (**radiotherapy**) or by certain drugs (**chemotherapy**). New methods of treatment are currently under research.

Review questions

1 Why does the cell cycle take so little time in some of the cells that line the gut?

2 In which other tissues would you expect cell division to proceed at a high rate and why?

3 A diploid cell can undergo mitosis or meiosis but a haploid cell can only undergo mitosis. Explain.

4 Distinguish precisely between homologous chromosomes, non-homologous chromosomes and chromatids.

5 What are the differences between cell division in animal cells and plant cells?

6 By means of a list, compare and contrast mitosis and meiosis.

7 Suggest how chemicals, radiation and viruses might each cause cancer.

8 Do you think there should be government health warnings on low fibre foods? Defend your answer.

9 Explain briefly the principles behind surgery, radiotherapy and chemotherapy as treatments for cancers.

10 Suggest why the incidence of most cancers increases with age.

Further reading

Chapter 13 on 'Cell Growth and Division' in *Molecular Biology of the Cell*, by Alberts et al. (Garland, 1989) is an extremely well written account of the cell cycle, mitosis and meiosis. However, it does go into a lot of detail.

Cancer by K. Sikora and H. Smedley (Heinemann Medical Books, 1988), provides a balanced and readable introduction to the subject of cancer.

CHAPTER 32   Patterns of reproduction

In the last chapter we looked at the cellular aspects of cell division and saw how cell division is necessary for reproduction as well as for growth and the replacement of old or damaged cells. In this chapter we shall look at reproduction, not at the cellular level, but from the perspective of the whole organism. We will concentrate on general aspects of reproduction, emphasising patterns rather than physiological details.

Asexual reproduction

Asexual reproduction does not involve combining genetic material from two different individuals. It therefore does not necessitate the production and fusion of gametes. Instead, one offspring produces near-identical copies of itself. The descendants produced asexually from a single individual belong to a **clone**. Unless mutation occurs, all the members of a clone share the same genetic constitution.

There is little doubt that asexual reproduction evolved long before sexual reproduction. However, it still occurs today. One reason is that it generally takes place very rapidly and so helps to maximise the production of offspring, particularly when environmental conditions are favourable.

For convenience, asexual methods of reproduction can be divided into a number of types:

- Fission.
- Spore formation.
- Budding.
- Fragmentation.
- Vegetative reproduction.
- Parthenogenesis.

Let us look briefly at each in turn.

Fission

In **fission** the organism divides into two or more equal-sized parts. **Binary fission**, the division of the organism into two or more daughter cells, is characteristic of prokaryotes and many protoctists (figure 32.1). The rate of multiplication achieved in this way can be prodigious: for example, in favourable conditions bacterial cells may divide once every 20 minutes, which means that in 24 hours a single cell can give rise to a population exceeding 4000 million million million (4×10^{21}).

This astronomical figure is achieved because the increase is exponential (see page 58): one cell divides into two, two into four, four into eight, and so on. In its early stages such exponential growth seems rather unimpressive, but it gains momentum as the numbers increase. To revert to bacteria dividing in two every 20 minutes, only eight exist at the end of the first hour, and only 512 by the end of the third hour. But by the end of a day ...! The principle is the same in compound interest. If 1p had been invested at just 1 per cent interest per year when Jesus was born, it would be worth over £4 million today.

Even higher reproductive rates are achieved by **multiple fission** which is shown by various protoctists, particularly parasitic ones. In this case the nucleus divides repeatedly and each daughter nucleus breaks away, together with a small portion of the cytoplasm. This splitting process is termed **schizogony**, and a cell that does it is called a **schizont** (see page 80).

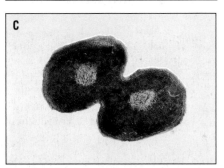

Figure 32.1 Electron micrographs showing three successive stages in the binary fission of the bacterium *Staphylococcus aureus*.

The details of schizogony vary, as do the number of offspring produced. In the malarial parasite, multiple fission will produce as many as 1000 merozoites from a single schizont during the parasite's asexual cycle in the liver. Multiple fission occurs again later when the merozoites divide inside the red blood cells. In this case multiplication is rather less prolific, not more than 24 daughter cells being formed from a single parent.

Spore formation

Spores are unicellular bodies formed by cell division in a parent organism. Having become detached from the parent they develop, directly or indirectly, into a new individual, provided environmental conditions are suitable. Spores are produced by prokaryotes, protoctists, fungi and many plants. They come in a wide range of forms, and are produced and dispersed in many different ways.

Spores are generally very small and light, which helps them to be distributed by wind, water or animals (figure 32.2). Some spores have thick resistant walls which enable them to survive unfavourable conditions, including drought (figure 32.3). They are usually numerous. The ability of fungi to produce vast numbers of airborne spores explains why members of this important group of saprobionts and parasites manage to spread so quickly. Spore formation in mosses and ferns will be considered in more detail later in this chapter.

Budding

In this method of reproduction an organism develops an outgrowth which, on detachment from the parent, becomes a self-supporting individual. Budding is characteristic of yeast cells (figure 32.4) and a wide variety of animals including *Hydra*, certain flatworms and several annelid groups. In multicellular animals like *Hydra* budding takes place by proliferation of undifferentiated cells which then develop into appropriate structures within the bud (figure 32.5).

Figure 32.2 Puffball releasing a cloud of spores.

Figure 32.3 During the Second World War experiments were carried out on Gruinard Island to investigate the possible use of spores of the bacterium *Anthracis* for biological warfare. This bacterium causes the deadly disease, anthrax. This photograph shows scientists decontaminating the island over forty years later, the spores having survived for this length of time.

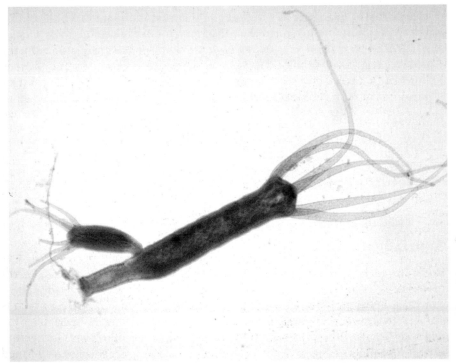

Figure 32.5 Budding in *Hydra*. The tiny perfectly formed bud can be seen on the left.

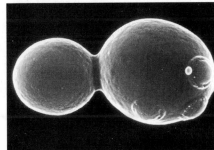

Figure 32.4 Scanning electron micrograph of a yeast cell budding.

569

Figure 32.6 The piggy back plant, a member of the saxifrage family, is a perennial herbaceous plant native to North America. New plants arise from the upper side of old leaves – hence the name 'piggy back plant'.

Fragmentation

Sometimes an organism may be broken into two or more pieces, each of which grows into a new individual. As a means of reproduction, fragmentation depends on the organism having good powers of **regeneration**. Sponges and hydroid coelenterates, for example, have astonishing powers of regeneration: if a sponge is macerated by passing it through fine gauze, the separated cells come together in groups and grow into new individuals. Given the right conditions, very small fragments of free-living flatworms will regenerate into new individuals, and in the marine nemertine worm *Lineus* dozens of individuals may be formed from a single worm.

Vegetative reproduction

Vegetative reproduction is the form of asexual reproduction in plants where parts of the body become detached and develop into new self-supporting individuals. Scores of examples could be given. One instance is provided by the piggy back plant. Here a new plant can sprout from a single leaf (figure 32.6). Vegetative reproduction is considered further in the next chapter.

Parthenogenesis

Parthenogenesis is the development of new individuals from an unfertilised egg. It is found in a number of animal and plant groups, even including some lizards.

- In **diploid parthenogenesis** the eggs, instead of being formed by meiosis, are formed by mitosis, with the result that they are diploid instead of haploid. The egg then divides by mitosis to give rise to a diploid adult. This is what happens at certain stages in the life cycle of aphids. In the summer months, wingless females produce further generations of mainly wingless females by diploid parthenogenesis, a rapid and efficient way of increasing numbers without necessitating the presence of males.

   In certain flowering plants an embryo may develop from a diploid cell in the ovule which has not undergone meiosis. As the embryo develops, the surrounding tissues form the seed and fruit in the usual way (see page 612). The formation of a plant embryo without the fusion of gametes occurs in a number of plants, including potatoes, citruses and dandelions. If you see a patch of dandelions it is quite likely to be the result of this kind of reproduction (figure 32.7).

- In **haploid parthenogenesis**, eggs are produced by meiosis in the usual way, and are therefore haploid. These develop, without being fertilised, into individuals whose cells are therefore haploid. A well known example of this type of parthenogenesis is seen in ants, bees and wasps (see page 547). In honeybees, for instance, haploid eggs laid by the queen develop into adult males (drones).

Sexual reproduction

In its broadest sense **sexual reproduction** is any process in which genetic material is transferred from one cell to another. Sexual reproduction generally involves the fusion of specialised sex cells called **gametes** which are derived from two different individuals. Gametes are always haploid, and they cannot develop further unless they fuse appropriately. However, sexual reproduction need not involve the production of gametes, as we can see in bacteria.

Figure 32.7 Despite the fact that they have bright flowers, most dandelion plants result not from sexual reproduction, but from the mitotic growth of a single diploid cell in the ovule.

Sexual reproduction in bacteria

Until the 1940s, bacteria were thought to be only capable of asexual reproduction. However, in 1946 Joshua Lederberg and Edward Tatum showed that the colon bacillus *Escherichia coli* can also reproduce sexually. They discovered that on coming into contact with another bacterium of the same species, an individual may develop one or more specialised tubes called **sex pili** (figure 32.8). One of these pili allows some of the DNA from the first bacterium to pass into the second. Experiments have shown that the longer the two bacteria are in contact, the more DNA passes from one to the other. Because this form of sexual reproduction requires two individuals to be in contact with each other, it is known as **conjugation** (literally 'joined together').

All *E. coli* look identical, so we cannot really talk about males and females. However, only some of them can produce sex pili. These particular bacteria have a special bit of DNA called an **F factor** (F standing for fertility). This is not part of the main bacterial DNA but a separate structure called a **plasmid**. The F factor carries genes for pili production and for the other functions needed to transfer DNA from the donor to the recipient bacterium. What happens is that this F factor can insert into the rest of the DNA and then cause some of it to pass into the recipient cell. Once in the recipient cell, some of the donor's genes may change places with corresponding genes of the recipient. This **recombination** may result in a bacterium with a new set of genes (figure 32.9).

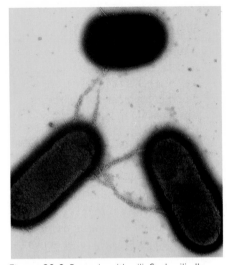

Figure 32.8 Bacteria with pili. Such pili allow DNA to pass between bacteria in a type of sexual reproduction known as conjugation.

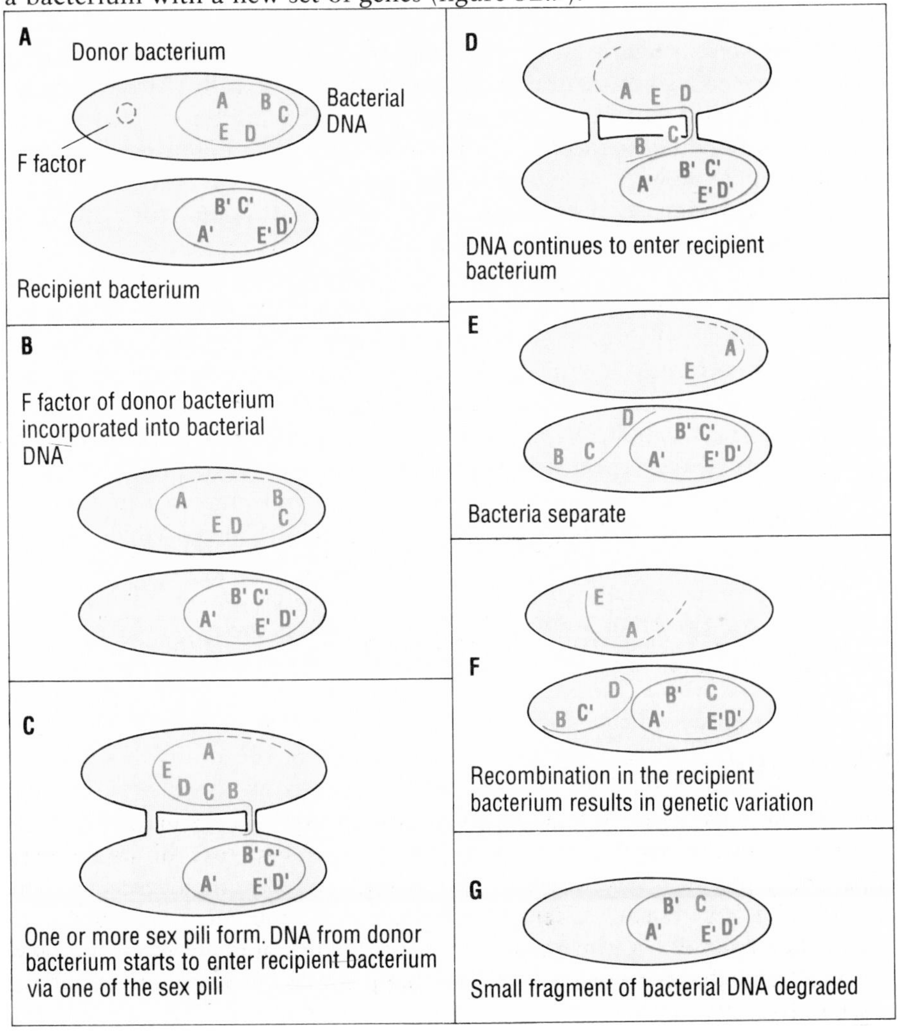

A
Donor bacterium
A B C E D — Bacterial DNA
F factor
B' C' A' E' D'
Recipient bacterium

B
F factor of donor bacterium incorporated into bacterial DNA
A B E D C
B' C' A' E' D'

C
A E D C B
B' C' A' E' D'
One or more sex pili form. DNA from donor bacterium starts to enter recipient bacterium via one of the sex pili

D
A E D
B C
A' B' C' E' D'
DNA continues to enter recipient bacterium

E
A E
D B C B' C' A' E' D'
Bacteria separate

F
E A
D B C B' C A' E' D'
Recombination in the recipient bacterium results in genetic variation

G
B' C A' E' D'
Small fragment of bacterial DNA degraded

Figure 32.9 Diagram to show the transfer of genetic material in bacterial conjugation.
A Each bacterium has a circular piece of DNA, shown here in the donor bacterium with genes ABCDE and in the recipient bacterium with genes A'B'C'D'E'. In addition, the donor bacterium has a small extra piece of DNA (a plasmid) known as an F factor.
B The F factor of the donor bacterium is incorporated into the bacterial DNA.
C One or more sex pili form between the donor and recipient bacteria, and the end of the donor DNA furthest from the F factor starts to pass into the recipient bacterium via one of the sex pili.
D More of the DNA from the donor bacterium enters the recipient bacterium.
E The link between the two bacteria breaks, leaving some of the DNA from the donor bacterium in the recipient cell.
F The genes C and C' swap over; this recombination in the recipient cell between the two homologous pieces of DNA results in genetic variation.
G The donor bacterium dies and disintegrates. Meanwhile, the fragments BC'D in the recipient are degraded, leaving a single bacterium with a new order of genes.

What are plasmids?

A plasmid is a small circular piece of DNA separate from the rest of a cell's DNA. They are found in bacteria and yeast and can replicate independently of the rest of the DNA. There may be several different plasmids in a single cell. Bacterial plasmids include the fertility factor (F factor), and plasmids that carry genes for resistance to antibiotics. Some plasmids may carry up to five resistance genes, each responsible for resistance to a different antibiotic.

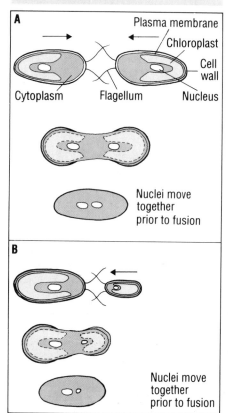

Figure 32.10 Gametes of the green alga *Chlamydomonas*.

A Most species produce gametes which are identical in structure, size and motility. They unite as shown: the gametes move towards each other, the cell walls are discarded, the chloroplasts break down, the gametes join and the nuclei fuse.

B *Chlamydomonas braunii* produces gametes which differ in size and the smaller gamete moves towards the larger one before they unite.

Another way in which sexual reproduction occurs in some bacteria is rather more straightforward. The bacterium simply takes up pieces of DNA from the environment across its cell wall in a process called **transformation**. On entering the cell the foreign DNA may, as in conjugation, be integrated into the bacterial DNA by recombination. Transformation falls within our definition of sexual reproduction because genetic material is transferred from one cell to another. The DNA might come, for instance, from an individual that has died and released its DNA to the environment.

Certain viruses provide a third way that the genes of different bacteria may be brought together. Essentially what happens is that the viruses carry bits of bacterial DNA from one bacterium to another in a process called **transduction**.

Evolutionary development of gametes

In most organisms, apart from bacteria, sexual reproduction involves the union of gametes, a process known as **syngamy** (literally 'joining together'). Generally the gametes differ from each other in structure, size and behaviour, for which reason they are known as **heterogametes**. Eggs and sperm, for example, are heterogametes. In organisms that have eggs and sperms syngamy takes place by the process of **fertilisation** in which a sperm penetrates an egg and donates its nucleus to it.

Some organisms, such as protoctists and fungi, produce gametes that are identical with each other (**isogamy**) or are only very slightly different (**anisogamy**) (figure 32.10). In many unicellular organisms, including the ones illustrated in figure 32.10, the gametes, as well as being identical with each other, are also structurally similar to the parent cells. At the simplest level there are no gametes at all, genetic material being transferred directly from one individual to another. This is essentially what happens in bacterial conjugation and, with certain elaborations, in some protoctists. We can therefore envisage a progression from bacterial conjugation through isogamy and anisogamy to heterogamy.

To be of genetic value syngamy must occur between gametes derived from different parents, and it is noteworthy that even in isogamous organisms fusion does not occur between gametes from the same parent. Although structurally identical, the gametes can recognise whether or not they come from the same parent, and react accordingly. In some protoctists and fungi, for example in pin mould (*Mucor*), it is possible to separate members of a single species into **plus** and **minus** strains: plus conjugates (fuses) with minus, but plus will not conjugate with plus, nor minus with minus. This foreshadows the existence of separate sexes which almost certainly arose later in evolution.

Some protoctists and fungi also show a tendency for one gamete to be migratory and the other stationary. This anticipates the existence of **sperm** and **eggs**. Fully differentiated eggs and sperm are found in organisms as different as seaweeds, mosses, cnidarians, insects and chordates. The sperm of different species differ somewhat in structure (figure 32.11). However, all sperm share the same fundamentals of smallness, the ability to swim and the posession of a haploid nucleus. Similarly, eggs always have a haploid nucleus, but are relatively large and non-motile. An egg receives genetic material from a sperm and provides nourishment for the developing embryo.

Sex is a risky business. Consider, for example, a female toad. When she mates she risks being drowned by the onslaught of male toads fighting amongst themselves to mate with her (figure 32.12). Not only that but she depends on her eggs being penetrated by sperms that contribute nothing but another individual's genes! Why doesn't she simply produce the same number of diploid eggs and avoid males altogether? In that way she would side-step the dangers of mating and produce offspring each of which would contain all her genes rather than only half her genes.

The answer is 'variation'. Although sex may be hazardous, it generates genetic variation. As we shall see in Chapter 43, much of this variation is harmful, but in the long run it provides the raw material for evolution. Organisms that reproduce asexually evolve more slowly than organisms that reproduce sexually. They therefore run the risk of their descendants being outcompeted by organisms resulting from sexual reproduction.

Cross fertilisation and self fertilisation

Two sorts of fertilisation are found in sexual reproduction:

- **Cross fertilisation** – the gametes come from two separate individuals.
- **Self fertilisation** – both gametes come from the same individual.

If sexual reproduction is geared towards generating genetic variation, we should expect organisms to favour cross fertilisation rather than self fertilisation. This is just what we see in nature. Some plants, such as certain violets for instance, can reproduce both by self fertilisation and by cross fertilisation. In such cases self fertilisation is used as a back up, only adopted if cross fertilisation fails to occur for some reason.

Evolution of reproductive methods

Fundamental to sexual reproduction is the method by which gametes are brought together. At its simplest this takes place by the gametes of both sexes being liberated into the surrounding water as occurs, for instance, in seaweeds and many fish. In animals this sort of fertilisation is known as **external fertilisation**. It is found in many aquatic organisms and in certain terrestrial ones, such as the toads in figure 32.12 that return to water for breeding. In most terrestrial animals, however, fertilisation occurs inside the body of the female (**internal fertilisation**). Generally internal fertilisation necessitates the use of some kind of **intromittent organ** (e.g. a **penis**) to introduce the sperm into the female's body.

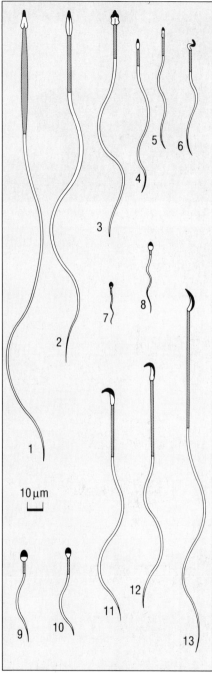

Figure 32.11 Structural variety in mammalian sperm. 1–6 are sperm of Australian marsupials; 7–13 are from placental mammals. 1 honey possum; 2 marsupial rat; 3 short-nosed brindled bandicoot; 4 tammar wallaby; 5 brush-tailed possum; 6 koala; 7 hippopotamus; 8 human; 9 rabbit; 10 sheep; 11 golden hamster; 12 brown rat; 13 Chinese hamster. Although the sperm shown differ considerably in structure, they all share the features of small size, motility and possession of a haploid nucleus. The detailed structure of sperm is described on page 586.

Figure 32.12 External fertilisation in the common toad. Several males are attempting to mate with the single female at the bottom of the pile.

Figure 32.13 Many mammals look after their young long after they are weaned. Here an adult female bear helps her three cubs learn how to fish.

Internal fertilisation has two advantages over external fertilisation:

- It is a surer method since, from the point of view of both the male and the female, there is less chance of gametes being wasted.
- It means that the fertilised egg can be enclosed within a protective covering before it leaves the female's body (**oviparity**). This is what happens in animals that lay eggs. Some animals take this idea further and the embryos develop within the female parent and derive nourishment from her (**viviparity**). This reaches its greatest development in those mammals which nourish their developing young before birth by means of a placenta.

Comparable mechanisms occur in terrestrial plants. They may not possess intromittent organs as such, but special techniques have evolved for transferring the male gametes to the egg cells, after which early development of the embryo takes place within the body of the parent plant.

Many organisms desert their offspring as soon as they have been produced as fertilised eggs. Others provide some sort of **parental care**. For example, the male stickleback looks after the fertilised eggs in a defended territory and fans them, to provide oxygen, until they hatch and swim away (see page 534).

By and large, the more parental care provided, the fewer the number of offspring produced. At one extreme, certain types of fish produce over 100 million eggs at a spawning. At the other, certain mammals, including ourselves, usually produce only one offspring at a time. Mammals continue to provide maternal care after birth in the form of milk production (**lactation**). Even after the offspring have been weaned, parental care may be provided by one or other parent, usually the mother, who protects the young as they grow up and helps them learn how to survive in their environment (figure 32.13).

The life cycle

An organism's **life cycle** is the sequence of events from fertilisation in one generation to fertilisation in the next generation.

In the course of its life cycle, an organism normally produces a new generation of individuals which repeat the process. New generations are produced by **reproduction**, which we have seen may be either asexual or sexual. We will start by looking briefly at the life cycle of the human which, despite the structural complexity of the adult, is comparatively simple (figure 32.14).

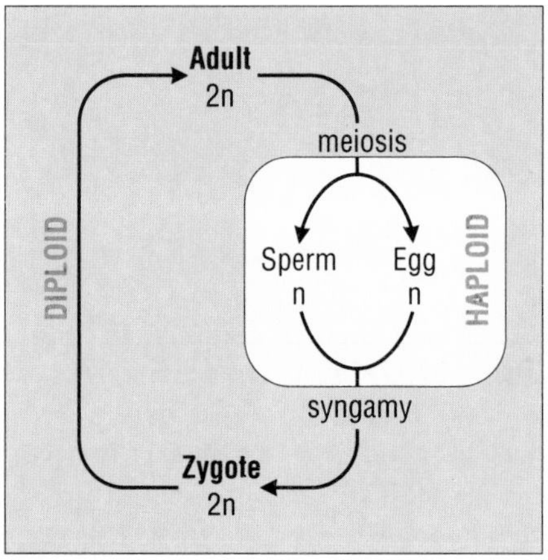

The life cycle of the human

An adult human produces either eggs or sperm. If these gametes fuse successfully, a **zygote** is formed which may develop into a new adult. The details of this complicated process are discussed in Chapters 33 and 35. At present we are only concerned with the overall picture. Almost all the cells of an adult human are diploid, the only exception being the gametes. These are formed by meiosis and are therefore haploid. When a sperm and an egg fuse as a result of fertilisation, a zygote results. Since it is formed by the union of two haploid gametes, the zygote is diploid; and as it divides mitotically, the adult to which it gives rise will also be diploid.

Meiosis and syngamy divide the life cycle into two distinct phases: the **diploid phase**, which spans the zygote and the adult, and the **haploid phase**, containing only the gametes. This is shown in figure 32.14.

The majority of animals have life cycles which conform to the same

Figure 32.14 The life cycle of the human and most other animals follows the plan outlined here. There is considerable variation in different animals as to the way the zygote develops into the adult, but the fundamental division of the life cycle into diploid and haploid phases is the same throughout.
n = haploid; 2n = diploid.

general plan seen in humans, though there are a number of variations on the theme. For example, one or more **larval stages** may be interpolated between the zygote and the adult, as in amphibians, certain insects and a number of parasites (see page 633). While the existence of larval stages increases the general complexity of the life cycle, it in no way affects the overall pattern seen in figure 32.14.

Alternation of generations

An important departure from the basic life cycle described above is seen in certain seaweeds and in mosses, liverworts and ferns. In these organisms gametes are produced by *mitosis* from a haploid **gametophyte** (literally 'gamete plant'). The gametophyte is sexually mature and the gametes that result are haploid, in the usual way. These gametes fuse to produce a diploid zygote, but this cannot, being diploid, develop into a new gametophyte. Instead it grows (by mitotic cell divisions) into another individual which is quite distinct from the gametophyte.

The function of this individual is to produce **spores**, for which reason it is referred to as the **sporophyte** (literally 'spore plant'). Formed by meiosis, and therefore haploid, spores are small, light and readily dispersed. When they alight on a suitable surface, they germinate and grow by mitosis into a gametophyte, which then repeats the sequence of events. This kind of life cycle is summarised in figure 32.15.

From this brief account it is clear that the life cycle of a moss or fern contains two distinct stages, a haploid gametophyte and a diploid sporophyte, which alternate with each other within the life cycle. This phenomenon is known as **alternation of generations**. These two generations are shown in figure 32.16. Let us now see how they fit together in the life cycles of mosses and ferns.

The life cycles of mosses and ferns

Figure 32.15 is a general outline of the life cycle of any organism showing alternation of generations and takes no account of the variations and complexities of individual species. Figures 32.17 and 32.18 show how the life cycles of a common moss and fern conform to this general pattern. We

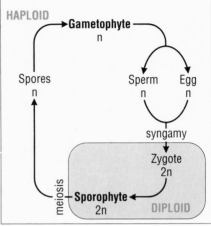

Figure 32.15 The life cycle of many plants, notably ferns and mosses, shows alternation of generations in which a haploid gamete-producing gametophyte alternates with a diploid, spore-producing sporophyte. Notice that, as in animals, meiosis and syngamy divide the life cycle into haploid and diploid phases.

Figure 32.16
A Moss showing the diploid sporophytes growing out of the leafy gametophytes.
B Fern showing the haploid gametophyte from which the young diploid sporophyte is beginning to grow.

advise you to concentrate on the overall picture, rather than the details. The two figure captions need be read only if you require a detailed understanding of the two life cycles.

As you can see from figures 32.17 and 32.18, in both mosses and ferns the gametophyte bears special gamete-forming organs:

- **Antheridia** which produce sperm;
- **Archegonia** which produce eggs.

Various methods exist by which sperm are released from the antheridia and brought into contact with the eggs. The result of the union of a sperm with an egg is a diploid zygote which grows into a sporophyte. In mosses this is attached to, and dependent on, the gametophyte; in ferns, though, the sporophyte is a separate self-supporting plant. In both cases the spores are formed in specialised spore-bearing structures called **sporangia** from which they are released by dispersal mechanisms which ensure that they are scattered over a wide area. The spores, if they germinate, grow into gametophytes.

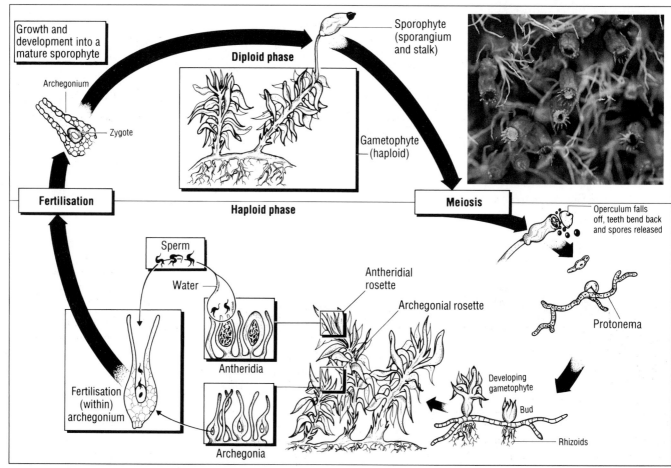

Figure 32.17 Life cycle of a moss such as *Funaria*. In spring, egg-containing archegonia and sperm-producing antheridia are found amongst the leaves of the haploid gametophyte. For fertilisation to occur, the antheridial and archegonial rosettes must contain water. Sperm are released by rupture of the antheridia. At the same time the necks of the archegonia open, creating an open passage through which the sperm can swim to the eggs. This movement of sperm from antheridia to archegonia is thought to be aided by rain-splash. After fertilisation, the zygote grows into the sporophyte which remains attached to, and dependent on, the gametophyte. Spores develop by meiosis within a spore sac inside the sporangium (capsule). In dry weather the operculum falls off and the flexible teeth bend outwards. The tissues near the opening of the capsule dry out and the haploid spores are released, to be dispersed by wind and air currents. On landing on moist ground, each spore germinates into a green filamentous protonema which produces buds that grow into the gametophyte, thus completing the life cycle.

The two life cycles are therefore basically similar but differ in detail. The most noticeable difference is the relative emphasis which each places on the gametophyte and sporophyte. In mosses the gametophyte is the dominant generation, the sporophyte being comparatively simple in structure, short-lived and dependent – almost parasitic – on the gametophyte. In ferns it is the other way round. The sporophyte is the dominant generation: it is large (some tree ferns are over seven metres high), differentiated into leaf, stem and roots with vascular tissues and a complex internal organisation on a level with that of a flowering plant. By comparison, the gametophyte of a fern (or **prothallus** as it is called) is quite insignificant. A mere millimetre or two in diameter, it is a flat plate of photosynthetic cells anchored to the soil by thin root-like rhizoids.

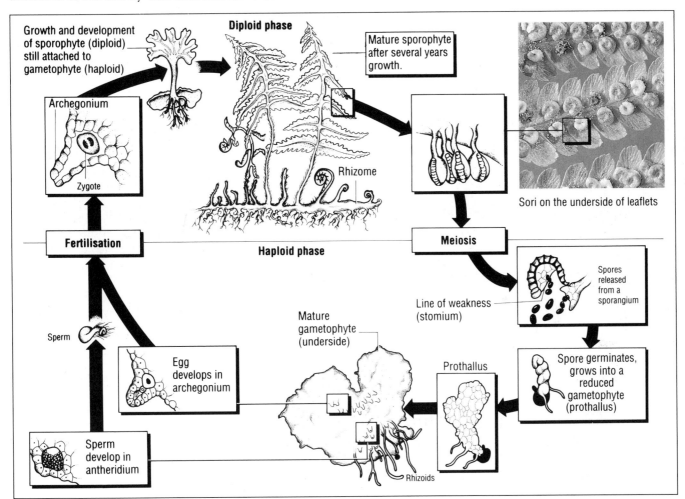

Figure 32.18 Life cycle of the fern *Dryopteris*. The prominent sporophyte (diploid) consists of a horizontal rhizome (underground stem) from which vertically-growing fronds (leaves) arise. The rhizome overwinters, new fronds being formed from it each year. On the undersides of sporophylls (spore-bearing leaflets), groups of sporangia develop. Each group, protected by an umbrella-like shield, is called a sorus, and inside the sporangia haploid spores are formed by meiosis. The mature sporangium (capsule) is topped by a row of cells which in dry weather readily lose water by evaporation. The resulting tension ruptures the capsule at the stomium, thereby releasing the spores. If moisture is present, each spore germinates into a simple heart-shaped prothallus, a flat plate of photosynthetic cells anchored to the soil by filamentous rhizoids. The prothallus is a reduced gametophyte: antheridia and archegonia, located on its underside, produce sperm and eggs respectively. The gametophyte depends on a damp environment, not only to prevent it drying out, but also for transference of sperm. After rupture of the antheridium, the ciliated sperm swim to an egg cell at the base of an archegonium where fertilisation occurs. The zygote grows into a young sporophyte which, once it has established roots and leaves, becomes self-supporting, thus completing the cycle. Note that in contrast to the life cycle of the moss, in ferns the sporophyte is the dominant generation, the gametophyte being much reduced.

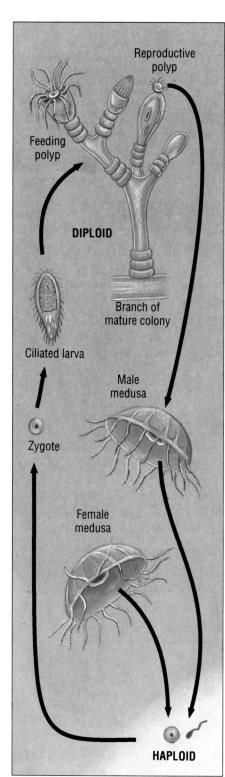

Reproductive polyp

Feeding polyp

DIPLOID

Branch of mature colony

Ciliated larva

Male medusa

Zygote

Female medusa

HAPLOID

Figure 32.19 Life cycle of the colonial hydroid *Obelia*. Can you see why, despite the general resemblance to figures 32.17 and 32.18, there is no true alternation of generations?

Reduction of the gametophyte

Alternation of generations is basic to the life cycle of almost all plant groups. It is most clearly seen in mosses, liverworts and ferns, where both generations can readily be seen. In other groups the pattern may be obscured by the gametophyte generation being reduced or absent and the sporophyte being correspondingly prominent.

We have already seen this to some extent in ferns where the gametophyte is dwarfed by the sporophyte. But it is in the conifers and flowering plants that the dominance of the sporophyte is seen most dramatically.

Flowering plants

Consider a flowering plant such as a buttercup or oak tree. The bulk of the plant is the sporophyte; the gametophyte is hidden away inside the sporophyte. We have seen that the function of a sporophyte is to produce spores, and this is precisely what happens in a flowering plant. In fact flowering plants, in common with conifers and certain fern-like groups, have two types of spores:

- Very small **microspores** from which male gametes are derived.
- Larger **megaspores** from which female gametes are derived.

The details of how these spores are produced and what happens to them will have to wait until we look at the way flowering plants reproduce – the subject of the next chapter. Here it is sufficient to note that flowering plants represent the end product of a line of evolution in which the gametophyte, a prominent self-supporting plant in groups such as the mosses, gradually degenerates until eventually it becomes incorporated into the body of the sporophyte. Meanwhile the sporophyte gains in structural importance, being very much the dominant generation in ferns, and even more so in flowering plants.

Exactly why this evolutionary trend towards the dominance of the sporophyte generation has occurred is far from clear. It may be because the sporophyte, being diploid, is able to 'hide' the effect of harmful recessive alleles (see page 679). Alternatively (or in addition) it may be an adaptation to life on land: the gametophyte, with its dependence on water, is suppressed and reproduction is based on the production of seeds. This is characteristic both of conifers and flowering plants.

Alternation of generations in animals?

Do animals show alternation of generations? At first sight the answer might appear to be yes. After all, butterflies and a number of other insects *appear* to show an alternation in their life cycles between the imago (adult) and the caterpillar (see page 634). But for this to be regarded as true alternation of generations, in the sense that we have been using the term here, it would have to be shown that the caterpillar, like the sporophyte, is capable of asexual reproduction and the imago, like the gametophyte, is haploid. In fact neither is true.

A seemingly more likely case is found in cnidarians. The colonial hydroids like *Obelia* show an alternation between a gamete-producing jellyfish-like medusa, and an asexually reproducing hydra-like polyp (figure 32.19). On grounds of reproduction this would seem to be a genuine alternation of generations. However, it does not qualify from the genetic point of view, for both the medusa and the polyp are diploid, meiosis occuring in the formation of the gametes. In fact, true alternation of generations is not known in the animal kingdom.

Summary

1 Reproduction can be **sexual** or **asexual**. Asexual reproduction produces offspring which, in the absence of mutations, are genetically identical to one another and to their parent. Sexual reproduction, in contrast, confers genetic variation.

2 The descendants produced asexually from a single individual belong to a **clone**.

3 Asexual methods of reproduction include **binary** and **multiple fission, spore formation, budding, fragmentation, vegetative reproduction** and **parthenogenesis**.

4 Sexual reproduction is any process by which genetic material is transferred from one organism to another.

5 Three sorts of sexual reproduction are found in bacteria: **conjugation** in which contact between two bacteria is required; **transformation** in which a single bacterium picks up a bit of DNA from its environment; and **transduction** in which the passage of genetic information from one bacterium to another is mediated by a virus.

6 Sexual reproduction usually involves the union of haploid **gametes** to form a diploid **zygote**. Gametes may be identical (**isogamy**), or they may differ from each other with respect to their structure, size and behaviour (**heterogamy**).

7 In some cases of isogamy, individuals cannot be separated into males and females, but can be classified into **plus** or **minus** strains. Plus and minus strains can mate with each other but not amongst themselves.

8 The structure of **eggs** and **sperm** is related to their functions: sperm are motile vehicles for the male's genetic material, eggs receive genetic material from sperm and provide nourishment for embryos.

9 Many aquatic animals show **external fertilisation**. Most terrestrial animals have **internal fertilisation** with **oviparity** or **viviparity**. In mammals nourishment of the embryo is provided by a **placenta, lactation** occurs after birth and there may be subsequent **parental care**.

10 The progressive sequence of changes which a species goes through from fertilisation in one generation to fertilisation in the next is known as the **life cycle**.

11 In organisms with sexual reproduction, **meiosis** (halving of the chromosome number) and **syngamy** (union of gametes) divide the life cycle into **haploid** and **diploid** phases.

12 In animals, the haploid phase is represented only by the gametes. However, in mosses, ferns and certain other organisms, the life cycle shows an **alternation of generations** between a haploid gamete-producing **gametophyte** and a diploid **sporophyte** that produces haploid **spores**.

13 In mosses the gametophyte is the dominant generation, the sporophyte being attached to, and dependent upon, the gametophyte. In ferns the sporophyte is the dominant generation, the gametophyte being reduced. In both groups wet conditions are needed for the gametophyte to reproduce.

14 Conifers and flowering plants continue the trend seen in ferns towards reduction of the gametophyte. The rise of the sporophyte as the dominant generation may be an adaptation to life on dry land. It may also provide a way of suppressing harmful recessive alleles.

15 Certain animals have an asexually reproducing stage in their life cycle, but alternation of generations in the genetic sense is not known in the animal kingdom.

Review questions

1 List and distinguish between the various types of asexual reproduction.

2 Why do you think multiple fission is found particularly in endoparasites?

3 Budding is rare in organisms that have a large number of different cell types. Why do you think this is?

4 What are the fundamental differences between sexual reproduction in bacteria and mammals?

5 Which do you think came first in evolution – isogamy or heterogamy? Suggest reasons for your answer.

6 Draw a graph to illustrate what you think might be the relationship between the number of offspring a female produces and the amount of energy she invests in each of them. How might you test your hypothesis?

7 Given the advantages of internal fertilisation, can you suggest reasons why external fertilisation has persisted to this day?

8 What are the essential similarities and differences between the life cycles of a moss and a fern?

9 'In plants, gametes are produced by mitosis'. Comment on this statement.

10 Can you suggest why alternation of generations is not found in animals?

Further reading

If you want to find out more about patterns of reproduction in bacteria, fungi, algae or plants, *Green Plants and their Allies* by Tim King (Nelson, 1983) is an excellent source.

For an original and extremely interesting approach to life cycles, read Geoff Harper's paper 'Teaching life cycles: the four-dimensional organism', *Journal of Biological Education* (1987) **21**, 107-116.

CHAPTER 33   Reproduction of the mammal

In the last chapter we looked at the general principles of reproduction as illustrated by a wide range of organisms. In this chapter we shall look at mammalian reproduction with particular reference to the human.

In delving into the problem of how mammals reproduce their kind, three issues need to be addressed:

- How and where are the gametes produced and what is their structure?
- How are the gametes brought into contact with each other?
- What happens to the zygote?

These questions cannot be answered without a sound understanding of the anatomy of the reproductive system so we shall start with that.

Anatomy of the human reproductive system

Before getting down to details, it is useful to remind ourselves of what the reproductive system has to do. The male system has to produce sperm and ensure that they reach the appropriate part of the female. The female system has to receive the sperm, enable them to fertilise an egg, and incubate and nourish the developing embryo.

The anatomy of the human male and female reproductive systems is shown in figures 33.1 and 2. Notice that both consist essentially of a tube – the **genital tract** – which runs from the **gonad** (**ovary** or **testis**) to the exterior. The gonads and the tubes leading from them are paired (one on each side of the body). The tubes converge in the midline to form a single median tube which leads to the exterior.

The genital tract is not a uniform tube but is differentiated into a series of parts. In the female these are:

Figure 33.1 The reproductive system of the human female in ventral view. In **A** the ovary and oviduct are shown in their natural positions on the left hand side of the picture. On the right side the oviduct has been deflected upwards so as to expose the whole of the ovary, and the organs have been sliced horizontally so as to show their internal structure. In **B** the hymen is still intact. Note that the urinary and vaginal openings, though separate, are very close to each other.

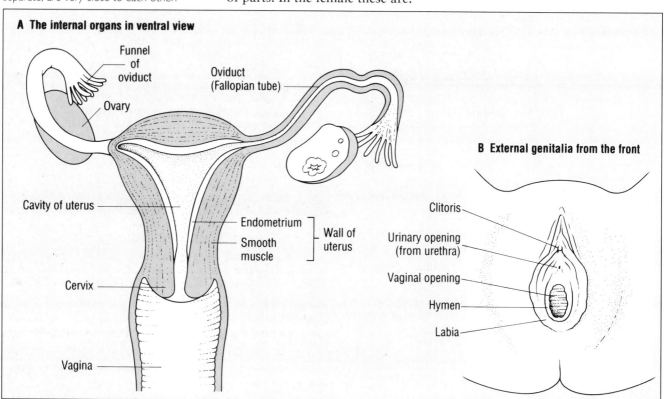

A The internal organs in ventral view

Funnel of oviduct

Ovary

Oviduct (Fallopian tube)

Cavity of uterus

Endometrium

Smooth muscle

Wall of uterus

Cervix

Vagina

B External genitalia from the front

Clitoris

Urinary opening (from urethra)

Vaginal opening

Hymen

Labia

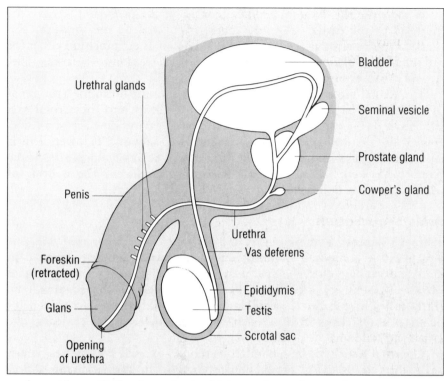

Labels in figure:
Bladder
Seminal vesicle
Prostate gland
Cowper's gland
Urethral glands
Penis
Urethra
Vas deferens
Foreskin (retracted)
Epididymis
Glans
Testis
Opening of urethra
Scrotal sac

Figure 33.2 The reproductive system of the human male in side view. Notice that the urethra receives the tube from the bladder as well as the vas deferens. It is therefore a common urinogenital duct carrying both urine and sperm to the exterior.

- the **oviducts** (**Fallopian tubes**) which run from the ovaries to
- the **uterus** whose lower end, the **cervix**, leads to
- the **vagina**, which runs to the exterior.

Primates are unusual in having a simple uterus of the sort depicted in figure 33.1. Most mammals have a Y-shaped uterus, with the two sides of the Y extending up towards the ovaries. The oviducts are correspondingly short. With its extra capacity, this kind of uterus can accommodate numerous embryos at the same time and is therefore well suited to the production of litters.

The main parts of the male genital tract are:

- the **vas deferens** which runs from each testis to
- the **urethra** which runs down the **penis** to the exterior.

Three important glands open into the vas deferens and urethra: they are the **seminal vesicles, prostate** (*not* 'prostrate'!) and **Cowper's glands**. We shall see what they do later.

Notice that the reproductive system is closely associated with the urinary system. Indeed, in the male the urethra is a common passage for both sperm and urine. For this reason the two systems are usually considered together as the **urinogenital system**. In the female the two systems are separate, but the urinary and genital (vaginal) openings are very close together and both form part of the **external genitalia**.

The external genitalia

The external genitalia are those parts of the urinogenital system which are visible externally. In the female they consist of the **vulva** which contains the urinary and vaginal openings. The vulva is flanked on either side by folds of skin called **labia** (literally 'lips') and at the anterior end by the **clitoris**. In the young female the vaginal opening is partly covered by a fold of tissue, the **hymen**, which is usually stretched and opened during adolescence or the first time intercourse occurs.

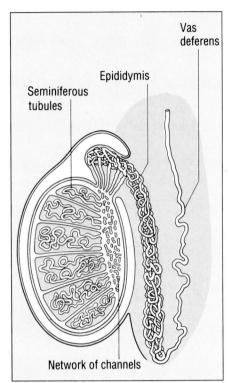

Figure 33.3 Internal structure of a human testis. Far more seminiferous tubules exist than are shown here. Each testis contains about 1000 of them, giving a total length of approximately 500 metres.

In the male the external genitalia consist of the **penis** and **scrotal sac**. The head of the penis, called the **glans**, is covered by the **foreskin**. The foreskin may be removed in the operation known as **circumcision** either for traditional or religious reasons or for medical reasons – for example, because the foreskin is tight.

The scrotal sac contains the testes. The testes start off in the abdominal cavity, but before or soon after birth they descend into the scrotal sac. Because of their position outside the abdominal cavity, they are at a lower temperature than the general body temperature – about 5°C lower. This is important because sperm will only form at this lower temperature. If the scrotal sac is kept too warm fewer sperm are produced. The wearing of tight Y-fronts has done nothing to improve male fertility!

Inside the scrotum

Figure 33.3 shows a human testis and associated structures in detail. The testis itself is composed of numerous **seminiferous tubules** arranged in bundles. It is here that the sperm are formed. The seminiferous tubules converge upon a network of interconnected channels which leads to a long, tightly coiled tube called the **epididymis**. The epididymis lies to one side of the testis and it leads to the much wider vas deferens which leaves the scrotal sac and joins the urethra.

The total length of the seminiferous tubules exceeds 500 metres, which makes the rate of sperm production prodigious. In normal circumstances the seminiferous tubules and epididymis will be full of sperm. How they are produced and what happens to them will be explained next.

Gametogenesis

The formation of gametes is called **gametogenesis**. The overall sequence of events is essentially the same in both sexes. Three stages are recognised:

- **Phase of multiplication**: diploid cells in the embryo, destined to give rise to gametes, divide repeatedly by mitosis.

- **Phase of growth**: the daughter cells resulting from the mitotic divisions grow in size.

- **Phase of maturation**: the products of the growth phase divide by meiosis, and the haploid daughter cells differentiate into the appropriate gametes (eggs or sperm).

Now let us look at the details of gametogenesis in the two sexes. Sperm-formation is called **spermatogenesis**, egg-formation **oogenesis**. Figure 33.4 shows the two processes side by side so that they can be compared.

In spermatogenesis the products of the initial phase of multiplication grow into **spermatocytes**. The latter divide by meiosis to form haploid **spermatids** which differentiate into **spermatozoa**. The way the sperms are formed by repeated cell divisions means that the total number of sperms is very great indeed.

Oogenesis is basically similar to spermatogenesis, but differs from it in detail. Most of the cells formed by the initial phase of multiplication degenerate, but some of them grow into **oocytes**. The amount of growth that takes place at this stage is much greater than in spermatogenesis – this is what makes eggs so much larger than sperms. The oocyte now undergoes meiosis, but the divisions are unequal resulting in four daughter cells that differ greatly in size. One of the cells remains large and becomes the egg cell

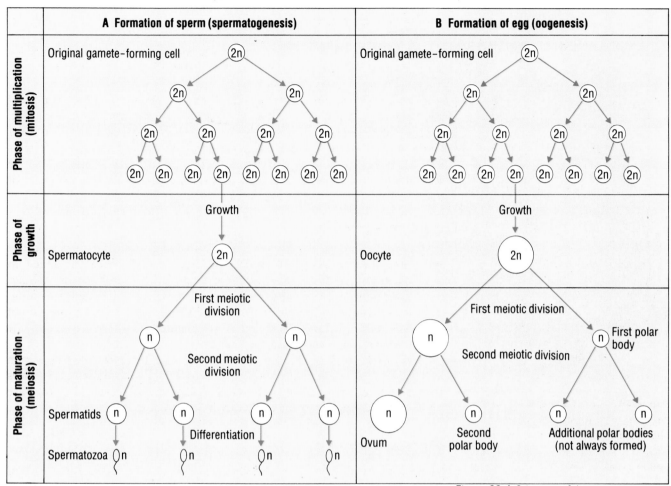

Figure 33.4 Summary of the way sperm and eggs are formed in a mammal (gametogenesis). Notice that the sequence of events is essentially the same in both cases. In spermatogenesis all the cells resulting from the phase of multiplication develop into spermatocytes. In oogenesis only some of the cells resulting from the phase of multiplication develop into oocytes; the rest degenerate. The second meiotic division in oogenesis usually occurs immediately after fertilisation.

(**ovum**). The other cells are small non-functional **polar bodies** which eventually degenerate.

In spermatogenesis all four products of meiosis become functional sperms, but in oogenesis only one becomes a functional egg. The polar bodies are the inevitable result of the fact that meiosis involves two successive divisions; they simply serve as a depository for unwanted chromosomes, thereby ensuring that the ovum is haploid.

Gametogenesis takes place in the gonads: spermatogenesis in the testes and oogenesis in the ovaries. To see gametes at various stages of formation it is necessary to look at sections of these organs under the microscope.

Microscopic structure of the testis

The testis is packed full of seminiferous tubules, and spermatogenesis takes place in their walls. Most of the initial cell multiplication takes place while the testis is still developing in the embryo, and the cells resulting from this can be seen in the outer part of the wall of the seminiferous tubules just beneath the surrounding connective tissue.

As cell divisions proceed, the daughter cells get pushed towards the lumen of the tubule, and spermatocytes can be seen undergoing meiosis into spermatids. The final transformation of spermatids to spermatozoa takes place in the part of the wall immediately adjacent to the lumen. At this stage the heads of the developing sperm are embedded in large **Sertoli cells,** and their tails project into the fluid-filled lumen of the tubule.

The Sertoli cells span the wall of the seminiferous tubule from the

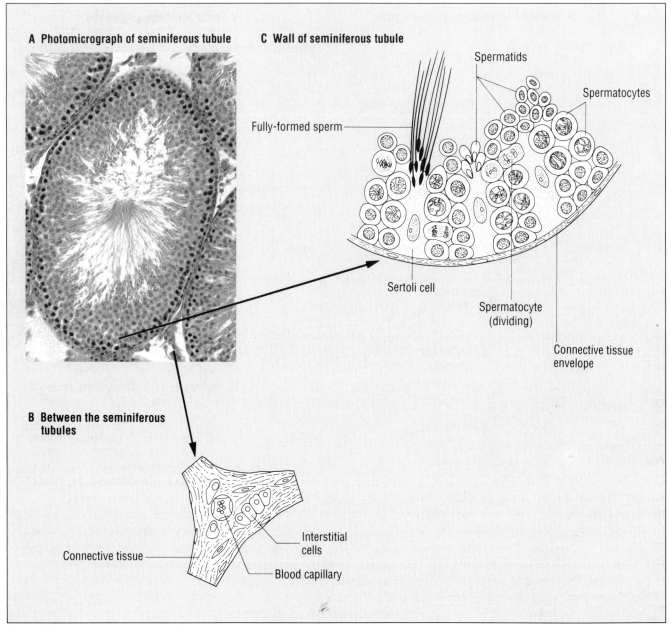

A Photomicrograph of seminiferous tubule

C Wall of seminiferous tubule

Spermatids

Spermatocytes

Fully-formed sperm

Sertoli cell

Spermatocyte
(dividing)

Connective tissue
envelope

B Between the seminiferous tubules

Connective tissue

Interstitial cells

Blood capillary

Figure 33.5 Microscopic structure of the mammalian testis.

A Section of the testis under the light microscope. One complete seminiferous tubule is visible, with parts of several others round the edge of the section. Notice the sperm tails projecting into the lumen of the tubule. Magnification × 300.

B Part of the wall of a seminiferous tubule showing spermatogenesis. Sperms can be seen in various stages of development, nourishment coming from the Sertoli cells.

C Tissue between adjacent seminiferous tubules showing the interstitial cells which secrete male hormones (androgens).

connective tissue envelope to the lumen. Their function is to nourish the sperm-forming cells and provide them with the right environment for undergoing meiosis. In addition they secrete the fluid which fills the lumen, and they phagocytose foreign particles.

Eventually the mature sperm become detached from the Sertoli cells and are released into the lumen of the seminiferous tubule. They are not yet motile as their tails cannot wave, so they move passively along the seminiferous tubules towards the epididymis. Motility is gradually acquired, and by the time the sperm reach the epididymis the tails are waving vigorously.

Sperm have a limited life span; if they are not discharged from the male genital tract, they degenerate and are either resorbed or, more usually, lost via the urine.

For spermatogenesis to take place **male sex hormones** are needed. These are secreted by prominent **interstitial cells** between the seminiferous tubules. You can see them in figure 33.5, together with the blood capillaries into which they release their secretion.

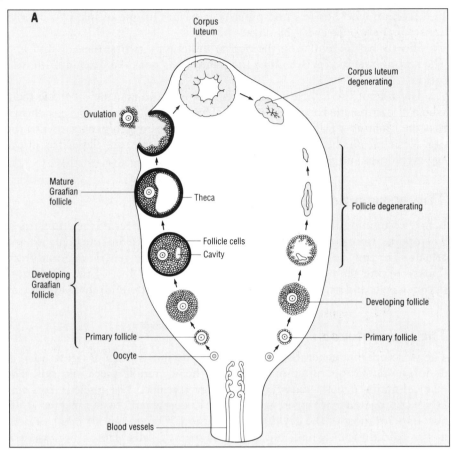

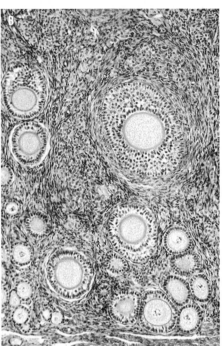

Figure 33.6 Microscopic structure of the mammalian ovary.

A Diagram of the whole ovary. On the left side of the diagram an oocyte is shown developing into a Graafian follicle which, after ovulation, turns into a corpus luteum (yellow body) and then degenerates. Only a small proportion of the oocytes develop into a corpus luteum. Most of them degenerate, as shown on the right side of the picture.

B Part of an ovary as it appears in a section under the microscope – not quite as neatly organised as the diagram! Magnification × 150.

Microscopic structure of the ovary

Compared with the testis, which is made up of numerous tubules, the ovary is a more solid mass of tissue (figure 33.6). Oocytes, resulting from cell multiplication and growth in the embryo, may be seen towards the edge of the ovary. Each oocyte is surrounded by a layer of **follicle cells**. The whole structure, about 50 μm in diameter, is called a **primary follicle**. At birth there are between 200 000 and 400 000 primary follicles in each ovary, but only 200 to 400 complete their development. The rest degenerate into cyst-like bodies which never produce eggs. One can be seen on the right hand side of figure 33.6.

You can see what happens to one of the viable follicles on the left hand side of figure 33.6. First the follicle cells surrounding the oocyte proliferate to form a wall many cells thick. As this occurs, a fluid collects between the cells, forming little pools. As more and more fluid accumulates, the pools coalesce, eventually forming one large fluid-filled cavity. The follicle grows and the oocyte finishes up embedded in a little hillock of follicle cells projecting into the cavity. Meanwhile connective tissue inside the ovary forms a protective sheath surrounding the follicle. It is called the **theca** and it has two layers: a vascular inner layer and a fibrous outer layer. The whole structure is called a **Graafian follicle** after the 17th century Dutch physician, Reinier de Graaf, who first described it.

As the Graafian follicle matures, it increases in size. From a mere 50 μm in diameter, it finishes up with a diameter of about 12 mm. As it develops, one side of it grows close to the edge of the ovary, causing a distinct bulge. When the time is ripe, the bulge ruptures and the oocyte is pinched off from its attachment to the wall of the follicle and extruded from the ovary, with some of the follicle cells still adhering to it. This process is called **ovulation**.

In a woman who has reached puberty it occurs in one of her two ovaries approximately once every 28 days.

Shortly before ovulation the oocyte undergoes its first meiotic division. The second meiotic division into the ovum does not take place until fertilisation.

The role of the follicle is to protect the egg and provide a vehicle from which it can be shed from the ovary. The electron microscope has shown that the innermost follicle cells have fine processes which penetrate into the egg. Vesicles, pinched off the ends of these processes, are deposited in the egg cytoplasm and provide it with nourishment.

The sperm and egg

Before examining the sperm and egg in detail, let us recall their functions. The sperm simply has to convey genetic material from the male to the female. The egg, on the other hand, has to receive the genetic material from the sperm and then develop into a new individual. Most of the differences between eggs and sperms can be explained by the different jobs they have to do.

The spermatozoon

The structure of a generalised mammalian sperm is shown in figure 33.7. It is differentiated into three main regions: **head**, **middle piece** and **tail**. The head contains genetic material in a large **nucleus**. The nucleus contains DNA conjugated with protein in a highly condensed form. In fact DNA accounts for most of the dry mass of the head. The amount of DNA present in the sperm nuclei is half that found in somatic cells. This is because it is haploid. The nucleus is surmounted by a thin cap – rather like those woolly caps which you can pull down over your ears. It is called the **acrosome**, and it contains enzymes which play an important part in fertilisation.

The rest of the sperm is concerned with propulsion, and our understanding of it is based largely on the electron microscope. Running down

Figure 33.7 Structure of a mammalian spermatozoon. The tail is really much longer than shown in **A**. **B** and **C** show the internal structure of the middle piece and tail as revealed by the electron microscope. Notice the '9+2' array of microtubules characteristic of eukaryotic flagella.

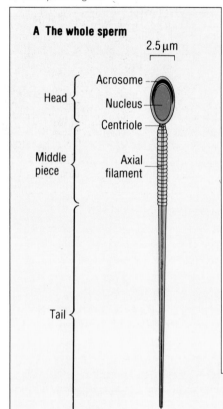

A The whole sperm

2.5 μm

Head { Acrosome, Nucleus, Centriole

Middle piece { Axial filament

Tail {

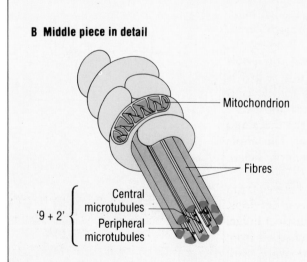

B Middle piece in detail

Mitochondrion

Fibres

'9 + 2' { Central microtubules, Peripheral microtubules

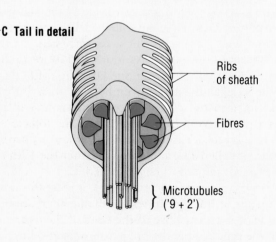

C Tail in detail

Ribs of sheath

Fibres

Microtubules ('9 + 2')

the centre of the middle piece and tail is an **axial filament** consisting of two central microtubules surrounded by a circle of nine peripheral ones. This is the 9+2 structure characteristic of cilia and flagella (see page 165). The sperm tail is therefore a modified flagellum. By lashing from side to side, it propels the sperm in the fluid medium through which it must swim to the egg. The microtubules are surrounded by a circle of solid fibres which provide strength, and the whole thing is enclosed in a sheath which is ribbed to permit flexibility.

In the middle piece the microtubules and strengthening fibres are surrounded by closely packed mitochondria arranged in spirals (figure 33.8). Mitochondria are, of course, associated with energy transfer, and the function of the middle piece is to provide the motive power for making the tail wave.

The egg

Since the egg does not have to propel itself, it has a simpler structure than the sperm. On the other hand it has to contain enough nutrients and metabolites to sustain itself through the earliest stages of its development. It is therefore much larger than the sperm. A human egg is just over 0.1 mm in diameter (100 μm), compared with the sperm whose head is only 2.5 μm across at the widest point.

Figure 23.9 shows a typical mammalian egg. A large haploid nucleus, situated slightly towards one end of the egg, is surrounded by cytoplasm which contains the usual organelles and enzymes found in cells generally. Just beneath the plasma membrane are numerous small vesicles called **cortical granules** whose function will be explained shortly.

Beyond the plasma membrane is a glycoprotein coat called the **zona pellucida** which literally means 'transparent zone'. This has a jelly-like consistency, for which reason we shall refer to it simply as the **jelly coat**. A small fluid-filled space separates the jelly coat from the plasma membrane, and in this space one or two polar bodies may be seen.

The jelly coat is produced by the ovary. In animals other than mammals it is referred to as the **vitelline membrane**. 'Vitelline' comes from the Latin word *vitellus*, meaning yolk, and its usage reflects the fact that most eggs contain yolk as a food supply. However, most mammalian eggs contain little or no yolk so the term is inappropriate for them.

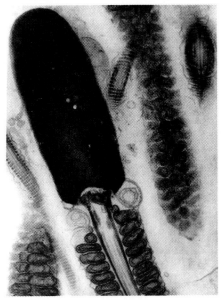

Figure 33.8 Electron micrograph of the head and middle piece of the spermatozoon of a bat. Notice the dense nucleus in the head, and the closely packed mitochondria in the middle piece. Magnification × 15 000.

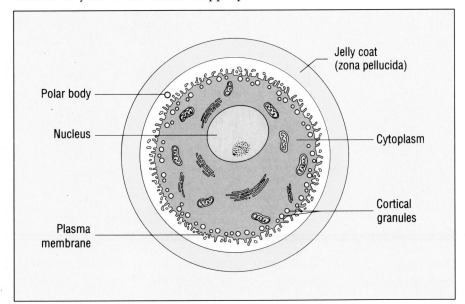

Figure 33.9 Structure of a mammalian egg. This picture, based on electron micrographs, shows an oocyte which is ready to be fertilised. Follicle cells have been omitted from the diagram.

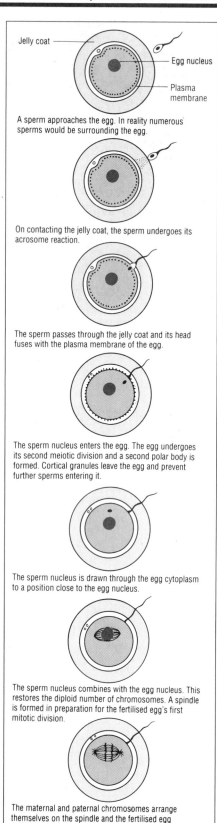

Jelly coat

Egg nucleus

Plasma membrane

A sperm approaches the egg. In reality numerous sperms would be surrounding the egg.

On contacting the jelly coat, the sperm undergoes its acrosome reaction.

The sperm passes through the jelly coat and its head fuses with the plasma membrane of the egg.

The sperm nucleus enters the egg. The egg undergoes its second meiotic division and a second polar body is formed. Cortical granules leave the egg and prevent further sperms entering it.

The sperm nucleus is drawn through the egg cytoplasm to a position close to the egg nucleus.

The sperm nucleus combines with the egg nucleus. This restores the diploid number of chromosomes. A spindle is formed in preparation for the fertilised egg's first mitotic division.

The maternal and paternal chromosomes arrange themselves on the spindle and the fertilised egg undergoes its first mitotic division.

Figure 33.10 Mammalian fertilisation
A Fertilisation in a generalised mammal showing the main sequence of events.

Fertilisation

To mature to the point that it is capable of fertilising an egg, a sperm must spend a certain amount of time in the female genital tract. This final part of the sperm's maturation process is called **capacitation**, and it probably involves biochemical changes taking place on the surface of the sperm.

The sperm come into contact with the eggs by random movements. There is no convincing evidence that in mammals (or indeed in any animals) the sperms are attracted to the eggs. However, in some plants this certainly happens. For example, in bracken (bracken has sperm, believe it or not), the eggs secrete malic acid to which the sperms are attracted. This is an example of **chemotaxis** (see page 533).

Fertilisation itself is illustrated in figure 33.10. Soon after the head of a sperm comes into contact with the jelly coat, the acrosome opens and releases its enzymes. The enzymes soften the glycoprotein at the point of contact, allowing the sperm to pass through it. The two most important enzymes are a trypsin-like protease and a carbohydrase called **hyaluronidase**. The whole process is called the **acrosome reaction**, and it enables the sperm to penetrate the egg. Meanwhile the vesicles in the outer part of the egg cytoplasm discharge their contents by exocytosis into the space between the plasma membrane and the jelly coat. This prevents other sperm entering the egg.

After a sperm has penetrated the egg membrane, its tail is usually discarded and the head and middle piece are drawn through the cytoplasm towards the nucleus. There is considerable variation in the way the two nuclei fuse. In many species the nuclear envelope breaks down, a spindle is formed, and the now visible sperm and egg chromosomes (the **paternal** and **maternal chromosomes** respectively) arrange themselves on the spindle as in mitosis. The diploid number of chromosomes is thus restored and the

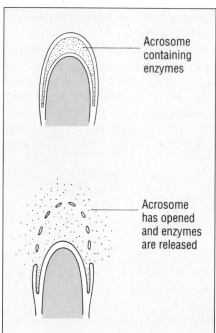

Acrosome containing enzymes

Acrosome has opened and enzymes are released

B Acrosome reaction of a mammalian sperm. The acrosome breaks open, releasing enzymes which soften the jelly coat of the egg and enable the sperm to pass through it.

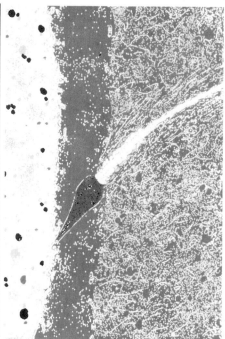

C Electron micrograph of a human egg being fertilised by a sperm. The sperm head has just penetrated the jelly coat (zona pellucida) and is resting in the space (dark) between the jelly coat and the egg.

fertilised egg, or **zygote**, is ready for its first mitotic division.

Normally eggs are only fertilised by sperm of the same species. What ensures that this happens? Research has shown that the sperm has a protein on its surface which binds to a specific protein binding site on the surface of the jelly coat, in much the same way as hormones bind to specific binding sites on the surface of their target cells. In this way the sperm *recognises* the egg, and specificity between sperm and egg is achieved.

Bringing sperm and eggs together

In aquatic animals the eggs and sperms are usually released into the surrounding water, and it is largely fortuitous as to whether or not they come into contact. Mammals, in common with most other terrestrial animals, have developed a more certain way of bringing the gametes together. This is achieved by the **penis** through which the sperms are introduced into the female in the act of **mating** (**sexual intercourse**).

For mating to take place, the penis must be **erect**. The penis contains three cylindrical bands of **erectile tissue** consisting of a three-dimensional network of connective tissue and smooth muscle permeated by blood spaces, rather like a sponge (figure 33.11). The arteries and veins serving the erectile tissue are equipped with muscular valves. Under conditions of erotic excitement, the arterial valves dilate and the venous valves constrict. The resulting high blood pressure causes the penis to become erect, enabling it to be inserted into the vagina.

Rhythmical moving of the penis in the vagina stimulates tactile receptors in the glans, triggering a reflex which causes repeated contractions of the vasa deferentia and urethra. The contractions sweep the sperm along these tubes where they become mixed with secretions from the seminal vesicles, prostate and Cowper's glands, the greatest contribution coming from the seminal vesicles. The secretions activate the sperm and keep them in a viable and motile state. The resulting milky suspension, **semen**, is expelled from the penis in the process of **ejaculation**.

The reflex mechanism which brings about ejaculation also inhibits urination, so there is no chance of the sperm being contaminated with urine. Ejaculation comes as the climax of the mating process and is accompanied by a pleasurable feeling, the **orgasm**. To describe an orgasm as a 'pleasurable feeling' is a masterpiece of understatement. It is a complex process whose physiological basis is still not understood. Of course women experience orgasms too. The female orgasm is particularly complex, but it is at least partly due to repeated tactile stimulation of the clitoris. The clitoris is homologous with the penis and, like the latter, is highly sensitive and can become erect.

It obviously takes a certain amount of time for the male to reach an orgasm, and this will determine how long mating lasts. In this respect there are marked differences between species. For example, the chimpanzee mates for less than ten seconds, the camel for 24 hours!

For mating to take place successfully the erect penis needs to be lubricated. This enables the penis to move easily and painlessly in the vagina, and prevents the epithelial lining of either being damaged by abrasion. Small amounts of a natural lubricant, secreted by the urethral glands, are discharged from the tip of the erect penis prior to ejaculation. The vagina itself is lined by stratified epithelium which does not contain secretory cells. However, glands in the cervix secrete copious quantities of mucus which flows over the surface of the vagina and serves as a lubricant.

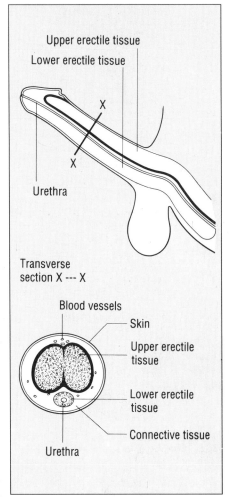

Figure 33.11 Internal structure of a human penis showing the tissues responsible for erection.

Movement of sperm in the female genital tract

Ejaculation usually occurs with sufficient force to propel the sperm to the upper end of the vagina and even into the cervix. They must now get from here to the upper end of an oviduct. By rhythmical undulations of the tail, they swim through the mucus. Round about the time of ovulation the mucus is thin and watery, and its glycoprotein chains run parallel with each other. This makes it relatively easy for the sperms to swim through it.

It has been suggested that a sperm swimming the full length of the female genital tract would be equivalent to a human swimming across the Atlantic – in treacle! How the sperm propel themselves is still not fully understood but the densely packed mitochondria provide the necessary energy, and the sperm can respire anaerobically as well as aerobically.

Nevertheless, it is doubtful if the sperm could ever complete the journey without the aid of muscular contractions of the genital tract. In fact the vagina, cervix, uterus and oviducts all undergo contractions which help to sweep the sperm along. Sperm have been detected in oviducts within minutes of ejaculation, and these could not have swum there unaided. Even inert particles injected into the vagina get into the oviducts. It seems that contractions of the female genital tract provide the main force, the sperm being responsible for only the last few millimetres.

Despite the help they receive, relatively few sperm reach the egg. A fertile man may produce as many as 500 million sperm in a single ejaculation. Of these probably fewer than 500 ever get to the part of the oviduct where the egg is located – less than one in a million.

From ovulation to pregnancy

Because of the way the reproductive system develops, the ovary and oviduct are not joined. In fact there is a gap between the ovary and the opening, (funnel) of the oviduct. When ovulation occurs the egg has to traverse this gap to get into the oviduct. How does it do it?

The oviduct and its funnel are lined with cilia. The beating of these cilia draws the egg into the funnel and propels it along the first part of the oviduct (figure 33.12). Follicle cells are still attached to the egg and they

Figure 33.12 The events which take place from ovulation to implantation. In the human it takes about a week for an egg which has just been released from the ovary to develop into a blastocyst and begin to implant. So typically implantation begins on the 21st day of the menstrual cycle and ends around what would have been the 28th day. This is when menstruation would have taken place. It is usually the missing of a menstrual period that tells a woman that she is, or may be, pregnant.

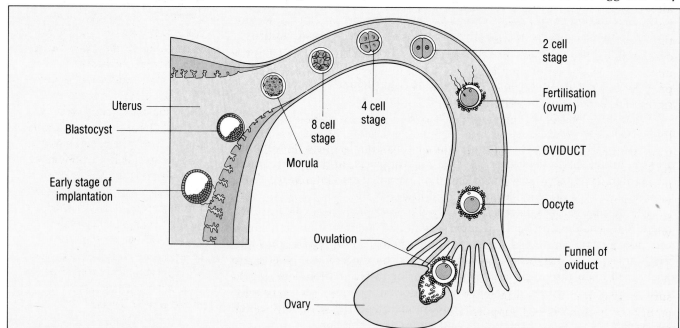

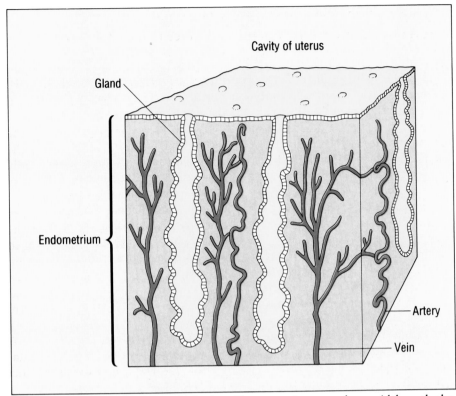

Cavity of uterus

Gland

Endometrium

Artery

Vein

Figure 33.13 The endometrium of the uterus when it is at its thickest, just before menstruation. Soft like a cushion, and permeated by glands and blood vessels, the endometrium is now ready to receive a blastocyst, if one is available.

provide a large surface on which the cilia can gain a purchase. Although the wall of the oviduct contains smooth muscle tissue, muscular contractions do not play much part, if any, in the transport of the egg at this stage, at least not in those species of mammal which have been studied.

Fertilisation usually occurs about a third of the way along the oviduct. After fertilisation, the zygote is pushed down the oviduct by gentle contractions of the circular muscle in the oviduct wall. Once the egg has been successfully fertilised, **conception** has been achieved.

Figure 33.12 shows the progress of the zygote along the oviduct. It takes about three days after fertilisation to reach the uterus. As it moves along, it divides to form a solid ball of cells called a **morula** which then becomes a hollow **blastocyst**. The follicle cells have disappeared by this time but the egg is still surrounded by the jelly coat. Eventually the blastocyst breaks out of the jelly coat and becomes attached to the lining of the uterus, a process called **implantation**. Once this happens, the woman is **pregnant**. In the human, implantation begins about eight days after fertilisation and takes about a week to complete.

As we shall see later, the uterus prepares itself for implantation beforehand. Its wall consists of two main layers: a layer of smooth muscle towards the outside, and a soft inner lining called the **endometrium**. By the time the blastocyst arrives, the **endometrium** is thick and contains numerous glands and blood vessels (figure 33.13). The glands secrete a wide range of nutrients and other substances which help the blastocyst to survive and continue its development. One of the nutrients is glucose from which the blastocyst obtains energy.

The outermost layer of cells of the blastocyst is called the **trophoblast**. This sends out finger-like outgrowths which project into the endometrium. As well as providing anchorage, these **trophoblastic villi** increase the surface area for the absorption of nutrients. In this way the developing embryo is nourished and supported during the early stages of its development.

Natural loss of embryos

In the human species, the number of embryos that fail to survive is surprisingly high. Of 100 fertilised eggs, as many as 50 to 55 per cent fail to implant successfully. Some never implant at all, others are lost during the implantation process. Of the embryos that do implant successfully, approximately ten per cent are spontaneously aborted at a later stage: they come away from the wall of the uterus and are born dead. Such miscarriages occur most commonly between the 7th and 10th weeks of pregnancy.

Why should so many embryos be lost? The answer is not known, though it may be nature's way of getting rid of defective embryos. This idea is supported by the observation that approximately fifty per cent of all spontaneously aborted embryos carry major genetic defects such as chromosome mutations. On the other hand, only about two per cent of newborn babies carry major genetic defects.

Sexually transmitted diseases

Any infectious disease may be transmitted by intercourse, but certain bacteria and viruses have evolved in such a way that they are normally *only* transmitted by this route. The diseases which they cause, **sexually transmitted diseases** (STDs), include syphilis, gonorrhoea and AIDS. The agents responsible for these diseases normally survive for only a very short time outside the body. It is therefore impossible to acquire them from, for example, a lavatory seat – convenient though this may be for explaining how one got the disease!

Syphilis, gonorrhoea and AIDS are serious diseases which can be fatal, and all three can be transmitted by pregnant mothers to their babies. Syphilis and gonorrhoea are both caused by bacteria and can be successfully treated with antibiotics such as penicillin. AIDS, however, is caused by a virus (HIV) which, like all viruses, cannot be destroyed by antibiotics. Although treatment with drugs can help, there is no cure for AIDS and a vaccine has not yet been developed against it.

Sexually transmitted diseases have been called 'hidden diseases'. This is because, in the early stages of infection, the symptoms may be very slight or even non-existent. For example, approximately half of all women with gonorrhoea experience no symptoms at all. However, the causative agent is there, and can cause trouble months or years later. Meanwhile, the person is a **carrier** and may transmit the disease to his or her sexual partner or partners. This is why STDs can spread so quickly through the community, and why STD clinics take pains to trace the partners of infected patients.

The term 'sexually transmitted diseases' includes a number of diseases which, though commonly transmitted by close sexual contact, can be caught in other ways too. Such diseases include genital herpes and viral hepatitis, both of which are serious (the type of hepatitis known as hepatitis B can be fatal), and a number of less serious but irritating infections such as thrush, genital warts and non-specific urethritis.

Until the early 1980s most people were not unduly worried about STDs. Serious ones like syphilis could be cured if treated early enough, and the others were relatively rare and mainly curable. But then came AIDS. The only *sure* way of avoiding AIDS (and any other STD for that matter) is to not have sexual intercourse with anyone. But this is patently ridiculous. We are therefore faced with a dilemma. It may be impractical to avoid intercourse altogether, but at least one can be guided by the dictates of common sense and avoid having casual sexual encounters with numerous different partners. And if a lifelong one-to-one relationship is not possible, or casual sex is too tempting to resist, then one can take the precaution of practising 'safe sex'.

What is 'safe sex'?

Let us consider the basic principle. HIV, the virus that causes AIDS, is usually transmitted by the blood of an infected person getting into another person's bloodstream. The amount of blood need only be very small for transmission to occur. This can happen during any kind of sexual activity which involves contact between delicate body surfaces that are, or might become, punctured. It is during intercourse that this is most likely to happen. 'Safe sex' (or 'safer sex' as more cautious people prefer to call it) avoids direct contact between such surfaces. One way of achieving this is by wearing a condom, though the reputation of this ubiquitous contraceptive for preventing AIDS is not entirely deserved.

HIV has also been found in semen and vaginal fluid, and infection can occur during the transfer of these fluids between sexual partners. Again, wearing a condom can reduce the chance of infection by this route.

HIV has also been detected in saliva, tears and urine. However, the virus is extremely dilute in these fluids and there has never been a reported case of someone being infected through them. The main method of transmission is through blood, semen and vaginal fluid, and preventive measures are based on this fact.

Brief notes on three important sexually transmitted diseases

- **AIDS**
  Caused by the immuno-deficiency virus (HIV) which attacks cells in the immune system rendering the person susceptible to opportunistic infections such as pneumonia. Symptoms may take years to develop. No vaccine, no cure. Some effective drugs have been developed but the side effects can be unpleasant.

- **Syphilis**
  Caused by a spiral bacterium, *Trepanoma pallidum*, which attacks the genital organs causing a sore on the penis or in the vagina (primary syphilis). Subsequent symptoms usually include skin rash and fever (secondary syphilis) and, years later, blindness, insanity, paralysis and heart failure (tertiary syphilis). Can be completely cured by antibiotics such as penicillin if treated early enough.

- **Gonorrhoea**
  Caused by a spherical bacterium, *Neisseria gonorrhoea* which attacks the genital organs causing discharge from the urethral opening and pain when urinating (described by Boswell as 'a most exquisite pain'). Later symptoms include general ill health, arthritis, emphysema and inflammation of the pericardium. Responds well to antibiotics such as penicillin but resistant strains of the bacterium have evolved, necessitating the use of stronger doses and/or other antibiotics.

In vitro fertilisation

In vitro fertilisation (IVF) can help infertile couples to have children. The following account of the technique is based on detailed information provided by scientists who work in this field.

In vitro fertilisation means fertilisation outside the body, and it leads to the production of what are popularly called 'test tube babies'.

The term 'test tube baby', coined by the media when the technique was first introduced, is decidedly misleading. Only fertilisation itself and the first few cell divisions take place outside the body, and the 'baby' that is placed back in the mother consists of eight cells at the most. From that point on, nature takes over and if all goes well the embryo will implant in the uterus and continue to develop in the normal way.

A key step in IVF is the removal of the egg. This has to be taken from the Graafian follicle in the ovary, for once ovulation has occurred and the egg has started its journey down the oviduct, it cannot be located. The aim is to collect the egg a few hours before ovulation. (At this stage it is, of course, an oocyte but for simplicty we shall refer to it as the egg.)

To increase the chance of success, doctors arrange for the woman to produce a larger number of eggs than the single one normally formed during each menstrual cycle. Having more than one egg means that:

- If one egg fails at some stage in the IVF procedure, another one may be successful.
- The strongest and most viable embryos can be selected for transfer back to the mother.
- Several embryos can be transferred back to the mother, thereby increasing the chance of her becoming pregnant.

The woman is made to produce several eggs at once by treatment with hormone-based drugs. This strategy not only increases the number of eggs produced but it also enables the doctors to control the time of ovulation so they know exactly when to collect the eggs.

Doctors achieve this control by first preventing the woman from producing her own hormones and then supplying first FSH then LH (see page 598). The doses are tailored and timed to obtain an optimal response.

Collecting the eggs is a relatively simple matter. The ovaries are only about 2 cm from the wall of the vagina – they are normally further away than this but following stimulation they become heavier due to the presence of the follicles, so they drop down nearer the vagina. Just before ovulation each mature follicle may be nearly 2 cm in diameter. The follicles are located by means of an ultrasound scanner. This instrument emits very high frequency waves which are reflected off solid structures but not fluids. Having been reflected, the sound waves are processed into an electrical image in which solids appear white and liquids and gases black. Each follicle shows up as a black shadow.

Using ultrasound guidance, a hollow needle is inserted into the vagina and through its wall into one of the follicles. The egg is then sucked out, together with the follicular fluid, and placed in a test tube containing a special medium. This procedure is repeated for the other follicles. The eggs are then maintained in separate test tubes at 37°C in an incubator.

Meanwhile the sperm are prepared. As well as normal sperm, the seminal fluid contains a large proportion of dead and abnormal sperm which must be removed. The semen is placed in a test tube and a layer of special medium is carefully placed on top. Strong motile sperm swim up into the medium from which they are easily harvested.

A few hours after collection, about 100 000 of the prepared sperm are added to each egg in a small petri dish. After 16 to 20 hours the eggs are checked to see if they have been fertilised. The embryos are then left in the incubator to develop for two or three days. By this time they will have reached the 4 or 8 cell stage and can be transferred back to the uterus. Up to three embryos are replaced, in the hope that one of them will implant successfully and develop into a new human being.

An important factor determining the success of IVF is the hormone treatment since this stimulates the ovaries to produce extra eggs. However, a small number of IVF clinics do not give hormone treatment. The reasoning behind this is that if the patient ovulates regularly and the semen is good enough to make fertilisation likely, there should be no need to stimulate the ovaries artificially. Instead it is left to the natural cycle to bring about the development of a single follicle from which the one egg can be recovered.

For this 'natural IVF' to be successful it is necessary to predict very accurately when ovulation is going to occur. This is achieved by monitoring the secretion of oestrogen by the ovary, and of LH by the anterior pituitary. Ovulation is preceded by a sudden increase in the concentration of LH. It is known that the time from the beginning of the LH surge to the moment of ovulation is about 36 hours. This information is corroborated by obtaining an image of the follicle itself with an ultrasound scanner. From the diameter of the follicle the doctors can assess when ovulation is likely to occur.

The amnion and placenta

Within a few weeks the job of nourishing the embryo is taken over by the **placenta**. At the same time the embryo becomes enveloped by a membrane called the **amnion**. The cavity enclosed by the amnion (the **amniotic cavity**) is full of fluid. How these structures arise is explained in Chapter 35. Here we are only concerned with their functions.

The function of the fluid-filled amniotic cavity is to cushion the embryo and protect it from physical disturbance. The amniotic cavity gradually expands to accommodate the growing embryo, and eventually it fills the entire uterus. By this stage all the organs and systems of the body have been laid down and the embryo is referred to as a **fetus** (also spelled **foetus**). This is the stage reached in figure 33.14A.

The placenta is intimately associated with the endometrium of the uterus, and is connected to the fetus by the **umbilical cord**. The latter contains two blood vessels: an **umbilical artery** which carries blood from the aorta of the fetus to the placenta, and an **umbilical vein** which carries blood from the placenta to the posterior vena cava of the fetus. Within the placenta numerous tree-like **chorionic villi**, containing capillary loops derived from the umbilical artery, project into a large **maternal blood space** in the wall of the uterus (figure 33.14B). This space is kept charged with blood from branches of the mother's uterine artery.

The fetal and maternal bloodstreams flow very close to each other. Across the thin barrier separating them exchange of materials takes place:

- Soluble food substances, oxygen, water and salts pass from the mother's blood into the fetal blood.
- Carbon dioxide and nitrogenous waste pass from the fetal blood into the mother's blood.
- In addition, antibodies pass from the mother's blood into the fetal blood, thereby conferring on the fetus **passive immunity** against various diseases.

The placenta is therefore the fetus' gaseous exchange surface, source of food, source of antibodies, and excretory organ. The relationship between the two bloodstreams is extremely intimate. However, they do not mix. The mother and fetus may belong to different blood groups, and if their bloods were to mix coagulation might occur. Moreoever, the mother's blood pressure would be far too high for the fetus.

The placental villi are well adapted to their function. Their branched arrangement gives them a large surface area, and the capillary loops within them are extensive. The barrier between the blood in the capillaries and the mother's blood in a fully developed placenta is extremely thin. As shown in figure 33.14C, it consists of three layers:

- The endothelium of the fetal capillary.
- A thin layer of connective tissue.
- The epithelial lining of the villus.

The epithelium lining the villus bears microvilli which increase its surface area, and it contains numerous mitochondria which provide energy for active transport. Exchanges occur by a combination of diffusion, active transport and pinocytosis. It is said that the villi can pulsate, creating a stirring effect and bringing them into contact with substances in the mother's blood. Absorption of oxygen by the fetus is aided by fetal haemoglobin having a higher affinity for oxygen than maternal haemoglogin (see page 320).

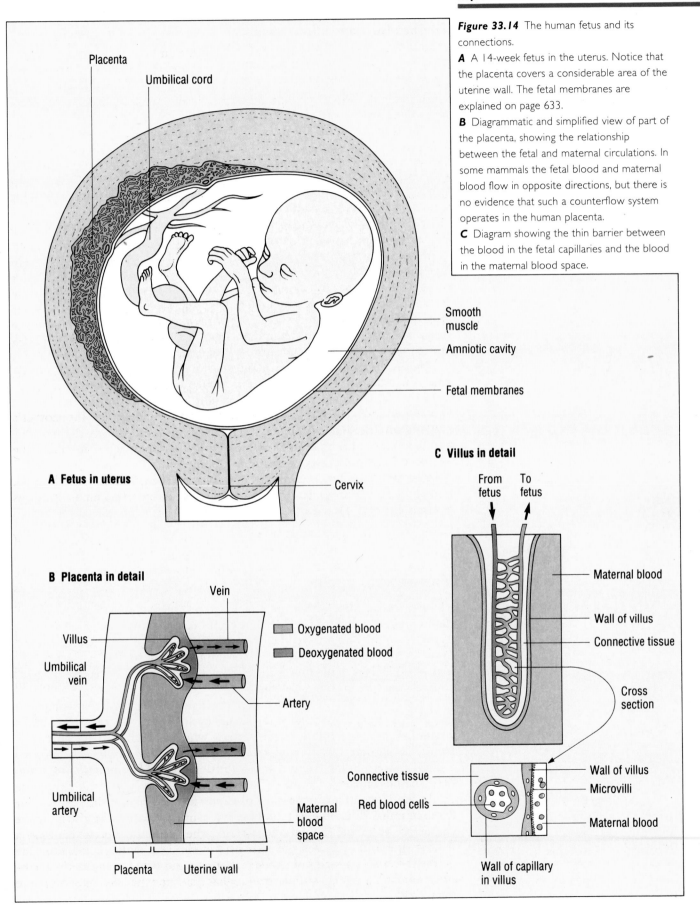

Placenta

Umbilical cord

Figure 33.14 The human fetus and its connections.

A A 14-week fetus in the uterus. Notice that the placenta covers a considerable area of the uterine wall. The fetal membranes are explained on page 633.

B Diagrammatic and simplified view of part of the placenta, showing the relationship between the fetal and maternal circulations. In some mammals the fetal blood and maternal blood flow in opposite directions, but there is no evidence that such a counterflow system operates in the human placenta.

C Diagram showing the thin barrier between the blood in the fetal capillaries and the blood in the maternal blood space.

Smooth muscle

Amniotic cavity

Fetal membranes

A Fetus in uterus

Cervix

C Villus in detail

From fetus

To fetus

Maternal blood

Wall of villus

Connective tissue

Cross section

B Placenta in detail

Vein

Villus

Umbilical vein

Oxygenated blood

Deoxygenated blood

Artery

Umbilical artery

Maternal blood space

Connective tissue

Red blood cells

Wall of villus

Microvilli

Maternal blood

Wall of capillary in villus

Placenta

Uterine wall

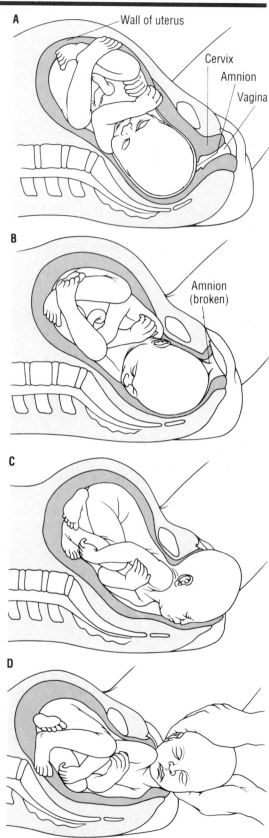

A
Wall of uterus

Cervix
Amnion
Vagina

B
Amnion (broken)

C

D

Figure 33.15 Birth (parturition). The cervix dilates and the uterine muscle contracts, forcing the baby through the vagina ('birth canal').

The placenta is a superbly efficient device for providing the fetus with everything it needs. And yet its very efficiency can cause problems, for if the mother takes undesirable things into her bloodstream they too will be taken up by the fetus. This is why pregnant women are advised not to smoke and to avoid potentially harmful drugs – including alcohol.

Birth

During pregnancy, the uterus expands enormously to accommodate the steadily growing fetus. At the same time, the muscular part of the uterine wall thickens and the endometrium becomes more and more richly vascularised. When the fetus reaches a certain size relative to the uterus, birth (**parturition**) takes place (figure 33.15).

Birth starts with rhythmical contractions of the uterine muscle ('going into labour'). Next the amnion bursts and the amniotic fluid flows out through the vagina ('breaking of the waters'). Then the fetus is forced out through the cervix and vagina by powerful contractions of the uterine muscle. The placenta comes away from the uterine wall and is expelled as the 'afterbirth'. The now redundant umbilical cord is tied and cut in the human but in other mammals it may be chewed through by the mother.

By this time the **mammary glands** in the breasts have developed greatly and at the time of birth they start secreting milk in the process known as **lactation**. This provides the newborn baby with nourishment (milk is an almost perfect food) and a continued source of antibodies until it builds up a supply of antibodies of its own. The milk produced during the first few days of lactation is called **colostrum** (Latin for 'first milk'). It has a high protein content and is particularly rich in antibodies.

The time from conception to birth is called the **gestation period**. In the human it lasts approximately nine months, but in other mammals it ranges from as little as 18 days in the house mouse to 18 months in the Indian elephant.

The sexual cycle

The impressive thing about the female's reproductive physiology is that all the events are synchronised, so that each occurs at the right moment. For example, in the human, well before ovulation is due to take place the lining of the uterus starts to prepare itself for implantation, so that by the time the blastocyst arrives in the uterus the endometrium is ready to receive it. What controls the timing of these events?

The answer lies in the fact that the female's reproductive behaviour occurs in a cycle. This is called the **sexual cycle**. The events that occur in the course of the cycle follow a set pattern which is regulated by hormones from the pituitary gland and ovaries. If pregnancy occurs, the normal cyclical pattern is interrupted and a third source of hormones comes into play: the placenta.

In the human female the most obvious outward sign of the sexual cycle is the monthly discharge of blood known as **menstruation**. Menstruation is characteristic of the human and certain other primates, for which reason their sexual cycle is called the **menstrual cycle**. In a woman, menstruation marks the end of a series of changes that have occurred in her body during the previous 28 days. To understand what has happened we must return to the ovary.

Puberty, sex hormones and the menopause

In a young child the gonads, though present, do not function. This situation continues until the onset of **puberty** at the age of about 12 years in girls, 14 in boys, when eggs and sperm start being produced. Girls experience their first menstrual period towards the end of puberty (the **menarche**). Boys find that their external genitalia grow considerably, and ejaculation becomes possible.

At puberty the **secondary sexual characteristics** develop: breasts and wide hips in the female; body hair and broken voice in the male. Growth also speeds up, giving the well known **adolescent growth spurt** when parents find themselves buying new clothes for their offspring more often than they may have bargained for (see illustration).

The changes which occur at puberty. They happen gradually over about a year. They are brought on by **sex hormones** secreted by the gonads: **androgens** (principally **testosterone**) by the testes, and **oestrogens** by the ovaries. The

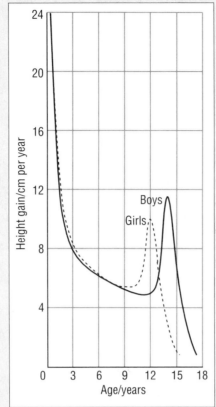

Growth rate curves for girls and boys before, during and after puberty.

production of these hormones is in turn controlled by **gonadotrophic** hormones from the anterior lobe of the pituitary gland.

Although androgens are regarded as male hormones and oestrogens as female hormones, small amounts of each are found in the opposite sex. For example, androgens in women cause development of pubic hair. The function of oestrogen in males is not known.

The sex hormones continue to be produced in adult life. In the female they control the menstrual cycle. In the male they maintain the steady production of sperm, and they stimulate muscular growth.

Synthetic androgens have been used (illegally) by athletes to enhance their performance, and by farmers to stimulate the growth of muscle in livestock. Some of these **anabolic steroids** are remarkably powerful and selectively stimulate the growth of skeletal muscle.

Men can go on producing sperm well into old age, but women stop ovulating at the age of about 45 to 50 when they reach the **menopause**. At this stage the production of sex hormones declines and no more Graafian follicles are produced.

The ovary and uterus working together

During the first 14 days following the beginning of menstruation, a Graafian follicle develops in one of the ovaries, as described earlier. After ovulation, the empty follicle undergoes certain changes. The follicle cells enlarge considerably, and a yellow pigment accumulates in them. Eventually they will fill the cavity of the original follicle, turning it into a solid **corpus luteum** ('yellow body'). You can see a corpus luteum in figure 33.6 on page 585. If the egg is *not* fertilised, the corpus luteum remains in the ovary for the next week or ten days and then degenerates.

While the Graafian follicle is developing, the wall of the uterus prepares itself for receiving a blastocyst. The endometrium thickens and becomes permeated by blood vessels and glands in readiness for implantation (see figure 33.13 on page 591). If, however, fertilisation does not occur, the unfertilised egg simply degenerates. Under these circumstances the corpus luteum regresses, and the endometrium of the uterus breaks down and sloughs off. The discarding of the endometrial tissue, accompanied by the loss of blood, takes place intermittently over several days and constitutes menstruation.

Hormonal control of the cycle

These changes, occurring in the ovary and uterus, are synchronised by hormones. Basically two groups of hormones are involved:

- **Pituitary hormones** secreted by the anterior lobe of the pituitary gland under the influence of the hypothalamus (see page 468). They are called **gonadotrophic hormones** because they bring about changes in the gonads, in this case the ovaries. There are two such hormones: **follicle stimulating hormone (FSH)** and **luteinising hormone (LH)**.

- **Ovarian hormones** secreted by the ovary itself. These hormones are **oestrogen** and **progesterone**, and they bring about changes in the uterus.

The details are summarised in figure 33.16. Just after menstruation, the anterior lobe of the pituitary gland, starts secreting FSH. FSH causes a Graafian follicle to develop in the ovary, and it stimulates the ovary to secrete oestrogen.

Oestrogen is secreted by the wall of the Graafian follicle, specifically the inner layer which, you will recall, is vascular (see page 585). Its immediate effect is to bring about the healing and repair of the uterine endometrium following menstruation. In the course of the next 11 days or so the amount of oestrogen in the bloodstream steadily increases. Then, shortly before ovulation is due to take place, LH is released by the anterior pituitary in a sudden surge. LH causes ovulation, and makes the Graafian follicle change into a corpus luteum.

The corpus luteum secretes progesterone. This, along with oestrogen, causes the continued thickening and vascularisation of the uterine endometrium in preparation for implantation. The section of the uterus in figure 33.13 was prepared at this stage.

Figure 33.16 The menstrual cycle of the human female showing the events occurring in the ovary and endometrium of the uterus, together with the relative levels of oestrogen and progesterone in the blood. How these events are synchronised is explained in the text.

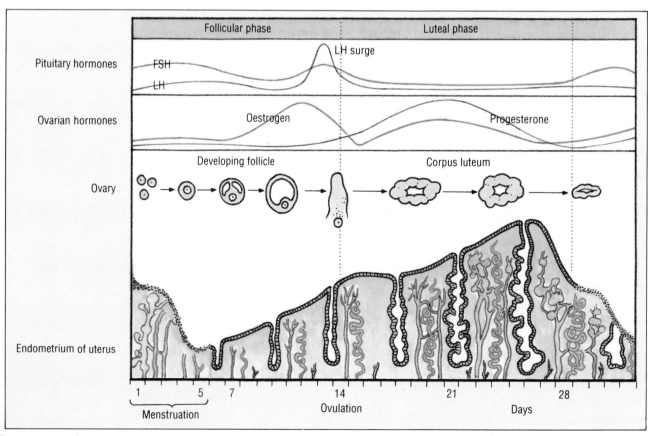

For a week or so after ovulation the concentrations of progesterone and oestrogen gradually increase, and then suddenly decrease. With the fall in the level of these two hormones, the uterine endometrium begins to disintegrate and menstruation starts. Several days later, when menstruation is over, the anterior pituitary starts secreting FSH again and the cycle is repeated.

What causes oestrogen and progesterone levels to fluctuate the way they do? The answer is feedback. Just before ovulation, the concentration of oestrogen reaches a point when it inhibits the secretion of FSH by the pituitary and stimulates the secretion of LH. In the second half of the cycle, the gradual build-up of progesterone inhibits the secretion of FSH and LH by the pituitary. This in turn stops the ovary secreting oestrogen and causes the corpus luteum to degenerate and stop secreting progesterone.

These hormonal interactions are illustrated in figure 33.17. We can sum up by saying that the two pituitary hormones, FSH and LH, stimulate the ovary to secrete oestrogen and progesterone. These hormones, in turn, regulate the production of the pituitary hormones by feedback. In achieving their feedback effects, oestrogen and progesterone act on the pituitary direct and also on the hypothalamus which then adjusts the activity of the pituitary. The way the hypothalamus communicates with the pituitary is explained on page 468.

In some women the pituitary fails to produce enough FSH, with the result that Graafian follicles do not develop in the ovary and ovulation does not occur. This can be remedied by injections of FSH or a synthetic equivalent, the so-called **fertility drug**. This can cause several eggs to be produced at the same time, resulting in twins, triplets, quadruplets or more. The technique is also used when eggs are required for *in vitro* fertilisation (see page 593).

Figure 33.17 Scheme summarising the interaction of hormones controlling the female sexual cycle. Solid arrows signify stimulation, broken arrows inhibition. Feedback takes place via the hypothalamus.

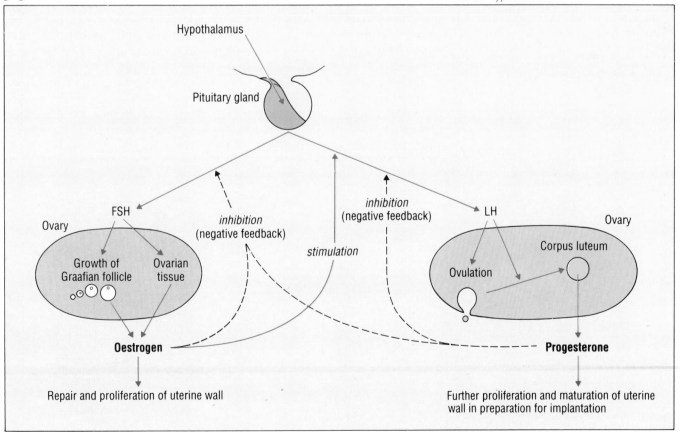

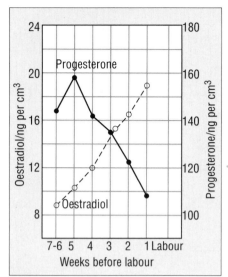

Figure 33.18 Mean concentrations of progesterone and oestradiol (an oestrogen) in the blood of 33 pregnant women during the seven weeks before the onset of labour. Notice the fall in the level of progesterone and the rise in the level of oestrogen. The unit ng is a nanogram, which is one thousand millionth of a gram.

In the event of pregnancy

The sequence of events described above is what happens if fertilisation does *not* take place. If, however, the egg is fertilised and implantation occurs, a different course is followed. Under these circumstances the corpus luteum, instead of degenerating, persists. In humans this is due to a hormone called **chorionic gonadotrophin** which is secreted by the developing placenta. This hormone signals to the mother's body that an embryo is present in the uterus. It is the basis of **pregnancy tests**: excess chorionic gonadotrophin is excreted, and its presence in the urine is detected and used as an indication that the woman is pregnant.

The corpus luteum continues to secrete progesterone which, coupled with a small but steady secretion of oestrogen, maintains the continued development of the uterus and, of course, prevents menstruation. The ovarian hormones also inhibit the anterior pituitary from producing FSH, thus preventing further follicles developing in the ovary. This fact was exploited in developing the **contraceptive pill**. The pill contains progesterone plus varying amounts of oestrogen, depending on the brand. It works by suppressing the development of follicles in the ovary.

After the first three or four months of pregnancy the corpus luteum begins to regress and the job of secreting oestrogen and progesterone is taken over by the placenta. In this way the endometrium of the uterus is maintained in a suitable state throughout pregnancy.

The hormonal control of birth and lactation

Towards the end of pregnancy the level of oestrogen in the blood rises while that of progesterone falls (figure 33.18). It has been suggested that this plays some part in bringing about birth. Certainly oestrogen promotes uterine contraction, and progesterone inhibits it. Premature births sometimes occur when the progesterone level falls too low, and if this happens before about the seventh month of pregnancy a **miscarriage** may ensue. The chance of a miscarriage occurring during a subsequent pregnancy can be reduced by injections of progesterone.

But the most direct cause of birth is another hormone, **oxytocin**, secreted by the posterior lobe of the pituitary gland. This causes the uterine muscle to contract. Oestrogen achieves its effect on the uterus by making the uterine muscle more sensitive to oxytocin. Progesterone has the reverse effect. This is illustrated in figure 33.19.

Figure 33.19 Actions of the female hormones during and immediately after pregnancy. Solid arrows signify stimulation, broken arrows inhibition. Inhibition of prolactin takes place via the hypothalamus.

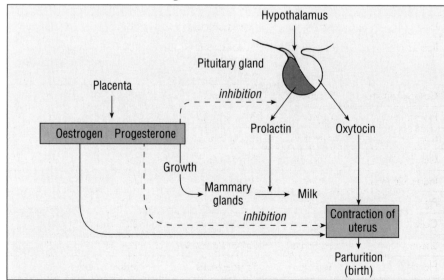

Oestrogen and progesterone are also responsible for the growth of the mammary glands in readiness for milk-production (lactation). After birth has taken place the flow of milk is induced by yet another hormone, **prolactin**, secreted by the anterior lobe of the pituitary. Before birth, prolactin secretion is inhibited by oestrogen and progesterone. The sudden fall in the level of these two hormones with the loss of the placenta at the end of pregnancy permits the onset of lactation. This too is illustrated in figure 33.19.

The sexual cycle of other mammals

The breeding habits of a number of mammals are summarised in table 33.1. In most mammals the time of ovulation is marked by heightened sexual excitement and is called **oestrus**. Oestrus comes from the Greek word *oistros* meaning 'mad desire' and the animal is described as being 'on heat'. At this stage the female may produce various secretions which act as **pheromones**, inducing sexual activity in the male. This ensures that mating takes place at the right time. In some species, rabbits for example, ovulation is delayed until about ten hours after mating has occurred by which time the sperm will have reached the oviducts and will be ready to fertilise the eggs.

In humans and other primates, however, no such safeguards exist. Indeed, there is no evidence that women show greater sexual awareness at the time of ovulation, despite the hormonal changes that are taking place in her body. It is therefore largely fortuitous as to whether or not mating happens at the right time.

In the human female ovulation occurs approximately midway between one menstrual period and the next, and as the sexual cycle lasts about 28 days a woman will ovulate some 12 or 13 times in the course of a year. In few other mammals is the frequency so low. Even in large mammals like

Name	Breeding time	Type of cycle	Gestation period (days)	Number of offspring
Human	Any time	Polymenstrual	267	1
Chimpanzee	Any time	Polyoestrous	228	1
Dog	Seasonal	Monoestrous	61	7
Domestic cat	Seasonal	Polyoestrous with induced ovulation	63	4
Lion	Any time	Polyoestrous	108	3
Rabbit	Any time	Polyoestrous with induced ovulation	28	6
Golden hamster	Seasonal	Polyoestrous	16	6
House mouse	Any time	Polyoestrous	19	6
Rat	Any time	Polyoestrous	22	8
Guinea pig	Any time	Polyoestrous	68	3
Indian elephant	Any time	Polyoestrous	624	1
Pig	Any time	Polyoestrous	113	3
Cow	Any time	Polyoestrous	282	1
Sheep	Seasonal	Polyoestrous	148	3
Horse	Seasonal	Polyoestrous	350	1

Table 33.1 Breeding patterns of some well-known mammals. Induced ovulation means that ovulation is delayed until mating occurs. The number of offspring (litter size) is variable and in some cases may be much greater than the figure given. For example, the domestic rabbit may have 12 or 13 offspring in a litter, and certain breeds of dog can have as many as 17.

Figure 33.20 Actions of the male hormones. In the male, luteinising hormone is also known as 'interstitial cell stimulating hormone' (ICSH), on account of its stimulating effect on the interstitial cells in the testis. However, it is chemically the same as LH. Feedback takes place via the hypothalamus. Solid arrows signify stimulation, broken arrows inhibition.

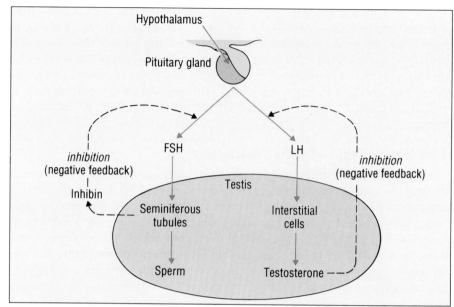

cows the sexual cycle only lasts about three weeks, and in small mammals like rats and mice oestrus occurs at approximately four to five day intervals. Menstruation does not occur in these mammals and it is usual to refer to their sexual cycle as the **oestrous cycle** ('oestrus' is the noun, 'oestrous' the adjective).

Rats, mice, cows and women can reproduce at any time of the year, but in many other mammals there are definite **breeding seasons**. During the breeding season the female may come into oestrus once (**monoestrous**) or many times (**polyoestrous**). The number and timing of the breeding seasons are also variable: commonly there is only one, occurring in the spring or summer, but some mammals have two.

Breeding seasons are closely related to the environment. However, the natural pattern seen in animals in the wild may be severely disrupted by domestication. The environmental stimuli which bring wild animals into season may not apply to an animal that spends most of its time curled up on a hearth rug. The way breeding is controlled by the environment is discussed on page 668.

Sexual activity in the human male

In the human male, the production of sperm by the testes is regulated by gonadotrophic hormones identical with those produced by the female. The anterior pituitary secretes FSH and LH. FSH promotes the growth of the seminiferous tubules in the testes and stimulates spermatogenesis. LH stimulates the interstitial cells between the seminiferous tubules to secrete male sex hormones (**androgens**). These are steroids, and the main one is **testosterone**. This is needed, along with FSH, for spermatogenesis.

Both FSH and LH are controlled by feedback mechanisms. LH is controlled directly by testosterone. FSH is controlled by a hormone called **inhibin** which is thought to be secreted by the Sertoli cells in the walls of the seminiferous tubules.

The way these hormones interact is summarised in figure 33.20. You will notice a number of parallels with the female system. However, there is one fundamental difference. In the female the hormones are produced in waves, which give rise to the menstrual cycle. However, in the male they are produced more or less uniformly all the time. Consequently there is no sexual cycle in the male.

Family planning, principles and practice

There are times when couples may wish to prevent pregnancy. This can be achieved by **family planning** or **birth control**, and generally it involves some form of **contraception**. Contraception is any procedure which *prevents* conception.

There are many different methods of birth control. Some are easy to use, others more difficult; some are reliable, others less so; and some carry health risks or may be disapproved of by particular religious or cultural groups. Choosing the right method is therefore an important matter and depends on many factors – personal, medical and social. **Family planning clinics** provide advice on the different methods available.

From the biological point of view, birth control methods fall into three categories:

- Methods that prevent sperm reaching the egg.
- Methods that prevent eggs being produced (ovulation).
- Methods that prevent the blastocyst implanting.

The various methods are summarised in the table below. From the table you will be able to see which category each method belongs to.

A distinction can be made between **barrier methods** and **chemical methods**. Barrier methods involve setting up a block in either the male or female system which stops the sperm getting through. Chemical methods involve the use of substances, usually hormonal, which interfere with the body's normal physiology and either prevent ovulation or stop the blastocyst implanting.

Not all the methods shown in the table involve using artificial devices or procedures. Some of the methods are natural. They appeal to people who, for religious or other reasons, object to artificial methods. The main natural method is the **rhythm method**. As this illustrates some important biological principles, we shall look at it in detail.

The rhythm method, a natural method of contraception

The time when a woman can conceive is round about the time of ovulation, which is approximately 14 days after the beginning of the preceding menstrual period. The length of time during which fertilisation is possible depends on how long the egg and sperm remain viable in the female genital tract. The egg can survive in the oviduct for several days, but it is only capable of being fertilised successfully for up to about 24 hours after ovulation. Sperm can live in the oviduct for a week or more, but their ability to fertilise an egg declines after about 48 hours.

From this we may conclude that a woman should conceive only if she has intercourse within a day or so on either side of ovulation. The rhythm method of contraception is based on the premise that if a woman avoids having intercourse at this time, she should not become pregnant.

The rhythm method depends on knowing when ovulation is going to occur, but in some women this is very difficult to determine. A number of subtle changes occur in the body at or around the time of ovulation – for example, the basal body temperature increases very slightly by about 0.2°C and there may be a slight discharge of mucus from the vagina. If these and other changes are monitored over many months, they may be used to predict when ovulation is likely to occur in future menstrual cycles. Once this information has been obtained, a calendar can be drawn up indicating when the 'safe periods' are likely to be.

Unfortunately, variations in the time of ovulation make this an imprecise method of contraception. It can also be a source of stress to some couples, particularly if they are experiencing sexual or emotional difficulties. However, it does have the advantage of being a natural method.

Abortion: termination of pregnancy

Despite the wide range of contraceptive methods available, women sometimes become pregnant when they do not wish to. The only way of avoiding giving birth is to have an **abortion** or – in medical parlance – **termination of pregnancy**. Countries have strict laws on abortion. In Britain an abortion is permitted only if the fetus is less than 24 weeks old and two doctors agree that by continuing the pregnancy the woman's physical or mental health is at risk.

Abortions are also given when the fetus is found to be severely abnormal or when the mother's life is placed in jeopardy by having the baby. In such circumstances abortions up to the end of pregnancy may be permitted.

The moral and ethical issues involved in abortion will be well known to you and we shall not go into them here, except to say one thing. A central question which must influence one's attitude to abortion is: when does a human life begin – or, putting it another way, when does an embryo or fetus become a human being with rights? Is it at conception, or at a later stage? And if the answer is a later stage, then should it be ten weeks, 24 weeks, at birth – or what? On this question a biologist can make useful contributions based on a knowledge of the human embryo and how it develops. There is more about this on page 628.

Method	Description	Comments
METHODS WHICH PREVENT SPERMS REACHING THE EGG		
Natural methods		
Coitus interruptus	Penis withdrawn from vagina before ejaculation	Very unreliable because pre-ejaculation lubricating fluid may contain sperm. Also it requires considerable self-control
Rhythm method	Intercourse avoided at times when ovulation is likely to occur	Unreliable except under expert guidance of doctor or counsellor
Artificial methods		
Vaginal douche	Vagina flushed out with soapy water after intercourse	Extremely unreliable because sperm may reach uterus before douche is given
Spermicide	Cream or pessary, available from pharmacy, placed in vagina before intercourse	Unreliable unless used with condom or diaphragm (see below)
Condom	Rubber sheath placed over penis	Very reliable if used correctly. Most condoms are coated with a spermicidal lubricant
Diaphragm	Rubber diaphragm placed over cervix	Very reliable so long as it stays in place and is combined with a spermicide
Male sterilisation	Vasa deferentia tied and cut by surgeon (vasectomy)	Very reliable but must be regarded as irreversible; semen still produced but without sperm
Female sterilisation	Oviducts tied and cut by surgeon (tubal ligation)	Very reliable but must be regarded as irreversible
METHODS WHICH PREVENT OVULATION		
Oral contraceptive (the 'pill')	Tablet (hormone preparation), prescribed by doctor, taken daily	Very reliable but prolonged use may cause high blood pressure and thrombosis in women who are predisposed to such disorders. May marginally increase the risk of breast cancer
Injectable contraceptive (eg Depo-provera)	Single intramuscular injection, given by doctor, stops ovulation for three months	Very reliable but prolonged use may cause irregular bleeding and possibly other health hazards
METHODS WHICH PREVENT IMPLANTATION		
Intra-uterine device (IUD)	Plastic or metal object placed in uterus by doctor; normal fertility resumed when IUD is removed	Reliable without ill efects though menstrual bleeding may be more severe than usual
Morning-after pill	Tablet taken within three days after intercourse	Reliable but may cause nausea; normally used only as emergency measure
Intra-vaginal ring	Ring-shaped polymer placed in vagina, slowly releases progesterone-like substance	Very reliable though this is a new method and long-term health effects have yet to be fully assessed

The main methods of birth control. Notice that some methods require the expertise of a doctor. Other methods can be carried out by the users themselves. Male and female sterilisation, though generally regarded as irreversible, can sometimes be reversed if, for example, people re-marry and decide they want a family. The success rate for reversing sterilisation is about 50 per cent. The theory behind the oral contraceptive is explained on page 600. The rhythm method is discussed on page 603.

Summary

1 Sexual reproduction starts with **gametogenesis**, the formation of gametes: **spermatogenesis** in the male, and **oogenesis** in the female. Both involve mitosis, growth and meiosis.

2 The microscopic structure of the **testis** and **ovary** is directly related to their functions of producing eggs and sperm respectively. Eggs are shed from the ovary in the process of **ovulation**.

3 The structure of sperms and eggs can be related to their functions. The sperm conveys the genetic material of the male to the egg; the egg receives the male's genetic material and develops into an embryo.

4 In mammals, as in many other animals, internal fertilisation is achieved by **mating (sexual intercourse)**.

5 Certain **sexually transmitted diseases** are associated with intercourse or close sexual contact.

6 In the process of **fertilisation**, a spermatozoon, aided by its **acrosome reaction**, penetrates the jelly coat and fuses with the plasma membrane of the egg. Its haploid set of chromosomes (**paternal chromosomes**) unites with those of the egg (**maternal chromosomes**).

7 After fertilisation, the **zygote** develops into a **blastocyst** which becomes **implanted** in the endometrium of the uterus.

8 In the human female, the **sexual cycle (menstrual cycle)** follows a monthly pattern, ovulation alternating with **menstruation**. The sequence of events is controlled by **gonadotrophic hormones** from the pituitary gland interacting with **ovarian hormones** from the ovary.

9 In the event of fertilisation and implantation, the hormonal balance is altered in such a way that menstruation and ovulation are temporarily suspended and the uterine endometrium continues to grow.

10 A **placenta** develops in association with the uterine endometrium. Connected to the fetus by an **umbilical cord**, it permits exchange of materials between the fetal and maternal bloodstreams.

11 During pregnancy, the placenta takes over the function of secreting the hormones formerly secreted by the ovary. They promote the continued growth of the uterine endometrium.

12 The placental hormones, together with certain hormones produced by the pituitary gland, ensure that **parturition** and **lactation** occur at the appropriate time.

13 In the male, **testosterone**, (**androgen**), stimulates spermatogenesis. Its secretion is maintained by pituitary hormones identical to those produced by the female.

14 As well as initiating egg and sperm production, the sex hormones cause the development of **secondary sexual characteristics** at **puberty**.

15 Some mammals, including the human, can reproduce at any time of the year. Others have specific **breeding seasons** the timing of which is controlled by a combination of environmental and hormonal factors.

16 Various methods of **birth control**, natural and artificial, are available to those who want them.

17 Childless couples may be helped to have children by *in vitro* fertilisation.

Review questions

1 Make a list of all the structures, in the right order, through which a human .perm has to pass from where it is formed to where fertilisation takes place.

2 In what respects are oogenesis and spermatogenesis (a) similar, and (b) different?

3 Compare the testis and ovary from a structural and functional point of view.

4 What ensures that in the human an egg is shed from an ovary only once every 28 days?

5 What do you see as the purpose of menstruation? Not all eutherian mammals menstruate. How do you think it is avoided?

6 Select three important features of a mammalian spermatozoon and explain how each feature helps the sperm to fertilise an egg.

7 List all the reasons you can think of why a woman who has been having frequent intercourse with her husband over many months does not become pregnant.

8 Suggest hypotheses to explain why an implanted blastocyst is not rejected by the mother's immune response.

9 List those substances which pass across the placenta (a) from the mother to the fetus, and (b) from the fetus to the mother.

10 It is claimed that testosterone stimulates male aggression. What sort of investigations would need to be carried out to test this idea?

Further reading

A comprehensive source of reference on all aspects of mammalian reproduction is Austin and Short's eight-volume treatise, *Reproduction in Mammals* (Cambridge University Press, 1980 – 1986). It is not as daunting as it sounds. The individual volumes are not particularly long and they are written in a surprisingly informal style.

Some important social aspects of human reproduction are addressed by Henry Leese in a short book, *Human Reproduction and in vitro fertilisation* (Macmillan Education, 1988). In addition to IVF and its ethical aspects, Henry Leese discusses infertility, artificial insemination and surrogacy.

CHAPTER 34

Reproduction of the flowering plant

Having discussed mammalian reproduction in Chapter 33, we turn for comparison to flowering plants (angiosperms). We shall see that in fundamental respects they are similar: haploid gametes fuse to form a diploid zygote which develops via an embryo into a new plant. However, the flowering plant has special features connected with the fact that it is stationary. This necessitates having devices for bringing the gametes together and for dispersing the reproductive products.

In Chapter 32 we saw how, in the life cycles of many plants, a haploid gamete-producing gametophyte alternates with a diploid spore-producing sporophyte. The flowering plant represents the end product of a line of evolution in which the gametophyte, a self-supporting plant in groups such as mosses, gradually degenerates until eventually it becomes enclosed within the body of the sporophyte. The sporophyte is thus very much the dominant generation in flowering plants (figure 34.1).

The success of flowering plants as a group can be attributed to many factors, but two of the most important are undoubtedly the suppression of the gametophyte with its dependence on water and the development of that unique feature of the group – the **flower**.

The flower

A flower is best considered as a shoot, produced by the sporophyte, which is specially modified for the purpose of sexual reproduction. As we shall see later, the flower contains the relics of the gametophyte.

Flowers show tremendous variety in their structure. There is therefore no such thing as a 'typical' flower. However, all flowers possess certain fundamental features which will now be described.

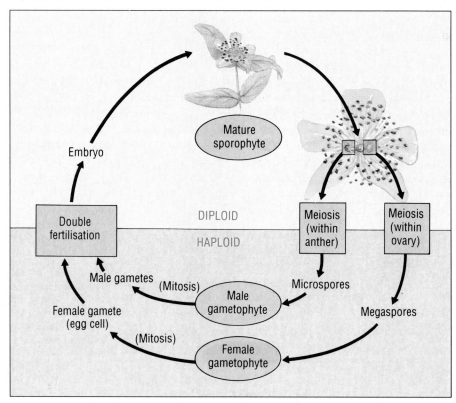

Figure 34.1 The life cycle of a flowering plant showing alternation of the gametophyte and sporophyte generations. The gametophyte generation is greatly reduced and incorporated into the sporophyte. Later we shall see what the microspores and megaspores represent and where the male and female gametophytes are to be found. We shall also see why fertilisation is described as 'double'.

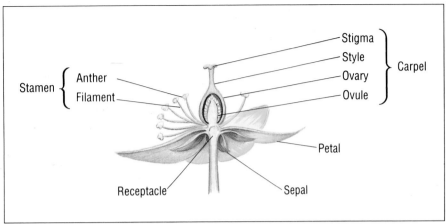

Structure of the flower

A flower typically consists of a series of modified leaves arranged in four circlets called **whorls** around a central stem (figure 34.2). The outermost whorl is usually, but not always, composed of small green leaf-like **sepals**, which together constitute the **calyx**. Unlike the rest of the flower, the sepals can photosynthesise.

The next whorl of leaves may be modified in both shape and colour to form the **petals**, which together form the **corolla**. Neither sepals nor petals are involved in the production of gametes; their function is to attract insects or other pollinating agents by their colour, scent or production of nectar. They may also provide some protection to the other parts of the flower. The sepals are particularly important in protecting the flower bud before it opens. In some cases the sepals have hairs and secrete gums and toxic substances which protect the bud from predators.

The next whorl as we pass from the outside inwards comprises the **stamens**. These modified leaves consist of a stalk or **filament** which supports the **anther**. When ripe, the anther splits open to release the **pollen grains** which contain the male gametes.

Finally, the central whorl is represented by modified leaves called the **carpels**. There may be one or many carpels which may be separate or fused together. Each carpel contains an **ovary**, which encloses one or more **ovules** inside which are the female gametes. The top of the ovary extends into the **style** which ends in a sticky and sometimes hairy **stigma** on which the pollen grains land during pollination.

The flowers of different plants show great diversity. For example, the number of parts in each whorl varies and sometimes the parts are fused together or indistinguishable from each other. For example, in flowers such as lilies and tulips both of the outer whorls are coloured and petal-like. Some of these variations are illustrated in figure 34.3.

Figure 34.2

A *Hypericum* flower showing the parts of a typical flower.

B Drawing of a section of a *Hypericum* flower showing the arrangement of the four whorls of specialised leaves.

Figure 34.3 There are many variations in the basic four-whorl arrangement of the parts of a flower.

A In the lily (*Lilium* sp) the perianth is not distinguished into sepals and petals (a feature of monocotyledons), the six stamens are separate but the three parts to the stigma suggest that the styles have become fused.
B In the hellebore (*Helleborus* sp) the sepals look like petals, the petals are modified as nectaries and there are many separate stamens and carpels.
C In the passion flower (*Passiflora* sp) the petals and sepals are joined to form a bowl from which radiate fine thread-like outgrowths. There are five separate stamens and, in the centre, three separate styles each with a stigma.

Figure 34.4 Holly trees (*Ilex sp*) are an example of a unisexual plant which means that all the flowers on a tree are either male or female. This is why some holly trees never bear berries. *Left* Male flowers with stamens but no carpels. *Right* Berries formed from female flowers.

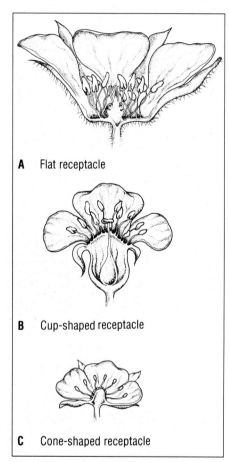

A Flat receptacle

B Cup-shaped receptacle

C Cone-shaped receptacle

Figure 34.5 The shape of the receptacle affects the position of the ovary, or ovaries, in relation to the other parts of the flower.
A The flowers of cinquefoils, *Potentilla sp*, have a flat receptacle.
B In the cherry flower, *Prunus sp*, the receptacle is cup-shaped.
C In the strawberry flower, *Fragaria sp*, the receptacle is cone-shaped.

Figure 34.6 Sections of two flowers to illustrate different types of symmetry.
A a buttercup flower in which the arrangement of the parts shows radial symmetry .
B a foxglove flower in which the arrangement of the parts shows bilateral symmetry.

In some species a whorl may be missing altogether. For example, the stamens or carpels may be absent, thus making the flower **unisexual**. If the stamens are missing and only the carpels are present the flower is female. If only stamens are present then the flower is male (figure 34.4).

Another variation is seen in the **receptacle**, the end of the stem on which the parts are arranged. It may be flat, cup-shaped or cone-shaped (figure 34.5).

There is also much variation in the shape and symmetry of the flower. The parts of the flower may be arranged in a **radially symmetrical** way as in the buttercup, or they may be arranged in a **bilaterally symmetrical** manner as in a foxglove (figure 34.6).

The enormous diversity in the colour, size and shapes of flowers can be related to the way in which the pollen is transferred, a subject we shall return to later. But first let us consider the events that take place inside the male and female parts of a 'typical' flower.

Gamete formation

The male gametes are formed in the anthers of the stamens. Each anther contains four pollen-producing chambers called **pollen sacs** (figure 34.7). In terms of the life cycles of plants described in Chapter 32, the pollen sacs are **microsporangia**. Inside the pollen sacs a large number of diploid **pollen mother cells** are produced as a result of a series of mitotic cell divisions. Each pollen mother cell then divides by meiosis to give a **tetrad** of four

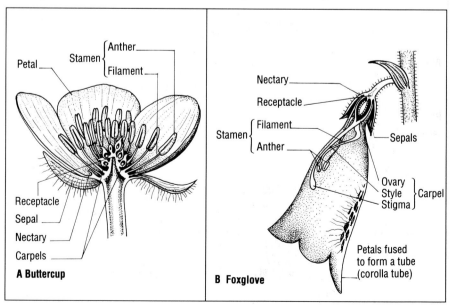

A Buttercup

B Foxglove

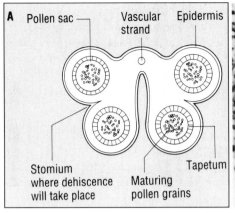

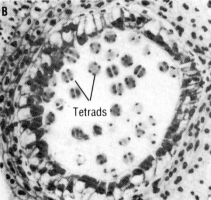

Tetrads

Figure 34.7

A Diagram of a transverse section of a lily anther with the pollen grains inside.

B Photomicrograph of a single pollen sac showing the tetrad stage of pollen-formation in a lily.

haploid cells which separate from each other and become the **pollen grains** (**microspores**). Each pollen sac is lined with a layer of cells called the **tapetum** which provides the developing pollen cells with nourishment. The filament which holds up the anther also contains a vascular strand which supplies the anther with water and nutrients.

While these events are taking place an inner wall, made largely of cellulose, is formed around each pollen cell. By the time the cells of the tetrad have separated, various other substances, mainly proteins, are deposited on the surface of the inner wall to form an outer wall. The outer wall is often beautifully sculptured and its detailed features are unique to each species of plant (figure 34.8).

The proteins in the outer wall provide a recognition system whereby a stigma can recognise pollen of its own species or even from the same plant. This is crucial in preventing self-fertilisation and fertilisation by another species. These proteins are also responsible for the unpleasant allergic reaction we call hay fever.

The way the pollen grains develop is illustrated in figure 34.9. In the tetrad stage each cell contains a single haploid nucleus. After separation, the nucleus of each cell divides by mitosis into a **generative nucleus** and a **tube nucleus**. These nuclei and the cytoplasm surrounding them represent the male gametophyte. So in flowering plants the male gametophyte is totally enclosed within the pollen grain.

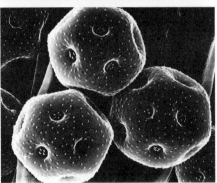

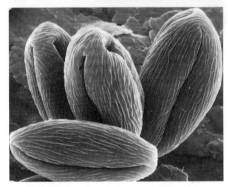

Figure 34.8 Scanning electron micrographs of the pollen grains of three different species. The outer wall is water-repellent and can become extremely resistant to decay. Indeed, pollen grains have been found in peat bogs after thousands of years, providing interesting information about which species existed on the site in the past.
Top Hollyhock × 1000.
Middle Carnation × 2000.
Bottom Cornflower × 1000.

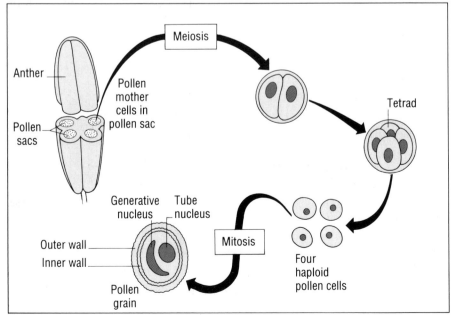

Figure 34.9 The development of a pollen grain. As a result of the meiotic division the pollen cells are haploid.

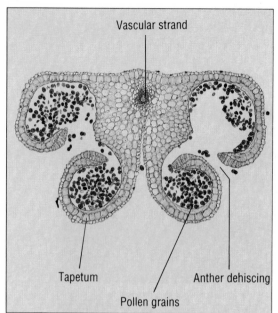

Figure 34.10 Photomicrograph of a transverse section of a lily anther which has split (dehisced), releasing the pollen grains from the pollen sacs.

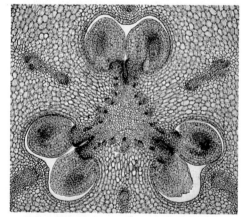

Figure 34.11 Photomicrograph of ovules in the ovary of a lily. Each ovule is attached to the ovary by a stalk (funicle) through which nutrients pass from the parent plant to the ovule. These nutrients will be stored in the seed.

Figure 34.12 A mature ovary containing a single ovule, in the centre of which is the embryo sac. The ovule is attached to the wall of the ovary by a stalk, the funicle. The part of the ovary wall to which the funicle is attached is called the placenta. The chalaza is the part of the ovule where the funicle merges with the nucellus and integuments.

When the anther dries out it splits down both sides. This is known as **dehiscence** and it results in the pollen grains being released (figure 34.10). The pollen grains are not motile and depend on other agents to carry them to the receptive stigmas of the same flower or a different flower of the same species.

The formation of the female gametes takes place in the ovary of the carpel. The ovary is hollow and contains one or more ovules (figure 34.11). The ovule starts as a small bulge of tissue called the **nucellus** on the inside of the ovary wall. Two folds of tissue called **integuments** grow up and over the nucellus leaving a small pore, the **micropyle**, at one end (figure 34.12).

The ovule is a **megasporangium**. Inside it a single cell, called the **embryo sac mother cell**, undergoes meiotic cell division to form a row of four haploid cells (**megaspores**). Three of these cells usually disintegrate. The remaining one expands and its nucleus undergoes three successive mitotic cell divisions to form an immature **embryo sac** containing eight nuclei (figure 34.13).

Inside the embryo sac the eight nuclei become arranged in a 3:2:3 pattern. Three remain at the micropylar end where they become separated from each other by cell walls and form one **egg cell** and two similar 'helper' or **synergid cells**. The three at the other end become the so-called **antipodal cells**. The remaining two nuclei occupy a central position and do not become surrounded by cell walls. They are called the **polar nuclei**.

The mature embryo sac represents the female gametophyte. It is surrounded by the ovule which in turn is enclosed within the ovary. So here, as in the male parts of the flower, the gametophyte is hidden away inside the sporophyte. The ovule is now ready for fertilisation. The style and stigma will have developed and the flower will usually be open so that pollination can take place.

Although the sequence of events just described is typical of many flowering plants, there are a number of variations. You will find such details in a botanical textbook.

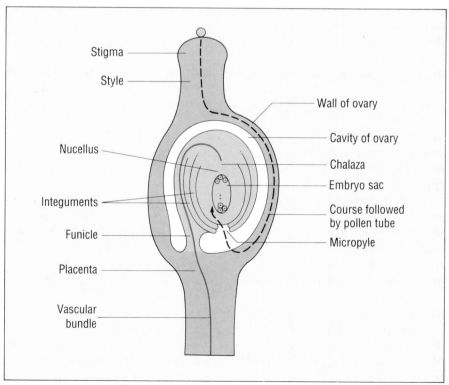

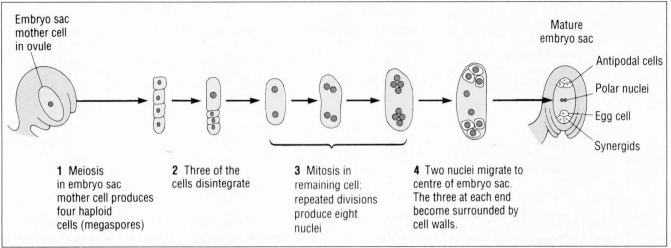

1 **Meiosis** in embryo sac mother cell produces four haploid cells (megaspores)

2 **Three of the** cells disintegrate

3 **Mitosis in** remaining cell: repeated divisions produce eight nuclei

4 **Two nuclei migrate to** centre of embryo sac. The three at each end become surrounded by cell walls.

Figure 34.13 The development of the embryo sac. Notice that all the nuclei in the embryo sac are haploid.

Pollination and the growth of the pollen tube

Pollination takes place when pollen is transferred from an anther to a stigma. Sometimes the pollen grains fall onto the stigma of the same flower (**self-pollination**) but more often they are conveyed either by wind, insects or some other agent to a flower of another plant (**cross-pollination**).

When a pollen grain lands on a compatible stigma it sticks to it because the stigma cells secrete a sugary solution. The sugar solution also promotes further development of the pollen grain. Because the embryo sac is embedded within the tissues of the carpel, a channel has to be provided to carry the pollen nuclei to it. In large flowers the distance may be as far as five centimetres. Fertilisation is therefore preceded by a process in which an outgrowth from the pollen grain, called the **pollen tube**, grows down to the embryo sac taking the pollen nuclei with it.

The pollen tube starts as a small outgrowth, lined by the inner wall of the pollen grain, which protrudes through the outer pollen wall. The pollen tube penetrates the surface of the stigma and then grows into the tissues of the style, deriving nourishment from the surrounding tissues (figure 34.14). Exactly what causes it to do this is uncertain but most pollen tubes are negatively aerotropic, i.e. they grow away from air where there is a higher concentration of oxygen. There is also some evidence that they are guided to the ovule by a chemical produced by the embryo sac.

When the pollen grain germinates, the tube nucleus occupies a position at the tip of the growing pollen tube. It controls the growth of the tube. The growth of the pollen tube is remarkably rapid; a rate of between 20 and 30 mm an hour has been recorded under laboratory conditions so that in some species the tube reaches the ovule in a matter of minutes.

By this time the generative nucleus has divided into a pair of **male nuclei** and these follow behind the tube nucleus as the pollen tube grows down the style (figure 34.15). On reaching the ovary the pollen tube enters the ovule, usually through the micropyle. It then enters the embryo sac and releases its contents near the egg cell and polar nuclei. The tube nucleus now disintegrates and fertilisation follows.

In ovaries with numerous ovules each ovule is fertilised by a male gamete from a different pollen tube.

The pollen grain, with its ability to withstand dry conditions and deliver the male gamete to the female gamete via the pollen tube, has been of great significance in the evolution of angiosperms as it has freed them from a dependence on external water for fertilisation.

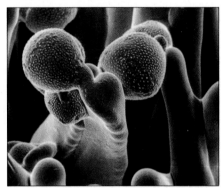

Figure 34.14 Scanning electron micrograph of pollen grains of poppy with tubes growing into a stigma. Magnification × 900.

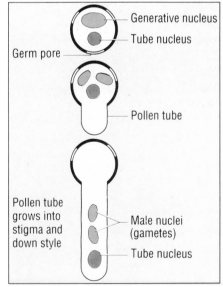

Figure 34.15 The germination of the pollen grain and growth of the pollen tube. The wall of the pollen tube is continuous with the inner wall of the pollen grain.

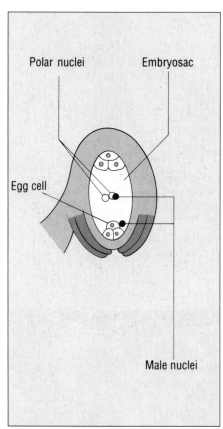

Figure 34.16 Fertilisation in a flowering plant. One male gamete fuses with the female gamete (egg cell) giving rise to a diploid zygote which develops into the embryo. The other male gamete fuses with the two polar nuclei giving rise to a triploid cell which develops into the endosperm tissue.

Figure 34.17 Photomicrograph of an embryo showing the row of cells called the suspensor by which it is attached to the wall of the embryo sac.

Fertilisation

Fertilisation is illustrated in figure 34.16. We have already noted that there are two male nuclei in the pollen tube. One of these nuclei fuses with the egg cell to form a diploid zygote. This is the first cell of the new sporophyte and will give rise to the **embryo**.

The second male nucleus fuses with both polar nuclei to form a *triploid* nucleus. This gives rise to a tissue called the **endosperm**. This tissue is very important because the food reserves of all cereals such as maize, wheat, rice, barley and oats are stored in it. Endosperm is, without question, the most important single source of food in the world. In the seeds of many dicotyledonous plants, however, the endosperm is absorbed by the developing cotyledons which then provide the main food reserve. This is the case in legumes (peas and beans etc).

The events just described constitute a **double fertilisation**, in the sense that *two* male nuclei fuse with female cells. This is unique to flowering plants.

After fertilisation

Following fertilisation, certain changes take place in the floral parts of the plant. Although the details vary from one species to another, the pattern is essentially the same in all flowering plants.

- The zygote divides mitotically, growing and developing into the **embryo**. The embryo consists of a **radicle** (young root), **plumule** (young shoot) and either one or two **cotyledons** (seed leaves). The embryo is attached to the wall of the now expanding embryo sac by a row of cells called the **suspensor** through which it may derive nourishment (figure 34.17).

- The endosperm nucleus divides by mitosis into a mass of nuclei which eventually become separated from one another by thin cell walls. This forms the endosperm, the food storage tissue which surrounds the embryo and provides it with nourishment. In order to accommodate the developing endosperm the nucellus becomes crushed out of existence, so the embryo and endosperm come to fill the whole space inside the integuments.

- The ovule develops into the **seed**, the outer integument becoming the **seed coat**. While this is happening the ovary develops into the **fruit**. The wall of the fruit (**pericarp**) is derived from the ovary wall. The sepals, petals, styles and stamens often wither and fall off after fertilisation, although they may contribute to the formation of the fruit as may the receptacle and even the bracts. Fruits formed from parts of the flower other than the ovary are called **false fruits**, for example apple and strawberry in which the fleshy part of the fruit is formed from the receptacle.

Fruits come in a wide range of shapes and forms but they all have a common function, which is to protect the seeds and aid their dispersal. We shall return to this later.

The final transformation of the ovule into the seed involves the removal of water from an initial 90 per cent to a mere 15 per cent, thus forming a dormant, resistant structure that can withstand adverse conditions.

Self versus cross fertilisation

The majority of plants are **hermaphrodite**. This means that both male and female organs are present in the same flower. This has the advantage that every flower is a potential producer of fertilised eggs, which increases the chances of a large number of offspring being produced. The disadvantage is that the plant runs the risk of **self fertilisation**.

Self fertilisation is the most extreme form of **inbreeding**. It precludes the possibility of genetic mixing between different individuals, and if carried out on a large scale over many generations it may lead to a decline of the species. In general, the offspring resulting from self fertilisation are less vigorous and productive than those resulting from cross fertilisation. It is not surprising to find that hermaphrodite organisms generally have anatomical and physiological mechanisms which promote **outbreeding** and prevent, or at least reduce, the chances of self fertilisation (see page 804).

In flowering plants this means having mechanisms that encourage **cross pollination** and prevent **self pollination**. The surest way of preventing self pollination is to have male and female flowers on separate plants, as in holly. In hermaphrodite flowers it is usual to find either the stamens maturing first and the carpels later or vice versa. Also the relative positions of the stamens and stigma may be such that self pollination is unlikely to happen while cross pollination is promoted. Some plants are self sterile, i.e. the plant's pollen fails to germinate on its own stigmas. As we shall see in the next section there are many devices which favour cross pollination.

Methods of pollination

Flowering plants are usually rooted in the soil and may be some distance from each other. Even if they are near to one another there is no way the male gametes can be transferred to another plant without the assistance of an outside agent. The agents which carry the pollen grains from one plant to another include wind, animal vectors (usually insects) and, in a few aquatic plants, water.

The characteristics of flowers are closely related to the way their pollen is transferred. In wind pollinated plants the pollen grains are small, dry and produced in great abundance, and the flowers lack large highly coloured petals or sepals. The stamens or the whole flower or inflorescence may hang in a pendulous fashion, as in hazel catkins, which ensures that the pollen is scattered as far away from the parent plant as possible (figure 34.18). In grasses the flowers are small but the anthers are borne on long flexible filaments (figure 34.19).

The disadvantage of wind as a vector is that the direction of pollen movement cannot be controlled; also, to be effective, the pollen must land on the stigma of the correct species. Much pollen is therefore wasted. The

Figure 34.18 The catkins of silver birch, *Betula pendula*. A catkin is a cluster of male flowers and is found in many wind-pollinated plants. There are no petals and the stamens hang loosely, producing large amounts of smooth light pollen which is easily carried by the wind.

Figure 34.19 Grass flowers are pollinated by wind. The long filaments with large anthers dangle in the wind, and the hairy stigmas are prominent and ideally placed for 'catching' pollen. In the photograph the dangling anthers are white, and some of them have split open. This particular grass is perennial rye, *Lolium perenne*.

Figure 34.20 Bloody cranesbill, *Geranium sanguineum*, an insect pollinated flower. The colour of the large petals with nectar guides, together with the scent and sticky pollen, are typical features of insect-pollinated flowers. Nectar is a sugary solution used as food by bees and other insects. It is secreted by glands called nectaries at the base of the petals.

Figure 34.21 A bee visits the bright flowers of a composite plant. The small flowers are massed together into a colourful inflorescence at the end of each shoot. Within each flower the stigmas are higher than the surrounding stamens. The bee will brush against the stigmas before it touches the anthers. Any pollen which has been picked up from another flower will be transferred to the stigmas.

stigmas of wind-pollinated flowers usually have a large and hairy surface on which the wind-borne pollen grains are trapped.

Insect-pollinated plants are quite different. They have special features which attract insects, for example the possession of brightly coloured sepals and/or petals, the emission of scent and the secretion of nectar (figure 34.20). In some species a large number of small flowers are clustered together at the end of a shoot to form an inflorescence. This can provide a bright splash of colour and a concentrated source of scent and nectar for insect pollinators. The common shrub *Buddleia*, much visited by butterflies, is an example.

Amongst insect-pollinated flowers there are sometimes elaborate mechanisms for promoting cross pollination. In many flowers the stigma is higher than the surrounding stamens, thus making it impossible for pollen to fall onto the stigma of the same flower. Moreover, if a large insect, such as a bee, visits the flower, its body will brush against the stigma before it reaches the anthers. Any pollen the bee has picked up from another flower will therefore be deposited on the stigma (figure 34.21). The pollen grains of insect-pollinated plants are usually sculptured or sticky, enabling them to adhere to the body of the insect.

Surprisingly few plants are pollinated by water. Those that are usually have small petals and the stigmas are large but smooth. The most familiar example is probably the Canadian water weed, *Elodea canadensis*. This plant is unisexual and the pollen grains from the male flowers are dispersed across the water surface to the stigmas of the female flowers. However, the male plants are so rarely found in Britain that sexual reproduction is not known to occur, Instead this plant reproduces by an entirely different method which is the subject of the next section.

Asexual reproduction

There are two basic types of asexual reproduction in flowering plants. The first one occurs when new individuals are formed from tissues which are not normally involved in sexual reproduction. This is called **vegetative propagation**. In the second type embryos are formed without prior fertilisation, that is by **parthenogenesis** (see page 570).

Vegetative propagation

Vegetative propagation depends largely on the possession in various parts of the plant of meristematic cells which are capable of dividing and differentiating into new tissues. This is what happens in the plant embryo, so in a

Traps and trickery

The varied ways in which animals are involved in pollination include some of the most fascinating mechanisms found in the living world. To the human onlooker some of the devices appear to trap or deceive the animal, usually an insect, in order to achieve pollination. Here we look at a few examples to illustrate the principles involved.

In Britain a highly specialised insect-trapping mechanism is found in the wild arum, *Arum maculatum*. The inflorescence of this extraordinary plant consists of two main parts, the spadix which is the axis of the inflorescence and the leaf-like spathe (illustration 1). The female flowers, which consist of just ovaries and stigmas, are at the base of the spadix. Immediately above them is a ring of hair-like sterile flowers. Above them is a mass of male flowers consisting of short-stalked stamens, the uppermost ones being hair-like and sterile. Above this the spadix extends as a club-shaped structure which is usually purplish in colour and generates

much energy with the result that at times it feels warm.

The spathe opens about midday and, although most people do not notice it, a smell of rotting carrion is produced by the spadix. Certain species of flies which would normally lay their eggs in dung are attracted to the flowers by the smell. They crawl to the bottom of the spadix where the nectar is produced. There they are trapped, unable to climb out because of the hairs and the slippery surface of the spadix and spathe. If the insects happen to be covered with pollen from another *Arum*, they pollinate the female flowers. The stigmas then wither and become non-receptive. The next day the spadix no longer produces a smell, and the male flowers open and release their pollen with which the insects become covered. The hairs, which prevented escape, then wither and the insects fly to another inflorescence where the female flowers are ready for pollination. By this ingenious mechanism cross-pollination is ensured and self-pollination prevented.

Another strategy is found in orchids. In many species of orchids

Illustration 2 A wasp pollinating a broad-leaved helleborine orchid. Notice the pollinia.

the stamen contains two curiously shaped structures called **pollinia** which consist of masses of pollen grains joined together by delicate threads. As soon as an insect alights on the flower and starts to search for nectar, a kind of explosion takes place and a small drop of sticky liquid is ejected which fixes the pollinia to the visiting insect. The liquid sets in a second or so, and the startled insect flies off with the pollinia to another flower. If the flower is more mature than the one just visited, the first structure it will encounter is the stigma. Pollen grains from the pollinia then become attached to the sticky stigma (illustration 2).

A further elaboration of this exists in a number of the orchids, such as the bee orchid and fly orchid. The males of certain species of insect are tricked into copulating with the flower because the lip of the orchid flower resembles the female insect. This happens before the female insects have emerged from pupation. In attempting to copulate with the flower the male insect removes pollinia from it. As soon as the females emerge, the males stop visiting the flowers. The visits of the male insects coincide exactly with the flowering of the orchid.

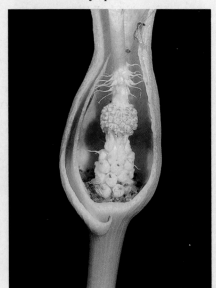

Illustration 1 The wild arum, *Arum maculatum*. *Left* The leaf-like spathe shielding the spadix. *Right* Close-up of the spadix showing the specialised inflorescence. Trapped flies can be seen at the base.

Figure 34.22 *Elodea* (Canadian water weed). The slender stem may break up into numerous pieces, each of which grows into a new plant.

sense meristems represent a continuation of the embryonic stage in the adult plant.

The spread of the Canadian water weed, *Elodea canadensis*, referred to at the end of the last section, is a classic example of how successful vegetative propagation can be. The slender stems of this plant are brittle and snap very easily, setting free pieces of stem which then grow and live independently. This simple but effective method of vegetative reproduction is called **fragmentation**. Its success as a method of propagation is demonstrated by the rapid spread of *Elodea* in the last century. The Curator of the Cambridge Botanic Garden was given some in 1847 and introduced it into a tributary of the river Cam in 1848. By 1852 it had spread into the river to the extent that it prevented fishing, swimming and rowing and made the towing of barges difficult. This plant spread so rapidly throughout parts of the country along rivers and canals that it was considered a pest (figure 34.22). No successful plan was ever discovered for dealing with it. However, by the beginning of the twentieth century it had fortunately declined in vigour and was no more luxuriant than any other water plant, so it ceased to cause a problem. This sort of thing is not unusual in water plants. In warmer climates water hyacinth and water lettuce are even more vigorous examples of the rapid spread of a species by vegetative means.

Vegetative propagation in land plants often takes place by means of modified stems. For example, a side branch, known as a **runner**, can grow out from one of the lower axillary buds of the parent plant. At its nodes small axillary buds and adventitious roots grow and develop into new plants. (An adventitious root is a root that grows out of a stem.) Later the new plants become separated from the parent and each other by decay of the internodal portions of the runner. Creeping buttercup and strawberry are examples (figure 34.23).

In the Mexican hat plant, *Bryophyllum daigremontianum*, numerous small **plantlets** grow on the edges of the leaves and if they fall off they establish themselves as new plants. In some cases, jade plant for example, a new plant is formed when a leaf falls or is torn from the parent plant.

Vegetative propagation may involve the formation of some sort of storage organ, which lies in the soil over the winter and develops into one or more plants the following year. Such devices are known as **perennating organs**. They may be formed from a modified stem, root or bud, depending

Figure 34.23 A strawberry plant with a runner. The runner is a horizontal stem which grows from an axillary bud and forms roots at a node.

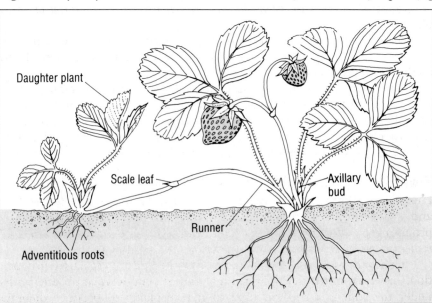

Daughter plant

Scale leaf

Axillary bud

Runner

Adventitious roots

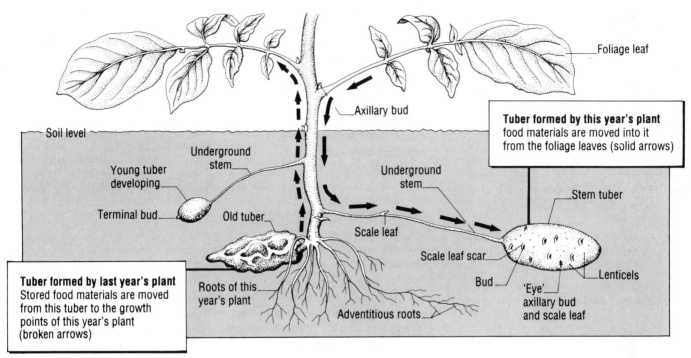

Foliage leaf

Axillary bud

Tuber formed by this year's plant
food materials are moved into it
from the foliage leaves (solid arrows)

Soil level

Underground stem

Young tuber developing

Underground stem

Terminal bud

Old tuber

Stem tuber

Scale leaf

Scale leaf scar

Lenticels

Tuber formed by last year's plant
Stored food materials are moved
from this tuber to the growth
points of this year's plant
(broken arrows)

Roots of this year's plant

Bud

'Eye' axillary bud and scale leaf

Adventitious roots

on the plant in question. Thus the potato is a swollen stem, as is the **corm** of a plant like the crocus and the **rhizome** of an iris. Like any normal stem, these structures have adventitious roots, apical buds and nodes with leaves and axillary buds. It is from the buds that new plants are formed. The basic principles involved in the formation and subsequent growth of a perennating organ are illustrated in figure 34.24.

In the case of root structures, the storage organ is formed from adventitious roots, as in dahlia and lesser celandine. Such structures are called **root tubers** in contrast to the **stem tubers** of, for example, potato plants.

Bulbs are swollen buds in which food is stored in thick fleshy leaves projecting from a much shortened vertical stem. Apical and axillary buds, situated amongst the leaves, develop into new plants either directly or via further bulbs. In some species, particularly lilies, small buds called **bulbils** are produced in the axils of the leaves and these fall off and grow into new plants.

These are but a few examples of vegetative propagation; the main point to note is that many different parts of a plant can contribute towards this method of reproduction.

Vegetative propagation is also important from an ecological point of view. Some of the most pernicious weeds have creeping rhizomes and can spread into, and colonise, new areas extremely rapidly. Couch grass, *Elymus repens*, can produce a new plant every fourteen days and ground elder, *Aegopodium podograria*, is a gardener's nightmare.

Vegetative propagation in horticulture and agriculture

Humans exploit the natural vegetative propagation of plants in horticulture and agriculture using in particular bulbs, corms and tubers as a means of propagating plants more rapidly than from seed. As the process is asexual, it ensures genetic uniformity and therefore consistent quality.

In addition we have developed artificial methods of vegetative propagation. **Layering**, in which a stem from a plant is bent downwards and buried under the soil, is a method used to induce plants to produce daughter

Figure 34.24 The general principle of the formation of perennating organs is illustrated by a potato plant. Towards the end of the growing season, the plant forms swollen tubers at the ends of horizontally growing underground stems. The tubers lie dormant in the soil until the following year when the axillary buds give rise to new plants. In the drawing only one new plant is shown growing out of the old tuber: but in fact all the axillary buds are capable of producing new plants. The old tuber shrivels as the food store is depleted.

Cloning the oil palm

Oil palm oil is used in large quantities in the manufacture of margarine and detergents. When grown under ideal conditions some oil palms (*Elaeis guineensis*) will yield 6 tonnes of oil per hectare. When seeds of high yielding plants are sown not all the plants are high yielding – there is a great deal of variation. The obvious solution is to clone the high yielding oil palm plants.

There is nothing new about cloning plants. Indeed, it is an ancient art which was practised by the earliest horticulturists. It is usually quite easy and amateur gardeners do it when they want to increase the numbers of a valued plant, for example by taking cuttings.

There are now laboratory techniques by which parent plant tissue can be induced to form large numbers of new plants. It relies on the fact that certain cells in the plant remain unspecialised and are capable of further development. It is possible to stimulate these cells to undergo mitosis and form clumps of cells called a **callus** (illustration 1). All the cells in a callus are identical and each one can be grown by the technique of tissue culture into a new plant identical to the parent. In this way thousands of identical plants can be created all belonging to the same clone (illustration 2).

The theoretical significance of this is explained on page 732. Here we are concerned with its commercial importance. It took scientists at Unilever ten years to find a way of cloning oil palms by this method. Besides using a sterile technique, it is essential to have a culture medium on which the plant tissue will grow. It must contain the right nutrients in the correct amounts. Oil palms reared in this way are now growing in plantations in Unipanwe Kluang in Malaysia (illustration 3) and all

Illustration 2 Young cloned oil palms in Colombia.

the plants are capable of a producing a high yield.

Other food plants such as pineapples and bananas are being cloned, and attempts are being made to clone forest trees such as the Norway spruce which is resistant to acid rain. For the gardener, orchids and roses and many other ornamental plants are being cloned, using tissue culture.

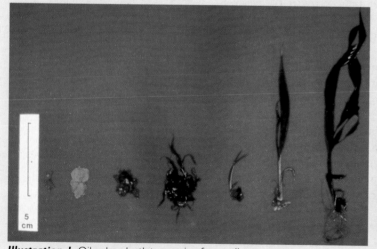

Illustration 1 Oil palm plantlets growing from callus.

Illustration 3 An oil palm plantation in Malaysia.

plants. Adventitious roots grow from the buried portion of the stem and eventually the offspring can be separated from the parent by cutting the connecting stem. All the daughter plants formed from one plant are members of the same clone.

The cut stems of plants (**cuttings**) can also be induced to form roots if they are placed in well watered soil.

Some of the most important methods of artificial vegetative propagation are **grafting** and **budding**. In these procedures a twig or bud of one plant is attached to the stem or roots of another. The method is based on the principle that the cambium tissues of different plants will unite and give rise to normal conducting tissue. (Cambium tissue is explained on page 640.) The plant whose root is used is called the **stock** and the twig or bud is called the **scion**. The way they may be joined is shown in figure 34.25. These methods of propagation are of economic importance to the growers of fruit trees and roses because the desirable qualities of root stock and scion can be combined. For example, a scion of a good eating apple can be grafted to a dwarf root stock making it a more suitable garden tree. Or the bud from a fragrant rose can be grafted to a disease-resistant root stock. Fortunately, the problem of rejection which bedevils grafting in animals does not apply to plants.

Parthenogenesis in flowering plants

The other type of asexual reproduction occurs when embryos and seeds are formed without meiosis or fertilisation taking place. A familiar example is the production of viable seeds with asexual embryos identical to the parent such as those often found in citrus fruits – oranges, grapefruits and tangerines and in their hybrids. It comes about either because a diploid embryo sac is formed or because the embryo is formed from a diploid cell of the nucellus or inner integument of the ovule. In either case meiosis is sidestepped and an embryo develops without fertilisation, so the plant can be said to reproduce by parthenogenesis.

Parthenogenesis has some of the same consequences as persistent selffertilisation in that the offspring are genetically similar to the parent and new genotypes are unlikely to occur. The flowers of parthenogenetic plants are apparently still able to function for pollination. However, in many cases it seems that the formation of the embryo takes place without any outside stimulus such as pollination. The method does, of course, have the advantage of retaining the same dispersal mechanism associated with sexual production of seeds.

Dispersal

Earlier in the chapter we encountered an example of the successful dispersal of a plant by vegetative means. Canadian water weed. Another often quoted example of dispersal is that of the Oxford ragwort, *Senecio squalidus* which was introduced to the Oxford Botanic Garden from Sicily in 1794. It is a vigorous weed and, with the coming of the railways to London, it spread on railway ballast. It is now seen in many parts of the country. The difference between its method of dispersal and that of Canadian water weed is not just that it used railways instead of canals but that it was dispersed by means of its fruits.

On 14 November 1963 a volcanic eruption occurred on the ocean floor several kilometres off the south coast of Iceland and the new island of Surtsey was formed. The first flowering plant appeared in 1965 and the island is still being colonised.

These examples serve to show that mechanisms are built into the reproductive processes of flowering plants ensuring wide dispersal of the progeny. Plants are sessile and wide dispersal is important, otherwise the offspring may compete with one another, and indeed with the parents, thus lowering the survival rate. Moreover wide dispersal enables the species to gain a foothold in new unexploited localities.

Flowering plants may be dispersed as **seeds** and **fruits** by natural agents such as wind, water and animals. To this end they are adapted appropriately. For example, many seeds are extremely small and light, aiding airborne dispersal. Heavier seeds and fruits are equipped with devices such

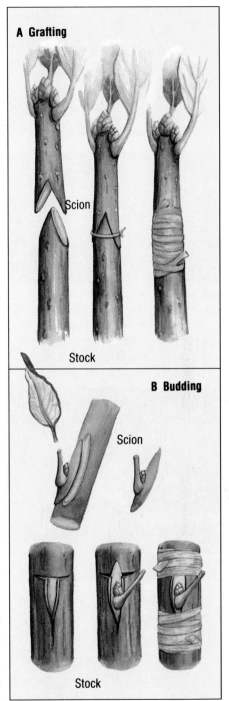

Figure 34.25

A Grafting. There are several ways of grafting. Here the scion and stock have been cut so that the two surfaces fit neatly together and the join is bound with tape.

B Budding. A scion bud is scooped out of the selected variety and inserted into a T-shaped cut in the bark of the stock which is bound with tape. The binding is loosened as growth begins.

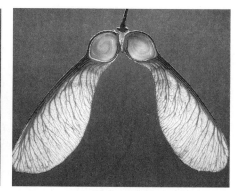

Figure 34.26 Wind dispersed fruits and seeds.

Left The hairy seeds of creeping thistle, *Cirsium arvense*.

Right The wings on a sycamore fruit are an extension of the outer part of the fruit wall pericarp.

Figure 34.27 *Top* Pods of *Laburnum anagyroides*, splitting open and dispersing the seed. *Bottom* Fruits of Indian Balsam, (*Impatiens glandulifera*). When mature and dry they suddenly split and catapult the seeds a considerable distance from the parent plant.

as wings and hairy parachutes which keep them airborne for longer (figure 34.26).

Dispersal is further aided by seeds being discharged from the parent plant by an 'explosive' mechanism involving the sudden splitting of the seed-containing body. This is called **dehiscence** (figure 34.27). Alternatively, they may be scattered from an ovary borne at the end of a long flexible stalk that sways in the wind or is knocked by passing animals. Such 'pepper pot' mechanisms are seen in the dispersal of poppy seeds.

The role of animals in dispersal is equally varied. **Hooked fruits** such as cleavers may cling to their bodies as they brush past (figure 34.28). Other fruits are fleshy and often shiny or brightly coloured, making them attractive to birds as food (figure 34.29). The hard seeds are indigestible so they pass out with the faeces, unharmed and still capable of germination. In fact germination may be stimulated by the passage of the seed through the gut. The seeds may be dropped a long way from the parent plant.

Water is also important in the distribution of certain plants such as palms, the coconut palm for instance. The fruits have thick fibrous walls containing air pockets, enabling them to float. Undoubtedly this has been important in the colonisation of previously unoccupied land masses during evolution (figure 34.30).

Despite these mechanisms to aid dispersal, most seeds do not get far away from the parent plant. However, the occasional ones that do so have had significant effects on the distribution of the species and the colonisation of new habitats.

Figure 34.28 *Top* The fruits ('burrs') of burdock (*Arctium sp*) have hooks which catch onto the coats of passing animals. When the animal scratches in a attempt to remove these burrs the seeds drop out. *Bottom* The hooked fruits of cleavers (*Galium aparnie*).

Figure 34.29 A hedgerow with ripe fruits of the blackberry in autumn.

Figure 34.30 A fruit of the coconut palm (*Cocos nucifera*) being washed ashore.

Summary

1 In flowering plants the reproductive organs are contained within the flower.

2 A flower typically consists of four whorls of modified leaves: **sepals, petals, stamens** and **carpels.** Flowers show great diversity in their structure.

3 The male gametes are formed within the anthers of the stamens. A meiotic division in each **pollen mother cell** gives rise to a tetrad of haploid **pollen grains.**

4 A mitotic division of the pollen grain gives rise to a **tube nucleus** and a generative **nucleus** which divides again into two **male nuclei.**

5 The female gametes are formed in the ovary of the carpel. The **embryo sac mother cell** divides meiotically to give four haploid cells one of which develops into the **embryo sac.**

6 **Pollination** is the process by which pollen is transferred from the male to the female parts of flowers. Sometimes **self pollination** occurs but more often **cross pollination** takes place.

7 After a pollen grain has landed on a compatible stigma a **pollen tube** grows down to the embryo sac taking the male nuclei with it.

8 The pollen tube enters the ovule, and **fertilisation** takes place when one of the male nuclei fuses with the egg cell to give rise to the **zygote.**

9 The other male nucleus fuses with two **polar nuclei** in the embryo sac to form the triploid **endosperm** nucleus which develops into the **endosperm tissue.**

10 After fertilisation the zygote develops into an embryo consisting of radicle, plumule and one or two cotyledons. Meanwhile the ovule develops into the **seed** and the ovary into the **fruit.**

11 Self fertilisation leads to inbreeding which may cause a decline in the species. Cross fertilisation leads to outbreeding and the offspring are generally more vigorous.

12 Flowering plants usually have mechanisms which prevent self pollination and promote cross pollination.

13 Because plants are sessile they depend on outside agents to carry the pollen from one individual to another. The most usual agents are wind and insects.

14 Many features of flowering plants can be related to their methods of pollination.

15 Because plants possess meristematic tissue they are able to reproduce asexually by **vegetative methods** such as runners, bulbs and corms.

16 In some cases embryos are formed **parthenogenetically,** i.e. without fertilisation taking place.

17 Humans have exploited the natural vegetative reproduction of plants as well as developing artificial methods.

18 Tissue culture has enabled scientists to **clone** economically important plants.

19 Although plants may be dispersed by asexual structures they are more usually dispersed by their fruits and seeds. Fruits and seeds have features to aid their dispersal by agents such as wind, animals and water.

Review questions

1 Explain how events in the life cycle of flowering plants relate to the functions carried out by the different parts of the flower.

2 Explain the differences between:

  (a) Megaspore and microspore.
  (b) Pollen grain and male gametophyte.
  (c) Ovule and female gametophyte.

3 It is incorrect to call the pollen grain the male gamete. Why?

4 Describe what happens, during and after fertilisation, to the eight nuclei formed in the embryo sac.

5 In what ways is endosperm tissue unusual? Why is it unlike other tissues?

6 Explain what is meant by double fertilisation in a flowering plant.

7 Summarise the changes that occur in a flower after fertilisation.

8 What are the advantages of cross pollination as opposed to self pollination?

9 Give examples to illustrate how flower structure reflects the method of pollination.

10 Explain the underlying principle on which most methods of vegetative propagation in plants depends.

Further reading

A comprehensive and fascinating account of pollination mechanisms can be found in *The Pollination of Flowers* by Michael Proctor and Peter Yeo (Collins, 1973).

In *Biology, Advanced Topics* there is further information on cross-fertilisation in flowering plants.

CHAPTER 35 Patterns of growth and development

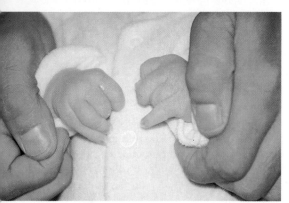

Figure 35.1 The hands of a ten day old baby compared with those of the father.

In the course of its life cycle an organism changes from a fertilised egg into an adult. As development proceeds, all sorts of changes take place. The most obvious change is **growth**. One has only to compare the hands of a human adult with those of a baby to appreciate the effectiveness of growth as a biological process (figure 35.1).

But development involves more than just growth. The egg gives rise first to a ball of cells that does not look at all like the adult organism. Somehow this ball of cells is transformed into a complex body with all the different structures arranged in the right positions. This is achieved by cell movement and cell specialisation.

The progressive changes which are undergone before an organism acquires its adult form constitute **embryonic development**, and the study of these changes is called **embryology**. Studying the embryology of any animal or plant entails asking two basic questions: what changes take place, and how do they occur? In this chapter we shall be mainly concerned with the structural changes that occur, starting with growth.

Growth

Three distinct processes contribute to growth: **cell division, assimilation** and **cell expansion**.

Cell division is the basis of growth in all multicellular organisms, but plainly to grow to the size of the parent cell, the daughter cells must be able to synthesise new structures from raw materials which they absorb from their surroundings. This is what is meant by assimilation, and it results in cell expansion.

In plants, cell expansion may be aided by vacuolated cells taking up water by osmosis and swelling up. This is the basis of how stems and roots increase in length, about which we shall have more to say later.

Measuring growth

Growth can be quantified by measuring some feature of the organism, such as height or mass, at suitable intervals over a known period of time. This is not always easy, because of difficulties in selecting the right feature. Commonly a linear dimension such as height or length is measured. Because growth usually takes a long time, a slowly revolving **kymograph** (see page 494) or **time-lapse photography** may be used for making a continuous record of the changes that occur. A continuous record also has the advantage of showing up any variations in the rate of growth that may occur at different times.

The drawback with measuring a single linear dimension such as height, is that it takes no account of growth in other directions, which in some cases may be considerable. One can sometimes get round this by measuring changes in volume. However, this may call for considerable mathematical ingenuity if the organism has an irregular shape.

A feature often used is mass, but this may not necessarily be a measure of growth as such, and can be particularly influenced by fluctuations in the fluid content of the body. To overcome this one may resort to estimating *dry* mass, that is the mass after all moisture has been driven off by heating. The trouble here is that it kills the organism, so measurements must be obtained by taking random samples at intervals from a large population of individuals. The latter should be the same age, growing under constant

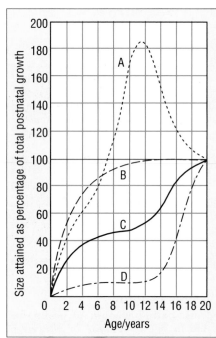

Figure 35.2 Growth rates of different parts of the human body between birth and maturity. The sizes on the vertical axis are expressed as percentages of the total gain between birth and maturity (20 years). Thus the size of any given part of the body is 100 per cent at age 20.

Curve **A**: lymph tissue.

Curve **B**: brain and head.

Curve **C**: general, i.e. legs, arms, lungs, kidneys, muscles etc.

Curve **D**: reproductive organs.

conditions, and preferably all identical genetically, that is members of the same clone. This technique is commonly adopted with plants.

Allometric growth

One problem with measuring growth is that different parts of the organism may grow at different rates and stop growing at different times. For example, in humans the head grows rapidly at first and then slows down, virtually stopping altogether soon after the age of about five years. However, the legs and arms continue to grow for another 15 years or so, as do most of the other organs (figure 35.2).

The growth of different parts of the body at their own particular rates, higher or lower than the growth rate of the body as a whole, is known as **allometric growth**. Most organisms show allometric growth to some extent. A full description of an organism's growth must obviously take this into account.

The growth curve

If an organism's measurements (height, mass or whatever) are plotted against time, a **growth curve** is obtained. Despite difficulties in measuring growth, the general pattern turns out to be the same for most organisms. If measured from an early enough stage, you get an S-shaped curve of the kind shown in figure 35.3A: growth is slow at first, then it speeds up, and finally it slows down as the adult size is reached.

In humans and certain other vertebrates, growth stops altogether when the adult size is reached (in the early twenties in most humans). However, in the majority of organisms growth continues in adult life, though slowly.

The rate of growth

The growth curve enables us to express the growth of an organism in terms of the **growth rate**. This can be done by estimating the increase in size that takes place during successive intervals of time. The increases (i.e. **growth increments**) are then plotted against time.

In an organism with a growth curve like the one in figure 35.3A, the growth rate increases steadily until it reaches a maximum, after which it gradually falls, giving the bell-shaped curve shown in figure 35.3B.

Relative growth rate

It was said earlier that multicellular organisms grow by cell division. Each generation of daughter cells then undergoes assimilation and expansion. In other words the products of the growth process are themselves capable of growing. This is quite different from, say, the growth of a crystal, in which new material is added to the surface of the existing crystal from the outside. Different, too, from the building of a house in which new bricks, obtained from an outside source, are added one by one to the existing structure.

In contrast, an organism's growth is essentially an internal process, taking place from *within* the organism. This means that the amount of growth which takes place at any stage is dependent on the bulk of tissue already present, i.e. on how much growth has already occurred. This is taken into account by measuring the **relative growth rate**, in which the increase in growth over a period of time is expressed as a percentage of the amount of growing matter already present.

Let us take an example. Between the ages of one and two years, a baby's body mass might increase from 10 to 12 kg. The absolute increase is

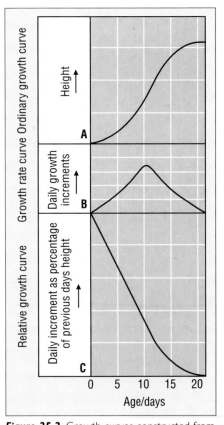

Figure 35.3 Growth curves constructed from data on lupins. The shape of the curve depends on how you express the growth. See text for details.

therefore 2 kg, but the relative increase, expressed as a percentage, is 2/10 x 100 = 20 per cent. Now, in the same period of time the mass of a teenager might go up from 50 to 55 kg, giving an absolute increase of 5 kg. However, the relative increase is only 5/50 x 100 = 10 per cent, half that of the baby. So the baby, though it puts on less mass in a year, has a higher *relative* growth rate.

If relative increase is plotted against time, we get a curve of the sort shown in figure 35.3C. Represented this way, the growth rate does not rise and then fall. On the contrary, growth is fastest at the beginning of life (in the human while the fetus is in the uterus), after which it gradually slows down. This is true of most organisms, plants as well as animals.

Intermittent growth in arthropods

The smooth growth curve shown in figure 35.3A is typical of most organisms, but there is one notable exception: arthropods. Look at figure 35.4, for instance. These curves were obtained by plotting the body masses of two different types of insect against time. Instead of increasing smoothly, growth takes place in a series of jumps. These correspond to the sequence of stages, or **instars**, in the insect's development (see page 634).

This **intermittent growth** is made necessary by the **cuticle** (**exoskeleton**) which, because of its hardness, prevents the body from growing. Periodically the cuticle is shed, a process called **moulting** (**ecdysis**). Only then – while the new cuticle underneath is still soft enough to allow the body to expand – can any significant amount of growth take place.

In some cases rapid expansion is achieved by the insect swallowing air or water. The waterboatman, from which the growth curve in figure 35.4A was obtained, expands by swallowing water – that is why its mass increases so abruptly each time it moults. The distension of the gut when water or air are swallowed pushes the new cuticle outwards. The cuticle then hardens and the tissues inside can grow to fill the space available. After that, further growth is impossible until the cuticle is shed again. At the final shedding of the cuticle, the wings expand.

Animal development

The changes which occur as an animal develops are brought about by the cells rearranging themselves and taking up new positions. This is achieved partly by cells migrating from one place to another, and partly by layers of cells becoming folded in various ways.

Cell migration is possible because the embryonic cells are able to move about by a process which looks superficially like amoeboid movement (see page 528). Once the cells have got into the right positions, they lose the ability to move. They then differentiate into particular types of tissue.

Embryonic development is normally triggered by **fertilisation**. In the majority of animals the subsequent changes fall into four main stages:

- **Cleavage**, the division of the zygote into daughter cells.
- **Gastrulation**, the arrangement of these cells into distinct layers.
- **Neurulation**, the formation of a central nervous system.
- **Organogenesis**, the formation of organs and organ systems.

Development is, of course, a continuous process and to some extent these four stages may overlap.

The following account is based mainly on amphibians such as the African clawed toad, *Xenopus*, whose development has been studied extensively. Amphibians belong to the chordate phylum and their early develop-

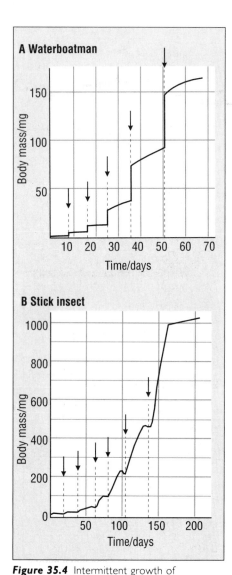

Figure 35.4 Intermittent growth of arthropods illustrated by two species of insect. Graphs showing the increase in mass of **A** a waterboatman *Notonecta glauca* and **B** a stick insect *Carausius morosus* with time. The times of moulting are indicated by the arrows. The reason why the mass rises so abruptly in graph **A** is that the waterboatman swallows water when it moults. Why do you think the body mass *decreases* slightly when the stick insect moults?

ment illustrates many of the basic principles of chordate development in general.

Cleavage

During cleavage, the zygote divides repeatedly into progressively smaller cells. The cell divisions are mitotic, so all the cells have the same genetic constitution.

In amphibians a moderate amount of yolk is present towards the bottom of the egg (the vegetal pole). The presence of the yolk makes the lower part of the egg relatively inert and slows down the rate of cell division. The result is that the cells at the top of the egg (the animal pole) are smaller than the ones beneath.

Cleavage is a highly organised process in which a series of successive divisions occur in planes at right angles to each other. Typically two vertical divisions at right angles to each other are followed by a horizontal division; thereafter alternate vertical and horizontal divsions take place (figure 35.5A). As the cells at the top divide faster than the yolky cells beneath, they come to be more numerous as well as smaller.

The result of cleavage is a ball of cells which, as no assimilation and cell growth have yet taken place, is the same size as the original fertilised egg. At first the ball of cells is solid, but as cleavage continues a fluid-filled cavity is formed in the middle. The resulting hollow ball of cells is known as a **blastula**, and its cavity is called the **blastocoel** (figure 35.5B).

Gastrulation

The key event in gastrulation is the formation of the gut (gastrulation means literally 'formation of a stomach'). The exact way this happens varies from one animal group to another. At its simplest it takes place by the hollow blastula invaginating at one end, rather like a hollow rubber ball being pushed in on one side (figure 35.6).

This process of invagination results in the virtual obliteration of the blastocoel and its replacement by a new cavity, the **archenteron** (literally 'primitive gut'). Its opening to the exterior, where invagination occurred, is called the **blastopore**. The blastopore represents the future posterior end of the embryo.

Gastrulation produces a two-layered structure, essentially a cup within a cup. The outer layer of cells is called the **ectoderm** and the inner layer of cells is called the **endoderm**. The ectoderm is destined to give rise mainly to the skin, the endoderm to the lining of the gut. This is what happens in invertebrate chordates (see page 116). In vertebrate chordates the process is more complicated. In amphibians, for example, invagination occurs just

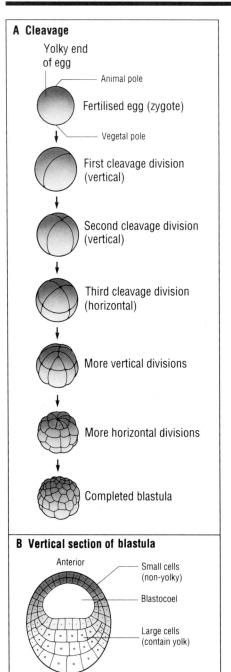

A Cleavage

Yolky end of egg

Animal pole

Fertilised egg (zygote)

Vegetal pole

First cleavage division (vertical)

Second cleavage division (vertical)

Third cleavage division (horizontal)

More vertical divisions

More horizontal divisions

Completed blastula

B Vertical section of blastula

Anterior

Small cells (non-yolky)

Blastocoel

Large cells (contain yolk)

Posterior

Figure 35.5 Cleavage in an amphibian. **A** Successive vertical and horizontal mitotic divisions of the fertilised egg result in the formation of a hollow blastula. Amphibian eggs are typically pigmented towards the upper side, as shown here. In **B** anterior and posterior refer to the future axis of the embryo.

Figure 35.6 Gastrulation in an invertebrate chordate takes place by invagination of the hollow blastula, as shown here. It results in the formation of a two-layered gastrula.

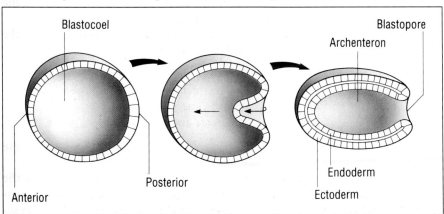

Blastocoel

Blastopore

Archenteron

Anterior

Posterior

Endoderm

Ectoderm

above the large yolky cells on the lower side of the blastula, and is accompanied by migration of cells in various directions.

As gastrulation proceeds, a third layer of cells makes its appearance between the ectoderm and endoderm. Because it is located between the other two layers of cells, it is called the **mesoderm**. The mesoderm gives rise to most of the body's organs and organ systems: muscles, skeleton, blood vessels and so on. It is therefore an important part of the embryo.

The way the mesoderm is formed varies between different species. In amphibians it is formed by cells migrating inwards into the blastocoel from the blastopore region. The same applies, with certain modifications, to birds and mammals. In these animals the inward migration of cells occurs on either side of a deep indentation called the **primitive streak** which extends forward from the blastopore on the dorsal side of the embryo. In the early 1980s the primitive streak hit the headlines because it was decided that its appearance in the human embryo should be taken as the point when embryo research should stop (see box on page 628).

However formed, the mesoderm of all chordates comes to lie between the ectoderm and endoderm. The embryo is therefore composed of three layers of cells: ectoderm, mesoderm and endoderm. These are called the **germ layers**. Having three layers of cells like this is a fundamental feature of the ground plan of most animals. Indeed, the only major group of animals that do not have three cell layers are the cnidarians – *Hydra* and its relatives. They have only two layers – ectoderm and endoderm (see page 112).

The appearance of the three germ layers in the right positions marks the end of gastrulation and paves the way towards the next important event: neurulation.

Figure 35.7 Neurulation in an amphibian. The left hand diagrams are transverse sections of the developing neurula; the right hand diagrams are dorsal views. In all chordates, neurulation takes place by the neural plate on the dorsal side of the embryo sinking downwards and becoming first a groove and then a tube. Notice that by the time neurulation starts, the mesoderm almost completely fills the space between the ectoderm and endoderm.

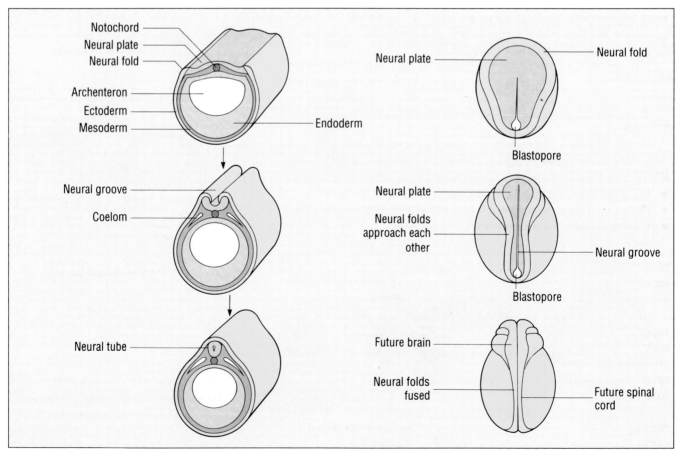

Neurulation

Neurulation, the formation of the central nervous system (CNS) is shown in figure 35.7. First, the cells in the mid-dorsal line immediately above the gut from a structure called the **notochord**. This is a skeletal rod which stiffens and strengthens the dorsal side of the embryo. In *Amphioxus* it persists in the adult. However, in the vertebrates it is replaced later on in development by the vertebral column.

If you look at figure 35.7A, you will see that the ectoderm immediately above the notochord differentiates into a flat area called the **neural plate**. This is destined to form the central nervous system. The way it does so is essentially the same in all chordates and is shown in figure 35.7B and C. First the neural plate sinks downwards, forming a longitudinal groove. The folds on either side of the groove (called **neural folds**) then grow towards each other until they meet in the mid-dorsal line. They then fuse together, forming a **neural tube**.

The anterior end of the neural tube expands to form the brain, while the rest remains narrow and becomes the spinal cord. The cavities of the brain and the central canal of the spinal cord are relics of the cavity in the neural tube.

At the stage when the neural tube is forming, the embryo is known as a **neurula**. By this time, the embryo has increased in length. The ectoderm indents at the anterior end to form a small pouch-like invagination which eventually breaks through into the archenteron as the mouth. Meanwhile, the blastopore closes up, and the archenteron acquires a new connection with the exterior just below the blastopore. This new opening becomes the anus.

Further development of the mesoderm

The way the mesoderm continues its development is shown in figure 35.8. These diagrams are based on amphibians but essentially the same events take place in other chordates too.

First, notice the small slit-like cavity inside the mesoderm on each side of the body. This is called the **coelom** and it is going to become the **body cavity**.

Gradually the coelom extends downwards on each side of the body. Then the mesoderm, and the coelomic cavity inside it, divide up into three parts on each side. These three parts of the mesoderm are:

- The **somite mesoderm** on either side of the neural tube and notochord.
- The **intermediate mesoderm** just below the somite mesoderm.
- The **lateral plate mesoderm** enveloping the gut.

The somite mesoderm splits up transversely into a series of identical blocks on either side of the body. Known as **somites**, they impose on the embryo a serially repeated pattern. This is called **metameric segmentation** and it is a fundamental feature of all chordates and many other animals.

The intermediate mesoderm also becomes segmented into a series of repeated parts on either side of the body. Each part sends out tubules which unite to form a longitudinal tube. This tube grows back to the **cloaca**, the common cavity which receives the anus and openings of the reproductive system. Further elaboration of the intermediate mesoderm results in the formation of the **kidney**.

The lateral plate mesoderm behaves quite differently. It remains unsegmented and the coelomic cavity inside it expands to form the general body cavity. As the coelomic cavities on either side of the body expand, their

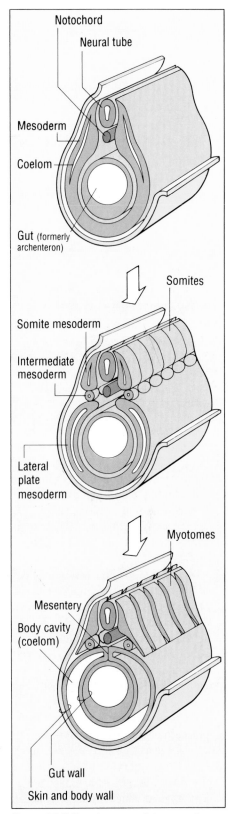

Figure 35.8 Development of the mesoderm based on transverse sections through the trunk region of amphibian embryos. The way the mesoderm develops is fundamentally the same in all vertebrates, including the human.

mesodermal walls approach each other above the gut and eventually meet in the midline. The vertical strand of mesoderm so formed becomes the **mesentery** by which the gut is suspended in the body cavity. Below the gut the coeloms on the two sides join to form one large **abdominal cavity**.

So we now have a large coelomic body cavity completely surrounded by mesoderm. The outer part of the mesoderm lies against the ectoderm, the inner part against the endoderm. The part lying against the ectoderm becomes the body wall and its muscles. The part lying against the gut becomes the muscle layers of the gut wall. The superficial mesodermal tissue lining the body cavity itself forms the **peritoneum**.

While the lateral plate mesoderm has been developing in this way, two important things have been happening to the somites. Cells from the inner face of each somite migrate inwards, surrounding – and eventually replacing – the notochord where they become the **vertebral column**. Most of the remainder of the somite becomes a solid block of muscle called a **myotome**.

Why fourteen days?

Research on human embryos is only permitted for fourteen days following fertilisation. Here, guest author Mary Warnock explains why the committee which she chaired on this matter decided on fourteen days.

There were good biological reasons for picking on this particular number of days. These reasons give grounds for a moral distinction which justifies our adopting a different attitude towards a human embryo before fourteen days after fertilisation from that which we adopt towards later embryos or fetuses.

Let me explain our reasoning. Up to fourteen days, the embryo consists of a collection of dividing cells which ae loosely clustered together. These cells are not yet differentiated into particular tissues or organs. Nor will all of them become part of the embryo itself: some of them will become part of one of the extra-embryonic structures such as the placenta or the amnion. Moreover, it is possible at this stage for two or even three embryos to develop from the cluster of cells. It is in fact the last stage at which twins or triplets may be formed.

The pre-fourteen day embryo is therefore not yet a single individual living organism: it may be one or two or three individuals. Indeed, such is its lack of differentiation that it has been suggested that the cluster of cells should not be called an embryo, but a 'pre-embryo'. However, at about the fourteenth day a definite change takes place: a groove appears on the upper side of the embryo – the **primitive streak**. This marks the beginning of gastrulation. It is at this stage that the cells begin to differentiate into specialised types, some taking up their role as part of the placenta, others coming together to form what will become the brain or spinal cord of the embryo itself. From this time onwards we must recognise that the cluster of cells has become an individual embryo which will become a fetus and then a child.

Our committee sought evidence from many different quarters, and a range of opinions was expressed. For example, The Royal College of Obstetricians and Gynaecologists suggested that embryos should not be allowed to develop *in vitro* beyond a limit of seventeen days, as this is the point when early neural development begins. The British Medical Association favoured a limit of fourteen days whilst certain other groups, including the Medical Research Council and the Royal College of Physicians, suggested that the limit should be the end of the implantation stage – that is, about 15 days after fertilisation. Some groups suggested that the limit should be the *beginning* of the implantation stage – about eight days after fertilisation.

To summarise, although the pre-fourteen day embryo contains all the genetic material that the child will ultimately have, in another sense it is not the same individual as that child: indeed it is not an individual at all. It has the potential to develop into several individuals, and its nervous system has not yet started to develop. These were the main biological reasons why Parliament decided that research of certain kinds might be carried out on the early human embryo.

The law states that by the fourteenth day the embryo must either be placed in a woman's uterus to develop in the normal way, or be frozen so that it may be placed in the uterus later. In practice embryo transfers are carried out by the fifth or sixth day at the latest, and usually by the second day. If transfer or freezing does not take place, the embryo may be used for research but must be destroyed by the fourteenth day. In practice any research will have been completed long before the fourteenth day.

Human embryo research

Research on human embryos is permissible until the fourteenth day after fertilisation. Here guest author Henry Leese explains the kind of research that is carried out.

The main types of research which can be carried out on human embryos are as follows:

Research on culture media for IVF

The development of a suitable culture medium in which to grow human embryos was a major hurdle facing early researchers in their pioneering work on IVF. Improvements to the media have been made over the last thirty years, and continue today. Obviously embryos are needed to test the efficacy of the various culture media under trial.

Research on improving the success of embryo transfer

The major point of failure in IVF therapy is at the embryo transfer stage. Embryos are assessed for transfer on the basis of their appearance under the microscope and on how well they develop in culture. Research is being carried out to devise more rigorous ways of assessment.

One approach is based on the observation that those embryos which implant successfully have a higher glucose consumption than those which do not. The aim, then, would be to analyse the culture medium using ultra-sensitive techniques and choose those embryos which take up most glucose.

Research on improving methods of storing embryos

Further experiments are aimed at improving the procedures for freezing and storing embryos so that a woman can have the opportunity of receiving an embryo at a later date.

Research on assisted fertilisation

Over 30 per cent of infertile couples owe their infertility to some kind of disorder of sperm production or function, and in most cases the problems are untreatable. Hope for infertile men may come from research into ways of helping sperm to cross the jelly coat (zona pellucida) of the egg. Techniques are being developed for making a fine hole in the jelly coat through which sperm may enter unaided or be injected with a very fine pipette. The first human pregnancy achieved by sperm microinjection occurred in 1986.

Research on a contraceptive vaccine

The sperm of a given species will only bind to the jelly coat of an egg belonging to the same species. This provides the key to developing an immunological method of contraception. The strategy would be to immunise the woman against the recognition proteins located on the egg or sperm. The antibodies against the egg or sperm would prevent fertilisation and act as a long-lasting contraceptive.

Research on chromosome abnormalities

Careful observation of human embryos created by IVF has revealed that about one third of the embryos have an abnormal chromosome content, preventing them developing into blastocysts capable of implanting, or leading to the births of abnormal babies. It is thought that these sorts of chromosome abnormalities are responsible for about 50 per cent of the 75 000 miscarriages that occur in the UK each year.

Research on the diagnosis of genetic disease

Perhaps the most exciting area of human embryo research is that aimed at diagnosing genetic abnormalities.

About 14 000 babies are born in the UK each year with such defects as cystic fibrosis, haemophilia, Huntingdon's chorea and β-thalassaemia. Half the babies born with genetic defects die in early infancy.

Embryo research offers the possibility of diagnosing genetic disorders at a very early stage of development.

Embryo screening

Diagnosis of many genetic disorders has been possible for some time by the techniques of **amniocentesis** and, more recently, **chorionic villus sampling** (**CVS**) (see page 791). The trouble is that these procedures cannot be carried out until well into pregnancy. If the diagnosis of genetic disorders could be carried out before implantation occurs, affected embryos could be discarded and only the healthy ones put back in the uterus.

Couples identified as 'at risk' of passing on genetic defects to their children can now attend for IVF and have their embryos screened. Techniques are available which make it possible to remove one or more cells at an early stage of development – usually the 8-cell stage three days after fertilisation. The embryo is unharmed by this. In the meantime, the DNA in the isolated cell(s) is amplified by making it replicate repeatedly to a level at which standard methods for diagnosing genetic disorders can be applied. The healthy embryos can be placed in the uterus immediately, or frozen for embryo transfer on a future occasion. Any unhealthy embryos may then be discarded.

All these remarkable developments culminated in the birth, in 1990 and 1991, of five babies whose embryos had been screened at the 8-cell stage. The women given this treatment had all had previous terminations of pregnancy.

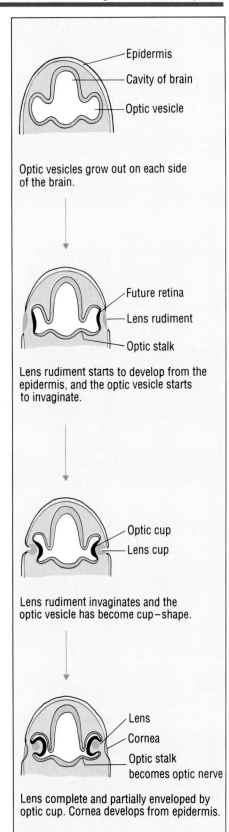

Optic vesicles grow out on each side of the brain.

Lens rudiment starts to develop from the epidermis, and the optic vesicle starts to invaginate.

Lens rudiment invaginates and the optic vesicle has become cup–shape.

Lens complete and partially enveloped by optic cup. Cornea develops from epidermis.

Figure 35.9 Transverse sections through the head of a generalised chordate showing the development of the eye.

In fishes the segmental pattern of the myotomes is very apparent (see page 522), but in terrestrial chordates such as amphibians and mammals the segmental pattern is obscured by the development of limbs.

Organogenesis

By the late neurula stage, the basic organisation of a chordate is laid down. Subsequent development involves the further differentiation of the three germ layers, particularly the mesoderm, into specific organs.

The limbs develop as outgrowths from the sides of the body. Their muscles are formed from mesodermal cells which migrate into them from the ventral sides of the somites.

The **gut** increases in length and becomes differentiated into various regions: pharynx, intestine and so on. The intestine increases greatly in length and becomes coiled, and various accessory organs such as the **liver** and **pancreas** develop as outgrowths from it.

The **lungs** arise as an outgrowth from the back of the **pharynx**, and **blood vessels** are moulded out of the mesoderm. The tadpole has feathery **external gills** to begin with, but later these are replaced by **internal gills**. The latter develop as pouches of the pharynx which eventually break through to the exterior on either side of the body.

The ventral mesoderm towards the anterior end of the body arranges itself into the shape of a large tube which expands to become the **heart**. The part of the coelom surrounding the heart becomes the **pericardial cavity**.

The anterior end of the neural tube expands to form the brain. The rest of the neural tube becomes the **spinal cord**. **Peripheral nerves** grow out of the brain and spinal cord, linking up with the body's receptors and effectors. **Special sense organs** (nose, eye and ear) develop in close association with the brain.

It is impossible to cover the formation of all these individual organs. However, let us look briefly at the development of the eye to see some of the principles involved.

Development of the eye

The way the eye develops is outlined in figure 35.9. By this stage the anterior part of the embryonic brain, known as the **forebrain**, is expanding to form what in mammals will become the cerebral hemispheres.

The first step in the development of the eye is the formation of an outgrowth from the posterior part of the forebrain on each side of the head. This is called the **optic vesicle** and at this stage it is hollow, its cavity being continuous with that of the brain. As it develops, the optic vesicle invaginates to become cup-shaped. The inner lining of the optic cup becomes the **retina**. In the meantime the epidermis lying alongside the optic cup invaginates to form the **lens**, and the epidermis lying alongside the lens obligingly forms the **cornea**. The optic vesicle never loses its connection with the brain – it becomes the **optic nerve**.

Here, as in earlier stages of development, we find layers of cells growing in various directions and folding in relation to each other. The question naturally arises: what causes the cells to do the right thing at the right time? This is discussed on page 740.

The extra-embryonic membranes

Although there are many detailed differences in the way they are formed, the embryos of all chordates are fundamentally similar. In fact a transverse section through the trunk region of *any* chordate embryo after neurulation looks more or less like the diagrams in figure 35.8. However, reptiles, birds

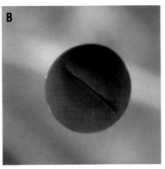

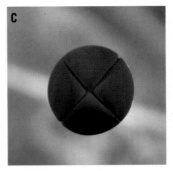

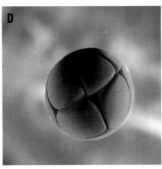

A

B

C

D

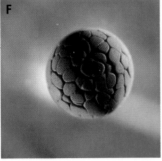

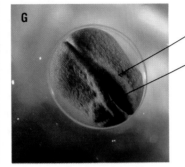

E

F

G

Neural fold

Neural groove

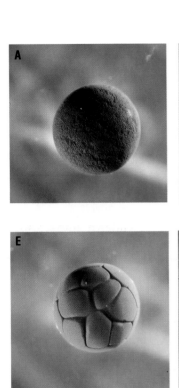

Figure 35.10 Early chordate development illustrated by the common frog, *Rana temporaria*.
A The egg soon after fertilisation.
B to **F** Cleavage, viewed from above, i.e. from the animal pole.
G Formation of the neural tube following gastrulation.
H Longitudinal vertical section after completion of the neural tube.
I Transverse section through the trunk region after completion of the neural tube. This stage is reached approximately one week after fertilisation.

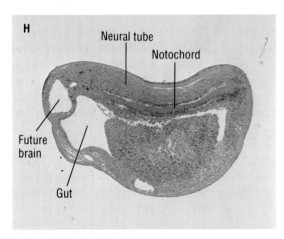

H

Neural tube

Notochord

Future brain

Gut

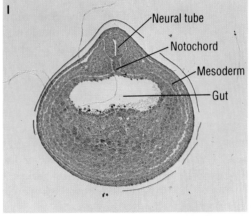

I

Neural tube

Notochord

Mesoderm

Gut

and mammals differ from other chordates in one important respect: they possess a system of membranes which are located *outside* the embryo. They are called **extra-embryonic membranes**.

The first extra-embryonic membrane to be formed is the **yolk sac** which is particularly well developed in reptiles and birds. Because the eggs of these animals contain so much yolk, cleavage is confined to the animal pole. This results in the embryo being situated on top of the yolk. As development proceeds, the embryo becomes lifted off the yolk sac to which it remains connected by a stalk. So the yolk sac is outside the embryo itself. The lining of the yolk sac is well supplied with blood vessels from the embryo (figure 35.11). The embryo derives nourishment from the yolk via these blood vessels.

Mammals, too, have a yolk sac though it is generally very small compared with that of reptiles and birds. It does not contain any yolk and provides no nourishment for the embryo.

The way the other extra-embryonic membranes are formed is shown in figure 35.12. The diagrams are based on the bird, but they are broadly

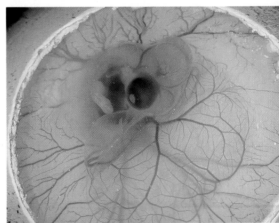

Figure 35.11 A six day old chick embryo as seen under the light microscope. Notice the vitelline arteries ramifying over the yolk sac.

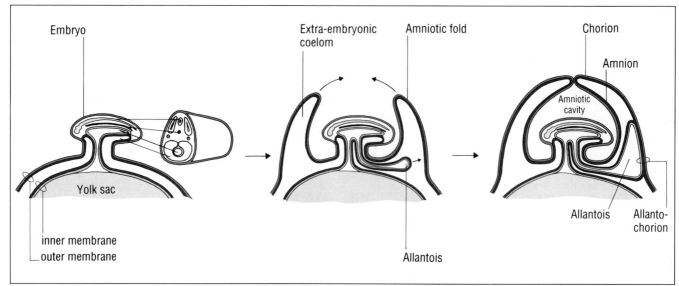

Figure 35.12 Development of the extra-embryonic membranes. The diagrams are based on birds, but also apply with only minor modifications to mammals including the human. The functions of the various membranes and the cavities which they enclose are explained in the text.

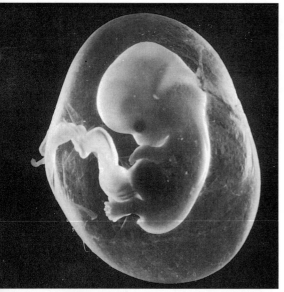

Figure 35.13 In this photograph of a human fetus, taken through a tube introduced into the uterus, the amnion can be seen surrounding the fetus. The fetus is just over 8 weeks old and is approximately 20 mm in length.

applicable to reptiles and mammals as well. First look at the top diagram and notice how the yolk sac is attached to the embryo. You will see that the yolk sac itself is surrounded by two membranes, an inner one which is continuous with the gut of the embryo, and an outer one which is continuous with the body wall of the embryo. Between these two membranes there is a coelomic cavity which, because of its position outside the embryo, is called the **extra-embryonic coelom**.

Now look at the lower two diagrams in figure 35.12, and see what happens. The outer membrane of the yolk sac becomes thrown into a circular fold which grows up and encloses the embryo in a fluid-filled **amniotic cavity**. Being formed from a fold, it is lined by two membranes. The inner one is called the **amnion**, and the outer one is called the **chorion**. The space between them is extra-embryonic coelom.

While the amniotic cavity is forming, a further cavity develops which you can see in the two right hand diagrams in figure 35.12. This cavity arises as an outgrowth from the lower side of the gut, and it pushes its way into the extra-embryonic coelom. Known as the **allantois**, it expands into a balloon-like sac whose lining fuses with the chorion to form the **allanto-chorion**.

The possession of an amnion and the other extra-embryonic membranes described above is fundamental to the embryos of all reptiles, birds and mammals. For this reason these three vertebrate groups are described as **amniotes**.

Functions of the extra-embryonic membranes

In all amniotes the fluid-filled amniotic cavity cushions the delicate embryo and protects it from physical disturbance. If you want to prevent a fragile object from breaking, one of the best ways is to suspend it in a fluid.

The function of the allantois differs in the various groups. In reptiles and birds it becomes a depository for nitrogenous waste. Since the embryo is surrounded by a shell there is no way of getting rid of nitrogenous waste, so it has to be stored out of harm's way. As the embryo grows and develops, the allantois becomes full of solid crystals of uric acid. Meanwhile the allanto-chorion develops into a highly vascular surface for gaseous exchange. Located just beneath the porous shell, it allows oxygen and carbon dioxide to diffuse between the blood of the embryo and the surrounding atmosphere.

In mammals the allanto-chorion develops into the **placenta**. The chorion develops finger-like outgrowths which become the **chorionic villi** described in Chapter 33. They become invaded by blood capillaries and project into blood spaces which develop in the wall of the mother's uterus. Across their thin walls, exchange of materials takes place between embryonic and maternal blood (see page 594). As the placenta grows and expands, the yolk sac gradually diminishes. At the same time the amniotic cavity expands, pushing the amnion and chorion outwards until finally the amnion fuses with the chorion, and the chorion with the inner surface of the uterus.

The net result of these changes is that the fluid-filled amniotic cavity completely fills the uterus, and the embryo (by now a **fetus**) lies in the middle of it. The only connection between the fetus itself and the wall of the uterus is the stalk of the allantois, and its associated mesoderm, which becomes the **umbilical cord**. This, you will remember, contains the **umbilical artery** and **vein** which carry fetal blood to and from the placenta. Because of their association with the fetus, the extra-embryonic membranes of a mammal are referred to as the **fetal membranes**.

The above description applies to *eutherian* mammals (see page 117). It does not apply to marsupials and monotremes. Marsupials, such as the kangaroo, have a placenta which arises differently from, and is much simpler than, the allantoic placenta of eutherian mammals. Monotremes, such as the spiny anteater, lay eggs and have no placenta at all.

The fetal circulation

The placenta is the means by which the fetus obtains oxygen. Because of this, the fetal circulation has to be different from that of the adult.

The basic plan of the fetal circulation is shown in figure 35.14. The umbilical artery carries deoxygenated blood from the dorsal aorta of the fetus to the placenta where the blood is oxygenated. The umbilical vein then carries the oxygenated blood from the placenta to the posterior vena cava of the fetus, whence it enters the right atrium of the heart. The lungs are functionless at this stage, and most of the blood bypasses them by flowing through a hole in the heart, the **foramen ovale**, which connects the right and left atria. Blood which misses it can take an alternative bypass, the **ductus arteriosus**, a short vessel which connects the pulmonary artery with the aorta. The foramen ovale is guarded by a valve which prevents blood flowing back from the left to the right atrium.

At birth the placenta is replaced by the lungs as the organ of gaseous exchange. This means that blood must now start flowing to them fully. Within a few minutes after birth, the ductus arteriosus constricts so that from now on all the blood in the right ventricle is sent to the lungs. This, coupled with the closure of the umbilical vein, results in the blood pressure in the left atrium exceeding that in the right atrium. This has the effect of closing the valve of the foramen ovale, like the slamming of a door. Within a few days after birth, the foramen ovale becomes sealed up by the fusion of its valve with the atrial wall. With the loss of the placental circulation, and the closure of the ductus arteriosus and foramen ovale, the adult circulation becomes established.

Larval forms

In the type of development described so far, the embryo develops into the adult without any breaks in the continuity. In some animals, however, the egg develops first into a **larva** which then changes into the adult. The larva

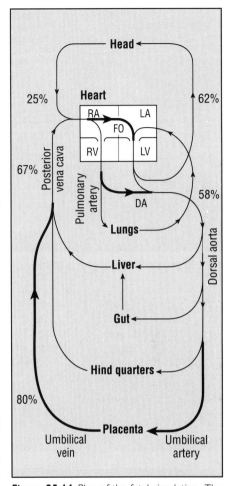

Figure 35.14 Plan of the fetal circulation. The thick arrows indicate routes taken by the blood in the fetus which are absent in the adult. The figures give the percentage saturation of the blood with oxygen in some of the major vessels. Investigations on the fetal circulation of the sheep have shown that about half the blood entering the right atrium of the heart from the venae cavae passes through the foramen ovale into the left atrium. Of the blood which enters the right ventricle nearly 80 per cent flows via the ductus arteriosus to the aorta. **RA** right atrium, **LA** left atrium, **RV** right ventricle, **LV** left ventricle, **FO** foramen ovale, **DA** ductus arteriosus.

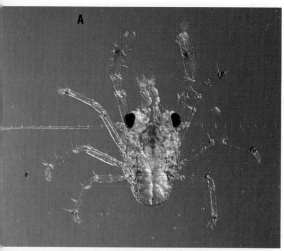

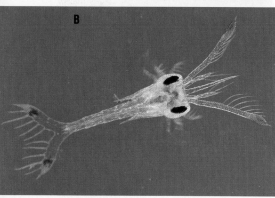

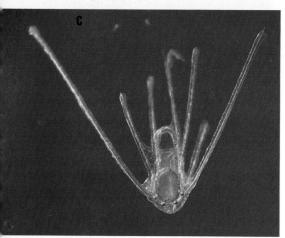

Figure 35.15 Some microscopic larvae commonly found in plankton.
A Nauplius larva of a lobster.
B Zoaea larva of a crab.
C Pluteus larva of a brittle star.

is usually very different from the adult in form and habit, and the process by which it is transformed into the adult is called **metamorphosis.**

The way a larva fits into an animal's development is seen particularly clearly in amphibians. The larval stage is the **tadpole,** and it differs from the adult not only in its structure but also in its habitat, food and behaviour.

Amphibians are the only vertebrates to have larvae. Larvae are more common amongst invertebrates. The best known are those of insects, such as the caterpillars of butterflies and moths, the maggots of flies and the grubs of ants and beetles. These larvae are all adapted to life on land.

Other invertebrates have aquatic larvae. For example, crustaceans such as lobsters and crabs have larvae with jointed legs for swimming, and marine annelids and molluscs have larvae which are wafted through the water by beating cilia. Ciliated larvae are found in a number of other invertebrate groups including cnidarians, echinoderms and parasitic flukes (see page 85). And the sea squirt, an invertebrate chordate, has a larva like a little tadpole which swims through the water by undulations of its tail (see page 774).

Though varied in structure, all these larval forms have three basic features in common:

- They are markedly different from the adult so that in some cases it is difficult to see any connection between them.
- They are self-supporting and lead an independent life, fending for themselves in ways that are generally different from those adopted by the adult.
- They cannot reproduce sexually, and only in certain specialised instances can they reproduce asexually.

It is desirable that the adult of a species should not compete with one of its own developmental stages. The fact that larvae and adults are so different means that they can exploit different habitats and never come into direct competition with each other.

The functions of larvae

Looking at animals in general, larvae have four basic functions:

1 Motile larvae help to distribute the species. This is particularly important to slow-moving or sessile animals such as sea anemones and corals.
2 In the case of parasitic species, the larva may enable the parasite to get from host to host. For example, the ciliated larvae of the blood fluke *Schistosoma* swim through the water and infect new human hosts.
3 In some species the larva is primarily responsible for feeding and growth, prior to the formation of the adult whose principal function is to reproduce sexually. Such is the case with insects, particularly butterflies and moths.
4 In certain specialised cases, notably parasitic flukes, the larvae may be capable of asexual reproduction, thereby increasing the number of offspring produced (see page 85).

Metamorphosis

Metamorphosis, the change from larva to adult, generally involves a profound reorganisation of the body. Nowhere can this be better seen than in insects. Insects show two types of metamorphosis:

- **Incomplete metamorphosis.** We see this in such insects as locusts, grasshoppers, cockroaches, termites and dragonflies. The egg develops into the adult via a series of **nymphs** which are essentially miniature adults lacking wings. Moulting and growth take place between each nymphal stage (instar), giving the intermittent stepwise growth described on page 624. 'Incomplete' is not a very apt adjective for this kind of metamorphosis – 'gradual' might be better, since each moulting brings the animal closer to the adult form (figure 35.16).

- **Complete metamorphosis.** We see this in such insects as butterflies, moths, beetles, flies, bees, wasps and ants. The egg develops into a **larva** which is completely different from the adult. After an active life of feeding and growth, typically with several moults, the larva changes into a **pupa.** Though usually immobile and seemingly inactive, the pupa is the site of considerable internal activity. The larval tissues are broken down by phagocytes into a fluid mass. The only structures to escape this dissolution are the central nervous system and small groups of cells called **imaginal discs.** From the imaginal discs the adult organs are formed: the cells multiply and differentiate, nourishment coming from the now dissolved remains of the other larval tissues. Once the adult body is complete, and provided environmental factors are favourable, the insect emerges from the pupa as the adult or **imago.**

The change of a tadpole into a frog is another example of metamorphosis. However, it does not entail complete destruction of the larval tissues – except for the tail which is digested by lysosome action. Amphibian metamorphosis involves more a modification of existing structures than their total replacement. These changes are associated with the move from water to dry land: the tail is lost, the gills are replaced by lungs, and the legs (already present in rudimentary form) develop fully. Meanwhile changes take place in the heart and blood vessels, and a double circulation is established (see page 313).

Development of the flowering plant

In flowering plants, development begins with the growth of the zygote into a simple **embryo** inside the seed. This has already happened by the time the seed is fully formed, and is described on page 612. The embryo itself is differentiated into an embryonic shoot (**plumule**), an embryonic root (**radicle**) and one or two 'seed leaves' (**cotyledons**). The embryo may be surrounded by **endosperm tissue**, and the whole is enclosed and protected within the tough **seed coat.**

The structure of a generalised seed, showing the parts mentioned above, is illustrated in figure 35.17. Notice the **epicotyl** and **hypocotyl.** The epicotyl is the base of the shoot above the point where the cotyledons are attached; the hypocotyl is the base of the radicle below the point where the cotyledons are attached. Their significance will become clear in a moment.

Not all seeds are exactly like the one in figure 35.17 – there are many variations on the theme. In the first place there may be either one or two cotyledons depending on whether the plant is a monocotyledon or dicotyledon (see page 111). There are also variations in the size and thickness of the cotyledons, and in the amount of endosperm tissue present.

The function of the endosperm is to nourish the embryo. If there is a lot of endosperm in the seed, it may nourish not only the embryo but also the young plant when it grows out of the seed. In some species the endosperm nutrients are absorbed by the cotyledons which then provide nourishment for the newly emerging plants.

The size of the cotyledons and the amount of endosperm in a seed are therefore related to the way the young plant is nourished during the early

Figure 35.16 The final moult of a dragonfly into the adult. From the shape of the old cuticle you can see that the adult is really an enlarged version of the preceding nymphal stage. Apart from size the only major difference is that the adult has wings. The cuticle of the newly emerged adult is soft enough to allow an immediate increase in size. The abdomen expands by the swallowing of air, the wings by blood being pumped into them from the thorax. Once the adult's cuticle hardens, no further growth can take place.

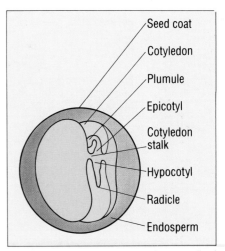

Figure 35.17 The main parts of a generalised seed. The seeds of different species differ in the number and size of the cotyledons, and the amount of endosperm present.

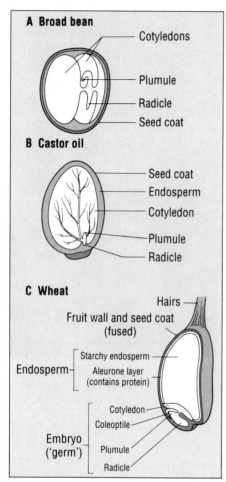

A Broad bean
- Cotyledons
- Plumule
- Radicle
- Seed coat

B Castor oil
- Seed coat
- Endosperm
- Cotyledon
- Plumule
- Radicle

C Wheat
- Hairs
- Fruit wall and seed coat (fused)
- Endosperm
  - Starchy endosperm
  - Aleurone layer (contains protein)
- Cotyledon
- Coleoptile
- Embryo ('germ')
  - Plumule
  - Radicle

Figure 35.18 The seeds of three different species of plant to illustrate the kind of variations which can be observed.

Figure 35.19 A broad bean seed germinating. Root hairs are evident on the radicle, and two lateral roots are just beginning to sprout. One of the cotyledons is just visible beneath the ruptured seed coat.

stages of its growth. To appreciate this, compare the three different seeds illustrated in figure 35.18:

- In the broad bean the mature seed has two large thick cotyledons full of stored food (starch), but no endosperm. In this type of seed, the cotyledons provide nourishment for the newly emerging plant.
- In contrast, the castor oil seed has two thin scale-like cotyledons and a relatively large amount of endosperm with oil as the food reserve. In this case the endosperm nourishes the newly emerging plant.
- In the wheat seed (the so-called 'grain'), the single cotyledon is reduced to a small scale-like structure, and the bulk of the seed is filled with endosperm which contains starch. Here too, the newly emerging plant is nourished by the endosperm.

Germination

The process by which a new plant emerges and grows out of the seed is called **germination**. The radicle appears first and grows downwards into the soil. Then the shoot appears and grows upwards out of the soil. Once the shoot is in the light, green leaves develop. Meanwhile lateral roots grow out from the main root, anchoring the plant and absorbing water and nutrients. The young plant is called a **seedling**.

Figure 35.19 shows a young broad bean seedling on which the above description is based. Notice that the shoot emerges in such a way that the plumule is bent back on itself. This protects the delicate growing points and young leaves, preventing them from getting damaged as the shoot pushes its way up through the soil. In the seedlings of wheat and other grasses the plumule is protected by a sheath, the **coleoptile**, which breaks open when the first leaves appear.

Types of germination

There are two types of germination which differ from each other in what happens to the cotyledons:

- In **hypogeal germination** (figure 35.20A) the epicotyl elongates, with the result that the plumule is thrust upwards out of the soil, leaving the cotyledon(s), still enclosed within the ruptured seed coat, in the soil (*hypogeal* means 'below the ground'). Seeds germinating this way include broad bean and wheat. During its early growth the seedling is nourished by food reserves in the seed – in the cotyledons of the broad bean, and the endosperm of the wheat seed.
- In **epigeal germination** (figure 35.20B) the hypocotyl elongates, with the result that the plumule *and* cotyledons are thrust upwards out of the soil (*epigeal* means 'above the ground'). Seeds germinating this way have thin cotyledons which, once exposed to light, develop chlorophyll and start to photosynthesise. Before this happens nourishment is provided by the endosperm which is usually extensive in this kind of seed. Examples of seeds showing epigeal germination are sunflower and castor oil.

What happens during germination?

Germination starts with a rapid uptake of water by the seed, usually through the micropyle. This results in a dramatic increase in mass – more than 1.5 times the original mass of the seed in the case of the broad bean.

How is the water taken up? You will recall that the final event in the formation of the seed is the drying out of the embryonic tissues inside.

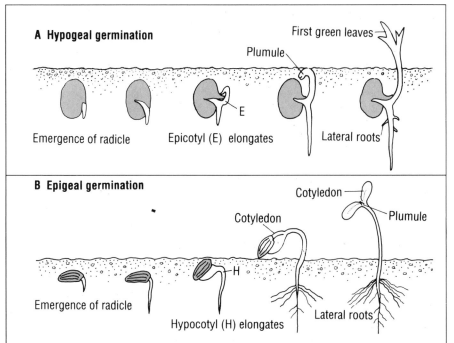

Figure 35.20 Diagrams showing the two types of germination. In hypogeal germination the epicotyl (**E**) elongates, so the cotyledons remain below the ground. In epigeal germination the hypocotyl (**H**) elongates, so the cotyledons are thrust up above the ground taking the seed coat with them. In these diagrams, hypogeal germination is based on the broad bean, epigeal on the sunflower.

This creates a massive water potential gradient acting inwards. When the time comes, water is absorbed by the dried-out cells and cell walls, first in the seed coat and then in the endosperm and embryo itself. This is called **imbibition**. With the hydration of the tissues, the soluble substances in the seed go into solution creating a solute potential which results in water being taken up by osmosis.

The uptake of water by the embryonic tissues causes the embryo to swell. This ruptures the seed coat, allowing the growing root to emerge. The shoot follows shortly after. By this time the enzymes are in solution and have started working, and the rate of respiration may increase a thousandfold. The stored food materials in the seed (e.g. starch) are hydrolysed into soluble products which are capable of being translocated to the tip of the root and shoot where growth occurs. This rapid mobilisation of food reserves is a requirement for successful germination.

What sort of conditions are needed for germination to occur? Controlled experiments can be carried out in which seeds are deprived of the various conditions thought to be necessary for germination, and the effects observed. Such experiments indicate that seeds require, in addition to water, a suitably high temperature, oxygen and appropriate illumination. These and other aspects of how germination is controlled are discussed in the next chapter.

Growth and development of the shoot and root

In plants, growth is achieved by cell division in certain localised regions called growing points or **meristems**. Figure 35.21 shows the positions of the meristems and related structures in a young plant. The principal meristems are at the tips of the shoot and root (**apical meristems**), and at the sides of the shoot (**lateral meristems**). The meristems of the shoot are enclosed in **buds**, the apical meristem in an **apical bud** and the lateral meristems in **axillary buds**. This latter name derives from the fact that they occur in the angle or **axil** between the stem and a leaf – or what may become a leaf. Leaves and axillary buds occur at regular intervals

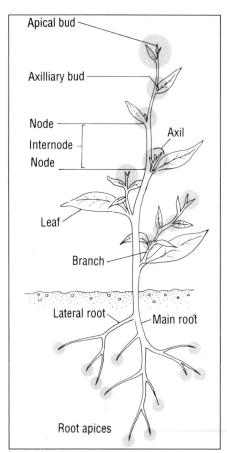

Figure 35.21 Diagram showing the positions of the primary meristems (growing points) of a plant. The meristems are ringed.

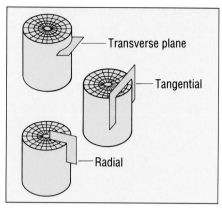

Figure 35.22 The planes in which cell divisions occur in a growing shoot or root.

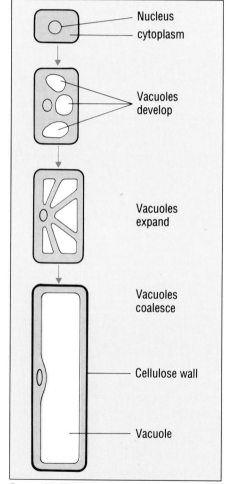

Figure 35.23 Expansion of a cell in the growing region of a flowering plant takes place by the osmotic uptake of water into the developing vacuole. To begin with only the primary cell wall has been formed (see page 152). This is soft and stretchable, allowing the cell to expand as shown. When the cell reaches its full size the secondary wall is added, making the cell wall tougher and preventing any further expansion.

called **nodes**; the region of the stem between two successive nodes is called an **internode**.

Meristematic cells are potentially capable of dividing in three different planes, and this determines the direction in which growth takes place (figure 35.22). Divisions in the **transverse plane** increase the length of the stem or root; divisions in the **radial plane** increase the circumference; and divisions in the **tangential plane** increase the diameter, i.e. the thickness. In the apical meristems most of the cell divisions are in the transverse plane, so the emphasis is on increase in length.

As new cells are formed, the older ones further back expand. Figure 35.23 shows how this happens. At first, the cell is full of cytoplasm with the nucleus in the middle. Then several small vacuoles appear in the cytoplasm. These soon coalesce to form the large, sap-filled vacuole typical of mature plant cells. Expansion takes place by the osmotic uptake of water into the developing vacuole.

The shape acquired by the cell depends on the thickening of its cellulose walls, and this is the first step towards differentiation. The process is rather like blowing up differently shaped balloons. If cellulose is laid down uniformly all round the cell, expansion occurs equally in all directions and a more or less spherical cell results. This is how parenchyma cells develop. If cellulose is laid down unevenly, expansion occurs more in one direction than another and an elongated cell may be formed. This is what happens in the formation of, for example, xylem vessels. A plant cell may increase in length by as much as forty times during its development.

Differentiation of the cells into particular types involves further elaboration of the cell wall: excessive deposition of cellulose at the corners results in the formation of collenchyma cells, and impregnation of the cellulose with lignin results in the formation of vessels, tracheids and sclerenchyma fibres.

Stem and root apices

The apex of a shoot or root can therefore be distinguished into three zones from the tip backwards:

- **Zone of cell division** where the cells are dividing.
- **Zone of cell expansion** where the cells are expanding.
- **Zone of cell differentiation** where the cells are developing into specialised types.

These three zones in a dicotyledonous plant are shown in figure 35.24. One of the first tissues to start differentiating, apart from the epidermis, is the vascular tissue. In fact the first-formed xylem and phloem tissues, known as **protoxylem** and **protophloem**, make their appearance in the zone of expansion. The later vascular tissues are called **metaxylem** and **metaphloem**, and they make up the bulk of the vascular tissues eventually. The protoxylem cells are generally smaller than the metaxylem cells and can readily be discerned in transverse sections of mature dicotyledonous stems. Where, within the vascular tissue, would you expect to see the protoxylem in the transverse sections on the left hand side of figure 35.24? And the protophloem?

In the shoot apex, **leaf primordia** arise on either side. These grow up and envelop the tip, forming an apical bud. In this way the delicate meristematic tissues are afforded protection. In the angle between each leaf (or leaf primordium) and the main stem an **axillary bud** may be found. Axillary buds have meristematic cells at the tip with the potential to form side branches or flowers.

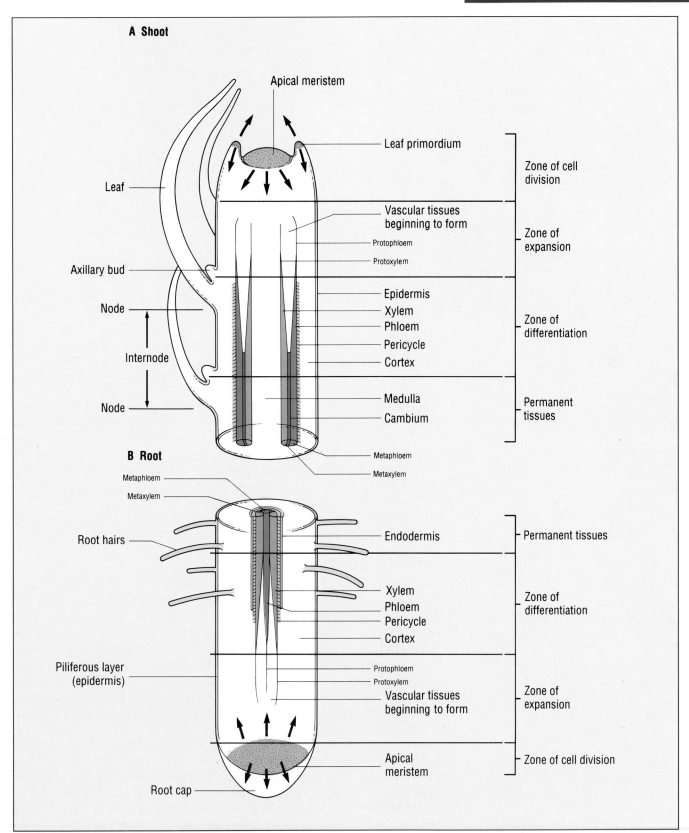

Figure 35.24 The internal structure of a dicotyledonous shoot and root apex to show how they grow and develop. Cell divisions in the apical meristem produce daughter cells which, with continued formation of new cells at the tip, enter the zone of expansion.

Further back the cells differentiate into specific types of tissue: xylem, phloem, pericycle and so on. There is no sharp distinction between the zones of expansion and differentiation; the cells begin to differentiate while they are still expanding.

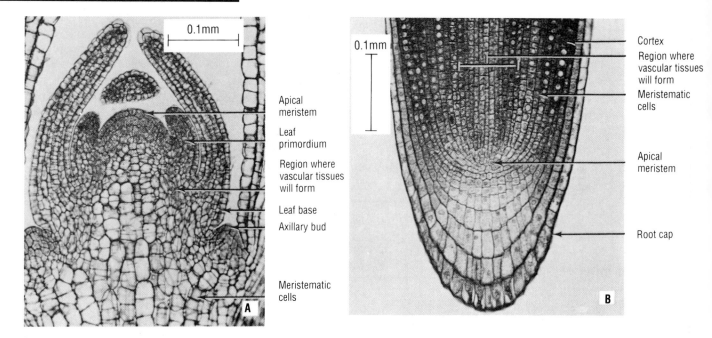

Figure 35.25 Photomicrographs of the apex of a shoot (*left*) and a root (*right*).

In the root the meristematic tissue at the tip is protected by the **root cap**. Further back, the root is covered by delicate **root hairs** which increase the surface area for the absorption of water and mineral nutrients (see page 335).

Photomicrographs of shoot and root apices are shown in figure 35.25. The zones of cell division, expansion and differentiation are particularly clear in the photomicrograph of the root apex.

The tissues formed so far are the result of **primary** or **apical growth** and constitute the primary structure of the stem or root.

Secondary growth

Primary growth, as just described, increases the length of stems and roots of dicotyledonous plants of dicotyledonous plants, but it does not add to their width. How, then, is the girth of such plants increased? This is achieved by a process of **secondary growth**. Such growth takes place extensively in woody perennials like trees and shrubs, but only slightly, if at all, in annuals and herbaceous perennials which die back each year.

Secondary growth is illustrated diagrammatically in figure 35.26. It depends on the presence, within the primary tissues, of meristematic cells which retain the capacity to divide long after all the other cells have become fully differentiated. These meristematic cells comprise the **cambium** – or, more properly, the *vascular* cambium because it is destined to give rise to new vascular tissues.

Initially the vascular cambium is restricted to a series of small groups of cells wedged between the primary xylem and phloem – you can see them in the left hand diagrams in figure 35.26. In the first step of secondary growth these isolated groups of cambium cells link up to form a ring or, more exactly, a cylinder. The formation of this **cambium ring** is achieved by radial divisions of the individual cambium cells. The primary xylem is situated on the inside of the ring, the primary phloem on the outside.

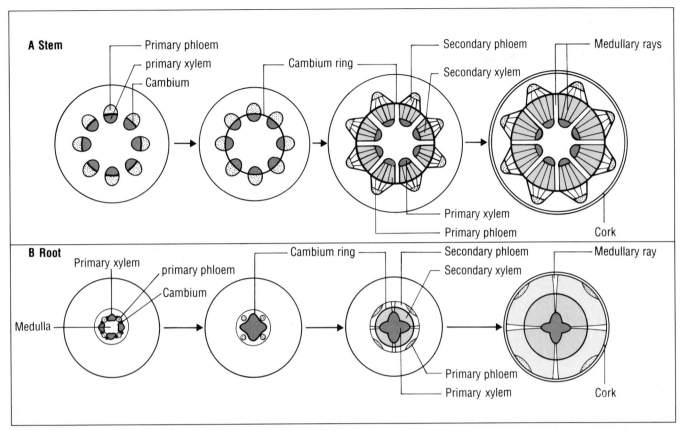

Figure 35.26 Secondary growth in a dicotyledonous stem and root. Only the first year of secondary growth is shown. In both cases the cambium tissue (shown in green) forms a complete ring which proliferates inwards to form secondary xylem and outwards to form secondary phloem. Further explanation in text.

The cells of the cambium ring now divide tangentially to form **secondary xylem** on the inside, and **secondary phloem** on the outside. In places, the cambium cells form parenchyma, rather than vascular tissue, thus creating a series of radiating **medullary rays** within the mass of vascular tissue. The medullary rays are composed of living cells – unlike the xylem, most of whose cells die eventually.

Figure 35.27 shows how the cambium cells divide to form the secondary vascular tissues. Cells cut off towards the outside become secondary phloem, whereas those cut off towards the inside become secondary xylem. In practice many more cells are cut off towards the inside than the outside, so the stem and root finish up with much more xylem than phloem. The result is that the phloem tissue and cambium ring gradually get pushed outwards. Periodically, radial divisions of the cambium cells occur to keep pace with its ever increasing circumference. This is made clear towards the right hand side of figure 35.27.

Figure 35.27 Diagrams illustrating how divisions of a cambium cell produces secondary xylem and phloem in a dicotyledonous stem or root. The figures illustrate a hypothetical sequence in which new cells might be cut off by successive divisions: 1 represents the original cambium cell; 2, 4, 6 and 7 are secondary xylem cells; 3, 5 and 8 are secondary phloem cells. In practice many more xylem cells are produced than phloem cells, roughly one phloem cell for every six xylem cells. Occasional radial divisions produce new cambium cells (1a and 1b) which increase the circumference of the cambium ring.

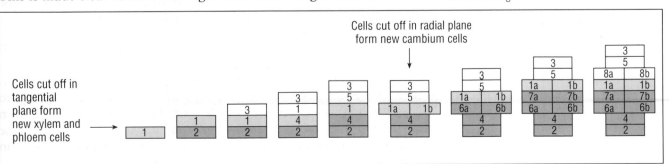

The fact that the cambium ring divides more on its inside than on its outside means that the great bulk of tissue formed is xylem. In fact the phloem is restricted to a thin layer just under the hard part of the bark. The xylem, when fully developed, is dead and comprises the wood. Its functions are to provide strength and carry water and mineral salts from the soil to the leaves. The phloem, on the other hand, is very much alive. It carries soluble products of photosynthesis from the leaves to the roots and other parts of the plant.

Annual rings and big trees

In temperate regions, secondary growth takes place between spring and autumn. The spring xylem contains a high proportion of large vessels with relatively thin walls to carry the spring flow of the transpiration stream. As the summer progresses, the vessels become narrower and thicker-walled, and an increasing number of sclerenchyma fibres are formed (figure 35.28). The summer wood is therefore harder and denser than the spring wood.

The result of this seasonal growth is the formation of a series of concentric **annual rings**. These can be counted if a tree trunk is severed, and they can provide an accurate method of measuring the ages of trees. For example, counting the annual rings of some of the giant conifers in California has shown these trees to be over 3000 years old.

Figure 35.28 Photomicrograph of a small part of the secondary xylem of a redwood tree (*Sequoia sempervirens*) as seen in a transverse section. Notice the marked contrast between the thin-walled, large-celled spring wood and the thick-walled, small-celled summer wood. Five rings are included, representing five successive years of growth. The area covered by the photomicrograph is shown by the rectangle in the diagram on the left.

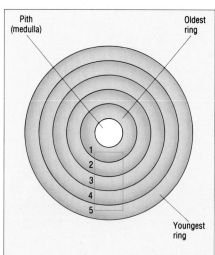

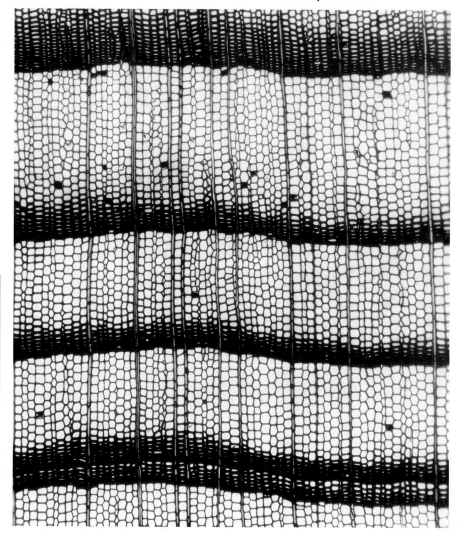

For the tree the importance of secondary growth is that it greatly increases the strength of the trunk, enabling the canopy to be raised to a much greater height than would otherwise be possible. Figure 35.29 bears this out.

Sapwood and heartwood

If you look at the cut end of the trunk of a felled tree, you will notice a difference between the old wood at the centre and the younger wood further out (figure 35.30). The younger wood is relatively light in colour and is called the **sapwood**. Its cells are not fully lignified and many of them are still alive. It is the physiologically active part of the wood, transporting water and mineral salts from the roots to the leaves.

The older wood at the centre is called the **heartwood**. It is often dark in colour due to the presence of tannins, resins and dyes. Its cells are completely dead and they no longer transport water and mineral salts. Their only function is to support the plant.

The trunk is permeated by radiating medullary rays. Their function is to transport soluble food substances from the phloem to the living cells in the sapwood, to store starch, and to carry the tannins, resins and dyes to the heartwood. The heartwood is much denser and harder than the sapwood, and the tannins and resins make it resistant to decay and to attack by insects. As you can imagine, this is the part of the wood that is favoured by the timber industry.

Secondary growth occurs in conifers and dicotyledonous angiosperms. However, it does not occur in monocotyledons. There is no secondary wood in monocots and that is why there are virtually no trees in this group of plants. One of the few exceptions are palm trees. However, their stems are supported, not by secondary tissues, but by numerous fibres and scattered vascular bundles formed as a result of primary growth.

Figure 35.29 The General Sherman tree (*Sequoiadendron gigantea*) in the Sierra Nevada, California. Reputed to be the largest tree in the world, it is well over 80 metres tall, and the base of the trunk has a mean diameter of over 11 metres. At 66 m above the ground the trunk is still over 4 m wide. The tree is estimated to be over 3000 years old. Fortunately, from the conservation point of view, the wood of these massive trees does not make good timber for building. It is, however, suitable for making toothpicks: there is enough wood in a tree of this size to make 5000 million toothpicks!

Figure 35.30 The cut surface of the trunk of a felled tree showing the distinction between the heartwood and the sapwood. Notice that the trunk has split along the medullary rays. Why do you think this has happened?

Cork and bark

The great increase in girth resulting from secondary growth would rupture the surface tissues were it not for the fact that they too undergo a secondary growth process. Between the epidermis and the cortex, there is another layer of meristematic cells called the **cork cambium**. The cells of the cork cambium divide tangentially to form new surface tissues (figure 35.31).

Those cells which are cut off towards the inside of the cork cambium form **secondary cortex** which, like the primary cortex, is composed of living parenchyma tissue. Those cells which are cut off towards the outside form a layer of tightly packed **corky cells**. Their walls become impregnated with **suberin**, a fatty substance which renders them impermeable to water and gases. They form the dead corky tissue characteristic of **bark**. (Bark, in the proper botanical sense, includes *all* the tissue, living and dead, outside the wood. This includes the phloem.)

By the continued meristematic activity of the cork cambium, the bark is kept intact and the living tissues underneath are protected against physical damage, attack by parasites and herbivores, and winter frosts.

Cork is impermeable to oxygen and carbon dioxide, so how do the living tissues undergo gaseous exchange? The answer is that here and there the suberised cells of the cork, instead of being tightly packed, form a loose mass called a **lenticel**. Here intercellular spaces allow gaseous exchange to take place freely between the inside and outside of the stem. This is particularly important for the phloem whose transport activities require energy from respiration.

Figure 35.31 The formation of cork at the surface of a stem or root depends on the meristematic activity of the cork cambium beneath the epidermis. In the diagram the numbers indicate the order in which the cork cambium divides to form new cells. The cells on the immediate outside of the cambium layer are the youngest; they have cellulose walls and are alive. The older cells further out have impermeable walls impregnated with suberin and are therefore dead. They form the corky part of the bark. In the lenticel the corky cells are loosely packed, permitting gaseous exchange. The photomicrograph is a section through the bark of a tree and shows the same structures that are visible in the diagram.

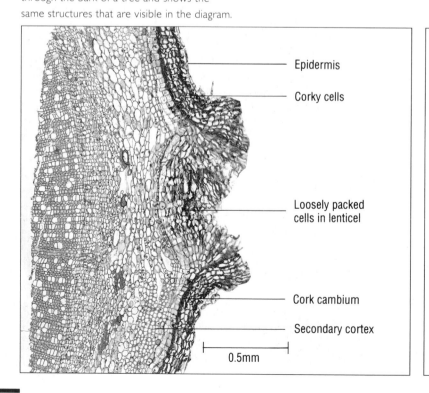

Epidermis

Corky cells

Loosely packed cells in lenticel

Cork cambium

Secondary cortex

0.5mm

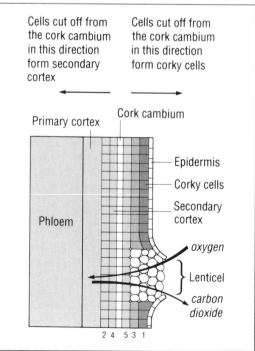

Cells cut off from the cork cambium in this direction form secondary cortex

Cells cut off from the cork cambium in this direction form corky cells

Primary cortex

Cork cambium

Phloem

Epidermis

Corky cells

Secondary cortex

oxygen

Lenticel

carbon dioxide

2 4   5 3 1

Wood and the timber industry

Guest author Tim King looks at the properties of wood and how they relate to the way we use this ubiquitous material.

The secondary xylem of trees – that is, **wood** – is light, strong, durable, flammable, easily shaped and relatively resistant to decay. Because of these properties, it is in great demand as timber and is of considerable economic importance. If you are in any doubt about this, think how many well known objects are made of wood.

Softwood and hardwood

A basic distinction can be made between **softwood** and **hardwood**. Softwood comes from coniferous trees, whereas hardwood comes from angiospermous trees (see page 111). Softwood is less dense than hardwood, and has a higher proportion of cellulose relative to lignin. Most of the cells in softwoods are relatively thin-walled tracheids whose primary function is to conduct water, whereas most of the cells in hardwoods are thick-walled, heavily lignified sclerenchyma fibres, providing support.

Rapidly-growing conifers are grown on a renewable basis in many parts of the northern hemisphere. One of the most widely grown is the robust Sitka spruce, native to North America but introduced on a large scale into Europe. The softwoods produced by these conifers are suitable for building, making cheap furniture and paper-making. Angiospermous trees, on the other hand, tend to be slower-growing and longer-lived. Most of those that are used for timber, oaks for example, are extracted from semi-natural communities and are not replaced. The hardwoods they yield are used to make expensive furniture and veneers. Veneers are thin polished sheets of wood, showing the characteristic hardwood grain, which can be stuck onto the surfaces of cheaper woods to make them look more attractive.

Special woods for special jobs

Many trees produce wood which is used for specialised purposes. For example, matchsticks are made from a variety of poplar which is grown in large even-aged plantations in southern Britain. Hazel has strong flexible stems suitable for making hurdles. This has been grown for centuries in coppices: the straight vertical stems are cut near the ground on an approximate 15 year rotation. In the USA, wood for pencils is produced mainly from the reddish wood of a certain species of juniper.

What makes particular woods suitable for particular functions? In some cases it is because of their chemical composition. For example, flammable woods such as the American torchwood have a high resin content which makes them ideal for firewood; and the Australian turpentine is particularly useful for underwater construction because its high silica content makes it resistant to the shipworm, a marine mollusc which bores into wood and can do untold damage.

In other cases the structure and arrangement of the xylem elements is the important factor. Here are three examples:

- Cricket bats are made from a certain variety of willow. The willow's xylem elements are resilient, having an ability to rebound after deformation – like a pneumatic tyre. If lighter woods were hit by cricket balls, the thinner-walled xylem elements would shatter; and if heavier woods were used, their thicker-walled xylem elements would not be flexible enough to be deformed.

- Pencils are made from the pencil cedar. The wood of this tree has an even texture without marked annual rings, making it easy for narrow grooves to be made in it for accommodating the lead. It can be sharpened obliquely with a relatively blunt instrument, takes paint and varnish well, presents a smooth surface comfortable to hold, and – last but not least – it does not taste unpleasant to those who chew their pencils!

- Elm wood is cross-grained, some of the xylem fibres being arranged horizontally. This makes it tough, enabling it to resist splitting and shearing. It is therefore ideal for chair seats, mallet heads, butchers' blocks, archery bows and the hubs of wheels.

Paper making

This is one of the most important uses of wood. In Britain, for example, over 150 kg of paper products are used per person per year. These include writing paper, cardboard boxes, packaging, wallpaper, paper handkerchiefs and tickets. The major trees used in paper-making are pine, spruce, eucalyptus and birch. The walls of their xylem elements consist of cellulose impregnated with up to 25 per cent lignin by mass.

Paper consists of a meshwork of cellulose fibres bound together. The way it is produced is outlined in the illustration. First, the wood is ground into pulp. The cellulose is then separated from the lignin by chemical digestion carried out in a giant pressure cooker. Next, the bleached pulp is suspended in water over a fine sieve and, as the water drains away, the cellulose fibres begin to bind. After gradual dehydration in a complex mechanised paper mill, the paper is treated in various ways to suit its purpose.

Summary

1 **Growth** results from **cell division**, **assimilation** and **cell expansion**.

2 You can measure growth by estimating the increase in a linear dimension (e.g. height), volume, total mass or dry mass. Each has its difficulties, one being that different parts of the organism may grow at different rates (**allometric growth**).

3 Growth may be expressed graphically by a **growth curve** from which the **absolute** or **relative growth rate** may be derived.

4 In most organisms growth takes place smoothly, but in arthropods growth is **intermittent**. This is caused by the presence of a hard cuticle which must be shed (**moulting, ecdysis**) before the body can expand.

5 The embryonic changes through which a chordate passes as it develops can be divided into **cleavage**, **gastrulation**, **neurulation** and **organogenesis**.

6 Organogeny, the formation of organs, can be illustrated by the development of the eye.

7 Birds and mammals possess **extra-embryonic membranes** which include the **amnion** and **allanto-chorion**. In eutherian mammals the allanto-chorion becomes the **placenta**.

8 Fundamental changes occur in the circulatory system of a newborn mammal associated with the replacement of the placenta by the lungs as the organ of gaseous exchange.

9 Some animals have a **larva** in the course of their development. The larva develops into the adult by **metamorphosis**.

10 In flowering plants the embryo develops into a **seedling** when the seed **germinates**.

11 Two types of germination are recognised: **hypogeal** and **epigeal**. In hypogeal germination the cotyledons remain in the soil, whereas in epigeal germination they are lifted out of the soil.

12 Conditions required for germination include water, suitable illumination, warmth and oxygen. Internally a rapid mobilisation of food reserves takes place.

13 **Primary growth** of the stem and root take place by cell division in **apical meristems** followed by cell expansion and differentiation.

14 **Secondary growth** takes place by means of a **secondary meristem** (the vascular cambium) which produces, amongst other things, **wood**.

15 Secondary growth is accompanied by the formation of **cork** and associated tissues from a cork cambium. Cork constitutes the outer part of the bark.

16 Wood is made use of in the timber industry. **Softwood** comes from coniferous trees and **hardwood** from angiospermous trees. Both have their uses, paper making being one of them.

Review questions

1 Account for the different growth rates in figure 35.2. In the text it says that an organism's growth is usually slow at first and then speeds up. Why is this not apparent in the growth curves in figure 35.2?

2 Explain why in an arthropod growth occurs in jumps.

3 Without resorting to diagrams give brief definitions of the following: blastula, gastrulation, neurula, notochord, somites.

4 Write brief explanatory notes on the structure and functions of the amnion and allanto-chorion of a mammal.

5 The existence of extra-embryonic membranes can be seen as an adaptation to life on land. Use the information presented in this chapter to explain this statement.

6 Which two blood vessels in a human fetus are connected by the ductus arteriosus? Why is it useful for these two blood vessels to be connected in the fetus?

7 What is the endosperm, where would you expect to find it and of what use is it to a plant?

8 If you observe certain types of seed germinating you will notice that the seed coat finishes up on top of the shoot. Explain.

9 Explain the difference between the primary and secondary growth of a plant, making clear the function of each.

10 If you remove a complete ring or bark from around a tree trunk, the tree will die. What causes its death?

Further reading

You will find a colourful account of human development in *Illustrated Human Embryology* by Tuchmann-Duplessis, David and Haegel (Chapman and Hall, 1972 – 1982). There are three slim volumes, of which Volume 1 (Embryogenesis) is most relevant to A-level studies.

If you are interested in growth and not frightened of mathematics, try reading *The Allometry of Growth and Reproduction* by Michael Reiss (Cambridge University Press, 1989). It addresses aspects of growth and size that go well beyond this chapter.

The complexities of allometric growth are also discussed in *Biology, Advanced Topics*, along with the functions of larvae and the formation of plant cell walls.

The control of growth

In the last chapter we saw that growth is brought about by cell division, cell expansion and assimilation. Obviously any factor that directly or indirectly affects these three processes will influence growth.

In this chapter we shall look at some of the main factors influencing the growth of plants and animals. We shall be concerned with the growth of the whole organism and of specific structures such as flowers.

For convenience we can make a distinction between **internal** and **external factors** affecting growth.

External factors affecting growth

External factors include a whole host of environmental influences: light, temperature, oxygen, food supply and so on. One of the most important is **food supply**. An organism such as the human has to be supplied with the chemicals from which to make its structures and obtain energy. If the diet is deficient, either in a major constituent such as protein, or an essential vitamin or trace element, poor growth will result.

Protein and nitrogen

Protein forms the structural foundation of the body. For a growing child laying down tissues, at least 20 per cent of the food taken in should be protein. Even in a fully grown person the figure is around 15 per cent, for protein is needed for the maintenance and repair of the tissues. Because of the relatively low protein content of most plant foods, a person on an exclusively vegetarian diet may have difficulty getting the required amount.

Receiving the right amount of protein is a particular problem in those parts of the world where populations are dense and livestock scarce. Assuming that the diet cannot be supplemented by dairy products, the only thing a person can do in these circumstances is to consume very large amounts of vegetable food. If this too is in short supply the person may suffer from **protein deficiency disease (kwashiorkor)**. A child suffering from this condition is physically weak and shows retarded growth (figure 36.1).

These principles apply no less to plants than to animals. Unless they possess special adaptations, plants growing in nitrogen-deficient soil cannot synthesise enough protein. Consequently they show stunted growth and development (see page 123).

Light

One of the most important external factors influencing plant growth is **light**. Light is needed for the synthesis and action of chlorophyll without which photosynthesis cannot take place. A seedling grown in the dark becomes **etiolated**. The plant is yellow, due to lack of chlorophyll, the leaves fail to expand, and the stem is long and spindly, the distance between successive nodes being greater than usual.

Plants become naturally etiolated if they happen to be growing in a dark place (figure 36.2). Later we shall look at the mechanism by which light influences plant growth.

Temperature

Temperature can be very important. An organism's metabolic rate is increased by a rise in temperature. It is therefore not surprising to find that growth and development take place more rapidly the higher the temperature. Provided other conditions are favourable, a plant will grow more

Figure 36.1 These children are suffering from protein deficiency disease (kwashiorkor). The disease is most common in developing countries where children are undernourished. Notice the swollen abdomen which at first sight might give the impression that the children are well fed. It is caused by severe retention of fluid in the tissues (oedema), which is one of the symptoms of protein deficiency.

Figure 36.2 Etiolated bluebells growing out from beneath a board that was lying on the soil.

quickly in warm weather than in cold weather, and a tadpole will develop faster in a warm pond than in a cold pond.

Temperature is one of several factors controlling germination and flowering, as we shall see later. It also affects secondary thickening. Because of its effect on the rate of cell division, more secondary xylem is formed in warm conditions than in cooler conditions. This means that warm summers tend to give thicker annual rings than cool summers. By carefully analysing the annual rings in a felled tree scientists can work out the climatic changes which have occurred in the past, and this provides a useful way of studying long-term weather patterns.

Tree rings and past climates

The thickness of the annual rings of trees can give us information about climates in the past. Guest author Jenny Chapman explains.

If a tree is cut down, concentric annual rings may be seen in the wood. Each ring represents secondary xylem produced during one growing season from spring to summer (see page 642). The width of each ring depends on the weather that year. As a result, trees over a wide area have similar ring patterns. Rings in British trees for 1975 and 1976, for example, are very narrow because the summers in those two years were so dry that trees did not have enough water to grow well.

A tree's annual rings, therefore, give us a record of the climate throughout its life. Archaeologists use long-lived trees such as the bristlecone pine of Arizona, and the trunks of dead trees preserved in bogs, to compile a tree ring record going back about 10 000 years. If a piece of timber is found at an archaeological site, its rings can be matched with this tree ring record and dated more accurately than by other methods such as radiocarbon dating. In fact analysis of ring-dated wood has shown that radiocarbon dating is inaccurate: radiocarbon dates from 500 BC to 1300 AD are often about 100 years too old, while radiocarbon dates older than 3000 BC are about 800 years too recent.

Annual rings are also found in wood which was preserved by fossilisation in calcite or silica. If a very thin slice

Cross section through a fossil tree from Antarctica. This particular tree was quite small, with a trunk about 10 cm in diameter. Larger trunks, a metre or more across, have also been found.

of this petrified wood is cut, and light shone through it, the individual xylem cells which make up the rings can still be seen. The section in the illustration is from a fossil tree which grew in Antarctica about 100 million years ago. Despite being very close to the South Pole, Antarctica was covered with forest in those days. This shows that the region must have been much warmer than it is today.

The Antarctic tree rings vary in width from a maximum of about 0.5 cm down to tiny rings so narrow that they can only be seen clearly using a microscope. Notice how varied the rings are in the illustration. Narrow rings indicate unfavourable growing seasons, perhaps due to cold or dry summers, or severe drought. Many of these Antarctic trees have damaged rings indicative of late winter frosts

and fluctuating growing conditions.

New recording methods are being developed to study these very old tree rings in an attempt to reconstruct past climates. Sophisticated computer models, based on the position of continents and mountain ranges and on estimates of sea temperatures, can be used to construct world climate maps for periods in the past. These models can give day by day changes in the temperature, rainfall and wind speeds for a climate hundreds of millions of years ago. The information locked up in the trees which grew at the time, and other climatic indicators such as the size and shape of fossil leaves, can be used to check the predictions of such models.

A project of this kind is now in progress at Reading and Oxford Universities: the climates of 100 and 150 million years ago are being modelled by computer, and information about the vegetation of the whole world for these two times is being collected to check the models.

Preliminary information from both the computer models and the fossil plants indicate that the climate at higher latitudes was warmer and more favourable for growth than it is today. Understanding how plants grew in these warmer conditions may help us to predict how the vegetation may change in the future as a consequence of the greenhouse effect. Perhaps once again trees may be able to grow in Antarctica and northern Alaska – but that will not happen unless the ice caps melt.

Oxygen

Another factor which can influence plant growth is **oxygen**. Oxygen does not directly affect the growth of the above-ground parts of a plant because there is always enough of it available. However, it can have a pronounced effect on the growth of roots as figure 36.3 clearly shows, and this in turn may affect the rest of the plant. So, well aerated soil is normally essential for good growth. This is a major concern of farmers in managing their soil. Waterlogged soil has a greatly reduced oxygen content, so efficient drainage is essential.

Internal factors affecting growth

Internal factors affecting growth include the genetic constitution of the organism and the concentration of certain chemicals, including hormones, in the body. These two factors are connected, for the genes generally influence growth through the action of such chemicals – and the latter, in turn, may affect the expression of genes.

Internal chemicals may of course be influenced by external factors. For example, lack of iodine in the diet results in stunted growth because iodine is an essential constituent of the hormone **thyroxine** (see page 465).

The general principle here is that growth, like so many other aspects of an organism's functioning, depends on an interaction between external and internal factors. Nowhere can this be seen better than in the way growth is controlled in flowering plants.

The control of plant growth

Consider the basic problem: after a seed has germinated the shoot grows upwards and the root downwards. What makes the shoot and root behave in this way? Over the years a large number of experiments have been done in an attempt to answer this fundamental question.

Evidence for the involvement of a growth substance

Three crucial experiments, first carried out in the early years of the 20th century, are shown in figure 36.4. Look first at experiment 1. The tip of a coleoptile is cut off just in front of the zone of elongation. The result is that growth stops. If, however, the tip is put back, growth resumes. This simple experiment suggests that the tip of the coleoptile exerts an influence over the region further back, causing growth to take place.

What form might this influence take? One possibility is that it is a chemical which passes down the coleoptile from the tip, causing growth to occur further back. This hypothesis is supported by experiment 2. The tip is cut off a coleoptile, and then put back so that it covers only half the cut end. The result is that growth stops on the side of the coleoptile which lacks the tip, but continues on the other side so the coleoptile bends.

Experiment 3 lends further support to the idea that the tip produces a chemical which stimulates growth. The tip of a coleoptile is cut off and placed on a small block of agar jelly. Agar jelly does not affect the tissues and soluble substances can diffuse through it freely. After about two hours the tip is discarded and the agar block placed on the cut end of the coleoptile. The result is that growth, temporarily inhibited by removal of the tip, resumes. We conclude that a growth-stimulating substance, produced in the tip, has accumulated in the agar and diffused back into the stump. Of course this experiment needs a control – what should it be?

We have here a chemical – or *suspected* chemical – which appears to stimulate growth. Such substances are referred to as **plant hormones** or **plant growth substances**.

Figure 36.3 The effect of oxygen concentration on the growth of tomato roots. The plants were grown in separate culture solutions. The percentage concentration of oxygen in the air was, from left to right: 1, 3, 5, 10 and 20 per cent. The normal oxygen content of atmospheric air is approximately 20 per cent. Notice the pronounced retardation of growth resulting from the lower oxygen concentrations.

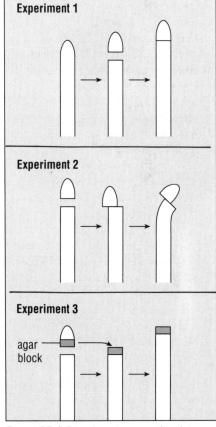

Figure 36.4 Experiments supporting the hypothesis that a growth-promoting chemical is produced in the tip of a coleoptile. The experiments are explained in the text. The coleoptile is the sheath which covers the young shoot of members of the grass family. It lends itself readily to experiments of this sort.

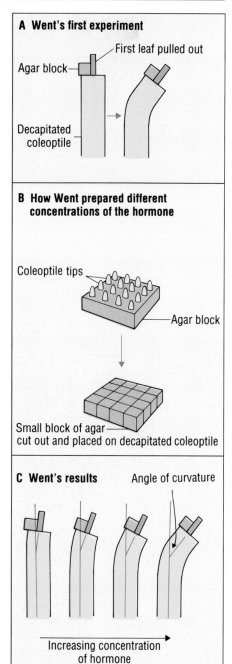

A Went's first experiment

First leaf pulled out

Agar block

Decapitated
coleptile

**B How Went prepared different
concentrations of the hormone**

Coleptile tips

Agar block

Small block of agar
cut out and placed on decapitated coleoptile

C Went's results   Angle of curvature

Increasing concentration
of hormone

Figure 36.5 Experiments performed by Fritz
Went confirming the growth substance
hypothesis.
A The effect of placing an agar block
containing the growth substance on one side
of the cut end of a decapitated coleoptile.
B How Went prepared an agar block
containing the growth substance at a particular
concentration.
C The effect of increasing concentrations of
the growth substance on the curvatures
developed by decapitated coleoptiles.
Measuring the angle of curvature is the basis
of Went's coleoptile curvature test.

Further experiments confirming the growth substance idea

In the late 1920s, Fritz Went, a young Dutch botanist, did an experiment which further supported the growth substance hypothesis. First he collected the substance in an agar block, as in experiment 3 in figure 36.4. Then he placed the agar block on top of a decapitated coleoptile so that it covered only half the cut end (figure 36.5A). The result was that more growth took place on the side with the block on it than on the other side, so the coleoptile bent.

This experiment is not as easy as it sounds. For one thing, an agar block placed on one side of a decapitated coleoptile has an irritating tendency to fall off. Went got round this in an ingenious way. The first leaf of the shoot is just under the tip of the coleoptile. After decapitating the coleoptile, Went carefully pulled this leaf out slightly and cut the end off. In this way he made a natural partition which could be used to stabilise the agar block.

Went predicted that the more concentrated the growth substance was in the block, the more the coleoptile should bend. He tested this idea by measuring the degree of curvature produced by different concentrations of the substance. He prepared different concentrations by standing varying numbers of coleoptile tips on identical blocks of agar for a given period of time (figure 36.5B). By spreading through the relatively large volume of agar, the hormone became diluted. The final concentration depended on how many tips were placed on the agar: the greater the number of tips, the more concentrated the substance. The large blocks of agar were then cut up into smaller blocks, and placed on the cut ends of decapitated coleoptiles as before.

Went took great pains to ensure that the conditions were the same for all the coleptiles used. The tests were carried out at constant temperature, high relative humidity (to prevent the agar block drying out) and in dim red light of uniform intensity. Curvature was assessed after two hours, the angle being measured from photographs.

Went found, as predicted, that the greater the concentration of the growth substance, the larger was the degree of curvature (figure 36.5C). In fact, *provided the concentration was not too great, the degree of curvature of the coleoptiles was directly proportional to the concentration of the growth substance.*

Went's technique provides a convenient way of estimating the concentration of a growth substance which has been collected from a coleoptile or shoot: the biological activity of the substance is expressed in terms of the curvature of the coleoptile. Known as the **coleoptile curvature test**, it is still the most sensitive way of assessing the activity of this substance.

Auxin and its effect on shoots and roots

The growth substance whose actions are described above is known as **auxin** from the Greek word *auxein* meaning 'to grow'. Early attempts to find out what it consists of chemically were fraught with difficulty because it occurs in plants in such minute quantities. However, in 1934 a successful analysis was made and it turned out to be a ring compound called **indoleacetic acid** or IAA for short.

This compound has an extremely powerful effect on growth. A solution of 0.01 mg in a litre of water applied to the side of a shoot is sufficient to cause bending. IAA has now been isolated from a wide variety of plant tissues, and in addition many substances with similar effects have been synthesised in the laboratory. These synthetic auxins are known as **plant growth regulators**. They are used extensively in regulating the growth of plants in agriculture and horticulture. Some plant species respond very readily to them (figure 36.7). The commercial aspects of these and other growth regulators are discussed in the box on page 655.

With a ready source of auxins at hand, quantitative experiments can be carried out to show the precise effects of different concentrations on the growth of shoots and roots. The results of one such experiment are shown graphically in figure 36.8. First look at the curve for the shoot. Provided that the concentration falls between a certain range, auxin invariably *stimulates* growth. Now look at the curve for the root. At very low concentrations the auxin appears to stimulate growth slightly, but at higher concentrations it *inhibits* growth.

Experiments with radioactively-labelled auxin suggest that it is formed at the tip of the shoot (in the meristematic region) and is then transported downwards to the roots. As it passes down the plant, it becomes more and more dilute. As a result, there is a concentration gradient along the main axis of the plant, the concentration being highest at the tip of the shoot and lowest in the tip of the root.

From these observations we might conclude that in the living plant auxin stimulates growth in the shoot *and* root. However, whilst auxin certainly stimulates shoot growth, there is serious doubt as to whether it stimulates root growth. The suggestion in the graph in figure 36.8 that it does so at low concentrations should be treated with caution because the evidence is very slender and depends on the species.

Why does auxin become more and more dilute as it passes down the plant? After all, if it is always on a downward move you would expect it to accumulate in the root and be most concentrated there. The reason is that there is a progressive loss of auxin in transit because it is readily destroyed with time. For this reason commercial preparations are usually not auxin itself but a synthetic substitute.

How do auxins work?

The auxin produced at the tip of a shoot is transported down the shoot where it stimulates growth, causing the shoot to lengthen. How does auxin

Figure 36.6 Photograph showing the bending response of oat coleoptiles as induced by different concentrations of auxin in agar blocks.

Figure 36.7 Some plants respond particularly quickly to growth substances and are used for testing the effectiveness of different chemicals. Application of the substance in a suitable carrier such as lanolin to the stems or leaves of the test plant (**A**) may induce a marked growth response within a matter of hours (**B**).

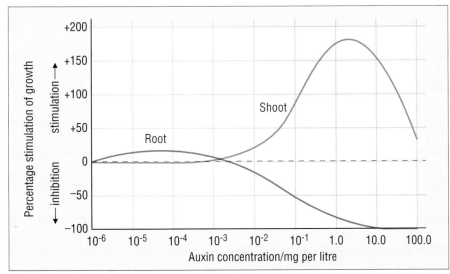

Figure 36.8 The effect on growth of applying different concentrations of auxin to the shoots and roots of oat seedlings. The results are expressed as percentage stimulation of growth compared with untreated controls. A positive result means relative stimulation compared with the control, a negative result means relative inhibition. Notice that the concentration which produces maximum growth in the shoot (about 1.0 mg per litre) inhibits growth in the root. The stimulating effect of low concentrations of auxin on the root is questionable.

Figure 36.9 The effect of removing the shoot apex of *Coleus*. The top photograph shows the plant shortly after the apex had been cut off. The lateral buds lower down are just beginning to develop into side branches. The lower photograph shows the same plant four weeks later. Notice how bushy it has become as a result of the growth of side branches.

Figure 36.10 Adventitious roots sprouting from the cut end of a stem of busy Lizzie (*Impatiens* sp), an auxin-induced response.

achieve this effect? There are two possibilities: it might increase the rate of cell division or it might facilitate cell expansion.

Evidence suggests that auxin promotes growth mainly by facilitating cell expansion. It seems to enable the cell walls to be stretched more easily by the pressures which develop in the vacuoles. It is thought that auxin stimulates the production of hydrogen ions by the plasma membrane. The resulting acidification of the cell wall then activates hemicellulase enzymes which break the hemicellulose links between the cellulose microfibrils. This allows the cellulose microfibrils to slide readily past each other.

Does auxin have *any* effect on cell division? The answer is yes, but the effect is only very slight unless another growth substance is present. We shall meet this substance presently.

Other auxin effects

Auxin is now known to exert many other effects on plants besides shoot and root growth. For example, it inhibits the development of lateral buds into side branches. This can be demonstrated by removing the apical bud from the top of a plant stem. After a short time one or more lateral buds give rise to side branches. If, however, auxin is applied to the cut end of the main stem immediately after the apical bud has been removed, no such branching occurs.

So the shoot apex appears to suppress the lower parts of the plant. This is known as **apical dominance**. Only if the inhibitory influence of the apex is removed will lateral growth take place. This, of course, is the theory behind **pruning**: cutting the top off the main stem removes the source of auxin, thus encouraging the sprouting of side branches lower down (figure 36.9).

Although auxin inhibits the growth of side branches, it stimulates the growth of adventitious roots – roots which grow out of the stem. Cuttings can be encouraged to 'take' by dipping the cut end of the stem or branch in auxin or a synthetic substitute. Of course cuttings will often sprout roots without the assistance of externally applied auxin, but applying auxin facilitates the process (figure 36.10).

Another important function of auxin is the formation of vascular tissue in developing shoots and roots. This has been demonstrated by placing an agar block impregnated with IAA in contact with a sample of undifferentiated callus tissue: the IAA, particularly if accompanied by sucrose, induces cells in the callus to develop into xylem and phloem.

Auxin is also involved in the formation of fruit. You will remember from Chapter 34 that fruits develop from the ovary or receptacle. Normally this will only happen if fertilisation has taken place: auxin is produced by the embryo and this then causes the fruit to develop. Sometimes, however, fruit formation occurs in the absence of fertilisation. The resulting fruit is normal in appearance, but seedless. This phenomenon which is known as **parthenocarpy** happens naturally in some plants – banana, for example. It can also be induced artificially by treating unpollinated flowers with synthetic auxin, a procedure which is sometimes used by commercial fruit-growers to increase the quantity and quality of their fruit.

Auxin plays an important part in the bending of shoots, and possibly roots, in response to external stimuli, a function which we shall return to later. It is also involved in secondary thickening, the ripening of fruit and falling of leaves. However, in carrying out these functions auxin works in conjunction with other plant growth substances which will now be described.

Other plant growth substances

Although auxin was the first plant growth substance to be discovered, a number of other growth substances are now known to exist in plants. They play an important part in plant growth and development, often in conjunction with auxin. Let us look at them briefly.

Gibberellins

Way back in the 1920s a Japanese farmer found that his rice seedlings suddenly started growing fantastically tall. He called these plants 'foolish seedlings'. It was discovered subsequently by Japanese research workers that this condition was caused by a fungus, *Gibberella fujikoroi*, which secretes a mixture of related compounds called **gibberellins**. We now know that plants produce their own gibberellins in varying quantities and these have a very powerful effect on growth. The main one is **gibberellic acid (GBA)**.

The most noticeable effect of gibberellins, and one which immediately distinguishes them from auxins, is the stimulation of rapid growth in dwarf varieties of certain plants. If treated with gibberellic acid a dwarf plant can be made to grow to the normal height. The dwarf condition is under genetic control and is thought to be caused by a shortage of gibberellin. The tall varieties on the other hand have enough gibberellin to make them grow to full height. Gibberellin achieves this effect by increasing the length of the internodal regions (figure 36.11).

A spectacular demonstration of the way gibberellin stimulates stem elongation is seen in a phenomenon called **bolting**, the precocious growth and flowering of certain plants. For example, the cabbage plants in figure 36.12 were each treated with less than one milligram of gibberellin. As a result they developed stems five metres long with flowers at the top!

Like auxins, gibberellins exert their growth-promoting effects mainly by causing cell elongation, though they stimulate cell division too. They can cause parthenocarpy in certain plants, possibly by initiating the synthesis of auxin. Unlike auxins, they *stimulate* the growth of side branches from axillary buds. Gibberellins are also involved in the breaking of dormancy of seeds and buds, and in mobilising food reserves during germination.

Certain growth effects are brought about by gibberellin and auxin working together. We see this, for example, in the formation of secondary vascular tissue. This has been shown by applying these two growth substances to short pieces of stems from which the buds (the normal source of growth substances) have been removed.

- If neither growth substance is applied, the cambium cells do not divide and no vascular tissue is formed.
- If auxin alone is applied, the cambium cells divide, at least to a limited extent, and some xylem elements are formed.
- If gibberellic acid alone is applied, the cambium cells divide and mainly phloem is formed.
- If auxin *and* gibberellic acid are applied, the cambium cells divide prolifically and abundant xylem and phloem are formed.

Detailed experiments suggest that the rate of division of the cambium cells, and the relative amounts of xylem and phloem formed, depend on the ratio of auxin to gibberellin.

From these and other findings a general principle emerges, namely that in flowering plants the pattern of development is determined to a large extent by the relative amounts of, and interactions between, a limited number of growth substances.

Figure 36.11 The effect of gibberellin on stem elongation of bean plants. The left hand plant, the control, was treated with 250 micrograms of lanolin at the point marked a. The right hand plant was treated with 250 micrograms of lanolin containing 63 trillionths of a gram of gibberellic acid. The photographs were taken four days after treatment.

Figure 36.12 Bolting in cabbages. The three plants on the right were treated with 0.1 mg of gibberellic acid weekly. The control pair on the left received no such treatment. Normally cabbages do not flower until the second year. However, first year plants treated with gibberellin show enormous elongation and produce flowers, as shown here. With the cabbage plants is S.H. Wittwer of Michigan State University. He discovered this particular response and kindly supplied the photograph.

Cytokinins

Another group of active growth substances was discovered in 1956. Known as **cytokinins** (or just **kinins**), they were first extracted from coconut milk but are now known to occur more widely in flowering plants. They are all purines related to adenine, one of the bases in DNA.

Cytokinins occur in very small quantities in plants but are most abundant in tissues where rapid cell division is taking place. They promote cell division but only do so in the presence of auxin. Neither auxins nor cytokinins alone will stimulate cell division to any significant extent.

But cytokinins do more than simply promote cell division. In conjunction with auxin they also bring about cell differentiation. This has been strikingly demonstrated by immersing undifferentiated callus tissue in a series of solutions containing different proportions of IAA and a synthetic cytokinin called kinetin. The callus can be induced to form shoots or roots, to continue proliferating into callus tissue, or to stop growing altogether, depending on the relative quantities of auxin and kinetin provided. Here again we see that the interaction between two different substances is critical in determining the growth of specific structures in the plant. There is an important commercial point here too, for these growth substances can be used in the propagation of plants (see page 655).

Cytokinins promote cell division and differentiation in roots, stems, leaves and flowers. They also promote cell expansion in leaves, and stimulate the growth of lateral buds by releasing them from the suppressive influence of apical dominance. In addition they release certain seeds from dormancy and are involved in the mobilisation of food materials in leaves.

Abscisic acid

In the mid-1960s two scientists at the University of California found high levels of a substance in cotton plants which appeared to cause the leaves to fall off. The falling of leaves and fruits is called abscission, so this newly discovered substance was called **abscisin**. Its chemical structure is now known, and it is called **abscisic acid (ABA)**.

At first it was thought that this substance was responsible for the natural falling of leaves and fruits that occurs in deciduous plants in the autumn, and there was some experimental evidence to support this idea. For example, applying abscisic acid to the leaves or fruits of some species of plants was found to cause abscission.

However, subsequent research has indicated that abscission is the one thing that this substance is *not* responsible for – at least not in natural circumstances. Evidence suggests that it may be involved in the germination of seeds, dormancy of buds and perhaps the response of roots to gravity. These possibilities will be examined shortly. But the most established role of abscisic acid is to bring about the closure of stomata in leaves suffering from severe water shortage: it stimulates the expulsion of potassium ions from the guard cells, which causes the stomata to close (see page 251). Since this has nothing to do with leaf and fruit fall, the name abscisic acid now seems rather inappropriate.

Ethene

All the plant growth substances mentioned so far are complex compounds. However, plants also produce small quantities of the simple gas **ethene** (C_2H_4). This is involved in a wide range of developmental processes.

One of ethene's most important functions is the ripening of fruit. It promotes the conversion of starch to soluble sugar and triggers a sudden

Commercial aspects of plant growth substances

Plant growth substances or their synthetic equivalents have all sorts of uses. Their main uses are summarised here by guest author John Land.

Ever since the chemical structure of auxin (IAA) was discovered in 1934, scientists have explored the possibility of using it, and other growth substances, in agriculture and horticulture.

The same approach has been adopted as in the search for medical drugs: a naturally occurring substance is discovered, its possible uses are explored, and attempts are then made to synthesise it – or an equivalent substance – in the laboratory.

Over the years numerous artificial growth substances have been made in the laboratory and are now produced commercially. Although these **analogues**, as they are called, differ chemically from the natural substances, they share certain features in common, as you can see if you compare natural IAA with its analogues in illustration 1.

In assessing the usefulness of an analogue, various criteria must be taken into account. In particular, the substance should be effective for its chosen purpose but of low toxicity to other organisms. It should be rapidly destroyed after being released into the environment, that is non-persistent.

Humans have a responsibility not to release persistent, broad spectrum toxic chemicals into the environment. This is where plant growth substances can be a great help because, as naturally occurring chemicals, they meet many of the requirements which environmentally sensitive manufacturers expect them to have.

What then are their main uses?

- **As selective herbicides**
  This is probably the best known

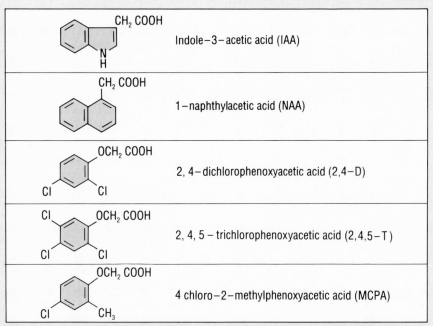

Illustration 1 The molecular structure of natural auxin (IAA) and its analogues. The names given are those currently used in the industry. Notice that the aromatic ring (coloured) is common to all the substances.

use of plant growth substances. 'Hormone weedkillers', as they are often called, are taken up by the leaves and translocated to all parts of the plant. They therefore kill the roots as well as the leaves. As you might expect, they exert their effect by interfering with the growth and metabolism of the plant.

The beauty of these herbicides is that, when applied in the right concentration, they kill the broad-leaved (dicotyledonous) weeds but have no adverse effect on the narrow-leaved (monocotyledonous) plants. MCPA and 2, 4-D are often used to remove broad-leaved weeds from lawns or cereal stands (illustration 2).

Woody plants are killed by 2, 4, 5-T, another chemical related to IAA. During the Vietnam war, the United States Air Force applied vast quantities of this substance to the forests in Vietnam to remove the natural cover.

- **As growth promoters**
  NAA, as an analogue of IAA,

induces root formation in cuttings. It is an ingredient of **rooting powders**. When applied to the cut surface of a stem or branch it supplements the plant's own IAA, increasing its concentration relative to cytokinins. This change of balance encourages the undifferentiated callus tissue which forms at the cut surface to develop into roots. Conversely, the

Illustration 2 The effects of a selective weedkiller which was sprayed onto a mixture of grass and broad-leaved plants two days earlier.

addition of a cytokinin analogue prevents the formation of roots, so that only a mass of simple cells is formed.

As growth retardants

Some artificial growth regulators are antagonists to naturally occurring gibberellins, and they have the effect of reducing the length of the internodes. When such a substance is applied to a cereal crop such as wheat or barley, it stops the stalks growing too long. This prevents the plants falling over (lodging), making them easier and cheaper to harvest.

When sprayed onto house plants such as chrysanthemums these growth retardants restrict growth, making the plant more compact and attractive, and easier to manage.

As flower inducers

Gibberellin antagonists have another use: they induce flowering in woody perennials such as apple and pear trees which do not normally flower until they are several years old. Application of the substance causes the vegetative apex to become floral in the first year, thus ensuring a supply of fruit even when the tree is young.

By contrast, biennials such as sugar beet and cabbage, which do not normally flower until the second year, can be made to flower at the end of the first year by applying gibberellin or one of its analogues.

Ethene is also used to induce flowering. For example, when applied to commercial pineapple plants it causes simultaneous flowering of the whole crop.

As fruit inducers

Normally a signal passes from the developing embryo to the ovary wall or receptacle, encouraging it to develop into a fruit – or, in the case of the receptacle, a 'false fruit'. This signal is IAA, and it can be mimicked by NAA. When applied to the unpollinated flowers of, say, a tomato plant or pear tree, fruits are formed without prior fertilisation (parthenocarpy). These fruits look very similar to the ones produced naturally when the plant's own IAA provides the stimulus. However, there is one notable difference – they are pipless!

Producing pipless fruit is now a big industry. In California, for example, giberellic acid and its analogues are used for producing seedless grapes on a large scale. Seedless fruits such as grapes and satsumas are favourites in supermarkets.

When pollination of a flower is poor and some of the ovules escape being fertilised, the quantity of IAA released may be insufficient to cause full development of the fruit. Application of NAA can supplement the natural IAA and ensure the production of high quality fruit (illustration 3).

As fruit ripeners

Ethene is given off naturally by many types of ripening fruit, and it accelerates the ripening process. A substance such as ethephon which releases ethene can be used for ripening fruit. This is particularly useful for fruits such as bananas which are picked and shipped green but have to be sold yellow. The fruit is sprayed with ethephon in the ship's hold and ethene is gradually released, encouraging the ripening process.

What about the future? In an ideal world we need crop plants which are highly responsive to growth regulators, but not susceptible to damage by herbicides. Producing such plants necessitates combining normal plant breeding practice with the skills of the genetic engineer. If one could produce a type of wheat, for example, which is tailor made to respond maximally to a specific growth regulating substance, the benefits would be enormous.

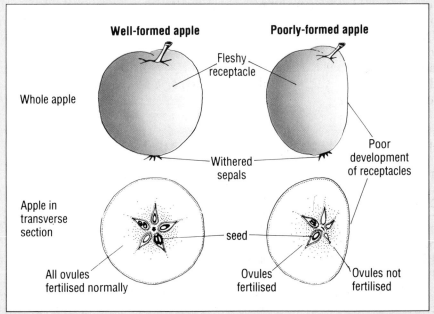

Illustration 3 An apple is a 'false fruit' formed by expansion of the receptacle of the flower (see page 612). When only some of the ovules are fertilised, a lopsided apple may form. This can be avoided by spraying the flowers with NAA which causes the receptacle to develop into an apple without prior fertilisation (parthenocarpy).

and dramatic increase in the respiration rate which leads to ripening. Fruit growers sometimes make use of this by supplying extra ethene to speed up the ripening process, as explained on the opposite page.

Another important function of ethene is wound-healing. If a plant is damaged, ethene is released at the site of the wound. The gas then stimulates the formation of callus tissue which plugs up the wound.

Ethene has been found to have a number of other functions. For example, it causes the rapid increase in length, and thin stem, of etiolated plants. It also promotes leaf and fruit fall, and releases the buds and seeds of certain plants from dormancy – more about those functions later. In plants whose stems grow under water it causes the formation of aerenchyma tissue (see page 183).

As a plant growth substance ethene is unique in that it exists as a gas at normal temperatures. The idea of a growth substance being a gas may strike you as odd, but in fact it is rather sensible because it can diffuse rapidly from the place where it is formed to its site of action.

Plant growth responses

Plants often respond to an external stimulus acting from a particular direction by a bending movement which involves growth. Such growth responses are called **tropisms** from the Greek word *tropos*, meaning 'turn'. Two types of stimulus are particularly important in evoking growth responses in plants: light and gravity.

Response to light

Growth responses to light are called **phototropisms**. In general shoots grow towards light, i.e. they are **positively phototropic**. Roots, if they respond to light at all, are **negatively phototropic**, i.e. they grow away from light.

The response shown by shoots to directional illumination can be seen in figure 36.13. More growth takes place on the dark side of the shoots than on the light side with the result that they bend over towards the light. Quantitative experiments in which coleoptiles are subjected to lights of varying intensity and duration suggest that the response is generally proportional to the total amount of light received. Thus strong light of short duration generally produces the same degree of curvature as weak light of long duration.

The survival value of the phototropic response is obvious: it enables shoots to grow towards places where there is plenty of light for photosynthesis. But what is the mechanism?

The mechanism of phototropism

One of the earliest investigations into this question was carried out by Charles Darwin. Darwin is so famous for his theory of evolution that his many other contributions to biology are often overlooked. In 1880, shortly before his death, he produced a book called *The Power of Movement in Plants* in which he describes an experiment which he did with his son Francis. The experiment is illustrated in figure 36.14.

The Darwins experimented on grass seedlings. They found that a coleoptile failed to bend towards light if its tip was covered with a light-proof cap. However, if a coleoptile was completely covered *except* for the tip, it bent towards light in the usual way. The Darwins concluded that the stimulus of light was detected by the tip of the coleoptile and that some kind of influence was then transmitted to the lower part where it caused the bending to occur.

Figure 36.13 Positive phototropism in the shoots of cress seedlings. In the top photograph the seedlings were illuminated from above. In the bottom photograph the seedlings were illuminated from the right hand side. Notice that the plants have bent towards the light.

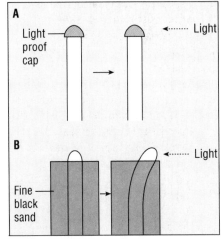

Figure 36.14 An experiment carried out by Charles Darwin and his son Francis on the cause of the phototropic response of coleoptiles. They illuminated a seedling of ornamental canary grass from one side, **A** with the tip of the coleoptiles shielded from light, and **B** with all parts of the coleoptile shielded from light except the tip. In **B** the coleoptile was buried in fine black sand with only the tip protruding.

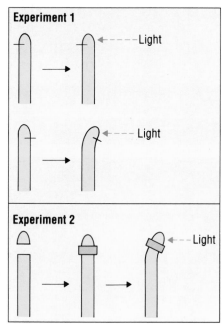

Experiment 1

←---Light

←---Light

Experiment 2

←---Light

Figure 36.15 Two experiments, carried out by Boysen-Jensen in 1913, which support the hypothesis that the phototropic response of coleoptiles is caused by a chemical produced in the tip. In the first experiment the thin piece of mica acts as a barrier: it is impermeable to chemicals in the coleoptile but has no adverse effect on the tissues. In the second experiment the agar blocks are shaded.

The idea that this influence might be a chemical is suggested by the two experiments illustrated in figure 36.15. These experiments were first performed in the 1920s by a scientist called Boysen-Jensen.

In the first experiment a thin piece of mica is inserted into the side of a coleoptile just behind the tip. The mica creates a barrier preventing any chemicals passing back from the tip, but it does not affect the surrounding tissues. It is found that if the mica barrier is inserted into the coleoptile on the dark side, the coleoptile fails to bend towards the light. However, if the mica is inserted on the illuminated side, bending occurs in the usual way. It seems that the mica prevents a growth-promoting hormone passing back from the tip on the dark side of the coleoptile.

The second experiment supports this idea. The tip of a coleoptile is cut off. The decapitated coleoptile does not bend towards light – indeed it is completely unresponsive and does not grow at all. However, if an agar block is inserted between the tip and the lower part of the coleoptile, the latter bends towards light in the usual way. We may conclude that a chemical from the tip has diffused through the agar into the lower part of the coleoptile where it accelerates growth on the dark side, thus bringing about the bending response. The chemical is, as you might guess, auxin.

Why does more growth occur on the dark side of the coleoptile?

In the phototropic response, more growth occurs on the dark side of the coleoptile than on the light side. How can we explain this in terms of auxin?

One possibility is that light causes an unequal distribution of auxin in the tip of the coleoptile, more on the dark side than on the light side. To test this hypothesis the experiment in figure 36.16 can be done. The tip of a coleoptile is cut off and placed on an agar block divided in two by a thin piece of mica. The excised tip is then illuminated from one side. After a time the tip is discarded and the divided agar block placed on the cut end of a decapitated coleoptile. The latter bends towards the right. We may conclude that the left half of the agar block contained more auxin than the right half.

This experiment was originally carried out in the 1920s by Fritz Went whom we met earlier in connection with his coleoptile curvature test. He used the test to compare the concentrations of auxin on the dark and light sides of numerous unilaterally illuminated coleoptiles, and he found that approximately two thirds of the auxin accumulated on the dark side. With Went's discovery, the explanation of phototropism in terms of auxin became generally accepted.

Figure 36.16 An experiment, carried out by Fritz Went in 1928, investigating the effect of directional illumination on the distribution of auxin in the tip of a coleoptile. Explanation in text.

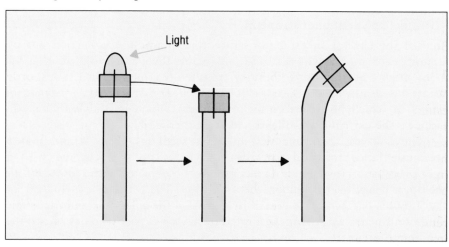

Light

Is auxin destroyed or does it move?

Directional light causes an unequal distribution of auxin, but how is this brought about? Is it caused by destruction of auxin on the illuminated side of the coleoptile, or by the auxin moving across to the darker side? Information on this question is provided by the experiment illustrated in figure 36.17. Auxin is collected from intact coleoptiles and from coleoptiles which have been partially or completely divided down the middle by mica barriers. Study the diagrams carefully and draw your own conclusions.

The results, taken at their face value, support the idea that light affects the distribution of auxin within the coleoptile but does not destroy it – at least not at the relatively low light intensities used in this experiment. So it seems that when a shoot is illuminated from one side, auxin is transported laterally to the other side where it causes the bending to occur.

What causes the bending?

Bending is caused by more growth occurring on the dark side of the coleoptile than on the light side. The actual bending itself occurs behind the apex, in the zone of elongation. The higher concentration of auxin on the dark side causes the cells to elongate more on that side of the coleoptile, thus making it bend in the other direction.

Response to gravity

Consider the experiment in figure 36.18. A young broad bean seedling is placed horizontally in a dark chamber and left to continue its development. After a day or so it is found that the shoot has bent upwards and the root downwards. This is a plant's normal response to gravity, and it is called **geotropism** (or **gravitropism**). Roots grow towards gravity and are described as **positively geotropic**. Shoots grow away from gravity and are therefore **negatively geotropic**.

As with phototropism, the survival value of these geotropic responses is obvious: it means that, however the seed is orientated in the soil, the shoot will always grow upwards towards the light, and the roots downwards into the soil.

The mechanism of shoot geotropism

We can explain the negative geotropism of shoots by proposing that in a horizontally orientated seedling, like the one in figure 36.18, auxin accumulates on the lower side of the shoot. This will cause growth to occur faster on the lower side than the upper side, resulting in an upward curvature.

This hypothesis is consistent with the results of the experiment, mentioned earlier, on the effects of applying auxin to shoots: except at very low concentrations, auxin was found to accelerate shoot growth (see figure 36.8, page 651).

The mechanism of root geotropism

What is responsible for the root's positive response to gravity? An interesting discovery was made in the mid-1970s implicating the **root cap** in the response. Root caps were carefully removed from the roots of maize seedlings, and the seedlings were then orientated so that the roots were horizontal. It was found that the roots continued to grow horizontally instead of bending downwards. In other words, removing the root cap had abolished the geotropic response.

Further experiments were carried out in which half the root cap was removed and the effect on the geotropic response observed. The effect of inserting barriers behind the root cap was also investigated. The results are

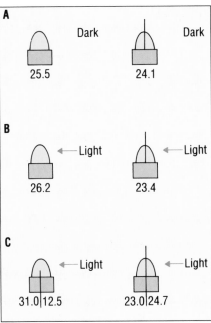

Figure 36.17 The effect of **A** darkness, and **B** and **C** directional illumination on the distribution of auxin in intact and divided maize coleoptiles. Explanation in text. The auxin concentrations were determined by Went's coleoptile curvature test. The figures represent degrees of curvature obtained when the agar blocks were placed on top of decapitated oat coleoptiles.

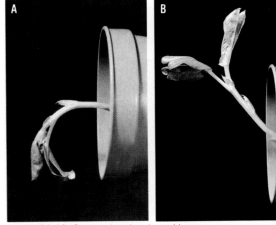

Figure 36.18 Geotropism in a broad bean seedling.

A The seedling, previously growing to one side, was orientated horizontally so that its shoot pointed downwards.

B Its appearance 24 hours later.

Figure 36.19 Experiments investigating the role of the root cap in geotropism. The root cap is shown in black. Removal of half the root cap encourages growth on that side, as does the insertion of a barrier just behind the root cap.

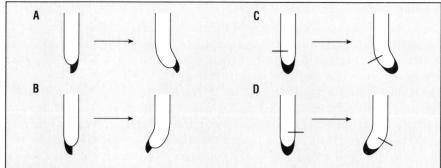

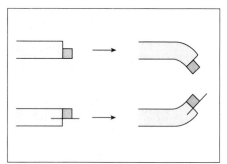

Figure 36.20 Another experiment on geotropism. If an agar block containing abscisic acid is placed in contact with one side of the cut end of a decapitated root, growth is inhibited on that side.

Figure 36.21 Positive thigmotropism in young grapevine tendrils. The top photograph shows part of a grapevine with young tendrils. Immediately after this photograph was taken a twig was placed in contact with one of the tendrils, and this is shown in the middle photograph. The bottom photograph shows the same tendril one hour later. Notice that the tendril has curved round the twig.

shown in figure 36.19, and they suggest that a growth inhibitor is produced by the root cap. In a horizontally orientated root this inhibitor accumulates on the lower side, causing downward bending. Indirect evidence of the kind outlined in figure 36.20 suggests that this inhibitor may be **abscisic acid**.

Although roots are generally positively geotropic and stems negatively so, there are some interesting exceptions. For example mangroves, which grow in tropical swamps where there is little or no oxygen, have 'breathing' roots which grow vertically upwards and project from the surface of the water where they can absorb oxygen from the air.

Other plant responses

Plants respond to other directional stimuli besides light and gravity. For example, roots appear to grow towards moisture (**hydrotropism**) and towards certain chemical substances in the soil (**chemotropism**). However, it is very difficult to show that roots respond positively to such stimuli and some botanists question the validity of these tropisms. (Why do you think hydrotropism is difficult to demonstrate?) An undisputed example of chemotropism, encountered in Chapter 34, is the growth of the pollen tube towards the ovary in flowering plants.

Some plants show tropic responses to touch (**thigmotropism**). An example is provided by the tendrils of climbing plants such as grape vines and sweet peas which bend round solid objects with which they come into contact. Growth is slowed down on the side of the tendril experiencing the stimulus of touch (figure 36.21). In plants such as honeysuckle the stems and branches respond to touch, and this enables them to grow spirally round objects such as drainpipes.

Plants respond to a variety of stimuli that do not come from any particular direction, for example temperature, humidity and the general level of illumination. These are called **nastic responses**. The opening and closing of flowers provides a good example. For instance, crocus flowers open when it is warm and close when it is cold (**thermonasty**), and the flowers of certain daisies open in the light and close in the dark (**photonasty**). In these cases the response involves differential growth or cell expansion in one part of the plant, resulting in a localised bending movement. In crocuses, for example, a rise in temperature causes accelerated expansion on the inner side of the petals, so the petals bend outwards and the flower opens.

Much faster nastic responses, comparable to those of animals in their speed, are seen in the spectacular closing of the leaves of the sensitive plant, *Mimosa pudica*, in response to touch, and the rapid reactions of insectivorous plants such as Venus flytrap when small animals such as flies alight on them.

In these responses little is known about how the message is transmitted from the site of stimulation to the part of the plant which responds, though some interesting findings are reported in the box on page 460.

Is the auxin story correct?

In recent years doubt has been cast on the conventional explanation of phototropism. Tim King explains.

The explanation of why coleoptiles bend towards light proposes that auxin moves across the tip of the coleoptile to the darker side where it stimulates elongation, thus bringing about curvature towards the light.

Let us ask some awkward questions about the proposed movement of auxin. For example, it has been estimated that in a single coleoptile, 200 million particles of light (photons) cause the movement of 2 million million molecules of auxin. How can one light photon possibly make 4000 auxin molecules move? And if auxin *does* move, how does it do it? The cells in a shoot apex are relatively unspecialised, and there are no obvious transport cells. Presumably the auxin molecules move through cells via the endoplasmic reticulum. Within the endoplasmic reticulum, however, what propels the auxin in a particular direction? What happens when auxin reaches a *dividing* cell, in which the normal structure of the endoplasmic reticulum is disrupted?

The answers to these and other questions may become clearer when more research has been done on plant cells. However, important evidence, inconsistent with the usual explanation of phototropism, has recently come to light which simply cannot be explained away. This evidence is of three types:

- Time-lapse photography has shown that for the first half hour or so after a coleoptile is illuminated from one side, growth markedly *slows down* on the light side. This response, which is too rapid to be accounted for by changes in auxin concentration, can be induced by blue light on its own and it obviously contributes to the curving of the coleoptile.

- Oat coleoptiles and sunflower shoots will bend towards light even when their apices have been cut off, or when their tips have been covered with light-proof caps.

- The distribution of auxin in directionally illuminated coleoptiles has recently been investigated using Went's coleoptile curvature test *and* three different modern techniques which measure auxin concentration directly. The results of the coleoptile curvature tests closely resembled those obtained by Went. However, when the auxin concentrations were measured directly, they turned out to be *the same* on the light and dark sides of the coleoptiles, just as they were in dark-grown controls!

This last experiment was repeated on sunflower and radish seedlings, with similar results. One possible explanation is that cells exposed to light make an inhibitor which inactivates auxin molecules. If this happens on the illuminated side of a coleoptile, the latter would be expected to bend towards the light. This suggestion overcomes many of the difficulties, mentioned earlier, of explaining how auxin moves across the tip of the coleoptile or shoot. Perhaps auxin does not move at all! The blue light growth reaction could be caused by a rapid synthesis of an auxin inhibitor, and the positive phototropism of decapitated coleoptiles could occur in seedlings which are capable of manufacturing the inhibitor well below the apex.

Some progress has been made towards identifying such an inhibitor. In radishes, for example, a compound called raphanusin, which binds IAA, can cause radish shoots to bend when applied to the side of the apex in microgram quantities. Compounds like this might have considerable economic importance. For this reason the search is now on to identify this auxin inhibitor.

How do plants detect stimuli?

We have seen how shoots and roots respond to light and gravity, but how do they *detect* these stimuli?

Until a relatively short time ago the answer was not known, but thanks to recent research we are now gaining an insight into these matters. Let us begin with the way shoots and roots detect gravity.

Gravity detection

Certain cells in shoots and roots contain special starch grains which are believed to give the plant its gravitational sense. On account of their function, these starch grains are called **starch statoliths**. When a seedling is laid on its side, the statoliths fall under gravity to the lower side of the cells (figure 36.22). It is thought that this initiates the geotropic response.

Evidence for this idea comes from the observation that if a vertically growing seedling is placed in a horizontal position and then returned to the

Figure 36.22 The electron micrograph shows two starch statoliths in a root cap cell: each statolith consists of a group of starch grains surrounded by a membrane. The diagrams show the positions of the statoliths in the root cap cells.

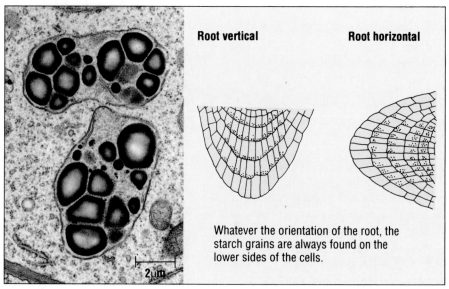

Root vertical   **Root horizontal**

Whatever the orientation of the root, the starch grains are always found on the lower sides of the cells.

2µm

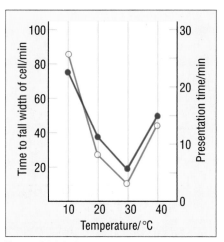

Figure 36.23 The results of an experiment on the stem of a pea plant. The graph shows the effect of temperature on the time taken for the starch statoliths to fall to the bottom of the cells, and on the presentation time required for the gravity-induced bending response. Statolith movement, red; presentation time, blue.

Figure 36.24 An experiment on geotropism using a klinostat. A broad bean seedling is attached to the cork inside the perspex cylinder. The filter paper is soaked in water to keep the atmosphere moist. Rotation of the cylinder at the speed used in this particular experiment resulted in the root growing straight. If the speed of rotation had been significantly slower, the root would have become twisted like a corkscrew.

vertical, a bending response is given only if the seedling was horizontal for a certain minimum period of time. This is called the **presentation time**. Now it has been found that if you raise the temperature, the time taken for the statoliths to fall and the presentation time both decrease. Indeed there is an almost perfect correlation between the two, as you can see in figure 36.23. Furthermore, if you destroy the statoliths (by keeping the seedling at 35°C for a couple of days), the root will no longer respond to gravity.

These ideas fit in with experiments which have been carried out for many years using an apparatus called a **klinostat**. A cylindrical chamber is attached to a horizontal spindle which can rotate at various speeds. A seedling is fixed in position inside the chamber and rotated. The effect of this on its growth is then observed.

In one experiment a broad bean seedling is placed in a klinostat as shown in figure 36.24. The result depends on the speed of rotation. If the speed of rotation is very slow, the root becomes twisted like a corkscrew. This is because each side of the root is exposed to the gravitational stimulus for sufficiently long for a response to begin. On the other hand if rotation is fast, the root does not become twisted and grows straight. In this case each side of the root is exposed to the gravitational stimulus for such a short period that there is not time for a response to be given.

Light detection

In Chapter 27 we saw that animals can only respond to light if the light is first absorbed by a photoreceptor substance. The same applies to plants. The first clue as to the nature of the photoreceptor substance in plants came from studies on germination.

It has been known for a long time that the seeds of certain plants, Grand Rapids lettuces for example, will germinate only if they are exposed, at least briefly, to light. Sometimes only a quick flash of light is needed. In the early 1950s research workers in the United States Department of Agriculture carried out systematic tests on Grand Rapids lettuce seeds to find out which particular wavelengths of light were effective in bringing about germination. They discovered that red light in the range 580 to 660 nm was the most effective, whilst far-red light between 700 and 730 nm, inhibited germination. Far-red light is at the end of the visible spectrum, almost at the beginning of the infra-red band. It is barely visible to us, indeed some people cannot see it at all.

The interesting thing is that if a flash of red light is followed immediately by a flash of far-red, the stimulating effect of the red light is cancelled and germination in inhibited. In fact if seeds are exposed to alternating flashes of red and far-red light, the response is determined by the last flash in the series: the seeds germinate if the last flash is red, but fail to do so if the last flash is far-red.

On the basis of these and other experiments it was suggested that light is absorbed by a single photoreceptor substance which can exist in two forms, one capable of absorbing red light and the other capable of absorbing far-red light. This hypothetical substance was given the name **phytochrome** which means 'plant pigment'.

Subsequent research showed that such a substance really does exist. It occurs in extremely small amounts, about 1 part in 10 million, in the tips of growing shoots. Despite the tiny quantities involved, it was successfully extracted and isolated around 1960 and was shown to be a pale blue-green compound consisting of a pigment molecule attached to a protein.

The absorption spectrum of phytochrome corresponds nicely with the results of the germination experiments described above. It does indeed exist in two forms. One absorbs red light and has its absorption peak at 665 nm; the other absorbs far-red light with its peak at 725 nm (figure 36.25). These two forms of phytochrome are interconvertible and are designated P_r and P_{fr} respectively.

Now when P_r absorbs red light it is rapidly converted into P_{fr}, and when P_{fr} absorbs far-red light it is rapidly converted into P_r. In the dark P_{fr} is slowly converted into P_r:

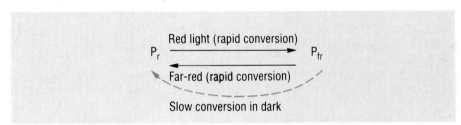

In natural sunlight P_r is converted into P_{fr}, and P_{fr} into P_r. However, the former reaction predominates because sunlight contains more red than far-red light and in any case less energy is needed to convert P_r into P_{fr} than *vice versa*. So P_{fr} tends to accumulate during daylight hours, whilst at night it is converted slowly back into P_r:

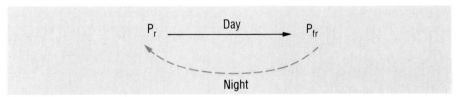

The significance of this is that P_{fr} is biologically active, possibly because it initiates enzyme action, whereas P_r is inactive. This does not mean that P_{fr} invariably stimulates growth. On the contrary, it sometimes inhibits growth, as we shall see later.

Returning now to the lettuce experiment, we can see why far-red light inhibits germination. Treatment with red light causes the conversion of inactive P_r to active P_{fr}. But if red treatment is followed immediately by far-red, the P_{fr} is converted back into P_r before it has had time to act.

The phytochrome system is now known to be involved in many other plant responses besides germination. In some cases red light is the effective

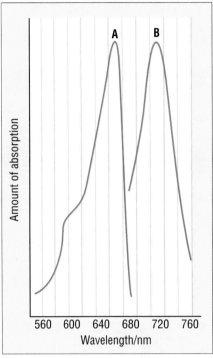

Figure 36.25 Absorption of light by phytochrome.

A Red-absorbing form with maximum absorption at 665 nm wavelength.

B Far-red absorbing form with maximum absorption at 725 nm.

Figure 36.26 Experiment to show the effect of red- and far-red light on stem elongation in bean plants. Stem elongation is stimulated by far-red light but inhibited by red light. All three bean plants received eight hours of daylight each day. The centre plant was given an additional five minute exposure to elongation-promoting far-red light during the night. The plant on the right was given the five minutes of far-red light plus a five minute exposure to elongation-suppressing red light. Notice that red light has counteracted the effect of the far-red.

Figure 36.27 The influence of daylength on the flowering of *Kalanchoe*. The plant on the left was given 14 hours of light and 10 hours of darkness per day. The plant on the right was given 10 hours of light and 14 hours of darkness per day. In all other respects the conditions were the same. The two plants were genetically identical, having been grown from cuttings taken from the same parent plant. *Kalanchoe* is a tropical succulent which is grown as a pot plant in temperate countries. The photograph was kindly provided by Dr Jack Hannay.

stimulus, in other cases far-red. Phytochrome-controlled responses include stem elongation, leaf expansion, leaf fall and the growth of lateral roots. An experiment illustrating its involvement in stem elongation is shown in figure 36.26.

The phytochrome system also initiates the changes that occur when a newly-germinated seedling emerges from the soil (see page 636). When the shoot is exposed to sunlight, P_r is converted to P_{fr} and this triggers the straightening of the plumule, thickening of the stem, expansion of the leaves and formation of chlorophyll. The same thing happens when an etiolated plant which has been growing in the dark is re-exposed to sunlight: red light counters the etiolating effects of ethene (see page 657).

But perhaps the most dramatic role of the phytochrome system is in the control of flowering. Flowering depends on alternating periods of light and dark, and the way this is synchronised by the phytochrome system demonstrates the delicate interplay between external and internal factors in the behaviour of plants.

The control of flowering

Why do some plants in temperate regions flower in the spring and others in the summer or autumn? The principal factor is the relative duration of day and night. Figure 36.27 shows a striking example. Many other responses shown by both animals and plants are regulated by daylength, i.e. the duration of the **photoperiod**. The general term for this phenomenon is **photoperiodism**.

Let us consider the basic principle before we get into the details. In order to respond to daylength, the plant must be able to 'measure' the duration of the light period or the dark period – or both. It is now known that the critical factor is the duration of the **dark period**, in other words the time that elapses between two consecutive light periods.

On the basis of their differing responses to the photoperiod, flowering plants can be divided into three groups:

- **Long-day plants**, e.g. petunias, spinach, radishes and lettuce, only flower if the period of uninterrupted darkness *is less* than a certain critical length each day. Long-day plants can be induced to flower by nights that are shorter than the critical length. On the other hand, they can be prevented from flowering by nights that are longer than the critical length.
- **Short-day plants**, e.g. chrysanthemums, poinsettias and orchids, only flower if the period of uninterrupted darkness *is more* than a certain critical length each day. Short-day plants can be induced to flower by nights that are longer than the critical length. Conversely, they can be prevented from flowering by nights that are shorter than the critical length.
- **Day-neutral plants**, e.g. geranium, tomato, cucumber and snapdragon, are indifferent to day length and will flower irrespective of the relative durations of light and dark which they receive each day.

There is no sharp dividing line between long- and short-day plants. For example, some species only flower if they are exposed first to long days and then to short days, others if they are exposed first to short days and then to long days.

Long-day plants tend to inhabit temperate regions where, at least in summer, days are long and nights short. Short-day and day-neutral plants, on the other hand, tend to live nearer the equator where days and nights are about the same length all the year round. Within the temperate zone long-day plants tend to flower in the summer whereas short-day plants flower in the autumn.

The dependence of flowering plants on the photoperiod is important commercially. For example, plants like chrysanthemums and poinsettias can be made to flower early by giving them extra darkness. In this way horticulturalists can ensure that there is a good supply of colourful plants at Christmas. Again, by careful adjustment of the photoperiod, early- and late-flowering varieties of particular species can be made to flower at the same time, thereby enabling plant breeders to cross them.

The role of the phytochrome system in flowering

Many experiments, too numerous to describe in detail, indicate that the phytochrome system is involved in the photoperiodic control of flowering. To mention the results of one experiment, it has been found that only red light inhibits the flowering of short-day plants, and this inhibitory effect can be cancelled by following the red treatment with far-red light. Bearing in mind that far-red light reconverts P_{fr} back into P_r, it seems that a short-day plant will only flower if a sufficient proportion of its phytochrome is in the P_r form. The trigger to flowering could be either a high enough concentration of P_r or a low enough concentration of P_{fr}. Current opinion favours the latter view, i.e. P_{fr} inhibits flowering and its conversion back to P_r removes the inhibition, thus allowing flowers to develop. In other words, flowering of short-day plants is promoted by the absence of P_{fr} rather than the presence of P_r.

In long-day plants the reverse seems to be true: accumulation of P_{fr} resulting from long exposure to light, stimulates flowering.

For both short-day and long-day plants the critical factor is not just the amount of P_{fr} or P_r which is present, but also the duration of its presence. Rarely is phytochrome all P_{fr} or all P_r; both will be present together and how much there is of each will depend on the quality of the light. In natural conditions there is a dynamic equilibrium between these two forms of phytochrome and their relative proportions will determine whether or not flowering occurs.

How does phytochrome exert its effects on flowering? In the first place the photoperiodic stimulus is detected by the leaves. This has been shown by covering the whole of a plant with a light-proof cover except for one leaf which is then subjected to light/dark treatment. Under these conditions the flowering response still takes place.

From the leaves the message is transmitted to the buds, some of which respond by changing into flower buds. The latter, instead of giving rise to vegetative structures such as side branches and leaves, develop into flowers. In other words, on receipt of the message, a potentially vegetative apex is turned into a floral apex.

The message itself takes the form of a chemical substance. This has been demonstrated ingeniously by grafting a short-day plant which has been induced to flower by exposure to short days to another short-day plant which has been prevented from flowering by being kept in long-day conditions. The result is that the latter blooms. The substance has been named **florigen**, but it has not yet been isolated and identified chemically. Functionally it seems to behave just like a hormone. A scheme incorporating these ideas is given in figure 36.28.

Temperature and flowering

In view of its importance in influencing growth and development generally, it would be surprising if temperature did not play a part in the flowering

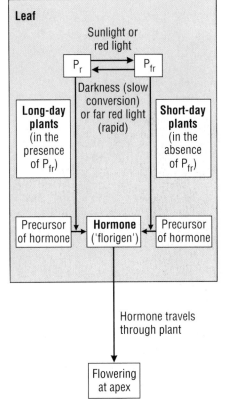

Figure 36.28 Scheme summarising the probable sequence of events that occurs in the photoperiodic control of flowering. Some of the research on which this scheme is based is described in the text.

process. Flowering is usually favoured by an increase in temperature, the optimum temperature being related to the part of the world that the plant comes from. In general, tropical plants tend to germinate and subsequently flower at higher temperatures than temperate, arctic and alpine plants.

Some plants need to experience a period of cold before they will come into flower. This is called **vernalisation**. Plants of this sort need to go through the winter before they will flower. In other words, the plant will not flower in its first year but will do so in the second year. This is typical of biennials such as foxgloves and cabbages. We also find it in winter varieties of wheat and other cereals. The seeds are sown in the autumn and the seedlings survive the winter before resuming their growth and flowering the following year. Most root vegetable such as carrots, turnips and sugar beet, produce a large store of food in their first year. If this is left instead of being eaten by humans, the plant will use the stored food as a reserve for flowering in the spring or summer of the second year.

Many plants can be induced to flower early by vernalising them artificially. This is done by exposing the germinating seeds to a period of cold. The cold has to be applied just as the radicle starts to emerge, and it should be continued for several weeks. A temperature just above freezing ($1 - 10°C$) is required. By chilling seeds like this you can get plants to flower in the same year that the seeds are sown. In other words you trick the plant into thinking that it has been through the winter! In parts of Russia where wheat seedlings cannot survive the freezing temperatures of winter, the partially germinated seeds are artificially vernalised by keeping them in cold storage. They are then planted in the spring and will flower in the summer a few months later.

How do plants respond to cold treatment in this way? The stimulus is detected by the apical meristem. Grafting experiments suggest that the meristem then produces a substance which, directly or indirectly, initiates flowering. In most cases gibberellic acid will substitute for the cold treatment, suggesting that it might be the substance involved. In many biennials vernalisation is only effective if it is followed by exposure to long periods of light each day, such as would happen in the spring and early summer. This has led to the suggestion that cold treatment may cause the production of a precursor which is subsequently activated by light.

Some plant species need to be exposed to a very *high* temperature before they will flower. Such is the case with cotton. This is one reason why such plants can only be grown in parts of the world with a hot climate.

The control of animal growth

We have seen that plant growth is regulated by chemicals. The same is true of animals. In humans and other mammals the main chemical that fulfils this function is **growth hormone (somatotrophin)** produced by the anterior lobe of the pituitary gland. Having been secreted, it is carried in the bloodstream to the epiphyses of the bones and other sites where growth takes place. It then stimulates growth by increasing the metabolic rate, the extra energy being diverted to cell division and protein synthesis.

The secretion of growth hormone by the pituitary gland is normally kept under tight control. Its release is triggered by a **releasing factor** from the hypothalamus (releasing factors are explained on page 468). Moment to moment control of growth hormone secretion is achieved mainly by variations in the amount of releasing factor produced. If for some reason much too much growth hormone is present in the bloodstream, its secretion is inhibited by another hormone called **somatostatin**. This too comes from the hypothalamus.

Despite these natural control mechanisms, a person's pituitary may persistently secrete too much growth hormone. If this happens in a child who is still growing, the rate of growth increases uniformly throughout the body resulting in a very large but correctly proportioned individual. This condition is called **gigantism**. Occasionally over-secretion of growth hormone occurs in adult life, in which case new bone tissue is laid down in the body's extremities, particularly the hands, feet and jaws. These parts become greatly enlarged, a condition called **acromegaly** (from the Greek *akros*: end, *megas*: great).

If the pituitary secretes too little growth hormone in the adult there are few noticeable effects. However, if this happens while the person is still growing, the rate of growth may be severely reduced and the person becomes short and stunted. Intelligence and reproductive functions are, however, unimpaired. This condition cannot be rectified once adulthood is reached, but during childhood it can be treated by regular injections of growth hormone obtained from human sources or genetically engineered bacteria (see page 743). Gigantism and dwarfism are illustrated in figure 36.29.

Pituitary growth hormone is not the only hormone that promotes growth in mammals. Insofar as it increases the general metabolic rate, **thyroxine** does so too, and under-secretion of it during childhood can result in stunted growth (see page 466).

Another hormone that affects growth is the male hormone **testosterone**. Injections of testosterone can enhance the growth of muscles. This fact has been exploited by meat-producers for increasing the mass of their livestock, and by certain over-ambitious athletes for improving their performance. Although many people feel that there is nothing unethical about treating livestock with hormones, the procedure has been banned in the European Community. What do you feel about the ethical and safety aspects of this practice?

Action of a growth hormone illustrated by insects

Insects are particularly interesting in this respect because they enable us to see how growth hormones may exert their action. The control of growth (and moulting which is an integral part of the growth process) has been investigated in a number of insects.

The research has shown that a hormone is secreted by neurosecretory cells in the brain. This flows into the thorax where it stimulates a gland to secrete a second hormone. This does not happen at once; it is necessary for a certain amount of the brain hormone to accumulate before it can trigger the thoracic gland. This second hormone, known as **moulting hormone** (or **ecdysone**), brings about shedding of the cuticle and growth.

It is thought that the moulting hormone exerts its effects by switching on the genes needed to produce the enzymes necessary for growth. Evidence supporting this theory comes from the observation that certain regions of the chromosomes swell up to form **chromosome puffs** when exposed to the hormone. This can be seen clearly in the giant chromosomes of *Drosophila*. The puffs represent the site of RNA synthesis through which the genes exert their action (see page 734). It is likely that growth hormones in general exert their effects through the action of genes, and this notion is consistent with what we know about how other hormones work (see page 470).

The control of metamorphosis in insects

Moulting is associated with **metamorphosis**, the gradual or sudden transformation of a juvenile insect (nymph or larva) into the adult. This is controlled by a **moulting hormone** secreted by a gland in the thorax.

Figure 36.29 Pituitary dwarfism and gigantism.

Top A scene from the film *The Wizard of Oz*. Dorothy, played by the then 16 year old Judy Garland, has just arrived in the Land of Oz. The Munchkins were played by pituary dwarfs. *Bottom* An exceptionally tall woman is seen here with her family and pet poodle. Her tallness was caused by excessive production of pituitary growth hormone during childhood.

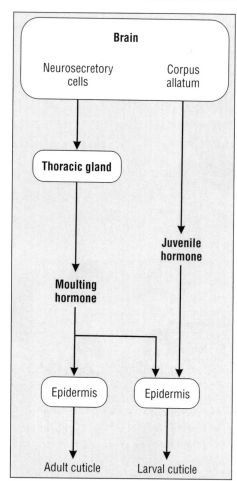

Figure 36.30 Scheme summarising the hormonal control of growth in an insect. For shedding of the cuticle the moulting hormone is required. Moulting hormone accompanied by juvenile hormone causes the epidermis to produce a larval cuticle. Moulting hormone alone, without the juvenile hormone, causes the epidermis to produce an adult cuticle.

Figure 36.31 Red deer have their mating season in the autumn and produce offspring the following year. Here a stag can be seen with a harem of females (hinds). Mating usually occurs in October and the calves are born in June.

Metamorphosis is suppressed by a **juvenile hormone** secreted by a gland called the **corpus allatum** in the brain. So long as this hormone is present in the blood, the epidermal cells – under the influence of the moulting hormone – produce a cuticle characteristic of the juvenile stage. At metamorphosis the corpus allatum stops secreting its juvenile hormone, and the moulting hormone – in the absence of the juvenile hormone – causes the epidermal cells to lay down the adult type of cuticle. These events are summarised in figure 36.30.

The involvement of the corpus allatum has been shown by simple experiments. For example, a larva whose corpus allatum has been removed develops adult characteristics precociously. Conversely, if the corpus allatum from a third or fourth stage larva is implanted into the abdomen of a fifth stage larva, the latter fails to pupate and undergo metamorphosis. Instead it develops into a giant larva.

The juvenile hormone therefore inhibits metamorphosis and causes the retention of juvenile characteristics. How it achieves this is uncertain but it is likely that it suppresses the genes responsible for producing adult structures. Once the inhibitory influence is removed, the genes leap into action.

The control of metamorphosis in amphibians

The development of a tadpole culminates in its undergoing metamorphosis into the adult (see page 634). This process involves extensive changes in the animal's anatomy and physiology.

Amphibian metamorphosis is controlled by the hormone **thyroxine** secreted by the **thyroid gland**. Injecting thyroxine into a tadpole results in premature metamorphosis. Conversely, removing the thyroid from a tadpole prevents metamorphosis and results in an oversized tadpole. It is therefore clear that thyroxine is essential for metamorphosis.

More precise data have been obtained by treating tadpoles with radioactive iodine. These experiments are based on the principle that thyroxine contains iodine; tracing what happens to radioactive iodine should therefore tell us what the thyroid gland is doing at different times. It turns out that at metamorphosis there is a marked decrease in the radio-iodine content of the gland. This is caused by the discharge of the hormone from the gland. The hormone then causes metamorphosis.

Further research suggests that metamorphosis is brought about partly by an increase in the amount of thyroxine in the bloodstream and partly by an increased ability of the tissues to respond to it. Here, as in insects, the hormone probably exerts its effects by influencing the genes responsible for the production of adult structures.

Control of breeding in animals

We saw earlier that the flowering of plants is controlled by daylength, in other words the stimulus is a photoperiodic one. The same applies to many animals which have a breeding season, including numerous species of mammals and birds. It is obviously important that such animals should produce offspring at a time of the year when environmental conditions are favourable and there is plenty of food available. Generally this is the spring or summer.

In animals which mate and produce offspring in the spring or early summer, increased daylength acts as the stimulus which brings them into the breeding condition. However, some animals mate in the autumn and produce offspring the following year. In these animals decreased daylength is the effective stimulus. Such is the case with red deer (figure 36.31).

Numerous investigations have shown that the photoperiodic response is mediated by the hypothalamus and pituitary gland (see page 468). The sequence of events is outlined in figure 36.32. The stimulus is received by the eyes from which nerve impulses are sent to the hypothalamus. The latter then produces a releasing factor which passes to the anterior lobe of the pituitary gland. The pituitary responds by secreting **gonadotrophic hormones** into the bloodstream. These hormones cause the ovaries and testes to grow to maturity.

What exactly constitutes the stimulus in this photoperiodic response? Is it the duration of the light period each day, or the duration of the dark period? In plants we saw that the critical factor is the duration of the dark period, i.e. the interval between two consecutive light periods. The same applies to animals – at any rate to the Japanese quail which has been much used for studies on this topic. For quails to come into breeding condition, successive light periods must be separated by about 14 hours. In the laboratory you can get quails to breed at any time of the year by giving them light periods separated by this amount of darkness.

It seems that the animal can 'measure' the time between the light periods. In flowering plants we saw that this is achieved by the phytochrome system. In animals like the quail it is achieved by the hypothalamus functioning as a 'clock'. When successive light periods are separated by the correct interval, the activity of the hypothalamus – and hence the pituitary gland – is such that the animal is brought into season.

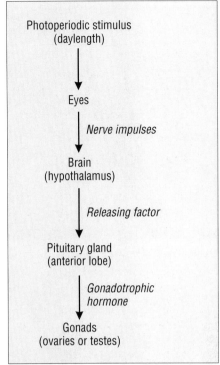

Figure 36.32 Many species of birds and mammals have a breeding season whose timing is controlled by daylength. This scheme summarises the chain of events which brings such animals into breeding condition.

Dormancy and suspended growth

In certain conditions an organism may enter a state of **dormancy** either as an adult or at some stage in its life cycle. Growth and development cease, and the metabolic rate may fall to the point that it is only just sufficient to keep the cells alive. In this way the organism can survive for many months, even years, without exhausting its food reserves.

Dormancy is closely geared to the environment. It enables organisms to withstand unfavourable conditions such as drought, food shortage and winter cold. It also allows time for dispersal by agents such as wind and water, whilst at the same time permitting any necessary internal changes to take place.

Seeds, buds, spores, eggs and plant storage organs can all be dormant. So can insect nymphs, larvae, pupae, and adults. The dormancy of seeds is usually associated with the hard, resistant **seed coat**. The fertilised eggs (zygotes) of many fungi and protoctists secrete a thick wall around themselves, thereby becoming resistant **zygospores** which may remain formant for long periods of time. Much the same applies to asexually produced spores, including those produced by bacteria.

Plant storage organs such as tubers and bulbs enable plants to survive the winter from one growing season to the next, for which reason they are known as **perennating organs**. Buds provide a means whereby new leaves and flowers can develop after a period of suspended growth. This is important in deciduous trees and shrubs which shed their leaves before winter sets in, and form new leaves the following spring (figure 36.33).

The mechanism of dormancy

The phenomenon of dormancy raises two fundamental questions: what induces it, and what brings it to an end? The general answer is that dormancy is brought on, and subsequently ended, by environmental factors, particularly temperature and light, acting via internal chemicals. As

Figure 36.33 A horsechestnut bud opening in the spring. Factors that induce this response are discussed in the text.

a broad statement this would apply equally to animals and plants. One can further predict that there may be two interacting chemicals, one for promoting dormancy and the other for breaking it. With these general ideas in mind let us look at dormancy in certain specific structures.

Seeds

Seed dormancy may be caused by a variety of environmental factors including oxygen lack, drying out, or the presence of inhibitory substances which prevent germination. Also it may be necessary for the embryo within the seed to undergo further development before it can germinate, or the seed coat may be so hard and impervious to water or oxygen that germination simply cannot occur. In some cases it may be necessary for the seed coat to be abraded or partially digested in an animal's gut before it will germinate.

The seeds of many types of plant, particularly in temperate regions, must be subjected to a period of cold before they can germinate. This is known as **stratification** (not to be confused with *vernalisation* which is the exposure of plants to a period of cold before they will flower (see page 666). Seed merchants stratify the seeds of some species before packaging them so that they will germinate as soon as they are sown.

Inside the seed, growth substances have a role to play. For example, it has been discovered that the reluctance of certain seeds to germinate is caused by the presence of high concentrations of abscisic acid which acts as a germination inhibitor. On the other hand, dormancy can often be broken by treatment with gibberellic acid. This suggests that the germination inhibitor may be opposed by gibberellic acid, an idea which is supported by the observation that the concentration of gibberellic acid rises towards the end of dormancy.

Buds

Experimental evidence suggests that the cessation of growth and the formation of dormant buds in deciduous trees and shrubs is induced by the longer nights of autumn, so the stimulus is a photoperiodic one. As with seeds, a period of low temperature, typical of winter, is generally necessary before growth can be resumed and the buds open the following spring. The lengthening days (or shortening nights) as spring approaches may be the trigger that breaks dormancy. However, increase in temperature is also important towards the end of the dormant period. Horsechestnut buds, if brought into a warm house in the spring, will open much earlier than if they are left on the tree.

Physiologically, three growth substances seem to be involved in dormancy: auxin, gibberellic acid and abscisic acid. Abscisic acid has been extracted from buds and shown to inhibit growth. This suggests that this hormone may induce dormancy. Conversely, bud dormancy can often be released by treatment with IAA or gibberellic acid, suggesting that one or other, or both, of these hormones may be responsible for breaking dormancy.

Perennating organs

Perennating organs are formed by the swelling up of roots, stems or leaves (see page 616). The formation of a swollen structure from one that is normally long and thin involves a suppression of the normal elongation process and its replacement by lateral expansion. Once formed, the organ becomes dormant and remains so until the following year.

The development of perennating organs such as tubers can be induced by a photoperiodic stimulus similar to that which induces bud formation. There is evidence that the stimulus is detected by the leaves from which one or more hormone-like substances are translocated to the parts of the plant where the perennating organs are formed.

For subsequent development perennating organs need to experience a period of cold, similar to that which is required by seeds. Bulbs sold in garden shops have usually been 'prepared' by chilling so that they will sprout into new plants in the same year that you plant them.

Leaf fall

Leaf fall, or **abscission**, is associated with the formation of buds and winter dormancy in deciduous trees. The details vary from one species to another. However, the central event, common to most species, is the development of a layer of cells, the **abscission layer**, at the base of the leaf stalk (figure 36.34). In the course of time the primary wall of the abscission cells dissolves under the action of enzymes, and the cementing effect of the middle lamella is lost. The result is that the cells separate from one another and the leaf becomes loose. At the same time the cells expand sideways, and this causes the leaf stalk to slough off the stem. Meanwhile, a layer of corky cells forms across the stump of the leaf stalk, protecting it from invasion by micro-organisms and reducing water loss. This corky layer becomes the **leaf scar**.

At one time it was thought that abscisic acid was responsible for leaf fall. However, it now seems that ethene is responsible. Ethene becomes highly concentrated towards the base of the leaf stalk at the time of abscission. Moreover, placing a jacket of ethene round the base of the stalk can cause premature abscission. Ethene makes the cells of the abscission layer expand sideways, breaking the leaf stalk. The ethene response is stimulated by long nights via the phytochrome system.

Auxin is also involved in leaf fall. If the leaf blades are removed from a deciduous tree before autumn, leaving the leaf stalks still attached to the tree, the leaf stalks soon fall off. However, if auxin is applied to the cut ends of such leaf stalks, they stay on the tree. These observations suggest that during the summer auxin passes from the leaf blade down the stalk and inhibits abscission. It therefore seems that the action of ethene is opposed by auxin. During the life of a leaf, auxin production gradually decreases until eventually leaf fall occurs. Here we have yet another process which seems to be controlled by two antagonistic hormones.

Dormancy in animals

Amongst animals, a type of dormancy akin to that seen in plants is shown by many species of insects. It is called **diapause**, and can occur at any stage in the life cycle: egg, larva, pupa or adult. In the dormant state, the animal may survive and remain viable for months or even years. Typically it occurs during the winter, which is why you don't see many insects around at that time of the year.

Diapause shares the same kind of cause as that underlying dormancy in plants, i.e. internal chemicals regulated by the environment. An insect's growth and development is promoted by a hormone secreted by its brain (see page 667). Diapause seems to be caused by this growth-promoting hormone not being produced, at any rate in adequate quantities.

The hormonal changes which induce diapause are related to daylength. As soon as the hours of daylight fall below a certain critical level, diapause sets in. The critical amount of daily light varies from one species of insect to

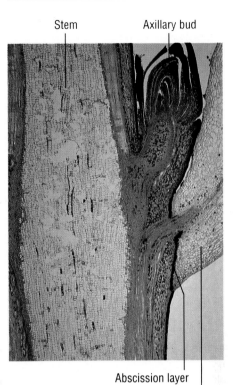

Stem   Axillary bud

Abscission layer

Leaf stalk

Figure 36.34 Photomicrograph of a vertical section through the leaf stalk of an old leaf showing the abscission layer.

another. In the cabbage white butterfly it is about 12 hours. When the light falls below this level, the pupae enter diapause and do not resume their development until the following spring. Surprisingly, insects do not register the photoperiodic stimulus with their eyes: covering their eyes does not abolish the diapause response. The light penetrates the cuticle and acts directly on the brain.

How is diapause ended? In some species the change to longer days may be the effective stimulus, but in many insects a period of cold has been found to be necessary before growth can be resumed – another parallel with plants.

Hibernation is superficially similar to diapause. It occurs on a seasonal basis in many animals, including certain mammals (see page 409). As in diapause and other forms of dormancy, the metabolic rate falls to a low level with the result that the animal draws on its reserves only very slowly. Some hibernating animals, bats for example, wake up to feed from time to time, but otherwise all activities including growth are suspended.

Hibernation is brought on mainly by the fall in environmental temperature at the beginning of winter, and it is primarily a means of avoiding the need to maintain a high body temperature during the winter cold. To do so would necessitate keeping up a consistently high metabolic rate, a task which would require the consumption of more food than the animal could reasonably obtain during the winter.

Hibernation comes from the Latin word *hiberna*, meaning 'winter', and this reflects the fact that it normally occurs during the winter. Another kind of seasonal dormancy is **aestivation** which occurs in summer (aestivation comes from the Latin word *aestas*, meaning 'summer'). This type of dormancy is a response to drought or excessive heat and some examples are given on page 388.

The distinction between hibernation and aestivation is not always clear. Many animals go into a state of partial or complete dormancy (or **torpor** as it is sometimes called) at any time of the year, and for periods of varying duration, depending on environmental conditions. The important point, from the survival point of view, is that the animal should respond appropriately to changes in the environment whenever they occur.

Survival during dormancy

There is much variation in the length of time a dormant organism can survive and remain viable. Seeds of lotus plants have been found embedded in peat on the site of an ancient lake in Manchuria. After their coats had been softened by brief immersion in concentrated sulphuric acid, most of them germinated successfully. Radioactive carbon dating showed them to be over 1000 years old. The current record is held by seeds of the Arctic lupin found in frozen silt in the Yukon. The seeds germinated successfully and were estimated to be between 8000 and 13 000 years old!

On the animal side, the record for longevity in the dormant state is probably held by the beetle *Buprestis aurulenta* whose larva can survive for well over 40 years. The pupa of the gall midge *Sitodiplosis mosellana* is known to remain viable for at least 18 years.

There is also considerable variation in the severity of the conditions which can be endured by dormant tissues. Overwintering buds and perennating organs can of course endure freezing, and spores and seeds can survive long periods of drought. Dry seeds can survive freezing in liquid nitrogen (–250°C), and cysts of the unicellular ciliate

Colpoda can withstand boiling. Dormancy is therefore an efficient way of coping with adverse conditions. Freezing is now used for the long-term storage of seeds.

It is interesting to speculate on how the tissues inside these dormant structures manage to survive. In seeds, the water content declines to a very low level, mitochondria and other organelles shrivel up and respiration can hardly be detected even with the most sensitive apparatus. If the tissues are dry, the formation of ice crystals within the cells, normally damaging, ceases to be a problem.

Summary

1 Growth is influenced by a variety of external and internal factors.

2 In flowering plants the growth substance **auxin** (indoleacetic acid, IAA) promotes growth of the shoot and performs other functions as well.

3 Other plant growth substances include **gibberellins, cytokinins, abscisic acid** and **ethene**. All have specific functions.

4 Plant hormones, or synthetic substitutes, are important commercially as growth regulators and, in the case of auxins, selective herbicides.

5 Plants respond to directional stimuli by growth movements (**tropisms**), e.g. **phototropism** and **geotropism**. Evidence suggests that these responses are brought about by an unequal distribution of hormone within the responding structure.

6 Plants also respond to stimuli which do not come from a particular direction (**nastic responses**).

7 Plants detect light by means of the photoreceptor substance **phytochrome** .

8 Phytochrome is involved in many light-induced responses including germination, stem growth, leaf expansion, leaf fall and flowering.

9 Flowering depends on the daylength and is an example of **photoperiodism**. Flowering plants can be divided into **long-day**, **short-day** and **day-neutral** plants.

10 In the photoperiodic control of flowering, it is the length of the dark period (night) rather than the length of the light period (day) that matters. The link between the stimulus and the response appears to be hormonal.

11 Temperature is also important in flowering. In some species flowering will only occur if the plants or germinating seeds are subjected to a period of cold beforehand (**vernalisation**).

12 In animals growth is controlled by hormones e.g. pituitary **growth hormone** and **thyroxine**.

13 Evidence suggests that the hormones controlling growth exert their influence by suppressing or activating the relevant genes.

14 Animals with breeding seasons are brought into breeding condition by changes in daylength, another example of photoperiodism. As in flowering, it is the length of the dark period (night) that matters.

15 Growth and development may be temporarily interrupted by **dormancy**. Dormancy is initiated and terminated by a combination of external and internal factors.

16 The dormant seeds of some plants require a period of cold before they will germinate (**stratification**).

17 In insects **diapause** is comparable to dormancy in plants. **Hibernation** and **aestivation** are types of dormancy found in certain animal groups.

Review questions

1 Describe one experiment which, in your opinion, provides the most convincing evidence that the growth of a coleoptile is promoted by a chemical produced in the tip.

2 Give one example of a situation where two plant growth substances oppose each other's action, and one example of a situation where two plant growth substances augment each other's action.

3 Describe one experiment which supports the hypothesis that the phototropic response of a coleoptile is caused by an unequal distribution of a growth substance within the coleoptile.

4 Suggest three stimuli to which a climbing plant such as a honeysuckle may respond which enable the stem to grow upwards.

5 Study the experiment illustrated in figure 36.19 (page 660) on the role of the root cap in geotropism. What other experiments might be done to test the hypothesis that the root cap produces a growth inhibitor?

6 Do you think the plant in figure 36.27 (page 664) is a short-day plant or a long-day plant? Relate your answer to the plant's normal environment.

7 In photoperiodism what matters is the length of the dark period rather than the length of the light period. Describe one experiment which supports this idea in *either* a flowering plant *or* an animal.

8 What is phytochrome? Explain one function which phytochrome is known to perform in plants. How would you attempt to find out if phytochrome is involved in phototropism?

9 Explain the difference between stratification and vernalisation. In what ways are they important commercially?

10 Suggest one environmental stimulus which may initiate hibernation in a mammal such as the dormouse. How might your suggestion be tested?

Further reading

W.M.M. Baron's *Organisation in Plants* (Arnold, 1979) contains an excellent account of the physiology of plant growth which is just right for A-level studies.

More detail on many aspects of plant growth and development can be found in *Growth and Differentiation in Plants* by P.F. Waring and I.D.J. Phillips (Pergamon, 1981).

On the animal side, *The Triumph of the Embryo* by Lewis Wolpert (Oxford University Press, 1991) makes fascinating reading.

In *Biology, Advanced Topics* the growth substances involved in root geotropism and the physiology of seed germination are discussed.

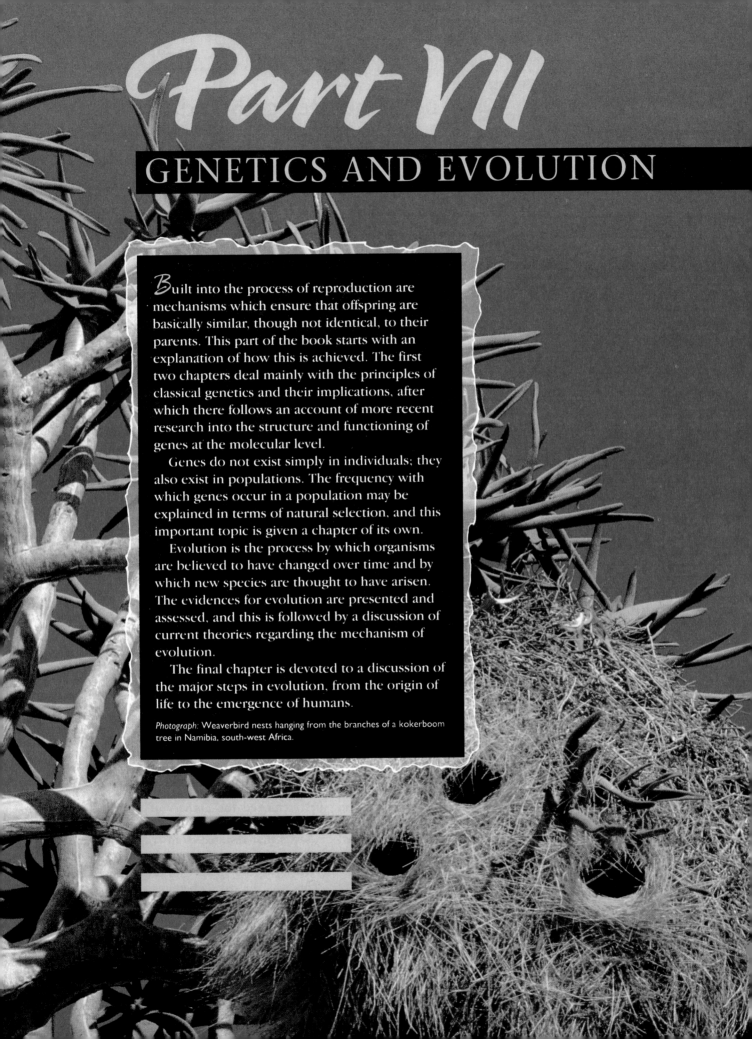

Part VII

GENETICS AND EVOLUTION

$\mathcal{B}$uilt into the process of reproduction are mechanisms which ensure that offspring are basically similar, though not identical, to their parents. This part of the book starts with an explanation of how this is achieved. The first two chapters deal mainly with the principles of classical genetics and their implications, after which there follows an account of more recent research into the structure and functioning of genes at the molecular level.

Genes do not exist simply in individuals; they also exist in populations. The frequency with which genes occur in a population may be explained in terms of natural selection, and this important topic is given a chapter of its own.

Evolution is the process by which organisms are believed to have changed over time and by which new species are thought to have arisen. The evidences for evolution are presented and assessed, and this is followed by a discussion of current theories regarding the mechanism of evolution.

The final chapter is devoted to a discussion of the major steps in evolution, from the origin of life to the emergence of humans.

Photograph: Weaverbird nests hanging from the branches of a kokerboom tree in Namibia, south-west Africa.

CHAPTER 37

The principles of heredity

Figure 37.1

A Einkorn wheat, an ancient species of wheat known from over 11 000 years ago before the cultivation of wheat began.

B Modern wheat, a result of applied genetics.

Figure 37.2 Gregor Mendel, who first put the study of heredity on a firm scientific basis.

Figure 37.3 Hand pollination of a petunia.

What do giraffes have that no other organisms have? The answer is not long necks – ostriches have long necks – but baby giraffes (or parent giraffes). No one can help being struck by the often remarkable similarity between parents and their offspring, but it is just as noticeable that parents and offspring differ from each other in many respects. The science of heredity, or **genetics**, attempts to explain both the similarities and the differences between parents and offspring. Genetics began as 'pure' science, but applied genetics soon developed, and today the subject is of central importance to agriculture and medicine (figure 37.1).

We now know that information is contained in the chemicals that make up the structures called **genes** which are located along the **chromosomes**. In recent years spectacular advances have been made in understanding the structure and functioning of these genes. But the first major breakthrough in the study of heredity took place over a hundred years ago, long before genes or even chromosomes had been recognised. The person responsible for this was a Moravian monk, Gregor Mendel, and the story of heredity starts with him (figure 37.2).

Mendel was born in 1822 and entered the monastery in Brünn, Moravia (now Brno, Czechoslovakia) in 1843. The monastery was an unusual one and the young monks were encouraged to continue their academic studies. Mendel went to Vienna University where he became interested in plant breeding.

Starting in about 1856, Mendel carried out a vast number of breeding experiments in the garden of his monastery. He concentrated on the garden pea which has a number of pairs of clearly distinguished characteristics, for example, long versus short stems and smooth versus wrinkled seeds. With great perseverance and diligence he carefully isolated plants, transferred pollen from one to another, collected and sowed the seeds, and laboriously counted and recorded the different types of offspring. The conclusions he drew from his studies form the foundations on which the study of heredity is built.

Monohybrid inheritance

In the early stages of his work Mendel studied the inheritance of just one pair of contrasting characteristics, which is nowadays called **monohybrid inheritance**. In one such experiment he took a pure-breeding tall pea plant and crossed it with a pure-breeding short pea plant. (Pure-breeding plants are ones which, when crossed among themselves, always give rise to offspring which are like the parents.) The way Mendel crossed plants was to take pollen grains from one plant and dust them onto the stigma of another plant, having first removed the anthers of this second plant to ensure that it could not pollinate itself (figure 37.3).

Mendel collected the seeds that resulted from crosses between tall pea plants and short ones, and sowed them. He found that the seeds, once they had germinated and grown into adult plants, always developed into tall offspring (figure 37.4). This was the case whether pollen grains from tall plants were placed on the stigmas of short plants, or pollen grains from short plants were placed on the stigmas of tall plants.

In these crosses, the original pure breeding parent plants are referred to as the **parental generation** (or **P** for short), and the offspring belong to what is called the **first filial generation** (or F_1). Mendel then took these tall F_1

plants and self-pollinated each of them, precautions again being taken to prevent them being pollinated by any other kind of pollen. The resulting seeds were sown and the offspring (belonging to the **second filial** or F_2 **generation**) were examined. Mendel found that some of these F_2 plants were tall and some short. Overall he counted 1064 plants. Of these, 787 (74 per cent) were tall and 277 (26 per cent) short. It seemed as though approximately three-quarters (75 per cent) of the F_2 generation were tall and one-quarter (25 per cent) short. In other words, the ratio of tall to short plants was approximately 3:1.

The results of these crosses can be summarised as follows:

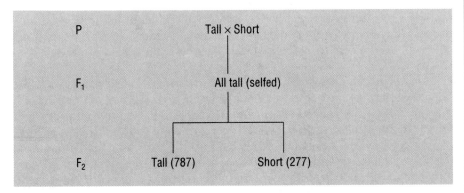

Other monohybrid crosses that Mendel carried out produced very similar results as you can see from table 37.1.

Conclusions from Mendel's monohybrid crosses

What conclusions can we draw from these results? The first striking fact to notice is that in neither the F_1 nor the F_2 generations are there any medium-sized plants, that is plants intermediate between the tall and the short parents. From this we conclude that inheritance is not a process in which the features of the two parents are blended together to produce an intermediate result, like the mixing of black and white paints to produce grey. Rather, it is a process in which definite structures, or particles, which may or may not show themselves in the outward appearance of the organism, are transmitted from parents to offspring.

That such particles exist is borne out by the observation that they can be combined in one generation but separated in the next, as is witnessed by the recovery of the short form in the F_2 generation despite its absence in the F_1 generation. For these reasons inheritance may be described as **particulate**.

Nowadays we call these particles genes, but Mendel simply referred to them as factors. Although he never saw them, nor knew what they were

Figure 37.4 Mendel found that tall garden peas (1.9–2.2 m) crossed with short garden peas (0.3–0.5 m) always gave rise to tall garden peas (1.9–2.2 m).

Table 37.1 Summary of Mendel's experiments on the inheritance of single pairs of characters in the garden pea *Pisum sativum*. Notice that for all the characters investigated, a ratio close to 3:1 was obtained.

Character investigated	Cross	F_2 products	Ratio
Form of seed	Smooth × wrinkled	5474 smooth, 1850 wrinkled	2.96:1
Colour of cotyledons	Yellow × green	6022 yellow, 2001 green	3.01:1
Colour of petals	Purple × white	705 purple, 244 white	3.15:1
Form of pods	Inflated × constricted	882 inflated, 299 constricted	2.95:1
Colour of unripe pods	Green × yellow	428 green, 152 yellow	2.82:1
Position of flowers	Axial × terminal	651 axial, 207 terminal	3.14:1
Height of stem	Tall × short	787 long, 277 short	2.84:1

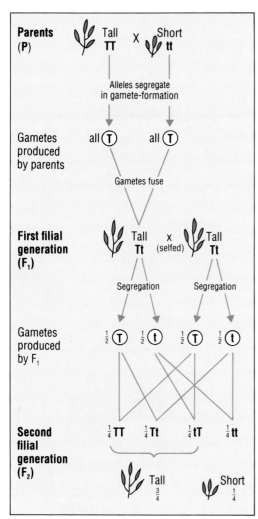

Figure 37.5 Interpretation of what happens when a pure-bred tall pea plant is crossed with a pure-bred short plant. Gametes are circled. This is an example of monohybrid inheritance.

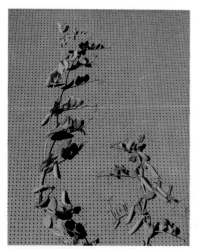

Figure 37.6 A tall and a short pea plant.

made of, he appreciated their existence and is rightly credited with their discovery.

The second conclusion that can be drawn derives from the observation that there were no short plants in the F_1 generation, despite the fact that one of the parent plants was short. However, short plants did reappear in the F_2 generation. From this we can conclude that although the F_1 plants are tall, they must receive from their short parent a factor for shortness which remains 'hidden' in the F_1 plants and does not reveal its presence in the outward appearance of the plants until the F_2 generation.

A third conclusion is that, as the factor for shortness fails to show itself in the F_1 generation, it must in some way be swamped by the factor for tallness. Only in the absence of this factor will the factor for shortness show itself in the outward appearance of the plant. In other words, the factor for tallness is **dominant** to the factor for shortness. Shortness is described as **recessive**.

Although Mendel knew nothing of chromosomes and genes, he suggested that his factors must be transmitted from parents to offspring via the gametes. If we are right in assuming that the F_1 plants contain factors for shortness as well as for tallness, it is reasonable to suppose that each F_1 plant receives via the gametes one factor for tallness from its tall parent and one factor for shortness from its short parent. That is, *the gametes contain only one of the two factors for size, while the plants to which these gametes give rise contain a pair of such factors.*

Genes and their transmission

All these ideas are summarised in the genetic diagram shown in figure 37.5. The gene controlling height in the pea plant exists in two forms. One functions normally and is responsible for producing a tall plant. The other, however, influences development in such a way that, if two are present together, a short plant is produced. These different forms of a gene are known as **alleles**, from the Greek *allos*, 'other'. Alleles, therefore, are alternative forms of a gene. The place on a chromosome where a gene is found is known as its **locus**, *locus* being the Latin for place.

In figure 37.5 the allele for tallness is represented by T, and the allele for shortness by t. For reasons that will become clear shortly, we shall assume that each parent plant (or, more strictly, each cell of each parent plant) contains a pair of identical alleles: **TT** in the case of the tall parent, **tt** in the case of the short parent. When an organism contains identical alleles like this, it is said to be **homozygous**. In making this statement we are describing the genetic constitution of the parent plants, or at least that part of it which determines their size. The genetic constitution of an organism is known as its **genotype**. The outward appearance of the organism, i.e. the way the genes express themselves in the structure of the organism, is known as its **phenotype** (figure 37.6). So in the case of the parent pea plants, the genotype of the tall parent is TT, its phenotype being 'tall'; the genotype of the short parent is tt, its phenotype being 'short'.

Now each of the gametes produced by the tall parent will contain one **T** allele, and each of the gametes produced by the short parent one **t** allele. Fertilisation brings the **T** and **t** alleles together so that all the F_1 offspring have the genotype **Tt**. Phenotypically they are all tall, as the **T** allele is dominant to the **t** allele. When an organism contains two dissimilar alleles, as here, it is said to be **heterozygous** (contrasting with the homozygous condition when the two alleles are identical). In this particular instance the **T** allele is dominant and expresses itself in the phenotype. The **t** allele, however, being swamped by the dominant **T** allele, is described as recessive.

A dominant allele, by definition, can express itself whether it occurs in the homozygous or the heterozygous condition. A recessive allele, however, can only express itself when in the homozygous condition. An individual homozygous for a recessive allele is said to be **homozygous recessive**, and an individual homozygous for a dominant allele is described as **homozygous dominant**.

To return to our example, each of the F_1 plants, being heterozygous, produces two types of gamete: half the gametes will contain the T allele, the other half the t allele. On self-pollinating the F_1 plants, these two types of gamete will fuse randomly to produce offspring possessing all three possible genotypes: **TT**, **Tt** and **tt**.

There are various ways of showing how this comes about. One was illustrated in figure 37.5. Another, which avoids having lots of lines crossing each other, is shown in figure 37.7. This is the **Punnett square**, so called because it was first used by the Cambridge geneticist R. C. Punnett (figure 37.8). In this device the gametes of one parent are written along the top of a series of boxes, and the gametes of the other parent are written down the side. The products of the various fusions are written in the appropriate boxes and their relative numbers can be estimated.

In our example, the T allele is possessed by half the male gametes and half the female gametes. The proportion of zygotes which end up **TT** will therefore be ½ × ½ = ¼. The same reasoning applies to the t alleles: half the male gametes and half the female gametes contain the t allele so the proportion of zygotes receiving **tt** will be ¼.

In the case of the heterozygous (**Tt**) offspring there are two possibilities. Such offspring can either result from the fusion of a male **T** gamete with a female **t** gamete, the probability of which is ½ × ½ = ¼, or they can result from the fusion of a male **t** gamete with a female **T** gamete, the probability of which is again ½ × ½ = ¼. Thus the total proportion of **Tt** zygotes will be ¼ + ¼ = ½.

To summarise: ¼ of the F_2 offspring will have **TT** as their genotype, ½ will be **Tt** and ¼ will be **tt**. As **T** is dominant to **t**, the plants whose genotype is **TT** and those whose genotype is **Tt** will all be tall. Thus ¾ will be tall and ¼ short, which agrees with the 3:1 ratio found by Mendel.

Probability and the role of chance in genetic ratios

It is important to be clear about what we mean when we say that ¾ of the F_2 generation will be tall and ¼ short. For one thing, this only applies when quite a large number of F_2 individuals have their phenotypes described. Another way of putting it is to say that if an F_2 plant is selected at random, there is a 3 in 4 chance of its being tall and a 1 in 4 chance of its being short. In other words, the **probability** of its being tall is ¾, and of its being short is ¼.

Now, even if we looked at a large number of F_2 plants, we would not expect the ratio of tall to short individuals to be exactly 3:1. Rather, we would expect *approximately* three-quarters of the plants to be tall. It *is* true that exactly half of the gametes (or potential gametes) will be **T** and exactly half **t**. However, many of these gametes will fail to develop, or die, or fail to give rise to a zygote.

Another point is that even if exactly half of the gametes that gave rise to the F_2 plants were **T** and exactly half **t**, the random fusion of gametes would mean that we *could* end up with all the offspring being heterozygous and so being tall.

For all these reasons the actual ratios obtained in genetic crosses only approximate to the expected ratios. However, the more individuals that are

Punnett square to show fusion of F_1 gametes

		♂ gametes	
		½ (T)	½ (t)
♀ gametes	½ (T)	¼ TT	¼ Tt
	½ (t)	¼ tT	¼ tt

Figure 37.7 A monohybrid cross with pea plants. A Punnett square can be used to show the fusion of gametes when the F_1 individuals of figure 37.5 are selfed and give rise to the F_2 generation.

Figure 37.8 R.C. Punnett in his youth. It was he who devised what is now known as the Punnett square for summarising the fusion of gametes in genetic crosses. Punnett was Professor of Genetics at Cambridge. He wrote a large number of papers between 1900 and 1958, most of which helped to confirm and extend Mendel's work. He worked mainly on poultry, but also investigated the genetics of rabbits and sweet peas. He is said to have had an inordinate fondness for Chelsea buns.

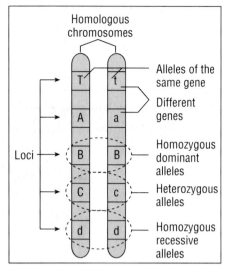

Figure 37.9 Diagram summarising the relationship between the genes and chromosomes of a diploid organism, and the terms used to describe them. The loci (singular: locus) are the positions along the length of the chromosomes where the genes occur. Alleles of the same genes therefore occur at the same locus. Only one allele can be present at any particular locus on one chromosome.

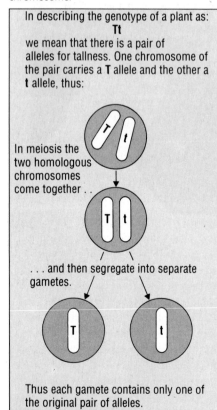

Figure 37.10 The segregation of alleles in inheritance corresponds to the segregation of homologous chromosomes in meiosis.

counted, the closer the observed ratios tend to be to the expected ones. This is why Mendel looked at so many thousands of pea plants. Only then was he convinced that the ratios he observed were the ones he expected.

Why did Mendel get a 3:1 ratio?

Why did Mendel get a 3:1 ratio in the F_2 generation of his monohybrid crosses? The answer lies in the behaviour of the chromosomes at meiosis, although Mendel himself knew nothing of this process.

You will remember that in meiosis homologous chromosomes separate from each other, as a result of which the haploid gametes receive only one of each type of chromosome instead of the two present in diploid cells. In diploid cells alleles occur in pairs, each of the pair being located on one of two homologous chromosomes (figure 37.9). When homologous chromosomes separate in meiosis they take their alleles with them, and thus each gamete receives only *one* of a pair of alleles – just as they receive only one of a pair of homologous chromosomes (figure 37.10). Historically, it was the striking similarity between the segregation of Mendel's factors in inheritance and the separation of homologous chromosomes in meiosis as observed under the light microscope that provided evidence that genes are carried on chromosomes.

Breeding true

One of the facts to emerge from Mendel's monohybrid crosses is that a particular phenotype may be produced by more than one genotype. For example, a tall pea plant may be **TT** (homozygous) or **Tt** (heterozygous). Either way it will be tall, and there is no way of distinguishing between the two genotypes from their external appearance.

One way of establishing whether a given tall plant is homozygous or heterozygous is to self-pollinate it. If the resulting offspring are all tall, we can conclude that the parent plant has the genotype **TT**. If, however, we get a mixture of tall and short plants, the parent plant must have the genotype **Tt**.

The point is that when an organism which is homozygous at a particular locus is self-fertilised it produces offspring all of which are identical with the parent. Exactly the same result occurs if the organism is crossed with another organism that is homozygous at the same locus. In both cases the organism is said to **breed true**. The organisms are said to belong to a **pure line** for the characteristic in question.

Test crosses

In the last section we saw that one way of establishing whether an organism is homozygous dominant or heterozygous at a particular locus is to self-fertilise it, but what do we do when confronted with an organism that is incapable of self-fertilisation, as most animals are? A technique that is much used by geneticists is to cross the individual whose genotype is unknown with an individual that is homozygous recessive at the locus in question. We can illustrate this by reference to an animal which is much used in genetic experiments, the fruit fly *Drosophila melanogaster*.

Drosophila melanogaster is known to exist in a large number of variants or forms. For instance, most individuals have red eyes, but some have white eyes. Similarly, most individuals have long wings, but some have vestigial wings which are short and functionless (figure 37.11). The allele for the long-winged condition (**Vg**) is dominant to the allele for vestigial wing (**vg**). Accordingly, if a pure-bred long-winged fly is mated with a vestigial-winged fly, the F_1 individuals are all heterozygous at this locus and have long wings. If two of these F_1 flies mate with each other, a mixture of long-winged and vestigial-winged flies are produced in a ratio of approximately 3:1:

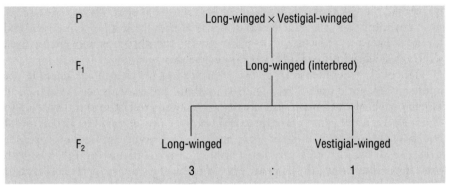

P   Long-winged × Vestigial-winged

F_1 Long-winged (interbred)

F_2 Long-winged   Vestigial-winged

     3   :   1

Figure 37.11

Top Normal-winged *Drosophila*.
Bottom Vestigial-winged *Drosophila*.

This is what we would expect by analogy with Mendel's experiments. But how can we decide whether a given F_2 long-winged fly is homozygous dominant (**Vg Vg**) or heterozygous (**Vg vg**)? The simplest way is to cross it with a vestigial-winged fly. We know that a vestigial-winged fly must be **vg vg** (homozygous recessive) – it cannot be anything else. If the long-winged fly whose genotype we wish to determine is **Vg Vg**, then crossing it with a vestigial-winged fly will give nothing but long-winged flies. If, however, the unknown fly has the genotype **Vg vg**, then the cross will give a mixture of long- and vestigial-winged flies in approximately equal numbers. This is summarised in figure 37.12.

Because this experiment is carried out in order to determine the organism's genotype, it is called a **test cross**. Test crosses with individuals known to be homozygous recessive at the locus in question are a routine method of establishing an organism's genotype.

Figure 37.12 The principle underlying a test cross. How can we establish the genotype of a long-winged fruit fly? One way is to cross it with a vestigial-winged fly, which must be homozygous recessive, **vg vg**. If the 'unknown' fly is homozygous, **Vg Vg**, all the offspring will be long-winged (left). If the 'unknown' fly is heterozygous, **Vg vg**, there will be approximately equal numbers of long-winged and vestigial-winged flies in the offspring (right).

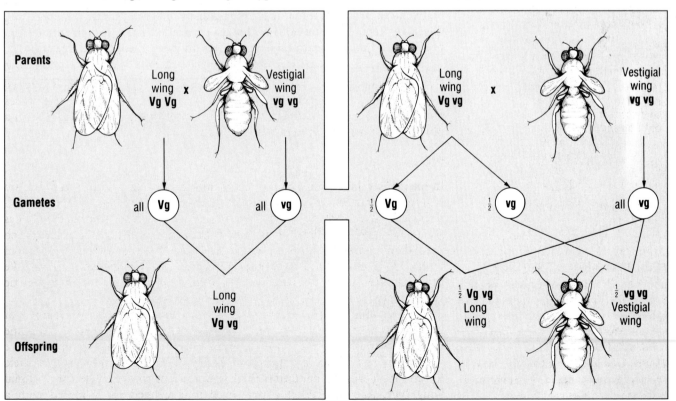

Parents

Long wing **Vg Vg** x Vestigial wing **vg vg**

Long wing **Vg vg** x Vestigial wing **vg vg**

Gametes

all **Vg**   all **vg**

$\frac{1}{2}$ **Vg** $\frac{1}{2}$ **vg**   all **vg**

Offspring

Long wing **Vg vg**

$\frac{1}{2}$ **Vg vg** Long wing

$\frac{1}{2}$ **vg vg** Vestigial wing

Albinism in history

Albinism is probably the earliest recorded human genetic condition. According to the Book of Enoch, which dates from the second century BC, Noah had 'flesh as white as snow and red as a rose; the hair of his head was white like wool, and long; and his eyes were beautiful'.

Figure 37.13 An albino boy from Kavango, Namibia. He shows some of the classic problems that an albino person has in a hot country – his skin is burnt and blistered, in particular the lips.

Figure 37.14 Albinism, an example of monohybrid inheritance in humans. The diagram shows the genotypes and phenotypes of the children that might result from a union between two carriers of the albino allele. Note that there is a one in four chance of any child being an albino. If a carrier marries an albino what is the probability of a child of theirs being an albino?

Monohybrid inheritance in humans

A number of human conditions are known to be associated with single pairs of alleles which are inherited in a Mendelian fashion. One of these is **albinism**, a condition in which the skin is pink and fails to tan, the hair white and the iris pink (figure 37.13). The reason is that albinos are unable to make the black pigment **melanin** because they lack an enzyme required for its synthesis. They therefore lack the protection from ultraviolet light which this pigment normally confers on the skin.

The allele for albinism is recessive (**a**) and so only exerts its effect in the homozygous state (**aa**). The allele for melanin production (**A**) is dominant. The genotype of a person with normal pigmentation is therefore **AA** or **Aa**.

Suppose a couple each with normal pigmentation have an albino child. For this to happen, the child must have the genotype **aa**. Therefore, aside from the possibility of a rare mutation, each parent must be heterozygous (**Aa**). In other words the parents, though not themselves albino, carry the albino allele, for which reason they may be described as **carriers**.

If this happened in practice, the couple would probably want to know the likelihood or probability of their next child also being an albino. The answer to this can be worked out quite easily (figure 37.14). Both parents are heterozygous (**Aa**), so each produces **A** and **a** gametes in about equal numbers. These fuse randomly to produce three types of genotype: **AA**, **Aa** and **aa**. The phenotypes are in the ratio 3:1. In practical terms this means that the probability of any of their subsequent children being an albino is ¼, one chance in four.

Albinism has an incidence of about 1 in 40 000. Fortunately, albinism is not too serious a condition, though albinos are susceptible to sunburn, have difficulty seeing in strong light, and have a higher than average incidence of skin cancer. In some societies they may be ostracised.

A number of other inherited conditions are more serious. For example, **cystic fibrosis** is a distressing condition in which a person produces abnormally large amounts of mucus, particularly in their lungs, pancreas and digestive tract. Vigorous physiotherapy is needed daily to help the person breathe, and they have to take enzymes with every meal to aid digestion.

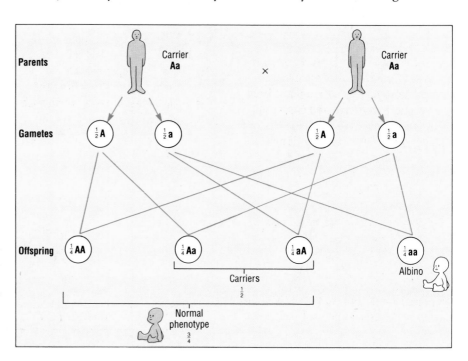

Thankfully cystic fibrosis is caused by a recessive allele, like albinism, so that only people who are homozygous recessive are actually affected by the condition. However, one in 24 white Europeans carries the allele which means that one in 2000 children born to white European parents has cystic fibrosis. Many do not live beyond their twenties, though a tremendous amount of medical research is currently underway which it is hoped will soon improve the survival rate and quality of life for people with the condition.

Not all examples of monohybrid inheritance in humans are caused by recessive alleles. One of the more common sorts of restricted growth in humans is called **achondroplasia** (figure 37.15) which is caused by a dominant allele. Heterozygotes have a mean height of about 130 cm. Achondroplasics often get bad backache, but a more significant problem is the discrimination they suffer from many taller people.

Actually, there are not many examples of monohybrid inheritance known in humans. One that appears in almost every textbook is eye colour. Most books state that brown eye colour is dominant to blue eye colour, blue eye colour therefore being due to the presence of a pair of recessive alleles. In fact it is now known that the inheritance of human eye colour is

Figure 37.15 Gerald Steddan, an actor with achondroplasia.

Genetics and agriculture

Plant breeding has been important since prehistoric times and in many respects the techniques used then are still valid today.

Let us imagine that a plant breeder has two varieties of wheat, both of which breed true. One variety is tall stemmed and relatively resistant to mildew; the other is short stemmed and relatively susceptible to mildew. Let us suppose that the breeder wants to create a new variety which is short stemmed but relatively resistant to mildew.

The obvious first step is to cross a plant from the tall stemmed and resistant variety with a plant from the short stemmed and susceptible variety. Now let us suppose that all the F_1 offspring that result are tall stemmed and resistant to mildew. The simplest assumptions to make are that tallness is dominant to shortness, that resistance to mildew is dominant to susceptibility to mildew, and that the two genes are inherited independently.

If this is the case, then calling **T** the allele for tallness, **t** the allele for shortness, **R** the allele for resistance, and **r** the allele for susceptibility, we can presume that the tall resistant variety has the genotype **TTRR** and the short susceptible variety the genotype **ttrr**. The F_1 offspring that result when these two varieties are crossed will have the genoytpe **TtRr**.

Now suppose that the breeder crosses the F_1 offspring among themselves. There are nine possible genotypes which may occur in the F_2 generation (see illustration).

Our plant breeder wants to end up with a pure line of short resistant plants with the genotype **ttRR**. Just two of the F_2 genotypes have the required phenotype: **ttRR** and **ttRr**. These two genotypes can be distinguished either by selfing the plants, or by test crossing them with short susceptible plants. Only the

ttRR genotype will breed true. Thus a new pure breeding line can be established within three generations.

Of course, most plant and animal breeding is much more complicated than this, but this illustrates the general principles.

What do you suppose might be the advantages of short-stemmed over tall-stemmed wheat?

How might these basic techniques be modified to allow a breeder to obtain a herd of hornless cows with low fat milk from crosses between two breeds of cattle, one that has cows with horns and low fat milk, and one that has hornless cows and rich creamy milk?

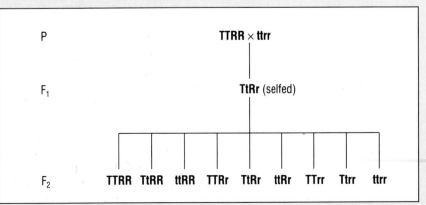

P	TTRR × ttrr
F₁	TtRr (selfed)
F₂	TTRR TtRR ttRR TTRr TtRr ttRr TTrr Ttrr ttrr

Figure 37.16

Top A pea plant with purple flowers.
Bottom A pea plant with white flowers.

more complicated than this. For example, it *is* possible for you to have brown eyes even if both your parents have blue eyes.

Dihybrid inheritance

So far we have considered the inheritance of only one pair of contrasting characteristics. But Mendel did not stop at this. He went on to study the inheritance of two pairs of characteristics, i.e. a **dihybrid cross**.

In one experiment Mendel crossed a pure-bred tall pea plant possessing purple flowers with a short plant possessing white flowers (figure 37.16). In the F_1 generation all the plants produced were tall and had purple flowers. These were then self-pollinated. In the F_2 generation four different phenotypes were observed: tall plants with purple flowers; tall plants with white flowers; short plants with purple flowers; and short plants with white flowers. In other words, the offspring showed the two pairs of characteristics (tall – short, purple – white) combined in every possible way.

As before, Mendel counted the different types of plant and in one particular case he got 96 tall purple, 31 tall white, 34 short purple and 11 short white, giving a ratio of approximately 9:3:3:1. The experiment can be summarised as follows:

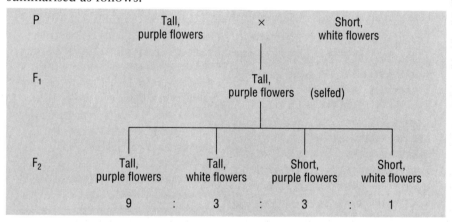

Conclusions from the dihybrid cross

What conclusions can we draw from these results? To begin with, the fact that all the F_1 plants are tall and possess purple flowers confirms that tall is dominant to short and purple flower is dominant to short flower. This is as expected from the results of the monohybrid crosses (table 37.1).

Figure 37.17 shows how the alleles are transmitted in this dihybrid cross. **T** represents the allele for tallness, **t** for shortness, **P** for purple flower and **p** for white flower. Mendel always started his experiments with pure-bred plants, so the parent plants must be homozygous for both genes. The genotype of the tall plant with the purple flowers is therefore **TTPP**, and that of the short plant with white flowers **ttpp**. From Mendel's earlier work we know that the gametes produced by the parent plants are **TP** from the tall purple parent and **tp** from the short white parent. All the F_1 offspring will therefore have the genotype **TtPp**, heterozygous for both genes.

The next step in the argument is crucial. If all four possible combinations of characteristics are to show up in the F_2 generation, we must conclude (as Mendel did) that the F_1 plants produce four kinds of gamete: **TP, Tp, tP** and **tp**. The Punnett square in figure 37.17 shows the different ways these gametes can fuse, together with the genotypes of the F_2 offspring. To be tall, the genotype of the plant must contain at least one

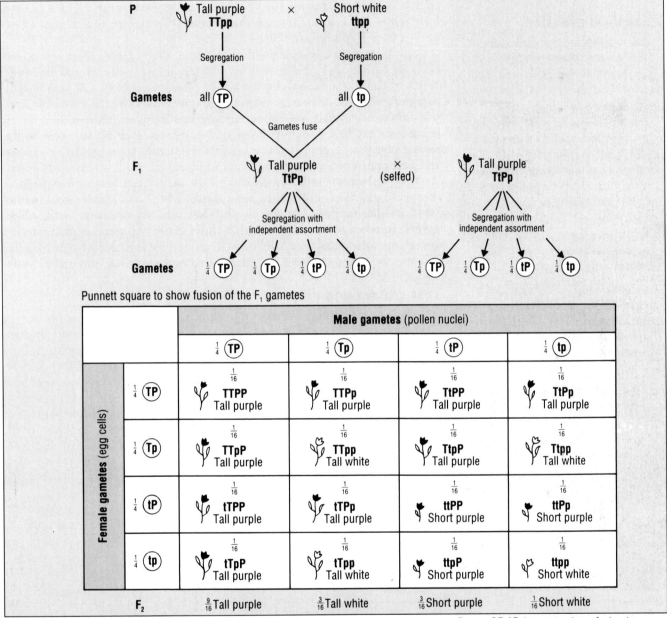

Punnett square to show fusion of the F₁ gametes

Figure 37.17 Interpretation of what happens when a pure-bred tall pea plant with purple flowers is crossed with a short plant with white flowers. **T** is the allele for tallness, **t** for shortness, **P** for purple flowers and **p** for white flowers.

T allele; to be purple, it must contain at least one P allele. From the Punnett square it can be seen that there are 16 possible fusions. Of these, 9 give tall purple plants, 3 tall white, 3 short purple, and 1 short white. The observed 9:3:3:1 ratio can be accounted for if all the possible fusions occur with equal likelihood.

What general conclusion emerges from all this? The main one, surely, is that the alleles of the two genes are transmitted independently of each other from parents to offspring, and therefore assort freely. In other words, *each of the alleles of one gene may combine independently with each of the alleles of another gene.*

Interpreting dihybrid ratios in terms of probability

Expressed in terms of probability, transmission of the genes determining stem height and flower colour in the garden pea are **independent events**. If we consider the alleles for height on their own, the probability of any one F₂ plant being tall is ¾, and of its being short is ¼. You can see this in figure

Haploid genetics

Everything we have discussed in this chapter about genetics applies to diploid organisms. You might suppose that haploid genetics would complicate matters. Not a bit of it. Consider an organism, such as a moss or a yeast, which is haploid throughout much or all of its life cycle. The organism has in each of its nuclei only one allele for each gene, not two. The notion of dominance does not arise, nor does homozygosity or heterozygosity.

Imagine crossing a yeast which has a higher than average yield of alcohol with a yeast which has an average yield of alcohol. What genetic ratios might you predict?

37.17: $\%_{16}$ of the plants are tall and have purple flowers, and $\frac{3}{16}$ are tall and have white flowers. Combining these figures we can see that a total of $^{12}\!\!/_{16}$, i.e. $\frac{3}{4}$, of the F$_2$ plants are tall.

Similarly if we consider the flower colour alleles alone, there is a probability of $\frac{3}{4}$ that an F$_2$ plant will be purple, and of $\frac{1}{4}$ that it will be white. What, then, is the probability of an F$_2$ plant being both tall and purple? Assuming that the alleles are transmitted independently, the answer is $\frac{3}{4}$ x $\frac{3}{4}$ = $\%_{16}$. This means that the chance of any one F$_2$ plant, chosen at random, being both tall and purple is 9 out of 16, slightly over 50 per cent. It also means that in a large random sample of F$_2$ plants, approximately 9 out of 16 of them can be expected to be tall and purple.

We can apply similar reasoning to the other possible combinations of characteristics. The probability of an F$_2$ plant being tall and white is $\frac{3}{4}$ x $\frac{1}{4}$ = $\frac{3}{16}$; short and purple is $\frac{1}{4}$ x $\frac{3}{4}$ = $\frac{3}{16}$; and short and white is $\frac{1}{4}$ x $\frac{1}{4}$ = $\frac{1}{16}$. These figures agreee with those obtained by the Punnett square method and with the results of Mendel's experiments. They can be explained by postulating that the two pairs of alleles are transmitted independently and assort freely.

Test crosses and dihybrid ratios

It is clear from the Punnett square in figure 37.17 that the same phenotype may result from several different genotypes. For example, a tall purple plant may have one of four possible genotypes: **TTPP** (homozygous for both genes), **TTPp** (homozygous tall, heterozygous for colour), **TtPP** (heterozygous for height, homozygous purple) or **TtPp** (heterozygous for both genes).

The easiest way of establishing the genotype of a tall purple plant is to cross it with a short white one (**ttpp**). You will appreciate that if the 'unknown' plant is homozygous for both characters, all the offspring from the test cross will be tall and purple (note why).

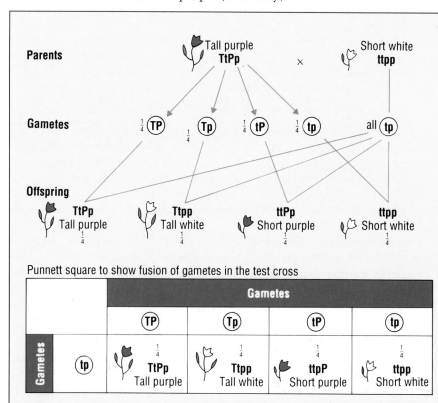

Figure 37.18 Diagram showing the result of test-crossing a pea plant heterozygous for both height and flower colour with the homozygous recessive. Four possible types of offspring may result.

Now consider the outcome if the unknown plant happens to be heterozygous for both genes. In this case it will produce four types of gametes: **TP, Tp, tP** and **tp**. The short white plant, however, produces only one type of gamete: **tp**. The fusion of the gametes is shown in figure 37.18 from which it is clear that four types of offspring should be produced in approximately equal numbers: tall purple, tall white, short purple and short white. Mendel carried out this experiment and this is precisely what he found. In one case, for instance, he obtained 47 tall purple plants, 40 tall white, 38 short purple and 41 short white.

There are two other possible genotypes for a tall purple plant: **TTPp** and **TtPP**. What should be the result of test-crossing each of these with a dwarf white plant?

Explanation of dihybrid ratios

The observation that characters like height and flower colour are inherited independently of each other is known as **independent assortment**. The explanation lies in the behaviour of the chromosomes at meiosis, just as was the segregation of alleles that Mendel observed in his monohybrid crosses.

Independent assortment requires that the genes concerned are carried on different chromosomes: for example, the alleles of the gene for flower colour are located on one pair of chromosomes and the alleles of the gene for height on another pair of chromosomes (figure 37.19). Now in metaphase of the first meiotic division, homologous chromosomes line up side by side on the spindle prior to separating at anaphase. In doing this, different pairs of homologous chromosomes behave independently of each other: the way one pair of homologous chromosomes arrange themselves on the spindle and subsequently separate has no effect whatsoever on the behaviour of any other pair of chromosomes.

The consequence of the independent behaviour of non-homologous chromosomes in meiosis is shown in figure 37.19 which illustrates how the four different types of gametes (**TP, Tp, tP** and **tp**) can be formed from a plant that is heterozygous for height and flower colour (**TtPp**). We can summarise the situation by saying that the alleles for height and flower colour segregate and assort independently because they are carried on separate chromosomes which themselves segregate and assort independently in meiosis.

Mendel's laws

Mendel summarised his conclusions in two general statements, now known as **Mendel's Laws**.

- **Mendel's First Law** came from his work on monohybrid inheritance and is known as the **Law of Segregation**. It says that an organism's characteristics are determined by internal 'factors' which occur in pairs. Only one of a pair of such factors can be represented in a single gamete. Restated in modern terms, Mendel's First Law states that the characteristics of organisms are controlled by alleles occurring in pairs. Of a pair of such alleles, only one can be carried in a single gamete.

- **Mendel's Second Law** followed from his work on dihybrid inheritance and is known as the **Law of Independent Assortment**. It states that each of a pair of contrasted characters may be combined with either of another pair. In today's language we would say that either of the two alleles of a gene is equally likely to be inherited with either of the two alleles of another gene.

In describing the genotype of a plant as:

TtPp

we mean that there are two pairs of chromosomes, one pair carrying the alleles of the gene for tallness and the other pair carrying the alleles of the gene for flower colour.

The two chromosomes carrying the 'tallness' alleles are homologous with one another, and the two chromosomes carrying the 'flower-colour' alleles are homologous:

In meiosis the homologous chromosomes come together (**assort**) but they arrange themselves on the spindle **independently** of each other. Thus they may arrange themselves ...

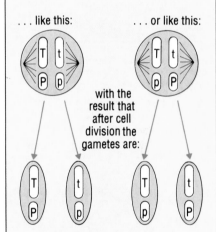

... like this: ... or like this:

with the result that after cell division the gametes are:

Thus meiosis results in the formation of four types of gamete which, since the process is random, occur in approximately equal numbers.

Figure 37.19 Meiosis provides the explanation for the independent assortment Mendel found in his dihybrid crosses. The free assortment of alleles in inheritance corresponds to the free assortment of chromosomes during meiosis.

Figure 37.20 An ebony-bodied fruit fly.

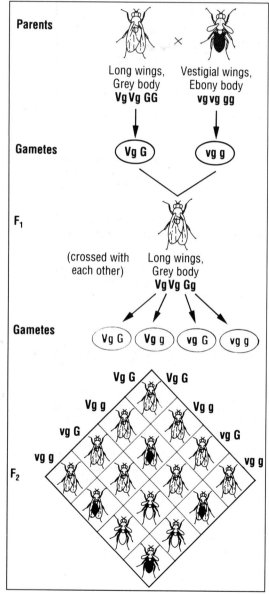

Figure 37.21 A dihybrid cross with fruit flies. In this case a diamond shaped checkerboard, a modification of the Punnett square, is used to show how a 9:3:3:1 ratio can result in the F₂. Allele symbols: **Vg**, long wing; **vg** vestigial wing; **G**, grey body; **g**, ebony body.

Independent assortment in the fruit fly

As with segregation, independent assortment can be demonstrated in other organisms beside peas. Take *Drosophila* for example. As well as flies with long wings and vestigial wings, there are flies with grey-coloured bodies and ebony-coloured bodies (figure 37.20).

The allele for the usual grey colour is dominant to the allele for ebony colour. If we cross a fly possessing long wings and a grey body with one possessing vestigial wings and an ebony body, the F₁ offspring are all long-winged and grey-bodied. If two of these are crossed, the F₂ generation yields four types of fly: long-winged and grey-bodied, long-winged and ebony-bodied, vestigial-winged and grey-bodied, and vestigial-winged and ebony-bodied. These occur in a ratio of 9:3:3:1 respectively (figure 37.21).

From these results we can conclude that the genes determining wing length and body colour are located on different pairs of chromosomes. The genes segregate and assort freely, just as the genes for height and flower colour did in Mendel's experiments with peas.

Mendel in retrospect

Mendel's research reveals the mind of a genius. There are three main reasons for this. First, he saw the importance of studying one phenomenon at a time. He did not attempt to follow the inheritance of the many characteristics of pea plants simultaneously, but started by confining himself to one pair of characteristics. Secondly, he was not content merely to *describe* the different types of offspring produced; he *counted* them as well. In other words, he realised the importance of expressing his results quantitatively. Thirdly, and this is where his greatest insight lay, he interpreted his results and drew general conclusions from them. It is all the more impressive that he managed to do this without any knowledge of chromosomes or meiosis.

Mendel worked on inheritance in the garden pea for ten years. During this time he examined, classified and counted over 28 000 garden peas. In 1866 he published his results in the journal of his local scientific society. However, it received little publicity and made no impact on the scientific world. Until recently historians of science assumed that this was because hardly anyone read Mendel's work. We now know that this is not the case. Many scientists including Charles Darwin read his paper. Why then was Mendel's work ignored? The truth is simply that Mendel was ahead of his time. It is difficult for us to realise how unimportant the mechanism of heredity seemed to 19th century biologists. Mendel's work was not ignored because it was not understood; rather it was thought to be irrelevant.

Before he died in 1884 Mendel told a close friend 'my time will come'. He was convinced that his research was important. However, it wasn't until 1899 that three biologists, Hugo de Vries, Carl Correns and Erich von Tschermak, independently recognised the pioneering importance of Mendel's work. Only then, 33 years after its publication, was the full significance of Mendel's work realised.

Although Mendel's work forms the basis of heredity, it does not cover all situations: if it did, genetics would be far easier and less interesting than it is! The fact is that Mendel's work applies to diploid organisms, and not all organisms are diploid. Moreover, a gene may have more than two alleles, and it is not always the case that one is dominant to another. Further, some characteristics are determined by several genes, not just by one. Finally, genes do not always assort independently. We will look at these exceptions in the next chapter.

Summary

1 The first quantitative experiments on heredity of any significance were carried out in the middle of the nineteenth century by Gregor Mendel on the garden pea.

2 In his first investigations Mendel studied the inheritance of a single pair of contrasting characteristics (**monohybrid inheritance**).

3 From monhybrid crosses it can be concluded that:

- Inheritance is particulate (nowadays the particles or factors are called **genes**).
- Alleles occur in pairs and may be **dominant** or **recessive** with respect to one another (from which the concepts of **homozygosity** and **heterozygosity** emerge).
- Only one allele of a gene may be carried in a single gamete.

4 The conclusion that only one allele of a gene may be carried in a single gamete is enshrined in Mendel's First Law, the **Law of Segregation**.

5 Examples of monohybrid inheritance in humans include albinism, cystic fibrosis and achondroplasia (a form of growth restriction).

6 In later experiments on the garden pea Mendel studied the inheritance of two pairs of characteristics (**dihybrid inheritance**).

7 From dihybrid crosses it can be concluded that each allele of one gene is equally likely to be inherited with each allele of another gene. This conclusion is enshrined in Mendel's Second Law, the **Law of Independent Assortment**.

8 Mendel's Laws and conclusions can be interpreted in terms of the structure of chromosomes and their behaviour during meiosis.

9 Mendel's work was published in 1866 but its significance was not realised until 1899 when it was rediscovered by de Vries and others.

Review questions

1 Mendel started all his experiments with pure-bred lines? Why was this a wise choice?

2 Explain as clearly as you can why a cross between tall and short pea plants does not result in pea plants of intermediate height.

3 Suggest why less is known about human genetics than about the genetics of fruitflies.

4 Domestic hamsters show some variation in the length of their fur. Describe how you might test the hypothesis that this variation has a genetic basis.

5 Distinguish between the following pairs of terms:

Monohybrid inheritance and dihybrid inheritance.
Homozygous and heterozygous.
Dominant and recessive.
Genotype and phenotype.

6 In the F_2, a monohybrid cross between pure-bred lines results in a 3:1 ratio, and a dihybrid cross in a 9:3:3:1 ratio. Can you predict what ratio would be expected in a *trihybrid* cross? You can test your prediction by working out what would be expected in the F_2 generation from a cross between tall pea plants with purple flowers and smooth seeds and short pea plants with white flowers and wrinkled seeds (see table 37.1).

7 Outline what is meant by the term *independent assortment* and relate it to the ratios which Mendel obtained.

8 Imagine yourself in conversation with a group of dog breeders convinced that a knowledge of genetics is of no use in breeding champion dogs. How might you attempt to change their minds?

9 With reference to table 37.1, explain how you could determine the genotype of a tall pea plant with green, constricted pods.

10 Suppose that treatments for cystic fibrosis improve to the point where people with the condition often survive to be parents. Discuss what phenotypic ratios might be seen among their children.

Further reading

If you are interested in reading more about the life and work of Gregor Mendel, there is a good 100 page biography called *Mendel* written by V. Orel (Oxford University Press, 1984).

Lynn Burnet's *Essential Genetics: A course book* (Cambridge University Press, 1986) and her companion volume *Exercises in Applied Genetics* (Cambridge University Press, 1988) are excellent volumes which go into genetics in more depth than is possible here.

Are Mendel's ratios too good to be true? This question is discussed in *Biology, Advanced Topics*.

CHAPTER 38

Chromosomes and genes

In the last chapter we considered examples of monohybrid and dihybrid inheritance where the genetic ratios produced agreed with Mendel's findings. However, this is not always the case. Apart from their intrinsic interest, these situations are important because they tell us much about the relationship between chromosomes and genes.

Linkage

One of the many inherited characteristics in *Drosophila* concerns the width of the abdomen. Most flies have a broad abdomen but some have a narrow one. The allele for broad abdomen is dominant to the allele for narrow abdomen.

If a long-winged, broad-abdomened fly is crossed with a vestigial-winged, narrow-abdomened fly, the F_1 offspring all have long wings and broad abdomens, as we would predict. But if two of these flies are mated, the F_2 generation fails to yield the 9:3:3:1 ratio we expect. Instead about ¾ of the offspring have long wings and a broad abdomen and nearly all the remaining flies, about ¼ of the total, have vestigial wings and a narrow abdomen, thus:

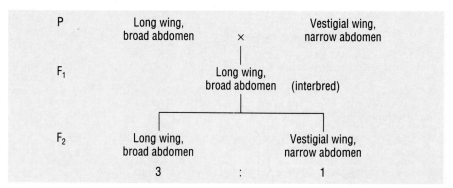

The explanation is that the genes determining the length of the wings and the width of the abdomen are located on the *same* chromosome. This results in their being transmitted together (figure 38.1). Such genes are said to be **linked**, and the general phenomenon is known as **linkage**. It does not, however, follow that the alleles of linked genes can never be separated. If one looks at a very large number of F_2 flies in the example cited above, one finds that a few show independent assortment, i.e. a few long-winged narrow flies and vestigial-winged broad flies turn up in the F_2 generation.

The reason for this will be considered later. For the moment it is sufficient to appreciate that if, in a breeding experiment, the transmission of two (or more) characters show independent assortment, then it is very likely that the genes are carried on different chromosomes. If, however, little or no independent assortment is shown, we can conclude that the genes are located on the same chromosome. It is now known that an individual chromosome may contain as many as several thousand genes controlling a wide variety of characteristics. Genes linked together on the same chromosome constitute a **linkage group**.

Linkage groups and chromosomes

Our knowledge of the relationship between chromosomes and genes is based on experiments started in the early part of the 20th century by

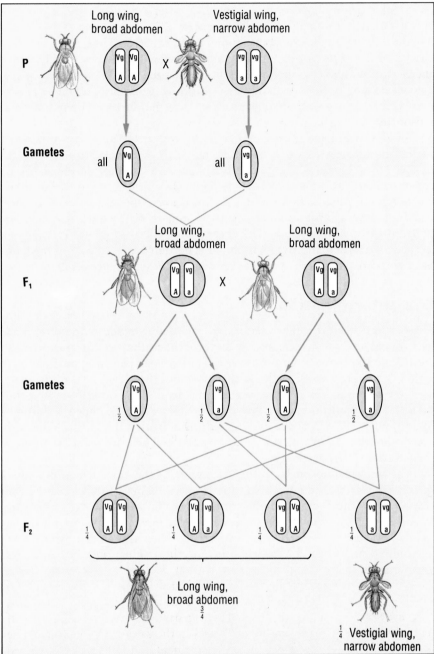

Figure 38.1 Linkage in the fruit fly. The genes for wing length and abdomen width are located on the same chromosome with the result that they are transmitted together and fail to show independent assortment. Allele symbols: vestigial wing (recessive), **vg**; long wing (dominant), **Vg**; narrow abdomen (recessive), **a**; broad abdomen (dominant), **A**.

T.H. Morgan and his co-workers in the United States. Morgan's influence on the science of genetics is hardly less great than Mendel's. He trained as an embryologist and only started breeding *Drosophila* because he was sceptical about Mendel's results. However, he soon became convinced that Mendel's Laws were essentially correct. In further studies Morgan discovered linkage. He hypothesised that genes which failed to show the ratios characteristic of independent assortment were located on the same chromosome. For this and other related work Morgan was awarded the Nobel Prize for physiology and medicine in 1933.

From a long series of experiments it became established that *Drosophila melanogaster* has four linkage groups. The genes in any one linkage group are transmitted together but independently of the genes in the other linkage groups. The interesting thing is that there are also four pairs of chromosomes (figure 38.2), evidence that genes are located on chromosomes.

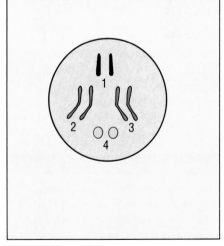

Figure 38.2 The fruit fly *Drosophila melanogaster* has four pairs of chromosomes which are distinguished from each other by their size. There are also four linkage groups whose sizes differ from each other in the same way as the chromosomes. The medium-sized pair of chromosomes (black in the diagram) are the sex chromosomes about which there is more information on the next page.

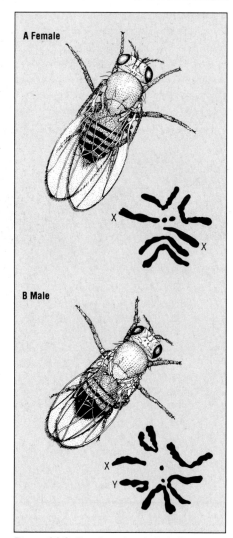

Figure 38.3 Female and male fruit flies and their chromosomes. In the female the two medium-sized chromosomes are the **X** chromosomes. The male has the same complement of chromosomes as the female except that one of the **X** chromosomes is replaced by a hook-shaped **Y** chromosome.

Figure 38.4 Sex determination in the human. An individual's sex is determined by his or her sex chromosomes. Females possess two **X** chromosomes; males an **X** and a **Y**. The sex chromosomes are transmitted in the normal Mendelian fashion as shown here. In determining an individual's sex, the **X** and **Y** chromosomes are only important at a relatively early stage of development when the gonads (ovaries and testes) are developing. Once the gonads have been formed, a process completed before birth, sex hormones controlled by autosomal chromosomes take over. The symbols **X** and **Y** do not refer to alleles, but to the chromosomes.

Similar results have been obtained in other organisms. In all cases it appears that the number of linkage groups found in a species equals the haploid number of chromosomes found in that species. Thus in the different species of *Drosophila* the haploid number varies from three to six, and in each case the number of linkage groups is the same. For obvious reasons an extensive study of linkage in humans is difficult to undertake, but it is now known that there are 23 linkage groups, corresponding to 23 pairs of chromosomes.

Studies of linkage groups enable us to predict not only the number of chromosomes in a particular species, but their relative sizes as well. If a linkage group contains a large number of genes, we expect the chromosome concerned to be relatively large. This is borne out by *Drosophila melanogaster* in which two of the linkage groups are large (i.e. each contains quite a large number of genes), one is of medium size, and the remaining one is very small. The chromosomes bear a similar relationship to each other: there are two pairs of large chromosomes, a pair of medium-sized chromosomes and a pair of very small ones (see figure 38.2).

Sex determination

The medium-sized chromosomes in *Drosophila melanogaster* determine the individual's sex, for which reason they are called the **sex chromosomes**. In the female the two sex chromosomes, both rod-shaped in appearance, are identical and are known as the **X chromosomes** (figure 38.3A). In the male, however, the two sex chromosomes differ from each other: one is a rod-shaped **X** chromosome, the other is hook-shaped, the so-called **Y chromosome** (figure 38.3B). Sex is determined in humans in much the same way except that the **Y** chromosome is not hooked, but simply smaller than the **X** chromosome (see page 701).

The sex chromosomes are an exception to the rule that homologous chromosomes are identical in appearance. Being different, they are described as **heterosomes** (Greek for 'different bodies'). All the other pairs of chromosomes, which are identical in appearance, are called **autosomes** ('same bodies'). Despite this difference, the sex chromosomes are transmitted in a normal Mendelian manner, as is illustrated in figure 38.4 for humans.

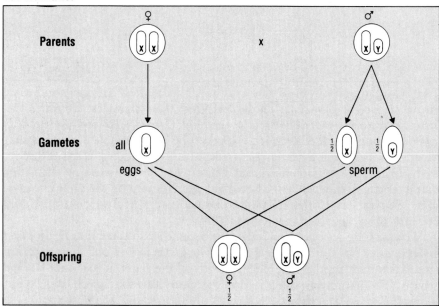

Clearly, a female produces only one kind of gamete as far as the sex chromosomes are concerned: all her eggs contain an **X** chromosome. For this reason in humans, and many other species, the female is said to be **homogametic** ('same gametes'). A male, on the other hand, produces two kinds of gamete as far as the sex chromosomes are concerned: half the sperm contain an **X** chromosome, the other half a **Y**. The male is therefore **heterogametic** ('different gametes'). On fusing randomly, approximately half the zygotes receive two **X** chromosomes and develop into females; the rest receive an **X** and a **Y** chromosome and give rise to males.

The male is not invariably the heterogametic sex. For example, in birds, males are **XX** and females **XY**. A further pattern of sex determination is seen in some insects. You may remember from page 547 that female honey bees develop from fertilised eggs, and males from unfertilised eggs. This means that in honey bees females are diploid and males haploid, the so-called **haplodiploid** condition. The same pattern of sex determination is found in certain other social insects.

In some insects females are **XX** and males **XO**. This means that females have two sex chromosomes, but males only one. It is possible that this evolved from a system where females were **XX** and males **XY**. As we shall see later, the **Y** chromosome has very few functional genes on it. To evolve from an **XX / XY** determining system to an **XX / XO** one, all that has to happen is that **XY** males lose their **Y** chromosome but remain male. The **XX / XO** system should not be confused with the haplodiploid system. In the former, females have one more chromosome than males; in the latter, twice as many.

A quite different system of sex determination is found in alligators and crocodiles. Here the sex of the offspring is determined entirely by environmental factors (figure 38.5). There are no differences between males and females in terms of their chromosomes. Instead there is a critical period in the early development of the fertilised egg during which the ambient temperature determines the sex of the individual! In some species high temperatures lead to males; in others, high temperatures result in females.

Sex linkage

In organisms with sex chromosomes, such as *Drosophila* and ourselves, all the genes carried on the sex chromosomes are transmitted along with those determining sex – that is they are **sex-linked**. Consider, for example, the inheritance of eye colour. In *Drosophila* there are red-eyed and white-eyed strains. The result of crossing a red-eyed fly with a white-eyed fly depends on which parent is red-eyed and which is white-eyed. If the father is white-eyed, the F₁ gives nothing but red-eyed flies, half of which are males and half of which are females:

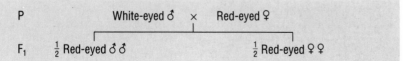

There is nothing surprising in this. The allele for red eyes is evidently dominant to the allele for white eyes. If, however, the father has red eyes and the mother white eyes, half the F₁ flies have red eyes and half white, all the red-eyed ones being females, and all the white-eyed ones, males:

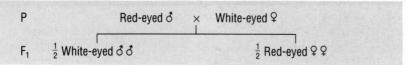

Figure 38.5 A female estuarine salt water crocodile, *Crocodilus porosus*, building a nest mound with her hind limbs. In this species the sex of the offspring is determined by the temperature at which the eggs are incubated during a critical period.

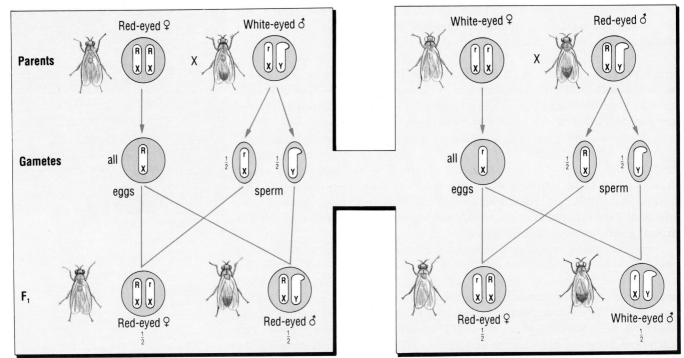

Figure 38.6 Sex linkage in the fruit fly (*Drosophila*). The gene controlling eye colour is located on the **X** chromosome, and so is sex-linked. The result of crossing red- and white-eyed flies depends on which parent is red-eyed and which white. This can be seen by comparing the two genetic diagrams above. Allele symbols: red eye (dominant), **R**; white eye (recessive), **r**.

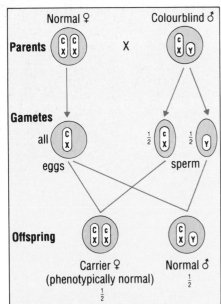

Figure 38.7 Red-green colour blindness, an example of sex linkage in humans. Allele symbols: allele for colour vision (dominant), **C**; colour blind allele (recessive), **c**.

At first sight these results may seem extraordinary, but they can be explained by assuming that the gene controlling eye colour is carried on the **X** chromosome, but not on the **Y** chromosome. Indeed, in *Drosophila* and humans, the **Y** chromosome carries very few genes, compared to over a thousand carried on the **X** chromosome. A full explanation of the sex-linked inheritance of eye colour in *Drosophila* is given in figure 38.6.

Note that in *Drosophila* and in humans, indeed in all species where females are **XX** and males **XY**, males never inherit their father's **X** chromosome. To all intents and purposes, the **Y** chromosome carries no genes and all sex-linked genes are therefore carried on the **X** chromosome. Because fathers never pass their **X** chromosomes to their sons, a male cannot inherit his father's sex-linked traits. Daughters, however, always receive their father's **X** chromosome. Subsequently there is a 50 per cent chance that they will transmit this chromosome to their offspring. These offspring may show their grandfather's sex-linked traits, but only if he is their maternal grandfather.

If all this sounds complicated, some examples may help.

Colour blindness

In humans **red-green colour blindness** is inherited as a sex-linked characteristic. The allele for this form of colour blindness is carried on the **X** chromosome and is recessive in females. (Notice that it is meaningless to say that it is recessive in males as males are functionally haploid for sex-linked genes.)

A colourblind man, married to a woman with two alleles for normal colour vision, transmits his allele for colour blindness to his daughters (figure 38.7). As his daughters receive a normal functioning allele from their mother, and since this allele is dominant to the allele for colour blindness, they will not be colourblind themselves. However, they will carry the defective allele. The sons of the colourblind man will have normal colour vision as they cannot receive their father's defective allele, but instead receive their mother's functioning allele.

Now consider what happens if one of the daughters marries a man with normal colour vision. If they have a son, there is a probability of ½ that he will be colourblind. Any daughters will be phenotypically normal for this trait, but will have a probability of ½ of being carriers.

As you might expect, red-green colour blindness is more common in males than in females (figure 38.8). The only way a female can be red-green colourblind is for her to have two copies of the faulty allele. Males, though, only need one copy of the faulty allele to be colourblind. About eight per cent (1 in 12) of males are colourblind, but fewer than one per cent of females.

Haemophilia

Another sex-linked trait in humans, much more serious than red-green colour blindness, is **haemophilia**. In this condition the blood takes an abnormally long time to clot, resulting in profuse and prolonged bleeding from even minor knocks and wounds.

Haemophilia, like red-green colour blindness, is caused by the recessive allele of a gene which is carried on the **X** chromosome. As can be seen in figure 38.9, if a man who does not have haemophilia is married to a woman who happens to carry the allele for haemophilia, there is a probability of ½ that if they have a son he will be a haemophiliac. If they have a daughter, she will be phenotypically normal, but has a 50 per cent chance of being a carrier.

This is precisely what has happened in the royal families of Europe during the last hundred years (figure 38.10). It seems that a haemophilia allele arose by mutation in one of the gametes (it might have been the egg or the sperm) which gave rise to Queen Victoria. Of her nine children, one was a haemophiliac (Leopold) and two were carriers (Beatrice and Alice). As a result of marriages between the various royal families, the defective allele spread to several European countries. Beatrice transmitted the haemophilia

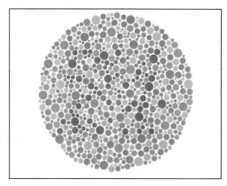

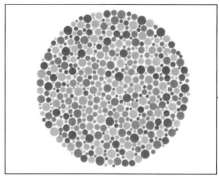

Figure 38.8 Colour blindness can be tested using simple diagrams like this. People with normal colour vision can read the number embedded in the dot pattern. Those with red-green colour blindness cannot distinguish the number or see a different one.

Figure 38.10 Photograph of Queen Victoria and some of her relatives. Three of the women here were carriers of haemophilia, namely Victoria herself (seated left of centre and wearing a crown), one of her daughters, Beatrice (seated slightly right of centre with a cluster of children one of whom has his arm on her right shoulder), and one of Queen Victoria's granddaughters, Alice (standing almost at the extreme right of the photograph with the hands of a Prince of Schleswig-Holstein on her shoulders).

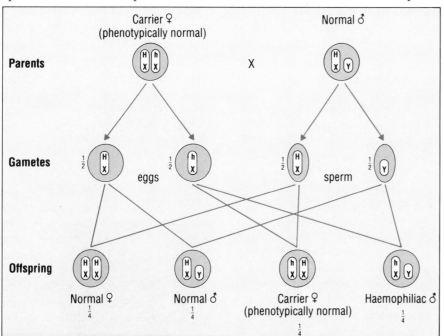

Figure 38.9 Haemophilia, another example of sex linkage in humans. If a man whose blood clots normally and a woman who carries the allele for haemophilia have children, there is a probability of ¼ that any given conception will result in a son with haemophilia. Allele symbols: haemophilia allele (recessive), **h**; allele for normal blood clotting (dominant), **H**.

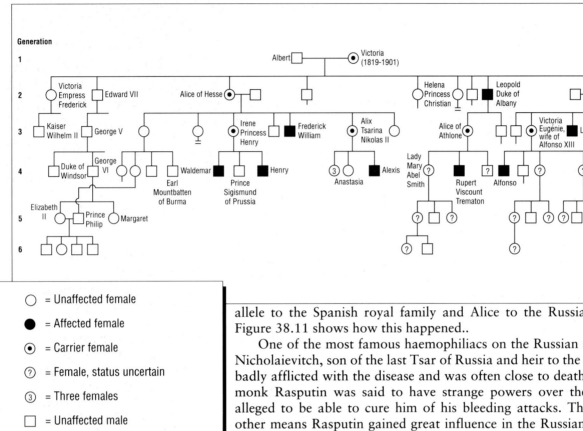

Generation

Legend:

- ○ = Unaffected female
- ● = Affected female
- ◉ = Carrier female
- ⊘ = Female, status uncertain
- ③ = Three females
- □ = Unaffected male
- ■ = Affected male
- ⊡ = Male, status uncertain

Figure 38.11 A pedigree chart showing the transmission of the allele for haemophilia from Queen Victoria into several of the Royal families of Europe.

allele to the Spanish royal family and Alice to the Russian royal family Figure 38.11 shows how this happened..

One of the most famous haemophiliacs on the Russian side was Alexis Nicholaievitch, son of the last Tsar of Russia and heir to the throne. He was badly afflicted with the disease and was often close to death. However, the monk Rasputin was said to have strange powers over the boy and was alleged to be able to cure him of his bleeding attacks. Through this and other means Rasputin gained great influence in the Russian court, to such an extent that for a short period just before the 1917 revolution he was virtually the ruler of Russia.

Do women ever suffer from haemophilia? For a woman to suffer from haemophilia, she would need to be homozygous for the malfunctioning allele, as it is recessive to the normal allele. However, the haemophilia allele is so rare that the chances of having two copies of it are extremely remote. It is not known for certain whether there have ever been women with haemophilia. Before the advent of modern medicine, any such women

Hairy ears and Y-borne inheritance

In parts of India, Israel and Australia a high percentage of men have hairy ears (see illustration) and it has been suggested that this may be caused by a gene carried on the **Y** chromosome.

What then is the evidence that the gene for hairy ears is **Y**-linked? Let us assume that it is. If our assumption is correct, fathers who have hairy ears should pass the condition to *all* their sons. This will not be the case if the allele responsible is autosomal or **X**-linked.

This was investigated by the

American geneticist Curt Stern in a study done in the early 1960s on men in the Indian police force. He found that sons did *not* always inherit the condition from their father.

You might think that this disproves the theory of **Y**-linked inheritance. However, the condition might be one in which the allele does not *always* give rise to the expected phenotype, possibly due to an inhibitory influence by other genes. Cases of this are known and are referred to as **incomplete penetrance**.

In one Israeli study, 37 male relatives of men with hairy ears were looked at and 28 of them had hairy

ears. These data are consistent with the hypothesis of **Y**-linked inheritance combined with incomplete penetrance, and are difficult to explain by any other genetic model. Can you think of any alternatives?

would have had little chance of surviving for long beyond puberty, once menstruation had begun.

Crossing over

We have seen that linked genes are carried on the same chromosome. This being so, we might expect that their alleles would always stay together and never separate. However, this is not the case. When studying the inheritance of linked genes it is unusual to find complete linkage. More often that not, a certain proportion of the offspring show new combinations, as in independent assortment. We will illustrate this with maize which, like *Drosophila*, is a favourite in genetic research.

In maize a single cob is covered with several hundred kernels. Each kernel is the product of a single fertilisation. The kernels show several clear-cut characteristics including colour and shape (figure 38.12). If a maize plant from a pure line for kernels which are coloured and smooth is crossed with one from a pure line having colourless and shrunken kernels, the F$_1$ all have coloured smooth kernels. Evidently coloured is dominant to colourless, and smooth to shrunken.

Now what might we expect to happen if one of the F$_1$ plants is test-crossed with the double recessive? If the genes for colour and shape are on separate chromosomes, we would expect the test cross to produce all four combinations of characteristics in approximately equal numbers. If the two genes are on the same chromosome we might expect the progeny to show only two types of kernel: coloured smooth and colourless shrunken.

In fact, neither of these two possibilities turns out to be the case. What we get are mainly coloured smooth and colourless shrunken kernels, but there are a few coloured shrunken and colourless smooth ones as well:

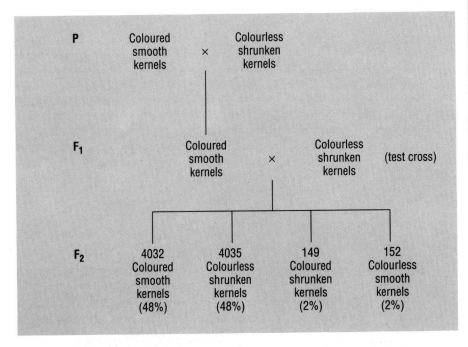

In other words, all four combinations of characteristics are found, but not in the proportions we would expect if the two genes were located on separate chromosomes.

How can we explain this? The answer is that the genes are situated on the same chromosome and for the most part they are transmitted together

Figure 38.12 Part of a maize cob with kernels that differ in colour and shape.

Sex linkage and the Y chromosome

If a gene is **Y**-linked, we would expect its effects to show themselves only in men. Can you think of a definite example of such a trait? The answer is 'maleness'. To be more specific, we now know that the **Y** chromosome has several copies of a **testicular differentiating gene**. The effect of this gene is to act on the undifferentiated gonads of the young embryo and cause them to differentiate into the testes. In the absence of the product made by these testicular differentiating genes, the gonads develop into ovaries.

There are no other conclusive examples of **Y**-linked inheritance in humans, though some fish and mice species show several instances of **Y**-linked inheritance.

One of the most notable cases of possible **Y**-linked inheritance in humans was the famous 'porcupine man' of eighteenth century England. This unfortunate character had patches of hard, spiny skin rather like a porcupine and is alleged to have transmitted this condition to all his sons. However, much doubt has been cast on the validity of the records and there is little evidence that the condition was associated with the **Y** chromosome.

Figure 38.13 Diagram showing the result of crossing maize homozygous for coloured smooth kernels with maize having colourless shrunken kernels. The genes controlling colour and shape of the kernels are linked. The small percentage of recombinants in the progeny can be explained by postulating that crossing over takes place between homologous chromosomes during gamete formation. Allele symbols: coloured (dominant), **C**; colourless (recessive), **c**; smooth (dominant), **S**; shrunken (recessive), **s**.

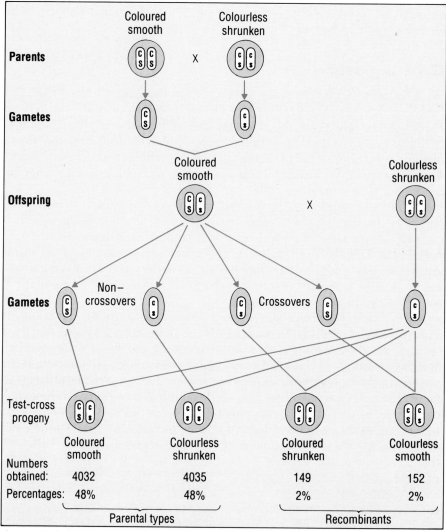

through the gametes to the offspring. However, in the formation of a small proportion of the gametes the alleles of these genes, instead of staying on their own chromosome, change places. This is called **crossing over** and it has the effect of separating alleles that were previously linked, allowing them to recombine. The result is that, while the majority of offspring have the same combination of characteristics as the parents, a few show new combinations; they are known as **recombinants**. This is summarised in figure 38.13.

Explanation of crossing over

In seeking an explanation for crossing over, it helps to remember two facts:

- In meiosis homologous chromosomes become intimately wrapped round each other.
- The alleles of a particular gene occupy the same positions (loci) on their respective chromosomes and therefore lie alongside each other when the homologous chromosomes come together.

During prophase of the first meiotic division, when homologous chromosomes become intertwined, the chromatids of homologous chromosomes can be seen to be in contact with each other at certain points along their length (see page 562). At these points, known as **chiasmata** (singular: **chiasma**), the chromatids break and rejoin. The result is that portions of the chromatids belonging to the two homologous chromosomes change places, taking their alleles with them. So the chiasmata result in crossing over. Eventually the chromatids finish up in separate gametes and, after fertilisation, give rise to new combinations of alleles in the offspring – the so-called recombinants (figure 38.14).

The number of chiasmata formed in a bivalent during meiosis, and therefore the amount of crossing over, varies from one species to another and, within a species, from one pair of homologous chromosomes to another. Occasionally no chiasmata are formed, sometimes as many as eight. Generally the longer the chromosomes in a homologous pair, the greater the number of chiasmata.

The importance of crossing over is that by establishing new allelic combinations it is an important source of genetic variation. The significance of this is discussed in Chapter 43.

Locating genes on chromosomes

A useful incidental consequence of crossing-over is that it enables geneticists to work out the relative positions of genes on a chromosome. In 1911 the same T H Morgan who discovered linkage (see page 690) suggested that the extent of recombination that occurs between genes on the same chromosome is a measure of the distance between them.

To see how this works, imagine two linked genes **A** and **B**. The further apart **A** and **B** are on their chromosome, the more likely it is that during meiosis the chromosome will break and rejoin at some point between them. Conversely, the closer they are, the less likely it is that breakage and crossing over will occur between them. So if in a breeding experiment we find that a relatively large percentage (say 20 to 40 per cent) of the offspring are recombinants, we can conclude that the genes are relatively far apart on the chromosome. If, though, only a low percentage (say one to five per cent) of the offspring are recombinants, we can conclude that the genes lie quite close together. The percentage of offspring which show recombination is called the **cross over value (COV)**.

By looking at figure 38.13, can you see what the highest cross over value could be? The answer is 50 per cent. Even in the extreme case where crossing over always takes place between two genes, half the offspring show the parental genotypes and a 1:1:1:1 ratio results in which the parental and recombinant types are equally frequent. This is the same ratio we get when two genes are unlinked, that is when they occur on non-homologous chromosomes. The reason why the COV is limited to 50 per cent is that even if all four chromatids in a bivalent form chiasmata, on average half the cross overs are between sister chromatids which means that linked alleles remain linked.

Mapping chromosomes

Imagine that in a breeding experiment it is found that the COV of **A** and **B** is 14 per cent. This means that the genes **A** and **B** are 14 map units apart on their chromosome, thus:

Remember that we only know the *relative* positions of A and B. We do not know precisely where on the chromosome they lie. For example, they might lie in the middle of the chromosome or at one end of it.

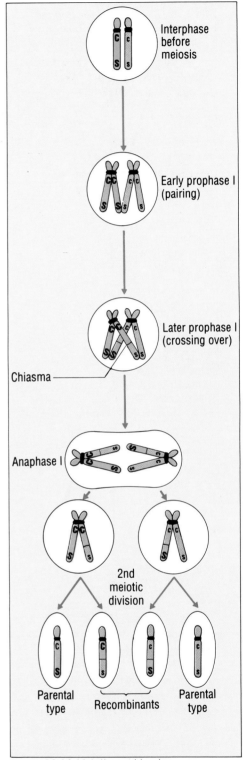

Figure 38.14 Meiosis provides the explanation for crossing over. In prophase I of meiosis homologous chromosomes become intimately associated with one another and adjacent non-sister chromatids may break and rejoin as shown here. The result is that previously unlinked alleles may become joined and new combinations established.

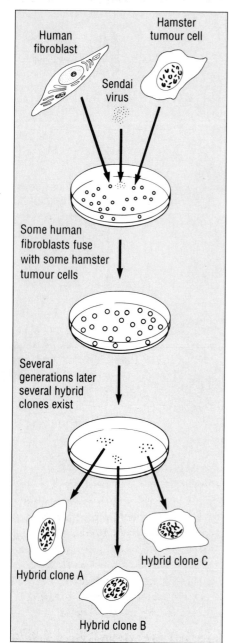

Figure 38.15 The technique of cell fusion. Human fibroblasts and hamster tumour cells are placed with Sendai viruses and various chemicals. Fused hybrid cells result. These cells give rise to hybrid clones which differ in the chromosomes they contain. The clones can be used to assign genes to particular chromosomes as described in the text.'

Suppose now that we investigate the transmission of these genes (**A** and **B**) with a third linked gene **C**. If we find that **A** and **C** give a COV of 20 per cent, whereas **B** and **C** give only six per cent, we can conclude that **B** is located between **A** and **C**, as follows:

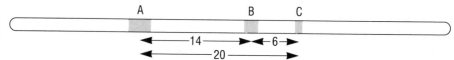

If, on the other hand, **A** and **C** give a COV of eight per cent, and **B** and **C** of 6 per cent, we conclude that **C** lies between **A** and **B**:

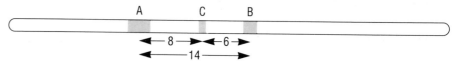

Another possibility is that **A** and **C** might again give a COV of eight per cent, but the COV between **B** and **C** might be 22 per cent. From this we can conclude that **A** lies between **B** and **C**:

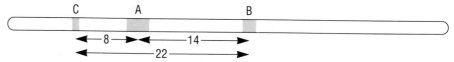

Although this may look like a very powerful technique for **mapping chromosomes**, difficulties may arise. There are three main reasons for this:

- First, the approach only works if you can look at very large numbers of offpsring. It is therefore much easier to determine the positions of *Drosophila* genes than human genes, for instance.
- Secondly, even in organisms like *Drosophila* and maize, it may be difficult to determine the relative positions of genes that lie very close to one another.
- Thirdly, if two genes are widely separated on a chromosome, recombinations may take place at two points between them, resulting in a **double cross over**. This will go undetected and means that the distance between widely separated genes will be underestimated.

From data collected over many years from numerous breeding experiments, **chromosome maps**, showing the positions of the various genes on the appropriate chromosomes, have been built up for several organisms, notably *Drosophila* and maize. In *Drosophila* many hundreds of gene loci have been established in this way.

Mapping human chromosomes

One way of finding out whether two human genes are linked or not is to follow the inheritance of the characteristics which they determine over two or more generations. This technique is called **pedigree analysis** and we have already come across it in our consideration of haemophilia (figure 38.11).

We can be confident that haemophilia is caused by a gene on the **X** chromosome for two reasons: first, because haemophilia is far more common in males than in females; and secondly, because males may pass the allele on to their daughters but never to their sons. These characteristics are typical of genes carried on the **X** chromosome, so it is relatively easy to find out which human genes are sex-linked. Of the 1500 human genes whose chromosomes have been identified, about 500 are on the **X** chromosome. Among these are genes for haemophilia, red-green colour blindness and Duchenne muscular dystrophy, a distressing condition in which the muscles progressively waste away, eventually leading to an early death.

But how can human geneticists determine on which autosomal chromosomes genes occur? Until recently this was extremely difficult. However tremendous progress has been made thanks to a technique known as **cell fusion**. To use this technique, you must first establish a colony of human cells which will reproduce themselves in the laboratory. Such **cell lines** are commonly derived from **fibroblasts**, one of the principal cells found in connective tissue (see page 177).

Once a cell line of fibroblasts is established, one of the cells is placed with a diploid cell from a hamster or other small mammal in the presence of various chemicals and a certain virus. The virus enhances the fusion of the two kinds of cell to form a 'hybrid' cell (figure 38.15). The result is that the cytoplasms of the two cells coalesce but their nuclei at first remain separate. The cell then undergoes mitosis. A spindle is formed and chromosomes from both cells become attached to it. However, not all the chromosomes succeed in doing this. As a consequence, some of the daughter cells end up with fewer chromosomes than others.

Over successive generations, more and more chromosomes may be lost. Eventually cells may result that contain only one human chromosome and a number of hamster chromosomes. It may then be possible to detect proteins made by the cell which are known to be produced by humans but not by hamsters. In such a case, the one human chromosome must be producing the protein. The next step is to examine the cell under the microscope and identify the human chromosome. This is done by comparing it with a prepared set of human chromosomes: a **karyotype**, as it is called. In a human karyotype the 23 different chromosome pairs can be distinguished on the basis of their size and reaction with certain stains (figure 38.16). Thus this method allows geneticists to determine the precise chromosome on which the gene is located.

Figure 38.16 Human chromosomes can be individually recognised by their size, position of centromere and banding pattern with certain stains. The bands correspond to large groups of genes. The photomicrograph shows a full set of human chromosomes arranged and numbered according to size and centromere position in a male. The diagram shows the banding patterns in detail.

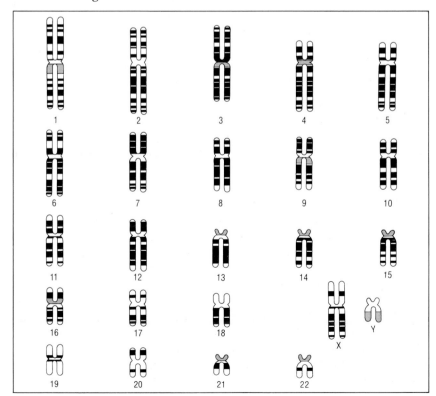

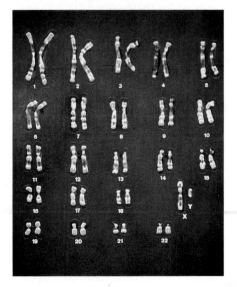

Pedigree analysis, cell fusion and other techniques of cell and molecular biology are making it possible to map the entire human **genome**, genome being a collective word for the genetic material of an organism. Mapping all of the human genome will undoubtedly take many years and may cost several billion pounds. If this sounds like a lot of money, it should be remembered that humans have somewhere between 50 000 and 100 000 genes and that it takes considerable time and effort to map just one of these. The project will require unprecedented international cooperation among the participating geneticists. It is hoped that what is learnt will not only increase our understanding of the nature of inheritance, but also lead to cures being found for some of the distressing human diseases caused by faults in the genetic material. Approximately 60 million people world-wide are affected by these.

Degrees of dominance

Mendel's experiments might lead us to conclude that alleles are always either dominant or recessive. You will remember that Mendel never found offspring with phenotypes midway between their parents. For example, the pea plants that resulted from a cross between a pure line of tall peas and one of short peas were all tall. However, this does not always happen.

Take flower colour in snapdragons, for example. Here, a cross between two pure bred individuals of differing genotypes results in offspring which are identical with neither parent but are intermediate between the two. A snapdragon with red flowers crossed with a snapdragon with white flowers gives plants with pink flowers in the F_1, a result which contrasts sharply with those obtained by Mendel for the garden pea (figure 38.17). The snapdragons with pink flowers are heterozygous for the allele for flower colour, but instead of one allele being dominant to the other, both express themselves equally in the phenotype. Such alleles are said to be **codominant**.

When codominance occurs, the gene should be designated by an upper case letter and the alleles by appropriate superscript upper case letters. In the snapdragon example, we might call the gene C for colour. The red allele will then be C^R and the white allele C^W. Crossing snapdragons with pink flowers among themselves gives a phenotypic ratio of approximately 1 red : 2 pink : 1 white (figure 38.18).

Between the extremes of complete dominance and no dominance (codominance) are various shades of **partial dominance**. In such cases an offspring's phenotype resembles one parent more than the other for a given characteristic.

Figure 38.17 Crosses between red-flowered and white-flowered snapdragons can give rise to pink-flowered individuals. Snapdragons also occur in other colours.

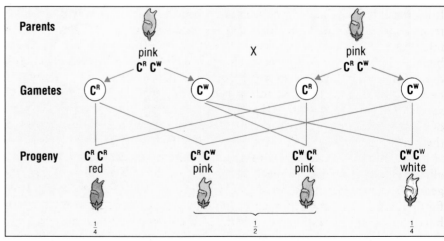

Figure 38.18 Diagram showing the result of crossing snapdragons with pink flowers among themselves. A phenotypic ratio of approximately 1 red : 2 pink : 1 white results.

Multiple alleles

So far we have looked at situations in which a gene may have only two alleles. Sometimes, however, there may be more than two alleles that can occur at a given locus. Of course, in any one individual only two alleles can be present.

A clear example of such **multiple alleles** is provided by the alleles controlling the **ABO blood group system** in humans. The ABO system is controlled by three alleles generally referred to as I^A, I^B and I^O. The physiology of the ABO system is explained in Chapter 24 and here we are only concerned with the alleles responsible for determining the different blood groups, and their transmission.

The I^A allele is responsible for the production of type A antigens in the person's red blood cells, and the I^B allele for the production of type B antigens. The third allele in the series, I^O produces neither antigen. As only two of the three alleles can be present at any one time, an individual may possess any of the following six genotypes: I^AI^A, I^AI^O, I^BI^B, I^BI^O, I^AI^B or I^OI^O. The I^A and I^B alleles show equal dominance with respect to one another (i.e. they are codominant), but each is dominant to I^O. Thus:

- A person with the genotype I^AI^A or I^AI^O belongs to blood group A.
- A person with the genotype I^BI^B or I^BI^O belongs to blood group B.
- A person with the genotype I^AI^B belongs to blood group AB.
- A person with the genotype I^OI^O belongs to blood group O.

The fact that there are more than two alleles responsible for determining the blood groups makes no difference to their transmission, which takes place in a normal Mendelian fashion. Thus a child whose parents are both blood group O must be blood group O (note why). However, consider what happens when two people, one of whom is blood group A and the other blood group O, have children. The genotypes of the children depend on the genotype of the A parent. If he or she is homozygous with the genotype I^AI^A, the children can only have the genotype I^AI^O and be blood group A. However, if the group A parent is heterozygous with the genotype I^AI^O, each child has a 50:50 chance of being blood group A or blood group O.

An interesting aspect of multiple alleles is that offspring may result whose genotypes differ from both of their parents. Work out, for example, the phenotypes that can result when a couple with the genotypes I^AI^O and I^BI^O have children (see figure 38.19).

Lethal alleles

It is probably true that in genetic studies more has been learned about genes from abnormal ratios than from normal ones. Consider, for example, the inheritance of fur colour in mice. In mice the allele for yellow fur (**Y** – not to be confused with the Y chromosome with which it is quite unconnected) is dominant to the allele for grey (**y**). Now if a pair of yellow mice known to be heterozygous for the coat colour gene are mated, the result is always the same: two thirds of the offspring are yellow, and one third grey. Yet from our knowledge of monohybrid ratios, we naturally expect three quarters of the mice to be yellow and only a quarter to be grey. What is going on?

A possible explanation is that individuals homozygous for the yellow allele (i.e. with the genotype **YY**) die before birth. In other words, the genotype **YY** represents a lethal combination of alleles. As can be seen from figure 38.20, the death of such individuals in the embryonic state would have the effect of removing a quarter of the offspring from the litter. The dead embryos would represent a third of the potential yellow offspring,

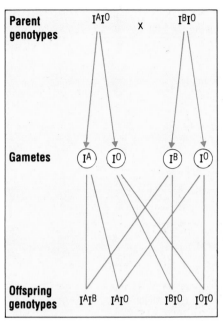

Figure 38.19 The children of parents with the genotypes I^AI^O and I^BI^O may have genotypes that differ from both their parents. What are the *phenotypes* of the parents and the offspring in the cross outlined above?

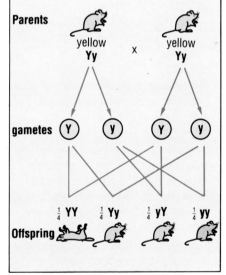

Figure 38.20 Inheritance of fur colour in mice. The allele for yellow coat (**Y**) is dominant to that for grey (**y**), at least as far as coat colour is concerned. Mice that are homozygous **YY** die before birth. As a result, a cross of two mice with the **Yy** genotype fails to produce the 3:1 ratio typical of monohybrid crosses.

thus reducing the proportion of yellow offspring from what would have been ¾ to ⅔.

Evidence for this hypothesis comes from two observations:

- Crossing yellow with yellow never produces exclusively yellow offspring; a ratio of two yellow to one grey always results. In other words, it is impossible for a pair of yellow mice to breed true. This can be explained by assuming that viable yellow mice are always heterozygous and that a living homozygous yellow mouse is an impossibility.

- Examination of the uteri of yellow female mice which have mated with yellow males usually reveals one or more dead embryos. Few if any dead embryos are found either in the uteri of yellow females which have mated with grey males or in the uteri of grey females which have mated with yellow males. This is presumably because in neither case can an offspring arise with the genotype **YY**.

There is therefore good evidence to support the hypothesis that the **YY** combination is lethal. However it seems incredible that being homozygous for the colour yellow simply kills mice. Presumably the allele we have called **Y** has two effects, one on coat colour, the other on viability.

An allele which has two or more effects is said to show **pleiotropy**. We met an earlier instance of this when we considered the allele for cystic

The inheritance of intelligence

Few topics cause as much argument in human heredity as the genetics of intelligence. On the one hand some people argue that intelligence is a polygenic trait which, though influenced by the environment, is essentially inherited. At the other extreme there is the view that, with the exception of people with moderate or severe learning disabilities, a person's upbringing is overwhelmingly the most important determinant of his or her intelligence. Between these two extremes is the general feeling that it is difficult to agree on precisely what is meant by intelligence and that even if a compromise definition can be agreed, intelligence is very difficult to measure.

Some of the best data supporting a strong genetic component to inheritance come from studies of identical twins reared apart. Not surprisingly, there are not many such twins. However, in several countries careful studies have been made of the **intelligence quotient (IQ)** of identical twins adopted into

different families from very early childhood. The twins' IQs can be measured by giving them special **IQ tests**. These tests are meant to quantify how intelligent a person is, though there is considerable disagreement about whether they are valid or not.

If intelligence lacks any genetic component, there should be no relationship between the IQs of separated identical twins. In other words, the **correlation coefficient** between the IQs of the two twins should be zero. On the other hand, if intelligence lacks any environmental component, the correlation coefficient should be 1. In fact it varies from 0.49 to 0.78, which is quite high for a correlation coefficient. (These data do not include the results obtained by the English geneticist Cyril Burt, as there is some controversy about whether he made up some of his data.)

This looks like strong evidence for a genetic *and* an environmental component to intelligence. However, it has been pointed out that just because the twins were brought up in different homes, it does not

necessarily mean that their environments will have been dissimilar. After all, a child who is adopted is not sent randomly into any family, but goes to carefully selected parents who have to fulfil certain criteria showing that they can care for the child. Indeed, most adoption agencies try to 'match' children and the families in which they are placed.

Adoption studies provide some of the strongest evidence that the environment plays a more important role than heredity in the determination of intelligence. If you look at the intelligence of unrelated children adopted into the same family, correlations between the childrens' IQs vary from 0.12 to as high as 0.65. The extreme view that intelligence is innately determined and uninfluenced by the environment would predict a correlation of 0.

Perhaps the most valid conclusion to draw is that both heredity and environment play a role in determining intelligence and that it is impossible to assess their relative importance.

fibrosis (see page 682). You may remember that cystic fibrosis is a condition in which the affected person produces abnormally large amounts of mucus. One consequence of this is that the mucus blocks the alveoli and bronchioles in the lungs, leading to severe problems with breathing. A second consequence is that mucus in the pancreas blocks the exit for digestive enzymes, leading to inadequate digestion. A third consequence is that these enzymes, unable to leave the pancreas, may result in autodigestion – that is, they start to eat away the pancreas itself. One result is that the person may have much of their islets of Langerhans destroyed, with the consequence that diabetes develops. Thus you can see how the cystic fibrosis allele has a whole series of phenotypic effects.

Returning to the mice, should the **Y** allele be described as dominant or recessive? The answer is that it depends on how we look at it. As the allele controlling fur colour it is dominant, but as a **lethal allele** it is recessive, exerting its effects only when in the homozygous state.

In most cases, lethal alleles are recessive, for which reason they are called **recessive lethals**. Occasionally, though, the presence of an allele in the heterozygous state is sufficient to cause death. Such alleles are known as **dominant lethals**. An example of a medical condition in humans caused by a dominant lethal is Huntington's disease, characterised by deterioration of the nervous system. Here, individuals with a single copy of the malfunctioning allele die, usually after reaching adulthood. The population genetics of Huntington's disease are discussed further on page 747.

Lethal alleles are known to exist in a wide range of organisms. Each of us, on average, carries four lethal alleles. Fortunately they are all recessive, so problems do not arise provided they are in the heterozygous state. Exactly which four lethal alleles we carry varies from one person to another, so if two people reproduce, the children are unlikely to be homozygous for any of these lethals. However, children produced by matings between close relatives are more likely to be homozygous for these alleles. We shall return to this when looking at **inbreeding** (see page 804).

Genetic counselling

Suppose a couple have had a child with haemophilia and want to know if there is a risk of any other children they may have also having haemophilia. They can go a **genetic counsellor** for advice. Genetic counsellors need to have a sound understanding of human genetics and must also be able to explain their knowledge clearly and sensitively. People often go for **genetic counselling** feeling worried or guilty. A good genetic counsellor will help to ease their worries and allay any feelings of guilt.

Sometimes a pregnant woman goes to a genetic counsellor having had a diagnostic test (see page 791) which showed that, if she has her child, the baby runs a significant risk of having an abnormality. In such circumstances the genetic counsellor needs to explain all the medical and legal options available, which may include termination of the pregnancy. However, this needs to be done in such a way as to allow the woman to make her own decision.

A genetic counsellor needs to able to explain genetic ratios and probabilities so that they can be understood by non-specialists. For example, it is no good telling a couple that their children have a one in four chance of suffering from cystic fibrosis if the couple do not understand what this really means. For example, a couple may assume that because their first child has cystic fibrosis, the next three are certain not to.

What might a genetic counsellor say to a couple who have a boy with haemophilia and are thinking of having another child?

The following pedigree shows the inheritance in a family of a type of blindness. Indicate whether each of the following is consistent with the pedigree:

(a) Autosomal recessive.
(b) Autosomal dominant.
(c) **X**-linked recessive.
(d) **X**-linked dominant.
(e) **Y**-linkage.

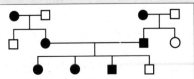

The circles are females and the squares are males; filled-in circles and squares are affected individuals, empty circles and squares are normal individuals.

Figure 38.21 In wheat, seed colour is determined polygenically. A total of three genes are involved. This diagram illustrates the complicated phenotypic ratios that can result when characters show polygenic inheritance.

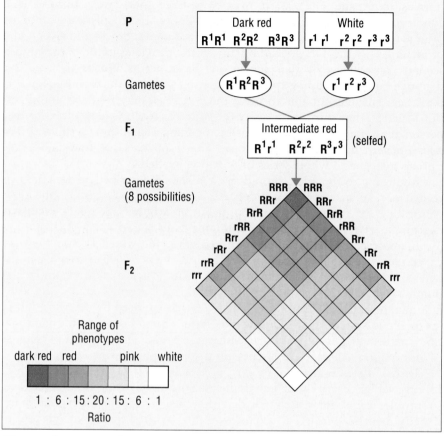

Gene interaction

So far we have dealt only with cases where a characteristic is controlled by the alleles of one gene. Sometimes, however, a single characteristic is controlled by the alleles of two or more genes interacting with one another. A character controlled by more than one gene is known as a **polygenic character**, and its transmission is called **polygenic inheritance**.

An example of polygenic inheritance is found in the wheat *Triticum vulgare*. In wheat seeds, colour is determined by three genes, each on a different chromosome. Each of these genes has two alleles. Seeds with dark red coats have the genotype $R^1R^1R^2R^2R^3R^3$. At the other extreme, seeds with white coats have the genotype $r^1r^1r^2r^2r^3r^3$. The colour of a wheat seed is simply determined by how many of the **R** as opposed to the **r** alleles it has. Seeds can have any number of **R** alleles from zero to six. For example, a seed with five **R** alleles is fairly red but not quite as red as one with all six **R** alleles.

If a wheat plant which has all six **R** alleles is crossed with one that has all six **r** alleles, the resulting offspring have seeds that are an intermediate red colour, as you would expect. What is interesting, though, is what happens when these offspring are crossed among themselves. As you can see from figure 38.21, the full range of seed colours is seen in the F_2 with an expected ratio of 1:6:15:20:15:6:1! Can you work out what ratio would have been expected if only two genes, not three, had been involved?

Many characters are polygenic, and it is the basis of **continuous variation** (figure 38.22). A character is said to vary continuously if individuals show a *range* of phenotypes with a smooth graduation from one extreme to another, rather than falling into a small number of discrete categories. An example in humans is height.

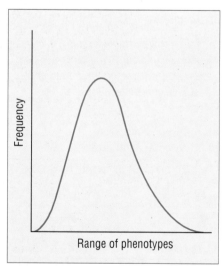

Figure 38.22 An example of continuous variation in a character. Continuous variation may be due to polygenic inheritance, environmental effects or even multiple alleles.

Characters that show continuous variation, if they have a genetic basis at all, are usually polygenic. Other characters, such as those that Mendel studied in his garden peas, show **discontinuous variation**. Mendel could unambiguously assign all his pea plants to a small number of phenotypes, such as tall or short (figure 38.23). This is quite different from the continuous variation in height seen in humans and occurs because only one gene is involved.

You may be able to think of other explanations for continuous variation apart from polygenic inheritance. One possibility is the presence of multiple alleles. It is important not to confuse polygenic inheritance with multiple alleles. Multiple alleles all occur at one locus, whereas in polygenic inheritance several loci are involved. However, there are cases of polygenic inheritance where one or more of the loci involved have multiple alleles.

In continuous variation **environmental effects** may be particularly important. This can be seen in human height. People's heights depend not only on their genotypes but also on the environments in which they grow up. The environment has an even greater effect on a person's body mass.

Epistasis

Another sort of gene interaction is seen when one gene modifies or masks the action of another gene. This is known as **epistasis**, and it can give rise to unusual ratios in genetic crosses. We are not talking about dominant and recessive *alleles* which, by definition, occur at the same loci on homologous chromosomes. The genes involved in epistasis occur at different loci.

An example of epistasis is provided by the inheritance of certain coat colours in mice. Most mice have a coat colour described as agouti, a grayish pattern formed by alternating bands of pigment on each hair (figure 38.24). However, some mice are black and others white. The allele for agouti coat colour (**A**) is dominant to the allele for black (**a**). White coat colour is due to the presence of a recessive allele (**w**) at a separate locus, so that white mice are homozygous recessive (**ww**). A mouse that is homozygous recessive has a white coat irrespective of the alleles at the other locus. Thus **AAww**, **Aaww** and **aaww** are all white. The relationship between the genotypes and phenotypes is summarised in table 38.1.

One way to explain these results is to suppose that the following pathway determines coat colour:

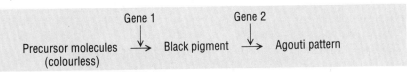

Lack of the product made by gene 1 leads to a white coat colour, irrespective of the actions of gene 2, because the colourless precursor molecules accumulate unless the product made by gene 1 is present.

You might find it instructive to consider the outcome of crossing the various genotypes listed in table 38.1. For example, try crossing two mice with the genotypes **AaWw**. You should get a 9:3:4 ratio. One can't help thinking that if Mendel's crosses had produced such ratios, he would have found them rather difficult to explain.

We ended the last chapter by saying that there are a number of situations where the conclusions that Mendel reached do not hold. We now know that these situations arise from the way genes are carried on the chromosomes and the way they assort and interact with each other. This reflects the intricate mechanisms by which genes control an organism's characteristics. The basis of these mechanisms is the subject of the next two chapters.

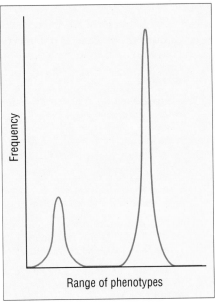

Figure 38.23 An example of discontinuous variation in a character. Discontinuous variation usually occurs because a character is influenced by just one gene.

Figure 38.24 Adult female house mouse with her 12 day old young. Notice the agouti coat colour described in the text.

Phenotype	Genotypes
Agouti	AAWW, AaWW, AAWw, AaWw
Black	aaWW, aaWw
White	AAww, Aaww, aaww

Table 38.1 The relationship between genotype and phenotype in the determination of mice coat colour. For a possible explanation of these results, see text.

Summary

1 In dihybrid crosses genes sometimes fail to assort independently. This can be explained by postulating that such genes are carried on the same chromosome (**linkage**).

2 Genes linked together on the same chromosome constitute a **linkage group**. In *Drosophila* the number of linkage groups equals the haploid number of chromosomes, and the number of genes in the linkage groups corresponds to the lengths of the chromosomes.

3 Homologous chromosomes are normally identical in appearance (**autosomes**). In many species an exception is provided by the **sex chromosomes** (**heterosomes**).

4 In mammals and birds sex is determined by the presence of the **X** and **Y** chromosomes. In mammals females are **homogametic** (**XX**) and males **heterogametic** (**XY**).

5 In humans genes are carried on all the autosomes and on the **X** chromosome (**sex linkage**). Examples of **X**-linked inheritance include red-green colour blindness and haemophilia.

6 Crosses involving linked genes usually produce a small proportion of offspring with new combinations (**recombinants**) in addition to the parental combinations. This can be explained by the formation of **chiasmata** and **crossing over** during meiosis.

7 Crossing over enables geneticists to work out the relative positions of genes on a chromosome. In general the distance between two genes is proportional to their **cross over value** (**COV**). In this way **chromosome maps** can be established.

8 In recent years the technique of **cell fusion** has been used to identify which chromosomes carry particular human genes.

9 In **codominance** two alleles both exert a phenotypic effect when present together in the heterozygous state.

10 Some characteristics are controlled by **multiple alleles**. In the case of the **ABO blood group system**, three alleles are involved, although only two may be present in any one individual. These alleles are inherited in a normal Mendelian manner.

11 Sometimes the presence of two particular alleles at a locus results in the death of an organism. Such alleles are **recessive lethals**. Occasionally the presence of just one allele is sufficient to cause death, in which case the allele is a **dominant lethal**.

12 When an allele affects two or more characteristics of an organism it is said to show **pleiotropy**. The allele for yellow fur colour in mice and the cystic fibrosis allele in humans are both examples of **pleiotropic alleles**.

13 A character, such a height in humans, which is influenced by the presence of two or more genes is known as a **polygenic character** and its transmission is called **polygenic inheritance**.

14 Polygenic characters generally show **continuous variation** as do characters strongly influenced by the **environment**. In contrast, characters such as height in Mendel's pea plants, which are caused by single genes, show **discontinuous variation**.

15 Sometimes one gene modifies or masks the action of another gene. This is known as **epistasis**.

Review questions

1 What sorts of phenotypic ratios in a genetic cross would lead you to suspect that linkage was involved?

2 List the ways may be in which the sex of an organism may be determined by its genetic make up.

3 Explain why colour blindness is less common in women than in men.

4 Suppose that you breed mice for a hobby and a new coat colour (speckled) turns up in all the male mice of a litter. How might you investigate whether it is Y-linked or not?

5 What sorts of phenotypic ratios in a genetic cross would lead you to suspect that crossing over had occured?

6 How could you produce a pure bred line of snapdragons with pink flowers?

7 Do you think the money that may be spent on the human genome project will be worth it? Defend your answer.

8 Genetics is said to explain why offspring resemble their parents. Yet a child born to parents, one of whom is blood group AB and the other blood group O, can never have the same phenotype as either of its parents. Explain this apparent paradox.

9 Distinguish between the following pairs of terms:
Multiple alleles and polygenes.
Partial dominance and epistasis.

10 Does the existence of continuous variation make the job of a geneticist attempting to breed new crop varieties easier or more difficult? Explain your answer.

Further reading

Heredity and Human Diversity by Stephen Tomkins (Cambridge University Press, 1989) is a short, beautifully written book on human genetics.

A more advanced text is Sam Singer's *Human Genetics: An Introduction to the Principles of Heredity* (W. H. Freeman, 1985). It is clear and well illustrated.

The nature of the gene

In this chapter we shall explore the chemical nature of the gene, and we shall see that an understanding of how it works lies in its molecular structure. This is not of purely academic interest. It has practical applications too – see figure 39.1 for example. But before getting down to details let us see what general predictions we can make about the nature of the gene.

Genes, as we have seen in the last two chapters, help determine an organism's characteristics. This means that genes must contain **information**, a set of instructions if you like, telling the organism how to develop. It also follows that genes must be able to reproduce themselves, or **replicate**, without losing this information, otherwise the instructions they carry will be progressively diluted in successive generations.

In searching for the chemical nature of the gene scientists therefore looked for molecules that contain information and are capable of replication. Nowadays everyone accepts that **nucleic acids** fulfil this role. However, for many years proteins were considered the only possible candidates because they alone seemed to have the structural diversity necessary for carrying information. But in 1944 Oswald Avery of the Rockefeller Institute in New York produced evidence that nucleic acids rather than proteins are the carriers of genetic information. Let us look briefly at what he did.

Avery's demonstration

The bacteria that cause pneumonia, *Pneumococcus*, exist in two different strains: capsulated and non-capsulated. The former are characterised by a thick capsule which surrounds the cells. In the non-capsulated strain this capsule is missing. Avery and his colleagues prepared a sample of dead capsulated bacteria. They then extracted the polysaccharides from these cells and added them to a medium in which non-capsulated bacteria were growing.

Nothing remarkable happened. The non-capsulated bacteria simply gave rise to more non-capsulated bacteria. Exactly the same result followed when lipids, proteins or ribonucleic acid (RNA) were tried. However, when deoxyribonucleic acid (DNA) was extracted from the dead capsulated bacteria and added to the medium, capsulated bacteria appeared amongst the non-capsulated ones. This showed that DNA carries the information that determines whether the bacteria are capsulated or non-capsulated.

The structure of nucleic acids

Although the chemical building blocks of nucleic acids have been known since the turn of the 20th century, it is only in the last forty years that we have come to understand how they are fitted together to form nucleic acid molecules. We now know that nucleic acids occur in all living cells and in viruses. Unravelling their structure has been one of the most exciting adventures in modern science. It has brought us to a better understanding of heredity and development, and has opened the doors to understanding the nature of life itself.

Two types of nucleic acids are found in cells: **deoxyribonucleic acid (DNA)** and **ribonucleic acid (RNA)**. By means of chemical tests on eukaryotic cells, it can be shown that DNA is found in the nucleus, mitochondria and chloroplasts, whereas RNA is found in the nucleus and the cytoplasm,

Figure 39.1 In 1988 this man was sentenced to life imprisonment for the rape and murder of two 15-year-old girls. He was found guilty as a result of evidence gained from the structure of his genetic material. The procedure, called genetic fingerprinting, is explained on page 795.

Griffith's discovery

Avery's work was foreshadowed almost 20 years earlier by similar experiments carried out by Frederick Griffith, a medical officer in the British Ministry of Health. It happens that the non-capsulated strain of *Pneumococcus* is non-virulent when injected into mice; in other words, it does not kill the mice. On the other hand, the capsulated bacteria are virulent. They are virulent because their capsules make it difficult for the mice's phagocytes to destroy them. Griffith found that if he injected mice with live non-virulent bacteria to which heat-killed virulent bacteria had been added, the mice died. However, the injection of heat-killed virulent bacteria on their own had no harmful effect on the mice. Plainly an agent was present in the heat-killed virulent bacteria which could *transform* the live non-virulent bacteria into a virulent strain.

though mainly in the latter. Like proteins, nucleic acids are long chain molecules, but the chains are mostly longer than those of proteins and the sub-units more complicated than amino acids.

The building blocks of a nucleic acid are called **nucleotides**. A nucleotide consists of three molecules linked together: a **pentose (5-carbon) sugar**, an **organic base** and **phosphoric acid**. Let us look at these three constituents in turn.

First, the **sugar**. You will recall that a hexose sugar such as glucose consists of five carbon atoms and one oxygen atom which form a six-membered ring to which various side groups are attached, including one which contains a single carbon atom. A pentose sugar has basically the same structure except that there is one less carbon atom in the ring with the result that the molecule is constructed as follows:

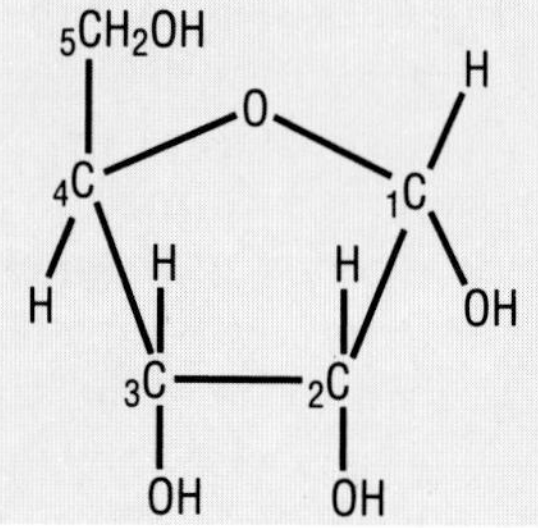

This particular sugar is **ribose** and it is found in ribonucleic acid. Deoxyribonucleic acid has a different sugar, **deoxyribose**, which differs from ribose only in that the hydroxyl group at position 2 is replaced by a hydrogen atom. In other words, deoxyribose has one less oxygen atom than ribose:

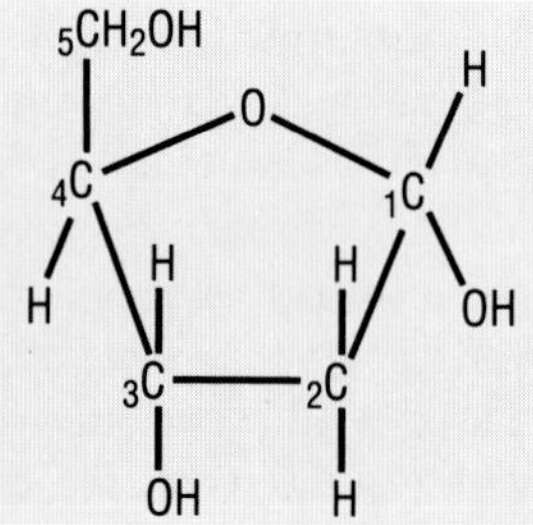

The second constituent of a nucleotide is **phosphoric acid** (H_3PO_4) which has the structural formula:

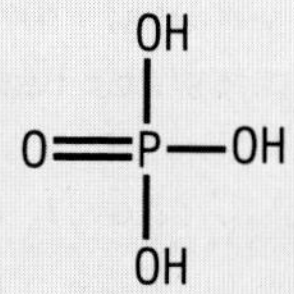

The third component is the **organic base**. DNA contains four different organic bases: **adenine, guanine, cytosine** and **thymine**, abbreviated respectively to **A, G, C** and **T**. RNA also contains adenine, cytosine and guanine, but has **uracil** (abbreviated to **U**) rather than thymine. All these five bases are ring compounds, the rings being composed of carbon and nitrogen atoms which for simplicity we can represent thus:

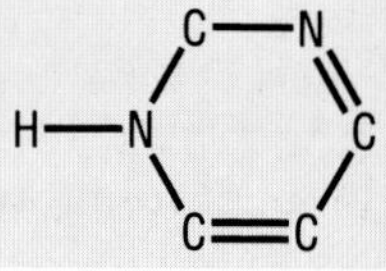

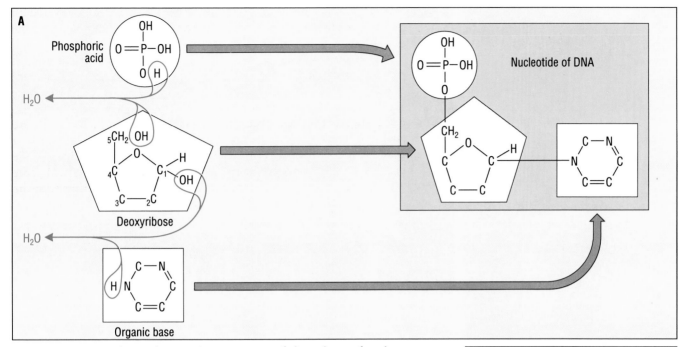

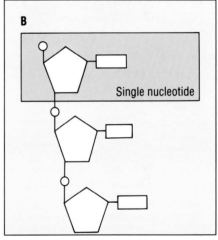

Don't worry about the precise structure of these bases for the moment, but notice the hydrogen atom projecting from the nitrogen on the left: this plays an important part in the building up of a nucleotide.

How do the three components link up to form a nucleotide? As in the construction of so many other organic compounds, the process is one of condensation (figure 39.2A). A sugar attaches itself to a phosphoric acid molecule at position 5, and to one of the five bases at position 1. Two molecules of water are removed in the process.

To form a nucleic acid, the nucleotides are then strung together. This also involves condensation. The sugar of one nucleotide joins to the phosphate radical of another nucleotide at position 3, a molecule of water is released and a **dinucleotide** is formed. The addition of further nucleotides produces a long **polynucleotide chain** whose backbone consists of alternating sugar and phosphate groups with the bases projecting sideways from the sugars (figure 39.2B).

The sugar and the phosphate groups are identical all the way along the chain; in other words the backbone is absolutely uniform and shows no variation in structure. In RNA the sugars are all ribose; in DNA they are all deoxyribose. The phosphate groups are the same in RNA and DNA. The bases, however, show no such uniformity. We have already noted that there are five different ones: **A, G, C, T** and **U**. DNA contains **A, G, C** and **T;** RNA **A, G, C** and **U**. Now the sequence in which these bases occur along the length of the nucleic acid chain varies from species to species and from individual to individual. It is in this sequence of bases that the nucleic acid carries information controlling the organism's development.

At first sight it seems incredible that all the instructions required to produce an organism as complicated as, say, a human being, should be conveyed by only four kinds of base. However, it should be borne in mind that a single molecule of DNA may contain five million nucleotides, and the number of possible combinations is almost infinite. The bases are, in fact, like letters in a four-letter alphabet. From these four letters innumerable words can be constructed. It is worth remembering that computers use only two 'letters' (0 and 1) so perhaps it is not too surprising that four letters are enough to specify a human.

Figure 39.2 How a nucleic acid is built up.
A A pentose sugar, in this case deoxyribose, unites with a phosphoric acid molecule and an organic base to form a nucleotide.
B Nucleotides join through their phosphate groups to form a chain of nucleotides. As well as being the building blocks of nucleic acids, nucleotides are the basis of ATP and enter into the structure of NAD, NADP and FAD, coenzymes involved in respiration and photosynthesis (see pages 234 and 300).

Figure 39.3 James Watson (*left*) and Francis Crick with their model of DNA. Watson and Crick worked together in the Cavendish Laboratory at Cambridge in the early 1950s when Watson, an American, was on a post-doctoral visit to Europe. Their collaboration led to the discovery of the structure of DNA, for which, together with Maurice Wilkins, they were awarded a Nobel Prize in 1962. Crick, after working for many years in Cambridge, is now a Professor at the Salk Institute for Biological Studies in California. Watson is Director of the Cold Spring Harbor Laboratory, Long Island, New York.

Figure 39.4 Rosalind Franklin worked on the structure of DNA at King's College, London in the early 1950s. An expert X-ray crystallographer, she showed in 1952 that the phosphate groups of DNA must lie on the outside of the molecule. Her work was pivotal in enabling Watson and Crick to propose their hypothesis for the structure of DNA. After the elucidation of the structure of DNA she worked on the structure of viruses. Her career was cut short when she died tragically of cancer at the age of 37 in 1958, four years before Crick, Watson and Wilkins were awarded the Nobel Prize. Nobel Prizes cannot be awarded posthumously.

But we are leaping ahead of the story, for although the chemical components of nucleic acid were known at the time that Avery did his experiments on *Pneumococcus*, the way they are joined to make up DNA was not known. In fact even after Avery's work, some biologists were reluctant to accept that nucleic acids were the genetic material.

The Watson-Crick hypothesis

In 1953 the whole situation changed when James Watson and Francis Crick, working together at the Cavendish Laboratory in Cambridge, put forward a possible structure for DNA. How did Watson and Crick arrive at their conclusions?

Some years earlier an American chemist, Erwin Chargaff, had used chromatography to separate the four bases in DNA samples from various organisms. Quantitative techniques were then used to work out the amounts of the four bases. Some of Chargaff's original data are given in table 39.1. What do you notice about his results? You can see that the ratio of adenine to thymine is close to one, as is the ratio of guanine to cytosine. How can this be explained? With a flash of insight Watson and Crick suggested that DNA might consist of two parallel strands held together by pairs of bases; adenine being paired with thymine, and guanine with cytosine.

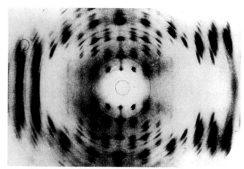

Figure 39.5 An X-ray diffraction photograph of DNA.

Source	Approximate per cent			
	A	C	G	T
Yeast	32	17	18	33
Avian tubercle bacilli	16	34	36	14
Ox thymus	30	18	24	28
Ox spleen	30	18	24	29
Human sperm	30	19	19	32

Table 39.1 Chargaff's original data on the base composition of DNA from several sources.

Meanwhile attempts had been made to work out the structure of DNA by X-ray diffraction analysis (see page 144). Despite formidable technical difficulties, mainly caused by DNA's reluctance to crystallise, some clear X-ray photographs were obtained by Rosalind Franklin and Maurice Wilkins at King's College, London. One such photograph is shown in figure 39.5.

Interpreting X-ray diffraction patterns is no easy matter at the best of times and for a large and complex molecule like DNA it is particularly difficult, especially when the patterns are rather diffuse. However, Watson and Crick set to work on the X-ray patterns, and after months of work they suddenly realised that both Chargaff's results and the X-ray diffraction data could be explained if DNA consists of two chains twisted round each other to form a **double helix**.

From the relative positions of certain spots in the X-ray photographs Watson and Crick concluded that the two chains are cross-linked at regular intervals corresponding to the nucleotides, and that there are ten nucleotides for one complete turn of the helix. Watson and Crick thus envisaged DNA as a kind of twisted ladder, the two uprights consisting of chains of alternating sugar and phosphate groups, the rungs as pairs of bases sticking inwards towards each other and linked up in a specific relationship: A with **T**, C with **G** (figure 39.6).

What is the evidence that **A** bonds with **T** and **C** with **G**? There are two main lines of evidence. First, such a relationship would explain Chargaff's results that cells contain the same amount of **A** as **T**, and the same amount of **C** as **G**. Secondly, when Watson and Crick made accurate cutout models of the four different nucleotides with all their atoms and bonds in the right places, they found that the only way in which they could make a model of DNA was to have the two strands running in opposite directions (i.e. antiparallel) with the bases linked **A** to **T** and **C** to **G** by hydrogen bonds.

Thymine and cytosine are **pyrimidine** bases consisting of a single hexagonal ring. Adenine and guanine, on the other hand, are **purine** bases consisting of a hexagonal ring joined to a pentagonal ring (figure 39.7). The

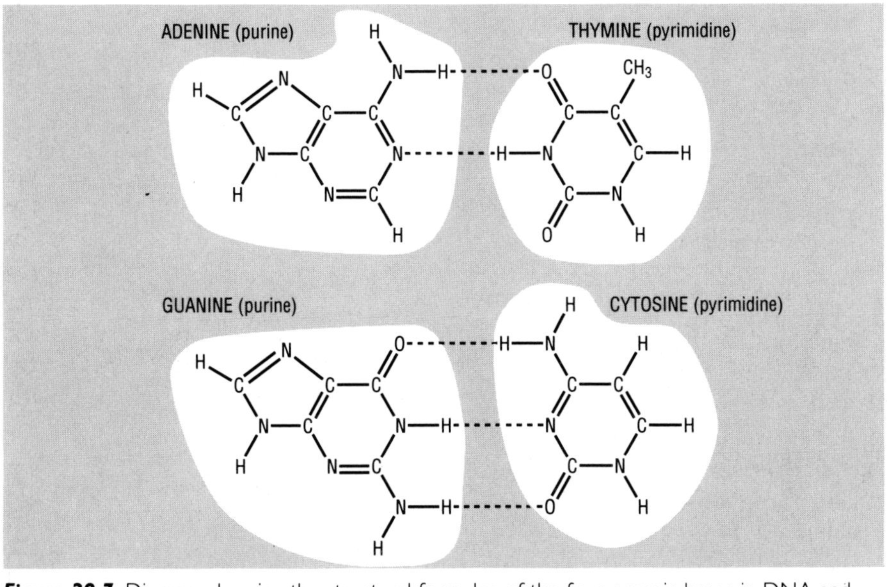

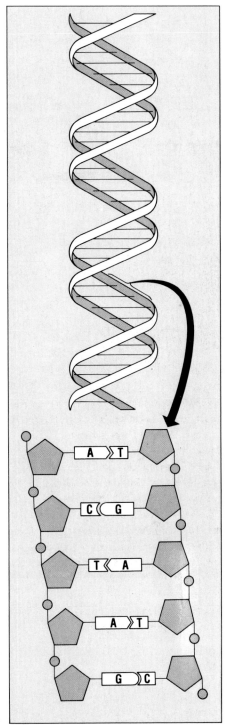

Figure 39.6 The Watson-Crick model of DNA. At the top is shown a short length of the double helix: the two strands are cross-linked at intervals by hydrogen bonds, ten cross-linkages for every complete turn of the spiral. Below is shown a short length of the DNA helix untwisted to show the positions of the sugars, phosphates and organic bases (**A**, **C, G** and **T**) in the two strands. Note that **A** pairs with **T**, and **C** with **G**.

Figure 39.7 Diagram showing the structural formulae of the four organic bases in DNA and how they form hydrogen bonds with one another. The configuration of the molecules is such that two hydrogen bonds are formed between **A** and **T**, and three between **C** and **G**. In RNA uracil replaces thymine. Uracil's structure is the same as thymine's except that the CH₃ group of the latter is replaced by H. **U** therefore links with **A** just as **T** does.

rungs in the DNA ladder can only be formed by linking a purine with a pyrimidine. The sizes of the four bases are such that there would be insufficient room for two purines and too much room for two pyrimidines. The bases in each rung are held together by hydrogen bonds. The positions of the hydrogen atoms in relation to the shape of the molecule ensure that **A** links with **T**, and **C** with **G**, rather like the fitting together of complementary pieces in a jig-saw puzzle. The net result is two long intertwined chains of nucleotides as shown in the computer graphics image of DNA in figure 39.8.

Figure 39.8 A computer graphics image of DNA showing the carbon (white), nitrogen (blue), oxygen (red) and phosphorus (green) atoms in their correct positions. Can you follow the two strands as they coil around one another?

The double helix

Model-building played an essential part in Watson and Crick's discovery of the structure of DNA. Here Watson reflects on the events which led to the building of their final model.

The following morning I felt marvelously alive when I awoke. On my way to the Whim I slowly walked toward the Clare Bridge, staring up at the gothic pinnacles of the King's College Chapel that stood out sharply against the spring sky. I briefly stopped and looked over at the perfect Georgian features of the recently cleaned Gibbs Building, thinking that much of our success was due to the long uneventful periods when we walked among the colleges or unobtrusively read the new books that came into Heffer's Bookstore. After contentedly poring over *The Times*, I wandered into the lab to see Francis, unquestionably early, flipping the cardboard base pairs about an imaginary line. As far as a compass and ruler could tell him, both sets of base pairs neatly fitted into the backbone configuration. As the morning wore on, Max and John successively came by to see if we still thought we had it. Each got a quick, concise lecture from Francis, during the second of which I wandered down to see if the shop could be speeded up to produce the purines and pyrimidines later that afternoon.

Only a little encouragement was needed to get the final soldering accomplished in the next couple of hours. The brightly shining metal plates were then immediately used to make a model in which for the first time all the DNA components were present. In about an hour I had arranged the atoms in positions which satisfied both the X-ray data and the laws of stereochemistry. The resulting helix was right-handed with two chains running in opposite directions.

Only one person can easily play with a model, and so Francis did not try to check my work until I backed away and said that I thought everything fitted. While one interatomic contact was slightly shorter than optimal, it was not out of line with several published values, and I was not disturbed. Another fifteen minutes' fiddling by Francis failed to find anything wrong, though for brief intervals my stomach felt uneasy when I saw him frowning. In each case he became satisfied and moved on to verify that another interatomic contact was reasonable. Everything thus looked very good when we went back to have supper with Odile.

From *The Double Helix* by James D. Watson (Weidenfeld and Nicolson, 1968).

The Francis to whom Watson refers is of course Francis Crick. Max and John are Max Perutz and John Kendrew who discovered the molecular structure of haemoglobin and myoglobin respectively. Odile is Francis Crick's wife and the Whim is a restaurant in Cambridge.

DNA replication

It was said at the outset of this chapter that an essential property of the genetic material is that it should be able to replicate accurately. Watson and Crick realised that an attractive feature of their model was that it provided a possible method of replication. This is illustrated in figure 39.9.

It isn't difficult to imagine the two chains separating from each other rather like a zip unfastening – it should be remembered that hydrogen bonds (which link the bases of one chain with the bases of the other) are not very strong. Any free nucleotides would then come along and form hydrogen bonds with each of the two chains. If these nucleotides then joined together through their sugar and phosphate groups, two DNA molecules would result. The complementary relationship between the bases would ensure that each of these DNA molecules was identical to the original one. Because the sequence of bases in the two daughter molecules is exactly the same as in the parent molecule, accurate replication will have occurred, just as is required.

What evidence is there that accurate replication of DNA does indeed take place? If the hypothesis is correct then we should be able to demonstrate DNA synthesis *in vitro* outside the cell. All that should be needed for this is a liberal sprinkling of the four types of nucleotide, an energy source (ATP), the enzyme needed to join together neighbouring nucleotides and a quantity of intact DNA to act as the **template** for the synthesis of new DNA.

The first successful attempt to replicate DNA in a test tube in this way was carried out by Arthur Kornberg, then at the University of Washington. This was a triumph of molecular biology. Kornberg's greatest difficulty was isolating the enzyme that joins the nucleotides together, but after overcoming great technical problems he managed to extract and purify the necessary enzyme from the colon bacillus *Escherichia coli*. He called the enzyme **DNA polymerase**. The stage was now set for the synthesis of DNA.

Kornberg and his colleagues found, just as predicted, that if intact DNA was added to a solution containing nucleotides, DNA polymerase and ATP, new DNA molecules were formed. Not only that, but on analysis the new DNA was found to have the same proportions of the four bases in its structure as the original parent DNA, a strong indication that accurate replication had occurred.

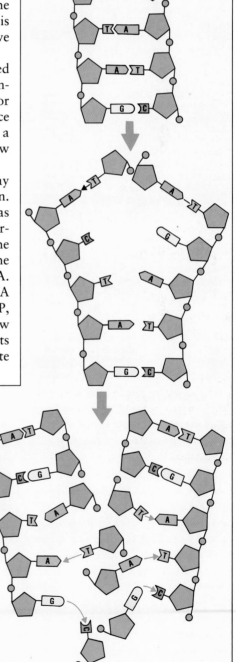

Figure 39.9 Replication of DNA. The two strands of the double helix part company and free nucleotides align themselves in relation to each of the two strands. The specific relationship between **A** and **T** and between **C** and **G** ensures that the sequence of bases in the daughter DNAs is exactly the same as in the parent DNA.

Parent DNA

Daughter DNA

Figure 39.10 Diagram comparing the two ways in which DNA might replicate. The original DNA is shown as thick lines, the new DNA strands as thin lines.

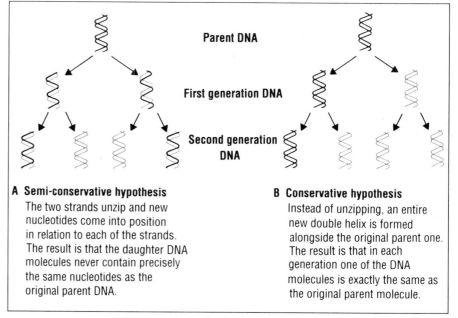

Parent DNA

First generation DNA

Second generation DNA

A Semi-conservative hypothesis
The two strands unzip and new nucleotides come into position in relation to each of the strands. The result is that the daughter DNA molecules never contain precisely the same nucleotides as the original parent DNA.

B Conservative hypothesis
Instead of unzipping, an entire new double helix is formed alongside the original parent one. The result is that in each generation one of the DNA molecules is exactly the same as the original parent molecule.

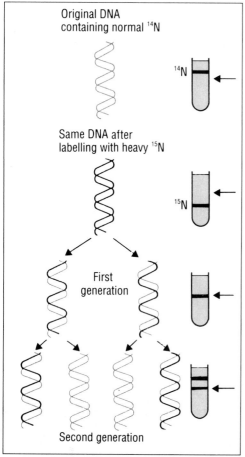

Original DNA containing normal ^{14}N

^{14}N

Same DNA after labelling with heavy ^{15}N

^{15}N

First generation

Second generation

Figure 39.11 The Meselson-Stahl experiment. On the right are shown the results of centrifuging the DNA from bacteria grown for many generations in ^{15}N and then transferred to ^{14}N. A band above the arrow indicates normal 'light' DNA; a band below the arrow indicates 'heavy' DNA , i.e. DNA containing ^{15}N; a band situated right on the arrow indicates equal amounts of 'light' and 'heavy' DNA. On the left is the interpretation in terms of DNA replication: the 'heavy' DNA (containing ^{15}N) is shown by thick lines, the normal DNA by thin lines. Notice that the interpretation supports the idea of semi-conservative replication and satisfactorily explains the results of the centrifugation.

Conservative versus semi-conservative replication

The zip-fastener idea is a neat and economical way of explaining replication, but it is not the only one. For instance, another possibility is to suppose that the double helix remains intact and in some way stimulates the synthesis of a second double helix identical with the first.

These two alternative hypotheses were put to the test in the late 1950s by Matthew Meselson and Franklin Stahl in a classic investigation which admirably demonstrates the scientific principles of hypothesis-making and testing.

If the zip-fastener hypothesis is correct neither of the products of DNA replication should be completely new; rather, in both daughter DNA molecules one of the two strands should be new, while the other should be one of the two parental strands. On the other hand, if the second hypothesis is correct, one of the two daughter DNAs will be completely new, while the other one will be the original parent molecule.

These two hypotheses are sumarised in figure 39.10 and are known as the **semi-conservative hypothesis** and **conservative hypothesis** respectively. To decide between these two hypotheses, Meselson and Stahl designed an elegant experiment involving *E. coli*.

Cells of *E. coli* were grown for many generations on a medium in which normal nitrogen, ^{14}N, was replaced with the heavy isotope, ^{15}N. Once enough time had passed for most of the nitrogen atoms in the DNA molecules of *E. coli* to be of the heavy type, the bacteria were introduced into a new medium containing normal ^{14}N. Samples of bacteria were then withdrawn at time intervals equal to the generation time, and the relative amounts of the two types of nitrogen estimated by a technique which relied on the fact that molecules containing ^{15}N are very slightly heavier than those containing ^{14}N. Ultracentrifugation was used to separate the DNA molecules according to the ratio of ^{14}N to ^{15}N that they contained.

The results, shown in figure 39.11, give unequivocal support to the semi-conservative (zip-fastener) hypothesis. In the first generation after being switched back to normal ^{14}N, the DNA was found to have a density midway between what it would have if it contained only ^{14}N or only ^{15}N; in other words it contained equal amounts of each. In the second generation, two sorts of DNA were detected: one sort contained only ^{14}N; the other sort was the same as that obtained in the first generation, i.e. it contained equal amounts of ^{14}N and ^{15}N. These results fit in perfectly with what we would expect from the semi-conservative hypothesis.

DNA replication and mitosis

It has long been known from special staining techniques and isotope labelling that in eukaryotes DNA occurs in the chromosomes. In fact a chromosome is essentially an enormously long length of double-stranded DNA coiled on itself and accompanied by certain special proteins and some RNA (see page 736). From the well established fact that the amount of DNA in the nucleus doubles during interphase, it is known that DNA replication takes place before mitosis, i.e. before the chromatids become visible. By the time prophase of mitosis begins, each of the two chromatids that make up a chromosome contains a single double helix derived by DNA replication from the parent chromosome. By separating the chromatids into two daughter cells, mitosis ensures that the products of cell division contain exactly the same complement of DNA as the parent cell did before DNA replication.

The essential role of DNA

So far in this chapter we have considered the evidence that DNA is the molecule of heredity. But how are the instructions that are embodied in DNA translated into action?

To answer this question we must first appreciate what exactly responds to DNA's instructions. An analogy may be helpful here. An architect's plan may contain all the information for building a house. The complete set of instructions may be contained on a few sheets of paper. However, if the house is to be built, these instructions must be interpreted and put into action by a builder. With nothing more than the building blocks of the house and the architect's blueprint, the builder must be able to construct the house exactly as the architect intended. In the same way the coded information in DNA must be interpreted and translated into action in the cell.

DNA and protein synthesis

There is every reason to believe that the essential link between DNA and the functioning cell is provided by proteins. In earlier chapters we have seen how everything a cell does – what it develops into, what it synthesises and how it operates – is determined by, more than anything, its enzymes and other proteins. It is not surprising therefore that the central role of DNA, apart from replicating itself, is to tell the cell what proteins to make.

As long ago as the 1940s George Beadle and Edward Tatum showed that genes control the production of enzymes. Beadle and Tatum, then at Stanford University in California, were interested in the genetics of the bread mould *Neurospora crassa* (figure 39.12). They found that this mould would thrive on a minimal medium containing nothing but minerals, sucrose and the vitamin biotin. Evidently the mould could synthesise all its other organic compounds from these few precursors.

Beadle and Tatum subjected samples of this mould to radiation treatment and found as a consequence that some of the progeny failed to grow on the minimal medium. By systematically testing the growth of these mutants on different media, Beadle and Tatum discovered that each had acquired an inability to synthesise one specific organic compound. For instance, one mutant could only grow if provided with the amino acid

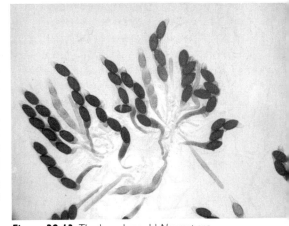

Figure 39.12 The bread mould *Neurospora crassa* showing its reproductive bodies (asci) with spores inside. In a classic experiment in the 1940s, George Beadle and Edward Tatum used *Neurospora* to show that genes control the production of enzymes.

arginine; another mutant could only grow if the medium contained ornithine.

When Beadle and Tatum crossed these mutants with normal moulds able to grow on the minimal medium, they found that the inability to synthesise the extra chemical was transmitted in a normal Mendelian manner. Beadle and Tatum suggested that the mutants lacked specific enzymes. For example, they hypothesised that the mould that could only grow on the medium supplemented with arginine lacked an enzyme required for the synthesis of arginine from simpler precursors. Beadle and Tatum therefore put forward the hypothesis that a single gene controls the production of a single enzyme, the **one gene-one enzyme hypothesis**.

Beadle and Tatum's experiment, a classic in the history of genetics, is summarised in figure 39.13.

Figure 39.13 Beadle and Tatum's experiment on the bread mould *Neurospora crassa*, on which the one gene-one enzyme hypothesis is based. Irradiation with X-rays occasionally produces mutant strains which are incapable of growing on a minimal medium because they cannot synthesise one of their required organic compounds, such as an amino acid. The particular organic compound may be identified by systematically testing the mutant's growth on a series of media each of which is supplemented with a different organic compound. In the case illustrated here, the mutant fails to grow on the first 19 media, but grows on the 20th, indicating that the organic compound added to the minimal medium to make up this medium, compound T, is the one which the mutant cannot make for itself. Like many other micro-organisms, *Neurospora* is haploid, each individual possessing a single allele rather than a pair as in diploid organisms. Crossing this mutant with a normal mould able to grow on the minimal medium produces spores, half of which are able to grow on the minimal medium and half of which can only grow on a medium to which T has been added. The defect is therefore transmitted in a Mendelian fashion, suggesting that the enzyme responsible for the synthesis of T is controlled by a single gene.

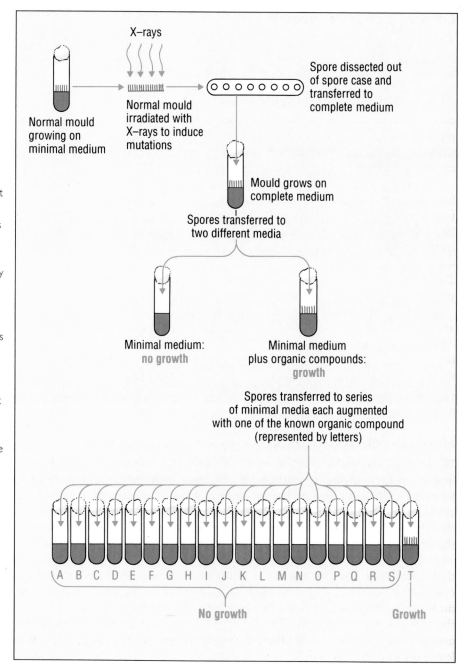

Numerous experiments on the biochemistry and genetics of micro-organisms have confirmed the general validity of this idea. Indeed we now know that the same is true of *all* organisms including ourselves. For example, albinism in humans (see page 682) has been shown to be the result of the absence of a specific enzyme.

From studies of proteins such as haemoglobin it is now realised that genes control the production not only of enzymes but of other proteins as well. Moreover, a single protein may contain several polypeptides. Unless they are identical, these polypeptides will be the result of different genes. In view of this it would be more accurate to restate Beadle and Tatum's hypothesis as the **one gene-one polypeptide hypothesis**. Even this is an over-simplification as it is now known that not all genes code for polypeptides. Some carry out other functions, as we shall see later.

DNA as a code for proteins

The principal role of DNA, then, is to instruct the cell to make specific proteins. How might this be done? A protein may contain up to 500 amino acids of 20 different types. It is the order in which these amino acids are arranged and their relative abundance that gives a particular protein its individuality. Somehow the DNA with its four different bases has got to determine the sequence in which the 20 different types of amino acid are put together in the protein. The question is: how can a four-letter code (for that is what DNA amounts to) specify a protein which at any given point can contain one of 20 different amino acids?

Clearly a single base cannot specify a single amino acid, for then only four different amino acids could be coded for, and proteins containing only four kinds of amino acids would be formed. Nor is it feasible for just two bases to specify a single amino acid since only 16 amino acids could be coded for (4 x 4 = 16). But three bases is sufficient: with these a total of 4 x 4 x 4 = 64 bases can be specified, more than enough to account for the 20 different amino acids commonly found in cells. Of course, four bases would give even more possibilities (how many?), but this is unnecessary.

Clearly the minimum number of bases which between them can specify an amino acid is three. We are thus faced with the proposition that a combination of three bases codes for one amino acid. This suggestion was first put forward by Francis Crick on purely theoretical grounds, but since then a firm body of experimental evidence has been established to support it. A triplet of bases is known as a **codon**; codons form the basis of the genetic code.

How does DNA communicate with the cytoplasm?

We are now confronted with the problem of how the instructions embodied in this **triplet code** are carried out by the cell. Look at it this way. DNA is located in the chromosomes in the nucleus, yet proteins are made in the cytoplasm on ribosomes (see page 156). Somehow the information held by the triplets of bases in the DNA has got to be conveyed from the nucleus to the sites of protein synthesis in the cytoplasm.

How might this happen? There are really only two possibilities. One is that the DNA itself, or part of it, moves out from the nucleus into the cytoplasm. The other is that the DNA stays in the nucleus and another molecule, acting as a go-between or messenger, carries instructions from the DNA to the cytoplasm. The first hypothesis may be discounted on the grounds that chromosomal DNA is never detected in the cytoplasm, which leaves us with the second.

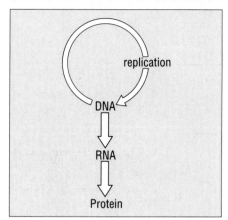

Figure 39.14 The central dogma of molecular genetics is that information flows from DNA to RNA and from RNA to protein. In addition DNA is capable of self-replication.

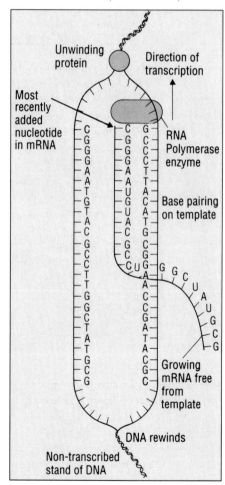

Figure 39.15 Diagrammatic representation of the synthesis of messenger RNA by DNA. When the DNA molecule unwinds, RNA nucleotides pair with one of the exposed strands of DNA which serves as a template. These nucleotides are then joined together by the enzyme RNA polymerase, resulting in messenger RNA.

We now know that DNA in the nucleus acts as the basis or **template** for the production of another sort of nucleic acid called **messenger RNA**. Messenger RNA gets its name from its ability to convey the instructions needed for protein synthesis from the nucleus to the cytoplasm. It is similar in structure to DNA in that it is made up of a string of nucleotides. However, it differs from DNA in four ways:

- It contains the sugar ribose instead of deoxyribose.
- It is single-stranded rather than double-stranded.
- It contains the base uracil instead of thymine.
- It is much shorter than DNA, usually containing fewer than a thousand nucleotides.

The idea that DNA makes protein via an intermediate, RNA, is known as the **central dogma of molecular genetics** (figure 39.14). Enshrined in this law is the notion that information can only flow from DNA to proteins, not from proteins to DNA. In other words, changes in DNA may change the resulting proteins, but changes in proteins cannot feed back and change the DNA.

Formation of messenger RNA

How is messenger RNA formed? Before attempting to answer this question let us think about what messenger RNA has to do. A typical polypeptide might contain 200 amino acids. The instructions required for assembling such a molecule will involve 600 bases. However, a typical chromosome contains millions of bases. This means that a given messenger RNA molecule is required to carry instructions from only a very short section of a DNA molecule. The sequence of bases in the messenger RNA must exactly match the sequence of bases in this short section of DNA.

Bearing in mind how DNA replicates (see page 715) you may be able to suggest how DNA makes RNA. The process is illustrated in figure 39.15. The double-stranded DNA first untwists and then unzips in the relevant region. Free RNA nucleotides then align themselves opposite one of the two strands. Because of the complementary relationship between the bases in DNA and free nucleotides, cytosine in the DNA attracts a guanine, guanine a cytosine, thymine an adenine, and adenine a uracil. An enzyme called **RNA polymerase** then joins these nucleotides together, resulting in the synthesis of messenger RNA. The whole process is known as **transcription**: *DNA has been transcribed into RNA*.

Once assembled, the messenger RNA molecule peels off its DNA template and moves out of the nucleus into the cytoplasm via the pores in the nuclear envelope. Meanwhile the relevant section of the DNA zips up and twists itself back into a helix again. Note that the sequence of bases in the messenger RNA molecule is the same as that of one of the two strands of the DNA – the one which did not act as the template. The only difference is that RNA has uracil where DNA has thymine.

Protein synthesis

When messenger RNA gets out into the cytoplasm it attaches itself to a ribosome where it causes amino acids to assemble in the right order. This it does with the help of yet another kind of nucleic acid called **transfer RNA**.

Transfer RNAs take their name from their function: they *transfer* or carry amino acids to ribosomes. They are comparatively small molecules and, unlike messenger RNA which is usually linear in shape, they are folded back on themselves to form a compact three-dimensional structure shaped rather like a clover leaf (figure 39.16). Their most important property is that they can bind to amino acids at one end and to messenger RNA at the other.

It has been shown that cells possess over 20 different types of transfer RNA – more than enough for the different amino acids. What happens is shown in figure 39.17. The **amino acid binding site** of the transfer RNA is attached by an enzyme to a specific amino acid. The transfer RNA and accompanying amino acid then move to the messenger RNA on the ribosome. The three bases at the **messenger RNA binding site** then form hydrogen bonds with the appropriate three bases in the messenger RNA molecule. The three bases in the messenger RNA are the codon, and the corresponding bases in the transfer RNA comprise the **anticodon**.

In this way the amino acids are linked up in an order corresponding to the sequence of base triplets in the messenger RNA. As the latter is determined by the sequence of base triplets in the original DNA, it follows that the base sequence in the DNA determines the order in which amino acids line up on the ribosome.

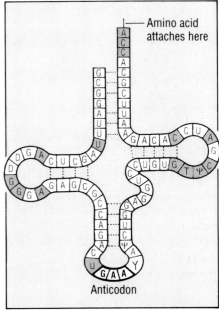

Figure 39.16 The structure of a transfer RNA. The molecule has been untwisted, so it appears here as a flat molecule shaped like a clover leaf. In all there are over 20 different sorts of transfer RNAs in each cell. Some nucleotides occupy the same positions in all transfer RNAs; these are shown in grey. The other nucleotides vary according to the particular transfer RNA. The symbols D, γ, Ψ and T represent unusual nucleotides characteristic of transfer RNAs. Base pairings occur only in certain regions as shown. The three bases at the bottom constitute the messenger RNA binding site, or anticodon. They form hydrogen bonds with the appropriate triplet of bases in messenger RNA. The amino acid binding site is at the top of the molecule.

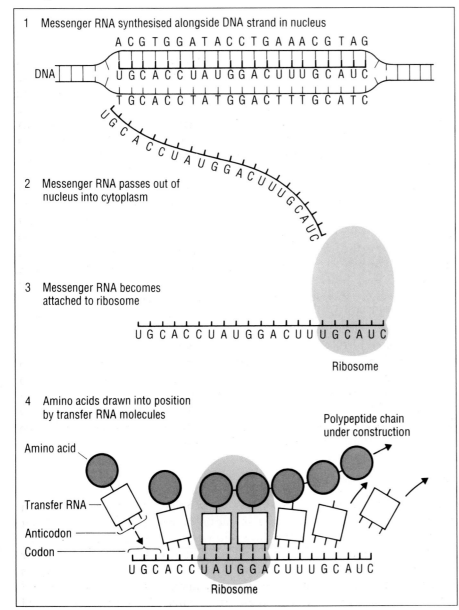

Figure 39.17 Diagram summarising how DNA in the nucleus controls the assembly of a polypeptide in the cytoplasm. Through the action of transfer RNA, the messenger RNA dictates the order in which amino acids link up to form the polypeptide chain. The anticodons at the ends of the transfer RNA molecules complement the codons (base triplets) in the messenger RNA. Thus the anticodon belonging to the left-hand transfer RNA molecule in this diagram is ACG. In this diagram the transfer RNA molecules are represented as squares; in reality they are shaped like clover leaves as shown in figure 39.16.

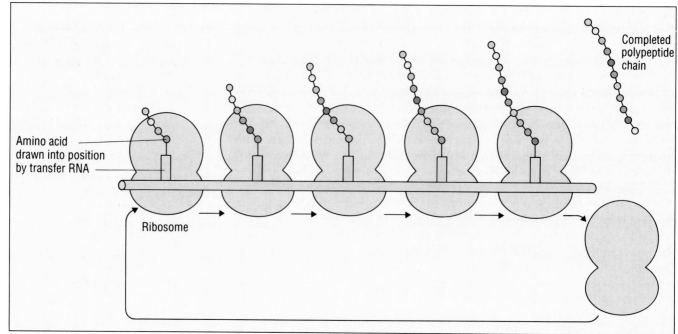

Figure 39.18 How a polyribosome works. A series of ribosomes moves along a messenger RNA molecule (or the messenger RNA moves along a chain of ribosomes – depending on how you look at it). Each ribosome synthesises a polypeptide molecule as it moves along the mesenger RNA. Transfer RNA molecules draw the appropriate amino acids into position as the ribosome passes each triplet of bases in the messenger RNA. When the ribosome reaches the end of the RNA strand it releases its polypeptide chain and returns to the beginning.

Once aligned, peptide bonds are formed sequentially between adjacent amino acids and a polypeptide chain is eventually formed. The process of assembly starts at one end of the chain, the end with a free amino group, and proceeds, amino acid by amino acid, to the other end - the end with a free carboxyl group. As the amino acids join up, the completed polypeptide chain peels off from the transfer RNA molecules. The job of the transfer RNAs complete, they detach themselves from the messenger RNA and return to the pool of transfer RNAs in the cytoplasm, from which they can be drawn upon again when required.

As might be expected, the process described above requires energy and this is provided by ATP and related compounds. A large proportion of the fuel our bodies burn up is needed for protein synthesis. Enzymes too are involved at various stages, for instance to attach the amino acids to the transfer RNAs, and to join the adjacent amino acids together.

Earlier we said that the synthesis of messenger RNA from DNA is known as transcription. The synthesis of proteins from messenger RNA is known as **translation**: *messenger RNA has been translated into protein.*

The role of the ribosomes

The function of the ribosomes is to provide a suitable surface for attachment of messenger RNA and the assembly of protein. But there is more to them than this. Ribosomes may occur in chains called **polyribosomes**. Under the electron microscope a polyribosome is seen to consist of five to 50 individual ribosomes. Special staining techniques show that they lie on a single strand of messenger RNA.

How does a polyribosome function in protein synthesis? What seems to happen is that a ribosome attaches itself near one end of a messenger RNA strand and then progresses towards the other end (figure 39.18). As the ribosome passes a triplet of bases the appropriate transfer RNA molecule takes up position, bringing its amino acid with it. The ribosome then moves on to the next section of the messenger RNA strand and another amino acid is drawn into position, and so on. As the ribosome moves along the messenger RNA, more and more amino acids are added to the growing polypeptide chain. Meanwhile the other ribosomes follow suit so that several ribosomes may move along the messenger RNA strand simultaneously, each synthesising a polypeptide chain as it does so. On reaching the end of the messenger RNA strand the ribosome drops off and releases its polypeptide chain.

The advantage of polyribosomes is that they allow a large number of polypeptides to be made from a single messenger RNA strand in a comparatively short time. It has been calculated that in red blood cells, for example, the time required for a single ribosome to travel the full length of a messenger RNA strand and produce a completed polypeptide chain is about one minute. By having ten or more ribosomes at any one time making proteins from a single messenger RNA strand, the rate of protein synthesis is greatly increased. In bacterial cells protein synthesis happens even more rapidly. This is because prokaryotes lack a nucleus and protein synthesis can begin even before messenger RNA synthesis is complete.

Is the code overlapping or non-overlapping?

Consider the following hypothetical sequence of bases in a short length of messenger RNA:

ACUGAC

If the code is non-overlapping, this sequence would consist of two codons one after the other like this:

ACUGAC

and obviously only two amino acids could be coded for. However, it is possible that the codons might overlap like this:

ACUGAC

in which case four amino acids would be coded for. A less compact sort of overlapping code would be one in which the codons overlap like this:

AGUGAC

The main advantage of an overlapping code is that it would permit a small number of bases to code for a relatively large number of amino acids, and this would enable an entire polypeptide to be programmed by a relatively short length of DNA. On the other hand, an overlapping code would impose a constraint on the sequencing of the amino acids. For instance, in the first example of an overlapping code above, as the first amino acid is coded by ACU, the second one will have to be coded by a triplet whose first two bases are CU, and so on. Obviously this will limit the flexibility of the code.

This limitation is the main theoretical argument against the code being an overlapping one. But there is convincing empirical evidence against it too. Geneticists have been able to make synthetic RNAs in the laboratory. If, for example, synthetic messenger RNA consisting only of uracil nucleotides is added to a cell-free suspension of ribosomes, ATP, the necessary enzymes and a large number of amino acids, the resulting polypeptide consists of nothing but the amino acid phenylalanine.

Now this does not tell us whether or not the code is non-overlapping. It just means that the triplet UUU codes for phenylalanine. However, when the experiment is repeated with a messenger RNA possessing the base

More about ribosomes

Ribosomes consist of protein combined with a type of RNA known as **ribosomal RNA**. The structure responsible for the manufacture of ribosomes is the **nucleolus**. Abnormal cells lacking nucleoli fail to manufacture ribosomal RNA, and are thus unable to make ribosomes.

Ribosomes usually exist in the cytoplasm in two sub-units, a smaller one called a **40 S sub-unit**, and a larger one called a **60 S sub-unit**. (S is a unit of size.) Both contain numerous protein molecules together with ribosomal RNA.

The illustration shows a eukaryotic ribosome bound to rough endoplasmic reticulum. Unbound ribosomes are also found throughout the cytoplasm. Generally proteins which are secreted from cells are synthesised on bound ribosomes, whereas those which remain in the cytosol are made on free ribosomes.

Ribosomes are also found in prokaryotes and in mitochondria and chloroplasts. They are smaller than the ribosomes found in the cytoplasm of eukaryotic cells, though they too consist of two sub-units and are involved in protein synthesis.

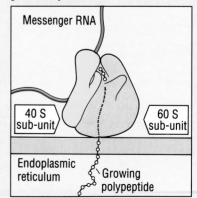

A ribosome attached to the endoplasmic reticulum helping to synthesise a polypeptide.

sequence GUAGUAGUAGUA and so on, the polypeptide that results consists only of valines. This suggests that the code is a non-overlapping one, being read in this instance as GUA, GUA, GUA, GUA. Had the code been overlapping it would have been read as GUA, UAG, AGU, GUA ... or perhaps as GUA, AGU, UAG, GUA ... In either case we might have expected the resulting polypeptide to consist of more than one amino acid.

The genetic dictionary

Painstaking work of the sort just described resulted, in 1966, in the complete elucidation of the genetic code, a triumph of modern biology. Table 39.2 summarises the **genetic dictionary**. It shows the relationship between the triplets of bases in messenger RNA (i.e. the codons) and the amino acids that are translated from the messenger RNA code. From this you should be able to work out the relationship between the bases in the original DNA and the amino acids that result.

You can see that most of the amino acids are coded for by more than one codon. So the code contains more potential information than is actually used by the cell: to use the cybernetic term, the code is **degenerate**. Three of the codons do not actually code for an amino acid. Instead they stop the polypeptide chain at that point, acting as **termination signals**. These stop codons play an essential role in the cell, allowing polypeptides of precisely the right length to be produced.

Although the code is non-overlapping, certain viruses have found ways to squeeze additional information out of their relatively small supply of DNA. In some cases, genes overlap. That is, the start of one gene overlaps with the end of another, allowing the overlapping portion to be used both

Table 39.2 The genetic dictionary. The messenger RNA codons corresponding to the twenty amino acids made by translation on the ribosomes are shown in this genetic dictionary. Three codons act as stop codons, and under certain conditions the codon AUG initiates protein synthesis. The dictionary is known to hold for almost all organisms. Other, rarer, amino acids are made by cells from the amino acids listed here.

Ala	=	alanine
Arg	=	arginine
Asn	=	asparagine
Asp	=	aspartic acid
Cys	=	cysteine
Gln	=	glutamine
Glu	=	glutamic acid
Gly	=	glycine
His	=	histidine
Ile	=	isoleucine
Leu	=	leucine
Lys	=	lysine
Met	=	methionine
Phe	=	phenylalanine
Pro	=	proline
Ser	=	serine
Thr	=	threonine
Try	=	tryptophan
Tyr	=	tyrosine
Val	=	valine

Second base

First base

First base	U	C	A	G	Third base
U	UUU, UUC } Phe; UUA, UUG } Leu	UCU, UCC, UCA, UCG } Ser	UAU, UAC } Tyr; UAA Stop; UAG Stop	UGU, UGC } Cys; UGA Stop; UGG Trp	U C A G
C	CUU, CUC, CUA, CUG } Leu	CCU, CCC, CCA, CCG } Pro	CAU, CAC } His; CAA, CAG } Gln	CGU, CGC, CGA, CGG } Arg	U C A G
A	AUU, AUC, AUA } Ile; AUG Met	ACU, ACC, ACA, ACG } Thr	AAU, AAC } Asn; AAA, AAG } Lys	AGU, AGC } Ser; AGA, AGG } Arg	U C A G
G	GUU, GUC, GUA, GUG } Val	GCU, GCC, GCA, GCG } Ala	GAU, GAC } Asp; GAA, GAG } Glu	GGU, GGC, GGA, GGG } Gly	U C A G

for the end of one protein and the beginning of another. In at least one case an even more remarkable adaptation is found. The same piece of DNA is read in one direction to produce one sort of protein and in the *other* direction to produce another sort of protein.

To illustrate this latter adaptation suppose that part of the DNA sequence is ACTTCGCAGGCA. Now work out the messenger RNA that results and then use table 39.2 to determine the two amino acid sequences that this messenger RNA can be translated into, depending on whether it is read forwards or backwards. As the primary structure of this second protein is effectively determined by the primary structure of the first, it seems extraordinary that both proteins serve a useful function, but they do.

Introns and exons

In 1977 the exact sequence of bases in the gene that codes for the ß chain of haemoglobin was determined for the first time. Much to everyone's surprise it turned out that the β-haemoglobin gene contains two regions of DNA whose base sequence did not correspond to the known amino acid sequence of β-haemoglobin. Further study revealed that the entire gene is transcribed into messenger RNA, but some of the RNA is cut out and discarded before translation occurs. Altogether, 670 of the 1660 bases are discarded as shown in the illustration.

In the illustration, the portions of the DNA that end up coding for amino acids are shown in white. These *expressed* portions of DNA are known as **exons**. The pieces of DNA that code for those sections of messenger RNA that are removed before translation are shaded. These unused pieces of messenger RNA are, in a sense, *interruptions* and are called **introns**.

What is the function of these introns? The simplest hypothesis is to suppose that they are parasitic bits of DNA, of no benefit to the rest of the cell, but just hanging in there, ensuring that they get reproduced generation after generation. Another interpretation is to suppose that they have some function, even if it is not to code for the amino acids in β-haemoglobin.

What, then, might be their function? We now know that there is a type of blood disease that can result from a mutation in one of the introns of the β-haemoglobin gene. The abnormal allele has a thymine instead of the usual guanine 19 bases away from the junction of the first intron with the second exon. The presence of the thymine does not affect transcription but causes the messenger RNA to be improperly edited and spliced before it is exported from the nucleus to the cytoplasm for translation. The net result is that although the first 29 amino acids of the polypeptide are correct, there then follow 6 incorrect amino acids and then the polypeptide stops. A normal β-haemoglobin molecule contains 141 amino acids. So the incorporation of a single faulty base in one of the introns causes a short defective β-haemoglobin to be released. A person homozygous for this mutation suffers from **thalassemia major** which results in severe anaemia, growth retardation and a number of other abnormalities. This tells us that, at least in this case, the intron does serve a useful function.

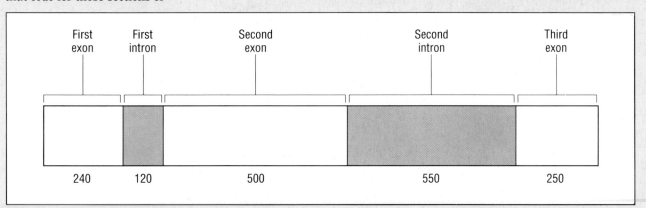

Diagrammatic representation of the region of human DNA that codes for β-haemoglobin. The white areas are exons, the shaded areas introns. The figures refer to the number of bases in each exon or intron.

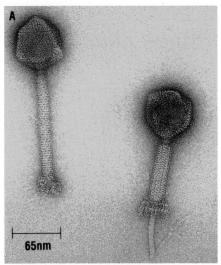

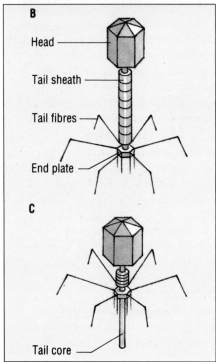

Figure 39.19

A Electron micrograph of bacteriophages before and after injecting their genetic material into the host.

B Diagram of a bacteriophage before injecting its genetic material into its host. The head, a bipyramidal hexagonal prism, contains a long coiled thread of DNA. The tail consists of a hollow tube (core) surrounded by a sheath. Attached to the distal end of the sheath is a hexagonal end plate from which six tail fibres project.

C Diagram of a bacteriophage after injecting its DNA into its host. The tail sheath has contracted, causing the tail core to be thrust into the body of the bacterium.

Viral reproduction and genetics

Much of the evidence for the role of DNA has come from the study of viruses that attack bacteria. These viruses are known as **bacteriophages** or just **phages**, from the Greek word for 'to eat' – meaning that they 'eat' bacteria. One species of bacteria readily infected by bacteriophages is the colon bacillus *Escherichia coli* which lives in the mammalian large intestine and can be quite easily cultured in the laboratory.

The structure of one sort of bacteriophage is shown in figure 39.19. Chemical analysis and electon microscopy show it to consist of DNA surrounded by a protein coat. A long thread of DNA containing about 150 genes is packed into a **head** from which a short **tail** projects. Though larger than the majority of viruses, bacteriophages are nevertheless exceedingly small, the head being only 65nm wide.

When a phage attacks a bacterium it adheres to the bacterial surface by its tail (figure 39.20). By a process which is analagous to the action of a hypodermic syringe, the DNA thread is injected into the bacterium where it proceeds to replicate prolifically. Under the influence of the viral DNA, new virus heads and tails are manufactured and then assembled within the

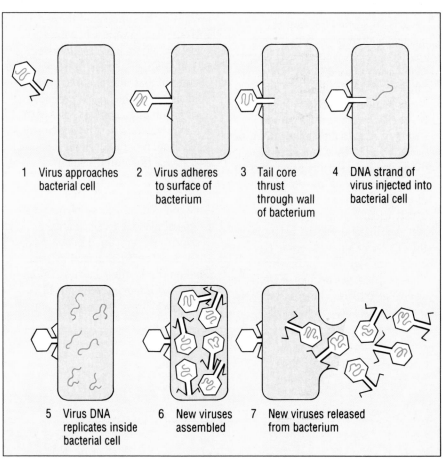

Figure 39.20 Life cycle of a bacteriophage. Only the viral DNA enters the bacterial cell, the protein coat remains outside. The viral DNA contains all the necessary instructions for directing the synthesis of new viruses within the bacterium. In reality far more viruses are formed than are shown here. All viruses work by taking over the biosynthetic machinery of their hosts, though the ways in which they do this are many. In the case of certain small viruses which attack animal cells, the whole virus enters the cell and then releases its nucleic acid strand. Plant viruses may be injected through the cell walls of the host's cells by insect vectors such as greenflies.

bacterial cell. After about 30 minutes the bacterium may burst open, releasing some 300 viruses which then repeat the process in other bacteria. Steps in the process can be followed in electron micrographs: two are shown in figure 39.21.

That the viral DNA alone is responsible for directing operations in the bacterial cell was demonstrated in 1952 by the American scientists Alfred Hershey and Martha Chase. In order to work out what was going on they took two samples of bacteriophage. In one they labelled the viral DNA with radioactive ^{32}P; in the other they labelled the protein of the head and tail with ^{35}S. This was made possible because DNA contains phosphorus but not sulphur, whereas protein contains sulphur but not phosphorus.

Hershey and Chase then took two cultures of *E. coli*. As shown in figure 39.22 they infected one of these cultures with phages that had their DNA labelled, and the other culture with phages that had their proteins labelled. After the phages had been given enough time to infect the bacteria, the bacteria were agitated in a blender so as to separate them from any viral coats attached to them. Centrifugation was then used to isolate the viral coats from the bacteria: the bacteria were thrown down to the bottom of the centrifugation tubes, whereas the viral coats stayed in the supernatant fluid.

Hershey and Chase found that in the ^{32}P experiment the infected bacteria contained a considerable amount of ^{32}P and were therefore highly radioactive. However, the supernatant fluid, containing the viral protein,

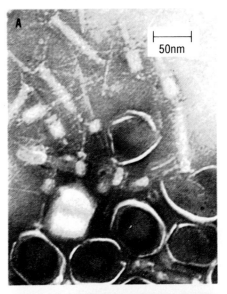

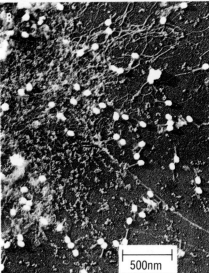

Figure 39.21

A Electron micrograph showing the component parts of bacteriophages before they are assembled in a bacterial cell.
B Electron micrograph showing the release of newly assembled viruses following rupture of the bacterial cell: notice the phage particles lying among the remains of the bacterial cytoplasm.

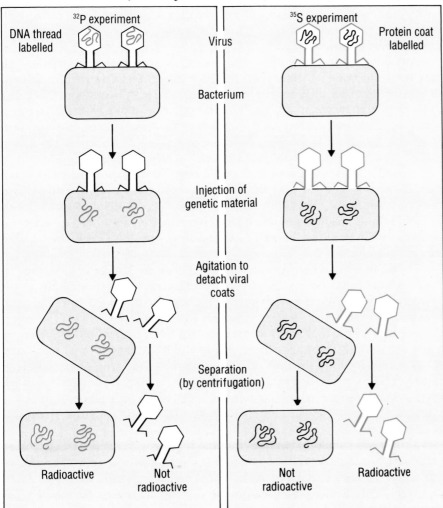

Figure 39.22 A summary of the experiments by Hershey and Chase which showed that DNA is the hereditary material of a virus. Radioactively labelled molecules are shown in red. These experiments showed that the DNA of the virus was injected into the host while the protein coat remained outside. This demonstrates that the DNA molecule contains all the information for the manufacture of new viral particles.

contained very little ^{32}P. On the other hand, in the ^{35}S experiment most of the labelled sulphur and radioactivity was confined to the virus coats, and very little was present in the infected bacterial cells.

The conclusion to be drawn from these results is that on infection only the viral DNA enters the bacterium, the protein coats being left behind. So the DNA alone must be responsible for directing the synthesis of new virus particles within the bacterial cell. The viral DNA takes over the entire metabolic machinery of the bacterium, suppressing its normal metabolism and causing it to manufacture new protein coats and nucleic acid threads identical with those of the invading phage.

More recent research has shown that not all viruses inject their DNA into the cell they attack. In some cases the whole virus enters the cell. Either way it is easy to see why viruses are often associated with disease.

Proviruses and the role of viruses in cancer

Viruses which actively attack and proliferate in cells are described as **virulent**. Sometimes, however, a virus may infect a cell and then remain in a quiescent state for a long period of time. Instead of replicating, the viral DNA inserts itself into the host's DNA, replicating only when the host's own DNA replicates. In this temperate state the virus is known as a **provirus**. A provirus exerts little influence over the cell, though it may prevent reinfection by another virus. Later on, the virus may lose its benign nature and give rise to a crop of new viruses which burst out of the cell. This is why some virus diseases, such as herpes, tend to recur even in the absence of reinfection.

As described in Chapter 31, some cancers are caused by viruses. You may remember that a cancer is basically a mass of cells that are growing out of control and dividing too much (see page 564). Viruses seem to cause cancers in two ways. First, some of the viral genes may make proteins which coincidentally affect the regulation of the host's genes, causing them to produce more of a certain type of messenger RNA. This may result in a protein being produced that causes the cell to grow and divide more.

Secondly, some viruses carry genes that they do not require for the manufacture of their own proteins. Rather, these genes cause the host cell to become cancerous. They do this by producing proteins which closely resemble those produced by the host to increase the rate of cell growth and division. Such genes are known as **oncogenes**, after the Greek word *onkos* meaning tumour.

How can a virus end up carrying genes that are almost identical to the host's genes? It has been suggested that some viral oncogenes are the result of messenger RNA from the host becoming incorporated into the viral genetic material, which in these viruses is RNA not DNA.

We now know that many viruses contain RNA instead of DNA as their genetic material. In some of these viruses the RNA functions as messenger RNA once it gets into the host cell, directing the production of viral protein. Other RNA viruses, known as **retroviruses**, possess an enzyme called **reverse transcriptase** which transcribes their RNA into DNA. The newly synthesised viral DNA then enters the host's DNA as a provirus, remaining in a temperate state for months or years.

Retroviruses include **Human Immunodeficiency Virus (HIV)** which can cause AIDS (see page 420). They do not conform to the central dogma of molecular genetics that DNA makes RNA makes protein (see figure 39.14 on page 720). Rather, they cause the central dogma to be modified as shown in figure 39.23.

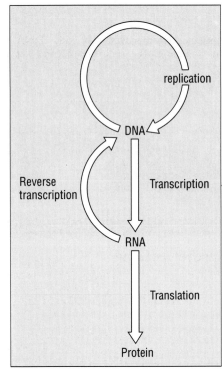

Figure 39.23 Some viruses have RNA instead of DNA as their genetic material. Such RNA viruses may contain the enzyme reverse transcriptase which allows them to make DNA from RNA. These viruses are known as retroviruses. The existence of such viruses causes the central dogma of molecular genetics to be modified – compare with figure 39.14 on page 720.

Summary

1 Experiments carried out by Avery on the bacterium *Pneumococcus* pointed to **deoxyribonucleic acid** being the carrier of genetic information.

2 Two types of **nucleic acid** exist in cells: **deoxyribonucleic acid (DNA)** and **ribonucleic acid (RNA)**. Both consist of chains of **nucleotides**. Each nucleotide consists of a **pentose sugar, phosphate group** and one of five **organic bases (A, C, G, T and U)**. DNA contains **A, C, G** and **T**; in RNA, **T** is replaced by **U**.

3 According to the **Watson-Crick hypothesis**, DNA is a **double helix** consisting of two coiled chains of alternating phosphate and sugar groups, the latter being connected by pairs of bases which form hydrogen bonds with each other in a specific way: **A** with **T**, and **C** with **G**.

4 During interphase, prior to cell division, DNA undergoes accurate **replication**, the mechanism being **semi-conservative**.

5 A **gene** can be looked on as a segment of the DNA chain. In general a single gene is responsible for the synthesis of a single polypeptide chain (originally known as the **one gene-one enzyme hypothesis**).

6 DNA controls protein synthesis by determining the order in which amino acids are linked together on the ribosomes. Each amino acid is coded for by a **triplet** of bases in the DNA.

7 In controlling protein synthesis, the relevant portion of DNA in the nucleus is first **transcribed** into **messenger RNA**. This then moves to the cytoplasm where, with the help of transfer **RNA**s, it is **translated** into protein. This is summed up in the **central dogma of molecular genetics** which says that DNA makes RNA makes protein.

8 Ribosomes are often found in chains called **polyribosomes**. These help to speed up the assembly of amino acids into polypeptides by moving in convoy along the mesenger RNA strand.

9 Ribosomes are made in the **nucleolus**.

10 Most amino acids are coded for by more than one triplet. The genetic code is therefore **degenerate**. Of the 64 base triplets, 61 code for amino acids; the other three act as **termination codons**.

11 The genetic code is **non-overlapping**, i.e. a given triplet codes for one amino acid, and none of its constituent bases codes for any other amino acid.

12 Generally only part of the DNA within a gene is expressed, i.e. used for protein synthesis. The parts that are expressed are called **exons**; the unused parts are called **introns**.

13 The potency of DNA in controlling protein synthesis can be seen in **viruses**, notably bacteriophages, whose nucleic acid can take over the metabolic machinery of the host cell.

14 Some viruses, known as **retroviruses**, can make DNA from RNA, thus causing the central dogma of molecular genetics to be modified.

Review questions

1 What are the essential features of DNA that make it suitable as the genetic material? Why are proteins unsuitable?

2 Why is DNA replication described as semi-conservative?

3 DNA exists as a double helix, yet in any one gene only one of the two strands is transcribed into messenger RNA. Why do you think DNA exists as a double rather than a single helix?

4 If Watson and Crick had not discovered the structure of DNA, someone else would have, possibly within a matter of months. Do you think they deserved a Nobel Prize for their work?

5 Outline the essential steps in DNA replication.

6 How many bases would there probably be in a codon if only two different bases existed and there were still 20 amino acids?

7 Suggest an advantage to a eukaryotic cell of having some of its ribosomes on the endoplasmic reticulum and some free in the cytosol.

8 By means of a table, summarise the differences between DNA, messenger RNA and transfer RNA in terms of structure and function.

9 Outline the essential steps in protein synthesis.

10 What do you think should be the status of the central dogma of molecular genetics? Should it be a law, a theory, an hypothesis or what?

Further reading

James D. Watson's *The Double Helix* (Penguin, 1968) is the classic and very personal account of the discovery of the structure of DNA. If you are doing biology and like reading, this is the book for you.

Francis Crick's *What Mad Pursuit: A Personal View of Scientific Discovery* (Penguin, 1988) is well worth reading partly because it gives his side of the DNA story and partly because it is more up to date than Watson's book.

Experimental evidence for the triplet code is presented in *Biology, Advanced Topics*.

CHAPTER 40   Gene action

In this chapter we shall look at how genes work. We shall see that although tremendous advances have been made in our understanding of the mechanism of gene action at the molecular level, we are still a long way from understanding the link between the working of individual genes and the development of whole organisms.

The development of a complex organism from the fertilised egg to the adult involves three things:

- An increase in the size of the organism.
- A progressive addition of visible complexity as **cell differentiation** proceeds.
- A highly ordered sequence of events in which the various cells, interacting with one another, differentiate at just the right time and in precisely the right place within the embryo.

For development to proceed appropriately, there must be an elaborate mechanism by which it is controlled both in space and time. To elucidate the nature of this mechanism is one of the central problems of developmental biology, and in this chapter we can do no more than touch on some of the basic issues involved.

The importance of the nucleus

Nowadays we are used to the idea that the genes on the chromosomes are responsible for a cell's structure and functioning. It is difficult to realise that the central role played by the nucleus only became apparent to biologists fairly recently. In the 1930s some elegant experiments were carried out by the German biologist Joachim Hämmerling who clarified the relative importance of the nucleus and the cytoplasm in determining a cell's shape.

Hämmerling worked on a marine alga called *Acetabularia* (figure 40.1). The advantage of this organism is that although it is unicellular, it is large. The cell consists of a 'cap', a stalk about 40 mm long, and a 'foot' which contains the nucleus. If the cap is removed, the cell soon regenerates a new one. Different species of *Acetabularia* have caps of different shapes. Hämmerling worked on *A. mediterranea* which has a cap shaped rather like an umbrella (figure 40.1), and on *A. crenulata* whose cap looks rather like a bunch of petals.

Figure 40.1 *Acetabularia mediterranea* used by Hämmerling in his studies on the roles of the nucleus and the cytoplasm in development.

This picture is about twice the natural size, so *Acetabularia* is quite a large organism. And yet it consists of only one cell with a single nucleus. So here we have a unicellular organism which is easy to see and experiment on.

Hämmerling took the stalk of *A. mediterranea* and grafted it onto a foot, containing the nucleus, of *A. crenulata*. The result was that a new cap grew with a shape intermediate between those of the two species. When this cap was removed, another cap was formed which had the shape of *A. crenulata* (figure 40.2). Hämmerling then did the reverse experiment: he took the stalk of *A. crenulata* and grafted it onto a foot of *A. mediterranea*. The new cap that grew was again intermediate between the two species. When this cap was removed, the next cap that formed had the shape of *A. mediterranea*.

Hämmerling concluded that chemicals which determine the shape of the cap are produced by the nucleus. These chemicals travel through the cytoplasm, which is why the first cap produced after the transplant is intermediate between the two species. By the time the second cap grows, the chemicals present in the cytoplasm from before the original transplant have been used up. As a result the new cap is entirely under the influence of the new nucleus.

The role of genes in development

Given that the nucleus plays a fundamental role in determining the structure and functioning of a cell, we come to the question of the part played by the genes during development. The problem is this. The cells of an adult multicellular organism, even those of an embryo, are highly specialised in structure and function. And yet all these cells are derived from one original single cell, the fertilised egg. In the last chapter we saw that the polypeptides made by a cell depend on its genetic code, that is on the sequence of nucleotides in the DNA in its nucleus. Now if we assume, as we did in Chapter 39, that DNA replicates completely and accurately prior to cell division, then it follows that all the cells of an adult should have exactly the same genetic make-up. So we are faced with a paradox. The cells of an adult differ from each other, yet their genes are the same.

There are two ways of getting round this difficulty. One is to suppose that the replication of DNA is not in fact complete and different genes are passed on to different cells at cell division. The second way is to suppose that all the cells in an adult do in fact contain the same genetic material, but that different genes are expressed in different cells at the various stages of development.

In order to decide between these two hypotheses an experiment can be done which is attractive in its simplicity and directness. Let us consider the theory behind the experiment before we get involved with the practical details. If it is true that the genetic code remains unaltered during development, a direct consequence is that all the nuclei of an embryo, or even an adult, must contain all the necessary genetic information required for producing a complete adult organism. This being so, it follows that if a nucleus is extracted from an embryo or adult and implanted into an egg which has had its own nucleus removed, the egg should give rise to a normal individual. All this assumes, of course, that such a finicky operation can be done without unduly damaging either the nucleus or the egg into which it is implanted.

By now you will have gathered that the ingenuity of biologists is almost boundless. It will therefore not surprise you to learn that this experiment has been done, and indeed is now a commonplace procedure in the laboratory. The operation was first performed successfully in 1952 by two American biologists, Robert Briggs of the University of Indiana and Thomas King of the Institute for Cancer Research in Philadelphia. They

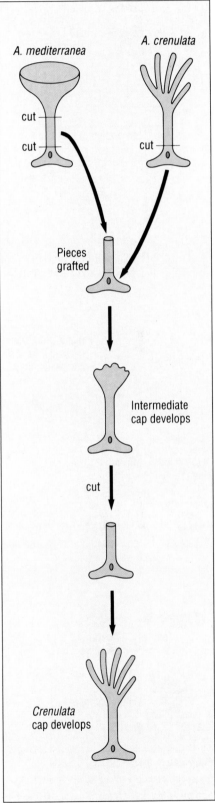

Figure 40.2 One of Hämmerling's experiments with the unicellular organism *Acetabularia*. The results suggest that cap shape is determined by the nucleus via a chemical which is carried in the cytoplasm.

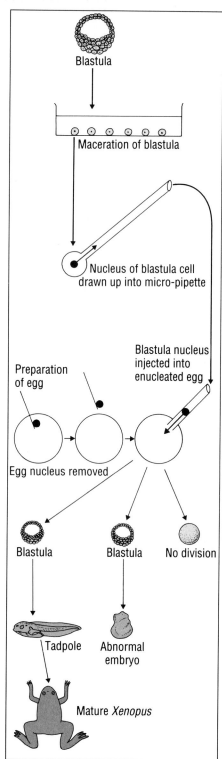

Figure 40.3 Briggs and King's method of transplanting nuclei in the toad *Xenopus*. A nucleus is extracted from a blastula cell and injected into an enucleated egg. The latter is found to develop normally in a significant number of cases though sometimes it gives rise to an abnormal embryo or does not develop at all.

used toads for their experiments.

Briefly, what Briggs and King did was to take a toad embryo at the late blastula stage (see page 625) and immerse it in a fluid which caused the cells to separate from one another (figure 40.3). A nucleus was then extracted from one of the cells by means of a micropipette. Meanwhile an egg was prepared for receiving the nucleus. Its nucleus was removed by means of a fine glass needle. This procedure was helped by the fact that at this stage the nucleus lies close to the edge of the egg cell. Now it only remained for the donor nucleus to be implanted into the enucleated egg. The egg was then left to develop.

This experiment has been repeated many times since Briggs and King first did it in 1952. Despite a high mortality rate at first, the results are now reasonably consistent. In general, nuclei obtained from late blastulae are capable of sustaining normal embryos which, on occasions, develop right through to adults. The conclusion is that at least up to the late blastula stage no irreversible changes occur in the genetic information contained within the nucleus.

But might it not be possible that genetic changes occur after the blastula stage? The most obvious way of testing this possibility is to repeat the experiment with nuclei taken from later stages. The technical difficulties are considerable, due partly to the delicacy and small size of the cells involved. However, in the late 1960s J.B. Gurdon of Oxford University found that when he took nuclei from the skin of an adult toad and injected them into enucleated eggs, a few of the eggs developed into tadpoles which subsequently metamorphosed into perfectly normal adults. In other words, a nucleus taken from a fully differentiated adult cell can direct the development of a complete animal.

The individuals produced by this technique are genetically identical to the individual from which the nucleus was taken: that is, the individuals are part of a **clone** (see page 568). This technique is therefore known as **nuclear cloning**. Such cloning cannot be done with humans. However, the time will no doubt come when it is feasible, though whether it is desirable is another matter.

A rather different kind of experiment has shown that in plants too adult cells contain the same genetic information as does the fertilised egg cell. In the 1950s F.C. Steward of Cornell University took mature cells from a carrot root and cultured them on their own. When reared in the right conditions they grew into complete new carrot plants (figure 40.4). In other

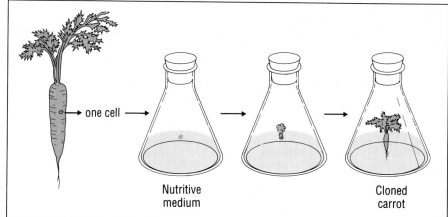

Figure 40.4 A single cell taken from a mature carrot can give rise to a new carrot plant. This suggests that the single adult cell contains the same genetic information as a newly fertilised egg cell.

words, a cell from a mature organ can go through the cell divisions and differentiations neccesary for the production of an entire adult plant. This technique is now of great commercial importance in plant breeding (see page 618).

What these experiments indicate is that the genetic code does not change during development. We may conclude that differentiation is brought about by different parts of the genetic code being used at different times and in different cells of an organism.

Gene switching

If different parts of the genetic code come into operation at different times as differentiation takes place, there must be a mechanism which ensures that the right parts of the code operate at the correct time. Such a mechanism must, in effect, *switch* the appropriate genes on or off, as and when they are required.

Before considering the evidence for this, it will help to look at an example to illustrate the basic idea. When adult, we have two sorts of haemoglobin chains in our red blood cells, α chains and β chains. In the fetus, however, γ chains are produced instead of β chains. The differences betwen the β and γ chains, though slight, are sufficient to confer the markedly different oxygen-carrying powers discussed in Chapter 19. At birth, the production of fetal haemoglobin (which consists of two α and two γ chains) ceases and is replaced over the next three months by adult haemoglobin (which consists of two α and two β chains) (figure 40.5).

Now there is strong evidence from genetic studies that the formation of each of these polypeptide chains is controlled by a single gene. This evidence comes mainly from studying people with abnormal sorts of haemoglobin. In every case the abnormalities are associated with a difference in the amino acids in one or other of the polypeptide chains. Pedigree analyses show that these abnormal haemoglobins are inherited in a normal Mendelian manner.

From these studies a hypothesis can be put forward to explain in genetic terms the replacement of fetal with adult haemoglobin at birth:

- The gene which specifies the α chain works all the time, that is, both before and after birth.
- The gene which specifies the γ chain works only before birth, and is then switched off.
- The gene specifying the β chain is inactive during embryonic life, and is then switched on around the time of birth.
- We can also postulate the existence of one or more other genes, responsible for switching the γ gene off and the β gene on.

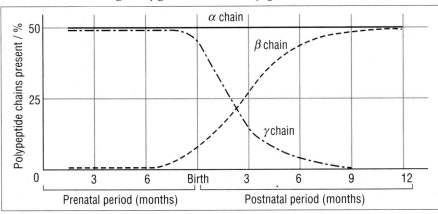

Figure 40.5 The four polypeptide chains, which together with four haem groups make up a single haemoglobin molecule, change during development. Before birth each haemoglobin molecule consists of two α and two γ chains. Around the time of birth, production of the γ chain ceases and is replaced by the β chain.

Chromosome puffs

Evidence supporting the idea that differentiation is brought about by different parts of the genetic code being used at different times comes from observations on the **giant chromosomes** of flies. In 1933 it was found that chromosomes in the salivary glands of *Drosophila* (fruit-fly) larvae are thousands of times broader than those found elsewhere in the body. What happens is that during the larval stage of the insect these cells do not divide. However, the chromosomes continue

Illustration 1 Giant chromosomes from the salivary glands of *Drosophila*. These chromosomes are formed by DNA replicating repeatedly into a large number of double helices which, instead of separating, stay together.

to replicate, over and over again. As a result the chromosomes contain thousands of DNA double helices lying side by side (illustration 1). The significance for geneticists of the 1930s and 1940s was that these giant chromosomes could clearly be seen under the light microscope. This was a great advantage as the electron microscope had not yet been invented.

How does the existence of giant chromosomes help in our understanding of cell development and differentiation? Well, occasionally the DNA strands which make up these chromosomes become less tightly packed in certain regions, and sections of the chromosomes puff up. The regions where this occurs are called **chromosome puffs** (illustration 2).

Experiments with special stains and radioactive tracers have shown that chromosome puffs are the sites of messenger RNA synthesis. Moreover, puffing occurs in different parts of the chromosomes at different times as the insect develops, suggesting that different parts of the

DNA in the chromosome are being used at different times. For example, puffing has been observed in a particular part of the chromosome just before the larva moults. Moulting is brought about by a hormone called ecdysone (see page 667). If this hormone is experimentally injected into an immature larva, puffing occurs prematurely in this very part of the chromosome.

All this makes sense, but how can a hormone cause a particular region of the DNA in a chromosome to start producing messenger RNA? One possibility is that the hormone might switch on the relevant part of the DNA. The concept of **gene switching** is explained on page 733.

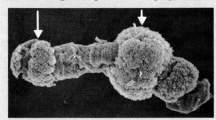

Illustration 2 Scanning electron micrograph of a giant chromosome from the salivary glands of a chironomid fly showing chromosome puffs (arrowed).

The Jacob-Monod hypothesis of gene action

The idea of genes being switched on and off may seem rather fanciful but over the years considerable evidence has come to hand to support it. During the late 1950s François Jacob and Jacques Monod of the Institut Pasteur in Paris carried out a series of brilliantly designed experiments on the genetic control of enzyme-synthesis in the bacterium *E. coli*. Briefly, what they found was this. *E. coli* only synthesises certain enzymes if and when it is appropriate for the bacterium to do so. For example, it produces enzymes for breaking down sugar for the release of energy. One such sugar is lactose. If lactose is present in the nutrient medium in which the bacteria are growing, they produce an enzyme, β **galactosidase**, to break it down. But if lactose is absent from the medium, this enzyme is not produced. If lactose is added to a medium which previously lacked it, then, and only then, will the bacteria start synthesising the enzyme.

From these experiments, together with other investigations into the genetics and biochemistry of *E. coli*, Jacob and Monod put forward a theory to explain how the gene responsible for the production of β galactosidase is regulated. The basic scheme is outlined in figure 40.6A.

The section of the DNA strand which codes for the enzyme is called the **structural gene**; through the intermediacy of messenger RNA it brings about synthesis of the enzyme. Situated close to the structural gene is another section of the DNA strand called the **promotor region**. At times

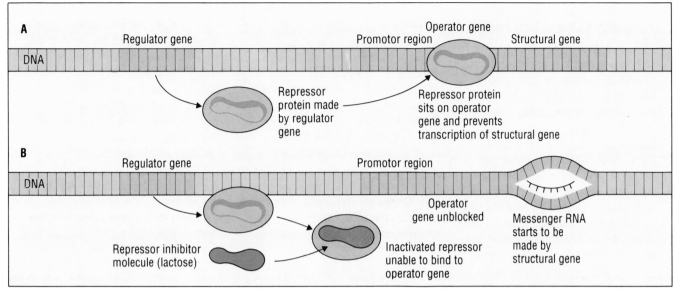

A

Regulator gene

Operator gene

Promotor region

Structural gene

DNA

Repressor protein made by regulator gene

Repressor protein sits on operator gene and prevents transcription of structural gene

B

Regulator gene

Promotor region

DNA

Repressor inhibitor molecule (lactose)

Operator gene unblocked

Inactivated repressor unable to bind to operator gene

Messenger RNA starts to be made by structural gene

Figure 40.6 The Jacob-Monod theory of the control of messenger RNA synthesis.

A Structural gene inactivated as a result of repressor protein made by a regulator gene.

B Structural gene making messenger RNA as a result of inactivation of the repressor protein by a repressor inhibitor molecule such as lactose. Full explanation in text.

when the enzyme is needed, the promotor region activates the structural gene, causing it to produce the messenger RNA which is then translated into β galactosidase. However, between the promotor region and the structural gene lies an **operator gene**. Now the operator gene, according to Jacob and Monod's theory, comes under the influence of yet another gene, the **regulator gene**, situated further along the DNA chain. The regulator gene codes for a **repressor substance** which inhibits the operator gene when the enzyme is not required, thereby preventing the structural gene from doing its bit. When the enzyme is required the repressor substance is inhibited (in this case by lactose), the operator gene becomes unblocked, the promotor region becomes functional, the structural gene is activated and the enzyme is produced (figure 40.6B).

If you find all this rather heavy going, don't lose heart. It took Jacob and Monod years to unravel it, and they got a Nobel Prize for it!

The original version of the Jacob-Monod hypothesis postulated that the structural gene is switched off except when needed. More recent evidence suggests that micro-organisms also possess other systems in which the structural gene is switched *on* except when it is *not* needed.

Gene regulation in eukaryotes

Precisely how gene regulation occurs in eukaryotes such as ourselves is still far from clear. It is known that transcription is regulated by proteins that bind to specific sites on the DNA molecule, just as for *E. coli*. However, it seems that gene regulation is far more complicated in eukaryotes than in prokaryotes, particularly when multicellular eukaryotes are considered. For instance the sites at which proteins made by regulator genes bind to the DNA may be thousands of base pairs away from the promotor gene, quite different from the situation in *E. coli* as depicted in figure 40.6.

What is clear is that eukaryotes have a number of types of gene control which are absent from prokaryotes. For instance, about 5 per cent of the cytosine bases in eukaryotic DNA have methyl ($-CH_3$) groups added to them. This is known as **DNA methylation**. When one looks at the same gene in cells from different tissues, it is usually found that the genes are more heavily methylated in those cells where they are *not* expressed. Further, drugs that inhibit methylation often cause genes to start synthesising messenger RNA. So DNA methylation may be a mechanism for gene regulation in eukaryotes.

How DNA is packed into chromosomes

Measured from end to end, the DNA in a human chromosome is about 100 000 times longer than a chromosome at metaphase. This means that when a cell divides in two its DNA is packed incredibly tightly, far more tightly than, say, a ball of string. The reason for this should be clear if you imagine what cell division would otherwise be like. The DNA belonging to the different chromosomes would get in the most hopeless tangle and there would be no chance of cell division resulting in the genetic material being evenly apportioned between the daughter cells.

So how is DNA packed in the chromosome of a dividing cell? The answer is that it is tightly wrapped around special protein molecules called **histones**. Histones are basic proteins that are present in very large numbers in a cell. There are five types of histones, rather unimaginatively called H1, H2A, H2B, H3 and H4. There are about 30 million molecules of H1 per cell, and about 60 million molecules of each of the other four types. As a result, chromosomes are mainly protein; the DNA makes up less than half the mass of each chromosome.

The histones serve two main functions. First, they protect the DNA from damage; secondly, they allow the long length of DNA to be packaged in such a way that it can be moved around the cell at cell division.

Careful studies using the electron microscope, X-ray diffraction and a battery of biochemical techniques have helped to elucidate the relationship between the histones and the DNA. The complex of DNA, protein and RNA in a chromosome is called **chromatin**. The fundamental unit of chromatin is the **nucleosome**. A nucleosome is composed of DNA wrapped around a group of histone molecules (illustration 1). These units occur at regular intervals along the length of the DNA, like a string of beads. Illustration 2 shows how it is thought that the nucleosomes are clustered together in a chromosome.

During interphase the chromosomes uncoil which allows messenger RNA to be made by the appropriate genes. However, the histones remain associated with the DNA.

Illustration 1 The structure of a nucleosome, the basic unit of chromatin.

Cluster of eight histone molecules

Rod—like histone molecule

DNA

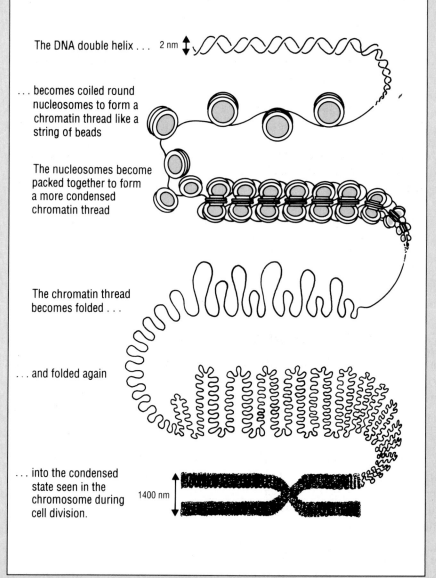

The DNA double helix . . . 2 nm

. . . becomes coiled round nucleosomes to form a chromatin thread like a string of beads

The nucleosomes become packed together to form a more condensed chromatin thread

The chromatin thread becomes folded . . .

. . . and folded again

. . . into the condensed state seen in the chromosome during cell division.

1400 nm

Illustration 2 The structure of a chromosome shown at different magnifications. Notice the different scales and follow the diagrams from top to bottom.

Gene switching and the germination of barley seeds

Guest author Tim King discusses a commercially important example of gene switching, the germination of barley seeds.

In the brewing of beer from barley, the barley seeds (strictly they are fruits) are induced to germinate. During the early stages, the starch stored in the endosperm is hydrolysed to the sugar maltose which is an ideal substrate for yeast to ferment to alcohol. Once the barley seeds contain a high enough concentration of maltose, they are killed and the 'malt' is extracted. Because of its economic importance, much time has been spent working out the details of this process.

To understand what happens you need to be familiar with the structure of this kind of seed: on page 636 there is a diagram of a wheat seed which is very similar to barley.

A couple of days after the seed has begun to absorb water, prior to germination, the shoot tip of the embryo releases the plant growth substance gibberellic acid (see page 653). This travels through the embryo and is released into the endosperm. When it reaches the aleurone layer, a mixture of enzymes is secreted from the aleurone cells into the endosperm. These enzymes break down large insoluble storage molecules in the endosperm into smaller soluble molecules suitable for transporting to the germinating embryo. One of the enzymes is β-amylase which converts starch into maltose.

By isolating various parts of a barley seed, it has been shown that only the cells of the aleurone layer secrete β-amylase, and that gibberellic acid triggers this process. Is the enzyme, which of course is a protein, already present and merely released under the stimulus of gibberellin, or is it synthesised from scratch by the aleruone cells?

This question has been investigated by adding radioactively-labelled amino acids to aleurone tissue. The labelled amino acids are rapidly incorporated into new molecules of β-amylase under the influence of gibberellin. This process can be prevented, however, by drugs such as actinomycin D which inhibit messenger RNA synthesis on the DNA template. It seems therefore that molecules of gibberellin, which are lipid-soluble, pass across the plasma membranes of the aleurone cells and then act on the DNA, switching on the genes responsible for synthesis of the enzyme.

This theory has been confirmed by several elegant experiments. For example, when isolated nuclei of aleurone cells are exposed to gibberellic acid, their rate of synthesis of messenger RNA increases by a factor of between six and fourteen. If this messenger RNA is isolated and added to a cell-free preparation of ribosomes, transfer RNA and the necessary enzymes and amino acids, a protein identical to β-amylase is produced.

So, next time you drink a pint of beer, spare a thought for the intricate genetic and biochemical mechanisms which occur in the organisms on which brewing depends!

Suggest how the molecules of gibberellic acid might switch on the genes for β-amylase when they reach the aleurone cells. What sort of experiments might be carried out to test your suggestion(s)?

Cytoplasmic control of gene expression

In the type of regulation considered so far, unwanted genes are prevented from being transcribed. In other words, regulation takes place in the nucleus at the **level of transcription**. However, cells have another avenue of control, namely in the cytoplasm at the **level of translation**. The idea here is that the cytoplasm exerts some control over the rate at which messenger RNA is translated.

However, there is no evidence that the cytoplasm can control *which* proteins are synthesised. This fundamental element of control seems to reside at the level of transcription in the nucleus. Cytoplasmic control should therefore be seen as a supplement, rather than as an alternative, to nuclear control.

Cytoplasmic inheritance

Nevertheless there are some cases where specific proteins are determined by the cytoplasm rather than by the nucleus. For instance, in 1909 Carl Correns reported some surprising results from breeding experiments he had carried out on four-o'clock plants (*Mirabilis jalapa*). These plants have

Figure 40.7 Leaf variation in the four-o'clock plant *Mirabilis jalapa*. Flowers may be found on green, white or variegated branches. The results of crossing these flowers cannot be explained by conventional Mendelian genetics. The genes involved are carried in the chloroplasts, not in the nucleus.

three sorts of leaves on their branches. Some branches carry only green leaves, others only white leaves and others variegated leaves (figure 40.7). Flowers occur on all three types of branches. When Correns crossed plants, he found that the phenotypes of the progeny depended only on the phenotype of the maternal branch from which the flower came. The phenotype of the paternal branch was irrelevant (table 40.1). This sort of inheritance is known as **maternal inheritance**.

Phenotype of branch bearing egg parent (♀)	Phenotype of branch bearing pollen parent (♂)	Phenotype of progeny
White	White	White
White	Green	White
White	Variegated	White
Green	White	Green
Green	Green	Green
Green	Variegated	Green
Variegated	White	Variegated, green or white
Variegated	Green	Variegated, green or white
Variegated	Variegated	Variegated, green or white

Table 40.1 Results of crosses of four-o'clock plants showing the significance of maternal inheritance.

The white plants produced in Correns' crosses soon died, through their inability to photosynthesise. However, the variegated and green plants grew well and were used in further breeding experiments. Again, maternal inheritance was found.

How can these results be explained? The different leaf colours are due to the presence or absence of chloroplasts. What seems to happen is that leaf colour is determined not by nuclear genes, but by genes carried in the chloroplasts. The egg cell contains chloroplasts, but the pollen grain does not. Accordingly, the phenotype of the offspring, as far as its chloroplasts go, is determined by the mother's chloroplasts.

We now know that both chloroplasts and mitochondria carry their own circular DNA. This DNA is involved in the replication of the organelles, though chloroplasts and mitochondria are not entirely autonomous: nuclear genes also play a part in their synthesis. The inheritance of characteristics through structures in the cytoplasm is known as **cytoplasmic inheritance**.

Mitochondrial DNA, human evolution and the mother of us all

Because sperm are so much smaller than eggs, they contribute no organelles to the zygote that results from the fusion of a sperm and an egg. It is a fascinating thought that all our mitochondria are derived from our mothers, none from our fathers. Similarly, for each of us, our mother got her mitochondria from her mother, and so on. Geneticists have studied the DNA carried by human mitochondria. The more closely related two people are, the more similar their mitochondrial DNA.

From analyses of human mitochondrial DNA, some geneticists have calculated that the entire human race is descended from a single woman, a sort of proto-Eve, who lived about 220 000 years ago. This does not mean that this person was the first human. As we shall see in Chapter 44, humans have been around for longer than this. What it does suggest is that about 220 000 years ago the human race may have been greatly reduced in size, perhaps to only a few dozen individuals. Although several of the women among these individuals may have had offspring, it seems that only one of the women had a line of descendants that survived. If this is correct, then we are all descended from this one woman.

The role of the environment

A well known case of environmental control is provided by fur colour in the Himalayan rabbit. The Himalayan rabbit has a white body with black ears, nose, feet and tail (figure 40.8). At first glance it might be thought that this pattern is under genetic control, but a simple experiment shows that this is not the case. If a cold pad is fixed to the rabbit's back, left in position for a few weeks and kept cold, black hair starts to develop beneath the pad.

What seems to be happening is that the heat prevents the development of the black pigment. Only in those parts of the body which are cool enough, i.e. the extremities, does black fur grow. The same thing happens in seal-point siamese cats. Owners of such cats sometimes find that in winter the black areas enlarge, only to regress in warmer weather.

There are many other cases of the environment influencing an organism's development. For example, in plants, chlorophyll will only develop if light is available, and flowers will only appear if the day-length is right and the temperature suitable, and so on. These and other examples are discussed in Chapter 36.

It is easy to underestimate the importance of the environment on the development of organisms and to assume that everything is under genetic control. In reality, development is the result of a subtle and complex inter-action between heredity and the environment. Consider, for instance, communication in humans. Even blind babies smile, which strongly suggests that smiling is largely genetically determined. Yet the way we use our hands in communication, our facial expressions and above all the language we speak are the result of both genetic and environmental influences.

Figure 40.8 Influence of environment on development. In the Himalayan rabbit, black fur develops at the extremities such as the ears and nose due to the lower temperature of these exposed parts of the body. The two youngsters in this picture have not yet developed their dark fur.

The control of animal development

Having seen how genes can be switched on and off, and examined the importance of the cytoplasm and the environment in the development of organisms, we can now look in more detail at how these various influences combine to produce a complete multicellular organism.

The fate of cells in the blastula

In Chapter 35 we saw how in animals a fertilised egg divides repeatedly to give rise to an embryo which consists of a number of distinct tissues. What makes this so remarkable is that the developing embryo receives no infor-mation from the outside world. We are forced to conclude that everything required for the formation of a differentiated multicellular embryo is present in the single fertilised egg from the time of fertilisation.

In chordate embryos there are three germ layers – ectoderm, endoderm and mesoderm (see page 626). Their origin can be traced back to certain formative cells in the blastula – the fluid-filled ball of cells that results from the repeated division of the zygote. The way this is done is to mark specific cells of the blastula or gastrula with harmless dyes. The movements of the stained cells can then be followed during subsequent development, and their fate determined.

This kind of study was first carried out by the German embryologist W. Vogt who constructed **fate maps** to illustrate the eventual destiny of the different regions in the wall of the blastula and early gastrula of amphibians (figure 40.9). These regions are called **presumptive areas** and the cells in each area give rise to predictable tissues in later stages of development. The question we have to answer is whether the fate of a particular area is fixed

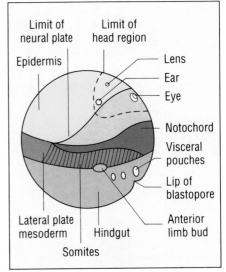

Figure 40.9 Vogt's fate map showing which parts of the late blastula of an amphibian give rise to which parts of the adult. Notice how the part that eventually gives rise to the eye is quite some way from the part that will give rise to the lens. The anterior end of the future embryo is to the left, the posterior end to the right.

and unalterable from an early stage, or dependent on influences arising within the embryo itself as development proceeds.

Tissue culture and grafting

The answer to these questions has come from two different types of experiment: **tissue culture** and **grafting**. In tissue culture a small cluster of cells from, say, the region of the blastula known normally to develop into ectoderm, is removed from a blastula and transferred to a petri dish in the laboratory. Here it can be kept alive, at least for a while, if provided with salts and water at the appropriate pH.

If conditions are satisfactory the cells of the **explant** (as it is called) divide and development occurs in isolation from other tissues. The results of such experiments indicate that in most cases the cluster of cells develops along the lines it would have done if left in place in an intact blastula. By and large this is true of cells that develop into epidermal tissue, mesoderm, notochord and gut.

So, it seems that for most tissues their fate is sealed, or **determined** to use the technical term, as far back as the blastula stage. However, there is one outstanding exception to this and that is the **neural plate**, the region of ectoderm destined to become the central nervous system (see page 626). When isolated and grown in tissue culture, neural plate cells develop not into nervous tissue but into epidermis. Some kind of influence from neighbouring tissue is required if the neural plate is to give rise to nervous tissue.

Which particular tissue in the intact embryo exerts an influence on the neural plate causing it to develop into nervous tissue? This is where grafting experiments come in. By careful surgery it is possible to cut out small pieces of tissue from one embryo (the **donor**) and graft them into another (the **host**). The effect of the graft on the host's tissues is then noted. Numerous experiments of this type were carried out in the 1920s, mainly on amphibian embryos. The experiments showed that one tissue, in particular, has a powerful influence on neighbouring tissues. This is the prospective **notochord**. If this is grafted into another embryo so that it lies just under the ectoderm, the latter is transformed into nervous tissue. In fact in a normal embryo it is notochord tissue that causes the neural plate to develop into nervous tissue.

Tissues which have a particularly powerful influence on neighbouring tissues, causing them to develop in a particular way, are called **organisers**. Prospective notochord tissue is a prime example of an organiser. However, we now know that most tissues are capable of exerting an effect on their neighbours at *some* stage of development. Typically the ability of a tissue to be an organiser changes during development. Equally, a tissue which is particularly sensitive to an organiser at one stage of development may be relatively insensitive at other stages. This applies, for instance, to ectoderm. Once the neural tube has been formed, the ectoderm loses its capacity to respond to the influence of the underlying notochord and will only develop into epidermis.

Senescence

So far in this chapter we have considered the processes leading to the formation of a fully efficient adult organism. But in many species a process of **senescence** ensues in which the smooth functioning of the organism declines, culminating in **death** (figure 40.10).

The manifestations of senescence in humans are well known and include:

Figure 40.10 One person, F.S. (1899–1981), at different times in her life. From top to bottom, aged 3, 12, 21, 40 and 79 years.

- Greying and loss of hair.
- Wrinkling of the skin.
- Loss of cardio-vascular efficiency and capacity resulting in faster, shallower breathing and a decrease in activity.
- Reduction in libido.
- Muscular weakness due to the replacement of muscle fibres by connective tissue.
- Sensory impairment including a decrease in visual acuity, a tendency towards long-sightedness, an inability to hear high frequencies or to appreciate some tastes and smells.
- Slower reaction times.
- Reduction in body size due to progressive atrophy of the bones and other tissues.
- Inefficient homeostasis as the body adjusts less effectively to variations in temperature, blood sugar and so on.

In addition, old age *may* ultimately be accompanied by mental senility, brittle bones or incontinence.

It should be appreciated that there is no precise age at which senescence begins. Many of the changes listed above start in one's twenties, others much later. The question is, what causes senescence?

What causes senescence?

There is no simple answer to this question but research in recent years has suggested that senescence results from the gradual accumulation of genetic and biochemical defects. Some of these are listed below.

- **Mistakes in protein synthesis.** Old age appears to be accompanied by changes in the metabolic processes occurring in cells, particularly those involved in protein synthesis. In most species as individuals get older there is a gradual decline in the accuracy of DNA replication with the result that the genetic make-up of the cells formed in mitosis is abnormal. Since these abnormalities arise as a result of errors in the production of the body (somatic) cells as opposed to the reproductive (germ) cells, they are called **somatic mutations** (see page 794).

  Many somatic mutations are not too serious, but some lead to cellular misfunction. In some cases this results in the death of a cell. In other cases quite the opposite may happen: a cell may go out of control and divide repeatedly, possibly because it is no longer making the repressor molecules which prevent excessive division. The cell has become cancerous (see page 564). This is the reason why most cancers are more common in older people.

- **Cell loss.** In most tissues new cells are formed by mitosis throughout life, with the result that dead cells are constantly replaced by new ones. However, there are certain tissues, notably muscle and nerve, whose cells are not replaced. Once you reach your early twenties, your brain loses about 100 000 neurones a day! Inevitably there comes a time when such continued losses contribute to senescence.

- **Chemical changes in tissues.** As one gets older the formation of extra cross-linkages in structural proteins such as collagen and elastin result in the loss of suppleness in one's limbs. Arteries too become harder and less elastic.

- **Auto-immunity.** There is evidence that as people get older they may start to produce antibodies against their own antigens. The explanation lies

Why don't we live for ever?

Cells taken from a human fetus go through about 50 cycles of cell division before they die. The older you are, the fewer the number of cell divisions your cells have left in them.

In 1990 Dr Calvin Harley, of McMaster University in Canada, and his colleagues reported a study on specialised pieces of DNA, called telomeres, that occur at the end of chromosomes. They found that telomeres shorten in proportion to the number of cell cycles a cell has gone through. This suggests that loss of telomere DNA might be related to senescence.

It is known that an enzyme called telomerase can *lengthen* telomeres. As Harley points out, this raises the possibility that methods might be found to boost telomerase and so lengthen lifespan.

Do you think it is desirable for people's lifespan to be lengthened any more than it is already?

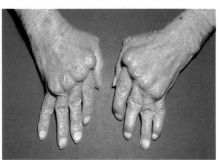

Figure 40.11 A severe case of rheumatoid arthritis, a disease resulting from auto-immunity.

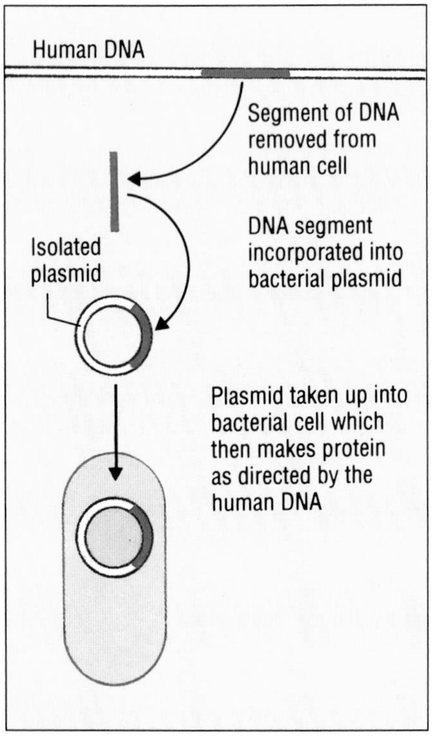

Figure 40.12 The principle behind genetic engineering (recombinant DNA technology). A short piece of DNA, in this case from a human, is transferred to a bacterial cell which then makes the protein coded for by this foreign bit of DNA.

Human DNA

Segment of DNA removed from human cell

Isolated plasmid

DNA segment incorporated into bacterial plasmid

Plasmid taken up into bacterial cell which then makes protein as directed by the human DNA

partly in the fact, already mentioned, that ageing is accompanied by mistakes in protein synthesis. Since the protein molecules so formed are new to the body, they may be treated by the immune system as foreign and attacked accordingly.

Another explanation for auto-immunity is that the suppressor T lymphocytes, which normally prevent the body from attacking its own cells, stop functioning properly. The result is that the person's own cells get destroyed. (T lymphocytes are explained on page 418.)

Certain diseases associated with old age are due to auto-immunity. These include diabetes, motor neurone disease and rheumatoid arthritis (figure 40.11).

Genetic engineering

Are there any ways by which we can alter an organism's genetic constitution so that it develops differently? The answer is, of course, yes. Such manipulations have been carried out for centuries in **selective breeding** of crop plants and farm animals. However, a more direct approach has been made within the last decade by what is popularly called **genetic engineering**, or more properly **recombinant DNA technology**.

Techniques of recombinant DNA technology

The first step in recombinant DNA technology usually involves inserting a short piece of foreign DNA into the DNA of a host organism, usually a bacterium. This host organism then acquires the ability to synthesise certain proteins characteristic of the donor. In practical terms the technique involves breaking open the DNA ring of a bacterial plasmid and inserting a piece of DNA from a donor species into it (figure 40.12). This procedure is called **gene splicing**.

Gene splicing relies on an important group of naturally occurring enzymes called **restriction endonucleases**. A given restriction endonuclease cuts the bacterial plasmid open at a specific site which is determined by the sequence of bases in that region. The same enzyme will cut foreign DNA wherever an identical base sequence occurs.

Now it is characteristic of most restriction endonucleases that they cut the two strands of the DNA at slightly different points. The result is that the two ends of the foreign DNA segment have a short row of unpaired bases which match the complementary bases at the two ends of the opened up plasmid. These are referred to as 'sticky ends'. In suitable conditions the unpaired bases of the foreign DNA and the plasmid join up, and so the foreign DNA gets incorporated into the plasmid (figure 40.13). The bonding is made secure by another enzyme, **DNA ligase**. Once in position,

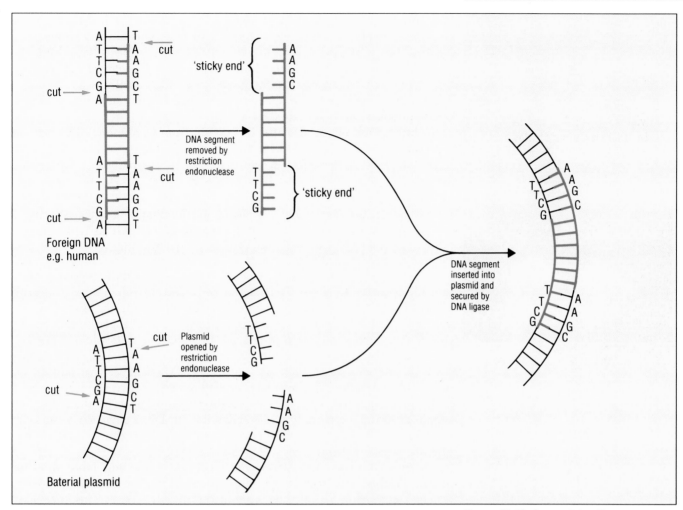

A
T
T
C
G
A

cut

T
A
A
G
C
T

cut

'sticky end'

A
A
G
C

DNA segment removed by restriction endonuclease

'sticky end'

T
T
C
G

A
T
T
C
G
A

cut

T
A
A
G
C
T

cut

Foreign DNA
e.g. human

DNA segment inserted into plasmid and secured by DNA ligase

A
A
G
C

T
T
C
G

T
T
C
G

A
A
G
C

A
T
T
C
G
A

cut

T
A
A
G
C
T

cut

Plasmid opened by restriction endonuclease

T
T
C
G

A
A
G
C

Baterial plasmid

Figure 40.13 Gene splicing. The particular restriction endonuclease depicted here cuts DNA between the bases T and A in the sequence TAAGCT, and between G and A in the sequence ATTCGA. The sequence of unpaired bases in the segment of foreign DNA and the opened up plasmid allow the foreign DNA to become incorporated into the plasmid as shown. Only a small part of the plasmid is shown in these diagrams.

the foreign DNA replicates along with the rest of the plasmid every time the bacterial cell divides.

The enzymes needed for DNA splicing – restriction endonucleases and DNA ligase – did not evolve for the benefit of genetic engineers; they occur naturally both in prokaryotes and eukaryotes and have important functions in their own rights. For example, in bacteria they are responsible for cutting and rejoining the DNA ring during sexual conjugation, and in eukaryotes they enable the chromosomal DNA to break and rejoin during chiasma-formation. What genetic engineers have done is to exploit these enzymes, extracting them and using them as tools in genetic manipulation.

Once a bacterium has taken up a piece of foreign DNA successfully, it may divide repeatedly and give rise to a large population of bacterial cells all of which contain replicas of the foreign DNA. The latter has thus been cloned and can be used for the large-scale synthesis of the particular protein for which it codes. The production of large quantities of identical genes by means of genetic engineering is called **gene cloning**.

Applications of recombinant DNA technology

Genetic engineering has opened up all sorts of exciting possibilities. True, some of the earlier results were more spectacular than useful, but by now some very valuable results have been achieved. For example, important human proteins such as insulin and growth hormone are now routinely made by recombinant DNA technology.

Figure 40.14 Tobacco plant glowing like a firefly. Fireflies are insects the males of which produce bursts of light by which they attract females. The light is produced by the action of the enzyme luciferase on the chemical luciferin. The plant figured here carries the gene for luciferase production as a result of recombinant DNA technology. When watered with a solution of luciferin the plant glows. Although this particular example of genetic engineering is unlikely to be commercially significant, it does illustrate the way in which genes can now be moved from one species to another.

However, a word of caution. Some diabetics who switched from bovine or porcine insulin to the new genetically engineered insulin have found that its effects are slightly different. In particular, it may be more difficult for the diabetics to realise when their blood sugar levels are getting dangerously low. In a few cases this has unfortunately led to the death of diabetics. So genetically engineered products are not necessarily superior to those obtained by traditional methods.

Genetic engineering of plants is becoming more common. An intriguing example is given in figure 40.14. Rather more usefully, several companies have developed strains of crop plants that make the plant resistant to the powerful herbicide glyphosate (trade name Roundup or Tumbleweed). The idea is that glyphosate could then be applied to crops, killing the weeds but not damaging the crops. This would be advantageous for farmers *and* be environmentally friendly as glyphosate is non-toxic to animals and quickly breaks down to harmless components. These two advantages are not shared by many other herbicides.

It is also hoped that it may be possible to take the DNA responsible for, say, nitrogen-fixation out of bacterial cells and introduce it into a crop plant such as wheat, thereby conferring on the wheat the ability to fix atmospheric nitrogen. This would save a fortune on nitrogen fertilisers and reduce the problem of high nitrate levels in water due to fertiliser runoff.

In medicine it is hoped that related techniques may one day cure people with genetic disorders such as cystic fibrosis, sickle-cell anaemia and muscular dystrophy. This would be called **gene therapy**. The hope is that faulty genes may be repaired, or that their missing gene products may be supplied. At the moment, however, recombinant DNA technology can only be used to diagnose genetic abnormalities early in pregnancy. It cannot provide cures for them.

Numerous firms throughout the world are investing large sums of money in this new branch of biotechnology (figure 40.15). However, genetic engineering may not be without certain dangers. For instance, new pathogens might be created accidentally – or even deliberately for use in warfare. Accordingly there are very strict guidelines currently in place on this area of research.

Figure 40.15 The Constant Environment Growth Room, where genetically engineered plants are reared, at Twyford Plant Laboratories. Absolute cleanliness is maintained, together with an appropriate controlled environment. Such facilities are expensive, but the payoffs can be immense.

Summary

1 Development involves a highly ordered sequence of events, carefully controlled in space and time.

2 Experiments on unicellular organisms indicate that the nucleus is not only necessary for development to proceed, but that it also determines what sort of structure the cell develops into.

3 The cytoplasm can also play an important part in controlling development.

4 Nuclear-cloning experiments in amphibians show that the DNA content of the nucleus of a particular cell remains unaltered during development. Differentiation is brought about by different parts of the genetic code being used at different times and in different cells as an organism develops.

5 At a given moment only a proportion of the genes in a cell are synthesising messenger RNA; other genes are in some way masked or 'switched off'. This concept is supported by Jacob and Monod's work on the synthesis of sugar-splitting enzymes in the colon bacillus *Escherichia coli*.

6 In eukaryotes the control of gene regulation is still far from being understood. Most control probably resides at the level of transcription (messenger RNA synthesis), though control at the level of translation (protein synthesis from messenger RNA) may also be involved.

7 In eukaryotes DNA is found in close association with positively charged **histone** proteins.

8 In chordate embryos the origin of certain structures can be traced back to specific **presumptive areas** in the blastula.

9 Although the destiny of most tissues is determined as early as the blastula stage, some tissues show considerable flexibility in what they can develop into. The fate of such tissues is determined by neighbouring tissues (**organisers**) which induce them to develop in a particular way.

10 An organism's genetic make-up can now be altered by **genetic engineering (recombinant DNA technology)**. The basic technique involves removing genes from one species and inserting them into another. These techniques are already being used to enable large-scale production by bacteria of human insulin and growth hormone.

11 **Senescence**, a natural process of decline culminating in death, is caused by a combination of factors including somatic mutations, mistakes in protein synthesis, cell loss, chemical changes in tissues and auto-immunity.

Review questions

1 All the cells of an organism have a complete copy of the organism's DNA rather than just those bits they need for their own functioning. Discuss the implications of this.

2 In his experiments on toads (page 732) Gurdon had more difficulty getting nuclei from adult toads to give rise to new individuals than nuclei from tadpoles. Can you suggest why this was?

3 Explain the applied benefits of plant cloning.

4 List the evidence that the characteristics of eukaryotes are not determined solely by the nucleus.

5 What precisely can be learned about gene regulation from the structures of fetal and adult human haemoglobin?

6 Summarise the fundamental principles of recombinant DNA technology.

7 Do you feel there are any ethical limits for biotechnology? How would you feel, for instance, about parents being able to determine the mental or physical characteristics of their children?

8 Humans and chimpanzees have over 99 per cent of their DNA in common. What conclusions can you draw from this?

9 Discuss the extent to which medical research funds should be targeted at the problems of senescence.

10 It has been calculated that all species of mammal, irrespective of their size, live for approximately the same number of heartbeats. Can you suggest why this is so?

Further reading

Tom Maniatis and Mark Ptashne's paper 'A DNA operator-repressor system' in the January 1976 issue of *Scientific American* goes into the control of messenger RNA synthesis in more detail than this chapter does. The paper is reprinted in the collection of *Scientific American* articles entitled *Genetics*, introduced by C. I. Davern (W.H. Freeman, 1981).

Biotechnology Topics for A-level edited by Alan Cadogan (Institute of Biology, 1989) contains eight chapters each written by a different expert in the field of biotechnology.

Genetic Engineering by P. E. O. Wymer for the National Centre for School Biotechnology (Hobsons) is pitched at exactly the right level for A and AS level study.

For the classic fictional account of cloning in humans read Aldous Huxley's *Brave New World*.

CHAPTER 41 | Population genetics

Why do some people have blue eyes, others brown and others grey? In this chapter we will be concerned with the factors that determine the frequencies of alleles in populations of organisms. We will also look at the connection between allele frequency and phenotype frequency. If, for example, 20 per cent of the loci for eye colour in a population of humans are occupied by alleles for blue eye colour, what percentage of people will have blue eyes? As we shall see, the answer is *not* 20 per cent!

Populations and allele frequencies

In Chapter 5 we defined a population as a collection of individuals able to breed with one another. This means that not only must the individuals all belong to the same species, but they must live in the same geographical area: rabbits in Yorkshire do not belong to the same population as rabbits in Norfolk. Indeed, there are no doubt many different rabbit populations both in Norfolk and in Yorkshire.

Geneticists refer to a population that is genetically isolated from other populations as a **deme**. A good example of a deme would be a collection of woodmice in a small wood surrounded by agricultural land (figure 41.1). Other examples might be frogs in a pond, beech trees in a copse or *Paramecium* in a ditch.

Although there may be considerable movement of individuals to and from individual demes, a deme generally perpetuates itself by the inter-breeding of the individuals within it. It thus represents a genetic unit, and what happens to it in evolutionary terms depends on the genes it contains. The genetic constitution of a deme, i.e. the sum total of all the different genes in the population, is known as the **gene pool**. Just as the future of an individual organism depends to a large extent on its genetic constitution, so the evolutionary future of a deme depends on its gene pool.

The frequency of any given allele in a population, relative to other alleles at the same locus, is known as the **allele frequency**. Sometimes, rather confusingly, allele fequencies are called **gene frequencies**, although the former term is to be preferred. Consider, for instance, a population of fruit flies, such as those whose inheritance we studied in Chapters 37 and 38. Suppose a population contains 100 flies and we want to know the frequencies of the alleles that determine wing length.

In arriving at an answer, we must bear in mind that fruit flies are diploid and that each cell therefore contains two alleles for wing length. Imagine that 160 of the 200 alleles are alleles for normal wings and that 40 are alleles for vestigial wings. Then the proportion of the alleles that are alleles for normal wings equals 160 divided by 200, i.e. 0.8. The proportion of the alleles that are alleles for vestigial wings equals 40 divided by 200, i.e. 0.2. As we expect, the sum of these two proportions, 0.8 and 0.2, equals 1.0, as all the alleles at this particular locus are either alleles for normal wings or alleles for vestigial wings.

Allele frequencies are sometimes expressed as proportions, in which case they lie betwen 0 and 1, and sometimes as percentages, in which case they lie between 0 per cent and 100 per cent. Converting from a proportion to a percentage simply involves multiplying by 100 and adding a percentage symbol (%). In the above case, the allele for normal wings has a frequency of 0.8 or 80 per cent, while the allele for vestigial wings has a frequency of 0.2 or 20 per cent.

Figure 41.1 Aerial photograph showing patches of woodland, many of which are connected by hedges. The more isolated geographically a patch of woodland is, the more likely it is that organisms in it are isolated genetically from organisms of the same species in another patch of woodland. Of course, two small woods may be genetically isolated from each other for some species (e.g. slugs), but not for others (e.g. songbirds).

Factors that change allele frequencies

Under certain conditions, allele frequencies may remain constant over time. However, there are a number of factors that can lead to changes in allele frequencies. They are as follows:

- **Allele-specific mortality or emigration** Let us return to our example of a population of fruit flies containing alleles both for normal wings and for vestigial wings. Suppose that vestigial-winged individuals are more likely to die. We saw in Chapter 37 that vestigial-winged individuals are homozygous for the vestigial-winged allele. Greater mortality among vestigial-winged individuals would therefore lead to a decrease in the frequency of the allele for vestigial wings and a corresponding increase in the frequency of the allele for normal wings.

  In the same way, if one of the two phenotypes is more likely to emigrate than the other, allele frequencies will change. Note that mortality or emigration by themselves have no effect on allele frequencies; only if such mortality or emigration is allele-specific, that is, more likely for one allele than another, will mortality or emigration lead to changes in allele frequencies.

- **Allele-specific reproduction or immigration.** In the same way, if one allele is associated with a higher probability of reproduction or immigration, allele frequencies will change accordingly. For example, normal-winged fruit flies might be more likely to immigrate into other fruit fly populations than vestigial-winged fruit flies simply because the latter cannot fly. Of course, immigration into one population is always balanced by an emigration from another one. Immigration and emigration may therefore change allele frequencies within individual populations – but for the species as a whole they are of no consequence.

- **Chance.** Suppose, for the sake of argument, that colour blindness is not associated with a decrease or increase in mortality, emigration, reproduction or immigration. Nevertheless, different populations of humans might still differ in the frequencies of their alleles for colour blindness and normal colour vision purely by chance. Suppose that in one population, a woman homozygous for the colour blind allele had a very large family for reasons quite unconnected with her possession of two alleles for colour blindness. The next generation would see an increase, albeit a small one, in the frequency of the allele for colour blindness. Chance increases or decreases in allele frequencies over time are known as **genetic drift**.

  The importance of genetic drift is greatest when population sizes are very small. This is most clearly seen when a group of individuals founds a new population. If the group is large, then its gene pool will probably be very similar to that of the parent population. If, however, only a few individuals found a new population, the gene pool of the new deme may be quite distinct from that of the parent deme. This phenomenon is known as the **founder effect**.

- **Mutation.** Consider a population in which a particular locus can be occupied by one of two alleles, **A** and **a**. Suppose that the two alleles have no differences in their effects on an individual's survival, reproduction, immigration or emigration. Despite this, it is still possible that, for example, **A** may steadily increase at the expense of **a**, if the frequency with which **A** mutates to **a** is less than the frequency with which **a** mutates to **A**. In real life such a reason for a change in allele frequency is probably rarely important, simply because mutation rates are usually very low.

The founder effect in humans

A clear instance of the founder effect in humans is provided by the geographical distribution of a rare neurological condition known as **Huntington's disease**, which is characterised by the degeneration of the nervous system. Affected people find motor coordination difficult so their hands shake and they have problems with balance. As the condition worsens they find it more and more difficult to look after themselves. The disease usually manifests itself in people aged between 30 and 50, and death generally follows within five to ten years. The condition is caused by the possession of a mutant autosomal dominant allele. This means that individuals homozygous or heterozygous for the allele are affected.

Fortunately, Huntington's disease is uncommon. In Britain, for instance, the average incidence of people with the mutant allele is about seven per 100 000. However, in the Moray Firth area in Scotland the figure is 560 per 100 000, while there are villages in Venezuela where the figure is over 1000 per 100 000, i.e. in excess of one per cent. The condition was probably introduced into the Venezuelan state of Zulia in the 1860s by a sailor aboard a German trade ship. A particularly large number of descendants resulted from a relationship between the sailor and a Venezuelan woman, and many of these descendants inherited the harmful allele.

Allele and phenotype frequencies

The factors that can change allele fequencies will obviously change phenotype frequencies. But what is the precise relationship between allele frequencies and phenotype frequencies? To return to the question posed at the beginning of this chapter, if 20 per cent of the loci for eye colour in a population of humans are occuped by alleles for blue eye colour, what percentage of the population will have blue eyes?

Note, first of all, that if we were haploid organisms, the answer to this question would be 20 per cent, as individuals with a copy of the allele for blue eye colour would have blue eyes and individuals with alleles for other eye colours would have brown or green or grey eyes, depending on the allele they possessed. However, we are, of course, diploid, not haploid and this makes the relationship more complex.

The Hardy-Weinberg formula

Let us make the simplifying assumption that a particular population of humans has eye colour alleles only for blue or for brown eyes, and that the allele for blue eye colour is recessive to the allele for brown eye colour. If we let **B** stand for the allele for brown eyes and **b** for the allele for blue eyes, individuals will have the following genotypes and phenotypes:

Genotype	Phenotype
BB	Brown eyes
Bb	Brown eyes
bb	Blue eyes

We can represent the frequency of the allele for brown eyes by the symbol p, and the frequency of the allele for blue eyes by the symbol q. As we have made the assumption that the population in question has eye colour alleles only for brown or for blue eyes, no other alleles can be present at the locus for eye colour. Therefore, p and q are related to one another by the simple equation:

$$p + q = 1$$

What we need is an equation which will relate the allele frequencies p and q to the phenotype frequencies given by the percentage of people who are blue-eyed and brown-eyed.

It was this relationship between allele frequencies and phenotype frequencies that bothered the geneticist R. C. Punnett, the originator of the Punnett square, as he travelled back to Cambridge on a train from a Royal Society of Medicine meeting in London in 1908. Fortunately he was a close friend of the mathematician G. H. Hardy, with whom he used to play cricket (figure 41.2). On his return to Cambridge, Punnett sought out Hardy and explained the problem to him. Hardy at once replied "p^2 to $2pq$ to q^2".

Punnett assured Hardy that although he might find the solution to the problem trivial, he had made an important contribution to genetics. Hardy was persuaded to publish his result. In the same year the German physician W. Weinberg independently published the same conclusion, for which reason it is now known as the **Hardy-Weinberg principle**.

Put less succinctly, the Hardy-Weinberg principle states that if the frequency of one allele, which we may call **A**, is p, while the frequency of the other allele, **a**, is q, then the frequencies of the three possible genotypes **AA**, **Aa** and **aa** are given respectively by p^2, $2pq$ and q^2. A population for which this is the case is said to be in **Hardy-Weinberg equilibrium**.

What is the explanation of this relationship? Consider what happens at

Figure 41.2 G. H. Hardy. Although his name is nowadays most widely known for his derivation of the Hardy-Weinberg equation, Hardy was a leading pure mathematician during the first half of the 20th century. At the age of 15 he read a novel called *A Fellow of Trinity* and decided that he wanted to be one. He duly arrived at Trinity College, Cambridge as an undergraduate and spent the rest of his life there. His daily routine altered little throughout his adult life. Over breakfast he read *The Times*, paying particular attention to the cricket scores. From nine to one, unless he was giving a lecture, he worked at his own mathematics. 'Four hours creative work a day is about the limit for a mathematician' he used to say. After lunch he spent the afternoon watching cricket, unless it was winter in which case he would play a game of real tennis. About two to three weeks before his death he heard from the Royal Society that he was to be given their highest honour, the Copley Medal. He grinned and remarked to a close friend, the novelist C. P. Snow, 'Now I know that I must be pretty near the end. When people hurry up to give you honorific things there is exactly one conclusion to be drawn.'

meiosis and at fertilisation with respect to the two alternative alleles, **A** and **a**. As a result of meiosis, a proportion p of the gametes will carry the **A** allele, simply because gametes are haploid and a proportion p of the alleles at the locus in question are **A** alleles. Similarly, a proportion q of the gametes will carry the **a** allele. Now we can construct a Punnett square to see what happens to these gametes on fertilisation:

Gametes _Frequency_	**A** p	**a** q
A p	**AA** p^2	**Aa** pq
a q	**Aa** pq	**aa** q^2

You can see that the frequency of the **AA** genotype is p^2, that of the **Aa** genotype is $pq + pq = 2pq$, and that of the **aa** genotype is q^2.

This gives us the relationship between allele frequencies and _genotype_ frequencies. The relationship between allele frequencies and _phenotype_ frequencies is now easily worked out. Suppose that **A** is dominant to **a**. In that case, there are only two phenotypes to consider, one displayed by the homozygous recessive genotype, **aa**, and the other by the genotypes **AA** and **Aa**. The frequency of the recessive phenotype is simply q^2, while that of the dominant phenotype is equal to $2pq + q^2$.

Using the Hardy-Weinberg formula

To illustrate how the Hardy-Weinberg formula can be used, consider the inheritance of ear lobes in humans. Human ear lobes may be attached or free (figure 41.3). This difference is largely controlled by the actions of a single gene. The allele for free ear lobes, **F**, is dominant to the allele for attached ear lobes, **f**. As a result, people with free ear lobes are either homozygous dominant for the allele in question (**FF**) or heterozygous (**Ff**); people with attached ear lobes are homozygous recessive (**ff**).

Suppose that in a population 84 per cent of people have free ear lobes whereas the remaining 16 per cent do not. Using the Hardy-Weinberg formula we can calculate the frequencies of the **F** and **f** alleles and also work out the frequencies of the three different genotypes.

The genotypes will be distributed according to the Hardy-Weinberg equation:

$$p^2 + 2pq + q^2 = 1$$

where p^2 is the frequency of the homozygous dominant individuals (**FF**), $2pq$ the frequency of heterozygous individuals (**Ff**) and q^2 the frequency of the homozygous recessives (**ff**).

Now the 16 per cent of the population with attached ear lobes must have the genotype **ff**. So:

$$q^2 = 0.16$$

Therefore:

$$q = \sqrt{0.16}$$
$$= 0.4$$

But:

$$p + q = 1$$

Therefore:

$$p = 1 - 0.4$$
$$= 0.6$$

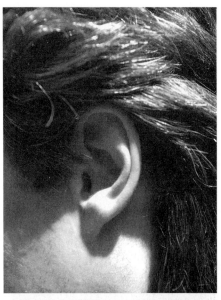

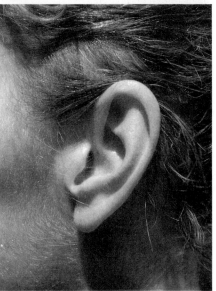

Figure 41.3
Top Attached ear lobe.
Bottom Unattached ear lobe.

When to use the Hardy-Weinberg equation

Phenylketonuria (PKU) is a hereditary disease found in 1 in 10 000 people in Britain who are homozygous recessive at a particular locus. People with the disease lack an enzyme which acts on the amino acid phenylalanine. As a result, phenylalanine in the diet is converted instead into a toxic compound which impairs brain development. Fortunately, mental subnormality can be avoided if a phenylalanine-free diet is taken during early childhood. Because of this, all children born in Britain are routinely tested for PKU and placed on such a diet if the test proves positive.

Question

What percentage of people in Britain are carriers of PKU?

Answer

Carriers are heterozygotes. Assuming Hardy-Weinberg equilibrium, we therefore need to calculate $2pq$. We know that 1 in 10 000 people are homozygous recessive. So:

$$q^2 = 1 \text{ in } 10\ 000$$
$$= 0.0001$$

which means that:

$$q = 0.01$$

So:

$$p = 0.99$$

Therefore:

$$2pq = 0.0198$$
$$\approx 0.02$$
$$\approx 2\%$$

We conclude that approximately two per cent of people in Britain carry the allele for phenylketonuria.

So by using the Hardy-Weinberg equation we have determined both q, the frequency of the recessive allele, and p, the frequency of the dominant allele.

Note that we used proportions when working out q from the information that $q^2 = 0.16$. You are advised always to use proportions, rather than percentages, when using the Hardy-Weinberg equation. This is because most people tend to assume that the square root of 16 per cent is 4 per cent, when in fact it is 40 per cent! Remember that 'per cent' is the Latin for 'out of a hundred', so that 16 per cent equals 16/100, the square root of which is 4/10, not 4/100.)

Having worked out the values of p and q, the proportion of the population who have the genotype **FF** can easily be calculated as it equals p^2. So:

$$p^2 = 0.6 \times 0.6$$
$$= 0.36$$

Similarly the frequency of the heterozygotes equals $2pq$. So:

$$2pq = 2 \times 0.6 \times 0.4$$
$$= 0.48$$

As a check, the frequencies of these three different genotypes should, of course, add up to 1, as each individual in the population must have one of these three genotypes. So:

$$p^2 + 2pq + q^2 = 0.36 + 0.48 + 0.16$$
$$= 1$$

as expected.

Assumptions made by the Hardy-Weinberg principle

Although the Hardy-Weinberg principle is a powerful tool in the study of population genetics, it does make a number of assumptions, and these need to be appreciated if the principle is not be used inappropriately.

First assumption: the population consists of diploid sexually reproducing organisms

As we said earlier, if a population is haploid, then genotype frequencies simply equal allele frequencies. The Hardy-Weinberg principle considers the relationship between these two variables for a diploid population. It also assumes that reproduction is sexual. Indeed, the whole question of what a population is takes on a new meaning if reproduction is asexual. To a large extent, species that reproduce only by asexual means consist of large numbers of clones (see page 568). Each clone contains individuals that are genetically identical with one another, apart from the occasional mutation. Over time clones gradually diverge from one another through the slow accumulation of distinct mutations.

Second assumption: the allele frequencies do not change over time

Earlier we saw that allele-specific mortality, reproduction, immigration or emigration all lead to changes in allele frequencies over time. Clearly any of these could invalidate the Hardy-Weinberg principle.

To take an extreme example, let us suppose that people with attached ear lobes always die in their early twenties (fortunately this does not happen). Were this to happen, then in the population we were considering on the previous page, the genotype frequencies would be as follows:

	FF	Ff	ff
People aged under 20	36%	48%	16%
People aged over 30	43%	57%	0%

Although people aged under 20 are in Hardy-Weinberg equilibrium, this is not the case for people aged over 30. In the same way as allele-sepecific mortality can invalidate the Hardy-Weinberg principle, so can allele-specific emigration, reproduction and immigration.

Third assumption: the population size is large

In very small populations, chance effects may generate ratios that appear not to conform with the predictions of the Hardy-Weinberg principle. Just as a family of six children might consist of five girls and a single boy, or even of six girls, so small populations may have genotypic and phenotypic ratios that differ from those expected from the allele frequencies. Statistical procedures can be used, however, to see whether such ratios can be accounted for by small population sizes.

Fourth assumption: mating is random with respect to genotype

Suppose that people with free ear lobes tend not to marry people with attached ear lobes. In that case the population will show a deficit of heterozygotes. The easiest way to see this is to make the rather extreme assumption that people always marry others with the same genotype for ear lobe attachment as themselves. In that case children can result from one of three sorts of mating:

1 FF x FF
2 Ff x Ff
3 ff x ff

Now matings **1** and **3**, in the absence of mutations, lead only to homozygotes. In the case of mating **2**, one quarter of the children that result are **FF**, one quarter **ff** and a half **Ff**. So in one generation the frequency of heterozygotes has halved, although there has been no change in allele frequencies. In the next generation the frequency of heterozygotes will again halve if children always result only from the union of people with the same genotype.

You might suppose that this example is completely fanciful. However, for almost every physical and mental characteristic, people do tend to marry individuals more similar to themselves than would be expected by chance. By and large tall people marry tall people, people with blue eyes marry people with blue eyes and people with outgoing happy-go-lucky personalities marry people with outgoing happy-go-lucky personalities. This is the way most dating agencies work. Once you have paid your fee, all the computer does is to arrange for you to meet someone of similar age, physical appearance and interests who doesn't live too far away – though most dating agencies do ensure that you and your date are of opposite sex.

The tendency for individuals to mate with individuals of similar phenotypes is called **assortative mating**. One of the very few examples known where people are more likely to marry individuals who *differ* from them in appearance occurs in respect of redhairedness. For some reason red-heads are less likely to marry red-heads than chance predicts.

Non-random mating with respect to genotype occurs in **inbreeding** when individuals are more likely to mate with relatives. Relatives, of course, are more likely to have the same genotypes, so that from the point of view of upsetting the Hardy-Weinberg equilibrium, assortative mating and inbreeding lead to similar consequences. The difference is that assortative mating usually disrupts the Hardy-Weinberg equilibrium at only a few loci, whereas inbreeding leads to a loss of heterozygosity at a very large number of loci.

When not to use the Hardy-Weinberg equation

In the MN human blood group system alleles **M** and **N** are codominant. Individuals with the genotype **MM** have the phenotype M, those with the genotype **MN** have the phenotype MN, and those with the genotype **NN** have the phenotype N.

Question

Suppose that 26 per cent of the population are blood group M and 44 per cent are blood group MN. What is the frequency of the **N** allele?

Answer

This is a population genetics question that should be answered *without* the use of the Hardy-Weinberg principle. The reason is that the two alleles, **M** and **N**, are codominant, which means that heterozygotes can be distinguished from both sorts of homozygotes. The best way to answer this question is as follows:

Consider 100 people in this population. 26 of them will have the genotype **MM** and 44 the genotype **MN**. Between them the 100 people have a total of 200 of the alleles in question: each **MM** person has two **M** alleles, each **MN** person one **M** and one **N** allele, and each **NN** person two **N** alleles. Of these two hundred alleles, the total number of M alleles is:

$(2 \times 26) + 44 = 96$

The frequency of the **M** allele is therefore:

$96/200 = 0.48$

Therefore the frequency of the **N** allele is:

$1 - 0.48 = 0.52$

$= 52\%$

After all this you might suppose that the assumptions of the Hardy-Weinberg principle are so strict that it can hardly ever be used in real life. In practice, however, it turns out that unless the assumptions of the principle are violated quite substantially, allele frequencies can usually be used to determine genotype and phenotype fequencies with some accuracy, and *vice versa*.

Population genetics in nature

Having seen how allele frequencies, genotype frequencies and phenotype fequencies are interrelated, we shall now look at two instances where these may change over time or space.

Colour variation in the peppered moth

One of the best studied examples of population genetics in nature is furnished by the peppered moth (*Biston betularia*) which has been studied by Bernard Kettlewell and others for over forty years.

The peppered moth is very common in Britain and normally rests in shaded sites on trees either under horizontal branches or where branches join the main trunk. Here it depends on its cryptic coloration to blend in with the background. The normal or *typica* form of the moth is speckled white, but another form is very much darker. This is called the **melanic** or *carbonaria* form.

The first melanic moths were reported in 1848 near Manchester. After that the number increased prodigiously in various parts of Britain. In the 1950s Kettlewell conducted an extensive survey on the relative abundance and distribution of the normal and melanic forms in different parts of the country (figure 41.4). The interesting fact that emerged was that the

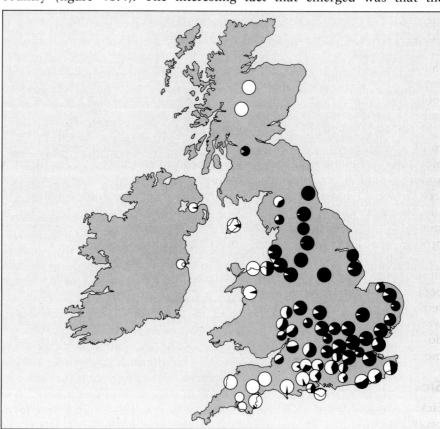

Figure 41.4 Map summarising the relative frequencies of the dark and light forms of the peppered moth (*Biston betularia*) in different parts of Britain in the 1950s. In each disc the white sector represents the light form and the black sector the dark form. The sizes of the discs indicate the number of moths examined at each locality. The dark form predominates in areas which are blackened by industrialisation.

melanic form abounded in industrial regions where smoke and soot from factory chimneys had blackened the bark of trees and killed off pale lichens. Around Manchester, for example, the frequency of the melanic form exceeded 95 per cent. In non-polluted areas, however, the light form predominated. In the north of Scotland and the extreme south-west of England it even reached 100 per cent.

How can we explain this distribution? The peppered moth is preyed upon by birds, such as great tits, which peck them off the trees. In polluted areas the dark form is almost invisible against the darkened branches, whereas the light form stands out like a beacon. In clean areas the reverse is true: the light form is admirably camouflaged against the background of unsooted lichens, but the dark form is very clearly seen (figure 41.5). Kettlewell showed that in polluted woods, such as occurred near Birmingham, far more light moths were picked off the trees by birds than the better camouflaged dark forms. As a result the frequency of dark moths was significantly higher. In non-polluted Dorset woods, however, it was mainly the dark moths that fell prey to the birds, so the frequency of the light moths was higher.

In each case differential mortality was achieved by **selective predation**. The darkening of trees with the coming of the industrial revolution meant that the dark body colour was favoured over light. In the last thirty years, however, there has been a significant reduction in industrial pollution in Britain. As a result the frequency of melanic moths has started to decline in industrial areas.

Genetics of the peppered moth

What about the genetics of the two forms? Breeding experiments have shown that the normal and the melanic forms differ at a single locus. The *carbonaria* allele is dominant to the *typica* allele so that heterozygotes are melanic. However, the story is more complicated than first appears to be the case. Kettlewell noted that in the 19th century the dominance of *carbonaria* over *typica* was not complete, so that heterozygotes were lighter than moths homozygous for the *carbonaria* allele. What seems to have happened as the *carbonaria* allele spread is that the darker a heterozygote looked, the more it was favoured. As a result the *carbonaria* allele evolved to be dominant to the *typica* allele.

Perhaps the easiest way to understand why the *carbonaria* allele evolved to be dominant is to consider the position of an unfortunate heterozygous moth that looked intermediate between the melanic and typical forms. Such a moth would be conspicuous both on a lichen-covered tree and on a dark tree. It would have the worst of both worlds. Understanding *how* the *carbonaria* allele has evolved to be dominant is more complicated and is still not fully understood. It involves genetic changes at other loci which produce proteins that modify the effects of the *carbonaria* allele.

Recent work by Mike Majerus at the University of Cambridge has shown that there is still a great deal to be learned about melanism in peppered moths and in other insects. For example, peppered moths tend to settle on backgrounds that camouflage them. Clearly this makes sense – it would be no good a melanic moth settling on a pale background. But how do the moths 'know' on what sort of background to rest? Also, do the moths mate at random or are melanics more likely to mate with melanics?

Sickle cell anaemia in humans

Sickle cell anaemia is a blood condition which is found in some blacks, peoples of Mediterranean countries, Arabs and Indians. In sickle cell

Figure 41.5 The light and dark forms of the peppered moth (*Biston betularia*) at rest on trees, *top* on a soot-covered oak tree near Birmingham, *bottom* on a lichen-covered tree in Dorset.

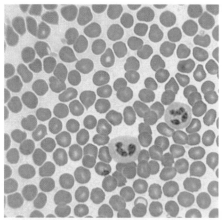

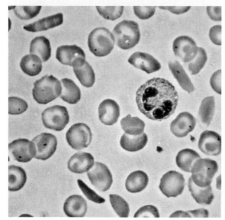

Figure 41.6

Top Light micrograph showing normal biconcave disc-shaped red blood cells. *Bottom* Light micrograph showing both sickle-shaped and disc-shaped red blood cells.

anaemia the normal haemoglobin in the red blood cells is entirely replaced by an abnormal haemoglobin known as **haemoglobin S**. Haemoglobin S is much less soluble than normal haemoglobin and it begins to crystallise when the oxygen concentration falls, as it does in the blood capillaries. This causes the red blood cells, normally biconcave disc-shaped, to assume the shape of a sickle or crescent (figure 41.6).

With their abnormal haemoglobin, the sickled red cells are less efficient at carrying oxygen. Not only that, but they may block the smaller arterioles and capillaries (figure 41.7). This can lead to acutely painful attacks called **crises**. The pain, rather like the pain of a heart attack, results from the lack of oxygen at the affected parts (see box opposite).

In Britain sickle cell anaemia is found in about 1 in 200 babies of West African origin, and in about 1 in 300 babies of Afro-Caribbean origin. Although some people with the disease live to a ripe old age, many die before reaching adulthood and few have any children.

What causes sickle cell anaemia? Following the discovery that people with sickle cell disease have a different form of haemoglobin, intensive research centered on finding the precise biochemical difference between haemoglobin S and normal haemoglobin. The difference was discovered in 1956 and turned out to be extremely slight: in haemoglobin S there is one position in each of the two β polypeptide chains in the haemoglobin molecule where the amino acid valine takes the place of glutamic acid. By causing this seemingly trivial change, the defective allele has far-reaching effects on the individual's physiology.

Recent studies of haemoglobin S using techniques such as X-ray diffraction and electron microscopy have shown that as haemoglobin S crystallises, the growing crystals distort the shape of the red blood cell. If a way could be found to prevent haemoglobin S from crystallising, then we would have a cure for sickle cell anaemia. This is not as far fetched as it may sound. For example, the amino acid phenylalanine delays crystallisation. However, the levels required are toxic. But hopefully a non-toxic substance will eventually be found which will prevent the crystallisation of haemoglobin S.

Global distribution of sickle cell anaemia

There are countries where sickle cell anaemia is much more frequent than in the United Kingdom. In parts of Africa as many as 1 in 25 children are born with the condition. Given that someone with sickle cell anaemia has two copies of the recessive sickle cell allele, you should be able to use the Hardy-Weinberg equation to show that if 1 in 25 people have the condition, the frequency of the allele responsible must be 1 in 5 (0.2 or 20 per cent).

Why is it that the sickle cell allele is so common when people with sickle cell anaemia usually die young, having left few if any children? A clue can be found by comparing the geographical distribution of the sickle cell allele with the geographical distribution of malaria (figure 41.8). Places with a high incidence of malaria also have a high frequency of the sickle cell allele.

It turns out that people who are heterozygous for the sickle cell condition are at an advantage in areas where malaria is common. This is because they are less susceptible to malaria than people who lack the sickle cell allele. This may sound surprising until you remember that the parasite responsible for malaria spends part of its life cycle in the human red blood cell (see page 80). Presumably it is less well adapted to living in red blood cells half of whose haemoglobin is haemoglobin S. Confusingly, however,

Section through small blood vessel showing normal flow of blood

Section through small blood vessel showing consequence of sickling

Figure 41.7 Sickled red blood cells cannot flow through very narrow blood vessels. They often get stuck and prevent the blood flowing freely. This is both painful and dangerous.

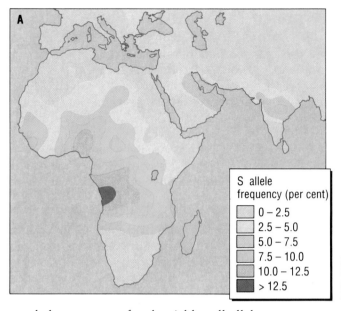 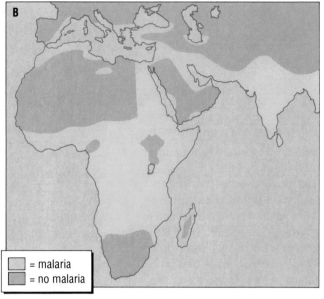

S allele
frequency (per cent)

☐ 0 – 2.5
☐ 2.5 – 5.0
☐ 5.0 – 7.5
☐ 7.5 – 10.0
☐ 10.0 – 12.5
☐ > 12.5

☐ = malaria
☐ = no malaria

people homozygous for the sickle-cell allele are very susceptible to malaria.

Heterozygotes are said to show **sickle cell trait** although phenotypically they are the same as people who are homozygous for the normal allele. Only by exposing their blood to unnaturally low oxygen concentrations can their red blood cells be made to sickle. Such a state of affairs is known as **heterozygous advantage** because the heterozygote is fitter than either of the homozygotes. It is because of heterozygous advantage that both the sickle cell allele and the normal allele persist. All this is summarised in table 41.1.

Figure 41.8 **A** The distribution of the sickle cell allele throughout Africa, southern Europe, the Middle East and India. Notice how this correlates with **B** the distribution of malaria in this region.

Genotype	Name given to genotype	Suffers from sickle cell anaemia?	Susceptible to malaria?
Hb^{A}Hb^A	Normal	No	Yes
Hb^{A}Hb^S	Sickle cell trait	No	Slightly
Hb^{S}Hb^S	Sickle cell anaemia	Yes	Very

Table 41.1 The relationship between genotype and phenotype at the sickle cell locus. **Hb^A**, normal allele; **Hb^S**, sickle cell allele.

A sickle cell crisis

"I had just ridden into town on my bike. It was quite cold and on my return my teeth were on edge. Like I'd just eaten an ice cream. Three hours later, the pain was quite bad. It settled for a while and then went to my back and jaw. So my friends decided that it was Casualty time. I followed reluctantly. I always reached Casualty at all hospitals with a mixed feeling of relief and dread. On this occasion I had good reason to feel dread, I didn't see a doctor for another one and a half hours. He quickly looked me over and then stalked out mumbling something about haematologists and their responsibility.

Two hours later I was still waiting. I was trying desperately to stop myself from crying out in front of my friends. However, I couldn't help it and I started to bawl like a baby. Twice my friends asked what the hold-up was and at one point I fell off the trolley. I got up, saying that I had had enough. I went out and asked: 'How much longer?' I was calmly told that 'Doctor was on his way.' My jaw had clamped shut with the pain by this time. After four and a half hours, I was finally admitted to the ward and given pethidine, a pain-killer.

On the ward, I was constantly told off for all the noise that I was making. I felt guilty enough without being told; I didn't want to keep everyone awake. After about two hours I was moved to another bay to keep some other patients awake. By morning I had a temperature of 39.5 and I was delirious. Nothing else existed except the agony I was experiencing. When the doctors came, they asked stupid questions like, how bad was the pain? Christ, how I hate that question, and they all ask it. Pain is pain, never mind what kind. How in God's name do you describe the kind of pain that you are experiencing?

I was only a patient for six days. It felt like six months."

(Abstracted from *Pain in Sickle Cell Disease*, a Sickle Cell Society Publication)

Genetic polymorphism

The peppered moth (*Biston betularia*) and many other animal and plant species exhibit the phenomenon of **polymorphism**. Literally this means 'having many forms' and it may be defined as the existence within a particular species of two or more distinct types of individual. In some cases the different types may result from differences of environment, but in **genetic polymorphism** the different forms, or **morphs** as they are termed, have a genetic basis and their distinctive characteristics are transmitted in a Mendelian manner. A genetic polymorphism occurs when two or more alleles in a population are maintained at levels above those that can be accounted for by mutations alone. An example in humans is the ABO blood group system (see page 703).

The difference between a genetic polymorphism and one which results from environmental factors is seen in the different sorts of individuals found in a honey bee colony. As we saw in Chapter 30, a honey bee colony contains a queen, a number of drones and a very large number of workers. The queen and workers are all females and the differences between them result from the way they are reared as larvae. However, drones are males and differ genetically from the other members of the hive.

With the exception of sex, which is usually determined by the possession of one or more specialised chromosomes, genetic polymorphisms usually result from the possession of alternative alleles by the various morphs. One, or at most a few, loci are involved. In the case of colour variation in the peppered moth, just one locus (i.e. one gene) is involved. This is also true for sickle cell anaemia in humans.

Two types of genetic polymorphism are recognised: **transient** and **balanced**. In the former a genetically-controlled morph is in the process of spreading through a population. Eventually the population may become uniform and the polymorphism disappear. In industrial areas the spread of the melanic form of the peppered moth provides us with an example of a transient polymorphism.

In a balanced polymorphism the different morphs – and thus the alleles responsible for them – occur in fairly constant proportions within a given population. A balanced polymorphism is achieved by the existence of relative advantages and disadvantages, each morph being favoured in the particular conditions that occur within a varied environment. The sickle cell condition in humans provides an example of a balanced polymorphism.

Often in a genetic polymorphism the various forms possess what appear to be trivial differences which one can hardly imagine would be of any significance in terms of survival and reproduction. However, it can sometimes be demonstrated that the various forms are associated with more important differences, such as viability and fecundity. For example, there would at first sight appear to be no advantage to having a particular blood group within the ABO system. But in fact there is evidence that people belonging to blood groups A and AB were more susceptible to smallpox (now extinct) than people belonging to groups O and B. On the other hand, members of group O are about 40 per cent more likely to develop duodenal ulcers than members of the other two blood groups. The present global distribution of the three alleles, I^A, I^B and I^O is probably due partly to such factors and partly to migrations of people from one place to another.

In this chapter we have seen how the genotype of an individual can affect its chances of survival and reproduction. But what is the evidence that over time changes in allele frequencies can lead to the evolution of new species? To answer this question we need first to look at the evidence for evolution itself, and this is the subject of the next chapter.

Cyanogenesis in clover

Most populations of white clover (*Trifolium repens*) are polymorphic at two particular loci. Between them these loci are responsible for the production of **hydrogen cyanide**. In 1954 the geneticist H. Daday showed that the occurrence of the cyanogenic phenotypes across Europe correlated closely with mean January temperatures. The warmer the winters, the more clover plants contain hydrogen cyanide.

Subsequent studies have shown that slugs, snails and voles prefer to eat clover plants that lack the ability to produce hydrogen cyanide. As cyanide is a poison which inhibits respiration, this is hardly surprising. However, clover plants that can produce hydrogen cyanide are more susceptible to frost damage.

There are thus two opposing ecological pressures. The action of herbivores favours hydrogen cyanide production, but the occurrence of frost favours the *absence* of hydrogen cyanide production. The result is a more or less uniform change of gene frequencies across Europe. The milder the winters, the greater the proportion of clover plants that produce hydrogen cyanide.

A regular correlation between the occurrence of a particular genotype and some geographical feature such as latitude or altitude is known as a **cline**. The European distribution of hydrogen cyanide production in white clover is therefore an example of a cline.

Summary

1 A population genetically isolated from other populations is called a **deme**, and the sum total of all the different genes in a deme is known as the **gene pool**.

2 The frequency of any given allele in a population is known as the **allele frequency**.

3 Over time, allele frequencies can be changed by **allele-specific mortality, emigration, reproduction** or **immigration** and by **genetic drift** and **mutation**.

4 If only a few individuals start a new population, the gene pool of the new population may differ from that of the parent population, a phenomenon known as the **founder effect**.

5 The **Hardy-Weinberg principle** states that, provided certain conditions are met, if the frequency of allele **A** is p, and of the alternative allele **a** is q, then the frequencies of the three genotypes **AA**, **Aa** and **aa** are given respectively by p^2, $2pq$ and q^2.

6 The assumptions made by the Hardy-Weinberg principle are that the population consists of diploid sexually reproducing organisms, that there are no changes in allele frequencies over time, that the population size is large and that there is random mating with respect to genotype.

7 Provided its assumptions are met, the Hardy-Weinberg principle can be used to work out allele frequencies from phenotype frequecies, or *vice versa*.

8 The peppered moth provides an example of natural variation in populations which have been extensively studied by population geneticists.

9 **Sickle cell anaemia** is a blood condition in which the normal haemoglobin in the red blood cells is replaced by abnormal **haemoglobin S**. The allele responsible is recessive, though heterozygous individuals are less likely to die from malaria than either of the two homozygotes.

10 A **genetic polymorphism** occurs when two or more alleles in a population are maintained at levels above those that can be accounted for by mutation alone. They may by **transient (unstable)** or **balanced (stable)**.

11 Balanced genetic polymorphisms often result from **heterozygous advantage** in which heterozygotes are fitter than either homozygote.

Review questions

1 Distinguish clearly between allele frequency, genotype frequency and phenotype frequency. How are these three variables interconnected?

2 Which of the following would you expect to *fail* to show Hardy-Weinberg equilibria, and why:

(a) Rabbits in Australia?
(b) Pedigree labrador dogs?
(c) *Spirogyra* in a pond?
(d) An angiosperm capable of both cross- and self-pollination growing on a small island without any pollinators?

3 Why do you think people usually end up marrying people much like themselves? Answer as scientifically as you can!

4 Can you produce a non-mathematical approximation of the Hardy-Weinberg formula?

5 Many species of ladybirds show considerable variation. How might you determine whether such variation is the result of genetic polymorphism?

6 Can you suggest why the peppered moth has not evolved into two species, one adapted to polluted environments and the other to unpolluted ones?

7 Cystic fibrosis is a disease of humans caused by the possession of a recessive allele in the homozygous state. If about 1 in 2000 children in the UK are born with the condition, what percentage of people are carriers for the disease?

8 Explain what is meant by the term *heterozygous advantage*.

9 Discuss why some genetic polymorphisms are transient and others balanced.

10 Why do you think human eye colours vary so much?

Further reading

The 61st volume in the Collins New Naturalist series is called *Inheritance and Natural History* and was written by Professor R.J. Berry. Although published in 1977 it is well worth consulting as it provides a fascinating account of genetic variation in the animals and plants of the British Isles.

Population Genetics by J.S. Gale (Blackie, 1980) is worth looking at if you are interested in quantitative aspects of population genetics.

'Moths, melanism and clean air' by J.A. Bishop and L.M. Cook, *Scientific American* **232**(1) 90–99 (1979) gives a beautifully clear summary of research carried out on the peppered moth.

The concept of race

Within a species there may be sub-divisions of individuals which share common biological characteristics that distinguish them from other such groups. Such sub-divisions are often referred to by biologists as **races**. For example, the herring gull (*Larus argentatus*) is divided into several races, among which are the Western European race (*L. argentatus argentatus*) and the Eastern Scandinavian race (*L. argentatus omissus*). These two races differ in that the Western European form has a pale silver grey back and pink legs, while the Eastern Scandinavian race has a dark slate grey back and yellow legs (illustration 1). However, both races belong to the same species, as they produce viable offspring when interbred.

How great do the differences between the sub-divisions of a species have to be for them to be described as races? It is difficult to answer this categorically. Certainly no one would describe the melanic and pale morphs of the peppered moths as belonging to distinct races as only one locus is involved and the two morphs regularly interbreed in nature. For two morphs to be classified as distinct races, several loci must be involved and the morphs must usually be geographically separated in nature so that interbreeding, though possible, is rare.

To what extent can races be identified in humans? Until the 1960s most biologists classified humans into a number of distinct races. In 1962, for instance, the anthropologist C.S. Coon recognised five racial groupings (illustration 2):

- **Capoids** – cape bushmen of southern Africa;
- **Negroids** – other black people south of the Sahara;
- **Caucasoids** – white people indigenous to Europe and West Asia;
- **Mongoloids** – people indigenous to East Asia and North and South America;
- **Australoids** – aboriginal people of Australia and New Guinea.

Over the last twenty years, however, many people have increasingly felt it unhelpful to classify people into races. For a start, the genetic diversity *within* each of the above five racial groupings is considerably greater than the genetic distance *between* them. Secondly, over the last few centuries travel has been such that in almost every country of the world, significant numbers of people are to be found belonging to more than one of these racial groupings, thus blurring the distinctions between them. Thirdly, the concept of race in humans has on occasions been abused for political ends, as in apartheid in South Africa, so that the concept is now felt by many to be distasteful.

Illustration 1 Two races of herring gull.
A Western European race.
B Eastern Scandinavian race.

A Cape bush woman from Namibia.

B Zulu woman and baby.

C Caucasian woman of Celtic and Polish/Russian descent.

D Tamang woman from Nepal.

E Aboriginal woman from Australia.

Illustration 2

Evolution in evidence

As far as we know, our planet is unique in possessing living organisms. Of course, life may yet be discovered elsewhere in the Universe, but it is possible that life exists only on the planet Earth. Here it is certainly found in abundance, often in inhospitable places. There are an estimated twenty to thirty million species in existence today, while from the air most land looks green, witnessing to the presence of countless photosynthetic autotrophs. The question to which all biologists seek an answer is: how did such tremendous diversity of life come to exist on this planet?

Darwin and the theory of evolution

The person whose name is most closely associated with this question is Charles Darwin (1809–1882). Ever since his days as a Cambridge undergraduate Darwin had been a keen naturalist, devoting much of his time to collecting animals and plants, especially beetles. But his real opportunity came in 1831 when he was offered a berth on HMS *Beagle*, a small ship which was to sail round the world on a map-making survey. The journey took nearly five years and the many stops, some of them several months long, gave Darwin an unparalleled opportunity to explore the flora and fauna of many different parts of the world.

During his long voyage Darwin was gradually forced towards the conclusion that organisms have **evolved** by a slow and gradual change over successive generations, this being brought about by **natural selection**. For twenty years after returning from his voyage Darwin consolidated his data and filled in the details of his theory, seeking support for his ideas from geology, embryology and other branches of biology. On 24 November 1859 his book *The Origin of Species by means of Natural Selection or the Preservation of Favoured Races in the Struggle for Life* was published. The entire first edition sold out on its day of publication and a second edition was quickly produced. The book has been in print ever since and is without serious doubt the most important biology book ever written.

The reason for the importance of Darwin's book was that it was the first theory of evolution to be fully supported by evidence and backed up by a credible theory to explain the mechanism by which evolution occurs. This was not in fact the first announcement of the theory, as the previous year Darwin had published a short paper with Alfred Russel Wallace who had independently thought of the same mechanism for evolution as Darwin. However, despite the fact that they published their theory jointly, Darwin is the person better remembered for the theory, partly because of the huge mass of evidence he collected in its defence, and partly because he published his ideas in the form of a book.

Darwin and society

Nowadays most people take evolution for granted, but it should be remembered that the climate of opinion in the middle of the 19th century far from favoured the notion. Although the idea had been in the air for some time, most people preferred to believe that animals and plants had arisen by a supernatural act of **special creation** – each kind of organism being formed separately. It had even been calculated by the ingenious Dr Lightfoot, vicar of the University Church at Cambridge, that the world had been created at 9 a.m. on 23 October 4004 BC. Although many people felt that the exact date could not be determined as precisely as this, it was generally thought

Figure 42.1 A lone kokerboom tree in the Namib Desert, south-west Africa. How did life come to exist in such an inhospitable environment?

Figure 42.2 Charles Darwin at the age of 40.

Why did Darwin take so long to publish his theory?

In 1831 Darwin set out on his Beagle voyage believing that species were created separately in much the form as they exist today. By 1838 he was convinced that all species, including humans, had evolved by natural selection.

Darwin realised the importance of his ideas and in 1842, and again in 1844, wrote them out in detail leaving strict instructions with his wife to publish them should he die. Yet he didn't publish his ideas until 1858 when Wallace's independent discovery forced his hand.

So why did Darwin take so long to publish his theory?

Conventional wisdom has it that he spent the time gathering evidence for his ideas. No doubt there is some truth in this, but twenty years!

Another explanation is that he was afraid of public reaction. It is difficult for us nowadays to recognise the impact of his ideas on Victorian England. When an entire society, tens of millions of people, believe that they are recently descended from Adam, a perfect, sinless immortal created by God in his own image out of the dust of the Earth, it takes courage to publish a theory which implies that we are descended from an endless series of animal forms that date back countless millions of years to the beginnings of life itself.

By all accounts Darwin was a quiet and relatively shy man. Though not a recluse, he seems to have cared little for the cut and thrust of academic debate and public life, preferring instead the company of his family. It is an intriguing question whether he would ever have published his theory had it not been for Wallace.

that the Earth was no more than ten thousand years old. Darwin's theory required the Earth to be many millions of years old and this was widely held to be ridiculous, particularly as the chronologies of the Old Testament, if interpreted literally, required Adam and Eve to have been created by God only about six thousand years ago.

Darwin therefore found himself immediately at the centre of controversy. He was opposed not so much by the Church, for many leading theologians had little difficulty in accepting his ideas, but by Victorian society in general. The idea that humans were descended from other animals was felt to be insulting, even blasphemous.

Darwin was a shy man. However, the biologist T.H. Huxley, a close friend, soon became known as 'Darwin's bulldog' as he tirelessly defended Darwin's theories both in print and in public debate. The most famous confrontation Huxley experienced was with the Bishop of Oxford, Dr Samuel Wilberforce, whose fluency as a speaker earned him the nickname of Soapy Sam. In a public debate the bishop asked Huxley if he traced his descent from an ape through his grandfather or his grandmother; whereupon Huxley replied that he would rather be descended from an ape than from an intelligent being 'who uses his gifts to discredit and crush humble seekers after truth'.

The newspapers of the day were divided as to whether Huxley or Wilberforce had won the argument, but despite these stormy beginnings Darwin's theory is generally held to have stood the test of time and, with certain modifications, is accepted today by practically all biologists.

What did Darwin do?

In essence Darwin did two things. First, he marshalled powerful evidence supporting the proposition that species have not remained largely unaltered through time, but have gradually changed from one form into another. This was by no means an entirely new idea – it is found in the writings of some earlier naturalists and philosophers – but Darwin was the first person to put it on a sound scientific basis. Some of Darwin's evidence was based on the geographical distribution of the animals and plants he had observed during his five-year voyage.

Darwin then went on to argue that if species have arisen by gradual change it should be possible to learn something about their ancestry from the similarities and differences between them, and from their embryology and fossil record. This he set out to do with painstaking care and thoroughness. The result was that he gave a new purpose and direction to much of biological enquiry. The old disciplines of comparative anatomy and palaeontology took on a new form. No longer purely descriptive, these subjects increasingly became concerned with tracing the ancestral history of organisms and this helped to establish the essential correctness of Darwin's theory.

The second thing Darwin did was to put forward a plausible theory explaining the mechanism by which species have changed. As a naturalist Darwin was enormously impressed with the remarkable way organisms are adapted to their surroudings (see Chapters 3 and 5). Darwin explained this by postulating that individuals of a species differ from each other in the degree to which they are suited to their environment. The poorly adapted ones, he argued, perish while the well adapted ones survive and hand on their beneficial characteristics to their offspring. This is what is meant by natural selection, nature as it were selecting the 'fit' and rejecting the 'unfit'.

To Darwin natural selection provided an explanation of the extinct forms seen so clearly in the fossil record. We shall return to this in Chapter

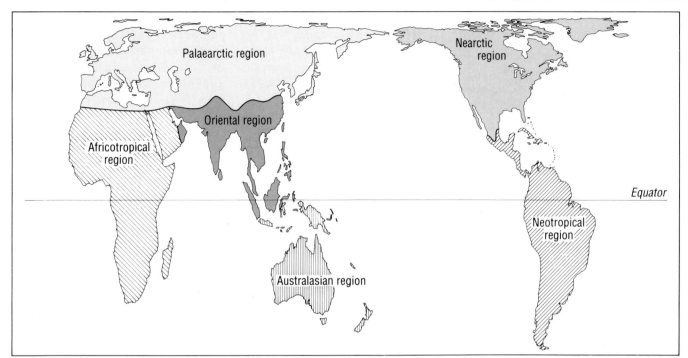

Figure 42.3 The major biogeographical regions of the world.

43. In the present chapter we shall be concerned with the way evolution reveals itself – or *appears* to reveal itself – in different areas of biology. The areas we shall discuss are:

- Geographical distribution.
- Comparative anatomy.
- Molecular biology.
- Embryology.
- Taxonomy.
- Palaeontology.

Geographical distribution studies

Travellers to foreign countries are often struck by the fact that a country with a similar climate to their own may nevertheless have different animals and plants. To illustrate this let us look at the general distribution of mammals in the continents of the world.

Continental distribution

The world can be divided into a number of **biogeographical regions** (figure 42.3). The exact number varies from one authority to another, but around six can be recognised, corresponding more or less to the world's continents.

First consider Africa and South America. Both contain approximately the same range of latitude, and both have much the same variety of habitats – humid jungles, dry plains, high mountain ranges and so forth – and yet each supports a different fauna. True, many of the same major groups are found on both continents, but for the most part the individual species and genera are different. Thus Africa has short-tailed (Old World) monkeys, anthropoid apes, the African elephant, the dromedary (one-humped) camel, antelopes, the giraffe and the lion, to mention but a few of the mammals. South America, however, has none of these. Instead we find such mammals as long-tailed (New World) monkeys, llamas, tapirs, the puma ('mountain lion') and the jaguar. A tapir is shown in figure 42.4.

Figure 42.4 Baird's tapir from Venezuela, one of a number of mammals indigenous to South America which contrast sharply with the mammals found in other continents of the Southern Hemisphere.

Alfred Russel Wallace

Alfred Russel Wallace was born on 7 January 1823. He was one of eight children and left school at the age of 14 because of his family's financial difficulties. In 1843 he became a teacher at a Leicester boarding school. There he had a stroke of good fortune: he met the naturalist Henry Bates (remembered today for Batesian mimicry – see page 90).

As a result of this meeting Wallace found himself at the age of 25, despite his lack of biological education, deep in the Amazon basin with Bates on a four year expedition. Despite being short of food, and suffering periodically from malaria, tropical ulcers and other infections, Wallace collected nearly 15 000 animal species, some 8000 of which were new to science.

Then disaster struck. On the return journey in 1852 the ship caught fire and Wallace lost all his specimens and most of his notes. Undeterred, he set off in 1854 for what was to prove to be an eight year expedition

to the Malay Archipelago. It was here in 1858 that, as he lay ill with fever, he wondered 'Why do some die and some live? ... from the effects of disease, the most healthy escape; from enemies, the strongest, the swiftest, or the most cunning; from famine, the best hunters or those with the best digestion.' On his recovery Wallace wrote a 12 page paper on his ideas and sent it to Darwin asking him to forward it to the geologist Sir Charles Lyell.

Darwin received Wallace's letter on 18 June 1858 and was stunned. Its basic argument was identical to his own. Sixteen years before, in 1842, Darwin had sketched out his theory of natural selection and two years later had expanded it into a 160 page manuscript. However, he had published neither his sketch nor the essay. Wallace's letter came out of the blue. Darwin wrote in confusion to Lyell, the botanist Joseph Hooker and others. The result was that a meeting of the Linnean Society in London was presented with Wallace's letter together with a five

page summary of Darwin's theory. For these reasons we should think of the theory of natural selection not just as Darwin's theory, but as the Darwin-Wallace theory.

Wallace returned from his eight year expedition in 1862, having collected an incredible 125 660 specimens. For the rest of his long life he remained in England, writing and lecturing. He seems to have been a very modest man, calling, for instance, his book on natural selection *Darwinism*.

He had a great belief in social reform, exposing, for example, the greed of absentee English landlords in Ireland and Scotland. His passion for social reform brought him into conflict with the establishment and he wasn't elected a Fellow of the Royal Society until he was 69 years old.

He lived for another 21 years, dying in 1913. By that time the Darwin-Wallace theory of natural selection had become almost universally accepted as the cornerstone of modern biology.

If we take Australia into consideration as well, we find even greater differences despite the fact that it, too, lies on the same latitude as much of South America and Africa. In Australia we find pouched mammals (**marsupials**), such as kangaroos, which are totally absent from Africa and are represented in South America only by opossums. It is in Australia that we find the duck-billed platypus and spiny anteater, the only living representatives of the **prototherians**, a group of egg-laying mammals found nowhere else in the world. So distinctive are these animals that when the first stuffed duck-billed platypus was brought back to Europe in 1798, it was widely believed by reputable zoologists to be a fake, made by stitching together parts of a duck with parts of a mammal.

Australia is also distinctive in the mammals it *lacks*. It has very few placental (eutherian) mammals, except for those that have been introduced by humans, their place being taken by the many different marsupials (figure 42.5). The marsupials have evolved to occupy the ecological niches filled on other continents by eutherian mammals.

Africa, South America and Australia are all in the Southern Hemisphere. If, however, we examine the mammals of the Northern Hemisphere, we find that the differences are far less pronounced. In both North America and Eurasia we find reindeer, red deer (called wapiti or elk in North America), bison, beavers, hares, wild goats, mountain sheep, bears and the lynx. In some cases the same species is found in North America and Eurasia, e.g. the lynx (figure 42.6). In other cases, one species occurs in

North America and another very similar species in the same genus is found in Eurasia, as is the case with beavers (figure 42.7).

Explanation of continental distribution

We are left, then, with the general picture of the two great continents of the Northern Hemisphere having very similar mammals, whereas the three southern continents have sharply contrasting mammals. How can we explain this? A glance at a map of the world will remind you that whereas South America, Africa and Australia are separated from one another by great bodies of water, North America and Asia are separated only by a shallow strait (the Bering Strait), less than 100 km wide. Moreover, there is evidence that in the geological past a continuous land bridge linked these two northern continents across what is now the strait.

Figure 42.5 Australasian marsupials.
A Great grey kangaroos.
B Spotted cuscus.
C Koala and young.
D Marsupial wolf (now almost certainly extinct).
E Sugar glider possum.

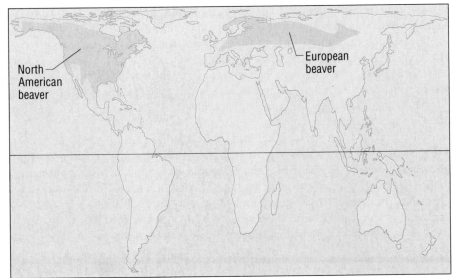

Figure 42.7 Many of the mammals of North America are closely related to those found in Eurasia. The map shows the non-overlapping distributions of the North American beaver (*Castor canadensis*) and the European beaver (*C. fiber*).

Figure 42.6 The lynx, a species found throughout the northern latitudes.

A possible hypothesis to explain the geographical distribution of mammals is that evolution gave rise to new species and genera, some of which moved from North America to Eurasia, or *vice versa*. In other words, different mammals evolved in these two continents, but the geographical closeness of the two regions kept their faunas together and prevented them from diverging very greatly. On the other hand, the wide separation of the three continents of the Southern Hemisphere meant that only very rarely was there any exchange of mammals between them, so the mammals of each evolved independently along their own lines.

How can we test this hypothesis? One way is to look at the distribution of fossil organisms such as the camel family, the Camelidae. The oldest fossils of this group, belonging to the Eocene early in the Tertiary period, have been found in North America. Their distribution suggests that this is where they originated and that later, during the Pliocene, they migrated southwards into South America, and westwards into Asia and thence North Africa. Fossil evidence supports the idea that here, in these separate continents, they evolved along their own lines. Today the Camelidae are represented by the modern camels in Afro-Asia, and the llama in South America, both fundamentally similar but different in detail.

Continental drift

The fossils of the southern continents have revealed some interesting things. Such is the case with the fossil reptile, *Mesosaurus* (figure 42.8). *Mesosaurus* lived about 270 million years ago. Measuring about a metre in length, it had webbed feet, a long tail and numerous sharp teeth. It appears to have been well adapted to living in freshwater where it probably fed on small fish.

In itself, *Mesosaurus* is of no great importance, unless you are interested in fossil reptiles. However, its geographical distribution is striking. It is found in fossil deposits in only two places: the eastern side of South America and the western side of South Africa (figure 42.9). How can we explain this? It is unlikely that this reptile could have migrated from one of these two continents to the other via a northern land route without leaving any fossil remains in between; and it seems unlikely that it could have swum over 3000 miles across the Atlantic. There is, however, another possible explanation which would help to explain the distribution not only of *Mesosaurus*, but of many other animals and plants as well.

If you look at a map of the modern world (figure 42.9), the complementary shapes of South America and Africa are striking. If you bring them into close proximity, they fit together quite snugly like the pieces of a jigsaw puzzle. This has led to the suggestion that at one time South America and Africa were joined together. But if this was indeed the case, how come they are now so far apart?

One theory is that America and Africa have gradually moved apart. This theory of **continental drift** was proposed by the geologist Alfed Wegener in 1912. At the time very few scientists took his ideas seriously, mainly because they could not envisage a mechanism for continental drift. However, since the 1960s more and more geophysical and oceanographic evidence has come to light suggesting that the continents, far from being fixed in their present positions, have indeed moved about the surface of the globe and are still doing so. Further, the theory of **plate tectonics** provides an understanding of how continents move and allows geologists to reconstruct what the surface of our planet may have looked like in previous eras (figure 42.10).

You can see from figure 42.10 that when *Mesosaurus* existed, South

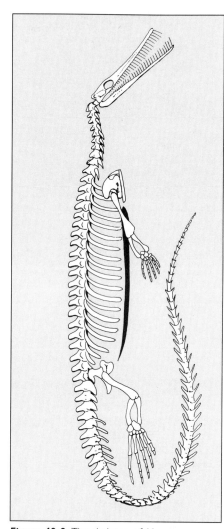

Figure 42.8 The skeleton of *Mesosaurus*, a fossil reptile about a metre in length that lived around 270 million years ago. This animal is found in fossil deposits in the eastern side of South America and the western side of South Africa. One possible explanation for its distribution is that when this animal lived, South America and South Africa were joined together.

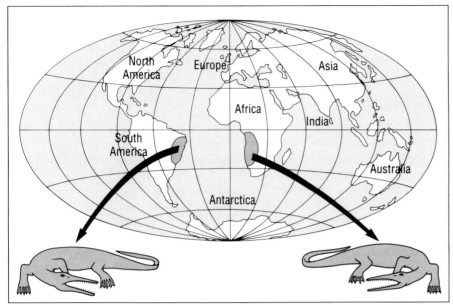

America and Africa may well have been united, along with the other land masses, into a single supercontinent called **Pangea** ('all the earth'). There is considerable argument over the timing, but it is generally agreed that South America, Antarctica and Australia had separated from the other continents but were still joined to each other when the first marsupials were evolving. Fossil marsupials have recently been found on Antarctica, exactly as this would predict.

Oceanic islands

If the effects of geographical isolation are well shown by the three great southern continents, they are even more clearly seen in the faunas of oceanic islands. An oceanic island is one which has never had any connection with the mainland. Most of them are formed by a submerged volcanic mountain erupting and pushing up above the surface of the sea. This has happened at intervals throughout geological time and still takes place today (figure 42.11). Once it has broken the surface, the exposed mountain peak cools down and in the fullness of time becomes an island available for colonisation by any organisms that can get there.

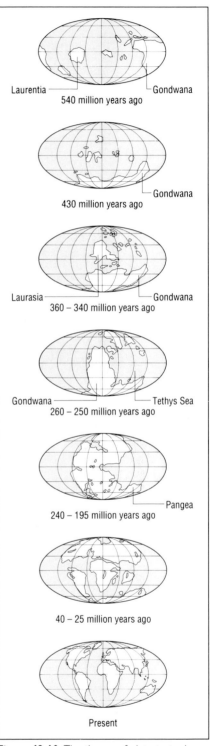

Laurentia — Gondwana
540 million years ago

Gondwana
430 million years ago

Laurasia — Gondwana
360 – 340 million years ago

Gondwana — Tethys Sea
260 – 250 million years ago

Pangea
240 – 195 million years ago

40 – 25 million years ago

Present

Figure 42.10 The theory of plate tectonics predicts that the continents have slowly moved and changed shape over time. This diagram shows what the distribution of land and sea is thought to have been at various times over the last 540 million years.

Figure 42.11 Surtsey, a volcanic island which erupted into existence 30 km south of Iceland on 14 November 1963.

Organisms reach volcanic islands in a variety of ways. Some are blown there by the wind, as spores for example; others are carried by ocean currents, sometimes clinging to drift-wood; still others arrive on the bodies of other organisms – plant seeds, for instance, may be carried in mud on the feet of birds.

The Galapagos Islands

On his voyage aboard the *Beagle*, Darwin visited the Galapagos Islands. These islands are situated on the equator some 900 km west of Ecuador in South America (figure 42.12). It is thought that the islands were formed by volcanic action and so were at first devoid of life. Later they became colonised by organisms from the mainland. These then evolved along their own lines into species which, though fundamentally similar to the mainland forms, differ from them in certain respects.

Despite the harmful effects of animals that have been introduced there by humans within the last few hundred years, the Galapagos Islands are a biologist's paradise. This is not because of their climate, for it is generally exceptionally hot on the islands, and some of them lack fresh water. Rather it is because the islands demonstrate the effect that isolation can have on subsequent evolution.

What Darwin saw on the Galapagos Islands during the month that the *Beagle* anchored there shaped his ideas about evolution more forcibly than any other single experience during his five-year voyage. As he himself wrote: 'Here, both in space and time, we seem to be brought somewhat near to that great fact – that mystery of mysteries – the first appearance of new beings on this earth'. The Galapagos flora and fauna are unique and, seen against the background of volcanic rock and twisted larva, it makes a visit to the islands seem like stepping back into a past geological age.

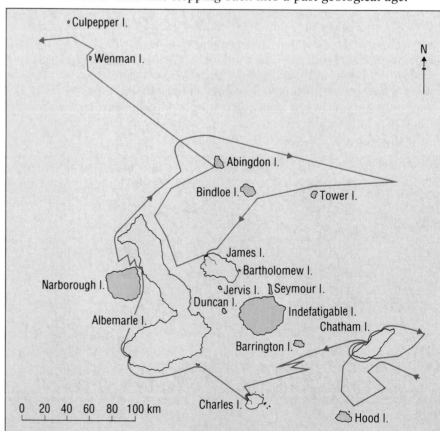

Figure 42.12 The Galapagos Islands lie some 900 km west of Ecuador. The arrowed line shows the path taken by the *Beagle* on Darwin's voyage. The four islands coloured green are the ones Darwin visited.

Among the more prominent inhabitants of the islands at the time Darwin visited them were the **giant iguana lizards** (figure 42.13). About 1¼ metres long, there are two species, one terrestrial and the other marine. The marine species is the only known aquatic lizard, and is adapted for living in water by having webbed feet and a laterally-flattened tail which it uses for propelling itself like a newt. The terrestrial species was extremely abundant at the time that Darwin visited the islands, and it is thought that the marine form evolved from it as a result of overcrowding and competition for food on land. Both species are herbivorous, the land species feeding on leaves and other types of vegetation, the marine species on seaweed.

Darwin's finches

While on the Galapagos Islands Darwin also collected a number of small birds – all finches of one kind or another. At the time these did not interest him as much as some of the other organisms he had seen on the islands, but later he saw in these finches the key to uderstanding the evolutionary process. Darwin was familiar with similar finches on the mainland of South America. There they all possess short straight beaks which they use to crush seeds. On the Galapagos islands, however, there are a total of thirteen species of finch which fall into six main types, each having a beak specially adapted for dealing with a particular kind of food (figure 42.14).

Between them, the Galapagos finches exploit a wide range of ecological niches which on the mainland are mainly occupied by other types of bird. The **ground finches**, the closest to the mainland finches in form and habit,

Figure 42.13 Giant iguana lizards on the Galapagos Islands.
Top The terrestrial iguana.
Bottom The marine iguana.

Woodpecker finch

Warbler finch

Insectivorous tree finches

Vegetarian tree finch

Ground finches

Cactus finches

Figure 42.14 The heads of the 13 species of finches found on the Galapagos Islands arranged according to their possible evolutionary relationships.

have typical finch-like beaks for crushing seeds. In contrast, the **cactus finches** have long straight beaks and split tongues with which they obtain nectar from the flowers of the tree-sized prickly pear cactus which grows in abundance on the islands. The **vegetarian tree finch**, on the other hand, has a curved parrot-like beak with which it feeds on buds and fruits. The **insectivorous tree finches** have similar beaks which they use for feeding on beetles and other small insects. Then there is the **warbler finch** which is so like a true warbler that at first it was thought to be one. It uses its slender beak for feeding on small insects which it catches on the wing just as true warblers do.

Perhaps the most remarkable of all the Galapagos finches is the **woodpecker finch** (figure 42.15). This resembles a true woodpecker in its ability to climb up vertical tree trunks and bore holes in wood in search of insects. But whereas true woodpeckers use their long tongues to seek out insects, the woodpecker finch, which lacks a long tongue, picks up a cactus spine in its beak and pokes this into holes. When the insect emerges, the bird drops the spine and devours the insect. Although the operation is time-consuming compared to the way a true woodpecker feeds, the technique allows the woodpecker finch to exploit a niche that would otherwise be vacant as there are no true woodpeckers on the Galapagos islands. Quite apart from its evolutionary implications, the woodpecker finch is remarkable for being one of the few species other than ourselves to use a tool.

The Galapagos finches afford an excellent example of **adaptive radiation**. It is assumed that a stock of ancestral finches reached the islands from the mainland and then, in the absence of much competition, evolved to fill many of the empty ecological niches occupied on the mainland by species absent from the islands. Presumably, given more time, the various Galapagos finches might diverge even further.

The Galapagos tortoises

Further inland on the Galapagos Islands, where the vegetation becomes more lush and plentiful, **giant land tortoises** are found. These unique organisms give their name to the islands, as galapagos is the Spanish for tortoise. The first fact about them to strike Darwin was simply their size. They may reach a metre in height and weigh up to 225 kg. However, at dinner one evening, Mr Lawson, an Englishman who was acting as vice-governor of the Galapagos archipelago, remarked to Darwin that he could tell by looking at a tortoise which island it had come from. Thus the tortoises on Albemarle Island have a different sort of shell from those on Chatham, and both differ again from those on James. What was Darwin to conclude from this? Had a different form of tortoise been created on each island, or had a single ancestral form evolved into distinct forms on the islands, isolated as they are from one another by deep water?

Isolating barriers

It is clear from this brief review of continental and island faunas that the distribution of animals and plants, and the form they take in different localities, depend to a considerable extent on migration and isolation. These in turn depend on the existence of **natural barriers** which restrict movement in one direction or another. Barriers limiting the movement of terrestrial organisms include water, mountain ranges, deserts, temperature differences and other environmental factors. Aquatic organisms are limited by such factors as salinity, oxygen concentration, currents and tides.

Isolating barriers do not remain static throughout geological time but change from one period to another. Routes that have served as a pathway

Figure 42.15 A woodpecker finch on the Galapagos islands using a cactus spine to obtain insects from under bark.

for the migration of animals during one period may become closed in a subsequent period, thus isolating groups of organisms from each other and allowing them to evolve independently.

Comparative anatomy

If it is true that widely separated groups of organisms share a common ancestor, as their geographical distribution suggests, we would expect them to have certain basic structural features in common. In fact the degree of resemblance between them should indicate how closely related they are in evolution: groups with little in common are assumed to have diverged from a common ancestor much earlier in geological history than groups which have a lot in common. Establishing evolutionary relationships on the basis of structural similarities and differences is the business of **comparative anatomy**.

In deciding how closely related two organisms are, a comparative anatomist looks for structures which, though they may serve quite different functions, are fundamentally similar in structure, suggesting a common origin. Such structures are described as **homologous**. In deciding whether or not two structures are homologous many considerations must be taken into account: their relative positions, gross morphology, histological appearance and so on. In cases where the structures serve different functions in the adult, it may be necessary to trace their origin and development in the embryo if fundamental similarities are to be discerned.

The pentadactyl limb

One of the clearest examples of homology is shown by the **pentadactyl limb**, so called because typically it has five digits (figure 42.16). It is found in all four classes of terrestrial vertebrates (amphibians, reptiles, birds and mammals) and some of the limb bones can even be traced back to the fins of certain fossil fishes from which the first amphibians are thought to have evolved.

Throughout the terrestrial vertebrates the structure of the pentadactyl limb is fundamentally the same, conforming to a greater or lesser extent to the generalised pattern shown in figure 42.16. However, if we look at individual animals we find that the limbs of different vertebrates have become

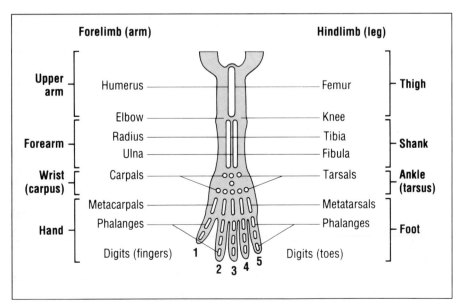

Figure 42.16 A generalised pentadactyl limb. This kind of limb is possessed by most terrestrial vertebrates. The edge of the limb that generally points towards the main axis of the body is to the left. The forelimbs and hindlimbs both conform to the pattern illustrated: the nomenclature used for each is shown to the left and right of the diagram respectively.

adapted for different functions, in some cases involving major structural modifications. Something of this can be seen in figure 42.17 which shows how the forelimb is modified for grasping, walking, swimming and flying in a selection of vertebrates.

In some cases evolution has resulted in extreme reduction, even total loss, of a structure. In a bird's wing, for instance, the third digit is very much reduced and the fourth and fifth are missing altogether. Structures which are greatly reduced are known as **vestigial**, and their existence has been used as evidence for evolution: it is thought that vestigial structures performed a function in the ancestor but have since been reduced to such an extent that they have lost or greatly changed their original function. Well known examples are the wings of the kiwi and other flightless birds, the muscles that go to our ear lobes, and the reduced pelvic girdles and hind limbs of whales and pythons (figure 42.18).

Figure 42.17 The principle of homology illustrated by the adaptive radiation of the forelimb of a selection of vertebrates. All conform to the basic pentadactyl pattern shown in the centre of the diagram but are modified for different uses.

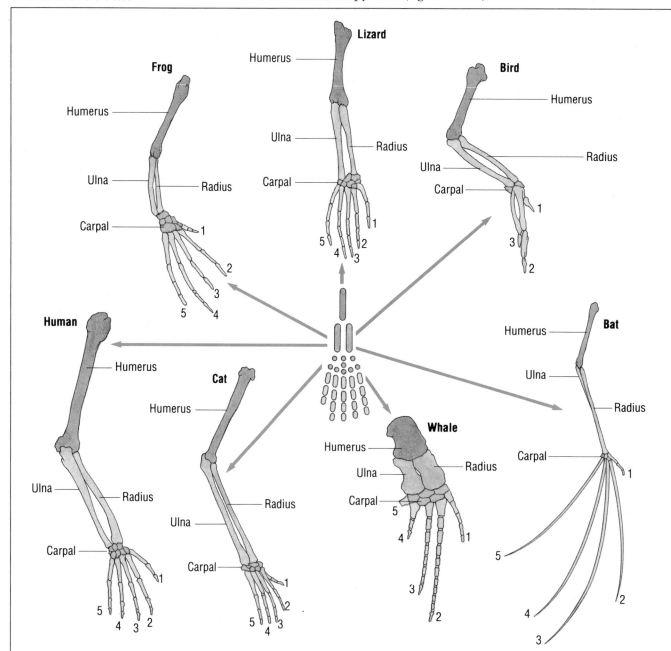

Divergent evolution

We can explain variations in the pentadactyl limb within a group such as the vertebrates by postulating that from an ancestral stock numerous lines of evolution led to modification of the basic pattern to serve different functions, thus enabling the descendants to fill a wide variety of ecological niches. This is described as **divergent evolution**, and clearly it results in adaptive radiation. The end products have certain structural features in common with each other and with the ancestral stock from which they arose. These structural similarities are the basis of homology.

Comparative anatomy permits evolutionists to do more than relate a handful of diverse organisms to a common ancestor. In certain situations it allows **evolutionary trees** to be constructed. The principle is quite straight-forward. The more similar two organisms are, the more recently they are assumed to have diverged. However, there is a possible danger here, namely the occurrence of convergent evolution.

Convergent evolution

Consider a shark and a porpoise. They look very similar, and one might suppose that they are closely related. Yet one is a cartilaginous fish and the other a mammal. The similarity in their shapes is the result of **convergent evolution**. This is when complete organisms (or their parts) come to resemble each other more closely than their ancestors (or ancestral structures) did, as a result of their sharing similar environments (figure 42.19).

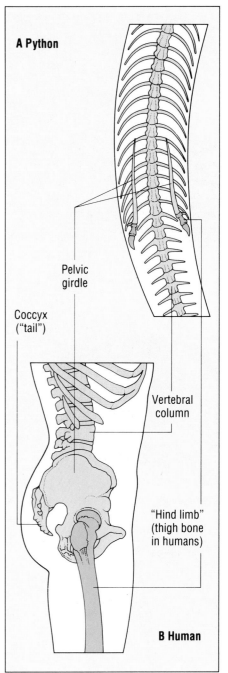

Figure 42.18 The vestigial pelvic girdle and hind limbs of a python compared with the homologous bones in a human.

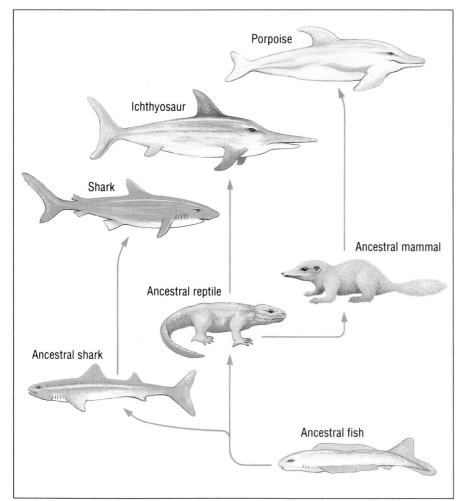

Figure 42.19 Convergent evolution in three marine carnivores brought about by adaptations for sustained rapid swimming in the same environment, the sea. Ichthyosaurs were reptiles that lived at the same time as the dinosaurs. Like sharks and porpoises, they had a streamlined shape and 'fins' and were probably excellent swimmers.

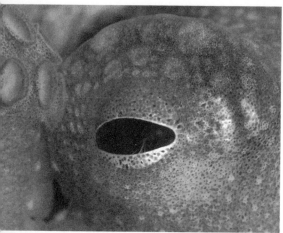

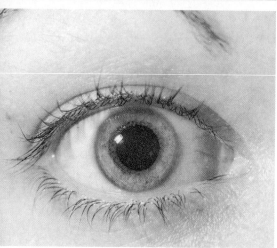

Figure 42.20 The eyes of octopuses and vertebrates are very similar, yet they are the products of two distinct lines of evolution. The top picture shows the eye of an octopus, the bottom picture the eye of a human.

Much of the anatomical similarity between species is caused not by a common ancestry but by the fact that structures performing the same function are bound to resemble one another to a degree. Such structures are described as **analogous**. Examples of analogous structures include the legs of spiders and mammals, and the wings of butterflies and birds. It can easily be seen that the legs of spiders and mammals, though performing the same tasks, have quite different structural organisations. Similarly, the wings of butterflies and birds, though both used for flight, are constructed on different principles.

In these two cases of analogy a cursory glance is enough to tell us that the structures bear no fundamental resemblance to each other. But this is not always the case. The eyes of octopuses and vertebrates, for instance, are remarkably similar even down to fine points of detail and an observer might well conclude that they are homologous (figure 42.20). However, there is one telling difference between them: in the vertebrate eye the nerve fibres lie in front of the sensory cells of the retina, whereas in the octopus eye they lie behind them. Because of this, the vertebrate eye has a 'blind spot' where the optic nerve emerges from it, whereas the octopus eye lacks one. The reason for this difference lies in the ways the two eyes develop, and tells us at once that they are the products of two distinct lines of evolution, resembling each other as a result of convergent evolution.

Careful study can uncover cases of convergent evolution and prevent us from attributing evolutionary relationships when they do not exist. Even so, there is a limit to how much conventional comparative anatomy can tell us about evolutionary relationships. Major advances in establishing evolutionary relationships had to wait until the 1960s when techniques of cell and molecular biology began to be used to determine evolutionary pathways.

Molecular biology

Research carried out on the structure and function of cells leads to the conclusion that the cells of different organisms are remarkably alike in many details of their biochemistry and fine structure. Chemicals such as nucleic acids, ATP and cytochrome, and certain organelles including ribosomes, appear to be of almost universal occurrence. This supports the view that all living things have had a common ancestry. Even viruses, which at first sight appear very different from living organisms, possess nucleic acid and proteins.

However, many structures and chemical substances are not ubiquitous but are confined to specific groups of organisms. For example, most plants contain chlorophyll, cellulose and starch, all of which are absent from the tissues of animals; vertebrates possess adrenaline and thyroxine, neither of which is found in other groups, and the brown algae are the exclusive possessors of the orange pigment fucoxanthin.

Organisms sharing the same chemical characteristics are considered to be more closely related than those lacking such affinities. This principle, known as **biochemical homology**, has been used in recent years to identify and confirm evolutionary relationships. The analysis of proteins and DNA has been particularly revealing.

Protein and DNA structure

Since Sanger developed a technique for working out the sequence of amino acids in proteins (see page 144), **amino acid sequence analysis** has become an important tool in establishing possible evolutionary affinities. For example, the sequence of amino acids has been analysed in part of the fibrinogen molecule of various mammals. It turns out that the sequence differs in varying degrees from one species to another, and this has enabled scientists to draw up a possible evolutionary tree for mammals (figure 42.21).

It is not always necessary to do a full sequence analysis of proteins to uncover evolutionary affinities. Sometimes all that is required is to use chromatography and electrophoresis to separate and compare particular chemical substances present in different species. This may reveal similarities or differences which indicate how closely related the species are. For example, electrophoresis has been used to compare the density of egg-white protein from different species of birds. The comparison has enabled a possible pattern of evolution to be worked out in a group in which considerable uncertainty existed about how evolution had proceeded.

Another way of determining possible evolutionary relationships is to compare the sequence of bases in the DNA of different organisms. The more alike the sequences, the closer the organisms are presumed to be in evolution. The comparison is normally carried out by the technique of **DNA hybridisation**.

First you extract the DNA from one species and separate the two strands by heat treatment. You then do the same thing with another species. The single strands of the two species are then mixed together, whereupon they join up, sometimes with the complementary strand from their own species, but sometimes with the complementary strand from the other species.

On heating the mixture, the DNA separates into two strands. However, the double-stranded DNA that contains one DNA strand from one species and its other strand from the other species separates into two strands at a lower temperature. This is because the hydrogen bonding holding the two strands together is weaker as some of the bases fail to pair up.

The closer the temperature at which such hybrid DNA separates compared to the temperature at which the double-stranded DNA of each of individual species separates, the more closely related the two species are thought to be.

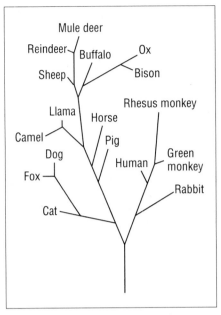

Figure 42.21 An evolutionary tree for a selection of mammals based on a comparison of the sequence of amino acids in part of their fibrinogen molecules. Mammals with similar fibrinogen molecules are assumed to be more closely related than mammals with dissimilar fibrinogen molecules.

Embryology

There are times when it is necessary to study an organism's embryological development in order to establish evolutionary relationships. Sometimes the embryonic stages give us an insight into what the ancestors may have been like. Used in this way, embryology becomes a special type of comparative anatomy.

However, there is a problem. Although embryology can be indispensible in establishing evolutionary relationships, there has been a tendency in the past to take it too far. Thus Ernst Haeckl (1843–1919) suggested that during its embryological development an organism repeats its ancestral history, or, to use Haeckl's own way of putting it, 'ontogeny recapitulates phylogeny'.

There is a grain of truth in this: the presence of branchial grooves and segmental myotomes in the human embryo, for example, is suggestive of a fish ancestry. But it is quite wrong to assume that an animal literally 'climbs up its family tree' during its development. After all, many of the steps in its ancestral history will have no usefulness in embryological development and will have long since dropped out of the developmental sequence, if indeed they were ever there. Besides, there is every reason to suppose that embry-

Figure 42.22 A group of adult sea squirts. Despite their modest appearance, these creatures belong to the phylum Chordata, just as we do.

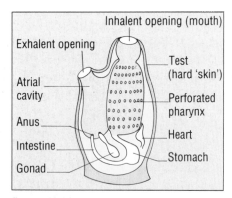

Figure 42.23 The adult sea squirt bears little resemblance to a chordate. There is no trace of a notochord and, except for the perforated pharynx, none of the other chordate characteristics are seen. The inhalent and exhalent openings, perforated pharynx and atrial cavity are associated with this animal's filter feeding habits.

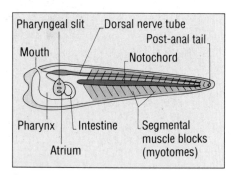

Figure 42.24 The evolutionary affinity of sea squirts with the chordates is revealed by its free-swimming 'tadpole' larva which shows the characteristic features of a chordate.

ological stages, particularly later ones, have themselves evolved and may be markedly different now from what they were in the past. This is particularly well illustrated by insects, whose larvae show almost as much diversity of form as the adults.

Bearing in mind these provisos, let us see how embryology helps us to place an organism in a particular group. As an example we shall consider the evidence that sea squirts (tunicates) belong to the phylum Chordata.

The tadpole larva of sea squirts

You may remember from Chapter 8 that chordates are characterised by the presence of a notochord, a hollow dorsal nerve cord, visceral clefts and a post-anal tail. Included in the phylum are sea squirts, fish, amphibians, reptiles, birds and mammals.

At first it seems extraordinary that sea squirts are included in the chordates. After all, the adult sea squirt looks nothing like the other members of this phylum (figure 42.22). It is a sessile filter feeder and lacks any trace of a notochord (figure 42.23).

However, a detailed examination of its motile larva makes its affinity with the other chordates abundantly clear (figure 42.24). Not only is there a notochord but there are pharyngeal clefts, a dorsal tubular nerve chord, segmental myotomes and a post-anal tail. In fact this little creature so resembles the larva of an amphibian that it has been called the 'tadpole larva'. Eventually the larva attaches itself to a rock or piece of weed by its head and undergoes metamorphosis into the sessile adult, thereby obscuring its evolutionary relationships.

Taxonomy

As we saw in Chapter 7, taxonomy is the study of the principles, rules and methods of classification. Modern classification dates from the time of the Swedish biologist Carl Linnaeus (1707–1778). Along with virtually all his contemporaries, Linnaeus believed in the fixity of species. Yet his classification system, worked out a hundred years before Darwin's *Origin of Species* was published, is in many places very close to the evolutionary relationships thought to hold by most modern biologists. How could this be?

The answer is that Linnaeus classified organisms into common groups, or **taxa**, if they shared certain essential characteristics. Mammals, for instance, were classified together on the grounds that they possess fur, have adult females that produce milk and are warm-blooded. Exactly the same principles are used today by biologists attempting to discern evolutionary relationships. Viewed this way, taxonomy is not so much evidence for evolution as the inevitable result of it.

Taxonomy only reflects evolutionary affinities when a natural system of classification is used. As discussed in Chapter 7, other classification systems exist. Indeed, even Linnaeus had some groupings that failed to reflect evolution. For example, his major zoological divisions were *Mammalia* (mammals), *Aves* (birds), *Amphibia* (amphibians and reptiles), *Pisces* (fish), *Insects* (including crustaceans) and *Vermes* (which included anything that resembled a worm).

The problem with grouping everything that looks like a worm into one division is that shape is a highly adaptive feature which has evolved convergently in many different groups. If a natural classification is to reflect evolutionary, or **phylogenetic,** relationships it must be based on homologous and not on analogous structures. Determining whether similar structures are analogous or homologous is sometimes difficult, though molecular biology and embryology can help, as can fossils.

Palaeontology

The evidences for evolution presented so far are based on studying organisms living today. Further evidence comes from studying the animals and plants of the past as seen in the fossil record, a branch of biology known as **palaeontology**.

How fossils are formed

Fossils are generally preserved in **sedimentary** rock, which is formed by the deposition of silt, sand or calcium carbonate over millions of years. Silt deposits give **shales**, sand gives **sandstone,** and calcium carbonate (derived from the shells of animals or precipitated from solution) gives **limestone**.

The most common method of fossilisation involves the ultimate conversion of the hard parts of the body (such as shells, bones or teeth) into rock. What happens is that when an animal such as a bivalve mollusc dies, the organic material in its shell gradually decays away, resulting in the shell becoming porous. If the animal subsequently becomes buried in mud, mineral particles may infiltrate into the shell and slowly fill up the pores. If and when the mud turns into rock, the shell hardens and may be preserved for hundreds of millions of years.

On occasions dead animals become covered by wind-blown mineral-enriched sand or volcanic ash, and if this is followed by flooding or heavy rain, the same process of mineral infiltration may occur. Fortunately sedimentary rock is comparatively soft, so that it may not be too difficult for a palaeontologist, armed with hammer and chisel, to separate the fossil from the softer rock or **matrix** surrounding it.

Fossilisation is not confined to animals. Given the right circumstances plants can also become fossilised. For example, there are instances of entire tree trunks being preserved in fossilised forests in Arizona, Antarctica and elsewhere (figure 42.25). In the case of the famous 'Petrified Forest' of Arizona the original organic matter of the wood became replaced, particle by particle, by silica which was carried into the logs by water from the sediment in which the trees were buried. The result was that the wood was literally turned into rock, a process called **petrifaction**. So detailed is the transformation that the individual xylem elements and annual rings can clearly be seen. It is even possible to measure the widths of the individual rings and determine what the climate was like at the time (see box on page 648).

Sometimes an organism, particularly when buried in rapidly hardening mud, decays completely and the space it occupied – the **mould** – becomes filled with another kind of material. This process results in the formation of a **cast**. For instance, in the case of many shells the cast is composed of silica while the surrounding rock is made of limestone. Recovery of the fossil can then be carried out by chemical means, the limestone being removed by hydrochloric acid.

Occasionally footprints or other marks made by animals on mud become covered over by a layer of deposit which subsequently hardens. If a line of weakness between the two layers splits, it may reveal the marks as **trace fossils**. Although the information they provide may be fragmentary, such impressions can tell us quite a lot about the organisms that made them (figure 42.26).

In certain circumstances an organism may be preserved by being immersed in some kind of natural preservative. A spectacular example is provided by insects trapped in **amber**. Such creatures were caught in resin exuding from coniferous trees. On hardening, the resin turned to amber,

Figure 42.25 View of the 'Petrified Forest' in north-eastern Arizona, USA. These great logs are the remains of trees that flourished about 160 million years ago. The trees were washed downstream in flood waters and rapidly buried, their wood subsequently becoming replaced by silica.

Figure 42.26 An example of a trace fossil. Footprints of an upright primate made in soft, damp, volcanic ash some 3.7 million years ago at Laetoli, Tanzania, as found by Mary Leakey. Can you suggest what exactly these fossils show?

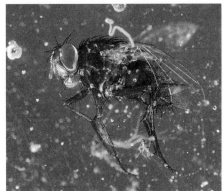

Figure 42.27 A dipteran fly fossilised in amber.

Figure 42.29 Dinosaur bones exposed in the famous quarry in north-eastern Utah, USA. Parts of over 300 individual dinosaurs, belonging to ten different species, have been excavated from the quarry which dates from approximately 140 million years ago.

Figure 42.28 Lindow Man died approximately 1900 years ago. His remains were well preserved in the anoxic acid peat of a Cheshire bog. The body was sufficiently well preserved for a forensic pathologist to determine that death was caused by strangulation with a rope, while his last meal consisted of a flat unleavened griddle cake made from Emmer wheat, Spelt wheat and barley cooked over a heather fire at a maximum temperature above 300°C.

preserving the animals intact (figure 42.27). Subsequent serial sectioning of the embedded specimens can enable their internal anatomy to be described in detail.

Another natural preservative is the asphaltic oil found in **tar pits** and **asphalt lakes** in various parts of the world. Complete skeletons of the sabre-toothed tiger and other extinct mammals have been obtained from the tar pits at Rancho La Brea in southern California.

Yet another means of preservation is **freezing**. Complete specimens of mammoths and woolly rhinoceroses have been found preserved in the frozen soil of northern Siberia. The mammoth's flesh is said to have been in such a good state of preservation that it was eaten by wolves.

In 1984 the preserved body of a man, now known as **Lindow Man**, was found in a **peat bog** in Cheshire (figure 42.28). His skin, hair and main internal organs were all intact, thanks to the preservative effects of the anoxic acid peat. Radiocarbon dating showed the body to be 1900 ± 100 years old.

What are the chances of an organism ending up as a fossil?

From the foregoing account the impression may have been given that fossilisation is a common process. On the contrary it is a very rare occurrence, requiring precisely the right circumstances. Only a very small percentage of organisms become preserved after they have died and this, coupled with the fact that many fossils get destroyed by erosion or are inaccessible, means that the geological record is for the most part scanty and incomplete. Further, the fossils we have provide us with a very biased account of life long ago. Organisms with shells, bones or teeth are much more likely to be preserved than those whose bodies lack hard parts. This means that our knowledge of, for instance, fossil fungi or flatworms is extremely patchy.

Despite the small chances of fossils being preserved and subsequently uncovered, there are certain places, such as the famous **Ludlow Bone Bed** in Shropshire and the great **dinosaur beds** in Utah and Colorado, where large numbers of fossils have been found concentrated together in a comparatively small area (figure 42.29). It is thought that in these cases large populations of animals met a sudden end as the result of a cataclysmic change in the environment.

The Ludlow Bone Bed contains innumerable fragments of armoured fish which are thought to have perished as a result of a sudden change in the

salinity of the water. In the case of the American dinosaur beds it is believed that the animals were drowned and then washed downstream after a sudden flood. Excavation of these fossils and careful reconstructions have enabled palaeontologists to build up a partial picture of the flora and fauna that have existed on this planet during past ages (figure 42.30).

Reconstructing evolutionary pathways from the fossil record

By arranging extinct animals and plants into some kind of geological sequence, it is possible to suggest how one group may have evolved into another. The fact that fossils are formed in sedimentary rocks helps palaeontologists to do this. In the formation of sedimentary rock a layer of silt, sand or calcium carbonate hardens and another layer is subsequently formed on top of it, and so on. The resulting rock consists of a series of

Finding a fossil

Some advice to would-be fossil collectors is given here by guest author Arthur Cruickshank, a research palaeontologist.

Many of us have come across fossils accidentally when out walking, or when on holiday, but the chance of anything actually becoming fossilised is very low. Having died, the most important thing, if an organism is to be fossilised, is for it not to get scavenged or decomposed but to get buried quickly.

Fossils deserve to be collected and treated very carefully. What you may find by chance is a rare relic of a past era, an ecosystem which has for ever disappeared from the face of this planet, and can only be reconstructed by painstaking analysis.

If you go out to collect fossils deliberately (or even if you find them by chance) it is necessary to bear in mind that the ground you are walking on may be private property. If you like the idea of collecting fossils, and you want to learn something from them, then your local Geological Society will be the best body to contact; subscriptions are modest and the local knowledge unsurpassed.

Once you are ready to start collecting, there are some simple procedures to follow. To fix the specimen in time and space you need to know its Grid Reference, its height

above sea level and its position relative to the rock strata which contain it. If the fossil has an obvious orientation, then you should also record that by compass. It is very useful to know if the specimen is lying upside down, or on its side, relative to the sediment.

You will need maps (Ordnance Survey and Geological Survey), an orienteering-type compass, old newspapers (to wrap the fossils in) and sellotape to secure your parcels. You will also need a waterproof felt-tip pen to mark, on both the fossil and the outside of the package, the Field Number you have given it, alongside a sketch to explain anything that might seem unusual about its position. All this information should be entered in your Field Note Book, whose numbering should start with number one and run sequentially. When you get home, you will have the chance to clean your specimens carefully and make a more accurate identification of your prizes. For cleaning, water and an old toothbrush are recommended: they will not do too much damage except to the most delicate specimens.

Join your local Geological Society or become a junior member of the Geological Association – there are branches in all regions of the United Kingdom and you will find their addresses in your local museum or library. Read the following books:

R. Black, *The Elements of Palaeontology*, (Cambridge University Press); and M.J. Benton, *Vertebrate Palaeontology*, (Unwin Hyman). Both are up-to-date texts, with paperback editions. Your local museum will be the place to look for help in identifying your finds, and the place to look for advice on matters of collecting in general. You may have to talk fast to keep your better material! Yours may be the first of a new species, and important fossils of this kind ought to be in publicly accessible collections so that interested scientists can examine them at their convenience.

Fossils can be found in chalk pits, limestone quarries (where there are Carboniferous Limestone outcrops) and along the foot of cliffs (especially where Mesozoic sediments are found as in Dorset and Yorkshire). Fossils can also be found in lumps of coal, if you look carefully! However, do take care when out in the field, and ask for permission and advice on entering even disused quarries. Working quarries are unlikely to welcome you, and are dangerous places anyway. Be sensible when selecting places to visit; watch out for cliff edges and falling rocks; do not climb on cliffs, and wear the correct footwear, a hardhat and the right clothing for the weather you are likely to meet – and don't get cut off by the tide. Good luck with your fossil hunting!

Figure 42.30 An artist's reconstruction of some of the different animals and plants to be found at various times in the fossil record. The left hand half is the older, dating from about 240 to 200 million years ago; the right hand half dates from about 170 to 100 million years ago.

horizontal layers or **strata** (singular **stratum**), each containing fossils typical of the time when it was laid down. The oldest rocks, and therefore the earliest fossils, are contained in the lowest strata; the youngest rocks, and most recent fossils, are in the highest strata.

But how do we get at the lowest layers? Fortunately nature has come to our aid by eroding sedimentary rock in such a way that the different strata are exposed. Nowhere can this be seen better than in the Grand Canyon in Arizona (figure 42.31). Almost two kilometres deep, the canyon has been cut by the eroding action of the Colorado River which has exposed a series of strata spanning some 500 million years of geological history.

Studying the fossil inhabitants of different strata in places such as these has made it possible to trace the evolution of successive groups of animals and plants during geological time. In order, though, for the scientists to obtain the maximum information from any fossil, it is necessary for that fossil to be dated.

Dating fossil remains

How can fossils be dated? Very rough estimates can be made on the basis of how long it takes for sedimentary rocks to be laid down, but such estimates may be very wide of the mark. More accurate methods are based on the fact that the older a rock is, the less radioactive it is. Strata can often be dated by analysis of radioactive isotopes contained in crystals of igneous rock. Such rock is formed from the molten material beneath the Earth's surface. The radioactive clock starts once the crystalline rock is formed, so the older the rock, the less of the original radioactive material remains.

By estimating the rate at which uranium decays to lead, or potassium to argon, it is possible to make reasonably accurate datings of rocks and fossils. The **potassium-argon method** is particularly useful because potassium is a common element found in all sorts of rocks, and it decays into argon extremely slowly. In this way it is even possible to date rocks that are over three billion years old.

For younger fossils which still contain some organic material, radioactive **carbon dating** can be used. This method is based on the fact that after an organism dies the radioactive carbon (^{14}C) it contains gradually disintegrates into nitrogen (^{14}N). As disintegration is rapid, this method can only be used for dating recent fossils not more than about 50 000 years old. However, it is an accurate method and has been used to make precise datings not only of fossils but also of archaeological remains. Carbon dating was used to age Lindow Man (see page 776).

What kind of evolutionary sequences have been established from the fossil record? There are obviously far too many for us to look at all of them, so we shall choose one for detailed discussion: the evolution of horses.

Figure 42.31 The Grand Canyon in Arizona. At its greatest width the canyon measures 28 km from rim to rim. It has a depth of over 1700 m. Horizontal strata can be seen clearly and these consist of sedimentary rocks which span some 500 million years of geological history.

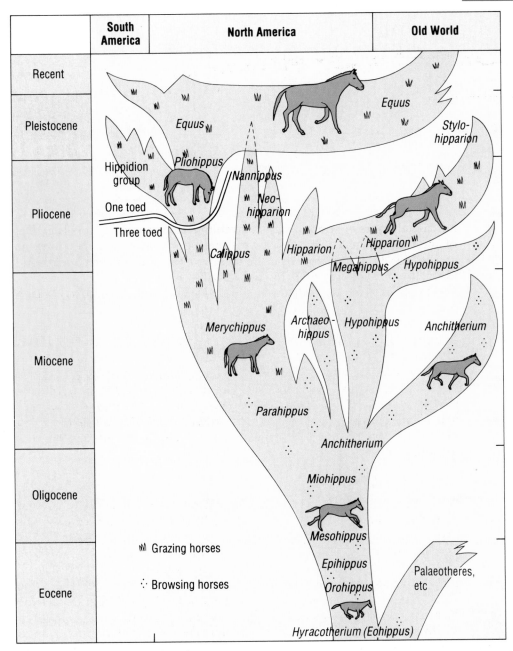

Figure 42.32 A detailed evolutionary history of the horse family, showing the possible relationships between the various genera.

The evolution of horses

The evolution of horses can be followed through a series of fossils obtained from successively younger rock strata. The series starts with a small animal called *Hyracotherium* (old name *Eohippus*), which lived in North America in the Eocene epoch about 50 million years ago and then spread across to Europe and Asia. It finishes up with the modern horse *Equus*. In between, there are a great many intermediate forms, with numerous offshoots from the main line (figure 42.32).

Compared with most fossil sequences, the record for horses is pretty complete, though it is pieced together from a number of different sites: there is no one place where the whole sequence in figure 42.32 can be seen in its entirety. Further, palaeontologists believe that there were numerous complications. For one thing, the rate at which evolution took place was probably not uniform, but sporadic and irregular. For another, there are

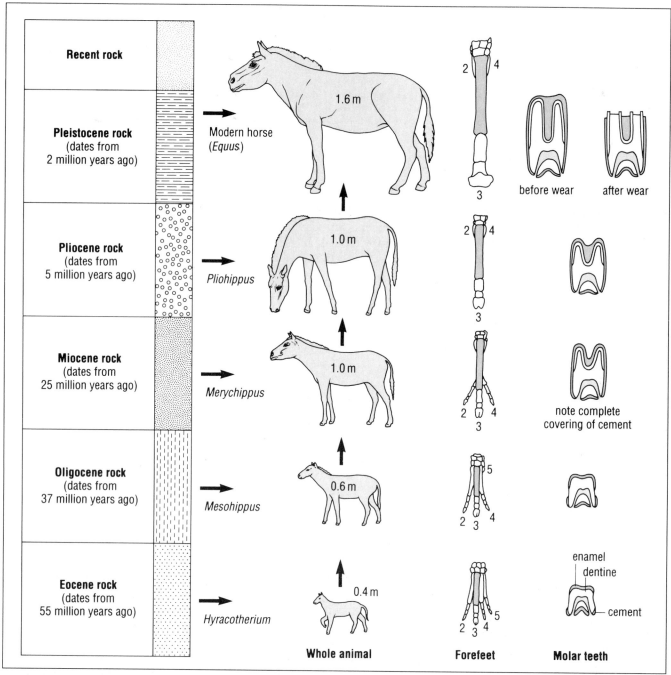

Figure 42.33 The main steps in the evolution of the horse, showing reconstructions of the fossil species obtained from successive rock strata. The foot diagrams are all front views of the left forefoot. The 3rd metacarpal is shaded throughout. The teeth are shown in vertical section.

thought to have been times when certain of the trends were reversed – when, for instance, horses became smaller for a short period.

With these cautions in mind, we can now turn to the overall changes in this particular evolutionary story. They are summarised in figure 42.33. Fossil remains of *Hyracotherium* obtained from Eocene rocks in North America show it to have differed from modern horses in three important respects: it was very much smaller, had well developed digits (four on the forefoot, three on the hindfoot), and possessed low-crowned molar teeth lacking the serrated surface typical of modern horses. We know that it lived in rather marshy well-wooded country in which its spreading toes would have afforded it much better support than a hoof. It probably fed on soft vegetation and fruit, for which its non-grinding molars would have been perfectly adequate.

In the subsequent evolution of horses three major changes took place:

- The animals increased in size. *Hyracotherium* was barely 0.4 m tall. The later fossils show a progressive increase in size, finishing up with the modern horse which typically stands a good 1.5 m off the ground.

- The third digit got stouter and longer; meanwhile the remaining ones were reduced or lost so that by the Pliocene epoch, some five million years ago, they no longer touched the ground. The lengthening of the third digit was brought about by great elongation of the metacarpal and metatarsal, this being accompanied by the conversion of the distal phalange (strictly, its nail) into a hoof. Thus the modern horse stands on the tip of its third digit.

- The molar teeth, from being low-crowned in *Hyracotherium*, acquired higher crowns with a complete covering of cement. Subsequent wearing of the surface resulted in the serrated structure typical of the modern horse. These changes were accompanied by a transformation of the premolars into molar-type teeth.

These three changes can be related to changes in the environment. The fossil plants found in the different strata tell us that the marshy, wooded country in which *Hyracotherium* lived was gradually replaced by a drier type, and the Miocene descendants of *Hyracotherium* found themselves living in open prairie offering little concealment from predators.

Survival now depended on the head being in an elevated position for gaining a good view of the surrounding countryside, and on a high turn of speed for escape from predators – hence the increase in size and replacement of the splayed-out foot by the hoofed foot. The drier, harder ground would make the original splayed-out foot unnecessary for support.

The changes in the teeth can be explained by a change in diet from soft vegetation to grass. Grass has a high silica content which wears down teeth. This is why evolution from *Hyracotherium* to *Equus* was accompanied by enlargement of the grinding area and deepening of the teeth.

Descended from apes!

On hearing of Darwin's theory, the wife of the Bishop of Worcester is said to have exclaimed:

'Descended from apes! My dear, let us hope it is not so; but if it is, that it does not become generally known.'

Is 'Descended from apes' a fair conclusion to be drawn from Darwin's theory?

Why do you think the Bishop's wife hoped this would not become widely known?

Scientific arguments against evolution

The theory of evolution differs from many other scientific theories in the extent to which it is testable. After all, there is no way we can directly test the hypothesis concerning the evolution of horses.

Despite this, the theory of evolution *is* a scientific theory. It makes predictions which can be tested, at least indirectly. For instance, if a single fossilised human were ever found in the same sedimentary rocks as dinosaurs, this would disprove the hypothesis, currently accepted by most biologists, that humans evolved long after the dinosaurs had become extinct. In this sense evolution is a science much as astronomy is.

Scientists cannot directly experiment on the history of the universe, but they can make predictions about what we should see today *if* certain astronomical theories hold.

Granted that the theory of evolution is a scientific theory, what can we say about the evidence for and against it? Perhaps the best evidence in favour of evolution is the fossil record; yet fewer than 300 000 fossil species have been described. This is almost certainly fewer than one in a thousand of the species that have existed.

There are some quite major difficulties with the theory of evolution. How did DNA replication and protein synthesis get going, for example? Without these processes it is difficult to imagine any form of life, however simple, and yet even in the smallest prokaryotes the biochemical sophistication required for these metabolic processes is immense. Are they really the blind product of chance? Can natural selection, which we shall explore in more detail in the next chapter, account for the evolution of humans? Has the human brain really evolved from the inorganic precursors of life?

Although the great majority of scientists alive today would answer 'yes' to these questions, it must be admitted that such an answer requires an element of faith in evolution. The evidence for evolution is less good than, say, the evidence that the Sun does not go round the Earth.

Summary

1 Charles Darwin and Alfred Russel Wallace were the first people to propose a plausible mechanism for evolution.

2 Darwin's contribution was twofold: he collected a large mass of data supporting the idea of evolution, and he proposed a reasonable hypothesis explaining the mechanism.

3 Evolution reveals itself in the geographical distribution of organisms, comparative anatomy, molecular biology, embryology, taxonomy and palaeontology.

4 Evidence for evolution is seen in the **geographical distribution** of both fossil and modern-day species. For example, the present-day Australian fauna can be understood if it is assumed that marsupials evolved there to occupy the ecological niches filled elsewhere by eutherian mammals.

5 The theory of **plate tectonics** explains **continental drift** which in turn allows the continental distribution of organisms to provide evidence for evolution.

6 Darwin visited the Galapagos islands during his voyage on the *Beagle* and the finches, tortoises and other species there provided him with some of his clearest evidence of evolution.

7 From **comparative anatomy** the principle of **homology** emerges. This can be explained in terms of **divergent evolution** amd **adaptive radiation** and provides evidence for evolution. A clear example is the vertebrate pentadactyl limb.

8 Groups with separate evolutionary origins may appear to be similar as a result of **convergent evolution**. Superficially similar structures shared by such groups are called **analogous structures**, an example being the vertebrate and octopus eye.

9 **Cell biology** and **molecular biology** also provide evidence for evolution. The fundamental similarities in the structure and functioning of all cells and the ubiquitous occurrence of many biochemicals suggests a common ancestry for all organisms.

10 **Biochemical homology**, established by techniques such as amino acid sequence analysis and DNA hybridisation studies, provides further evidence for evolutionary affinities within certain groups.

11 Sometimes **comparative embryology** can provide evidence for evolutionary affinities which are not evident from studying the adult forms.

12 **Taxonomy**, the classification of organisms, is not so much evidence for evolution as a consequence of it. The purpose of a natural classification is to reflect the degree of evolutionary affinity between different groups.

13 The most direct evidence for evolution derives from **palaeontology**, the study of fossils. Fossils may be preserved in a variety of ways and the rocks in which they occur can often be dated by estimating the decline in radioactivity.

14 The fossil record can be used to trace evolutionary pathways in detail as in the case of the evolution of horses.

15 The theory of evolution is testable, and is therefore a scientific theory. However, the evidence in favour of it, although generally held to be convincing, is not foolproof.

Review questions

1 Both Darwin and Wallace hit upon the theory of evolution while studying islands in the tropics. Why were tropical islands so helpful?

2 Explain precisely how fossils provide evidence for evolution.

3 Suppose evolution has not taken place. How could you explain the similarities between organisms in a non-evolutionary way?

4 To what extent is the theory of evolution testable?

5 Distinguish, with brief examples, between convergent and divergent evolution.

6 How might you investigate the hypothesis that birds are more closely related to reptiles than to mammals?

7 What conditions need to be fulfilled if fossils are to be formed, preserved and collected?

8 Outline the essential principles by which fossils are dated using radioactive methods.

9 The general trend in evolution is for species to get larger rather than smaller. Can you suggest why this is?

10 Do you think the fossil remains of humans, such as Lindow Man, should be examined scientifically or buried? Explain your answer.

Further reading

No author writes about evolution in a more stimulating way than Stephen Jay Gould. Several of his books are available as Penguin paperbacks. Perhaps the best known is *Ever Since Darwin: Reflections in Natural History*, first published in 1978.

For a well written attack on the theory of evolution by natural selection, try Francis Hitching's *The Neck of the Giraffe or Where Darwin Went Wrong* (Pan, 1982).

Biology, Advanced Topics takes a critical look at the traditional evidences for evolution and includes a discussion of the timing of changes in relation to phylogenetic trees.

The mechanism of evolution

Natural selection, as proposed by Darwin and Wallace, is still held to be the driving force for evolution. In this chapter we shall start by looking at the theory of natural selection in outline and then explore its various propositions in detail. We shall see that although Darwin and Wallace's ideas are still thought to be correct in their essentials, a great deal more is now known about how evolution takes place. This is partly because the mechanism of heredity is now much better understood, and partly because population geneticists know more about the workings of natural selection in the field.

Summary of the theory of natural selection

The theory of natural selection is so simple that when Darwin's close friend, T.H. Huxley, read of it, he said 'how stupid of me not to have thought of it first'.

Darwin and Wallace realised that within a species not all individuals are exactly the same; rather there are slight differences between individuals in their appearance, how fast they grow and so on. Some of the individuals will be more successful than others. As a result they are more likely to survive and reproduce. Now the offspring organisms produce resemble their parents. Because more individuals are born than survive to reproduce, the successful individuals pass on their characteristics to their offspring, and so the characteristics of a species change over time.

The theory can be summarised by means of four propositions and two conclusions.

Propositions

- 1 Individuals differ from one another (figure 43.1).
- 2 Offspring generally resemble their parents (figure 43.2).
- 3 More offspring are born than can possibly survive to maturity and reproduce (figure 43.3).
- 4 There is a **struggle for existence**, some individuals being better suited for this than others (figure 43.4).

Figure 43.1 Individual variation within a species of snail (*Cepaea hortensis*).

Figure 43.2 In all species, offspring usually resemble their parents.

Figure 43.3 The chance of all these young blue tits surviving to adulthood is very small.

Figure 43.4 A group of elm trees some of which have succumbed to Dutch Elm disease.

Conclusions

- 1 Individuals that survive and reproduce pass on to their offpsring the characteristics that have enabled them to succeed.
- 2 In time, a group of individuals that once belonged to the same species may give rise to two different groups that are sufficiently distinct to belong to separate species.

If any of these four propositions fail to hold, then neither of the conclusions follow. For example, suppose that proposition 4 does not hold, whereas the other three do. This would mean that although more offspring are born than can survive and reproduce, and although individuals differ from one another and offspring resemble their parents, *exactly which* individuals reproduce is random as all individuals are equally well suited to the conditions in which they live. The result is that there is no overall change in characteristics over time, and hence no evolution.

You should similarly be able to show that no evolution will take place if any of propositions 1, 2 or 3 fail to hold.

Lamarck's theory

A central tenet of the theory of natural selection is that the variations which form the 'raw material' for natural selection arise spontaneously. They are in no way dictated by the environment or purposefully geared towards making the organism better adapted. This idea is in direct contrast to an alternative theory put forward in 1809 (coincidentally, the year of Darwin's birth) by the French naturalist Jean-Baptiste Pierre Antoine de Monet, Chevalier de Lamarck, generally referred to as Lamarck.

Lamarck proposed that when an organism develops a need for a particular structure, this induces the appearance of the structure. The idea was based on the observation that structures which are subjected to constant use become well developed, whereas those that are not used tend to degenerate.

This in itself is not an unreasonable proposition; after all, everyone knows the effect that exercise and training can have on the development of muscles in an athlete or swimmer. But Lamarck went on to suggest that these beneficial characteristics, acquired during an individual's lifetime, could be handed on to the progeny. In other words, evolutionary change could be achieved by the **transmission of acquired characteristics**. This implies that a swimmer who has developed large powerful arm muscles would produce children born with specially large powerful arm muscles.

The Darwinian and Lamarckian theories compared

To illustrate the difference between the Darwinian and Lamarckian theories consider the case of the giraffe (figure 43.5). Palaeontologists are confident, from fossil evidence, that the ancestors of the modern giraffe had quite short necks, and that in the course of geological history the neck gradually got longer and longer. How do we explain this?

A Lamarckian explanation would go something like this. The ancestors of the giraffe fed on the leaves of bushes and trees and, competing with each other for a limited food supply, stretched their necks in order to reach the higher branches. This condition was transmitted to the offspring who therefore started with somewhat longer necks and repeated the process. Hence the descendants of the original stock acquired progressively longer necks.

The Darwinian explanation is based on a quite different premise, namely that the occasional occurrence of a giraffe with a longer than average neck was a spontaneous event and not the result of environmental

Figure 43.5 Giraffes browsing the top of an acacia tree in East Africa. Alternative explanations as to how the long necks evolved were offered by Lamarck and by Darwin.

need. In past generations some individuals *happened* to have longer necks than others. Since they could reach the leaves on higher branches than their shorter-necked contemporaries, such individuals were more successful in the struggle for existence and passed on this characteristic to their offspring.

Darwin and Lamarck today

How do the Darwinian and Lamarckian theories stand today? In the course of the last hundred years a mass of evidence has been marshalled in support of the Darwin-Wallace theory of natural selection. On the other hand, with possibly one or two exceptions, no decisive evidence has been found in favour of Lamarck's theory. This is not to say that the environment plays no part at all in directing the course of evolution. It certainly does, though not by dictating what structures an organism should or should not *develop* during its lifetime, but by *selecting* those individuals which by chance happen to be better adapted.

Before we go on to look at the theory of natural selection in more detail, it is worth emphasising that just because Lamarck's theory is now thought to be incorrect, it does not mean that the theory is worthless or that Lamarck was somehow to blame for this! It is the way of science that most theories, however successful they are for a while, eventually become superseded. Lamarck's theory is perfectly reasonable. It just doesn't happen to be supported by the evidence. In its time it was a valuable theory, not least because it helped Darwin to propose an alternative one.

When Lamarck and Darwin put forward their ideas, practically nothing was known about heredity. Subsequent research by geneticists, including the pioneering work of Mendel reviewed in Chapter 37, has provided a clearer understanding of inheritance and firm support for the Darwinian theory. This reappraisal of the theory of natural selection in terms of modern genetics is sometimes called **neo-Darwinism**. Let us now look at the key points in neo-Darwinism one at a time.

Variation

In Chapter 38 we reviewed the reasons why individuals of the same species differ from each other, i.e. show variation. Both environmental and genetic differences contribute to variation. From the evolutionary point of view, genetic variation (i.e. the kind that can be transmitted from parents to offspring) is what is important, not environmental variation (figure 43.6). With this in mind, let us look into the causes of genetic variation and assess their role in evolution.

The causes of genetic variation

There are several causes of genetic variation, and it is important to be clear about each of them.

In the first place **meiosis** allows genes to be 'reshuffled'. This can occur in two ways. First, as explained in Chapter 31, during metaphase of the first meiotic division homologous chromosomes come together in pairs and subsequently segregate into the daughter cells independently of each other. The result of this **independent assortment** is the production of a wide variety of different gametes depending on which particular chromosomes end up with one another in each daughter cell. This in turn depends on the way the various chromosomes line up on the spindle prior to separating.

Figure 43.6 Some of the differences in the appearance of these trees will be genetic in origin, others environmental. For instance, trees at the edge of a wood experience greater differences in environmental factors such as light intensity and wind strength than those trees inside the wood. Even if all the trees in a wood are genetically identical, as can happen with large clones of elm trees, we expect to see differences in their growth form.

Figure 43.7 These diagrams show how different kinds of gametes can be formed even in the absence of crossing over, depending on how homologous chromosomes segregate during meiosis. The parent cells show the different ways chromosomes can arrange themselves on the spindle prior to separating. The gametes show the different combinations of chromosomes resulting from meiosis. Note that up to eight different gametes may be produced, 2 to the power of 3 – three being the haploid number in this example. The two members of each pair of homologous chromosomes are here given different colours (red and yellow). Although homologous chromosomes look identical, they may differ in the complement of dominant and recessive alleles that they carry.

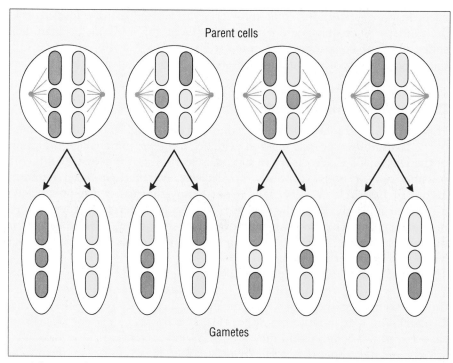

Parent cells

Gametes

The number of possible different combinations depends on how many pairs of chromosomes there are in the parent cell. To illustrate this, consider three pairs of chromosomes. From figure 43.7 you can see that the various ways in which they can segregate give a total of eight possible combinations in the gametes. In general terms, the number of different combinations that can occur is 2^n, where n is the haploid number of chromosomes, in this case three. In humans, with a haploid number of 23, the number of combinations is 2^{23}, almost ten million.

The mechanism described above, though important in promoting genetic variety, can only mix up alleles of genes carried on different chromosomes. It can play no part in separating and recombining alleles carried on the same chromosomes. This second sort of reshuffling in meiosis is provided by **crossing over**.

In prophase of the first meiotic division, when homologous chromosomes are in intimate contact with one another, the chromatids of homologous chromosomes may break and rejoin at any point along their length. The places where this happens are called **chiasmata** (see page 698). The number and positions of the chiasmata relative to the sequence of genes determines the different combinations possible in the gametes (figure 43.8). As each chromatid typically carries hundreds or thousands of alleles, and as the number of chiasmata per chromatid may vary from zero to as many as eight, you can see that the amount of variation that may result from crossing over is effectively infinite.

A third source of variety is achieved on **fertilisation**. Union of gametes results in the alleles present in one gamete being united with the gametes in another gamete. If a population consists of large numbers of outbreeding individuals, the amount of variation that may result from this is again virtually infinite.

Despite the tremendous amount of variation that these three processes may generate, they play only a limited role in evolution. The reason is that although they may establish a new combination of alleles in one generation, they do not *generate* long-lasting variation of a novel kind. This kind of genetic variation is the result of mutations to which we now turn.

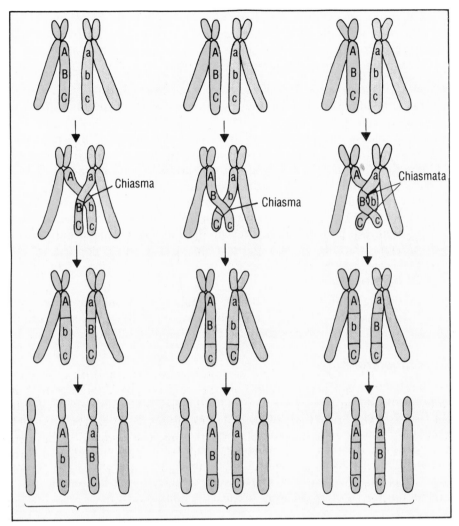

Figure 43.8 These diagrams show how crossing over between the chromatids of homologous chromosomes can lead to new combinations of alleles. The exact genotypes produced depend on the number of chiasmata and the positions of the genes relative to the sites of crossing over (chiasmata). The letters represent alleles on the chromosomes.

Figure 43.9 Bugle normally has purple flowers. The plants with white flowers are mutants.

Mutagen	Effect
X-rays	Gene and chromosome aberrations
UV light	Structural distortion of DNA
Colchicine	Prevents spindle-formation in mitosis and so doubles chromosome number
Cyclamate	Chromosome aberrations
Mustard gas	Guanine in DNA replaced by other bases
Nitrous acid	Adenine in DNA deaminated so it behaves like guanine
Acridine orange	Addition and/or removal of bases in DNA

Table 43.1 Some mutagens and their effects. Colchicine is a drug extracted from the autumn crocus *Colchicum autumnale*. Its effects are discussed in more detail on page 793. The mutagenic effects of mustard gas (bis-2-chloroethyl sulphide) were discovered in the 1940s when it was being investigated as a possible chemical warfare agent. Cyclamate is an artificial sweetener, now banned. Acridine orange is a dye used as a biological stain and in the dyeing industry.

What are mutations?

Every now and again a natural population of organisms throws up an individual with some characteristic that is strikingly different from the rest of the population (figure 43.9). Examples include haemophilia and cystic fibrosis in humans, white eyes and vestigial wings in *Drosophila*, resistance to penicillin in bacteria and to DDT in flies – the list is unending. It can be shown from studies of inheritance that these conditions are nearly always transmitted in a Mendelian fashion. The genetic mechanism producing the change is known as a **mutation**. Individuals showing the new characteristic are referred to as **mutants**.

It is characteristic of mutations that they are comparatively rare, at least from the perspective of a particular gene. In most organisms the mutation rate at any given locus varies between 1 and 30 mutations per million gametes. The exact number is variable since genes at different loci have different **mutation rates**. Low mutation rates bear witness to the tremendous accuracy with which DNA replicates.

Low mutation rates made it difficult for geneticists to investigate mutations until the discovery in 1927 by the American biologist H.J. Muller that the mutation rate in *Drosophila* can be greatly accelerated by irradiation with X-rays. Since then it has been found that other factors also speed up the mutation rate. These **mutagens** include gamma rays, ultraviolet light and a number of chemicals including mustard gas (table 43.1).

The discovery of mutagens made it easier to study the cause and transmission of mutations. Most experiments are carried out on bacteria and plants, though animal cells may be used in tissue culture experiments.

From these studies three main facts emerge:

- Mutations arise spontaneously and are in no sense 'directed' by the environment. Environmental influences can greatly affect the mutation rate but they cannot induce a particular mutation to occur.
- Mutations are persistent. They tend to be transmitted through many generations without further change, though there is always the possibility that they may mutate again, either producing another novel characteristic or reverting to the original condition.
- The vast majority of mutations confer disadvantages on the organisms that inherit them. The occurrence of a useful mutation is an extremely rare event. Natural selection prevents harmful mutations accumulating but ensures that beneficial mutations spread through the population.

Types of mutation

We can distinguish between two types of mutation: **chromosome mutations** and **gene mutations**. The former involve changes in the gross structure of chromosomes. The latter are chemical changes in individual genes.

Chromosome mutations

During meiosis when chromosomes become intertwined, there is plenty of opportunity for various kinds of structural aberration to take place (figure 43.10). For example, a chromosome may break in two places and the section in between may drop out, taking all its genes with it. If the two ends then join up, a shorter chromosome results with a chunk missing in its middle. This is called a **deletion** and, as it leads to an absence of certain genes, it can have a profound effect on the development of an organism. In fact all but the shortest deletions are usually fatal.

Figure 43.10 Diagrams showing four different types of chromosome mutation. Each type of mutation results in an alteration in the number and/or sequence of genes (represented by letters) on the chromosome.

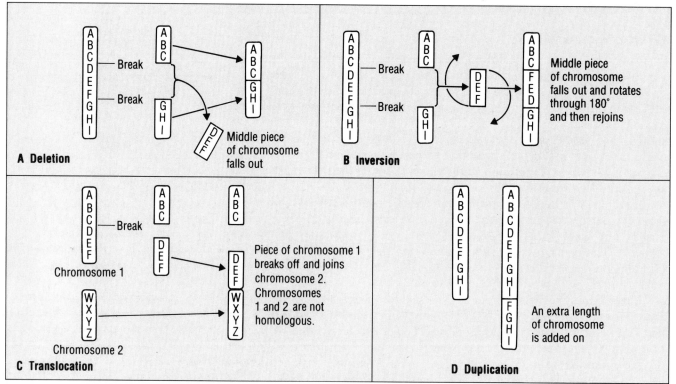

788

Another kind of chromosome abnormality occurs if a chromosome breaks in two places and the middle piece then turns round and joins up again, so that the normal sequence of genes is reversed. This is called an **inversion**.

Sometimes a section of one chromosome breaks off and becomes attached to another chromosome. This is known as a **translocation**.

Inversions and translocations result in neither the loss nor the gain of genetic material, but change the order in which genes occur on chromosomes. Often this disrupts gene regulation and very occasionally the resulting change in gene expression may benefit the organism.

Yet another abnormality occurs when a section of a chromosome replicates so that a set of genes is repeated: this is **duplication**. Again, duplication is frequently harmful. However, on occasions it may be selected for. The various genes that control the different haemoglobins produced in human red blood cells are thought to have arisen by duplications.

Another kind of chromosome abnormality is caused by the addition or loss of one or more whole chromosomes. To understand how this comes about we must return to meiosis for a moment. Normally in meiosis homologous chromosomes come together and then segregate into separate cells, so that the gametes finish up with only one of each type of chromosome. However, on some occasions the two homologous chromosomes, instead of separating, go off into the same cell.

This phenomenon is known as **non-disjunction** and it results in the formation of two types of gametes in equal proportions: one type has two of the chromosomes whilst the other type has none (figure 43.11). The fusion of the first kind of gamete with a normal gamete gives a zygote with three such chromosomes, i.e. the normal pair plus an extra one. This condition is called **trisomy**. Fusion of the second kind of gamete with a normal gamete gives an individual with only one of this particular type of chromosome in each cell.

Chromosome mutations and meiosis

Each of the four sorts of chromosome mutations described in the adjacent text (deletion, inversion, translocation and duplication) produces a characteristic effect when homologous chromosomes are viewed at prophase I of meiosis. Since equivalent loci line up alongside each other, any change in the sequence of genes prevents the chromosomes lying parallel with one another. For example, a deletion will cause a loop, an inversion a twist, and so on.

It was the unusual appearance of the chromosomes under the microscope during meiosis that first alerted geneticists to the fact that these sorts of mutations can take place.

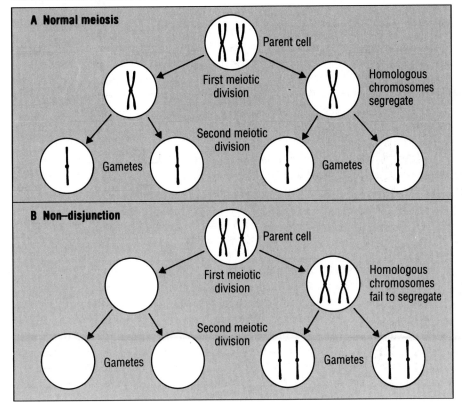

A Normal meiosis

Parent cell

First meiotic division

Homologous chromosomes segregate

Second meiotic division

Gametes

Gametes

B Non–disjunction

Parent cell

First meiotic division

Homologous chromosomes fail to segregate

Second meiotic division

Gametes

Gametes

Figure 43.11 Diagram comparing normal meiosis with non-disjunction for one pair of chromosomes. In normal meiosis the homologous chromosomes segregate, so the gametes each contain one chromosome. In non-disjunction the chromosomes fail to segregate, so half the gametes contain two chromosomes each and the other half contain no chromosomes at all. Generally non-disjunction takes place with respect to just one pair of homologous chromosomes, the rest behaving normally. It can occur during either the first or the second meiotic division.

Figure 43.12 The chromosomes of a male with Down's syndrome. Notice that there are three copies of chromosome 21, giving a total of 47 chromosomes instead of the usual 46.

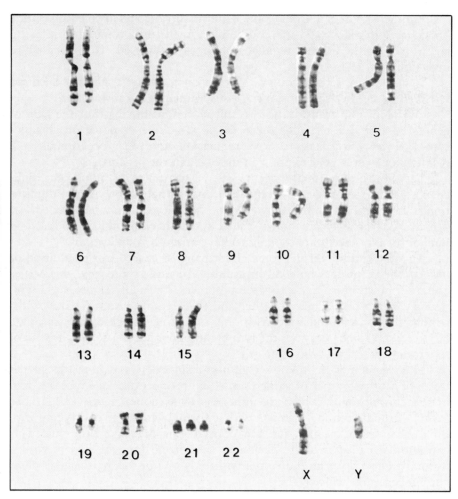

Figure 43.13 A young boy with Down's syndrome. In recent years considerable advances have been made in caring for people with Down's syndrome. The education of children with Down's syndrome is now much more appropriate, and many children with this syndrome have surprised their parents and teachers by showing how much they can learn. Better medical care also means that the prognosis for adults with Down's syndrome has improved significantly.

Maternal age at birth of child	Risk of child having Down's syndrome
20 years	1 in 1925
25 years	1 in 1205
30 years	1 in 885
35 years	1 in 365
40 years	1 in 110
45 years	1 in 32
50 years	1 in 12

Table 43.2 The risk of a child being born with Down's syndrome increases the older the mother becomes.

Chromosome mutations in humans

Quite how important non-disjunction has been in generating useful genetic novelty is uncertain, but there is no doubt that it can have a profound effect on an organism's development. For example, **Down's syndrome** in humans is caused by the presence of an extra chromosome in each cell, chromosome number 21 to be precise (figure 43.12). This is one of the smallest of the human chromosomes, yet its presence plays havoc with the individual's normal development.

Children with Down's syndrome have a characteristic appearance with almond-shaped eyes and a roundish face (figure 43.13). Such children are mentally retarded and can rarely read or write more than a limited number of words. They often die before they are 30 years old as they are susceptible to infections and frequently have congenital heart disease. On the other hand, they are usually delightful children, happy and affectionate, enjoying both home life and school.

Since Down's syndrome affects one of the autosomes, i.e. the non-sex chromosomes, it is known as *autosomal* trisomy. It is by far the commonest autosomal trisomy in humans. Its incidence increases the older the mother is (table 43.2). However, as most women have their children in their 20s or early 30s, the majority of babies with Down's syndrome are born to women under the age of 40. Approximately a quarter of Down's syndrome cases are the result of non-disjunction in the father, and in these cases too age has a significant effect: older men are more likely to father a Down's syndrome child.

Prenatal diagnosis

A number of techniques are now available to test for chromosomomal and genetic mutations in human fetuses. At the moment these techniques are used to detect abnormalities, on the basis of which the parents may be offered the option of a termination of pregnancy. However, in the future some of the techniques may be developed to allow certain genetic disorders to be treated.

The best known technique for prenatal (before birth) diagnosis is **amniocentesis** (illustration 1A). A long hollow needle with a fine point is inserted through the mother's abdominal wall into the amniotic cavity in the uterus, and a sample of amniotic fluid is drawn off. This fluid contains fetal cells, some of which are alive and can be cultured. The cultured cells are then stained to show up the chromosomes and reveal any chromosome abnormalities, such as that responsible for Down's syndrome. The procedure is usually carried out around 14–16 weeks into gestation and it takes about three to four weeks for the cells to be cultured and chromosome mutations revealed. The risk that the procedure will induce a miscarriage is about 0.5 per cent. It is also possible to test the amniotic fluid for a number of gene mutations.

Another, more recent, approach to prenatal diagnosis is that of **chorionic villi sampling** (illustration 1B). Here a narrow tube is inserted through the cervix and a tiny sample of the chorionic villi from the placenta is taken. This is embryonic, rather than maternal, in origin, so that chromosome staining and examination can be carried out to test for chromosome mutations in the fetus. More fetal cells are obtained in chorionic villi sampling than in amniocentesis, which means that this technique can be done

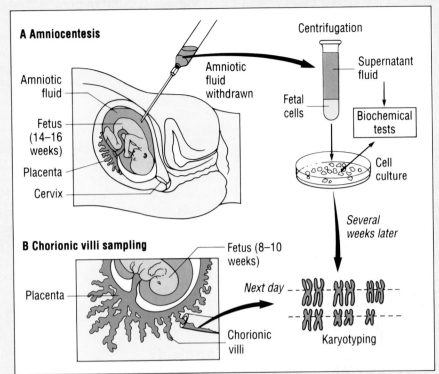

Illustration 1 The techniques of amniocentesis and chorionic villi sampling compared.

earlier (from around eight to ten weeks into gestation) and the results obtained more quickly (within a couple of days). However, the risk that the procedure will induce a miscarriage is higher than for amniocentesis, being about 2 per cent.

A quite different approach is provided by **α fetoprotein screening**. In this procedure the concentration in the *mother's* blood of a particular protein called α fetoprotein is determined. About 80 per cent of cases of open neural tube defects (spina bifida) and over 90 per cent of cases of anencephaly (in

which a part of the skull and brain fail to develop) can be detected by an increased maternal serum concentration of α fetoprotein. On the other hand, an unusually *low* α fetoprotein concentation in the mother's blood is associated with an increased risk of Down's syndrome. This technique obviously carries no risk to the fetus.

A final approach involves **ultrasound** (illustration 2). This technique carries no risk to the fetus and can be used to test for a wide range of morphological abnormalities including hydrocephaly (water on the brain), various types of congenital heart disease, clefts of the lip and palate and bone abnormalities. Ultrasonography also tells the mother whether or not she is carrying twins.

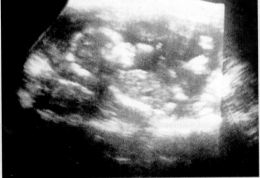

Illustration 2 Ultrascan showing a healthy human fetus around 20 weeks gestation. The head is to the left, the feet to the right.

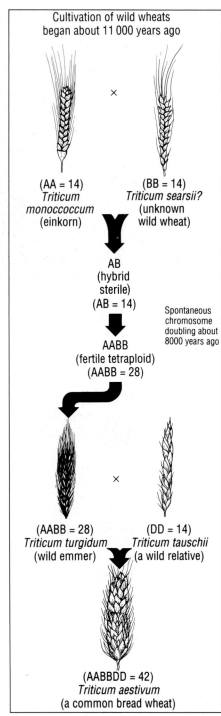

Cultivation of wild wheats
began about 11 000 years ago

(AA = 14)
Triticum monoccoccum
(einkorn)

×

(BB = 14)
Triticum searsii?
(unknown wild wheat)

AB
(hybrid sterile)
(AB = 14)

Spontaneous chromosome doubling about 8000 years ago

AABB
(fertile tetraploid)
(AABB = 28)

(AABB = 28)
Triticum turgidum
(wild emmer)

×

(DD = 14)
Triticum tauschii
(a wild relative)

(AABBDD = 42)
Triticum aestivum
(a common bread wheat)

Figure 43.14 Probable evolutionary history of modern wheat over the last ten thousand years or so as revealed by a combination of archaeology and genetics. The letters A, B and D each refer to a different set of seven chromosomes. For example, *Triticum monoccoccum* has two sets of A chromosomes while *Triticum aestivum* has two sets of A chromosomes, two sets of B chromosomes and two sets of D chromosomes, making a total of 42 chromosomes.

Various sex chromosome abnormalities in humans are also caused by non-disjunction. For example, approximately two in a thousand men have the genetic constitution **XXY** – **Klinefelter's syndrome**. This may result either from the fusion of a **Y** sperm with an **XX** egg, or from the fusion of an **XY** sperm with an **X** egg. Although **XXY** individuals are phenotypically men, they have very small genitals and are infertile; in addition, they may develop breasts. However, the condition is not usually associated with below-average intelligence and testosterone therapy at puberty can often help alleviate the symptoms.

Another sex chromosome abnormality is due to the absence of one of the sex chromosomes. Fetuses with 22 normal pairs of autosomes and a single **Y** chromosome never survive to birth – can you suggest why? However, children may be born with 22 normal pairs of autosomes and a single **X** chromosome. Such individuals have the genetic constitution **XO**. They are females and occur with an incidence of approximately 0.4 per 1000 liveborn girls. The condition is known as **Turner's syndrome** and the phenotypic effects are relatively minor. Individuals are usually shorter than normal with a characteristic webbed neck. Intelligence is not usually affected, but the person is infertile. Oestrogen replacement therapy can allow normal pubertal development, and growth can be stimulated with growth hormone.

Polyploidy

Sometimes cell division fails altogether, resulting in half the gametes having two of each type of chromosome (i.e. being diploid), the rest having none. If a diploid gamete fuses with a normal haploid gamete the resulting individual is **triploid**, i.e. it has three of each type of chromosome. If two diploid gametes fuse, a **tetraploid** individual results. It is thus possible for an organism to acquire one or more complete extra sets of chromosomes, a phenomenon called **polyploidy**.

Polyploidy also occurs if the whole chromosome set doubles after fertilisation. In this case the chromosomes replicate as they would prior to mitosis. Sometimes, however, the spindle fails to form and the cell does not divide, finishing up with twice the normal number of chromosomes. If this happens to a diploid cell, a tetraploid results; if it happens to a triploid cell, a hexaploid results.

Such post-fertilisation polyploidy can be particularly important in cases where two different, but closely related species, are crossed. The diploid offspring will be incapable of producing gametes, and are therefore sterile, because the chromosomes, being non-homologous, will be unable to pair during meiosis. (If you find it difficult to follow this explanation, try drawing what happens at anaphase I of meiosis in a cell with, say, four chromosomes, two from one species and two from another, remembering that none of the chromosomes will be homologous.) However, if the diploid number is doubled, giving the tetraploid condition, each chromosome will have a homologous one with which it can pair. As a result, successful meiosis will be possible.

Polyploidy is thought to have been important in the evolution of wheat. Modern wheat – the type we use for bread making – is believed to have evolved from a sterile hybrid whose chromosome number doubled about 8000 years ago (figure 43.14).

A more recent example of polyploidy is provided by the evolution of the cord grass *Spartina anglica*. In 1829 a plant with the name of *S. alterniflora* (2n = 62) was first recorded in the British Isles after being introduced to Southampton Water in shipping ballast. This species hybridised with *S.*

maritima (2n = 60), a plant which on the south coast of England is at the northern limit of its natural distribution. The result was a sterile hybrid called *S. x townsendii* (2n = 61) which first appeared in Southampton Water around 1870.

About 1890 *S. x townsendii* doubled its chromosome number and gave rise to *S. anglica*, a fertile tetraploid with 122 chromosomes. *S. anglica* is a tough vigorous halophyte which uses the C4 pathway in photosynthesis. It spread rapidly both vegetatively and by seed, outcompeting the other species. It is now widely distributed around the coast of the British Isles. Indeed, certain areas are choked with it (figure 43.15). There is some evidence that the number of overwintering birds, dunlin for example, have declined as a result (figure 43.16). This is because such birds find it difficult to penetrate the dense sward to reach their invertebrate food supply in the nutrient-rich intertidal sediment. This illustrates the far-reaching ecological consequences of an organism doubling its chromosome number.

Polyploidy is rare in animals, but common in plants. In fact, approximately half of all plant species are polyploid. Polyploidy is often associated with advantageous characteristics such as increased size and greater hardiness, though such advantages are sometimes offset by reduced fertility.

Reduced fertility is particularly common when individuals are triploid (3n), or when tetraploidy (4n) results not from the crossing of individuals from two different species, but simply from a doubling of the chromosome number in one species. Infertile triploids and tetraploids are often of great commercial significance precisely because they *are* infertile. Many of the seedless bananas, grapes and other fruit we eat are the result of such polyploidy (figure 43.17).

Polyploidy can be induced experimentally by heat or cold shock or by various chemical agents, notably **colchicine**, an alkaloid substance extracted from the crocus *Colchicum*. Applied in the correct amounts, colchicine prevents spindle-formation during mitosis. The chromosomes replicate in the usual way but the absence of a spindle means that anaphase fails and when the nuclear envelope reforms, cells often result with twice the normal number of chromosomes.

Figure 43.15 Cord grass (*Spartina anglica*), a vigorous halophyte, is here seen flourishing in the salt marshes around Poole Harbour, Dorset. The way it has evolved is explained in the text.

Figure 43.16 Overwintering dunlin feeding on a mudflat.

Figure 43.17
Top A diploid orange with seeds.
Bottom A seedless triploid orange.

Why do people with HIV take so long to develop AIDS?

One of the unusual things about infection with HIV (human immunodeficiency virus) is that it typically takes years before any symptoms are seen. Indeed, some people infected with HIV never seem to progress to AIDS. (The symptoms of AIDS are described on pages 419 and 420.)

Why does it take so long for HIV to progress to AIDS, and why do some people infected with HIV never show any symptoms? Recent research suggests that the answer may be related to the extraordinarily high mutation rate of HIV. HIV mutates up to a million times faster than other viruses. In a person infected with HIV, the virus replicates and, because the mutation rate is so high, sooner or later the host's antibodies fail to recognise the viral antigens. Eventually enough of these mutant viruses accumulate to start attacking the person's immune system. That is approximately when the first symptoms of AIDS appear.

Support for this theory comes from observations on a group of Scottish haemophiliacs thought to have been infected with the same strain of HIV via contaminated blood products. Several years later all were infected with *different* strains of HIV.

If this theory turns out to be correct, then finding a cure for AIDS is going to be even harder than previously thought, and finding a vaccine virtually impossible. From the biological point of view, it is an impressive example of just how rapidly evolution can take place.

Gene mutations

Gene mutations are thought to have been very important in generating evolutionary change. A gene mutation arises as a result of a chemical change in an individual gene. An alteration in the sequence of nucleotides in the part of a DNA molecule that corresponds to a particular gene may change the order of amino acids making up a protein. This may have far-reaching consequences on the fitness of an organism, as we saw earlier in our examination of sickle cell anaemia (see page 753).

The kind of gene mutation that causes sickle cell anaemia is called a **substitution**. This is because the mutation results from the substitution of one base for another in the DNA. In sickle cell anaemia, instead of the triplet coding for the sixth amino acid of β haemoglobin being CTT, it is CAT – in other words thymine is replaced by adenine at this particular point in the DNA molecule. As a result, the sixth amino acid is valine rather than the usual glutamic acid.

When a gene mutation involves a change in only a single base, as in the case just mentioned, it is called a **point mutation**. However, some gene mutations involve a change in two or more bases.

If we look upon DNA as a conveyor of coded information, we can see at once that even a very slight change may be enough to alter completely its information content. As an analogy, consider the faulty information which might be conveyed by a sentence in which a single incorrect letter is substituted for the intended one:

Intended message: SUSAN IS NOW ARRIVING BY AIR FROM NEW YORK.
Actual message: SUSAN IS NOT ARRIVING BY AIR FROM NEW YORK.

Let us consider some other misprints. Here is a example of an extra letter creeping into a message. A geneticist would call it an **insertion**:

Intended message: PLEASE SAY WHERE YOU ARE.
Actual message: PLEASE STAY WHERE YOU ARE.

On the other hand a letter might be left out (**deletion**) as in the following example:

Intended message: I WILL SEND A FRIEND TO COLLECT YOU.
Actual message: I WILL SEND A FIEND TO COLLECT YOU.

Another possibility is that two or more letters might be printed the wrong way way round, resulting in an **inversion**:

Intended message: GUERILLAS ARE SENDING ARMS TO HELP RIOTERS.
Actual message: GUERILLAS ARE SENDING RAMS TO HELP RIOTERS.

Somatic mutation

Sometimes a mutation occurs in a non-reproductive (i.e. somatic) cell of an organism. This is called a **somatic mutation**. The resulting genetic change will be present in all the cells descended from the original mutant cell and, as such, may profoundly affect the individual. However, as the genetic change is only in non-reproductive cells, it will not appear in the gametes and so cannot be transmitted to future generations. Of course, a somatic mutation may affect the reproductive success of the individual, and in this way make its presence felt in evolution.

Somatic mutations cause such phenomena as birth marks in humans. Whatever their manifestations, somatic mutations result in some cells of the organism having a different genetic constitution from the rest. Such an individual is described as a **genetic mosaic**. The proportion of cells affected

Genetic fingerprinting

It has long been known that no two people have precisely the same pattern of dermal ridges on their fingers: our fingerprints are unique. This fact is often used by the police in detective work. The reason why our fingerprints are unique is that each of us has our own unique DNA.

Of course, your DNA is pretty similar to anybody else's, but mutations, independent assortment and crossing-over combine to make your DNA unique to you. In 1984 Alec Jeffreys, a geneticist at Leicester University, discovered a technique that could readily distinguish one person's DNA from another's. This is the basis of **genetic fingerprinting**.

The essence of the method is to take some of a person's DNA and cut it up into lots of bits with restriction endonucleases. These enzymes recognise specific sequences in the DNA (see page 742). Because each of us has a unique sequence of nucleotides in our DNA, the lengths of these bits will vary from person to person. Electrophoresis is then used

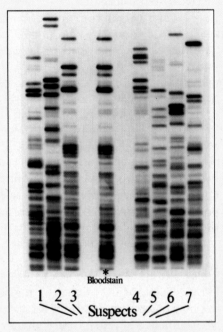

1 2 3   4 5 6 7
Suspects
Bloodstain *

to separate out these bits according to their size and charge. The net result is a pattern unique to each of us. The only exceptions are identical twins – they share the same pattern.

So much for the technique. How can it be used? Here's an example that became known as the 'Babes in the Wood' trial. In 1988 a girl came down from Durham to see the

pantomime at The London Palladium. She was picked up by a student on the underground, taken back to his flat, plied with drink and then raped. After escaping from his flat she appealed to two men in a red Cortina to drive her to a police station. Instead they drove her to a park where they both raped her.

Eventually she did get to a police station and a vaginal swab produced enough semen for DNA fingerprinting. The analysis confirmed that she had indeed had intercourse with three men that day. The police caught one of them and he was sent to prison for 12 years. The other two have not yet been caught but their DNA fingerprints are on permanent record.

Some DNA fingerprints from another criminal investigation (a murder case) are shown in the illustration. You can see at once which suspects are unlikely to have committed the crime.

How could you explain the technique of genetic fingerprinting to a jury with no knowledge of biology?

depends on how early in development the mutation occurs: obviously, more cells will show the genetic change if the mutation occurs in the early embryo rather than in the adult. Somatic mutations can occur at any stage in life and an accumulation of them in older individuals is thought to contribute to senescence (see page 740).

The struggle for existence

If you turn back to the four propositions of the Darwin-Wallace theory of natural selection (see page 783), you will see that they include the idea that more offspring are born than can possibly survive to maturity and reproduce, and that there is a struggle for existence, some individuals being better suited for this struggle than others.

Let us consider these propositions in more detail. First, see if you can answer the following question. In a species consisting of sexually reproducing males and females, how many offspring would each female need to produce during her lifetime for the population to remain constant in numbers, assuming no infant mortality?

The answer is two. Now there is no species in the world in which adult females only produce two offspring during their lifetime. Even in elephants, a female typically produces about eight young during her lifetime. This means that in every species more offspring are born than can possibly

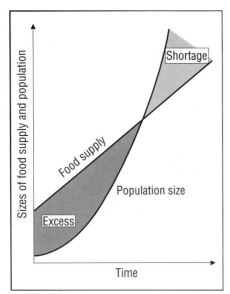

Figure 43.19 An African elephant with calf. A healthy adult female elephant only produces a single calf every five years. Even an animal that reproduces as slowly as this has the potential to explode in numbers, as Darwin showed in *The Origin of Species*.

survive to reproduce.

The first person to realise the importance of this was Thomas Malthus, an English clergyman, who in 1798 argued that while the human population increases geometrically, the food supply only grows arithmetically, as shown in figure 43.18. This means that in time the number of people alive will always tend to outstrip the available food supply, leading to 'famine, pestilence and war'.

It was a grim doctrine which challenged the optimism of the time. Many of Malthus' contemporaries disagreed with his argument, partly because England was then enjoying a period of prosperity and sustained population growth. Indeed, with hindsight it is difficult to see why food supply should only increase arithmetically. However, despite any logical imperfections of the argument, both Darwin and Wallace were much impressed with it. They each saw that it applied to all organisms, not just humans. In the Malthusian argument they could see the seeds of a mechanism for evolution.

Populations and evolution

How does the Malthusian doctrine help our understanding of evolution? In the first place it is clear that all species produce more individuals than the environment can possibly support. In *The Origin of Species* Darwin tried to determine how many elephants would result from a single pair if all the offspring survived. He calculated that after five hundred years some fifteen million elephants would result (figure 43.19).

Clearly the world would soon be covered with elephants if such unrestrained geometric (exponential) growth went on for ever. But, as we saw in Chapter 5, exponential growth cannot continue for long. Soon an increase in mortality or a reduction in fecundity sets in. However, the mortality that keeps population sizes from increasing for ever is not random, i.e. it does not affect all individuals equally. It strikes more fiercely as those individuals that are least well adapted for survival. In other words the population is kept in check by a process of *differential* mortality.

As well as keeping the population on an even keel, differential mortality favours the perpetuation of beneficial characteristics. However, it does not necessarily follow that the individuals which are the fittest physically are also the fittest genetically. Only if there is a genetic basis to differential survival and reproduction can evolution by natural selection occur, as we shall now see.

Natural selection

From the evolutionary point of view differential mortality is important because, if it occurs before the individual has had a chance to reproduce, it eliminates unfavourable alleles from the population. However, death is not the only way of achieving this. Any process that encourages the transmission of favourable alleles and hinders the transmission of unfavourable ones contributes towards evolution. Given enough time, an allele which is associated with only a very slight reduction in viability, fertility or fecundity will usually be eliminated from the population.

Natural selection as an agent of constancy as well as change

A central conclusion from Darwin's theory is that species change over time. In proposing his theory, a major difficulty Darwin had to contend with was that species appear to remain remarkably constant. This was seized upon by some of his critics as a weakness in the argument.

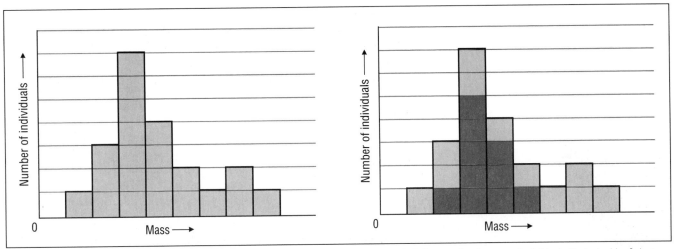

Figure 43.20 A Hypothetical diagram showing a frequency distribution curve for the mass of individuals in a population.

B Hypothetical diagram for the same individuals illustrated in **A**, but showing (by shading) which individuals breed.

But in fact natural selection is responsible both for maintaining the constancy of species and for changing them. To see how this works, imagine that we construct a frequency distribution curve for mass in a population of organisms and obtain the result shown in figure 43.20A. Now suppose that we identify those individuals that reproduce and leave viable offspring. These individuals are shown in figure 43.20B. You can see how only those individuals whose mass is close to the average reproduce. None of the very light nor any of the very heavy individuals contribute to the next generation. This kind of selection is known as **stabilising selection** because it maintains the constancy of species over generations.

Stabilising selection normally occurs when the environment remains constant over time. If, however, the environment changes, for instance by becoming colder in winter, then it may be an advantage to be larger than before. A new mass becomes the 'ideal' or 'optimum' and the result is that the frequency curve of the breeding individuals becomes shifted to the right. The net effect is to achieve an overall increase in the mean size of individuals in the population – provided, of course, that mass is at least partly heritable. This kind of selection clearly favours the emergence of new forms and is called **directional selection**.

A hypothetical example of a population subjected to alternative periods of stabilising and directional selection is shown in figure 43.21. However, in reality such evolution would usually take hundreds or thousands of generations, rather than the very few shown here.

Natural selection in action

Another weakness in Darwin's original theory was that he was unable to demonstrate natural selection actually taking place. This is understandable, for palaeontologists calculate that it often takes over a million years for one species to evolve into another!

Today, though, we do have examples of natural selection in action. Remember, for example, the evolution of the cord grass *Spartina anglica* which we discussed earlier in this chapter. Here, within 150 years, a new species evolved and spread hundreds of miles, outcompeting other species as it did so. A more modest example of natural selection was discussed in detail in Chapter 41, namely the evolution of melanism in the peppered moth (*Biston betularia*). Other, more recent examples are given in the box on page 800.

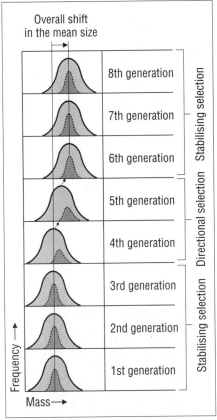

Figure 43.21 Diagram showing alternate periods of stabilising and directional selection. Stabilising selection is responsible for maintaining the constancy of species. Directional selection causes a shift in the mean mass by, in this case, favouring heavier individuals. In each generation the frequency curve for all individuals born is shown as a continuous line. The curve for breeding individuals is shown as a broken line.

The origins of species

A species can be defined as a group of organisms which are potentially able to breed amongst themselves but not with any other species. Often, though, we cannot employ this definition directly. Palaeontologists, for instance, never have the opportunity to see whether their fossils can breed with one another or not. In such situations a different criterion is used, one of **morphological similarity**.

Morphological similarity makes use of the common observation that species can be distinguished by their appearance – a song thrush looks recognisably different from a blackbird, for instance. However, there are dangers in using morphological similarities as the sole criterion for what constitutes a species. Female blackbirds, for instance, look different from male blackbirds, yet they obviously belong to the same species (figure 43.22).

The importance of isolation

Over time one species may evolve into another. If, however, one species is to evolve into *two*, it is necessary for the species to become split up into at least two separate demes, each with its own gene pool (see page 746). These demes must be almost totally isolated from each other because if more than a tiny amount of gene exchange occurs between them they will effectively behave as one population and any genetic differences which might arise between them will not be perpetuated. If they are isolated, mutation and selection can take place independently in the two populations and each may develop into a distinct species.

Isolation is often geographic in origin. Such isolation provides the opportunity for each population to evolve along its own lines. If the two populations subsequently come together, each may have changed to such an extent that for physiological or genetic reasons interbreeding is impossible. If this is the case, the two populations have become separate species. In time it is likely that they will diverge even further, unless one of them becomes extinct.

Isolating mechanisms

The kinds of **isolating mechanisms** that can lead to the emergence of new species are of two main types:

- **Geographical isolation between populations.** Good examples of this are provided on oceanic islands, such as the Galapagos Islands (see page 766). When a population becomes geographically split into separate demes, the evolution of new species is very probable, given the passage of enough time. This sort of speciation is known as **allopatric speciation** (literally 'speciation in different countries').

- **Reproductive isolation within a population.** This occurs when ecological, behavioural or genetic barriers arise within a population and lead to the formation of new species. Suppose, for instance, that within a diurnal species of insect a mutation occurs that causes a few individuals to be nocturnal. Ninety nine times out of a hundred the mutation will be disadvantageous. However, there is always the small chance that such a mutation might lead to a new niche being exploited. If individuals carrying the nocturnal mutation never meet the diurnal individuals to mate with them, this could result in the evolution of a new species. This sort of speciation is known as **sympatric speciation** ('speciation in the same country').

Figure 43.22 The song thrush (*Turdus philomelos*) and the blackbird (*Turdus merula*) look distinct and are classified as separate species. However, despite belonging to the one species, male and female blackbirds can be easily distinguished.
A Song thrush.
B Female blackbird.
C Male blackbird.

In plants, both sympatric and allopatric speciation are important, while in animals allopatric speciation is probably the more important. One of the most important sorts of sympatric speciation is polyploidy, which we discussed earlier (see page 792).

Whatever the type of speciation, two species will only remain as separate entities if interbreeding is either impossible or very rare. Often interbreeding is prevented by geographical isolation. In this case the two species may interbreed if brought together. For example, the wild cat (*Felis silvestris*) found in Scotland will interbreed with the domestic cat (*Felis catus*) and there is little doubt that the gene pool of the wild cat is being infiltrated by genes from domestic cats. A Scottish wild cat is shown in figure 43.23.

Apart from geographical isolation, interbreeding between separate species may be prevented by a lack of attraction between males and females of the two species or by physical non-correspondence of the genitalia. In the case of flowering plants it may be due to the fact that pollination is impossible between the two species. In animals with elaborate behaviour patterns it may be because the courtship behaviour of one fails to stimulate the other (figure 43.24).

Even if mating is possible, fundamental differences in genetic constitution may prevent reproduction being successful. Thus, the gametes may be prevented from fusing, as, for example, when the pollen grains of one species of plant fail to germinate on the stigmas of another (figure 43.25). Even if fertilisation does occur the zygotes may be inferior in some way and fail to develop properly. Sometimes offspring are produced but the hybrids may die before reaching adulthood. Or they may be sterile, as in the famous case of the mule, formed by crossing a donkey with a horse.

The emergence of new species

It is clear that, far from being fixed and immutable, species change and may evolve into new species. The process by which new species are formed is called **speciation.**

This raises a practical difficulty, for if a species shows signs of evolving into a new species, what do we call the intermediate forms? Normally, recognisably distinct forms within a species are called **sub-species** (see page 94). Only when such sub-species fail to interbreed are they said to have evolved into separate species.

Gradual change or sudden jumps?

Our discussion of the origin of species has been based on the idea that species gradually change over long periods of time from one form to another. This is known by the formidable name of **phyletic gradualism,** ('phyletic' meaning evolutionary). Darwin regarded this as the main way in which evolution has taken place, and until recently almost all biologists took a similar position. If this idea is correct, one would expect to find intermediate forms between one fossil species and the next in successive rock strata. However, intermediate forms in the fossil record are surprisingly rare.

The rarity of intermediate forms is seen by **creationists,** who believe in special creation rather than in the evolution of species, as evidence that evolution has not occurred. However, two American palaeontologists, Niles Eldredge and Stephen Gould, put forward a different interpretation. They suggest that new species may arise rapidly, perhaps within a few thousand years, and then remain almost unchanged for millions of years

Figure 43.23 Scottish wild cat, *Felis silvestris*. This species can interbreed with the closely related domestic cat, *Felis catus*.

Figure 43.24 In the wild, different species of ducks rarely interbreed, partly because each species has its own characteristic courtship behaviour.

Figure 43.25 Where many species of flowering plant co-exist, it is vital that they do not interbreed. Usually interbreeding is prevented because pollen grains can only germinate on the stigmas of the same species.

Recent examples of natural selection

Natural selection is not just a process of the past. It still happens and is responsible for a continuous process of evolution. In this box some recent examples are given.

Heavy metal tolerance in plants

One of the most convincing examples of natural selection is provided by the evolution in certain grasses of tolerance to heavy metals, such as copper, zinc and lead, enabling them to flourish on the spoil from mines (illustration 1).

Various physiological mechanisms have evolved to allow these plants to grow and reproduce in soils where heavy metals are present at concentrations that kill normal plants. In some species the toxic metals bind to organic molecules in the cell walls where they remain trapped, unable to harm the cell's

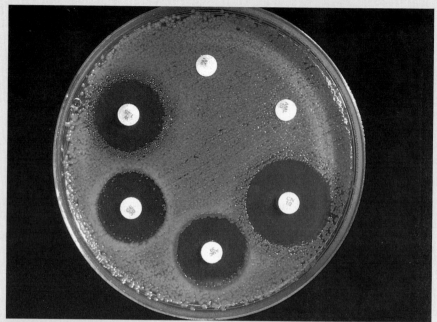

Illustration 2 Bacteria growing on an agar plate on which have been placed six different antibiotics (white disks). Notice that the bacteria fail to grow in the presence of four of the antibiotics but *can* grow in the presence of two of them.

Illustration 1 A classic photograph taken by A.D. Bradshaw of the University of Liverpool showing the grass *Agrostis tenuis* growing on the spoil from a lead and zinc mine in mid-Wales. Bradshaw found that in this and other species of grass, tolerance to metals such as lead, zinc and copper evolved in less than 30 years. Normal genotypes of the same species of grass die if transplanted into such areas. Tolerant varieties are now used in industrial regions for covering slag heaps and turning them into recreational areas.

contents. In other species the metals are stored in the vacuole, again out of harm's way. Other species trap the metals at special membrane sites. Some plants simply export the metals from their cells to the external environment.

Whatever the mechanism, the net result is the same: these plants are able to flourish in an environment which would otherwise remain unexploited. Indeed, the plants have become so well adapted to living in such conditions that on unpolluted soil they do not fare so well and are outcompeted by normal plants.

Antibiotic resistance in bacteria

A more sinister example of the power of natural selection is provided by the evolution of antibiotic resistance by certain bacteria. Antibiotics are widely used in medicine and veterinary practice to kill pathogenic bacteria. However, bacteria have very short generation times, are haploid and can reproduce sexually in a variety of ways (see page 571) and are haploid. These features

enable bacteria to evolve rapidly in response to changes in their environment. (Can you see why?)

With the widespread use of antibiotics over the last forty years, many bacteria have evolved cellular mechanisms enabling them to grow in the presence of a great many antibiotics (illustration 2). A few bacteria have even evolved the ability to feed off certain antibiotics! Nowadays doctors tend to be more restrained than they were about how many different antibiotics they prescribe. That way, a few really effective ones can be kept in reserve to be used only if a bacterium is resistant to all the more common antibiotics.

DDT resistance in insects

The widespread use of DDT to control insect pests has lead to the evolution of resistance to this chemical by many species. One Nigerian survey of mosquitoes in the species *Anopheles gambiae* found that in unsprayed villages almost no flies were resistant to DDT.

However, in villages which had been subject to regular spraying, approximately 90 per cent of the flies were homozygous for resistant alleles.

In house flies, several mechanisms are known which permit resistance. Four genes are involved and each has a distinct function. Two of the DDT-resistant genes enable the poison to be detoxified, each by a different route. Another gene reduces the rate at which DDT penetrates the cuticle. The fourth gene acts by an unknown route.

Warfarin resistance in rats

In much the same way, many rat populations are now resistant to the rat poison warfarin. Warfarin was first used as a rat poison in Britain in 1950. It works by interfering with blood clotting, so that the poisoned animals suffer fatal haemorrhages.

Warfarin resistance is determined by a single dominant allele. Rats with this allele have a slightly different biochemical mechanism that enables blood clotting to take place even in the presence of warfarin. However, there is a disadvantage to carrying the resistant allele. Such animals need a very high intake of vitamin K. This means that in areas without warfarin, warfarin-resistant rats are at a disadvantage.

Many more examples of natural selection in action could be given, though it has to be admitted that the clearest instances, such as those given above, generally result from the activites of humans. It is widely believed, however, that over time natural selection has been the prime mechanism driving evolution and still operates today.

Evolution: a gene's eye view

Are we just vehicles for our genes? Guest author Richard Dawkins suggests that we are, and briefly explains his reasoning.

Why are we living things so good at doing what we do? It is because we are descended from an unbroken line of successful ancestors. Almost all individuals die young, but not a single, solitary one of your ancestors did. From an unbroken line of successful ancestors, all living things inherit what it takes to be successful. This tells us what adaptation really is. An adaptation is a device for becoming an ancestor.

We inherit what it takes to be successful and this means, of course, successful genes. Adaptations are devices created by successful, as opposed to unsuccessful, genes. Udders exist, and are well-adapted for suckling, for one reason only: genes that give mothers good udders save copies of those very same genes in the bodies of the young suckled. Penises are well adapted for inserting sperms into females because genes that make good penises have shot their way down the generations through a long succession of ancestral good penises, and that is why those genes are still around. Genes that made ineffective penises are no longer present in the world. Of course many adaptations work by fostering individual survival – strong teeth, sharp claws, swift limbs, keen eyes – but this is not the end; it is a means to the end of preserving copies of the genes inside the individual.

An adaptation – it might be an organ or an entire body – is best seen as a device for preserving and propagating the genes that made it. You can usually get away with saying that an adaptation is a device for enhancing the 'fitness', in the sense of reproductive success, of an individual. But even this is incorrect for worker ants, termites and bees which, being sterile, have no offspring but only brothers and sisters, nephews and nieces. This difficulty disappears the moment we take a gene's eye view of evolution.

Genes that make sterile bees work and sacrifice themselves for their hive are preserved, not in the workers' own bodies nor, obviously, in their offspring, but in the young queens and drones emerging from the hive. Those new queens and drones will begin new hives, and produce new sterile workers driven to similar action by copies of those very same genes.

Natural selection, if it is to have a long-term effect on evolution, must choose between alternative entities that aspire to being long-term. These entities must have at least the potential to survive indefinitely through generation after generation in the form of copies. Genes have this potential immortality. Bodies, even the best of them, are mortal. The most natural view of adaptive evolution is the gene's eye view. A body is the genes' way of making more genes. A body is a 'throwaway survival machine' for its genes.

Do you agree that the human body is simply a throwaway survival machine for its genes?

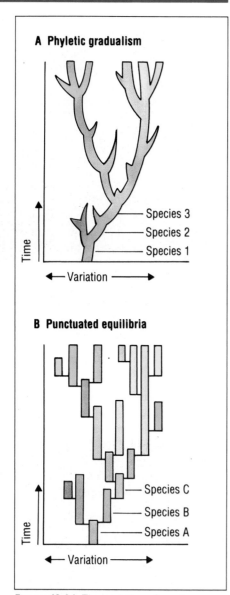

A Phyletic gradualism

Time

← Variation →

Species 3
Species 2
Species 1

B Punctuated equilibria

Time

← Variation →

Species C
Species B
Species A

Figure 43.26 The evolution of species according to two contrasting models: phyletic gradualism and punctuated equilibria models. Phyletic gradualism proposes that species change gradually in the course of evolution, whereas the punctuated equilibria model proposes that species change suddenly and then remain pretty constant for long periods before changing again.

Figure 43.27 The coelacanth. In 1938 a trawler fishing off the coast of South Africa caught one of these fish. Until then the species had been thought to be extinct for 70 million years. Because it has changed so little over so long a period, it is called a 'living fossil'.

before changing again. Moreover, the sudden evolution of a new species may occur in a marginal part of the population, containing only a small number of individuals.

In these circumstances we would not usually expect to find a gradation between successive species in the fossil record. This idea is embodied in the term **punctuated equilibria** – 'punctuated' referring to the short periods of rapid evolution, 'equilibria' to the long periods of almost no change.

Phyletic gradualism and punctuated equilibria are compared diagrammatically in figure 43.26. Some people have felt that the idea of punctuated equilibria is contrary to Darwinism. However, it can be explained in terms of natural selection, and Darwin himself recognised that it could happen. It is quite possible that both processes have occurred in the course of geological history.

The rate of evolution

The rate at which evolution occurs varies enormously. At one extreme are so-called **living fossils** such as the coelacanth and ginkgo tree (figures 43.27 and 43.28). These organisms have remained almost unchanged for tens of millions of years or longer. At the other extreme are organisms such as the banana-feeding moths in the genus *Hedylepta* found only in Hawaii. There are five species of this moth. Bananas were only introduced to Hawaii approximately 1000 years ago, so it seems likely that these five species have evolved from a common ancestor within the last thousand years.

Another example of the rapid evolution of new species is provided by a lake which was cut off from Lake Victoria in Uganda approximately 4000 years ago. This lake contains five species of cichlid fish, each similar to, but distinct from, one of the cichlid species in Lake Victoria.

Extensions of natural selection

Darwin extended the Darwin-Wallace theory of natural selection in two ways. First, he asked how worker sterility could have evolved in social insects such as honey bees. You may remember from Chapter 30 that the answer he came up with is still thought to be the correct one, namely **kin selection**. This happens when a characteristic is favoured in evolution not for the benefit it confers on the individual that possesses it, but for the

benefit it confers on its relatives. For example, the stinging behaviour of worker bees does not benefit the individual workers, but it does benefit the offspring of the queen.

The second way in which Darwin extended the theory of natural selection was by suggesting that certain characteristics are the result of **sexual selection**. In most mammals, for instance, males are larger than females. Why is this? The reason is that adult males often compete amongst themselves for access to females. The result is that some adult males never get to breed. Instead, other males monopolise the breeding. This leads to selection for large, strong males. Such species show a marked difference in size between the males and females.

It is hardly surprising that these successful males tend to be the largest and strongest ones. But there is a cost to pay for being very large. In species where males are larger than females, males die younger than females. Because of this a balance exists between the advantages to a male of being larger (more reproduction) and the accompanying disadvantages (shorter lifespan). As a result, the greatest differences in size between males and females occurs in species where a few males monopolise the breeding of an entire population (figure 43.29).

There is a second way in which sexual selection can occur and this is by **female choice**. In a number of birds, males are more brightly coloured than females and may display bizarre courtship behaviour or possess exotic plumage (figure 43.30). In 1930 the English geneticist R.A. Fisher suggested that *if* such males are more likely to breed, a runaway form of sexual selection will occur. Suppose, for instance, that females are more likely to notice a male with a long tail. This might make a particular male marginally more likely to attract the female into mating with him. Then this male will breed more successfully than other males and pass on his long tail to his sons who will in turn be more attractive to females. Sexual selection for increased tail length will continue until the advantage of having an exceptionally long tail is cancelled out by a *dis*advantage: for example, a very long tail might make the male poorer at flying, or the bright plumage might make him more vulnerable to predation.

Figure 43.28 Leafy branch of a gingko tree. This tree is native to China but is grown as an ornamental tree in mild climates all over the world. Plants that look virtually identical to this tree are found in the fossil record over 150 million years ago.

Figure 43.29 Two male southern elephant seals fighting over females. In this species the males can weigh up to eight times as much as the females.

Figure 43.30 A peacock with dazzling plumage attempts to attract the attention of a peahen.

The idea of evolution by female choice may sound fanciful, but evidence in support of this hypothesis is accumulating. For example, the Swedish ornithologist Malte Andersson studied widow birds in Kenya. These birds are sparrow-sized, but while females have tails about 7 cm long, males have tails up to 50 cm in length! Andersson studied 36 males which he treated in four ways. One group had most of their tail feathers cut off; another group had these tail feathers stuck on with glue so that their tails appeared to be some 75 cm in length; a third group had its tail feathers cut off and then reglued (why?); the final group was left untouched.

The results were striking. The males with the extra long tails had between two and four times the reproductive success of the other males.

Artificial selection

For thousands of years humans have altered certain species by imposing on them a process of **artificial selection**. This forms the basis of **animal and plant breeding**. Breeders select individuals with the characteristics that are wanted, and allow them to interbreed. Individuals lacking the desired qualities are prevented from breeding. By rigorous selection over many generations special breeds or varieties may be developed for particular purposes.

Animals that have been subjected to artificial selection include cattle for milk and beef, sheep for wool and meat, horses for racing and hauling, pigs for bacon and lard production, pigeons for flight capacity and plumage type, poultry for egg and meat production and dogs for hunting, retrieving, racing and appearance.

Amongst plants, crops such as wheat, barley and potatoes have been bred for higher yield, greater resistance to disease and so on. In all these cases the different varieties, each with its distinctive characteristics, have arisen by a process of artificial selection in which humans play the role normally performed by nature.

Because artificial selection, like natural selection, relies on genetic variation, an important part of being an animal or plant breeder is recognising and selecting individuals with advantageous characteristics. A plant breeder, for example, who wants to develop a variety of wheat tolerant to salty soils might grow large numbers of young wheat plants in salty soils and then select those plants that survive and grow best.

The next stage of any artificial breeding programme is to multiply up the numbers of the new variety and check that it does not have any disadvantageous characteristics. The temptation here may be to use only a few individuals to give rise to a new variety. The problem with this approach is the danger associated with the crossing of closely related individuals, namely **inbreeding**.

Inbreeding leads to a loss in fitness known as **inbreeding depression**. This is because an individual produced as a result of the crossing of two close relatives is more likely to have two copies of a harmful or even lethal recessive allele. So damaging is inbreeding depression that animal and plant breeders may try to produce **hybrids**.

A hybrid is the result of a cross between individuals belonging to two different varieties (**outbreeding**). Such individuals show **hybrid vigour**. This is because hybrids tend to be heterozygous at many of their loci. Any harmful alleles therefore have their effects masked by healthy ones. Gardeners often grow F_1 hybrid plants. These are the result of crossing two different parent lines, each parent line having been inbred for about six or seven generations beforehand (figure 43.31). On the animal side, many of

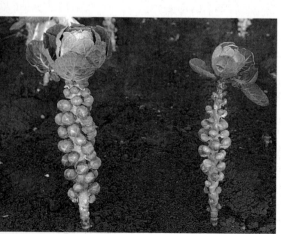

Figure 43.31 An F_1 hybrid Brussels sprout plant (*left*) with one of its inbred parents (*right*).

the lambs produced in Britain are hybrids.

In farm animals, **artificial insemination** is fequently used as a rapid means of spreading the beneficial characteristics of a particular male throughout the stock. For example, the semen from a single bull can be used to sire as many as 90 000 cattle a year. With so large a number it becomes extremely important for farmers to maintain accurate breeding records if they are to avoid the problems of inbreeding.

Artificial selection in humans

Could the kind of artificial selection we have been discussing be imposed on humans? To most people this idea seems repugnant, conjuring up visions of selective breeding and compulsory birth control. But in fact it already happens to a slight degree as when, for example, a couple with a history of abnormality in their children or close relatives decide, perhaps on the basis of information given them by a genetic counsellor, not to have any more children. There is nothing intrinsically evil about wanting to improve the quality of the human race, especially when it involves minimising the frequency of deleterious alleles, such as those that cause haemophilia and certain mental defects. The theory and practice of improving the human species by means of selective breeding is known as **eugenics**, and despite its sinister undertones many people feel it should not be dismissed as totally unacceptable provided of course that it is carried out on a voluntary basis.

Just as important as the ethical question of the acceptability of eugenics is the scientific question as to whether or not it could ever be very effective. By using the Hardy-Weinberg formula it is possible to calculate the effect which might be achieved if individuals possessing deleterious alleles were prevented from having children. Until recently the answer was that eugenics would never be very effective at eliminating deleterious alleles because such alleles are usually recessive and could only be detected when homozygous.

Recently, though, advances in molecular genetics and in the study of human reproductive physiology have given us a different perspective. It is already possible, at several loci, to detect carriers (i.e. heterozygotes) as well as individuals homozygous for a recessive allele. Further, if *in vitro* fertilisation is accompanied by suitable biochemical tests carried out at the 8-16 cell stage, doctors may be able to determine whether the embryo will develop into a healthy baby or show any genetic abnormalities.

This information could then be made available to the woman before a decision has to be taken as to whether or not to implant the embryo into her womb (figure 43.32). However, the majority of human babies will no doubt continue to be conceived and carried to term as before.

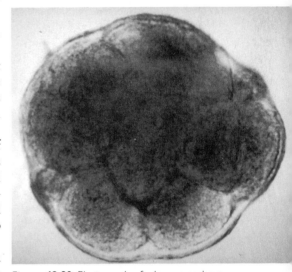

Figure 43.32 Photograph of a human embryo at the 8 – 10 cell stage.

The green revolution

Over the last twenty to thirty years agriculturalists have produced many new varieties of the world's major food crops, such as rice, wheat, maize and barley. This process has been called the **green revolution**. In general, these new varieties display some or all of the following advantages over the older ones:

- Their stems are shorter, resulting in dwarf varieties which are less likely to be flattened by wind and rain and can be more easily harvested.
- They give a higher yield per unit area.
- They show a greater response to water and fertilisers.
- They are relatively insensitive to day length and/or temperature, with the result that two or even three crops may be grown per year.
- They are more resistant to pests and diseases.

In developing countries the green revolution has had a pronounced effect on food production. For example, the wheat harvest in India and Pakistan in 1968 was over 35 per cent higher than in any preceding year. However, one trouble is that these new varieties require high levels of fertiliser which are expensive and not always available in developing countries. This has led some economists to question the benefits of the green revolution. It has been argued that the introduction of these varieties concentrates wealth in the hands of the minority of farmers able to afford artificial fertilisers.

Whatever happened to real dogs?

The domestic dog has been the subject of more artificial selection than any other animal. Until about a hundred years ago, each breed was bred for a particular purpose. For example, St Bernard's were bred for mountain rescue, Old English sheepdogs for rounding up sheep, poodles for retrieving ducks. But then fashion took over and people started to breed these and other types of dogs either to show or to keep as pets. The result is that today many pedigree dog breeds have been exposed to extremes of selection, are inbred, unhealthy and mere shadows of their ancestors.

Take the basset hound, for instance. As you can see from the print in illustration 2, done in 1880, this breed once had drooping but not excessively long ears. However, today's version has ears that are so long that the dogs sometimes trip over them. The floppy lower eyelids expose the eyes to an increased risk of infection, while back problems are common.

Other breeds face worse difficulties. Some bulldogs and pugs find it so hard to breathe through their squashed noses that their owners even provide them with oxygen masks. Yorkshire terriers and toy poodles suffer from slipping kneecaps, collapsing hip joints, deformed tear ducts and progressive loss of vision.

This sorry catalogue shows that artificial selection can have unintended as well as intended results. Whether the problem gets

Illustration 1 Typical basset hound in 1992. The modern breed has short legs, very long ears and sagging eyelids.

Illustration 2 Typical basset hounds in the 1870s. In those days they had short legs and long ears but neither was excessive.

better or worse may depend on the Kennel Club, which has a 'breed standard' for each breed of dog, and on judges at dog shows. Unless something decisive is done, tens of thousands of pedigree dogs will continue to display hereditary disorders rarely found in mongrels.

Explain precisely why so many modern breeds of dogs show genetic disorders.

Summary

1 According to the Darwin-Wallace theory, evolution occurs by **natural selection** of chance variations. In contrast, Lamarck's theory suggests that evolution occurs by the **transmission of acquired characteristics**.

2 Of the two theories, natural selection has stood the test of time far better. The modern reinterpretation of the Darwinian theory is called **neo-Darwinism**.

3 The variation on which natural selection depends arises by **mutations**, but is aided by the reshuffling of genes in meiosis through **independent assortment** and **crossing-over**, and by **fertilisation**.

4 Mutations may be caused by changes in the gross structure of chromosomes (**chromosome mutations**) and by changes in the structure of genes (**gene mutations**).

5 Mutation frequencies are generally very low. However, the mutation rate can be increased by various **mutagenic agents**.

6 Mutations occur spontaneously and are relatively persistent. Usually they are harmful but occasionally they may confer beneficial characteristics on the individual.

7 Types of chromosome mutation include **deletion, inversion, translocation** and **duplication**. The gain or loss of one or more entire chromosomes may result from **non-disjunction** during meiosis.

8 Sometimes an organism may gain a complete set of extra chromosomes. This is known as **polyploidy**. In certain situations polyploidy is associated with beneficial characteristics.

9 Gene mutations involve changes in the sequence of the nucleotide bases in DNA. These may be brought about by the **substitution, insertion, deletion** or **inversion** of one or more bases. Seemingly trivial changes may have far-reaching effects.

10 Mutations sometimes occur in an organism's non-reproductive cells. These are called **somatic mutations** and result in **genetic mosaics**.

11 The conflict between organisms and their environment, physical or biotic, has been described as the **struggle for existence**.

12 The fact that more offspring are born than can possibly survive is the basis of **differential mortality**, an essential requisite for natural selection.

13 Natural selection is instrumental in holding species constant (**stabilising selection**), but if the evironment changes it favours the emergence of new forms (**directional selection**).

14 For new species to arise (**speciation**) some degree of **genetic isolation** is necessary. Isolation may result from geographical isolation between populations (**allopatry**) or from reproductive isolation within a population (**sympatry**).

15 There is much variation in the rate at which evolution occurs. Gradual evolutionary change is known as **phyletic gradualism**; sudden evolutionary changes alternating with long periods of almost no change are known as **punctuated equilibria**.

16 In many species males and females differ as a result of **sexual selection**.

17 The principles of genetics and evolution are employed by humans in **animal and plant breeding**, in which natural selection is replaced by **artificial selection**.

Review questions

1 How could you test the hypothesis that the occurrence of heavy metal tolerance in grasses that grow on mine spoils is the result of *Lamarckian* evolution?

2 Can you suggest why maternal age is more important than paternal age in affecting the chances of a baby being born with Down's syndrome?

3 Why do you think polyploidy is more common in plants than in animals?

4 Explain how modern wheat is believed to have evolved.

5 Most examples of natural selection in action result from human activity. Discuss.

6 Distinguish between sympatry and allopatry.

7 Why do some species evolve more rapidly than others?

8 Is creationism a scientific theory? Explain your answer.

9 Can you suggest why male birds are generally more brightly coloured than female birds?

10 Discuss the ethical implications of human sperm and egg banks.

Further reading

Charles Darwin's *The Origin of Species* (John Murray, 1859) is definitely worth looking at. A Penguin reprint is available or you can try Richard E Leakey's *The Illustrated Origin of Species* (Faber and Faber, 1979).

Pat Brookfield's *Modern Aspects of Evolution* (Stanley Thornes, 1986) is an excellent introduction to evolution.

For a highly original and superbly written modern account of natural selection you can't do better than read Richard Dawkins' *The Blind Watchmaker* (Longman, 1986).

John Bowman's *An Introduction to Animal Breeding* (Edward Arnold, 1984) provides a concise account of the principles of artificial selection as seen in animal breeding.

Evolution and Pollution by A.D. Bradshaw and T. McNeilly (Edward Arnold, 1981) summarises much of the classic work done on the evolution of pollution tolerance in plants.

A discussion of the species concept and further details as to how evolution may have occured can be found in *Biology, Advanced Topics*.

CHAPTER 44 | Major steps in evolution

There is something remarkable about the thought that you, the person sitting reading this chapter, and we, the authors of it, are – if current scientific opinion is to be believed – the products of an evolutionary process that began some thirteen billion years ago with the birth of the Universe itself. In this chapter we will survey some of the major events in the history of life. We shall start by going back some three and a half to four billion years, to the time when it is thought that life first arose on this planet.

The origin of life

In 1953 Stanley Miller, then a 23 year-old graduate student at the University of Chicago, succeeded in synthesising amino acids, the building blocks of proteins, by putting a spark across a mixture of simple gases in a closed system. This was a momentous achievement, not because he synthesised amino acids as such, but because he managed to produce them under the primitive conditions that it is thought might have existed on this planet some 4×10^9 years ago. We shall return to this later, but in the meantime let us see why Miller's achievement hit the scientific headlines.

Ever since the beginning of recorded history people have speculated on the origin of life. Of course, people have always known that ducklings only come from ducks, lambs from sheep and babies from women, but common experience seemed to suggest that maggots came from rotting meat and worms from the soil. It was even widely supposed that rats came from garbage and mice from stored grain.

Until the 17th century it was almost universally believed that some organisms were generated spontaneously from non-living matter – the **theory of spontaneous generation**. However, in 1668 Francesco Redi, an Italian physician, argued that the maggots which appeared on decaying meat were introduced from the outside in some way, not spontaneously generated within the meat itself. By covering meat with a very fine gauze, which prevented female flies from laying their eggs on the meat, he showed that maggots did not arise from meat.

Rather surprisingly, Redi did believe that grubs could appear spontaneously in decaying *vegetable* matter. For the next 200 years the question as to whether life could arise spontaneously or not was one of the great intellectual debates of the time. Evidence in favour of the theory of spontaneous generation was obtained in the middle of the 18th century by John Needham, an English scientist who became the first director of the Royal Academy of Belgium. It was known that boiling killed organisms, so Needham boiled some mutton gravy and sealed it in a glass flask. After some days the gravy was swarming with life. Surely here was proof that life could arise spontaneously.

It was not until 1862 that the theory of spontaneous generation was finally disproved in a series of experiments performed by the French chemist and microbiologist Louis Pasteur. Pasteur performed much the same experiment as John Needham had a hundred years earlier, except that he boiled the nutrient broth *after* it had been placed in its glass container, not before. Can you see why this made all the difference? Pasteur found that it was not even necessary to seal the flask. If the neck of a flask containing broth was drawn out into a long S-shaped tube, and the broth then boiled, micro-organisms often failed to develop. If, later, the tube was broken off close to the flask, micro-organisms quickly multiplied. Pasteur

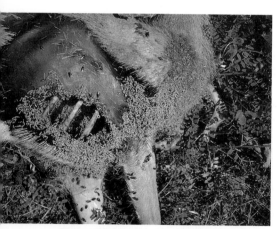

Figure 44.1 Maggots on a rotting deer carcass. Until the seventeenth century almost everyone thought that maggots were spontaneously generated by meat itself.

Figure 44.2 *left* Louis Pasteur in his laboratory in Paris.
Below One of Pasteur's swan-necked flasks. Notice the nutrient broth inside the flask. Pasteur found that if the broth was boiled inside the flask, it would remain fresh indefinitely. At the Pasteur Institute in Paris there is a swan-necked flask containing broth which has remained fresh ever since it was set up over a hundred years ago.

reasoned that micro-organisms entered the flask from the atmosphere. In the first case they became trapped on the walls of the tube and so failed to reach the broth (figure 44.2).

From Pasteur's work grew the idea that all life comes from pre-existing life, and all notions of spontaneous generation died a quiet death. In fact this theory became so unfashionable that some people could not even accept that the first organisms on this planet arose from non-living matter, preferring to believe that life was brought here by meteorites from other planets. Most scientists think this theory unlikely and in any case it merely begs the question as to how life began in the first place.

What were the first organisms like?

Before discussing how life might have arisen, it is worth asking what form the first organisms might have taken. What would they have used as a source of energy?

There are really only two possibilities: they must have been either **autotrophs** or **heterotrophs**. At first sight autotrophism might seem more likely as we are used to food webs with autotrophs at the base supporting a mass of heterotrophs. However, the metabolic equipment required to synthesise organic substances from inorganic raw materials, which is what an autotroph does, is generally more complicated than that needed by a heterotroph which feeds on ready-made organic matter. On these grounds it is generally believed that the first organisms were heterotrophs.

This immediately raises a whole host of questions. If the first organisms were heterotrophs, how did the organic substances, on which they were dependent for food, come into being? How did these first organisms originate? How did they metabolise these organic substances to release energy? And so on!

The hypothesis that the first organisms were heterotrophic was first put forward by the Russian scientist Alexander Oparin in the 1930s and, subject to various additions and refinements, it is still largely adhered to today. Let us examine its various propositions, step by step.

Synthesis of organic molecules

The age of the Earth has been calculated to be about 4.6×10^9 years, and the first indications of primitive life, as revealed in the fossil record, occurred about 3.5×10^9 years ago. In the early stages of its existence the Earth would have been too hot for life to exist, and we can therefore narrow down the origin of life to around 3.8×10^9 years ago, give or take a couple of hundred million years!

Figure 44.3 Stanley Miller in his laboratory in 1990 with a replica of the apparatus with which he showed, 37 years earlier, how the first organic chemicals might have evolved.

Geochemical evidence suggests that at this time the Earth's atmosphere was dominated by four simple gases: **methane** (CH_4), **ammonia** (NH_3), **hydrogen** (H_2) and **water vapour** (H_2O). It is thought that oxygen was probably not found as a gas (O_2) since the atmosphere was too hot: it would have combined with other substances, such as iron and silicon, whose oxides form much of the earth's crust. Water vapour is thought to have been formed mainly from volcanic activity: about 10 per cent of the material in a modern volcanic eruption is water.

The first step towards the origin of life must have been the synthesis of simple organic molecules. Many suggestions have been put forward to explain how this might have happened, but the most generally accepted theory is that they were formed by the action of lightning and ultraviolet radiation, or possibly gamma radiation, on the four simple gases mentioned above. Evidence for this rests on the fact that scientists have been able to repeat such syntheses in the laboratory. A photograph of the apparatus used by Stanley Miller in his experiment, with which we started this discussion, is given in figure 44.3. Figure 44.4 shows a diagram of the apparatus, emphasising its main features.

Since Miller's original work, several other steps in the synthesis of organic molecules have been carried out under primitive earth conditions. Miller himself sythesised amino acids from the four gases using an electric spark. From the same raw materials Melvin Calvin, using gamma radiation, managed to produce a mixture of amino acids, simple 6-carbon sugars, and also purines and pyrimidines which, you will recall, enter into the composition of nucleic acids.

Since then more complex organic molecules have been made: polypeptides have been synthesised from amino acids simply by heating to melting point and then cooling; nucleic acids have been formed from nucleotides merely by heating under pressure. These laboratory syntheses do not, of course, prove that similar events happened millions of years ago, but they do suggest that such events *could* have taken place.

Assuming that the synthesis of organic molecules took place in the atmosphere, it is supposed that they were subsequently brought down to the Earth's surface in heavy rain and that, in the course of time, they accumulated in primitive oceans and lakes. One can imagine that these great bodies of water may have been teaming with organic molecules, a kind of 'organic soup'.

Figure 44.4 Diagram of the apparatus which Stanley Miller used to synthesise organic compounds under primitive earth conditions. Some 15 amino acids were synthesised in the apparatus including glycine, alanine, glutamic acid and aspartic acid.

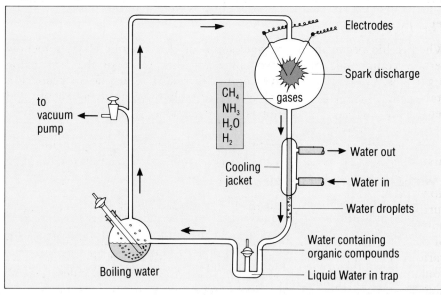

Life from clay?

Since Miller's work, some earth scientists have questioned whether the Earth ever had a reducing atmosphere lacking oxygen, and whether it really was as hot as had previously been supposed. The existence of an 'organic soup' has also been questioned, as has the idea that life arose from it.

These doubts have led to the formulation of alternative hypotheses. One of the most fascinating of these is the notion that the first organisms arose on land from clay crystals. At first this idea sounds far-fetched, but it has been championed over the years by its original proponent, A.G. Cairns-Smith, a chemist from Glasgow.

Cairns-Smith begins by pointing out that the ordinary clays found in soils are astonishingly diverse in structure. Scanning electron micrographs and X-ray studies reveal a tremendous number of different sorts of clay crystals. They are mostly built up from silicic acid, $Si(OH)_4$, a compound of silicon whose tetrahedral shape is much the same as that of methane, CH_4. Silicic acid easily polymerises, again in much the same way that methane polymerises to give a carbon chain.

Clays are by no means simple homogeneous crystals. Rather they contain many irregularities. These irregularities may be in the pattern of polymerisation – whether, for instance, the silicic acids join in a straight line or in a branching arrangement. Irregularities also arise depending on the occasional presence of ions such as Mg^{2+}, Al^{3+} or Fe^{2+}. These irregularities are akin to mutations in a genetic code. Further, clays, being crystalline, can be said to replicate, in the sense that they grow and then break into smaller units. Not only that, but the precise pattern they display depends on the elements they contain and on the way these elements are arranged.

Finally, clays can behave as catalysts. This should not surprise us. We saw earlier (see page 214) that inorganic substances such as iron and platinum can act as catalysts. In much the same way clays can catalyse chemical reactions; indeed, the variety of their structures allows them to be quite specific as to which chemical reactions they catalyse. For example, Aharon Katchalsky of the Weizman Institute of Science in Israel has found that montmorillonite clays will faithfully catalyse the formation of polypeptides from amino acids.

By now a significant minority of scientists think that there may be something in Cairns-Smith's ideas. However, it is difficult to see precisely how life based on carbon could have evolved from life based on silicon.

The first organisms

Whether life began in an 'organic soup' or as inorganic clays, somehow certain compounds must have come together to form the first living organisms, i.e. they must have combined in such a way as to produce a stable and integrated chemical system capable of transferring energy and replicating itself. However, this is an enormous step and one about which very little is known.

A possible clue to how certain compounds came together to form the first living organisms comes from the study of certain macromolecules such as proteins and carbohydrates. When mixed together in the right conditions, they form aggregates called **coacervates** (figure 44.5). When surrounded by water, a coacervate droplet is remarkably stable and shows a number of properties similar to living matter. For example, in the presence of certain oils it may become coated with a lipid membrane through which various substances are selectively absorbed. Moreover, if a coacervate contains appropriate enzymes it will absorb certain molecules such as glucose and convert them into more complex polymers such as starch.

The origin of carbon

All organisms rely on carbon for their organic compounds. Carbon is made inside stars by fusion reactions which can only take place at tremendous temperatures and pressures. The essence of the reaction is that three helium nuclei, each with two protons and two neutrons, fuse to form a single carbon nucleus with six protons and six neutrons.

It is thought that when a star gets to the end of its life it either collapses inwards under gravitational pressure or explodes, scattering its contents to an enormous distance. Planets form from the scatterings of exploded stars. As John Polkinghorne, a former Cambridge Professor of Mathematical Physics who is also a member of the Anglican clergy, puts it: 'We are made from the ashes of dead stars'.

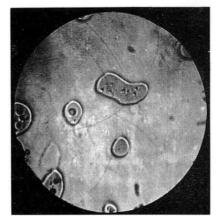

Figure 44.5 Coacervates are polymer-rich colloidal droplets which form spontaneously under certain conditions. The droplets show a number of similarities to cells and may provide a clue as to how the first living organisms were formed.

However it was put together, there are certain things that the earliest organisms must have been able to do if they were to qualify as living beings. First and foremost they must have been able to obtain energy, presumably by the breakdown of organic molecules. If there was little or no oxygen present at this time, their respiration would have been anaerobic. Secondly, they must have been able to reproduce. Presumably at this early stage of evolution reproduction was a simple asexual process involving nothing more than the synthesis of new macromolecules and the splitting of the organism in two.

It seems likely that replication of whatever chemical made up the genetic material in these early days of life would not be absolutely accurate. Any inaccuracies would allow natural selection to proceed. The likely result would be the rapid evolution of more complex and better adapted forms. Any early form of sexual reproduction would hasten this evolution.

Today all organisms use DNA (or RNA in the case of some viruses) as

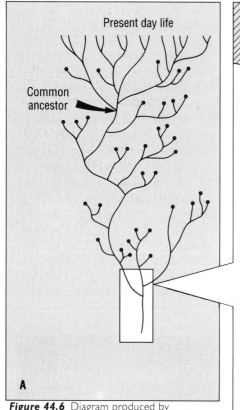

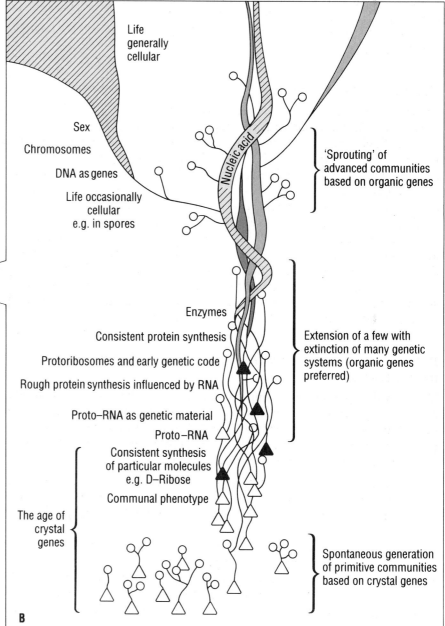

Figure 44.6 Diagram produced by Cairns-Smith to represent his theory that the earliest genes were crystal genes based on silicic acid. These may then have paved the way for the subsequent evolution of organic genes, based first on RNA and then on DNA. The important thing is not to get bogged down in the details, but to appreciate the way in which organisms based on organic genes may have replaced earlier organisms based on crystal genes. △ represents the appearance of a new crystal genetic material; ▲ the appearance of a new organic genetic material; ○ represents an extinction: **B** is a close up of part of **A**.

their genetic material. So how did the first DNA arise, and how did the familiar pattern '*DNA makes RNA makes protein*' become established? The problem is that, on its own, DNA is a rather delicate molecule, susceptible to mechanical damage and to chemical alteration by ultraviolet radiation. One possibility is that DNA only evolved *after* RNA, which is a more robust molecule.

Cairns-Smith argues that the presence of crystal genes, based on silicic acid, paved the way for organic genes, such as those based on RNA or DNA (figure 44.6). Other biologists, such as James Watson, the discoverer with Francis Crick of the structure of DNA, agree that RNA preceded DNA. One reason is that ribose, the sugar in RNA, is much more readily synthesised than deoxyribose, the sugar in DNA, under simulated prebiotic conditions. Another reason is that RNA can act as a catalyst. It is now known that relatively short stretches of just 52 RNA nucleotides can catalyse the synthesis of a complementary RNA chain. Other RNA molecules can synthesise a variety of other reactions. In other words, it is possible that early organisms relied on RNA both for their genetic material and for their enzymes. A genetic material made of DNA and enzymes made of protein may have evolved later.

Evolution of autotrophs

So we envisage that the first organisms were heterotrophs which evolved either from clays or from 'organic soup'. What happened next?

It is likely that the supply of organic molecules, originally present in vast quantities in the primitive oceans, was gradually exhausted by the ever-growing population of heterotrophs. The competition must have been increasingly fierce, and this would have placed a premium on any organisms capable of an alternative method of feeding. In other words the evolution of autotrophs would be strongly favoured.

Of course we have no certain idea what kind of autotrophism the first autotrophs indulged in. It may have been a form of **chemosynthesis** akin to that used by certain present day bacteria. Or it may have been **photosynthesis**, perhaps similar to that performed by present-day green and purple sulphur bacteria which, living in anaerobic conditions, use hydrogen sulphide as the source of hydrogen for reducing carbon dioxide.

Aerobic respiration and the further evolution of heterotrophs

The arrival of photosynthesising autotrophs would have led to the production of oxygen (O_2). At first this probably resulted in the oxidation of Fe^{2+} to Fe^{3+}, giving rise to vast tracts of Banded Iron Formations. But eventually photosynthesis would have resulted in oxygen gas accumulating in the atmosphere. This was important for three reasons:

- It resulted in the formation of a layer of ozone (O_3) high in the Earth's atmosphere. This forms a barrier to the sun's radiation and would have reduced the chances of further organic compounds being synthesised in the atmosphere.
- In subsequent stages of evolution ozone would have protected organisms from exposure to harmful radiation.
- The presence of oxygen allowed some organisms to evolve so as to utilise this free oxygen for aerobic respiration, thereby achieving a more thorough breakdown of organic substances with the release of additional energy (see page 237).

Life found deep beneath the earth

Scientists have discovered live bacteria several miles below ground that have apparently lived off energy from the Earth's core for millions of years. Other researchers have previously reported microbes living at about 200 metres below the seabed, but this is the first time that live bacteria have been discovered at great depths in ancient granite rock. The discovery of the deepest living organisms could upset existing theories on the origin of life, which invoke the importance of the Sun's energy in sustaining organisms. Unlike life-forms on the surface of the planet, the subterranean bacteria seem not to have relied on the Sun's energy for their survival. They could be a model for possible underground life on other planets, Thomas Gold, emeritus professor of astronomy at Cornell University, New York, said yesterday.

The amount of life existing deep underground could exceed that living on or near the Earth's surface, he said. "We do not know at present how to make a realistic estimate of the subterranean mass of material now living, but all that can be said is that one must consider it possible that it is comparable to all the living mass at the surface . . . . There are certainly very major life-forms down there."

Because the rock is granite, and not sedimentary deposits such as sandstone, it is unlikely the microbes originated from life on the surface, Professor Gold said. The bacteria do not need oxygen and live at very high temperatures of about 100°C.

By Steve Connor, Science Correspondent, *The Independent*, Thursday 2 July, 1992.

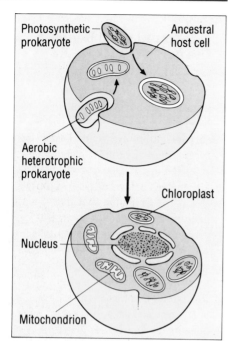

Figure 44.7 Diagrammatic representation of the endosymbiotic theory in which the eukaryotic cell is envisaged as a consortium of prokaryotes that established a particularly intimate symbiotic relationship. A photosynthetic prokaryote is here depicted becoming a chloroplast, and an aerobic heterotrophic prokaryote is depicted becoming a mitochondrion.

Figure 44.8 Lynn Margulis, the leading advocater of the endosymbiotic theory of the origin of eukaryotes. Marginalised by the established scientific community for much of her life, her views are now widely accepted. Now professor of Biology at Boston University in the USA, she is also responsible, with Karlene Schwartz, for the five kingdom classification system outlined on page 101.

The presence of autotrophs and heterotrophs would have led to natural selection for **predation**. Predatory heterotrophs would have attacked other organisms rather than relying on the presence of free organic molecules in their environment.

So we end up with autotrophs and a range of heterotrophs coexisting side by side. These provide the basic components of a balanced ecosystem. Both were presumably unicellular at this early stage of evolution. It is thought that the photosynthetic autotrophs eventually gave rise to the plant kingdom. The heterotrophs were presumably the ancestors of the fungi and animal kingdoms. It is supposed that bacteria (both autotrophic and heterotrophic) and the eukaryotic protoctists also arose from this early stock.

From prokaryotes to eukaryotes

In tracing the evolution of life we must assume that at some point eukaryotes evolved from prokaryotes, that is, a prokaryotic cell acquired organelles. How might this have happened?

One possibility is that a heterotrophic prokaryote may have ingested an autotrophic prokaryote which, instead of being digested, became a symbiont inside the heterotroph, enabling it to carry out photosynthesis. Equipped with its own DNA, the symbiont may have divided inside the host cell every time the host cell itself divided, and in this way the symbiont may have become a chloroplast inside the host cell.

This **endosymbiotic theory**, as it is called, may also explain the origin of mitochondria. The ancestors of mitochondria may have been bacteria that were aerobic heterotrophs. Perhaps they first gained entry into a larger prokaryote as undigested prey or internal parasites. One can imagine how the 'capture' of appropriate prokaryotes might lead to a large prokaryote having protochloroplasts and protomitochondria (figure 44.7).

The endosymbiotic theory has been passionately advocated over the last 25 years by the biologist Lynn Margulis (figure 44.8). There are several lines of evidence for it:

- It explains why mitochondria and chloroplasts, unlike other organelles, have a double membrane. The inner membrane in each case presumably belonged to the original free-living organism. The outer membrane is assumed to be comparable to the membrane that surrounds a food particle in phagocytosis.
- Mitochondria and chloroplasts have their own DNA and this is in the form of a ring, just as in present day prokaryotes.
- The inner membranes of mitochondria and chloroplasts have several enzymes and transport systems that closely resemble those found in the cell membranes of modern prokaryotes.
- Mitochondria and chloroplasts divide by a splitting method reminiscent of binary fission in bacteria.
- The ribosomes in mitochondria and chloroplasts are the same size as those found in modern prokaryotes, and significantly smaller than those found in the cytosol of a eukaryote.

Other cell structures, such as the endoplasmic reticulum and nuclear envelope, may have originated as infoldings of the plasma membrane. Simple infoldings are found in some present-day bacteria (see page 153) and it is not difficult to imagine them folding in various ways and eventually pinching off from the plasma membrane to become separate structures (figure 44.9).

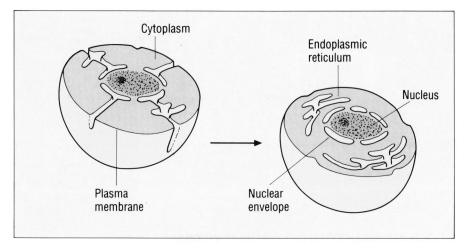

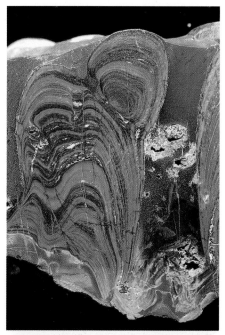

The relationship between prokaryotic and eukaryotic cells is uncertain, but there is one interesting piece of evidence which suggests that prokaryotes represent an early step in evolution. The earliest fossils that have ever been found – estimated by the potassium-argon method to be over 3000 million years old – are very similar in structure to some modern prokaryotes (figure 44.10).

Origin of multicellular organisms

Like so many other aspects of early evolution, this is a controversial matter and we can do no more than touch on the possibilities. One obvious possibility is that the first multicellular organisms may have arisen as a result of a unicellular organism dividing and the daughter cells then failing to separate. We see this today in the green protoctist *Pleurococcus* which lives on damp tree trunks and in other moist places. When the cell divides a cross-wall is formed, but frequently the daughter cells, instead of separating, remain attached to one another in small groups as shown in figure 44.11. It is possible that simple multicellular organisms may have originated in this kind of way.

An alternative possibility is that the nucleus of an ancestral unicellular organism may have divided repeatedly to give a **multinucleate cell**. If

Figure 44.10 A Cross-section through a rock dated to over 3000 million years old. The resulting image looks very similar to cross-sections through modern-day stromatolites. Stromatolites are dome-shaped calcareous formations laid down in shallow sea water. They can be seen in surface view in **B**. Each one consists of a stack of photosynthetic prokaryotes.

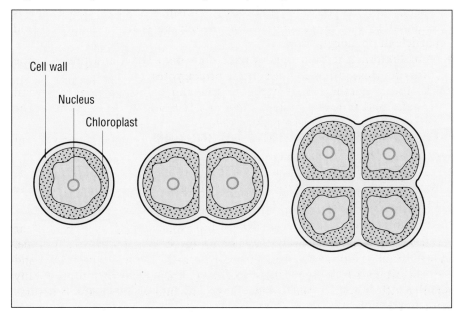

Figure 44.11 The green protoctist *Pleurococcus* occurs singly or, if the daughter cells fail to separate after cell division, in small groups. Might some multicellular plants have arisen in this way?

Figure 44.12 Diagrams illustrating how a simple multicellular animal may have arisen in evolution from a multinucleate protoctist.

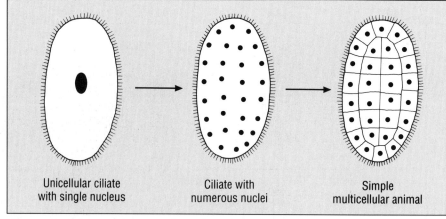

| Unicellular ciliate with single nucleus | Ciliate with numerous nuclei | Simple multicellular animal |

plasma membranes were to form between the nuclei, a simple multicellular organism would result (figure 44.12). One piece of evidence in favour of this theory is that multinucleate protoctists do exist, and indeed this condition is quite common among ciliates. Furthermore, there are certain flatworms in which the plasma membranes between adjacent cells are incomplete. Like other free-living flatworms, these animals are ciliated, and it is just possible that they may have arisen from a multinucleate ciliate which developed membranes between its nuclei.

The divergence of animals and plants

The theory just propounded assumes that animals and plants had a common ancestry, a belief that is substantiated by their many biochemical similarities. If this is so, might we not expect to see, even today, unicellular organisms capable of existing both autotrophically and heterotrophically?

In fact such organsims do exist. For instance, we find them among the protoctists in the phylum **Euglenophyta** (euglenoid flagellates). Euglenoid flagellates are generally green (because they contain chlorophyll) and have one or two flagella. Most of them feed exclusively by photosynthesis and will die if kept in the dark. However, some of them can thrive in darkness. This is because they can feed heterotrophically by absorbing soluble organic matter through their cell wall. Certain species can even feed on solid matter by phagocytosis (figure 44.13).

However multicellular organisms arose (and they may well have arisen in more than one way) once they existed there must have been an explosion of evolution, as witnessed by the fossil record. Although the first multicellular organisms appeared only about 600 million years ago, they quickly diversified into a tremendous variety of forms. A brief history of the principal events in the history of the Earth is given in table 44.1.

The colonisation of land by animals

We have seen that in all probability life began in the oceans. Even if the very first organisms were crystal clays, there is little doubt that the early carbon-based organisms were restricted to water. Many millions of years later, armed with the appropriate adaptations, organisms began to forsake their aquatic home and move onto land.

This migration from water to land seems to have happened on several occasions in evolutionary history, in both plants and animals. The best known instance, well documented by fossils, is the movement onto land by a group of fishes in Devonian times some 380 million years ago. Known as **crossopterygians**, they, and the early amphibians to which they gave rise,

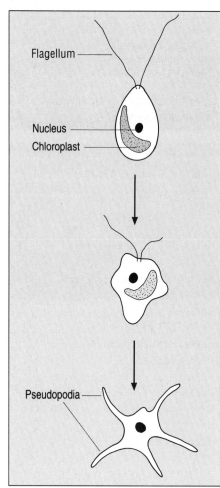

Figure 44.13 The green flagellate *Ochromonas* can change from a photosynthetic flagellated form into a heterotrophic amoeboid form. The latter takes in solid particles of food by phagocytosis.

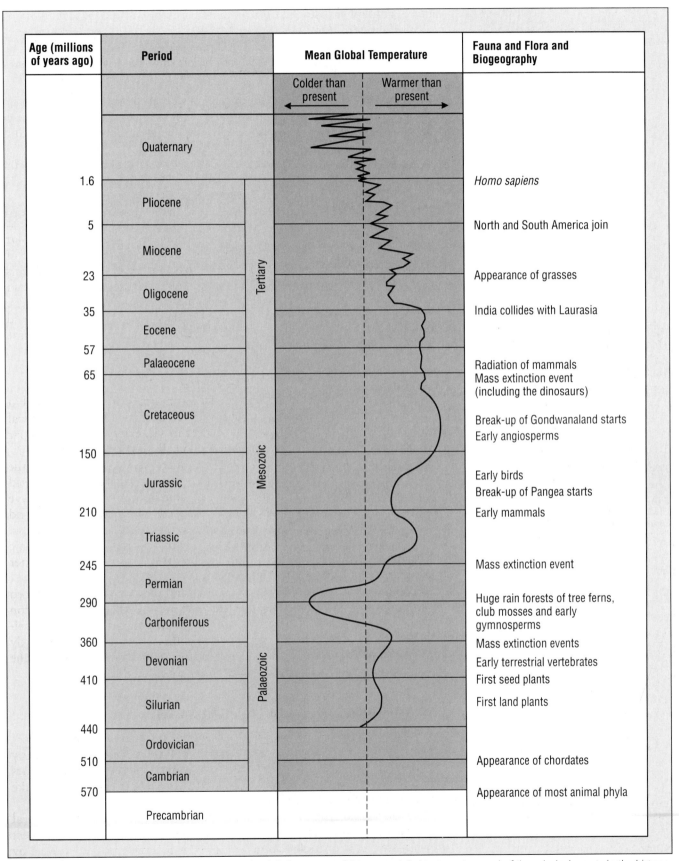

Age (millions of years ago)	Period		Mean Global Temperature	Fauna and Flora and Biogeography
			Colder than present ← → Warmer than present	
	Quaternary			
1.6	Pliocene	Tertiary		*Homo sapiens*
5	Miocene	Tertiary		North and South America join
23	Oligocene	Tertiary		Appearance of grasses
35	Eocene	Tertiary		India collides with Laurasia
57	Palaeocene	Tertiary		Radiation of mammals
65	Cretaceous	Mesozoic		Mass extinction event (including the dinosaurs)
				Break-up of Gondwanaland starts
				Early angiosperms
150	Jurassic	Mesozoic		Early birds
				Break-up of Pangea starts
210	Triassic	Mesozoic		Early mammals
245	Permian	Mesozoic		Mass extinction event
290	Carboniferous	Palaeozoic		Huge rain forests of tree ferns, club mosses and early gymnosperms
360	Devonian	Palaeozoic		Mass extinction events
				Early terrestrial vertebrates
410	Silurian	Palaeozoic		First seed plants
				First land plants
440	Ordovician	Palaeozoic		
510	Cambrian	Palaeozoic		Appearance of chordates
570	Precambrian			Appearance of most animal phyla

Table 44.1 Table of geological periods together with a brief summary of the mean global temperature and of the principal events in the history of the Earth.

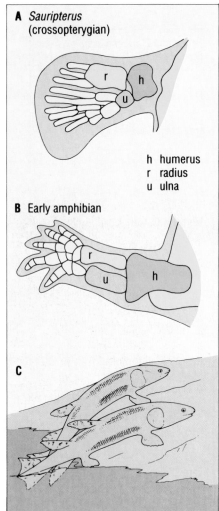

A *Sauripterus* (crossopterygian)

h humerus
r radius
u ulna

B Early amphibian

C

Figure 44.14 Fossil evidence suggests that animal migration from water to land took place in the Devonian period about 380 million years ago when a group of fresh water fishes, the crossopterygians, gave rise to the first amphibians. The crossopterygians had lobed fins, constricted at the base, which in some cases showed a marked tendency towards the pentadactyl limb. It is thought that these were used for locomotion on land. The Devonian included long periods of seasonal droughts and any fishes capable of struggling overland from one body of water to another would have been at an advantage.

A Pectoral fin of a crossopterygian showing its likeness to the pentadactyl limb.

B Forelimb of an early amphibian for comparison.

C Artist's reconstruction of a lobe-finned crossopterygian clambering out of water.

show a gradual transformation of paired fins into the pentadactyl limbs typical of modern tetrapods (figure 44.14).

Let us consider the anatomical and physiological changes that would be required for any animal to move from water onto land. The chief changes can be summarised as follows:

- Air is a much less dense medium than water, so there would have to be new means of movement and support. This particularly applies to large land-dwelling vertebrates, in which the skeleton holds the head and abdomen clear of the ground (see Chapter 29).
- Aquatic animals like fish breathe by means of gills, but these are totally unsuitable on land – can you think why? Terrestrial animals have evolved air-breathing organs such as lungs (see Chapter 15).
- Terrestrial animals are liable to lose water by evaporation. As explained in Chapter 22, both active and passive mechanisms have evolved for coping with this. The passive technique of developing an impermeable cuticle is common to animals and plants.
- Water, particularly in the oceans, is a comparatively stable medium, not liable to the wide fluctuations in temperature which characterise the terrestrial environment. Land animals, whether endothermic or ectothermic, must have structural, physiological or behavioural means of controlling their body temperature (see Chapter 23).
- The low resistance to movement that is characteristic of air means that higher speeds can be achieved. Almost all birds can fly faster than the swiftest of fish can swim. It does not of course follow that all terrestrial animals are fast movers; some, such as worms and snails, withdraw instead to protected environments.
- In many aquatic animals fertilisation is external, eggs and sperm being shed into the surrounding water. As this is impossible on land, terrestrial animals have other means by which females can obtain sperm. In many cases this involves the use of an intromittent organ such as the penis by which sperms are deposited inside the female. However, some terrestrial animals, such as amphibians, still have external fertilisation and return to water for breeding purposes.
- With internal fertilisation comes the possibility of internal development and viviparity. This is an enormous advantage to a terrestrial animal, for the environmental hazards that plague an adult can have an even more devastating effect on its helpless eggs and young. Of course, birds still produce eggs, though these have a hard protective shell and are looked after carefully by one or both parents (figure 44.15).

Figure 44.15 A male emu keeps guard over his eggs.

Evolutionary trends in animals

Some animals, such as *Hydra*, are constructed of two layers of cells: the **ectoderm** lines the outside of the body, and the **endoderm** lines the 'gut' (enteron). These two layers are separated by a jelly-like mesogloea which is virtually devoid of cells. Such animals are described as **diploblastic**.

In more complex animals there are three layers of cells: ectoderm (lining the outside), endoderm (lining the gut) and, between these two, a third layer of cells, the **mesoderm**. Such animals are described as **triploblastic**. The development of the mesoderm has been a most important step in evolution because in the embryology of triploblastic animals it is the

Evolution of flight

Many animals, including even one species of snake, have evolved the ability to glide downwards from tree to tree or from tree to ground. However, true powered flight is found in only four groups: insects, birds, bats and the extinct pterosaurs. Rather little is known from the fossil record about how flight evolved in insects or bats. Fossil bats are extremely scarce, while even the earliest insect wings seem superbly adapted for flight.

More, though, is known about the evolution of flight in birds. In 1861, just two years after Darwin's *Origin of Species* was published, a remarkable fossil was found at Solnhofen in present-day Germany. This fossil appeared to be a 'missing link' between reptiles and birds. Given the name *Archaeopteryx* (literally 'ancient wing'), it was found in rocks from the Upper Jurassic, some 150 million years old.

By now a total of six relatively complete specimens have been found, all belonging to the same species. *Archaeopteryx* was about the size of a small chicken. It combined features found in reptiles of the time and in present-day birds. Its jaws bore teeth, as in a reptile, and it lacked the keeled extension of the sternum to which, in modern birds, the flight muscles are attached. Other reptilian features include the retention of abdominal ribs, the presence of a long vertebral column in the tail and three fingers on each

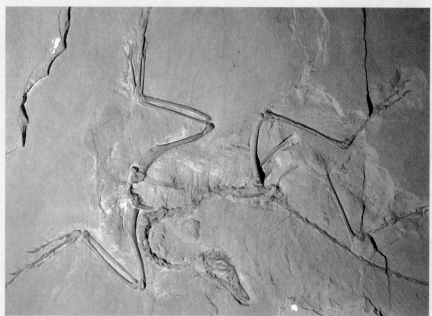

Archaeopteryx, a fossil bird showing a combination of reptilian and avian characteristics. The skull is 52mm in length.

forelimb which were not incorporated into the wings but were freely movable as claws.

Despite this abundance of reptilian features, *Archaeopteryx* had one vital feature which immediately distinguishes it from all other reptiles: it had feathers. Indeed, the feathers were so well developed that they are indistinguishable in structure and distribution on the body from the flight feathers of modern birds. There is little doubt that feathers evolved from reptilian scales, but no reptile has feathers.

Archaeopteryx existed at the same time as a group of flying reptiles, the **pterosaurs**. Close relatives of the dinosaurs, these were the first backboned animals to fly. They had

light hollow bones and their wings were made of skin that stretched from the tail to an immensely elongated fourth finger. The presence of an enlarged cerebellum, as revealed by the shape of their skulls, presumably helped them to maintain their balance. The smaller pterosaurs were the size of sparrows and probably flew actively by flapping their winds; the largest ones glided over prehistoric lakes and oceans and may have fed on surface fish.

Some of these pterosaurs were huge. The record is held by *Quetzalcoatlus*, a recently discovered pterodactyl that stood over 3 metres tall and had a wing span of 15 metres!

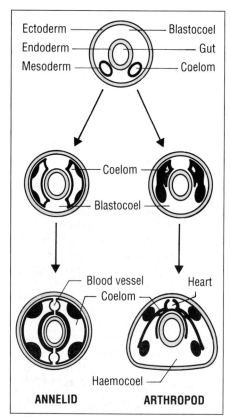

Figure 44.16 Diagrams showing the embryological development of the body cavity in annelids and arthropods. Both groups start the same way, with a block of mesoderm containing a small coelomic cavity on either side of the gut. In annelids the coelom expands until the mesoderm on each side of the body meets above and below the gut. In consequence the original space between the ectoderm and endoderm, the blastocoel, gets obliterated except in certain places where it remains as the blood vessels. The layer of mesoderm lining the ectoderm becomes the body wall muscles, and the layer of mesoderm lining the endoderm becomes the gut muscles. Meanwhile the coelom, filled with watery fluid, becomes the main body cavity. In arthropods the coelom remains small and the blastocoel becomes the main body cavity. It contains blood and is known as the haemocoel. It forms the open blood system typical of insects.

mesoderm that gives rise to most of the individual's organs (see page 627).

In flatworms the mesoderm forms a solid mass of tissue between the ectoderm and endoderm. In all other animals a **body cavity** develops in this region, though the way it is formed varies in different phyla. In annelids and chordates the body cavity is enclosed by mesoderm and is known as the **coelom**; in arthropods it lies between the ectoderm and endoderm and becomes a blood-filled **haemocoel** (figure 44.16).

The development of a body cavity, be it a coelom or haemocoel, is yet another important advance because it provides a space in which the organs can be suspended and it permits the body wall and gut to move independently. Moreover, in certain soft-bodied animals such as the earthworm it serves as a hydrostatic skeleton which is important in locomotion (see page 526).

You will remember that in chordates the dorsal part of the mesoderm splits up into a series of identical units called somites. This results in certain structures and organs being repeated along the length of the body, a phenomenon known as **metameric segmentation**. Metameric segmentation is fundamental to the organisation of most animals including chordates (see page 627). It is seen particularly clearly in the chaetae of the earthworm and the muscle blocks (myotomes) of fish where its main advantage is to provide an effective means of locomotion. In birds and mammals metameric segmentation has become obscured, but traces of it can still be seen in, for example, the repeated pattern of the spinal nerves.

By and large evolution has led to an increase in complexity. When we look at the phylogenetic tree of the animal kingdom we see a general trend towards more sophisticated nervous, circulatory and feeding systems, not to mention musculo-skeletal arrangements, sense organs and so on.

To say that evolution tends to produce more complex forms is not to imply that it is never regressive. There are many instances of what are thought to have been quite active animals taking up a sedentary or parasitic existence. Resorting to such passive modes of life generally involves the degeneration or even total loss of many organs, which puts them in sharp contrast with their free-living relatives. However, parasitic organisms frequently show complex biochemical adaptations to their hosts.

Evolutionary trends in plants

Because of the scantiness of the fossil record, it is not easy to reconstruct the evolutionary history of the plant kingdom. However, analysis of what fossils there are, and examination of modern algae and plants, enables us to detect certain trends.

For example, in some multicellular green algae, such as certain members of the colonial Volvocales and the filamentous *Spirogyra*, all the cells are alike and all have the capacity to reproduce sexually. But in other green algae the cells have become differentiated into those that reproduce (**gonadic cells**) and those that carry out non-reproductive functions such as photosynthesis (**somatic cells**). The rudiments of such differentiation are seen even in *Volvox*, but the process is carried much further in plants. The separation of 'sex and soma' is one of the earliest and most fundamental evolutionary trends in the plant kingdom.

In Chapter 32 we saw that in the majority of plants there is a distinction between **sporophyte** and **gametophyte generations**. The diploid sporophyte undergoes meiosis to produce haploid spores; and the haploid gametophyte produces haploid gametes. Among the tracheophytes (club mosses, horsetails, ferns, conifers and flowering plants) there has been a trend

Early land plants

The colonisation of the land by plants was one of the most important events in Earth history. Here guest author Dianne Edwards takes a look at some fossil plants.

The colonisation of the land by plants was probably a gradual process with origins in the early Palaeozoic or even in the Precambrian, but there is no direct fossil evidence for these early stages. It seems likely that most terrestrial surfaces were initially coated by mats of cyanobacteria and algae. However, it was the advent of the vascular plants in the Silurian which was of major importance in changing the face of our planet, both in modifying geological processes and in creating a diversity of ecological niches and habitats on land.

Vascular plants exhibit a number of biochemical and anatomical adaptations that allow them to grow in a wide range of environments – from moist to arid. This is because they maintain their own internally hydrated environment. The cuticle is a waterproofing layer that drastically reduces evaporation from these hydrated tissues. Stomata permit exchange of gases for photosynthesis and respiration and connect to an extensive system for their diffusion. Specialised absorption regions (e.g. root hairs) developed on extensive rooting systems result in the exploitation of large volumes of soil for water and mineral nutrients. Once plants had colonised the land, taller individuals were probably at an advantage for the dispersal of spores by air currents. However, an increase in height necessitates the presence of water-conducting systems. The best developed is the xylem of vascular plants composed of tracheids or vessels. These utilise the complex polymer lignin to resist collapse under tension, and to provide structural support.

The early vascular plants are exemplified by *Rhynia gwynne-vaughanii* from the Rhynie Chert which shows all the anatomical 'inventions' associated with the invasion of the land. The Rhynie Chert deposit offers a unique window into the plant life of a wetland in Lower Devonian times (illustration 1). Earlier representatives, such as *Cooksonia*, in the lowermost Devonian and late Silurian, are smaller and even simpler, but – being preserved as thin films of coal – they usually lack anatomical detail (illustration 2). Thus, although we know that *Cooksonia* possessed a cuticle with stomata on its upright forking axes, there is no good evidence that it was a vascular plant.

Questions about the ancestry of vascular plants cannot be answered just by reference to the fossil record. It is likely that within the next twenty years DNA hybridisation studies and amino acid sequencing will reveal much about the origin and subsequent evolution of land plants.

Illustration 1 Reconstruction of early land plants growing in the vicinity of hot springs in Lower Devonian times in what is now Scotland.

Illustration 2 A fossil *Cooksonia* from Wales, one of the first land plants (×16). With simple branched stems ending in sporangia the shape and size of small pinheads, it would have looked like a mossy green carpet; very unassuming compared with the land vegetation we know today.

Figure 44.17 *Brachiosaurus*, one of the largest herbivorous dinosaurs. Whether it supported its huge mass by spending most of its time half submerged in water (as in the foreground) is still controversial, though the consensus is that they could walk on dry land.

towards suppression of the gametophyte. Eventually, in flowering plants (angiosperms), the gametopyte becomes incorporated into the body of the sporophyte itself (see page 577). This is associated with the development of pollination, enclosed egg cells and production of seeds. As such it may be seen as an adaptation to life on land.

Many of the fundamental trends in the evolution of plants relate to the colonisation of land, just as was the case for animals. These trends are discussed in the box on page 821.

Size and its implications

In both plants and animals there have been trends towards larger size over the course of evolutionary history. Some of the problems attendant on this are discussed on page 821. Increase in size generally goes hand in hand with the development of ever more complex tissues and organs.

A tendency towards increased size has evolved in many groups. California boasts of having the world's largest and smallest trees. The largest is the giant coastal redwood (*Sequoia sempervirens*) which can be 120 m tall. The smallest is a tiny alpine willow, *Salix petrophila*, only 200 mm tall at its largest.

In the course of evolution many remarkable forms appeared. Most of them have long since gone extinct. One of the classic examples is provided by the **dinosaurs**, a group of reptiles some of whose members carried size to its ultimate conclusion. These great animals were the dominant fauna for over 100 million years during the Mesozoic era. Some, like *Tyrannosaurus rex*, were savage carnivores; others, like *Apatosaurus* (which used to be known as *Brontosaurus*) were vegetarian. Although some dinosaurs were only the size of a domestic cat, others reached fantastic sizes: *Brachiosaurus*, for instance, was about 22 m long, stood 13 m tall and had a mass of some 75 000 kg!

The main problem facing enormous terrestrial animals is how to support the body. The largest male elephants, for instance, only lie down (to go to sleep) on ground that slopes; otherwise they find it extremely difficult to get up again.

The mass of an animal varies with the cube of its linear dimensions. In other words, if the animal's size doubles in all directions (length, height and breadth), its mass increases by about eight times. But the strength of its legs varies with their cross-sectional area. If a large animal had legs that were proportionately the same size as a smaller animal, the strength of its legs would fail to keep up with the mass of the animal. This is because an eight-fold (2 × 2 × 2) increase in mass would be accompanied by only a four-fold (2 × 2) increase in the cross-sectional area of the legs.

The result of this argument, which was appreciated by the seventeenth century Italian scientist Galileo Galilei, is that for a large animal to support itself, the width of its legs must increase at a greater rate than the rest of the body. Judging by their fossils, the legs of the larger dinosaurs were indeed extremely thick, rather like elephants' legs are today.

Even so, some zoologists are doubtful if the legs could have supported such heavy bodies. For this reason, it has been suggested that the largest dinosaurs spent much of their time wallowing in lakes and lagoons where the water would buoy up their massive bodies (figure 44.17). This idea seems to be supported by evidence from fossil footprints which sometimes appear to show the animals on tip toe. However, it has been calculated that if they were aquatic creatures the water pressure at such depths would have collapsed their lungs.

Extinction of the dinosaurs

By the end of the Mesozoic era, some 65 million years ago, none of these mighty dinosaurs remained: they had all died. What led to their extinction? We do not know for certain, but at the last count there were over one hundred separate theories! There is good evidence that the end of the Mesozoic saw marked changes in climate: land levels changed and there may have been a pronounced drop in temperature over much of the world. Large animals, such as dinosaurs, may have been particularly sensitive to such climatic changes, partly because of the large amounts of food they required and partly because their huge size may have made thermoregulation more difficult.

However, this latter explanation assumes that dinosaurs were ectothermic. A number of dinosaur experts now believe that dinosaurs were in fact endothermic. The evidence for this comes from a variety of sources. Anatomical details of bone structure suggest that dinosaurs were fast moving and agile, while there are indications from fossil dinosaur nests that juvenile dinosaurs had growth rates typical of mammals and birds and far in excess of reptiles (figure 44.18).

Another factor contributing to the extinction of the dinosaurs may have been changes in the composition of the vegetation. It has even been suggested that the change from ferns, with their distinctly laxative action, to flowering plants may have caused them to die of constipation!

Another theory was proposed by Luis Alvarez, a Nobel laureate, and his son, Walter, a geologist, in 1980. They argued that an asteroid 10 km in diameter crashed into the Earth 65 million years ago. The impact could have triggered volcanic eruptions leading to the release of copious amounts of dust that might have blocked out the sun for a few years, leading to massive starvation, particularly among larger animals. Evidence in favour of this theory comes from the unusually high abundance of the element **iridium** in rocks that date from precisely this period. It is known that asteroids contain considerably more iridium than the Earth's crust.

Figure 44.18 In 1987 Wendy Sloboda, a farm hand who is also an amateur palaeontologist, found some hadrosaur nests in southern Alberta, Canada. This discovery suggests that these dinosaurs incubated their eggs in carefully constructed nests, as shown in this artist's reconstruction. The adults weighed from four to six tonnes. The eggs are about 20 cm in length. There is some evidence from the remains of young hadrosaurs that they grew by as much as 280 cm in their first year after birth. Such dramatic growth suggests that the animals were endothermic.

Figure 44.19 Why did the dinosaurs become extinct? Chris Nichols of the Department of Earth Sciences at Cambridge puts forward four ideas.

Two brains are better than one

Being one of the larger dinosaurs presents problems. For instance, how do you overcome the length of time taken for nervous impulses initiated by the brain to reach your tail? One solution was described by Bert Taylor, an American rather fond of dinosaurs:

Behold the mighty dinosaur,
Famous in pre-historic lore,
Not only for his power and strength
But for his intellectual length.
You will observe by these remains
The creature had two sets of brains
One in his head (the usual place),
The other at his spinal base.
Thus he could reason *a priori*
As well as *a posteriori*
No problem bothered him a bit;
He made both head and tail of it.
So wise was he, so wise and solemn,
Each thought filled a spinal column.
If one brain found the pressure strong
It passed a few ideas along.
If something slipped his forward mind
'Twas rescued by the one behind.

Some of the larger dinosaurs did indeed have an enlargement of the spinal cord at the base of the spine, as revealed by their fossil remains. In *Stegosaurus*, this bundle of nerve tissue was some twenty times the size of the brain in the head. It was presumably used to control the massive hindlegs and spiked tail (see illustration).

The dinosaur *Stegosaurus*. The plates sticking up on the animal's back may have been used for thermoregulation.

Whatever the cause of the extinction of the dinosaurs, their disappearance allowed another group of animals to blossom forth. This group had been around for upwards of 100 million years, remaining small and insignificant, probably living in caves and trees and feeding on insects and buds. But as soon as the great age of dinosaurs came to an end, they underwent an explosion of adaptive radiation and in a short period of time gave rise to the many species that we know as **mammals**. Humans, of course, are members of this group.

The emergence of humans

By any account, humans are a remarkable species. In 1945 the American anthropologist George P. Murdock listed the following characteristics that have been recorded in every human society:

Athletic sports, Belief in the afterlife, Bodily adornment, Calendars, Cleanliness training, Community organisation, Cooking, Cooperative labour, Cosmology, Courtship, Dancing, Decorative art, Division of labour, Dream interpretation, Education, Etiquette, Faith healing, Family feasting, Fire making, Folklore, Food taboos, Funeral rites, Games, Gestures, Gift giving, Government, Greetings, Hair styles, Hospitality, Housing, Hygiene, Incest taboos, Inheritance rules, Joking, Kin groups, Language, Law, Magic, Marriage, Mealtimes, Medicine, Obstetrics, Penal sanctions, Personal names, Population policy, Property rights, Puberty customs, Religion, Sexual restrictions, Superstitions, Surgery, Tool making, Trade, Visiting, Weaving and Worship.

From time to time people have tried to single out just one or two characteristics that make humans unique – such as tool use or worship. One problem with this approach is that the characteristic may be shared by other species. For example, chimpanzees and the Galapagos finch both use tools. Another problem is that there are some individual humans fail to display the particular characteristic in question, such as worship.

A more fruitful approach is to look at some of the ways in which we differ from our close evolutionary relatives, gorillas and chimpanzees:

- We walk on two legs, that is we are *bipedal*.
- Our hands have opposable thumbs which make it easier to perform very fine manipulations.
- Our brains are extremely large (1350 cm^3 on average).
- Our gestation period is unusually long (40 weeks).
- We remain highly dependent on our parents for a very long time (10 – 20 years).
- We have a long lifespan (often 60 years or more).
- We have a highly evolved communication system (most people have a vocabulary of about 5000 different words).
- We are almost hairless (Desmond Morris's 'naked ape').
- Females have no oestrous period and breeding may occur at any time of year.
- We sometimes live in very large societies (over 20 million people exist in Mexico City).
- We can control our environment to an unparalleled degree.
- We are found throughout the world (figure 44.20).

How did all this come about? A combination of the fossil record and evolutionary trees derived from DNA hybridisation studies and analysis of the amino acids in certain proteins suggests that we shared a common ancestor

Figure 44.20 Humans are found throughout the world and have adapted to many different environments and life styles. *Left to right* An Eskimo (Inuit) from northern Canada; a Bedouin Arab who lives in Beersheba, Israel; a businesswoman originally from South Africa now living in England.

with chimpanzees from which we split about 5 – 8 million years ago. Unfortunately the fossil record is not at all clear about exactly what happened subsequent to this split. Conclusions have to be drawn from a limited number of fossil remains, none of which is complete. As one scientist has put it: 'deciphering the course of evolution from those fragments is like trying to follow the story of *War and Peace* from twelve pages torn randomly from the book'.

Fossil remains of early humans

In 1924 the British anthropologist Raymond Dart announced the discovery of a fossil skull from a South African quarry. The fossil was named *Australopithecus africanus* (Southern ape). Subsequent discoveries indicated that *Australopithecus* walked fully erect and had human-like hands and teeth. However, the brain of *Australopithecus* was only about one-third the size of a modern human's.

The genus has by now been split into several species. One of these is called *A. afarensis* because the first fossil of this species was found in the Afar region of Ethiopia (figure 44.21). This fossil was discovered in 1974 by a team led by the American palaeoanthropologist Don Johansen. Its significance lies partly in the fact that it is 40 per cent intact, making it one of the most complete fossil hominids known. The fossil is known as 'Lucy' after the Beatles' track 'Lucy in the sky with diamonds' which was playing in camp on the night of her discovery.

Lucy lived some three million years ago. She stood only 110 cm tall and weighed about 30 kg. The shape of her pelvis identifies her as an adult female. Her cranial capacity was only about 400 cm^3 and, although she was bipedal, her walk was probably more rolling than ours. There are differences between modern-day humans and *Australopithecus* in foot anatomy and leg musculature.

Between Austalopithecus and ourselves – *Homo sapiens* (literally 'wise man') – lie a number of other species including *Homo habilis* and *Homo erectus*. Of these two, *H. habilis* is the older, existing about two million years ago (figure 44.22). *H. erectus* evolved about 1.5 million years ago, probably in Africa, from where it migrated to Asia, where the first fossils were found (Java Man and Peking Man). Judging by the artefacts found in the vicinity of the fossils by Mary Leakey and others, both species used tools. *H. erectus* individuals seem to have lived in huts and caves, built fires and clothed themselves in animal skins.

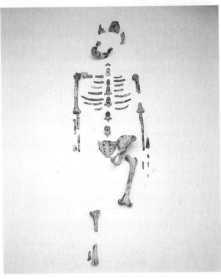

Figure 44.21 Fossil remains of Lucy, a member of the species *Australopithecus afarensis*, which dates from some three million years ago. This species may have been a direct ancestor of our own species.

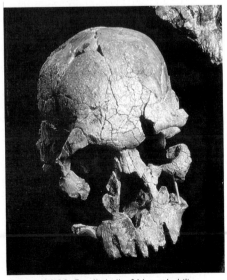

Figure 44.22 Fossil skull of *Homo habilis* dating from almost two million years ago.

Figure 44.23 Evidence suggests that we have been burying our dead for a very long time. The picture shows Silbury Hill in Wiltshire. It is the largest man-made mound in Europe, having a height of 39 metres and a base area of 2 hectares. Dated at around 2745 BC, it was probably a burial chamber though there is no certain evidence for this.

The oldest fossils classified as *H. sapiens* date from about 130 000 years ago. *H. sapiens* is distiguished from *H. erectus* by a number of precise anatomical differences, including the possession of a significantly larger brain. In addition archaeological remains show that the early members of *H. sapiens* buried their dead (figure 44.23).

How did humans evolve?

The details of human evolution are unclear, particularly the early stages (figure 44.24). Indeed, although most anthropologists think we evolved on the savannahs of Africa, Alister Hardy and Elaine Morgan have championed the idea that we are 'aquatic apes'. This theory argues that we passed through a semi-aquatic phase during which we lost most of our body hair, acquired large amounts of subcutaneous fat, became bipedal, began to copulate face to face, learned to cry and began to talk. Elaine Morgan writes most convincingly and her books *The Descent of Woman* and *The Aquatic Ape* are well worth reading.

Whether we evolved on land or at the sea's edge, the evolution of the delicate muscles that control our fingers and thumbs must have been of paramount importance. Hands probably originated in primates long ago as prehensile grasping devices for climbing trees. In early humans they became efficient manipulative devices for making tools and hurling weapons. Today, of course, they provide the means by which we show our creativity and transmit our achievements down the generations (figure 44.25).

Full use of the hands would not have been possible had it not been for our ancestors becoming bipedal. This necessitated major changes in the musculo-skeletal system, particularly the vertebral column and pelvis.

Larval forms and evolution

In trying to reconstruct evolutionary pathways one generally endeavours to derive an organism from the *adult* form of a group known to have been present earlier in the fossil record.

However, there are reasons for believing that on more than one occasion during evolution, a group may have evolved not from an adult ancestor, but from its larva. On first consideration this may seem absurd; after all, larvae cannot, by definition, reproduce. However, it is thought that in the course of evolution certain larval forms may have acquired sexual maturity, and then evolved into other forms. On this hypothesis, the original adult would have become redundant and disappeared from the life cycle.

This may have happened in the evolution of the chordates. For example, the chordates may have evolved from the 'tadpole' larva of the sea squirts (see page 774). The evidence for this is circumstantial and indirect, but it is certainly true that larvae can, on occasions, become sexually mature. Such is the case with the axolotl, a native of certain Mexican lakes. A favourite feature in many aquaria, this giant tadpole is the larval form of the salamander *Amblystoma* (illustration). Reaching over 15 cm in length, it becomes sexually mature and is able to reproduce without undergoing metamorphosis into the adult. This process is called **neoteny**, and it makes one suspect that evolution from a larval form may not be as unlikely as it might appear at first sight.

It is even possible that a mild form of neoteny has been important in the recent evolution of humans. After all, compared with other mammals we are relatively hairless and dependent on our parents for a remarkably high percentage of our lifespan. Moreover, as adults we have relatively large heads and often play, characteristics typical of *juvenile* primates. In short, maybe we are just overgrown babies!

An axolotl, the larval form of a species of salamander.

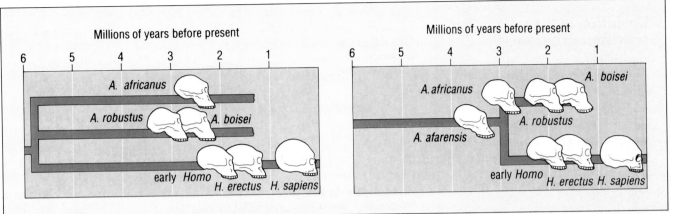

Figure 44.24 Exactly how humans evolved is still shrouded in doubt. Here are two possible phylogenetic trees tracing the evolution of *Homo sapiens* from species in the genus *Australopithecus*.

These changes are part of the reason why many people get backache and why childbirth is painful for mothers. However, the evolution of bipedalism freed the hands from their former function of locomotion and allowed them to be used for other purposes. We owe much to our bipedal stance. Precisely *why* bipedalism evolved is another question. It may have helped our ancestors to see predators at a distance. Or perhaps it prevented overheating, by exposing a smaller surface area to the tropical sun. Can you think of any other ideas?

In the emergence of *Homo sapiens* as a dominant species, the development of **speech** has been extremely important. Of course, many organisms can make a variety of sounds and communicate thereby. What is unique to our species is the ability to produce such an extensive repertoire of sounds by subtle movements of the lips and tongue. Human speech depends on the production of sound by the larynx. In the sound-producing process two elastic strands of tissue, the vocal cords, are vibrated by blasts of air emitted from the lungs. Pitch is determined by the tension on the vocal cords, together with the size of the glottal aperture; loudness by the strength of the blast of air. Our hands and voice are coordinated by complex neural mechanisms initiated by the brain. In fact while all these developments were taking place there was a dramatic increase in brain size (figure 44.26). The increased **mental ability** which this would have allowed must have helped our ancestors to think rationally, predict the behaviour of others, foresee the outcome of their actions, solve problems and appreciate the difference between right and wrong.

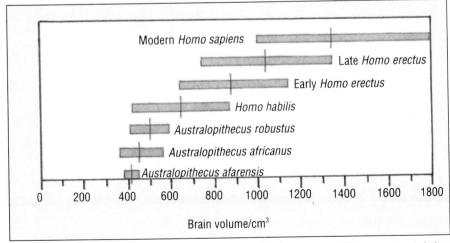

Figure 44.26 Brain volumes of various hominids showing the mean and 95 per cent population limits in each group.

Figure 44.25 *Top* Bushman cave art from at least 15 000 years ago, Inanke cave, Matopos, Zimbabwe. *Bottom* Illuminated manuscript depicting a knight on horseback, French 13th/14th Century. The dexterous use of hands made these artefacts possible.

Evolution of the mammalian ear ossicles

Much of the success of humans as a species depends on the possession of exquisitely adapted structures which have evolved in mammals as a whole. One of these is the ear. Here we trace the evolution of the mammalian ear ossicles from their earliest beginnings in fishes and amphibians.

This evolutionary sequence, well documented by fossils, is extraordinary because it illustrates how structures can radically change their function in the course of evolution. The sequence, illustrated alongside, starts with a fish and ends up with a mammal.

Fishes, both living and fossil, have no middle ear. The backs of the jaws are held in position by a brace, the hyomandibular, which runs from the point of articulation between the upper and lower jaws to the back of the cranium just by the auditory capsule.

In amphibians and early reptiles the first of a series of remarkable changes takes place. The upper jaw, previously slung from the cranium by ligaments, becomes fused to the floor of the cranium. The hyomandibular, now released from its function of supporting the jaws, goes into the newly-developed middle ear chamber as the stapes. Its function is to transmit sound waves from the tympanic membrane to the inner ear.

In present-day amphibians, reptiles and birds the stapes is the only ossicle in the middle ear. But in mammals two others are present: the malleus and incus (see page 485). Where do they come from? Fossil evidence, supported by comparative anatomy and embryology, indicates that they are derived from, of all places, the upper and lower jaws.

In amphibians and reptiles the jaws articulate between the quadrate bone at the back of the upper jaw and the articular bone at the back of

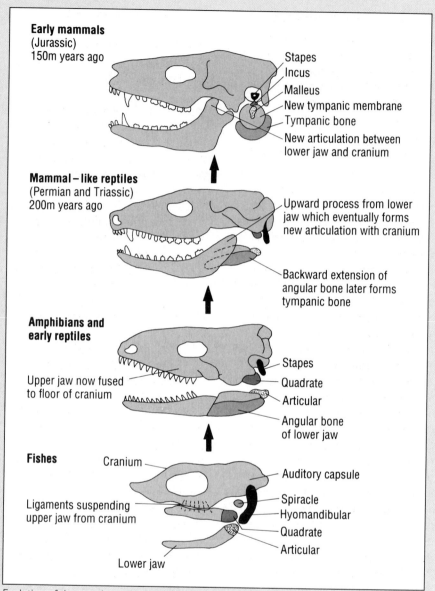

Evolution of the vertebrate ear ossicles. The diagrams are based on fossils which show the incorporation of the hyomandibular of fishes into the amphibian middle ear cavity as the stapes (black in the diagram). In the evolution of the mammal-like reptile the stapes is joined by the articular and quadrate bones from the back of the jaws. These become the malleus and the incus respectively (stippled and grey).

the lower jaw. A very complete series of fossil mammal-like reptiles shows that the articular and quadrate gradually became 'pinched off' the back of the lower and upper jaws and incorporated into the middle ear as the malleus and incus respectively. Meanwhile a new jaw articulation is set up between an upward process from the lower jaw and the region of the upper jaw just in front of the

quadrate. The angular bone of the lower jaw grows back in an arc and finally loses its connection with the lower jaw, becoming the tympanic bone whose function is to support the tympanic membrane.

The middle ear is now complete with its full complement of ossicles, and a new jaw articulation has been established.

The 11th Commandment

The harsh realities of evolution by natural selection have created ethical problems for humans. Garrett Hardin, Emeritus Professor of Human Ecology at the University of California, Santa Barbara, questions the morality of sending food aid to countries afflicted with recurrent famine.

Can anyone watch children starve on television without wanting to help? Naturally sympathetic, we all want to do unto others as we would have them do unto us.

But wanting is not doing. Forty years of attempts to feed the world's starving have produced mixed results. Before we respond to the next appeal we should ask, 'Does what we call 'aid' really help?'

Some of the shortcomings of food aid can be dealt with briefly. Waste is unavoidable: because most poor countries have wretched transportation systems, food may sit on a dock until it rots. Then there are the corrupt politicians who take donated food away from the poor and give it to their political supporters. In Somalia in the 1980s, fully 70 per cent of the donated food went to the army.

But there is another kind of loss. Before we jump on to the next 'feed-the-starving' bandwagon we need to understand how well-intentioned efforts can be counterproductive.

Briefly put, it is a mistake to focus only on starving people while ignoring their surroundings. Where there is great starvation there is usually an impoverished environment: poor soil, scarce water and wildly fluctuating weather. As a result, the 'carrying capacity' of the environment is low. The territory simply cannot support the population that is trying to live on it. Yet if the population were much smaller, and if it would stay smaller, the people

would not need to starve.

Let us look at a particular example. Nigeria, like all the central African countries, has increased greatly in population in the last quarter-century. Over many generations, Nigerians learned that their farmlands would be most productive if crop-growing alternated with 'fallow years' – years in which the land was left untilled to recover its fertility.

When modern medicine reduced the death rate, the population began to grow. More food was demanded from the same land. Responding to that need, Nigerians shortened the fallow periods. The result was counterproductive. In one carefully studied village, the average fallow period was shortened from 5.3 to 1.4 years. As a result, the yearly production (averaged over both fallow and crop years) fell by 30 per cent.

Are Nigerian farmers stupid? Not at all! They know perfectly well what they are doing. But a farmer whose family has grown too large for his farm has to take care of next year's need before he can provide for the future. To fallow or not to fallow translates into this choice: zero production in a fallow year or a 30 per cent shortfall over the long run. Starvation cannot wait. Long-term policies have to give way to short-term ones. So the farmer plows up his overstressed fields, thus diminishing long-term productivity.

Once the carrying capacity of a territory has been transgressed, its capacity goes down, year after year. Transgression is a one-way road to ruin. Ecologists memorialise this reality with an 11th Commandment: 'Thou shalt not transgress the carrying capacity'.

Transgression takes many forms. Poor people are poor in energy resources. They need energy to cook their food. Where do they get it? Typically, from animal dung or trees and bushes. Burning dung deprives

the soil of nitrogen. Cutting down trees and bushes deprives the land of protection against eroding rain. Soil-poor slopes cannot support a crop of fuel-plants. Once the soil is gone, water runs off the slopes faster and floods the valleys below. First poor people deforest their land, and then deforestation makes them poorer.

When we send food to a starving population that has already grown beyond the environment's carrying capacity we become a partner in the devastation of their land. Food from the outside keeps more people alive; they demand more food and fuel; greater demand causes the community to transgress the carrying capacity more, and transgression results in lowering the carrying capacity. The deficit grows exponentially. Gifts of food to an overpopulated country boomerang, increasing starvation over the long run. Our choice is really between letting some die this year and letting more die in the following years.

Only one thing can really help a poor country: population control. Having accepted disease control the people must now accept population control.

What the philosopher-economist Kenneth Boulding has called 'lovey-dovey charity' is not enough. 'It is well to remember', he said, 'that the symbol of Christian love is a cross and not a Teddy bear'. A good Christian should obey the 11th Commandment, refusing to send gifts that help poor people destroy the environment that must support the next generation.

Reproduced from *Morality in Practice*, James P. Sterba (ed), (Wadsworth, 1991).

Do you agree with Garrett Hardin's '11th Commandment'? If we don't send food aid to countries where people are starving, then what should we do to help them?

Extinction

The evolution of species has been accompanied by extinction. Guest author Tim Halliday explains why animals become extinct and how this relates to conservation.

The extinction of animal and plant species is of considerable concern at the present time, because of the very high rate at which species are being exterminated by the direct and indirect effects of human activities, such as habitat destruction and pollution. It is important to remember, however, that extinction is also a natural process and that it is the ultimate fate of all species to become extinct or evolve into new species. The 30 million species that inhabit the Earth today represent only a minute fraction of all the species that have existed; the history of life on Earth has involved a process of continuous turnover, in which new species replace previous ones. From time to time, however, the rate of turnover has shown dramatic increases, leading to mass extinctions, the best known being the demise of the dinosaurs. At the present time there is a comparable mass extinction caused, not by natural events, but by the harmful activities of humans.

A species will inevitably become extinct if mortality among existing individuals persistently exceeds the addition of young individuals to the population. While this is self-evident, it provides the essential basis for effective conservation of endangered species, since it is necessary to decide whether efforts should be directed towards reducing mortality or enhancing reproduction. The great auk, for example, was exterminated by the uncontrolled slaughter of adult birds, whereas the decline of many large birds of prey, such as the peregrine falcon, has been caused by pesticides like DDT that caused them to lay eggs with very thin shells.

Active conservation of several birds of prey has involved efforts to enhance their reproductive rate whereas protection of other species, such as the once endangered elephant seal and polar bear, has been achieved through restrictions on hunting.

Naturally-occurring extinctions are primarily the result of two interacting processes: competition between species and environmental change. As environments change, they impose pressures on species to adapt to such changes. Species that cannot adapt are replaced by species that can. For example, the ice ages in Britain caused widespread changes in the fauna and flora. What were once semi-tropical forests were replaced by coniferous and deciduous woodlands which were better able to survive in the changed environment.

A distinction can be made between real extinctions and **pseudo-extinctions**. All the species existing at a particular time are direct descendants of ancestral species, and it will often be the case that an ancestral species is no longer present. In a sense it did not become extinct but became transformed into a different species over a long period of time. For example, the direct ancestors of *Homo sapiens* did not suffer real extinction but pseudo-extinction. In other instances, however, species and entire groups of organisms have gone extinct without leaving any descendants. Contemporary extinctions, caused by human activities, are real extinctions because they do not involve the transformation of existing species into new ones.

Clearly, certain kinds of species are more prone to extinction than others. One such category are large, predatory species, such as eagles and other birds of prey. Because they are at the top of a food chain, they tend to exist in low numbers and to be adversely affected by any disturbance at lower levels in the chain. Another

The Everglades kite whose specialised diet made it vulnerable to extinction.

group are species with very specialised habits. For example, the Everglades kite (see illustration) is adapted to feed exclusively on a particular species of snail, and it is endangered because its prey species has declined. The corollary of this is that species with very generalised habits, such as starlings and sparrows, prosper and spread as a result of habitat changes brought about by humans.

The highest rates of extinction in recent times have occurred among species endemic to small oceanic islands. Because of their isolation, such islands commonly contain species that are uniquely adapted to the local conditions and are found nowhere else. Because islands are often small, they are quickly devastated by human activities and the resident species have no escape. The classic example of a recent extinction, the dodo, provides an example of a common pattern among birds. In adapting to life on the island of Mauritius, where there were no ground-living predators, it lost the ability to fly. As a result it was helpless when hunted by humans and the predators that humans brought with them, such as rats and cats.

The future course of evolution

Today, in many human societies, natural selection is not the potent force that it is in other species, or indeed used to be in human communities. Modern science and medicine have seen to that.

Does this mean that the human species is no longer evolving? The answer is no. Natural selection still operates, though on a more limited scale and in more subtle ways than in past ages. But, more importantly, humans have entered a new phase in their evolution, a phase in which advances depend not so much on structural changes in the body as on the transmission of accumulated experience from one generation to the next (figure 44.27). This can be termed **cultural evolution**.

We are such a dominant species on this planet that the Earth's entire future may depend on what we do within the next generation or two. At one extreme, we have the potential to destroy the majority of the world's population through the use of nuclear weapons. A nuclear war could herald a **nuclear winter** in which enormous amounts of dust generated by the explosions might block out the Sun's rays for years.

In much the same way that the dust caused by an asteroid impact may have caused the extinction of the dinosaurs (see page 823), the dust from nuclear explosions might lead to a collapse in agricultural production with accompanying mass starvation. It is unclear whether the human species would become extinct, or whether sufficient individuals would survive to repopulate the Earth.

Even in the absence of a nuclear winter, there are other ways in which our activities may threaten ourselves and other species. As we saw in Chapter 4, global warming and the destruction of the ozone layer are recent phenomena, the outcome of which is still unclear. However, where there is the greatest potential for harm, there is also the greatest potential for good. We are unique as a species. At any event, the next fifty years are likely to show whether we are heading towards heaven or hell.

Figure 44.27 Learning from previous generations has enabled *Homo sapiens* to undergo a process of cultural evolution which hopefully will continue in the future.

Figure 44.28 We may yet be able to plan ahead and avoid catastrophe. Delegates at the Earth Summit in Rio de Janeiro in 1992 discuss ways of averting an ecological crisis which threatens the future of life on our planet.

Summary

1 Pasteur, in his famous swan-necked flask experiment, disproved, once and for all, the **theory of spontaneous generation**.

2 The first step in the formation of living organisms may have been the synthesis of organic molecules from simple gases. This has been repeated in the laboratory under anaerobic conditions thought to resemble those found on Earth four billion years ago.

3 Another possibility is that the first organisms arose on land from clay crystals.

4 Whether life began in an '**organic soup**' or as inorganic clays, somehow certain compounds must have come together to form the first living organisms. **Coacervates** provide a clue as to how this may have happened.

5 The first organisms were probably **heterotrophs**. **Autotrophs** evolved later, eventually releasing oxygen into the atmosphere and paving the way for **aerobic respiration**.

6 The transition from a **prokaryotic** to a **eukaryotic** cell structure may have occurred largely as a result of **endosymbiosis**.

7 **Multicellular organisms** probably arose either as a result of the failure of cells to separate after cell division, or from a multinucleate ancestor.

8 A major development in the evolution of both animals and plants has been the exploitation of dry land. For this to take place various anatomical and physiological changes were necessary to cope with the shortage of water, loss of buoyancy and other environmental problems.

9 Evolutionary trends in animals include the evolution of **triploblastic organisation**, **body cavities** (**coelom** and **haemocoel**) and **metameric segmentation**.

10 On the plant side, an early trend led to the separation of **reproductive** and **somatic** cells, and a later trend to the distinction between **sporophyte** and **gametophyte**.

11 In both animals and plants there have been trends towards larger size. The largest ever terrestrial organisms were certain of the dinosaurs. The reason the dinosaurs became extinct some 65 million years ago is still hotly debated.

12 Although extinction of species is a natural process, the rate of extinction has greatly increased recently as a result of human activities.

13 Humans probably shared a common ancestor with chimpanzees from which we diverged five to eight million years ago.

14 The evolution of the human species (*Homo sapiens*) has been marked by **bipedalism, increased intelligence, manipulative hands, speech, prolonged parenting, loss of body hair** and a **sense of right and wrong**.

15 Over the last few thousand years we have become increasingly dependent on the transmission of accumulated experience, termed **cultural evolution**.

16 The future of the planet is largely in our hands.

Review questions

1 Why did Pasteur conclude that spontaneous generation was not possible when Needham had earlier concluded exactly the opposite from nearly the same experiment?

2 Do you think it will ever be possible to prove whether life began as inorganic clays or in an organic soup? Explain your answer.

3 What are the arguments in favour of the theory that DNA evolved after RNA?

4 This chapter argues that heterotrophs evolved before autotrophs. Argue the opposite case.

5 What problems are faced by terrestrial organisms such as angiosperms, mammals and birds, when they attempt to go back to the sea?

6 To what extent is extinction a *natural* process? Why do you think evolution has often favoured the development of larger organisms?

7 How might palaeontologists try to determine whether the dinosaurs were endothermic or ectothermic?

8 Why do you think there was strong selection for increased mental capacity in *Australopithecus* and *Homo*?

9 Is it a good thing that natural selection is less important in many human societies than it was? Argue your case.

10 Suppose that humans still exist in fifty million years. What course may evolution have taken by then?

Further reading

The Scientific American book *Evolution* (Freeman, 1978) contains nine fascinating articles ranging from 'Chemical evolution and the origin of life' to 'The Evolution of Man'.

Stephen Tomkins', *The Origins of Mankind* (Cambridge University Press, 1984) provides an excellent short account of the evolution of humans over the last few million years.

David Lambert's *Dinosaur Data Book* (Facts on File, 1990) provides a comprehensive up-to-date A-Z coverage of dinosaurs, describing every known genus.

The Life Puzzle by A.G. Cairns-Smith (Oliver and Boyd, 1974) is a most readable account of Cairns-Smith's ideas about the evolution of life. He also describes his theory in *Seven Clues to the Origin of Life* (Cambridge University Press, 1990).

Photographs

The authors and publisher are grateful to the following for permission to reproduce copyright material. If any acknowledgement has been inadvertently omitted, this will be rectified at the earliest possible opportunity.

Cover: Humpbacked whale: Ardea/François Gohier

Chapter 1
1.1 By permission of The Syndics of Cambridge University Library; 1.2 A Science Photo Library/Geoff Thompkinson; B ICCE/ Philip Steele; 1.4 A Science Photo Library/Morley Reed; B Heather Angel; C Heather Angel; 1.5 *Left* Heather Angel; *Top* Ardea/Keith and Liz Laidler; *Bottom* Walter Singer, New York.

Part I: Pictor International

Chapter 2
2.1 Science Photo Library; 2.5 Bruce Coleman Ltd/Erwin and Peggy Bauer; 2.6 Bruce Coleman Ltd/Hans Reinhard; 2.7 Bruce and Cherry Alexander; 2.8 Penni Bickle; 2.10 Heather Angel; 2.11 Heather Angel; 2.16 Heather Angel; 2.17 Science Photo Library/Sinclair Stammers; 2.18 Bruce Coleman Ltd/Eugene Schumacher; 2.19 BC Ltd/Erwin and Peggy Bauer.

Chapter 3
3.1 Heather Angel; 3.2 Heather Angel; 3.3 Bruce Coleman/Philip H Evans; 3.4 Science Photo Library/John Heseltine; 3.5 Penni Bickle; 3.6 Dr Z. Glowacinski; 3.7 Bruce Coleman/ M.P. Kahl; 3.15 Bruce Coleman/D. Houston; 3.17 Bruce Coleman/Gunter Zeisler; 3.21 Silver Springs IGGZ.

Chapter 4
4.1 Bruce Coleman/Gerald Cubitt; p.43 Greenpeace/Ferraris; 4.8 Science Photo Library/Simon Frazer; 4.14 *Top* Panos/David Reed, *Bottom* Panos/ Jeremy Hartley; 4.15 Bruce Coleman; 4.16 Heather Angel; 4.19 Biofotos/Brian Rogers; 4.20 Biofotos/Brian Rogers; 4.21 Bruce Coleman/Steve Kaufmann; 4.22 Penni Bickle; p.55 Bruce Coleman/Frances Furlong.

Chapter 5
5.1 Bruce Coleman/Patrick Clement; 5.6 Bruce Coleman/Jane Burton; 5.13 Australian News and Information Bureau; 5.14 Australian News and Information Bureau; 5.15 Biofotos/C A Henley; 5.16 *Top* and *bottom* Heather Angel; 5.17 A and B Bruce Coleman/Frieder Sauer; 5.19 *Top* Bruce Coleman/ Leonard Lee Rue III; *Bottom* Bruce Coleman/Erwin and Peggy Bauer; 5.25 Bruce Coleman/Leonard Lee Rue III; 5.26 Bruce Coleman/Jane Burton; p.73 Heather Angel.

Chapter 6
6.1 Bruce Coleman/Hans Reinhard; 6.2 Heather Angel; 6.3 Science Photo Library/M.I. Walker; 6.6 Harry Smith Collection; 6.9 Science Photo Library/Omikron; 6.10 Bruce Coleman/Hans Reinhard; 6.11 Frank Lane; 6.12 M. Brooke/Dept of Zoology/ University of Cambridge; 6.13 *Left* Gene Cox; *Middle* Science Photo Library/London Scientific Films; *Right* M.M. Wong/ University of California School of Veterinary Medicine; 6.16 Dr H.J. Hudson/Dept of Botany/University of Cambridge; 6.17 Bruce Coleman/C.B. Frith; 6.18 Science Photo Library/Dr Jeremy Burgess; 6.20 Bruce Coleman/J.L.G. Girande; 6.22 A Biofotos/Brian Rogers; B Biofotos/Brian Rogers; 6.23 Oxford Scientific Films/Michael Fogden. 6.24 Heather Angel; 6.25 A and B Bruce Coleman/Michael Fogden.

Chapter 7
7.3 *Top* and *bottom* Biofotos/Jeremy Thomas; 7.4 *Top* Bruce Coleman/ Hans Reinhard; *Bottom* Bruce Coleman/S. Nielsen; p.97 Biophoto Associates; 7.14 Biophoto Associates.

Chapter 8
8.1 Science Photo Library/Dr Jeremy Burgess; 8.2 Science Photo Library/Sinclair Stammers; 8.3 Science Photo Library/Professor David Hall; 8.4 Science Photo Library/CNRI; 8.5 Science Photo Library/A.B. Dowsett; 8.6 Science Photo Library/CNRI; 8.7 Science Photo Library/A.B. Dowsett; p.105 Courtesy of Upjohn Ltd; 8.8 Science Photo Library/Michael Abbey; 8.9 *Top* Bruce Coleman/Frieder Sauer; *Bottom* Science Photo Library/Andrew Syred; 8.10 Biophoto Associates; 8.11 Heather Angel; 8.12 Heather Angel; 8.13 Heather Angel; 8.14 Science Photo Library/Bruce Iverson; 8.15 Dr Maurice Grindle/University of Sheffield; 8.16 Heather Angel; 8.17 Bruce Coleman/Hans Reinhard; 8.18 Bruce Coleman/Hans Reinhard; 8.19 Heather Angel; 8.20 Bruce Coleman/Hans Reinhard; 8.21 *Top* Science Photo Library/Dr Morley Reed, *Bottom* Ardea/John Mason; 8.22 *Left* Heather Angel, *Right* Heather Angel; 8.23 *Top* Bruce Coleman/Jack Stein Grove; *Bottom* Bruce Coleman/Dr Frieder Sauer; 8.24 *Top* Bruce Coleman/Felix Labhardt; *Bottom* Heather Angel; 8.25 Science Photo Library/Sinclair Stammers; 8.26 Heather Angel; 8.27 Heather Angel; 8.28 Heather Angel; 8.29 Bruce Coleman/Jane Burton; 8.30 Bruce Coleman/ Mr P. Clement; 8.31 Heather Angel; 8.32 Bruce Coleman/Hector Rivarola; 8.33 Bruce Coleman/Jane Burton; 8.34 Bruce Coleman/Dr Frieder Sauer; 8.35 Heather Angel; 8.36 Oxford Scientific Films/London Scientific Films; 8.37 Bruce Coleman/Jane Burton; 8.38 Heather Angel; 8.39 Science Photo Library/Dr Morley Reed; 8.40 Bruce Coleman/Frieder Sauer; 8.41 Bruce Coleman/Jan van der Kam; 8.42 *Left* Heather Angel; *Middle* Bruce Coleman/Fritz Prenzel; *Right* Bruce Coleman/Hans Reinhard;

Below Bruce Coleman/Jane Burton/Kim Taylor.

Part II: Biophoto Associates
Chapter 9
9.1 Bruce Coleman/Kim Taylor; 9.2 Heather Angel; 9.3 Oxford Scientific Films/Lewis Trusty; 9.4 Dr G. Bond and Dr E.J. Hewitt, University of Glasgow; 9.9 Tate and Lyle; 9.12 A Gene Cox, B Middlesex Hospital Medical School; 9.14 R.D Preston/University of Leeds; 9.19 Gene Cox; 9.20 Heather Angel; 9.30 Bruce Coleman/G.D Plage; 9.31 Sir John Randall; 9.32 Dr S.D. Dover/King's College London; 9.36 Frederick Sanger; 9.37 and 9.38 J.D. Kendrew/MRC Laboratory of Molecular Biology, Cambridge; 9.41 Science Photo Library/Biophoto Associates; p.147 Wellcome Institute Library; 9.43 National Medical Slide Bank; p.149 Royal Society of Chemistry/Geoffrey Argent.

Chapter 10
10.5 Biophoto Associates; 10.6 Audrey M. Glauert/Strangeways Research Laboratory, Cambridge; p.154 Wellcome Institute Library; 10.7 Biophoto Associates; 10.10 B K.R. Porter, Harvard University; 10.11 A K.R. Porter, Harvard University; B Dr Daniel Branton/ University of California, Berkeley; p.158 *Illustration 1* Science Photo Library; *Illustration 2* Science Photo Library; p.159 *Illustration 3* Biophoto Associates; *Illustration 4* Science Photo Library/David Scharf; 10.12 Biophoto Associates; 10.14 Professor Ruth Bellairs/Dept of Anatomy and Embryology/University College London; 10.15 A.R. Akester/Dept of Veterinary Anatomy/University of Cambridge; 10.17 A.C. MacDonald, University of Aberdeen; 10.18 Br Brij Gupta/University of Cambridge; 10.19 *Left* Science Photo Library/Marshall Sklar; *Right* Science Photo Library/Biophoto Associates; 10.20 V. I. Barber, Patricia Holborow and M. S. Laverick, Universities of Bristol and St Andrews; 10.21 *Left* Dr A. Boyde/ Department of Anatomy, University College London; *Right* A. V. Grimstone/University of Cambridge; 10.22 B.E. Juniper/ University of Oxford; 10.23 B.E. Juniper/University of Oxford; 10.27 A.R. Akester/ University of Cambridge.

Chapter 11
11.1, 11.3, 11.9, 11.10, 11.14 A, 11.16, 11.17 and 11.18 Gene Cox; 11.20 Bruce Coleman/Gerald Cubitt; 11.21 Frank Lane; 11.22 *Top* Bruce Coleman/Jane Burton; *Bottom* Heather Angel; 11.24 *Left* Dr Nick Evans; *Middle* Science Photo Library/Dr T Anderson & Dr Lee Simon; *Right* Science Photo Library/NIBSC; p.109 Science Photo Library/Omikron.

Chapter 12
p.95 Dr Jens Skou; 12.9 Gene Cox; 12.12 CR Photography; 12.14 Biophoto Associates; 12.16 Biophoto Associates.

Chapter 13
13.2 CR Photography; 13.4 Michael Roberts; 13.6 *Top* Zefa/F.D. Book; *Bottom* Science Photo Library/Keith Kent; 13.7 B.J.W Heath; 13.16 Science Photo Library/Philippe Plailly.

Chapter 14
14.2 A Michael Roberts; B Dr Kenneth Dickstein; 14.4 Wellcome Institute Library; p.235 Estate of Sir Hans Krebs; 14.10 Young and Co Brewery plc; 14.15 A Bruce Coleman/Wayne Lankinen; B Bruce Coleman/Jane Burton;

Part III: Bruce Coleman/Dragesco
Chapter 15
15.1 Gene Cox; 15.2 B.E. Juniper/ University of Oxford; 15.4 Dr C.M Williams/Dept of Biological Science, University of Stirling; 15.9 *Top* Biofotos/S. Summerhays; *Bottom* Heather Angel; 15.17 Gene Cox; p.260 Grace Monger; 15.20 *Bottom* Dr J. Clarke/Dept of Anatomy and Physiology, St Bartholomew's Hospital; 15.23 Royal Geographical Society/A Gregory; p.266 Science Photo Library/James Stevenson;

Chapter 16
16.1 A Heather Angel; B Penni Bickle; C Science Photo Library/Martin Dohrn; D Heather Angel; E Bruce Coleman/Jean Burton; 16.2 B.J.W. Heath; 16.3 CR Photography; 16.4 Science Photo Library/Andrew Syred; 16.5 Oxford Scientific Films/David Thompson; 16.7 Bruce Coleman/Erwin and Peggy Bauer; 16.8 Heather Angel; 16.9 B.J.W. Heath; 16.10 Heather Angel; 16.11 A Science Photo Library/Sinclair Stammers; B Oxford Scientific Films/G. Bernard; C Science Photo Library/Claude Nuridsany and Marie Perennou; 16.12 Heather Angel; 16.13 Science Photo Library/Claude Nuridsany and Marie Perrenou; 16.14 Oxford Scientific Films/Peter Parks; 16.21 B Biophoto Associates; 16.24 Dr Henry Leese/University of York; 16.25 Science Photo Library/ Fawcett/ Hirokawa/Heuser; 16.28 Gene Cox.

Chapter 17
17.9 A-C Heather Angel; 17.10 Heather Angel; 17.15 Professor Rachel Leech/Dept of Biology/ University of York; 17.17 Dr Daniel Branton; 17.20 A and B Gene Cox; 17.21 CR Photography; 17.27 *Left* Lawrence Berkeley Laboratory/ University of California; *Right* Lawrence Berkeley Laboratory/ University of California; 17.32 Heather Angel; 17.33 O.N. Allen/University of Wisconsin.

Chapter 19
19.2 Science Photo Library; p.321 Science Photo Library/NIBSC; p.324 Illustration 1 Mansell Collection; Illustration 2 Parke, Davis & Company; 19.10 B.J.W Heath; 19.18 Biophoto Associates; 19.22 Biofotos/J.W.H. Conroy.

Chapter 20
20.1 Biophoto Associates; 20.3 A and B Biophoto Associates; 20.7 Biophoto Associates; 20.8 Gene Cox; 20.9 Left Biophoto Associates; Right Biophoto Associates; 20.11 Dr Peter Gasson/Jodrell Laboratory, Royal Botanic Gardens, Kew; 20.13 A and B Biophoto Associates; 20.14 Left J.F. Crane, Right Biophoto Associates; 20.21 Bruce Coleman/Paul Meitz; 20.23 K. Esau and V.I. Cheadle/ University of California; 20.26 Heather Angel; 20.27 Biophoto Associates; 20.28 Tjallingll Hogen Esch 1993.

Part IV: Bruce Coleman

Chapter 21
21.1 W.B. Saunders Company; 21.3 Science Photo Library; 21.5 A Dr C.S. Foster/Department of Histopathology, Royal Postgraduate School, Hammersmith Hospital, B Science Photo Library/Astrid and Hans Frieder-Michler; 21.10 Top Science Photo Library; Bottom Science Photo Library/James Stevenson; 21.12 Gene Cox; 21.14 Biophoto Associates.

Chapter 22
22.3 Biophoto Associates; 22.5 C.D. Pease/University of California; p.383 Science Photo Library/Simon Frazer; 22.11 Oxford Scientific Films/P. Kent; 22.13 Bruce Coleman/Frieder Sauer; 22.18 Ardea/ A. Greensmith;22.20 Bruce Coleman/ John Cancalosi; 22.21 Bruce Coleman/ Gerald Cubitt; 22.22 Heather Angel; 22.23 Science Photo Library/John Craddock; 22.24 A and B Gene Cox; 22.25 Bruce Coleman/John Shaw; 22.26 Heather Angel; p.393 Illustration 1 Bruce Coleman/ Peter Davey; Illustration 2 Panos/J Hartley.

Chapter 23
23.3 A Science Photo Library/Manfred Kage; 23.4 Bruce Coleman/Jane Burton; 23.7 T.H. Benzinger Naval Medical Research Inst. Bethseda, Maryland; 23.13 A Bruce Coleman/ Johnny Johnson, B Penni Bickle; 23.14 A Bruce Coleman/Jane Burton; B Bruce Coleman/Hans Reinhard; C Bruce Coleman/Steven Kaufman; p.407 Professor M. Stock/St George's Hospital and Dr N. Rothwell/ University of Manchester; 23.16 Bruce Coleman/Nicholas De Vere III; 23.18 Bruce Coleman/David Hughes; 23.20 Michael Roberts; 23.21 Heather Angel; p.411 Heather Angel.

Chapter 24
24.1 Dr M.W. Jennison, Syracuse University, New York, courtesy of the Society of American Bacteriologists; 24.3 Wellcome Institute Library; 24.4 Science Photo Library/Alexander Tsiaras; 24.6 A.R. Akester/University of Cambridge; 24.7 Science Photo Library/CNRI; 24.11 Science Photo Library/S. Nagendra; 24.12 Wellcome Institute Library; 24.14 Top Science Photo Library/St Mary's Medical School; Bottom Science Photo Library/St Mary's Medical School; 24.15 Top Science Photo Library/NASA; Bottom Science Photo Library/Philippe Plailly; p.427 Illustration 1 Sir Roy Calne; Illustration 2 British Heart Foundation; 24.17 Sir Peter Medawar/National Institute for Medical Research; 24.20 Long Ashton Research Station/Dr J.A. Bailey; p.432 Wellcome Institute Library

Part V: Allsport/Peter Duffy

Chapter 25
25.5 Zefa; 25.7 Michael Roberts; 25.14 B O.N. Allen, University of Wisconsin; 25.15 Biophoto Associates; 25.20 B Science Photo Library/CNRI; p.460 Heather Angel.

Chapter 26
26.2 B Science Photo Library/Astrid and Hans Frieder-Michler; 26.4 St Mary's Hospital Audio Visual Unit; 26.5 St Mary's Hospital Audio Visual Unit.

Chapter 27
27.1 A Boyde/University College London; 27.9 Gene Cox; 27.10 B Professor John Marshall/ Opthalmology Department, St Thomas' Hospital; p.484 Illustration 2 Gene Cox; 27.16 Science Photo Library/Dr Goran Bredburg; p.491 Illustration 1 Geoffrey Curtis; Illustrations 2–4 Siemens Hearing Instruments.

Chapter 28
28.4, 28.5, 28.7 H.R. Huxley MRC Laboratory of Molecular Biology, Cambridge; p.506 Illustration 1 Gene Cox; Illustration 2 Heather Angel; Illustration 3 Peter Herring/Biofotos.

Chapter 29
29.2 Royal College of Surgeons; 29.6 John Topham; p.513 Illustration, 2 Top Mr Glyn Evans; Bottom Science Photo Library/Alexander Tsiaras; 29.12 Bernard Knowles; 29.14 B Allsport/Bob Martin; C Allsport/Ann Guichaoua; 29.15 Bruce Coleman/Gerald Cubitt; 29.16 CR Photography; 29.19 Ardea/Jean-Paul Ferraro; 29.20 Bruce Coleman/Fritz Prenzel; 29.25 Bruce Coleman/Frans Lanting; 29.26 B.J.W. Heath; p.528 Illustration 1, Bottom Biophoto Associates.

Chapter 30
30.1 Bruce Coleman/Uwe Walz; 30.5 B.J.W. Heath; 30.7 Ardea/Peter Lumb; 30.14 Michael Roberts; 30.17 CR Photography; p.543 Jane Goodall Institute, UK; 30.21 A Michael Reiss; B Bruce Coleman/ Campbell; 30.23 Jane Goodall Institute, UK; 30.24 BIPAC.

Part VI: Bruce Coleman/Hans Reinhard

Chapter 31
31.3 P. Motta/Department of Anatomy, University 'Lasapienza', Rome; 31.4 Dr Andrew Bajer; 31.6 Daniel Mazia/University of California; 31.8 Br Brij Gupta/ University of Cambridge; 31.10 Dr Peter Brandham/Jodrell Laboratory, Royal Botanic Gardens, Kew; 31.11 Science Photo Library/Dr Jeremy Burgess; 31.13 Biophoto Associates; 31.14 Bernard John/ Australian National University; 31.16 Biophoto Associates; 31.19 Science Photo Library/Novosti; 31.20 Science Photo Library/Martin Dohrn.

Chapter 32
32.1 Audrey M. Glauert/University of Cambridge; 32.2 Oxford Scientific Films/Richard Packwood; 32.3 CDDE; 32.4 Gene Cox; 32.5 Gene Cox; 32.6 CR Photography; 32.7 Heather Angel; 32.8 Science Photo Library/Dr L. Caro; 32.12 Bruce Coleman/Andy Purcell; 32.13 Bruce Coleman/Erwin and Peggy Bauer; 32.16 A Bruce Coleman/Jane Burton; B Heather Angel; 32.17 Heather Angel; 32.18 Heather Angel.

Chapter 33
33.5 A Science Photo Library/Andrew Syred; 33.6 B Gene Cox; 33.8 Don Fawcett/Harvard University; 33.10 C Science Photo Library/Petit Format/CSI.

Chapter 34
34.2 A Heather Angel, B Heather Angel,C Gene Cox; 34.3 A Heather Angel; 34.4 Left Bruce Coleman/ Adrian Davies, Right Heather Angel; 34.7 B J.F. Crane; 34.8 Top Biophoto Associates; Middle Biophoto Associates; Bottom Biophoto Associates; 34.10 Biophoto Associates; 34.11 Science Photo Library/Andrew Syred; 34.14 Oxford Scientific Films/Dr L.E. Jeffree; 34.17 Science Photo Library/Dr Jeremy Burgess; 34.18 Heather Angel; 34.19 Heather Angel; 34.20 Bruce Coleman/Hans Joachim Flugel; 34.21 Bruce Coleman/A.J. Deane; p.615 Illustration 1, Left Heather Angel, Right Heather Angel, Illustration 2 Heather Angel; 34.22 Ardea/John Clegg; p.618 Illustrations 1–3 Unilever; 34.26 Left Heather Angel; Right Science Photo Library/Claude Nuridsany and Marie Perennou; 34.27 Top Heather Angel, Bottom Heather Angel; 34.28 Top and bottom Premaphotos Wildlife/K.G. Preston Mafham; 34.29 Bruce Coleman/Hans Reinhard; 34.30 Heather Angel.

Chapter 35
35.1 Hutchinson Library/Christine Pemberton; 35.10 A-G Oxford Scientific Films/G Bernard, H and I Biophoto Associates; 35.11 Oxford Scientific Films/Peter Parks; 35.13 Science Photo Library/Dr M.A. Ansary; 35.15 A-C Oxford Scientific Films/Peter Parks; 35.16 Oxford Scientific Films/Terry Heathcote; 35.19 B.J.W. Heath; 35.25 A and B Katherine Esau; 35.28 B Gene Cox; 35.29 Science Photo Library/Tony Craddock; 35.30 Penni Bickle; 35.31 Biophoto Associates.

Chapter 36
36.1 Hutchinson Library/Liba Taylor; 36.2 Heather Angel; p.648 Dr Jenny Chapman/Dept of Earth Sciences, Cambridge University; 36.3 L.C. Erickson/University of California; 36.6 Dr Kenneth V. Thiman/ University of California; 36.7 A and B United States Department of Agriculture; 36.9 A and B Michael Roberts; 36.10 Heather Angel; 36.11 US Dept of Agriculture, Dept of Information; 36.12 Dr S.H. Wittwer/Michigan State University; p.655 Illustration 2 John Land; 36.13 B.J.W. Heath; 36.18 Michael Roberts; 36.21 Patrick H. Wells, Occidental College, Los Angeles; 36.22 A Michael Roberts; 36.24 B.J.W. Heath; 36.26 US Dept of Agriculture, Office of Information; 36.27 Dr J.W. Hannay; 36.29 Top The Kobal Collection; Bottom Science Photo Library/Bettina Cirone; 36.31 Oxford Scientific Films/Jim Hallett; 36.33 Heather Angel (3 pics); 36.34 Biophoto Associates.

Part VII: Penni Bickle

Chapter 37
37.1 A and B Heather Angel; 37.2 Science Photo Library; 37.3 Harry Smith Collection; 37.6 G.P. Dent Processors and Growers Research Association; 37.8 Wellcome Institute Library; 37.11 A Ardea/John Clegg; B Heather Angel; 37.13 Bruce Coleman/Gerald Cubitt; 37.15 Uglies Model Agency; 37.16 Top G.P. Dent Processors and Growers Research Association, Bottom Bruce Coleman/ J Fennell; 37.20 Ardea/John Mason.

Chapter 38
38.5 Bruce Coleman/C.B. and D.W. Frith; 38.10 Mary Evans Picture Library; p.696 Curt Stern/University of California; 38.12 Biophoto Associates; 38.16 Science Photo Library/CNRI; 38.17 Ardea; 38.24 Ardea/Liz and Tony Bamford.

Chapter 39
39.1 Science Photo Library/Neville Chadwick; 39.3 Hulton Deutsch Collection; 39.4 Mrs Jennifer Gunn; 39.5 Science Photo Library/Science Source; 39.8 Science Photo Library; 39.12 Biophoto Associates; 39.19 A Science Photo Library/S Heggeler/ Biozenzum University of Baden; 39.21 A R.W. Horn/John Innes Institute, B E. Kellenberger/ University of Geneva.

Chapter 40
40.1 Oxford Scientific Films/Z.G. Leszczynski/Animals Animals; p.734 Illustration 1 Dr Bruce Reed/Dept of Genetics, Cambridge University; Illustration 2 Biophoto Associates; 40.8 Bruce Coleman/Jane Burton; 40.10 Herbert Reiss; 40.11 Science Photo Library/James Stevenson; 40.14 Keith Wood/University of California, San Diego; 40.15 Twyford Plant Laboratories.

Chapter 41
41.1 Heather Angel; 41.2 Royal Society; 41.3 A and B Penni Bickle; 41.5 A and B Heather Angel; 41.6 Top and bottom Science Photo Library/Eric Graves; p.758 Illustration 2 A Bruce Coleman/Gerald Cubitt; B Bruce Coleman/Christian Zuber;

C Penni Bickle; D Bruce Coleman/ Gerald Cubitt; E Panos Pictures/ Penny Tweedie.

Chapter 42
42.1 Penni Bickle; 42.2 Science Photo Library/National Library of Medicine; 42.4 Bruce Coleman/Erwin and Peggy Bauer; 42.5 A Bruce Coleman/Jen and Des Bartlett; B Bruce Coleman/Gerald Cubitt; C Bruce Coleman/John Cancalosi; D Australian News and Information Bureau; E Bruce Coleman/Francisco Futi; 42.6 Bruce Coleman/Hans Reinhard; 42.11 Frank Lane; 42.13 *Top* Bruce Coleman/ Konrad Wothe; *Bottom* Bruce Coleman/Hans Reinhard; 42.15 Bruce Coleman/Alan Root; 42.20 *Top* Bruce Coleman/Kjeil Sandved; *Bottom* Bruce Coleman; 42.22 Bruce Coleman/Bill Wood; 42.25 Bruce Coleman/Michael Freeman; 42.26 Science Photo Library/John Reader; 42.27 Oxford Scientific Films/Harry Taylor; 42.28 British Museum; 42.29 US National Park Service; 42.31 Science Photo Library/ Tony Craddock.

Chapter 43
43.1 Bruce Coleman/Jane Burton; 43.2 Dr Kenneth Dickstein; 43.3 Bruce Coleman/Kim Taylor; 43.4 Heather Angel; 43.5 Bruce Coleman/Masood Qureshi; 43.6 Penni Bickle; 43.9 Heather Angel; 43.12 Science Photo Library/L Willatt, East Anglian Regional Genetics Service; 43.13 Science Photo Library/Hattie Young; p.791 Illustration 1 National Medical Slide Bank; 43.15 Heather Angel; 43.16 Bruce Coleman/Jan van der Kam; 43.17 CR Photography; p.795 Michael Roberts; 43.19 Bruce Coleman/William S Paton; 43.22 A Bruce Coleman/George McCarthy; B Bruce Coleman/Gordon Lanesham; C Bruce Coleman; 43.23 Bruce Coleman/Jane Burton; 43.24 Heather Angel; 43.25 Premaphotos Wildlife/K G Preston Mafham; p.800 Illustration 1 A.D. Bradshaw/University of Liverpool; Illustration 2 Science Photo Library/John Durham; 43.27 Bruce Coleman/Michael Viard; 43.28 Bruce Coleman/Leonard Lee Rue III; 43.29 Bruce Coleman/Jen and Des Bartlett; 43.30 Bruce Coleman/Frans Lanning; 43.31 Dr Chris Wood/ Horticulture Research International, Wellesbourne; 43.32 Science Photo Library/Omikron; p.806 Illustration 1 Zefa; Illustration 2 L.C. Thomas.

Chapter 44
44.1 Bruce Coleman/Leonard Lee Rue III; 44.2 Wellcome Institute Library; 44.3 Science Photo Library/Roger Ressmeyer/Starlight; 44.8 Richard Howard; 44.10 A Science Photo Library/Sinclair Stammers; B Bruce Coleman/Patrick E. Baker; 44.15 Ardea/Jean-Paul Ferraro; p.819 Science Photo Library/Sinclair Stammers; p.821 Illustration 2 Dianne Edwards; 44.20 *Left* Zefa/E. Hummel; *Middle* Pictor International, *Right* Penni Bickle; 44.21 Science Photo Library/John Reader; 44.22 Science Photo Library/John Reader; 44.23 Ancient Art and Architecture

Collection; p.826 Science Photo Library/ Claude Nuridsany and Marie Perrenou; 44.25 *Top* Penni Bickle; *Bottom* British Library; p.830 Tim Halliday; 44.27 Sally and Richard Greenhill; 44.28 Rex Features/Chaim Mendes.

Illustrations
Certain material in this book is based on already published sources as follows:

Chapter 2
2.2 and 2.3 A. Friday and D.S. Ingram (eds), *The Cambridge Encyclopaedia of Life* (Cambridge University Press); 2.4 P. Colinvaux, *Ecology* (John Wiley); 2.9 B. Moss, *Ecology of Fresh Waters: Man and Medium* (Blackwell Scientific Publications); 2.12 R.S.K. Barnes and R.N. Hughes, *An Introduction to Marine Ecology* (Blackwell Scientific Publications); 2.14 T.R.G. Gray and S.T. Williams, *Soil Micro-organisms* (Longman); 2.15 David Waugh, *Geography, An Integrated Approach* (Nelson).

Chapter 3
3.9 P.R. and A.H. Ehrlich, *Population, Resource, Environment* (W.H. Freeman); 3.12 C.J. Krebs, *The Message of Ecology* (Harper and Row); 3.13 J.P. Kimmins, *Forest Ecology*, (Macmillan/Collier Macmillan); 3.22 T.J. King, *Ecology, 2nd edn* (Nelson) taken from E.P. Odum, 'Trophic structure and productivity of Silver Springs Florida, *Ecological Monographs* 27, 1957.

Chapter 4
4.3 Dr C.D. Keeling, Scripps Institution of Oceanography, University of California at San Diego, La Jolla, California; 4.4 J. Krebs; 4.5 Data by Moore and Walker; 4.6 and 4.11 K. Mellanby,*The Biology of Pollution* (Edward Arnold); 4.7 J. Lee, 'Acid rain' (*Biological Sciences Review*) 1 (4), 15–18, 1988); 4.10 H. Pearson, 'Muck an' brass': The sewage story' (*Biological Sciences Review* 1 (4), 1989); 4.13 B. Howard and N. Beresford, 'Chernobyl – the long shadow' (*Biological Sciences Review* 1 (3), 1989); 4.17 and 4.18 Based on Barnes and Hughes;

Chapter 5
5.3 J.W. Silvertown, *Introduction to Plant Population Ecology* (Longman); 5.5 G.E. Hutchinson, *An Introduction to Population Ecology* (Yale University Press); 5.7, 5.18 and 5.20 M. Begon, J.L. Harper and C.R. Townsend, *Ecology: Individuals, Populations and Communities* (Blackwell Scientific Publications); 5.9 S.P. Johnson, *World Population and the United Nations: Challenge and Response* (Cambridge University Press); 5.10 United Nations Demographic Yearbook, 1986; 5.12 B. Knapp, *Systematic Geography* (Collins);

5.22 and 5.24 P. Gadd, *Individuals and Populations* (Cambridge University Press);

Chapter 6
Page 76 G.H. Harper; 6.4 G.N. Agrios, *Plant Pathology* (Academic Press); 6.8 W.C. Marquardt and R.S. Demaree, *Parasitology* (Macmillan/Collier Macmillan); 6.19 P.H. Raven, R.F. Evert and H. Curtis, *Biology of Plants* (Worth); 6.21 D. MacDonald (ed), *The Encyclopaedia of Mammals: 2* (BookClub Associates by arrangement with George Allen and Unwin).

Chapter 7
7.16 G. Monger and M. Sangster, *Systematics and Classification* (Longman).

Chapter 8
Page 108 G. Monger and M.Sangster.

Chapter 9
9.13 C. Starr and R. Taggart, *Biology: The Unity and Diversity of Life* (Wadsworth); 9.15 B. Alberts, D. Bray, J. Lewis, M. Raff, K. Roberts and J.D. Watson *Molecular Biology of the Cell* (Garland Publishing); 9.21 A.L. Lehninger, *Principles of Biochemistry* (Worth Publishing); 9.23, 9.26B and 9.27 F.B. Armstrong, *Biochemistry* (Oxford University Press); 9.25A J.Simpkins and J.I. Williams, *Advanced Biology* (Unwin Hyman); 9.25B P. Sheeler and D.E. Bianchi, *Cell and Molecular Biology* (John Wiley & Sons,); **Table 9.3** Slightly modified from F.B. Armstrong;

Chapter 10
10.8 Modified after Brachet; 10.24 J.A. Ramsay, *The Experimental Basis of Modern Biology* (Cambridge University Press; 10.25 and 10.26 S.J. Singer and G.L. Nicholson, *Science* 175, 1972; 10.26 Modified after Singer and Nicholson.

Chapter 11
11.4 A.W. Ham, *Histology* (Pitman); 11.5 W.H. Freeman and B. Bracegirdle, *An Atlas of Histology* (Heinemann); 11.13 W. Bloom and D.W. Fawcett, *A Textbook of Histology* (Saunders). **Page 186** K. Vickerman and F.E.G. Cox, *The Protozoa* (John Murray);

Chapter 12
12.3 and 12.4 B. Alberts et al, *The Molecular Biology of the Cell* (Garland Publishing); 12.6 Based on J.F. Sutcliffe.

Chapter 13
13.3 G.H. Harper,*Tools and Techniques* (Nelson); 13.5 G.G. Simpson and W.S. Beck, *Life, An Introduction to Biology* (Harcourt Brace Jovanovich); 13.17 M. Boxer and Z. Towalski, *New Scientist*, 19 January 1984;

Chapter 14
14.1 D.G. Mackean, *Experimental Work in Biology No 7: Respiration and Gaseous Exchange* (John Murray);

14.12 M. Yudkin and R. Offord, *Comprehensive Biochemistry* (Longman). 14.16 S. Davidson and R. Passmore, *Human Nutrition and Dietetics* (Churchill-Livingstone).

Chapter 15
15.5 After Noel, 'Some New Techniques in Plant Physiology', *School Science Review*, 142, 1959; 15.6 S. Boussiba and A. Richmond, 'Abscisic acid and the after-effect of stress in tobacco plants', *Planta*, 129, 1976. 15.12 and page 255 G.M. Hughes,*Comparative Physiology of Vertebrate Respiration* (Heinemann); 15.14 C. Starr and R. Taggart; 15.16 D.G. Mackean, *Introduction to Biology* (John Murray); 15.17 Teresa Tetley, 'Holy Smoke: Smoke Damage in the Lungs', *Biological Sciences Review* Vol 2, No 5, May 1990; **Page 260** T. Turvey, *Revised Advanced Science Biology*, Practical Guide 1 (Longman); 15.20 G. Monger (ed), *Revised Nuffield Advanced Science Biology* (Longman); 15.24 and 15.25 V.B Wigglesworth, *The Principles of Insect Physiology* (Methuen); Pages 266–7 Graphs reproduced by courtesy of the Health Education Authority.

Chapter 16
16.17 A.W. Ham; 16.19 G. Monger (ed), *Revised Nuffield Advanced Science Biology* (Longman); 16.21A G.L. McCulloch, *Man Alive* (Aldus Books); **Page 286** K. Schmidt-Nielson, *How Animals Work* (Cambridge University Press);

Chapter 17
17.5 After Haxo and Blinks; 17.8 Data by Gaastra; 17.12 Mainly after Clayton; 17.14 Professor Rachel Leech, University of York;

Chapter 18
18.2 Professor M.F. Perutz; 18.4 J.A. Ramsay, *A Physiological Approach to the Lower Animals* (Cambridge University Press); 18.6–8 G. Monger (ed), *Revised Nuffield Advanced Science Biology* (Longman).

Chapter 19
19.46 G. Monger (ed), *Revised Nuffield Advanced Science Biology* (Longman); 19.8 G.J. Tortora, *Principles of Human Anatomy* (Canfield Press); 19.9, 19.11, 19.13, 19.19 C. Starr and R. Taggart; 19.12 Winton and Bayliss, *Human Physiology* (Churchill-Livingstone)

Chapter 20
20.4 G. Monger (ed), *Revised Advanced Science Biology* (Longman); 20.13C K. Esau, *Plant Anatomy* (John Wiley and Sons); 20.15 Data after Professor J.F. Sutcliffe; 20.17 After Zimmerman; 20.19 Data by Hoagland;

20.20 Data provided by Dr Richard Gliddon;
20.24 F.A.L. Clowes and B.E. Juniper, *Plant Cells* (Blackwell);
20.29 and 29.30 M. Willkins, *Plant Watching* (Macmillan);
20.31 R. Thaine, 'A protoplasmic streaming theory of phloem transport', *Journal of Experimental Biology*, 15, 470–84, 1964.
20.32 M. Richardson, *Translocation in Plants* (Edward Arnold).

Chapter 21
21.4 Data after T.E. Isles and Hazel Barker.

Chapter 22
22.1 C.H. Best and N.B. Taylor, *The Living Body* (Chapman and Hall);
22.5 G. Monger (ed), *Revised Nuffield Advanced Science Biology*, (Longman);
22.17 Data after Sir James Beament;
22.19 H.G.Q Rowett, *Dissection Guides V Invertebrates*, (John Murray);
Page 382 Illustration 1 A.C. Guyton, *Basic Human Physiology* (Saunders); Illustration 2 G. Monger (ed), *Revised Nuffield Advanced Science Biology* (Longman);
Page 383 Illustration 3 R. Gabriel, *A Patient's Guide to Dialysis and Transplantation* (MTP Press Ltd).

Chapter 23
23.1 Data after C.J. Martin;
23.2 A.C. Guyton, *Physiology of the Human Body* (Saunders);
23.5 J.R. Levick, *An Introduction to Cardiovascular Physiology* (Butterworth);
23.8 Data after T.H. Benzinger;
23.10 Data after F.G. Benedict and E.P. Slack;
23.11 M.S. Gordon, *Animal Physiology* (Macmillan);
23.12 P.F. Scholander et al, *Biological Bulletin*, Vol 99;
23.19 H. Swan, *Thermoregulation and Bioenergetics* (Elsevier, 1974).

Chapter 24
24.2 and 24.10 L. Gamlin, 'The Human Immune System', Part 1, *New Scientist*, 1603, 10 March 1988
24.8 L. Gamlin, 'The Human Immune System', Part II, *New Scientist*, 1605, 24 March 1988
24.16 G. Monger (ed), *Revised Nuffield Advanced Science Biloiogy* (Longman)

Chapter 25
25.4 G.L. McCulloch, Man Alive (Aldus Books);
25.6C and 25.16 B. Alberts et al;
25.19 P. R. Wheater et al, *Functional Histology*, (Churchill-Livingstone);
25.22 W. Penfield and T. Rusmussen, *The Cerebral Cortex of Man*, (Macmillan);
Page 457 C. Blakemore, *The Mind Machine* (BBC Books).

Chapter 26
26.1 G. J. Tortora, *Principles of Human Anatomy* (Canfield Press).
26.8 and 26.9 R. Guillemin and R. Burgus in D. Emslie-Smith et al (eds) *Textbook of Physiology* (Churchill-Livingstone);

Chapter 27
27.4 W.R. Lowenstein;
27.13 George Wald and others;
Page 483 Illustration 1 E. G. Boring; Illustration 2 Barbara Gillam, 'Geometrical illusions', *Scientific American*, January 1980;
Page 484 V.B. Wigglesworth, *The Life of Insects* (Weidenfeld and Nicholson);
27.16 W. Bloom and D. W. Fawcett, *A Textbook of Histology* (Saunders);
Page 488 Lippold and Winton, *Human Physiology* (Churchill Livingstone);
27.17 D. Emslie Smith et al, *Textbook of Physiology* (Churchill-Livingstone);
27.18 R. F. Schmidt (ed) *Fundamentals of Sensory Physiology* (Springer-Verlag)
27.19a and 27.20A G.L. McCulloch, *Man Alive* (Aldus Books);
Page 492 Illustration 3, A. and M. Hearing Aids Ltd.

Chapter 28
28.8 and 28.10A C.Starr and Taggart;
28.9 Peter G. Kohn;

Chapter 29
29.1 G.J. Tortora *Principles of Human Anatomy* (Canfield Press);
29.4 and 29.7 C. Starr and R. Taggart;
Page 512 Based on G.J. Tortora;
29.9A Henry Gray, *Anatomy, Descriptive and Surgical* (Running Press, Philadelphia); B L. Peterson and P. Renstrom, *Sports Injuries – Their Prevention and Treatment* (Martin Dunitz);
29.22 A J.Z. Young, *The Life of Vertebrates* (Oxford University Press);
29.28 Sir James Gray.

Chapter 30
30.2 R.A.Hinde, *Biological Bases of Human Social Behaviour* (McGraw-Hill);
30.3 and 30.15 F. Huntingford, *The Study of Animal Behaviour* (Chapman and Hall);
30.4 A.J. Premack and D. Premack, *Teaching Language to An Ape* (Scientific American);
30.6 J. Alcock, *Animal Behaviour: an Evolutionary Approach* (Sinauer Associates, Inc);
30.9 N. Tinbergen, *The Study of Instinct* (Oxford University Press);
30.10A N. Tinbergen;
30.11 A.P. Brookfield, *Animal Behaviour* (Nelson);
30.12 Drickamer and Vessey and A.P. Brookfield
30.16 Data taken from I.C.T. Nisbet, 'Courtship-feeding, egg-size and breeding success in common terns' *Nature*, 241, 141–142;
30.18–20 M.J. Reiss and Harriet Sants, *Behaviour and Social Organisation* (Cambridge University Press);
30.22 E.O. Wilson, *Sociobiology: The New Synthesis* (Belknap Press of Harvard University Press).

Chapter 31
31.9 B. Alberts et al;
31.19B V. Rich, 'An ill wind from Chernobyl' (*New Scientist* **20 April**, 1991, 26-8).

Chapter 32
32.11 C.R. Austin and R.V. Short (eds), *Reproduction in Mammals* (Cambridge University Press)
32.17 C. Starr and R. Taggart (as previously) and N. A. Campbell, *Biology* (Benjamin/Cummings);
32.18 and 32.19 C. Starr and R. Taggart.

Chapter 33
33.1, 33.2, 33.14 and 33.15 R.J. Demarest and J.J. Sciarra Conception, *Birth and Contraception* (McGraw-Hill/Hodder and Stoughton);
33.3 M. Dym in L. Weiss and R.O. Greep (eds), *Histology* (McGraw-Hill);
33.5B B.I. Balinsky, *An Introduction to Embryology* (Holt Saunders);
33.6 R. Meadows, *Pocket Atlas of Human Histology* (Oxford University Press);
33.7 D.W. Fawcett, *The Cell*, (Saunders)
33.11 Side view based on John Bancroft in C.R. Austin and R.V.Short (eds) *Human Sexuality* (Cambridge University Press) Transverse section based on A.W. Ham;
33.12 H. Tuchmann-Duplesses, G. David and P. Haegel, *Illustrated Human Embryology, Vol 1 Embryogenesis* (Springer Verlag/Chapman and Hall), C.R. Austin and R. V. Short (eds), *Germ Cells and Fertilisation and Embryonic and Fetal Development* (Cambridge Unversity Press);
33.16 Henry Leese, *Human Reproduction and In Vitro Fertilisation* (Macmillan);
Page 597 J. M. Tanner, *Fetus into Man* (Open Books);
33.18 Flint, Jeremy, Patten, Keirse and Anderson in *The Lancet*, Vol I, No 101, 1974.
Table 33.1 A.S. Asdell and others.

Chapter 34
34.1, 34.2 and 34.13 C. Starr and R. Taggart;
34.5 G. Beckett, *The Secret Life of Plants* (Octopus) based on an original text by J. Pazourek;
34.23 and 34.24 R.B. Whellock, *General Biology* (Harrap);
34.25 A. Gemmell and P.Swindells, *Your Gardening Questions Answered* (Reader's Digest).

Chapter 35
35.2 J.M. Tanner, *Growth and Adolescence* (Blackwell);
35.3 G.G. Simpson and W.S. Beck, *Life: An Introduction to Biology* (Harcourt Brace Jovanovich);
35.4 Data after G. Teissier;
35.7 B.I. Balinsky, *An Introduction to Embryology* (Holt Saunders)
35.21 A.S. Foster and E.M. Gifford, *Comparative Morphology of Vascular Plants* (W.H. Freeman);
35.24 K. Esau, *Anatomy of Seed Plants* (John Wiley and Sons).

Chapter 36
36.8 Data after L.J. Audus;
Page 656 J.B. Land and R.B. Land, *Food Chains to Biotechnology* (Nelson);
36.22 K. Esau, *Anatomy of Seed Plants*, (John Wiley and Sons);
36.17 Data after Briggs et al;
36.19 M. B. Wilkins;
36.23 Data after L. Hawker.
36.25 After Hendricks;
36.30 Based on V.B.Wigglesworth.

Chapter 38
38.3 A.M. Srb and R.D. Owen, *General Genetics* (W.H. Freeman);
38.11 and 38.15 S. Singer, *Human Genetics: An Introduction to the Principles of Heredity* (W.H Freeman);

Chapter 39
39.15 S. Singer;
39.16, 39.19B and C and 39.22 H. Curtis and N.S. Barnes, *Biology* (Worth);
39.18 After Rich;

Chapter 40
40.3, 40.7 and table 40.1 D.T. Suzuki, A.J.F. Griffiths, J.H. Miller and R.C. Lewontin, *An Introduction to Genetic Analysis* (W. H. Freeman);
40.5, 40.6 and 40.9 H. Curtis and N.S. Barnes;

Chapter 41
41.7 E.N. Anionwu and H.B. Jibril, *Sickle Cell Disease: A Guide for Families* (Collins International Textbooks);
41.8A and B S. Singer.

Chapter 42
42.3 J.M. Barrett, P. Abramoff, A.K. Kumaran and W.F. Millington, *Biology* (Prentice-Hall);
42.7 D. MacDonald (ed), *The Encyclopaedia of Mammals* (Guild Publishing);
42.8 A.S. Romer, *Vertebrate Paleontology* (University of Chicago Press);
42.9 Based on Hallam;
42.10 and 42.18 C. Starr and R. Taggart;
42.12 F.J. Sulloway, 'Darwin and the Galapagos', in *Biological Journal of the Linean Society* 21, 29–59;
42.16 Grove and Newell, *Animal Biology*, (University Tutorial Press);
42.17 and 42.19 M.W. Strickberger, *Evolution* (Jones and Bartlett);
42.21 After Eck and Dayhoff;
42.24 R. Buchsbaum;
42.32 H. Curtis and N.S. Barnes;
42.33 Sir Gavin de Beer.

Chapter 43
Page 791 Illustration 1 N.A. Campbell, *Biology* (Benjamin/Cummings);
43.14 C. Starr and R. Taggart;
43.26 G.H. Harper and A. Cruickshank.

Chapter 44
44.4 C. Starr and R. Taggart after Stanley Miller;
44.6 R.E. Dickerson, 'Chemical evolution and the origin of life', in *Scientific American* 239(3) 70–86;
44.7 and 44.9 N.A. Campbell;
44.13 After Pascher;
44.14 A and B Mainly after A.S. Romer, C The American Museum of Natural History;
44.16 J.A. Ramsay, *Physiological Approach to the Lower Animals*, (Cambridge University Press);
44.24 C. Starr and R. Taggart;
44.26 S. Tomkins;
Page 828 After Simpson.